APB No.	Date Issued		*Accounting Principles Board (APB) Opinions*, AICPA (1962–73)
22	Apr.	1972	Disclosure of Accounting Policies
23	Apr.	1972	Accounting for Income Taxes—Special Areas
24	Apr.	1972	Accounting for Income Taxes—Equity Method Investments
25	Oct.	1972	Accounting for Stock Issued to Employees
26	Oct.	1972	Early Extinguishment of Debt
27	Nov.	1972	Accounting for Lease Transactions by Manufacturer or Dealer Lessors
28	May	1973	Interim Financial Reporting
29	May	1973	Accounting for Nonmonetary Transactions
30	June	1973	Reporting the Results of Operations
31	June	1973	Disclosure of Lease Commitments by Lessees

SFAC No.			**Financial Accounting Standards Board (FASB),** *Statement of Financial Accounting Concepts* (1978–97)
1	Nov.	1978	Objectives of Financial Reporting by Business Enterprises
2	May	1980	Qualitative Characteristics of Accounting Information
3	Dec.	1980	Elements of Financial Statements of Business Enterprises
4	Dec.	1980	Objectives of Financial Reporting by Nonbusiness Organizations
5	Dec.	1984	Recognition and Measurement in Financial Statements of Business Enterprises
6	Dec.	1985	Elements of Financial Statements (a replacement of *FASB Concepts Statement No. 3*, incorporating an amendment of *FASB Concepts Statement No. 2*)

SFAS No.			**Financial Accounting Standards Board (FASB),** *Statements of Financial Accounting Standards* (1973–97)
1	Dec.	1973	Disclosure of Foreign Currency Translation Information
2	Oct.	1974	Accounting for Research and Development Costs
3	Dec.	1974	Reporting Accounting Changes in Interim Financial Statements (an amendment of *APB Opinion 23*)
4	Mar.	1975	Reporting Gains and Losses from Extinguishment of Debt
5	Mar.	1975	Accounting for Contingencies
6	May	1975	Classification of Short-Term Obligations Expected to Be Refinanced
7	June	1975	Accounting and Reporting by Development Stage Enterprises
8	Oct.	1975	Accounting for the Translation of Foreign Currency Transactions and Foreign Currency Financial Statements
9	Oct.	1975	Accounting for Income Taxes: Oil and Gas Producing Companies (an amendment of *APB Opinions 11* and *23*)
10	Oct.	1975	Extension of "Grandfather" Provisions for Business Combinations (an amendment of *APB Opinion 16*)
11	Dec.	1975	Accounting for Contingencies: Transition Method (an amendment of *FASB Statement 5*)
12	Dec.	1975	Accounting for Certain Marketable Securities
13	Nov.	1976	Accounting for Leases
14	Dec.	1976	Financial Reporting for Segments of a Business Enterprise
15	June	1977	Accounting by Debtors and Creditors for Troubled Debt Restructurings
16	June	1977	Prior Period Adjustments
17	Nov.	1977	Accounting for Leases: Initial Direct Costs (an amendment of *FASB Statement 13*)
18	Nov.	1977	Financial Reporting for Segments of a Business Enterprise—Interim Financial Statements (an amendment of *FASB Statement 14*)
19	Dec.	1977	Financial Accounting and Reporting by Oil and Gas Producing Companies
20	Dec.	1977	Accounting for Forward Exchange Contracts (an amendment of *FASB Statement 8*)
21	Apr.	1978	Suspension of the Reporting of Earnings per Share and Segment Information by Nonpublic Enterprises (an amendment of *APB Opinion 15* and *FASB Statement 14*)
22	June	1978	Changes in the Provisions of Lease Agreements Resulting from Refundings of Tax-Exempt Debt (an amendment of *FASB Statement 13*)
23	Aug.	1978	Inception of the Lease (an amendment of *FASB Statement 13*)
24	Dec.	1978	Reporting Segment Information in Financial Statements that Are Presented in Another Enterprises's Financial Report (an amendment of *FASB Statement 14*)
25	Feb.	1979	Suspension of Certain Accounting Requirements for Oil and Gas Companies (an amendment of *FASB Statement 19*)
26	Apr.	1979	Profit Recognition on Sales-Type Leases of Real Estate (an amendment of *FASB Statement 13*)
27	May	1979	Classification of Renewals or Extension of Existing Sales-Type or Direct Financing Leases (an amendment of *FASB Statement 13*)
28	May	1979	Accounting for Sales with Leasebacks (an amendment of *FASB Statement 13*)
29	June	1979	Determining Contingent Rentals (an amendment of *FASB Statement 13*)
30	Aug.	1979	Disclosure of Information about Major Customers (an amendment of *FASB Statement 14*)
31	Sept.	1979	Accounting for Tax Benefits Related to U.K. Tax Legislation Concerning Stock Relief
32	Sept.	1979	Specialized Accounting and Reporting Principles and Practices in AICPA Statements of Position and Guides on Accounting and Auditing Matters (an amendment of *APB Opinion 20*)
33	Sept.	1979	Financial Reporting and Changing Prices Illustrations of Financial Reporting and Changing Prices
34	Oct.	1979	Capitalization of Interest Cost

SFAS No.	Date Issued		Financial Accounting Standards Board (FASB), *Statements of Financial Accounting Standards* (1973–97)
35	Mar.	1980	Accounting and Reporting by Defined Benefit Pension Plans
36	May	1980	Disclosure of Pension Information (an amendment of *APB Opinion 8*)
37	July	1980	Balance Sheet Classification of Deferred Income Taxes (an amendment of *APB Opinion 11*)
38	Sept.	1980	Accounting for Preacquisition Contingencies of Purchased Enterprises (an amendment of *APB Opinion 16*)
39	Oct.	1980	Financial Reporting and Changing Prices: Specialized Assets—Mining and Oil and Gas (a supplement to *FASB Statement 33*)
40	Nov.	1980	Financial Reporting and Changing Prices: Specialized Assets—Timberlands and Growing Timber (a supplement to *FASB Statement 33*)
41	Nov.	1980	Financial Reporting and Changing Prices: Specialized Assets—Income-Producing Real Estate (a supplement to *FASB Statement 33*)
42	Nov.	1980	Determining Materiality for Capitalization of Interest Cost (an amendment for *FASB Statement 34*)
43	Nov.	1980	Accounting for Compensated Absences
44	Dec.	1980	Accounting for Intangible Assets of Motor Carriers (an amendment of Chapter 5 of *ARB 43*, and an interpretation of *APB Opinions 17* and *30*)
45	Mar.	1981	Accounting for Franchise Fee Revenue
46	Mar.	1981	Financial Reporting and Changing Prices: Motion Picture Films
47	Mar.	1981	Disclosure of Long-Term Obligations
48	June	1981	Revenue Recognition When Right of Returns Exists
49	June	1981	Accounting for Product Financing Arrangements
50	Nov.	1981	Financial Reporting in the Record and Music Industry
51	Nov.	1981	Financial Reporting by Cable Television Companies
52	Dec.	1981	Foreign Currency Translation
53	Dec.	1981	Financial Reporting by Producers and Distributors of Motion Picture Films
54	Jan.	1982	Financial Reporting and Changing Prices: Investment Companies (an amendment of *FASB Statement 33*)
55	Feb.	1982	Determining Whether a Convertible Security Is a Common Stock Equivalent (an amendment of *APB Opinion 15*)
56	Feb.	1982	Designation of AICPA Guide and SOP 81–1 on Contractor Accounting and SOP 81–2 on Hospital-Related Organizations as Preferable for Applying *APB Opinion 20* (an amendment of *FASB Statement 32*)
57	Mar.	1982	Related Party Disclosures
58	April	1982	Capitalization of Interest Cost in Financial Statements that Include Investments Accounted for by the Equity Method (an amendment of *FASB Statement 34*)
59	April	1982	Deferral of the Effective Date of Certain Accounting Requirements for Revision Plans of State and Local Government Units (an amendment of *FASB Statement 35*)
60	June	1982	Accounting and Reporting by Insurance Enterprises
61	June	1982	Accounting for Title Plant
62	June	1982	Capitalization of Interest in Situations Involving Certain Tax-Exempt Borrowings and Certain Gifts and Grants (an amendment of *FASB Statement 34*)
63	June	1982	Financial Reporting by Broadcasters
64	Sept.	1982	Extinguishment of Debt Made to Satisfy Sinking Fund Requirements (an amendment of *FASB Statement 4*)
65	Sept.	1982	Accounting for Certain Mortgage Bank Activities
66	Oct.	1982	Accounting for Sales on Real Estate
67	Oct.	1982	Accounting for Costs and Initial Rental Operations of Real Estate Projects
68	Oct.	1982	Research and Development Arrangements
69	Nov.	1982	Disclosures about Oil and Gas Producing Activities (an amendment of *FASB Statements 19, 25, 33,* and *39*)
70	Dec.	1982	Financial Reporting and Changing Prices: Foreign Currency Translation (an amendment of *FASB Statement 33*)
71	Dec.	1982	Accounting for the Effects of Certain Types of Regulation
72	Feb.	1983	Accounting for Certain Acquisitions of Banking or Thrift Institutions (an amendment of *APB Opinion 17*, an interpretation of *APB Opinions 16* and *17*, and an amendment of *FASB Interpretation 9*)
73	Aug.	1983	Reporting a Change in Accounting for Railroad Track Structures (an amendment of *APB Opinion 20*)
74	Aug.	1983	Accounting for Special Termination Benefits Paid to Employees
75	Nov.	1983	Deferral of the Effective Date of Certain Accounting Requirements for Pension Plans of State and Local Governmental Units (an amendment of *FASB Statement 35*)
76	Nov.	1983	Extinguishment of Debt (an amendment of *APB Opinion 26*)
77	Dec.	1983	Reporting by Transferors for Transfers of Receivables with Recourse
78	Dec.	1983	Classification of Obligations that Are Callable by the Creditor (an amendment of *ARB 43*, Chapter 3A)
79	Feb.	1984	Elimination of Certain Disclosures for Business Combinations by Nonpublic Enterprises (an amendment of *APB Opinion 16*)
80	Aug.	1984	Accounting for Futures Contracts
81	Nov.	1984	Disclosure of Postretirement Health Care and Life Insurance Benefits
82	Nov.	1984	Financial Reporting and Changing Prices: Elimination of Certain Disclosures (an amendment of *FASB Statement 33*)
83	Mar.	1985	Designation of AICPA Guides and Statement of Position on Accounting by Brokers and Dealers in Securities, by Employee Benefit Plans, and by Banks as Preferable for Purposes of Applying *APB Opinion 20* (an amendment of *FASB Statement 32* and *APB Opinion 30,* and a rescission of *FASB Interpretation 10*)
84	Mar.	1985	Induced Conversions of Convertible Debt (an amendment of *APB Opinion 26*)

INTERMEDIATE ACCOUNTING

VOLUME II

The Irwin/McGraw-Hill Series in Intermediate Accounting and Financial Reporting

Brownlee, Ferris, and Haskins
Corporate Financial Reporting: Text and Cases
Third Edition

Chasteen, Flaherty, and O'Connor
Intermediate Accounting
Sixth Edition

Dyckman, Dukes, and Davis
Intermediate Accounting
Fourth Edition

Ferris
Financial Accounting and Corporate Reporting: A Casebook
Fourth Edition

Hawkins
Corporate Financial Reporting and Analysis: Text and Cases
Fourth Edition

Louwers and Pasewark
Athletronics, Inc.: A Practice Set for Intermediate Accounting

Mansuetti and Weidkamp
Wild Goose Marina, Inc.
Second Edition

Smith and Birney
Interactive Intermediate Accounting Lab
Second Edition

Spiceland and Sepe
Intermediate Accounting

Zeff and Dharan
Readings and Notes on Financial Accounting: Issues and Controversies
Fifth Edition

To place an order or for more information, call our Customer Service Department at (800) 338-3987 or visit us at
http://www.mhhe.com/business/accounting/

INTERMEDIATE ACCOUNTING

Fourth Edition

Volume II

Thomas R. Dyckman

Ann Whitney Olin Professor of Accounting
Cornell University

Roland E. Dukes

University of Washington

Charles J. Davis

California State University—Sacramento

Boston   Burr Ridge, IL   Dubuque, IA   Madison, WI   New York   San Francisco   St. Louis
Bangkok   Bogotá   Caracas   Lisbon   London   Madrid
Mexico City   Milan   New Delhi   Seoul   Singapore   Sydney   Taipei   Toronto

To our wives and families:
Ann, Daniel, James, Linda, David
Phyllis, Peter, Anna
Susan, Nicole, Michael

Irwin/McGraw-Hill

A Division of The McGraw-Hill Companies

INTERMEDIATE ACCOUNTING

This book is printed on acid-free paper.

1 2 3 4 5 7 8 9 0 VNH/VNH 9 0 9 8 7 (USE)
1 2 3 4 5 7 8 9 0 VNH/VNH 9 0 9 8 7 (ISE)

ISBN 0-256-16825-3 (combined volume)
ISBN 0-256-16864-4 (volume I)
ISBN 0-256-16867-9 (volume II)

Vice president and editorial director: *Michael W. Junior*
Publisher: *Jeffrey J. Shelstad*
Sponsoring editor: *George Werthman*
Developmental editor: *Tracey Klein Douglas*
Marketing manager: *Heather L. Woods*
Project manager: *Paula M. Buschman*
Production supervisor: *Karen Thigpen*
Senior designer: *Laurie J. Entringer*
Compositor: *GTS Graphics, Inc.*
Typeface: *10/12 Times Roman*
Printer: *Von Hoffmann Press, Inc.*

Library of Congress Cataloging-in-Publication Data

Dyckman, Thomas R.
    Intermediate accounting / Thomas R. Dyckman, Roland E. Dukes,
Charles J. Davis.—4th ed.
        p. cm.—(The Irwin/McGraw-Hill series in intermediate
accounting and financial reporting)
    Includes bibliographical references and indexes.
    ISBN 0-256-16825-3 (alk. paper)
    1. Accounting.   I. Dukes, Roland E.   II. Davis, Charles Joseph.
1950-   III. Title.   IV. Series.
HF5635.D985   1998
657'.044—dc21   97-25532

INTERNATIONAL EDITION

When ordering the title, use ISBN 0-07-115237-7.

http://www.mhhe.com

ABOUT THE AUTHORS

Thomas R. Dyckman, Ph.D., is Ann Whitney Olin Professor of Accounting and Quantitative Analysis and Associate Dean for Academic Affairs at Cornell University's Johnson Graduate School of Management. In addition to teaching accounting and quantitative analysis, he teaches in Cornell's Executive Development Program. He earned his doctorate degree from the University of Michigan.

He is a former member of the Financial Accounting Standards Board Advisory Committee and the Financial Accounting Foundation, which oversees the FASB. He was president of the American Accounting Association in 1982 and received the association's *Outstanding Educator Award* for the year 1987. He also received the AICPA's *Notable Contributions to Accounting Literature Award* in 1966 and 1977.

Professor Dyckman has extensive industrial experience that includes work with the U.S. Navy and IBM. He has conducted seminars for Cornell Executive Development Program and Managing the Next Generation of Technology, as well as for Ocean Spray, Goodyear, Morgan Guaranty, GTE, Southern New England Telephone, and Goulds Pumps.

Professor Dyckman has coauthored several books and written over 50 journal articles on topics from financial markets to the application of quantitative and behavioral theory to administrative decision making. He has been a member of the editorial boards of *The Accounting Review, The Journal of Finance and Quantitative Analysis, The Journal of Accounting and Economics, The Journal of Management Accounting Research,* and *The Journal of Accounting Education.*

Roland E. (Pete) Dukes, Ph.D., is professor of accounting at the University of Washington where he teaches intermediate and advanced financial accounting at the undergraduate and graduate levels. He has served as chairman of the department of accounting from 1983 to 1992. He received his doctorate from Stanford University.

A member of the American Accounting Association, Professor Dukes has chaired the Annual Meeting Technical Program Planning Committee, the Doctoral Consortium Committee, the Notable Contribution to Accounting Literature Committee, and the Corporate Accounting Policy Seminar Committee. He has also served as a Distinguished Visiting Faculty for the Doctoral Consortium, as Director of the Doctoral Consortium, and as the Puget Power Affiliate Program Professor of Accounting at the University of Washington from 1986 to 1990. In 1993, Professor Dukes was named the William R. Gregory Accounting Faculty Fellow at the University of Washington.

Professor Dukes has published numerous articles in accounting journals, including *The Accounting Review, Journal of Accounting Research,* and the *Journal of Accountancy.* He has served on the editorial boards of *The Accounting Review, Journal of Accounting Research,* and *Journal of Accounting Literature.* He has been a consultant to the Financial Accounting Standards Board and authored the *FASB Research Report,* which investigated the effect of *SFAS No. 8* on security return behavior. Professor Dukes also has served as a consultant to the Securities and Exchange Commission and to industry and government.

Charles J. Davis, Ph.D., C.P.A., is professor of accounting at California State University, Sacramento, and has served as Department Chair. He received his doctorate in accounting from the University of Illinois at Urbana.

Professor Davis has taught in the areas of financial and managerial accounting and auditing at both the intermediate and advanced levels. He has also been active in CPA review programs and has taught internationally. Professor Davis received excellence in teaching awards from both the University of Illinois at Urbana and California State University, Sacramento. In addition, he has been active in student accounting groups on campus.

Professor Davis has written journal articles in accounting and related business fields that appear in *Advances in Accounting, Issues in Accounting Education, Journal of Accounting and Public Policy,* in several health-care fiscal management journals, and in international accounting journals. He worked as a staff auditor for Peat, Marwick, Mitchell and Company and has served as a consultant to industry and government. Professor Davis is a member of the American Accounting Association.

INTRODUCTION

We continue to revise *Intermediate Accounting* with the student in mind. Our mission is to present critical concepts in a clear, concise way that is most helpful to learning and to enhancing the student's interest. The major changes we have made have this goal in mind. This revision was driven by extensive research into the preferences of current users as well as faculty who were not adopters of the *Third Edition* of this text. Instructors tell us they prefer a text that is user-friendly and that fosters the learning process.

We believe this edition reflects the views of both non-adopters and our faithful group of repeat users. We have learned a great deal. We thank them for their support and their suggestions. Our hope is that our text truly is a book that students will want to read and one from which they will learn a great deal.

As the authors of this text, we have put our many years of practical experience in teaching intermediate accounting to work in designing what we feel is an outstanding text for intermediate accounting. We have learned what works and what does not in the classroom and have exercised special care when covering those areas that are especially troubling for students. We involve the student in the learning process by developing the logic for important and controversial principles and by integrating real-world examples of financial reporting into the text.

By starting each chapter with a short introduction involving the main issues of the chapter in a real-world context, we first catch the student's interest and then hold it to the end of the chapter. We welcome your comments on how to improve continually the learning process for our students and add value for our adopters.

OVERALL OBJECTIVES AND CHANGES FOR THE FOURTH EDITION

The fourth edition builds on the foundation of the third edition and maintains its:

- Comprehensive and up-to-date coverage of accounting principles.
- Use of examples to illustrate procedure.
- Clear writing style.
- Thorough end-of-chapter material.
- Emphasis on critical thinking.
- Real-world emphasis in both text and end-of-chapter material.
- Flexible organizational structure.
- Diverse set of pedagogical features.

Curriculum Concerns   We believe that the curriculum should continue to respond to issues pertaining to encouraging students to learn how to learn. Rather than emphasize rote learning of rules and regulations, we underscore how important it is for users and preparers of financial statements to understand accounting principles and how they are applied in financial reporting decisions. We also believe that without a firm grounding in accounting principles, the more user-oriented features would be of little value. Once the basics are internalized, the focus is on the process of inquiry in which the student learns to identify problem situations, search for relevant information, analyze and interpret the information, and reach valid conclusions.

The text presents GAAP as the current solution to a continually evolving host of financial reporting questions. By acquainting the student with the political nature of standard setting, the reader becomes aware that both users and preparers are affected by the outcome of the standard-setting process. Therefore each of us should have input into the deliberations that establish reporting standards. A fair number of the end-of-chapter cases require students to adopt this perspective in making recommendations on reporting issues. We hope this text stimulates a more interactive and involved learning process on the part of students as they learn.

Appearance and Exposition   The design of this text should make reading and learning more interesting and pleasant for the student. More important, we have made much greater use of examples, diagrams, tables, flowcharts, and other visuals in an effort to use graphical material as much as possible in place of pure textual discussion to facilitate the learning process. A short example is often better than using a verbal approach. We have introduced the "Crystal Clear Connections" icon to show the integration of critical topics throughout the text.

We have found in our teaching that visual aids and examples help students get over the initial introduction to new material, increase their interest and enthusiasm, and improve retention. Use of graphical material also is more efficient in terms of the space required to present a concept. The interaction of several components of a complex procedure often is more easily assimilated visually. You will find fewer long paragraphs compared to earlier editions, and fewer pages without page breaks of some kind.

Critical Chapters   From discussions with our reviewer panel and colleagues at several universities across the country, we have identified eight topics that are critical to understanding intermediate accounting. These are integrated throughout the text and clearly indicated by the use of linking icons. The topics are *cash flows, pensions, inventory, leases, revenue recognition, taxes, bonds,* and *earnings per share* and are concentrated in nine chapters:

Chapter	Topic
7	Revenue Recognition
10	Inventory, Alternative Valuation Methods
14	Investments in Debt and Equity Securities
16	Long-Term Liabilities
17	Accounting for Leases
18	Accounting for Pensions
19	Accounting for Income Taxes
22	Earnings per Share
23	Statement of Cash Flows

We have made a special effort in these chapters to proceed from the less difficult and more conceptual material to the more complex procedural and technical material. Our aim here is to build the student's confidence while emphasizing the conceptual and theoretical underpinnings. We believe that with this foundation, the student is better equipped to tackle the more difficult accounting procedures and longer examples that characterize the material in each of these chapters. An added benefit of this approach is that instructors who wish to deemphasize the more complex mechanics of applying GAAP to practical situations may do so without compromising accounting theory. To provide complete coverage and to help students master the more difficult technical material, we have added a number of review problems after major sections within each of these chapters.

User Emphasis   Where appropriate, we have added a short section on financial ratio effects to selected chapters. Rather than devote an entire chapter to financial statement analysis and the use of financial statement information (as was the case in a previous edition of this text), we have integrated the discussion of ratios in relevant chapters. By integrating ratio coverage and specific GAAP, we are able to discuss the effects of GAAP choices and other aspects of financial reporting in a more dynamic context. We believe that the student will learn more about the usefulness and limitations of ratios while simultaneously studying the major substantive issues of a chapter.

Up-to-Date Coverage   Another goal of this edition is to maintain up-to-date and comprehensive coverage of accounting principles while not significantly increasing the size of the text. The coverage of relevant professional pronouncements is current as of the date of publication. It includes discussion of all recently published FASB statements and exposure drafts that affect intermediate accounting. However, while recognizing the necessity of maintaining comprehensive coverage, the realities of the marketplace and the ever-increasing number of professional standards have caused us to reevaluate the relative importance of certain topics, resulting in some deletions and reductions of coverage in other areas.

In addition, we have updated most introductions, often shortening them to focus on the chapter issues within a real-world context. Most of the real-world examples within the text and end-of-chapter material have been updated. Global views were rewritten where necessary to reflect major changes in international accounting.

End-of-Chapter Material   The problem material for each chapter has been reordered and organized into two parts:

Part I: Understanding and Applying Concepts and Standards.

This part includes questions, exercises, and problems and stresses the basic understanding of relevant GAAP and application of those standards. These items typically are more staightforward and structured than those in Part II.

Part II: Analysis, Judgment, and Communication

This part includes cases, financial statement analysis problems, and comparative analysis problems. As such, this part of the end-of-chapter material stresses more open-ended situations, writing, and real-world contexts. One of the benefits of real-world problems is that students are exposed to more complex and realistic situations. These contexts often do not lend themselves as readily to solution as do the items in Part I. Significant exposure to this type of material is, we believe, an important part of the education of an accountant.

Specific end-of-chapter changes include:

1. **Quantity of items.**   In the nine chapters designated as critical chapters, we have added several more exercises and problems, with particular emphasis on the application of GAAP and required procedures. With the addition of these exercises and problems, our text should exceed the coverage in other intermediate texts in terms of the quantity and variety of end-of-chapter material. Other exercises and problems, and especially our cases and analysis problems probe more conceptual issues.

For all chapters, completely new items have been added, both in areas for which accounting principles have changed and in areas where they haven't. In addition, roughly one-quarter of existing items that were retained have been modified so that the previous homework solution will no longer apply. This should help ease the transition to this edition. We are grateful to Professor Loyd Heath of the University of Washington who contributed problems to selected chapters. His problems are typically longer writing cases involving more complex financial reporting situations.

2. **Financial statement analysis.**   Several problems addressing ratio analysis and financial statement analysis have been added. A common theme of these problems is to ask the student to address the effects of alternative

measurement choices on financial ratios. These problems require a broader knowledge of the effects of GAAP choice because aggregate measures typically are involved in the ratios considered in these problems. These ratio problems complement the chapters that have sections devoted to ratio analysis in them, but also appear in other chapters.

3. **Comparative analysis.** We have added more comparative financial statement problems in response to favorable comments by adopters. These items address specific aspects of accounting principles within the chapter by comparing the reporting practices of two firms, often in the same industry. More chapters now have a comparative problem, and some have more than one. We have found that the comparative problem is a convenient avenue to discuss GAAP choice, ratios, and other aspects of financial statement analysis in a real-world context.

4. **Group items.** We have added new items and modified some of the longer, existing items that are conducive to a team solution. The goal of these problems is to encourage students to work together, share ideas, and learn from one another.

We suggest that the instructor plan the group work before assigning these items. For example, the instructor can assign primary responsibility for one part of these items to each class group. Each group then reports to the class. Each group also should be aware of the remaining parts of the problem and evaluate other groups' reports. Another strategy for group application is for each group to perform all parts of each item, then have the leader of each group provide a brief report on the answer. After each group reports, the groups re-form and discuss the aspects of the discussion they missed, and what aspects they alone discovered. For additional strategies on group work, see Peek, Winking, and Peek, "Cooperative Learning Activities: Managerial Accounting," *Issues in Accounting Education,* Spring 1995, v. 10, no. 1, pp. 111–25.

5. **World Wide Web Problems.** In a few selected chapters we have added problems that make use of the World Wide Web portion of the Internet. As such, students can put the Web to work in the context of an intermediate accounting issue. These problems provide an important exposure to actual financial statements because the entire statement is at their disposal. None of the data is given in the text. The student retrieves the 10-K report of the firm identified in the problem from the SEC's EDGAR database. The solutions given in the answer manual reflect the most recent statements available. We would appreciate your comments on this and other possible uses of information technology for improving the text.

6. **Accuracy.** We have checked and rechecked each end-of-chapter item. In addition, to increase the accuracy of the problems and solutions, Jim Emig of Villanova University checked each item independently. We are confident that you will find the text essentially error-free.

TOPICAL CHANGES IN THE FOURTH EDITION

Along with the overall changes in this edition, the fourth edition has been updated to reflect changes in accounting and reporting principles since the previous edition and to fine-tune the coverage. The following list highlights the substantive changes made to each chapter.

Chapter 2   *Conceptual Framework*
A new Global View covering the IASC's conceptual framework has been added which compares and contrasts the U.S. and international frameworks. A new appendix on comprehensive income, currently on the FASB's agenda, replaces the Future Directions Appendix.

Chapter 3   *Accounting Cycle*
A new section explaining in greater detail the differences between the cash and accrual bases of accounting has been added. This section appears near the adjusting entry section and reinforces the importance of the adjusting process. The discussion also explains how concepts from Chapter 2, Conceptual Framework, affect the more procedural recording process.

Chapter 4   *Income Statement*
The section on accounting for discontinued operations has been rewritten to clarify when gains and losses on disposal are recognized. The sections dealing with multiple versus single-step reporting formats have been condensed. We added a short discussion of the Jenkins Committee report and its possible implications for changes in the income statement. In addition, a number of new analysis problems have been added.

Chapter 5   *Balance Sheet and Statement of Cash Flows*
A new section on ratio analysis has been added and illustrates how balance sheet and income statement information is used by analysts in developing several types of financial ratios.

Chapter 7   *Revenue Recognition*
The chapter has been reorganized to focus attention earlier on accounting for long-term contracts. This change reflects the relative importance of the topic. The section has been supplemented with more analysis and examples.

Chapter 8   *Cash and Receivables*
This chapter includes newly written material covering relevant portions of two new pronouncements: *SFAS No. 125,* "Accounting for Transfers and Servicing of Financial Assets and Extinguishments of Liabilities," and *SFAS No. 118,* "Accounting by Creditors for Impairment of a Loan." The discussion and examples on factoring with recourse have been changed to reflect the new criteria for determining when a transfer of financial assets is recorded as a sale or as a loan *(SFAS No. 125).* The section on loan impairments also was revised to accommodate the choices now open to creditors for recognizing interest revenue on impaired loans *(SFAS No. 118).* New examples were added to illustrate these recognition choices.

Chapter 9 *Inventory*
The example applying LIFO in a perpetual inventory system has been removed. The discussion on LIFO liquidation has been extended. The DV-LIFO section has been rewritten and now includes both a simple and a more involved example.

Chapter 11 *Plant Assets*
This chapter was modified significantly in two areas. First, the FASB Exposure Draft "Accounting for Certain Liabilities Related to Closure and Removal of Long-Lived Assets" has been incorporated into the early part of the chapter. This proposed standard would alter the amount capitalized for assets requiring significant closure costs and require liability recognition. A section on the effect of capitalized interest on financial ratios has been added. This material enhances the discussion of the effect of interest capitalization on the quality of earnings. The material on exchanges of plant assets was rewritten to replace the "tentative" gain discussion on similar assets with a method we believe is easier to follow and more consistent with general accounting principles.

Chapter 12 *Depreciation*
A section on financial ratios contrasts the effects of straight-line and accelerated depreciation methods on profitability ratios including rate of return on assets and equity. A discussion on early warning disclosures incorporates material from AICPA *SOP 94-6*, "Disclosure of Certain Significant Risks and Uncertainties," which requires disclosure of information about risk-related items including uncertainties and the use of estimates in financial statements. The most significant change in the chapter is the incorporation of *SFAS No. 121*, "Accounting for the Impairment of Long-Lived Assets and for Long-Lived Assets to Be Disposed Of." Related to this discussion is another new section about restructuring charges which highlight a recent EITF ruling on accounting for these costs.

Two structural changes include (1) placement of casualty insurance losses (coinsurance) into an appendix and (2) the addition of a new appendix on the effects of price-level changes on financial statements. This short appendix restores material that had been removed from the previous edition and emphasizes the effects of inflation. We chose Chapter 12 as the appropriate place for this material because of the relatively large effect of price-level changes on depreciation expense, and therefore on earnings and total assets. Purchasing power gains and losses from holding monetary items also are discussed.

Chapter 13 *Intangible Assets*
The section on measuring and accounting for goodwill has been rewritten to clarify measurement issues and to illustrate accounting for goodwill. The section on restoration costs has been de-emphasized because it is covered in detail in Chapter 11. More end-of-chapter exercises and problems have been added dealing with accounting for computer software development costs.

Chapter 14 *Investments*
New material on disclosures for financial instruments has been added to correspond with *SFAS No. 119*, "Disclosure about Derivative Financial Instruments and Fair Value of Financial Instruments." A new appendix on how financial instruments are used in managing risk highlights options, futures, and swaps. A new example illustrating how derivatives can be used to reduce the risk of foreign currency exchange rate fluctuations, commodity price changes, and interest rate fluctuations brings the area to life and explains the incentives for both parties in these transactions.

Chapter 16 *Long-Term Liabilities*
The section of the chapter discussing debt retirement has been modified to incorporate *SFAS No. 125*'s new definition of what constitutes an extinguishment of debt. For example, in-substance defeasance no longer meets the definition. Also, Appendix A on troubled debt restructure and Appendix C on debt securities held to maturity were modified to reflect changes brought about by *SFAS Nos. 118, 121,* and *125.*

Chapter 17 *Leases*
Appendices A and B are now combined and include only leases involving land and buildings, as well as leveraged leases.

Chapter 18 *Pensions*
A new summary diagram was added early in the chapter as a big picture of the major issues in pension accounting and includes the important effects on financial statements and a summary of the journal entries required each period. The summary allows students to keep in mind the overall objective of pension accounting as the details are studied. The sections on component five of pension expense (pension gains and losses) and additional minimum pension liability were completely rewritten with simplification in mind. New examples have been added to explain the effect of gains and losses on pension expense and how amounts are rolled forward to future periods without being amortized. The alternative approach to computing pension expense, involving the use of actual return on plan assets, has been deemphasized.

Chapter 19 *Income Taxes*
This chapter has been rewritten and reorganized to emphasize the conceptual underpinnings of interperiod tax allocation with new and shorter examples. The approach uses a step-by-step method leading to the tax accrual entry. Each new issue is addressed separately before merging several concepts together. The more complex examples are placed later in the chapter. The valuation allowance is not introduced until later in the chapter for example. Several new examples are added to complement the new organization.

The conceptual basis for each aspect of interperiod tax allocation is fully developed.

Chapter 20　*Contributed Capital*

A new section on financial statement analysis has been added. This section discusses the use of ratios involving owners' equity in the evaluation of a firm's performance and risk. The use of leverage as measured by debt to equity ratios is examined. The uses and limitations of book value per share also are discussed.

Chapter 21　*Retained Earnings*

A major rewrite of this chapter covers accounting for compensation-based stock options in accordance with *SFAS No. 123.* Coverage of stock appreciation rights is clarified. The discussion on alternative ways to account for stock splits and stock dividends has been rewritten.

Chapter 22　*Earnings per Share*

This chapter underwent the most significant change as a result of the adoption of *SFAS No. 128,* "Earnings per Share and Disclosure of Information about Capital Structure." The new standard replaces primary and fully diluted EPS with basic (historical) EPS and diluted EPS (reflecting full dilution). EPS no longer involves common stock equivalency testing. The chapter uses completely new examples to illustrate the new reporting requirements. The cooperation between the FASB and IASC aimed at achieving greater cross-border agreement in EPS reporting is briefly discussed in a global view. The end-of-chapter material also incorporates the proposed new standard and is completely revised.

Chapter 23　*Statement of Cash Flows*

The similarities and differences between the direct and indirect methods of presenting the statement of cash flows have been clarified. In particular, the logic underlying the determination of items to include in the operating activities section for both methods has been improved. The student is walked-through several examples of operating items and is shown how to report the resulting cash flows in the direct method operating section as well as in the reconciliation of earnings and operating cash flows. This is probably the most challenging aspect of preparing the statement for students.

Chapter 24　*Accounting Changes*

To emphasize the major concepts, less involved examples of current and retroactive changes, as well as error corrections were placed in the first half of the chapter. Once the student learns the overall goal of reporting for accounting changes, they can proceed to longer, more complex examples involving comparative statements which now appear in the latter half of the chapter. Instructors may wish to limit the coverage of the chapter to the more basic material. In this way, the student will learn the most important material without struggling through the longer examples.

Chapter 25　*Special Topics*

The growing importance of line-of-business reporting highlights the new version of this chapter. We also have added a brief discussion of the Jenkins Committee report and its implications for financial reporting.

▌KEY PEDAGOGICAL FEATURES

We continue many of the pedagogical features from our previous edition that have received positive reviews from current adopters. The purpose of these features is to facilitate the learning process and to provide variety in the text and end-of-chapter material. Also, the previous section on changes to the fourth edition highlights several more. A brief discussion of each follows. Many of these are denoted with an icon, in either the text or end-of-chapter material. The icons for those features are shown in the list below.

Text Features

Crystal Clear Connections.　Extensive customer research has driven the fourth edition, resulting in clearer presentation of topics determined to be difficult for students. A new icon clearly indicates the integrated treatment of topics throughout the text.

Ratio Analysis.　Sections covering ratio and financial statement analysis in selected chapters integrate the effects of major accounting principle choices on financial ratios. This feature is discussed in greater length in the section on changes to the fourth edition.

Review Problems.　Each chapter ends with a solved review problem to provide additional practice on the technical aspects in that chapter. In addition, the nine critical chapters also have review problems after each major section, adding further reinforcement to more complex topics.

Real-World Examples.　We use examples of financial reporting practices of actual companies throughout the text. These examples not only place the subject matter squarely in the real world but also illustrate how firms interpret GAAP and put these principles into practice. To catch the student's interest, we start each chapter with a short introduction. The foundation of each is an example of an actual reporting situation. In addition, we make liberal use of the financial press including *The Wall Street Journal, Financial Executive,* and other publications. Frequent use of the AICPA's *Accounting Trends and Techniques* brings further real-world perspective to the text.

Coca-Cola Financial Statement.   The 1995 statements and footnotes of the Coca-Cola Company appear in an appendix to the text. This edition integrates these statements throughout the text discussion to a greater extent than the previous edition.

Global Views.   This boxed element provides insights into international accounting issues pertaining to main issues in the chapter. Students learn that most countries have their own set of accounting principles, that groups of countries such as the European Union have other principles, and that the International Accounting Standards Committee is yet another source for accounting principles.

On the Horizon.   This boxed element appears in several chapters and summarizes issues in progress and those that are just emerging. These elements connect to and extend the subject matter and remind the student that the process of generating accounting principles is never complete.

Concept Reviews.   To reinforce major concepts, we have placed three short review questions at the end of each major section of each chapter. The questions are answerable directly from the text and serve the same function as a short quiz. The answers are provided in the solutions manual for the convenience of the instructor.

Learning Objectives.   Each chapter starts with a list of the objectives for the chapter. The objectives are the key recognition, measurement, and reporting issues for the chapter area. The summaries and end-of-chapter material are tied back to the learning objectives.

Summary of Key Points.   Each chapter ends with a list of major points discussed in the chapter. The summary is in list form. Each is keyed to the appropriate learning objective from the beginning of the chapter.

End-of-Chapter Material Features

Ratio Problems.   Many chapters have one or more problems or exercises that require the student to analyze the effect of major measurement rules and GAAP choices on ratios most affected by the rules and choices. We believe a more meaningful coverage of ratios is possible by integrating the coverage of ratios throughout the chapters. A closer linking of topical area with relevant ratios is thereby achieved.

Comparative Analysis.   These problems appear in many of the chapters and use excerpts from the financial statements of two or more firms to highlight different measurement and reporting practices. These also provide a context for financial statement analysis including the use of ratios.

Group Problems.   Many chapters use longer problems and cases as a context for group work. This feature is discussed in greater length in the section on changes to the fourth edition.

Analysis of Financial Statements.   Several of these problems appear in almost every chapter and help bring the subject matter to life within the context of an actual firm. These typically are less structured and the data is less organized relative to the exercises and problems in Part I of the end-of-chapter material.

Comprehensive Problems.   Found in most chapters, these problems cover several of the chapter's learning objectives and bring together several issues in one problem. These problems help reduce the inherent modularization in coverage of intermediate accounting topics.

Writing Cases.   Appearing in every chapter, these cases require students to write specific documents such as memos and reports. The solutions to several of the writing cases have been rewritten to exemplify a more conversational tone and to add realism to the exchange of ideas between the writer and the audience.

You Make the Call.   These appear in several chapters and present a reporting issue that either has yet to be considered by the FASB or one that continues to provide an excellent context for students to develop their own analysis of the appropriate accounting treatment.

Ethics Problems.   These cases appear in several chapters and focus on the ethical implications of particular actions and reporting decisions.

Coca-Cola Problems.   Similar to Analysis of Financial Statement problems, these problems use the Coke financial statements as the database. Often, these items are more involved because we can draw on a much larger database of financial statement and footnote information. Also, more years of data are present than can be provided in other real-world problems in this text.

World Wide Web Problems.   The web provides the data for these problems similar to Analysis of Financial Statement problems. But like the Coca-Cola problems, a richer database can be used to develop more elaborate items. This feature is discussed in greater length in the section on changes to the fourth edition.

Spreadsheet Problems.   Called SPATS problems, these problems and exercises are designed to be solved with a computer spreadsheet. Templates are provided for these problems.

ANCILLARIES AND SUPPLEMENTARY MATERIALS

For the Professor:

We have provided you with two different ways to purchase *Intermediate Accounting.* You can purchase *Intermediate Accounting, Chapters 1–14 and Chapters 15–25* in two separate volumes, or *Chapters 1–25* in one volume.

Intermediate Accounting, Fourth Edition, offers numerous teaching aids to assist the instructor.

Solutions Manual, Chapters 1–14 and 15–25 Done in two volumes, this comprehensive solutions manual provides complete solutions and explanations for all end-of-chapter questions, cases, exercises, and problems. The estimated completion time for each item is given in the assignment assistance schedule at the beginning of each chapter. Answers to the concept review questions are included at the end of each volume of the solutions manual.

Test Bank, Chapters 1–14 and 15–25 Prepared by Doris deLespinasse of Adrian College and revised and expanded with this edition, the test bank offers approximately 4,000 questions and problems from which to choose in preparing examinations. This test bank contains true-false, short-answer, problems, and cases.

Solutions Transparencies, Chapters 1–14 and 15–25 Acetate transparencies of solutions to all exercises, problems, and cases are free to adopters. Now increased in clarity, these transparencies are especially useful when covering problems in large classroom settings.

Teaching Transparencies, Chapters 1–14 and 15–25 Selected lecture transparencies based on material from the textbook and based on material from outside the book.

Instructor's Resource Manual, Chapters 1–14 and 15–25 This manual includes overviews, learning objectives, lecture outlines, problem analysis, and transparency masters. It was prepared by Craig Bain, Northern Arizona University.

Computerized Testing Software This microcomputer test generator program allows the instructor to select and edit exam questions from the test bank database. Questions can be selected using several criteria, such as chapter, type of question (e.g., multiple choice, true-false, problem solving), and level of difficulty. The software is menu-driven, requiring little computer knowledge. It comes with a program disk, data disks containing the Test Bank database, and clearly written documentation. It provides password protection, can be used on a network, and is available on both 5.25″ and 3.5″ diskettes for IBM compatible microcomputers.

Teletest Irwin is happy to serve those customers without access to administrative support or a computer system. Simply choose your questions from the Test Bank and call Irwin/McGraw-Hill College New Media. By calling a toll free number, users can specify the content of exams and have a laser printed copy of the exam mailed to them within one day.

Ready Shows Ready Shows is a package of multimedia lecture enhancement aids that uses PowerPoint® software to illustrate chapter concepts.

The following item is intended for student use at the option of the instructors.

Spreadsheet Applications Template Software (SPATS) Selected exercises and problems in each chapter, identified by a spreadsheet symbol, can be solved using SPATS. The software contains innovatively designed templates based on Lotus 1-2-3 and includes a very effective Lotus 1-2-3 tutorial. SPATS is available on 5.25″ and 3.5″ disks. Upon adoption, this package is available for classroom or laboratory use.

For the Student:

Several support materials have been designed especially for the student.

Study Guides, Chapters 1–14 and Chapters 15–25 The study guides provide the student with a summarized look at each chapter's issues. Included are outlines, chapter overviews, key concepts, review questions, true-false, multiple choice questions, and critical thinking exercises. The study guides were prepared by Craig Bain of Northern Arizona University.

Working Papers, Chapters 1–14 and Chapters 15–25 Two sets of working papers are available for completing assigned problems and exercises. In many instances, the working papers are partially filled in to reduce the "pencil pushing" required to solve the problems, yet not so complete as to reduce the learning impact.

Manual Practice Set Video One Wholesalers, a manual practice set, can be assigned after Chapter 6 as a review of the accounting cycle.

Computer Supplement Wild Goose Marina, Inc. offers a complete corporate simulation and is intended for use after coverage of stocks, bonds, and cash flows. The corporate simulation is prepared by Leland Mansuetti and Keith Weidkamp, both of Sierra College.

Ready Notes This booklet of Ready Show screen printouts enables students to take notes during Ready Show presentations.

Check Figures A list of check figures for selected end-of-chapter items is available.

ACKNOWLEDGMENTS

This text would not have been possible without the help of a great many people. We recognize and appreciate all of their efforts.

We wish to thank our colleagues at Cornell University, the University of Washington, and California State University, Sacramento. We greatly appreciate the time they took to let us know of potential changes, improvements, and different ways of approaching certain topics. We also thank our outstanding faculty reviewer panel for this edition. Their comments and suggestions were instrumental in making the text more complete, accurate, and understandable. These reviewers are:

Jim Gray, *Northern Virginia Community College–Alexandria;* Barbara Greogrio, *Nassau Community College;* Loyd Heath, *University of Washington;* Doug Johnson, *Southeast Community College;* John Mills, *University of Nevada, Reno;* Craig Bain, *Northern Arizona University;* Charles Baril, *James Madison University;* Robert Brown, *Strayere College–Alexandria;* Dennis Coates, *Florida Atlantic University;* Parveen Gupta, *Lehigh University;* John Hillman, *Southwest Texas State University;* Ed Nelson, *University of New Hampshire;* Anthony George Petrie, *University of Texas-Pan Am;* Morton Pincus, *University of Iowa;* Will Snyder, *San Diego State University.*

We also wish to thank the reviewer panel who did such a fine job on the previous edition. These reviewers are:

Suzanne C. Abbe, *Baylor University;* Diane Adcox, *University of North Florida;* Michael D. Akers, *Marquette University;* W. David Albrecht, *Bowling Green State University;* Sudro Brown, *Suffolk University;* Mike Doran, *Iowa State University;* Kathy J. Dow, *Bentley College;* Jack R. Ethridge, *Stephen F. Austin State University;* Larry Falcetto, *Emporia State University;* Paul Foote, *California State University at Fullerton;* Sharron M. Graves, *Stephen F. Austin State University;* Chula G. King, *University of West Florida;* Susan A. Lynn, *University of Baltimore;* Emeka Ofobike, *University of Akron;* Herbert Olivera, *Towson State University;* Paul Schwinghammer, *Mankato State University;* Brian P. Shapiro, *University of Arizona;* David H. Sinason, *University of North Florida;* Loren K. Waldman, *Franklin University*

We would like to thank Jim Emig of Villanova University for his work in checking the end-of-chapter material. We are especially grateful for the assistance and support from the people at Irwin/McGraw-Hill. In particular, Tracey Douglas worked very hard as the developmental editor, keeping us on schedule and telling us when we were not. Tracey handled the manuscript and day-to-day details which kept us on course. Marc Chernoff also helped out with the details. We also thank Mark Pfaltzgraff and George Werthman for their efforts as sponsoring editors. Special thanks as well to Jeff Shelstad, publisher, and to Paula Buschman, the project manager. Finally, we thank Mike Junior, vice president and editorial director, whose vision and direction helped shape this edition.

The contributions of all these people have made it possible for us to feel confident in assuring you of the highest quality of this text.

Thomas R. Dyckman (trd2@cornell.edu)
Roland E. Dukes (rdukes@u.washington.edu)
Charles J. Davis (daviscj@csus.edu)

The most important goal of a text is to assist you in learning the material of the course. The learning process is more effective when the ideas are presented in real-world contexts. Thus, each chapter begins with an actual situation.

The subject matter of this book, financial accounting, is critically important to many of the major decisions made in this country and abroad. Financial accounting information impacts the decisions that lead to resource allocation, the distribution of wealth, and the comparative competitive strengths of firms, industries, and economies.

Financial accounting is the study of the public information that organizations publish about their economic performance. This information is disseminated to those outside the organization for evaluation and action. Investors decide which firms' stocks or bonds they will buy. Other organizations use the data to decide whether to acquire them. Unions use the data in contract negotiations. Governments develop tax and trade policies based in part on financial reporting information, and these are only a few of the major types of decisions that rely heavily on accounting data.

It is our aim to develop the subject matter of this area so that you will be aware of the types of information that are made available, the rules that govern its composition and disclosure, and the limitations to current financial reporting practice.

Financial reporting is a dynamic field. It is changing daily. Issues of comparability, relevance, reliability, and practicality underlie the choices that must be made in preparing financial statements. Critical thinking and judgment are essential. Ethical and international considerations are often involved. We will be considering all these issues in the chapters ahead and in the problems, cases, and exercises you will be asked to complete.

Our adventure through the window of this book into the world of financial accounting will, we hope, be exciting, challenging, and rewarding. With your instructor's help, you should be able to master the material soon to be placed at your fingertips. Let the voyage begin!

BRIEF CONTENTS

CONTENTS

OWNER'S EQUITY   1025

PART V

Special Topics   1185

23   Statement of Cash Flows   1186

24   Accounting Changes and Error Corrections   1259

25   Disclosures, Segment Reporting, and Interim Reporting   1303

III

LIABILITIES

15 SHORT-TERM LIABILITIES

LEARNING OBJECTIVES

After you have studied this chapter, you will:

1   Be able to define a liability and specify its characteristics.

2   Know how to distinguish short-term (current) from long-term liabilities.

3   Know when it is appropriate to recognize a liability in a firm's accounts and how to measure the amount to be recognized.

4   Understand the accounting for interest-bearing and noninterest-bearing current liabilities as well as how to treat notes with unrealistic interest rates.

5   Be able to explain why cash collected in advance of delivery of a good or service creates a liability for the firm.

6   Be able to properly account for the incurrence and payment of short-term liabilities.

7   Know what contingent and estimated liabilities are and the accounting appropriate to such liabilities.

INTRODUCTION

The first frequent flyer program was introduced by American Airlines in 1981. Today all major U.S. airlines, and many foreign ones (e.g., Kiwi International Air Lines introduced its first frequent flyer program September 9, 1996) offer similar programs. By early 1995, the estimate of free travel miles earned in the United States alone was three trillion miles. Yet the airlines recognize a liability for only about a third of the miles earned. The airlines rationalize this practice on the basis that a liability exists only after sufficient mileage has been earned to allow members to claim a free ticket.[1]

In 1994 American Airlines began the practice of selling frequent flyer miles to other firms, such as Citicorp's credit card operation and Allied Van Lines—a major moving company—as well as other nontravel or marketing partners, that later granted them to their customers. The estimate is that 40 percent of all frequent flyer miles are now obtained by firms in this way. These frequent flyer miles are being sold at an estimated two cents per mile with actual airline costs amounting to less than one-fifth of that amount.

---

[1] *Forbes,* June 13, 1988, p. 62. Also see "Free Airline Miles Become a Potent Tool for Selling Everything," *The Wall Street Journal,* April 15, 1996, pp.A1 and A8; and "Frequent Flyer Program Will Begin Next Week," *The Wall Street Journal,* September 4, 1996, p.A4.

The April 15, 1996, *Wall Street Journal* reported that 7 to 8 percent of all passenger miles were flown on frequent flyer programs, up from 3 to 4 percent just a few years ago. United, a major U.S. airline, used to disclose no liability for its frequent flyer program. Today, airlines are required to disclose their potential frequent flyer liability in SEC filings.

Do frequent flyer programs produce liabilities exceeding the amounts currently recognized? Are there difficulties associated with measuring either the amount or the timing of a liability for these miles? What disclosure options are available, if this liability is recognized? If a liability is recognized, would a catch-up adjustment be required?

WHAT IS A LIABILITY?

A liability is an obligation requiring a company to convey assets or services to someone else. Generally, this simple description serves quite well, but it is not sufficient for certain difficult situations. A good example is provided by the case of frequent flyer awards made by United and other airlines. Should a liability be recorded? United's frequent flyer example is not the only case. In 1982, the Manville Corporation, a supplier of asbestos insulation, filed for reorganization under the bankruptcy laws based on expected claims that might arise from potential lawsuits that had not yet been litigated. This action would apparently not have been taken except for the passage of *SFAS No. 5,* "Accounting for Contingencies," which requires balance sheet recognition of these potential payments. A.H. Robins, a pharmaceutical company, experienced similar complications connected with its Dalkon Shield. Problems with this intrauterine device surfaced by the mid-1970s, yet a liability was not recorded until 1984, and then it was only about 25 percent of the final amount required. Corning, a producer of specialty materials and consumer products, recently incurred legal costs associated with its silicone implants. Other situations where accountants wrestle with whether a liability exists and, if so, in what amount, include coupons that have not been presented for redemption and potential requirements to clean up toxic waste dumps.

In *SFAC No. 6,* the FASB defines **liabilities** as

> probable future sacrifices of economic benefits arising from present obligations of a particular entity to transfer assets or provide services to other entities in the future as a result of past transactions or events.

Thus, a liability possesses three essential characteristics:

1. An obligation exists that can be satisfied only by the transfer of an asset or a service to another entity.[2]
2. The event that gave rise to the obligation has occurred.
3. The obligation must be probable and unavoidable.

When a liability conforming with the definition given above is incurred, it should be immediately recognized and recorded. The FASB definition is specific about the essential characteristics defining a liability. Prior to *SFAC No. 6,* the accounting definition of a liability was vague. Conceptually, the amount of a liability is the present value of all future cash payments (or the cash equivalent of noncash assets and services to be transferred), discounted at the interest rate consistent with the risks involved. A liability involves a principal amount to which interest is added as time passes.

Accounting recognition of a liability should take place on the date the liability is incurred. The transaction that creates a liability usually identifies the date the obligation comes into existence. However, the recognition date of a liability is not always clear-cut. In the case of an injury to an employee or an outsider, the final determination of liability may depend on the decision of a court of law.[3]

---

[2] A liability can also be satisfied by creating another liability, as, for example, when a note replaces an account payable.

[3] From an auditing standpoint, identification of existing liabilities is a critical problem because many liabilities are easy to hide or overlook. This issue—determining the existence of liability—is precisely the one faced by United Airlines in deciding whether to record the liability for frequent flyer awards.

Furthermore, current liabilities can influence operations in a different manner than long-term liabilities because current liabilities represent a claim on current resources, making these assets unavailable for day-to-day operations. These claims differ from those that mature years into the future, such as bonds. This distinction is critical to the classification of liabilities as either current or long-term.

Measuring the amount of a liability is sometimes difficult. The transaction that creates a liability usually provides the basis for measuring it. Transactions lead to one or more debits that balance the liability credit. That is, the debit side of the transaction usually provides the clue to measuring the related liability. For example:

Cause of Liability	Type of Account Debited
Inventory purchased on account.	An asset.
A note signed for an account due and indicated on the balance sheet as an account payable.	Another liability.
Cash dividends declared.	Retained earnings.
Repair services received.	An expense.
A litigation award against the company.	A loss.
Magazine subscriptions to be delivered over the coming year.	Cash collected in advance of service rendered.

When an asset is acquired on credit, the asset and related liability are recognized at cost under the cost principle. The cost of the asset received measures the amount of the liability. Sometimes, the relationship between the cost of the asset and the valuation of the liability is not clear-cut.

Example Assume that a company acquires a machine and promises to pay the quoted price (a single amount) of $10,000 one year from the date of purchase, with no separate interest payments specified. The amount of the liability is less than $10,000. The liability, and the cost of the asset, should be measured as the present value of the future cash payment. If the market interest rate for transactions involving similar risk is 15 percent, the present value is:

$$\$10,000(PV1, 15\%, 1) = \$10,000(.86957) = \$8,696 \text{ (rounded)}$$

The appropriate journal entries are:

Purchase date:

Machine	8,696	
Note payable, 15% (face, $10,000)		8,696

Payment date:

Note payable	8,696	
Interest expense ($8,696)(.15)	1,304	
Cash		10,000

Interest that is not explicitly specified, such as the $1,304 in the above example, is called **implicit interest.** Implicit interest on short-term liabilities (particularly those involving accrued liabilities and accounts payable of one to three months) need not be recognized. *APB No. 21* (par. 3a) states that the requirement to account separately for interest does not apply to "receivables and payables arising from transactions with customers or suppliers in the normal course of business, which are due in customary trade terms not exceeding approximately one year." This is an application of the materiality and cost–benefit constraints discussed in Chapter 2. Companies usually measure, record, and report short-term liabilities at their maturity amount because the cost of the asset received and the maturity amount of the liability coincide. Aside from cases covered by the materiality and cost–benefit constraints, short-term liabilities should be recorded and reported at their present value when they are incurred.

CONCEPT REVIEW

1. What are the three essential characteristics of a liability?
2. When should a liability be recognized?
3. Most accountants would agree that the amount of a liability incurred is the present value of all future payments. Why, then, is the gross amount to be paid at the future date typically recorded for short-term liabilities?

WHAT IS A CURRENT LIABILITY?

Current (short-term) liabilities are defined as "obligations whose liquidation is reasonably expected to require the use of existing resources properly classifiable as current assets, or the creation of other current liabilities."[4] Current assets are those assets that are expected to be converted to cash or used in normal operations during the operating cycle of the business, or one year from the balance date, whichever is longer.[5] The time dimension that applies to current assets also generally applies to current liabilities. Liabilities that do not conform to this definition are called *long-term,* or *noncurrent, liabilities.* Long-term liabilities are discussed in the next chapter.

Common current liabilities are

- Accounts payable.
- Short-term notes payable.
- Cash and property dividends payable.
- Accrued liabilities related to expenses.
- Advances and returnable deposits.
- Unearned revenues collected in advance (e.g., cash collected before service is rendered, such as rent).
- Taxes (sales, property, and payroll).
- Conditional payments (income taxes and bonuses)
- Compensated-absence liabilities.
- Current maturities of long-term debt.
- Obligations callable on demand by the creditor.

Special accounting problems related to current liabilities are discussed in the following sections.

Accounts Payable

Accounts payable—more descriptively, *trade accounts payable*—are obligations arising from the firm's ongoing operations, including the acquisition of merchandise, materials, supplies, and services used in the production and sale of goods or services.[6] Current payables that are not trade accounts (such as income taxes and the current portion of long-term debt) should be reported separately from accounts payable.

Short-Term Notes Payable

Short-term notes payable include trade notes payable that arise from the same source as accounts payable, nontrade notes payable that arise from other sources, and the current payment due on long-term notes. A short-term note is either secured (by a mortgage or another type of lien that specifies particular assets pledged as security), or unsecured if repayment is based only on the general creditworthiness of the debtor. Disclosure for a secured note payable should specify the primary terms of the debt agreement, including any pledged assets.

---

[4]"Restatement and Revision of Accounting Research Bulletins," *Accounting Research Bulletin 43* (New York: AICPA, 1961), chapter 3, par. 7.

[5]The normal operating cycle of a business is the average period of time between the expenditure of cash for goods and services and the time that those goods and services are converted back to cash. For a manufacturing company, this cash-to-cash cycle is the sequence: cash expenditure to buy inventory, inventory converted into finished product, product sold on account, account collected in cash.

[6]In determining the amount of the liability, the accountant must adjust for purchase discounts, allowances, and returns.

A note payable may be either interest-bearing or noninterest-bearing. An interest-bearing note explicitly states a rate of interest. This rate is called the **stated rate of interest.** Notes designated as noninterest-bearing do not state an explicit interest rate but, instead, implicitly reflect a rate of interest called the **effective rate,** or **yield.** In other words, regardless of designation, all commercial debt instruments implicitly or explicitly require the debtor to pay interest because the cost of using money over time cannot be avoided. (For example, in the case of the machinery acquisition for $10,000 paid one year hence, discussed earlier in this chapter, the effective interest rate is the implicit rate of 15 percent.) The stated rate determines the amount of cash interest that will be paid on the principal amount of the debt. In contrast, the **effective rate of interest** is the market interest rate based on the actual cash, or cash equivalent, amount due. The effective rate is used to discount the future cash payments on a debt to the cash equivalent borrowed.

Interest-Bearing Notes   Interest-bearing notes specify a rate of interest. The debtor receives cash, other assets, or services and pays back the face amount of the note plus interest at the stated rate on one or more interest dates. When the stated rate appropriately reflects the note's risk, the stated and effective interest rates are the same. This is the usual case.

Example   Assume that on October 1, 1998, Biloxi Company borrows $10,000 cash on a one-year note with 12 percent interest payable at the maturity date.[7] The accounting year ends December 31, and the maturity date of the note is September 30, 1999. This transaction requires the following accounting and reporting:

Entries during 1998:

October 1, 1998—To record the interest-bearing note at its present value:

```
Cash .............................................  10,000
    Note payable, short term ................................      10,000
```

December 31, 1998—Adjusting entry for accrued interest:

```
Interest expense ($10,000)(.12)(3/12) ...............................  300
    Interest payable ........................................      300
```

Reporting at December 31, 1998—Interest-bearing note payable:

```
            Income statement:
                Interest expense  . . . . . . . . . .   $   300

            Balance sheet:
                Current liabilities:
                    Note payable, short term  . . . . .   $10,000
                    Interest payable   . . . . . . . .        300
```

Entry at maturity date:

September 30, 1999—Payment of face amount plus interest at maturity:

```
Interest payable . . . . . . . . . . . . . . . . . . . . . . . . . . . . . . . .     300
Interest expense ($10,000)(.12)(9/12) . . . . . . . . . . . . . . . . . . . . . . .     900
Note payable, short term . . . . . . . . . . . . . . . . . . . . . . . . . . . .  10,000
    Cash  . . . . . . . . . . . . . . . . . . . . . . . . . . . . . . . . . . . .         11,200
```

Noninterest-Bearing Notes   The label "noninterest-bearing" is a misleading description because such notes do, in fact, bear interest. The face amount includes both the amount borrowed and interest as a single amount to be paid back at the maturity date. The

---

[7] The present value of the two cash flows of this interest-bearing note is equal to the cash borrowed because the stated rate and the effective rate are the same.

```
Maturity amount: $10,000 (PV1, 12%, 1) = $10,000(.89286) . . . . .   $ 8,929
Interest: $1,200 (PV1, 12%, 1) = $1,200(.89286) . . . . . . . . . .     1,071
    Total present value (cash borrowed)  . . . . . . . . . . . . . .   $10,000
```

borrower receives the difference between the face amount and the interest on the note. The cash received is the discounted value of the face amount using the effective interest rate.[8] The difference between the discounted cash value and the face amount of the note is the interest. The effective interest rate is determined by reference to market rates for instruments of similar risk rather than specified on the note.

Example   Assume that on October 1, 1998, Brite Lite Company signs an $11,200, one-year, noninterest-bearing note but receives only $10,000 cash. The effective rate of interest is, therefore, 12 percent ($1,200 ÷ $10,000). The present value of this note is $10,000:

$$\$11,200(PV1, 12\%, 1) = \$11,200(.89286) = \$10,000$$

This debt should be recorded at its present value, either by recording the note using the net method or by recording it using the gross method offset with a discount account, a contra-note payable account.

Accounting Entries and Reporting

Entries during 1998:

October 1, 1998—To record a noninterest-bearing note payable at its gross (face) amount:[9]

	Gross Method		Net Method	
Cash	10,000		10,000	
Discount on note payable, short term	1,200			
Note payable, short term		11,200		10,000

December 31, 1998—Adjusting entry for accrued interest:

	Gross Method		Net Method	
Interest expense ($1,200)(³⁄₁₂)	300		300	
Discount on note payable, short term		300		
Note payable, short term				300

Reporting at December 31, 1998—Noninterest-bearing note payable:

	Gross Method		Net Method	
Income statement:				
Interest expense		$ 300		$ 300
Balance sheet:				
Current liabilities:				
Note payable	$11,200			$10,300
Less: Unamortized discount	900	$10,300		

Entries at maturity date:

September 30, 1999—Payment of the face amount of the note:

	Gross Method		Net Method	
Interest expense ($1,200)(⁹⁄₁₂)	900		900	
Note payable, short term	11,200		10,300	
Discount on note payable, short term		900		
Cash		11,200		11,200

Accounting for Short-Term Notes Payable Having Unrealistic Stated Interest Rates

Sometimes a noncash asset is acquired and a note is given with a stated rate of interest that is less than the current market rate (the effective rate) of interest for the level of risk involved. When this happens, the stated rate is unrealistic for measuring interest expense. The correct cost of the asset is the present value of the future cash payments discounted at the current market rate of interest rather than at the stated interest rate.

---

[8]A noninterest-bearing note is also called a *discounted note* because the cash received is less than the face amount of the note.

[9]The amount of interest expense and the net liability balances are the same whether the note is recorded at net or gross.

Example   Assume that a machine is purchased on January 1, 1998, with a one-year, $1,000, 6 percent interest-bearing note. The current market rate of interest for obligations with this level of risk is 12 percent.

1. Cost of the machine:

$$(\$1,000 + \$60)(PV1, 12\%, 1) = (\$1,060)(.89286) = \$946.43$$

2. Entries (net method):

January 1, 1998—Acquisition date:

Machine	946.43	
Note payable, short term		946.43

December 31, 1998—Payment date:

Note payable, short term	946.43	
Interest expense ($946.43)(.12)	113.57	
Cash ($1,000 + $60)		1,060.00

The current market interest rate for similar notes with the same risk is used as the effective rate. If the competitive cash price of the noncash asset received is known, it could also be used to establish the effective rate of interest.

Cash and Scrip Dividends Payable

Cash dividends declared but not yet paid are reported as a current liability if they are to be paid within the coming year or operating cycle. Declared dividends are reported as a liability between the date of declaration and payment because declaration gives rise to an enforceable contract.[10]

Liabilities are not recognized for undeclared dividends in arrears on preferred stock or for any other dividends not formally declared by the board of directors. Dividends in arrears on cumulative preferred stock should be disclosed in the notes to the financial statements. These dividends must be paid before any common dividends can be paid. Scrip dividends payable are reported as a current liability unless there is no intention to make payment in the next fiscal year.[11]

Accrued Liabilities

Examples of accrued liabilities include wages and benefits earned by employees and interest earned by creditors but not as yet paid. Accrued liabilities are recorded in the accounts by making adjusting entries at the end of the accounting period. For example, any wages that have not yet been recorded or paid at the end of the accounting period must be recorded by debiting wage expense and crediting wages payable. Recognition of accrued liabilities is consistent with the definition of a liability.

Advances and Returnable Deposits

A company may receive advances or cash deposits from customers as guarantees for payment of future obligations or to guarantee performance on a contract or service. For example, when an order is taken, a company may require an advance payment to cover losses that would be incurred if the order is canceled. Such advances create liabilities for the company receiving the payment until the underlying transaction is completed. Advances are recorded by debiting cash and crediting a liability account such as customer deposits.

Deposits may also be made as guarantees in case of noncollection or for possible damage to property. For example, deposits required from customers by gas, water, light, and other public utilities are liabilities of such companies to their customers. Employees may also make returnable deposits to ensure the return of keys and other company property, for locker privileges, and for club memberships. Deposits should be reported as current

---

[10]Stock dividends payable are not liabilities but rather merely a division of the assets into more ownership shares.

[11]A dividend payable in scrip is a promise by the corporation to pay the dividend at a later date. Scrip dividends are declared when the corporation wishes to keep its record of continuous dividend payments uninterrupted and has the necessary retained earnings to declare the dividend legally but is currently short of cash.

or long-term liabilities depending on the time involved between date of deposit and expected termination of the relationship. If the advances or deposits are interest bearing, an annual adjusting entry is required to accrue interest expense and to increase the related liability.[12]

Unearned Revenues

Cash collected in advance of the delivery of a good or service creates a liability, but it does not yet qualify for recognition as revenue. Examples of revenues collected in advance include gift certificates, college tuition, rent, ticket sales, and magazine subscriptions. Such transactions are recorded as a debit to cash and a credit to an appropriately designated current liability account. This account is often titled *unearned revenues* and may be given a modifying adjective, for example, *unearned subscription revenues* in the case of subscriptions. Another title is *subscription revenue collected in advance*. The phrase *deferred revenues* is also occasionally encountered but is not the preferred description of the account.

Subsequently, when the product or service is delivered and the revenue is earned, the liability account is decreased and the appropriate revenue account is credited. This entry is typically one of the year-end adjusting entries (see Chapter 3 on adjusting entries).

Example   Assume that on November 1, 1998, Zorex Company collects rent of $6,000 for the next six months. The accounting period ends December 31. The entries are:

November 1, 1998—Rent collected in advance:

Cash	6,000	
Rent revenue collected in advance [or unearned rent revenue]		6,000

December 31, 1998—Adjusting entry for the portion earned:

Rent revenue collected in advance [or unearned rent revenue]	2,000	
Rent revenue ($6,000)(%)		2,000

The remaining unearned rent revenue of $4,000 is reported as a current liability because Zorex has an obligation to provide the space during the following four months.

Example   Another example of an obligation to render future service is newspaper and magazine subscriptions for which the cash has been collected prior to delivery. This liability is illustrated by the 1995 financial statements of Dow Jones & Company, a major producer and distributor of financial services and information. In their Summary of Significant Accounting Policies (note 1), the company states

> Unearned revenue is recorded as earned, pro rata on a monthly basis over the life of subscriptions. Costs in connection with the procurement of subscriptions are charged to expense as incurred.

The company titles the current liability *unearned revenue.*

Taxes

State and federal laws require businesses to collect certain taxes from customers and employees for remittance to governmental agencies. These taxes include sales taxes, income taxes withheld from employee paychecks, property taxes, and payroll taxes. Similar collections are made on behalf of unions, insurance companies, and employee-sponsored activities. Collections made for third parties increase both cash and current liabilities. The collections represent liabilities that are settled when the funds are remitted to the designated parties. Common examples of such taxes are

- Sales taxes
- Payroll taxes
- Property taxes

---

[12]Employees also have portions of their wages withheld for savings bond purchase programs, stock purchase plans, medical insurance premiums, and retirement programs. These withholdings constitute liabilities until either the amounts are delivered to a trustee or the service (delivery of the savings bond, for example) is completed.

Sales Taxes   In most states, retail businesses are required to collect a sales tax at the time of sale and to remit the tax to the taxing authority. Summary entries, assuming a 6 percent sales tax and $500,000 of sales, are:

1. At date the tax is assessed (point of sale):

Cash and accounts receivable	530,000	
Sales revenue		500,000
Sales tax payable ($500,000)(.06)		30,000

2. At date of remittance to taxing authority:

Sales tax payable	30,000	
Cash		30,000

These entries assume that the sales tax is separately recognized at the point of sale. Some companies simply include the sales tax in sales revenue. In that case, an adjusting entry is required at the end of the accounting period to debit sales revenue and credit sales tax payable (or cash if remitted at that time).

Payroll Taxes   Companies must pay various payroll taxes in addition to the wages and salaries paid to employees. Also, companies must deduct amounts from their employees' pay for federal income taxes, social security taxes, union dues, insurance premiums, and the like. The primary federal payroll taxes are the FICA and FUTA taxes.

FICA payroll tax is authorized by the social security laws. The employer must deduct this tax from the pay of each employee under specified conditions. In addition to the tax paid by the employee, the employer must usually match the contribution of the employee and remit both amounts to the U.S. Treasury. FICA taxes, so called because the enabling legislation is the Federal Insurance Contribution Act (also known as the Federal Old-Age Survivor and Disability Insurance, or OASDI), include the Federal Hospital Insurance tax. Together these two taxes are commonly referred to as the social security tax. Rates for these taxes change from time to time. For example, for 1997, employers and employees each paid a tax of 7.65 percent on the first $65,400 earned by the employee. The purpose of the social security tax is to provide retirement pay and medicare for retirees and death benefits for retirees' survivors.

FUTA payroll tax, authorized by the Federal Unemployment Tax Act, is used to finance the cost of the federal-state unemployment compensation program. In most but not all states, this payroll tax is paid only by the employer. The state portion of this tax is commonly referred to as SUTA. Assume that for 1998 the FUTA rate is 6.2 percent on the first $7,000 in wages paid to each employee, with 5.4 percent the maximum payable to the state and the remaining 0.8 percent payable to the U.S. Treasury.

Example   Thor Company paid January 1998 salaries of $100,000. Income tax withholding was $20,000, and the FICA and FUTA rates applied to all salaries paid (the rates listed above are used):

a. To record salaries and employee deductions:

Salary expense	100,000	
Federal income tax payable (from a tax table)		20,000
FICA tax payable, employees ($100,000)(.0765)		7,650
Cash		72,350

b. To record payroll taxes payable by the employer:

Expense, payroll taxes	13,850	
FICA tax payable, employer ($100,000)(.0765)		7,650
FUTA tax payable, ($100,000)(.008)		800
SUTA tax payable, ($100,000)(.054)		5,400

c. To record remittance of payroll taxes:

Federal income tax payable	20,000	
FICA tax payable, employees*	7,650	
FICA tax payable, employer*	7,650	
FUTA tax payable[†]	800	

(*continued on page 723*)

SUTA tax payable	5,400	
Cash		41,500

*These taxes are usually recorded in one account, FICA tax payable, with no distinction between the employee and employer contributions. The taxes are paid as frequently as within three working days after release of the employee paychecks but no less frequently than once a quarter.

†Usually paid quarterly. The higher the state portion of the FUTA rate, the lower the federal portion: the total rate is constant.

Property Taxes   Property taxes paid directly by the company are based on the assessed value of real and personal property and are levied to support school, city, county, and other designated activities. Unpaid taxes constitute a lien on the assessed property.

The typical sequence of assessing property taxes is:

By Mid-Year

Development of tentative taxable valuations
together with estimated tax rates.

By Year-End

Property owner receives:
- Actual taxable valuation.
- The tax rate.
- Resulting property tax bill.

Early Following Year

Payment made to taxing authority

Therefore, 1998 property taxes would typically be assessed late in 1998 and paid in 1999. The accounting period during which these taxes should be recognized, therefore, precedes the period in which the taxes are paid. Correct matching of the property tax expense with the period benefited means that the expense must be accrued before the actual amount of tax is known. Therefore, estimates must often be used. Most businesses accrue property tax expense each month, using estimates, and handle revisions as changes in estimates (i.e., prospectively). At year-end, the estimated amounts that have been recorded in the related expense and liability accounts are adjusted to agree with the actual amount assessed, which must be used for annual accounting and reporting purposes.

Example   To illustrate accounting for property taxes, consider a situation that involves quarterly recognition of property taxes during 1998. The following sequence of events and their accounting treatment are appropriate:

1. January 1998—*Estimate* of 1998 quarterly property tax based on an expected 20 percent increase over the actual 1997 annual tax of $2,061:

$$(\$2,061 \times 1.20) \div 4 = \$618 \text{ (Use \$600 per quarter as the estimate.)}$$

   March 31, 1998—Accrued tax for first quarter based on original estimate:

Property tax expense	600	
Property tax payable		600

2. June 30, 1998—Second-quarter entry, identical to the entry made March 31, 1998.
3. September 30, 1998—In September the taxing authority forwards its tentative tax valuation for 1998 based on a property valuation of $190,076 and the current tax rate of $1.447 per $100 of assessed valuation. This report suggests an updated estimate of the tax assessment for 1998 to be $1,900.76 × 1.447, or $2,750. The amount of the entry on September 30 is [$2,750 − 2($600)] ÷ 2 quarters left, or $775:

Property tax expense	775	
Property tax payable		775

4. December 31, 1998—In December the taxing authority's bill arrives indicating a final assessed valuation of $197,076 and a rate of $1.45 per $100 of assessed valuation. The amount of the entry on December 31 is ($1,970.76 × 1.45) − (2 × $600 + $775), or $883:

Property tax expense	883	
Property tax payable		883

5. January 1999—Payment of 1998 property tax:

```
Property tax payable (2 × $600 + $775 + $883) . . . . . . . . . . . . . . . . .  2,858
   Cash . . . . . . . . . . . . . . . . . . . . . . . . . . . . . . . . . . . . . . . . . . . . .         2,858
```

The December 31, 1998, financial statements would show:

```
Income statement:
   Property tax expense  . . . . . .   $2,858

Balance sheet:
   Current liabilities:
      Property tax payable  . . . . .   $2,858
```

Regardless of the particular tax and accounting fiscal periods, the accounting approach can be adapted to conform to GAAP.[13]

Conditional Payments

Some liabilities are established on the basis of a firm's periodic income. Two examples are bonuses or profit-sharing payments to employees and income taxes based on taxable income. These items can be established at year's end, but the liability must be estimated quarterly. Until paid, they represent current liabilities of the organization.[14]

Income Taxes Payable   Quarterly reports require a provision for both federal and state income tax liabilities, so estimates are required. The estimated liability should be reported as a current liability based on the firm's best estimates. Periodic payments, which will change through the year as the estimated tax changes, are required. Income taxes are covered in a later chapter.

Bonuses   Many companies pay cash bonuses, which depend on earnings. Accountants should insist that any agreement be specific. For example, if earnings are involved, it should be clear whether the earnings measure is before or after taxes. Further, when earnings are involved, the adjusting entry to recognize the bonus cannot be established until all other adjusting entries affecting earnings have been made.

Bonus payments to employees are considered wages in the year earned. Bonuses therefore increase the period's wage expense and establish a concurrent liability, properly considered a current liability.

Computing bonuses can be complex because the bonus is an expense and hence deductible from income. In addition, the bonus affects the computation of the company's tax expense and, thereby, also income.

Example   Aldar Corporation has pretax income of $500,000 in 1997 before establishing the year's bonus. The bonus agreement specifies that the employees are to be paid 10 percent of net income as this year's bonus. The bonus is an expense and must be deducted in determining the income on which the bonus is to be paid. For the moment, ignore income taxes. Then the bonus is 10 percent of income, with income first reduced by the bonus:

$$\text{Bonus} = .10(\$500,000 - \text{Bonus})$$

Solving:

$$\text{Bonus} = \$50,000 - .1(\text{Bonus})$$
$$1.1(\text{Bonus}) = \$50,000$$
$$\text{Bonus} = \$45,455$$

---

[13]When property taxes are levied in advance of the taxing jurisdiction's fiscal year, the appropriate accounting would use the prepaid method. Cash (or a liability) is credited, and prepaid property tax expense is debited. The prepayment is written off to expense over the period covered by the assessment.

[14]Royalty agreements are another example of a conditional payment that creates a current liability for the payor.

Now assume a 40 percent tax rate. If the bonus were known, the tax expense would be

$$\text{Tax} = .40(\$500,000 - \text{Bonus})$$

And if the tax were known, the bonus would be

$$\text{Bonus} = .10(\$500,000 - \text{Tax} - \text{Bonus})$$

These two equations, involving two unknowns, can be solved simultaneously to yield both the bonus and the tax expense. Simplifying these two equations:

$$\text{Tax} = \$200,000 - .4(\text{Bonus})$$
$$\text{Bonus} = \$\ \ 50,000 - .1(\text{Tax}) - .1(\text{Bonus})$$

Now substituting the expression for tax into the simplified expression for the bonus gives

$$\text{Bonus} = \$50,000 - .1[\$200,000 - .4(\text{Bonus})] - .1(\text{Bonus})$$

or

$$\text{Bonus} = \$50,000 - \$20,000 + .04(\text{Bonus}) - .1(\text{Bonus})$$
$$\text{Bonus} = \$50,000 - \$20,000 - .06(\text{Bonus})$$
$$1.06\ \text{Bonus} = \$30,000$$

giving a bonus of \$28,302. Using this figure for the bonus:

$$\text{Tax} = \$200,000 - .4(\$28,302)$$
$$\text{Tax} = \$188,679$$

The entry to record the bonus is:

Wage expense (employee bonus)	28,302	
Bonus payable		28,302

Compensated-Absence Liabilities   Companies often grant employees paid vacations and holidays. When employees can carry over unused time to future years, *SFAS No. 43,* "Accounting for Compensated Absences," requires that any expense due to compensated absences must be recognized (accrued) in the year in which it is earned, provided that all the following criteria are met:

- The absence from work relates to services already rendered.
- The benefits accumulate (carryover), or vest.
- The payment is probable (the absence will occur).
- The amount (i.e., cost) can be reliably estimated.

A benefit vests when it is no longer contingent on continuing employment. However, a benefit that accumulates does not necessarily vest. For example, an employee with six weeks of earned vacation pay accumulated over the last two years loses this benefit if it is unvested and the employee leaves the firm before using the paid vacation time. Also, most employers limit the amount of benefits that can be accumulated.[15]

Implementing the accrual of compensating absences involves an adjusting entry at the end of each fiscal year to accrue all of the compensation cost for the vacation and holiday time that is carried over. An expense and a current liability are recorded. When the vacation or holiday time is taken, the liability account is debited at the time the employee is paid. These entries recognize the cost of the compensated absences as an expense in the period earned rather than when taken because the firm has a probable obligation to transfer assets in the future as a result of events in the current period.

Example   Consider the carryover of vacation time of the Conway Company, which has 500 employees. Each employee is granted three weeks' paid vacation time each year. Vacation time, up to a maximum accumulation of four weeks, may be carried over to subsequent years prior to termination of employment. At the end of 1998, the end of the annual accounting period, personnel records revealed the following information concerning carryover vacation amounts:

---

[15]In the case of accumulated rights to receive nonvesting sick pay benefits, accrual is not required but is permitted. A strong case can be made that the illness (when it occurs) is the event causing the expense rather than the employee's previous service. However, if unused sick pay benefits are paid as a matter of course, say at retirement, the benefits must be accrued in the period earned.

	Number of Employess	Weeks per Employee	Carryovers from 1998*	
			Total Weeks	**Total Salaries**
Wage class A	10	2	20	$30,000
Wage class B	3	1	3	6,000

*These are carryovers from 1998 to future years.

Disregarding payroll taxes, which are excluded here to simplify the analysis, the indicated entries are:

December 31, 1998—Adjusting entry to accrue vacation salaries not yet taken or paid:

```
Salary expense  ..............................................  36,000
    Liability for compensated absences  ............................       36,000
```

During 1999—Vacation time carryover taken and salaries paid (one person did not take two weeks, carried over at $3,000):

```
Liability for compensated absences  ............................  33,000
    Cash ($36,000 − $3,000)  ....................................       33,000
```

The balance remaining in the liability account is $3,000.

This illustration assumes that there was no change in the rate of pay from 1998 to 1999 (when the carryover was used) for those employees who had the carryover. If there were rate changes, the pay difference would be debited (if an increase) or credited (if a decrease) to salary expense during 1999. The change is considered a change in estimate.[16] For example, if the 1999 salaries relating to the employees who used their carryovers during 1999 increased by $1,000, the 1999 entry would have been:

```
Liability for compensated absences  ............................  33,000
Salary expense (1999)  ........................................   1,000
    Cash ($36,000 + $1,000 − $3,000)  ..........................       34,000
```

The balance in the liability account is $3,000 after this entry. This reduces by $3,000 the expense that otherwise would be recognized in the 1999 compensated absences adjusting entry.

Current Maturities of Long-Term Debt

How should a debt that is part current and part noncurrent be reported? The issue arises when periodic payments are to be made on a debt, one in the next accounting period and additional payments in later accounting periods. If the next payment is to be made from current assets, that portion of the debt should be reported as a current liability.

Example   The following accounts would appear in a balance sheet dated December 31, 1998, for a $500,000 debenture with $100,000 due in 1999.

```
Current liabilities:
    Current payment on bond issue (due in 1999)  ......................  $100,000

Long-term liabilities:
    Bonds payable (less current portion: $100,000)  ...................  $400,000
```

The current payment is often combined with other current liabilities rather than reported separately.

Obligations Callable on Demand by the Creditor

SFAS No. 78, "Classification of Obligations that Are Callable by the Creditor," amends *ARB No. 43,* Chapter 3A, to specify certain kinds of debt that must be included in the current liability classification:

Case 1—obligations that are payable on demand (i.e., callable) or will be due on demand within one year from the balance sheet date, or the operating cycle, if longer, even though liquidation within that period is not expected.

Case 2—long-term obligations that are or will be callable by the creditor either because of a violation of the terms of the debt at the date of the balance sheet or because a violation, if not cured within a specified grace period, will make the debt callable.

---

[16]In practice, many firms would simply recalculate the liability at the next year-end and adjust it through salary expense.

The rationale that supports this classification is that debtors subject to such obligations cannot control the payment date.

SHORT-TERM OBLIGATIONS EXPECTED TO BE REFINANCED

A company may want to reclassify liabilities from current to long term to improve its reported working capital position. One justification for such reclassifications is the intention to refinance the liability, and the resulting expectation that current assets will not be used for payment. *SFAS No. 6*, "Classification of Short-Term Obligations Expected to Be Refinanced," establishes guidelines intended to prevent abuses. Current liabilities expected to be refinanced can be reclassified as long-term liabilities only if the debtor

1. Fully intends to refinance the specific short-term liability.
2. Shows an ability to do so by
   a. Actually refinancing it on a long-term basis *before the financial statements are issued.*
   b. Entering in good faith into a long-term, noncancelable refinancing agreement supported by a viable lender.
   c. Issuing an equity instrument.

Reporting abuses have occurred when firms financed new plant and equipment with short-term commercial paper, expecting to finance it later on a long-term basis, and then reported the debt as long term. Penn Central, a specialized property, railroad, casualty insurance, and defense services company, had extensive debt classified as long term because the railroad felt it was covered by refinancing commitments from lenders. When the commitments did not materialize, Penn Central went bankrupt. In the meantime, current liabilities were understated substantially.

When a financing agreement is relied on to support classification of short-term obligations as long-term debt (2*b* above), it must meet the following criteria of *SFAS No. 6:*

1. The agreement must be noncancelable by all parties (except for violations by the debtor) and extend beyond one year from the balance sheet date or from the start of the operating cycle, whichever is longer.
2. At the balance sheet date and the issue date, the company must not be in violation of the agreement (unless a waiver is obtained).
3. The lender must be financially capable of honoring the agreement.

Replacement of one short-term obligation with another is not sufficient to avoid classification as a current liability. A revolving credit agreement cancelable at any time by the creditor, for example, does not fulfill the requirements of *SFAS No. 6*.

The amount of the short-term debt that can be classified as long term cannot exceed the amount available under the agreement, must be adjusted for any limitations in the agreement, and cannot exceed a reasonable estimate of the minimum amount expected to be available (if the amount available for refinancing will fluctuate). If any of these three amounts cannot be estimated, the entire amount of the short-term debt must remain a current liability.

Short-term obligations liquidated *after* the balance sheet date but *before* the statement issue date must be reported as short-term obligations if the funds used in refinancing were short term, even if long-term financing is ultimately obtained before the financial statement issue date. Furthermore, short-term obligations extinguished with current assets that are replenished with long-term financing *before* the statement sheet issue date also are classified as current liabilities.

Example   Rell Company liquidates a $30,000 short-term note by paying cash in February 1998, before the 1997 financial statements are published. Even if Rell replaces the $30,000 cash used to pay the note with long-term debt before the issue date, the short-term debt is *not* classified as long term in the 1997 balance sheet. *FASB Interpretation No. 8* reaffirmed the concept that short-term obligations requiring the use of current assets for payment are current liabilities.

Some long-term debt agreements contain a subjective clause permitting the creditor to accelerate the due date. Are these liabilities classified as current? *FASB Technical Bulletin 79–3* states that if the likelihood of acceleration is remote, the debt is not reclassified as current. If the debtor is experiencing financial difficulties, and if a reasonable probability exists that the due date may be accelerated to within a year of the balance sheet date, reclassification is warranted.

The following disclosure is required for current liabilities: total current liabilities and a general description of the financing arrangements of short-term obligations excluded from current liabilities, and terms of any new debt or equity securities issued to replace the short-term obligation.

If a short-term obligation is to be excluded from current liabilities under a financing agreement, footnote disclosure is required and should include:
- A general description of the financing agreement.
- The terms of any new obligation to be incurred.
- The terms of any equity security to be issued.

In certain specialized industries (including broker-dealers, real estate, and stock life insurance companies) the current-noncurrent distinction is not useful. These firms prepare unclassified balance sheets and are thus not covered by *SFAS No. 6*. Short-term obligations that satisfy the requirements to be shown as long term can be given a specific and distinct caption if desired, such as *short-term debt expected to be refinanced*.

CONCEPT REVIEW

1. Why might a company want to reclassify a liability from short to long term?
2. Under what conditions can a short-term liability be reclassified as a long-term liability?
3. When a short-term obligation is excluded from current liabilities under a financing agreement, what footnote disclosure is required?

ACCOUNTING FOR CONTINGENCIES

Liabilities must often be estimated because while a known liability exists, the ultimate amount is uncertain or a contingency exists. A **contingency** is defined in *SFAS No. 5*, "Accounting for Contingencies," as

> an existing condition, situation, or set of circumstances involving uncertainty as to possible gain (hereinafter, 'gain contingency') or a loss (hereinafter, 'loss contingency') to an enterprise that ultimately will be resolved when one or more future events occur or fail to occur. Resolution of the uncertainty may confirm the acquisition of an asset or the reduction of a liability or the loss or impairment of an asset or the incurrence of a liability.

In 1995, 70 percent of the firms surveyed in *Accounting Trends and Techniques* reported loss contingencies due to litigation alone. *SFAS No. 5* is the basic pronouncement on contingencies and estimated liabilities. It defines contingencies and specifies particular accounting treatments on the basis of whether the contingency is

1. **Probable** The future event (or events) is likely to occur.
2. **Reasonably possible** The chance of occurrence of the future event (or events) is more than remote but less than likely.
3. **Remote** The chance of occurrence of the future event (or events) is slight.

The provisions in *SFAS No. 5* relating to contingencies are summarized in Exhibit 15–1.

EXHIBIT 15–1
Summary of Accounting for
Contingencies

The Contingent Event Is	Amount Can Be Reasonably Estimated	Amount Cannot Be Reasonably Estimated
Loss Contingency		
Probable	1. Accrue both a loss and a liability, and report them in the body of the statements.	2. Do not accrue; report as a note in the financial statements.
Reasonably possible	3. Do not accrue; report as a note in the financial statements.	4. Do not accrue; report as a note in the financial statements.
Remote	5. No accrual or note is required; however, a note is permitted.	6. No accrual or note is required; however, a note is permitted.
Gain Contingency		
Probable	7. No accrual is required except in unusual circumstances. Note disclosure is required.	8. Note disclosure is required; exercise care to avoid misleading inferences.
Reasonably possible	9. Note disclosure is required; exercise care to avoid misleading inferences.	10. Note disclosure is required; exercise care to avoid misleading inferences.
Remote	11. Disclosure not recommended.	

Loss Contingencies that Require Accrual and the Recognition of a Liability

SFAS No. 5 requires that a loss contingency must be accrued if *both* of the following conditions are met:

1. Information received before issuance of the financial statements indicates that it is *probable* that an asset has been impaired or a liability has been incurred at the date of the financial statements. It must be probable that one or more future events will or will not occur confirming the fact of the loss.
2. The amount of the loss can be reasonably estimated.[17]

This situation corresponds to the box numbered 1 in Exhibit 15–1.

Such a loss contingency must be reported on the balance sheet as a liability and on the income statement as an expense or loss in the period in which these two criteria are first met. Liabilities that meet these two criteria also meet the definition of a liability in *SFAC No.6.*

SFAS No. 5 identifies a number of loss contingencies that must be given appropriate disclosure. These contingencies include estimated losses on receivables (allowance for doubtful accounts); estimated warranty obligations; litigations, claims, and assessments; and anticipated losses on the disposal of a segment of the business. Three examples illustrate the accrual of a loss contingency and recognition of a liability.

Case A—Product Warranty Liability   Rollex Company sells merchandise for $200,000 cash in 1998. Experience has indicated that warranty and guarantee costs will approximate 0.5 percent of sales. The indicated entries are as follows:

1. In 1998:

Cash	200,000	
Sales revenue		200,000
Warranty expense	1,000	
Warranty liability ($200,000)(.005)		1,000

---

[17]If the two conditions mentioned are met but the information available indicates only that the loss is within some range (no single amount in the range being a better estimate than any other amount), the minimum amount is accrued. The exposure to an additional amount (up to the maximum in the range) should be disclosed in the notes.

2. In 1999, actual warranty expenditures of $987 are made during the warranty period:

Warranty liability	987	
Cash (and other resources used)		987

3. Instead, if the actual expenditure were $1,100, the entry would be

Warranty liability	1,000	
Warranty expense	100	
Cash (and other resources used)		1,100

Under the entry in (2), $13 remains in the liability account. This means the warranty expense recognized in previous periods was overstated by $13. No attempt is made to correct prior years' accounts. The situation is treated as a change in estimate. Warranty expense for 1999 would simply be $13 less than the amount otherwise recognized.

Example Champion Enterprises, Inc. reported accrued warranty obligations of $12,589,000 in its 1995 annual report.

Case B—Frequent Flyer Programs Many airlines now offer frequent flyer programs and accrue the expense once the award level is reached.

Continental Airlines, Inc., a major U.S. airline, reports the following accounting for frequent flyer miles in the Summary of Significant Accounting Policies footnote of its 1995 10-K report:

> Passenger revenues are recognized when the transportation is provided, rather than when a ticket is sold. The amount of passenger ticket sales not yet recognized as revenue is reflected in the consolidated balance sheets as air traffic liability. The Company performs a periodic evaluation of this estimated liability, and any adjustments resulting therefrom which can be significant, are included in the results of operations.
>
> Continental sponsors a frequent flyer program (OnePass) and records an estimated liability for the incremental cost associated with providing the related free transportation at the time a free travel award is earned and awards redeemed.

Suppose that in 1998 Continental provided transportation services under its frequent flyer program equivalent to $5 million, of which $1 million was for miles sold to others participating in the program. Also during 1998, customers earned awards of $7 million. The entries below shift the recognition of the expense and liability of the frequent flyer program to the year in which the awards are earned.

1. To record transportation earned:

Operating expenses	7m	
Air traffic liability		7m

2. To record transportation services provided:

Cash	1m	
Air traffic liability	4m	
Passenger revenues		1m
Inventories, payables, etc.		4m

Case C—Liability from Litigation Assume that Solon Company is sued during the last quarter of the current year because of an accident involving a vehicle owned and operated by the company. The plaintiff is seeking $100,000 damages. If, in the opinion of management and company counsel, it is probable that damages will be assessed and a reasonable estimate is $50,000,[18] the indicated entry is:

---

[18]Management is unlikely to disclose a belief that a contingent loss is probable and can be reliably estimated. Doing so could imply that it may be advisable to settle out of court. To disclose a tacit expectation of loss in advance may prejudice the outcome of the trial. For this reason, lawyers vehemently object to such disclosures. The information would appear, if at all, in the notes to the financial statements. Even then, it is unusual for a firm to mention specific amounts unless court judgments have already been rendered. A study of 126 lawsuits lost by publicly traded companies found that 7 (5.6 percent) were accrued in prior years' financial statements before the suit was decided, 45 (35.7 percent) were not mentioned in prior years' financial statements, 74 (58.7 percent) were mentioned in a footnote. Of those mentioned in a footnote, 9 (7.1 percent) were with a strong disclaimer of liability, 60 (47.6 percent) conceded the possibility of a liability, and only 5 (4 percent) provided an estimated amount. R. Fesler, "Disclosure of Litigation Contingencies Faulted," *Journal of Accountancy,* July 1990, p. 15.

Estimated loss from pending lawsuit   50,000
   Estimated liability from pending lawsuit   50,000

Estimated liabilities may ultimately require expenditures that differ from the amount originally estimated to satisfy the actual liability. When the estimated liability varies from the actual, the difference is accounted for as a change in estimate under the provisions of *APB No. 20*. The loss or expense is increased or decreased when the amount becomes known.

Potential loss contingencies, such as guarantees of indebtedness, accommodation endorsements, threat of expropriation of assets, standby letters of credit (guarantees of the credit of a third party), and risks due to fire, flood, and other hazards, must also be assessed and accounted for in conformity with *SFAS No. 5*.

Example   The Harley Davidson Company, a maker of motorcycles, reported the following in a note to their 1995 financial statements:

> The company self-insures its product liability losses in the United States up to $3 million (catastrophic coverage is maintained for individual claims in excess of $3 million).

Loss Contingencies that Are Disclosed Only in Notes

A loss contingency and the related liability are accrued and reported only when the loss is probable and the amount can reasonably be estimated (box 1 of Exhibit 15–1). In contrast, Exhibit 15–1 identifies three situations involving loss contingencies for which disclosures in the notes are required (accrual is not permitted):

- Box 2: The loss is probable but cannot reasonably be estimated.
- Box 3: The loss is reasonably possible and can reasonably be estimated.
- Box 4: The loss is reasonably possible but cannot reasonably be estimated.

The note must describe the nature of the contingency and disclose any amount of loss that can be estimated and that is at least reasonably possible.[19]

Example   The 1995 financial statements of the Danaher Corporation include the following note in part:

> A former subsidiary of the company is engaged in litigation in multiple states with respect to product liability. . . . The plaintiffs seek compensatory and punitive damages. The cases are in preliminary stages of discovery and pleading. The company's maximum obligation under the contract is approximately $85,000,000. The outcome of this litigation is not currently predictable.

Gain Contingencies

For a gain contingency to be disclosed, the characteristics of a contingency must be present: there must be a probable increase in assets or a decrease in liabilities, and the change must depend upon the occurrence of future events.

Contingent gains are rarely accrued, but they are accorded note disclosure, provided the note does not give misleading implications. The different treatment accorded gain contingencies compared with loss contingencies is justified by the conservatism constraint. *Accounting Trends and Techniques,* reports that 64 percent of the surveyed firms reported contingent gains in 1995.

Example   General Dynamics Corporation reports in a note to its 1995 financial statements:

> The Company has filed refund claims for approximately $275 million (plus interest) in additional research and experimentation tax credits for the years 1981–1990. . . . As the ultimate allowance of these claims is expected to be dependent upon the outcome of the litigation, no benefits will be recognized until the completion of the litigation.

Executory Contracts

Executory contracts, or agreements, occur when two parties agree to transfer resources or services, but neither party has yet performed. For example, a purchase agreement has been made, but no assets have been received and no payments have been made. Other examples include lines of credit and promises of future compensation prior to any transfer of

---

[19]*FASB Interpretation No. 14* to *SFAS No. 5.*, par 5.

resources. When a transfer of resources occurs, the contract or agreement is no longer executory. Executory contracts are usually not recorded because a transfer of assets or liabilities has not yet occurred. If the anticipated considerations are material, full disclosure should be made.

ACCOUNTING FOR ENVIRONMENTAL LIABILITIES[20]

The magnitude of private-sector environmental liabilities is growing steadily. Rockwell International alone was expected to report environmental liabilities of $130 million in 1993.[21] Estimates of the total cost to clean up the environment range up to $750 billion. In 1982, an average of 2 percent of capital spending was for environmental purposes. Ten years later the proportion had grown to 20 percent. Under existing law, past or present owners of a hazardous waste site can be held liable without regard to responsibility. In general, concerns about environmental liability affect investment by and in many types of businesses.

Chevron Corporation discovered environmental risk when the firm put two of its oil refineries up for sale:

> Moreover, environmental liabilities and cleanup costs at refinery sites have reached staggering proportions and are a major impediment to transactions. Chevron may not even be able to give the refineries away, unless they assume the environmental liabilities.[22]

Many firms are increasing the amount of information they report, including Monsanto and Niagara Mohawk Power. PPG Industries, Inc., plans to publish an entire annual report on its environmental performance listing penalties and the amount of hazardous waste produced, a topic many companies prefer to avoid. Some companies have little choice. A 1993 settlement between the EPA and United Technologies Corporation requires the company to undergo extensive environmental audits by outsiders.[23]

Some companies are working hard to provide more and better information. Polaroid, for example, reports on all the toxic chemicals and other pollutants it releases, even in parts of the world where such reporting isn't required.[24] Yet "a recent survey of the S&P 500 by the Washington-based Investor Responsibility Research Center found that 80% of the respondents conduct some sort of environmental auditing, but just 6% release summaries to shareholders, and then only on special request."[25] Another recent study by Price Waterhouse, the big six accounting firm, "found that 62% of 523 companies surveyed said they have known environmental exposures that haven't been recorded in their financial statements."[26]

The growing environmental liability problem may require new accounting standards or greater enforcement of existing standards. The Financial Accounting Standards Advisory Council met in January 1992 to discuss whether, with environmental liabilities increasing, the FASB should address the significant accounting questions that are arising.

At present, *SFAS No. 5,* "Accounting for Contingencies," requires recognition of a liability when it is probable that an obligation exists and can be estimated. Firms may concede the existence of an obligation when it is identified as potentially responsible for an environmental problem under the Comprehensive Environmental Response, Compensation and Liability Act (Superfund Act). In many cases, however, the liability is difficult if not impossible to measure, and most firms therefore record at most only a partial liability.

On June 8, 1993, the Securities and Exchange Commission issued *Staff Accounting Bulletin No. 92,* which requires companies to increase their disclosure of potential liabilities.

---

[20]This section, and quoted statistics, are based primarily on *Overview of Environmental Regulation in the United States and Nature of Environmental Liabilities,* Financial Accounting Standards Advisory Council, January 1992.

[21]L. Berten, "SEC Rule Forces More Disclosure," *The Wall Street Journal,* December 13, 1993, p. B1.

[22]"Chevron to Sell Nearly a Third of U.S. Refining," *The Wall Street Journal,* May 28, 1993, p. A3.

[23]See T. Aeppel, "Firms Reveal More Detail on Environmental Efforts but Still Don't Tell All," *The Wall Street Journal,* December 13, 1993, p. B1.

[24]Ibid., p. B2.

[25]Ibid., p. B1.

[26]L. Berton, Op. cit.

The SEC regulations now require various disclosures related to environmental costs and obligations. Firms must disclose the effects of compliance with environmental laws on capital expenditures, earnings, and competitive position. Other requirements include disclosures of pending judicial proceedings under environmental law, estimates of future compliance costs if they are expected to increase, and a discussion of material environmental costs in the management's discussion and analysis section. The SEC has also endorsed the consensus reached by the Emerging Issues Task Force at its May 20, 1993, meeting with respect to potential recoveries and criteria for discounting environmental liabilities. Under the consensus, any loss arising from recognition of an environmental liability should be reduced by a potential claim for recovery (insurance) only when realization is probable. Further, discounting an environmental liability for a specific cleanup site to reflect the time value of money is appropriate only if the aggregate amount of the obligation and the amount and timing of the cash payments are fixed or reliably determinable for that site.

Major issues confronting the accounting profession in this area include

- How to develop standards to guide the timing of recognition of the cost and obligation.
- Whether to require advance recognition of cleanup costs.
- What criteria should guide mandated disclosures about environmental liabilities.
- Whether, given the magnitude of the problem, separate *SFASs* should be promulgated, or whether existing accounting standards are sufficient.
- How to distinguish between remedial expenditures required under the Superfund Act and voluntary expenditures on leading-edge technology for preventing future environmental problems.

In 1996, the AICPA issued *SOP 96–1, "Environmental Remediation Liabilities,"* which addresses recognition, measurement, and disclosure of environmental liabilities. A firm is liable for environmental remediation if it has an obligation for an existing environmental hazard.

The *SOP* provides benchmarks when evaluating the probability that a loss has been incurred and whether it can be estimated. When losses are accrued, the amount recognized should include the incremental direct costs of the remediation effort and related compensation costs. The measure of the liability should consider:

- Relevant laws and regulations.
- The technology to be used in the remediation effort.
- An estimate of the cost of the effort at the time the work will be performed. (Discounting is permitted.)

Environmental remediation costs can be substantial. In footnote 19 to its 1996 annual report, Oryx Energy Company, an oil and gas exploration company, reports an environmental cleanup liability of $20 million. This amount is about 15% of the firm's net income.

┃ *CONCEPT REVIEW*

1. When must a loss contingency be accrued?
2. When is it necessary to report a loss contingency in the notes? What value, if any, should be reported?
3. How are executory contracts treated in the accounting records?

┃ *SUMMARY OF KEY POINTS*

(L.O. 1)
1. A liability has three essential characteristics:
   a. An obligation exists that can be satisfied only by the transfer of an asset or a service to another entity.
   b. The event that gave rise to the obligation has occurred.
   c. The obligation is probable and unavoidable.

(L.O. 2)
2. Current liabilities are obligations whose liquidation is reasonably expected to require the use of existing resources properly classified as current assets, or the creation of other current liabilities.

(L.O. 3)   3. A liability is measured as the present value of all future cash payments discounted at the interest rate consistent with the risks involved. However, there is no requirement to account separately for interest that is not explicit on liabilities to be paid within one year.

(L.O. 4)   4. All obligations with terms beyond normal trade terms explicitly or implicitly involve interest.

(L.O. 5)   5. Cash or other assets received in advance of the delivery of goods or services create liabilities for the receiving firm.

(L.O. 3, 6)   6. Short-term obligations expected to be refinanced on a long-term basis can be classified as long-term only if the debtor (*a*) fully intends to refinance, and (*b*) shows an ability to refinance either by so doing or by entering into a noncancelable refinancing agreement with a viable lender.

(L.O. 7)   7. A loss contingency must be accrued if (*a*) before issuance of the financial statements, information implies that it is probable that an asset has been impaired or a liability incurred as of the balance sheet date, and (*b*) the amount of the loss can reasonably be estimated.

(L.O. 7)   8. Loss contingencies for guarantees of indebtedness, standby letters of credit, and related events are reported in the notes if either they are probable but cannot reasonably be estimated or they are reasonably possible.

(L.O. 7)   9. Gain contingencies are usually not accrued but rather are reported in the notes if probable or reasonably possible.

REVIEW PROBLEM

Answer each of the following questions:

1. Should United Airlines show a liability for its frequent flyer miles? Assuming the company is required to recognize a liability, how would you measure it?
2. A firm buys a delivery bus, giving as payment a noninterest-bearing note for $20,000 to be paid one year hence. The bus could be purchased for $18,182 in cash today. What entries are appropriate today and when payment is made?
3. The firm selling the bus in (2) agrees to cover the cost of all repairs for the year, estimated to be $1,500. Assume the bus is inventory to the seller. What entry should the seller make at the time of sale?
4. Suppose the locality in which the bus sale was made has a total sales tax of 8 percent, of which 6 percent goes to the state. What entry by the seller is appropriate at the time of sale to recognize the tax? (Assume that the tax is included in the cash price.)
5. The owner of the selling firm earns a bonus equal to 2 percent of the firm's net income over $1,000,000. The firm's pretax income for the year is $3,500,000, and the firm's tax rate is 40 percent. What is the owner's bonus?
6. During the year, a bus driver stopped the bus suddenly and without warning. One passenger was injured and brought a suit against the company for $1 million. The suit is pending. The company expects to be held liable and estimates that the final settlement will be between $100,000 and $500,000. What entry, if any, is appropriate?

SOLUTION

1. Yes, it meets the test of a liability. Transfer of a service is required, the causal event has occurred and the obligation is unavoidable on United's part. Estimates based on the historic use of existing mileage estimates or trips earned could be used to estimate the liability. In the case of some airlines, the materiality of the item may be sufficiently small to justify no accrual.
2. Entry today:

Asset: bus	18,182	
Note payable		18,182

Entry one year hence:

Interest expense	1,818	
Note payable	18,182	
Cash		20,000

3.

Note receivable	18,182	
Warranty expense	1,500	
Liability for warranty		1,500
Sales revenue		18,182

4.

Sales revenue	1,347	
Sales tax payable: state (.06)($16,835)		1,010
Sales tax payable: local (.02)($16,835)		337

Let R = Sales revenue
$R + .08 R = \$18,182$
$R = \$16,835$
Total tax = $\$18,182 - \$16,835 = \$1,347$

5.

$$B = \text{Bonus} \qquad T = \text{Tax} \qquad NI = \text{Net income after tax}$$
$$NI = \$3,500,000 - B - T$$
$$B = .02 \, (NI - \$1,000,000)$$
$$B = .02 \, (\$3,500,000 - B - T - \$1,000,000)$$
$$B = .02(\$2,500,000 - B - T)$$
$$T = .4(\$3,500,000 - B)$$

Therefore,

$$B = .02[\$2,500,000 - B - .4(\$3,500,000 - B)]$$
$$B = \$50,000 - .02B - .02(.4)(\$3,500,000 - B)$$

Solving, $B = \$21,739$.

6.

Expense 100,000	
Liability	100,000

The claim is probable and the lower end of the range is accrued. The event may be infrequent, but it is not unusual and should appear in the expenses for the year. The liability should be described, if material, in a note. Lawyers might convince the company to omit the liability until the trial is over and the award established.

APPENDIX   SFAS No. 112—Employers' Accounting for Postemployment Benefits

SFAS No. 112, "Employers' Accounting for Postemployment Benefits," (November 1992) amends *SFAS No. 5* and *SFAS No. 43.* Financial statements for fiscal years beginning after December 15, 1993, must report postemployment benefits for former and inactive employees on the accrual basis. The standard establishes uniform accounting requirements for a topic area formerly characterized by diverse reporting practices including accrual of benefits as well as cash basis accounting.

Scope of *SFAS No. 112*

SFAS No. 112 establishes standards for recognizing the cost of *postemployment benefits* (distinguished from *postretirement* benefits) provided to former or inactive[27] employees *after employment but before retirement,* and to their beneficiaries and covered dependents regardless of whether the employee is expected to return to active employment. Postemployment benefits include but are not limited to

- Salary continuation.
- Supplemental unemployment benefits.
- Severance benefits.
- Workers' compensation.
- Job training and counseling.
- Continuation of health and life insurance coverage.
- Disability benefits.

Benefits may be paid as a result of disability, layoff, death, and other events. They may be paid immediately upon conclusion of employment or over time.

Postemployment benefits were specifically excluded from both *SFAS No. 5,* "Accounting for Contingencies," and *SFAS No. 43,* "Accounting for Compensated Absences." *SFAS No. 112* extends to postemployment benefits the applicability of

- The "probable and estimable" criteria for recognizing contingencies in *SFAS No. 5.*
- The criteria for recognizing compensated absences in *SFAS No. 43.*

The standard does not apply to

- Pension and postretirement benefits, which are currently covered by *SFAS No. 87, No. 88,* and *No. 106.*
- Individual deferred compensation arrangements, which are covered by *APB Opinion No. 12.*
- Stock compensation plans, which are currently covered by *APB Opinion No. 25* and *SFAS No. 123.*
- Allocation of the cost of compensated absences, including postemployment benefits, to interim periods.

---

[27]Inactive employees have not been terminated but are not currently rendering service. Employees who have been laid off or are on disability leave, regardless of whether they expect to return to service, are considered inactive.

Accounting for Postemployment Benefits

The FASB concluded that postemployment benefits are part of the compensation earned by employees in exchange for services rendered. The central focus of *SFAS No. 112* is the principle that the event creating a liability and establishing the amount of future benefit cost is the rendering of service by employees. An expense and a liability are accrued for the amount of future payments to be made based on services rendered in the past.

Example   If for each year of service, employees receive credit for one week of severance pay, an expense and a liability are accrued for the cost of expected future severance pay as measured by employee credits earned each year through the balance sheet date.

Other benefits create an obligation for the employer as a result of a specific event. For example, upon announcing a layoff affecting a group of employees, an employer promises to provide supplemental unemployment benefits based on an employee's years of service. In this case, the event giving rise to the future benefits is the layoff. Therefore, the entire cost of the unemployment benefits is recognized at the time of layoff, rather than accrued over time.

SFAS No. 112 establishes criteria for recognizing postemployment benefit expense and obligation. A liability must be accrued for postemployment benefits that meet all of the following criteria:[28]

1. The employer's obligation relating to employees' rights to receive compensation for future absences is attributable to employees' service already rendered.
2. The obligation relates to rights that vest (the employer's obligation is not contingent on continuing service by the employee) or accumulate (unused rights carry over to future periods although limits may apply).
3. Payment of the compensation is probable.
4. The amount can be reasonably estimated.

The expense applicable to benefits earned *before* initial application of the standard is reported as a change in accounting principle similar to the cumulative effect of an accounting change, except that pro forma effects of retroactive application are not required. Previously issued financial statements are not restated.

Example   Assume that Henley Boats, Inc., estimates that total unfunded postemployment benefits at December 31, 1994, based on services rendered by employees to that date, the transition date, are $100,000. Henley then records the resulting accounting change and obligation upon adopting *SFAS No. 112:*

December 31, 1994

Cumulative effect of change in method of		
accounting for postemployment benefits	100,000	
Accrued postemployment benefit obligation		100,000

The cumulative effect reduces pretax earnings in 1994, and as benefit payments are made, the obligation is reduced.

Each year, Henley will recognize postemployment benefit expense and an obligation as current employees earn postemployment benefits that meet the four criteria of *SFAS No. 112*. Also, changes in benefits to former or inactive employees are recognized in current postemployment benefit expense. Both these benefit costs may be accrued or recognized as the result of a specific event, depending on the type of benefit.

If Henley recognizes $20,000 of additional postemployment benefit cost based on services rendered in 1998, or because estimates of prior benefits are changed, the cost is recognized as follows:

December 31, 1995

Postemployment benefit expense	20,000	
Accrued postemployment benefit obligation		20,000

Measuring the Cost and Liability   *SFAS No. 112* provides no specific guidance on measuring the amount to be accrued. Measurement approaches used in accounting for pension and postretirement benefits are applied where relevant. Discounting of future postemployment

---

[28]*SFAS No. 112*, par. 6. (These are the same criteria that apply to compensated absences in *SFAS No. 43*, par. 6.)

benefits is appropriate although not required by the standard. Firms must make assumptions about life expectancy, current and future pay rates, interest rates, and many other factors when determining the amount to accrue, depending on the type of benefit promised.

However, delayed recognition of the postemployment expense and obligation, one of the fundamental aspects of both pension and postretirement benefit accounting, is not permitted. The FASB reasoned that the magnitude of the postemployment expense does not warrant delayed recognition and that unnecessary complexity and reduced comparability would result from delayed recognition. Therefore, the entire estimated expense and obligation must be accrued in the year of estimation. Consequently, there is no off-balance-sheet financing of the postemployment benefit obligation.

Postemployment benefits that do not meet the four criteria of *SFAS No. 112* are subject to the "probable and estimable" criteria of *SFAS No. 5* (the last two of the four criteria of *SFAS No. 112*). This means that benefits that do not vest or accumulate may still be accrued if payment is probable and the amount can be reasonably estimated.[29]

Benefits that are not accrued because the amount cannot be reasonably estimated are disclosed in footnotes to the financial statements. The additional disclosure requirements of *SFAS No. 5,* such as those for reasonably possible obligations, do not apply to postemployment obligations.

Effect of *SFAS No. 112*   The effect of *SFAS No. 112* on earnings is considerably less than the magnitude of *SFAS No. 106* (on postretirement benefits other than pensions); nor has *SFAS No. 112* received the volume of objections leveled at *SFAS No. 106*. However, many firms experienced significant earnings effects, particularly in the transition year.

A survey conducted by the management consulting firm Towers Perrin found that, on average, pretax earnings would be reduced by $20 million for a firm with 10,000 employees.[30] In addition, some benefits experts estimated that the total effect on corporate profits would be as high as $30 billion.[31]

Others feared that the yearly change in earnings caused by the annual accrual of postemployment benefits would increase earnings variability. However, many other companies had been accruing postemployment costs for years, lessening the overall impact of *SFAS No. 112.*

UNDERSTANDING AND APPLYING CONCEPTS AND STANDARDS

QUESTIONS

1. Give a conceptual definition of a liability.
2. Conceptually, how should a liability be measured?
3. Explain how the measurement of a liability is related to its cause.
4. Why are most liabilities recognized at maturity value at the beginning of their term?
5. Compute the present value of a $10,000, one-year note payable that specifies no interest, although 10 percent would be a realistic rate. What is the amount of the principal and the interest?
6. In evaluating a balance sheet, some bankers say the liability section is one of the most important parts. What are the reasons justifying this position?
7. Some liabilities are reported at their maturity amount. In general, when should liabilities, prior to maturity date, be reported at less than their maturity amount?
8. How is the cost principle involved in accounting for current liabilities?
9. Define a current liability.
10. Differentiate between secured and unsecured liabilities. Explain the reporting procedures for each.
11. Distinguish between the stated rate of interest and the effective rate of interest (yield) on a debt.
12. Briefly define the following terms related to a note payable: principal, face, and maturity amounts.
13. Distinguish between an interest-bearing note and a noninterest-bearing note.

---

[29]For nonvesting plans, the accrual of benefits may be seen by employees as tantamount to vesting. However, there is no legal requirement that such nonvested accrued liabilities be paid.

[30]"*SFAS No. 112* Will Siphon Millions in Profits," *Accounting Today,* December 21, 1992.

[31]"Companies Face New Accounting of Benefit Costs," *The Wall Street Journal,* November 13, 1992, p. A3.

14. Assume that $4,000 cash is borrowed on a $4,000, 10 percent, one-year note payable that is interest-bearing and that another $4,000 cash is borrowed on a $4,400 one-year note that is noninterest-bearing. For each note give the following:
    a. Face amount of the note.
    b. Principal amount.
    c. Maturity amount.
    d. Total interest paid.
15. Are all declared dividends a liability between declaration and payment dates? Explain.
16. Why is an unearned revenue classified as a liability?
17. What is a compensated absence? When should the expense related to compensated absences be recognized?
18. What is the accounting definition of a contingency? What are the three characteristics of a contingency? Why is the concept important?
19. How does the accountant measure the likelihood of the outcome of a contingency? In general, how does this affect the accounting for and reporting of contingencies?
20. Briefly explain the accounting and reporting for loss contingencies.
21. What costs are being recognized by at least some firms for environmental obligations?

EXERCISES

E 15–1
(L.O. 3, 6, 7)

Multiple Choice

1. On January 17, 1998, an explosion occurred at a Cord Company plant causing extensive property damage to area buildings. Although no claims had yet been asserted against Cord by March 10, 1998, Cord's management and counsel concluded that it was reasonably possible Cord would be responsible for damages, and that $2,500,000 would be a reasonable estimate of its liability. Cord's $10,000,000 comprehensive public liability policy has a $500,000 deductible clause. In Cord's December 31, 1997, financial statements, which were issued on March 25, 1998, how should this item be reported?
   a. No footnote disclosure or accrual is necessary.
   b. As a footnote disclosure indicating the possible loss of $500,000.
   c. As an accrued liability of $500,000.
   d. As a footnote disclosure indicating the possible loss of $2,500,000.
2. Tone Company is the defendant in a lawsuit filed by Witt in 1997 disputing the validity of a copyright held by Tone. At December 31, 1997, Tone determined that Witt would probably be successful against Tone for an estimated amount of $800,000. Appropriately, a $800,000 loss was accrued by a charge to income for the year ended December 31, 1997. On December 15, 1998, Tone and Witt agreed to a settlement providing for cash payment of $500,000 by Tone to Witt and transfer of Tone's copyright to Witt. The carrying amount of the copyright on Tone's accounting records was $120,000 at December 15, 1998. What would be the effect of the settlement of this liability on Tone's income before income tax in 1998?
   a. No effect.
   b. $120,000 decrease.
   c. $180,000 increase.
   d. $300,000 increase.
3. A manufacturer of household appliances has potential costs due to the discovery of a possible defect in one of its products. The occurrence of the loss is reasonably possible and the costs can be reasonably estimated. This possible loss should be

	Accrued	**Disclosed in Footnotes**
a.	No	No
b.	No	Yes
c.	Yes	Yes
d.	Yes	No

4. An expropriation of assets which is imminent and for which the amount of loss can be reasonably estimated should be

	Accrued	**Disclosed in Footnotes**
a.	No	No
b.	No	Yes
c.	Yes	Yes
d.	Yes	No

(AICPA adapted)

E 15–2
(L.O. 3, 6, 7)

Multiple Choice

1. On December 31, 1998, Beal Company was involved in a tax dispute with the IRS. Beal's tax counsel believed that an unfavorable outcome was probable and a reasonable estimate of additional taxes was $275,000, with a chance that the additional taxes could be as much as $425,000. After the 1998 financial statements were issued, Beal accepted the IRS settlement offer of $325,000. What amount of additional taxes should have been accrued in 1998?
   a. $425,000.
   b. $325,000.
   c. $275,000.
   d. $0.

2. On November 5, 1997, a Dunn Corporation truck was in an accident with an auto driven by R. Bell. Dunn received notice on January 12, 1998, of a lawsuit for $350,000 in damages for personal injuries suffered by Bell. Dunn Corporation's counsel believes it is probable that Bell will be awarded an estimated amount in the range between $100,000 and $225,000, and that $150,000 is a better estimate of potential liability than any other amount. Dunn's accounting year ends on December 31, and the 1997 financial statements were issued on March 2, 1998. What liability should Dunn accrue at December 31, 1997?
   a. $0.
   b. $100,000.
   c. $150,000.
   d. $225,000.

3. The following information pertains to a fire insurance policy in effect during the calendar year 1998, covering Vail Company's inventory:

Face amount of policy	$400,000
Deductible	25,000
Amount of premium	2,000
Coinsurance clause	80%

   Vail's inventory averages $500,000 uniformly throughout the year. Vail's income tax rate is 40 percent. How much of a contingent liability should Vail accrue at December 31, 1998, to cover possible future fire losses?
   a. $0.
   b. $15,000.
   c. $23,000.
   d. $60,000.

4. When the occurrence of a gain contingency is reasonably possible and its amount can be reasonably estimated, the gain contingency should be
   a. Included in net income and disclosed.
   b. Included as an appropriation of retained earnings.
   c. Disclosed, but not included in net income.
   d. Neither included in net income nor disclosed.

(AICPA adapted)

E 15–3
(L.O. 3, 5, 6)

Multiple Choice

1. Robb Company requires advance payments with special orders from customers for machinery constructed to their specifications. Information for 1998 is:

Customer advances—balance 12/31/97	$590,000
Advances received with orders in 1998	920,000
Advances applied to orders shipped in 1998	820,000
Advances applicable to orders canceled in 1998	250,000

   At December 31, 1998, what amount should Robb report as a current liability for customer deposits?
   a. $0.
   b. $440,000.
   c. $690,000.
   d. $740,000.

2. Cobb Company sells appliance service contracts to repair appliances for a two-year period. Cobb's past experience is that, of the total amount spent for repairs on service contracts, 40 percent is incurred evenly during the first contract year and 60 percent evenly during the second contract year. Receipts from service contract sales for the two years ended December 31, 1998, are $250,000 in 1997 and $300,000 in 1998. Receipts from contracts are credited to unearned service contract revenue. Assume that all contract sales

are made evenly during the year. What amount should Cobb report as unearned service contract revenue at December 31, 1998?

a. $180,000.

b. $235,000.

c. $240,000.

d. $315,000.

3. In packages of its products, Curran Co. includes coupons that may be presented at retail stores to obtain discounts on other Curran products. Retailers are reimbursed for the face amount of coupons redeemed plus 10 percent of that amount for handling costs. Curran honors requests for coupon redemption by retailers up to three months after the consumer expiration date. Curran estimates that 70 percent of all coupons issued will ultimately be redeemed. Information relating to coupons issued by Curran during 1998 is as follows: consumer expiration date, December 31, 1998; total face amount of coupons issued, $300,000; and total payments to retailers as of December 31, 1998, $110,000. What amount should Curran report as a liability for unredeemed coupons at December 31, 1998?

a. $0.

b. $100,000.

c. $121,000.

d. $154,000.

4. An employer's obligation relating to employees' rights to receive compensation for future absences is attributable to employees' services already rendered. The payment of compensation is probable and the amount of compensation can be reasonably estimated. Employees' compensation should be

a. Accrued if the obligation relates to rights that vest or accumulate.

b. Accrued if the obligation relates to rights that do not vest or accumulate.

c. Expensed when paid.

d. Disclosed, but not accrued if the obligation relates to rights that vest or accumulate.

(AICPA adapted)

E 15–4
(L.O. 3, 6)

Multiple Choice

1. Bloy Company pays all salaried employees on a biweekly basis. Overtime pay, however, is paid in the next biweekly period. Bloy accrues salaries expense only at its December 31 year-end. Data relating to salaries earned in December 1998 are:

- Last payroll was paid on December 26, 1998, for the two-week period ended on that day.
- Overtime pay earned in the two-week period ended December 26, 1998, was $8,400.
- Remaining work days in 1998 were December 29, 30, and 31, on which days there was no overtime.
- The recurring biweekly salaries total $150,000.

Assuming a five-day workweek, Bloy should record a liability at December 31, 1998, for accrued salaries of

a. $45,000.

b. $53,400.

c. $90,000.

d. $98,400.

2. On September 1, 1997, Pine Company issued a note payable to National Bank in the amount of $900,000, bearing interest at 12 percent, and payable in three equal annual principal payments of $300,000. On this date the bank's prime rate was 11 percent. The first interest and principal payment was made on September 1, 1998. At December 31, 1998, Pine should record accrued interest payable of

a. $22,000.

b. $24,000.

c. $33,000.

d. $36,000.

3. Pam, Inc. has $500,000 of notes payable due June 15, 1999. At the financial statement date of December 31, 1998, Pam signed an agreement to borrow up to $500,000 to refinance the notes payable on a long-term basis. The financing agreement called for borrowings not to exceed 80% of the value of the collateral Pam was providing. At the date of issue of the December 31, 1998, financial statements, the value of the collateral was $600,000 and was not expected to fall below this amount during 1999. In its December 31, 1998, balance sheet, Pam should classify notes payable as

	Short-term Obligations	Long-term Obligations
a.	$ 0	$500,000
b.	$ 20,000	$480,000
c.	$100,000	$400,000
d.	$500,000	$ 0

4. Which of the following is classified as an accrued liability?

	Liability for Federal Unemployment Taxes	Liability for Employer's Share of FICA Taxes
a.	Yes	Yes
b.	Yes	No
c.	No	No
d.	No	Yes

(AICPA adapted)

E 15–5
(L.O. 1)

Characteristics of Liabilities   Listed below are five characteristics that may be associated with any liability:

a. The transfer of an asset or the obligation to provide a service is assured.
b. The magnitude of the obligation must be material relative to the firm's assets.
c. The obligation to transfer assets or provide services must be unavoidable if the existence of the obligation is at least probable.
d. The obligation arises from a past event.
e. An explicit interest rate must be stated.

Required

Indicate which of the above are necessary characteristics for the item to be a liability. Explain.

E 15–6
(L.O. 1, 2)

Identifying Liabilities and Current Liabilities   Five items discussed in the chapter are listed here:

a. Coupons that may be redeemed for merchandise or service.
b. Frequent flyer miles earned by airline passengers.
c. Probable requirements to clean up toxic wastes.
d. Company contract promises to pay postretirement health benefits.
e. Probable awards based on product liability suits.

Required

Which of these items, if any, should be considered liabilities and recognized on the balance sheet? Should any of them or portions thereof be recognized as current liabilities? Explain.

E 15–7
(L.O. 2)

Identifying Current Liabilities   Consider the following five items:

a. Bank overdraft.
b. Retained earnings.
c. Long-term debt.
d. Cash dividends declared but not paid.
e. Customer payments for magazine subscriptions not yet delivered.

Required

Identify the current liabilities among these five items.

E 15–8
(L.O. 2)

Identifying a Current Liability   Suppose a firm has an obligation that requires it to pay another organization $500,000 two years from today.

Required

Normally such a liability would be considered long term. Is there any situation in which this obligation could be considered a current liability? Explain.

E 15–9
(L.O. 4)

Interest-Bearing and Noninterest-Bearing Notes Compared

a. On January 1, 1998, a heavy-duty truck was purchased with a list price of $35,500. Payment included $5,500 cash and a two-year, noninterest-bearing note of $30,000 (maturity date, December 31, 1999). A realistic interest rate for this level of risk is 12 percent. The accounting period ends December 31.
b. On January 1, 1998, a small truck was purchased and payment was made as follows: cash, $5,000, and a one-year, 6 percent, interest-bearing note of $15,000, maturity date December 31, 1998 (which also is the end of the accounting period). A realistic interest rate for this level of risk is 12 percent.

Required

Give all entries for each case from purchase date through maturity date of each note. Disregard depreciation. Round to the nearest dollar.

E 15–10
(L.O. 4)

Interest-Bearing Note: Entries and Reporting   On May 1, 1998, Reo Meters borrowed $400,000 cash and signed a one-year, 12 percent interest-bearing note for that amount. Reo's accounting period ends December 31.

Required

1. Give all of the required entries from May 1, 1998, through the maturity date of the note. Disregard reversing and closing entries.
2. Show how all amounts related to the note should be reported on the debtor's balance sheet at December 31, 1998, and on the 1998 income statement.

E 15–11
(L.O. 4)

Analysis of Two Noninterest-Bearing Notes—One Has an Unrealistic Rate   On March 1, 1998, Mongo Lumber borrowed $50,000 cash from SP Bank and signed a one-year note for $60,000 (designated note A); no interest was specified in the note. On June 1, 1998, Mongo borrowed additional cash and signed a one-year note, face amount, $18,000 (designated note B). No interest was specified in the note; however, the going rate of interest for this level of risk was 10 percent. The accounting period ends December 31.

Required

	Note A	Note B
1. How much cash was received?	$______	$______
2. What was the face amount of the note?	$______	$______
3. What was the principal of the note?	$______	$______
4. How much interest expense should be reported in		
1998	$______	$______
1999	$______	$______
5. What was the stated interest rate?	______%	______%
6. What was the yield or effective interest rate?	______%	______%

E 15–12
(L.O. 4)

Analysis and Comparison of Interest-Bearing and Noninterest-Bearing Notes   On September 1, 1998, Dyer Company borrowed cash on a $100,000 note payable due in one year. Assume the going rate of interest was 12 percent per year for this particular level of risk. The accounting period ends December 31.

Required

Complete the following tabulation; round to the nearest dollar.

	Assuming the Note Was	
	Interest-Bearing	Noninterest-Bearing
1. Cash received	$______	$______
2. Cash paid at maturity date	$______	$______
3. Total interest paid (cash)	$______	$______
4. Interest expense in 1998	$______	$______
5. Interest expense in 1999	$______	$______
6. Amount of liabilities reported on 1998 balance sheet:		
Note payable (net)	$______	$______
Interest payable	$______	$______
7. Principal amount	$______	$______
8. Face amount	$______	$______
9. Maturity value	$______	$______
10. Stated interest rate	______%	______%
11. Yield or effective interest rate	______%	______%

E 15–13
(L.O. 4)

Noninterest-Bearing Note: Entries and Reporting   On April 1, 1998, Martin Manufacturing purchased a heavy machine for use in operations by paying $20,000 cash and signing an $80,000 (face amount) noninterest-bearing note due in one year (on March 31, 1999). The going rate of interest for this type of note was 14 percent per year. The company uses straight-line depreciation. The accounting period ends on December 31. Assume a five-year life for the machine and 10 percent residual value.

Required

1. Give all entries from April 1, 1998, through March 31, 1999 (round amounts to the nearest dollar).
2. Show how all of the related items would be reported on the 1998 income statement and balance sheet.

E 15–14
(L.O. 4, 5, 6)

Current Liabilities: Original and Adjusting Entries   Vintage Sales Company, a large retail outlet, completed the following selected transactions during 1998 and 1999:

a. At the end of 1998, accrued wages that have not yet been recorded amounted to $40,000. These accrued wages were paid in the January 15, 1999, payroll, which amounted to $190,000 (disregard payroll taxes).
b. On November 1, 1998, rent revenue for the following six months was collected, $9,600.
c. On October 1, 1998, Vintage received $400 as a deposit from a customer for some special containers that are to be returned on or about March 31, 1999. Vintage agreed to "give the customer credit at an annual rate of 6 percent interest on the deposit." The containers were returned on April 1, 1999.

Required   Give all of the required entries (omit closing and reversing entries) during 1998 and 1999 for each of the above transactions. The accounting period of Vintage ends on December 31.

E 15–15
(L.O. 4, 6)   **Reporting Liabilities: Dividends and Secured Notes**   The records of the Fisk Corporation provided the following information at December 31, 1998.

a. Notes payable (trade), short term (includes a $4,000 note given on purchase of equipment that cost $20,000; assets were mortgaged in connection with purchase)	$ 30,000
b. Bonds payable ($30,000 due each April 1)	120,000
c. Accounts payable (including $3,000 owed to president of the company)	50,000
d. Accrued property taxes (estimated)	1,000
e. Stock dividends issuable on 3/1/1999 (at par value)	26,000
f. Cash dividends declared, payable 3/1/1999	20,000
g. Long-term note payable, maturity amount ($14,500 carrying value)	16,000
h. Accrued interest on all bonds and notes	13,500

Required   Assuming that the fiscal year ends December 31, show how each of the above items should be reported on the balance sheet at December 31, 1998.

E 15–16
(L.O. 6)   **Entries to Record Payroll and Related Deductions**   Ryan company paid salaries for the month amounting to $120,000. Of this amount, $30,000 was received by employees who had already been paid the $53,400 maximum amount of annual earnings taxable in one year under FICA laws (FICA rate, 7.65 percent).

Of the $120,000, $14,000 was paid to employees who had already reached the $7,000 maximum wages subject to unemployment taxes (rates: 5.4 percent state and 0.8 percent federal). Withholding taxes amounted to $36,000, and $1,450 was withheld from the $120,000 for investment in company stock per an agreement with certain employees.

Required   Give entries to record (*a*) salary payment and the liabilities for the deductions, (*b*) employer payroll expenses, and (*c*) remittance of the taxes.

E 15–17
(L.O. 6)   **Recording Payroll and Related Deductions**   Smiley Corporation paid salaries and wages of $143,800. Of this amount, $3,800 was paid to employees who had already exceeded the FICA maximum. Also, $43,800 was paid to employees who had already been paid the SUTA maximum. Use the FICA and FUTA rates given in the chapter. Income tax withholding was $35,000. Deductions: union dues (in conformity with the union agreement), $3,000, and insurance premiums, $12,000.

Required   Give the entries to record liabilities for payroll deductions, payroll expenses, and remittance of the deductions.

E 15–18
(L.O. 6)   **Compensated Absences: Entries and Reporting**   Tunacliff Mowers allows each employee to earn 15 paid vacation days each year with full pay while on vacation. Unused vacation time can be carried over to the next year; if not taken during the next year it is lost. By the end of 1998, all but 3 of the 30 employees had taken their earned vacation time; these three carried over to 1999 a total of 20 vacation days, which represented 1998 salary of $6,000. During 1999, each of these three used their 1998 vacation carryover; none of them had received a pay rate change from 1998 to the time they used their carryover. Total cash wages paid: 1998, $700,000; 1999, $740,000. There was no carryover of vacation time earned in 1999.

Required   1. Give all of the entries for Tunacliff related to vacations during 1998 and 1999. Disregard payroll taxes.
2. Compute the total amount of wage expense for 1998 and 1999. How would the vacation time carried over from 1998 affect the 1998 balance sheet?

E 15–19
(L.O. 7)   **Estimated Warranty Expense: Recording and Reporting**   Macy Furniture sells a line of products that carry a three-year warranty against defects. Based on industry experience, the estimated warranty costs related to dollar sales are the following: first year after sale, 1 percent of sales; second year after sale, 3 percent of sales; and third year after sale, 5 percent. Sales and actual warranty expenditures for the first three-year period were as follows:

	Cash Sales	Actual Warranty Expenditures
1998	$ 80,000	$1,000
1999	110,000	4,100
2000	120,000	9,800

Required   1. Give entries for the three years for (*a*) the sales, (*b*) the estimated warranty expense, and (*c*) the actual expenditures.
2. What amount should be reported as a liability on the balance sheet at the end of each year?

E 15–20
(L.O. 7)

Liability for Premiums: Entries and Reporting   Van Slyke Stereos has initiated a promotion program whereby customers are given coupons redeemable in $25 special savings certificates. Each certificate can be turned in to the savings company for its face amount at the end of the third year from its issuance to the customer. One coupon is issued for each dollar of sales. On the surrender of 500 coupons, one $25 savings certificate (cost $20) is given. It is estimated that 25 percent of the coupons issued will never be presented for redemption. Sales for the first period were $400,000, and the number of coupons redeemed totaled 210,000. Sales for the second period were $440,000 and the number of coupons redeemed totaled 300,000. The savings certificates are acquired as needed.

Required   Prepare journal entries (including closing entries) relative to the premium plan for the two periods. Show amounts that should be reported in the balance sheet and income statement for the two periods. Hint: Use the following accounts: cash, premium expense, estimated premium claims payable, and income summary.

E 15–21
(L.O. 7)

Loss Contingency—Three Cases: Entries and Explanation   Canseco Company is preparing the annual financial statements at December 31, 1999. During 1999, a customer fell while riding on the escalator and has filed a lawsuit for $40,000 because of a claimed back injury. The lawyer employed by the company has carefully assessed all of the implications. If the suit is lost, the lawyer's reasonable estimate is that the $40,000 will be assessed by the court.

Required   How should the contingency be handled during 1999 in each of the following cases? Give all necessary entries and any notes:

1. Assume that the lawyer and the management concluded that it is reasonably possible that the company will be liable, and it is reasonably estimated that the amount will be $40,000.
2. Assume, instead, that the lawyer, the independent accountant, and management have reluctantly concluded that it is probable that the suit will be successful.
3. Assume that the conclusion of the legal counsel and management is that the chance of a contingency loss is remote. They believe the suit is without merit.

E 15–22
(L.O. 7)

Property Taxes: Recording   Luxor Company is located in a relatively small town that has recently restructured its property tax procedures. During the past year (1998) the company experienced a significant increase in the property appraisal for taxes. The company paid property taxes of $100,000. However, it expects the tax for the current year, 1999, to decrease some because of citizen complaints. Both the city tax year and Luxor's accounting year end on December 31. The following events occurred during 1999:

January 20—paid the 1998 property taxes.

January 30—estimated a 10 percent decrease in property taxes for 1999. The company accrues property taxes each month.

July 10—received a tentative tax notice assessment for taxes, $2,280,000, preliminary tax rate per $100 valuation, $5.00. The company will revise its estimate to these assessments.

December 28—received final tax notice, 1999 tax assessed, $111,000, payable by January 24, 2000.

January 24, 2000—paid the 1999 property tax.

Required   Give the journal entries related to property taxes from January 1, 1999, through January 2000.

E 15–23
(L.O. 3, 4, 6)

Ratio Analysis   Suppose a firm issues short-term interest-bearing notes and uses the proceeds to purchase inventories. Assume, further, that the decision turns out to be a good one for the firm. Assume the firm's profits for the year remain unchanged.

Required   Indicate how the use of the notes would affect the indicated ratios immediately following the decision unless otherwise indicated by the symbol *, which means indicate the effect over the year but before any of the liability is repaid. Use the following symbols: U for up, D for down, and NC for no change.

| | | Effect on | |
Ratio	Numerator	Denominator	Ratio
a. Current ratio	______	______	______
b. Working capital to total assets	______	______	______
c. Net cash flow to current liabilities	______	______	______
d. Debt to equity	______	______	______
e. Debt to total assets	______	______	______
f. Times interest earned*	______	______	______
g. Cash flow per share*	______	______	______
h. Return on total assets*	______	______	______

E 15–24

Post Employment Benefits: Reporting and Entries (Appendix)   Alexes Supply and Rental Company estimates that on December 31, 1994, its total unfunded postemployment benefits obligation based on previous employee services is $6,837,500. The firm adopts *SFAS No. 112* on Dec. 31, 1994. The company intends to pay these benefits. Additional benefits are earned and vested during 1998 in the amount of $738,000. A third of this amount results from a change during 1998 in the labor contract. (Ignore taxes.)

Required

1. What entries, if any, are required on December 31, 1994? What is the effect on income before taxes?
2. What entries, if any, are required on December 31, 1998?
3. Should management discount any benefit amounts?
4. Would it matter whether the benefits were vested?
5. Suppose the amounts could not be reasonably estimated. What should Alexes do?

PROBLEMS

P 15–1
(L.O. 3, 5, 6)

Multiple Choice

1. Farr Company sells its products in expensive, reusable containers. The customer is charged a deposit for each container delivered and receives a refund for each container returned within two years after the year of delivery. Farr accounts for the containers not returned within the time limit as a sale at the deposit amount. Information for 1998 is (dollar amounts represent deposits received from customers):

Containers held by customers at December 31, 1997, from deliveries in		
1996	$150,000	
1997	430,000	$580,000
Containers delivered in 1998		$780,000
Containers returned in 1998, from deliveries in		
1996	$ 90,000	
1997	250,000	
1998	286,000	$626,000

What amount should Farr report as a liability for returnable containers at December 31, 1998?
   a. $494,000.
   b. $644,000.
   c. $674,000.
   d. $734,000.

2. Dunn Trading Stamp Company records stamp service revenue and provides for the cost of redemptions in the year stamps are sold to licensees. Dunn's past experience indicates that only 80 percent of the stamps sold to licensees will be redeemed. Dunn's liability for stamp redemptions was $24,000,000 at December 31, 1997. Additional information for 1998 is:

Stamp service revenue from stamps sold to licensees	$16,000,000
Cost of redemptions (stamps sold prior to 1/1/98)	11,000,000

If all the stamps sold in 1998 were presented for redemption in 1999, the redemption cost would be $9,000,000. What amount should Dunn report as a liability for stamp redemptions at December 31, 1998?
   a. $13,000,000.
   b. $20,200,000.
   c. $22,000,000.
   d. $29,000,000.

3. Grey operates as a retail furrier. Some customers pick out furs and place deposits with Grey to set the furs aside for future delivery. Grey records the cash receipts on these transactions as layaway plan sales. How-

ever, title to the fur passes to the customer only when the full sales price is received by Grey. The average gross margin on the furs is 75 percent of sales. The following pertinent data were taken from Grey's December 31, 1998, unadjusted trial balance:

Regular sales	$5,000,000
Layaway plan sales	$2,000,000
Deposits from customers	$ 0

An analysis of the layaway plan sales revealed that $1,200,000 was received in full payment for furs delivered to customers during 1998. In Grey's December 31, 1998, balance sheet, deposits from customers would be

a. $2,000,000.

b. $1,500,000.

c. $1,200,000.

d. $800,000.

4. During 1997, Ward Company introduced a new product carrying a two-year warranty against defects. The estimated warranty costs related to dollar sales are 2 percent within 12 months following sale and 4 percent in the second 12 months following sale. Sales and actual warranty expenditures for the years ended December 31, 1997 and 1998, are:

	Sales	Actual Warranty Expenditures
1997	$ 600,000	$ 9,000
1998	1,000,000	30,000
	$1,600,000	$39,000

At December 31, 1998, Ward would report an estimated warranty liability of

a. $57,000.

b. $45,000.

c. $17,000.

d. $10,000.

(AICPA adapted)

P 15–2
(L.O. 3, 6, 7)

Multiple Choice

1. A state requires quarterly sales tax returns to be filed with the sales tax bureau by the 20th day following the end of the calendar quarter. However, the state further requires that sales taxes collected be remitted to the sales tax bureau by the 20th day of the month following any month such collections exceed $1,000. These payments can be taken as credits on the quarterly sales tax return.

   Taft Corporation operates a retail hardware store. All items are sold subject to a 6 percent state sales tax, which Taft collects and records as sales revenue. The sales taxes paid by Taft are charged against sales revenue. Taft pays the sales taxes when they are due.

   Following is a monthly summary appearing in Taft's first-quarter 1998 sales revenue account:

	Debit	Credit
January	$ —	$21,200
February	$1,200	14,840
March	—	19,080
	$1,200	$55,120

In its financial statements for the quarter ended March 31, 1998, Taft's sales revenue and sales taxes payable would be

	Sales Revenue	Sales Taxes Payable
a.	$55,120	$3,120
b.	$53,920	$1,200
c.	$52,000	$3,120
d.	$52,000	$1,920

2. In March 1998, an explosion occurred at Nilo Company's plant, causing damage to area properties. By May 1998, no claims had yet been asserted against Nilo. However, Nilo's management and legal counsel

concluded that it was reasonably possible that Nilo would be held responsible for negligence and that $1,500,000 was a reasonable estimate of the damages. Nilo's $2,500,000 comprehensive public liability policy contains a $150,000 deductible clause. In Nilo's December 31, 1997, financial statements, for which the auditor's field work was completed in April 1998, how should this casualty be reported?

   a. As a footnote disclosing a possible liability of $1,500,000.

   b. As an accrued liability of $150,000.

   c. As a footnote disclosing a possible liability of $150,000.

   d. No footnote disclosure or accrual is required for 1997 because the event occurred in 1998.

3. The following information relating to compensated absences was available from Graf Company's accounting records at December 31, 1998.

   ■ Employees' rights to vacation pay vest and are attributable to services already rendered. Payment is probable, and Graf's obligation was reasonably estimated at $220,000.

   ■ Employees' rights to sick pay benefits do not vest but accumulate for possible future use. The rights are attributable to services already rendered, and the total accumulated sick pay was reasonably estimated at $100,000.

What amount is Graf required to report as the liability for compensated absences in its December 31, 1998, balance sheet?

   a. $320,000.

   b. $220,000.

   c. $100,000.

   d. $0.

4. Ruhl Company grants all employees two weeks' paid vacation for each full year of employment, up to six weeks. Unused vacation time can be accumulated and carried forward to succeeding years and will be paid at the salaries in effect when vacations are taken or when employment is terminated. There was no employee turnover in 1998. Additional information relating to the year ended December 31, 1998, is:

Liability for accumulated vacations at 12/31/97	$50,000
Pre-1998 accrued vacations taken from 1/1/98 to 9/30/98 (the authorized period for vacations)	30,000
Vacations earned for work in 1998 (adjusted to current rates)	40,000

Ruhl granted a 10 percent salary increase to all employees on October 1, 1998, its annual salary-increase date. For the year ended December 31, 1998, Ruhl should report vacation pay expense of

   a. $42,000.

   b. $45,000.

   c. $60,000.

   d. $70,000.

(AICPA adapted)

P 15–3
(L.O. 4)

Interest-Bearing and Noninterest-Bearing Notes Compared: Entries and Reporting   Ripkin Company borrowed cash on August 1, 1998, and signed a $33,300 (face amount), one-year note payable, due on July 31, 1999. The accounting period ends December 31. Assume a going rate of interest of 11 percent for this company for this level of risk.

Required   Round amounts to nearest dollar.

1. How much cash should Ripkin receive on the note, assuming two cases: Case A, an interest-bearing note; and Case B, a noninterest-bearing note?
2. Give the following entries for each of the two cases:
   a. August 1, 1998, date of the loan.
   b. December 31, 1998, adjusting entry.
   c. July 31, 1999, payment of the note, assuming no reversing entry was made.
3. What liability amounts should be shown in each case on the December 31, 1998, balance sheet?

P 15–4
(L.O. 4)

Interest-Bearing and Noninterest-Bearing Notes Compared: Entries   On October 1, 1998, Reed Travel Company borrowed $40,000 cash and signed a one-year note payable, due on September 30, 1999. The going rate of interest for this level of risk was 10 percent. The accounting period ends on December 31.

Required

1. Compute the face amount of the note assuming
   a. Case A—An interest-bearing note.
   b. Case B—A noninterest-bearing note.

2. Complete a tabulation as follows:

		Case A: Interest- Bearing	Case B: Noninterest- Bearing
a.	Total cash received	$ 40,000	$ 40,000
b.	Face amount of note	$______	$______
c.	Total cash paid	$______	$______
d.	Total interest	$______	$______
e.	Interest expense, 1998	$______	$______
f.	Interest expense, 1999	$______	$______
g.	Amount of liabilities reported on the 1998 balance sheet:		
	Note payable	$______	$______
	Interest payable	$______	$______
h.	Principal amount	$______	$______
i.	Stated interest rate	______%	______%
j.	Yield or effective interest rate	______%	______%
k.	Time to maturity:		
	October 1, 1998	Months______	Months______
	December 31, 1998	Months______	Months______

3. Give entries for each case from October 1, 1998, through maturity date (assume that reversing entries were not made).
4. Show how the liability and expense amounts should be reflected for each case on the December 31, 1998, balance sheet and the 1998 income statement.

P 15–5
(L.O. 4)

Two-Year, Noninterest-Bearing Note: Entries and Reporting   On January 1, 1998, Jump Construction Company acquired a machine (an operational asset) that had a list price of $40,000. Because of a serious cash problem, Jump paid $10,000 cash and signed a two-year note with a maturity amount of $30,000 due on December 31, 1999. The note did not specify interest. Assume that the going rate of interest for this company for this level of risk was 15 percent. The accounting period ends December 31.

Required

Round amounts to nearest dollar.

1. Give the entry to record the purchase of the machine.
2. Complete the following tabulation related to the note:

a.	Cash equivalent received on note	$______
b.	Face amount	$______
c.	Total interest to be paid	$______
d.	Interest expense:	
	1998	$______
	1999	$______
e.	Liability on the 1998 balance sheet	$______
f.	Depreciation expense (on cost) (10-year estimated life; no residual value; straight-line)	$______
g.	Effective interest rate	______%
h.	Stated interest rate	______%

3. Give all entries (exclude closing and reversing entries) from January 1, 1998, through the end of 1999. Use the net method.
4. Show how the liabilities and expenses would be reported on the 1998 and 1999 financial statements (assume that the company has a two-year operating cycle).

P 15–6
(L.O. 4)

Two-Year, Noninterest-Bearing Note: Entries and Reporting   On January 1, 1998, Therm Publishing Company purchased a large used machine for operations; the asking price was $46,000. Payment was $16,000 cash and a $30,000 (maturity value), two-year, noninterest-bearing note payable due on December 31, 1999. The note did not specify interest; however, for Therm, the rate for this level of risk was 15 percent. Assume straight-line depreciation, a five-year life, and no residual value. The accounting period ends on December 31.

Required

Round amounts to the nearest dollar.

1. Give the entry to record the purchase of the machine.
2. Complete the following tabulation related to the note:

a. Cash equivalent received	$________
b. Face amount of note	$________
c. Cash to be paid at maturity	$________
d. Total interest expense	$________
e. Interest expense:	
1998	$________
1999	$________
f. Depreciation expense	$________
g. Effective interest rate	________%
h. Stated interest rate	________%

3. Prepare a debt amortization schedule for this note. Use the following column headings: date, interest expense, and carrying value of the liability.
4. Give all entries (except closing and reversing entries) from January 1, 1998, through the end of 1999.
5. Show how the liabilities and expenses should be reported on the 1998 and 1999 financial statements (assume that the company's operating cycle is two years).

P 15–7
(L.O. 6)

Property Tax and Sales Tax: Recording and Reporting General Department Stores has asked you to assist in improving its accounting for taxes. The following selected transactions, which were completed during 1999, have been presented to you for analysis; the accounting period ends on December 31.

a. Property taxes—Property taxes for 1998 amounted to $24,000. During January 1999, General estimated that the property tax would increase approximately 10 percent for 1999. During June 1999, the company received a tentative property tax appraisal that indicated a property valuation of $2,100,000 and an estimated 1999 tax rate per $1,000 of $13.10. The final tax assessment notice was received December 9, 1999, and specified a 1999 property tax of $31,000. The 1999 property taxes were paid in full on January 17, 2000.

b. Sales revenue for 1999 amounted to $9 million; the sales tax rate is 6 percent, and 98 percent of all sales were subject to tax. Unremitted sales tax at the end of 1999 amounted to $20,000.

Required

Round to the nearest dollar.

1. Give all entries indicated for (*a*) the accrual of property tax (during 1999 on a monthly basis) and the payment on January 17, 2000, and (*b*) the sales tax (for 1999) transactions.
2. Show how the effects of the above tax transactions should be reported on the 1999 financial statements.

P 15–8
(L.O. 6)

Compensated Absences: Entries and Reporting Aloha Company has a personnel policy that allows each employee with at least one year's employment 20 days vacation time and two holidays with regular pay. Unused days are carried over to the next year. If not taken during the next year, the vacation and holiday times are lost. Aloha's accounting period ends December 31.
At the end of 1999, the personnel records showed the following:

Vacations Carried over to 2000		Holidays Carried over to 2000	
Total Days	**Total Salaries**	**Total Days**	**Total Salaries**
70	$16,800	10	$2,580

During 2000, all of the 1999 vacation time and eight days of the holiday time, which were carried over, were taken. Salary increases in 2000 for these employees relating to the days carried over amounted to $1,600. Total cash wages paid: 1999, $1,780,000; 2000, $1,860,000.

Required

1. Give all of the entries for Aloha Company related to vacations and holidays during 1999 and 2000. Disregard payroll taxes.
2. Show how the effects of the above transactions should be reported on the 1999 and 2000 financial statements of Aloha.

P 15–9
(L.O. 7)

Contingency Losses, Six Events: Explanations, Entries, Reporting Duker Corporation is preparing its first set of financial statements at December 31, 1998, along with the appropriate adjusting entries. Among the contingent losses under consideration are the following transactions and events:

a. Sales revenue for 1998 was $475,000. Unpaid credit sales at year-end amounted to $10,000, and it is probable that $1,000 of that amount will result in a loss.

b. Two of the major product lines sold during the year carry a two-year warranty for defects (both labor and parts cost). Sales of these items amounted to $20,000. On the average, warranty expenditures approximate 4 percent of sales price.

c. During 1998, Duker issued 5,000 "DC orange coupons." Each 10 coupons held can be turned in, within one year from the date on the coupon, for a $7.50 credit on any item sold by Duker that costs more than $25. Duker estimates that 25 percent of the coupons will be redeemed.

d. Duker was sued by a shopper for $30,000 damages due to an accident in the retail store. The shopper asserts a permanent back injury, characterized primarily by pain and stiffness. Legal counsel is of the opinion that it is probable that the plaintiff will prevail in court and that Duker will have to pay 10 percent of the claim; it is anticipated that the insurance company will pay the balance. The suit is expected to be resolved in mid-1999.

e. Duker Corporation endorsed and guaranteed a $15,000, 15 percent, one-year mortgage note given by a local supplier (of merchandise) to Duker. The bank required a guarantor. The bank indicated that the probability of default by the supplier was reasonably possible.

f. The comprehensive liability insurance policy carried by Duker Corporation covers all claims for damages to individuals or groups due to accident, negligence, and other injuries relating to the legitimate operations of the company. However, the insurance policy carries an escape clause that states, "When the insured is willfully negligent, as determined by an independent third party, 10 percent of the loss must be paid by the insured."

Required

1. Evaluate each of the above transactions and events and recommend appropriate accounting and reporting actions. Give any entry or note required for each item.
2. Identify each liability and the amount that should be reported on the 1998 balance sheet.

P 15–10
(L.O. 7)

Redeemable Coupons: Accounting and Reporting   For the purpose of stimulating sales, Carter Cereal Company places a coupon in each box of cereal sold; the coupons are redeemable in chinaware. Each premium costs the company 90 cents (the cost of printing the coupons is negligible). Ten coupons must be presented by the customers to receive one premium. The following data are available:

Month	Boxes of Cereal Sold	Premiums Purchased	Coupons Redeemed
January	650,000	25,000	220,000
February	500,000	40,000	410,000
March	560,000	35,000	300,000

It is estimated that only 50 percent of the coupons will be presented for redemption.

Required

1. Prepare entries for each event listed below for each of the three months:
   a. Premiums purchased.
   b. Premium expense and related liability.
   c. Coupons redeemed.
2. Complete the following schedule for each month:

Accounts	Ending Account Balances		
	January	February	March
Premiums—Chinaware			
Estimated premium claims payable			
Premium expense (monthly)			

P 15–11
(L.O. 7)

Estimated Warranty Costs: Entries and Reporting   Habek Hardware, Inc., provides a product warranty for defects on two major lines of items sold since the beginning of 1998. Line A carries a two-year warranty for all labor and service (but not parts). The company contracts with a local service establishment to service the warranty (both parts and labor). The local service establishment charges a flat fee of $60 per unit payable at date of sale.

Line B carries a three-year warranty for parts and labor on service. Habek purchases the parts needed under the warranty and has service personnel who perform the work and are paid by the job. On the basis of experience, it is estimated that for Line B, the three-year warranty costs are 3 percent of dollar sales for parts and 7 percent for labor and overhead. Additional data available are as follows:

	Year		
	1998	**1999**	**2000**
Sales in units, Line A	700	1,000	
Sales price per unit, Line A	$ 610	$ 660	
Sales in units, Line B.	600	800	
Sales price per unit, Line B	$ 700	$ 750	
Actual warranty outlays, Line B			
Parts	$3,000	$ 9,600	$12,000
Labor and overhead	$7,000	$22,000	$30,000

Required

1. Give entries for annual sales and expenses for 1998 and 1999 separately by product line. Assume that all sales were for cash.
2. Complete the tabulation below:

	Year-End Amounts		
Accounts	**Year 1998**	**Year 1999**	**Year 2000**
a. Warranty expense (on income statement)	$_______	$_______	
b. Estimated warranty liability (on balance sheet)	$_______	$_______	$_______

P 15–12
(L.O. 6)

Recording and Reporting Liabilities, Including Payroll Deductions   The following selected transactions of Mattingly Company were completed during the accounting year just ended, December 31, 1998.

a. Merchandise was purchased on account; a $10,000, one-year, 16 percent interest-bearing note, dated April 1, 1998, was given to the creditor. Assume a perpetual inventory system.
b. The company cosigned an $8,000 note payable for another party (no entry required).
c. On July 1, the company borrowed cash; a one-year, noninterest-bearing note with a face amount of $28,750 was signed. Assume a going rate of interest of 15 percent.
d. Payroll records showed the following (assume that amounts given are correct):

Gross Wages	Employee			Employer		
	Withholding	**FICA**	**Union Dues**	**FICA**	**SUTA**	**FUTA**
$50,000	$15,000	$3,100	$500	$3,100	$1,350	$350

   Remittances: withholding taxes, $13,000; FICA, $6,000; SUTA, $1,200; FUTA, $340; and union dues, $280.
e. The company was sued for $150,000 in damages. It appears a court judgment against the company that is reasonably estimated to be $125,000 is probable. For problem purposes, assume that this is an extraordinary item.
f. On November 1, 1998, the company rented some office space in its building to Zorn Company and collected rent in advance for six months; total $2,400.
g. Cash dividends declared but not yet paid were $14,000.
h. Accrued interest on the notes at December 31.

Required

1. Give the entry or entries for each of the above transactions and events.
2. Prepare a list (title and amount) of the disclosures related to the liabilities at December 31, 1998.

P 15–13
(L.O. 7)

Contingencies and Warranty Costs   Cope Company is a manufacturer of household appliances. During the year, the following information became available:

a. Probable warranty costs on its household appliances are estimated to be 1 percent of sales.
b. One of its manufacturing plants is located in a foreign country. There is a threat of expropriation of this plant. The threat of expropriation is deemed to be reasonably possible. Any compensation from the foreign government would be less than the carrying amount of the plant.
c. It is probable that damages will be received by Cope next year as a result of a lawsuit filed this year against another household appliances manufacturer.

Required

In answering the following, do not discuss deferred income tax implications.

1. How should Cope report the probable warranty costs? Why?
2. How should Cope report the threat of expropriation of assets? Why?
3. How should Cope report this year the probable damages that may be received next year? Why?

(AICPA adapted)

P 15–14
(L.O. 7)

 **Contingencies and Warranty Costs**   Spackenkill Company is a manufacturer of household appliances. During the year, the following information became available:

a. Potential costs due to the discovery of a safety hazard related to one of its products. These costs are probable and can be reasonably estimated.
b. Potential costs of new product warranties. These costs are probable but cannot be reasonably estimated.
c. Potential costs due to the discovery of a possible product defect related to one of its products. These costs are reasonably possible and can be reasonably estimated.

Required

1. How should Spackenkill report the potential costs due to the discovery of a safety hazard? Why?
2. How should Spackenkill report the potential costs of warranties? Why?
3. How should Spackenkill report the potential costs due to the discovery of a possible product defect? Why?

(AICPA adapted)

P 15–15
(L.O. 6)

Compensated Absences   Carol Company has many long-time employees who have built up substantial employee benefits. These employee benefits include compensation for future vacations.

Required

What conditions must be met for Carol to accrue compensation for future vacations? Include in your answer the theoretical rationale for accruing compensation for future vacations.

(AICPA adapted)

P 15–16
(L.O. 4, 6, 7)

Overview: Liabilities, Contingency Losses, Recording, and Reporting   The following selected transactions of Johnson Motors Company were completed during the current accounting year ended December 31, 1998.

a. March 1, 1997, borrowed $25,000 on a two-year, 12 percent, interest-bearing note. Interest is paid yearly.
b. April 1, 1997, borrowed cash and signed a $20,000, two-year, noninterest-bearing note (no interest was specified). The market rate of interest for this level of risk was 16 percent.
c. June 1, 1998, purchased a special truck with a list price of $33,000. Paid $3,000 cash and signed a $30,000, one-year, noninterest-bearing note (no interest was specified). The market rate of interest for this level of risk was 16 percent.
d. During 1998, sold merchandise for $30,000 cash that carried a two-year warranty for parts and labor. A reasonable estimate of the cost of the warranty is 1.5 percent of sales revenue. By December 31, 1998, actual warranty costs amounted to $250.
e. June 1, 1998, Johnson cosigned and guaranteed payment of a $50,000, 14 percent, one-year note owed by a local supplier to City Bank. The bank required a cosignature; however, they believe that default by the debtor is only reasonably possible.
f. October–November 1998, in order to promote sales during these two months, Johnson gave its customers 10,000 premium certificates based on cash sales. Each certificate turned in during December 1998 and January 1999 will reduce the price by 50 cents on all single items that sell above $20. A reasonable estimate is that 75 percent of the certificates will be redeemed. By December 31, 1998, 60 percent of those issued had been redeemed.
g. Property taxes of 1998 to be recorded monthly:
 (1) Prior-year property taxes, $2,087; expected to increase by 15 percent during 1998.
 (2) December 10, 1998, final tax assessment received, $2,500; paid on February 1, 1999, the latest payment date without penalty.
h. December 1998, dividends declared (not yet paid or issued):
 (1) Cash, $20,000 (use payable account).
 (2) Stock, $15,000 (use issuable account).
i. December 1998, sales revenue (excluding sales taxes collected) for the month, $400,000. Sales tax, 5 percent, applicable to 98 percent of the sales. No unpaid sales tax carried over from November 1998.
j. December 31, 1998, accrual of interest payable.

Required

Round to the nearest dollar.

1. For each of the 10 items, give all entries that Johnson should make in 1998 based on the data given.
2. List each current liability (account title and the amount) that should be reported on the 1998 balance sheet of Johnson Company (issued during 1999).

P 15–17

Postemployment Benefits: Reporting and Entries (Appendix)   R. L. Jump Construction adopted *SFAS No. 112* on December 31, 1994, at which time it computed an unfunded vested postemployment obligation balance of $2,432,000 for employee services rendered to that date. This balance has not been accrued previously.

During 1998 Jump incurred additional benefits under its employment plan of $640,000. During 1998 benefits paid amounted to $327,000. (Ignore taxes.)

Required

1. Give all entries for 1994 and 1998 on Jump's books.
2. How should the items be reported on the 1994 and 1998 statements of R. L. Jump?

ANALYSIS, JUDGMENT, AND COMMUNICATION

CASES

C 15–1
(L.O. 7)

Evaluation of a Liability: Recommendations   Evans Equipment Company sells new and used earthmoving equipment. Evans uses a perpetual inventory system, and its accounting period ends December 31. On December 28, 1998, Evans purchased a used backhoe for resale, at a list price of $80,000. Terms of the purchase: cash down payment, $40,000, plus a note payable, face amount, $40,000, maturity date, December 28, 2000. The company bookkeeper entered the equipment in the perpetual inventory account at $80,000 and reported no interest expense for 1998 because the note did not specify that any interest would be paid. In answer to a question by the newly engaged independent auditor, the bookkeeper said that the entry on maturity date of the note would be a debit to notes payable and a credit to cash of $40,000. The transaction was recorded on January 5, 1999, because it was on that date that Evans received the equipment and the check was drawn. Write a memo to the controller to address the two items below.

Required

1. Evaluate the accounting treatment of the purchase of the equipment. Consider both theoretical and GAAP issues. State any assumptions that you make.
2. If the company's accounting seems in error, give recommendations for what should be done, including reasons. Also provide all the necessary journal entries. State any factual assumptions made.

C 15–2
(L.O. 7)

Contingencies: Four Situations   Unlucky Company is preparing its annual financial statements at December 31, 1995, and is concerned about application of *SFAS No. 5,* "Accounting for Contingencies." Four unrelated situations are under consideration:

a. During 1998, a shopper sued the company for $500,000 for a claimed injury that occurred on the premises owned by Unlucky. No date for the trial has been set; however, the lawyer employed by Unlucky has completed a thorough investigation. Because it can be proven that the customer did fall on the premises, the legal counsel believes it will not be difficult for the plaintiff to prove injury. There is some evidence that it was due, at least partially, to negligence by the plaintiff. The attorney believes that it is not probable, but is reasonably possible, that the suit will be successful (for the plaintiff), but for a significantly smaller amount that cannot be reasonably estimated at this time.

b. The company held a $10,000, 8 percent, one-year note receivable from a customer. Unlucky discounted the note, with recourse, at the bank to obtain cash before its due date (due on June 1, 1999). If the maker does not pay the bank by the due date, Unlucky will have to pay it. The customer has an excellent credit rating (having never defaulted on a debt).

c. An outside party has filed a suit against Unlucky for $25,000 claiming that certain actions by Unlucky caused the party to lose a contract on which the estimated profit was this amount. In the opinion of the legal counsel engaged by Unlucky, the probability that the claim is successful is remote. Counsel does not believe it will ever be brought to trial. If necessary, Unlucky will defend itself in court.

d. The company owns a small plant in a foreign country that has a book value of $3 million and an estimated market value of $4 million. The foreign government has indicated its unalterable intention to expropriate the plant during the coming year and to reimburse Unlucky for 50 percent of the estimated market value.

Required

For each situation, write a memo to the CFO giving your ideas on what should be done, considering the following two points.

1. What accounting recognition, if any, should be accorded each situation at the end of 1998? Explain why and give journal entries.
2. Indicate how each situation should be reported on the balance sheet.

C 15–3
(L.O. 2)

Distinguishing Short-Term from Long-Term Liabilities   This case relates to Coca-Cola's financial statements located at the end of the book.

Required

1. What current liabilities does Coca-Cola list on its balance sheet? Indicate the type of liability according to the list in the section titled "What Is a Current Liability?" in this chapter.
2. Does Coca-Cola discuss any of its current liabilities in the notes to its financial statements? If so, describe.

C 15–4
(L.O. 3)

Liabilities: Football Contract   According to an article by Gordon Forbes reported on p. 3C of the July 13, 1993, issue of *U.S.A. Today* ("Big Benefits for Bledsoe Created by His Crafty Agent), Drew Bledsoe, who recently signed to play quarterback for the New England Patriots, will be well compensated for his services. The deal includes:

1. A $4.5 million signing bonus spread over six years.
2. Base salaries of

$1.025 million for 1993–94.	$1.793 million for 1996–97.
$1.281 million for 1994–95.	$2.050 million for 1997–98.
$1.538 million for 1995–96.	$2.306 million for 1998–99.

However, the contract is not as cut and dried as it appears. Only the first three years are guaranteed. If Bledsoe achieves certain measurable performance standards, the contract can be reexamined and changed after three, four, and five years. (Although the article does not state so, we assume that the contract salary may be negotiated upward but not downward. After three years Bledsoe may also elect to become a free agent and sign with any team.)

Required

1. Does the Patriot football organization have a liability to Mr. Bledsoe? Explain, indicating whether it meets the conditions of a liability.
2. Assuming it is liability,
   a. What parts, if any, constitute current liabilities?
   b. How should the amounts be measured?

C 15–5
(L.O. 3)

YOU MAKE THE CALL   Michael Schroeder reports in a recent *Business Week* article that "the tally of worker injuries and liability suits [from the use of polychlorinated biphenyls (PCBs) and other toxic chemicals] promises to grow ... From the 1930s to 1970, Westinghouse and General Electric Company were the biggest purchasers of PCBs as fire retardants and coolants in capacitors and transformers. Other big users have included electric-equipment companies such as McGraw Edison, ITE Imperial, and Sprague Electric. NCR used PCBs to make carbonless copy paper. Though no firm number is available, plantiff's attorneys estimate that tens of thousands of workers have handled PCBs."[32]

Required

Write a report explaining whether you believe firms that used PCBs and similar chemicals should recognize liabilities for either the potential cleanup process on prior disposals or for future claims by affected workers? Cite appropriate authoritative pronouncements. Do you see an ethical issue here? How might you resolve it?

ANALYZING FINANCIAL STATEMENTS

All questions in this section are based on information taken from the financial statements of actual companies.

A 15–1
(L.O. 1, 2, 3, 4, 6)

Analysis of Current Liabilities   Listed below are the current liability section and note 7 of the 1995 balance sheet of Amoco Corporation, a major oil firm.

	1995	1994
Current liabilities	*(millions of dollars)*	
Current portion of long-term obligations	$ 196	$ 94
Short-term obligations	226	112
Accounts payable	2,496	2,217
Accrued liabilities	948	1,124
Taxes payble (including income taxes).	672	665
	$4,538	$4,212

NOTES TO CONSOLIDATED FINANCIAL STATEMENTS

7. Short-Term Obligations
Amoco's short-term obligations consist of notes payable and commercial paper. Notes payable as of December 31, 1995, totaled $36 million at an average annual interest rate of 5.7 percent, compared with $7

---

[32]M. Schroeder, "Did Westinghouse Keep Mum on PCBs?" *Business Week,* August 12, 1991, pp. 68–70.

million at an average annual interest rate of 5.7 percent at year-end 1994. Commercial paper borrowings at December 31, 1995, were $699 million at an average annual interest rate of 5.7 percent compared with $217 million at an average annual interest rate of 5.9 percent as of December 31, 1994.

Bank lines of credit available to support existing commercial paper borrowings of the corporation amounted to $490 million at both December 31, 1995 and 1994. All of these were supported by commitment fees.

The corporation also maintains compensating balances with a number of banks for various purposes. Such arrangements do not legally restrict withdrawal or usage of available cash funds. In the aggregate, they are not material in relation to total liquid assets.

Required

1. What amount of Amoco's long-term debt reflected in its current liabilities did Amoco pay off in 1995?
2. Explain the origin of the $196 million figure.
3. During 1995, did Amoco reduce its average yearly interest requirements on its short-term obligations described in note 7? Do you observe any interesting issues you might want to learn more about? If so, what are they?
4. Do the lines of credit that Amoco holds at the end of 1995 appear as liabilities on its balance sheet? Explain.

A 15–2
(L.O. 2, 3)

 **Analysis of Restructuring Liability**   The current liabilities section of Tenneco's balance sheet and note 4 to its financial statements appear below. Tenneco is an oil company.

	1993	1992
Current liabilities	*(millions)*	
Short-term debt	**$1,274**	$1,696
Payables:		
Trade	**1,337**	1,405
Affiliated companies	—	—
Gas transportation and exchange	**136**	243
Taxes accrued	**158**	237
Interest accrued	**154**	201
Restructuring liability	**223**	298
Natural gas pipeline revenue reservation	**291**	156
Other	**1,337**	1,444
	$4,910	$5,680

4. *Restructuring Costs* (Taken from the 1991 annual report)
During 1991, Tenneco identified restructuring measures which resulted in a pre-tax restructuring charge of $552 million (after-tax $480 million or $3.91 per average common share) which was recorded as part of continuing operations. The charge reflects estimated costs of $287 million attributable to an 8,000 personnel reduction program; $122 million to plant closings; and $143 million to rationalization of product lines and the related write down to net realizable value of certain inventory, equipment and other assets.

The $143 million amount described above includes a $115 million provision for discontinued product lines, including costs associated with dealer discounts, other incentive programs and inventory write downs to net realizable value. The discontinuation of product lines represents a major departure from past business strategy of Tenneco's farm and construction equipment segment and although it periodically revises its levels of sales incentives and dealer discounts to reflect normal changes in competitive and market conditions, it believes its classification of the costs of disposing of remaining inventories of discontinued product lines as a restructuring charge is appropriate in view of the extraordinary nature and level of such costs.

The specific restructuring measures were based on management's best business judgement under prevailing circumstances, and on assumptions which may be revised over time and as circumstances change. In like manner, the estimated costs associated with such measures may require revision in the future. Accordingly, the Company intends to adjust such measures and revise its estimated costs as future circumstances may require, and will make such accounting entries as may be appropriate to reflect such adjustments and revisions, if any.

Required

1. Do you believe the restructuring liability was most appropriately valued at $478 million? If not, what would have been more reasonable? Explain. (Ignore tax issues.)
2. Did Tenneco report the restructuring charge in 1991 prior to determining net income before taxes, or was it treated similar to an extraordinary item (net of tax)?

A 15–3
(L.O. 1, 2)

An Unknown Company's Current Liabilities   The following is the liability section of a corporation's 1995 annual financial statement:

	December 31	
	1995	**1994**
Liabilities	*(millions)*	
Noninterest-bearing deposits in US offices	**$ 13,388**	$ 13,648
Interest-bearing deposits in US offices.	**36,700**	35,699
Noninterest-bearing deposits in offices outside the United States	**8,164**	7,212
Interest-bearing deposits in offices outside the United States	**108,879**	99,167
Total deposits	**$167,131**	$155,726
Trading account liabilities (Note 1)*.	**18,274**	22,382
Purchased funds and other borrowings (Note 1)*	**16,334**	20,907
Acceptances outstanding	**1,559**	1,440
Accrued taxes and other expenses (Note 8)*.	**5,719**	5,493
Other liabilities.	**9,767**	8,878
Long-term debt (Note 1)*	**17,151**	16,497
Subordinated capital notes (Note 1)*.	**1,337**	1,397

*The notes are not reproduced here.

Required

1. What is unusual about the items included in the disclosure?
2. What do you believe would be included in "purchased funds and other borrowings"?
3. What type of corporation is this? How do you know?

A 15–4
(L.O. 1, 2, 3, 7)

   Analysis of Current Liabilities   New York Gas and Electric Company (NYSEG) reports the following current liabilities:

	1995	**1994**
Current liabilities	*(millions)*	
Current portion of long-term debt	**$ 37,003**	$ 36,231
Current portion of preferred stock	**100,000**	—
Commercial paper	**28,620**	151,900
Accounts payable and accrued liabilities	**117,637**	107,356
Interest accrued	**24,093**	25,132
Taxes accrued.	**22,231**	12,414
Other	**68,027**	82,547
Total current liabilities	**$397,611**	$415,580

In the notes to its financial statements, NYSEG indicates the following obligations as of December 31, 1995:

    a. Obligations under capital leases . . . . $ 14,799
    b. Liability for environmental restoration   31,800
    c. Redeemable preferred stock redeemable solely at the option of the company 140.500
    d. Current sinking fund requirements at 1% of principal (amount not given) . . . .   ?
    e. Accumulated deferred investment tax credits (optional question)   80,868
    f. Commitments for capital expenditure programs (estimated 1996 expenditure)   215,000

Required   Which of the above six items (or portions thereof) do you believe are included as part of one of the figures in NYSEG's current liabilities given above? For each item identified as belonging with the current liabilities, indicate which account title contains the amount and whether the above balance is a debit or credit.

COMPARATIVE ANALYSIS

Relating Specific Liabilities to their Companies   This problem is amenable to being worked in groups. See the preface for suggestions on working group problems. The problem will also likely require some research to properly identify each specific current liability with the company reporting that liability.

Suggestion: in solving this problem, consider using the SEC's Electronic Data Gathering, Analysis and Retrieval System (EDGAR). Follow these steps:

1. URL: http//www.sec.gov/index.html
2. Click on EDGAR Database of Corporate Information
3. Click on search the EDGAR Data Base
4. Click on search the EDGAR Archives
5. Enter the company name in the search dialog box
6. Click on the listing for the most recent 10K annual report

Required   Identify each liability in the left-hand column with the reporting company in the right-hand column. Each liability attaches to one and only one company.

Current Liability	**Company**
1. Accrued advertising and merchandising	*a.* DeVry
2. Accrued broker-dealer liabilities	*b.* Circus Circus
3. Advances and billings in excess of related costs	*c.* Flight Safety International
4. Advance tuition payments	*d.* Krim Brewery Ltd.
5. Beer tax payable	*e.* Maxis
6. Construction commitments on foreign flag bulk vessels	*f.* McDonnell Douglas
7. Progress jackpots	*g.* Overseas Shipbuilding
8. Reserve for asbestos litigation claims	*h.* Owens Corning
9. Royalties payable	*i.* Princeton American Corporation
10. Unearned income for contract training	*j.* Quaker Oats

16 LONG-TERM LIABILITIES

Learning Objectives

After you have studied this chapter, you will:

1   Be familiar with long-term liabilities and how to value them for financial reporting purposes.

2   Understand the nature of bonds and how to compute the price of a bond at issuance.

3   Know how to account for basic and more complex bond situations.

4   Appreciate the accounting issues surrounding long-term debt instruments issued with equity rights.

5   Be familiar with the different ways long-term debt is extinguished.

6   Be able to value long-term notes payable and measure periodic interest.

Introduction

Noncurrent liabilities provide one of three major sources of long-term capital (the other two being earnings and shareholder investment). Debt, mainly through bond issuance, also is a popular source of governmental financing.

But how long is *long?*

A typical bond issue has a term of 20 to 40 years. Recently, several firms have lengthened the term of their indebtedness.

Example   Walt Disney and Coca-Cola issued *100-year* bonds in 1993. The purchaser of one of these bonds will not receive face value ($1,000) until the year 2093.

What advantages accrue to the issuer of such a bond? Are there greater risks for the investor? Why would anyone buy a 100-year bond? At what value will they appear in the issuer's balance sheet?

While some firms issue very long-term debt, others issue debt that pays no periodic interest. For example, a zero coupon bond pays no interest during the term of the bond.

Example   At the close of the New York Bond Exchange, September 27, 1996, Whirlpool Corporation's $1,000 zero coupon bonds were selling for $400. When the bonds were issued in 1991, the company received only $170 million on the $675 million (face value) issue, or $250 per $1,000 bond. The bonds were issued to yield a 7 percent return on the investment if held to maturity.

Why were the investors able to pay only 25 percent of face value for the bonds, and why were they selling for so much more five years later? At what value are these bonds reported in Whirlpool's balance sheet?

The proliferation of new financial instruments has broadened the variety of long-term debt instruments issued by firms and governments. Two particularly innovative bond issues were proposed by New York City. One issue is backed by delinquent property taxes. When the issue sold out in a few hours, the city received an immediate large cash inflow from investors who purchased the bonds and were willing to bear the risk of collecting the tax in return for a higher interest rate.

The second New York bond issue proposes to back bonds with the future payments of parents who are behind in their child-support payments. Again, the city will receive a much needed immediate influx of cash for support payments and will transfer the risk of default to the investors who buy the bonds.[1]

This chapter addresses the basic issues surrounding long-term debt accounting. Accounting principles for long-term debt are designed to help the financial statement user assess cash flow prospects and the relative risk of a firm's financial position. Later chapters consider additional long-term debt issues including income taxes, leases, and pensions.

CHARACTERISTICS AND VALUATION OF LONG-TERM LIABILITIES

A long-term liability is an obligation that does not meet the definition of a current liability. Most long-term liabilities extend beyond one year from the current balance sheet date or the operating cycle of the debtor (borrower), whichever is longer. However, some short-term liabilities due within one year of the balance sheet also are classified as long-term, as discussed in Chapter 15.

Debt capital is an attractive means of financing for the debtor. Creditors do not acquire voting privileges in the debtor company, and debt issuance causes no ownership dilution. Debt capital is obtained more easily than equity capital for many new and risky firms. Interest expense, unlike dividends, is tax deductible. Furthermore, a firm that earns a return on borrowed funds that exceeds the rate it must pay in interest is using debt to its advantage and is said to be successfully **leveraged.**

Debt financing often supplies the capital for expansion and takeover activities when issuance of new stock is difficult. The potential increase in profits from expansion can be sufficiently attractive to induce firms that traditionally avoid debt to increase liability levels.

Example   The Adolph Coors Company planned the first major debt issue in its 117-year history in order to expand and increase its market share.

However, leverage is dangerous if sales or earnings decline and interest expense becomes an increasing percentage of earnings. Business failures are frequently caused by incurring too much debt in expectation of high sales and profits. Such firms often attempt to restructure their debt by extending maturity dates or requesting a reduction in principal or interest.

Debt agreements often restrict the operations and financial structure of the borrower to reduce the risk of default. Restrictions include ceilings on dividends and future debt, maintenance of specific income and liquidity levels, and the establishment of sinking funds that will be available to extinguish the debt. A **sinking fund** is a cash fund restricted for a specific purpose and classified as an investment. Violation of the restrictions places the debtor in technical default, meaning that the debt is due at the creditor's discretion. Exhibit 16–12 (Dole Food Company), shown later in the chapter, includes an example of the kinds of restrictions imposed on borrowers.

Debt is an attractive investment for creditors by providing legally enforceable debt payments, eventual return of principal, and a prior claim to assets upon corporate liquidation.

---

[1]"Now They're Thinking of Investing in Deadbeat Dads," *The Wall Street Journal,* June 12, 1996, p. C1.

EXHIBIT 16–1
Cash Flows in a Bond Issue

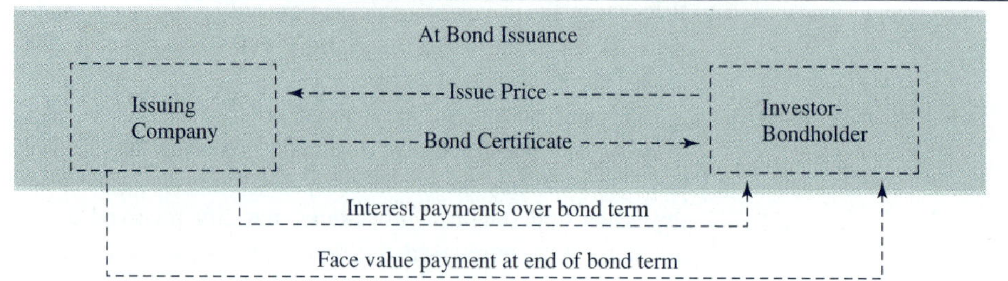

Although debt investments provide, on average, a lower overall return than equity investments, they are generally less risky. Debt securities with claims on specific assets further reduce the risk.

The Measurement and Valuation of Long-Term Liabilities

Three general principles are followed in measuring and recording most long-term liabilities and interest expense:

1. Long-term liabilities are recorded at the fair value of the goods or services obtained by incurring debt. The market rate of interest is the rate implicit in the transaction and equates the present value of the required future cash payments to the fair value of the goods and services. If the fair value of goods and services cannot be determined, the liability is recorded at the present value of required future cash payments discounted at the market interest rate for similar debt instruments.
2. Periodic interest expense is based on the market interest rate on the date of debt issuance and the liability balance at the *beginning* of the reporting period.
3. The book value of long-term debt at a balance sheet date is the present value of all remaining cash payments required, discounted at the market interest rate at issuance. The rate of interest used for this purpose is not changed during the term of the debt.

BONDS PAYABLE

A **bond** is a debt security issued by companies and government units to secure large amounts of capital on a long-term basis. A bond represents a formal promise by the issuing firm to pay principal and interest in return for the capital invested. Exhibit 16–1 illustrates the cash flows in a typical bond issue over the bond term.

A formal bond agreement, or **bond indenture,** specifies the terms of the bonds and the rights and duties of issuer and bondholder. The indenture specifies any restrictions on the issuing company, the dollar amount authorized for issuance, the interest rate and payment dates, the maturity date, and conversion and call privileges. An independent trustee appointed to protect the interests of both the issuer and the investors (usually a financial institution) maintains the necessary records and disburses interest and principal. The investors receive bond certificates, which represent the contractual obligations of the issuer to the investors.

Bonds are normally issued in small denominations, such as $1,000 and $10,000. The small denominations increase the affordability of the bonds and allow investors greater diversification in their portfolios.

Bonds are marketed in several ways. Typically, an entire bond issue is sold to investment bankers who underwrite (assist in selling and assume all or part of the risk) the bond issue at a specified price and then market the bonds at a higher price to individual investors. The underwriting firm may agree to buy any unsold portion of the issue at a specified price. Private direct placement with financial institutions and individual investors is an alternative to underwriting.

Many bond issues are offered through a prospectus. A **prospectus** includes the audited financial statements of the issuer, states the offering price, and describes the securities offered, the issuing company's business, and the conditions under which the securities will be sold. The investment bank publishes a "tombstone" advertisement announcing the issue and listing the underwriters in order to generate interest in the securities.

EXHIBIT 16–2   Bond Table Excerpt from *The Wall Street Journal*

NEW YORK EXCHANGE BONDS

CORPORATION BONDS
Volume, $16,056,000

Bonds	Cur Yld	Vol	Close	Net Chg.
AMR 8.10s98	7.9	4	102⅞	+ ¾
AMR 9s16	8.3	35	108½	+ 1½
ATT 4¾98	4.9	87	97¾	+ ⅛
ATT 4⅜99	4.6	21	95⅜	− ⅛
ATT 6s00	**6.2**	**25**	**97⅜**	**− ⅞**
ATT 5⅛01	5.5	30	93½	− ½
ATT 6¾04	6.8	109	98¾	+ ⅜
ATT 7s05	7.0	10	100	+ ½
ATT 7½06	7.3	10	103¼	...
ATT 8⅛22	7.9	21	102½	− ⅛
ATT 8⅛24	7.9	71	102⅜	− ⅞
ATT 8⅝31	8.2	17	104¾	− ¾
AcmeM 12½02	11.8	45	106	...
Advst 9s08	cv	13	104	− ½
AlskAr 6½05	cv	24	112½	+ 1½
AlskAr 6⅞14	cv	10	92¼	+ ¾
AlldC zr2000	...	30	77⅛	+ ⅝
AlldC zr07	...	50	46	+ ⅝
Alza 5s06	cv	24	97½	...
Amresco 03	...	11	100½	− ½
Anhr 8⅝16	8.5	5	102⅛	− ⅞
AnnTaylr 8¾00	9.2	36	95⅜	+ ⅜
Argosy 12s01	cv	30	90	− ¾
Arvin 7½14	cv	125	104	...
Ashlnd 6¾14	cv	15	102	...
AutDt zr12	...	25	57½	+ 1
BBN 6s12	cv	85	85	− 2
BkrHgh zr08	...	35	69¾	+ 1⅜
Bally 10s06f	cv	24	104	...
BellPa 7⅛12	7.4	1	95⅞	...
BellPa 7½13	7.6	5	98½	− 1¼
BellsoT 6½00	6.4	1	100⅞	+ ⅞
BellsoT 6¼03	6.5	60	96⅞	...
BellsoT 7s05	7.0	50	100	− ¼

Bonds	Cur Yld	Vol	Close	Net Chg.
BellsoT 8¼32	8.0	78	103½	+ 1
BellsoT 7½33	7.6	1	98⅜	+ 2¾
BellsoT 6¾33	7.6	20	89⅜	+ 1½
BstBuy 8⅝00	8.8	120	98⅝	− ¼
BethSt 8.45s05	8.6	8	98½	+ ⅜
Bevrly 7⅝03	cv	10	94	− ½
Bevrly 9s06	9.2	78	97¾	+ ½
Bevrly 5½18	cv	11	96	...
BorgWS 9⅛03	9.5	60	96¼	− ¼
CaterpInc 9⅜00	8.4	3	111½	+ 1½
ChsCp 8s99	7.8	10	102½	+ 1¼
ChsCp 6⅛08	7.0	25	87	+ 1
ChmWst zr10	...	6	42	...
CPWV 7¼13	7.5	1	96¼	+ 1⅝
Chryslr 10.4s99	9.9	41	104¾	+ ⅛
Chryslr 10.95s17	10.1	10	108½	...
ChryF 12¾99	10.9	5	116½	+ 1¼
ChryF 9½99	8.8	2	107¾	+ ¼
ChryF 6⅝00	6.7	14	98⅜	+ ¼
Clardge 11¾02	14.9	695	78¾	− ½
ClrkOil 9½04	9.3	3	102½	− ½
ClevEl 8¾05	8.8	60	99¼	− ½
ClevEl 9¼09	9.2	20	100½	...
ClevEl 8⅜11	8.9	68	94	− ⅝
ClevEl 8⅜12	8.9	26	93⅞	− ¼
Coastl 10s01	9.1	10	109⅞	+ 1⅞
Coeur 6⅜04	cv	8	88¾	− ⅝
ColeWld zr13	...	73	28¾	...
CmwE 7⅝03F	7.8	9	98	− ⅜
CmwE 7⅝03J	7.8	10	97¼	− 2¼
CompUSA 9½00	9.2	119	102⅞	+ ⅜
ConrPer 6¾01	cv	32	106	+ 1
ConrPer 6½02	cv	40	114¼	+ ¼
ConNG 7¼15	cv	10	108⅞	− ⅛
ConPort 10s06	10.2	2	98¼	+ 1¼
CntlHm 6⅞02	...	15	101	− 1½

Quotations as of 4 p.m. Eastern Time
Monday, September 30, 1996

Volume $16,579,000

	Domestic Mon.	Fri.	All Issues Mon.	Fri.
Issues traded	294	287	300	291
Advances	127	132	129	136
Declines	106	104	110	104
Unchanged	61	51	61	51
New highs	9	8	9	9
New lows	3	3	3	3

SALES SINCE JANUARY 1
(000 omitted)

1996	1995	1994
$4,267,099	$5,573,234	$4,524,541

Dow Jones Bond Averages

	−1995− High	Low	−1996− High	Low		−1996− Close	Chg.	%Yld	−1995− Close	Chg.
	105.34	93.63	106.09	100.99	20 Bonds	102.25	− 0.36	7.26	103.15	+ 0.06
	102.30	89.08	102.43	97.46	10 Utilities	99.21	− 0.32	7.36	99.59	+ 0.03
	108.96	98.08	109.94	104.06	10 Industrials	105.30	− 0.39	7.16	106.71	+ 0.08

Bonds	Cur Yld	Vol	Close	Net Chg.
DukePw 7s05	7.1	18	99	− ⅜
DukePw 7½25	7.8	335	96	+ ¼
EMC 4¼01	cv	10	119½	+ 1
Eckerd 9¼04	8.9	150	104⅛	− ⅝
EthAln 8¾01	8.5	15	102½	+ ¼

Bonds	Cur Yld	Vol	Close	Net Chg.
LgIsLt 7½07	8.4	5	89½	− ¼
LgIsLt 8.9s19	9.4	35	94⅝	...
LgIsLt 9¾21	9.8	325	100	− ⅛
LgIsLt 9s22	9.4	50	95½	− ⅛
LgIsLt 8.2s23	9.1	10	90⅜	+ ⅝
LgIsLt 9⅝24	9.6	20	99⅞	...

Explanation: The third listed bond issue of American Telephone and Telegraph Company (AT&T) has a 6 percent stated interest rate, matures in 2000 (00), and has a current yield (*Cur Yld*)—or effective interest rate—of 6.2 percent if purchased at the close of business, September 30, 1996, at the 97 3/8 closing price (.97375 × face value). The *Vol* column indicates the dollar amount of bonds that traded hands, in thousands. On this day, $25,000 of the 6 percent AT&T bonds were traded.

The *s* shown for several companies is a separator and has no further meaning. Also, *zr* refers to zero coupon bond. No current yield is provided for zeroes because interest is not paid on a periodic basis. The current yield as listed is a one-year approximation to the true compounded rate and equals the stated rate divided by the closing price. For the 6 percent bonds, 6.2% = 6% ÷ 97.375%.

Source: "New York Exchange Bonds," *The Wall Street Journal*, October 1, 1996, p. C22. Reprinted by permission of *The Wall Street Journal*, Copyright 1996, Dow Jones & Company, Inc. All Rights Reserved Worldwide.

Many bond issues are actively traded on a daily basis on bond exchanges. Trades between investors are not recorded by the issuing company. *The Wall Street Journal* publishes daily information about listed bonds (see Exhibit 16–2).

Information about the risk of bond issues is available from Standard & Poor's Corporation, Moody's Investor Services, and other rating services. These services use quality designations and ratings:

	Ratings	
Quality Designation	Standard & Poor's	Moody's
Prime	AAA	Aaa
Excellent	AA	Aa
Upper medium	A	A
Lower medium	BBB	Baa
Marginally speculative	BB	Ba
Very speculative	B	B, Caa
Default	D	Ca, C

A bond rating reflects the perceived ability of the issuing company to pay principal and interest and thus affects the ability of a firm to raise debt capital. Bond ratings change with financial circumstances.

Example   In late 1995, Moody's Investors Service downgraded the debt ratings of CBS Inc.'s long-term debt because of Westinghouse Electric Corp.'s proposed acquisition of

CBS. The concern was that the acquisition by Westinghouse, already burdened with significant debt, would increase the risk of default to holders of CBS debt.

Classification of Bonds

Investors have a wide variety of investment goals, preferences, and policies. As a result, many different types of bonds are issued. Bonds may be classified by

1. Issuing entity.
   a. *Industrial* bonds: issued by private for-profit companies.
   b. *Municipal* bonds: issued by governmental entities.

2. Collateral.
   a. *Secured* bonds: supported by a lien on specific assets; bondholders have first claim on the proceeds from sale of secured assets.
   b. *Debenture* bonds: unsecured; backed only by issuer's credit; upon bankruptcy of issuer, bondholders become general creditors for distribution of issuer's assets.[2]

3. Purpose of issue.
   a. *Purchase money* bonds: issued in full or part payment for property.
   b. *Refunding* bonds: issued to retire existing bonds.
   c. *Consolidated* bonds: issued to replace several existing issues.

4. Payment of interest.
   a. *Ordinary (term)* bonds: provide cash interest at a stated rate.
   b. *Income* bonds: interest is dependent on issuer's income.
   c. *Registered* bonds: pay interest only to the person in whose name the bond is recorded or registered.
   d. *Bearer* bonds: not registered; interest and principal are paid to the holder; transfers require no endorsement.
   e. *Coupon* bonds: pay interest upon receipt of coupons detached from bonds.

5. Maturity.
   a. *Ordinary (term)* bonds: mature on a single specified date.
   b. *Serial* bonds: mature on several installment dates.
   c. *Callable* bonds: issuer can retire bonds before maturity date.
   d. *Redeemable* bonds: bondholder can compel early redemption.
   e. *Convertible* bonds: bondholder can convert bonds to equity securities of the issuer.

Valuation of Bonds Payable

Bond Features Several bond features affect accounting for bonds. To illustrate, assume that late in 1997, Randolph Company plans to issue $100,000 of 10 percent debentures dated January 1, 1998.[3] Each bond has a $1,000 face value. The bonds mature December 31, 2007, and pay interest on June 30 and December 31. Five features specified in the bond indenture do not change:

1. The *face (maturity, principal, par)* value of a bond is the amount payable when the bond is due ($1,000 for Randolph).
2. The *maturity date* is the end of the bond term and the due date for the face value (December 31, 2007, for Randolph). The length of the bond term reflects the issuer's long-term cash needs, the purpose for which the funds will be used, and the issuer's expected ability to pay principal and interest.
3. The *stated (coupon, nominal, contractual) interest rate* is the rate that determines periodic interest payments (10 percent for Randolph). This rate is normally set to approximate the rate of interest on bonds of a similar risk class.

---

[2]A *junk* bond is a high-interest-rate, high-risk, unsecured bond. Junk bonds were used extensively in the 1980s to finance leveraged buyouts.

[3]Debenture bonds are used for the examples, but the general valuation principles apply to most bond issues.

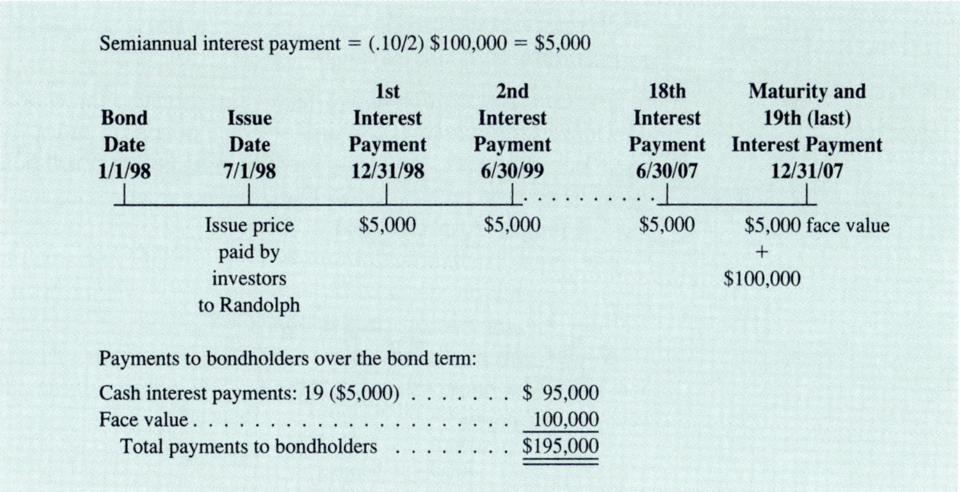

Bond Date 1/1/98	Issue Date 7/1/98	1st Interest Payment 12/31/98	2nd Interest Payment 6/30/99	18th Interest Payment 6/30/07	Maturity and 19th (last) Interest Payment 12/31/07
	Issue price paid by investors to Randolph	$5,000	$5,000	$5,000	$5,000 face value + $100,000

Payments to bondholders over the bond term:

Cash interest payments: 19 ($5,000)	$ 95,000
Face value	100,000
Total payments to bondholders	$195,000

4. The *interest payment dates* are the dates the periodic interest payments are due (June 30 and December 31 for Randolph). Semiannual interest payments are common.[4] Randolph pays $50 interest on these dates for each bond (.10 × $1,000 × 1/2), regardless of the issue price or market rate of interest at date of issue.

5. The *bond (authorization) date* is the earliest date the bond can be issued and represents the planned issuance date of the bond issue (January 1, 1998, for Randolph).

Two other features necessary for valuation are dependent on market factors:

6. The *market (effective, yield) interest rate* is the true compounded rate that equates the price of the bond issue to the present value of the interest payments and face value. This rate is not necessarily the same as the stated rate. The market interest rate depends on several interrelated factors, including the general rate of interest in the economy, the perceived risk of the bond issue, yields on bonds of similar risk, inflation expectations, the overall supply of and demand for bonds, and the bond term. (Assume that this rate is 12 percent for the Randolph issue.)

7. The bond *issue date* is the date the bonds are actually sold to investors. Bonds often are issued after the bond authorization date. (Assume that the issue date is July 1, 1998, for the Randolph issue.) When issuing bonds takes more time than expected, the bonds may be issued after the bond authorization date. The process includes registration with the SEC, negotiations with underwriters, and printing. Changes within the firm and in the economy can pose difficulties in marketing bonds. The issuing company also may delay issuance to take advantage of declining interest rates.

Exhibit 16–3 diagrams many of these bond features for the Randolph issue.

Bond Prices   The issue price of a bond depends on the relationship between the market and stated interest rates. The two rates are frequently different at issuance. There are three situations:

1. **Market rate = stated rate.** Here, the interest payments at the stated rate yield a return equal to the market rate for bonds of similar term and risk. The bonds sell at face value.

2. **Market rate > stated rate.** Here, the issue price must decline *below* face value to yield the investor a return equal to the market rate. The difference between face value and issue price is called **discount** on bonds payable.

The Randolph bonds sold at a discount because the market rate (12 percent) exceeds the stated rate (10 percent). Investors are unwilling to pay the $1,000 face value (a price that yields 10 percent) because competing debt securities of the same grade yield 12 percent.

---

[4]The decision to pay interest twice per year represents a trade-off between investors' desire for more frequent cash payments and the issuing company's desire to reduce administrative costs.

3. **Market rate < stated rate.** Here, the issue price rises *above* face value until the yield decreases to the market rate. The excess above face value paid by the investor is called **premium** on bonds payable.

Investors pay a price above face value because the stated rate exceeds the interest rate demanded by the market for similar grade bonds. In order for the Randolph bonds to yield 8 percent, an investor must pay more than $1,000 for each bond. The investor receives interest at 10 percent per year or $100 per bond, which yields less than 10 percent on the investment if the price for the bond exceeds $1,000.

The terms *discount* and *premium* do not imply negative or positive qualities of the bond issue. They merely describe adjustments to the selling price to bring the yield rate in line with the market rate on similar bonds.

A bond entitles the investor to two different types of cash flows: principal and interest. The price of a bond issue equals the present value of these payments discounted at the market rate of interest:

> **Randolph bonds:**
> Present value of principal
> [$100,000(PV1, 6%,* 19†) = $100,000(.33051)] $33,051
> Present value of interest payments
> [$100,000(.10)(1/2)(PVA, 6%, 19) = $5,000(11.15812)] . . . . $\underline{55,791}$
> Price of Randolph bonds, July 1, 1998 . . . . $\underline{\underline{\$88,842}}$
>
> Discount on bonds ($100,000 − $88,842) . . . . $\underline{\underline{\$11,158}}$
>
> *Market rate of interest: 12% (6% per semiannual period).
> †Bond term: July 1, 1998 through December 31, 2007 (19 semiannual periods)

Investors who purchase the Randolph bonds (at a discount) and hold them for the entire term earn 6 percent compounded semiannually on their original investment of $88,842. As shown in Exhibit 16–3, the investors will receive $195,000 from Randolph over the bond term in return for their $88,842 investment. The investment yields an annual return of 12 percent.

Accrued Interest Bond *prices* exclude accrued interest but the **proceeds** on bonds sold between interest dates include accrued interest at the stated rate since the last interest date.

Example If the Randolph bonds were to sell on August 1, 1998, at 90 percent of face value, total proceeds would be:

> Price .90($100,000) $90,000
> Accrued interest from 7/1/98
>   .10($100,000)(1/12). . . . . $\underline{833}$
> Bond proceeds . . . . $\underline{\underline{\$90,833}}$

An investor who purchases the bonds on August 1 and holds the bonds five months to December 31 earns only five months' interest. Yet the investor receives six months' worth of interest on December 31. Therefore, the investor must pay one month of interest at purchase. This system facilitates the trading of bonds and ensures that each bondholder ultimately receives interest for the period they hold the bonds.

After issuance Bond prices and interest rate changes are inversely related. If the general rate of interest in the economy decreases, all bonds on the market become relatively more attractive, and vice versa.

Example The Randolph bonds were sold to yield 12 percent. If the market interest rate on bonds similar to Randolph's falls to 10 percent, the price of a Randolph bond on the market will increase to $1,000 because they pay 10 percent interest.

Firm specific factors such as changes in income, financial position, and risk also affect bond prices. When firms release a disappointing earnings announcement, for example, the price of their bonds may decline due to a perception of increased risk.

Quoted bond prices   Bond prices are quoted as a percentage of face value to accommodate all denominations. A $1,000 bond quoted at 97 sells for $970 (.97 × $1,000).

Example   Exhibit 16–2 is an excerpt from a table of bond prices in *The Wall Street Journal*. The third AT&T bond issue listed sold below face value (at 97 3/8) on September 30, 1996, because the market rate on that day (6.2 percent) exceeded the stated rate (6 percent). However, the book value per bond in AT&T's accounts reflects the market rate of interest at the date the 6 percent bonds were issued. The book value of bonds on the issuing company's books is not adjusted to reflect the current market interest rate.

Although issuers usually attempt to set bond rates close to the expected market rate at issuance (minimizing the discount or premium), **deep discount bonds** and **zero coupon bonds** are exceptions. Deep discount bonds sell for a small fraction of the face value because the stated interest rate is much lower than the market rate. Zero coupon bonds provide no separate interest payments. The investor receives only one payment: face value at maturity.

Example   If the Randolph bonds were zero coupon bonds and were sold to yield 12 percent, the issue price would be $33,051, the present value of the maturity amount.

Deep discount bonds and zeros are issued for a variety of reasons.[5] Issuing companies find the reduced or nonexistent interest payments attractive. The issue price is small relative to face value, attracting investors. Zeros, and all bonds issued at a discount, generally increase in value each year as they approach maturity. For zeros, issuers can deduct this annual increase as interest expense even though no interest is paid. Although the annual increase in value of a zero is taxable, some investors can structure their investment to defer taxes until maturity (for example, through an individual retirement account). When so structured, zeros are a popular investment for parents wishing to save for their children's college education. Pension funds, which do not pay taxes, also find these investments attractive.

Fundamental Bond Accounting Principles

To demonstrate accounting for bonds, several cases illustrate different reporting situations. In these situations, bonds are issued on the bond date and at the beginning of the fiscal year. Three different effective (market) interest rates are illustrated.

Common Information: Bonds issued on bond date, the beginning of fiscal year   On January 1, 1998, Gresham Company, a calendar-year firm, issues $100,000 of 7 percent debentures dated January 1, 1998, which pay interest each December 31. The bonds mature on December 31, 2002.

Situation A: effective interest rate = 7 percent.

Situation B: effective interest rate = 6 percent.

Situation C: effective interest rate = 8 percent.

Situation A: Bonds sell at face value, market and stated rate = 7 percent

$$\text{Price} = \$100,000(\text{PV1, 7\%, 5}) + \$100,000(.07)(\text{PVA, 7\%, 5})$$
$$\$100,000(.71299) + \$7,000(4.10020) = \$100,000$$

When a bond is issued, the issuer records the maturity value of the bond in bonds payable, a long-term liability account. In this case, the maturity value equals the amount paid by the bondholders. Gresham makes the following entries during the bond term:

January 1, 1998—Issue bonds:

Cash	100,000	
Bonds payable		100,000

---

[5]Zero coupon bonds were first conceived in 1973 during the Arab oil embargo. Investment bankers worried that interest-bearing bonds would be difficult to market in the Middle East because the Koran prohibits interest. See "A Strange Breed of Bond," *Forbes*, May 25, 1981, p. 142.

December 31, 1998–2002—Interest payment:

```
Interest expense  . . . . . . . . . . . . . . . . . . . . . . . . . . . . . . . . . . . . . . . . .   7,000
    Cash($100,000 × .07)  . . . . . . . . . . . . . . . . . . . . . . . . . . . . . . .           7,000
```

December 31, 2002—Bond maturity:

```
Bonds payable  . . . . . . . . . . . . . . . . . . . . . . . . . . . . . . . . . . . 100,000
    Cash  . . . . . . . . . . . . . . . . . . . . . . . . . . . . . . . . . . . . . .         100,000
```

Interest expense for bonds issued at face value equals the amount of the interest payment. The book value of the bonds remains $100,000 to maturity. Subsequent changes in the market rate of interest are ignored for journal entry purposes.[6] Matured bonds are canceled to prevent reissuance.

Situation B: Bonds sell at a premium, market rate = 6 percent

$$\text{Price} = \$100,000(\text{PV1}, 6\%, 5) + \$100,000(.07)(\text{PVA}, 6\%, 5)$$
$$\$100,000(.74726) + \$7,000(4.21236) = \$104,213$$

The bonds sell at a premium because they pay a stated rate that exceeds the yield rate on similar bonds. The initial $4,213 premium is recorded in premium on bonds payable, an *adjunct* valuation account which *increases* the net bond liability (an adjunct account has an effect opposite that of a contra account). The present value (which equals book value) at issue date ($104,213) is the amount that, if invested by the issuing company at the effective interest rate, satisfies all payments required on the bond issue, including the face value. The following entry is made to record the issue.

January 1, 1998—Issue bonds:

```
Cash  . . . . . . . . . . . . . . . . . . . . . . . . . . . . . . . . . . . . . . . . . 104,213
    Bonds payable  . . . . . . . . . . . . . . . . . . . . . . . . . . . . . . . . . .         100,000
    Premium on bonds payable  . . . . . . . . . . . . . . . . . . . . . . . . . . .           4,213
```

Total interest expense over the term of a bond issue equals total cash payments required by the bond (face value and interest) less the aggregate issue price. Total interest expense is not equal to total cash interest when a bond is sold at a premium or discount, as shown for Gresham Company (situation B):

Face value	$100,000
Total cash interest .07($100,000)(5 years)	35,000
Total cash payments required by bond	135,000
Issue price	104,213
Total interest expense for bond term	$ 30,787

Gresham received $4,213 more than face value at issuance but will pay only face value at maturity. Therefore, the effective rate is less than the stated rate, and total interest expense for Gresham over the bond term is less than total interest paid.

Subsequent to issuance, the premium or discount is completely amortized over the bond term so that net book value equals face value at maturity. Amortized premium reduces periodic interest expense relative to interest paid, and amortized discount increases interest expense. The net bond liability equals face value plus the remaining unamortized bond premium or less the remaining unamortized bond discount.

Amortization Methods   Two methods of amortizing bond premium and discount are available: the **interest method** and the **straight-line method.** The following entries illustrate application of the two methods to the Gresham bonds:

---

[6]It can be argued that the current market interest rate should be incorporated into accounting for bonds. Otherwise, the book value of the debt does not equal its market value. However, it is assumed that the bond will be outstanding the entire term, in which case the market rate at issuance reflects the true interest rate over the bond term.

	Interest Method	Straight-Line Method	
December 31, 1998:			
Interest expense	6,253*	6,157	
Premium on bonds payable	747	843†	
Cash $100,000(.07)		7,000	7,000

*$104,213(.06)

†$4,213/5 years

	Interest Method	Straight-Line Method	
December 31, 1999:			
Interest expense	6,208*	6,157	
Premium on bonds payable	792	843	
Cash $100,000(.07)		7,000	7,000

*($104,213 − $747)(.06)

Under the interest method, the bonds are disclosed in the long-term liability section of Gresham's December 31, 1999, balance sheet as follows:

Bonds payable	$100,000
Unamortized premium on bonds payable ($4,213 − $747 − $792)	2,674
Net book value of bonds payable	$102,674

In practice, most firms disclose the unamortized premium or discount in a footnote or parenthetically in the balance sheet, as illustrated in Exhibit 16–4.

Interest expense under the interest method is the product of the effective interest rate (6 percent) and net liability balance at the *beginning* of the period. Interest expense is therefore a constant percentage of beginning book value. The investor receives part of the original investment back with each interest payment. In 1998, this amount is $747, which reduces the net investment and net bond liability at the beginning of 1999. Consequently, 1999 interest expense is less than that for 1998. The book value of the bonds at December 31, 1999, is the present value of the *remaining* cash flows:

$$\$102,674 = \$100,000(PV1, 6\%, 3) + \$100,000(.07)(PVA, 6\%, 3)$$
$$= \$100,000(.83962) + \$7,000(2.67301)(\text{rounded})$$

An **amortization table** often is prepared to support bond journal entries. The table gives all the data necessary for journal entries over the term of the bond and each year's ending net liability balance. An amortization table is shown in Exhibit 16–5 for the interest method.

The **straight-line method** is a popular alternative to the interest method that amortizes an equal amount of discount or premium each interest period. Interest expense equals the cash interest paid less premium amortized or plus discount amortized. This method produces a stable dollar amount of interest expense each period rather than a constant rate of interest each period.

The straight-line method recognizes the average amount of interest each year ($6,157 = $30,787/5), while the interest method reflects the changing debt balance. The straight-line method is allowed only when interest expense is not materially different under the two

Great Dane Holdings, Inc., 1995 Annual Report
Excerpt from Footnote F, Long-Term Liabilities

	December 31,	
	1994	**1995**
12¾% Senior Subordinated Debentures less debt discount of $9,725 (1994) and $7,311 (1995)	$122,315	$106,629
14½% Subordinated Discount Debentures less debt discount of $6,335 (1994) and $6,105 (1995)	55,012	55,242

Date	Interest Payment	Interest Expense*	Premium Amortization†	Unamortized Premium‡	Net Bond Liability§
1/1/98				$4,213	$104,213
12/31/98	$ 7,000	$ 6,253	$ 747	3,466	103,466
12/31/99	7,000	6,208	792	2,674	102,674
12/31/00	7,000	6,160	840	1,834	101,834
12/31/01	7,000	6,110	890	944	100,944
12/31/02	7,000	6,056	944	0	100,000
	$35,000	$30,787	$4,213		

*(Previous net liability balance)(.06)
 $6,253 = $104,213(.06) for 1998

†(Interest payment) − (Interest expense)
 $747 = $7,000 − $6,253 for 1998

‡(Previous unamortized premium) − (Current period amortization)
 $3,466 = $4,213 − $747 at December 31, 1998

§$100,000 + (Current unamortized premium)
 $103,466 = $100,000 + $3,466 at December 31, 1998

methods (*APB Opinion No. 21*, par. 15). For example, the method seriously misstates interest expense early in the term of a zero coupon bond. Similarly, very long bond terms magnify the differences between the two methods because the initial net liability can be considerably smaller or larger than face value.[7]

Situation C: Bonds sell at a discount, market rate = 8 percent; Accounting by Issuer and Investor

$$\text{Price} = \$100,000(PV1, 8\%, 5) + \$100,000(.07)(PVA, 8\%, 5)$$
$$= \$100,000(.68058) + \$7,000(3.99271) = 96,007$$

The Gresham bonds sell at a discount in this case because the stated rate is less than the yield rate on similar bonds. The discount is recorded in the discount on bonds payable account, a contra liability valuation account, which is subtracted from bonds payable to yield the net liability at present value. Although the primary focus of this chapter is on accounting for the debtor company, we illustrate accounting for the bondholder–investor (creditor) in this example. The investor classifies the bond holdings in an investment account that includes acquisition price and any commissions and taxes on purchase.

Example   The investor in this example is Elmhurst Company. When the creditor intends to hold the bonds to maturity (as is assumed here), the accounting for the creditor is parallel to that of the debtor, although the creditor typically uses the net method rather than separately report a premium or discount. Also, the amortization period for the creditor runs from the purchase date to maturity, which is often shorter than the issuing company's amortization period. Appendix 16C discusses in more detail the reporting requirements for investments in debt securities held to maturity.

The entries for the first two years after the sale of the Gresham bonds follow, along with an amortization table (see Exhibit 16–6) and the relevant portion of the balance sheet after two years. Only the interest method is illustrated, although the straight-line method could be used by either firm.

Gresham Company (issuer)	**Elmhurst Company** (investor)

January 1, 1998—Issue bonds:

Gresham Company (issuer)		Elmhurst Company (investor)	
Cash 96,007		Bond investment 96,007	
Discount on bonds payable 3,993		Cash	96,007
Bonds payable	100,000		

---

[7]For example, under the interest method, the issuer of 15 percent, $1,000, 25-year bonds yielding 10 percent ($1,454 issue price) recognizes $145 of interest expense in the first year per bond, 10 percent more than the $132 under the straight-line method.

EXHIBIT 16–6

Amortization Table for Gresham
Company Bonds Sold at
Discount—Interest Method

Date	Interest Payment	Interest Expense*	Discount Amortization†	Unamortized Discount‡	Net Bond Liability§
1/1/98				$3,993	$ 96,007
12/31/98	$ 7,000	$ 7,681	$ 681	3,312	96,688
12/31/99	7,000	7,735	735	2,577	97,423
12/31/00	7,000	7,794	794	1,783	98,217
12/31/01	7,000	7,857	857	926	99,074
12/31/02	7,000	7,926	926	0	100,000
	$35,000	$38,993	$3,993		

*(Previous net liability balance)(.08) $7,681 = $96,007(.08) for 1998

†(Interest expense) − (Interest payment) $681 = $7,681 − $7,000 for 1998

‡(Previous unamortized discount) − (Current period amortization) $3,312 = $3,993 − $681 at December 31, 1998

§$100,000 + (Current unamortized discount) $96,688 = $100,000 − $3,312 at December 31, 1998

December 31, 1998—Interest expense:

Interest expense	7,681*		Cash	7,000	
Discount on bonds			Bond investment	681	
payable		681	Interest revenue		7,681
Cash ($100,000 × .07) . .		7,000			

*7,681 = $96,007(.08)

December 31, 1999—Interest expense:

Interest expense	7,735*		Cash	7,000	
Discount on bonds			Bond investment	735	
payable		735	Interest revenue		7,735
Cash ($100,000 × .07) . .		7,000			

*$7,735 = ($96,007 + $681)(.08)

GRESHAM COMPANY
Portion of Long-Term Liability Section of Balance Sheet
December 31, 1999

Bonds payable	$100,000
Unamortized discount on bonds payable ($3,993 − $681 − $735)	(2,577)
Net book value of bonds payable	$ 97,423

The initial $3,993 discount is the amount in excess of the total bond price that the issuer must pay the investor at maturity. Therefore, the discount represents interest, in addition to the cash interest payments required over the bond term. A portion of the discount is recognized (amortized) each period, causing both interest expense and the net bond liability to increase. When completely amortized, the net bond liability and the bond investment account have increased to $100,000, the maturity amount. Total interest expense over the bond term is $38,993, the sum of cash interest payments ($35,000) and the bond discount ($3,993).

Exhibit 16–7 summarizes several aspects of bond accounting. The exhibit is designed for semiannual interest payments, the usual situation.

|CONCEPT REVIEW

1. How does a premium on bonds payable occur? What does it represent?
2. Why is interest expense increased by the amount of discount amortized?
3. Why is the straight-line method of amortization not appropriate for deep discount bonds?

EXHIBIT 16–7

Summary Table: Accounting for Bonds, Assuming Semiannual Interest Payments

Price of bond issue = Present value of principal and interest payments

= (Face value)(PV1, i, n) + (Face value)(s)(PVA, i, n)

where i = effective interest rate per six-month period.

n = number of semiannual periods in bond term.

s = stated interest rate per six-month period.

Initial discount = Face value − Price of bond issue

(effective rate exceeds stated rate)

Or:

Initial premium = Price of bond issue − Face value

(stated rate exceeds effective rate)

Net book value of bonds = Face value + Unamortized premium

Or: = Face value − Unamortized discount

	Premium	Discount
As maturity approaches:		
Unamortized amount	declines	declines
Net book value	declines	increases
Annual interest expense*	declines	increases

*Under interest method. Constant under straight-line method.

Two Methods of Amortizing Premium and Discount

	Interest Method	Straight-Line Method
Annual interest expense	Changes each year	Constant over term
Annual interest expense as a percentage of beginning book value	Constant over term	Changes each year

REVIEW PROBLEM

Kentucky Kernal issued 100, 9 percent, $1,000 bonds on July 1, 1998, yielding 12 percent. The bonds pay interest each December 31 and June 30. The bonds mature five years from the issue date. Kentucky's fiscal year ends June 30.

Provide:

1. The bond issue proceeds, expressed as a percentage of face value.
2. The journal entry to record the bond issue.
3. The journal entries to record the first two interest payments under both the interest method and straight-line method.
4. The balance sheet disclosure of the net bond liability at June 30, 1999, under both methods of amortization.

SOLUTION

The semiannual interest payment is $4,500 ($100,000 × .09/2).

1. Bond proceeds = $100,000(PV1,.06,10) + $4,500(PVA,.06,10)

= $100,000(.55839)   + $4,500(7.36009)

= $88,959

Proceeds as a percent of face value = 89.

2. July 1, 1998

Cash	88,959	
Discount on bonds payable	11,041	
Bonds payable		100,000

3. December 31, 1998

	Interest Method	Straight-Line Method
Interest expense	5,338*	5,604
Discount on bonds payable	838	1,104†
Cash	4,500	4,500

*$5,338 = .06($88,959)

†$1,104 = $11,041 ÷ 10 semiannual interest periods

June 30, 1999

Interest expense	5,388*		5,604
Discount on bonds payable		888	1,104
Cash		4,500	4,500

*$5,388 = .06($88,959 + $838)

4. Balance sheet, long-term liability section, June 30, 1999:

	Interest Method	**Straight-Line Method**
Bonds payable	$100,000	$100,000
Unamortized discount	9,315*	8,833†
Net bond liability	$ 90,685	$ 91,167

*$9,315 = $11,041 − $838 − $888

†$8,833 = $11,041 − $1,104 − $1,104

ADDITIONAL ISSUES IN ACCOUNTING FOR BONDS

Accounting for bonds is more involved when the issue date does not coincide with the first day of the fiscal year or with an interest payment date, and when bond issue costs are incurred.

Bond Issue Costs

Bond issue costs include legal, accounting, underwriting, commission, engraving, printing, registration, and promotion costs. These costs are paid by the issuer and reduce the net proceeds from the bond issue, thus raising the effective rate for the issuer.

Bond issue costs are classified as a deferred charge (long-term asset) rather than as a reduction of premium or increase in discount (*APB Opinion No. 21*). Over the bond term, the bond issue costs are amortized to expense. The rationale for gradual recognition is that the bond issue costs were necessarily incurred to obtain debt financing. The funds obtained presumably contribute to revenue over the bond term. Therefore, the bond issue costs should be recognized over that same period. The straight-line method is the most commonly used method but the interest method also may be used.

To illustrate accounting for bond issue costs, assume that $3,600 is incurred by Gresham to issue the bonds in the previous situations. The bond issue costs are amortized by the straight-line method at the rate of $720 per year ($3,600/5). Gresham makes the following entries *in addition to* those previously recorded.

January 1, 1998—Record bond issue cost:

| Bond issue cost . . . . | 3,600 | |
| Cash . . . . | | 3,600 |

December 31, 1998–2002—Amortize bond issue cost:

| Bond issue expense($3,600/5) . . . . | 720 | |
| Bond issue cost . . . . | | 720 |

Effects on Gresham Company's 1998 income statement and balance sheet:

| Income statement: bond issue expense. . . . . | $ 720 |
| Balance sheet: long-term deferred charge balance ($3,600 − $720) . . . . . . | $2,880 |

Bond issue costs do not meet the *SFAC No. 6* definition of an asset (par. 237) because they produce no future benefit. Rather, they reduce the funds derived from the bond issue. Treatment as an adjustment to the premium or discount, or as an expense in the borrowing period is suggested by this view. Although an *SFAC* does not constitute GAAP, the FASB is expected to develop new guidelines for reporting these and other deferred charges.[8]

---

[8]If the method of amortizing premium or discount and that of amortizing bond issue costs are the same, deferral and amortization of bond issue costs yields the same periodic income as does treating bond issue costs as a reduction of the proceeds. Only the classification of expense is different (interest expense versus bond issue expense). However, deferral and amortization (present GAAP) requires an asset to be recorded at issuance rather than a liability to be reduced.

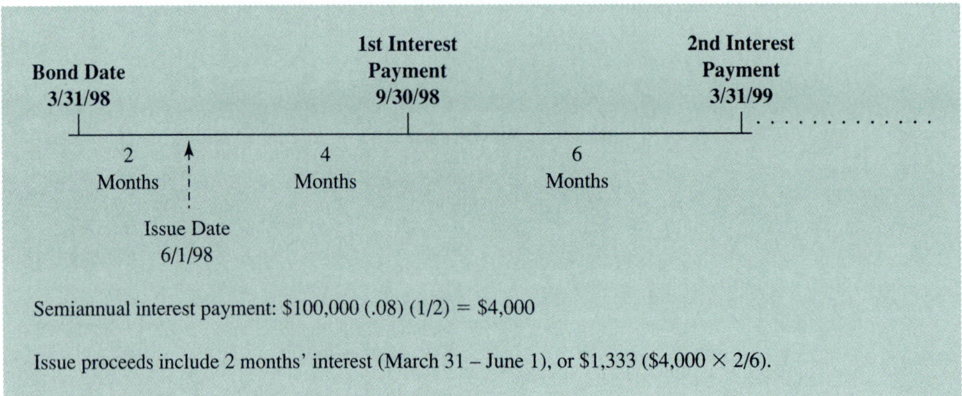

Semiannual interest payment: $100,000 (.08) (1/2) = $4,000

Issue proceeds include 2 months' interest (March 31 – June 1), or $1,333 ($4,000 × 2/6).

Bonds Issued between Interest Dates

In the previous examples, bonds were issued on an interest date, a schedule we chose to emphasize the accounting principles. However, bonds usually are not issued on an interest date, and semiannual interest payments are more typical. Two new problems arise: accounting for accrued interest from the most recent interest payment date and computing the issue price.

New information for Gresham bond issue:

1. The bond date is March 31, 1998, and the maturity date is March 31, 2003.
2. The issue date is June 1, 1998 (between interest dates).
3. The bonds pay interest each September 30 and March 31.
4. The stated rate is 8 percent, and the effective interest rate is 10 percent.
5. Face value is $100,000.

Exhibit 16–8 illustrates the issuance of the Gresham bond issue between interest dates.

The price of the Gresham bond issued between interest payment dates is calculated as follows:

Price of bond at immediately preceding interest date (3/31/98):		
Face value [$100,000(PV1, 5%, 10) = $100,000(.61391)	$61,391	
Interest [$100,000(.08/2) (PVA, 5%, 10) = $4,000(7.72173)]	30,887	
Total present value		$92,278
Growth in bond present value at yield rate, from 3/31/98 to 6/1/98		
[$92,278(.10) (2/12)]		1,538
Cash interest at stated rate from 3/31/98 to 6/1/98 [$100,000(.08) (2/12)] . . .		(1,333)
Price of bond at 6/1/98		$92,483

The $1,538 growth component is the normal growth in present value of the bond from March 31 to June 1 and is added for bonds issued at either a discount or a premium. The cash interest is the portion of that return due September 30 as a separate payment. Interest payments reduce the present value of a bond by the amount of the payment. Therefore, the two months' cash interest is deducted from the bond price.

Interpolation, using the bond prices at the two interest payment dates *bordering* the issue date, also can be used to determine the issue price:

Price at 3/31/98 (from previous calculation)		$92,278
Price at 9/30/98:		
Face value [$100,000(PV1, 5%, 9) = $100,000(.64461)].	$64,461	
Interest [$100,000(.08/2) (PVA, 5%, 9) = $4,000(7.10782)]	28,431	
Total present value.		$92,892
Interpolated price at 6/1/98:		

$$\$92{,}278 - 2/6(\$92{,}278 - \$92{,}892) = \$92{,}483$$

Or:

$$\$92{,}892 + 4/6(\$92{,}278 - \$92{,}892) = \$92{,}483$$

The bond issue date (June 1) is two months, or 2/6 of a semiannual period after March 31. Therefore, 2/6 of the difference between the March 31 and September 30 prices is subtracted from the March 31 price in the first interpolation. In the second interpolation, 4/6 of the difference is added to the September 30 price to account for the additional four months the bond is outstanding. This approach is followed whether the bond is issued at a premium or discount.

Accrued interest at the stated rate from March 31 to June 1 is collected from the investor, effectively an interest-free loan to the issuer. The initial discount or premium amount is independent of accrued interest and equals face value less the bond price, as usual. The following entry records the bond issuance by Gresham:

June 1, 1998—Issue bonds:

Cash	93,816*	
Discount on bonds payable	7,517†	
Interest payable		1,333‡
Bonds payable		100,000

*$92,483 + $100,000(.08)2/12

†$100,000 − $92,483

‡$100,000(.08)(2/12); two months' accrued interest from the bond date to the issue date is collected from the investor and then is reimbursed on the first interest payment date.

The entry to record the first interest payment after issuance (September 30) takes into account the partial interest period and accrues interest from the previous interest date (March 31). The amortization table constructed for the same bond but assuming issuance on *March 31, 1998* is constructed. The interest date immediately preceding the actual issue date is used as the basis for the September 30 entry under the interest method. Part of this table, as well as the September 30, 1998, interest entry follows:

Date	Interest Payment	Interest Expense	Discount Amortization	Unamortized Discount	Net Bond Liability
3/31/98				$7,722	$92,278*
9/30/98	$4,000†	$4,614‡	$614§	7,108‖	92,892#
3/31/99	4,000	4,645	645	6,463	93,537

*Price if sold on 3/31/98 to yield 10 percent (see text discussion).

†$100,000(.08)(1/2)

‡$92,278(.10)(1/2)

§$4,614 − $4,000

‖$7,722 − $614

#$92,278 + $614, or $100,000 − $7,108

September 30, 1998—Interest payment (interest method):

Interest payable	1,333	
Interest expense	3,076*	
Discount on bonds payable		409†
Cash ($100,000 × .08/2)		4,000

*The interest for four months based on the March 31 issue price: $3,076 = $92,278(.10)(4/12). Also, $3,076 = $4,614(4/6).

†The amortization for four months based on the March 31 issue price: $409 = $614(4/6). Also, the change in bond value from June 1 to September 30: $409 = $92,892 − $92,483.

After the first interest payment entry, the amortization table above (based on issuance at March 31) is used for the remaining entries during the bond term.

Under the straight-line method of amortization, the bond discount is amortized over the 58-month bond term at $129.60 per month ($7,517/58). The September 30 entry under the straight-line method follows:

September 30, 1998—Interest payment (straight-line method):

Interest payable	1,333	
Interest expense	3,185	
Discount on bonds payable		518*
Cash ($100,000 × .08/2)		4,000

*($7,517/58-month bond term)(4 months)

REVIEW PROBLEM

The Memphis Mart, a calendar-year firm, issued $50,000 of 6 percent bonds on October 1, 1998. The bonds are dated January 1, 1998, pay interest each June 30 and December 31, yield 4 percent, and mature December 31, 2007. $2,000 of bond issue costs were incurred. Provide:

1. The amount of the proceeds from the bond issue. Separate the accrued interest from the bond price.
2. The journal entry to record the bond issue.
3. The journal entry for the first interest payment under the interest method and the straight-line method.

SOLUTION

The semiannual interest payment is $1,500 ($50,000 × .06/2).

1. At July 1, 1998, 19 semiannual interest periods remain in the bond term. One-half of an interest period has elapsed at October 1, the issue date.

Price at
July 1, 1998 = $50,000(PV1, .02, 19) + $1,500(PVA, .02, 19)
= $50,000(.68643) + $1,500(15.67846) = $57,839

Growth in bond value to
  October 1, 1998 = .04($57,839) (3/12)   578

Cash interest at stated rate
  to October 1, 1998 = .06($50,000) (3/12) . . . .   (750)
Bond issue price at October 1, 1998. $57,667
Accrued interest to October 1, 1998: $1,500/2   750
Bond proceeds $58,417

2. October 1, 1998

Cash	58,417	
Interest payable		750
Premium on bonds payable		7,667
Bonds payable		50,000
Bond issue costs	2,000	
Cash		2,000

3. There are 9(12) + 3 = 111 months in the bond term.

	Interest Method	Straight-Line Method
December 31, 1998		
Interest payable	750	750
Interest expense	578*	543
Premium on bonds payable	172	207†
Cash	1,500	1,500

*$578 = (3/12)(.04)($57,839)

†$207 = (3/111)($7,667)

	Interest Method	Straight-Line Method
Bond issue expense	54	54
Bond issue costs	54	54

$54 = (3/111)($2,000)

CONCEPT REVIEW

1. What new accounting issues arise when bonds are issued between interest dates?
2. If bonds issued May 1, 1998, pay interest on June 30 and December 31, how many months of accrued interest does the issuer receive from the investor? What interest rate is used to compute the accrued interest?
3. Are bond issue costs an asset or a reduction of a liability? Defend both points of view.

DEBT SECURITIES WITH EQUITY RIGHTS

Firms issue debt securities that include rights to acquire capital stock. These rights enhance marketability and improve the terms to the issuer. The investor receives a potential right to become a shareholder and participate in stock price appreciation in addition to principal and interest payments. Two common examples of this type of hybrid security are nonconvertible bonds with detachable stock warrants and bonds convertible into capital stock.

Bonds with Detachable Stock Purchase Warrants

A **stock warrant** conveys the option to purchase from the issuer a specified number of shares of common stock at a designated price per share, within a stated time period (the exercise period). The warrant is valuable because it enables the holder to buy stock for less than market value if the market value rises above the designated price. Hence, warrants generally increase the bond price.[9]

APB Opinion No. 14 requires that a portion of the bond price be allocated to the warrants if they are detachable. The allocation is credited to a contributed capital (owners' equity) account calculated on the market values of the two securities on the date of issuance (the *proportional* method). If only the warrants have a readily determinable market value, the bonds are valued at the difference between the total bond price and the market value of the warrants (the *incremental* method).

In contrast, if the stock purchase warrants are *not* detachable, no separate market for them exists, and the entire bond price is allocated to the bonds.

Once the issue price is allocated to the bonds and detachable warrants, bond accounting is not affected by the warrants. Therefore, the following example of accounting for nonconvertible bonds with detachable stock purchase warrants does not illustrate interest recognition.

Example Embassy Corporation issues $100,000 of 8 percent, 10-year, nonconvertible bonds with detachable stock purchase warrants. Nuvolari Corporation purchases the entire issue. Each $1,000 bond carries 10 warrants. Each warrant entitles Nuvolari to purchase one share of $10 par common stock for $15.[10] The bond issue therefore includes 1,000 warrants (100 bonds × 10 warrants per bond). Assume the bond issue sells for 105 exclusive of accrued interest. Shortly after issuance, the warrants trade for $4 each.

1. **Proportional method** (Both securities have market values.) Shortly after issuance the bonds were quoted at 103 ex-warrants (without warrants attached).

Market value of bonds ($100,000 × 1.03)	$103,000
Market value of warrants ($4 × 1,000)	4,000
Total market value of bonds and warrants	$107,000
Allocation of proceeds to bonds [$105,000 × ($103,000 ÷ $107,000)] . . . $101,075	
Allocation of proceeds to warrants [$105,000 × ($4,000 ÷ $107,000)] . . . 3,925	
Total proceeds allocated $105,000	

---

[9] Warrants are either detachable or nondetachable. If detachable, the warrants are traded as separate securities. If nondetachable, the debt security must be surrendered to obtain the stock.

[10] *Par* value for common stock is the minimum stock issue price. It appears on the stock certificate, is used in certain dividend calculations, and constitutes the minimum capital per share to be retained. Common stock is credited with par value; contributed capital in excess of par is credited with proceeds in excess of par value.

Embassy Corporation (issuer)		**Nuvolari Corporation (investor)**	

Issuance entry:

Cash 105,000		Investment in bonds 101,075	
Bonds payable	100,000	Investment in detach-	
Detachable stock		able stock warrants . . . 3,925	
warrants (OE)	3,925	Cash	105,000
Premium on bonds			
payable	1,075*		

*$101,075 − $100,000

2. **Incremental method** (Only one security has a market value.) Assume now that no market value is determined for the bonds as separate securities. The warrants trade for $4 each.

Embassy Corporation (issuer)		**Nuvolari Corporation (investor)**	

Issuance entry:

Cash 105,000		Investment in bonds 101,000	
Bonds payable	100,000	Investment in detach-	
Detachable stock		able stock warrants . . . 4,000	
warrants	4,000*	Cash	105,000
Premium on bonds			
payable	1,000†		

*(1,000 warrants)($4).

†Value allocated to bonds − face value of bonds, or ($105,000 − $4,000) − $100,000.

Under the incremental method, the warrants are credited at market value. The remaining, or *incremental,* portion of the proceeds ($101,000) is allocated to the bonds. The amount of premium recorded equals the difference between the amount allocated to the bonds and face value. Nuvolari classifies its two investment accounts as trading securities or as securities available for sale, depending on the intended holding period.

The entries to account for exercise and expiration under the incremental method example, assuming no subsequent change in the market value of warrants, are as follows:

Embassy Corporation (issuer)		**Nuvolari Corporation (investor)**	

Entry to account for exercise of 900 warrants:

Cash (900 × $15) 13,500		Investment in common stock . . 17,100	
Detachable stock warrants . . 3,600*		Investment in detachable	
Common stock (900 × . . .		stock warrants	3,600
$10)	9,000	Cash	13,500
Contributed capital in			
excess of par	8,100		

*$4(900 warrants)

Entry to account for expiration of remaining 100 warrants:

Detachable stock warrants . . . 400*		Loss on investment 400	
Contributed capital from		Investment in detachable	
expiration of detach-		stock warrants	400
able stock warrants	400		

*$4(100 warrants).

Detachable stock warrants is reduced by the original amount allocated to it ($4 per warrant), and $3,600 of the resources allocated to warrants is allocated to other owners' equity accounts upon exercise.

An expiration entry is recorded at the end of the exercise period for any warrants that remain outstanding, whether through oversight or because of an unfavorable stock price. The issuing company retains the portion of the bond price originally allocated to the expired warrants.

Convertible Bonds

A **convertible bond** is exchangeable for capital stock (usually common stock) of the issuer at the *option of the investor.* Typically, convertible bonds are also *callable* at a specified redemption, or call, price at the *option of the issuer.* If the bonds are called, the holders either convert the bonds or accept the call price. Convertible bonds often are marketable at lower interest rates than conventional bonds because investors assign a value to the conversion privilege.

The primary attraction of convertibles to investors is the potential for increased value if the stock appreciates. If it does not, the investor continues to receive both interest and principal (although usually at a lower rate than nonconvertible bonds would provide).

Convertible bonds are advantageous to the issuer for several reasons:

- The prospect for raising debt capital often is improved.
- The bonds often pay a lower interest rate than nonconvertible bonds.
- If the bonds are converted, the face value is never paid.
- Fewer shares may be issued on conversion than in a direct sale of stock.
- The call option protects the issuer from having to issue stock with an aggregate value in excess of the call price.

Convertible bonds are not without disadvantages, however. If the stock price rises, the issuing company forgoes the higher proceeds that would be possible from a direct sale of stock. In the opposite case, the firm must continue to service the debt.

Example   Many Japanese firms experienced declining profits in the early 1990s and were burdened with huge amounts of maturing convertible bonds. In Japan, convertible bonds had been a very attractive means of financing because stock prices continued to rise throughout the 1980s. Issuing firms obtained low-rate debt financing and frequently did not have to pay the maturity value. By 1993, with prices of Japanese stocks at roughly half the value of 1990, few holders converted, thus forcing the issuing firms to refinance the debt at much higher rates.[11]

Accounting and Reporting   Accounting for the issuance of convertible bonds poses a conceptual problem. A popular view holds that the economic value of the conversion feature, reflected in the bond price, should be recorded as stockholders' equity, but *APB Opinion No. 14* specifies that convertible bonds be recorded only as debt. The APB reasoned that the debt and equity features of a convertible bond are inseparable and do not exist independently of each other.

A separate market does not exist for either the bond standing alone or the conversion privilege. There is no objective basis (such as a market or an exchange transaction) for allocating the bond price to the bond and the conversion feature. The value of the conversion feature is contingent on a future stock price that cannot be predicted.

Accounting for interest expense and amortization of premium or discount is not affected by convertibility. The entire bond term is used for amortization because the date of conversion cannot be anticipated. Accounting for interest is omitted in the example to follow.

Example   Assume that Tollen Corporation sells $100,000 of 8 percent convertible bonds for $106,000. Each $1,000 bond is convertible to 10 shares of Tollen Corporation $10 par common stock on any interest date after the end of the second year from date of issuance. (In practice, conversion is generally possible on any date within the conversion period. The restriction on conversion is used only to facilitate the example.)

Issuance entry:

```
Cash . . . . . . . . . . . . . . . . . . . . . . . . . . . . . . . . . . . . . . . . . . . . 106,000
    Premium on bonds payable  . . . . . . . . . . . . . . . . . . . . . . . . . . . .           6,000
    Bonds payable  . . . . . . . . . . . . . . . . . . . . . . . . . . . . . . . . . . .         100,000
```

When the bonds are converted, the issuer updates interest expense and amortization of premium or discount to the date of conversion. Then, bonds payable is closed. Two methods are acceptable for recording the stock issued upon conversion:

1. **Book value method** Record the stock at the book value of the convertible bonds; recognize neither gain nor loss.

---

[11]"Japanese Firms Are Losing One Key Advantage," *The Wall Street Journal,* March 29, 1993, p. A15.

2. **Market value method** Record the stock at the market value of stock or debt, whichever is more reliable. A gain or loss equal to the difference between the market value and the book value of debt is recognized.

The following entries illustrate both methods. Assume that the bonds are converted on an interest date. On the conversion date, the stock price is $110 per share, and $3,000 of premium remains unamortized after updating the premium account.

	Book Value Method	Market Value Method
Entry for conversion of bonds:		
Bonds payable	100,000	100,000
Premium on bonds payable	3,000	3,000
Loss on conversion of bonds		7,000‡
Common stock	10,000*	10,000
Contributed capital in excess of par	93,000†	100,000§

*(100 bonds)(10 shares per bond)($10 par).

†Book value of bonds is $103,000; $103,000 − $10,000 = $93,000.

‡Market value of stock issued ($1,000 shares × $110 = $110,000) less book value of bonds ($103,000) equals loss of $7,000.

§$110,000 (market value of shares issued) less $10,000 (par value of shares issued).

Under the book value method, the owners' equity accounts replace the bond accounts for the issuer. Under the market value method, the owners' equity accounts are credited at full market value, as if the issued stock were sold on the date of conversion. The gain or loss on conversion is not classified as extraordinary because the investor initiated the conversion. Tollen's $7,000 loss is the cash it forgoes by issuing shares on bond conversion, but it is not necessarily the economic loss because the market value of the bonds is not considered in the accounting.

If the book value of the bonds is less than the total par of stock issued on conversion, retained earnings is debited for the difference. For example, if the total par of Tollen stock issued is $105,000 (assume $105 par), retained earnings is debited for $2,000 under the book value method.

The book value method appears to be more popular. Many accountants view the conversion as the culmination of a single transaction that started when the convertible bonds were issued. The valuation of issued stock thus is restricted to the actual resources received on the bond issue, adjusted for amortization to date of conversion. Furthermore, this view holds that the gain (loss) under the market value method is not supported by the value of resources originally received on the bond issue. Others prefer the market value method because it uses current value to measure the conversion. The valuation of the stock issued is based on the value received if the shares were sold.

Induced Conversion of Convertible Debt Issuers of convertible debt sometimes change the conversion provisions after the issuance date to induce prompt conversion. The inducement is an incentive over and above the original shares to be issued on conversion. Common inducements include an increase in the number of shares issued per bond, issuance of stock rights, and cash or other consideration. Declining interest rates and a preference for lower debt levels can prompt an induced conversion.

SFAS No. 84, "Induced Conversions of Convertible Debt," requires that the issuer recognize an expense equal to the fair value of consideration in excess of the fair value of the securities issuable under the *original* conversion terms. The expense is not classified as an extraordinary item because the original debt agreement remains in effect during the inducement period, and the debt is extinguished at the bondholder's option rather than the issuer's. *SFAS No. 84* applies only to changes in conversion provisions exercisable for a limited time, that is, only changes made to induce prompt conversion.

The expense is recognized only for bonds converted during the limited time period, and the market value of consideration transferred is measured at the date the inducement is accepted. Consider an example:

Example Berlin Corporation issued 500, 6 percent convertible bonds issued at face value ($1,000). Each bond is convertible into 10 shares of $20 par common stock. Some time after issuance, Berlin offers two additional shares of common stock for each bond as an inducement to convert. The offer is open for a two-month period. The bondholders accept the inducement within the required period. The market price of the common stock on the acceptance date (also an interest date) is $110. The entries to record the induced conversion under the book value and market value methods are as follows:

| **Book Value Method** | **Market Value Method** |

Conversion entry:

Book Value Method		Market Value Method	
Bonds payable 500,000		Bonds payable 500,000	
Debt conversion		Debt conversion	
expense 110,000*		expense 110,000	
Common stock	120,000†	Loss on conversion . . . 50,000‡	
Contributed capital .		Common stock . . .	120,000
in excess of		Contributed capital	
par	490,000	in excess of	
. . . .		par	540,000§

*(12 − 10)(500)($110)—The market value of 2 additional shares per bond.

†12(500)($20)

‡Difference between market value of stock issued ($660,000) and book value of bonds converted ($500,000), less the cost of the inducement ($110,000)

§$660,000 − $120,000

The issuer recognizes the market value of the two additional inducement shares per bond as an expense under both methods. Under the book value method, the expense is effectively capitalized as an increase in owners' equity reflecting the issuance of additional common shares without proceeds.[12] Under the market value method, part of the total loss on conversion is reclassified as debt conversion expense. The increase to owners' equity is measured at the total market value of shares issued. Under either method, if cash is the inducement, the debt conversion expense equals the amount of cash paid.

One view of induced conversions holds that expense recognition is inappropriate for transactions involving a firm and its equity investors. Others see the inducement as an extinguishment, implying that market values should be recorded. Yet another view holds that the cost of the inducement should be treated as a reduction of the equity capital provided. However, in *SFAS No. 84,* the FASB reasoned that a firm incurs a cost not expected under the original agreement when inducing conversion. Were it not for the extra inducement, the conversion would not have occurred.

CONCEPT REVIEW

1. Why is a value recorded for detachable warrants, but not for the conversion feature of convertible bonds?
2. How is the premium (discount) computed for bonds issued with detachable warrants?
3. What is the rationale for the market value method of accounting for conversion of convertible bonds? And what does the gain or loss on conversion represent?

DEBT EXTINGUISHMENT

Firms typically use the proceeds of long-term debt instruments for the entire debt term. At maturity all discount or premium is fully amortized; gains and losses are not recognized on normal retirement. Firms can, however, retire debt before maturity. Early retirement of debt decreases the debt–equity ratio and can facilitate future debt issuances.

---

[12]The additional shares issued are similar to a stock dividend. A stock dividend is the issuance of shares to existing shareholders without proceeds to the issuing firm. Stock dividends reduce retained earnings, just as debt conversion expense does.

The incentives for retiring bonds differ depending on whether interest rates have increased or decreased since the bonds were issued:

1. If interest rates have *increased,* the bond's market price (the amount paid to retire the bonds early) has fallen, often below net book value. The result is a *gain* recognized by the issuer on retirement.
2. If interest rates have *decreased,* the bond's market price has increased. In this case, the issuing company retires higher interest rate bonds thus reducing future interest costs. However, a *loss* is recognized because the market price of the bond exceeds book value. Many firms take this opportunity to issue lower-rate debt in a refinancing of the higher-rate debt, just as homeowners do when they refinance their home mortgages when rates decline.

The main reporting issues are determining *what* constitutes a debt extinguishment, and *how* to classify the gain or loss on extinguishment. The gain or loss is the difference between the book value and market value of the debt on the date of extinguishment.

SFAS No. 125, "Accounting for Transfers and Servicing of Financial Assets and Extinguishments of Liabilities," states that a liability is derecognized (removed from the balance sheet) only if it is extinguished. A liability is extinguished only if one of the following two criteria is met:

1. The debtor pays the creditor and is relieved of its obligation (paying includes delivery of cash, other financial assets, goods, or services).
2. The debtor is legally released from being the primary obligor under the liability, either judicially or by the creditor. (par. 16)

Debtors may be released (criterion 2) from responsibility for a liability for a variety of reasons. A *legal* release is accomplished, for example, when a debtor sells a real-estate asset that serves as collateral for an assumable mortgage loan. When the buyer assumes the loan, the seller (original debtor) is legally released from the debt. The assumption of the loan by the seller extinguishes the debtor's liability.

The *creditor* also may release the debtor provided that a third party assumes the obligation and the original debtor becomes secondarily liable. This type of release also extinguishes the debtor's liability. However, the original debtor becomes a guarantor and may be required to recognize or disclose a contingent liability under *SFAS No. 5,* "Accounting for Contingencies." If a guarantee contingent liability is recognized (when probable and estimable), the guarantee liability reduces the gain or increases the loss on extinguishment of the original debt.

Classification of Gain or Loss   *SFAS No. 4* requires that gains and losses on debt extinguishment be classified as *extraordinary items* even though they might be frequent occurrences. In many instances, extinguishment gains have been significant in relation to operating income, and classification as extraordinary brings the gains into the open. Firms no longer are able to report a large extinguishment gain as a component of ordinary income.[13]

Extinguishment of debt is broadly defined and is not restricted to early retirement or to cash reacquisitions of debt.[14] Normal conversion and induced conversion of convertible bonds are not debt extinguishments for purposes of classifying the gain or loss because retirement occurs at the option of the investor, although retirement of debt accomplished through issuance of equity securities is considered a debt extinguishment.[15]

Required disclosures for extraordinary gains and losses from extinguishment include (*SFAS No. 4,* par. 9)

---

[13]For example, in 1973, United Brands refunded $125 million (book value) of 5½ percent bonds by issuing $75 million of 9⅛ percent bonds and paying $12.5 million cash. United Brands recognized a $37.5 million *ordinary* gain. The market value of the old bonds had fallen $37.5 million because of the rise in interest rates. The company had averaged only $6.6 million in earnings during the preceding five years!

[14]Some troubled debt restructures, discussed in Appendix 16A, result in debt retirement but are not considered debt retirements for purposes of classifying gains and losses.

[15]*FASB Technical Bulletin No. 80–1.*

- A description of the transaction, including the means used for extinguishment.
- The income tax effect of the gain or loss.
- The per share amount of the aggregate gain or loss net of related tax effect.

Another disclosure is required for some firms. *SFAS No. 76,* "Extinguishment of Debt," which was superseded by *SFAS No. 125,* allowed **insubstance defeasance** as a way to extinguish debt.[16] Although no longer permitted, disclosures for firms using this method of extinguishment before the effective date of *SFAS No. 125,* which is not retroactively applied, are required to disclose a general description of the defeasance transaction and the relevant debt amount, as long as the debt remains outstanding.

Debt extinguishment can be accomplished in a variety of ways, as illustrated in the following sections.

Accounting for debt extinguishment involves

- Updating interest expense, discount or premium, and related issue costs to the retirement date.
- Removing the liability accounts.
- Recording the transfer of cash, other resources, or debt securities.
- Recording an extraordinary gain or loss.

Extinguishment of Bonds by Open-Market Purchase or Exercise of Call Privilege

In an open-market purchase of bonds, the issuer pays the current market price as would any investor purchasing the bonds. If bonds carry a **call privilege,** the issuer may retire the debt by paying the call price during a specified period. The call price places a ceiling on the market price. Investors who purchase callable bonds are at a disadvantage if interest rates decline because they may have to surrender bonds that pay higher interest than noncallable bonds. For this reason, callable bonds often are issued with higher interest rates. In addition, the call price typically exceeds face value by the **call premium** that can decline each year of the bond term.

As a basis for an example, Exhibit 16–9 repeats a portion of the amortization table for the Gresham bonds in Exhibit 16–5. Assume that interest rates have increased since the bonds were issued, and assume that on March 1, 1999, Gresham purchases 20 percent ($20,000 face value) of the bonds on the open market at 90. The price decline reflects increased interest rates. If the issue were called instead, the call price would be used in lieu of market price. Otherwise, the accounting is the same. The entries to record the extinguishment under the effective and straight-line methods are as follows:

	Interest Method		Straight-Line Method	

March 1, 1999—On portion retired: update interest and premium amortization:

Interest expense	207*		205	
Premium on bonds payable	26		28†	
Interest payable		233‡		233

*.06($103,466)(2/12)(.20)
  (Market rate at issue)(Book value on 1/1/99)(2/12 year)(Portion of bond issue retired)

†$4,213(2/60)(.20)
  (Original premium)(2 months/60 months bond term)(Portion of bond issue retired)

‡$20,000(.07)(2/12)
  (Accrued interest from January 1, 1999)

March 1, 1999—Update bond issue expense:

| Bond issue expense | 24* | | 24 | |
| Bond issue cost | | 24 | | 24 |

*$3,600(2/60)(.20)
  (Total issue cost)(2 months/60 month bond term)(Portion of bond issue retired)

---

[16]A firm that insubstance defeased its debt placed risk-free securities into an irrevocable trust for the sole purpose of extinguishing the liability in the future. Although the liability was not currently paid, both the liability and assets used for the trust were derecognized.

Issue date: January 1, 1998
Stated interest rate: 7 percent
Interest payment date: December 31
Maturity date: December 31, 2002

Total face value: $100,000
Bond date: January 1, 1998
Yield rate at issuance: 6 percent
Bond issue costs: $3,600

**Partial Amortization Table for Gresham Company Bonds
Sold at Premium—Interest Method**

Date	Interest Payment	Interest Expense	Premium Amortization	Unamortized Premium	Net Bond Liability
1/1/98				$4,213	$104,213
12/31/98	$ 7,000	$ 6,253	$ 747	3,466	103,466
12/31/99	7,000	6,208	792	2,674	102,674

March 1, 1999—Remove relevant accounts and recognize gain:

Bonds payable	20,000		20,000
Premium on bonds payable	667*		646†
Interest payable	233		233
Cash		18,233‡	18,233
Bond issue cost		552§	552
Extraordinary gain, bond extinguishment		2,115‖	2,094#

*$3,466(.20) − $26
 (Unamortized premium 1/1/99)(Portion of bond issue retired) − (Amount of premium amortized on 3/1/99)

†$4,213(46/60)(.20)
 (Original premium)(46 months remaining/60 month bond term)(Portion of bond issue retired)

‡$20,000(.90) + $233 interest payable

§$3,600(46/60)(.20)
 (Total issue cost)(46 months remaining/60 month bond term)(Portion of bond issue retired)

‖Book value of bonds retired ($20,000 + $667 = $20,667) less price of bonds ($18,000) less unexpired bond issue cost on
 bonds retired ($552) equals the extraordinary gain of $2,115.

#Calculation is similar to interest method.

Extinguishment does not affect the accounting for the remaining 80 percent of the bond issue; 80 percent of the values in the amortization table would be used for the remaining bond term, as well as 80 percent of the bond issue costs.

The Nature of the Extraordinary Item   The extraordinary gain in the Gresham example is the difference between the total market price and the book value of the bonds, less the unexpired portion of the bond issue costs relating to the retired bonds. The remaining bond issue costs generate no future benefit. Brokerage fees and other costs of retiring the bonds also decrease the gain (increase the loss).

The extraordinary gain occurs because the market value of the bonds decreased below book value as a result of increased interest rates. However, it can be argued that the bond extinguishment does not alter Gresham's economic position because the debt was retired at market value. A more profitable alternative might be to apply the $18,000 to a higher-yield investment. Retiring low-cost debt when interest rates rise is questionable, especially if additional debt issuances are contemplated.[17]

The extraordinary gain or loss can be quite large.

Example   In late 1995 Black & Decker, a maker of power tools and household appliances, recognized a $30 million after-tax loss when it retired bonds that were to mature in 2016. The general level of interest rates in the economy had declined after the bonds were issued, causing the market price per bond to increase relative to book value. The loss represents the difference between market and book values of the bonds.

---

[17]Financial statement and footnote disclosures often do not provide sufficient information to completely analyze the economic effect of a bond retirement on the issuer. The economic gain or loss depends on the discount rate chosen. Only coincidentally will the reported gain equal the computed economic gain. See J. Dietrich and J. Deitrick, "Bond Exchanges in the Airline Industry: Analyzing Public Disclosures," *Accounting Review*, January 1985, pp. 109–26.

Sinking-Fund Retirements: Ordinary Gain and Loss Classification   Early retirement of bonds fulfills the sinking-fund requirements of some bond issues. Under *SFAS No. 64,* gains and losses from such extinguishments made to satisfy requirements that must be met within one year of the extinguishment are treated as ordinary income items, without regard to the means used to retire the debt.

Example   Assume that Gresham was required by the bond indenture to retire $20,000 of bonds by December 31, 1999, to satisfy a sinking-fund requirement. The date of retirement, March 1, 1999, is within one year of the deadline. Therefore, the gain is reported as ordinary. In contrast, if the sinking-fund retirement deadline is May 1, 2001, the gain is classified as extraordinary because retirement did not occur within one year of the required date.

This exemption recognizes the difference between required and discretionary extinguishments and allows one year to complete the necessary arrangements for bond retirement. If an issuer must retire bonds under the indenture and does so within a year of the deadline, it is difficult to argue that the purpose of the retirement is to manipulate income. If bonds are retired two years ahead of schedule, the issuer could have motivations other than meeting a distant deadline.[18]

Treasury Bonds   Regardless of the form extinguishment takes, if the issuer does not cancel its bonds after reacquisition but contemplates reissuance at a later date, treasury bonds, a contra bond payable account, is debited in lieu of bonds payable. When the bonds are reissued, treasury bonds is credited rather than bonds payable, and a new discount or premium is recorded. If bonds are canceled, treasury bonds is credited and bonds payable is debited. Like bonds payable, treasury bonds is debited or credited only with face value.

Retirement of Convertible Debt   When convertible bonds are converted, the gain or loss under the market value method is classified as ordinary. Occasionally, firms retire convertible bonds through open-market purchase or other methods. Gains and losses on these retirements are classified as extraordinary, consistent with the intent of *SFAS No. 4.*

Extinguishment of Bonds by Refunding

When a **refunding** takes place, one bond issue is replaced with another bond issue. One way of refunding is to issue new bonds in exchange for the old bonds. Cash is involved if the bond issues have different market values. More frequently, however, the proceeds from a new bond issue are used to retire the old issue because the holders of the old issue do not necessarily wish to become the new creditors. In both cases, the accounting for refunding is similar to all other forms of debt extinguishment. The following information illustrates the two situations involving refunding:

1. **Refunding by direct exchange of debt securities** On January 1, 1998, WestCal Corporation issues $100,000 of 10-year, 5 percent bonds at face value with interest payable each June 30 and December 31. On January 1, 2002, the bondholders agreed to exchange their bonds for $90,000 of 20-year, 8 percent bonds with the same interest dates as the 5 percent bonds. The market rate of interest on similar bonds is 8 percent.

   Analysis:
   a. The bondholders receive 10 percent less principal but 60 percent more in the interest rate.
   b. PV (market value) of new bonds $90,000
   PV (market value) of old bonds (12 semiannual periods remain in the old issue):
   Principal [$100,000(PV1, 4%, 12) = $100,000(.62460)] $62,460
   Interest [$2,500(PVA, 4%, 12) = $2,500(9.38507)]   23,463   85,923

   Difference: Economic loss to WestCal . . . . $ 4,077

---

[18]Some bond indentures specify serial retirement of bonds. These scheduled maturities are preplanned and do not qualify for the exemption from extraordinary classification under *SFAS No. 64.*

January 1, 2002—Refunding entry:

Bonds payable, 5%	100,000	
Bonds payable, 8%		90,000
Extraordinary gain, bond extinguishment		10,000

WestCal accepts the economic loss to extend the maturity 20 years and to avoid the costs of issuing the new bonds for cash. The creditors receive $2,200 more in interest each year ($7,200 − $5,000). WestCal records a $10,000 *accounting gain* yet sustains an *economic loss* of $4,077 because increases in interest rates allow new bonds with a lower face value but higher present value to replace the old bonds. By refunding the old bonds, WestCal has committed itself to making a new stream of future cash payments with an increased present value.

This is an example of the problems that arise from using the market rate at issuance to measure the book value of bonds. WestCal could invest $85,923 at 8 percent and satisfy the remaining payments on the 5 percent bonds. Many accountants view this value as a more appropriate current valuation of the 5 percent bonds, particularly if WestCal intends to extinguish the bonds early.

2. **Refunding by issuing new debt and purchasing old debt** On January 1, 1998, West-Cal Corporation issues $100,000 of 10-year, 5 percent bonds at face value with interest payable each June 30 and December 31. On January 1, 2002, WestCal issues at face value $86,000 of 20-year, 8 percent bonds with the same interest dates as the 5 percent bonds. The market price of the old bonds is 86. The old bonds are retired.

January 1, 2002—Issue 8 percent bonds:

Cash	86,000	
Bonds payable		86,000

January 1, 2002—Retire 5 percent bonds:

Bonds payable	100,000	
Cash		86,000
Extraordinary gain, bond extinguishment		14,000

The accounting gain is $14,000, but no economic gain or loss occurs because the 5 percent bonds were extinguished at market value.

Summary of Gain and Loss Classification

Exhibit 16–10 provides a summary of gain and loss classification for debt extinguishments and retirements.

REVIEW PROBLEM

This problem continues the Memphis Mart bond issue from the previous review problem. Recap of the data: Memphis is a calendar-year firm; $50,000 of 6 percent bonds were issued on October 1, 1998; the bonds are dated January 1, 1998, pay interest each June 30 and December 31, yielded 4 percent, and mature December 31, 2007. $2,000 of bond issue costs were incurred. The semiannual interest payment is $1,500, and there are 111 months in the bond term. *Additional information:* A short segment of the amortization table for the bonds follows (using the interest method):

Date	Payment	Interest Expense	Premium Amort.	Unamortized Premium	Net Bond Liability
1/1/02				$5,288	$55,288
6/30/02	$1,500	$1,106	$394	4,894	54,894

On May 1, 2002, Memphis Mart purchased and retired $20,000 of the bonds at 108. Provide:

1. A verification of the January 1, 2002, net liability balance of $55,288 in the preceding partial table.
2. The May 1, 2002, journal entry for the interest accrual on the bonds to be retired, and the entry for retirement, using the interest method.

EXHIBIT 16–10

Summary of Gain and Loss
Classification on Debt
Extinguishments and Retirements

Method of Extinguishment or Retirement	Classification of Gain or Loss
1. Conversion of convertible bonds	Ordinary
2. Induces conversion of convertible bonds (gain, loss, and conversion expense)	Ordinary
3. Direct payment to creditors	Extraordinary
4. Sinking-fund purchases made to satisfy sinking-fund requirements that must be met within one year of the purchase	Ordinary
5. Issuance of equity securities	Extraordinary
6. Retirement of convertible debt	Extraordinary
7. Call	Extraordinary
8. Refunding	Extraordinary
9. Legal release from obligation	Extraordinary

SOLUTION

1. Six years (12 semiannual interest periods) remain in the bond term at January 1, 2002. The net bond liability on that date is:

$$\$50,000(PV1, .02, 12) + \$1,500(PVA, .02, 12) =$$
$$\$50,000(.78849) + \$1,500(10.57534) = \$55,288$$

2. May 1, 2002

The percent of the bond issue retired is 40 percent ($20,000/$50,000). On this date, five years and 8 months or 68 months remain in the bond term.

Interest expense (.04)(4/12)(.40)$55,288	295	
Premium on bonds payable	105	
Interest payable $1,500(4/6)(.40)		400
Bond issue expense $2,000(4/111)(.40)	29	
Bond issue costs		29
Bonds payable	20,000	
Premium on bonds payable	2,010*	
Interest payable	400	
Cash 1.08($20,000)		21,600
Bond issue costs		490†
Extraordinary gain, bond retirement		320

*$2,010 = $5,288(.40) − $105

†$490 = $2,000(68/111)(.40)

CONCEPT REVIEW

1. If gains and losses on debt extinguishment are not unusual, why are they classified as extraordinary?
2. Why is the gain or loss on a debt retirement made June 30, 1998, to fulfill sinking-fund requirements that must be met by January 1, 1999, classified as ordinary?
3. If interest rates have increased since the issuance of a bond, what financial reporting incentive is created for early extinguishment of the bond?

LONG-TERM NOTES

A note is a formal document that specifies the terms of a debt. Long-term notes are often used for specific asset acquisitions, and bonds are more likely to be used to raise large amounts of capital for general purposes. Notes typically have shorter maturities than bonds and are not traded on organized exchanges. Present value techniques are used for valuation and interest recognition for long-term notes.

Example 1: Long-Term Note, Stated Rate and Market Rates Different   Fema Company purchased goods on January 1, 1998, and issued a two-year, $10,000 note with a 3 percent stated interest rate. Interest is payable each December 31, and the entire principal is payable December 31, 1999. The merchandise does not have a ready market value. The market rate of interest appropriate for this note is 8 percent. The present value of the note and its recorded value are computed as follows:

Present value of maturity amount
$10,000(PV1, 8%, 2) = $10,000(.85734) = ... $8,573
Present value of the nominal interest payments
$10,000(.03)(PVA, 8%, 2) = $300(1.78326) = ...   535
Present value of the note at 8%. $9,108

The present value of the note is less than its face value because the note pays less interest than is available elsewhere in the market. A higher face value must therefore be paid to compensate the seller for the lower interest rate. The difference between face value and present value ($892) represents the discount on the note, or interest in addition to the 3 percent cash payments. The accounting is similar to a bond issued at a discount (assume the interest method).

January 1, 1998—Issue note (gross method):

Inventory 9,108
Discount on long-term notes payable (contra note payable)   892
   Long-term notes payable   10,000

December 31, 1998—Interest payment

Interest expense ($9,108 × .08)   729
   Discount on long-term notes payable   429
   Cash   300

The straight-line method is acceptable if it yields results not materially different from the interest method. Under the straight-line method, Fema amortizes $446 ($892/2) of the discount and recognizes $746 of interest expense ($300 + $446) each period.

The remaining entries under the interest method for Fema are as follows:

December 31, 1999—Interest payment

Interest expense ($9,108 + $429).08   763
   Discount on long-term notes payable   463
   Cash   300

December 31, 1999—Note maturity

Long-term notes payable 10,000
   Cash   10,000

Example 2: Long-Term Note Issued for Noncash Consideration, Payments Include Interest and Principal   On January 2, 1998, Bellow Company purchased equipment by paying $5,000 down and issuing a $10,000, 4 percent note payable in four equal annual installments starting December 31, 1998. The current market rate on notes of a similar nature and risk is 10 percent. The market value of the equipment is not readily determinable. Fixed-rate mortgage notes secured by real property have longer terms than the Bellow note but are otherwise similar. Payments on mortgage notes include both interest and principal.

The payment (P) and present value of the note are determined to be

$$\$10,000 = P(\text{PVA, 4\%, 4}) = P(3.62990)$$
$$\$10,000/3.62990 = \$2,755$$

Present value of note:

$$\$2,755(\text{PVA, 10\%, 4}) = \$2,755(3.16987) = \$8,733$$

Note 18. Commitments

At December 31, 1994, the Company had contractual commitments to purchase coal which is primarily used to blend with Company mined coal. Based on the contract provisions these commitments are currently estimated to aggregate approximately $161,743 and expire from 1996 through 1998 as follows: 1996, $76,761; 1997, $57,929; 1998, $27,053. Purchases under the contracts were $83,532 in 1995, $53,097 in 1994, and $81,069 in 1993.

January 2, 1998—Issue note (net method):

Equipment ($5,000 + $8,733)	13,733	
Cash		5,000
Long-term notes payable		8,733

December 31, 1998—Interest expense:

Interest expense ($8,733 × .10)	873	
Long-term notes payable	1,882	
Cash		2,755

The entries for the remaining term of the note parallel those in the first example.

High and unstable interest rates gave rise to innovative mortgage notes. These include point-system mortgages, shared-appreciation mortgages, and adjustable rate mortgages.

The proceeds to the borrower are reduced in a **point-system mortgage** as a way of increasing the effective interest rate. The monthly payment is based on face amount of the note before the points are assessed. The interest rate on an **adjustable-rate mortgage (ARM)** fluctuates as market conditions change, periodically requiring a recalculation of the monthly payment based on the current loan balance, new interest rate, and remaining mortgage term. In a **shared-appreciation mortgage,** the lender charges a lower stated interest rate in return for a share of the market value appreciation on property financed with the note.

OFF-BALANCE-SHEET FINANCING AND DISCLOSURES FOR LONG-TERM LIABILITIES

Long-term liability measurement and disclosure are crucial to assessments of the risk and financial strength of companies, but the criteria for recognizing liabilities are imprecise. The *SFAC No. 6* definition of a liability allows substantial latitude in interpretation. Creative financial instruments that increase the opportunity for **off-balance-sheet financing** complicate liability recognition and measurement. Through off-balance-sheet financing, firms raise debt capital without reporting liabilities. Lease and postretirement benefit liabilities, once absent from corporation balance sheets, are now required to be disclosed. However, instances of off-balance-sheet obligations remain.

Unconditional Purchase Obligations

An **unconditional purchase obligation** is an arrangement obligating the borrower to transfer funds in the future for fixed or minimum quantities of goods and services. *SFAS No. 47,* "Disclosures of Long-Term Obligations," does not require recognition of such obligations. However, the following disclosures are required for unconditional purchase obligations that are noncancelable, have a remaining term of more than one year, and are not disclosed in the balance sheet:

1. The nature and term of the obligation.
2. The amount as of the balance sheet date and for the succeeding five balance sheet dates.

Disclosure of the amount of imputed interest necessary to reduce the obligations to present value is encouraged. If the obligation is recorded as a liability, only the relevant amounts for the succeeding five annual balance sheet dates must be reported.

Exhibit 16–11 provides an example of footnote disclosure of unconditional purchase obligations.

Disclosures for Financial Instruments

The 1980s ushered in an enormous number of new and creative financial instruments. Internationalization, deregulation, increased competition, inflation, changes in the financial services industry, tax law changes, and interest rate volatility contributed to this explosion of financial instruments. Many financial instruments were developed to reduce exposure to loss from interest rate and foreign exchange rate changes.

> A Rip Van Winkle who fell asleep in 1979 and just woke up would hardly recognize today's financial landscape. ... Arthur Andersen & Company has kept a list of new financial products since 1986; it now ... totals more than 600.[19]

An **exchangeable debenture** is one such innovative debt instrument. Pennzoil Company sold $402.5 million of debentures exchangeable into Chevron Corporation common stock owned by Pennzoil. Pennzoil's investment in Chevron had not appreciated as expected. The exchangeable debentures shift some of the stock ownership risk to the bondholders. Until the exchange, Pennzoil will continue to receive Chevron dividends. The bondholders can benefit from Chevron stock price appreciation. Several accounting issues arise. Is this one financial instrument or two? Does the exchangeable provision affect the reporting of Pennzoil's investment in Chevron stock? How is the income statement affected?

Another example is an **interest rate swap,** an arrangement between two companies agreeing to trade interest payments. One company may have variable-rate debt outstanding but prefer more stable, fixed-rate financing that it cannot obtain because of its poor credit rating. Another company with fixed-rate debt is willing to risk interest rate fluctuation and exchanges its fixed interest payments for the variable payments of the first company.

Off-Balance-Sheet Risk for Liabilities   *SFAS No. 105* states that if the potential obligation for a financial instrument exceeds the amount recognized as a liability, the financial instrument has off-balance-sheet risk of accounting loss. Off-balance-sheet risk arises from **credit risk, market risk,** or **physical risk.** Credit risk is the possibility of loss from failure of another party to perform according to the contract. Market risk is the possibility that market price changes will make a liability more costly to extinguish. Physical risk involves potential theft or damage.

An obligation with off-balance-sheet risk is a guarantee of indebtedness in which the guarantor agrees to pay the debt if a borrower defaults, in return for a fee from the borrower. No liability is recognized initially, but a future liability and loss is possible, depending on the outcome of a future event.

Example   R.H. Macy & Company secured significant loan commitments from several banks in the 1980s. Although Macy filed for bankruptcy, the loan commitments, obtained for a fee, require banks to continue lending to the troubled retailer. The resulting increased exposure to credit loss in the event that such debtor firms do not improve their financial condition underscores the off-balance-sheet risk of loan commitments:

> Banks have hundreds of billions of dollars in these credit commitments that periodically come back to haunt them.[20]

The following information for financial instruments with off-balance-sheet risk must be disclosed:

The face, contract, or notional[21] principal amount.

The nature and terms of the instrument.

A discussion of credit and market risk, any cash requirements, and accounting policies related to the instruments.

In addition, for those instruments with credit risk, firms must disclose the amount of accounting loss incurred by the holder if any party to the instrument fails to perform. The required information about financial instruments with off-balance-sheet risk describes characteristics not disclosed in the balance sheet and helps investors and creditors assess risk.

---

[19]"Is Financial Product Explosion Perilous for Investors?" *The Wall Street Journal,* December 21, 1989, p. C1.

[20]"Macy's Lenders Are Being Forced to Make Loans of $600 Million under Prior Pacts," *The Wall Street Journal,* January 30, 1992.

[21]The fictional amount upon which interest payments are computed by both parties, for example, in interest rate swaps.

EXHIBIT 16–12

Example of Disclosures for Long-Term Liabilities: Dole Food Company, Incorporated

Note 7—Debt (in thousands)	1995	1994
Unsecured debt		
Notes payable to banks at an average interest rate of		
6.8% (6.2%—1994)	$169,547	$ 835,598
6.75% notes due 2000	225,000	225,000
7% notes due 2003	300,000	300,000
7.875% debentures due 2013	175,000	175,000
Various other notes due 1996–2007 at an average		
interest rate of 5.4% (5.2%—1994)	17,085	7,840
Secured debt		
Mortgages, contracts, and notes due 1996-2012, at an		
average interest rate of 9.0% (9.6%—1994)	13,890	17,608
Unamortized debt discount and issue costs	(2,745)	(3,092)
	897,777	1,557,954
Current maturities	(1,779)	(3,450)
	$895,998	$1,554,504

In May 1994, the Company replaced its existing revolving credit facility with a $1 billion, five-year revolving credit facility ("Facility"). At the Company's option, borrowings under the Facility bear interest at a certain percentage over the agent's prime rate or the London Interbank Offered Rate. Provisions under the Facility require the Company to comply with certain financial covenants which include a maximum permitted ratio of consolidated debt to net worth and a minimum required fixed charge coverage ratio.

Disclosures about Market Value   *SFAS No. 107* requires that all entities disclose the market value of all financial instruments, both asset and liability, for which it is practicable to estimate their value. The quoted market price in the most active market for the instrument is the basis for determining market value, irrespective of the potential effect of subsequent sale or extinguishment on the market price. When a quoted price is not available, management's best estimate of fair value may be based on the price of a similar instrument or on the estimated present value of future cash flows.

Example   A firm would disclose the market value of its bonds payable outstanding under this requirement. This information would help users to identify the effects of interest rate changes on debt and to determine whether unrealized gains or losses have occurred. In general, disclosure of market value allows periodic evaluation of management's decisions as market conditions change. Footnote 9 to the 1995 Coca-Cola Company financial statements in the Appendix to this text indicates the following disclosure related to fair value of long-term debt:

> The fair values for marketable equity securities, investments, receivables, long-term debt and hedging instruments are based primarily on quoted prices for those or similar instruments.

	Carrying Value	Fair Value
Long-term debt ($ millions)	$1,693	$1,737

General Disclosure Requirements for Long-Term Liabilities   In general, footnotes supply information not conveniently disclosed in the balance sheet. Interest rates, maturity dates, debt restrictions, call provisions, and conversion privileges are usually disclosed in the footnotes. Any assets pledged as collateral for debt also are disclosed in the footnotes. In addition, a debtor firm may transfer collateral to the creditor as part of the terms of a secured debt agreement. Under *SFAS No. 125,* if the creditor is permitted to sell the collateral and the debtor does not have the right to redeem the collateral before sale by the creditor, then the debtor must reclassify and separately report the asset. The creditor recognizes the collateral as an asset at fair value and recognizes its obligation to return it.

SFAS No. 47, "Disclosure of Long-Term Obligations," requires disclosure of the aggregate amount of maturities and sinking-fund requirements for all long-term debt for each of the five years following the balance sheet date. Portions of the long-term liability footnote to the 1995 Dole Food Company annual report in Exhibit 16–12 illustrate several disclosure requirements mentioned in the chapter.

GLOBAL VIEW

The accounting principles for long-term liabilities in many countries are significantly different from those of the United States in at least two respects: the definition of long-term and valuation.

Under U.S. principles, liabilities are long term if they are due later than one year from the balance sheet date (assuming an operating cycle of one year or less) with some exceptions. The International Accounting Standards Committee uses the same criterion: current liabilities are

> obligations payable at the demand of the creditor and those parts of the following obligations whose liquidation is expected within one year of the balance sheet date. (IAS No. 13, "Presentation of Current Assets and Liabilities")

Several countries, however, have a completely different view of *current* as compared with *long-term*. For example, Spain uses an 18-month cutoff: liabilities with maturities exceeding 18 months are long term. Germany and the United Kingdom use four years as the cutoff point. Some European countries make no distinction between current and long-term liabilities. These different definitions create comparability problems for financial analysts concerned with the ability of international firms to pay short-term debt. Ratios measuring liquidity and solvency are affected similarly.

The results of comparing long-term valuation principles across countries may be more surprising: Not all countries record long-term liabilities at present value. In the United States, long-term liabilities are measured at the present value of future cash flows, discounted at the effective rate of interest on the date of issuance. Although this fundamental valuation principle makes considerable sense in terms of the present sacrifice and required investment to liquidate a long-term liability, not all countries have adopted it.

The IASC has no general statement on valuation of long-term liabilities with contractual cash flows. Many European countries carry long-term debt at face value, just as they do current liabilities. Firms in Sweden and Hungary carry debentures, mortgages, and long-term bank credit at face value. Firms in Luxembourg state liabilities at the amount due, and the Netherlands uses face value with supplemental disclosure of interest rates. Japanese firms immediately expense bond discount, making the subsequent valuation of bonds equal to face value.

Article 2 of the European Union's Fourth Directive states

> The annual accounts shall give a true and fair view of the Company's assets, liabilities, financial position and profit or loss.

However, there is no specific guidance on how to value long-term liabilities fairly, and discounted cash flow valuation is not mandated.

SUMMARY OF KEY POINTS

(L.O. 1) 1. Long-term liabilities are those fulfilling the *SFAC No. 6* definition of a liability, with a term extending more than one year from the balance sheet date or the operating cycle, whichever is longer. Some exceptions to this definition exist.

(L.O. 1) 2. Three basic principles are used for valuing long-term liabilities. The recorded value at date of issuance is the present value of all future cash flows discounted at the current market rate of interest for debt securities of equivalent risk. Interest expense is the product of the market rate at issuance and the balance in the liability at the beginning of the reporting period. And the book value of long-term debt at a balance sheet date is the present value of all remaining cash payments required, using the market rate at issuance.

(L.O. 2) 3. Bonds are long-term debt instruments that specify the face value paid at maturity and the stated interest rate payable according to a fixed schedule. A significant source of capital for many firms, different forms of bonds appeal to investor preferences.

(L.O. 2) 4. The price of a bond at issuance, which excludes accrued interest at the stated rate, is the present value of all future cash flows discounted at the current market rate of interest for bonds of a similar risk class.

(L.O. 3) 5. Bonds are sold at a premium if the stated rate exceeds the market rate and at a discount if the reverse is true. Bond premiums and discounts are amortized over the remaining life of the security under the straight-line method or the interest method (which is preferable because it is based on present value concepts).

(L.O. 3) 6. Accounting for bonds depends on the bond's particular features. Bonds issued between interest dates require payment of accrued interest by the investor and calculation of the bond price using present value techniques.

(L.O. 4) 7. Certain long-term debt instruments are issued with equity rights, including bonds issued with detachable stock warrants and convertible bonds. The equity feature is recorded by the issuer only if a separate market exists for the equity feature. Convertible bonds are accounted for by the issuer in the same way as nonconvertible bonds until they are converted because the conversion feature cannot be valued reliably.

(L.O. 5) 8. Extinguishment of debt is accomplished by paying the creditor or replacing the debt with another debt instrument; or by obtaining a legal release or a release from the creditor.

(L.O. 5) 9. The gain or loss from extinguishment, which is the difference between the market value of consideration used for extinguishment and book value of debt extinguished, is classified as extraordinary.

(L.O. 6) 10. Long-term note valuation follows the three general principles for valuing long-term liabilities. Notes are formal promises by a debtor to pay principal and interest.

REVIEW PROBLEM

On August 1, 1999, Pismo Corporation, a calendar-year corporation that records adjusting entries only once per year, issued bonds with the following characteristics:

1. $50,000 total face value.
2. 12 percent stated rate.
3. 16 percent yield rate.
4. Interest dates are February 1, May 1, August 1, and November 1.
5. Bond date is October 31, 1998.
6. Maturity date is November 1, 2003.
7. $1,000 of bond issue costs were incurred.

Required

1. Provide all entries required for the bond issue through February 1, 2000, for Pismo using the interest method.
2. On June 1, 2001, Pismo retired $20,000 of bonds at 98 through open market purchase. Provide the entries to update the bond accounts for this portion of the bond issue and to retire the bonds using the interest method.
3. Provide the entries required on August 1, 2001, under the following methods of discount amortization:
   a. Interest method
   b. Straight-line method

SOLUTION

1.

August 1, 1999—Issue bonds and incur issue costs:

Bond issue cost	1,000	
Cash		1,000
Cash	43,917*	
Discount on bonds payable	6,083	
Bonds payable		50,000

*Four and one-quarter years, or 17 quarters, remain in the bond term.
$$\$43,917 = \$50,000(PV1,\ 4\%,\ 17) + .03(\$50,000)(PVA,\ 4\%,\ 17)$$
$$= \$50,000(.51337) + \$1,500(12.16567)$$

November 1, 1999—Interest payment date:

Interest expense	1,757*	
Discount on bonds payable		257
Cash		1,500†
Bond issue expense	59‡	
Bond issue cost		59

*$1,757 = $43,917(.04)

†$1,500 = $50,000(.03)

‡$59   = $1,000/17

December 31, 1999—Adjusting entry:

Interest expense	1,178*	
Discount on bonds payable		178
Interest payable		1,000†
Bond issue expense	39‡	
Bond issue cost		39

*$1,178 = ($43,917 + $257)(.04)(2/3 of quarter)

†$1,000 = $1,500(2/3)

‡$39   = $59(2/3)

February 1, 2000—Interest payment date:

Interest expense	589*	
Interest payable	1,000	
Discount on bonds payable		89
Cash		1,500
Bond issue expense	20†	
Bond issue cost		20

*$589 = ($43,917 + $257)(.04)(1/3 of quarter)

†$20 = $59(1/3)

2. On May 1, 2001, the remaining term of the bonds is two and one-half years, or 10 quarters, and the \$20,000 of bonds to be retired have the following book value:

$$\$18,378 = \$20,000(PV1, 4\%, 10) + \$20,000(.03)(PVA, 4\%, 10)$$
$$= \$20,000(.67556) + \$600(8.11090)$$

On May 1, 2001, the remaining discount on the portion of bonds to be retired is therefore \$1,622 (\$20,000 − \$18,378).

June 1, 2001— Update relevant bond accounts before retirement:

Interest expense	245*	
Discount on bonds payable		45
Cash		200†
Bond issue expense	8‡	
Bond issue cost		8

June 1, 2001—Remove relevant bond accounts:

Bonds payable	20,000	
Extraordinary loss, bond extinguishment	1,404	
Discount on bonds payable		1,577§
Bond issue cost		227‖
Cash (.98 × \$20,000)		19,600

*\$245   = \$18,378(.04)(1/3 of quarter)

†\$200   = \$20,000(.03)(1/3)

‡\$8   = \$1,000(1/17)(1/3)(.40 of issue retired)

§§\$1,577 = \$1,622 − \$45

‖At June 1, 2001, nine and two-thirds quarters remain in bond term: \$227 = \$1,000(.40)(9⅔)/17

3. On May 1, 2001, the remaining term of the bonds is two and one-half years, or 10 quarters, and the remaining \$30,000 of bonds have the following book value:

$$\$27,567 = \$30,000(PV1, 4\%, 10) + \$30,000(.03)(PVA, 4\%, 10)$$
$$= \$30,000(.67556) + \$900(8.11090)$$

On May 1, 2001, the remaining discount is therefore \$2,433 (\$30,000 − \$27,567).

a. August 1, 2001—Interest payment date:

Interest expense	1,103*	
Discount on bonds payable		203
Cash		900†
Bond issue expense	35	
Bond issue cost		35‡

*\$1,103 = \$27,567(.04)

†\$900   = \$30,000(.03)

‡\$35   = (.60 of issue remaining)(\$1,000)/17

b. Under the SL method, the discount is amortized \$358 (\$6,083/17) per quarter on the entire bond issue.

August 1, 2001—Interest payment date:

Interest expense	1,115	
Discount on bonds payable		215*
Cash		900
Bond issue expense	35	
Bond issue cost		35

*\$215 = \$358(.60)

APPENDIX 16A   *Troubled Debt Restructure*

With increasing frequency during the 1980s, debtor firms (and nations) were unable to make interest and principal payments on long-term debt. Others experienced a related problem: violation of debt indentures. Rising interest rates, nonperforming loans, unsatisfactory return on investment, and lack of demand for a firm's products and services may contribute to troubled debt.

Rather than write off nonperforming loans or pursue legal action, creditors frequently agree to a debt restructure allowing the debtor to remain in operation, in the hope that the debtor can

EXHIBIT 16A–1   Summary of Accounting for Troubled Debt Restructures

BV: Book value of debt (receivable) to be restructured, including unpaid accrued interest.
MV: Market value of assets or equity securities of debtor used to settle the debt.
SUM: Sum of restructured cash flows, at nominal value.
PV: Present value of restructured cash flows.

Accounting by Debtors

| | Modification-of-Terms TDRs | |
Settlement TDRs	SUM ≤ BV	SUM > BV
Extraordinary gain = BV − MV. Other gain or loss on disposal of assets is possible. Debt is removed from debtor's books. Debtor records any stock issued at market value.	Extraordinary gain = BV − SUM. Carrying value of debt is reduced to SUM. All restructured payments are returns of principal. No further interest is recognized.	No gain or loss is recognized. Carrying value of debt = BV. Restructured payments include interest at the rate equating PV to BV.

Accounting by Creditors

Settlement TDRs	Modification-of-Terms TDRs
Loss = BV − MV, classified according to *APB Opinion No. 30.** Receivable is removed from creditor's books. Assets received are recorded at MV.*	Modification-of-terms TDRs are treated as loan impairments. The carrying value of the note is reduced to the present value of the restructured cash flows, discounted at the original effective interest rate (or reduced to market value).

*If the creditor intends to sell the assets, they should be recorded at market value less estimated direct costs to sell, consistent with accounting for any asset held for disposal. The loss recognized by the creditor is increased by the estimated selling costs. (*SFAS No. 121*, "Accounting for the Impairment of Long-Lived Assets and for Long-Lived Assets to Be Disposed of.")

resolve its financial difficulties. Creditors usually receive more on restructured debt than through bankruptcy by the debtor.

Typical provisions of restructure agreements include elimination or reduction of interest and principal payments, reduction of interest rates, extension of terms, and partial or complete settlement of the debt through cash payment or transfer of equity securities. In a troubled debt restructure (TDR), *the creditor grants a concession to the debtor that it would not otherwise consider.*

For a debt restructure to be troubled, the creditor must accept new debt or assets with an economic value less than the book value of the original debt. A creditor may accept $10,000 in full payment of a $15,000 receivable (a settlement TDR). Or a creditor may accept an extension of terms without compensation for lost interest (a modification-of-terms TDR). The portion of debt settled is not considered an extinguishment under *SFAS No. 76*, "Extinguishment of Debt." Also, a transfer of equity securities pursuant to the existing terms of convertible debt does not qualify as a TDR.

The accounting issues arising in a TDR include the measurement of the new liability and receivable (or consideration transferred in settlement) and the reporting of any gain or loss on restructure. *SFAS No. 15*, "Accounting by Debtors and Creditors for Troubled Debt Restructuring," and *SFAS No. 114*, "Accounting by Creditors for Impairment of a Loan," which amends *SFAS No. 15*, apply to TDRs.

Summary of Accounting for TDRs

The accounting and reporting for TDRs depends on whether (1) the debt is settled or (2) the terms are modified, in which case the debt is not terminated. Exhibit 16A–1 provides a summary of accounting for TDRs.

The accounting by the creditor for settlement TDRs is parallel to that of the debtor. The difference between the book value of the debt and the market value of consideration transferred is a gain to the debtor and a loss to the creditor. However, as Exhibit 16A–1 indicates, the different accounting requirements for modification-of-terms TDRs applying to the debtor and creditor result in a significant accounting asymmetry.

Debtor accounting for modification of terms TDRs is based on the *nominal* sum of restructured cash flows, whereas creditor accounting is based on the *present value* of restructured cash flows. The creditor treats a modification-of-terms TDR as a loan impairment (discussed in Chapter 8).[22]

Examples of Troubled Debt Restructuring

Four examples are used to illustrate debtor and creditor accounting for both types of TDRs. Each uses the following initial information:

> On January 1, 1998, Debb Company issues a 10 percent, two-year, $500,000 note paying annual interest each December 31 to Credex Company in exchange for $500,000 of merchandise at sales value. Debb is unable to make the December 31, 1998, interest payment. Both companies are calendar-year companies and accrue the 1998 interest.

Example 1: Settlement by Transfer of Assets   On January 1, 1999, Debb agrees to transfer a factory building and land to Credex in full settlement of the note, as follows:

	Land	Building
Market value, January 1, 1999	$100,000	$250,000
Original cost to Debb	75,000	300,000
Accumulated depreciation through January 1, 1999 . . .		100,000
Book value, January 1, 1999	75,000	200,000

This restructuring is a settlement TDR because the market value of the consideration transferred to the creditor ($350,000) is less than the $550,000 book value of the debt ($500,000 face value + $50,000 accrued interest). The entries to record the TDR for both companies are as follows:

Debb (debtor)			**Credex (creditor)**		
January 1, 1999:					
Land	25,000*				
Building	50,000†				
Gain on disposal of					
land and building . . .		75,000			
Note payable	500,000		Land	100,000	
Interest payable	50,000		Building	250,000	
Accumulated depreciation, .			Loss on debt restructure . .	200,000	
building	100,000		Interest receivable		50,000
Land		100,000	Note receivable		500,000
Building		350,000			
Extraordinary gain,					
debt restructure		200,000			

*$100,000 − $75,000

†$250,000 − ($300,000 − $100,000)

Transfer of assets in a TDR is a disposal requiring the same gain or loss recognition as a cash sale. The extraordinary gain to the debtor reflects the amount of liability excused and the improvement in its economic position.

The creditor removes the accounts related to the receivable, records the assets received at market value, and recognizes a loss equal to the difference between the book value of the receivable and the market value of the assets. Losses on unsuccessful investments and receivables are not generally considered extraordinary.[23]

Now if Credex intends to hold the land and building received in settlement for disposal, the assets' recorded values are reduced by estimated selling costs, and the loss on restructure is increased.

---

[22]The accounting principles for the creditor—modification of terms case in Exhibit 16A–1—do not apply to debt securities. If a loan meets the definition of a security in *SFAS No. 115*, "Accounting for Certain Investments in Debt and Equity Securities," and is restructured in a TDR, then the creditor follows the provisions of *SFAS No. 115*, rather than *SFAS No. 114* (see *FASB Technical Bulletin No. 94-1*, "Application of Statement 115 to Debt Securities Restructured in a Troubled Debt Restructuring").

[23]If the receivable was considered when bad debts were estimated, the allowance for doubtful accounts, rather than a loss, is debited. If the allowance is insufficient, a loss is debited for any excess.

Example   Assume that direct selling costs are estimated to be $10,000 and are allocated to the assets based on market value. The land comprises 29 percent of total market value ($100,000/$350,000) and the building is 71 percent of total market value ($250,000/$350,000). Credex would record the following entry in place of the preceding one:

Land $100,000 − .29($10,000)	97,100	
Building $250,000 − .71($10,000)	242,900	
Loss on debt restructure	210,000	
Interest receivable		50,000
Note receivable		500,000

Example 2: Settlement by Transfer of Equity Interest in Debtor

On January 1, 1999, Debb issues 2,500 shares of its $10 par common stock in full settlement of the note. The market price per share is $60 on January 1, 1999, and the increase in outstanding shares is not expected to affect the stock price appreciably.

The accounting for a transfer of an equity interest is essentially the same as for a transfer of assets except that the debtor recognizes no disposal gain or loss.

Debb (debtor)			**Credex (creditor)**		

January 1, 1999:

Note payable	500,000		Investment in common		
Interest payable	50,000		stock	150,000	
Common stock		25,000*	Loss on debt restructure	400,000	
Contributed capital in			Interest receivable		50,000
excess of par		125,000†	Note receivable		500,000
Extraordinary gain debt					
restructure		400,000‡			

*(2,500 shares × $10 par)

†2,500($60 − $10)

‡$550,000 book value of debt − $150,000 market value of stock

Example 3: Modification of Terms—Total Restructured Payments Are Less than Debt Book Value

On January 1, 1999, Debb and Credex agree to a debt restructure agreement with the following provisions:

    a. Face value of the note is reduced to $400,000.

    b. Accrued interest for 1998 is forgiven.

    c. Maturity is extended to January 1, 2001 (a one-year extension).

    d. The interest rate is reduced to 5 percent; interest payments are due December 31, 1999 and 2000.

Book value of debt, January 1, 1999.		$550,000
Sum of restructured cash flows:		
Face value payable January 1, 2001	$400,000	
December 31, 1999 interest payment (.05 × $400,000)	20,000	
December 31, 2000 interest payment	20,000	(440,000)
Extraordinary gain (debtor) on restructure.		$110,000

For Debb, the two $20,000 "interest" payments are in fact principal payments because the original principal and missed interest payment are not fully recovered by the creditor. For Credex, the TDR is treated as a loan impairment, which calls for a write-down of the note to the present value of expected future cash flows discounted at the original effective rate (10 percent). The net carrying value of the note for Credex after the restructure is

$$\$400,000(\text{PV}1, 10\%, 2) + \$20,000(\text{PVA}, 10\%, 2) =$$
$$\$400,000(.82645) + \$20,000(1.73554) = \$365,291$$

Credex recognizes an immediate charge to bad debt expense of $184,709 ($550,000 − $365,291) and then recognizes interest at 10 percent over the remaining term of the restructure agreement (the interest method). The following entries for Credex reclassify the note and interest receivable to a new note account, recognize a valuation account reducing the carrying value of the note to present value, and record subsequent cash receipts.

<table>
<tr><td colspan="2">Debb (debtor)</td><td colspan="2">Credex (creditor)</td></tr>
<tr><td colspan="4">January 1, 1999:</td></tr>
<tr><td>Note payable . . . .</td><td align="right">500,000</td><td>Note receivable . . . . . .</td><td align="right">550,000</td></tr>
<tr><td>Interest payable . . . .</td><td align="right">50,000</td><td>Bad debt expense . . . . . .</td><td align="right">184,709</td></tr>
<tr><td style="padding-left:2em">Note payable . . . . . .</td><td align="right">440,000</td><td style="padding-left:2em">Allowance for decline</td><td></td></tr>
<tr><td style="padding-left:2em">Extraordinary gain,</td><td></td><td style="padding-left:3em">in note value . . . . . .</td><td align="right">184,709</td></tr>
<tr><td style="padding-left:3em">debt restructure . . . .</td><td align="right">110,000</td><td style="padding-left:2em">Interest receivable . . . . .</td><td align="right">50,000</td></tr>
<tr><td>. . . . .</td><td></td><td style="padding-left:2em">Note receivable . . . . . .</td><td align="right">500,000</td></tr>
<tr><td colspan="4">December 31, 1999:</td></tr>
<tr><td>Note payable . . . .</td><td align="right">20,000</td><td>Cash . . . .</td><td align="right">20,000</td></tr>
<tr><td style="padding-left:2em">Cash . . . .</td><td align="right">20,000</td><td style="padding-left:2em">Notes receivable . . . . .</td><td align="right">20,000</td></tr>
<tr><td></td><td></td><td>Allowance for decline in</td><td></td></tr>
<tr><td></td><td></td><td style="padding-left:2em">note value . . . .</td><td align="right">36,529</td></tr>
<tr><td></td><td></td><td style="padding-left:2em">Interest revenue</td><td></td></tr>
<tr><td></td><td></td><td style="padding-left:3em">.10($365,291) . . . . . .</td><td align="right">36,529</td></tr>
<tr><td colspan="4">December 31, 2000</td></tr>
<tr><td>Note payable . . . .</td><td align="right">420,000*</td><td>Cash . . . .</td><td align="right">420,000</td></tr>
<tr><td style="padding-left:2em">Cash . . . .</td><td align="right">420,000</td><td style="padding-left:2em">Notes receivable . . . . .</td><td align="right">420,000</td></tr>
<tr><td></td><td></td><td>Allowance for decline in</td><td></td></tr>
<tr><td></td><td></td><td style="padding-left:2em">note value . . . .</td><td align="right">38,182</td></tr>
<tr><td></td><td></td><td style="padding-left:2em">Interest revenue</td><td></td></tr>
<tr><td></td><td></td><td style="padding-left:3em">.10($365,291 + $36,529</td><td></td></tr>
<tr><td></td><td></td><td style="padding-left:4em">− $20,000) . . . . . .</td><td align="right">38,182</td></tr>
<tr><td></td><td></td><td>Allowance for decline in</td><td></td></tr>
<tr><td></td><td></td><td style="padding-left:2em">note value . . . .</td><td align="right">110,000</td></tr>
<tr><td></td><td></td><td style="padding-left:2em">Notes receivable . . . . .</td><td align="right">110,000</td></tr>
<tr><td></td><td></td><td colspan="2">(Allowance balance has $2 debit balance after this entry due to rounding in the present value tables.)</td></tr>
</table>

*$420,000 = $400,000 new "principal" + $20,000 "interest."

SFAS No. 118, "Accounting by Creditors for Impairment of a Loan—Income Recognition and Disclosures," does not *require* a creditor to use the interest method (shown for Credex) to account for interest revenue after recording a loan impairment. The cost recovery and other methods also may be used. See Chapter 8.

In this example, Credex's loss (the charge to bad debt expense) and Debb's gain are quite different because the creditor records the note at present value while the debtor records the note at nominal value. In many cases, a creditor has recorded a loan impairment before the formal restructuring, because the conditions leading up to the restructure develop over a period of time. To the extent that the TDR changes the estimate of future cash flows to be received already reflected in the impaired note, the creditor adjusts the carrying value and bad debt expense in a normal reestimation of the impairment.

Example 4: Modification of Terms—Total Restructured Payments Exceed Debt Book Value
On January 1, 1999, Debb and Credex agree to a debt restructure agreement providing the following:

a. Accrued interest for 1998 is forgiven.

b. Maturity is extended to January 1, 2001 (a one-year extension) and regular interest payments are required December 31, 1999 and 2000.

Sum of restructured cash flows		
Face value payable January 1, 2001	$500,000	
December 31, 1999, interest payment (.10 × $500,000)	50,000	
December 31, 2000, interest payment	50,000	$600,000
Book value of debt, January 1, 1999		(550,000)
Excess of restructured cash flows over debt book value		$ 50,000

Although the sum of restructured cash flows equals the total cash flows under the original debt agreement, the entire cash flow schedule is shifted ahead one year, causing an economic loss to the creditor. Debb maintains the existing liability balance, recognizes no gain or loss, and computes the new effective interest rate for recognizing the interest component of the restructured cash payments. The new effective rate, *i,* is found by solving:

EXHIBIT 16A–2
Combination Settlement and
Modification of Terms TDR

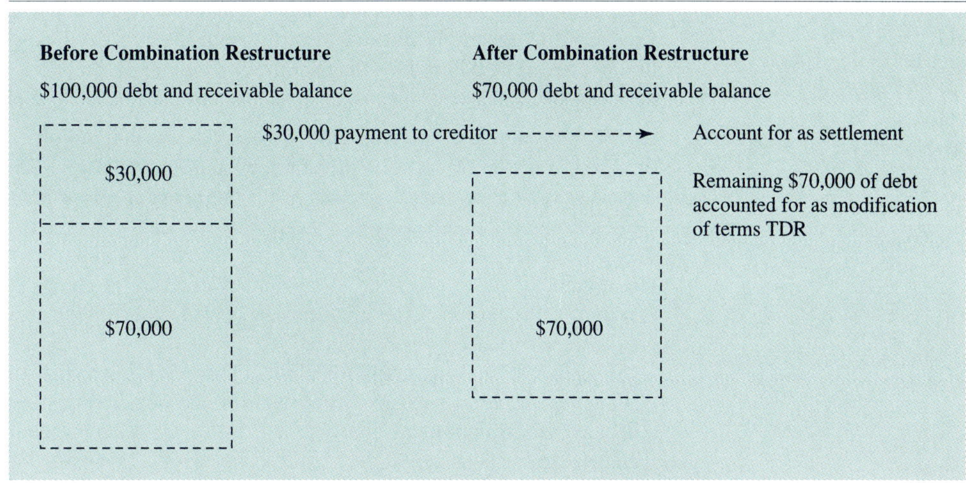

$$\$550,000 = \$500,000(PV1,\ i,\ 2) + \$50,000(PVA,\ i,\ 2)$$

By applying a computer program or business calculator to this equation, the new rate is found
to be 4.64875 percent. This rate confirms that the new agreement is a TDR—Credex receives a
significantly lower rate of interest as a result. Debb's remaining entries are as follows:

January 1, 1999:

Note payable	500,000	
Interest payable	50,000	
Note payable		550,000

December 31, 1999:

Note payable	24,432	
Interest expense	25,568*	
Cash		50,000

*$550,000(.0464875)

December 31, 2000:

Note payable	25,568	
Interest expense	24,432†	
Cash		50,000

†($550,000 − $24,432)(.0464875)

January 1, 2001:

Note payable	500,000	
Cash		500,000

Credex records a loan impairment using the same approach followed in Example 3.

Combination of Settlement and Modification of Terms

When only a portion of a debt is settled, the terms of the remaining portion may be modified.
The amount of debt settled is accounted for as a settlement, except that there is no gain or loss
on restructure (there could be a disposal gain or loss for the debtor). The remaining portion is
treated as a modification-of-terms TDR.

For example, assume that a $100,000 debt is restructured by transferring assets with a mar-
ket value of $30,000 and the terms of the remaining debt are modified. The debt and receivable
are reduced by $30,000; accounting for the remaining $70,000 portion of the original debt follows the modification provisions. Exhibit 16A–2 illustrates the allocation of a partial settlement.

Additional Measurement and Disclosure Requirements for TDRs

FASB Technical Bulletin 80–2 clarified the nature of a troubled debt restructure by confirming
that it is possible for only one party to have a TDR. This can occur if the book value of debt
and receivable differ.

Example   Debtor Company owes $25,000 to Creditor-A Company. Debtor Company experi-
ences financial difficulties, and Creditor-A Company sells its receivable to Creditor-B Company

for $15,000 on a nonrecourse basis. Subsequently, Debtor Company transfers $18,000 to Creditor-B Company in settlement of the debt. Debtor Company records a troubled debt restructure because $18,000 is less than the book value of its liability. However, Creditor-B Company does not because it receives more than the book value of its $15,000 investment.

Other asymmetries between the debtor and creditor involve estimation of the market value of assets transferred and classification of gains and losses. The debtor's gain on reduction of debt in a settlement is extraordinary, but the creditor's loss may not be.

Legal and other direct costs incurred by the debtor to restructure debt reduce the extraordinary gain unless an equity interest is transferred, in which case the equity interest is reduced by the amount of those costs. If no gain on restructure is recognized, the costs are recognized as expense in the period of restructure. Legal and other direct costs of restructuring borne by the creditor are expensed when incurred.

SFAS No. 15 does not apply to debtors involved in restructurings that require general restatement of liabilities, such as bankruptcy proceedings and quasi-reorganization restructurings. For example, a debtor may be able to pay only 40 percent of the dollar amount of all its liabilities. Because all liabilities are restated, *SFAS No. 15* does not apply. However, if a restructuring does not involve general restatement of all liabilities, the statement applies to isolated troubled debt restructurings that occur simultaneously with the restructure proceedings (*FASB Technical Bulletin 81–6*).

APPENDIX 16B   *Accounting for Serial Bonds*

A **serial bond** issue matures in a series of installments rather than in one maturity amount. The advantages of serial bonds to the issuer include
- Reduced need for a sinking fund.
- Less perceived risk.
- Improved marketability.
- Less burdensome debt retirement schedule.

Serial bonds are sold either as separate issues or as one aggregate issue. If the bonds are sold separately, it is possible to identify the yield rate on each, which normally increases with the length of the term to compensate for increased risk. An aggregate bond issue carries a single average yield rate. Either way, the price of serial bonds is the sum of the present value of each issue using the appropriate yield rate.

Three methods of accounting for premium and discount amortization on serial bonds are available:

1. **Interest method:** If the yield rate on each issue is known, each issue is treated as an individual bond issue. If not, the entire issue is treated as one bond issue, and the average yield rate is used to recognize interest. The book value of serial bonds payable is reduced by the face amount of serial bonds retired at each maturity date. Otherwise, procedures for amortizing discount and premium under the interest method are identical to ordinary bonds.
2. **Straight-line method:** An equal amount of premium or discount is allocated to each reporting period for each separate issue. Then the amounts for each issue are totaled by reporting period. Total amortization for a reporting period reflects each separate issue outstanding that period. This method is permitted only if it produces results not materially different from the interest method.
3. **Bonds outstanding method:** The discount or premium for each separate issue need not be identified under this method. A constant rate of discount or premium per dollar of bond outstanding per period is used for amortization. This is a modified straight-line method, permitted only if it produces results not materially different from the interest method.

All three methods relate the premium or discount to the total face value of bonds outstanding during the period. This amount decreases by the face value of each maturing issue. Consequently, relative to an ordinary bond, discounts and premiums are amortized on an accelerated basis.

The application of the straight-line and interest methods to serial bonds is equivalent to that for single-maturity bonds. The bonds outstanding method, a variation of the straight-line method, provides a convenient shortcut to computing amortization of premium and discount and produces similar results. We illustrate the bonds outstanding method in the following example. A short bond term simplifies the illustration.

Example   Michael Corporation issues $100,000 of 8 percent serial bonds on January 1, 1998. The bonds are sold as one issue to yield 10 percent, resulting in proceeds of $96,410 (this amount may be verified through the usual bond-price calculation.) The bonds pay interest each December 31 and mature according to the following schedule.

Maturity Date	**Maturity Amount**
January 1, 1999	$ 20,000
January 1, 2000	50,000
January 1, 2001	30,000
	$100,000

January 1, 1998—Issue serial bonds:

Cash	96,410	
Discount on serial bonds	3,590	
Serial bonds payable		100,000

The amount of discount allocated to each reporting period under the bonds outstanding method is the product of three amounts:

1. A constant rate of amortization per dollar of bond per period.
2. The dollar amount of bonds outstanding (at face value) during the period.
3. The length of the period.

A table is used to develop the rate of amortization:

Face Value of Bonds Outstanding During	**Rate of Discount Amortization per Dollar of Face Value per Year**
1998 . . . . $100,000	
1999 . . . . 80,000*	$\dfrac{\text{Initial discount}}{\text{Sum of bonds outstanding}} = \dfrac{\$3,590}{\$210,000} = \$.0171$
2000 30,000	
Sum $210,000	

*On January 1, 1999, $20,000 of bonds mature; therefore $80,000 of bonds are outstanding during 1999.

The amortization rate indicates that $.0171 of discount is associated with each dollar of bond face value each year in the term of the serial bonds. Selected entries follow:

December 31, 1998—Interest payment:

Interest expense	9,710	
Discount on serial bonds (.0171 × $100,000 × 1 year)		1,710
Cash (.08 × $100,000)		8,000

January 1, 1999—Retire bonds due 1/1/99:

Serial bonds payable	20,000	
Cash		20,000

Now assume that on January 1, 1999, Michael also retires $10,000 of the issue scheduled to mature January 1, 2001, on the open market at 99.

January 1, 1999—Retire $10,000 of the $30,000 of bonds due 1/1/01 at 99:

Serial bonds payable	10,000	
Extraordinary loss, bond extinguishment	242	
Discount on bonds payable		342*
Cash (.99 × $10,000)		9,900

*(.0171 × $10,000 × 2 years remaining in bond term) = $342

December 31, 1999—Interest payment:

Interest expense	6,797	
Discount on serial bonds (.0171 × $70,000 × 1 year)		1,197
Cash (.08 × $70,000)		5,600

The amortization rate can be applied to any amount of face value or any period length. For example, if $10,000 of the bonds scheduled to mature January 1, 2001, are retired March 1, 1999, rather than on January 1, 1999, the amount of discount to be removed from the accounts is $314 (.0171 × $10,000 × 1 10/12 years).

The complications arising when serial bonds are issued during a fiscal year are minimized by the bonds outstanding method. For example, assume that $100,000 of serial bonds are issued March 31, 1998, at a premium and that the amortization rate is $.02. If $25,000 of bonds mature on March 31, 1999, the total amount of premium amortized during 1999 is $1,625:

$$(.02 \times \$100,000 \times 3/12) + (.02 \times \$75,000 \times 9/12) = \$1,625$$

APPENDIX 16C *Accounting Principles for Investments in Debt Securities Held to Maturity*

Chapter 14 discusses the accounting for investments in debt securities classified as trading securities and securities available for sale.[24] Accounting for a third category of investments in debt securities, those held to maturity, is parallel to that of the issuing firm and is illustrated in this chapter (Elmhurst Company example). Such securities are carried at amortized cost. This appendix discusses the reporting requirements pertaining to these investments.

The Held-to-Maturity Category

Investments in debt securities (bonds of other corporations, for example) are classified as held to maturity (HTM) and are measured at amortized cost if the investing firm is *able* and *intends* to hold the securities to maturity.

Sale by the investor of a debt security classified as HTM for either of the following reasons is consistent with the classification and does not call into question the classification for other securities:

- Sale occurs near enough to maturity that interest rate risk is essentially eliminated (for example, within three months of maturity).
- Sale occurs after a substantial portion of the original principal amount (for example, 85 percent) has been collected.

Furthermore, the sale or transfer of an HTM security before maturity for any one of the following changes in circumstances is also not inconsistent with its original classification and does not call into question the classification of other securities as HTM:

- A significant change in the issuing company's ability to pay principal and interest.
- A change in tax law modifying the tax-exempt status of the interest.
- A business combination or disposition, requiring the sale of the security to maintain the holder's interest rate risk position or credit risk policy.
- A change in legal or regulatory requirements causing the holder to dispose of the security.

However, if the intent is to hold the security for only an indefinite period, this category does not apply. For example, if the investor might sell the debt securities to improve liquidity or in response to changes in interest rates, changes in yield in alternative investments, or changes in foreign currency risk, the securities are not considered HTM. Furthermore, if a firm classifies a bond issue as HTM but trades some of the bonds before maturity for reasons other than those listed above, the firm runs the risk of having to reclassify all the bonds because they were not held to maturity.

Also excluded from the HTM category are investments in securities

> that can contractually be prepaid or otherwise settled in such a way that the holder would not recover substantially all of its recorded investment. (*SFAS No. 125,* "Accounting for Transfers and Servicing of Financial Assets and Extinguishments of Liabilities," par. 14)

Such securities must be classified as trading securities or securities available for sale because the book value under the HTM assumption may overstate the actual investment value. Investments subject to risk of prepayment include mortgage-backed securities and callable securities purchased at a substantial premium.

Normally, a debt security purchased at a premium and categorized HTM is amortized over its term so the book value equals maturity value at the end of the term. The investor earns the yield rate implied by the purchase price and no gain or loss results. However, if the security is paid off well before maturity and the interest rate on similar debt has risen since the investor acquired the bonds, the investor may receive an amount less than substantially all of the recorded book value. The investor records a loss, and will have earned a rate of return other than the yield rate at purchase. This result is inconsistent with classification as HTM.

Changes in Investment Carrying Value

If a security in this category is sold before maturity, the recognized gain or loss is the difference between carrying value (net of any unamortized discount or premium) and proceeds from

---

[24]"Accounting for Certain Investments in Debt and Equity Securities," *SFAS No. 115,* provides the guidance for these investments.

sale. If a permanent decline in fair value below amortized cost occurs and the investor will probably not collect all contractual amounts, the investment is written down to fair value and a loss is recognized. The new cost basis is not changed for subsequent recoveries in fair value.

UNDERSTANDING AND APPLYING CONCEPTS AND STANDARDS

QUESTIONS

1. List and briefly explain the primary characteristics of long-term debt securities.
2. What are the primary distinctions between a debt security and an equity security?
3. Explain the difference between the stated rate of interest and the effective rate on a long-term debt security.
4. What is the issue price of a zero coupon bond?
5. Briefly explain the effects on interest recognized when the stated and effective rates of interest are different.
6. What are the primary characteristics of a bond? What distinguishes it from capital stock?
7. Contrast the following classes of bonds: (*a*) industrial versus municipal, (*b*) secured versus debenture, (*c*) ordinary versus income, (*d*) ordinary versus serial, (*e*) callable versus convertible, and (*f*) registered versus coupon.
8. What are the principal advantages and disadvantages of bonds versus common stock for (*a*) the issuer and (*b*) the investor?
9. Distinguish between the par amount and the price of a bond. When are they the same? When different? Explain.
10. Explain the significance of bond discount and bond premium to (*a*) the issuer and (*b*) the investor.
11. Assume that a $1,000, 8 percent (payable semiannually), 10-year bond is sold at an effective rate of 6 percent. Explain how to compute the price of this bond.
12. Explain why and how bond discount and bond premium effect (*a*) the balance sheet and (*b*) the income statement of the investor.
13. What is the primary conceptual difference between the straight-line and interest methods of amortizing bond discount and premium?
14. Under GAAP, when is it appropriate to use the (*a*) straight-line and (*b*) interest method of amortization for bond discount or premium?
15. When the end of the accounting period of the issuer is not on a bond interest date, adjusting entries must be made for (*a*) accrued interest and (*b*) discount or premium amortization. Explain in general terms what each adjustment amount represents.
16. When bonds are sold (or purchased) between interest dates, accrued interest must be recognized. Explain why.
17. What are convertible bonds? What are the primary reasons for their use?
18. Why is the accounting different for nonconvertible bonds with detachable stock purchase warrants and nonconvertible bonds with nondetachable stock purchase warrants?
19. Define extinguishment of debt.
20. When may extinguishment of debt occur? List the various ways that extinguishment of debt occurs.
21. Explain how an accounting gain or loss to the debtor may occur when a call privilege is exercised.
22. When the issuer purchases its own debt securities in the open market to extinguish the debt, two entries must usually be made. Explain.
23. What is meant by refunding?
24. Interest rates have increased since a company issued its bonds. Why would the firm want to refund the bonds with another issue of bonds paying a higher rate?
25. A firm retired a bond issue early, at a loss. Is the firm in an economically worse position after the retirement?
26. What is meant by troubled debt restructuring? What are some of the features of typical restructuring arrangements?
27. Explain the classification of gains and losses from troubled debt restructuring.
28. Differentiate between a debt restructure in which debt is settled and one in which it continues after the restructure.
 29. With respect to the classification and valuation of long-term liabilities, what are some major differences between reporting practices found in other countries and those of the United States?

EXERCISES

E 16–1
(L.O. 2, 3)

Bonds: Issue above, at, and below Par   Rowe Corporation authorized $600,000 of 8 percent (interest payable semiannually), 10-year bonds. The bonds were dated January 1, 1998; interest dates are June 30 and December 31.

Assume four different cases with respect to the sale of the bonds: *Case A*—Sold on January 1, 1998, at par; *Case B*—Sold on January 1, 1998, at 102; *Case C*—Sold on January 1, 1998, at 98; *Case D*—Sold on March 1, 1998, at par.

Required

1. For each case, what amount of cash interest will be paid on the first interest date, June 30, 1998?
2. In what cases will the effective rate of interest be (*a*) the same, (*b*) higher, or (*c*) lower than the stated rate?
3. After sale of the bonds, and prior to maturity date, in what cases will the carrying or book value of the bonds (as reported on the balance sheet) be (*a*) the same, (*b*) higher, or (*c*) lower than the maturity or face amount?
4. After the sale of the bonds, in Cases A, B, and C, which case will report interest expense (*a*) the same, (*b*) higher, or (*c*) lower than the amount of cash interest paid each period?

E 16–2
(L.O. 2)

Bonds: Compute Four Bond Prices   Compute the bond price for each of the following situations (show computations and round to nearest dollar):

a. A 10-year, $1,000 bond with annual interest at 7 percent (payable 3½ percent semiannually) purchased to yield 6 percent interest.
b. An eight-year, $1,000 bond with annual interest at 6 percent (payable annually) purchased to yield 7 percent interest.
c. A 10-year, $1,000 bond with annual interest at 6 percent (payable semiannually) purchased to yield 8 percent interest.
d. An eight-year, $1,000 bond with annual interest at 6 percent (payable annually) purchased to yield 6 percent interest.

E 16–3
(L.O. 2, 3)

Issue above, at, below Par, Issuer and Investor   Yale Corporation issued to Zepher Corporation a $60,000, 8 percent (interest payable semiannually on June 30 and December 31), 10-year bond dated and sold on January 1, 1998. Assumptions: *Case A*—Sold at par; *Case B*—Sold at 103; and *Case C*—Sold at 97.

Required

In parallel columns for the issuer and the investor (assume that Zepher intends to hold to maturity), give the appropriate journal entries for each case on (1) January 1, 1998, and (2) June 30, 1998. Assume that the difference between the interest method and the straight-line method of amortization is not material; therefore, use straight-line amortization.

E 16–4
(L.O. 2, 3)

Compute Bond Price, Interest Method, Issuer and Investor Entries   On January 1, 1998, New Corporation issued to Old Corporation a $20,000, 9 percent (interest payable semiannually on June 30 and December 31), 10-year bond, dated January 1, 1998. The bond was sold at an 8 percent effective rate (4 percent semiannually). Old intends to hold the bonds to maturity.

Required

1. Compute the price of the bond.
2. In parallel columns for the issuer and the investor, give the appropriate journal entries on (*a*) January 1, 1998, and (*b*) June 30, 1998. Assume the difference between the interest method and the straight-line method of amortization is material; therefore, use the interest method.

E 16–5
(L.O. 3)

Bonds at a Premium, Accrued Interest: Straight Line   On September 1, 1998, Golf Company issued to Youngblood Company $30,000, five-year, 9 percent (payable semiannually) bonds for $32,320 plus accrued interest. The bonds were dated July 1, 1998, and interest is payable each June 30 and December 31. The accounting period for each company ends on December 31.

Required

In parallel columns, give entries for the issuer and the investor for the following dates: September 1, 1998; December 31, 1998; and June 30, 1999. Assume that the difference between the interest method and straight-line method amortization amounts is not material; therefore, use straight-line amortization. Youngblood intends to hold the bonds to maturity.

E 16–6
(L.O. 3)

Bonds, Accrued Interest, Issuer Entries: Straight Line   Ryan Corporation sold and issued $75,000 of three-year, 8 percent (payable semiannually) bonds payable for $78,200 plus accrued interest. Interest is payable each February 28 and August 31. The bonds were dated March 1, 1998, and were sold on July 1, 1998. The accounting period ends on December 31.

Required

1. How much accrued interest should be recognized at date of sale?
2. How long is the amortization period?
3. Give entries for Ryan Corporation through February 1999. Use straight-line amortization.
4. Would the above amounts also be recorded by the investor if the intent was to hold the bonds to maturity? Explain.

E 16–7
(L.O. 2, 3)

Compute Bond Price: Amortization Schedule, Interest Method   Radian Company issued to Sievers Company $30,000 of four-year, 8 percent bonds dated June 1, 1998. Interest is payable semiannually on May 31 and November 30. The bonds were issued on March 1, 1999, for $28,371 plus accrued interest. The bonds would have sold at the effective rate on the next interest date for $28,478. The accounting period ends December 31 for both companies. The effective interest rate was 10 percent.

Required

Round to the nearest dollar.

1. Verify the bond price. Use straight-line interpolation between interest dates.
2. Prepare a bond amortization schedule. Use interest method amortization.
3. In parallel columns, give entries for the issuer and the investor for the following dates: March 1, 1999, and May 31, 1999. Use interest method amortization, and assume that Sievers will hold the bonds to maturity.

E 16–8
(L.O. 3)

Bond Issuance and Amortization Schedule, Interest Method   Mitchell, Inc., issued 40, 6 percent, $1,000 bonds on January 1, 1998. The bonds pay interest annually each December 31 and were issued to yield 7 percent. The bonds mature December 31, 2000.

Required

1. Prepare the complete amortization table for this bond issue using the interest method.
2. Explain why, in economic terms, the interest expense recognized each year exceeds the cash interest paid.

E 16–9
(L.O. 2, 3)

Multiple Choice: Accounting for Bonds   Choose the correct answer for each question.

1. A 6 percent bond issue has nine semiannual interest periods remaining in its term. Each $1,000 bond in the issue was sold to yield 10 percent. The bonds were sold at 79 between interest dates. What is the current book value under the interest and straight-line methods of amortization, as measured in percentage of face value?

	Interest Method	Straight-Line Method
a.	91.2	97.3
b.	85.8	Cannot be determined
c.	101.5	85.8
d.	87	Cannot be determined

2. On July 1, 1998, Center Company paid $599,000 for 10 percent, 20-year bonds with a face value of $500,000. Interest is paid on December 31 and June 30. The bonds were purchased to yield 8 percent. Center uses the interest method to recognize interest income from this investment. What is the carrying amount of this investment in bonds in Center's December 31, 1998, balance sheet if Center intends to hold the bonds to maturity?
   a. $603,950.
   b. $599,000.
   c. $597,960.
   d. $596,525.
3. Delia Company incurred costs of $6,600 when it issued, on August 31, 1998, five-year debenture bonds dated April 1, 1998. What amount of bond issue expense should Delia report in its income statement for the year ended December 31, 1998?
   a. $440.
   b. $480.
   c. $990.
   d. $6,600.
4. The following information pertains to Hike Tours, Inc., issuance of bonds on July 1, 1998:

Face amount	$400,000
Term	10 years
Stated interest rate	6%
Interest payment dates	Annually on July 1
Yield	9%

   What is the issue price for each $1,000 bond?
   a. $1,000.   *c.* $807.
   b. $864.   *d.* $700.

(AICPA adapted)

E 16–10
(L.O. 3)

Bond Issuance between Interest Dates   Setup Inc. sold an issue of 10 percent, $1,000 bonds dated January 1, 1998, on May 1, 1998, to yield 12 percent. The bonds pay interest every June 30 and December 31 and mature December 31, 2002.

Required

Write two different expressions showing how the price of the bond on May 1 is computed (excluding accrued interest), using general present value terminology (PVA, PV1). Use c = coupon rate and m = market rate. One of the expressions uses interpolation. Do not attempt to calculate the factors or the price.

E 16–11
(L.O. 4)

Nonconvertible Bonds with Detachable Warrants   Hardware Corporation issued $75,000 of 6 percent, 10-year, nonconvertible bonds with detachable stock purchase warrants. Each $1,000 bond carried 20 detachable warrants, each of which was for one share of Hardware common stock, par $20, at a specified option price of $60. The bonds sold at $102 including the warrants (no bond price ex-warrants was available), and, immediately after date of issuance, the detachable stock purchase warrants were selling at $4 each. The entire issue was acquired by Software Company as a long-term investment with the intent to hold to maturity. All indicated transactions occurred in the same fiscal year.

Required

1. Give entries for both the issuer and the investor at date of acquisition of the bonds.
2. Give the entry for the investor assuming a subsequent sale of all of the warrants to another investor at $5.50 each.
3. Disregard (2). Give the entries for the issuer and the investor assuming subsequent tender of all of the warrants by the investor for exercise at the specified option price. At this date, the stock was selling at $75 per share.

E 16–12
(L.O. 4)

Convertible Bonds: Entries, Issuer and Investor, Conversion   Stonewall Corporation issued $20,000 of 5 percent, 10-year convertible bonds. Each $1,000 bond was convertible to 10 shares of common stock (par $50) of Stonewall Corporation at any interest date after three years from issuance. The bonds were sold at $105 to Mason Corporation as a long-term investment, the firm intends to hold the bonds to maturity.

Required

1. Give the entry for both the issuer and the investor at the date of issuance.
2. Give entries for both the issuer and the investor assuming that the conversion privilege is subsequently exercised by Mason Corporation immediately after the end of the third year. Assume that 30 percent of any premium or discount has been amortized and that, at date of conversion, the common stock was selling at $125 per share. Show the entries for both the book value method and market value methods.

E 16–13
(L.O. 3, 5)

Debt Issuance and Early Retirement   On January 1, 1998, Quaid Company issued $100,000 of 10 percent debentures. The following information relates to these bonds:

Bond date	January 1, 1998
Yield rate	8%
Maturity date	January 1, 2003
Interest payment date	December 31
Bond issue costs incurred	$2,000

On March 1, 1999, Quaid retires $10,000 (face value) of the bonds when the market price is $110.

Required

Provide entries for Quaid on the following dates under both the interest and straight-line methods of amortization.

1. January 1, 1998, bond issuance.
2. December 31, 1998, first interest payment.
3. March 1, 1999, entries to update the portion of the bond issue retired and to extinguish the bonds.

E 16–14
(L.O. 2, 3, 5)

Bond Issuance, Interest, and Early Retirement   This exercise has three independent situations:

a. On April 1, 1998, Felly Company issued 800 of its 10 percent, $1,000 bonds at 97 plus accrued interest. The bonds are dated January 1, 1998, and mature on January 1, 2008. Interest is payable semiannually on January 1 and July 1.

b. On July 1, 1998, Center Company issued 9 percent bonds in the face amount of $500,000, which mature on July 1, 2008. The bonds were issued for $469,500 to yield 10 percent, resulting in a bond discount of $30,500. Center uses the interest method of amortizing bond discount. Interest is payable annually on June 30.

c. On July 1, 1999, Fondue Company issued 1,000 of its 9 percent, $1,000 callable bonds for $960,000. The bonds are dated July 1, 1999, and mature on July 1, 2009. Interest is payable semiannually on January 1 and July 1. Fondue uses the straight-line method of amortizing bond discount. The bonds can be called by the issuer at $101 at any time after June 30, 2004. On July 1, 2005, Fondue called in all the bonds and retired them.

Required
1. Compute the proceeds on the Felly bond issue.
2. Compute the unamortized discount on the Center bond issue on July 1, 2000.
3. Give the entry to record the extinguishment of the Fondue bond issue.

(AICPA adapted)

E 16–15
(L.O. 5)

Early Retirement of Bonds, Straight-Line Method   Sandollar, Inc., issued $30,000 of bonds paying 12 percent interest semiannually on June 30 and December 31, on March 1, 1998, at 105. The bonds are scheduled to mature December 31, 2001; $1,000 of bond issue costs were incurred by Sandollar. Unexpectedly, $10,000 of the bonds were retired September 1, 1998, when the bonds were selling at $89.

Required
Provide the entry to record the bond retirement. Assume the straight-line method to amortize bond discount and premium. Also provide the entries to recognize interest expense and bond issue expense for the portion of the bond issue retired.

E 16–16
(L.O. 5)

Bond Issuance and Retirement, SL Method   Durango, Inc., issued 40, 6 percent, $1,000 bonds on January 1, 1998. The bonds pay interest annually each December 31 and were issued to yield 7 percent. The bonds mature December 31, 2000. Durango decided to retire one-half of the bond issue one year early on January 1, 2000, when the yield rate had fallen to 5 percent. Durango uses the SL method to amortize premium and discount.

Required
1. Prepare the journal entry to record the issuance of the bonds.
2. Prepare the journal entry to retire the bonds.
3. Prepare the journal entries for the remaining bonds, to maturity.

E 16–17
(L.O. 5)

Bond Issuance and Retirement, Interest Method   Using the information in E 16–16, complete the requirements assuming Durango uses the interest method.

E 16–18
(L.O. 5)

Extinguishment by Call   On January 1, 1998, Radar Company issued $200,000 of bonds payable with a stated interest rate of 12 percent, payable annually each December 31. The bonds mature in 20 years and have a call price of 103, and are callable by Radar Company after the fifth year. The bonds originally sold at 105.

On December 31, 2009, the company called the bonds. At that time, the bonds were quoted on the market at a price to yield 10 percent. Radar Company uses straight-line amortization; its accounting period ends December 31.

Required
1. Give the issuance entry for Radar Company required on January 1, 1998.
2. Give the entry for extinguishment of the debt.

E 16–19
(L.O. 5)

Extinguishment by Call   On January 1, 1998, Sty Company issued $400,000 of bonds payable with a stated interest rate of 5 percent, payable annually each December 31. The bonds mature in 10 years and are callable after the fourth year at 101. The bonds originally sold on January 1, 1998, at 104.

On June 30, 2003, the bonds were called. The company uses straight-line amortization, and the accounting period ends December 31.

Required
1. Give the issuance entry on January 1, 1998.
2. Give any entries on the extinguishment (i.e., call) date.

E 16–20
(L.O. 5)

Extinguishment by Refunding   On January 1, 1998 Rocket Corporation issued $250,000 of 6 percent, 20-year bonds at 98. The interest is payable each December 31. Rocket uses straight-line amortization. Its accounting period ends December 31.

On January 1, 2009, Rocket issued $250,000, 9 percent, 20-year, refunding bonds at par. On this date, the old 6 percent bonds could be purchased in the open market at their present value based on the current effective rate of 9 percent. Rocket immediately purchased all of the 6 percent bonds.

Required
Round to the nearest dollar.

1. Give the entry for issuance of the 6 percent bonds.
2. Give the entry for issuance of the 9 percent bonds.
3. Give the entry to record the extinguishment of the old bonds by refunding.

E 16–21
(L.O. 5)

Extinguishment by Open Market Purchase   On January 1, 1998, Nue Corporation issued $200,000 of 10 percent, 10-year bonds at 98. Interest is paid each December 31, which also is the end of the accounting period. The company uses straight-line amortization. On July 1, 2003, the company purchased all of the bonds at 101 plus accrued interest.

Required

1. Give the issuance entry.
2. Give the interest entry on December 31, 1998.
3. Give the related entries on July 1, 2003.

E 16–22
(L.O. 6)

LT Noninterest-Bearing Note   Fox purchases goods on January 1, 1998, and issues a $20,000 noninterest-bearing note requiring $10,000 to be paid on December 31, 1998 and 1999. Each payment includes principal and interest. The market rate of interest is 10 percent. Use the gross method.

Required

1. Compute the amount to be recorded in purchases.
2. The entry to record the purchase.
3. The entry to record the 1998 payment on the note.
4. The entry to record the 1999 payment on the note.

E 16–23
(L.O. 6)

LT Note: Borrower and Lender   On May 1, 1998, Watt Company borrowed $24,000 cash from Tandy Bank on a $24,000, 10 percent, three-year note. Interest is payable each April 30, and the principal is payable on April 30, 2001. The accounting period ends on December 31 for each party.

Required

1. Give all current and adjusting entries through April 30, 1999, for both the borrower and the lender.
2. Show how this note and the related items would be shown on the 1998 financial statements of each party.

E 16–24
(L.O. 6)

LT Note: Point-System Mortgage   On January 1, 1998, Derek Company borrowed cash from Patricia Finance Company on a $30,000, 12 percent, two-year note. The note will be paid off in two equal installments each December 31. Patricia assessed Derek two points, which means that the proceeds to Derek are reduced by 2 percent of the face value of the note. The annual payment, however, is computed on the face value. Use interpolation to determine the effective rate. The accounting period for each company ends December 31.

Required

1. Compute the amount of each annual payment.
2. The effective rate is 13.55 percent. Show how this rate was computed.
3. Prepare a debt amortization schedule for the two parties.
4. Give all entries for each party from January 1, 1998, through the maturity date.

E 16–25
(L.O. 6)

LT Note: Borrower and Lender   The following data are available: on January 1, 1998, a borrower signed a long-term note, face amount, $100,000; time to maturity, three years; stated rate of interest, 8 percent. The effective rate of interest of 10 percent determined the cash received by the borrower. The note will be paid in three equal annual installments each December 31 (which is also the end of the accounting period for both parties).

Required

1. Compute the cash received by the borrower and prepare a debt amortization schedule.
2. Give the required entries for both the borrower and lender for each of the three years.

E 16–26
(L.O. 6)

LT Note: Borrower and Lender Entries   On January 1, 1998, a borrower signed a long-term note, face amount $100,000; time to maturity, three years; stated interest rate, 12 percent; and cash proceeds from the loan, $96,661. The note will be paid in equal annual installments each December 31 (this is also the end of the accounting period for both parties).

Required

1. Prepare a debt amortization schedule.
2. Give the required entries for both the borrower and lender for each of the three years.

E 16–27
(L.O. 6)

LT Note: Unrealistic Rate, Debtor and Creditor   Cathy Company purchased a machine at the beginning of 1998 with a three-year, $2,000, 5 percent note, payable in three equal annual payments of $734 (including principal and interest) at each year-end. The current market rate of interest for this level of risk was 12 percent.

Required

1. What was the cost of the machine to Cathy Company?
2. Give the entry by Cathy to record the purchase. Use the net approach.
3. Prepare the amortization schedule for the note.
4. Give the entries for both the debtor and the creditor at the end of each year (assuming that the accounting year-end for the debtor and creditor coincides with the note's year-end).

E 16–28   **Appendix 16A: Multiple Choice—Troubled Debt Restructure**   Choose the correct answer for each question.

1. Nano Corporation agreed to give Rewind Company a machine in full settlement of a note payable to Rewind. The machine's original cost was $70,000. The note's face amount was $55,000. On the date of the agreement,
   - The note's carrying amount was $52,500, and its present value at the current market rate was $48,000.
   - The machine's carrying amount was $54,500, and its fair value was $48,000.

   What amounts of gain (loss) should Nano recognize, and how should these be classified in its income statement?

	Extraordinary	Other
a.	$(2,000)	$ 0
b.	0	(2,000)
c.	2,500	(2,000)
d.	4,500	(6,500)

2. Wild Company, a debtor-in-possession under Chapter 11 of the Federal Bankruptcy Code, granted an equity interest to a creditor in full settlement of a $56,000 debt owed to the creditor. At the date of this transaction, which is considered an isolated transaction with respect to the bankruptcy proceedings, the equity interest had a fair value of $50,000. What amount should Wild recognize as an extraordinary gain on restructuring of debt?
   a. $0.
   b. $6,000.
   c. $50,000.
   d. $56,000.

3. During 1998, Camellia Company experienced financial difficulties and was likely to default on a $500,000, 15 percent, three-year note dated January 1, 1997, payable to Central National Bank. On December 31, 1998, the bank agreed to settle the note and unpaid 1998 interest of $75,000 for $410,000 cash payable on January 31, 1999. What is the amount of gain, before income taxes, from the debt restructuring?
   a. $0.
   b. $75,000.
   c. $90,000.
   d. $165,000.

4. In 1993, Marie Corporation acquired land by paying $37,500 down and signing a note with a maturity value of $500,000. On the note's due date, December 31, 1998, Marie owed $20,000 of accrued interest and $500,000 principal on the note. Marie was in financial difficulty and was unable to make any payments. Marie and the bank agreed to amend the note as follows:
   - The $20,000 of interest due on December 31, 1998, was forgiven.
   - The principal of the note was reduced from $500,000 to $475,000, and the maturity date was extended one year to December 31, 1999.
   - Marie would be required to make one interest payment totaling $15,000 on December 31, 1999.

   As a result of the troubled debt restructuring, Marie should report a gain, before taxes, in its 1998 income statement of
   a. $20,000.
   b. $25,000.
   c. $30,000.
   d. $45,000.

(AICPA adapted)

E 16–29   **Appendix 16A: Restructure, Transfer of Noncash Asset, Entries by Each Party**   Down Company owed Super Bank a $50,000, three-year, 10 percent (payable each December 31) note dated January 1, 1995. During 1997, Down Company experienced unusual financial difficulties and was unable to pay the note or interest for 1997 that had been accrued. On January 1, 1998, the bank agreed to settle the debt and interest (for 1997) for $2,000 cash plus land that had a current market value of $30,000. At December 31, 1997, the records of Down Company showed the acquisition cost of the land to be $20,000. Super intends to sell the land and estimates $3,000 of direct selling costs.

Required   Give all entries required on January 1, 1998, to record this debt restructure (*a*) for Down Company and (*b*) for Super Bank.

E 16–30   **Appendix 16A: Restructure, Transfer of Cash and Noncash Assets, Entries by Each Party**   Slow Company owed Quick Finance Company a three-year, $100,000, 10 percent (payable annually each December 31) note dated January 1, 1995. At December 31, 1997, Slow was experiencing serious financial problems and could not pay the principal and interest for 1997 that had been accrued. Quick agreed to settle the debt and interest in full for $12,000 cash plus a tract of land (Slow's acquisition cost was $7,000) plus 1,000 shares of Slow common stock, par $10, that had a current market price of $35 per share. The current market value of the land on January 1, 1998, was $20,000. The agreement was accepted by both parties, and settlement was effected on January 1, 1998.

Required　　Give all entries required to record the debt restructure for (*a*) Slow Company and (*b*) Quick Finance Company.

E 16–31　　**Appendix 16A: Restructure, Modification of Terms, Compute New Interest Rate, Entries for Both Parties**　Brown Company owed City Bank a $50,000, 10 percent (payable each December 31), four-year note dated January 1, 1995. Early in 1996, it became clear that Brown Company was experiencing difficulty in making the annual interest payment, although the company did manage to make the 1995 payment. Because of expected continuing difficulties, it appeared that there was a good chance the company would default on the note (as well as on other obligations). On January 2, 1997, the two parties agreed to restructure the debt by (*a*) reducing the remaining annual interest payments to $2,240 each and (*b*) reducing the principal amount (maturity amount) to $48,000. Brown paid the interest for 1996.

Required
1. Compute the new yield or effective rate of interest to be used by Brown.
2. Give all entries required on date of restructure (January 2, 1997) for each company. If no entry is required, explain the reason.
3. Give all entries required at December 31, 1997, and 1998, for each company. Assume that City Bank uses the interest method.

E 16–32　　**Appendix 16A: Restructure, Modification of Terms, Entries by Both Parties**　Orange Company owed National Bank a $60,000, 10 percent (payable each December 31), four-year note dated January 1, 1995. Orange Company has experienced severe financial difficulties and is likely to default on the note and interest during 1997 unless some concessions are made by the bank. Consequently, on January 2, 1997, the parties agreed to restructure the debt as follows: (*a*) interest payments each year to be reduced to $1,000 per year for 1997 and 1998, and (*b*) reduce the principal amount to $30,000. On December 31, 1996, Orange paid $6,000 interest for 1996.

Required
1. Does this restructure change the yield or effective interest rate? Explain. Is a new effective rate of interest needed for accounting purposes in this situation? Explain.
2. Give all entries required for each party on the date of restructure, January 2, 1997.
3. Give all entries required for each party on December 31, 1997 and 1998. National Bank uses the interest method.

E 16–33　　**Appendix 16B: Serial Bonds, Bonds Outstanding Method**　Minot Company issued $40,000 of 5 percent serial bonds on January 1, 1996, at 84; they mature as follows:

Series A	December 31, 1998	$20,000
Series B	December 31, 2000	$20,000

The bonds pay interest each December 31.

Required　　Give the entry to retire $5,000 of the series B bonds on August 1, 1997, at 98, using the bonds outstanding method. Include the interest accrual entry to August 1.

| PROBLEMS

P 16–1
(L.O. 2, 3)　　**Bonds: Price Computation, Interest Method**　Alpha Corporation sold and issued to Beta Corporation $400,000 of 8 percent (payable semiannually on June 30 and December 31), three-year bonds. The bonds were dated and sold on January 1, 1998, at an effective interest rate of 10 percent. The accounting period for each company ends on December 31. Beta intends to hold the bonds to maturity.

Required
1. Compute the price of the bonds.
2. Prepare a debt amortization schedule for the life of the bonds (use the interest method and round to the nearest dollar).
3. In parallel columns prepare entries for the issuer and the investor through December 31, 1998.
4. Show how the issuer and the investor would report the bonds on their respective balance sheets at December 31, 1998.
5. What would be reported on the income statement for each party for the year ended December 31, 1998?

P 16–2
(L.O. 3)

Bonds: Accrued Interest, Straight-Line Method   Foyt Corporation sold and issued to Mears Corporation $100,000 of bonds on June 1, 1998, for $102,640 plus accrued interest. Mears intends to hold the bonds to maturity. The bond indenture provided the following information:

Maturity amount	$100,000
Date of bonds	April 1, 1998
Maturity date	March 31, 2001
Stated interest rate	6½%, payable semiannually
Interest payments	March 31 and September 30

Required

1. In parallel columns, give entries for the issuer and investor from date of sale to maturity. Assume that the difference between the amortization amounts is not material; therefore, use straight-line amortization. Also assume that the accounting period for each company ends on December 31.
2. Show how the bonds would be reported on the balance sheet of each company at December 31, 1998.
3. What would be reported on the income statement for each company for the year ended December 31, 1998?

P 16–3
(L.O. 3)

Bonds: Interest Method, Adjusting Entries   Jones Corporation issued bonds, face amount $100,000, three-year, 8 percent (payable semiannually on June 30 and December 31). The bonds were dated January 1, 1998, and were sold on November 1, 1998, for $100,739 (including interest of $2,667 and a bond price of $98,072) at an effective interest rate of 9 percent. The bonds would have sold at the effective rate on December 31, 1998, for $98,206. The bonds mature on December 31, 2000. The bonds were purchased as a long-term investment by Smith Corporation, which intends to hold the bonds to maturity.

Required

1. In parallel columns, give the entries at November 1, 1998, for the issuer and the investor.
2. Prepare a bond amortization schedule using the interest method.
3. In parallel columns, give the entries for both the issuer and investor for interest and amortization at the interest date, December 31, 1998. Use the interest method of amortization.
4. Assume that the accounting period for each party ends on February 28. In parallel columns, give the adjusting entries for each party on February 28, 1999. Assume the interest method of amortization.
5. Compute the amount of amortization per month for each party, assuming that straight-line amortization is used (i.e., the difference between the amortization amounts is not material).

P 16–4
(L.O. 2, 3)

Bonds: Price Computation, Interest Method, Entries for Both Parties   Randy Corporation issued $200,000 of 8 percent (payable each February 28 and August 31), four-year bonds. The bonds were dated March 1, 1998, and mature on February 28, 2002. The bonds were sold on August 1, 1998, to yield 8½ percent interest. The bonds were purchased by Voss Corporation, which intends to hold the bonds to maturity. The accounting period for each company ends on December 31. The bonds were sold for $196,967 plus accrued interest of $6,667. They would have sold on August 31, 1998, for $197,027.

Required

1. Prepare an amortization schedule using the interest method of amortization.
2. In parallel columns, give entries for the issuer and the investor from date of sale through February 28, 1999. Base amortization on (1) above.
3. Compute the amount of amortization per month for each party, assuming that the straight-line method is used (because the difference between the amortization amounts is not material).

P 16–5
(L.O. 2, 3)

Bonds: Bond Price, Computation, Straight Line, Entries for Issuer and Investor   Koy Corporation sold and issued to Lott Corporation $100,000 of four-year, 11 percent bonds on September 1, 1998. Interest is payable semiannually on February 28 and August 31. The bonds mature on August 31, 2002, and were sold to yield 10 percent interest. The accounting period for both companies ends on December 31. Lott intends to hold the bonds to maturity.

Required

1. Compute the price of the bonds (show computations and round to nearest dollar).
2. In parallel columns, give all entries required through February 1999 in the accounts of the issuer and the investor. Assume that the difference between the interest method and the straight-line method of amortization is not material; therefore, use straight-line amortization.

P 16–6
(L.O. 3)

Valuation of Bonds Payable   Majors, Inc., has two bond issues outstanding today, each with (1) $1,000 face value, (2) a term of five years at issuance, (3) three years remaining to maturity, and (4) 10 percent yield rate at issuance. Bond A is a zero coupon bond; bond B pays 10 percent annually and just paid interest yesterday. The yield rate today on both bonds is 12 percent.

Required

1. Determine the bond for which book value and market value have changed the most since issuance. Assume the interest method.

2. Discuss the magnitude of the difference between the changes in the values of these two bonds.

P 16–7
(L.O. 3)

Bond Issuance between Interest Dates, Interest Method   Claremont, Inc., issued $50,000 of 6 percent bonds dated January 1, 1998, on November 1, 1998, to yield 8 percent. The bonds pay interest each June 30 and December 31 and mature December 31, 2002. Claremont uses the interest method.

Required

1. Compute the proceeds of the bond issue, separating the accrued interest from the bond price. Express the bond price in terms of percentage of face value.
2. Provide the journal entry for issuance.
3. Provide the journal entry for the first interest payment after issuance.
4. Provide the journal entry for the second interest payment after issuance.

P 16–8
(L.O. 3)

Bond Issuance between Interest Dates, SL Method   Using the information in P16–7, complete the requirements assuming that Claremont uses the SL method.

P 16–9
(L.O. 4)

Case A, Entries for Convertible Bonds; Case B, Detachable Stock Warrants   This problem involves two independent cases:

Case A
On January 1, 1996, when its $30 par value common stock was selling for $80 per share, Ancil Corporation issued $5,000,000 of 4 percent convertible debentures (i.e., bonds) due in 10 years. The conversion option allowed the holder of each $1,000 bond to convert the bond into five shares of the corporation's $30 par value common stock. The debentures were issued for $5,500,000. The present value of the bond payments at the time of issuance was $4,250,000, and the corporation believes that the difference between the present value and the amount paid is attributable to the conversion feature. On January 1, 1997, the corporation's $30 par value common stock was split 3 for 1. On January 1, 1998, when the corporation's $10 par value common stock was selling for $90 per share, holders of 40 percent of the convertible debentures exercised their conversion options. For convenience, assume that the corporation uses the straight-line method for amortizing any bond discount or premium.

Required

1. Give the entry to record the original issuance of the convertible debentures.
2. Give the entry to record the exercise of the conversion option, using the book value method. Show supporting computations.

Case B
On July 1, 1998, Salem Corporation issued $2,000,000 of 7 percent bonds payable due in 10 years. The bonds pay interest semiannually. Each $1,000 bond includes a detachable stock purchase right. Each right gives the bondholder the option to purchase, for $30, one share of $1 par value common stock at any time during the next 10 years. The bonds were sold for $2,000,000. The value of the stock purchase rights at the time of issuance was $100,000.

Required

Prepare the entry to record the issuance of the bonds.

(AICPA adapted)

P 16–10
(L.O. 4)

Bonds: Detachable Stock Warrants, Entries for Issuer and Investor   Friendly Corporation issued $1,000,000 of 6 percent, nonconvertible bonds with detachable stock purchase warrants. Each $1,000 bond carried 20 detachable stock purchase warrants, each of which called for the purchase of one share of Friendly common stock, par $50, at the specified option price of $60 per share. The bonds sold at 106, and the detachable stock purchase warrants were immediately quoted at $1 each on the market.

Goode Company purchased the entire issue as a long-term investment and intends to hold the bonds to maturity.

Required

1. Give the following entries for Friendly Corporation (the issuer):
   a. To record the issuance of the bonds.
   b. To record the subsequent exercise by Goode of the 20,000 stock purchase warrants.
2. Assuming that Goode did not exercise all 20,000 stock purchase warrants in requirement (1) above, give the following entries for Goode Company, assuming that all indicated transactions occurred in the same year.
   a. Acquisition of the bonds (including the stock purchase warrants).
   b. Subsequent sale to another investor of half of the stock purchase warrants at $1.50 each.
   c. Subsequent exercise of the remaining half of the stock purchase warrants (by tendering them to Friendly Corporation). The market value of the stock was $62 per share.

P 16–11
(L.O. 4)

Induced Conversion of Convertible Bonds   Convee Company issued $75,000 of 12 percent convertible bonds at face value on an interest payment date several years ago. The face value of each bond is $1,000, and each bond is convertible into 15 shares of $5 par common stock of Convee. Convee has embarked on a program of debt reduction; U.S. interest rates have declined during the term of the convertible bonds. Consequently, Convee offers the convertible bondholders $50 cash per bond as an inducement to convert. The market price of Convee stock is currently $70 per share. The bonds must be converted within a three-month period to receive the cash inducement. The bondholders accept the inducement and convert within the required period.

Required

1. Why did the bondholders convert?
2. Record the conversion; assume that Convee uses the book value method to record conversions of convertible bonds.
3. Record the conversion, but assume that Convee uses the market value method to record conversions of convertible bonds.
4. Explain why induced conversion is not treated as debt extinguishment for purposes of classifying the inducement cost.

P 16–12
(L.O. 5)

Bond Issuance and Early Retirement, Interest Method   Plenary, Inc., issued $100,000 of 8 percent bonds on January 1, 1998, to yield 6 percent. The bonds pay interest each June 30 and December 31, and mature 10 years from issuance. On January 1, 2006, when the bonds were yielding 12 percent, Plenary retired the bond issue. Plenary uses the interest method.

Required

1. Provide the entry for bond issuance.
2. Provide the entry for the June 30, 2004, interest payment without using an amortization schedule.
3. Provide the entry for bond retirement.

P 16–13
(L.O. 5)

Bond Issuance and Early Retirement, SL Method   Using the information in P16–12, complete the requirements assuming Plenary uses the SL method to amortize bond premium and discount.

P 16–14
(L.O. 5)

Extinguishment: Debtor Entries, Purchase in the Open Market   On July 1, 1995, Coputer Corporation issued $300,000 of 5 percent (payable each June 30 and December 31), 10-year bonds payable. The bonds were issued at 97, and issue costs of $1,000 were paid from the proceeds. Assume straight-line amortization of discount and bond issue costs.

Due to an increase in interest rates, these bonds were selling in the market at the end of June 1998 at an effective rate of 8 percent. Because the company had available cash, $100,000 (face amount) of the bonds were purchased in the market and retired on July 1, 1998.

Required

1. Give the entry by Coputer Corporation to record issuance of the bonds on July 1, 1995.
2. Give the entry by Coputer Corporation to record the extinguishment of part of the debt on July 1, 1998. How should the gain or loss be reported on the 1998 financial statements of Coputer Corporation?
3. Was the extinguishment economically favorable to the issuer, investor, or neither?

P 16–15
(L.O. 5)

Extinguishment by Refunding: Debtor Entries   Deenilli Corporation issued $100,000 of 4½ percent (payable each December 31), 10-year bonds on January 1, 1994. The issuer may call them at any time after 1997 at 104. The bonds sold on January 1, 1994, at 98. Straight-line amortization is used.

Due to a large increase in interest rates, the bonds were being sold in the market at the end of 1998 at 86 (i.e., at an effective rate of 8 percent). In view of this situation, Deenilli decided to issue a new series of bonds (a refunding issue) in the amount of $75,000 (8 percent payable annually, five-year term) on January 1, 1999. Deenilli had cash on hand sufficient to retire the old bonds.

Required

1. Give the entry for Deenilli Corporation to record issuance of the bonds at 98 on January 1, 1994.
2. Assume that the $75,000 refunding issue was sold at par; give the required entry for Deenilli.
3. Assume that all of the old bonds were immediately purchased in the open market at 86 on January 2, 1999. Give the required entry for Deenilli. How should the gain or loss be reported on the financial statements?
4. What was the economic gain or loss to the issuer and the investor?

P 16–16
(L.O. 5)

Extinguishment with Equity Securities; Call, Refunding, Entries   On January 1, 1994, Grand Corporation issued $100,000 of 9 percent (payable each June 30 and December 31), 10-year bonds payable (convertible and callable) at a 10 percent effective rate of interest. Each $1,000 bond is convertible, at the option of the holder, into Grand common stock (par $10) as follows: first five years—25 shares for each bond tendered; second five years—20 shares for each bond. The bonds can be called, at the option of Grand, after the fifth year at 101.

On July 1, 2000, the market interest rate on comparable bonds is 8 percent, and the common stock is quoted on the market at $52 per share.

Required

1. Give the entry to record the issuance of bonds on January 1, 1994. Show computation of the bond issue price.
2. Give the entry to record payment of bond interest and the amortization of bond premium or discount on June 30, 1994. Use the interest method.
3. Prepare the journal entries at July 1, 2000, to record each of the following separate assumptions (use straight-line amortization):

   Assumption A—All of the bondholders converted their bonds to common stock. Use the market value method to record the conversion.

   Assumption B—Grand called all of the bonds at the stipulated call price.

   Assumption C—Grand refunded all of the outstanding 9 percent bonds by purchasing them in the open market at the current yield rate of interest. Cash for the refunding was obtained by issuing new 8 percent bonds (interest payable semiannually) at par; cash proceeds were $103,000 (face amount of bonds sold).

4. Which of the three alternative means of retiring the old 9 percent bonds is most likely to occur if each were available to the investors? Why?

P 16–17
(L.O. 2, 3, 5)

Bond Accounting over Complete Term, Partial Extinguishment   McGill, Inc., a calendar-year firm, issued $20,000 of 6 percent bonds on January 1, 1998, to yield 8 percent. The bonds pay interest semiannually on June 30 and December 31 and mature on January 1, 2000. (An unrealistically short bond term is used for convenience). McGill incurred $1,200 of bond issue costs. On August 1, 1999, $5,000 of the bond issue was retired at 96.

Required

Prepare all journal entries during the bond term under both the interest and straight-line methods of amortizing bond premium and discount.

P 16–18
(L.O. 3, 4, 5)

Three Transactions: Bonds, Detachable Warrants, Extinguishment—Entries   This problem involves three independent situations.

   a. On January 1, 1998, Hopewell Company issued its 8 percent bonds that had a par value of $1,000,000. Interest is payable at December 31 each year. The bonds mature on December 31, 2007. The bonds were sold to yield a rate of 10 percent.
   b. On September 1, 1998, Junction Company issued at 104 (plus accrued interest) 4,000 of its 9 percent, 10-year, $1,000 par value, nonconvertible bonds with detachable stock purchase warrants. Each bond carried two detachable warrants; each warrant was for one share of common stock, at a specified option price of $15 per share. Shortly after issuance, the warrants were quoted on the market for $3 each. No market value can be determined for the bonds above. Interest is payable in December 1 and June 1. Bond issue costs of $40,000 were incurred and were deducted from the proceeds.
   c. On December 1, 1995, Cone Company issued its 7 percent, $2,000,000 par value bonds for $2,200,000 plus accrued interest. Interest is payable on May 1 and November 1. On July 1, 1998, Cone purchased and retired the bonds at 98 plus accrued interest. Cone uses the straight-line method for the amortization of bond premium because the results do not materially differ from those of the interest method; the total amortization period at the date of issuance was 50 months.

Required

1. Give the entry to record the issuance of the bonds by Hopewell Company. Show supporting computations.
2. Give the entry to record the issuance of the bonds by Junction Company. Show computations.
3. Give the entries required by Cone Company:
   a. At issue date.
   b. At reacquisition date.

(AICPA adapted)

P 16–19
(L.O. 6)

LT Note: Adjustable-Rate Note   On January 1, 1998, Baker Company borrowed cash from Alter Finance Company and signed a three-year, $30,000 note. Interest is payable each December 31 at a stated interest rate of "floating prime at January 1 of each year plus 2 percent." The principal is due on December 31, 2000. The following actual prime rates were used by Alter: January 1, 1998, 13 percent; January 1, 1999, 12 percent; and January 1, 2000, 15 percent. The accounting period for each company ends on December 31.

Required

1. Compute the total amount of interest paid, by year.
2. What was the difference between the stated and effective rates? Explain.
3. Give all entries for each company through maturity date.

4. Give the 1998 adjusting entry that would have been necessary had the accounting periods for each company ended on August 31 instead of December 31.

P 16–20
(L.O. 6)

Adjustable Rate Mortgage   On January 1, 1998, Five Vegetables Per Day, Inc., a health-food retailing firm, borrowed $90,000 to partially finance its purchase of a building for its retailing operations. The firm chose an adjustable-rate mortgage starting at 5 percent. The rate can be increased once per year on January 1. The term of the mortgage is three years and requires annual payments, which include principal and interest, each December 31. The mortgage payable is to be completely paid off at the end of the term. The annual payment for each year reflects the interest rate in effect that year. The interest rate on the mortgage was changed on January 1, 1999, to 6 percent, and on January 1, 2000, to 7 percent, to reflect changing economic conditions.

Required

Prepare the journal entries for the entire term of the adjustable-rate mortgage. For each change in interest rate, Five Vegetables, a calendar-year firm, recomputes the annual payment that will satisfy the remaining loan balance.

P 16–21
(L.O. 6)

Note with Share Appreciation: Borrower and Lender   On January 1, 1998, Cantral Company borrowed cash from Tenor Financing Company on a $60,000, 14 percent, three-year note. Interest is payable each December 31, and the principal is payable December 31, 2000. This note is designated note A.

On the same date, Cantral Company also borrowed cash from Tulare Commercial Loan Company on a $200,000, 9 percent, five-year note. This note, designated note B, will be paid with five equal annual payments each December 31 based on the $200,000 amount and 9 percent interest. Tulare granted a low 9 percent stated rate in exchange for a 10 percent share appreciation in an office building under construction. The current best estimate of the present value of the share appreciation at January 1, 1998, was $52,754. The annual payment for this note is based on the note's face value and the stated rate. However, the effective rate is the rate equating the face value reduced by the share appreciation value, to the present value of the above annual payments. This effective rate is used to recognize interest and is applied to the liability balance as reduced by the share appreciation value. The accounting period for each company ends on December 31.

Required

1. What is the amount of each annual payment on note B?
2. For each note, what is (*a*) the stated interest rate and (*b*) the effective interest rate?
3. Prepare a debt amortization schedule for note B.
4. For each note separately, give all entries for both the borrower and the lenders through December 31, 1998.
5. Show the items and amounts that would be reported on the December 31, 1998, financial statements, by each company under the following captions: revenues, expenses, assets, liabilities, and stockholders' equity (current and noncurrent classifications are not required).

P 16–22
(L.O. 6)

Note with Unrealistic Interest Rate   Sable Company purchased merchandise for resale on January 1, 1998, for $5,000 cash plus a $20,000, two-year note payable. The principal is due on December 31, 1999; the note specified 8 percent interest payable each December 31.

Assume that Sable's going rate of interest for this type of debt was 15 percent. The accounting period ends December 31.

Required

1. Give the entry to record the purchase on January 1, 1998. Show computations (round to the nearest dollar).
2. Complete the following tabulation:

    a. Amount of cash interest payable each December 31 . . . . $______
    b. Total interest expense for the two-year period . . . . $______
    c. Amount of interest reported on income statement for 1998 . . . . $______
    d. Amount of liability reported on the balance sheet at
        12/31/1998 (excluding any accrued interest) . . . . $______

3. Give the entries at each year-end for the debtor.
4. Give the entries at each year-end for the creditor.
5. Show how the debtor and creditor should report or disclose the data related to the note on the income statement and balance sheet at each year-end.

P 16–23

Appendix 16A: Restructure Entries, Assets, New Debt, and Equity Securities   Double Company owed Rohr Finance Company a $300,000, five-year, 18 percent (payable each year-end) note, dated January 1, 1995. Double has experienced serious financial problems and as a consequence has not paid the interest at December 31, 1997. However, each company included its accrual of interest in the adjusting entries at that date. On January 2, 1998, a debt restructure was agreed upon that provided that the principal and interest accrued will be paid in full as follows:

Cash, $10,000.

Transfer of land—original cost to Double, $45,000, and appraised value, $137,000.

Transfer of 20,000 shares of Double common stock, par $1; estimated current market value, $3.00 per share.

Transfer of $30,000 of accounts receivable; the related allowance for doubtful accounts on Double's books is $4,000 (this appears to be realistic).

Transfer of 5,000 shares of Wells Corporation stock held by Double as a long-term investment; cost to Double, and current market value, $10 per share.

Required   Give all entries to record the debt restructure for each company.

P 16–24   **Appendix 16A: Restructure by Modification of Terms, Entries by Both Parties**   Baker Company owed Cox Company a $20,000, 10 percent (annual interest payable each December 31), four-year note, dated January 1, 1995. Baker Company faced extreme financial difficulties. Both companies had accrued interest for the year 1996, but no interest was paid for 1996. On January 2, 1997, the parties agreed that the principal would be paid in full on maturity date and that the interest for 1996, 1997, and 1998 would be settled by payment of $3,340 cash on December 31, 1998 (maturity date).

Required   1. Compute the new effective rate of interest for Baker.
2. Give all entries required on date of restructure (January 2, 1997) for each company.
3. Give all entries required on December 31, 1997, and 1998, for each company. Cox uses the interest method.

P 16–25   **Appendix 16A: Combination Restructure, Entries by Both Parties**   On January 1, 1999, Day Corporation owed a $65,000 note payable to Cox Corporation that required the payment of 10 percent interest on each December 31; the note was due on December 31, 1999. Because of continuing serious financial difficulties, Day informed Cox that default (and discontinuance of the business) was probable unless a concession on terms could be negotiated. Day has paid interest through December 31, 1998. On January 1, 1999, Cox agreed to the following restructure of the debt:

a. Day will immediately transfer $15,000 of its accounts receivable to the creditor in settlement of $14,000 of the debt. The accounts of Day reflected $1,000 in the allowance for doubtful accounts that related to these receivables; thus, the current net realizable value of the receivables was reasonably stated at $14,000.
b. Day will immediately transfer its long-term investment in 800 shares of common stock (par $10) of Tye Corporation in partial settlement of the debt. Day accounts reflected a carrying value equal to the current market value of $32,000.
c. Day will pay $10,000 cash at the end of the fifth year from January 1, 1999, (date of restructure) to settle the remaining $19,000 of the principal. Therefore, the restructured maturity date is December 31, 2003.
d. Day will pay $5,000 total interest over the five-year period from January 1, 1999, to December 31, 2003 (i.e., $1,000 cash interest per year at December 31).

Required   1. Give any required entry of the debtor and the creditor on date of restructure, January 1, 1999.
2. Give the required entries for the debtor and the creditor on the first two interest dates. Cox uses the interest method.
3. Record the last restructured payment.

P 16–26   **Appendix 16A: Restructure by Modification of Terms, Entries for Both Parties**   On January 1, 1998, Overdue Corporation issued to Liquid Corporation a $100,000, 7 percent (payable annually on December 31), 10-year note to yield 8 percent interest. After paying interest for 1998 and 1999, Overdue Corporation encountered severe financial difficulties, which made it apparent that Liquid Corporation would have to make concessions as to the debt terms. Therefore, a debt restructure was agreed to on January 1, 2000, that provided that (*a*) the remaining term to maturity would be 20 years from January 1, 2000, and (*b*) interest would be reduced so that the same total dollar amount of interest would be paid over the new term to maturity (20 years) as would have been paid over the remaining portion of the old term (8 years).

Required   1. Give the entry by each party to record issuance of the note on January 1, 1998. Show computation of the original note issuance price. Overdue received cash from Liquid in exchange for the note. Use the net method.
2. Compute the carrying amount of the note for the debtor and creditor on January 1, 2000.
3. Compute the new effective rate of interest for Overdue (use straight-line interpolation to compute the approximate interest rate to two decimal places.)
4. Give any required entry for the debtor and the creditor on the date of restructure, January 1, 2000.

5. Give all entries for both the debtor and the creditor on the two interest dates, December 31, 2000, and December 31, 2001. Liquid uses the cost recovery method.
6. Give Liquid's December 31 entry for the first year in which interest revenue would be recognized.

P 16–27

Appendix 16A: Combination Restructure   Janco Inc. issued a five-year, 10 percent, $500,000 note on January 2, 1994, for a merchandise purchase. The stated interest rate reflects the market rate on similar notes. The note requires equal annual payments each December 31 beginning 1994. Each payment includes principal and interest.

Subsequently, Janco experienced financial difficulties and on January 1, 1997, reached an agreement with the creditor to restructure the loan. Janco did not make the payment due December 31, 1996. According to the restructure agreement, the remaining payments under the original loan agreement are replaced by the following:

An immediate payment of $200,000.

$200,000 due January 2, 2001, the revised maturity date.

Required

Use interpolation if a new effective interest rate is required and record the following entries for Janco:

1. Interest accrual on December 31, 1996.
2. Entry to record the troubled debt restructure on January 1, 1997, and to reclassify the remaining liability accounts.
3. Entry to record interest on December 31, 1997.
4. Entry to record the final payment on January 2, 2001.

P 16–28

Appendix 16B: Serial Bonds, Bonds Outstanding Method   A $700,000 issue of serial bonds dated April 1, 1998, was sold on that date for $707,600. The interest rate is 8 percent, payable semiannually on March 31 and September 30. Scheduled maturities are as follows:

Serial	Date Due	Amount
B	March 31, 1999	$100,000
C	March 31, 2000	200,000
D	March 31, 2001	200,000
E	March 31, 2002	200,000

Required

1. Prepare an amortization schedule for the issuer; use the bonds outstanding method.
2. Give all entries for the issuer relating to the bonds, including reversing entries, through March 31, 1999. The issuing company adjusts and closes its books each December 31.
3. Prepare the entry for the early retirement on June 1, 1999, of $50,000 of Serial E bonds at 98, and interest accrued to that date.

P 16–29

Appendix 16B: Serial Bonds, Interest Method   On January 1, 1998, Tobin Corporation sold serial bonds (dated January 1, 1998) due as follows: Serial A, $10,000, December 31, 2002; Serial B, $15,000, December 31, 2003; and Serial C, $25,000, December 31, 2004. The bonds carried a 3 percent coupon (stated) interest rate per semiannual period (each June 30 and December 31) and were sold to yield 4 percent interest per semiannual period.

Required

Round to the nearest dollar.

1. Compute the selling price of the bond issue.
2. Prepare an amortization schedule for Tobin for the life of the bond issue, assuming that the interest method is used. (Hint: Discount amortization—6/30/98, $306; 6/30/03, $352.)
3. Give Tobin's entry to record retirement of half of Serial C at 99½ on June 30, 2004. Assume that the accounting period ends December 31.

P 16–30
(L.O. 2, 3, 5)

Bond Issuance, Retirement   Westlawn Company issues $200,000 of 10 percent bonds on March 1, 1994. Additional information on the bond issue is as follows:

Bond date: January 1, 1994.

Maturity date: January 1, 2004.

Yield rate: 12 percent.

Interest payment dates: June 30, December 31.

Required

1. Record the bond issue and the first interest payment for Westlawn under the interest method.
2. On August 1, 1999, Westlawn purchased 30 percent of the bonds on the open market for 103. Record the entries necessary to update the portion of the bond issue retired and to record the extinguishment.
3. Have interest rates risen or fallen between the issuance of the bonds and the early extinguishment? (Assume no significant change in Westlawn's risk.)

4. Discuss the nature of the extraordinary item you recorded in (2). In explaining this item to a financial statement user, what cautions would you include in your discussion?

5. Record the entry to accrue interest expense on December 31, 1999, on the remaining bonds.

ANALYSIS, JUDGMENT, AND COMMUNICATION

CASES

C 16–1
(L.O. 4)

 **Convertible Bonds versus Detachable Stock Warrants**   Seton Corporation is considering the issuance of $100,000 worth of five-year bonds. Two alternatives are under consideration as follows:

Alternative A—At the beginning of 1998, issue 100 convertible bonds that would specify that each $1,000 bond can be tendered for conversion to 15 shares of Seton's common stock, par $10, at any time after the second year from the issue date of the convertible bonds. Seton's best estimate is that the convertible bonds can be sold to Investor X for $108,000 cash at the beginning of 1998 if the common stock is selling at that time for not less than $65 per share.

Alternative B—At the beginning of 1998, issue 100 nonconvertible $1,000 bonds with 15 detachable stock purchase warrants per bond. Each warrant can be tendered at any time after 1999 for one share of Seton's common stock, par $10, at an option price of $60 per share. Seton's best estimate is that the nonconvertible bonds can be sold to Investor X for $108,000 cash at the beginning of 1998 if the common stock is selling at that time for not less than $65 per share. The warrants are expected to have a market value of $2 each immediately after issuance of the bonds; the bonds do not have a listed market price.

Seton's management is considering which alternative to select. The management is concerned about several issues that may influence the decision. One such issue is the comparative impact of the two alternatives on the financial statements. Your assistance in selecting an alternative has been requested. Assume in each case that the investor intends to hold the bonds to maturity.

Required

1. Using Seton's best estimate, give the journal entries for each alternative that each party would make at the beginning of 1998. Explain any differences in accounting values between the two alternatives.

2. Give the entries for each alternative that each party would make at the beginning of 2001, assuming all of the bonds in alternative A are tendered for conversion and all of the warrants are turned in for shares in alternative B. Seton's common stock is selling for $75 per share. Use the market value method for alternative A. Assume straight-line amortization, and assume that the market value of the warrants has not changed.

3. Complete the following schedule, assuming that the transactions in (1) and (2) have taken place.

4. Outline your response to management's request for assistance in choosing between the two alternatives in a memo. Consider the results of requirement 2.

| | A—Convertible Bonds | | B—Detachable Warrants | |
Items	Issuer	Investor	Issuer	Investor
Gain (loss) conversion				
Investments:				
Bonds				
Common stock				
Liabilities				
Bonds payable				
Stockholders' equity:				
Common stock				
Contributed capital in excess of par				
Cash:				
Inflow				
Outflow				

C 16–2
(L.O. 3)

Zero Coupon Bonds and Amortization Methods   The Shelby Company issues $10 million of bonds maturing 25 years after issuance. The bonds yield 16 percent but pay no interest.

Required

1. Why would Shelby issue bonds paying no interest?
2. Why would investors buy them?
3. Compute the issue price (assume annual compounding periods and that issue date and bond date are the same).
4. Compute interest expense for the 1st, 16th, and 25th year under the interest method.
5. Compute interest expense for the 1st, 16th, and 25th year under the straight-line method.
6. Comment on your findings in (4) and (5). Why is the straight-line method inappropriate for the Shelby bonds?

C 16–3
(L.O. 1, 3)

Ethical Considerations: Reporting Liabilities   Write a short report regarding the following two situations from an ethical and financial reporting viewpoint. (Note: (*b*) requires knowledge of material from Chapter 15.)

a. "Accounting for an Albatross," *Forbes,* June 13, 1988, p. 62, states that American Airlines has accumulated a liability of 4 billion miles due to its frequent-flyer program. Its estimated liability for free flights amounts to $270 million but could be $40 million higher if the opportunity cost of lost revenue from displaced passengers is considered.

   The airlines argue that the actual cost of each free flight is only approximately $8—for food, insurance, and other miscellaneous costs. That is the cost of filling an otherwise empty seat. Furthermore, flyers with free tickets often bring along a paying customer, which more than offsets the negligible cost. Consequently, the average liability disclosed is only a fraction of the amount industry analysts insist exists.

b. In December, Mr. Wilson, the controller of Fargo Company, a calendar-fiscal-year company, is faced with a tough situation. The bond indenture of a major issue of Fargo bonds requires maintaining a 3-to-1 current ratio as measured at each balance sheet date. Fargo has recently experienced cash shortages caused by a downturn in the general economy and in the demand for Fargo's products. However, leading economic indicators suggest that an upturn is expected.

   A substantial account payable is due in January. Fargo does not have the cash to pay the debt before the end of the current year. Furthermore, the January cash budget based on a realistic estimate of sales and collections from accounts receivable indicates a cash shortage requiring short-term financing. The payable due in January is large enough to cause the current ratio at December 31 to fall below 3.0. The controller begins the search for a financial institution willing to refinance the payable on a long-term basis. If successful, the payable would be reclassified as long term, enabling Fargo to comply with the bond indenture. Several financial institutions are willing to refinance the payable, but none agree to do so on a noncancelable basis.

   The controller is quite stressed by the situation. Noncompliance with the bond indenture may lead to technical default. If the bondholders exercise their right and call the bonds, Fargo may be forced into bankruptcy. The controller is confident that Fargo will rebound in the coming year and reasons that more harm will come to the company, its employees, and its shareholders if he does not take action that will result in compliance with the bond indenture. Mr. Wilson therefore decides to refinance the payable on a long-term basis and to include in the footnotes a statement that the refinancing agreement complies with *SFAS No. 6,* "Classification of Short-Term Obligations Expected to Be Refinanced."

C 16–4
(L.O. 4)

Accounting for Convertible Bonds   Columbus Company's 10-year convertible bonds, issued and dated October 1, 1996, are convertible into 20 shares of Columbus' $25 par value common stock, at the holder's option. The bonds were issued at a premium when the common stock traded at $45 per share. After payment of interest on October 1, 1998, 30 percent of the bonds were tendered for conversion when the common stock was trading at $57 per share. Columbus uses the book value method to account for the conversion.

Required

In a short memo, discuss

1. How the issue price of Columbus's convertible bonds would be determined.
2. How Columbus should account for the issuance of the convertible bonds. Give the rationale for this accounting practice.
3. How Columbus should account for the conversion of the bonds into common stock.

(AICPA adapted)

C 16–5
(L.O. 1)

Liabilities: Off-Balance-Sheet Risk   The reported balances of certain liabilities carried on a corporation's books do not always indicate the maximum obligation potentially facing the firm as a result of past transactions. In addition, a firm may have potential obligations that are not recorded at all.

Required

For each of the following potential or actual liability items, briefly discuss in writing whether the firm is subject to off-balance-sheet risk of accounting loss and, if so, whether that risk arises from credit risk or market risk (or both), and why. Your discussion should be from the point of view of the company named.

1. Fixed-rate mortgage payable by Wellco, Inc., secured by real estate owned by Wellco.
2. The guarantee by Jolko, Inc., of a $4 million loan obtained by one of Jolko's subsidiaries.
3. Bonds payable issued by Samson, Inc., at a discount, due in five years.
4. Convertible bonds issued by Coastal Company, at a premium, due in two years.
5. Transfer of accounts receivable by Jenell Company, accounted for as a borrowing. The transfer is with recourse to Jenell.
6. Variable-rate mortgage payable by Angeles, Inc., secured by real estate owned by Angeles.
7. A loan commitment made by BCCJ Bank to a computer manufacturer, guaranteeing a fixed line of credit at a fixed rate of interest for one year from the commitment date.

ANALYZING FINANCIAL STATEMENTS

All questions in this section are based on information taken from the financial statements of actual companies.

A 16–1
(L.O. 3)

Zero Coupon Bonds   Baxter International, Inc., is a manufacturer of surgical and medical instruments. Following is author-adapted information from the footnotes to Baxter's 1995 annual report:

Note 7: Long-Term Debt and Lease Obligations (in part):

	December 31	
	1995	**1994**
	(millions)	
Zero coupon notes due 2000, effective rate 10%	$86	$78

The company had unamortized original issue discounts of $58 and $66 for the zero coupon notes due 2000, at December 31, 1995 and 1994 respectively.

Assume the notes were issued January 1 of a previous year and mature December 31.

Required

1. Reconstruct the 1995 interest expense entry rounding your computations to the nearest million. Also, verify the December 31, 1995, net note book value from the results of your entry.
2. Estimate the face value of the notes.
3. Using a present value approach, verify the December 31, 1995, net bond liability balance using your result in requirement 2. For this requirement only, use 10.7 percent as the effective rate.

A 16–2
(L.O. 2)

***Wall Street Journal* Bond Prices, Zero Coupon Bonds**   Two zero coupon bond listings for $1,000 bonds from the October 3, 1996, *Wall Street Journal* "New York Exchange Bonds" section follow. Shoney is a family-style restaurant chain, and Time Warner is a media company.

	Cur Yld	**Vol**	**Close**
Shoney zr04	—	6	43
TmeWar zr13	—	266	42

Required

Use Exhibit 16–2 to find the meaning of the abbreviations in this bond listing. Estimate the annual yield (effective interest rate) earned by the purchaser of one of these bonds at the closing price shown in the listing. This is the interest rate earned on the bond investment if held to maturity. (*The Wall Street Journal* does not provide a yield for zeroes because no periodic interest is paid.)

To simplify the computations, assume that maturity occurs on December 31 of the year indicated and use the nearest whole number of years for the term of the investment.

A 16–3
(L.O. 4)

Convertible Bonds   Part of International Paper Company's long-term liability footnote to its 1995 financial statements disclosed the following:

Note 12: Long-Term Debt (*millions*)	**1995**	**1994**
5 3/4% Convertible subordinated debentures		$199

In July 1995, the 5¾ percent debentures were called by the company and converted into 5.8 million shares of common stock.

Additional information:
1. The average market price per share of the firm's common stock was approximately $40 during 1995.
2. The par value of common stock is $1.

Required

1. Prepare the conversion entry, assuming the book value method is used.
2. Prepare the conversion entry, assuming the market value method.
3. Why might a company prefer to use the book value method? The market value method?
4. Why did the bondholders convert rather than accept the call price?

A 16–4
(L.O. 3)

Bonds Payable and Debt Retirement   A portion of the long-term liability footnote to the 1995 annual report of Alaska Air Group Inc. follows:

	December 31	
	1995	**1994**
	(millions)	
$7^3/4\%$ convertible subordinated debentures due 2006–2010	$10.8	$14.4

Additional assumptions:

a. The debentures were issued on January 1 in a previous year and pay interest each December 31.
b. The debentures retired were scheduled to mature December 31, 2008.
c. The retirement of the debentures occurred December 31, 1995. Alaska Air paid the market value of the bonds which reflected a yield rate of 5 percent.

Required

1. Prepare the December 31, 1995, interest payment entry.
2. Prepare the December 31, 1995, entry for bond retirement.
3. What factor may have contributed to the recognition of a loss on the early retirement?

A 16–5
(L.O. 1)

 **Long-Term Liabilities**   Refer to the 1995 financial statements of the Coca-Cola Company that appear at the end of this text, and respond to the following questions.

1. What was 1995 interest expense for Coca-Cola, and how much interest was paid in 1995?
2. Using 1995 interest expense and only the items listed in the long-term debt footnote, estimate an average 1995 interest rate using the 1994 balances in long-term debt. What factors might contribute to this rate's being considerably higher than the average rate implied by the interest rates listed for each component of long-term debt?
3. What are some of the specific debt issuances contributing to the 1995 statement of cash flows financing inflow "issuances of debt"?
4. What is the market value of Coke's long-term debt? What does this value imply about the current market rate of interest relative to the average effective interest rate on Coke's long-term debt?

COMPARATIVE ANALYSIS

 **Coca-Cola Company and Pepsico Inc: Debt Ratios and Leverage**   This item is amenable to a group or individual solution. Refer to the preface for additional details on using group items.

This problem compares Pepsico Inc. and Coca-Cola Company. The 1994 and 1995 comparative balance sheets and selected 1995 income statement and cash flow information for Pepsico Inc. follow. Use the Coca-Cola Company annual report reproduced at the end of this text along with this information:

Required

1. For each firm, compute the following ratios for 1995 (these ratios are discussed in Chapter 5):
   a. Current ratio.
   b. Quick or acid test ratio.
   c. Cash flow to current liabilities.
   d. Total debt to total owners' equity.
   e. Total debt to total assets.
   f. Times interest earned.
   g. Rate of return on owners' equity.
   h. Rate of return on assets.

For any ratio requiring a tax rate, use the firm's effective tax rate for 1995 (the ratio of income tax expense to pretax earnings). Also compute the ratio of after-tax interest expense to average total debt for both firms.

2. Using your findings in requirement 1, and any other available information, which firm appears to have employed debt financing more successfully in 1995?

Pepsico Inc. Comparative Balance Sheets

Assets	December 30	
	1995	**1994**
Current Assets:	*(millions)*	
Cash and cash equivalents	$ 382	$ 331
Short-term investments, at cost	1,116	1,157
	1,498	1,488
Accounts and notes receivable, less allowance:		
$150 in 1995 and $151 in 1994	2,407	2,051
Inventories	1,051	970
Prepaid expenses, taxes, and other current assets	590	563
Total Current Assets	5,546	5,072
Investments in unconsolidated affiliates	1,635	1,295
Property, plant, and equipment, net	9,870	9,883
Intangible assets, net	7,584	7,842
Other assets	797	700
Total Assets	$25,432	$24,792

Liabilities And Shareholders' Equity

	1995	1994
Current Liabilities:		
Accounts payable	$1,556	$1,452
Accrued compensation and benefits	815	753
Short-term borrowings	706	678
Accrued marketing	469	546
Income taxes payable	387	672
Other current liabilities	1,297	1,169
Total Current Liabilities	5,230	5,270
Long-term debt	8,509	8,841
Other liabilities	2,495	1,852
Deferred income taxes	1,885	1,973
Shareholders' Equity:		
Capital stock, par value 1 2/3 cents per share:		
authorized 1,800 shares, issued 863 shares	14	14
Capital in excess of par value	1,060	935
Retained earnings	8,730	7,739
Currency translation adjustment and other	(808)	(471)
	8,996	8,217
Less: Treasury stock, at cost:		
75 shares and 73 shares in 1995 and 1994, respectively	(1,683)	(1,361)
Total Shareholders' Equity	7,313	6,856
Total Liabilities and Shareholders' Equity	$25,432	$24,792

From the 1995 Pepsico Income Statement

	Millions
Interest expense	$ 682
Income from continuing operations before tax	2,432
Income tax expense	826
Net income	$1,606

From the 1995 Pepsico Statement of Cash Flows

Net cash flow from operations	$3,742

Note on financial leverage.   The degree to which a firm uses debt financing is a measure of its use of financial leverage. If leverage or debt financing has been used successfully, the rate of return on owners' equity (ROE) will exceed the rate of return on assets (ROA). This occurs if the firm can borrow at a rate less than it can earn on assets (i.e., if its after-tax borrowing rate is less than ROA). Successful use of leverage means that the firm is earning a higher rate of return on borrowed funds than it is paying for the borrowed funds.

17 ACCOUNTING FOR LEASES

LEARNING OBJECTIVES

After you have studied this chapter, you will:

1   Understand the nature of a lease and why the lessee may wish to keep the lease off the balance sheet, while the lessor may prefer to remove the leased asset from its records.

2   Know how to determine whether a lease is a capital lease or an operating lease.

3   Be able to distinguish sales-type and direct financing leases.

4   Be able to make the lessee's and lessor's entries for operating and capital leases.

5   Be able to make the lessee's and lessor's entries for direct financing-type and sales-type capital leases.

6   Know how to deal with special problems related to the accounting for leases, including bargain purchase and renewal options, residual value guarantees, the use of alternative interest rates by the lessee and lessor, lessee depreciation requirements, accounting for executory and initial indirect costs, and the classification of lease receivables and payables.

7   Understand sale–leaseback arrangements.

8   Be familiar with lease disclosure requirements.

INTRODUCTION

This chapter examines how firms account for leases. The topic is more complex than many described in this book and involves many rules.

Gino's pizza chain appeared to grow by leaps and bounds in the 1980s, seemingly without having to borrow money. Astute investors and accountants, however, knew that Gino's was using leases to finance its growth. Everything was leased—stores, baking ovens, restaurant seating, and delivery trucks—and none of the leased assets or liabilities incurred in conjunction with the leases was reported on Gino's balance sheet. But then the accounting rules changed, forcing Gino's to revise the debt it reported on its balance sheet from $30 million to $156 million. With a total stockholders' equity of $46 million, and the old $30 million in debt, Gino's debt-to-equity ratio was about two to three (65 percent), which many analysts would consider less than satisfactory debt coverage. With debt newly reported at $156 million, the ratio reversed to three to one (339 percent), a frightening ratio by anyone's standards.

Kmart Stores, one of the largest U.S. retailers, had a similar experience. After the change in accounting rules, the retailer's reported balance sheet debt grew from a rather modest $211 million to a towering $1.7 billion. Again, the increase reflected leases.

Indeed, the car-rental industry could not have achieved its present stature were it not for the leasing of cars from the automakers. If car-rental companies had to buy all the cars in their inventories, it would require enormous amounts of capital. Instead, they lease major portions of their car fleets from the automakers, usually for relatively short periods, such as 11 or 14 months. Incidentally, this is how the rental companies are able to advertise new, low-mileage models.

Many banks and Wall Street investment firms have been active in the lease investment market for the past two decades. Rather than investing in stocks or bonds, some investors prefer more exotic choices—like a $250,000 pooled participation investment in a Boeing 767, leased and operated by American Airlines, but owned jointly by 25 or more private investor–lessors. Instead of a jet airliner, the lease might involve a string of railroad freight cars or a 3-million-gallon liquid storage tank. Investment firms can arrange lease investments for all types of assets.

Millions of business assets will be leased this year by large and small companies alike. Assets such as construction equipment, computer mainframes, delivery vehicles, office furnishings, real estate, commercial aircraft, communications systems—even entire manufacturing plants, equipment included—will be leased at some point during the year. Although leasing, rather than buying, business assets has always been fairly common, in the late 1960s many companies discovered leasing, changing the face of asset acquisition forever.

From the relatively simple renting of space or equipment, leasing has become a complex proposition used to finance asset acquisitions, usually involving both economic and tax benefits.

BASIC LEASE ACCOUNTING ISSUES

A **lease** is "an agreement conveying the right to use property, plant, or equipment (land and/or depreciable assets), usually for a stated period of time."[1] In the commonly used sense of the term, a lease is a fee-for-usage contract between an owner of property and a renter. The owner of the property is referred to as the **lessor,** and the renter is the **lessee.** The lease specifies the terms under which the lessee has the right to use the owner's property and the compensation to be paid to the lessor in exchange.

Leased property can include both real and personal assets. Personal property includes both tangible assets (such as machinery, equipment, or transportation vehicles), and certain intangibles (such as patents).

Accounting for leases in this sense of the term is not complicated. The lessee makes periodic payments to the lessor, which are accounted for as normal expense items by the lessee. Meanwhile, the lessor credits the payments to an income account such as leasing revenue (or *other income* if leasing is not one of the company's mainstream business activities). If a lessee rents space for $1,000 a month, the entries would be:

Lessee's books—Entry to record payment of monthly rent expense:

Rent expense	1,000	
Cash		1,000

Lessor's books—Entry to record receipt of monthly rent payment as income:

Cash	1,000	
Leasing revenue		1,000

---

[1]This definition does not include "(*a*) agreements that are contracts for services that do not transfer the right to use property, plant, or equipment from one contracting party to the other . . . (*b*) lease agreements concerning the rights to explore for or to exploit natural resources such as oil, gas, minerals, and timber . . . (*c*) licensing agreements for items such as motion picture films, plays, manuscripts, patents, and copyrights." See *SFAS No. 13,* "Accounting for Leases," par 1.

<table>
<tr><td>The Lease from the Lessee's Viewpoint</td><td>

As the popularity of leasing grew, lessee companies were pleasantly surprised to find that leasing could afford them special economic and tax advantages if the lease were structured properly.[2] Specifically, lessees were quick to discern the key distinction between a capital lease and an operating lease.

</td></tr>
</table>

Capital Lease   A **capital lease** is a lease contract that transfers essentially all the risks and rewards of ownership in the leased asset from the lessor to the lessee. In this case, the lessee records the leased property on the balance sheet. The fair market value of the property involved is capitalized as a balance sheet asset, and the debt obligation incurred is recorded as a liability. From an accounting standpoint, this treatment is the same as if the property were purchased, with the acquisition being made possible by 100 percent debt financing. The lessee even recognizes depreciation expense on the leased asset.

The specific provisions of the lease contract, rather than the characteristics of the leased asset, determine whether the lease is a capital lease or an operating lease. An example of a lease provision that indicates the lease is a capital lease is the transfer of title to the leased asset from the lessor to the lessee at the conclusion of the lease term. Ownership *risk* involves the responsibility for casualty loss, wear and tear, obsolescence, and maintenance. Ownership *rewards* involve benefits such as the right of use, increases in the value of the leased asset, and ultimate transfer of title.

Operating Lease   All leases that do not transfer substantially all the risks and benefits of ownership from the lessor to the lessee are **operating leases.** The lessee does not report the property on the balance sheet. The lessee rents the property, and the rent payments are charged to expense as they come due.

SFAS No. 13 provides specific criteria (discussed shortly) for identifying a capital lease. All leases failing to meet these criteria are considered operating leases. Distinctions between capital and operating leases and the basic accounting treatments for both lease classifications are summarized in Exhibit 17–1.[3]

Before *SFAS No. 13,* the criteria for determining whether a lease transaction should be accounted for as a capital or operating lease were ambiguous. However, the central issue was then and still remains management's intent when the asset is leased. Consider two situations:

Situation 1 In conjunction with a one-time-only major building project, a construction company leases bulldozers for a period of two years to supplement its own equipment. The company intends to return the equipment to the lessor after this two-year period. This lease should be accounted for as an operating lease.

Situation 2 Working in close contact with a lending institution, a group of physicians arrange to have a medical clinic custom-designed and constructed for their medical practice. Their intention is to lease the property from the lending institution holding title to the property using a lease contract for a period of 30 years. This lease should be accounted for as a capital lease.

Off-Balance-Sheet Financing   By structuring leasing transactions as operating leases rather than capital leases (where management's intent points to capital lease accounting treatment), lessees can make full use of assets without capitalizing them or reporting the lease payment obligations as a balance sheet liability. This accounting treatment is an example of **off-balance-sheet financing.** Off-balance-sheet financing is attractive to lessee companies for two primary reasons:

- **Debt–equity ratio** Adding more debt to a company's capital structure increases the ratio and is considered an adverse development. If the debt–equity ratio is already considered

---

[2]Leasing activity can change rapidly with changes in the tax law. For example, the legislation that allowed and later rescinded the investment tax credit had immediate effects on the amount of leasing activity in the United States.

[3]Exhibit 17–1 implies a symmetry in the lessor and lessee entries. This symmetry is prevalent in other transactions, such as credit sales between a seller and buyer. But such symmetry is not always present in leasing. In some cases, a lease may be classified differently by the lessor and the lessee. Later in this chapter, cases are discussed in which the lessor records a capital lease while the lessee records the same lease as an operating lease.

EXHIBIT 17–1   Summary of Basic Lease Accounting Issues for Lessees and Lessors (assumed dollar amounts)

Lessee

Operating lease:

- Lessee is considered to be renting the asset from the lessor (not owning).
- Lessee makes periodic rent payments to the lessor that are accounted for as current operating expenses:

```
Rent expense . . . . . . . . . . . . . . .   100
    Cash . . . . . . . . . . . . . . . . .          100
```

- At end of lease term, the asset is returned to the lessor.
- Lessee *does not* record depreciation expense.

Capital lease:

- Lessee is considered to own the asset for accounting purposes.
- Lease is capitalized on lessee's books:

```
Leased asset . . . . . . . . . . . . . .   1,000
    Lease liability . . . . . . . . . . .          1,000
```

- Lessee recognizes periodic payment as part interest and part reduction of principal:

```
Interest expense . . . . . . . . . . . . . .    10
Lease liability . . . . . . . . . . . . . .     90
    Cash . . . . . . . . . . . . . . . . . .         100
```

- At the end of the lease term, the asset is often retained by the lessee.
- Depreciation expense *is* recorded on the asset.

Lessor

Operating lease:

- Lessor continues to own the asset that is leased to the lessee.
- Lessor collects periodic rent payments that are accounted for as current operating revenue:

```
Cash . . . . . . . . . . . . . . . . . .   100
    Leasing revenue . . . . . . . . . . .        100
```

- At end of lease term, the asset is returned to the lessor.
- Lessor records depreciation on the asset.

Capital (direct financing) lease:

- Asset is considered to be transferred permanently to the lessee at the inception of the lease, although lessor remains legal owner.
- Asset is removed from the lessor's books and replaced by receivable (direct financing lease):*

```
Lease receivable . . . . . . . . . . . .   1,000
    Asset . . . . . . . . . . . . . . .          1,000
```

- Lessor recognizes periodic collection of rent as part interest and part reduction of principal:

```
Cash . . . . . . . . . . . . . . . . . .   100
    Interest revenue . . . . . . . . . . .         10
    Lease receivable . . . . . . . . . . .         90
```

- At the end of the lease period, the asset is often retained by the lessee.
- No depreciation expense is taken during the time the asset is on lease.

*If an immediate recognition of profit is involved, the lease is called a capital (sales-type) lease and the accounting entry is as follows:

```
Lease receivable . . . . . . . . . . . . . . . . . . . . . . . . . . . . . . . . . . . . . . . . . . . . . . . . . . . . . . . . . . . . . . . . . . . . .   1,000
Cost of goods sold . . . . . . . . . . . . . . . . . . . . . . . . . . . . . . . . . . . . . . . . . . . . . . . . . . . . . . . . . . . . . . . . . . . .     800
    Sales revenue . . . . . . . . . . . . . . . . . . . . . . . . . . . . . . . . . . . . . . . . . . . . . . . . . . . . . . . . . . . . . . . . . . . . .      1,000
    Asset . . . . . . . . . . . . . . . . . . . . . . . . . . . . . . . . . . . . . . . . . . . . . . . . . . . . . . . . . . . . . . . . . . . . . . . . . .        800
```

high, stockholders might sell their shares, causing the stock price to decline, or creditors may refuse to extend credit (or call in loans).[4]

- **Existing debt covenants** Bond indentures on bank loan agreements may include restrictive covenants designed to protect the bondholders' investments. One such covenant prohibits a company from taking on additional debt without the consent of the present bondholders. Thus, a company may be prohibited from leasing if the lease obligation has to be capitalized.

Concerns over accounting for leases date back at least to 1949, when *ARB No. 38* was issued. But *ARB No. 38* set only loosely defined standards on how to account for leased assets. As a result, four subsequent pronouncements have now been adopted:

- *SFAS No. 13,* "Accounting for Leases," November 1976.
- *SFAS No. 23,* "Inception of the Lease," August 1978.
- *SFAS No. 91,* "Accounting for Nonrefundable Fees and Costs Associated with Originating or Acquiring Loans and Initial Direct Costs of Leases," December 1986, as amended.
- *SFAS No. 98,* "Accounting for Leases: Sale-Leaseback Transactions Involving Real Estate, Sales-Type Leases of Real Estate, Definition of the Lease Term, and Initial Direct Costs of Direct Financing Leases," May 1988.

---

[4]The appearance of more debt on the balance sheet can create the perception that the firm faces larger periodic interest charges and hence greater risk when business conditions deteriorate.

SFAS Nos. 13, 23, and *91* are the foundation for this chapter. The essence of these pronouncements is a set of tightly defined criteria for determining when and how a lessee must account for a leasing transaction as either an operating lease or a capital lease. These same pronouncements also set forth specific criteria for lessor accounting.

The Lease from the Lessor's Viewpoint

The popularity of business leasing is evident in the results of an AICPA survey of 600 companies in 1996 indicating that 544 of these companies (91 percent) engaged in leasing activities in one form or another.[5] The largest share of the lessor market is represented by banks, other lending institutions, and commercial leasing companies.[6] Other major lessors are manufacturers and distributors of industrial products that offer business buyers a choice of either buying their products outright or leasing them.[7]

Financial institutions and commercial leasing companies structure lease transactions as either operating or capital (direct financing or sales-type) leases. Direct financing leases account for the majority of these leasing transactions.

Direct Financing Capital Lease   The lessor in a **direct financing lease** purchases an asset to accommodate the leasing transaction and immediately leases it to the lessee. The purchased asset is on the lessor's books only momentarily. Conceptually, accounting for a direct financing lease is similar to accounting for a disposal of an asset on credit. But rather than reporting an account receivable, the lessor reports a lease receivable on the balance sheet. No asset depreciation is taken by the lessor, and the lessor's profit comes entirely from interest.

Sales-Type Capital Lease   **Sales-type leases,** used by manufacturers and distributors, are similar to direct financing leases. But unlike a direct financing lease, a sales-type lease does not involve purchase for immediate lease. The manufacturer instead leases out the asset directly from finished goods inventory, or the distributor leases the asset out of its inventory account. The key distinction is the way the lessor accounts for the transaction. As shown in the footnote to Exhibit 17–1, a lease receivable account is opened with entries made to cost of goods sold, sales revenue, and the asset. The lessor recognizes sales revenue and cost of sales just as if the asset were sold. Here the lessor's profit comes partly through selling the asset above cost and partly through interest.

This diagram depicts the relationship between a direct financing lease and a sales-type lease:

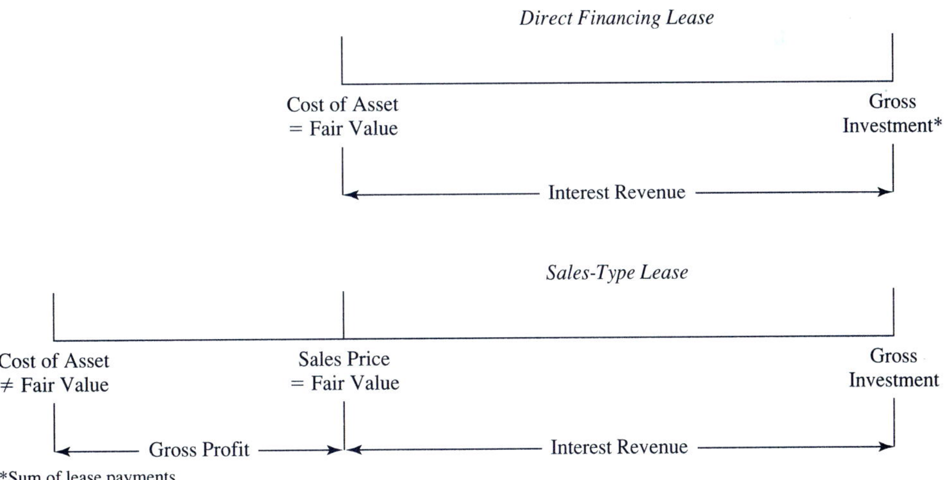

Operating Lease   The lessor in an **operating lease** acquires an asset and then leases it to a lessee in two separate transactions. The asset stays on the lessor's books throughout the term of the lease and is accounted for in the same way that other revenue-producing assets

---

[5]*Accounting Trends and Techniques—1996* (New York: AICPA, 1996), Table 2–28.

[6]Some of these nonbank commercial lessors are tiny one-person shops, while others are giant organizations such as Walter E. Heller & Co. and Commercial Credit Corporation.

[7]Manufacturers often set up subsidiary companies to handle leasing and other product financing arrangements. GMAC (General Motors Acceptance Corporation) and General Electric Capital Corporation are two such finance subsidiaries.

are accounted for on the balance sheet. When the asset is leased (which may or may not coincide with its acquisition), the lessor sets up a lease revenue account (income account) to record and account for rent receipts from the lessee. No lease receivable account (asset account) is used. The lessor depreciates the leased asset in the normal manner.

In summary, the types of leases considered so far are:

For the lessee:
1. Capital lease.
2. Operating lease.

For the lessor:
1. Capital lease.
   a. Direct financing.
   b. Sales type.
2. Operating lease.

Advantages of Leasing

Leasing affords a variety of advantages for lessees. The lessor profits by providing the use of an asset.

- Leasing may resolve a lessee's cash problems by making financing available for up to 100 percent of the leased asset value. Bank loans are typically limited to 80 percent of the asset's value.[8] Also, interest rates on leases may be negotiated at fixed rates, whereas some bank loans feature only variable rates.
- Leasing transactions can be structured as operating leases, providing off-balance-sheet financing not subject to debt covenant restrictions.
- In the case of industrial equipment that might need to be built to order and can require lengthy asset-implementation delays, leasing ready-to-use equipment can be attractive.
- Leasing may enable the lessee to avoid owning assets that are needed only temporarily, seasonally, or sporadically.
- Leasing assets for relatively short lease periods rather than owning them affords the lessee protection from equipment obsolescence.
- Leasing can provide income tax advantages derived from accelerated depreciation and interest expense.[9]
- In general, lease payment schedules can be tailored to dovetail with the lessee's expected cash inflows from operations.

On the lessor side of the market, manufacturers and dealer/distributors of industrial equipment use leasing to facilitate sales.[10] For lending institutions and commercial lessors, leasing is simply another part of their financial services product line.

Disadvantages of Leasing

Leasing has disadvantages as well as advantages. Some of these drawbacks parallel the advantages of leasing:

- The 100 percent financing of leased assets also means a higher total dollar outlay for interest.
- Off-balance-sheet financing merely masks the fact that new layers of debt are being assumed (a disadvantage to financial statement users).
- Leasing ready-to-use (as opposed to custom built) equipment may result in a lower-quality product and ultimately lost sales to the lessee.
- Seasonal leasing entails uncertainty that equipment will be available when needed. Also, leasing interest rates may be based on what the traffic will bear.
- Short-term leases may provide protection from product obsolescence, but short-term leasing rates are normally set at a premium over longer-term rates (to compensate the lessor for assuming the obsolescence risk).

---

[8]An important management decision for the lessee is the determination of whether to use bank financing to lease or buy the needed asset. Finance texts consider this issue in detail.

[9]Lease agreements are sometimes drawn up to shift tax advantages to the party (lessee or lessor) in the higher tax bracket. In exchange, the benefiting party compensates the forfeiting party in the form of either higher lease payments (if the lessee gains the tax benefits) or lower lease payments (if the lessor gains the tax benefits).

[10]Because of the high cost of such equipment, purchase financing is often a necessity. To ensure sales, many manufacturers offer product financing options, including leasing programs, in what have come to be known as full-service selling strategies. Today, this approach is common in selling new automobiles.

- Tax benefits may be temporary. A new tax provision can be enacted at any time, counteracting the provisions of the old code. This is a danger with all long-term leases featuring tax benefits.
- Long-term leases at fixed rates expose the lessor–lender to the risk of opportunity losses if interest rates advance.[11]

Leases and Ratios   We observed in the discussion of off-balance-sheet financing that capital leases (but not operating leases) increase debt-equity ratios for lessees. For lessors, the effect of a capital lease is on the firm's equity rather than on debt. This effect occurs because of the interest (and dealer profit on sales-type leases) accruing to the lessor. The effect on the lessor is to decrease the debt-equity ratio.

Leases, capital and/or operating, affect other ratios to the extent that either the numerator or denominator, or both, of these ratios change. The following changes are typical examples of components of ratios affected by lease accounting:

- Current assets: Current portion of capital lease receivable (lessor).
- Noncurrent assets: Asset leased (lessee and lessor).
- Current liabilities: Short-term portion of capital lease obligation (lessee).
- Long-term debt: Long-term portion of capital lease obligation (lessee).
- Expenses: Interest and depreciation on capital leases, and rent on operating leases (lessee).
                       Cost of sales on sales-type lease (lessor).
- Revenues: Interest and dealer profit on sales-type leases, and rent on operating leases (lessor).

CONCEPT REVIEW

1. What is the basic difference to the lessee between a capital lease and an operating lease?
2. What is the basic difference to the lessor between a direct financing capital lease and a sales-type capital lease?
3. List three advantages and three disadvantages of leasing.

ACCOUNTING FOR OPERATING LEASES

An example illustrates the characteristics of an operating lease. Assume that Grafixs Inc. (lessee) leases a computer from Comfast Inc. (lessor) for two years beginning March 1, 1998. Grafixs agrees to pay Comfast $4,800 a year, payable in advance on March 1 of each year. Comfast is responsible for ownership costs, such as maintenance, property taxes, and insurance. The lessee incurs only one risk, payment of the rentals, and obtains one benefit, temporary use of the asset. Since the risks and benefits of ownership are not transferred, this is an operating lease.

Assume that both firms' accounting periods end on December 31. Entries for the lessor (Comfast) to recognize receipt of the lease payments for 1998 are:

March 1, 1998—To record receipt of initial payment:

Cash	4,800	
Unearned rent revenue		4,800

December 31, 1998—To recognize revenue earned and depreciation of the asset:

Unearned rent revenue	4,000	
Rent revenue ($4,800 \times {}^{10}\!/_{12}$)		4,000
Depreciation expense*	3,000	
Accumulated depreciation		3,000

*Amount based on an assumed cost of $30,000, a life of 10 years, and straight-line depreciation with no salvage.

---

[11]This risk applies to financial institutions and commercial lessors that participate in direct financing leases and to manufacturers and distributors that engage in sales-type leases. The latter are susceptible to rising interest rates because most use bank borrowings or issue commercial paper (both sensitive to interest rates) to finance sales.

Unearned rent revenue is a liability of the lessor and reflects the lessor's obligation to make the computer available in the future.

Entries for the lessee (Grafixs) are:

March 1, 1998—To record payment of initial rent prepayment:

```
Prepaid rent ............................................  4,800
    Cash ...............................................         4,800
```

December 31, 1998—To recognize rent expense for 10 months:

```
Rent expense ...........................................  4,000
    Prepaid rent .......................................         4,000
```

In some cases, an operating lease provides that, in addition to the periodic rent, a nonrefundable down payment is made at the inception of the lease agreement. In this case, the lessor debits cash and credits unearned rent revenue when the down payment is received. The lessee debits an asset account called *leasehold* (or *prepaid rent*) and credits cash. Each party then amortizes the prepayment over the life of the lease on a systematic and rational basis. The straight-line method is used unless another is more appropriate.

Example   Grafixs makes a nonrefundable down payment March 1, 1998, of $720 to Comfast to cover both years. The lessor's (Comfast's) additional entries would be the following:

March 1, 1998—To record receipt of nonrefundable payment:

```
Cash ...................................................   720
    Unearned rent revenue .............................          720
```

December 31, 1998—To recognize rent revenue:

```
Unearned rent revenue ..................................   300
    Rent revenue ($720 × 10/24) .......................          300
```

The nonrefundable payment is recognized as additional rent when earned. The straight-line method is used here to recognize revenue as time passes. The benefits of the nonrefundable payment are assumed to be equal each period.

The lessee's (Grafixs) additional entries would be as follows:

March 1, 1998—To record payment of nonrefundable rent:

```
Prepaid rent ...........................................   720
    Cash ...............................................          720
```

December 31, 1998—To recognize rent expense:

```
Rent expense ...........................................   300
    Prepaid rent .......................................          300
```

ACCOUNTING FOR CAPITAL LEASES

Before the issuance of *SFAS No. 13,* most lessees accounted for leases as operating leases. Proponents of lease capitalization contend that in many cases the operating lease approach is improper because it results in off-balance-sheet financing; that is, obtaining financing without recording the contractual debt. In their view, a lease that transfers a material economic interest in the leased property creates an asset for the lessee that is more than a temporary right to use the leased property and that should be capitalized at the present value of the future lease rentals. Further, the lease creates a liability equal to the present value of the future payments, which also should be recognized by the lessee. Similar reasoning leads to the conclusion that, where a material economic interest in the property is transferred, the lessor should recognize a transfer of the asset. Thus, the lessor would both record a receivable and remove the cost of the asset from its records. Thereafter, the asset should be depreciated by the lessee rather than by the lessor. Moreover, the lease rental payments should be accounted for by both parties in the same manner as periodic payments on a long-term liability for which each rental payment is a combination of interest and debt reduction.

If the lease meets *any one* of the following four criteria at the inception of the lease, the lease is a capital lease to the lessee.*

1. The lease transfers ownership of the leased asset to the lessee by the end of the lease term.
2. The lease contains a bargain purchase option.
3. The lease term is equal to 75 percent or more of the remaining estimated economic life of the leased asset at the lease inception.
4. The present value of the minimum lease payments at the inception of the lease is at least 90 percent of the market value of the leased asset at that time.[†]

*Criteria 3 and 4 do not apply if the beginning of the lease term falls within the last 25 percent of the total economic life of the leased asset, land is the only asset leased, or the lease involves both land and building(s).

[†]The term *minimum lease payments* is defined in the text and in Exhibit 17–3.

The proponents of lease capitalization also point out that recognition of an asset and a liability on the lessee's financial statements makes its statements comparable with those of firms that purchase assets and finance the purchase with long-term debt. A company that leases properties under long-term leases and a company that owns similar properties financed by long-term debt are in the same economic position. Both companies are committed to a series of regular payments over a long term; lessees pay rents, and owners pay interest and principal on the debt. Also, in many long-term lease contracts, the lessee is committed to pay repairs and maintenance, property taxes and insurance, and similar **executory costs** associated with assets over their useful lives. If lessees can avoid recognition of assets and liabilities while owners cannot, their financial statements are not comparable even though they are in similar economic positions.

Lessees, however, point out that other long-term contracts are not recognized under GAAP and that lease contracts should not be singled out for different treatment.[12] Required recognition of large, previously unrecorded long-term lease liabilities could cause some lessees to be in technical default on long-term debt covenants that limit their indebtedness to a certain amount or require a specified debt–equity ratio. These loan covenants, specifying certain financial ratios, would not have considered the possible recognition of liabilities related to lease contracts. GAAP did not require such recognition. (In fact, altering accounting rules for leases caused some companies to change existing debt agreements.) The FASB moved ahead because it did not accept the lessees' arguments as persuasive, and it issued *SFAS No. 13* requiring recognition of many lease agreements.

Accounting for Capital Leases: Lessee

Because of the significant differences between accounting for operating and capital leases and the difficulty in determining when substantially all the risks and benefits of ownership have been transferred, *SFAS No. 13* specifies detailed criteria that qualify a lease contract as a capital lease. These criteria are outlined in Exhibit 17–2. Four criteria apply to lessees; if *any one* of these four criteria is met by the lessee, the lease qualifies as a capital lease for the lessee.

Transfer of Ownership (criterion 1) If a lease explicitly states that ownership of the asset transfers to the lessee at the end of the lease term, without payment of additional compensation to the lessor, the lease represents a capital purchase financing arrangement, similar to an installment purchase.

Bargain Purchase Option (criterion 2) A **bargain purchase option (BPO)** is an inducement for the lessee to buy the asset under lease at the end of the lease term. BPOs are often

---

[12]Employment contracts whereby employers agree to pay certain salaries for future services, purchase commitments that do not involve probable losses, and most postemployment benefits including pensions are but a few of the types of executory contracts for which an asset and corresponding liability were not recognized under GAAP at the time *SFAS No. 13* was being deliberated.

Minimum Lease Payments

Minimum lease payments are defined in *SFAS No. 13* to be "the payments that the lessee is obligated to make or can be required to make in connection with the leased property," including the following:*

- **Periodic rental payments (minimum rental payments):** The periodic rental payments are the base component. They are the periodic amounts paid to the lessor for use of a leased asset. In business leasing situations, periodic rental payments are ordinarily made annually, with the first payment at the inception of the lease, and subsequent payments on the lease anniversary date. *When lease payments are made at the front end of each lease period, present value annuity due (PVAD) tables are used rather than ordinary annuity tables to compute the present values of such payments.*
- **Bargain purchase option:** A BPO is an inducement offered to ensure that the lessee buys the leased asset at the end of the lease period. If a bargain purchase option is offered, the dollar amount is included in the minimum lease payments computation. *Because a BPO is a one-time-only payment at the end of the lease term, its present value is computed using the present value of 1 (PV1) table.*

Leases that do not feature BPOs (and that do not provide for transfer of ownership as a provision of the lease) may contain one or the other of the two following lease provisions—each of which is intended to protect the lessor's investment in the asset's residual value.

- **Guaranteed residual value:** The lessee may be required to guarantee to the lessor the leased asset's residual value at the end of the lease term. If so, the guaranteed amount is included in the minimum lease payments.
- **Failure to renew penalty:** Some leases feature a base lease term plus term extensions. At the end of the base term, the lessee has the option to renew or terminate the lease. In certain instances, failure to renew the lease may impose a penalty on the lessee, which compensates the lessor for the loss of leasing income and any decline in the asset's residual value. If a lease includes a penalty clause, the penalty is included in the minimum lease payments if it is expected that the lessee will reject the renewal option.

*Lease contracts may require the lessee to pay executory costs (insurance, maintenance, and taxes) to the lessor with the periodic rental payments. Any executory costs paid to the lessor are deducted from periodic rental payments to determine minimum lease payments since these payments merely maintain the asset. *Unless otherwise noted, periodic rental payment amounts included in all examples and illustrations are assumed to be net of executory costs.*

found in leases that do not explicitly transfer ownership. Essentially, the BPO serves the same purpose. If an asset's residual value is expected to be $10,000, for example, the BPO price might be $5,000 or even less. The lessee is not expected to pass up these savings, and the probability is high that the lessee will buy the asset at the BPO date.[13]

Lease Term Equal to 75 Percent or More of Asset's Remaining Useful Service Life (criterion 3)

If the remaining estimated useful economic life of an asset is 30 years at the lease's inception, for example, and the term of the lease is 25 years, then the lessee will have possession and unrestricted use of the asset for five-sixths (83 percent) of its remaining life. This control is considered equivalent to ownership. A **bargain renewal option (BRO),** which allows the lessee to renew the lease for a rental below the expected fair market rental at the time the BRO is exercisable, lengthens the lease term used in the comparison.

Minimum Lease Payments (at present value) at Least 90 Percent of the Asset's Market Value (criterion 4)

Minimum lease payments are the total dollars the lessee is obligated to pay the lessor over the course of the lease, including the BPO, if any. The bulk of the minimum lease payments take the form of periodic rental payments, meaning the amount to be paid each year for the use of the asset. A complete definition of minimum lease payments and their components appears in Exhibit 17–3.

Example   Assume that an asset is being leased for five years at a periodic rental payment of $25,000 each year paid in advance. Assume the appropriate interest rate on the lease is 10 percent. The present value of the $25,000 annual payments at 10 percent for five years is $104,247 = $25,000(PVAD, 10%, 5) = $25,000(4.16987). Next assume that the fair

---

[13]The BPO is not really a bargain. The payments built into the lease contract have been increased to compensate for the BPO.

market value of the leased asset is $110,000. In this case the present value of the minimum lease payments, $104,247, equals 94.8 percent of the asset's fair market value ($104,247 ÷ $110,000), meeting criterion 4 and requiring capital lease accounting treatment. Meeting criterion 4 indicates that the lessee is committed to a schedule of payments essentially equivalent to the asset's purchase price.

If any one of the four criteria in Exhibit 17–2 is met, the leased asset is considered to be purchased from the lessor at the inception of the lease, meaning the asset must be capitalized on the lessee's books (capital lease). If none of the criteria in Exhibit 17–2 is met, the transaction is accounted for as an operating lease.

The lessee records a capital lease at the date of inception of the lease at the lower of the asset's fair market value or the present value of the minimum lease payments.[14] The lessee records the lease by a debit to an asset account, with a title such as *leased property,* and a credit to lease liability for the present value of all future payments required in the lease agreement. Thus, the lessee's basic approach to lease valuation can be expressed as

$$\begin{pmatrix} \text{Valuation of leased} \\ \text{asset and related} \\ \text{liability at lease inception} \end{pmatrix} = \begin{pmatrix} \text{Periodic lease} \\ \text{payment} \end{pmatrix} \begin{pmatrix} \text{Present value of} \\ \text{annuity of } n \text{ payments} \\ \text{at rate of interest } i \end{pmatrix}$$

Example

1. On January 1, 1998, Lessor Company and Lessee Company sign a three-year noncancelable lease for an asset with an estimated economic life of three years.
2. The agreement involves no collection uncertainties, and the lessor's performance is complete (needed for lessor accounting, discussed later).
3. The three lease payments are $36,556 each, payable January 1, 1998, 1999, and 2000.
4. The fair market value of the asset at the inception of the lease is $100,000, which is also the carrying value (cost) on the lessor's books.
5. The lease does not contain a renewal or bargain purchase option, and the asset reverts to the lessor at the end of the three-year period.
6. The lessee's incremental borrowing rate is 10 percent.
7. Lessee Company and Lessor Company depreciate assets using the straight-line method for book purposes. The asset's residual value is estimated to be $0.
8. The accounting year ends December 31 for each party.
9. The lessor's **implicit interest rate** (target rate of return), the rate that equates the present value of the payments to the asset's market value, is 10 percent.

Because of item (1) of the example, the lease described in the example meets criterion 3 of Exhibit 17–2, which is sufficient to classify it as a capital lease. The lease also meets criterion 4, but not criteria 1 and 2 since there is neither a provision for transfer of ownership nor a bargain purchase option. The lease is a capital lease to the lessee because only one of the four criteria needs to be met.

Using the lessee's incremental borrowing rate of 10 percent, the lessee's computation of the valuation of the leased asset and the related lease liability is[15]

$$\$36,556(\text{PVAD, }10\%, 3) = \$36,556(2.73554) = \$100,000$$

The lessee's journal entries for the first year are:

January 1, 1998—To record the lease and initial payment:

Leased asset	100,000	
Lease liability		100,000

---

[14]*SFAS No. 13,* par. 5(k), requires that the recorded value of the leased asset not exceed its fair market value; that is, if the present value of the lease payments is greater than the market value of the leased asset at the lease inception date, both the asset and the liability must be recorded at the market value of the leased asset. In this case, the implied interest rate would have to be computed. For example, if the market value of the leased asset in the example were $96,375 instead of $110,000, the implicit interest rate would be computed as follows: $96,375 ÷ $25,000 = 3.855; reference to Table 6A–6, for $n = 5$, shows that the implicit interest rate is almost exactly 15 percent. The entries for the lessee would reflect the 15 percent rate based on the $96,375 value.

[15]Throughout this section, lease payments are assumed to be made on the first day of each period; thus, the present value of an annuity due is used. If the payments are not the same, each payment needs to be discounted separately.

EXHIBIT 17–4

Lease Amortization Schedule
(annuity due basis)

Date	Annual Lease Payments	Annual Interest at 10%	Decrease (Increase) in Lease Liability	Lease Liability Balance
1/1/98				$100,000
1/1/98	$ 36,556	—	$ 36,556	63,444
12/31/98	—	$6,344	(6,344)	69,788
1/1/99	36,556	—	36,556	33,232
12/31/99	—	3,324	(3,324)	36,556
1/1/00	36,556	—	36,556	–0–
	$109,668	$9,668	$100,000	

Lease liability	36,556	
Cash		36,556

December 31, 1998—To recognize interest and depreciation expense:

Interest expense: ($100,000 − $36,556)(.10)	6,344	
Lease liability		6,344
Depreciation expense: $100,000(⅓)	33,333	
Accumulated depreciation		33,333

The amortization schedule for the lease is shown in Exhibit 17–4.

Only the entries for 1998 are shown. The entries for each of the next two years are identical except for the accrual of interest expense. Interest expense for 1999 is $3,324, as shown in column 3 of the lease amortization schedule.

Lessee's Interest Rate   The interest rate used in the present value discounting directly affects the valuation of the leased asset and the related lease liability recorded at inception of the lease. The higher the interest rate, the lower the amount capitalized for the asset and recorded for the liability, and vice versa.

The lessee must compute the valuation of the asset leased and the lease liability by discounting the lease payments using *the lower* of its incremental borrowing rate or the discount rate used by the lessor (also called the lessor's implicit interest rate) *if known or determinable by the lessee*.[16] If the lessor's implicit interest rate is not known, or cannot be estimated reliably, the lessee must use the lessee's incremental borrowing rate. According to *SFAS No. 13*, this rate is "the rate that, at lease inception date, the lessee would have incurred to borrow (over a similar term) the funds necessary to purchase the leased asset." The choice of a specific interest rate by the lessee does not affect the total of interest expense plus depreciation expense over the life of the lease.[17] The timing of the recognition of each of these two expenses is affected, however.

Lessee's Depreciation   *SFAS No. 13* requires the lessee to depreciate this asset over the lease term (also here the economic life) of three years.[18] The residual value, any bargain purchase options, and any guaranteed residual value may affect the depreciation recorded by the lessee.

The lessee's entries parallel those that would be recorded for an actual purchase on a credit basis involving periodic payments that are part principal and part interest. For the current example, on December 31, 1998, the lessee reports:

1. Leased property at cost of $100,000 with accumulated depreciation of $33,333, reported with property, plant, and equipment.

---

[16]The problem of which rate to use is typically resolved by the limitation of market value. Only in the case of an unguaranteed residual value (discussed later) does a substantive recording issue emerge.

[17]For example, a higher interest rate increases interest expense but it also reduces the lease liability and asset. The two changes balance the total of interest expense and depreciation over the lease term.

[18]If the lease is capitalized because of either criterion 1 (title transfer) or 2 (BPO), the asset is depreciated consistent with the lessee's normal depreciation policy. Otherwise, the leased asset is depreciated over the term of the lease.

2. A lease liability of $69,788 ($100,000 − $36,556 + $6,344).
3. Interest expense of $6,344.
4. Depreciation expense of $33,333.

REVIEW PROBLEM

On January 1, 1998, Merick Inc. purchased an earth mover for $2 million to be leased. The machine is expected to have a 10-year life with no net residual value. The machine was leased immediately to Kregor Construction for $340,000 a year, payable January 1 of each year starting January 1, 1998. The lease term is for eight years with no renewal or bargain purchase option. Merick takes possession of the asset at the end of the lease term. Kregor uses 10 percent for lease capitalization purposes. Is this a capital lease or is it an operating lease? Why? If the lease is a capital lease, what is the value placed on the lease liability by Kregor on January 1, 1998? What expense would Kregor recognize on December 31, 1998? Assume SL depreciation and compute 1998 depreciation.

SOLUTION

The lease is a capital lease because it meets criterion 3 [(8-year term/10-year life) > .75]
Liability value: $340,000 (PVAD, 10%, 8) = $340,000 (5.86842) = $1,995,263
Interest expense: ($1,995,263 − $340,000) (.10) = $165,526
Depreciation expense: $1,995,263 ÷ 8 = $249,408

CONCEPT REVIEW

1. What entries does a lessee make for an operating lease?
2. What four criteria are used to determine whether a lease must be recognized on the lessee's balance sheet?
3. What is the important difference in disclosure between the accounting for an operating lease and the accounting for a capital lease?

Accounting for Capital Leases: Lessor

The criteria for determining whether the lessor must capitalize a lease include the criteria given in Exhibit 17–2. If the lease meets *any one* of the four criteria in Exhibit 17–2 *and both* criteria 5a and 5b in Exhibit 17–5, the lease must be capitalized by the lessor. These two additional criteria provide for risks and uncertainties that might make the first four criteria inoperative for the lessor.[19]

As we have seen, *SFAS No. 13* further defines capital leases for the lessor as either direct financing leases or sales-type leases. In the most simple terms, a sales-type lease involves a gross profit to the lessor, and a direct financing lease does not. There is no distinction between a direct financing lease and a sales-type lease for the lessee.

The lessor classifies a capital lease as a direct financing lease if there is no "manufacturer's or dealer's profit or loss." In this situation, the lessor's cost (or carrying amount, if different) of the leased asset equals its market value at the inception date, and the lessor uses this value to compute the lease rentals. Leasing companies typically have direct financing leases, rather than sales-type leases, because they purchase property for lease and not for resale. The lessor's profit objective is to set the lease rentals at a level sufficiently high to yield the target (implicit) rate of return on the investment in the leased asset by solving the following equation:

$$\text{Investment} = (\text{Lease rental})(\text{PVAD}, i, n)$$
$$\text{Lease rental} = \text{Investment}/(\text{PVAD}, i, n)$$

Direct Financing Leases   The lease in the previous Lessor, Lessee company example is a capital lease to the lessor because it meets criterion 3 from Exhibit 17–5 (see item 1 of

---

[19]Important uncertainties might include commitments by the lessor to guarantee performance of the leased asset beyond a typical product warranty or to protect the lessee from obsolescence of the leased asset. The necessity of estimating executory costs, such as insurance, maintenance, and taxes to be paid by the lessor, does not by itself constitute an important uncertainty.

If the lease meets *any one* of criteria 1 to 4 (of Exhibit 17–2 repeated here) and *both* criteria 5*a* and 5*b* below, the lease is a capital lease to the lessor.

1. The lease transfers ownership of the leased asset to the lessee by the end of the lease term.
2. The lease contains a bargain purchase option.
3. The lease term is equal to 75 percent or more of the remaining estimated economic life of the leased asset at the lease inception.
4. The present value of the minimum lease payments at the inception of the lease is at least 90 percent of the market value of the leased asset.
5*a*. Collectibility of the minimum lease payments is reasonably assured.
5*b*. No important uncertainties surround the amount of unreimbursable costs yet to be incurred by the lessor under the lease. (If uncertainties exist, they call into question whether the payments will be made and therefore the capitalizable amount.)

the example) and satisfies both additional criteria 5*a* and 5*b* (see item 2 of the example). It is a direct financing lease because (under item 4 in the example) the fair market value of $100,000 is equal to the cost on the lessor's books, implying that there is no dealer profit. The lessor's profit arises from the interest revenue earned in financing the transaction. The lessor's implicit interest rate is 10 percent (item 9). Therefore, the lessor's computation of the periodic lease rental is

$$\text{Rent} = \$100,000/(\text{PVAD}, 10\%, 3) = \$100,000/2.73554$$
$$= \$36,556$$

The lessor will receive three payments of $36,556, for a total of $109,668. This amount is entered as the gross receivable (*SFAS No. 98,* par. 22 h). The difference between the total payments of $109,668 and the leased asset's fair market value of $100,000 is the unearned interest revenue of $9,668 (*SFAS No. 98,* par. 22 i). The lessor records the total rentals as the gross receivable, and the net receivable is reported on the balance sheet. A portion of the receivable is reported as a current asset, the rest as long term. Periodic interest revenue is determined by applying the interest rate (10 percent here) to the net receivable at the beginning of the period.

The lessor's entries for this annuity-due payment lease are:

January 1, 1998—To record the lease:

Lease receivable	109,668	
Asset		100,000
Unearned interest revenue		9,668

January 1, 1998—First payment:

Cash	36,556	
Lease receivable		36,556

December 31, 1998—To recognize interest earned:

Unearned interest revenue: ($100,000 − $36,556)(.10)	6,344	
Interest revenue		6,344

Sales-Type Leases   The basic distinction between direct financing leases and sales-type leases is that a manufacturer's or dealer's profit (or loss) is recognized by the lessor in a sales-type lease at the inception of the lease. That is, the market value of the leased asset at the inception of the lease is greater (or less than) the lessor's cost (or carrying amount, if different).

Sales-type leases typically arise when a manufacturer or dealer uses leasing as one means of marketing its products. The lessor seeks to earn a profit on the sale of the leased asset and also to earn interest on the related lease receivable. Thus, two different profit amounts are recognized during the lease term for a sales-type lease:

- Manufacturer's or dealer's profit (gross margin or gross profit) is recognized in full at date of inception of the lease. This profit is:

$$\begin{pmatrix} \text{Normal sales price} \\ \text{(market value)} \\ \text{of the leased asset} \end{pmatrix} - \begin{pmatrix} \text{Cost (or carrying} \\ \text{amount, if different)} \\ \text{of the leased asset} \end{pmatrix} = \begin{pmatrix} \text{Manufacturer's or} \\ \text{dealer's profit or} \\ \text{loss} \end{pmatrix}$$

- Interest revenue on the lease receivable is recognized over the term of the lease. The total amount of interest is

$$\begin{pmatrix} \text{Gross lease} \\ \text{receivable (includes} \\ \text{the interest charge)} \end{pmatrix} - \begin{pmatrix} \text{Normal sales price} \\ \text{(market value)} \\ \text{of the leased asset} \end{pmatrix} = \begin{pmatrix} \text{Total interest} \\ \text{revenue over} \\ \text{the lease life} \end{pmatrix}$$

Example   To illustrate the accounting for a sales-type lease, we change item 4 in the previous Lessor Company, Lessee Company example to read:
- The fair market value of the asset at the inception of the lease is $100,000, and the carrying value on the lessor's books is $80,000.

This one change introduces a dealer's profit of $20,000. The periodic payment remains at $36,556 because it is based on the asset's market value.

The accounting entries for the lessor in 1998 are:

January 1, 1998—Inception of lease:

Lease receivable	109,668	
Cost of goods sold	80,000	
Sales revenue		100,000
Asset		80,000
Unearned interest revenue		9,668

January 1, 1998—First payment receipt:

Cash	36,556	
Lease receivable		36,556

December 31, 1998—To recognize interest earned:

Unearned interest revenue ($109,668 − $9,668 − $36,556)(.10)	6,344	
Interest revenue		6,344

The related amortization schedule from which the entries for future years can be obtained is the same as for the direct financing lease and is given in Exhibit 17–4.

In the December 31, 1998, financial statements, the lessor reports:

1. A net lease receivable of $69,788 [$109,668 − $36,556 − ($9,668 − $6,344)].
2. Sales revenue of $100,000, cost of goods sold of $80,000, and interest revenue of $6,344.

The lessor's entry at the inception date is similar to the entry that would be made if the leased asset had been sold outright on credit. That is, the lessor debits a net receivable and credits sales revenue for the sale price of the leased asset ($100,000), which is the same as the present value of the payments to be received. At the same time, the lessor debits cost of goods sold and credits the leased asset for its cost or carrying amount (in inventory), $80,000. The difference of $20,000 ($100,000 − $80,000) measures the lessor's dealer's gross profit on the sale. The subsequent entries by the lessor to record collections of periodic rent, interest revenue, and reduction of the lease receivable are the same as the lessor's entries under a direct financing lease.

The classification of leases by the lessor is diagrammed in Exhibit 17–6. A flowchart of the process for classifying leases for both the lessee and the lessor is provided in Exhibit 17–7.

Termination of Lease Agreements

A capital lease agreement may terminate due to a change of provisions in the lease, renewal or extension of the original lease, or expiration of the lease term. *SFAS No. 13* specifies the accounting for termination by the lessee and lessor as follows:
- *By lessor:* On termination, the net carrying value of the investment is removed from the accounts, and the leased asset is recorded at the lower of its original cost, present fair value, or present carrying amount.

EXHIBIT 17–6
Lease Classification: Lessor

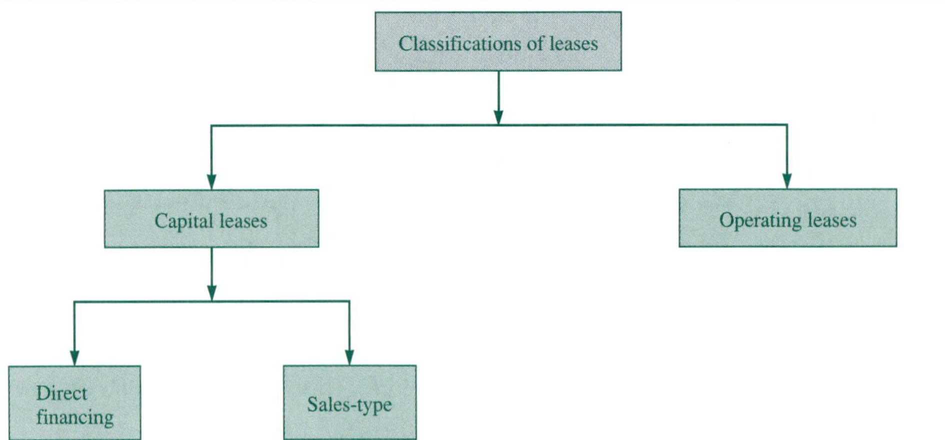

- *By lessee:* On termination, both the net carrying value of the leased asset and the lease liability are removed from the accounts. A gain or loss is recognized in the period of termination for any difference.

Example   Suppose the lease situation described in Exhibit 17–4 is terminated on January 1, 1999, and the January 1 payment is not made. Assume that the fair market value of the leased asset on this date is $61,000. The entries are as follows:

Lessor			Lessee		
Asset	61,000		Lease liability	69,788	
Unearned interest revenue . .	3,324		Accumulated		
Loss on lease			depreciation	33,333	
termination	8,788		Leased asset		100,000
Lease receivable		73,112*	Gain on lease		
			termination		3,121

*$109,688 − $36,556

Lease Entries under an Ordinary Annuity

While it is more common for the lease payments to be in the form of an annuity due, as illustrated in the prior example, the payments also can be in the form of an ordinary annuity. This would be true in the previous example if the payments were due December 31, 1998, 1999, and 2000. In this case, the payments would become

$$\$40,212 = \$100,000 \div (PVA, 10\%, 3) = \$100,000 \div 2.48685.$$

If the lease had involved an ordinary annuity, the *lessor's* entries for 1998 would have been the following:

January 1, 1998—Inception of lease:

Lease receivable ($40,212 × 3)	120,636	
Asset		100,000
Unearned interest revenue		20,636

December 31, 1998—Accrual of interest:

Unearned interest revenue: ($120,636 − $20,636)(.10)	10,000	
Interest revenue		10,000

December 31, 1998—First payment:

Cash	40,212	
Lease receivable		40,212

The lessor does not record depreciation because the asset is transferred and removed from the company's financial statements. The gross investment in this case is $120,636 = 3($40,212). The net investment is unchanged at $100,000. The entries for the following years are identical to those for 1998 except for the interest revenue, which declines each year. On December 31, 1998, *the lessor* would report

1. A net lease receivable of $69,788: ($120,636 − $20,636 + $10,000 − $40,212).

EXHIBIT 17–7   Lease Classification by Lessor and Lessee

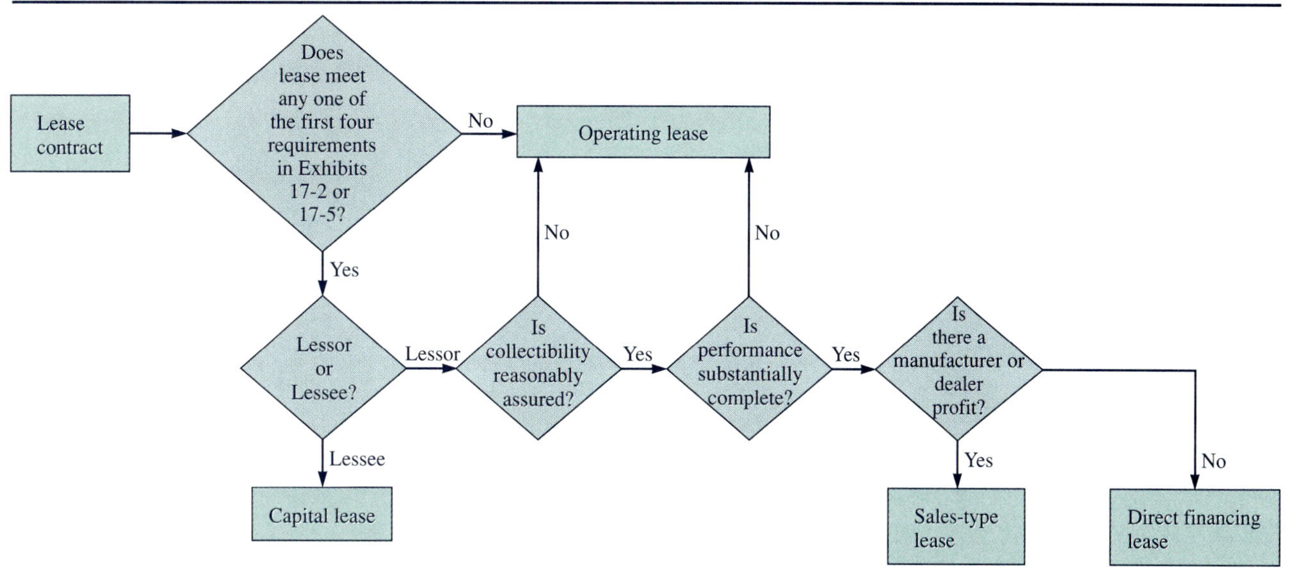

2. Interest revenue of $10,000.

The entries for 1998 on the *lessee's* books are:

January 1, 1998—Inception of lease:

Leased asset	100,000	
Lease liability		100,000

December 31, 1998—Accrual of interest:

Interest expense: $100,000(.10)	10,000	
Lease liability		10,000

December 31, 1998—First payment:

Lease liability	40,212	
Cash		40,212

December 31, 1998—Record depreciation:

Depreciation expense $100,000(1/3)	33,333	
Accumulated depreciation		33,333

For realism, annuities due are used throughout the rest of the chapter.

REVIEW PROBLEM

On January 1, 1998, Merick Inc. purchased an earth mover for $2 million to be leased. The machine is expected to have a 10-year life with no residual value. The machine was leased immediately by Kregor Construction for $340,000 a year payable January 1 of each year starting January 1, 1998. The lease payments are determined using the purchase price of $2 million. The lease term is for eight years with no renewal or bargain purchase option. There are no uncertainties surrounding collection and unreimbursable costs. What type of lease is this to Merick? What is the effect of the lease on Merick's balance sheet at the time the lease is signed? What revenues and expenses are recognized by Merick for the year 1998? (Approximate the answer.)

SOLUTION

This is a direct financing lease because it meets criterion 3 and there is no gross profit. The effect on Merick's balance sheet is to add a lease receivable of $340,000(7) = $2,380,000, an increase in cash by $340,000, a reduction in assets of $2,000,000, and the addition of unearned interest in the amount of $340,000(8) − $2,000,000 = $2,720,000 − $2,000,000 = $720,000.

The lessor's implicit interest rate here is derived by using the PVAD table for eight periods and the value $2,000,000 \div 340,000 = 5.88235$. This process yields an interest rate of approximately 10%. Therefore Merick will recognize only interest revenue in the amount of $.10(\$2,720,000 - \$2,000,000 - \$340,000) = .10(\$380,000) = \$38,000$ in 1998.

CONCEPT REVIEW

1. What two additional criteria must be met before a lease is capitalized by a lessor?
2. What type of annuity is most common for lease payments?
3. Does the lessor recognize depreciation on a sales-type lease or a direct financing lease?

SPECIAL ISSUES IN ACCOUNTING FOR CAPITAL LEASES

Additional issues beyond the fundamentals of accounting for leases include:

1. Bargain purchase options.
2. Bargain renewal options.
3. Residual values.
4. Different interest rates for the lessee and the lessor.
5. Depreciation of the leased asset by the lessee.
6. Executory and initial direct costs.
7. Sale–leaseback arrangements.
8. Classification of lease receivables and payables.
9. Lease disclosure requirements.

Exhibit 17–8 defines technical lease terms according to *SFAS No. 13*. These terms are used extensively in the remainder of this chapter.

Bargain Purchase Options

A bargain purchase option (BPO) permits a lessee to purchase the leased property, during a specified period of the lease term, at a price below the expected market value at that time. This price is set sufficiently low to ensure that the lessee will take advantage of the bargain. In effect, a BPO is viewed as a pending sale and transfer of ownership of the leased asset to the lessee at the specified bargain price. The definition of minimum lease payments in Exhibit 17–8 states (emphasis added)

> If the lease contains a BPO, *only the minimum rental payments* over the lease term and *the BPO payment* are included in the minimum lease payments.

This means that when there is a BPO, any residual values are disregarded when computing the lease rent amount. The residual value is used only to determine whether the purchase option is a bargain.

Including a BPO in a capital lease contract means that there are two sources of cash flows to the lessor from the lessee: one from the periodic rentals and the other from the BPO price. Thus, a BPO affects the amount of the annual rentals required to meet the lessor's target rate of return and the lessee's capitalizable cost of the leased asset. The annual rental in a lease with a BPO is less than in a lease without a BPO, because the lessor recovers part of its investment in the leased asset through the BPO price. The recovery reduces the amount that must be received through rental payments. The lessee includes the present value of the BPO price in computing the cost of the leased asset to be capitalized.

Example   We continue the original Lessor and Lessee company example to illustrate a lease with a BPO by changing items 1, 5, and 7:

1. The estimated life of the asset is four years rather than three years.
5. There is a BPO of $10,000 exercisable at the end of the three-year lease term.

Bargain purchase option (BPO) An option allowing the lessee to purchase the leased property for a price that is sufficiently lower than the expected market value of the property at the exercise date of the option so that exercise appears (at the lease inception date) to be reasonably assured.

Bargain renewal option (BRO) An option allowing the lessee to renew the lease for a rental that is sufficiently lower than the expected market rental of the property at the exercise date of the option so that exercise of the option appears (at the lease inception date) to be reasonably assured.

Estimated residual value of the leased asset The estimated market value of the leased asset at the end of the lease term.

Executory costs Costs of insurance, maintenance, and taxes. These are costs of ownership and use regardless of who pays them and are neither capitalized nor considered in the 90 percent test (criterion 4 in Exhibit 17–2).

Initial direct costs Costs incurred by the lessor in negotiating and consummating a lease agreement, including legal fees, cost of credit investigations, commissions, compensation, and clerical costs directly related to initiating the lease.

Interest rate implicit in the lease The interest rate that, at the lease inception date, equates the present value of (1) the minimum lease payments (excluding any executory costs to be paid by the lessor or lessee) and (2) the unguaranteed residual value.

Lease term The fixed noncancelable term of the lease plus periods covered by bargain renewal options and plus all periods covered by renewal options during which the lessee guarantees debt of the lessor, before the exercise date of a bargain purchase option. The lease term cannot extend beyond the exercise date of a bargain purchase option. In other words, the lease term is the period during which the lessee can reasonably be expected to continue leasing (due, in some cases, to a bargain renewal option or a penalty for nonrenewal such that, at inception, renewal appears reasonably assured).*

Lessee's incremental borrowing rate The interest rate that, at lease inception date, the lessee would have incurred to borrow (over a similar term) the funds necessary to purchase the leased asset.

Minimum lease payments—lessee The rental payments that the lessee is obligated (or can be required) to make in connection with the leased property, excluding executory costs (insurance, maintenance, and taxes) that the lessee is required to pay. If the lease contains a BPO, only the minimum rental payments over the lease term and the BPO payment are included in the minimum lease payments. If the lease does not contain a BPO, minimum lease payments include (1) the minimum rental payments called for by the lease over the lease term, (2) any residual value guaranteed by the lessee at the expiration of the lease term, and (3) any penalty payment the lessee can be required to make if the lease is not renewed or extended at the expiration of the lease term. If the lease term includes periods covered by a penalty for nonrenewal, the penalty is excluded from the minimum lease payments.

Minimum lease payments—lessor Same as the payments described for the lessee plus any residual value guaranteed by a third party unrelated to either the lessee or the lessor. (When there is a BPO, residual value is of no further concern to the lessor because the leased asset is expected to be retained by the lessee at the end of the lease term.)

Unguaranteed residual value The estimated residual value less any portion guaranteed by the lessee or by a third-party guarantor.

*As amended by *SFAS No. 98* (May 1988), par. 22.

7. The estimated residual value of the leased asset is \$15,000 at the BPO exercise date. The asset's residual value at the end of the fourth year is \$0.

The lease continues to be a *direct financing lease* to the *lessor* and a *capital lease* to the *lessee*. The lessor determines the annual lease payment, *P,* to be

$$\$100{,}000 = P(\text{PVAD}, 10\%, 3) + \text{BPO}(\text{PV1}, 10\%, 3)$$
$$\$100{,}000 = P(2.73554) + \$10{,}000(.75131)$$

$$P = (\$100{,}000 - \$7{,}513) \div 2.73554$$
$$P = \$33{,}809$$

As expected, the annual lease payment (\$33,809) is less than in the original example with no BPO (\$36,556). Exhibit 17–9 illustrates lessor and lessee accounting for this lease with a BPO.

If the lessee knows the market value of the asset, the lessee can determine the lessor's

EXHIBIT 17–9 Accounting for a Direct Financing Lease with a Bargain Purchase Option

Lessor			**Lessee**		
January 1, 1998—Inception of lease:					
Lease receivable	111,427*		Leased asset	100,000	
Asset		100,000	Lease liability		100,000
Unearned interest revenue		11,427			
January 1, 1998—First payment:					
Cash	33,809		Lease liability	33,809	
Lease receivable		33,809	Cash		33,809
December 31, 1998—Adjusting entries:					
Unearned interest revenue	6,619		Interest expense	6,619	
Interest revenue*		6,619	Lease liability		6,619
*Computations: See schedule below.			Depreciation expense	25,000	
			Accumulated depreciation		25,000
			($100,000 × ¼)		
December 31, 2000—Exercise of BPO:					
Cash	10,000		Lease liability	10,000	
Lease receivable		10,000	Cash		10,000
*3($33,809) + $10,000					

Lease Amortization Schedule with Bargain Purchase Option (annuity due basis): Lessor and Lessee

Date	Annual Lease Payments	Annual Interest at 10%	Decrease (Increase) in Lease Receivable/Liability	Lease Receivable*/Liability Balance
1/1/98				$100,000
1/1/98	$ 33,809	—	$ 33,809	66,191
12/31/98	—	$ 6,619	(6,619)	72,810
1/1/99	33,809	—	33,809	39,001
12/31/99	—	3,900	(3,900)	42,901
1/1/00	33,809	—	33,809	9,092
12/31/00	—	909	(909)	10,000 (rounded)
12/31/00	10,000	—	10,000	–0–
	$111,427	$11,428	$100,000 (rounded)	

*Net lease receivable.

implicit interest rate on the lease. Alternatively, the lessor may inform the lessee of the rate.[20] With these data, the lessee can compute the capitalizable cost of the leased asset:

$$\$33,809(PVAD, 10\%, 3) + \$10,000(PV1, 10\%, 3)$$
$$= \$33,809(2.73554) + \$10,000(.75131) = \$100,000$$

When there is a BPO, the lessee depreciates the leased asset (less any estimated residual value at the end of the asset's useful life) over its total expected useful life rather than over the lease term. The procedure assumes that the BPO will be exercised, which further implies that the lessee will receive title and permanent ownership of the leased asset.

If on December 31, 2000 (the BPO date), the lessee lets the bargain purchase option lapse, the lessor and the lessee remove all remaining balances related to the lease contract from their respective accounts and recognize a loss. Different entries on December 31, 2000, would replace those in Exhibit 17–9, assuming[21]

---

[20]Assumed here also to equal the incremental borrowing rate of the lessee.

[21]The lessor has a loss of $2,000 because the estimated $8,000 residual value on the BPO date, December 31, 2000, is less than the balance in the lease receivable account of $10,000.

1. A new estimated residual value of $8,000 instead of the original $15,000 estimate.
2. The lease is not renewed.

Lessor:

Asset (new estimated residual value)	8,000	
Loss on lapse of lease purchase option	2,000	
Lease receivable		10,000

Lessee:

Lease liability	10,000	
Loss on lapse of lease purchase option	15,000	
Accumulated depreciation ($25,000 $\times$ 3)	75,000	
Leased property		100,000

Bargain Renewal Options

Criterion 3 in Exhibit 17–2 requires that a lease be classified as a capital lease if the lease term is at least 75 percent of the remaining estimated economic life of the leased asset. One reason determining an asset's lease term is not a simple matter is that a fixed lease term can be extended by a bargain renewal option.[22] A bargain renewal offer (BRO) allows the lessee to renew the lease for a rental that is less than the expected fair market rental at the time the option is exercisable.

If it can be established at the inception of the lease that the rent under the renewal option is low enough at the option's exercise date to imply the exercising of the option, the lease term is extended to cover the additional period. With similar reasoning, *SFAS No. 98,* par. 22, specifies extension of the lease life if substantial penalties are specified for failure to renew or extend the lease for renewal periods preceding a BPO, for renewal periods during which the lessee is a guarantor of the lessor's debt, and for periods representing renewals or extensions of the lease at the lessor's option. However, the lease term never extends beyond the date a BPO becomes exercisable.

Residual Values

Residual values can affect the accounting for both parties in several ways, including computation of the minimum lease payments, the amount to be capitalized by the lessee, and the periodic depreciation expense. Two different estimates of residual value need to be considered when the lease term is shorter than the estimated useful economic life of the leased property: the value at the end of the lease term and the value at the end of the property's estimated useful life. For example, in Exhibit 17–9, the estimated residual value at the end of the three-year lease term is $15,000, whereas the estimated residual value at the end of the asset's four-year life is $0.

The accounting impact of an estimated residual value at the end of the lease term in a capital lease depends on whether the residual value is retained by the lessor or transferred to the lessee.

Residual Value Transferred to Lessee   The lessee receives the residual value in one of two ways:

1. If the lease provides for transfer of title to the lessee (criterion 1 in Exhibit 17–2), the leased property and its residual value at the end of the lease term belong to the lessee at no additional cost beyond the lease payments. This residual value affects neither the lessor's accounting nor the lessee's cost to be capitalized. Rather, the lessee depreciates the asset over its total economic life, using the estimated residual value at the *end* of that life in the calculation.
2. If the lease includes a BPO (criterion 2 in Exhibit 17–2), the asset is assumed to revert to the lessee. Therefore, the asset is depreciated as in point 1 above.

Residual Value Retained by Lessor   If only criterion 3 or 4 is met (Exhibit 17–2), the lessor retains the residual value and gets the leased asset back at the end of the lease term. To reduce the risk that the lessee will not properly maintain the leased asset, in which case

---

[22]Determining the economic life is also not simple, particularly for specialized assets. This issue is covered in Chapter 12.

the residual value would be less, the lease agreement may require the lessee to guarantee all or part of the estimated residual value. Thus, the estimated residual value retained by the lessor at the end of the lease term may be:

- Unguaranteed.
- Guaranteed in full by the lessee.
- Guaranteed in part by the lessee.
- Guaranteed by a third party for a fee depending upon the provisions of the lease agreement.

These four cases are discussed next.

Residual Value Unguaranteed   When the residual value of the leased asset is unguaranteed, the lessor computes the periodic rentals by deducting the present value of the estimated residual value from the market value of the asset. The lessee capitalizes only the lease payments, excluding any amount for residual value because the lessee does not guarantee the residual value, whereas the lessor capitalizes the residual value because it accrues to the lessor at the end of the lease term. (This creates a situation in which the entries by lessee and lessor are not symmetrical.)

Exhibit 17–10 illustrates a direct financing lease with a $10,000 **unguaranteed residual value** at the end of the lease term. The residual value replaces the BPO in the previous example. Otherwise the data are unchanged. The lessor's computation of the annual rentals in which the present value of the unguaranteed residual value is deducted yields $33,809, obtained by solving:

$$\$100,000 = P(PVAD, 10\%, 3) + \$10,000(PV1, 10\%, 3) \text{ for P.}$$

This is the same amount calculated for the lease when a $10,000 BPO was involved. Yet because the $10,000 residual value is not guaranteed by the lessee, the lessee capitalizes only the net asset cost of $92,487 = $33,809(PVAD, 10%, 3). The lessor capitalizes the three lease payments plus the residual value because the unguaranteed residual value is part of the asset's total value.

Exhibit 17–10 gives selected entries for the lessor and lessee and the lessee's computation of the cost of the leased asset. The entries (and amortization schedules) of the lessor and lessee differ (even though they are using the same implicit interest rate) because the estimated unguaranteed residual value appears in the lessor's accounts but is not capitalized in the lessee's accounts. The lessor's entry on January 1, 1998, the date of inception of the lease, removes the cost of the leased asset and records the receivable, which includes the $10,000 residual value. The last entry, made by the lessor at the termination of the lease, removes the residual value ($10,000) from the receivable account and returns it to its original asset account.

The lessor's amortization schedule shown in Exhibit 17–10, leaves an ending asset balance of $10,000 (the residual value) in the lessor's lease receivable account at the end of the lease term. The initial value in the lease receivable account (at net) for the lessor is the lessor's cost of the leased asset, $100,000, because the lessor plans to recover the total cost from the lessee's payments and the asset's residual value. In contrast, the lessee's amortization schedule starts with the lease liability amount ($92,487), which excludes the present value of the residual value, and ends with a zero balance. Because there is no transfer of title or BPO in this example, the lessee depreciates the leased asset over the lease term, disregarding the unguaranteed residual value.

For a sales-type lease with an unguaranteed residual value, *SFAS No. 13* requires that the lessor deduct the present value of the unguaranteed residual value from both sales revenue and cost of goods sold, to avoid overstating both. This does not affect the manufacturer's or dealer's profit, the lease receivable, or annual interest revenue.

Exhibit 17–11 shows the case of the sales-type lease used earlier, but now with an unguaranteed residual value of $10,000. (The value of the asset on the lessor's books before the sale is $80,000.) Both sales revenue ($92,487) and cost of goods sold ($72,487) are computed by deducting the present value of the unguaranteed residual value [$10,000(PV1, 10%, 3) = $10,000(0.75131) = $7,513] from the cash equivalent price ($100,000) and car-

EXHIBIT 17–10   Accounting for a Direct Financing Lease with a $10,000 Unguaranteed Residual Value

Lessor			**Lessee**	
January 1, 1998—Inception of lease:				
Lease receivable	111,427*		Leased asset	92,487[†]
Asset		100,000	Lease liability		92,487
Unearned interest revenue		11,427		

*This amount includes the $10,000 residual value in the lease receivable account. 3($33,809) + $10,000.

[†]Lessee's computation of cost of leased asset (the unguaranteed residual value is not capitalized by the lessee):
$$33,809(\text{PVAD}, 10\%, 3) = \$33,809(2.73554).$$

Lessor			**Lessee**	
January 1, 1998—First payment:				
Cash	33,809		Lease liability	33,809
Lease receivable		33,809	Cash		33,809
December 31, 1998—Adjusting entries:				
Unearned interest revenue	6,619		Interest expense	5,868
Interest revenue		6,619	Lease liability		5,868
See lessor's amortization schedule below.			See lessee's amortization schedule below.	
			Depreciation expense	30,829
			Accumulated depreciation ($92,487 × ⅓)		30,829
December 31, 2000—End of lease term: to remove the residual value from the lease receivable account:			To remove the asset from the accounts:	
			Accumulated depreciation	92,487
Asset	10,000		Leased asset		92,487
Lease receivable		10,000		

Lease Amortization Schedule (annuity due basis)

		Lessor			**Lessee**		
Date	**Lease Payments**	**Interest at 10%**	**Receivable Decrease (increase)**	**Net Receivable Balance**	**Interest at 10%**	**Liability Decrease (increase)**	**Liability Balance**
1/1/98	Initial value			$100,000			$92,487
1/1/98	$ 33,809	—	$33,809	66,191	—	$33,809	58,678
12/31/98	—	$ 6,619	(6,619)	72,810	$5,868	(5,868)	64,546
1/1/99	33,809	—	33,809	39,001	—	33,809	30,737
12/31/99	—	3,900	(3,900)	42,901	3,074	(3,074)	33,811
1/1/00	33,809	—	33,809	9,092	—	33,809	–0–*
12/31/00	—	909	(909)	10,000*			
	$101,427[†]	$11,427*	$90,000*		$8,942	$92,487*	

*Rounded.

[†]$10,000 could be added to reflect disposal of the leased asset.

rying value ($80,000), respectively. This approach results in the same manufacturer's or dealer's profit as when the residual value is guaranteed, but both sales revenue and cost of goods sold are reduced because the residual value reverts to the lessor. The residual amount, because it is not guaranteed, is the amount of the asset that cannot be considered sold at inception.

Residual Value Fully Guaranteed by Lessee   A lease agreement may require the lessee to guarantee some portion of the asset's residual value as motivation to take care of the asset during the lease period. If the residual value estimated at the inception of the lease is fully guaranteed by the lessee, the lessee must pay the cash equivalent to make up any residual value deficiency. The valuation is based on an appraisal (usually by an independent party) at the end of the lease term. Continuing the example used in Exhibit 17–10, assume that the actual residual value at the end of the lease term determined in accordance

EXHIBIT 17–11   Accounting for a Sales-Type Lease with a $10,000 Unguaranteed Residual Value

<table>
<tr><td colspan="3" align="center">Lessor</td><td colspan="3" align="center">Lessee</td></tr>
<tr><td colspan="6">January 1, 1998—Inception of lease:</td></tr>
<tr><td>Lease receivable . . . .</td><td>111,427</td><td></td><td>Leased asset . . . .</td><td>92,487*</td><td></td></tr>
<tr><td>Cost of goods sold . . . .</td><td>72,487*</td><td></td><td>Lease liability . . . .</td><td></td><td>92,487</td></tr>
<tr><td>Sales revenue . . . .</td><td></td><td>92,487†</td><td></td><td></td><td></td></tr>
<tr><td>Asset. . . . .</td><td></td><td>80,000</td><td></td><td></td><td></td></tr>
<tr><td>Unearned interest revenue. . . . . . .</td><td></td><td>11,427</td><td></td><td></td><td></td></tr>
</table>

*Lessor's cost of goods sold is the carrying value of the asset ($80,000) less the present value of the unguaranteed residual value $10,000(PV1, 10%, 3) = $7,513. Thus, ($80,000 − $7,513) = $72,487.

†Lessor's sales revenue: $100,000 − $7,513 = $92,487.

*Lessee's computation of leased asset cost excluding the unguaranteed residual value is $33,809(PVAD, 10%, 3) = $33,809(2.73554) = $92,487

<table>
<tr><td colspan="6">January 1, 1998—First payment:</td></tr>
<tr><td>Cash . . . .</td><td>33,809</td><td></td><td>Lease liability. . . . .</td><td>33,809</td><td></td></tr>
<tr><td>Lease receivable. . . . .</td><td></td><td>33,809</td><td>Cash . . . .</td><td></td><td>33,809</td></tr>
<tr><td colspan="6">December 31, 1998—Adjusting entries:</td></tr>
<tr><td>Unearned interest revenue . . . .</td><td>6,619</td><td></td><td>Interest expense. . . . .</td><td>5,868</td><td></td></tr>
<tr><td>Interest revenue . . . .</td><td></td><td>6,619</td><td>Lease liability . . . .</td><td></td><td>5,868</td></tr>
</table>

See lessor's amortization schedule in Exhibit 17–10.

See lessee's amortization schedule in Exhibit 17–10.

<table>
<tr><td>Depreciation expense. . . . .</td><td>30,829</td><td></td></tr>
<tr><td>Accumulated depreciation
($92,487 × ⅓) . . . .</td><td></td><td>30,829</td></tr>
</table>

<table>
<tr><td colspan="3">December 31, 2000—(end of lease term)—To remove the
residual value from the lease receivable account:</td><td colspan="3">To remove the asset from the accounts: . . . . .</td></tr>
<tr><td>Asset . . . .</td><td>10,000</td><td></td><td>Accumulated depreciation . . . .</td><td>92,487</td><td></td></tr>
<tr><td>Lease receivable. . . . .</td><td></td><td>10,000</td><td>Leased asset</td><td></td><td>92,487</td></tr>
</table>

Lease Amortization Schedule (annuity due basis)—Same as Exhibit 17–10

with the lease contract is $9,000, rather than the previously estimated $10,000. Assuming a fully guaranteed residual value, the lessee must pay the lessor $1,000 cash.

The lessor's accounting is the same whether the residual is guaranteed or not.

A capital lease with a residual value fully guaranteed by the lessee is illustrated in Exhibit 17–12, using the same data as in Exhibit 17–10 (direct financing lease). The lessor deducts the present value of the guaranteed residual value to compute the periodic rentals. The lessee capitalizes $100,000 (the same amount recognized by the lessor), which is the present value of the payments committed to by the lessee as well as the asset's market value. The lessee capitalizes the sum of these two amounts because the lease liability includes the guarantee.

At termination of the lease on December 31, 2000, the actual residual value is determined (independently and as specified in the lease agreement). This residual value then is compared with the guaranteed residual value to determine whether the lessee owes the lessor additional consideration. If, as is assumed here, the actual residual value at the end of 2000 is determined independently to be $9,000, the lessee is obligated to pay the lessor $1,000 cash ($10,000 − $9,000). If the guaranteed value is less than the actual value, the lessor has no obligation to make a refund to the lessee.

The estimated residual value of an asset under a capital lease must be reviewed annually to determine whether it is realistic. If the estimate is revised by a material amount, a change in estimate should be recognized and the subsequent lease entries (and schedules) revised accordingly.

A fully guaranteed residual value is accounted for in the same way for both direct and sales-type leases. Because there is neither a transfer of title at the end of the lease nor a BPO (neither criterion 1 or 2 of Exhibit 17–2 is met), depreciation is based on the term of the lease, three years in this example. The residual value reverts to the lessor; therefore, the lessee deducts the guaranteed residual when computing depreciation.

EXHIBIT 17–12   Accounting for a Direct Financing Lease with a $10,000 Residual Value Guaranteed by the Lessee

Lessor			Lessee		
January 1, 1998—Inception of lease:					
Lease receivable.	111,427		Leased asset	100,000*	
Asset		100,000*	Lease liability		100,000
Unearned interest revenue		11,427			
January 1, 1998—First payment:					
Cash.	33,809		Lease liability	33,809	
Lease receivable		33,809	Cash.		33,809
December 31, 1998—Adjusting entries:					
Unearned interest revenue	6,619†		Interest expense	6,619†	
Interest revenue		6,619	Lease liability.		6,619
			Depreciation expense	30,000	
			Accumulated depreciation		30,000
			($100,000 − $10,000) × ⅓		
December 31, 2000—Lease termination assuming an actual residual value of $9,000:					
Asset (market value)	9,000		Accumulated depreciation	90,000	
Cash ($10,000 − $9,000).	1,000		Lease liability	10,000	
Lease receivable		10,000‡	Loss on lease contract	1,000	
			Leased asset.		100,000
			Cash.		1,000

*$33,809(PVAD, 10%, 3) + $10,000(PV1, 10%, 3) =
$33,809(2.73554) + $10,000(0.75131).

†See amortization schedule below.

‡Guaranteed residual value.

Lease Amortization Schedule (annuity due basis)

Date	Lease Payments	Interest at 10%	Decrease (Increase) in Receivable/Liability	Net Lease Receivable/Liability Balance
1/1/98	Initial value			$100,000
1/1/98	$ 33,809	—	$33,809	66,191
12/31/98	—	$ 6,619	(6,619)	72,810
1/1/99	33,809	—	33,809	39,001
12/31/99	—	3,900	(3,900)	42,901
1/1/00	33,809	—	33,809	9,092
12/31/00	—	908	(908)	10,000 (guaranteed residual value)
	$101,427	$11,427	$90,000	

In the case of a sales-type lease, sales and cost of goods sold are not reduced by the present value of the residual if guaranteed by the lessee or a third party. The guarantee supports the recognition of the entire amount of sales and cost of goods sold.

Residual Value Partially Guaranteed by the Lessee   A lessee may guarantee only a part of the estimated residual value of the leased asset, but the lessor still bases the computation of the periodic lease payments (and the related amortization schedule) on the total estimated residual value. The lessee, however, capitalizes only the present value of the partially guaranteed amount. Again, the amounts recorded by the lessor and lessee would not be the same.

Residual Value Guaranteed by a Third Party   The residual value of a leased asset may be guaranteed in full or in part by a third-party guarantor, usually procured by the lessor for a fee. As in the case of the lessee guarantee of residual value, the lessor deducts the amount of the guarantee to compute the lease payments because the cash for any residual value deficiency will come from a different source. The lessor's receivable includes both the present value of the rental payments and the guaranteed residual value. The lessee, however, does not include the present value of the guaranteed residual value in the cost of the leased asset because the residual value is guaranteed by a third party (not the lessee). This again results in asymmetrical entries by the lessor and lessee.

Example   To illustrate this case, assume now that the $10,000 residual value is guaranteed by a third party (using the Exhibit 17–10 situation). The entries are the same as those shown in Exhibit 17–10. The procedure is the same for direct financing and sales-type leases. The calculations once again lead to rental payments of $33,809 by the lessee because the lessor is assured of the $10,000 from a third party.

The lessor includes the residual value as part of the lease payments, resulting in a lease receivable of 3($33,809) + $10,000 = $111,427. The present value of the lease payments including the guaranteed residual is $100,000. Because this present value is greater than 90 percent of the leased asset's market value at the inception of the lease [$100,000(.90) = $90,000], the lease satisfies criterion 4 in Exhibit 17–5 for a capital lease to the lessor. Since the present value of the lease payments, excluding the residual value, is $92,487, which also exceeds 90 percent of the leased asset's market value of $100,000, the lessee also treats the lease as a capital lease.

An interesting result occurs if the lessor has a third-party guarantee of $20,000 for the residual value. (Suppose, also, that the asset's economic life is now five years but the lease term remains unchanged at three years.) In this situation, the lessor reduces the rentals to $31,063 in recognition of the larger receivable guaranteed for the residual value:

$$[\$100,000 - \$20,000(\text{PV1, }10\%, 3)] \div (\text{PVAD, }10\%, 3) =$$
$$[\$100,000 - \$20,000(.75131)] \div (2.73554) = \$31,063$$

The lessor capitalizes the value of the lease payments plus the residual value to obtain $113,189: $31,063(3) + $20,000. The present value of the lease payments and the guaranteed residual is again $100,000. This amount exceeds 90 percent of the leased asset's fair market value (.9 × $100,000 = $90,000), and hence the lease satisfies criterion 4 in Exhibit 17–5 for a capital lease to the lessor. However, the guaranteed residual value by a third party is excluded from the minimum lease payments for the lessee, who computes only the present value of the $31,063 payments, obtaining $84,974 = $31,063(PVAD, 10%, 3) = $31,063(2.73554). This amount is *less* than 90 percent of the market value of the asset at lease inception = [$90,000 = .9($100,000)]. Because of this result, and the fact that the other criteria for a capital lease (Exhibit 17–2) are not met in this case, the lessee treats the lease as an operating lease. The lease term is only ⅗ of the asset's useful life, and there is no title transfer or BPO. The entries for this special case are given in Exhibit 17–13. Neither party records depreciation: The lessor now has a financial asset (receivable) but the lessee shows no recorded asset.

Using a third-party guarantor may thus allow a lessor to record a lease as a capital lease, while the lessee can record the lease as an operating lease, thereby circumventing the FASB's attempt to ensure accounting symmetry between lessor and lessee.[23] Unwittingly, the FASB, in publishing *SFAS No. 13,* can take credit for spawning a new submarket of third-party guarantor companies whose sole function is to guarantee, for a fee, the residual values of business leases.

One of the services many investment banking and securities firms now provide is assistance in structuring leases so that lessees can keep leases off their balance sheets while lessors account for them as direct financing leases. The use of a third-party guarantor is one way to accomplish this result. Investment bankers generally engage in this business as commission brokers and underwriters, not as principals in the leases themselves. Not all leases

---

[23]Lessors usually prefer to account for leases as capital leases, and lessees usually prefer to account for leases as operating leases. The two parties have engaged a third party to accept some of the lease transaction risks in regard to the ultimate value of the leased asset. Since the lessor has shifted a significant part of the risk to this third party, it can be argued that the economics of the transaction are different and the accounting should also be different.

EXHIBIT 17–13   Accounting for a Direct Financing Lease with a $20,000 Residual Value Guaranteed by a Third Party

Lessor (direct financing lease)		Lessee (operating lease)	
January 1, 1998—Inception of lease:			
Lease receivable 113,189*		No entry.	
Asset	100,000		
Unearned interest revenue.	13,189		
January 1, 1998—First payment:			
Cash 31,063		Rent expense.	31,063
Lease receivable.	31,063	Cash	31,063
December 31, 1998—Adjusting entries:			
Unearned interest revenue 6,894		No entry.	
Interest revenue	6,894		

See lessor amortization schedule below.

*3($31,063) + $20,000

Lessor's Lease Amortization Schedule (annuity due basis)

Date	Lease Payments	Interest at 10%	Decrease (Increase) in Receivable	Net Lease Receivable Balance
1/1/98	Initial value			$100,000
1/1/98	$31,063	—	$31,063	68,937
12/31/98	—	$ 6,894	(6,894)	75,831
1/1/99	31,063	—	31,063	44,768
12/31/99	—	4,477	(4,477)	49,245
1/1/00	31,063	—	31,063	18,182
12/31/00	—	1,818	(1,818)	20,000 (guaranteed residual value)
	$93,189	$13,189	$80,000	

handled by investment banks are split operating/direct financing deals. A typical lease deal might entail a $50 million equipment lease, with a Fortune 500 company as the lessee and a syndicate of institutional investors (primarily insurance companies and pension funds) as the lessors. The investment bank earns a fee for putting the deal together.

Exhibit 17–14 summarizes the accounting under different residual value situations.

Different Interest Rates

So far we have assumed that the lessor's implicit interest rate and the lessee's incremental borrowing rate are equal. For convenience and math ease, a 10 percent rate was used in most of the illustrations. Suppose, instead, that the lessor's implicit interest rate is 9 percent and the lessee's incremental borrowing rate remains at 10 percent. Which rate should be used?

This question in fact applies only to the lessee. The lessor knows the asset's cost and the amount and number of payments and thus can determine the interest rate implicit in the lease. Lessees must use their incremental borrowing rate unless the lessor's implicit interest rate is known to the lessee *and is lower* than the lessee's own borrowing rate.

The phrase *if it is known* in *SFAS No. 13* may seem to imply secrecy about the interest rate charged. In fact, most leasing transactions are quite open. Although the lessor's interest rate is not explicitly stated in the lease contract, it usually is communicated orally and may also be found in business documents accompanying the lease. The rate charged by the lessor is frequently subject to negotiation. Thus, in most cases, the lessee simply uses the lower of its incremental borrowing rate or the lessor's implicit interest rate.

In some cases, however, the implicit interest rate may not be known to the lessee's accounting staff (or external accountants). If, for example, the lessee uses independent business brokers to negotiate the lease, these outside representatives may be unavailable for questions or not attuned to the company's information needs. Accountants, therefore must rely on the lease contract for detailed accounting information.

Situation	Symmetrical Entries and Schedules?	Reason
1. No residual value	Yes	No residual value effect on either party.
2. Unguaranteed residual value (Exhibits 17–10 and 17–11)	No	Lessor includes the residual value in the capitalized lease asset. Lessee excludes the present value of the residual value from the leased asset.
3. Residual value fully guaranteed by lessee (Exhibit 17–12)	Yes	Lessor includes the residual value in the capitalized lease asset. Lessee includes the present value of the fully guaranteed residual in the leased asset.
4. Residual value partially guaranteed by lessee (not illustrated)	No	Lessor includes the total residual value in the capitalized lease asset. Lessee includes only the present value of the portion of residual value in the leased asset it guarantees.
5. Full or part residual value guarantee by third party (Exhibit 17–10, assuming the residual is guaranteed by a third party.)	No	Lessor includes the total residual value guarantee in the capitalized lease asset. Lessee excludes the present value of the residual value from the leased asset.

SFAS No. 13 is targeted to lessees who persist in treating lease transactions as operating rather than capital leases. Here's how interest rates fit into their plans: The higher the interest rate assigned to a leasing transaction, the lower is the dollar amount capitalized as a leased asset, given that the total dollar amounts of the minimum lease payments are fixed. If the capitalized portion can be kept below 90 percent of the leased asset's fair market value (and none of the other criteria for capitalization is met), the lessee can treat the transaction as an operating lease and omit the lease liability from the balance sheet.

Example   Assume that a lessee—for whatever reason—wishes to account for a leasing transaction as an operating lease rather than a capital lease. The same $100,000 example asset used throughout this chapter is also used here. Again, the lease term is three years, and the asset is assumed to have a $10,000 residual value at the end of the lease term. The minimum lease payments are $33,809 for three years, and the lessee does not know the lessor's implicit interest rate of 10 percent.[24]

The lessee knows that the market value of the asset being rented is $100,000, and the annual rental payments will be $33,809. The residual value is unknown to the lessee. Suppose the lessee determines that its incremental borrowing rate is 14 percent. The lessee then computes the present value to be

$$\$33,809(PVAD, 14\%, 3) = \$33,809(2.64666) = \$89,481$$

The calculations for both interest rates are:

Rate	Lease Payment		Present Value Annuity Due Factor		Present Value of Lease Payments	Percent of Asset's Market Value
10%	$33,809	×	2.73554	=	92,487	92.487%
14%	$33,809	×	2.64666	=	89,481	89.481%

---

[24]This example also assumes that the lease includes neither a transfer of ownership provision nor a bargain purchase option, and that the lease term is less than 75 percent of the asset's total useful economic life, criteria 1, 2, and 3 of Exhibit 17–2.

If left unchallenged, the lessee could account for the transaction as an operating lease because, using 14 percent, $89,481 is only 89 percent of the asset's market value, while the lessor accounts for it as a direct financing lease.

Lessees are normally aware of the fair market cost of the assets they lease, and they know the minimum lease payments and the term of the lease. They may not, however, know the leased asset's residual value as of the end of the lease term (a value that is included and discounted by the lessor in establishing the lease payments) because lessees are not interested in buying this portion of the asset's value. If the residual value is not known, the lessee cannot determine the implicit interest rate used by the lessor. In this case, lessees use their incremental borrowing rate as described previously.

The example illustrates a case in which the lessee can use a higher discount rate than the lessor's rate. If the lower (lessor) rate is known to the lessee, *SFAS No. 13* requires the lessee to use the lower rate. This not only makes it more likely the lessee will capitalize the lease but also prevents the lessee from understating the lease liability if capitalization is required.

Depreciation of a Leased Asset by the Lessee

The depreciable life and estimated residual value used by the lessee in computing periodic depreciation expense in a capital lease arrangement depend on the terms of the lease contract. If the lease does not provide for a transfer of ownership to the lessee at the end of the lease term or a BPO (criteria 1 and 2 in Exhibit 17–2), the period of depreciation must be the lease term rather than the life of the leased property. In this case, the lessee ignores any unguaranteed residual value when computing depreciation expense. However, the lessee deducts any portion of the residual it guarantees when computing depreciation.

If ownership of the leased asset is to be transferred from the lessor to the lessee at the end of the lease term or the lease contains a BPO, the lessee depreciates the capitalized cost over the total economic life of the leased asset to the lessee (rather than over the term of the lease). In this case, the lessee uses the estimated residual value as of the end of the asset's useful life (rather than as of the end of the lease term). The longer economic life and lower residual value are used in such cases because the lessee is assumed to retain the asset after the end of the lease term.

Executory and Initial Direct Costs

Two kinds of lease costs incurred by the lessor are given special accounting treatment. They are executory costs and initial direct costs.

Executory costs are expenses of ownership and use. They include insurance, property taxes, and maintenance. In the case of an operating lease, the executory costs are typically paid by the lessor and recovered by the lessor through the periodic lease rentals. In the case of a capital lease, a major part, if not all, of the executory costs are shifted by the lease contract to the lessee and are not included in the periodic rentals. To the extent that any executory costs incurred by the lessor are added to the current lease payment, they should be excluded from the present value of the periodic rentals for capitalization purposes by both parties. They are then reported as an expense when incurred. If such executory costs are not known by the lessee at the time the current lease payment is made, they should be estimated.

Example   Assume that the lessor in Exhibit 17–4 agrees to insure the leased asset at a cost of $1,000 per year and then to bill the lessee. The annual lease payment would then be $37,556. This amount is equal to the annual minimum lease payment required to yield a 10 percent rate of return to the lessor ($36,556) plus the annual executory costs ($1,000). The executory costs are *excluded* by the lessee in computing the amount capitalized. The interest revenue accruing to the lessor and the interest expense of the lessee are unaffected by the executory costs because the $1,000 is paid directly to the insurer.

Journal entries to reflect the annual executory costs incurred by the lessor on the date of the first rental are as follows:

January 1, 1998—First payment:

Lessor:

Cash	37,556	
Lease receivable		36,556
Insurance payable (or prepaid insurance if already paid)		1,000

Lessee:

Lease liability	36,556	
Insurance expense (or prepaid insurance)	1,000	
Cash		37,556

Initial direct costs are incremental costs incurred by the lessor in negotiating and consummating a specific lease agreement. They include legal fees, cost of credit and other investigations, commissions and employee compensation directly related to initiating the lease, and the clerical costs of preparing and processing the lease documents. These costs have no effect on the lessee's accounting but do affect the lessor's accounting. Initial direct costs exclude costs of advertising, soliciting potential lessees, and servicing existing leases.

In the case of an *operating lease,* the initial direct costs should be expensed by the lessor over the lease term on a reasonable basis (usually straight line) in order to match them with revenues that they helped earn. In the case of a *direct financing lease,* initial direct costs are included in the lessor's gross investment in the lease. This means that these costs must be added to the cost of the leased asset to compute the annual rentals. On this point *SFAS No. 91,* par. 23, states that

> Lessors shall account for initial direct costs as part of the investment in a direct financing lease. The practice of recognizing a portion of the unearned income at inception of the lease to offset initial direct costs shall no longer be acceptable.

The effect of this requirement is to spread the indirect costs over the term of the lease and thereby match the expenditures with the related interest revenue.

Example Suppose the lease in the continuing example (see Exhibit 17–4) involved initial direct costs of $6,000. The lease is a direct financing lease to the lessor. The investment to be recovered is now $100,000 plus $6,000, or $106,000. If the lessor continues to require a 10 percent return, the periodic payment will be

$$\$106,000 = P(\text{PVAD}, 10\%, 3)$$
$$P = \$38,749$$

The lessor's entries for the first year would be:

January 1, 1998—To record the lease:

Lease receivable	122,247*	
Asset		100,000
Cash		6,000
Unearned interest revenue		16,247

*3($38,749) + $6,000

January 1, 1998—First payment:

Cash	38,749	
Lease receivable		38,749

December 31, 1998—To recognize interest earned:

Unearned interest revenue*	6,725	
Interest revenue		6,725

*($106,000 − $38,749)(.10)

In the case of a *sales-type lease,* the initial direct costs should be expensed by the lessor in the year in which the lease is initiated (as an offset to the manufacturer's or dealer's profit) because these costs are considered to be a selling expense in the year of sale.

REVIEW PROBLEM

Consider again the Merick-Kregor data used in the two previous review problems:

On January 1, 1998, Merick Inc. purchased an earth mover for $2 million to be leased. The machine is expected to have a 10-year life with no residual value. The machine was leased immediately by Kregor Construction for $340,000 a year payable January 1 of each year starting January 1, 1998. The lease term is eight years with no renewal or bargain purchase option. There are no uncertainties surrounding collection and unreimbursable costs. Both firms use a 10 percent interest rate. Supply answers for the following questions treating each one independently of the others.

a. Suppose now that (1) the rental payment is changed such that the present value of the payments is $1.4 million and (2) the useful life of the equipment at the inception of the lease is 11 years. Would there be any effect on the lease classification for either party?

b. Retaining the change in part *a,* suppose the lease now includes an option to purchase the asset for a nominal $1. What type of lease would result for both parties? Would the accounting results change from the previous answers to the former review problems?

c. Return to the original data. Now suppose the lessee were to guarantee a positive residual value to the equipment at the end of the eighth year. Should the lessee include the present value of the residual in the initial value assigned to the lease obligation? Should the lessor include it in the value of the receivable?

d. Suppose in part *c* that the residual was instead guaranteed by a third party. What now is the answer to the two questions in *c* and why is this a particularly important issue?

SOLUTION

a. Yes, for both parties the lease is now an operating lease because none of the four criteria are met. Title is not transferred, there is no bargain purchase option, the ratio of lease term to useful life is $8/11$ (73 percent)—which is less than 75 percent, and the present value of the minimum lease payments is less than 90 percent of the market value of the asset at inception ($1.4/$2 = 70%$).

b. The lease would now be a capital lease for both parties. It meets criterion 2 of Exhibit 17–2 because the $1 purchase option is undoubtedly less than the residual value at the end of year eight (the asset has two years of life remaining at this point). The accounting would not change because the BPO is too small to affect the present values.

c. The answer is yes for both parties.

d. The lessor would include the guarantee in the receivable but the lessee would not because the lessee has no responsibility for the residual. This is important because this structuring of the lease agreement may allow the lessee to avoid meeting criterion 4, and therefore account for the lease as an operating lease. By not capitalizing the residual, the present value of the lessee's minimum lease payments may be less than 90 percent of the market value of the asset at inception.

CONCEPT REVIEW

1. Explain why, for a lessee, the present value of the residual value guaranteed by the lessee is included in the recorded lease obligation but is excluded if the guarantee is by a third party.
2. Under what conditions must the lessee use the lessor's implicit interest rate? Why does this requirement exist?
3. What are executory costs, and why does the lessee exclude them from the present value calculation of the lease liability?

Sale–Leaseback Arrangements

As the term indicates, the owner of an asset in a **sale–leaseback (SLB)** arrangement sells it to a leasing company or other party and immediately leases it back.[25] The asset itself never leaves the seller–lessee's possession.

---

[25]Sale–leaseback transactions are subject to the provisions of *SFAS No. 13,* par. 32–34, as amended by *SFAS No. 28.*

Like leasing in general, from the lessee's perspective, sale–leaseback transactions are essentially financing transactions and, in some cases, off-balance-sheet financing devices. Some of the reasons lessees engage in sale–leaseback transactions are:

- Fully depreciated assets afford no tax savings beyond maintenance and insurance expenses. *Action:* Sell the asset and lease it back. The lease payments will be tax deductible.
- In the majority of sale–leaseback transactions, the sale of assets generates immediate cash inflow. *Action:* If liquidity is a problem, or if expansion capital is needed, the sale–leaseback of assets (without giving up operating possession) provides an immediate inflow of cash equal to 100 percent of the asset's current market value. In contrast, asset-secured bank loans are typically limited to 75 percent or 80 percent of the asset's market value.
- A sale–leaseback often entails a gain on the sale of the asset, which normally must be deferred and amortized over the life of the accompanying leasing arrangement. However, if the total value of the leaseback (minimum lease payments at present value) is less than substantially all of the asset's total market value, a sizable portion of the gain may be recognized as current income.[26] *Action:* Buildings and other tangible assets that are owned but only partially occupied or used for business purposes, can be sold for a profit; only a portion of the building's space, or only a portion of a tangible asset's utility value, is leased back to the seller. Thus, a portion of the profits on the sale most likely would be reported as current income.[27]
- Sale–leaseback used as a refinancing tool can reduce interest expense. *Action:* If past asset acquisitions are being financed at a higher interest rate than now prevails, sale–leaseback is an effective means of refinancing at lower interest rates.
- Tax liabilities, such as those due to personal property taxes in some states, can result in serious drains of cash resources. *Action:* Sale–leaseback can alleviate the tax burden.

From the lessor's standpoint, sale–leaseback yields no special advantages or disadvantages; it is simply a financing transaction. The characteristics of a typical sale–leaseback arrangement may be diagrammed as follows:

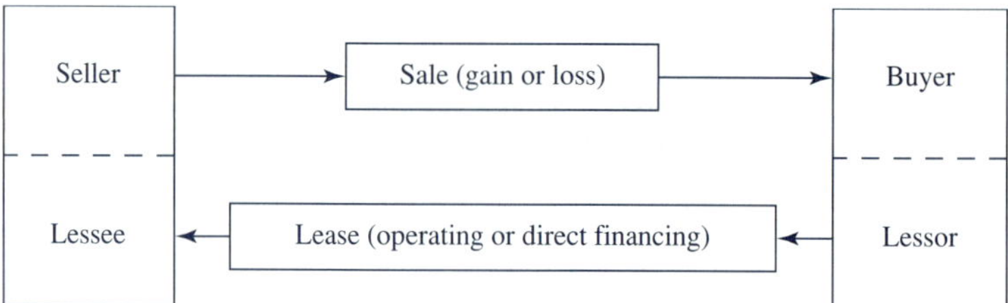

Accounting for Sale–Leaseback Transactions   Sale–leasebacks, like regular leases, are accounted for by lessees as either capital or operating leases depending on the criteria listed earlier. If the lease provisions meet any of the four criteria in Exhibit 17–2, the lessee must account for the transaction as a capital lease; if none of the criteria is met, the transaction is accounted for as an operating lease.

The same criteria apply to the lessor, plus the two additional criteria (5*a* and 5*b*, Exhibit 17–5) relating to lessors. Lessors account for sale–leaseback transactions as direct financing or operating leases. Sales-type leases are not permitted (as they would result in over-

---

[26]The phrase *substantially all* is generally interpreted to mean 90 percent of the asset's fair market value at the inception of the lease. *SFAS No. 28* calls for profits on the sale of assets included in a sale–leaseback transaction to be deferred and amortized up to the extent of the total minimum lease payments, computed at present value. Profits in excess of the minimum lease payments should be recognized and reported at the time of the sale–leaseback.

[27]An example of this application concerns large corporations that own major office buildings as corporate headquarters. In many of these office towers, the owner–tenant may occupy only 30 percent or 40 percent of the total space, renting out the remaining space to other businesses. Rather than keeping its capital tied up in owning real estate, the owner–tenant may find it advantageous to sell the property (usually at a sizable profit over the building's book value) and lease back only the space actually occupied. In many such instances, the sale profits will exceed the total minimum lease payments, with excess profits reported as additions to income for the year in which the sale takes place.

statement of sales revenue and gross margins). Accounting entries for lessors engaged in sale–leaseback are identical to those used to record regular leases.

For lessees, however, accounting entries for sale–leaseback transactions in most instances involve extra considerations:[28]

- For a capital lease, any gain or loss on the sale of the asset must be deferred and amortized over the term of the lease and in the same proportion as the leased asset itself is depreciated. Most sale–leasebacks are entered into for financing and tax purposes; the terms of the sale and leaseback are typically negotiated as a single unit. For example, the lessee might accept a loss on the sale in exchange for lower lease payments. In effect, the loss represents a prepayment of rent. The gain or loss on the sale is thus an integral part of the sale–leaseback transaction and should be recognized over the lease term. (Exceptions to this principle are noted later.)
- For an operating lease, essentially the same gain or loss deferral and amortization process applies, but the terminology and accounts change. The deferred gain or loss is amortized over the term of the lease in proportion to each year's gross rental expense.
- In amortizing deferred gains over the term of the lease, the credit side of the entry is normally to depreciation expense if a capital lease is involved, but to rent expense if it is an operating lease. In both cases, the effect is to reduce current expenses. When deferred losses are amortized, the opposite is true.

Sale–Leaseback Accounting Entries Illustrated   Assume the following case information:

- On January 1, 1998, a seller–lessee sells a warehouse to a buyer–lessor for $95,000. The warehouse is carried on the seller–lessee's books at $80,000 and has an estimated remaining useful economic life of 10 years, with no residual value. Its fair value is $110,000. There is no transfer of title or BPO.
- In conjunction with the sale of the warehouse, the seller–lessee and the buyer–lessor enter into a five-year lease. The buyer–lessor's implicit interest rate is 12 percent, which is the same as the seller–lessee's incremental borrowing cost.
- The sale of the warehouse produces a gain of $15,000 ($95,000 selling price less $80,000 carrying value). This gain is deferred and will be amortized over the five-year lease term.
- Annual lease payments, starting January 1, 1998, are $23,530, computed as $95,000 ÷ (PVAD, 12%, 5) = $95,000 ÷ 4.03735 = $23,530.
- Depreciation expense applicable to the leaseback portion of this transaction is computed using the straight-line method over 10 years, with no residual value.

Exhibit 17–15 shows the entries used to account for this sale–leaseback transaction over the first year of the lease. Since none of the criteria in Exhibit 17–2 is met, this lease is an operating lease for both parties. For example, the present value of the lease payments, $95,000, is less than 90 percent of the fair market value, $110,000. If we change the economic life of the warehouse to only five years, criterion 3 is met, and the lease is a capital lease for both parties. Exhibit 17–16 gives the accounting for this situation.

Exceptions to Deferral of Gain or Loss

- The first exception to the deferral of gain or loss on sale–leasebacks occurs when the seller–lessee relinquishes substantially all of the remaining use of the property sold—a "minor" leaseback. In this case, the sale and leaseback are accounted for as separate transactions, and the gain or loss is recognized immediately. If the present value of the lease payments is 10 percent of the fair value of the asset sold, or less, the leaseback part of the transaction is considered minor. Because the sale of the property is the dominant aspect of the transaction, the entire gain or loss is recognized immediately.

---

[28]Under the provisions of *SFAS No. 13* and *No. 28*, asset sale and leaseback transactions are treated as single financing transactions, similar to a loan, rather than as two independent transactions. The purpose of this single-transaction ruling is to prevent manipulative dealings. Without constraints, the seller–lessee could conceivably sell an asset to a buyer–lessor for an unrealistically high (or low) price purposely to report a gain (or loss) on the sale. The seller–lessee could then lease the asset back under an agreement with a present value equal to the sale price of the asset. Upon completion of both "independent" transactions, the seller–lessee would be in the same economic position as before, but a phantom gain or loss on the sale would be reported.

EXHIBIT 17–15   Accounting for Sale–Leaseback: Operating Lease

Seller–Lessee			Buyer–Lessor		
Jan. 1, 1998—Sale of warehouse:			Jan. 1, 1998—Purchase of warehouse:		
Cash	95,000		Warehouse	95,000	
Warehouse (net)		80,000	Cash		95,000
Unearned gain on SLB sale		15,000			
Jan. 1, 1998—To record first lease payment:			Jan. 1, 1998—To record the first lease receipt:		
Rent expense	23,530		Cash	23,530	
Cash		23,530	Rent revenue		23,530
Dec. 31, 1998—To record amortization of unrecognized gain:*			Dec. 31, 1998—To recognize depreciation:		
Unearned gain on SLB sale	3,000		Depreciation expense[†]	9,500	
Rent expense ($15,000 × ⅕ =			Accumulated depreciation		
$3,000)		3,000	($95,000 × ⅒)		9,500

*Straight-line method is used (over the lease life) because equal payments are made each year.

[†]Based on a 10-year economic life.

■ A second exception occurs when the fair value of the property sold in a sale–leaseback is less than the carrying value of the property. Any loss (carrying value less sales price) is recognized immediately up to the amount of the difference between carrying value and fair value. Consider two situations:

		Situation 1	Situation 2
Asset fair value		$120,000	
Asset carrying value		$140,000	$140,000
Sales price		120,000	110,000
Total loss on sale		$ 20,000	$ 30,000

In situation 1, the entire loss is explained by the $20,000 difference between carrying value and fair value and is recognized immediately rather than deferred. The asset was sold at fair value; the resulting loss cannot be considered a prepayment of rent by the lessee as the loss had occurred before the sale–leaseback.

In situation 2, only the amount up to the $20,000 difference between carrying value and fair value can be recognized immediately. The additional $10,000 of loss is explained by the fact that the asset was sold for $10,000 less than fair value. This amount can be considered a prepayment of rent and is deferred and amortized as discussed previously.

Classification of Lease Receivables and Payables

When a lessor has lease receivables (and the lessee has lease liabilities) extending beyond one year (or the operating cycle of the business, if longer), the amount to be reported as a current asset or liability must be determined. The lessor's total lease receivable, as well as the lessee's liability, should be reported at their present values using the interest rate applied to the lease. Two approaches are available to separate the current from the long-term portion. The first approach recognizes the present value of the next year's payment as the current portion. The second approach records the coming year's decline in the total lease receivable (payable) as the current portion. The amortization table in Exhibit 17–4 can be used to illustrate these two approaches.

The first approach would report on December 31, 1998, the next payment of $36,556, which is due January 1, 1996, as the current portion of the lease liability and net receivable and $33,232 ($69,788 − $36,556) as the long-term portion. If the 1999 payment were due December 31, the current portion for 1998 would be $36,556 (PV1, 10%, 1) or $33,233. The second approach reports the decline in the lease liability during 1999, $33,232 ($69,788 − $36,556), as the current portion.

Both approaches are reasonable. The next payment represents the sacrifice that must be made by the lessee and the payment to be received by the lessor in the next period. The present value is the current value of this amount. Alternatively, the coming year's decline

EXHIBIT 17–16   Accounting for Sale–Leaseback: Direct Financing Lease for the Lessor and Capital Lease for the Lessee

Seller–Lessee			**Buyer–Lessor**		
Jan. 1, 1998—Sale of warehouse:			Jan. 1, 1998—Purchase of warehouse:		
Cash	95,000		Warehouse	95,000	
Warehouse		80,000	Cash		95,000
Unearned gain on SLB sale		15,000			
Jan. 1, 1998—To record capital lease:			Jan. 1, 1998—To record direct financing lease:		
Leased asset	95,000				
Lease liability		95,000	Lease receivable ($23,530 × 5)	117,650	
			Warehouse (on lease)		95,000
			Unearned interest revenue		22,650
Jan. 1, 1998—Payment of first lease payment (see amortization schedule below):			Jan. 1, 1998—Receipt of first lease payment:		
Lease liability	23,530		Cash	23,530	
Cash		23,530	Lease receivable		23,530
Dec. 31, 1998—Adjusting entries:					
To record depreciation expense:					
Depreciation expense	19,000				
Accumulated depreciation ($95,000 × ⅕)		19,000			
To record amortization of unrecognized gain:					
Unearned gain on SLB sale	3,000				
Depreciation expense ($15,000 × ⅕)		3,000			
To record accrued interest on lease liability (see amortization schedule below):			Dec. 31, 1998—To record accrued interest on lease receivable:		
Interest expense	8,576		Unearned interest revenue	8,576	
Lease liability		8,576	Interest revenue		8,576

Lease Amortization Schedule (annuity due basis)

Date	Annual Lease Payment	Annual Interest at 12%	Lease Receivable/Liability Decrease (increase)	Net Receivable/Liability Balance
1/1/98				$95,000
1/1/98	$ 23,530		$23,530	71,470
12/31/98		$ 8,576	(8,576)	80,046
1/1/99	23,530		23,530	56,516
12/31/99		6,782	(6,782)	63,298
1/1/00	23,530		23,530	39,768
12/31/00		4,772	(4,772)	44,540
1/1/01	23,530		23,530	21,010
12/31/01		2,520	(2,520)	23,530
1/1/02	23,530		23,530	–0–
	$117,650	$22,650	$95,000	

in the lease is also a relevant measure of the current amount because it represents the change in the total liability in the next period. In practice, the prevailing approach is to show the coming year's decline in the lease liability as the current amount.[29]

---

[29]For a discussion of these issues, see R. Swieringa, "When Current Is Noncurrent and Vice Versa!" *Accounting Review*, January 1984, pp. 123–30, and A. Richardson, "The Measurement of the Current Portion of Long-Term Lease Obligations—Some Evidence from Practice," *Accounting Review*, October 1985, pp. 744–752.

Lessee disclosures:

1. For capital leases, disclose
   a. The gross amount of assets recorded under capital leases presented by major classes according to nature or function.
   b. Future minimum lease payments in the aggregate and for each of the five succeeding fiscal years, with separate deductions from the total for executory costs (including any profit thereon) included in the minimum lease payments and for the amount of the imputed interest necessary to reduce the net minimum lease payments to present value.
   c. The total of minimum sublease rentals to be received in the future under noncancelable subleases.
   d. Total contingent rentals (these amounts are dependent on some factor other than the passage of time)
2. For operating leases having initial or remaining noncancelable lease terms in excess of one year, disclose
   a. Future minimum rental payments required in the aggregate and for each of the five succeeding fiscal years.
   b. The total of minimum rentals to be received in the future under noncancelable subleases.
3. For all operating leases, disclose rental expense, with separate amounts for minimum rentals, contingent rentals, and sublease rentals.
4. Provide a general description of the lessee's leasing arrangements including, but not limited to, the following:
   a. The basis on which contingent rental payments are determined.
   b. The existence and terms of renewal or purchase options and escalation clauses.
   c. Restrictions imposed by lease agreements, such as those concerning dividends, additional debt, and further leasing.

Lessor disclosures:

1. For sales-type and direct financing leases, disclose
   a. The components of the net investment in sales-type and direct financing leases:
      (1) Future minimum lease payments to be received, with separate deductions for amounts representing executory costs (including any profit thereon) included in the minimum lease payments and the accumulated allowance for uncollectible minimum lease payments receivable.
      (2) The unguaranteed residual values accruing to the benefit of the lessor.
      (3) Unearned interest revenue.
   b. Future minimum lease payments to be received for each of the five succeeding fiscal years.
   c. Total contingent rentals included in income.
2. For operating leases, disclose
   a. The cost and carrying amount, if different, of property on lease or held for leasing by major classes of property according to nature or function, and the amount of accumulated depreciation in total.
   b. Minimum future rentals on noncancelable leases in the aggregate and for each of the five succeeding fiscal years.
   c. Total contingent rentals included in income.
3. Provide a general description of the lessor's leasing arrangements.

Lease Disclosure Requirements

SFAS No. 13 requires disclosure of many details concerning leasing arrangements in the financial statements or the accompanying notes. The primary lease disclosures are summarized in Exhibit 17–17. Firms usually provide information on their leases in the notes to their financial statements. The information differs according to the extent of the firm's leasing activity and the extent of disclosure it elects to provide. Two examples are provided by note 4 to the 1996 annual report of Boise Cascade, a producer of building and paper products, and note 8 to the 1995 annual report of Ameritech, a telecommunications company.

Boise Cascade Corporation and Subsidiaries:

3. Leases

Lease obligations for which the Company assumes substantially all property rights and risks of ownership are capitalized. All other leases are treated as operating leases. Rental expenses for operating leases, net of sublease rentals, were $36,354,000 in 1995, $31,714,000 in 1994, and $30,887,000 in 1993.

The Company has various operating leases with remaining terms of more than one year. These leases have minimum lease payment requirements, net of sublease rentals, of $25,139,000 for 1996, $22,029,000 for 1997, $20,222,000 for 1998, $19,304,000 for 1999, and $17,412,000 for 2000, with total payments thereafter of $175,240,000.

Substantially all lease agreements have fixed payment terms based upon the passage of time. Some lease agreements provide the Company with the option to purchase the leased property. Additionally, certain agreements contain renewal options averaging eight years, with fixed payment terms similar to those in the original lease agreements.

American Information Technologies Corporation and Subsidiaries:

8. Lease Commitments

The company leases certain facilities and equipment used in its operations under both operating and capital leases. Rental expense under operating leases was $200.0, $181.6 and $196.2 million for 1995, 1994 and 1993, respectively. As of December 31, 1992, the aggregate minimum rental commitments under noncancelable leases were approximately as follows:

Years	Operating	Capital
1996	$104.2	$ 54.7
1997	85.9	52.1
1998	66.1	20.7
1999	56.9	1.7
2000	44.8	1.5
Thereafter	245.0	5.4
Total minimum rental commitments	$602.9	136.1
Less: executory costs		2.5
interest costs		12.3
Present value of minimum lease payments		$121.3

A Continuing Issue

Many accountants believe that most, if not all, leases should be capitalized, but financial institutions often intentionally structure leases so that the *lessor* can treat the transaction as a sale or financing lease while the lessee treats it as an operating lease, thereby keeping the debt off the balance sheet.[30] The effect on lessee debt–equity ratios can be substantial, as we have seen. Avoiding capitalization also decreases expenses initially as book depreciation plus interest on capital leases will exceed the operating lease payment in the early years of the lease, generally without any mitigating tax benefit.

Example The lease described in Exhibit 17–4 provides the data. In the first year the lessee's total expense, using a capitalized lease, is $39,677, composed of $6,344 of interest and $33,333 of depreciation. Had the lease been accounted for as an operating lease, the expense would have been $36,556. In the third year of the capital lease, the lessee would record only depreciation expense of $33,333. (There is no interest expense because the last lease payment was made at the first of the year.) If the lease were accounted for as an operating lease, the expense again would be $36,556.

We discussed how lessees avoid lease capitalization in the discussion of residual values and interest rates. First, it is relatively easy to avoid transferring asset ownership, criterion 1, and to avoid selling the property at a bargain price, criterion 2. To ensure that the asset is leased for less than 75 percent of its economic life to avoid meeting criterion 3, the lessee usually signs a short-term lease.

The more difficult criterion to overcome is criterion 4, which states that the lease is a capital lease if the present value of the lease payments is at least 90 percent of the asset's fair value. It is this criterion that requires ingenuity to defeat. Use of a residual value guaranteed by a third party, and assuring the use of the lessee's incremental borrowing rate by making sure the lessor's interest rate is unknown to the lessee are the two primary means of keeping the present value of minimum lease payments below the 90 percent level and

---

[30]When acting as lessors, banks and other financial institutions normally prefer (if not insist) that leases be structured as direct financing leases, not operating leases. The logic behind this preference is that banks are in the business of financing the acquisition of business assets (direct financing leases) and not owning assets rented out to businesses (operating leases). Also, direct financing leases tend to be more profitable for banks and other lenders than operating leases, primarily because of the simpler nature of the lease-servicing work involved in a direct financing lease.

hence not recording the lease on the lessee's books.[31] Third-party guarantees of residual values are included in the payment calculations by the lessor (but are excluded by the lessee) and thereby lower the lease payment. Furthermore, if the lessee does not know the residual value guaranteed by the third party, the lessee will not be able to calculate the lessor's implicit rate. A higher discount rate for the lessee reduces the present value of the rental payments, thus enabling the 90 percent test to be circumvented.

Whenever very specific reporting requirements have been set down by accounting policymakers leading to undesired disclosures, some firms are able to modify their contracts and transactions to avoid those requirements. Lease reporting is an example.[32]

CONCEPT REVIEW

1. Why would the owner of an asset want to sell an asset and then lease it back?
2. Is the discounted value of the next year's payment typically shown as the current portion of a lessee's liability? If not, what is shown?
3. What are the primary disclosure requirements for capital and operating leases?

SUMMARY OF KEY POINTS

(L.O. 1)   1. A lease is an agreement that conveys the right from a lessor to a lessee to use property, plant, or equipment, usually for a stated period of time.

(L.O. 1)   2. Leasing is popular because it can conserve cash, protect against obsolescence and interest rate changes, and provide the lessee with a means of avoiding the recognition of liabilities.

(L.O. 1)   3. Lessees generally prefer to keep leases off their balance sheets to reduce their reported liabilities. Doing so makes debt ratios (such as debt to equity) appear more attractive. Lessors, on the other hand, prefer to treat leases as sales or as financing capital leases. In other words, lessees prefer to account for leases as operating leases, and lessors prefer to account for leases as capital leases.

(L.O. 2)   4. For accounting purposes, a lease is considered to be either an operating lease or a capital lease.

(L.O. 2)   5. An operating lease is equivalent to a rental agreement. The lessee pays a periodic fee for use of the asset. This fee is revenue to the lessor. The asset remains the property of the lessor, who depreciates the asset's cost.

(L.O. 2)   6. The lessee treats a lease as a capital lease if it meets any one of four criteria: (1) the lease transfers ownership, (2) the lease contains a bargain purchase offer, (3) the lease term equals or exceeds 75 percent of the estimated economic life of the asset, and (4) the present value of the minimum lease payments equals or exceeds 90 percent of the fair market value of the leased asset.

(L.O. 2)   7. The lessor treats the lease as a capital lease if in addition to satisfying any one of the criteria for lessees, it meets two additional criteria: (1) collectibility of all rentals is reasonably assured, and (2) future costs are reasonably predictable or the lessor's performance is substantially completed.

---

[31]Third-party guarantors, in effect, insure the market value of a leased asset. For a fee, they assume the risk that, for whatever reason, the asset's residual value at the end of the lease term will fall short of the original estimate made at the outset of the lease. Insurance losses for third-party guarantors can be substantial, as Lloyd's of London (a consortium of insurance companies) found out with its guarantee business in the computer-leasing field.

[32]See R. Abdel-khalik, "The Economic Effects on Lessees of *FASB Statement 13,* 'Accounting for Leases,'" Research Report (Norwalk, CT: FASB, 1981).

(L.O. 3) 8. The lessor treats a capital lease as a sales-type lease if a dealer profit (loss) accrues [the present value of the receivable obtained exceeds (is less than) the carrying value of the transferred asset]. Otherwise, the lease is accounted for as a direct financing lease, and the lessor recognizes only interest revenue.

(L.O. 4) 9. To the lessee, a capital lease is a means of financing an asset acquisition. The asset is recorded on the books of the lessee. The lessee also recognizes a liability for the contract lease payments and recognizes depreciation on the asset. The periodic payment by the lessee represents payment of principal and interest on the loan to the lessor.

(L.O. 5) 10. A direct financing lease results in removal of the asset from the lessor's books. Interest revenue is earned over the lease term.

(L.O. 5) 11. A sales-type lease results in removal of the asset from the lessor's books. Income is earned at the time the lease is signed equal to the difference between the present value of the lease and the carrying value of the leased asset on the lessor's books. Interest revenue is earned over the lease term.

(L.O. 6) 12. Since lessees capitalize only the residual values they guarantee but lessors capitalize all residual values, provisions for guarantees of the residual value by a third party can result in a lease accounted for as an operating lease by the lessee and as capital lease by the lessor. This asymmetry can also result if the lessee uses an interest rate higher than the lessor's.

(L.O. 7) 13. A sale–leaseback arrangement is an agreement in which the seller–lessee sells an asset and then leases back the asset. The seller–lessee obtains cash while incurring a (tax deductible) lease payment. The buyer–lessor receives the lease payments, depreciates the asset for tax purposes, and may also deduct for taxes any interest on debt used to finance the asset purchase. The seller–lessee accounts for the transaction as a sale and for the lease as a capital or operating lease as appropriate. The buyer–lessor accounts for the transaction as a purchase and for the lease as a direct financing lease or sales-type lease as appropriate.

(L.O. 8) 14. The portion of a lessee's lease liability typically reported as current is the decline in the present value of the total lease obligation that occurs during the next operating period.

(L.O. 8) 15. Lease disclosure requirements for both lessees and lessors include data on payments to be made and descriptions of lease arrangements for both capital and operating leases.

REVIEW PROBLEM

Orion leased a computer to the Lenox Silver Company January 1, 1998. The terms of the lease are:

1. Lease term (fixed and noncancelable)	3 years
2. Estimated economic life of the equipment	5 years
3. Fair market value at lease inception	$5,000
4. Lessor's cost of asset	$5,000
5. Bargain purchase offer	None
6. Transfer of title	None
7. Guaranteed residual value by lessee (excess to lessee)* 1/1/01	$2,000
8. Lessee's normal depreciation method	Straight line
9. Lessee's incremental borrowing rate	11%
10. Executory costs	None
11. Initial indirect costs	None
12. Collectibility of rental payments	Assured
13. Performance by lessor	Completed
14. Annual rental (1st payment January 1, 1998)	$1,620
15. Lessor's implicit interest rate	Unknown to lessee
16. Unguaranteed residual value (known only to lessor)	None

*The terms of the lease allow the lessee to sell the asset at the end of the lease term.

Required

1. Determine what type of lease this is for the lessee.
2. Determine what type of lease this is for the lessor.
3. Provide entries for the lessee and the lessor from January 1, 1998, through January 1, 1999.
4. Provide entries for the lessee and the lessor if the asset is worth $2,100 on January 1, 2001. Assume that interest was accrued on December 31, 2000.

SOLUTION

1. Discounting the minimum lease payments, which include the guaranteed residual value of $2,000, yields

$$\$1,620(\text{PVAD, } 11\%, 3) + \$2,000(\text{PV1, } 11\%, 3) =$$
$$\$1,620(2.71252) + \$2,000(.73119) = \$5,857$$

The lease qualifies as a capital lease to the lessee because the present value of the minimum lease payments, $5,857, exceeds 90 percent of the fair value of the leased property at the time of the lease inception: criterion 4. It does not satisfy any of the first three criteria. In this case, the lessor's implicit rate could not be used because it is unknown to the lessee. But even if it were known (or were estimated, assuming that the lessee knew there was no unguaranteed residual value) *and,* to be used by the lessee, if it was lower than 11 percent, the present value of the minimum lease payments would be even greater. (Lower discount rates increase present values.) Thus, this lease would still qualify as a capital lease to the lessee.

2. The lease is also a capital lease to the lessor for the same reasons and because criteria 5*a* and 5*b* are satisfied. The lessor records the lease at the asset's fair market value at the time of the lease's inception, $5,000. Since the asset's fair market equals the carrying cost of the asset on the lessor's books, there is no immediate profit on the transaction. Thus, this is a direct financing lease to the lessor.

3. **Lessee entries:** The leased asset value is limited to the lower of the discounted payments or the fair market value.

January 1, 1998—Inception of lease:

Leased asset	5,000	
Lease liability		5,000

January 1, 1998—First payment:

Lease liability	1,620	
Cash		1,620

December 31, 1998—Accrual of interest:

Interest expense [.2455 × ($5,000 − $1,620)]	830	
Lease liability		830

For reporting, the lessee must use the interest rate that equates the present value of the lease payments to the recorded value of the leased asset, here limited to the market value of $5,000 since that is less than $5,857, the discounted minimum lease payments.

The required interest rate is 24.55 percent and is found by solving the following equation for i using a business calculator or computer program:

$$\$1,620(PVAD, i, 3) + \$2,000(PV1, i, 3) = \$5,000$$

December 31, 1998—To recognize depreciation expense:

Depreciation expense	1,000	
Accumulated depreciation [($5,000 − $2,000)]/3		1,000

Because the capital lease did not meet criterion 1 or 2, the asset is depreciated over the term of the lease.

January 1, 1999—Second payment:

Lease liability	1,620	
Cash		1,620

Lessor entries:

January 1, 1998—To record sale:

Lease receivable 3($1,620) + $2,000	6,860	
Asset		5,000
Unearned interest revenue		1,860

January 1, 1998—To record first payment:

Cash	1,620	
Lease receivable		1,620

December 31, 1998—To record interest earned:

Unearned interest revenue	830	
Interest revenue		830

January 1, 1999—To record second payment:

Cash	1,620	
Lease receivable		1,620

4. Entries on disposal of asset:

Lessee:

January 1, 2001—Recognize disposal of asset:

Cash	100	
Lease liability	2,000	
Accumulated depreciation	3,000	
Leased asset		5,000
Gain on disposition		100

The lessee is assumed to sell the asset for $2,100, remit $2,000 to the lessor, and retain the $100 excess.

Lessor:

January 1, 2001—Recognize receipt of payment:

Cash	2,000	
Lease receivable		2,000

Although the problem did not ask what entries would be made if the lease were an operating lease, these entries are shown next for 1998 only.

Lessee:

January 1, 1998—To record the first payment:

Rent expense	1,620	
Cash		1,620

Although the lessee is owed the rent service at this moment, the service will be fulfilled by year's end, and thus the amount may be expensed immediately.

Lessor:

January 1, 1998—To record the first payment:

Cash	1,620	
Lease revenue		1,620

Although the lessor has not earned the revenue on January 1, it will be earned by the end of the year and may be credited to revenue now. The lessor would also recognize depreciation at this time. Sufficient data to establish the depreciation amount are not given in the problem.

APPENDIX   *Other Types of Leases*

Leases Involving Real Estate

Leases that involve real estate (land and buildings) are subject to special accounting treatment. The appropriate accounting is summarized in Exhibit 17A–1.

Leveraged Leases

A **leveraged lease** involves the use of borrowed capital to acquire assets that are then leased out to a business customer (lessee). Beyond this simple definition, a leveraged lease is a complex financial arrangement with lenders as principals in addition to the lessor and lessee. It is also a completely different type of lease in terms of its business motives. Leasing, in general, is an economically viable financial activity in which the lessor earns a return on capital invested in leases. In contrast, leveraged leasing is basically driven by tax benefits that accrue to high-income taxpayers who participate as lessors. Earning a competitive before-tax return on investment is usually of secondary importance to these taxpayer–lessors.

The key elements that make a leveraged lease arrangement work as a tax strategy are

- High-interest expense on a large loan principal balance during the early years of the lease.
- Use of accelerated depreciation methods for tax purposes, which results in higher expenses during the early years of the lease. (Virtually all leveraged leases are structured as direct financing leases, meaning that depreciation passes to the lessee. For tax purposes, however, the lessor uses depreciation on the leased asset as a deductible item.)
- Level lease payments collected from the lessee that result in income shortfalls (expenses exceed leasing revenue) during the early years and the reverse during the later years of a lease.

I. Criterion 1 or 2 is satisfied (transfer of title or BPO):
  A. Lessee—capital lease (building and land separated):
    1. The present value of minimum lease payments allocated to land and buildings in proportion to their fair market values.
    2. Building(s) depreciated over estimated useful life.
  B. Lessor (building and land treated as one unit):
    1. Criterion 1 met:
      a. Sales-type lease if there is dealer profit.
      b. Direct financing lease if there is no dealer profit and if the two additional lessor criteria (5*a* and 5*b*) are met.*
      c. Operating lease if there is no dealer profit and if either of the two additional lessor criteria (5*a* and 5*b*) is not met.
    2. Criterion 2 met:
      a. Direct financing lease if there is no dealer profit and if the two additional lessor criteria (5*a* and 5*b*) are met.
      b. Operating lease if there is no dealer profit and if either of the two additional lessor criteria (5*a* and 5*b*) is not met.
II. Neither criterion 1 nor 2 is satisfied, and the fair market value of the land is less than 25 percent of the total fair market value of the leased property. The land and building are treated as a single unit with the building life used to apply criterion 3:
  A. Lessee:
    1. Capital lease if either criterion 3 or 4 is met. The land and building are recorded as a single unit and amortized over the lease term.
    2. Operating lease if neither criterion 3 or 4 is met.
  B. Lessor:
    1. Direct financing or sales-type lease if either criterion 3 or 4 is met and the two additional lessor criteria (5*a* and 5*b*) are met, depending on whether or not there is a dealer profit.
    2. Operating lease if neither criterion 3 nor 4 is met or if either of the two additional lessor criteria (5*a* and 5*b*) is not met.
III. Neither criterion 1 nor 2 is satisfied, and the fair market value of the land equals or exceeds 25 percent of the total fair market value of the leased property.
  A. Lessor and lessee consider land and building separately for purposes of applying criteria 3 and 4. The portion of the minimum lease payments allocated to the land is the value of land divided by the appropriate present value factor. The remainder is allocated to buildings.
  B. Lessee:
    1. Capital lease if the building meets either criterion 3 or 4.
      a. The building is amortized over the lease term.
      b. The land is classified as an operating lease.
    2. Operating lease if the building meets neither criterion 3 or 4.
  C. Lessor:
    1. Building meets either criterion 3 or 4 and the two additional lessor criteria (5*a* and 5*b*) are met.
      a. The building is classified as a direct financing lease.
      b. The land is classified as an operating lease.
    2. Building meets neither criterion 3 nor 4 or it does not meet either of the two additional lessor criteria (5*a* and 5*b*). Building and land are classified as a single operating lease.

*Criteria 5*a* and 5*b* refer to the lessor's collectibility and uncertainty tests (Exhibit 17–5).

Source: *SFAS No. 13* (as amended), par. 26, and *SFAS No. 98.*

- Although investment tax credits were eliminated by the Tax Reform Act of 1986, tax-payer–lessors engaged in leveraged leases initiated prior to 1986 are entitled to 10 percent tax credits on those investments in tax-qualified business assets. Many pre-1986 leveraged leases remain in force today.

Thus, a lessor with high levels of taxable income from other sources is able to use losses, tax credits, and expenses from leveraged leasing operations to offset all or a portion of taxable income and thereby achieve tax savings. This is true of the early years only; during the later years when leasing revenue exceeds expenses, taxable income results.

Leveraged leases tend to be multimillion-dollar affairs, with many deals valued in the billions. Some are so large as to require a lending syndicate to accommodate the size of the loans, which can run as high as 80 percent of the value of the assets covered in the lease. Even if the lessor's investment in the lease is only 20 percent, if the assets are big-ticket items, such as Boeing jumbo jets worth over $1 billion, 20 percent is a substantial amount, over $200 million in this case. For this reason, the lessor (also known as the equity participant) is sometimes not an individual or a single company, but a limited partnership formed specifically for the purpose of engaging in leveraged leasing.

These limited partnerships normally consist of one or more general partners and a large pool of limited partners (public investors) who buy partnership interests in the deal. The same tax benefits that accrue to an individual lessor accrue to the limited partners.

Leveraged leases require special accounting treatment that pertains only to lessors. Lessees involved in leveraged lease arrangements account for these transactions in the usual manner— as capital leases in the vast majority of cases. Furthermore, while many lessors (commercial leasing companies, in particular) routinely borrow cash in order to acquire assets intended for the leasing market, this fact alone does not qualify a transaction as a leveraged lease. Such routine borrowings are equivalent to short-term inventory-financing loans, common to most dealer and retailing businesses.

UNDERSTANDING AND APPLYING CONCEPTS AND STANDARDS

QUESTIONS

1. Match the letter items immediately below with the numbered statements that follow by entering one letter in each blank space.

   A. Lessor; B. Capital lease; C. Lessee; D. Operating lease
   ______ (1) Contract in which lessor finances property leased.
   ______ (2) Lender in a lease contract transaction.
   ______ (3) Tenant in a lease contract transaction.
   ______ (4) Type of lease that requires capitalization.
   ______ (5) Type of lease that does not require capitalization.
   ______ (6) Property owner in a lease contract transaction during the lease term.

   Questions 2 and 3 are based on the following information (briefly explain your choices):

   Marne Company purchased a machine for leasing purposes on January 1, 1998, for $1,000,000. The machine has a 10-year life, no residual value, and will be depreciated on a straight-line basis. On March 1, 1998, Marne leased the machine to Dal Company for $400,000 a year for a five-year period ending February 28, 2003. During the year ended December 31, 1998, Marne incurred normal maintenance and other related expenses of $30,000 under the provisions of this assumed operating lease. Dal paid $400,000 to Marne on March 1, 1998.

2. Assuming an operating lease, what was the income before income taxes derived by Marne from this lease for the year ended December 31, 1998?
   a. $313,333.
   b. $286,667.
   c. $220,000.
   d. $225,000.

3. What was rent expense for Dal from this lease for the year ended December 31, 1998?
   a. $363,333.
   b. $430,000.
   c. $333,333.
   d. $400,000.

4. Give the primary GAAP concepts of accounting for an operating lease by lessors and lessees.

5. Advance rental payments often are received under operating lease contracts that extend well beyond a single fiscal year. Give the acceptable accounting procedures that should be used for advance rentals.

6. What is meant by capitalization of a lease from the viewpoint of the lessee?

7. From a lessee's standpoint, leases are classified as capital or operating leases. What criteria are used to identify a capital lease?

8. From a lessor's view, a capital lease involves two types of leases. Identify the types and distinguish between them.

9. Briefly define the following terms related to capital leases (refer to the technical definitions):
   a. Lease term.
   b. Bargain purchase option.
   c. Bargain renewal option.

d. Minimum lease payments from the standpoint of the lessee.
e. Minimum lease payments from the standpoint of the lessor.
f. Interest rate implicit in the lease.
10. How does a lessee determine what interest rate is appropriate for capitalization of a lease?
11. How does an unguaranteed residual value in a sales-type lease affect the lessor's accounting in recording the entries at date of inception of the lease?
12. Briefly explain how inclusion of a provision of residual value guaranteed by a third party in a capital lease can result in asymmetric accounting by lessor and lessee.
13. Define initial direct costs.
14. Define executory costs.
15. When computing annual depreciation, what residual value should the lessee use for a leased asset under a capital lease? Briefly explain each alternative.

EXERCISES

E 17–1
(L.O. 2, 6)

Multiple Choice

1. Rent should be reported by the lessor as revenue over the lease term as it becomes receivable according to the provisions of which of the following leases?

	Direct Financing Lease	**Operating Lease**	**Sales-Type Lease**
a.	Yes	Yes	Yes
b.	Yes	No	No
c.	No	Yes	No
d.	No	No	Yes

2. The present value of minimum lease payments should be used by the lessee in determining the amount of a lease liability under a lease classified by the lessee as which of the following?

	Capital Lease	**Operating Lease**
a.	Yes	Yes
b.	Yes	No
c.	No	No
d.	No	Yes

3. Lease Y does not contain a bargain purchase option, but the lease term is equal to 90 percent of the estimated economic life of the leased property. Lease Z does not transfer ownership of the property to the lessee by the end of the lease term, but the lease term is equal to 75 percent of the estimated economic life of the leased property. How should the lessee classify these leases?

	Lease Y	**Lease Z**
a.	Capital lease	Operating lease
b.	Capital lease	Capital lease
c.	Operating lease	Capital lease
d.	Operating lease	Operating lease

4. A lessee had a 10-year capital lease requiring equal annual payments. The reduction of the lease liability in year 2 should equal
a. The current liability shown for the lease at the end of year 1.
b. The current liability shown for the lease at the end of year 2.
c. The reduction of the lease obligation in year 1.
d. One-tenth of the original lease liability.

(AICPA adapted)

E 17–2
(L.O. 2, 3, 6)

Multiple Choice

1. The excess of the fair value of lease property at the inception of the lease over its cost or carrying amount should be considered by the lessor as
a. Unearned income from a sales-type lease.
b. Unearned income from a direct financing lease.
c. Manufacturer's or dealer's profit from a sales-type lease.
d. Manufacturer's or dealer's profit from a direct financing lease.

2. A lease is recorded as a sales-type lease by the lessor. The difference between the gross investment in the lease and the net receivable should be

a. Amortized over the period of lease as interest revenue by the interest method.

b. Amortized over the period of lease as interest revenue by the straight-line method.

c. Recognized in full as interest revenue at the lease's inception.

d. Recognized in full as manufacturer or dealer's profit at the lease's inception.

3. In a lease that is recorded as a sales type lease by the lessor, interest revenue

a. Does not arise.

b. Should be recognized over the life of the lease by the interest method.

c. Should be recognized over the life of the lease by the straight-line method.

d. Should be recognized in full as revenue at the lease's inception.

(AICPA adapted)

E 17–3
(L.O. 4, 5)

Multiple Choice

1. On January 1, 1998, Mill Corporation leased a machine to Ott Corporation for a five-year term at an annual rental of $50,000. The lease is an operating lease. At the inception of the lease, Mill received $100,000, covering the first year's rent of $50,000 and a security deposit of $50,000. This deposit will not be returned to Ott upon expiration of the lease but will instead be applied to payment of rent for the last year of the lease. Mill properly reported rental revenue of $100,000 in its 1998 income tax return. Mill's tax rate was 30 percent. In Mill's December 31, 1998, balance sheet, what portion of the $100,000 should be reported as a liability?

a. $50,000.

b. $40,000.

c. $35,000.

d. $28,000.

2. Beal, Inc., intends to lease a machine from Paul Corporation. Beal's incremental borrowing rate is 14 percent. The prime rate of interest is 8 percent. Paul's implicit rate in the lease is 10 percent, which is known to Beal. Beal computes the present value of the minimum lease payments using what rate?

a. 8 percent.

b. 10 percent.

c. 12 percent.

d. 14 percent.

3. On January 2, 1998, Ashe Company entered into a 10-year noncancelable lease requiring year-end payments of $100,000. Ashe's incremental borrowing rate is 12 percent, and the lessor's implicit interest rate, known to Ashe, is 10 percent. Ownership of the property remains with the lessor at expiration of the lease. There is no bargain purchase option. The leased property has an estimated economic life of 12 years. What amount (rounded) should Ashe capitalize for this leased property on January 2, 1998?

a. $1,000,000.

b. $614,500.

c. $565,000.

d. $0.

4. On December 30, 1997, Drew Company leased equipment under a capital lease for a period of 10 years. Drew contracted to pay $90,000 annual rent on December 31, 1997, and on December 31 of each of the next nine years. The capital lease liability was appropriately recorded at $608,400 on December 30, 1997, before the first payment. The leased equipment has a useful life of 12 years, and the interest rate implicit in the lease is 10 percent. Drew uses the straight-line method for depreciating all equipment. In recording the December 31, 1998, payment, Drew should reduce the capital lease liability by

a. $38,160.

b. $50,700.

c. $51,840.

d. $60,840.

(AICPA adapted)

E 17–4
(L.O. 6)

Multiple Choice

1. On January 1, 1997, Kerr Company signed a 10-year noncancelable lease for a new machine, requiring $20,000 annual payments at the beginning of each year. The machine has a useful life of 15 years, with no salvage value. Title passes to Kerr at the lease expiration date. Kerr uses straight-line depreciation for all of its plant assets. Aggregate lease payments have a present value on January 1, 1997, of $126,000, based on an appropriate rate of interest. For 1997, Kerr should record depreciation (amortization) expense for the leased machine at

a. $20,000.   *c.* $8,400.

b. $12,600.   *d.* $0.

2. The lessee should amortize the capitalizable cost of the leased asset in a manner consistent with the lessee's normal depreciation policy for owned assets for leases that do which of the following?

	Contain a Bargain Purchase Option	**Transfer Ownership of the Property to the Lessee by the End of the Lease Term**
a.	No	No
b.	No	Yes
c.	Yes	Yes
d.	Yes	No

3. A lease contains a bargain purchase option. In determining the lessee's capitalizable cost at the beginning of the lease term, the payment called for by the bargain purchase option would
   a. Not be capitalized.
   b. Be subtracted at its present value.
   c. Be added at its exercise price.
   d. Be added at its present value.

4. On January 2, 1995, Wayne, Inc., signed an eight-year lease for office space. Wayne has the option to renew the lease for an additional four-year period on or before January 2, 2003. During January 1997, two years after occupying the leased premises, Wayne made general improvements to the premises costing $360,000 and having an estimated useful life of 10 years. At December 31, 1997, Wayne's intentions as to exercise of the renewal option are uncertain because they depend upon future office space requirements. A full year's amortization expense is taken for calendar year 1997. Wayne should record amortization of leasehold improvements for 1997 at
   a. $30,000.
   b. $36,000.
   c. $45,000.
   d. $60,000.

(AICPA adapted)

E 17–5
(L.O. 4, 7)

Multiple Choice

1. In a sale–leaseback transaction the seller–lessee has retained the property. The gain on the sale should be recognized at the time of the sale–leaseback if the lease is classified as which of the following?

	Capital Lease	**Operating Lease**
a.	Yes	Yes
b.	No	No
c.	No	Yes
d.	Yes	No

2. On December 1, 1998, Barr Company leases office space for five years at a monthly rental of $60,000. On that date, Barr pays the lessors the following amounts:

First month's rent	$ 60,000
Last month's rent (Dec. 2003)	60,000
Security deposit (refundable at lease expiration)	80,000
Installation of new walls and offices	360,000

Barr's December 1998 expense relating to its use of this office space is
   a. $60,000.
   b. $66,000.
   c. $126,000.
   d. $200,000.

3. On December 31, 1997, Lane, Inc., sold equipment to Noll and simultaneously leased it back for 12 years. Pertinent information at this date is:

Sales price	$480,000
Carrying amount	$360,000
Estimated remaining economic life	15 years

At December 31, 1997, how much should Lane report as a deferred gain from the sale of the equipment?

a. $0.

b. $110,000.

c. $112,000.

d. $120,000.

4. The following information pertains to equipment sold by Bard Company to Kerr Company on December 31, 1997:

Sales price	$300,000
Book value	$100,000
Estimated remaining economic life	20 years

Simultaneously with the sale, Bard leased back the equipment for a period of 16 years. How much of the gain on the sale should Bard defer at December 31, 1997?

a. $200,000.

b. $12,500.

c. $10,000.

d. $0.

(AICPA adapted)

E 17–6

(L.O. 3)

Operating Lease: Leasehold Costs, Entries   Balsam Company signed an operating lease contract effective for five years from January 1, 1998. Balsam is to pay $120,000 at the start of the lease plus $16,000 monthly payments throughout the lease term. During January 1998, Balsam spent $60,000 renovating the lease property and built an addition to the leased property with the lessor's consent at a cost of $160,000. The estimated life of the addition is 20 years, and its residual value is zero. The lease contract does not contain a renewal option and may be terminated by the lessee with six months' notice.

Required

Give all entries on Balsam's books to reflect the renovation outlays, leasehold, and payments for 1998, including entries at the end of 1998, assuming that Balsam's accounting year is the calendar year. The straight-line method of amortization is to be used.

E 17–7

(L.O. 1, 2)

 **Explain Distinctions: Capital versus Operating, and Direct Financing versus Sales-Type Leases**

Part A

Capital leases and operating leases are the two classifications of leases that FASB pronouncements describe from the standpoint of the lessee.

Required

1. Describe how a capital lease would be accounted for by the lessee both at the inception of the lease and during the first year of the lease; assume that the lease transfers ownership of the property to the lessee by the end of the lease term.

2. Describe how an operating lease would be accounted for by the lessee both at the inception of the lease and during the first year of the lease; assume that equal monthly payments are made by the lessee at the beginning of each month of the lease. Do not discuss the criteria for distinguishing between capital leases and operating leases.

Part B

Sales-type leases and direct financing leases are two of the classifications of leases described in FASB pronouncements, from the standpoint of the lessor.

Required

Compare and contrast a sales-type lease with a direct financing lease as to

1. Net investment in the lease.
2. Recognition of interest revenue.
3. Manufacturer's or dealer's profit.

Do not discuss the criteria for distinguishing between the leases described above and operating leases.

E 17–8

(L.O. 2, 4, 5)

Lease: Apply Lease Criteria, Entries for Lessor and Lessee   Tam Leasing Company agreed with Lex Corporation to provide the latter with equipment under lease for a three-year period. The equipment cost Tam $120,000 and will have no residual value when the lease term ends. Tam expects to collect all payments from Lex and has no material cost uncertainties. The carrying value of the equipment was $120,000 at the inception of the lease. The three equal annual payments (amount to be determined) are to be paid each January 1, starting January 1, 1998 (at which time the equipment was delivered). Lex has agreed to pay taxes, maintenance, and insurance throughout the lease term as well as any other ownership costs. Tam expects a 20 percent return (known to Lex). The accounting year of both companies ends December 31.

Required

Round to the nearest dollar.

1. What kind of lease is this to Lex? To Tam?
2. Compute the annual payments and prepare an amortization schedule reflecting the interest and principal elements of Lex's payments over the three-year term of the lease. Give all journal entries relating to the lease for Lex Corporation for 1998 including year-end adjusting entries.
3. Give all journal entries for Tam Leasing Company relating to the lease for 1998 including year-end adjusting entries.

E 17–9
(L.O. 2, 5)

Lease: Financing or Sales Type, Schedule, Entries for Lessor   Green & Company uses leasing as a secondary means of selling its products. The company contracted with Lutz Corporation to lease a machine to be used by Lutz as an operational asset. The retail market value of the asset at the inception of the lease was $200,000; it cost Green $160,000 and is carried in its inventory at that value. Payments of $44,925 are to be made by Lutz at the end of each of the five quarters following inception of the lease. Green's implicit interest rate is 4 percent per quarter, which is known by Lutz. The lease qualifies as a capital lease for both parties.

Required

Round to the nearest dollar.

1. Classify the lease showing how the $44,925 rental payment was computed and prepare an amortization schedule for use by Green covering the five-quarter term of the lease.
2. Give Green's journal entries at the inception of the lease and upon receipt of the first payment. Assume that the first receipt coincides with the end of Green's accounting year.

E 17–10
(L.O. 2, 4, 5)

Lease: Financing or Sales Types, Schedule and Entries, Lessor and Lessee   Rex Corporation (lessor) and Lee Company (lessee) agreed to a noncancelable lease. The following information is available regarding the lease terms and the leased asset:

a. Rex's cost of the leased asset was $40,000. The asset was new at lease inception date.
b. Lease term is four years, beginning January 1, 1998. Lease payments are made each January 1, beginning January 1, 1998.
c. Estimated useful life of leased asset is four years. Estimated residual value at end of lease is zero.
d. Sales price of leased asset on January 1, 1998, was $46,000.
e. Rex's implicit interest rate is 15 percent on retail price (known to Lee).
f. Rex expects to collect all payments from Lee, and there are no material cost uncertainties.

Required

1. What kind of lease is this to Rex? To Lee?
2. Compute the annual lease payments.
3. Prepare an amortization schedule for the lease.
4. Give the journal entries for both parties on January 1, 1998, and December 31, 1998. Do not make closing entries.

E 17–11
(L.O. 2, 4, 5)

Lease: Analysis of Dealer's Profit or Loss   Jordin Company is an equipment dealer that sometimes uses leasing as a means to sell its products. On January 1, 1998, Jordin leased equipment to Easten Corporation. The lease term was four years, with annual lease payments of $11,538 to be paid on each December 31. The equipment has an estimated zero residual value at end of the lease term. The equipment was carried on Jordin's accounts at a cost of $40,000. Jordin expects to collect all rentals from Easten, and there were no material cost uncertainties at inception of the lease. The implicit interest rate on the lease was 11 percent on the selling price (known to Easten).

Required

1. What kind of lease is this to Jordin? To Easten?
2. What is the cost of the equipment to Easten?
3. What is the dealer's profit or loss recognized by Jordin?
4. Assume that the implicit interest rate is 4 percent (not 11 percent). What is the dealer's profit or loss recognized by Jordin?
5. Give the entries (based on the 11 percent rate) at date of inception of the lease for each party.

E 17–12
(L.O. 6, 8)

Overview of Special Lease Cases: Provide Explanations   Select the best answer in each of the following. Justify each choice that you make.

1. On the first day of its accounting year. Lessor, Inc., leased certain property at an annual payment of $200,000 receivable at the beginning of each year for 10 years. The first payment was received immediately. The leased property, which is new, cost $1,100,000 and has an estimated useful life of 12 years and no residual value. Lessor's implicit rate is 12 percent. Lessor had no other costs associated with this lease. Lessor should have accounted for this lease as a sales-type lease but mistakenly treated the lease as an operating lease. What was the effect on net income during the first year of the lease by having treated this lease as an operating lease rather than as a sales-type lease?

   a. No effect.

   b. Overstatement.

   c. Understatement.

   d. The effect depends on the accounting method selected for income tax purposes.

2. The appropriate valuation of leased assets under an operating lease on the balance sheet of a lessee is which of the following?

   a. Zero.

   b. The absolute sum of the lease payments.

   c. The sum of the present values of the lease payments discounted at an appropriate rate.

   d. The market value of the asset at the date of the inception of the lease.

3. What three types of expenses does a lessee experience with a capital lease?

   a. Rent expense, interest expense, amortization expense.

   b. Interest expense, amortization expense, executory costs.

   c. Amortization expense, executory costs, rent expense.

   d. Executory costs, interest expense, rent expense.

4. When the present value of future payments to be capitalized in connection with a capital lease is measured, how should identifiable payments to cover taxes, insurance, and maintenance be accounted for?

   a. Included with the future rentals to be capitalized.

   b. Excluded from future rentals to be capitalized.

   c. Capitalized, but at a different rate and recorded in a different account from that for future payments.

   d. Capitalized, but at a different rate and during a different period from the rate and period used for the future payments.

5. GAAP requires that certain lease agreements be accounted for as purchases. The theoretical basis for this treatment is that a lease of this type

   a. Effectively conveys most of the benefits and risks incident to the ownership of property.

   b. Is an example of form over substance.

   c. Provides the use of the leased asset to the lessee for a limited period of time.

   d. Must be recorded in accordance with the matching concept.

6. Your client constructed an office building at a cost of $500,000 and then sold this building to Jones for a large gain. The client leased it back from Jones for a stipulated annual payment. How should this gain be treated?

   a. Recognized in full as an ordinary item in the year of the transaction.

   b. Recognized in full as an extraordinary item in the year of the transaction.

   c. Amortized as an adjustment of the rental cost over the life of the lease.

   d. Amortized as an extraordinary item over the life of the lease.

(AICPA adapted)

E 17–13 (L.O. 5, 6)	**Direct Financing Lease with BPO: Schedule, Entries for Lessor** Lessor Marcy and lessee Lenox contract for the lease of a machine for five payments of $7,000 each. The $7,000 payments are to be paid at the end of each of five quarters. They also agree that at the time of the fifth payment, for an added $6,000 bargain purchase option payment, Lenox can buy the property. The interest rate is 4 percent per quarter. The lease qualifies as a direct financing lease.
Required	Round to the nearest dollar.
	1. Calculate the present value of the lease payments, and prepare an amortization schedule for the lease covering the five-quarter term. 2. Give the lessor's entries at the inception of the lease and at the time of the fifth payment if the lessee exercises the purchase option. Assume that it is a direct financing lease.
E 17–14 (L.O. 4, 5)	**Direct Financing Lease with BPO** Flint Company leased a computer to Land Company for a five-year period. Flint paid $46,965 for the computer (estimated useful life five years, no residual value). The lease started on January 1, 1998, and qualifies as a direct financing lease to the lessor and as a capital lease to the lessee. Flint

uses a target rate of return of 14 percent in all lease contracts. The first payment was on January 1, 1998, and the accounting periods end on December 31.

Required

1. Compute the annual payment for the lessor and the amount to be capitalized for the lessee. The computer reverts to the lessor at the end of the lease term.
2. Now assume, instead, that the lease contract contains a BPO stating that Land Company can purchase the computer for $14,000 on December 31, 2001, at which time its estimated residual value is $17,500. Compute the annual payment for the lessor and the amount to be capitalized for the lessee. Show whether the BPO is really a bargain.
3. Give the entries at inception date under requirements 1 and 2 for the lessor and lessee.

E 17–15
(L.O. 5)

Financing Lease: Unguaranteed Residual Value, Schedules, Ordinary and Annuity Due   The present value to a lessor of a lease on which the lessee is obligated to make a $40,000 payment at the end of each of the next three years and on which there is an unguaranteed residual value of $8,000 at the end of the lease term is $98,266 using the lessor's implicit interest rate of 14 percent. The lease qualifies as a direct financing lease.

Required

Round amounts to the nearest dollar.

1. Prepare an amortization schedule for the lessor covering the three-year lease term.
2. Compute the present value of a similar lease; assume that the lessor's implicit rate is 12 percent. Prepare an amortization schedule similar to the one required in (1) above.
3. Assume, instead, that each of the three $40,000 annual payments is paid at the beginning of each year, in advance, and that the $8,000 residual value is expected at the end of the lease term of three years. What is the present value of the lease payments at 14 percent? Prepare the lessor's amortization schedule for this lease.

E 17–16
(L.O. 2, 4, 5, 6)

Sales-Type Lease: Unguaranteed Residual Value, Inception Entries   On January 1, 1998, ABC Company signed a lease contract with Abel Company. The leased asset cost ABC $45,000 and had a normal selling price of $55,000. Three annual payments, based on the selling price, are payable by Abel on January 1, beginning in 1998. The asset reverts to ABC at the end of the lease term, December 31, 2000, and is estimated to have an unguaranteed residual value on that date of $3,000. ABC's implicit interest rate is 12 percent, which is known to Abel.

Required

1. What type of lease is this for ABC?
2. Compute the annual lease payments.
3. Give the lessor's entry on January 1, 1998.
4. Give the lessee's entry on January 1, 1998.
5. What amount will ABC show as its lease receivable balance on January 1, 2000, after receipt of the third and final lease payment?

E 17–17
(L.O. 2, 6)

Residual Value Guaranteed by Third Party: Lessor, Direct Financing; Lessee, Operating   Mike Leasing Company (lessor) and Ash Corporation (lessee) signed a four-year lease on January 1, 1998. The leased property cost Mike $50,000, which was also its carrying value at inception of the lease. The leased asset had an estimated life of six years, and the property reverts to Mike at the end of the lease term. Lease payments of $12,830 are payable on January 1 of each year and were set to yield Mike a return of 12 percent, which was known to Ash. The estimated residual value at the end of the lease term is $10,000 and is guaranteed by a third party. The lease contains no bargain purchase option. Mike is reasonably certain of the collectibility of the lease payments, and there are no additional costs to be incurred. The lease qualifies as a direct financing lease to the lessor, but an operating lease to the lessee.

Required

1. What evidence supports this as a direct financing lease for the lessor? Give Mike's journal entries at inception of the lease and to record the first lease payment.
2. What evidence supports this as an operating lease for Ash? Explain. Give Ash's journal entries at inception of the lease and to record the first lease payment.

E 17–18
(L.O. 4, 5, 6)

Direct Financing Lease: Residual Value Partially Guaranteed by the Lessee   Dunlap Company leased a large copier to Rust Company for a three-year period. Dunlap paid $30,000 for the copier and immediately leased it on January 1, 1998 (estimated useful life is four years and the estimated residual value at the end of the lease term is $6,000). Dunlap used an expected rate of return of 16 percent on cost (known by Rust). Because of inadequate maintenance, the lessee agreed to guarantee two-thirds ($4,000) of the residual value. The lease qualifies as a direct financing lease for the lessor and a capital lease for the lessee. The lessee uses straight-line depreciation. The first lease payment is on January 1, 1998, and the accounting periods for both parties end on December 31. At the lease termination date, an independent appraiser provided an estimated residual value of $3,000. The lessee immediately paid the difference of $1,000 ($4,000 guaranteed residual value minus $3,000, the actual residual value).

Required

1. Compute the minimum lease payment for the lessor and the amount to be capitalized by the lessee.
2. Give the entries for the lessor and lessee on January 1, 1998.
3. Give the entries for the lessor and lessee to record the lease termination.

E 17–19
(L.O. 4, 5, 6)

Accounting for Executory Costs   On January 1, 1998, Foxtrot leased a machine to Green on a three-year direct financing lease to the lessor and a capital lease to the lessee. The machine cost the lessor $84,000 and was immediately placed on lease at a 12 percent target rate of return (known by both parties). The lease did not contain a BPO, and there is no residual value. The rentals are payable each year starting on January 1, 1998. The accounting periods end December 31. All executory costs are to be paid by the lessee. However, insurance coverage was provided, at a cost of $174 per year, under the lessor's blanket policy. This amount is billed each year along with the lease payment.

Required

1. Compute the annual lease payment.
2. Give the entry for the lessor and lessee to record the inception of the lease (do not include the first rent payment).
3. Give the entry for the lessor and lessee to record the first rent payment.

E 17–20
(L.O. 7)

Sale–Leaseback, Direct Financing Lease   Rich Grocery owns the building it uses; it has a current carrying value on January 1, 1998, of $450,000, a 10-year remaining life, and no residual value. On this date it was sold to investor Lucky for $500,000 cash. Simultaneously, the two parties executed a 10-year direct financing lease with a 12 percent implicit interest rate; each annual payment is due on December 31 (end of their accounting periods).

Required

1. Compute the annual payments to be made by Rich to Lucky.
2. Give the entries for the seller–lessee (Rich Grocery) for 1998. Use straight-line depreciation.

E 17–21
(L.O. 2, 3)

Operating Lease: Amortization, Interest Method   Valley Company paid $50,000 on January 1, 1998, to Hill Properties as an advance lease bonus to secure a three-year lease on premises it will occupy starting from that date. Additionally, $60,000 will be paid on each December 31 throughout the term of the lease. The lease contains no specific renewal agreement. Valley's accounting period ends December 31. Hill will maintain the property and pay taxes and other ownership costs.

Required

Round to the nearest dollar.

1. What type of lease contract is involved? Explain.
2. Develop an interest method amortization schedule using a 14 percent rate (assume an ordinary annuity).
3. What is Valley's total occupancy cost for 1998 under the interest method used in your response to (2) above? What is the total occupancy cost using the straight-line basis for 1998?
4. What lease-related items should Valley's financial statements report as of December 31, 1998, if the amortization schedule developed in (2) above is used?

E 17–22
(L.O. 1)

Leases and Ratio Analysis   Suppose a firm were required to place its operating leases on its balance sheet; that is, the firm is required to capitalize its leases. What would be the impact on the following ratios:

- Current ratio
- Working capital to total assets
- Asset turnover
- Debt to equity
- Cash flow per share
- Return on investment
- Dividend payout

(Assume normal ratio values exist before capitalization, such as a current ratio of at least one.)

PROBLEMS

P 17–1
(L.O. 1, 8)

Lease Basis and Reporting   Lino Corporation's liability account balances at December 31, 1997 included the following:

Note payable to bank	$800,000
Liability under capital lease	280,000
Deferred tax liability	100,000

Additional information:

   a. The note payable, dated October 1, 1997, bears interest at an annual rate of 10 percent payable semiannually on April 1 and October 1. Principal payments are due annually on October 1 in four equal installments.

   b. The capital lease is for a 10-year period beginning December 31, 1992, with payment due in advance. Equal annual payments of $100,000 are due on December 31 of each year. The 16 percent interest rate implicit in the lease is known by Lino. At December 31, 1997, the present value of the four remaining lease payments discounted at 16 percent was $280,000.

   c. Deferred income taxes are provided in recognition of temporary differences between financial statement and income tax reporting of depreciation. For the year ended December 31, 1998, depreciation per tax return exceeded book depreciation by $50,000. Lino's income tax rate for 1998 (assume that no changes have been enacted for future years) was 30 percent.

   d. On July 1, 1998, Lino issued $1,000,000 face amount of 10-year, 10 percent bonds for $750,000, to yield 15 percent. Interest is payable annually on July 1. Bond discount is amortized by the interest method.

   e. All required principal and interest payments were made on schedule in 1998.

Required

1. What is the theoretical basis for requiring lessees to capitalize certain long-term leases? Do not discuss the specific criteria for classifying a lease as a capital lease.
2. Prepare the long-term liabilities section of Lino's balance sheet at December 31, 1998.
3. Prepare a schedule showing interest expense that should appear in Lino's income statement for the year ended December 31, 1998.

(AICPA adapted)

P 17–2
(L.O. 2, 3)

Lease: Determine Type, Entries for Lessor and Lessee   Crown leases a limo to Zap Productions for four years on January 1, 1998, requiring equal annual payments on each January 1 and, in addition, a single lump-sum prepayment of $3,000. The leased asset, recently purchased new, cost the lessor $50,000. The estimated unguaranteed value of the asset at end of lease term is $20,000.

   The annual lease payments were computed to yield Crown 12 percent (the implicit interest rate after considering that the residual value is known to Zap Productions). The leased asset has an eight-year life with zero residual value at the end of year 8. There is no bargain purchase option, and the asset is retained by Crown at the end of the lease term. Depreciation will be on the straight-line basis. The accounting period for both lessor and lessee ends December 31.

Required

1. Compute the annual lease payment.
2. What type of lease is this? Explain.
3. In parallel columns for the lessor and lessee, give:
   a. Entries at the inception of the lease, including the initial advance payment.
   b. Adjusting and closing entries for the year ended December 31, 1998. Use straight-line amortization for the prepayment.

P 17–3
(L.O. 3, 8)

Operating Lease: Down Payment, Entries for Both Parties   On July 1, 1998, Stanley Company leased a small building and its site to East Company on a five-year contract. The lease provides for an advance rental payment of $10,000 which does not reduce any other payment, plus an annual rental payment of $40,000 payable each July 1 starting in 1998. The lease can be terminated at any year-end by the lessee with a six-month advance notice. There is no renewal agreement. On July 8, 1998, East Company spent $20,000 on internal changes and painting. Stanley's accounts showed the following data on January 1, 1998: initial cost of the building, $250,000 (accumulated depreciation, $60,000); estimated remaining life, 15 years; and estimated residual value, $10,000. The accounting period for each company ends December 31. The lease is an operating lease to both parties.

Required

1. Give the entries for the lessor and lessee for 1998, 1999, and through July 1, 2000. Both companies will use straight-line depreciation and amortization of the advance rental. Closing entries are not required.
2. Give the amounts that each party should report on its 1998 and 1999 income statements and balance sheets.

P 17–4
(L.O. 4, 5)

Direct Financing Lease: Ordinary versus Annuity Due, Schedules, Entries for Both Parties   On January 1, 1998, Shell Leasing Company leased to Last Service Company a new machine that cost $45,500. The lease is a direct financing lease to Shell and a capital lease to Last. Last agrees to pay all executory costs and to assume other risks and costs of ownership. Shell computed the periodic payments at an amount that will yield an annual return on cost of 10 percent, and the lessee, being aware of this rate, also uses it to record the lease and calculate interest expense. The property is expected to have no residual value at the end of the four-year lease term. There are no collection or cost uncertainties. Both lessor and lessee have accounting years ending December 31.

Required   Round all amounts to the nearest dollar.

1. If the annual payments are payable at the end of each year, provide the following: (*a*) the amount of the periodic lease payments and (*b*) an amortization schedule for the lessor reflecting interest and recovery of investment throughout the four-year lease term.
2. Assume, instead, that the annual payments are payable at the start of the lease and annually thereafter. Provide the answers to (*a*) and (*b*) that were required in (1) above.
3. Last depreciates all assets using the straight-line method. Give entries under (1) above for both lessor and lessee relating to the lease for 1998 including adjusting and closing entries.

P 17–5
(L.O. 4, 5)

Sales-Type Lease: Amortization Schedules, Entries for Both Parties   Key Company uses leasing as a secondary means of selling its products. On January 1, 1998, it contracted with Lock Corporation to lease machinery for six years that had a sales price of $90,000 and that cost Key $60,000 (its carrying value in inventory). Equal annual lease payments of $18,786 are to be made each January 1, starting on January 1, 1998. Key's implicit interest rate, based on the sales price, is 10 percent (known to Lock). This lease qualifies as a capital lease for both parties. The accounting period for both companies ends on December 31.

Required   Round to the nearest dollar.

1. Prepare an amortization schedule for Key and Lock covering the six-year lease term.
2. Give the lessor's and lessee's entries at the inception of the lease. The lessee uses straight-line depreciation and zero residual value for the asset after six years. Also, give the adjusting and closing entries for both parties at December 31, 1998.

P 17–6
(L.O. 4, 5)

Direct-Financing and Sales-Type Leases Compared: Entries for Both Parties   On January 1, 1998, Sun Company leased to Marfa Corporation new equipment. The equipment cost Sun $38,000. The lease agreement specified that Marfa is to make five equal annual lease payments (on December 31, beginning December 31, 1998) to yield Sun a 14 percent return. The equipment has a five-year useful life with no residual value. Ownership of the leased asset transfers to Marfa at the end of the lease term. Marfa is aware of the implicit interest rate used by Sun. Straight-line depreciation will be used. Sun expects to collect all payments from Marfa, and there are no material cost uncertainties at inception of the lease. The accounting period for both Sun and Marfa ends December 31.

Required

1. If the equipment has a sales price of $42,000 on January 1, 1998, and the lease payments are based on this amount, what type of lease is this to the lessor? To the lessee? Explain. Compute the annual rental payments and prepare an amortization schedule for the lessor and lessee. Give all journal entries associated with this lease for the lessor and the lessee for the year ended December 31, 1998, including adjusting and closing entries.
2. If the equipment has a cost or carrying value of $38,000 on January 1, 1998, and the lease payments are based on this amount, what type of lease is this to the lessor? To the lessee? Explain. Compute the annual payments and prepare an amortization schedule for the lessor and the lessee. Give all journal entries associated with this lease for the lessor and the lessee for the year ended December 31, 1998, including adjusting and closing entries.

P 17–7
(L.O. 4, 5, 8)

Direct Financing Lease: Different Interest Rates Used by Lessor and Lessee, Entries   On January 1, 1998, lessor Hutton leased a machine to lessee Carmel on a three-year lease that qualifies as a direct financing lease. The machine cost Hutton $300,000 immediately prior to the lease. The machine has a three-year estimated useful life and no residual value. The lessor used an 11 percent target rate of return. The three annual lease payments start on January 1, 1998. The lessee uses straight-line depreciation, will retain the machine at the end of the lease term, and has a borrowing rate of 10 percent. The lessee knows both rates and therefore must use the lower of the two interest rates. The accounting period for each company ends on December 31.

Required

1. Compute the equal annual payments that the lessor will receive.
2. Prepare an amortization schedule for the lessor and give the related entries through December 31, 1998.
3. Compute the lease capitalization amount and prepare an amortization schedule for the lessee and give the related entries through December 31, 1998.

4. Complete the following 1998 comparative tabulation for the lessor and lessee and explain any differences:

Items	Lessor	Lessee
Income statement		
Interest revenue		
Interest expense		
Depreciation expense		
Balance sheet		
Lease receivable		
Lease liability		
Leased property		
Accumulated depreciation		

P 17–8
(L.O. 4, 5, 6)

Sales-Type Lease: BPO, Entries for Both Parties On January 1, 1998, lessor Onx and lessee Ryan signed a four-year lease that qualifies as a sales-type lease. The equipment cost Onx $900,000, and the cash sale price is $1,400,000. The equipment has a six-year estimated useful life. Estimated residual values were the following: end of 2001, $200,000, and end of 2006, $80,000. The lease gives Ryan an option to buy the equipment at the end of 2001 for $150,000 cash. The lease requires four equal annual payments starting on January 1, 1998. Onx's expected rate of return on the lease is 15 percent, and the incremental borrowing rate for Ryan is 16 percent. On December 31, 2001, the lessee exercises the purchase option, at which time a new estimate of residual value was $175,000. Ryan is aware of Onx's rate.

Required

1. Compute the annual payment and the amount the lessee should capitalize.
2. Prepare a lease amortization schedule for the lessor and lessee.
3. Give the entries for the lessor and lessee from the date of inception through the lease termination date.

P 17–9
(L.O. 1, 2, 3, 4, 5, 6)

Analysis to Classify Lease: Capital versus Operating, Unguaranteed Residual Value, Entries for Both Parties Lessor Sales Company and Lessee Manufacturing Company agreed to a noncancelable lease. The following information is available to both parties regarding the lease terms and the leased asset:

a. Lessor's cost of the leased asset was $30,000. The asset was new at the inception of the lease term.
b. Lease term is four years starting January 1, 1999.
c. Estimated useful life of the leased asset is six years. Estimated residual value at end of six years is zero.
d. On January 1, 2003, the estimated unguaranteed residual value of the leased asset one day after the end of the lease term is $4,000.
e. The straight-line depreciation method is used for the leased asset.
f. Lessee's incremental borrowing rate on January 1, 1999, is 18 percent. The lessee is considered a high-risk borrower.
g. Bank prime rate of interest on January 1, 1999, is 10 percent.
h. Purchase option price of leased asset exercisable one day after the end of the lease term is $4,500.
i. Title to the leased asset is retained by the lessor unless the purchase option is exercised.
j. Sales price of leased asset on January 1, 1999, is $40,000.
k. Lessor has no unreimbursable cost uncertainties.
l. Four annual lease payments are due on January 1 of each year during the lease term, and the first payment, due at the inception of the lease term, is $11,643.
m. The accounting period for the lessor and lessee ends on December 31.

Required

Round to the nearest dollar.

1. What was the lessor's implicit interest rate in this lease?
2. What type of lease was this to the lessee? To the lessor? Explain.
3. In parallel columns for the lessor and lessee, record the following:
    a. Entry, or entries, at inception of the lease on January 1, 1999, if appropriate.
    b. Adjusting and closing entries on December 31, 1999.

P 17–10
(L.O. 2, 4, 5)

Lease Classification: Entries for Lessor and Lessee The following data are available about a noncancelable lease that involves a leased asset that was new at the inception date of the lease term, January 1, 1998.

Lease term	6 years
Interest rate implicit in the lease	12%
Lessee's incremental borrowing rate	14%
Amount of each lease payment	$3,648
Lessor's cost of asset (market value)	$15,000
Lessee has no way of knowing the interest rate implicit in the lease.	
Each lease payment occurs at the end of each period (i.e., an ordinary annuity).	
Unreimbursable cost uncertainties of lessor	None
Credit standing of lessee	Excellent
Depreciation method, if needed	Straight line
Estimated useful life of asset	6 years
Estimated residual value at end of lease term	$–0–
Accounting period for both parties ends on December 31.	

Required   Round to the nearest dollar.

1. What type of lease is this to the lessee? To the lessor? Explain.
2. Give entries in parallel columns for lessor and lessee to record the following:
   a. The inception of the lease on January 1, 1998.
   b. All entries needed at year-end, December 31, 1998, for both parties to record lease payments (receipt), interest, and depreciation; include closing entries.

P 17–11
(L.O. 5, 6)

Direct Financing Lease: Unguaranteed Residual Value, Entries for Lessor   Jinx, Incorporated, purchased a machine (for leasing purposes) on January 1, 1998, for $270,000. By prior agreement the machine was delivered to Pine Company (lessee) under a direct financing lease whereby Pine made the first lease payment of $73,516 on January 1, 1998, and agreed to make three more such annual payments.

At the end of the four-year lease term, the machine will revert to the lessor, at which time it is expected to have a residual value of $20,000 (none of which was guaranteed by the lessee). The lessor's implicit interest rate was 10 percent on cost.

Required   Round amounts to the nearest dollar.

1. Show how the lessor computed the annual payment.
2. Prepare a lease amortization schedule for the lessor.
3. Give all of the entries for the lessor on the following dates:
   a. January 1, 1998—Purchase and other transactions.
   b. December 31, 1998—End of the accounting period.
   c. January 1, 2002—Return of the machine by the lessee at the termination of the lease. At this date the machine has an actual market value of $14,000 (instead of the $20,000 estimated residual value).
4. How would the lessor's entries differ at the end of the lease term if the actual market value of the machine turned out to be $23,000 (instead of the estimated residual value of $20,000)?

P 17–12
(L.O. 2, 4, 5, 6)

Capital Lease: Residual Value, Third-Party Guarantee, Schedules and Entries for Both Parties   The following data are available regarding a noncancelable lease:

a. Lease term is five years, beginning January 1, 1998.
b. The leased property cost the lessor $400,000, its market value, on January 1, 1998.
c. Estimated useful life of the asset is six years; residual value at the end of the six-year useful life is $20,000.
d. On January 1, 1998, the estimated residual value of the leased asset at the end of the lease term is $50,000. The residual value is guaranteed in full by a third-party guarantor (not the lessee).
e. The straight-line depreciation method is used for the leased asset.
f. No bargain purchase option is available to the lessee. Ownership is retained by lessor at the end of the lease term.
g. Five annual lease payments are payable on January 1 of each year (starting January 1, 1998) to yield the lessor a 14 percent return (implicit interest rate). Lessee does not know and cannot reliably estimate the lessor's yield rate. Lessee's incremental borrowing rate is 16 percent.
h. Lessor has no unreimbursable cost uncertainties. Lessee's credit rating is excellent.
i. The accounting year-end for both lessor and lessee is December 31.

Required   Round to the nearest dollar.

1. Compute the annual payments by the lessee.
2. What type of lease is this to the lessor? To the lessee? Explain.

3. Prepare an amortization schedule for the lessor. Give the following entries for the lessor:
   a. At the inception of the lease and for the initial lease payment on January 1, 1998.
   b. Adjusting and closing on December 31, 1998.
4. Prepare an amortization schedule for the lessee. Give the following entries for the lessee:
   a. At the inception of the lease and for the initial lease payment on January 1, 1998.
   b. Adjusting and closing on December 31, 1998.

P 17–13
(L.O. 6)

Direct Financing Lease: Change in Residual Value, Amortization Schedule   On January 1, 1998, Lansing Leasing Company leased equipment to a lessee for an eight-year term during which $90,000 is payable each January 1, starting on January 1, 1998. The unguaranteed residual value of the equipment at the end of the lease term is $40,000. The interest rate implicit in the lease is 15 percent. The accounting period for both the lessor and lessee ends on December 31. The lease qualifies as a direct financing lease.

Required

Round to the nearest dollar.

1. Compute the initial investment value (cost to the lessor) of the leased property and the total amount of interest to be earned by Lansing over the lease term.
2. Immediately after the fifth annual payment, the lease amortization schedule shows a lease receivable balance of $228,360. Prepare the amortization schedule for the lessor, using the value determined in (1) above to prove the correctness of that amount. For problem purposes, stop the amortization schedule after the January 1, 2002, payment.
3. Immediately after the fifth payment, Lansing determined that the expected unguaranteed residual value of $40,000 will probably be zero. This change in accounting estimate will decrease the unrecovered investment value by the present value of the previously estimated residual value. Prepare the journal entry to record this change. After adjusting the January 1, 2002, receivable balance, complete the lease amortization schedule developed in (2) above from the $228,360 value in view of this new determination.

P 17–14
(L.O. 5, 6)

Sales-Type Lease: Schedule, Entries for Lessor   On December 31, 1998, a lessor acquired a machine at a cost of $35,000 to be held for lease. The machine was leased on January 1, 1999, for five years in a sales-type lease that required annual payments of $14,099 at the end of each year. At inception of the lease, the sales value of the leased asset was $55,000. The machine will revert to the lessor at the end of the lease term, at which time the estimated residual value will be $2,500 (none of which is guaranteed by the lessee). The lessor's implicit rate of interest was 10 percent on the investment.

Required

Round amounts to the nearest dollar.

1. Show how the lessor computed the annual payment of $14,099.
2. Prepare a lease amortization schedule for the lessor.
3. Give the following entries for the lessor:
   a. To record acquisition of the machine on December 31, 1998.
   b. To record the inception of the lease on January 1, 1999.
   c. To record collection of the first payment and recognition of interest revenue on December 31, 1999 (end of the accounting period).
   d. To record, at termination of the lease on December 31, 2003, the last payment, interest revenue, and return of the asset, assuming the estimate of residual value is confirmed.
4. How would the lessor's entries differ at the end of the lease term assuming the market value of the returned machine was $2,000 (instead of the $2,500 estimated residual value)?

P 17–15
(L.O. 2, 4, 5)

Sales-Type Lease: Amortization Schedules, Entries for Both Parties   Lessor Company entered into a lease with Lessee Company on January 1, 1998. The following data relate to the leased asset and the lease agreement:

a. The asset leased was a large construction crane.
b. Cost to Lessor was $150,000.
c. Estimated useful life is 10 years.
d. Estimated residual value at end of useful life is $10,000.
e. Lessor's normal selling price is $200,000.
f. Lease provisions:
   (1) Noncancelable; the asset will revert to Lessor at the end of the lease term.
   (2) Estimated residual value at end of lease term is $20,000 (none guaranteed).
   (3) Ownership does not transfer to Lessee by the end of the lease term.

    (4) No bargain purchase option is included.
    (5) Lease term is six years starting January 1, 1998.
    (6) Lease payment at each year-end, starting December 31, 1998, is $43,329.
  g. Lessor's implicit rate of return is 10 percent (assume that Lessee knows this rate).
  h. Lessee's incremental borrowing rate is 12 percent (assume that this is evidence of a good credit rating).
  i. Lessor has no material cost uncertainties.

Required

Show computations and round to the nearest dollar.

1. What kind of lease was this to Lessee Company? Give the basis for your response.
2. What kind of lease was this to Lessor Company? Give the basis for your response.
3. For Lessor Company, give the entries to record (*a*) the lease at inception date and (*b*) the first payment.
4. For Lessee Company, give the entries to record (*a*) the lease at inception date and (*b*) the first payment.

P 17–16
(L.O. 2, 4, 5, 8)

Determine the Kind of Lease, Schedule, Entries for Both Parties   Lessor and lessee agreed to a noncancelable lease for which the following information is available:

  a. Lessor's cost of the asset leased was $25,000. The asset was new at the inception of the lease term.
  b. Lease term is four years starting January 1, 1998.
  c. Estimated useful life of the leased asset is six years.
  d. On January 1, 1998, lessor and lessee estimated that the residual value of the leased asset will be $6,000 on the purchase option date (see [*h*] below) and zero at the end of its useful life. The residual value is not guaranteed.
  e. The straight-line depreciation method is used for the leased asset.
  f. Lessee's incremental borrowing rate is 10 percent. Lessee has an excellent credit rating.
  g. Lessor's interest rate implicit in the lease is 10 percent.
  h. Purchase option price of leased asset exercisable on January 2, 2001, is $5,000.
  i. Title to the leased asset is retained by the lessor unless the purchase option is exercised.
  j. Sale value of leased asset on January 1, 1998, is $30,000.
  k. Lessor has no unreimbursable cost uncertainties.
  l. Four annual lease payments will be made each January 1 during the lease term, and the first payment, due at inception of the lease term, is $7,526.

Required

Round to the nearest dollar.

1. Show how the annual payment was computed.
2. Is this an operating lease or a capital lease to the lessee? Explain. Compute the lessee's capitalizable cost of the leased asset.
3. What type of lease is this to the lessor? Explain.
4. Prepare an amortization schedule. In parallel columns for the lessee and lessor, record the inception of the lease on January 1, 1998 (if appropriate), and the adjusting and closing entries on December 31, 1998.
5. Prepare the financial statement presentation of all lease-related accounts as they would appear in the financial statements of the lessee at December 31, 1998, for the year then ended. Disclosures are not required.

P 17–17
(L.O. 4, 5, 6)

Direct Financing Lease: Executory Cost, Partially Guaranteed Residual Value, Entries   Stockton Leasing Company (lessor) entered into a four-year noncancelable, direct financing lease with Acme Corporation (lessee) on January 1, 1998. The leased asset has a six-year life, with zero residual value at the end of the six years. On January 1, 1998, both lessor and lessee estimated the residual value of the asset at the end of the lease term to be $30,000, of which Acme guaranteed $20,000. The leased asset cost $500,000 (same as its market value). Lease payments are to be made on December 31 of each year, starting December 31, 1998, and are set to yield 16 percent to Stockton (implicit interest rate). This interest rate is known to Acme, which has an 18 percent incremental borrowing rate. Straight-line depreciation is used. Stockton agreed to pay annual executory costs of $3,000 and included this amount in the lease payments. There is no bargain purchase option, and ownership is retained by Stockton at the end of the lease term. The accounting period for both companies ends on December 31.

Required

Round to the nearest dollar.

1. Compute the annual lease payments.
2. Prepare amortization schedules for the lessor and lessee.
3. Record the following for the lessor and lessee:
  a. Entry at the inception of the lease.
  b. Adjusting and closing entries at December 31, 1998.

4. Assuming that the actual residual value of the leased asset on December 31, 2001 (end of lease term) was $15,000, prepare entries for lessor and lessee on December 31, 2001, to record the return of the asset to the lessor.
5. Ignore (4). Assuming that the actual residual value of the leased asset on December 31, 2001, was $25,000, prepare entries for lessor and lessee on December 31, 2001, to record the return of the asset to the lessor.

P 17–18
(L.O. 5)

Accounting for Initial Direct Lease Costs On January 1, 1998, lessor Loeb leased equipment to lessee Rao. The equipment cost the lessor $400,000, and the lessor's expected rate of return was 15 percent. The three annual payments are to start on December 31, 1998. The lease has no BPO and there is no residual value. The lessor incurred, and paid, initial direct costs of $6,000 in consummating the lease. The lessor recorded these costs as a credit to cash and a debit to a temporary holding account called *initial direct leasing costs*. The lease payments were indirectly set to cover such costs.

Required

1. Compute the annual payment (ordinary annuity basis) set by the lessor (where the payment includes the direct leasing costs) assuming the following cases:

   Case A: An operating lease.
   Case B: A direct financing lease.
   Case C: A sales-type lease if the normal or regular selling price of the leased asset is $600,000.

2. Give the lessor's entries for (*a*) the inception of the lease and (*b*) the payments related to the lease at the end of the first year, for each case.
3. Give any entry needed for each case that the lessor should make during the first year for the initial direct costs. (The lessee's entries are unaffected.)

P 17–19
(L.O. 7)

Sale–Leaseback: Operating and Direct Financing Leases Compared On January 1, 1998, Supergrocery, Inc., sold the building currently used to Diversified Investors for $9,000,000, its current market value. Prior to the sale the carrying value of the building was $7,000,000. The estimated remaining useful life of the building is 10 years, with no residual value at the time; straight-line depreciation is used.

On January 1, 1998, Supergrocery signed a 10-year noncancelable leaseback agreement that has a 15 percent implicit rate of return for the lessor. The lessee's incremental borrowing rate also is 15 percent. The annual payments start on January 1, 1998. During 1998 Supergrocery would pay $10,000 for executory costs (such as insurance, taxes, and maintenance) if this transaction qualifies as a direct financing lease. Alternatively, if it qualifies as an operating lease, this $10,000 would be paid by the buyer–lessor. For problem purposes only, two cases are assumed about the lease: Case A, an operating lease, and Case B, a direct financing lease.

Required

For practical reasons give all amounts in $000s.

1. Compute the annual lease payments and the gain or loss on the sale of the building.
2. Give the 1998 entries for the seller–lessee and the buyer–lessor in parallel columns for Case A, an operating lease.
3. (*a*) Prepare the lease amortization schedule through 1999 for Case B, a direct financing lease.
   (*b*) Give the 1998 entries for the seller–lessee and the buyer–lessor in parallel columns for Case B, a direct financing lease.

P 17–20
(L.O. 3)

Operating Lease: Advance Payment, Ordinary Annuity Basis In lieu of making four $40,000 rent payments spaced at one-year intervals with the first payment due at the end of the first year of the lease term, the lessee and the lessor agree that the lessee can make a lump-sum initial payment, the amount to be computed, at the start of the four-year lease term. This amount was calculated on the basis of an agreed 16 percent annual interest rate.

Required

Round all amounts to the nearest dollar.

1. Compute the lump-sum initial payment amount.
2. On the assumption that the lessee amortizes the prepayment on a straight-line basis, give the lessee's entries to record the initial payment and year-end adjustments if the lease year and lessee accounting year coincide.

P 17–21
(L.O. 3)

Operating Lease: Advance Payment, Annuity Due Basis A lessor and a lessee began negotiations that would have provided that the lessee pay six semiannual $16,000 payments for the use of property with the first payment to be at the beginning of the lease term. However, after agreeing that money was worth 14 percent per year at the time, the parties finally agreed that the lessee would instead pay a single advance payment at the outset in lieu of all other payments for the three-year term. Assume an operating lease.

Required   Round to the nearest dollar.

1. Calculate the advance payment and prepare an amortization schedule covering the entire term of the lease.
2. Assume that the lessor and lessee amortize the advance payment computed in (1) above by the straight-line method. Give entries for both parties to record amortization at the end of the year if the lease year and accounting year of the parties coincide.

ANALYSIS, JUDGMENT, AND COMMUNICATION

CASES

C 17–1
(L.O. 6)

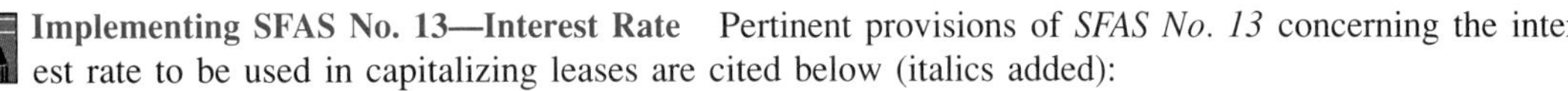 **Implementing SFAS No. 13—Interest Rate**   Pertinent provisions of *SFAS No. 13* concerning the interest rate to be used in capitalizing leases are cited below (italics added):

> A lessor shall compute the present value of the minimum lease payments using the *interest rate implicit in the lease*. . . . A lessee shall compute the present value of the minimum lease payments using his incremental borrowing rate . . . unless (*i*) it is practical for him to learn the implicit rate computed by the lessor, and (*ii*) the implicit rate computed by the lessor is less than the lessee's incremental borrowing rate. If both of these conditions are met, the lessee shall use the implicit rate.

> *Interest rate implicit in the lease* is defined as the discount rate that, when applied to the minimum lease payments (excluding executory costs) and to the unguaranteed residual value of the property to the lessor, causes the present value at the start of the lease term to equal the market value of the property to the lessor at the inception of the lease. (There are some qualifications to this abstracted definition, but they are not important for present purposes.)

> *APB Opinion No. 21,* which deals with the imputation of interest to receivables and payables, indicates that the choice of an interest rate "may be affected by the credit standing of the issuer, restrictive covenants, the collateral, payment and other terms pertaining to the debt, and, if appropriate, the tax consequences to the buyer and seller."

Required   Evaluate the foregoing criteria in light of the following assertions by writing a one-page memo to a superior:

1. Asking a lessor what interest rate is inherent in a lease transaction would be similar to asking a farmer what rate is implicit in the price the farmer can expect now for next fall's corn crop. There are varying degrees of risk in any operation having a distant future; the higher the farmer's future risks are thought to be, the higher the farmer will set his or her rate, and the lessor will do likewise.
2. The assumption that a lease has an implicit interest rate, in many cases, represents circular reasoning in that the market value of the leased asset itself (that is, the benchmark value used in determining the implicit rate) is determined by market forces. The value of the property stems from the payments it will command rather than the payments stemming from the value of the property.
3. One determinant of the implicit interest rate in a lease is the residual value of the property to be leased. This is a subjective judgment that, depending on the property, can be substantially in error. Lessors will not disclose what their guess is.

C 17–2
(L.O. 1, 2, 8)

YOU MAKE THE CALL   **Concern about Debt–Equity Ratio and Third-Party Residual Value Guarantees: Ethics**   Speedware Corporation has entered into a debt agreement that restricts its debt-to-equity ratio to less than two to one. The corporation is planning to expand its facilities, creating a need for additional financing. The board of directors is considering leasing the additional facilities but is concerned that leasing may violate its existing debt agreement; a violation would place the corporation in default. The potential lessor insists that the lease be structured in such a way that it can be accounted for as a capital lease by the lessor (the lessor is a dealer and wants to recognize the dealer's profit on the transaction immediately). In addition, the lessor requires that the residual value of the leased asset be guaranteed when it reverts to the lessor at the end of the lease term. Speedware's board has asked you to analyze the following alternatives:

Alternative A—Speedware would enter into a lease that qualifies as a capital lease (to Speedware). If this alternative is selected, Speedware's reported debt-to-owners'-equity ratio would be 1.9, and its ability to issue debt in the future would be seriously constrained.

Alternative B—Speedware would enter into a lease and pay a third party to guarantee the residual value of the leased property. The lease would be structured in such a way as to qualify as an operating lease to Speedware and as a capital lease to the lessor. In this case, Speedware's reported debt-to-equity ratio would be unaffected by the lease contract.

Required   Analyze and explain the consequences of each of the above alternatives in a one-page memo to your superior. Do you see any ethical considerations?

C 17–3
(L.O. 2, 4, 8)

Ameritech: Nature, Entries, and Disclosure of Leases   Notes 9 and 10 to Ameritech's 1994 annual report follow. Ameritech is a major player in the communications industry.

9. Long-Term Financing

LONG-TERM DEBT   Long-term debt consists principally of debentures issued by the Ameritech landline telephone subsidiaries. The following table sets forth interest rates and other information on long-term debt outstanding at December 31, after giving effect to refinancings in January 1994 reflected in 1993 amounts:

Interest Rates	Maturities	1994	1993
4.375%–6.0%*	1996–2025	$1,175.0	$ 755.0
6.125%–8.0%	2002–2024	2,345.0	2,345.0
8.125%–9.0%	1997–2026	333.7	340.7
9.1%–10.0%	1996–2016	205.8	207.6
		4,059.5	3,648.3
LESOP (Note 6).		341.2	416.5
Capital lease obligations		85.6	79.2
Other		1.5	0.8
Unamortized discount, net†		(39.9)	(54.4)
Total.		$4,447.9	$4,090.4

*Includes $450.0 million issued in 1994, tied to floating LIBOR rate.

†Change due principally to the discontinuation of *FAS 71*.

10. Lease Commitments

The company leases certain facilities and equipment used in its operations under both operating and capital leases. Rental expense under operating leases was $181.6, $196.2 and $196.3 million for 1994, 1993 and 1992, respectively. As of December 31, 1994, the aggregate minimum rental commitments under noncancelable leases were approximately as follows:

Years	Operating	Capital
1995	$101.2	$ 45.2
1996	82.7	42.8
1997	71.8	36.2
1998	65.0	13.1
1999	50.2	1.6
Thereafter	235.7	7.2
Total minimum rental commitments	$606.6	146.1
Less: executory costs		3.1
interest costs		20.2
Present value of minimum lease payments		$122.8

Required

1. Is the firm a lessee or lessor?
2. Where would the liabilities appear on the 1994 balance sheet and in what amounts?
3. Does Ameritech have any operating leases? How do you know? How are the payments accounted for by the firm?
4. What entries would Ameritech make to account for its leases during 1995, based on those leases currently on the books? (Ignore any executory costs.)

ANALYZING FINANCIAL STATEMENTS

All questions in this section are based on information taken from the financial statements of actual companies.

A 17–1
(L.O. 1)

Nature of a Lease   The following paragraphs are taken from an article appearing in *The Wall Street Journal* on April 7, 1993 (pp. A1 and A4), entitled "As IBM's Woes Grew, Its Accounting Tactics Got Less Conservative."

The Leasing Game

In 1982, IBM asked Merrill Lynch to perform a rare, inventive piece of financial surgery that directly affected its profits, though few shareholders or analysts ever heard of it.

When companies lease out equipment, they can account for it as an "operating" or a "sales-type" lease. An operating lease is conservative; revenues go on the books as they actually flow in each year. A sales-type lease is more liberal; all the revenue that will ever come in is recorded in the first year.

To restrain revenue-hungry companies the Financial Accounting Standards Board has extensive rules, running more than 100 pages, about sales-type leases. IBM's accountants zeroed in on a formula in paragraph 7D: Add up [the present value of] all the lease payments, plus the [present] value of the computer when the lease expires. If the total is 90% of the computer's value today, the lease can be considered a sales-type one.

In the hotly competitive market, IBM was offering terms that didn't add up to the 90% mark. Merrill's solution: It sold IBM "7D insurance" guaranteeing a certain value of the computer at the end of the lease—enough to push IBM over 90%.

"Helping IBM keep the accounting proper for these leases was a simple matter, and we were able to provide this service for them," says Federick Butler, a former Merrill director of lease financing.

"Without this guarantee, these leases would be just under the (90%) line and would have to be taken as operating leases." Mr. Butler says Merrill didn't offer the service to any other company. Asked later for further information about the arrangement, a Merrill spokesman declined to comment.

Required   Your company has a similar situation. Write a memo to your immediate supervisor commenting on the accounting, indicating both the acceptance of the approach under GAAP and its spirit. Bracketed words were added by the authors.

A 17–2
(L.O. 4, 8)
Estimating Lease Liability   Norfolk & Southern is a major transportation company. This is an excerpt of Note 8 to Norfolk & Southern's 1995 annual report:

8. Lease Commitments

NS is committed under long-term lease agreements, which expire on various dates through 2067, for equipment, lines of road and other property. Future minimum lease payments are as follows:

Years	Operating	Capital
	(millions)	
1996	$56.6	$ 15.0
1997	53.8	14.9
1998	45.5	14.9
1999	33.4	14.9
2000	31.8	14.8
2001 and subsequent years	583.8	80.5
Total	$804.9	155.0
Less: imputed interest on capital leases at an average rate of 8.4%		AO*
Present value of minimum lease payments included in debt		$100.9

*AO stands for amount omitted by authors.

Required   Given that lease payments occur evenly throughout the year, estimate the decline in the capital lease liability in 1995.

A 17–3
(L.O. 4, 8)
Lease Calculations and Disclosures   Turner Broadcasting Company sponsors CNN. Note 5 to Turner's 1994 annual statements, dealing with long-term debt, includes the following information in part:

Note 5: Long-Term Debt

Long-term debt consists of:

	December 31	
	1994	**1993**
	(thousands)	
Bank credit facilities	$1,490,000	$1,225,000
12% Senior Subordinated Debentures due October 15, 2001, net of		
unamortized discount of $3,268	—	536,732
8 3/8% Senior Notes due July 1, 2013, net of unamortized discount of $2,619		
and $2,675	297,381	297,325
7.4% Senior Notes due 2004, net of unamortized discount of $363	249,637	—
8.4% Senior Debentures due 2024, net of unamortized discount of $155	199,845	—
Zero coupon subordinated convertible notes, 7.25% yield, due February 13,		
2007, net of unamortized discount of $336,487 and $353,368	245,569	228,688
Convertible subordinated debentures of a wholly owned subsidiary	29,075	—
Obligations under capital leases due in varying amounts through 1999, net of		
imputed interest of $931 and $1,075.	6,200	6,353
Other debt, net of imputed interest of $1,175 and $29, due in varying		
amounts through 2009, interest at fixed rates ranging from 6.00% to 9.49%	1,386	2,510
	$2,519,093	$2,296,608
Less current portion	1,345	2,051
	$2,517,748	$2,294,557

Other information obtained from the notes to Turner Broadcasting Company's financial statements:

Included in the maturities of long-term debt amounts are obligations under capital lease of $1,299,000; $1,273,000; $1,261,000; $1,376,000; and $1,016,000 for each of the five years following December 31, 1994. Finally, assume that $565,000 of lease maturities exist for each of the years 2000, 2001, and 2002 respectively.

Required

Estimate the firm's average implicit interest rate on its lease obligations. Assume there are no further long-term lease obligations after December 31, 2002. All payments are made at the end of the year.

A 17–4
(L.O. 2, 4)

Lease Reporting and Entries   The United Airlines (UAL) liability section of its 1995 annual report and portions of note 9 are given below.

	December 31	
(in millions, except share data)	**1995**	**1994**
LIABILITIES AND SHAREHOLDERS' EQUITY		
Current liabilities:		
Short-term borrowings.	$ —	$ 269
Long-term debt maturing within one year	90	384
Current obligations under capital leases	99	76
Advance ticket sales	1,100	1,020
Accounts payable	696	651
Accrued salaries, wages and benefits	870	843
Accrued aircraft rent	771	825
Other accrued liabilities	807	838
	4,433	4,906
Long-term debt	2,919	2,887
Long-term obligations under capital leases	994	730
Other liabilities and deferred credits:		
Deferred pension liability	368	512
Postretirement benefit liability.	1,225	1,148
Deferred gains	1,214	1,363
Accrued aircraft rent	272	213
Other	336	272
	$3,415	$3,508

9) Lease Obligations

As of December 31, 1995, United leased 292 aircraft, 49 of which were under capital leases. These leases have terms of 4 to 26 years, and expiration dates range from 1999 through 2021. Under the terms of leases for 283 of the aircraft, United has the right of first refusal to purchase, at the end of the lease term, certain aircraft at fair market value and others at either fair market value or a percentage of cost. United has 29

Airbus A320-200 aircraft under 24- to 26-year operating leases that are cancelable upon 11 months' notice during the initial 10 years of the lease. Other leases include airport passenger terminal space, aircraft hangars and related maintenance facilities, cargo terminals, office and computer equipment and vehicles.

Future minimum lease payments as of December 31, 1995, under capital leases (substantially all of which are aircraft) and noncancelable operating leases having initial or remaining lease terms of more than one year are as follows:

| | Operating Leases | | Capital |
| | Aircraft | Non Aircraft | Leases |
(in millions)			
Payable during—			
1996	$ 866	$ 425	$ 182
1997	855	419	180
1998	862	410	183
1999	861	408	158
2000	878	397	136
After 2000	12,744	7,598	835
Total minimum lease payments	$17,066	$9,657	1,674
Imputed interest (at rates of 5.3% to 12.2%)			(581)
Present value of minimum lease payments.			1,093
Current portion			(99)
Long-term obligations under capital leases.			$ 994

Amounts charged to rent expense, net of minor amounts of sublease rentals, were $1.439 billion in 1995, $1.222 million in 1994 and $1.028 million in 1993. Included in rent expense was $22 million in contingent rentals, resulting from changes in interest rates for certain operating leases. United has entered into interest rate swap agreements.

Required

1. Does UAL show the current value of next year's capital lease payment or the decline in the present value of the lease obligation among its current liabilities? Justify your answer.
2. Provide UAL's journal entries as a lessee for 1996.
3. What was the value of the equipment acquired under capital lease obligations in 1995? What principal was paid on these new leases in 1995? (The cash flow statement reports principal payments under capital lease obligations of $80.0 million.)

A 17–5
(L.O. 1)

YOU MAKE THE CALL   **Capitalizing Operating Leases**   Currently, operating leases are not required to be shown on the balance sheet. If United Airlines' operating leases on December 31, 1995, were added to its liabilities, its current ratio would decline from 0.69 to 0.57 while its total debt would increase from $239 million to $1,105 million. There would also be significant changes in the measured return on assets because assets would be increased and the related increase in depreciation and interest expense exceeds the rent expense included in its 1995 income statement.

Required

Comment on this situation with regard to economic reality and the provision of useful information to decision makers. Do you believe operating leases should be capitalized? Why or why not? Put your answer in the form of a memo to the FASB.

A17–6
(L.O. 2, 4, 8)

Delta Airlines   This problem requires access to the World Wide Web portion of the Internet. You should use Delta's most recent 10-K annual report. To do so access the SEC's Electronic Data gathering, Analysis, and Retrieval System (EDGAR) using the following steps:

a. URL: http://www.sec.gov/index.html
b. Click on EDGAR Database of Corporate Information
c. Click on Search for EDGAR Database
d. Click on Search for EDGAR Archives
e. Enter the company name in the search dialog box
f. Click on the listing for the most recent 10K annual report

Required

(It is possible that some of the data you may need to answer the questions may not be available. If so, omit this portion of the requirements.)

1. What type of assets does Delta lease?
2. What method does Delta use to record rent expense on its operation leases? What entry did Delta make in the most recent year to recognize rent expense on its operating leases?

3. What is the amount of leasehold and operating rights (excluding flight equipment) held by Delta at the end of the last fiscal year?

4. What method does Delta use to measure the current portion of its capital lease obligation? How do you know?

5. Provide your best estimate of the entries Delta would make to recognize its capital lease payments for the coming fiscal year. (Use 10 percent as an estimate of Delta's average interest rate on its capital leases.) How would you estimate this rate if it were necessary to do so with only the information available on the 10-K?

COMPARATIVE ANALYSIS

CA 17–1
(L.O. 1, 2, 4, 8)

American Airlines and U.S. Air   This problem can be worked as a group exercise. See the preface for how to work group problems. Excerpts from the December 31, 1995, balance sheets of AMR Corporation (the parent company of American Airlines) and USAir Group, Inc., (the parent company of U.S. Air) regarding their respective lease obligations are:

(all amounts in millions)	American	U.S. Air
Assets:		
Owned property, plant, and equipment	$13,396	$6,325
Less: Accumulated depreciation	(3,544)	(2,301)
Net	$ 9,852	$4,024
Property, plant, and equipment acquired through capitalized leases	$ 2,624	$ 198
Less: Accumulated amortization	(875)	(140)
Net	$ 1,749	$ 57
Liabilities:		
Current obligation, capital leases	$ 122	$ 14
Long-term obligation, capital leases	2,069	51
Total capital lease obligation	$ 2,191	$ 65
Total stockholders' equity	$ 3,720	$ (836)
Total Assets	$19,556	$6,955

The notes to the financial statements provide the following additional disclosures regarding capital and operating leases:

AMR Corporation

The future minimum lease payments required under capital leases, together with the present value of net minimum lease payments, and future minimum lease payments required under operating leases that have an initial or remaining noncancelable lease term in excess of one year as of December 31, 1995, were (in millions):

Year Ending December 31	Capital Leases	Operating Leases
1996	$ 248	$ 879
1997	273	919
1998	268	926
1999	263	918
2000	328	874
2001 and subsequent	1,954	14,402
	3,334 (a)	$18,918 (a)(b)
Less amount representing interest	1,143	
Present value of net minimum lease payments	$2,191	

(a) Future minimum payments required under capital leases and operating leases include $205 million and $203 billion, guaranteed by AMR and American, respectively relating to special facility revenue bonds issued by municipalities.

(b) Future minimum lease payments required under operating leases include $6.2 billion guaranteed by AMR relating to special facility revenue bonds issued by municipalities.

USAir Group, Inc.

At December 31, 1995, obligations under capital and noncancelable operating leases for future minimum lease payments were as follows (in thousands):

	Capital Leases	Operating Leases
1996	$21,886	$ 761,281
1997	21,697	770,230
1998	10,687	735,035
1999	10,687	694,591
2000	7,586	666,841
Thereafter	20,094	6,651,858
Total minimum lease payments	92,637	$10,279,836
Less sublease rental receipts	27,141	90,133
Total minimum operating lease payments	$65,496	$10,189,703

Required

1. Both American and U.S. Air have capital leases. Which airline acquires a greater percentage of its property and equipment through capital leases? Which airline appears to have capital lease obligations that extend farthest into the future? Why might one airline have a greater reliance on capital leases than the other? State your assumptions, and show your analysis.
2. In addition to capitalized leases, both American and U.S. Air acquire property and equipment through operating leases. Which airline acquires the greater amount of its assets by operating leases, relative to the amount acquired through capital leases? Which airline has a greater obligation for operating leases that extend beyond 5 years into the future? Why might one airline have a greater reliance on operating leases than the other? State your assumptions, and show your analysis.
3. With the data given, for which airline can an estimate of the implicit interest rate used in the capital leases be estimated? Compute an estimated interest rate. Does this rate seem reasonable?
4. Assume that the operating lease payments for 2001 and thereafter for both airlines extend over the 10-year period from 2001 through 2010, in equal annual payments due at the end of each year. Also assume that the appropriate interest rate for capitalization of the operating leases is 10 percent for both airlines. Finally, use an average figure for the operating leases for the period 1996–2000 of $850 million for American Airlines and $725 million for U.S. Air. What effect would capitalizing the operating leases have on the balance sheets of the two airlines? Which company's balance sheet would be affected most? Why?

18 ACCOUNTING FOR PENSIONS & OTHER POSTEMPLOYMENT BENEFITS

After you have studied this chapter, you will:

1. Be familiar with fundamental pension concepts.

2. Understand the basic nature of pension expense and be able to determine the components of pension expense.

3. Be able to distinguish among the ways of measuring pension liability: projected benefit obligation, accumulated benefit obligation, vested benefit obligation, and accrued pension cost.

4. Understand unrecognized pension cost amounts and their effect on pension expense.

5. Understand and be able to compute additional minimum pension liability.

INTRODUCTION

The Coca-Cola Company's *obligation* for unpaid pension benefits promised to its employees was $1,313 million at the end of fiscal 1995. Yet the firm included only $187 million of that amount (14%) in its balance sheet (footnote 13). This amount was merged with other liabilities. Why is most of this significant liability kept off the balance sheet? Other firms in similar situations actually report a prepaid pension asset!

On the other hand, Coca-Cola's liability for other postretirement benefits (OPEB), which are mostly health care and insurance benefits for retirees, was $303 million at the same date, and $273 million of that amount (90%) was included in balance sheet liabilities (footnote 14). This amount was also merged with other liabilities. The underlying obligations for pensions and OPEB are similar yet their reporting appears to be quite different.

A closer look at Coca-Cola's footnotes reveals not just one but three amounts listed as obligations for future pension benefit payments:

Vested benefit obligation	$1,017 million
Accumulated benefit obligation	1,106 million
Projected benefit obligation	1,313 million

Will the real pension obligation please stand up! What do these different measures of Coca-Cola's pension liability represent and why are three different amounts reported?

Consider the problem of forecasting the pension benefit payments for employees who will retire 20 years from now. Many plans base benefit payments on salary levels near retirement. These salaries must be estimated. But when will employees actually retire? What about turnover? Inflation and interest rate changes also must be factored into the calculation. How long will employees live after retirement? What is their health status now? Do they smoke? Will they quit?

As you can see, a large number of estimates and assumptions must be made to ascertain a firm's pension liability. The uncertainty underlying OPEB liabilities is even greater, given the difficulty of forecasting future health care costs.

The pension and OPEB liabilities are measures at a point in time. What is the periodic cost or expense to be recorded? In other words, what is the measure of the cost of these plans for a given period? Coke reported the following expenses for 1995 in its footnotes. The amounts were merged with other operating expenses in the income statement:

<pre>
     Pension expense . . . . $66 million
     Other postretirement benefits expense . . . .   33 million
</pre>

What exactly do these amounts represent? Are these the benefit payments made in 1995, are they the amount placed in trust for future payment, or do they represent the present value of benefits earned in 1995?

Pension plan funding is yet another issue. Firms are required by law to fund their plans. But by some estimates, the pension plans of U.S. corporations in total are underfunded by at least $50 billion, meaning that if the present value of all benefits recognized to date was due today, the firms would be that much short. (By comparison, the federal government's pension plans are underfunded more than *$1 trillion*.) Coca-Cola's pension plan was underfunded $157 million at the end of 1995, while its OPEB plan was underfunded $261 million. These amounts are disclosed in the footnotes. Accounting principles play an important role in this measure of a firm's funded status because they define how the liability is to be measured. To many investors, the funded status of a plan (whether over or underfunded) is the single most important amount to be reported for a plan.

This chapter tackles the many challenging issues surrounding pension and OPEB accounting. The resulting corporate disclosures are among the least understood by users, and the most subject to management influence. As this chapter explains, the development of current GAAP in these areas is the result of compromises between preparer firms and accounting policymakers.

PENSION PLAN FUNDAMENTALS

Since the early 1900s public and private retirement programs have provided pension benefits for employees. These programs include Social Security, company retirement programs for employees, and tax-sheltered savings plans. Companies establish pension plans to increase employee motivation and productivity, reduce current demands for pay increases, reduce turnover, comply with union contracts, and maintain competitiveness in the labor market. Pension costs are a substantial percentage of total compensation costs, and pension benefits are a significant portion of total income for many retirees.

The **sponsor** of a **pension plan** agrees to make payments into a fund for future retirement benefits for employee services. A plan **participant** is any current or former employee (and beneficiaries) for whom the pension plan provides benefits. Pension plans provide participants with a degree of retirement security not otherwise attainable.

Many pension plans meet Internal Revenue Code requirements and hence qualify for tax advantages:

- Employers deduct contributions to the pension fund from taxable income, subject to certain limitations.

- Employers exclude pension fund earnings from taxable income.
- Employees exclude employer contributions from taxable income, subject to certain elections by the employee.
- Employees defer tax on benefits until after retirement.[1]

Types of Pension Plans

Employers generally establish one of two types of pension plans: **defined contribution** and **defined benefit** plans. This chapter is concerned primarily with defined benefit plans because the accounting is much more complex than for defined contribution plans.

Defined contribution plan *contributions* are established by formula or contract; the benefits are not specified. For example, some defined contribution plans require the employer to contribute a percentage of an employee's salary each month into an employee-directed investment fund. The employer makes no promise about the amount of retirement benefits. The employee bears the risk of pension fund performance in a defined contribution plan. In recent years, defined contribution plans have become increasingly popular because they shift the risk of investment performance to the employee and are more portable than defined benefit plans. The portability feature allows an employee to maintain full pension benefits when changing employers; it is particularly important given the increasing frequency with which employees currently change jobs.

A defined benefit plan, in contrast, commits the employer to specified retirement benefits. The *benefits* are established by a **pension benefit formula;** the contributions are not specified. The employer bears the risk of pension fund performance. Fund shortages caused by poor investment performance increase the employer's unfunded liability.

The variables in pension benefit formulas include number of qualified years of service credited to the employee, compensation levels, and age at retirement. An example of a *final-pay* pension benefit formula for a defined benefit plan is

$$\text{Annual benefit payment during retirement}$$
$$= 2.5\%(\text{Number of years service})(\text{Final salary})$$

Example   An employee with a $100,000 final salary who retires after 25 years of service receives $62,500 (.025 × 25 × $100,000) each year of retirement. The 2.5 percent term implies that 40 years of service must be rendered to achieve a pension equal to final salary. The annual benefit payment is a determinant of the investment required to satisfy the obligation and of the cost of the pension plan.

For purposes of the benefit formula, final salaries are estimated using an assumed annual rate of compensation increase that must be disclosed in the footnotes.

Example   Mary currently earns $30,000 per year and is expected to work another 15 years for her firm. The assumed annual rate of compensation increase is 6 percent. Therefore, Mary's estimated final salary is $71,897 [$30,000(FV1, .06, 15)]. This amount is used in the benefit formula to determine Mary's benefit payments.

---

[1]Tax deferral bestows two benefits on employees. The pension fund grows much faster during the years of employment, and employees may be in a lower tax bracket when they retire.

EXHIBIT 18–1

Relationships among Entities in a
Pension Plan

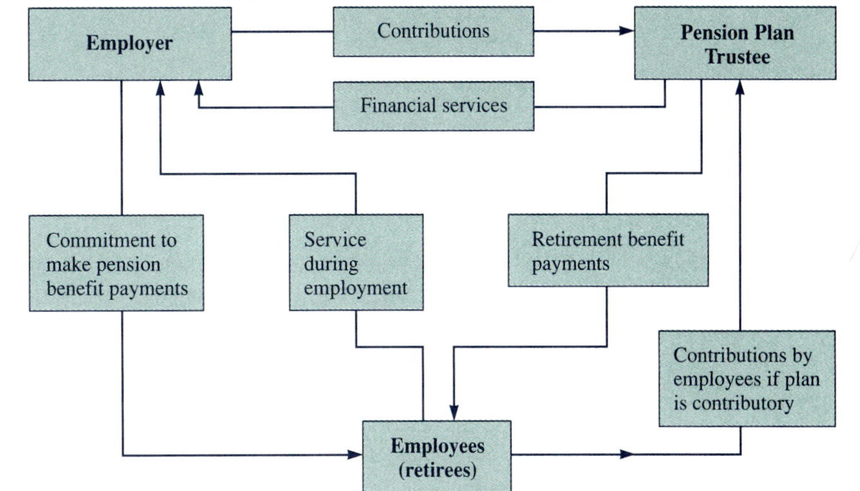

Vesting of Benefits

The right to receive earned pension benefits is **vested** when it is no longer contingent on continued employment. Most plans require a minimum employment term before benefits vest. Vesting provisions are especially important in a mobile labor force. Without vesting, workers who change jobs lose all their accumulated benefits. In some plans, vesting also guarantees benefits to the spouse of an employee who dies before retiring.

Pension Plan Funding

A pension fund is an accumulation of cash and other assets restricted for the payment of retiree benefits. Funding sources include employer contributions, fund earnings, and employee contributions. Pension fund earnings generally supply a significant portion of total required funding. Pension plans are **contributory** or **noncontributory.** A plan is contributory if the employees must pay part of the funding needed to provide the specified benefit or if the employees voluntarily make payments to increase retirement benefits.

Firms fund pension plans in one of three ways:

1. The firm maintains and administers the pension fund internally.
2. A bank or trust company, serving as the fund trustee, invests the employer contributions, makes retirement payments, and provides the employer with periodic information about the plan and investment performance.
3. The firm purchases a retirement annuity from an insurance company that accepts the responsibility for paying the pension benefits to the retirees.

The examples in this chapter assume an outside trustee. The trustee assumes ownership of the assets and bears the obligation for retirement payments. Exhibit 18–1 summarizes the relationships among the parties in a pension plan when an outside trustee is used.

Defined benefit pension plans are fully funded (or *overfunded*) if the market value of plan assets equals (or exceeds) the actuarial present value of all benefits earned to date by participants. Otherwise the plan is *underfunded.* Tax law, pension regulations, fund performance, current period pension benefits earned, general economic conditions, and cash flow constraints all affect the amount employers contribute each year to pension funds.

Role of Actuaries

Actuaries—professionals trained in a specific branch of mathematics and statistics—develop the estimates of future retirement benefit payments needed to compute the employer's pension expense and pension obligation. They use statistical models incorporating several variables including turnover, inflation, future compensation levels, final retirement age and life expectancy, the interest rate used for discounting benefit payments, and administrative costs.

The actuary works with the employer to develop the relevant historical data and expected changes in the employee population for this estimation process. Actuaries also give advice on the attributes of the plan most appropriate to an employer. Without the actuary, current pension accounting would not be possible.

Regulation of Private Pension Plan Funding

The Employee Retirement Income Security Act of 1974, as amended, known as **ERISA,** regulates the funding and administration of private (nongovernment) pension plans to protect employees. Before ERISA, underfunded pension plans were a major concern. Many employers funded plans on a pay-as-you-go basis, paying only those retirement benefits currently due.

ERISA sets minimum vesting and funding standards that require employers to back benefit promises with assets. It mandates extensive reporting to regulatory authorities that evaluate the plan's funded status, and it requires pension fund audits. Employers are subject to fines and denial of tax deductibility for noncompliance.

ERISA also created the Pension Benefit Guaranty Corporation (**PBGC**) to administer and make retirement payments for terminated plans. If a covered pension plan terminates with liabilities exceeding assets, the PBGC guarantees certain minimum benefits, including vested benefits and cost of living adjustments. The PBGC is financed by premiums from sponsoring companies and applies only to defined benefit plans.

Minimum Vesting Standards

Under ERISA, employee benefits must be vested according to one of two alternatives:[2]

1. One hundred percent vesting of employer contributions after five years of service ("cliff" vesting).
2. A vesting schedule:

Years of Service	Percent Vested
3	20%
4	40
5	60
6	80
7 or more	100

Example   Under the second alternative, 80 percent of an employee's promised pension benefits are vested after six years of service. Employee contributions to a pension plan vest immediately.

Minimum Funding Standards

The annual amount the employer contributes to the pension fund must cover at least the benefits earned in the current year, adjusted for the effects of plan amendments and changes in assumptions. Congress amends ERISA frequently. Changes in vesting and funding standards since 1974 have generally increased the protection of employee benefits.

CONCEPT REVIEW

1. What is the main difference between defined contribution and defined benefit plans?
2. What role does a pension benefit formula play in a defined benefit pension plan?
3. How does ERISA protect employee interests in pension benefits?

SUMMARY OF CURRENT PENSION ACCOUNTING

Accounting for a defined *contribution* plan does not involve new measurement or recognition issues. The employer debits pension expense for the amount of the required contribution, credits cash for the amount paid, and credits a liability for underpayments or debits a prepaid asset for overpayments.

The major issues in pension accounting involve defined *benefit* plans. They include how to measure and recognize pension expense and pension liabilities.

---

[2]*United States Code Annotated,* Title 29, Section 1053 (St. Paul, MN: West Publishing Company, 1996).

Measuring Pension Expense in Defined Benefit Plans

Pension expense is measured according to the concept of **attribution:** assigning pension benefits to periods of employee service as defined by the pension benefit formula.[3] Attribution takes into account the cost of pension benefits earned in the period, effects of previous over- or underfunding, return on the pension fund, and changes in the plan and underlying assumptions. The effects of these changes are recognized on a delayed basis.

Pension expense reflects future compensation levels if they are a factor in the benefit formula. However, only benefits attributable to service rendered through the reporting date are included in the measurement of pension expense and liabilities.

Recognizing Pension Liabilities in Defined Benefit Plans

The obligation to pay retirement benefit payments is based on past service by employees and the pension agreement. The existence of a future pension obligation is evident, although the amount is not known with certainty. Many accountants maintain that the employer's pension liability is extinguished when the actuarial present value of future benefits is funded. Under this view, the sponsoring firm does not own the assets contributed to the fund and has a liability only for underfunded pension benefits. The arrangement between the employer and trustee further supports this view. The trustee is a separate legal entity having title to the plan assets. Normally, the assets are restricted because the employer has access to the assets only on termination of the plan.

An alternative view holds that the employer extinguishes its liability only when benefit payments are made. This view requires recognition of the total obligation (present value of unpaid benefits) and pension fund assets in the balance sheet. Otherwise, the employer has significant off-balance-sheet debt, and employer assets are greatly understated. In addition, the economic substance, rather than the legal form of the employer–trustee relationship suggests that the employer, rather than the trustee, owes employees pension benefits. The employer's control over the plan, as exemplified by the ability to terminate the plan and reclaim surplus assets, supports this view. Again, the employer is liable for any underfunded amounts.

The profession has adopted a modified version of the latter view in *SFAS No. 87,* "Employers' Accounting for Pensions."[4] Both the fund asset balance and several liability measures are disclosed in the footnotes. But the FASB stopped short of requiring recognition of the total liability and plan assets in the accounts, favoring instead footnote disclosure.

Before launching into the details of pension accounting, we provide a summary of the issues and basic procedures in Exhibit 18–2. The exhibit provides a view of the major measurement and recognition issues as well as GAAP generalizations. The discussion that follows the exhibit expands on this summary and introduces the technical terms for defined benefit pension accounting.

MEASURING PENSION EXPENSE AND PENSION OBLIGATIONS

Example   Consider the defined benefit pension plan of the Lone Pine Corporation, a hypothetical software development company. This example focuses on one employee, Nicole Whitney, a software engineer, and develops the concepts of pension expense and liability for pension benefits.[5] Exhibit 18–3 gives the initial data for her pension plan.

Discount Rate

Employers use a discount rate to compute the actuarial present value of benefits, the pension expense, and the obligation of the employer under the plan. The discount rate is the rate at which pension obligations *could be settled* if sufficient funds were invested at that rate. The actuarial present value reflects not only the time value of money but also factors that affect the probability of payment, including life expectancy, turnover, and disability.

---

[3]The term *pension expense* denotes the pension cost recognized in a period. However, manufacturing firms capitalize part of total periodic pension cost to inventory for the portion relating to manufacturing personnel, pending sale.

[4]*SFAS No. 87* applies to all pension plans, whether written or implied. It does not apply to life and health benefits during employment or postemployment life insurance and health care benefits. The appendix discusses postretirement benefits other than pensions.

[5]In practice, the actuary analyzes data for the employee group and develops estimates of life expectancy, turnover, and other factors. It is generally not possible to predict the benefits payable to an individual employee, but we use one individual to simplify the presentation and focus on the concepts. Actuarial models are beyond the scope of this text.

EXHIBIT 18–2
Summary of Defined Benefit
Pension Accounting

All periods except period C in the time line represent several years.

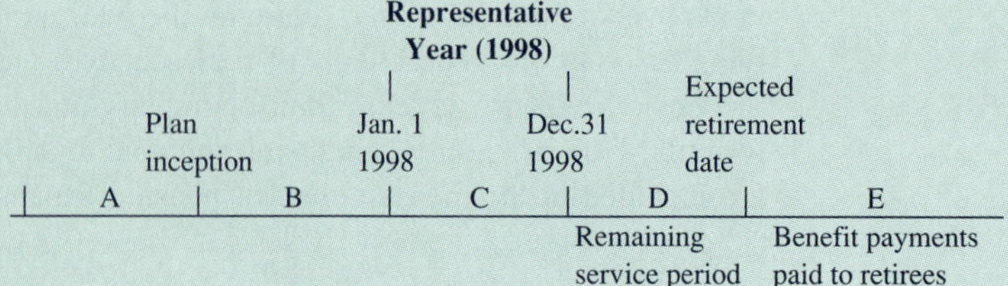

Summary of Pension Reporting for 1998 (a representative year):

1. Pension expense for 1998 (period C above) is the present value of the increase in benefit payments based on service credits earned in 1998, adjusted for factors *a* through *d* below. The benefit payments are based on service credits earned through period C only, but often reflect estimated salaries near the end of period D. Adjustments to periodic pension expense:
   a. Difference between growth in pension liability and growth in pension fund.
   b. Recognition of the cost of service credits retroactively granted for period A.
   c. Effects of changes in assumptions on pension liability and pension fund.
   d. Effect of transitioning to *SFAS No. 87* from previous accounting method.

2. The primary measure of total pension liability at December 31, 1998, is based on *future salaries*, and is the present value of benefit payments based on service credits earned in periods A through C. Typically only a small fraction of this amount is disclosed in the balance sheet. The entire amount is disclosed in the footnotes and is affected by estimated turnover, life expectancies, and many other factors.

Summary of the Annual End-of-Year Accounting Process (at most two journal entries)

Determine (1) pension expense, the net sum of six components, and (2) the funding amount.

Entry 1: Record pension expense and funding amount (1998 amounts assumed):

Pension expense		20,000
Accrued pension cost		5,000
Cash		15,000

The accrued pension cost account is the liability reported in the balance sheet, but is not the total pension liability. If cumulative funding has exceeded cumulative pension expense, the balance sheet account is an asset: prepaid pension cost.

In the footnotes to financial statements, disclose the Reconciliation of Funded Status report (1998 amounts assumed):

Total pension liability (based on future salaries)	$(100,000)
Total plan assets in fund (market value)	60,000
(Under) overfunded status	(40,000)
Adjustments relating to components 4–6 of pension expense	15,000
Balance in (accrued) prepaid pension cost (to balance sheet)	$(25,000)

This report explains why the balance sheet liability ($25,000) does not equal the total pension liability for the firm ($100,000), and discloses whether the plan is underfunded (total liability > fund assets) or overfunded (total liability < fund assets).

If the amount of underfunded obligation, using the total pension liability based on *current salaries,* exceeds the reported pension liability ($25,000 above), then an additional reported pension liability is recognized for the difference, in entry 2. Entry 1 is recorded annually; entry 2 is recorded only when needed. If needed, entry 2 is recorded after entry 1. (1998 amounts assumed: total liability based on current salaries, $90,000)

Entry 2: Record additional minimum pension liability

Intangible pension asset	5,000
Additional minimum pension liability	5,000

Underfunded status using $90,000 liability amount = $90,000 − $60,000	$30,000
Balance in accrued pension cost after entry 1 (see table above):	25,000
Required additional reported pension liability (assuming no beginning balance)	$ 5,000

EXHIBIT 18–3

Information for Lone Pine
Pension Plan and Employee
Nicole Whitney

Pension plan: Noncontributory defined benefit plan
Pension plan inception: January 1, 1998
Date Nicole Whitney joins Lone Pine: January 1, 1998
Starting salary for Nicole: $45,000 per year
Nicole's age on January 1, 1998: 40
Nicole's expected retirement date: December 31, 2022 (25 years of employment service expected)
Assumed annual rate of compensation increase: 5%. Nicole's final salary at retirement therefore is estimated
   at $152,386 [$45,000(FV1, .05, 25) = $45,000(3.38635)]. For this illustration, we have rounded her final
   salary to $150,000.
Pension benefit formula:

$$\text{Annual retirement benefit payment} = 2\%(\text{Number of years service})(\text{Final salary})$$

Lone Pine vests 10 percent of benefits after the first year, 15 percent of benefits after the second year, and
   then conforms to the present ERISA schedule (20 percent of total benefits vested after the third year, and
   so forth)
Discount rate and expected long-term rate of return on pension plan assets (assume that expected equals
   actual return): 10 percent
Nicole's expected retirement period: 10 years; payments are made at the end of each calendar year during
   retirement
Time line depicting service and retirement periods for Nicole:

	Service Period		**Retirement Period**	
1/1/1998		1/1/2023		12/31/2032
	25 years		10 years	

Contributions to pension plan (funding) are made at the end of service years:	Retirement benefit payments are made at the end of retirement years:
First contribution: 12/31/1998	First payment: 12/31/2023
Last contribution: 12/31/2022	Last payment: 12/31/2032

SFAS No. 87 requires that the discount rate approximates the market interest rate. When choosing the discount rate, firms consider the following factors:

- Rates implicit in annuity contracts offered by insurance companies.
- Information on interest rates from the PBGC.
- Returns on high-quality fixed-income investments expected during the accumulation period.

Firms also consider the average age of employees. For example, the discount rate for a plan covering mainly retirees might reflect a portfolio of investments with shorter maturities than those of a plan covering a younger workforce.

Pension Expense

Periodic pension expense is the **net cost** of six components.

1. Service cost.
2. Interest cost.
3. Return on plan assets.
4. Amortization of prior service cost.
5. Gain or loss recognized.
6. Amortization of transition asset or liability.

The first two components always cause periodic pension expense to increase, but the last four components may either increase or decrease pension expense, depending on the situation.

Service Cost: Component 1 of Pension Expense

Service cost is the actuarial present value of pension benefits attributed to employee service in a period, based on the pension benefit formula, which in this case uses Nicole's estimated final salary. The service cost for Nicole in 1998 is computed as follows: (see Exhibit 18–3):

$$\frac{\text{Annual retirement benefit}}{\text{earned by Nicole in 1998}} = .02(1 \text{ service year})(\$150,000) = \$3,000$$

Service cost, 1998
$$= \text{Present value of benefit payments earned in 1998}$$
$$= \$3,000(\text{PVA, }10\%, 10^*)(\text{PV1, }10\%, 24^\dagger)$$
$$= \$3,000(6.14457)(.10153)$$
$$= \underline{\underline{\$1,872}}$$

*Ten years of retirement payments.
†Retirement in 24 years, as of December 31, 1998. This factor discounts the 10-year annuity to December 31, 1998.

Nicole earned a retirement benefit of $3,000 *per retirement year* by working for Lone Pine during 1998.[6] Service cost for Nicole in 1998 is $1,872, the investment required at December 31, 1998 (the measurement date)[7] to settle the obligation for her future retirement payments *earned in 1998*. Service cost is not related to the amount contributed to the fund in 1998.[8]

For the first year only (assuming no amendments or transition gain or loss, and funding at the end of the year), pension expense equals service cost. No other components are involved. If Lone Pine contributes only $1,500 to the pension fund trustee because of liquidity problems,[9] the following entry records pension expense:

December 31, 1998—Record pension expense:

Pension expense	1,872	
Accrued pension cost		372
Cash		1,500

Accrued Pension Cost Account   The $372 balance in the liability account, accrued pension cost, is the amount by which the pension plan is underfunded. If Lone Pine plans to increase funding in 1999 to cover the deficiency, the liability is classified as current.

If Lone Pine contributed $1,900 (rather than $1,500) to the fund in 1998, an asset account, prepaid pension cost, would be debited for $28, the amount by which the plan would be overfunded.[10] The balance in accrued or prepaid pension cost equals the difference between cumulative pension expense recognized to date and cumulative funding to date.

Employer Pension Obligations   The **projected benefit obligation (PBO)** is the actuarial present value of the benefits attributed to employee service rendered to date, as measured by the benefit formula. Service cost for a period is the increase in PBO due to employee service during that period. Benefit payments reduce PBO.

PBO at the end of the first year of a pension plan (without amendments) equals service cost ($1,872 for Nicole) because service cost is also the present value of benefits earned in the first year. The FASB concluded that PBO is the most representationally faithful measure of the pension obligation because it is an estimate of a present obligation to make

---

[6]However, this amount is not guaranteed until both (*a*) the benefits vest and (*b*) Nicole attains her estimated final salary.

[7]In order to allow sufficient time to gather information, *SFAS No. 87* allows the measurement date, the date at which pension assets and liabilities are measured, to fall within the three-month period before the balance sheet date.

[8]In practice, the actuary determines service cost by considering productivity, seniority, promotion, turnover, life expectancy, and disability in the employee group.

[9]Underfunding is not allowed under ERISA, but is used for instructional purposes. Waivers of minimum funding requirements are available, however.

[10]It is common for firms to report a pension asset. For example, Ameritech Corporation reported $933 million of prepaid pension cost in 1995 on its defined benefit plans. Lone Pine's entry assuming $1,900 of funding would be:

Pension expense	1,872	
Prepaid pension cost	28	
Cash		1,900

future cash payments as a result of past events. In our example, the benefit formula incorporates future salaries. Therefore, PBO also reflects future salaries. The going-concern assumption supports the use of future compensation levels in calculating PBO.[11]

SFAS No. 87 requires disclosure of two additional liability measures: **accumulated benefit obligation (ABO)** and **vested benefit obligation (VBO).** The computation for each is similar to PBO except that ABO is based on current salary levels, and VBO is based on vested benefits, also measured at current salary levels. If the benefit formula does not incorporate future salary levels, ABO and PBO are equal. All three liability measures are disclosed in the footnotes to the financial statements.

ABO and VBO as of December 31, 1998, for Nicole are computed as:

Annual retirement benefit
earned by Nicole in 1998

$$
\begin{aligned}
\text{based on } \textit{current salary} &= .02(1 \text{ service year})(\$45,000) = \$900 \\
ABO &= \$900(\text{PVA}, 10\%, 10)(\text{PV1}, 10\%, 24) \\
&= \$900(6.14457)(.10153) \\
&= \underline{\underline{\$561}}
\end{aligned}
$$

Annual retirement benefit
earned by Nicole in 1998

$$
\begin{aligned}
\text{based on } \textit{vested benefits} &= .02(1 \text{ service year})(\$45,000)(.10)^* = \$90 \\
VBO &= \$90(\text{PVA}, 10\%, 10)(\text{PV1}, 10\%, 24) \\
& \$90(6.14457)(.10153) \\
&= \underline{\underline{\$56}}
\end{aligned}
$$

*Vesting percentage for first year.

If the benefit formula considers future compensation levels and not all benefits are vested, the following relationship generally holds:

$$ \text{PBO} > \text{ABO} > \text{VBO} $$

This relationship is illustrated below for Nicole:

Vested benefit obligation (VBO)	$ 56
Add nonvested benefit obligation	505
Accumulated benefit obligation (ABO).	561
Add effect of future compensation levels	1,311
Projected benefit obligation (PBO)	$1,872

PBO is the measure of the employer's obligation in a going concern; ABO and VBO provide a measure of the employer's potential obligation if the plan is discontinued. Some accountants consider ABO a more reliable measure of the employer's obligation because it is based on definite compensation levels. Others believe PBO is a more relevant measure because it uses compensation levels more likely to be in effect at retirement. The disclosure of several measures of the pension liability allows a more complete assessment of the employer's obligation.

Plan Assets   Plan assets include investments (primarily stocks, bonds, and other securities) and operational assets used in administering the pension fund. Plan assets are restricted to the payment of pension benefits and administering the pension plan. Except for plan terminations, the employer (sponsor) should not be able to access plan assets. Plan assets are maintained on the books of the trustee, not the sponsor, although footnote disclosure of the fair value of plan assets is required of sponsors.

Investment assets are valued at fair market value or market-related value. The fair market value is the amount realizable through a normal sale. Market-related value equals fair

---

[11]The rate of assumed annual compensation increase for computing PBO most commonly used by a sample of 600 major companies was 4.5 percent or less. See *Accounting Trends and Techniques—1996* (New York: AICPA, 1996), p. 314.

market value or a calculated value that recognizes changes in fair market value of plan investments in a systematic and rational manner over a period of not more than five years. The use of the market-related value reduces the volatility of periodic pension expense.

Operational pension assets are valued at book value and shown in the records of the fund trustee.[12] The sum of the plan investments (at fair market value or market-related value) and plan operational assets (at book value) is called *plan assets at fair value*. The trustee of the funding agency prepares an annual report showing the beginning balance in plan assets, all changes during the year, and the ending balance. For simplicity, we assume here that the pension fund consists entirely of investments and that fair value and market-related value are equal.

Example   Some companies have contributed noncash assets to pension funds in an attempt to maintain their own liquidity levels. In 1995 GM was given permission by the Labor Department to contribute $6 million in the Electronic Data Systems version of GM stock to the pension plan covering the company's U.S. auto workers.[13]

Funded Status, 1998   The **funded status** of a plan is the difference between PBO and the plan assets at fair value and indicates whether the plan is under- or overfunded. It is the critical measure of a pension plan. Lone Pine's plan is underfunded because PBO exceeds the pension fund's fair value, as indicated in the following table:

Reconciliation of Funded Status, Lone Pine Corporation, December 31, 1998

Projected benefit obligation.	($1,872)
Plan assets at fair value	1,500
Underfunded PBO (funded status)	($ 372)
Balance in accrued pension cost	($ 372)

PBO and fund assets describe separate characteristics of the pension plan. Although they are not related, they have two attributes in common. Neither is recorded in the accounts of the employer, and both are reduced by benefit payments. Benefit payments are paid from plan assets and reduce the employer's liability. They are recorded by the trustee rather than by the employer. The nonrecognition of PBO in the balance sheet is an example of off-balance-sheet financing.

The disclosure of funded status is an example of **offsetting.** In the example so far, the plan's funded status equals the balance in the accrued pension cost account. Therefore, Lone Pine's plan assets are offset against PBO for balance sheet reporting (accrued pension cost appears among the liabilities on the balance sheet). There are no reconciling items in this case. Reconciling items are those subject to delayed recognition, illustrated in later examples.

Nonrecognition of PBO is controversial. The FASB was sensitive to concerns that recognition of PBO in the balance sheet would greatly increase many companies' debt levels.

Example   Chrysler's 1995 balance sheet reported $42 billion in total debt. Its projected benefit obligation was an additional $14 billion. Although Chrysler's pension plans were slightly overfunded, PBO represents one-third of Chrysler's reported debt.

Interest Cost and Actual Return: Components 2 and 3 of Pension Expense, Second Year

Exhibit 18–4 presents information and pension calculations for 1999 and for the next two pension expense components.

Interest Cost   The second component of pension expense, **interest cost,** is the growth in PBO during a reporting period. At December 31, 1998, PBO equals $1,872. At 10 percent, interest cost for 1999 equals $187 ($1,872 × .10). The amount of the liability at December 31, 1999, for Nicole's first-year benefits *only* is $2,059:

---

[12]Book value is used because there is generally no intent to sell these assets, fair market value may be difficult to ascertain, and operational assets are generally unavailable to pay pension benefits.

[13]*The Wall Street Journal*, April 4, 1995, p. A14. There is concern that funding a pension with equity securities and assets whose value is tied to the performance of the sponsoring company abrogates the fundamental arm's-length relationship between sponsor and employee. See "Pension Raiding, 1983 Style," *Forbes*, June 20, 1983, p. 130. A 1993 U.S. Supreme Court decision upholding excise taxes on contributions of property in satisfaction of a funding obligation may reduce this practice.

EXHIBIT 18–4
New Information and Pension
Calculations, Lone Pine
Corporation, 1999

1999 compensation for Nicole: $47,250 (a 5 percent raise for 1999)
Estimated salary at retirement: $150,000 (unchanged)
Funding for 1999: $2,000
Service cost for 1999:

$$\text{Annual retirement benefit earned by Nicole in 1999} = .02(1 \text{ service year})(\$150,000) = \$3,000$$
$$\text{Service cost, 1999} = \$3,000(PVA, 10\%, 10)(PV1, 10\%, 23^*)$$
$$= \$3,000(6.14457)(.11168) \qquad = \underline{\underline{\$2,059}}$$
$$\text{PBO, 12/31/99} = \$6,000^\dagger(PVA, 10\%, 10)(PV1, 10\%, 23)$$
$$= \$6,000(6.14457)(.11168) \qquad = \underline{\underline{\$4,117}}$$

Nicole's vested benefits: .02(2 years)($47,250)(.15) = $284
Nicole's benefits based on current salary: .02(2 years)($47,250) = $1,890

VBO [$284(PVA, 10%, 10)(PV1, 10%, 23)]	$ 195
Add nonvested benefit obligation	1,102
ABO [$1,890(PVA, 10%, 10)(PV1, 10%, 23)]	1,297
Add effect of future compensation levels	2,820
PBO	$4,117

*23 years from December 31, 1999 to retirement.

†Nicole has earned two years of retirement benefits, or $6,000 according to the formula:
.02(2 years)$150,000 = $6,000.

$$\$2,059 = \$1,872(1.10)$$

Or:

$$\$2,059 = \$3,000(PVA, 10\%, 10)(PV1, 10\%, 23)$$
$$= \$3,000(6.14457)(.11168)$$

This means that Lone Pine must have $1,872 invested at December 31, 1998, to provide the benefits promised in 1998 and must have $2,059 invested at December 31, 1999, for the same benefits. The $187 difference is interest cost, the growth in PBO ($2,059 − $1,872).

PBO through the plan's second year ($4,117 in Exhibit 18–4) is the present value of benefit payments earned through December 31, 1999. Another way to compute PBO highlights certain pension expense components:

PBO, 12/31/99:	
Service cost through 12/31/99 ($1,872 + $2,059)	$3,931
Interest cost through 12/31/99	187
Benefits paid to Nicole through 12/31/99	(0)
PBO, 12/31/99	$4,118*

*$1 discrepancy due to rounding of present value factors.

Return on Plan Assets   The third component of pension expense, **return on plan assets,** is the increase or decrease in plan assets at fair value, adjusted for contributions and benefit payments. A schedule shows the changes in the fund during a period:

	Beginning fund balance
+	Return on assets
+	Employer contributions
−	Benefit payments
=	Ending fund balance

The return on assets generally reduces pension expense by partially or wholly offsetting the interest cost component, and it increases the pension fund.[14] Actual return includes

---

[14]With sufficiently high return, pension expense can be negative (an earnings increase). For example, in 1995, Pepsico Inc.'s actual return of $338 million was more than double the net sum of the other components of pension expense and 5.6 times the service cost.

| | | **Effect on** | |
| | | | |
Item	**Pension Expense**	**Projected Benefit Obligation**	**Plan Assets**
Service cost	Increase	Increase	No effect
Interest cost	Increase	Increase	No effect
Asset return†	Decrease	No effect	Increase
Contributions	No effect*	No effect	Increase
Benefit payments	No effect	Decrease	Decrease

*Contributions indirectly reduce future pension expense by increasing plan assets and (therefore) actual return.

†Assume positive return. If return is negative, the effects on pension expense and plan assets are opposite those listed.

dividends, interest, and realized and unrealized changes in plan assets at fair value. Assume that actual return is $150 in 1999 and equals the expected amount ($1,500 × .10).

Pension expense for 1999 is computed as follows:

Service cost, 1999	$2,059 (from Exhibit 18–4)
Interest cost, 1999	187
Asset return, 1999	(150)
Pension expense, 1999	$2,096

Lone Pine funds $2,000 in 1999 (Exhibit 18–4). The entry to recognize pension expense is as follows:

December 31, 1999—Record pension expense:

Pension expense	2,096	
Accrued pension cost		96
Cash		2,000

Pension expense increased in 1999 for three reasons: service cost reflects a shorter period to retirement, interest cost increases pension expense, and asset return is less than interest cost. The balance in accrued pension cost at December 31, 1999, is $468 ($372 from 1998 + $96 from 1999). The $96 increase represents an additional funding deficiency. Full funding would have required a contribution of $2,468 ($2,096 + $372 previous accrued pension cost balance) at the end of 1999.

Funding levels and pension expense are inversely related because asset return reduces pension expense. For example, if the plan were fully funded in 1998 ($1,872 contribution), pension expense in 1999 would be $2,059 (1999 service cost) because interest cost and actual return would exactly offset. Early full funding results in smaller subsequent pension expense.

Using the original information, the fund balance at the end of 1999 is as follows:

Fund balance, 1/1/99	$1,500
Asset return, 1999	150
Employer contributions, 1999	2,000
Benefits paid, 1999	(0)
Fund balance, 12/31/99	$3,650

The reconciliation of funded status for 1999 appears below. Relationships among several new terms introduced in this section are summarized in Exhibit 18–5.

Reconciliation of Funded Status: Lone Pine Corporation, December 31, 1998

Projected benefit obligation	$(4,118)
Plan assets at fair value	3,650
Underfunded PBO (funded status)	$ (468)
Balance in accrued pension cost	$ (468)

EXHIBIT 18–6

Pension Spreadsheet

LONE PINE COMPANY
Pension Plan Spreadsheet, 1999

	Informal Record		Formal Record	
	PBO (actuary)	Plan Assets (trustee)	Pension Expense	Accrued Pension Cost
Beginning balances, 1999.	$1,872	$1,500		$ (372)
Service cost	2,059		$2,059	
Interest cost	187		187	
Asset return		150	(150)	
Contributions		2,000		2,000
Benefits paid	0	0		
Ending balances:				
PBO	$4,118			
Plan assets		$3,650		
Underfunded PBO	$468			
Pension expense			$2,096	(2,096)
Accrued pension cost				$ (468)

Pension Spreadsheet   The spreadsheet in Exhibit 18–6 brings together the reports of the actuary and trustee. Service cost and interest cost appear in the PBO and pension expense columns as additions. Asset return increases assets but is entered as a negative amount in the pension expense column. The contribution is a positive entry in the assets column, yet is a decrease in the accrued pension cost column.

The spreadsheet distinguishes **formal** from **informal** records. The formal record includes accounts actually represented in the ledger including pension expense and accrued pension cost. The informal record includes those items not appearing in the balance sheet, such as pension plan assets, PBO, and items arising from delayed recognition (discussed later). These items are disclosed in the footnotes only.

⎸CONCEPT REVIEW

1. How is the benefit formula used in the calculation of service cost for a period?
2. Why are pension expense, service cost, and projected benefit obligation the same amount for the first year of Lone Pine's pension plan?
3. Why are the projected benefit obligation and plan assets not recorded in the accounts?

⎸REVIEW PROBLEM

The following data refer to the Hillsborough Company's defined benefit pension plan. The company's fiscal year ends December 31.

Balances, January 1, 1998		Information for 1998	
PBO	$400,000	Service cost	$40,000
Plan assets at fair value	300,000	Benefits paid	35,000
Accrued pension cost	100,000	Discount rate	8%
		Actual return on plan assets	
		(equals expected return)	30,000
		Funding (contribution)	50,000

Required

1. The December 31, 1998, entry to record pension expense.
2. The 1998 reconciliation of funded status.

SOLUTION

1. Pension expense, 1998:   December 31, 1998

Service cost	$40,000
Interest cost	32,000*
Actual return	(30,000)
Pension expense	$42,000

Pension expense	42,000
Accrued pension cost	8,000
Cash	50,000

*(.08)$400,000

2.

HILLSBOROUGH COMPANY

Reconciliation of Funded Status

December 31, 1998

PBO	($437,000)	($400,000 + $40,000 + $32,000 − $35,000)
		Beg. Bal. Service Interest Benefits
		Cost Cost
Plan assets at fair value	345,000	($300,000 + $30,000 − $35,000 + $50,000)
		Beg. Bal. Actual Benefits Funding
		Return
Underfunded PBO	($92,000)	
Accrued pension cost	($92,000)	($100,000 − $8,000 from 1998 entry)
		Beg. Bal.

Components 4, 5, and 6 of Pension Expense; General Considerations

The discussion to this point has emphasized the relationships among fundamental pension accounting concepts. Expected return on plan assets and delayed recognition of pension cost are two important concepts that affect the measurement of the remaining components of pension expense: amortization of prior service cost (component 4), gain or loss recognized (component 5), and amortization of transition amount (component 6).

Expected Return on Plan Assets   The expected return on plan assets is derived by multiplying the expected long-term rate of return on plan assets by the fair value of plan assets at the beginning of the reporting period. Current earnings rates on the fund and rates expected in the future are considered when estimating this rate.[15] Expected return in 1999 for Lone Pine is $150 (.10 × $1,500). When expected and actual returns differ, a pension gain or loss results, which may affect pension expense. For Lone Pine, we assumed both return measures were equal in 1999.[16]

The discount rate and the expected long-term rate of return on plan assets are not necessarily equal. The rate of return chosen reflects the sponsor's attitude toward risk and return. One employer might be willing to accept a higher degree of risk and demand a 12 percent expected rate of return. Another employer would accept a 9 percent expected rate of return with lower risk. Yet both employers could choose an 8 percent discount rate consistent with data from insurance companies or the PBGC. The discount rate reflects the rate at which the obligation could be settled. The rate of return more closely reflects the investment strategy of the sponsoring firm.

Many firms use an expected rate of return that exceeds the discount rate. The 1990s bull stock market encouraged many firms to increase those return rates and with good reason. Well-diversified portfolios of equity investments often turned in annual rates of return exceeding 25 percent.

---

[15]The long-term expected rate of return most commonly used by a sample of 600 major companies was 9 percent. See *Accounting Trends and Techniques—1996* (New York: AICPA, 1996) p. 314.

[16]When expected and actual returns differ, pension expense ultimately reflects expected return. The discussion on the fifth component of pension expense addresses this point.

Example   The expected rate of return for both PepsiCo and the Coca-Cola Company exceed their respective discount rates, with Coke's rate exceeding its discount rate by more than 2 percent in 1995. PepsiCo's actual return of $338 million in 1995 was almost three times its expected return.

Delayed Recognition   The last three components of pension expense are subject to **delayed recognition** of changes in pension obligations or assets. Changes are recognized in pension expense systematically over subsequent periods rather than immediately when incurred. The unamortized (unrecognized) amounts are carried forward to the following accounting periods.

One effect of delayed recognition is that the balance in accrued pension cost does not equal the plan's funded status. Reconciling items thus are required in the funded status report. For example, an increase in PBO resulting from a plan amendment is recognized only gradually in pension expense. Therefore, the balance in accrued pension cost reflects only the portion of the increase in PBO amortized to date.

The primary purpose of delayed recognition is to reduce the volatility of pension reporting by spreading changes in the pension plan over a number of years. Delayed recognition increased the business community's acceptance of *SFAS No. 87*. However, delayed recognition increases the likelihood that the accrued pension cost of employers with grossly underfunded plans will understate the actual obligation, an example of significant off-balance-sheet debt. Therefore, when underfunded ABO exceeds accrued pension cost, an additional minimum pension liability is recognized. This requirement partially reduces the effects of delayed recognition and appeases those not favoring the use of future compensation levels for measuring pension expense. (ABO is based on current and past salary levels.)

<table>
<tr><td>

Prior Service Cost: Component 4 of Pension Expense

</td><td>

Prior service cost (PSC) results from the granting of pension benefits for service rendered before the pension plan began or from plan amendments granting increased pension benefits for service rendered before the amendment.

Retroactive increases in pension benefits are common in collective bargaining agreements. For example, if an employer sets up a pension plan in 1998, employees who started in 1980 are at a disadvantage if they are not granted pension benefits for service rendered before 1998. Almost all plans recognize service rendered before the inception of the plan.[17]

PSC, the present value of retroactive benefits under the amendment, represents an increase in PBO. This expanded expression for PBO incorporates PSC:

</td></tr>
</table>

Sum of service cost to measurement date
+ Sum of interest cost to measurement date
+ PSC (present value at amendment date)
− (Benefits paid to measurement date)
= PBO at measurement date[18]

Assume that on January 1, 1999, Lone Pine Company amends its plan to award Nicole an additional annual $500 retirement benefit for service rendered in 1998. Nicole has 24 years of service remaining, and she is expected to draw 10 retirement payments. PSC is computed as follows:

$$\text{PSC, } 1/1/99 = \text{Present value of increased benefits granted by amendment}$$
$$= \$500(\text{PVA}, 10\%, 10)(\text{PV1}, 10\%, 24)$$
$$= \$500(6.14457)(.10153) = \underline{\$312}$$

Employers who increase pension benefits attributable to prior service are assumed to benefit in future periods from the resulting improved employee productivity and morale, reduced turnover, and reduced demand for pay raises. Therefore, the cost of retroactive grants is subject to delayed recognition and is matched against the periods

---

[17]M. Warshawsky, *The Funding of Private Pension Plans,* Board of Governors of the Federal Reserve System, 1987, p. 3.

[18]PSC will increase subsequent interest cost because it increases PBO.

SIERRA COMPANY

Date of amendment: January 1, 1998
Amendment: Increased the benefits attributable to service performed before January 1, 1998, for all active
 employees
PSC: Present value of increased benefits at 1/1/98 is $48,000
Active employees, and remaining estimated service years at 1/1/98:
Jim, 1; Frank, 2; Susan, 2; Katherine, 3; Bill, 4

Schedule of employee service years remaining at January 1, 1998:

	Employee Service Years				
Employee	1998	1999	2000	2001	Total
Jim	1				1
Frank*	1	1			2
Susan	1	1			2
Katherine	1	1	1		3
Bill	1	1	1	1	4
Service years per fiscal year	5	4	2	1	12

Average service period: 12 total years/5 employees = 2.4 years.

*Frank has two years of service remaining: 1998 and 1999.

of benefit to the firm. Rather than immediately expense the entire PSC amount, a portion of PSC is recognized each period through amortization as component 4 of pension expense. The unrecognized portion of PSC is carried forward as part of the informal pension record.

Amortization (recognition) of PSC, the fourth component of pension expense, generally increases pension expense.[19] PSC is amortized over the remaining service period of those employees active at the date of the amendment who are expected to receive benefits under the plan. Employees hired after that date do not affect the amortization. The number of years used for amortization is not subsequently changed except for a pension plan curtailment. If most of a plan's participants are inactive, PSC is amortized over the remaining life expectancy of those participants. Amortization of PSC is limited to amounts known at the beginning of the year.

Methods of Amortizing PSC   *SFAS No. 87* allows two approaches to amortizing PSC:

1. The straight-line method amortizes PSC over the average service period, resulting in quicker amortization than (2).
2. The service method allocates an equal amount of PSC to each employee service year and results in declining amortization as employees retire.

Exhibit 18–7 presents the data for an example of both approaches.

Straight-Line Method   The average remaining service period for the employee group is 2.4 years, as calculated in Exhibit 18–7. The straight-line method yields the following:

Year	Amortization Recognized	Unrecognized PSC at December 31
1998	$20,000 = $48,000/2.4	$28,000 = $48,000 − $20,000
1999	$20,000 = $48,000/2.4	$ 8,000 = $48,000 − $40,000
2000	8,000 (remaining)	$ 0 = $48,000 − $48,000

The straight-line method amortizes PSC more rapidly than the service method, resulting in greater pension expense in early years. Furthermore, this method fully amortizes PSC before the last covered employee retires. However, frequent plan amendments may imply

---

[19]A plan amendment can reduce PBO by reducing future benefits on a retroactive basis. The reduction is first used to reduce any existing unrecognized PSC. The amortization of the excess reduces pension expense.

EXHIBIT 18–8
Reconciliation of Funded Status

SIERRA COMPANY
Summary Pension Plan Information for Funded Status Report
December 31, 1998

PSC information applies from Exhibit 18–7, remaining data assumed
Unrecognized PSC, 12/31/98: $28,000
Service cost, 1998: $300,000
Interest cost, 1998: $80,000
Actual and expected return: $90,000
PBO, 12/31/98: $1,200,000 (includes $48,000 of PSC from 1/1/98 amendment)
Plan assets at fair value: $962,000
Accrued pension cost, 12/31/98: $210,000 cr. (after pension expense is recorded)

Pension expense, 1998:

Service cost	$300,000
Interest cost	80,000
Actual return	(90,000)
Amortization of PSC	20,000
Pension expense	$310,000

Reconciliation of funded status, 12/31/98:

Projected benefit obligation	$(1,200,000)
Plan assets at fair value	962,000
Underfunded PBO (funded status)	(238,000)
Unrecognized PSC	28,000
Balance in accrued pension cost	$ (210,000)

that the benefit period of each amendment is shorter than the entire service period of active employees.

Service Method   Under the service method, $20,000 of PSC (5/12 $\times$ $48,000) is amortized in 1998, when 5 of the total 12 service years are rendered. Pension expense is increased by $20,000 in 1998. At the end of 1998, $28,000 of PSC remains unamortized ($48,000 − $20,000). Amortization proceeds as follows:

Year	Amortization Recognized[20]	Unrecognized PSC at December 31
1998	$20,000 = $48,000(5/12)	$28,000 = $48,000 − $20,000
1999	$16,000 = $48,000(4/12)	$12,000 = $28,000 − $16,000
2000	$ 8,000 = $48,000(2/12)	$ 4,000 = $12,000 − $ 8,000
2001	$ 4,000 = $48,000(1/12)	$ 0 = $ 4,000 − $ 4,000

The service method is preferable because it logically relates PSC to years of service as rendered with more in the early years. The benefits the employer realizes are also greatest during those years. More employees are working and the effect of the grant on performance is at its peak soon after the award.

Reconciliation of Funded Status   Exhibit 18–8 presents complete data for the Sierra Company example. The exhibit shows $28,000 of unrecognized PSC as a reconciling amount at the end of 1998. Had Sierra recognized total PSC in pension expense immediately (rather than $20,000 in 1998), pension expense and the balance in the accrued pension cost account would have been $28,000 higher. The balance in accrued pension cost would have equaled $238,000, the underfunded PBO. Because PSC is subject to delayed recognition, accrued pension cost reflects only the amounts recognized as expense to date ($20,000 in 1998), whereas PBO reflects the entire amount of PSC. Thus, reconciling items explain why the reported liability (accrued pension cost) does not equal the plan's funded status.

---

[20]The two methods always produce the same amortization in the first year.

Gains and Losses: Component 5 of Pension Expense

The funded status of a pension plan (PBO − plan assets at fair value) is the critical value for evaluating the financial position of the plan. The first three components of pension expense measure the change in the funded status for the current period. Service cost and interest cost are the annual increases in PBO arising from service credits earned in the year and from the growth in PBO over time. The actual return on plan assets (which to this point is assumed to equal expected return) is the portion of the annual cost of the plan provided by fund earnings. The effects of prior service cost on pension expense were discussed in the previous section.

Two additional measurement issues affect funded status:

1. The amount disclosed for PBO at any balance sheet date is the result of estimates and assumptions about turnover, life expectancy, interest rates, and other factors. How should changes in these assumptions and deviations of actual experience from prior estimates— both of which cause a change in PBO—be incorporated into periodic pension expense?
2. What measure of return on plan assets (component 3) is most appropriate to use in determining pension expense? Investment returns are volatile from year to year. Is actual return in a given year representative of fund performance in the long run? Can it be used to measure the annual reduction in net pension expense?

SFAS No. 87 provides the following general guidelines for these issues:

- Changes in PBO are not immediately recognized in pension expense. Rather, they are subject to **delayed recognition** and amortized (recognized) gradually into pension expense. Furthermore, changes that increase PBO in one period are allowed to offset changes that decrease PBO in another period, thus reducing the reported effect on pension expense.
- **Expected return** rather than actual return for the period is used for component 3. In this way, volatility in pension expense arising from short-term market price fluctuations is reduced. The FASB believes that the actual return in any one period is not representative of the long-run return on the fund.[21] However, reported pension expense over the life of the plan must *ultimately* reflect the actual returns earned by the pension fund. Therefore, the difference between expected and actual return each year is merged with the PBO changes in the previous discussion and gradually amortized into pension expense.

PBO increases from changes in assumptions and experience are called **PBO losses** because the cost of the pension plan has increased. PBO decreases are called **PBO gains.** An **asset loss** occurs when expected return exceeds actual return, and vice versa for an **asset gain.** The effect of these items on funded status and pension expense (when amortized) is summarized below. An improvement in the funded status column means that the plan is less underfunded or more overfunded as a result of the item.

	Effect on	
Item	**Funded Status (PBO-Assets)**	**Pension Expense (When Item Is Amortized)**
PBO gain	Improvement	Decrease
PBO loss	Decline	Increase
Asset gain	No effect	Decrease
Asset loss	No effect	Increase

Asset gains and losses have no effect on funded status because only the actual return is reflected in plan assets at fair value.

---

[21]The previously cited case of PepsiCo, Inc., in 1995 is a good example. (Actual return of $338 million was almost three times expected return.) The returns of the mid-90s bull stock market are not indicative of average returns to stock investments over the long run.

PBO Gains and Losses   The value of PBO at any date reflects an assumption, for example, about the magnitude of expected future employee turnover. If a reexamination of expected turnover finds that turnover will be more frequent than previously expected, PBO is reduced because total pension benefit payments will decrease. This is a PBO gain. The reverse situation yields a PBO loss because PBO would be increased. This type of PBO change is called an **actuarial gain or loss.**

Another type of PBO change is called an **experience gain or loss.** An experience gain (loss) occurs when actual results are more (less) favorable than originally estimated. For example, when the average life expectancy of retirees exceeds previous expectations, an experience loss has occurred because pension benefits must be paid for a longer period than originally estimated. Thus PBO increases. The opposite holds true for an experience gain.

For purposes of pension accounting, both categories of PBO changes are referred to as actuarial gains and losses or PBO gains and losses and are treated the same for reporting purposes. To illustrate calculation of an actuarial loss, reconsider the Nicole Whitney example. Lone Pine used a 10 percent discount rate to compute PBO at December 31, 1999, as follows:

$$\text{PBO, } 12/31/99 = \$6{,}000(\text{PVA, } 10\%, 10)(\text{PV1, } 10\%, 23)$$
$$= \$6{,}000(6.14457)(.11168) = \underline{\underline{\$4{,}117}}$$

Suppose at the beginning of January 2000, on the advice of its actuary, Lone Pine reduces the discount rate to 8 percent because of changing market conditions. PBO is recalculated as follows:

$$\text{PBO, } 1/1/00 = \$6{,}000(\text{PVA, } 8\%, 10)(\text{PV1, } 8\%, 23)$$
$$= \$6{,}000(6.71008)(.17032) = \underline{\underline{\$6{,}857}}$$

The resulting $2,740 actuarial loss is the difference between the original and adjusted PBO ($6,857 − $4,117).

In each accounting period, the actuary supplies information about PBO gains and losses and the trustee supplies information about asset gains and losses. The gains and losses from both sources are combined to form a net gain or loss for accounting purposes. The net gain or loss is subject to delayed recognition and is amortized to periodic pension expense. The unamortized net gain or loss is carried forward as part of the informal pension record.

Gains and losses are subject to offset by future losses and gains. For example, future PBO increases from changing life expectancy and turnover can offset previous PBO decreases. Under these circumstances, immediate recognition of gains and losses under the time period assumption does not necessarily provide the most relevant information about long-run pension costs. Immediate recognition of the huge losses suffered by many pension funds from the stock market's Black Monday (October 19, 1987) would have dramatically increased pension expense for many firms. Within a relatively short time, however, the market recovered most of its loss.

Specific Reporting Requirements: Component 5   We use a two-year example to illustrate the details of reporting and recognition involving component 5.

Example   WestCom Inc., a calendar-year firm, reports the following:

Reconciliation of Funded Status: December 31, 1997

PBO	($100,000)
Plan assets at fair value	70,000
Underfunded PBO	(30,000)
Unrecognized PSC	10,000
Accrued pension cost	($ 20,000)

Assumed data for 1998:

Service cost	$12,000	Expected long-term rate of	
Interest cost	9,000	return on plan assets.	10%
Actual return on assets.	6,000	Annual PSC amortization	$ 1,000
Funding amount	12,000	Actuarial loss, determined 12/31 . . .	25,000

For accounting purposes:

PBO and asset gains and losses are combined to form one net unrecognized amount at the beginning of each period. Component 5 of pension expense is the *amortization* (recognition) of the net unrecognized gain or loss at the *beginning* of the year.

WestCom has no unrecognized gain or loss at January 1, 1998, as indicated in the reconciliation (only PSC is listed as an unrecognized amount). Therefore, the firm has no component 5 of pension expense for 1998. However, WestCom must compute the net unrecognized gain or loss at December 31, 1998, for the 1998 reconciliation of funded status and to help determine amortization in 1999.

The first part of that ending 1998 net unrecognized amount is a $1,000 asset loss for 1998. Actual return of $6,000 falls short of expected return of $7,000 (.10 × $70,000). Yet under *SFAS No. 87,* annual pension expense reflects expected return for the period (component 3). Thus for WestCom, pension expense is reduced by $7,000 (expected return) when the fund actually earned only $6,000. Ultimately however, pension expense over the long term must reflect actual costs and actual asset returns. This result is accomplished by including the $1,000 loss in the net unrecognized amount. Recognition through amortization beginning in 1999 increases pension expense gradually over many future periods. The asset loss is not amortized in 1998 because it was not known at the beginning of the year.

The second part of the ending 1998 net unrecognized amount is the $25,000 actuarial loss, an increase in PBO. The loss could be caused, for example, by an increase in assumed life expectancy of retirees causing benefits to be paid for a longer time than originally assumed. The amount, like the asset loss, was not known at the beginning of 1998. Therefore, it also is not subject to amortization until 1999. This is the computation of the ending net unrecognized loss, pension expense, and the 1998 reconciliation of funded status:

Net unrecognized gain or loss, January 1, 1998	$ 0
1998 asset loss	1,000
Actuarial loss, 12/31/98	25,000
Amortization of net unrecognized amount at 1/1/98	0
Net unrecognized loss, December 31, 1998	$26,000

Pension Expense, 1998

Service cost	$12,000
Interest cost	9,000
Expected return on assets	(7,000)
PSC amortization	1,000
Amortization of net unrecognized amount	0
Pension expense, 1998	$15,000

Entry to Record Pension Expense, 1998

Pension expense	15,000	
Accrued pension cost		3,000
Cash		12,000

Reconciliation of Funded Status: December 31, 1998

PBO	($146,000)	$100,000 + $12,000 + $9,000 + $25,000
		Beginning Service Interest Actuarial
		Balance Cost Cost Loss
Plan assets at fair value	88,000	$70,000 + $6,000 + $12,000
		Beginning Actual Funding
		Balance Return Amount
Underfunded PBO	($ 58,000)	
Unrecognized PSC	9,000	$10,000 − $1,000
		Beginning 1998
		Balance Amortization
Net unrecognized loss	26,000	From previous calculation
Accrued pension cost	($ 23,000)	$20,000 + $3,000
		Beginning 1998
		Balance Increase

The accrued pension cost (balance sheet liability) is *less* than the plan's funded status by $35,000 ($9,000 + $26,000). This difference occurs because PSC and the net unrecognized loss are subject to delayed recognition. Had these two amounts been recognized in 1999, both pension expense and accrued pension cost would have increased $35,000 assuming no increase in funding (refer to the preceding entry for pension expense). The result would have been accrued pension cost being reported in the balance sheet at $58,000, an amount equal to funded status. Delayed recognition thus contributes to the off-balance-sheet financing aspect of pension reporting.

Assumed Data for 1999

Service cost $16,000	Average remaining service period	
Interest cost 13,000	(assume constant each year) . . . . . 10 years	
Actual return on assets 10,000	Annual PSC amortization $1,000	
Funding amount 19,000	Actuarial gain, determined 12/31 24,000	

WestCom opens 1999 with a net unrecognized loss of $26,000 from the previous year. This is the amount subject to amortization in 1999. The amortization is component 5 of 1999 pension expense. *SFAS No. 87* requires minimum amortization under certain circumstances but also allows other methods of computing amortization if followed consistently. We illustrate both approaches for WestCom.

1. Corridor or Minimum Amortization   Under this approach, amortization is not required unless the beginning unrecognized amount is outside a defined **corridor,** that is, if the unrecognized amount exceeds the corridor limit of:

10% of the greater of 1. PBO at the beginning of the year ($146,000 for WestCom)
2. Plan assets at the beginning of the year ($88,000).

For WestCom, the corridor limit is $14,600 (.10 × $146,000). The opening amounts for PBO and assets for the year are used because the net unrecognized amount subject to amortization also is computed at the beginning of the year. The corridor for WestCom at January 1, 1999, is:

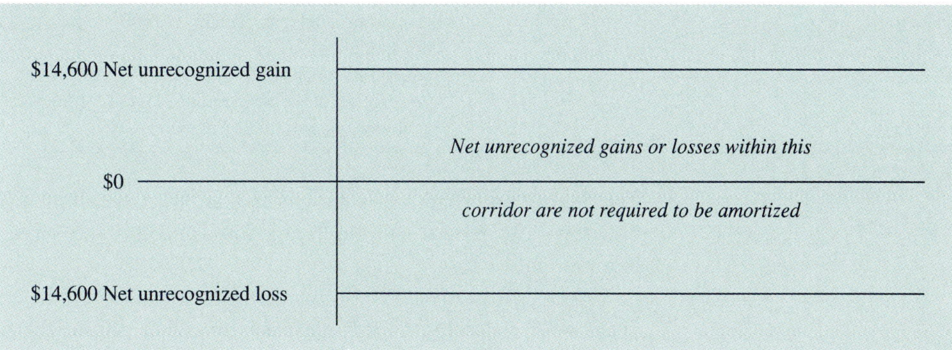

The width of the corridor is 20 percent of PBO for this firm. The net unrecognized gain or loss at January 1, 1999, can vary from a net loss of $14,600 to a net gain of $14,600 before amortization is required. WestCom's net unrecognized loss is $26,000, which is *outside* the corridor. The minimum required amortization to be recognized is computed as:

$$\frac{\text{Net unrecognized gain or loss at beginning of year} - \text{Corridor limit}}{\text{Average remaining service period of active employees expected to receive benefits under the plan}}$$

For WestCom, 1999 minimum or corridor amortization is:

$$\frac{\$26,000 \text{ net unrecognized loss} - \$14,600 \text{ corridor limit}}{10 \text{ years}} = \$1,140$$

If WestCom chooses corridor amortization, component 5 of pension expense for 1999 is $1,140. The amount increases pension expense because the amount being amortized is a loss. The amortization of a net unrecognized gain would decrease pension expense. The FASB chose 10 percent of the greater of the two components of funded status as the materiality threshold beyond which at least a portion of the net unrecognized amount must be recognized in pension expense. When the net unrecognized amount becomes significant (more than the corridor limit), amortization is appropriate.

2. Alternative Amortization   WestCom must amortize at least $1,140 of the net unrecognized loss. However, *SFAS No. 87* allows any systematic method provided it is used consistently and is disclosed. A common alternative to corridor amortization is the straight-line method that simply divides the net unrecognized amount by the average remaining service period. Under this alternative, WestCom would amortize $2,600 ($26,000/10). If WestCom chooses this alternative, component 5 of pension expense for 1999 is $2,600.

Example   Let's assume that WestCom chooses corridor amortization. Pension expense is increased by the smaller amount, $1,140, as the amortization of net unrecognized loss:

Pension Expense, 1999

Service cost	$16,000
Interest cost	13,000
Expected return on assets 10($88,000)	(8,800)
PSC amortization	1,000
Amortization of net unrecognized loss	1,140
Pension expense, 1999	$22,340

Entry to record pension expense, 1999

Pension expense	22,340	
Accrued pension cost		3,340
Cash		19,000

WestCom now computes its ending net unrecognized amount, that will be subject to amortization in 2000. The firm has a $1,200 asset *gain* in the year 1999 because actual return ($10,000) exceeds expected return ($8,800).

Net unrecognized loss, January 1, 1999	$26,000
1999 asset gain	(1,200)
Actuarial gain, 12/31/99	(24,000)
Amortization of net unrecognized loss at 1/1/99	(1,140)
Net unrecognized gain, December 31, 1999	$ (340)

The $1,140 amortization is shown as a subtraction along with the gains because amortization serves to reduce the beginning loss, and has the same effect as a gain that offsets a like amount of loss.

1999 began with a $26,000 net unrecognized *loss* and ended with a $340 net unrecognized *gain*. Allowing gains and losses to offset minimizes their effect on pension expense and therefore earnings. Corridor amortization supports this objective by minimizing the amount of amortization to be recognized. Less amortization is recognized before offsetting can take place. Earnings volatility is reduced as a result. These two factors, offsetting and corridor amortization, are consistent with the long-run nature of pension costs.

Most of the $26,000 net loss at the beginning of 1999 will never be amortized because the 1999 actuarial gain absorbed most of the loss. Actuarial and asset gains and losses, therefore, typically are not fully amortized in the usual sense. The $340 net unrecognized gain at the end of 1999 is not subject to amortization in 2000 because it is within the corridor. Although WestCom experienced substantial changes in PBO and asset gains and losses during 1998 and 1999, through corridor amortization and offsetting, the firm will amortize *only* $1,140 over the three years 1998–2000 under minimum amortization. Pension expense will increase only $1,140 as a result over this period.

Reconciliation of Funded Status: December 31, 1999

PBO.	($151,000)	$146,000 + $16,000 + $13,000 − $24,000
		Beginning Service Interest Actuarial
		Balance Cost Cost Loss
Plan assets at fair value.	117,000	$88,000 + $10,000 + $19,000
		Beginning Actual Funding
		Balance Return Amount
Underfunded PBO	($ 34,000)	
Unrecognized PSC	8,000	$9,000 − $1,000
		Beginning 1999
		Balance Amortization
Net unrecognized gain	(340)	From previous calculation
Accrued pension cost	($ 26,340)	$23,000 + $3,340
		Beginning 1999
		Balance Increase

The delayed recognition of the $340 net unrecognized gain serves to increase the accrued pension cost balance relative to funded status. The $340 amount is an improvement in funded status that has not yet reduced pension expense, and therefore accrued pension cost does not yet reflect the decrease.

Alternative Approach for Reporting Components 3 and 5   An alternative approach to reporting components 3 and 5 of pension expense is commonly encountered in practice because *SFAS No. 87* requires actual return to be disclosed. WestCom's pension expense under this approach is (amounts affected are in boldface type):

Pension Expense, 1999

Service cost.		$16,000
Interest cost.		13,000
Actual return on assets		**(10,000)**
PSC amortization		1,000
Amortization and deferral		
Amortization of net unrecognized amount	**$1,140**	
Actual less expected return	**1,200**	**2,340**
Pension expense, 1999		$22,340

Under this alternative approach, actual rather than expected return is used for component 3, and component 5 has two parts or elements. Because pension expense must reflect expected return for the period, and because pension expense is reduced by an amount greater than expected return ($10,000 in the above tabulation), component 5 is increased by the $1,200 asset gain. The net effect is to reduce pension expense by $10,000 − $1,200 or $8,800, the expected return. The $1,140 amount appears in both disclosure alternatives.

The total amount of pension expense is unaffected by the reporting alternative chosen. For simplicity, this text employs the approach illustrated previously (using expected return for component 3) except when discussing required footnote disclosures later in the chapter.

REVIEW PROBLEM

Information for the Jenkins Company defined benefit pension plan follows. All data relate to 1998 unless otherwise indicated. Jenkins is a calendar-year firm.

Beginning balance, PBO	$700,000
Beginning balance, pension fund at fair value	500,000
Discount rate	8%
Expected long-term rate of return on plan assets	10%
Prior service grant approved 1/1/96; present value of retroactive benefits at grant date	$120,000
Average remaining service period of active plan participants; assume this period remains constant across periods and is used for all amortization calculations	10 years

Jenkins uses the SL method to amortize prior service cost and corridor amortization for gains and losses

Service cost, 1998	$60,000
Net unrecognized gain, 12/31/97	160,000
Actuarial loss determined 12/31/98	40,000
Actual return on plan assets, 1998	55,000
Funding, end of 1998	88,000

Required

1. The December 31, 1997, reconciliation of funded status.
2. The entry to record 1998 pension expense.
3. The December 31, 1998, reconciliation of funded status.
4. Determine whether amortization of net unrecognized gain or loss is required for 1999.

SOLUTION

1.

JENKINS COMPANY

Reconciliation of Funded Status

December 31, 1997

PBO	$(700,000)
Plan assets at fair value	500,000
Underfunded PBO	$(200,000)
Unrecognized prior service cost	96,000*
Net unrecognized gain	(160,000)
Accrued pension cost	$264,000

*8 years remaining in the amortization period for PSC at 12/31/97
$96,000 = $120,000(8/10)

2. Pension expense, 1998

Service cost	$60,000
Interest cost (.08)$700,000	56,000
Expected return on plan assets (.10)$500,000	(50,000)
Amortization of prior service cost $120,000/10	12,000
Amortization of net unrecognized gain	(9,000)*
Pension expense	$69,000

$$*\$160,000 - \frac{.10(\text{greater of }\$700,000 \text{ and } \$500,000)}{10}$$

December 31, 1998

Pension expense	69,000	
Accrued pension cost	19,000	
Cash		88,000

3.

JENKINS COMPANY
Reconciliation of Funded Status
December 31, 1998

PBO.	$(856,000)	$700,000 + $60,000 + $56,000 + $40,000
		Beginning Service Interest Actuarial
		Balance Cost Cost Loss
Plan assets at fair value.	643,000	$500,000 + $55,000 + $88,000
		Beginning Actual Funding
		Balance Return
Underfunded PBO	$(213,000)	
Unrecognized PSC	84,000	$96,000 − $12,000
Net unrecognized gain	(116,000)*	
Accrued pension cost	$(245,000)	$264,000 − $19,000 (decrease from pension expense entry)

*Net unrecognized gain 1/1/98	($160,000)
Amortization of gain, 1998	9,000
Actual − expected return, 1998	(5,000)†
Actuarial loss, 1998	40,000
Net unrecognized gain, 12/31/98	($116,000)

†$55,000 − .10($500,000)

4. The net unrecognized gain of $116,000 at the beginning of 1999 exceeds 10 percent of the greater of PBO ($856,000) and plan assets ($643,000) at that date. Therefore, amortization of the $116,000 amount will be required as a component of 1999 pension expense.

Transition Amount: Component 6 of Pension Expense

Sponsors of pension plans were to comply with the provisions of *SFAS No. 87* for reporting years beginning after December 15, 1986. To reduce the impact of the accounting changes brought about by *SFAS No. 87,* a phase-in period was established. Under *APB Opinion No. 8* (superseded by *SFAS No. 87*), employers frequently reported a pension asset or liability account (similar to accrued or prepaid pension cost under *SFAS No. 87*). The transition asset or liability is the bridge between the requirements of the two pronouncements.

The periodic amortization (under delayed recognition) of this transition amount is the sixth and final component of pension expense. The sixth component is unique because it results from a transition asset or liability that occurs only once, and after the transition amount is fully amortized, the sixth component no longer appears in pension expense. The transition asset is also called transition gain; the transition liability is also called transition cost. The unrecognized portion of the transition amount is carried forward as part of the informal pension record.

Transition Asset or Liability   The **transition asset** or **transition liability** is the amount that equates the pension asset or liability balance reported under *APB Opinion No. 8* and the plan's funded status at transition date:

$$\begin{array}{c}\text{APB Opinion No. 8}\\ \text{account balance}\end{array} + \begin{array}{c}\text{Transition asset}\\ \text{or liability}\end{array} = \text{PBO} - \begin{array}{c}\text{Plan assets at}\\ \text{fair value}\end{array}$$

For firms with no pension asset or liability account under *APB Opinion No. 8,* the plan's funded status at transition is the transition asset or liability. The transition asset or liability affects neither PBO nor plan assets, and it is not recognized immediately. The account balance under *APB Opinion No. 8* continues as the accrued or prepaid pension cost account under *SFAS No. 87.* The next table presents several cases where all amounts except the transition asset or liability are assumed. The transition date is January 1, 1987.

Amounts at Transition	Case 1	Case 2	Case 3
PBO	($200,000)	($1,400,000)	($426,000)
Assets at fair value.	170,000	1,600,000	300,000
Funded status asset (liability)	(30,000)	200,000	(126,000)
APB Opinion No. 8 asset (liability)	(10,000)	(150,000)	15,000
Transition asset (liability)	($ 20,000)	$ 350,000	($141,000)

In case 1, the employer has a $30,000 underfunded plan (PBO − assets) at transition but is reporting only a $10,000 liability. A $20,000 transition liability is therefore required to account for the difference between accrued pension cost ($10,000 liability) and funded status ($30,000 liability):

$$\$10,000L \; + \; \text{Transition amount} \; = \; \$200,000L \; - \; \$170,000A$$
$$\text{Transition amount} \; = \; \$30,000L \; - \; \$10,000L \; = \; \$20,000L$$

The letter A denotes an asset, and L denotes a liability.

A T-account also can be used to determine the transition amount, shown in **boldface** type:

Underfunded PBO

	APB Opinion No. 8 balance	10,000
	Transition liability	**20,000**
	Funded status	30,000

The transition amount reconciles funded status and the accrued or prepaid pension cost account at transition. The remaining cases are analyzed the same way.

In case 3 the employer is reporting a $15,000 asset, yet the plan is underfunded in the amount of $126,000. The transition amount is therefore a $141,000 liability. *APB Opinion No. 8* did not require recognition or disclosure of PBO. In certain instances, funding was ahead of expensing (and hence the asset account), but the plan remained underfunded.

A transition liability is similar to PSC because it represents the cost of benefits promised *before* transition to *SFAS No. 87* and often reflects unrecognized past retroactive grants. In the discussion on additional minimum pension liability to follow, the transition liability is treated as if it were unrecognized PSC.

Amortization of Transition Amount   The amortization of a transition asset reduces pension expense; the opposite is true for a transition liability. In case 1 the $10,000 pre-*SFAS No. 87* liability represents $10,000 of recognized, but unfunded, pension expense. The remaining $20,000 of underfunded liability not yet recognized in expense will be amortized, gradually increasing pension expense.

The transition asset or liability is amortized on a straight-line basis over the average remaining service period of employees expected to receive benefits under the plan, beginning in the transition year.[22] If the average period is less than 15 years, the employer can elect to use 15 years for amortization to avoid excessive amortization. Otherwise, a plan with a four-year average remaining service period (for example) and large transition liability would experience a substantial increase in pension expense during the four years after transition.

In case 3 ($141,000 transition liability), if the average remaining service period is 10 years, the employer increases annual pension expense by one of the following two amounts:

$$\text{Amortization based on 10 years:} \; \$141,000/10 = \underline{\$14,100}$$
$$\text{Amortization based on 15 years:} \; \$141,000/15 = \underline{\$\ 9,400}$$

Rationale for Delayed Recognition of Transition Amount   The unrecognized transition asset or liability includes various amounts existing before transition: unrecognized costs of past retroactive plan amendments, the net unrecognized gain or loss, and the cumulative effect of past accounting standards. These factors combined to create large transition

---

[22]If all or almost all employees are inactive, the inactive participants' average remaining life expectancy is used for amortization.

EXHIBIT 18–9
Coca-Cola's Pension Expense

COCA-COLA COMPANY
Pension Expense Components
For the Year Ended December 31, 1995
(millions)

Service cost—benefits earned during the period	$ 43
Interest cost on projected benefit obligation	89
Actual return on plan assets	(211)
Net amortization and deferral	145
Net periodic pension cost	$ 66

liabilities for many firms. Respondents to the exposure draft preceding *SFAS No. 87* argued that immediate recognition of both the liability and resulting expense could adversely affect the perception of these firms' financial health. This view was adopted even though delayed recognition runs counter to the retroactive treatment afforded the transition to many new accounting principles.

Amortization of transition assets is a contributing factor to the general decline in pension expense under *SFAS No. 87*. A study of 100 firms employing over 10 million people found that pension expense decreased an average of 64 percent for those firms adopting the new standard in 1986.[23]

Example   McDonnell Douglas's amortization of transition asset was $106 million in 1989, causing the firm to record $95 million of pension *income* (that is, negative pension expense). Without amortization of the transition asset, the company would have recognized $11 million in pension *expense*.

CONCEPT REVIEW

1. Explain how the transition amount is computed.
2. What does the transition amount represent?
3. How is the transition asset or liability unique among the three pension amounts subject to delayed recognition?

Coca-Cola's Pension Expense

Exhibit 18–9 is adapted from footnote 13 of the Coca-Cola financial statements reproduced at the end of this text. Coke separately discloses its pension expense for its domestic and international pension plans. The exhibit aggregates the pension expense components across these two categories.

Interest cost on PBO was more than twice the service cost for 1995 indicating a large total pension obligation for benefits already earned relative to one year's increase in the obligation. Coke discloses actual rather than expected return and combines components 4 through 6 into one net amount. However, additional disclosures in the footnote allow users to identify the individual components 4–6. The 1995 bull stock market caused actual return to exceed expected return. Footnote 13 indicates that total pension expense for all pension plans amounted to $81 million for 1995, implying that Coke's expense for its *defined contribution* plans was $15 million ($81 million − $66 million).

ADDITIONAL MINIMUM PENSION LIABILITY

The accrued pension cost liability for most firms is only a small fraction of PBO and falls short of the plan's underfunded status. Delayed recognition of pension costs frequently causes the accrued pension cost liability to understate funded status significantly. As a result, the true debt position of the plan is not reported in the balance sheet. To prevent serious

[23]S. Bleiberg, "Less than Zero" (in "Pension Fund Perspective"), *Financial Analysts Journal,* March–April 1988, pp. 13–15.

underreporting of liabilities, *SFAS No. 87* requires recognition of an additional liability amount under certain circumstances. When required, a second journal entry is recorded after pension expense is recognized, increasing reported debt and creating additional ledger accounts for the formal pension accounting record.

Total Minimum Liability

The FASB, in a compromise decision, mandated the use of ABO (accumulated benefit obligation) rather than PBO for use in computing the required **total minimum liability** (also called *minimum pension liability* or *net pension liability*) to be reported in the balance sheet. Using ABO produces a smaller measure of the obligation, because ABO is based on current salary levels rather than future salary levels.[24] The amount of pension liability that firms must disclose in reported liabilities is:

$$\text{Total minimum liability} = \text{ABO} - \text{Plan assets at fair value}$$

Additional Minimum Pension Liability

Total minimum liability equals underfunded ABO. End-of-year amounts, *after* recording pension expense, are used in computing the total minimum liability. When the accrued pension cost liability balance is less than the total minimum liability (or when the firm is reporting a prepaid pension cost account) the difference is recorded in **additional minimum pension liability (AMPL):**

$$\begin{bmatrix}\text{Required ending} & = & \text{Total} \\ \text{AMPL balance} & & \text{minimum} \\ & & \text{liability}\end{bmatrix} \begin{array}{l} - \ \text{Accrued pension cost balance} \\ \qquad\qquad (\text{or}) \\ + \ \text{Prepaid pension cost balance}\end{array}$$

Therefore, AMPL records the extra liability amount required if the accrued pension cost account is less than total minimum liability. If the accrued pension cost is at least equal to total minimum liability, or if ABO is overfunded, no AMPL balance is required. The entry to record AMPL is made after the entry for pension expense because the accrued pension cost balance is updated in the pension expense entry. The accrued or prepaid pension cost account is maintained in a ledger account separate from AMPL for internal reporting purposes, but for external purposes they are combined into a single net pension liability (total minimum liability).

Example   The reconciliation of funded status and other pension account information follows for Holly, Incorporated:

HOLLY, INC.
Reconciliation of Funded Status
December 31, 1998
(Amounts assumed)

PBO	$(100,000)
Plan assets at fair value	65,000
Underfunded PBO	(35,000)
Unrecognized PSC	2,000
Net unrecognized loss	18,000
Unrecognized transition liability	3,000
Accrued pension cost	$(12,000)

Additional data at December 31 (assumed):

AMPL	$ 0
ABO	85,000

Total Minimum Liability and AMPL, December 31, 1998:

ABO	$ 85,000
Plan assets	65,000
Total minimum liability (underfunded ABO)	20,000
Less accrued pension cost balance	12,000
Required ending AMPL balance	$ 8,000

---

[24]The resulting total reported pension liability reflects current salary levels, whereas service cost, pension expense, and PBO reflect future salary levels. This inconsistency is the result of a compromise between the view that no liability beyond accrued pension cost should be reported, and the view that funded status (underfunded PBO) should be reported.

Holly reports a net pension liability of $20,000 in the 1998 balance sheet, and maintains two separate liability accounts internally:

Accrued pension cost $12,000
AMPL   8,000
Total minimum liability $20,000

Holly's accrued pension cost balance of $12,000, the cumulative shortfall of funding relative to pension expense, is less than the total minimum liability of $20,000 that must be reported. Therefore, Holly must recognize $8,000 of additional minimum pension liability bringing the total recognized liability to $20,000.[25] AMPL helps to reduce the off-balance-sheet feature of pension liability reporting but only to a limited extent. Holly's plan is $35,000 underfunded (PBO of $100,000 less plan assets of $65,000), yet only $20,000 of liability is recognized in the balance sheet:

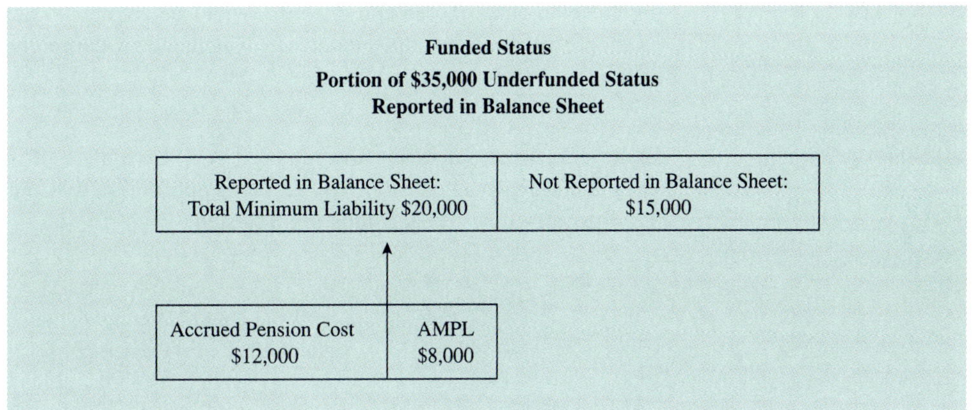

The underfunding of ABO occurs when firms do not fund the plan at a sufficient level or when investment returns are inadequate. Both underfunding of ABO and delayed recognition contribute to the need for AMPL. Holly has a total of $23,000 of unrecognized pension cost ($2,000 unrecognized PSC, $18,000 net loss, and $3,000 transition liability). If these amounts were recognized in pension expense, accrued pension cost would reflect a $35,000 balance, an amount more than sufficient to meet the total minimum liability requirement of $20,000. Holly would not recognize AMPL under these circumstances.

Recording AMPL   Holly records its $8,000 AMPL after recording pension expense. But what account is debited? Recording a like amount of additional pension expense would run counter to delayed recognition. *SFAS No. 87* requires a new account, **intangible pension asset,** to be recorded. This account is reported along with other intangible assets but is subject to a maximum balance:

Maximum intangible pension = Unrecognized PSC + Unrecognized transition
Asset balance   liability

Maximum intangible pension = $2,000   + $3,000   = $5,000
Asset for Holly at 12/31/98

A new account, **unrealized pension cost,** is debited for the excess of AMPL over the maximum intangible pension asset. Unrealized pension cost is a contra-owners' equity account. For Holly, this account is debited for $3,000:

Increase in AMPL for 1998 . . . . $8,000
Less maximum intangible balance   5,000
Increase in unrealized pension cost for 1998 . . . . . . $3,000

---

[25]If Holly were reporting *prepaid pension cost* of $12,000 instead of accrued pension cost, the required AMPL to be recognized would be $32,000 ($20,000 + $12,000). Combining the $32,000 AMPL with the $12,000 pension asset yields a net pension liability of $20,000, the required minimum.

December 31, 1998, entry to record AMPL (after recording pension expense):

```
Intangible pension asset  . . . . . . . . . . . . . . . . . . . . . . . . . . . .   5,000
Unrealized pension cost   . . . . . . . . . . . . . . . . . . . . . . . . . . . .   3,000
   AMPL  . . . . . . . . . . . . . . . . . . . . . . . . . . . .                          8,000
```

The $5,000 intangible asset represents the value of benefits to be received by the firm from retroactive grants, to the extent that such grants contribute to underfunded ABO. Hence, unrecognized PSC is included in the maximum intangible amount. The unrecognized transition liability also is included because in many cases the transition liability represents the cost of retroactive grants before transition to *SFAS No. 87.* The intangible pension asset is not amortized in the same way as other intangibles, but instead is reduced as PSC and transition liability are reduced over time.

The unrealized pension cost account represents pension costs not associated with retroactive grants and not yet recognized in pension expense. It is the reduction in the net worth of the company caused by the excess of AMPL over the intangible asset. Again, recognizing these amounts in pension expense would be counter to delayed recognition. Unrealized pension cost is an example of an item included in comprehensive income but not in net income as currently computed.

Adjusting the Accounts

Each year, firms determine the required AMPL balance, if any, and adjust the intangible asset and unrealized pension cost accounts appropriately. Continuing the Holly, Inc., example illustrates how the accounts are adjusted:

HOLLY, INC.
Reconciliation of Funded Status
December 31, 1999
(Amounts assumed)

```
PBO . . . . . . . . . . . . . . . . . . . . . . . . . . . . . .   $(130,000)
Plan assets at fair value . . . . . . . . . . . . . . . . . . .      79,000
Underfunded PBO . . . . . . . . . . . . . . . . . . . . . . .       (51,000)
Unrecognized PSC . . . . . . . . . . . . . . . . . . . . . .         1,000
Net unrecognized loss . . . . . . . . . . . . . . . . . . . .       30,000
Unrecognized transition liability. . . . . . . . . . . . . . .       2,000
Accrued pension cost . . . . . . . . . . . . . . . . . . . .     $ (18,000)

Additional data at December 31 (assumed):
ABO . . . . . . . . . . . . . . . . . . . . . . . . . . . . . .   $ 116,000
```

Total Minimum Liability and AMPL, December 31, 1999:

```
ABO . . . . . . . . . . . . . . . . . . . . . . . . . . . . .    $116,000
Plan assets . . . . . . . . . . . . . . . . . . . . . . . . .      79,000
Total minimum liability (underfunded ABO) . . . . . . . .          37,000
Accrued pension cost balance . . . . . . . . . . . . . . .         18,000
Required ending AMPL balance . . . . . . . . . . . . . .           19,000
Current AMPL balance (from 1998) . . . . . . . . . . . .            8,000
Increase in AMPL for 1999 . . . . . . . . . . . . . . . . .     $  11,000
```

December 31, 1999 entry to record AMPL (after recording pension expense):

```
Unrealized pension cost  . . . . . . . . . . . . . . . . . . . . . . . . . . . .   13,000
   Intangible pension asset . . . . . . . . . . . . . . . . . . . . . . . . . .             2,000*
   AMPL  . . . . . . . . . . . . . . . . . . . . . . . . . . . . . . . . . . .              11,000
```

```
*Intangible balance from 1998 . . . . . . . . . . . . . . . . . . . . . . . . . . . . . . . . . . . . . . .$5,000
   Maximum intangible balance at 12/31/99: $1,000 unrecognized PSC + $2,000 unrecognized transition obligation   3,000
   Decrease in intangible asset . . . . . . . . . . . . . . . . . . . . . . . . . . . . . . . . . . . . . . . .$2,000
```

Holly's total pension liability recognized in the balance sheet at December 31, 1999, is $37,000, consisting of:

COCA-COLA COMPANY
Reconciliation of Funded Status
December 31, 1995
(millions)

Projected benefit obligation	$(1,313)
Plan assets at fair value	1,156
Underfunded PBO	(157)
Unrecognized net asset at transition	(3)
Unrecognized prior service cost	63
Unrecognized net gain	(30)
Accrued pension cost	(127)
Additional minimum pension liability	(60)
Net pension liability in balance sheet	$ (187)

Accrued pension cost	$18,000
AMPL	19,000
Total minimum liability	$37,000

Other related ending 1999 balances:

Intangible pension asset	$ 3,000*
Unrealized pension cost	16,000†

*Maximum computed above

†1998 increase of $3,000 + 1999 increase of $13,000

Exhibit 18–10 illustrates footnote disclosure of the pension liability for the Coca-Cola Company. In footnote 13 of the annual report, Coke's funded status report is divided into four sections by domestic and international plans, and by plans with assets exceeding benefits and those with benefits exceeding assets. The exhibit aggregates this data into one combined funded status report.

Coke discloses $187 million of pension liability in its balance sheet, an amount somewhat greater than its underfunded status ($157 million). The minimum liability requirement partially mitigates the off-balance-sheet financing aspect of pension reporting. In Coke's case, the critical value for the pension fund, funded status, is reflected in total reported liabilities. However, most of Coke's total pension liability ($1,313 million) is kept off the balance sheet. The required offsetting of PBO and plan assets is one of the few remaining instances of offsetting of assets and liabilities allowed in financial reporting and results in substantial understatement of total recognized liabilities for many firms. Ratios such as debt to equity and debt to total assets are understated and reflect an overly favorable picture of the firm's relative debt position.

CONCEPT REVIEW

1. Explain the relationship between total minimum liability and additional minimum pension liability.
2. What is the maximum intangible pension asset account balance?
3. Interpret unrealized pension cost.

REVIEW PROBLEM

Pfennig Inc., a calendar-year firm, adopted *SFAS No. 87,* on January 1, 1988. At that date the firm had computed the following amounts:

Balance sheet liability from pre-*SFAS No. 87* accounting:	$40,000
PBO	420,000
Plan assets at fair value	300,000

At transition, the average remaining service period of employees expected to receive benefits under the plan was 12 years. Pfennig elected to use the maximum available period to amortize its transition amount. Years later, at the end of 1998, *after* recording pension expense but before recording additional minimum pension liability (AMPL), Pfennig's formal and informal pension plan records reflected the following:

		Record
PBO	$800,000	Informal
Plan assets at fair value	530,000	Informal
ABO	710,000	Informal
Accrued pension cost	60,000	Formal
Unrecognized prior service cost	13,000	Informal
Intangible pension asset	40,667	Formal
AMPL balance	90,000	Formal

Required

1. The amount of component 6 of pension expense, amortization of transition amount, to be included in 1998 pension expense.
2. The effect of this amount on 1998 pension expense.
3. The entry to adjust AMPL and related accounts at the end of 1998.

SOLUTION

1. The initial transition amount (T) in 1988 is an $80,000 liability:

$$\$40,000L + T = \$420,000L - \$300,000A$$
$$T = \$80,000L$$

Component 6 of pension expense = $80,000/15 = $5,333. The firm chose 15 years, the maximum period for amortization when the average remaining service period at transition is less than 15 years.

2. Pension expense for 1998 is increased by $5,333 because the transition amount is a liability.
3. Unrecognized transition liability at the end of 1998 is $21,333: $80,000(4 years remaining/15). Unrecognized prior service cost is $13,000. Therefore, the maximum allowable intangible asset balance is $34,333 ($21,333 + $13,000).

ABO	$710,000
Plan assets at fair value.	530,000
Total minimum liability	180,000
Balance, accrued pension cost	60,000
Required balance, AMPL	120,000
Current balance, AMPL	90,000
Increase in AMPL	$ 30,000

December 31, 1998 (entry 2 after recording pension expense):

Unrealized pension cost	36,334	
Intangible pension asset		6,334*
AMPL		30,000

*($40,667 − $34,333)

ADDITIONAL ISSUES IN PENSION ACCOUNTING

SFAS No. 87: A Compromise

SFAS No. 87 was adopted after lengthy debate in a four to three vote. The FASB vote reflects the controversial nature of the subject. The Board rejected the notion that the pension plan bears the obligation for pension benefits and concluded that plan assets are controlled by the employer. The frequent raiding of excess assets by employers supports this view. Yet the Board was unwilling to mandate recognition of PBO and assets in the balance sheet.

Certain board members believed that the use of a market-related asset value and an expected rate of return allows too much flexibility in the measurement of pension expense. The resulting lack of comparability and uniformity runs counter to the objectives of *SFAS No. 87*. Other members noted the inconsistency of requiring an additional minimum pension liability but not permitting an additional pension asset.

The Board acknowledged that delayed recognition excludes current and relevant information from the employer's balance sheet, but it concluded that immediate recognition of unrecognized pension amounts is impractical and too great a departure from previous accounting principles. Accrued pension cost, additional minimum pension liability, and expanded footnote disclosures, however, partially mitigate the effects of delayed recognition. At a minimum, underfunded ABO is disclosed in the balance sheet. Furthermore, although delayed recognition reduces the volatility of pension expense, it does not prevent disclosure of PBO or plan assets in the footnotes.

Certain reporting effects are unintended. For example, some plans with assets in excess of PBO disclose a liability. When the pension fund assets increase in value faster than expected, gains are recognized only on a delayed basis. Therefore, pension expense is larger than under immediate recognition of these gains. Under these circumstances, the firm might reduce its contributions, thereby increasing accrued pension cost. The gradual amortization of a transition asset adds to this effect.

The opportunities for income manipulation continue under *SFAS No. 87*. Future salaries, the expected rate of return on plan assets, and the discount rate are variables that can be adjusted for a desired income effect. For example, a study found that the profitability of a company and the rate used for discounting pension obligations are inversely related. Firms with lower profitability chose higher discount rates, resulting in lower pension obligations.[26]

Both pension expense and PBO are particularly sensitive to small changes in the discount rate, primarily because the relevant cash flows are projected far into the future. On average, pension expense increases 4 to 7 percent for each *one quarter* percent decrease in the discount rate. The response of PBO to the same change in the discount rate is roughly half that of pension expense.[27] Thus the opportunity for management to alter pension expense and liabilities is considerable.

In 1993, the SEC became concerned that firms were not responding quickly enough to the general decline in interest rates and began urging registrants to reduce discount rates for pension accounting. As firms gradually reduced their discount rates, PBOs increased. One result was that in 1995, the PBOs of U.S. plans increased approximately 40 percent overall while plan assets increased only 29 percent during that year.[28] Many firms found their funded status deteriorating even though funding levels had not been reduced.

Example   General Motors found that placing $10.4 billion into its pension fund was insufficient to wipe out its $9.3 billion underfunding at the beginning of 1995 because its PBO had risen more than plan assets at fair value, notwithstanding the strong bull market.

Settlements, Curtailments, Termination Benefits, and Asset Reversions

Some changes to defined benefit plans cause immediate recognition of amounts that are normally subject to delayed recognition. For example, plan termination or a plant closing resulting in a significant reduction in personnel can require immediate recognition of unrecognized pension amounts. Future benefit payments, and therefore PBO, are reduced. *SFAS No. 88,* "Employers' Accounting for Settlements and Curtailments of Defined Benefit Pension Plans and for Termination Benefits," provides guidelines for accounting for these events.

Pension Plan Settlements   A **settlement** is an irrevocable transaction that relieves the plan of primary responsibility for all or a portion of a pension plan obligation. Examples are lump-sum cash payments to replace future pension benefits and purchase of an annuity to cover pension benefits.

A settlement reduces PBO and is viewed as the realization of a portion of the net unrecognized gain or loss and of a portion of the unrecognized transition asset. A gain results in a reduction of accrued pension cost, and a loss results in an increase.

Pension Plan Curtailments   A **curtailment** either reduces the length of future employee service or eliminates the accrual of benefits for some or all future services. Curtailments occur when employees terminate earlier than expected or when a business contracts. Curtailments often reduce PBO, resulting in a gain, which reduces accrued pension cost.

---

[26]Z. Bodie, J. Light, R. Morck, and R. Taggart, Jr., "Corporate Pension Policy: An Empirical Investigation," *Financial Analysts Journal,* September–October 1985, pp. 10–16.

[27]A. Blankley and E. Swanson, "A Longitudinal Study of *SFAS No. 87* Pension Rate Assumptions," *Accounting Horizons,* December, 1995, p. 2.

[28]"How Pension Funds Lost in Market Boom," *The Wall Street Journal,* February 1, 1996, p. C1.

Termination Benefits   **Termination benefits** include special benefits offered only for a short period and contractual benefits required by the pension plan when a special event, such as a plant closing, occurs. These benefits may be provided when employment ends before the expected retirement date or to encourage employees to retire voluntarily.

Example   US West offered early-retirement incentives to 20,000 of its managers as part of a cost-cutting program. Pension payments were increased 15 percent for five years or until age 65, whichever occurred first.[29]

Employers who offer special termination benefits recognize a loss and related liability when employees accept the offer and the benefits are estimable. When the terminations are contractual, a loss and liability are recognized when it is probable that the employees are entitled to benefits and the amounts are estimable.

Pension Asset Reversion   An **asset reversion** occurs when an employer with an overfunded pension plan withdraws excess assets for purposes other than paying pension benefits. A pension plan must be terminated, and accumulated employee benefits must be satisfied through payment or purchase of an insurance company annuity, before assets are reverted.

Asset reversions were prevalent in the 1980s. The bull market increased the market value of many pension funds well beyond the pension obligation. Increases in interest rates lowered the cost of insurance company annuities purchased when plans were terminated and assets reverted. In some cases, asset reversions supplied the cash needed to service the higher debt levels resulting from corporate takeovers.

Example   In the period 1980 to 1989, 1,897 defined benefit pension plans, each with more than $1 million in excess assets, were terminated. The employer companies recovered $19.9 billion in excess assets after purchase of retirement annuities from insurance companies. Reversions reached a peak in 1985, when 582 plans were reverted.[30] Asset reversions became a matter of public concern as plan terminations reduced the number of healthy contributors to the Pension Benefit Guaranty Corporation. Legislation was introduced to limit asset reversions.

The fundamental question underlying asset reversions is, Who owns the excess—the sponsoring company or the employees? Those opposed to asset reversions argue that the fund belongs to the participants and that excess funds should be maintained as a cushion against leaner times. They maintain that reversions reduce the security of the plan and lower employee morale.[31] In addition, nonvested benefits become vested on termination, raising the ultimate cost of the pension plan by the amount of benefits that would otherwise be forfeited through normal turnover.

Those in favor of reversions argue that ERISA allows the employer to remove excess funds. Legally, the company's responsibility to employees ends when the employer extinguishes the liability by purchasing an annuity. In addition, investing the pension surplus in productive assets increases U.S. employment. Furthermore, restricting access to excess funds could contribute to a decline in the voluntary nature of pension plans. Employers also can reduce funding levels to offset the restrictions. A 1986 Department of Labor study of 97 pension-plan terminations found that no loss of benefits occurred to participants as a result of reversions.[32]

COMPREHENSIVE CASE AND PENSION DISCLOSURES

This section presents a three-year case showing how pension accounts and unrecognized amounts change over time as well as required disclosures. A fifth column is added to the spreadsheet for the beginning and ending unrecognized amount balances, changes during the year, and amortizations.

Comprehensive Case

Initial Data   On January 1, 1987, Owens Valley Company made its transition to *SFAS No. 87* for its noncontributory defined benefit pension plan. On that date, the firm had a $9,667 accrued pension liability account recorded under *APB Opinion No. 8*. Also on that date, PBO

---

[29]"US West to Set Pension Plan to Cut Costs," *The Wall Street Journal,* December 1, 1989, p. A6.

[30]"The Battle over Pension Surpluses," *Nation's Business,* August 1989, pp. 66–67.

[31]"Overfunded Plans," *Financial Executive,* November 1986, pp. 29–30.

[32]"The Battle over Pension Surpluses." op. cit.

EXHIBIT 18–11

Information for Three-Year Pension Case

OWENS VALLEY COMPANY

Pension Plan Information

Beginning 11 Years after Transition

From Actuary's Report	1998	1999	2000
Discount rate used by actuary	10%	10%	10%
Rate of compensation increase	6%	6%	6%
Average remaining service period of employees (years)	10	10	12
PBO, January 1	$100,000	$120,000	$194,000
Service cost	40,000	50,000	60,000
Interest cost (10% of PBO at Jan. 1)	10,000	14,000*	19,400
PSC (determined January 1)		20,000	
Actuarial loss (December 31)†		30,000	
Experience gain (December 31)‡			(12,000)
Benefit payments to retirees	(30,000)	(40,000)	(40,000)
PBO, December 31	$120,000	$194,000	$221,400
ABO, December 31	$ 96,000	167,000	177,000
VBO, December 31	42,000	67,000	125,000

From Trustee Report			
Expected long-term rate of return on plan assets	10%	9%	8%
Plan assets at fair value, January 1	$ 80,000	$ 95,000	$116,000
Actual return on plan assets	9,000	11,000	8,200
Contributions by Owens Valley (end of year)	36,000	50,000	55,000
Benefit payments to retirees (end of year)	(30,000)	(40,000)	(40,000)
Plan assets at fair value, December 31	$ 95,000	$116,000	$139,200
Expected return on plan assets (rate of return × beginning asset balance):	$ 8,000	$ 8,550	$ 9,280

Company Assumptions

The net unrecognized gain or loss is amortized on a straight-line basis over average remaining service period.

Unrecognized PSC is amortized over the average remaining service period at a date of grant (10 years). Transition amount is amortized over 26 years.

*Includes interest on PSC determined January 1, 1999: .10($120,000 + $20,000) = $14,000.

†Increase in life expectancy estimates.

‡Increase in actual turnover, relative to previous expectations.

was $53,000 and plan assets at fair value totaled $26,000. The resulting $17,333 transition liability bridged the gap between the pre-*SFAS No. 87* account and funded status at transition:

$$\text{Pre-}\textit{SFAS No. 87}\text{ liability} + \text{Transition liability} = \text{Funded status at transition}$$
$$\$9,667 \qquad + \qquad \$17,333 \qquad = \qquad \$53,000 - \$26,000$$

Owens Valley amortizes the transition obligation over 26 years, or $667 per year ($17,333/26). Eleven years after transition, at the beginning of 1998—the first year covered in this case—$10,000 of unrecognized transition liability remains to be amortized ($17,333 × (26 − 11)/26). At January 1, 1998, the accrued pension cost balance has grown to $10,000 and Owens has no unrecognized prior service cost or unrecognized gain or loss.

Exhibit 18–11 presents required information for 1998 through 2000. Exhibits 18–12, 18–13, and 18–14 are the completed pension spreadsheets.

1998   In Exhibit 18–12 the actuary supplies the beginning PBO, and the trustee's report is the source of plan assets at fair value. The employer provides the unrecognized pension cost amounts. The beginning 1/1/98 unrecognized pension cost amount of $10,000 is the remaining unrecognized portion of the transition liability. The pension expense column can accommodate six entries corresponding to the six pension expense components. The last column, accrued or prepaid pension cost, starts with the beginning balance. Additional minimum pension liability is determined outside the spreadsheet.

EXHIBIT 18–12   Pension Spreadsheet, 1998

OWENS VALLEY COMPANY
Pension Plan Spreadsheet, 1998

	Informal Record			Formal Record	
	PBO (actuary)	Plan Assets (trustee)	Unrecognized Pension Cost	Pension Expense	Accrued Pension Cost
Balances, 1/1/98	$100,000	$80,000	$10,000*		$(10,000)†
Service cost	40,000				
Interest cost	10,000			40,000	
Expected return				10,000	
Unrecognized loss:				(8,000)	
Beginning balance			$ 0		
1998 amortization			0‡		
Change from assets			G 1,000§		
Ending balance			G $ 1,000		
Unrecognized transition liability:					
Beginning balance			L $10,000*		
1998 amortization			(667)‖		
Ending balance			L $ 9,333	667	
Actual return		9,000			
Contributions		36,000			36,000
Benefits paid	(30,000)	(30,000)			
Ending balances:					
PBO	$120,000				
Plan assets		$95,000			
Underfunded PBO	$25,000				
Unrecognized pension costs			$ 8,333#		
Pension expense				$42,667	(42,667)
Accrued pension cost					$(16,667)

Note: L = loss, liability, or cost; G = gain or asset.

*Remaining unrecognized transition liability at 1/1/98.

†Account balance at 1/1/98, assumed.

‡No beginning unrecognized gain or loss; therefore, no amortization.

§Actual return ($9,000) − expected return ($8,000).

‖($17,333 initial transition liability)/26 = $667.

#$9,333 − $1,000.

For ease of illustration, expected return is used as component 3 of pension expense; therefore component 5 is the amortization of beginning unrecognized gain or loss. The beginning and ending balances in the unrecognized pension cost column are each the net sum of all three unrecognized amounts (PSC, net unrecognized gain or loss, and transition liability). The beginning balance does not enter into the calculation of the ending balance. For example, the 1998 ending net balance, $8,333, is the net sum of the $1,000 unrecognized gain and $9,333 unrecognized transition liability. The ending balances of the three unrecognized amounts are netted to form the beginning balance of unrecognized pension cost for the next period.

Owens Valley records the following entry:

December 31, 1998—Record pension expense:

Pension expense	42,667	
Accrued pension cost		6,667
Cash		36,000

The spreadsheet computes pension expense and automatically reflects the reconciliation of funded status, both at the beginning and at the end of the period. At the beginning of

1998, the funded status ($20,000 liability) and the $10,000 accrued pension cost account are reconciled by the $10,000 unrecognized transition liability. At the end of 1998, underfunded PBO ($25,000) less net unrecognized pension cost ($8,333) yields the ending accrued pension cost balance ($16,667).

No additional minimum pension liability is required at the end of 1999. Plan assets are nearly sufficient to cover ABO, as shown in the following schedule:

ABO, 12/31/98.	$96,000
Plan assets at fair value, 12/31/98	95,000
Total minimum liability	1,000
Balance, accrued pension cost, 12/31/98	16,667*
Required additional minimum pension liability	$ 0

*$10,000 (bal. 1/1/98) + $6,667 (from above entry).

1999 In Exhibit 18–13, the ending balances from 1998 carry over to 1999. The actuarial loss increases PBO and results in a net unrecognized loss at the end of 1999. The net unrecognized loss at the end of 1999 reflects the unamortized difference between actual and expected return in 1999. Component 5 of pension expense is restricted to amortization of the beginning $1,000 gain. Owens Valley records pension expense as follows:

December 31, 1999—Record pension expense:

Pension expense	58,017	
Accrued pension cost		8,017
Cash		50,000

Additional minimum pension liability is required in 1999:

ABO, 12/31/99.	$167,000
Plan assets at fair value, 12/31/99	116,000
Total minimum liability	51,000
Balance, accrued pension cost, 12/31/99	24,684*
Required additional minimum pension liability	26,316
Current balance, additional minimum pension liability	0
Required increase, additional minimum pension liability	$ 26,316

*$24,684 = $16,667 (bal. 1/1/99) + $8,017 (from above entry).

The maximum intangible asset allowed, $26,666, is the sum of unrecognized PSC ($18,000) and unrecognized transition liability ($8,666) at the end of the year. This amount exceeds the required additional minimum pension liability; therefore, unrealized pension cost is not recorded. The following entry records the additional minimum pension liability:

December 31, 1999—Record additional minimum pension liability:

Intangible pension asset	26,316	
Additional minimum pension liability		26,316

The net pension liability reported in the balance sheet is $51,000.

2000 As a result of the spreadsheet analysis in Exhibit 18–14, Owens Valley records these entries at the end of 2000:

December 31, 2000—Record pension expense:

Pension expense	75,008	
Accrued pension cost		20,008
Cash		55,000

December 31, 2000—Reduce additional minimum pension liability:

Additional minimum pension liability	26,316	
Intangible pension asset		26,316

The second entry, which reduces the additional minimum pension liability and intangible to zero, is based on the following schedule:

EXHIBIT 18–13　Pension Spreadsheet, 1999

OWENS VALLEY COMPANY
Pension Plan Spreadsheet, 1999

	Informal Record			Formal Record	
	PBO (actuary)	Plan Assets (trustee)	Unrecognized Pension Cost	Pension Expense	Accrued Pension Cost
Balances, 1/1/99	$120,000	$ 95,000	$ 8,333		$(16,667)
Service cost	50,000			$50,000	
Interest cost	14,000			14,000	
Expected return				(8,550)	
Unrecognized PSC:					
Beginning balance	20,000		L $20,000		
1999 amortization			(2,000)*	2,000	
Ending balance			L $18,000		
Unrecognized loss:					
Beginning balance			G $(1,000)		
1999 amortization			100†	(100)	
Change from assets			G (2,450)‡		
Actuarial loss	30,000		L 30,000		
Ending balance			L $26,650§		
Unrecognized transition liability:					
Beginning balance			L $ 9,333		
1999 amortization			(667)‖	667	
Ending balance			L $ 8,666		
Actual return		11,000			
Contributions		50,000			50,000
Benefits paid	(40,000)	(40,000)			
Ending balances:					
PBO	$194,000				
Plan assets		$116,000			
Underfunded PBO	$78,000				
Unrecognized pension costs			$53,316**		
Pension expense				$58,017	(58,017)
Accrued pension cost					$(24,684)

Note: L = loss, liability, or cost; G = gain or asset.

*($20,000 beginning PSC)/(10 year service life at date of grant)

†($1,000 unrecognized gain at 1/1/99)/10 = $100. Corridor amortization: 10% of greater of PBO, assets at 1/1/99 = .10($120,000) = $12,000. This amount exceeds the net unrecognized gain at 1/1/99; minimum amortization = 0. Owens amortizes unrecognized gains and losses on the straight-line basis rather than amortize the minimum amount.

‡Actual return ($11,000) − expected return ($8,550) = $2,450 G.

§This is an example of beginning the year with a gain, ending with a loss.

‖($17,333 initial transition liability)/26 = $667.

**$18,000 + $26,650 + $8,666.

ABO, 12/31/00	$177,000
Plan assets at fair value, 12/31/00	139,200
Total minimum liability	37,800
Balance, accrued pension cost, 12/31/00	44,692*
Required additional minimum pension liability	0
Current balance, additional minimum pension liability	26,316
Required decrease, additional minimum pension liability	$ 26,316

*$44,692 = $24,684 (bal. 1/1/00) + $20,008 (from above entry).

EXHIBIT 18–14   Pension Spreadsheet, 2000

OWENS VALLEY COMPANY
Pension Plan Spreadsheet, 2000

	PBO (actuary)	Plan Assets (trustee)	Unrecognized Pension Cost	Pension Expense	Accrued Pension Cost
		Informal Record		Formal Record	
Balances, 1/1/00	$194,000	$116,000	$53,316		$(24,684)
Service cost	60,000			$60,000	
Interest cost	19,400			19,400	
Expected return				(9,280)	
Unrecognized PSC:					
Beginning balance			L $18,000		
2000 amortization			(2,000)*	2,000	
Ending balance			L $16,000		
Unrecognized loss:					
Beginning balance			L $26,650		
2000 amortization			(2,221)†	2,221	
Change from assets			L $ 1,080‡		
Experience gain	(12,000)		G (12,000)		
Ending balance			L $13,509		
Unrecognized transition liability:					
Beginning balance			L $ 8,666		
2000 amortization			(667)§	667	
Ending balance			L $ 7,999		
Actual return		8,200			
Contributions		55,000			55,000
Benefits paid	(40,000)	(40,000)			
Ending balances:					
PBO	$221,400				
Plan assets		$139,200			
Underfunded PBO		$82,200			
Unrecognized pension costs			$37,508‖		
Pension expense				$75,008	(75,008)
Accrued pension cost					$(44,692)

Note: L = loss, liability, or cost; G = gain or asset.

*($20,000 beginning PSC)/(10 year service life at date of grant) = $2,000.

†$26,650/12 = $2,221. Corridor amortization: 10% of greater of PBO, assets at 1/1/00 = .10($194,000) = $19,400. Excess of unrealized loss over corridor threshold = $26,650 − $19,400 = $7,250. Minimum amortization = $7,250/12 = $604. Owens chooses to amortize more than the minimum.

‡Expected return ($9,280) − actual return ($8,200) = $1,080 L.

§($17,333 initial transition liability)/26 = $667.

‖$16,000 + $13,509 + $7,999

Pension expense increased considerably in 2000 without a corresponding funding increase. Therefore, accrued pension cost increased enough to eliminate the need for the additional minimum pension liability.

Financial Statement Disclosures   Owens Valley discloses the following account balances related to pensions in its financial statements. Long-term classification for pension liabilities is assumed. Owens Valley does not plan to increase funding in the near future.

	1998	1999	2000
Income statement:			
Pension expense (a component of an operating expense,			
such as cost of goods sold or wages and salaries)	$42,667	$58,017	$75,008
Balance sheet:			
Intangible assets: Intangible pension asset	0	26,316	0
Long-term liabilities: Net pension liability	16,667	51,000	44,692
Owners' equity: Unrecognized pension cost	0	0	0

Required Footnote Disclosures for Defined Benefit Plans

SFAS No. 87 specifies five categories of required disclosures for defined benefit plans. These are illustrated for Owens Valley by fiscal year. The spreadsheet provides most of the required quantitative information.

1. Description of the pension plan:
   a. Employees covered: all employees with at least one year of full-time employment.
   b. Type of benefit formula: defined benefit, final-pay formula—retirees are paid benefits based on years of service and final salary.
   c. Funding policy: annual contributions to approximate ERISA minimum standards are sent to the trustee. Basic investment policy: 55 percent equity securities, 30 percent debt securities, and 15 percent other investments. (Owens Valley does not meet the minimum funding standard in 1998 and 2000 because funding is less than service cost in those years.)
   d. Nature and effect of significant matters affecting comparability of information for all periods presented: none.
2. Amount of pension expense for each period with separate disclosure of service cost, interest cost, actual return on plan assets, and net total of other components. (Actual return is a required disclosure. Therefore, both elements of component 5 appear in the net total of other components, also called net amortization and deferral.)

	1998	1999	2000
Service cost	$40,000	$50,000	$60,000
Interest cost	10,000	14,000	19,400
Actual return on plan assets	(9,000)	(11,000)	(8,200)
Net total of other components	1,667*	5,017†	3,808‡
Pension expense	$42,667	$58,017	$75,008

Note: L = liability or loss; G = gain or asset.

*Component 5:		
Unrecognized gain (assets)		$1,000 L[33]
Amortization of transition liability		667 L
		$1,667 L
†Amortization of PSC		2,000 L
Component 5:		
Unrecognized gain (assets)	$2,450 L	
Amortization, previous gain	100 G	2,350 L
Amortization of transition liability		667 L
		$5,017 L
‡Amortization of PSC		$2,000 L
Component 5:		
Unrecognized loss (assets)	$1,080 G	
Amortization, previous loss	2,221 L	1,141 L
Amortization of transition liability		667 L
		$3,808 L

3. A schedule reconciling the funded status of the plan with amounts reported in the employers' balance sheet showing separately (*a*) plan assets at fair value, (*b*) PBO, (*c*) unrecognized PSC, (*d*) amount of unrecognized net gain or loss (*e*) unrecognized transition asset or liability, (*f*) additional minimum pension liability, and (*g*) the amount of net pension asset or liability recognized in the balance sheet.

---

[33]From the earlier discussion, the gain is listed as a loss in this schedule because actual return (component 3) reduced pension expense by $1,000 more than expected return. To compensate, pension expense is increased by $1,000. Hence the loss.

	1998	1999	2000
Vested benefit obligation	$ (42,000)	$ (67,000)	$(125,000)
Accumulated benefit obligation	$ (96,000)	$(167,000)	$(177,000)
Projected benefit obligation	$(120,000)	$(194,000)	$(221,400)
Plan assets at fair value	95,000	116,000	139,200
Underfunded PBO (funded status)	(25,000)	(78,000)	(82,200)
Unrecognized PSC	0	18,000	16,000
Unrecognized (gain), loss	(1,000)	26,650	13,509
Unrecognized transition liability	9,333	8,666	7,999
Accrued pension cost	(16,667)	(24,684)	(44,692)
Additional minimum pension liability	0	(26,316)	0
Net pension liability, disclosed in balance sheet	$ (16,667)	$ (51,000)	$ (44,692)

4. The assumed weighted average discount rate (10 percent each year) and rate of compensation increase (6 percent each year) used to measure PBO, and the weighted average expected long-term rate of return on plan assets (10 percent, 9 percent, and 8 percent from 1998, 1999, and 2000, respectively).

5. Amounts and types of employer securities included in plan assets (none).

Note disclosures provide information not recorded in the accounts and help compensate for the effects of delayed recognition. Information about funding policies helps users assess the future cash flows of the plan. The disaggregation of pension expense clarifies the nature of pension cost. For most plans, pension expense does not equal the amount funded during the period or the increase in cost attributable to benefits earned in the period.

The breakdown of pension liabilities into PBO, ABO, VBO, and net pension liability allows a more comprehensive appraisal of the effect of pension liabilities on the riskiness of the employer. Disclosure of the assumptions under which pension expense and liabilities are measured also aids in the assessment of pension cost and obligation.

Other Pension Disclosures

Multiple Pension Plans   When an employer sponsors more than one plan, *SFAS No. 87* is applied separately to each. Unless the employer has the right to commingle funds, assets and liabilities are not offset.

Annuity Contracts   A pension annuity contract is a contract between an employer and an insurance company that unconditionally requires the insurance company to provide pension benefits for a fixed fee or premium. The contract must be irrevocable and transfer the risk of the pension plan to the insurance company. If the contract covers all the benefits for a service period, service cost equals the periodic contract cost. Benefits covered by contracts are excluded from the employer's pension liabilities, and annuity contracts are excluded from plan assets.

Multiemployer Plans   Many employers participate in a multiemployer pension plan, in which contributions are commingled and used for retirees of all participating companies. Pension expense equals the required annual contribution to the plan. Liabilities are recognized only to the extent of unpaid contributions. Employers are required to disclose a description of the plan along with information on the benefits provided and the effect of significant matters on comparability of information for all periods presented.

Disclosures for Defined Contribution Plans   The following disclosures are required for employers with defined contribution plans:
- A description of the plan, employee groups covered, basis for determining contributions, and information affecting the comparability of information for all periods presented.
- The amount of cost (expense) recognized during the period.

SUMMARY OF KEY POINTS

(L.O. 1)   1. Employers bear the risk of providing the specified retirement benefit in a defined benefit plan, in which the benefit formula defines the amount of retirement benefit. The employee bears the risk in defined contribution plans.

(L.O. 1)   2. ERISA and the PBGC play an important role in regulating pension plans and protecting employee benefits. The actuary provides much of the data for measuring pension expense and liabilities, using present value analysis and estimates of life expectancy, turnover, retirement age, future compensation levels, interest rates, and other variables in measuring a plan's cost and obligations.

(L.O. 2)   3. Pension expense is based on attribution of benefits to periods of employee service as measured by the benefit formula. Pension expense has six components.

(L.O. 2)   4. Service cost, component 1 of pension expense, is the actuarial present value of pension benefits attributed by the benefit formula to services rendered in a period.

(L.O. 2)   5. Interest cost, component 2 of pension expense, is the growth in projected benefit obligation due to the passage of time.

(L.O. 2)   6. Actual return on plan assets, component 3 of pension expense, consists of interest, dividends, and realized and unrealized changes in fair value of plan assets.

(L.O. 3)   7. *SFAS No. 87* requires disclosure of three liability measures. Projected benefit obligation is the actuarial present value of all benefits attributed by the formula to employee service rendered to date using future compensation levels if incorporated in the benefit formula. The difference between projected benefit obligation and fair value of plan assets is the plan's funded status.

(L.O. 3)   8. Accumulated benefit obligation is the actuarial present value of all benefits attributed by the formula to employee service rendered to date, based on current compensation levels.

(L.O. 3)   9. Vested benefit obligation is the actuarial present value of vested benefits. It is the investment required to satisfy all vested benefits.

(L.O. 3)   10. The change for the period in accrued or prepaid pension cost is the difference between the amount funded and pension expense.

(L.O. 4)   11. Prior service cost is the present value of benefits granted for service rendered before the plan's inception or before a plan amendment date. Gains and losses result from changes in projected benefit obligation and differences between actual and expected return. Transition asset or liability is the difference between the pension asset or liability under *APB Opinion No. 8* and the plan's funded status at the date of adopting *SFAS No. 87*. All three are subject to delayed recognition and generate components 4 through 6 of pension expense.

(L.O. 4)   12. The reconciliation of funded status highlights the delayed recognition concept in pension accounting. The funded status is critically important for the evaluation of a pension plan. The reconciliation explains why the balance sheet account does not equal funded status, and it discloses the remaining unrecognized pension cost amounts.

(L.O. 5)   13. When accumulated benefit obligation exceeds plan assets at fair value, the employer must disclose this difference in the balance sheet as a liability. This is accomplished by combining additional minimum pension liability and accrued or prepaid pension cost. When the additional minimum pension liability is recorded, an intangible pension asset is also recorded.

REVIEW PROBLEM

Each of the following five independent cases illustrates a different aspect of pension accounting:

1. **Present value: computation of pension expense, projected benefit obligation, and accumulated benefit obligation** Raymond is a participant in a pension plan. Information on the plan and Raymond's involvement follows:

> Plan inception: 1/1/98
> Funding: $3,000 per year for the first three years (end of year payments)
> Raymond's first day with the company: 1/1/98
> Raymond's expected service period: 20 years
> Raymond's expected final salary: $100,000
> Retirement period: 10 years
> Raymond's salary for 1998 and 1999: $30,000
> Discount rate, expected return rate, actual return rate: 10 percent
> Pension benefit formula: Yearly benefit during retirement =
> (number of years worked)(final salary)/25

Required

a. Compute pension expense for 1998.

b. Compute accumulated benefit obligation at 12/31/99.

c. Compute projected benefit obligation at 12/31/99.

2. **Six components of pension expense** The following data relate to a defined benefit pension plan:

PBO 1/1/98, not including any items below	$20,000
Actuary's discount rate	8%
PSC from amendment dated 1/1/98 (10 years is the amortization period)	10,000
Unrecognized transition liability, original initial value: $8,500 at 1/1/89,	
the transition date, unrecognized amount at 1/1/98	4,000
Gain from change in actuarial assumptions, computed as of 1/1/98,	
straight-line amortization, 15-year period	3,000
Actual return on plan assets, 1998	2,000
Fair value of plan assets, 1/1/98	16,000
Long-run expected rate of return on plan assets	10%
Contributions to plan assets in 1998	4,000
Benefits paid to retirees in 1998	5,000
Service cost for 1998	9,000

Required

a. Compute pension expense for 1998.
b. Compute PBO at 1/1/99.
c. Compute fair value of plan assets at 1/1/99.

3. **Unrecognized gains and losses** Mountain Oak Company presents the following information related to its pension plan, for 1998, before recording pension expense.

Projected benefit obligation, 1/1/98	$300,000
Net unrecognized gain, 1/1/98	12,000
Actuarial loss, determined at 12/31/98	4,000
Plan assets at fair value, 1/1/98	280,000
Expected long-term rate of return	10%
Plan assets at fair value, 12/31/98	295,000
1998 contribution to pension fund	10,000
Benefits paid in 1998	15,000
Average remaining service period of employees . . .	20 years
Projected benefit obligation, 12/31/98	325,000

Required

a. Determine the amortization of the unrecognized gain for 1998, using (1) corridor, or minimum, amortization and (2) straight-line amortization based on average remaining service period.
b. Determine the unrecognized gain or loss at January 1, 1999, assuming straight-line amortization.
c. By what amount is 1998 pension expense decreased because of component 5 and return on assets, assuming straight-line amortization?
d. Amortization of unrecognized gain or loss for 1999, assuming straight-line amortization.

4. **Additional minimum pension liability** At the end of 1998, after recording pension expense but before determining the change in additional minimum pension liability, Furnace Company has the following balances in its ledger accounts for its pension plan:

December 31, 1998

Intangible pension asset	$ 6,000 dr.
Unrecognized pension cost	8,000 dr.
Accrued pension cost account	18,000 cr.
Additional minimum pension liability	14,000 cr.

Unrecognized PSC remaining at December 31, 1998, is $4,000 after pension expense for 1998 is recognized. Also at December 31, 1998, PBO is $98,000, ABO is $72,000, and plan assets at fair value are $48,000.

Required

Record the entry to adjust additional minimum pension liability.

5. **Transition asset or liability** The following pension-related values are measured at date of transition to *SFAS No. 87:*

PBO	$100,000
ABO	60,000
Plan assets at fair value	80,000
APB Opinion No. 8 pension asset balance	30,000

Required

Determine the transition asset or liability.

|SOLUTION

1. *a.* Benefit based on future salary levels, earned in 1998:

$$1(\$100,000)/25 = \$4,000$$
$$\text{Pension expense, 1998} = \text{Service cost, 1998}$$
$$= \$4,000(\text{PVA, } 10\%, 10)(\text{PV1, } 10\%, 19)$$
$$= \$4,000(6.14457)(.16351) = \$4,019$$

   b. Benefits based on current salary levels, earned through 1999:

$$2(\$30,000)/25 = \$2,400$$
$$\text{Accumulated benefit obligation}$$
$$= \$2,400(\text{PVA, } 10\%, 10)(\text{PV1, } 10\%, 18)$$
$$= \$2,400(6.14457)(.17986) = \$2,652$$

   c. Benefits based on future salary levels, earned through 1999:

$$2(\$100,000)/25 = \$8,000$$
$$\text{Projected benefit obligation}$$
$$= \$8,000(\text{PVA, } 10\%, 10)(\text{PV1, } 10\%, 18)$$
$$= \$8,000(6.14457)(.17986) = \$8,841$$

2. *a.* Pension expense, 1998:

Service cost	$ 9,000
Interest cost (.08 × $27,000)*	2,160
Expected return (.10 × $16,000)	(1,600)
Amortization of PSC $10,000/10	1,000
Amortization of unrecognized gain $3,000/15	(200)
Amortization of transition liability	500†
Pension expense, 1998	$10,860

*$27,000 = $20,000 + $10,000 (PSC) − $3,000 (gain).

†From the information given, ($8,500 − $4,000)/9.

   b. PBO, January 1, 1999:

PBO, 1/1/98	$20,000
PSC	10,000
Actuarial gain	(3,000)
Revised PBO, 1/1/98	27,000
Interest cost [.08($27,000)]	2,160
Service cost, 1998	9,000
Benefits paid, 1998	(5,000)
PBO, 1/1/99	$33,160

   c. Plan assets at fair value, January 1, 1999:

Plan assets at fair value, 1/1/98	$16,000
Actual return, 1998	2,000
Contributions, 1998	4,000
Benefits paid, 1998	(5,000)
Plan assets at fair value, 1/1/99	$17,000

3. *a.*

   (1) $$\frac{\$12,000 - 10\% \times \text{greater of } (\$300,000 \text{ or } \$280,000)}{20 \text{ years}} = \text{corridor amortization} =$$

   $0 because the calculation yields a negative amount (there is no excess of unrecognized gain over the corridor).

   (2) Straight-line amortization based on average service period = $12,000/20 = $600, decreases pension expense.

b.

$$\text{Expected return} = .10(\$280,000) = \$28,000$$

Actual return is determined as follows:

$$\$280,000 + \text{actual return} + \$10,000 - \$15,000 = \$295,000$$
$$\text{actual return} = \$20,000$$

Calculation of unrecognized loss at January 1, 1999:

Unrecognized gain, 1/1/98	$(12,000)
1998 amortization of unrecognized gain	600
Actuarial loss, 12/31/98	4,000
Excess of expected over actual return, 1998	8,000
Unrecognized loss, 1/1/99	$ 600

c. 1998 pension expense includes the following:

Service cost	not given
Interest cost	not given
Expected return	$(28,000)
Amortization of net unrecognized gain at 1/1/98	(600)
Pension expense	$ xx,xxx

1998 pension is decreased $28,600 as a result of return on plan assets and component 5, amortization of net unrecognized gain.

d. Amortization of unrecognized loss in 1999 is $600/20 = $30, an increase in pension expense for 1999.

4. Determination of additional minimum pension liability:

ABO	$(72,000)
Plan assets at fair value	48,000
Total minimum liability	(24,000)
Balance, accrued pension cost (cr.)	(18,000)
Required balance, additional minimum pension liability	(6,000)
Current balance, additional minimum pension liability	(14,000)
Required reduction, additional minimum pension liability	$ 8,000

December 31, 1998:

Additional minimum pension liability	8,000
Unrealized pension cost	6,000
Intangible pension cost	2,000*

*Maximum intangible is $4,000, the amount of unrecognized PSC. Therefore, the intangible is reduced by $2,000.

5. The transition liability is $50,000:

Underfunded PBO			
APB Opinion No. 8 asset	30,000		
		Transition liability	**50,000**
		Funded status	20,000

APPENDIX   *Accounting for Postretirement Benefits Other than Pensions*[34]

Introduction

The combined 1992 earnings of the Fortune 500 industrial firms was $10.5 million (*an average of $21,000 per firm*), the lowest since the rankings began in 1955. The culprit was the adoption of *SFAS No. 106,* "Employers' Accounting for Postretirement Benefits Other than Pensions." The new standard allowed firms to choose how they would recognize the cost of such benefits earned

---

[34]This appendix assumes knowledge of pension accounting. Accounting for nonpension postretirement benefits is similar to accounting for pensions in many respects.

by employees before the standard's adoption; many large firms chose to recognize the entire amount in 1992 earnings. Postretirement benefits other than pensions (called OPEB in the financial literature) are a significant cost for many firms but the size of the resulting charges surprised many in the financial community.

Example   General Motors broke all corporate earnings records when it reported the largest single-year loss in U.S. corporate history: $23.5 billion! The one-time charge of $20.8 billion from adopting *SFAS No. 106* explained most of the loss. The $20.8 billion figure was mainly the present value of postretirement health-care benefits already promised to current and former GM employees. GM estimates that medical costs alone account for $1,500 of the cost of each vehicle it manufactures.[35]

Nonpension postretirement benefits include all benefits, other than pensions, that an employer promises to provide retirees. Health care and other benefit costs are difficult to predict. Factors affecting these costs include the health care services needed by retirees, changes in technology and in government reimbursement policies, Medicare coverage, geographic location, age and general health, future pay increases, and coverage for spouses and dependents.

SFAS No. 106 requires accrual of the cost and obligation of postemployment benefits as employees render services. The statement treats postretirement benefits as part of the compensation paid to employees for services rendered, and incorporates three fundamental aspects characteristic of pension accounting: delayed recognition, net cost, and offsetting.

Before the new standard, most employers accounted for nonpension postretirement benefits on a pay-as-you-go cash basis, recognizing as expense only the payments made to retirees during a period. This method significantly understated both the expense and the liability for benefits to retirees and constituted a significant form of off-balance-sheet financing.

Scope of *SFAS No. 106*   *SFAS No. 106* applies to all postretirement benefits expected to be paid to current and former employees (and their spouses, dependents, and beneficiaries) other than pension benefits or life insurance benefits provided through a pension plan. These benefits include health care coverage, life insurance, tuition assistance, day care, legal services, and housing subsidies. For many employers, health care benefits are the most significant benefit. *SFAS No. 106* does not apply to accounting for similar benefits provided to employees during their working years or to individual contracts for postemployment benefits.[36]

SFAS No. 106 focuses on defined benefit postretirement plans and applies to unwritten as well as to contractual plans. It presumes that an employer providing regular postretirement benefits in the past will continue to do so, even if no contract exists. Benefits are defined in terms of specific monetary amounts or specific benefit coverage. Examples include coverage of up to $200 per day for hospitalization, 70 percent of the cost of dental work, or complete (open-ended) health-care coverage during retirement.

Full Eligibility   An employee is *fully eligible* for postretirement benefits when the employee renders the service necessary to receive all *expected* benefits. Full eligibility is attained by fulfilling age and service requirements, depending on the plan.

Some plans require both age (for example, age 55) and service requirements (for example, 20 years of service) to attain full eligibility. Other plans provide proportional benefits according to age and service.

Example   Assume that a plan promises 50 percent of full postretirement health-care coverage for 15 years of service after age 40, 75 percent for 20 years' service after age 40, and 100 percent for 25 years' service after age 40. The full eligibility date for an employee hired at age 40 and expected to retire at age 63 is age 60, at which time the employee is eligible for 75 percent coverage during retirement. The full eligibility date for pay-related plans is generally the retirement date because benefits are based on final salary.

Service beyond the full eligibility date does not increase future benefits. However, if the employee continues to earn material benefits for each year of service until retirement date (such as in a pay-related plan), the full eligibility date is the retirement date.

---

[35]"GM Retirees to Be Charged for Insurance," *The Wall Street Journal*, September 9, 1993, p. A3.

[36]*SFAS No. 106* amended *APB Opinion No. 12* to require that the employer's obligation for the latter plans be accrued according to the terms of the contract. *SFAS No. 112*, "Employers' Accounting for Postemployment Benefits," applies to benefits provided to active and inactive employees after employment but before retirement.

EXHIBIT 18A–1

Factors Leading to Estimates of Future Payments to Retirees under a Postretirement Health-Care Plan

1. **Per capita claims cost by age** The current cost of providing postretirement health-care benefits for one year at each age plan participants are expected to receive benefits under the plan. Past and present claims data for the plan, or the experience of other employers or insurance companies and consultants if such data are unavailable, are used to determine these amounts.
2. **Health-care cost trend rates** Assumptions about the annual rate of change of health-care costs for the benefits provided by the plan. These assumptions include health-care inflation, changes in utilization, technological advances, and health-care status of participants.
3. **Assumed per capita claims cost by age** The per capita claims cost by age adjusted for health-care cost trend rates.
4. **Plan demographics** The characteristics of the plan population, including geographical distribution, age, gender, and marital status
5. **Future gross eligible charges** Assumed per capita claims cost adjusted by plan demographics.
6. **Net incurred claims cost by age** The employer's share of the cost of providing postretirement health care. The cost equals future gross eligible charges reduced by expected Medicare reimbursement, expected employee contributions (cost sharing), and deductibles. The net incurred claims cost amounts by age are the cash flow inputs into the actuarial present value models.

Employer Obligations for Postretirement Benefit Plans

An employer's obligation under a postretirement benefit plan is the actuarial present value of expected future payments to retirees. The estimates of the amount and timing of payments for postretirement health care depend on a combination of factors, listed in Exhibit 18A–1. The actuarial present value also incorporates estimates of turnover and life expectancy, and benefits under pay-related plans are affected by salary increases. The discount rate used for present value purposes is based on the rate of return on high-quality fixed-income investments currently available to settle the obligation, and interest rates implied by contracts with third-party insurers.

The **expected postretirement benefit obligation (EPBO)** is the actuarial present value of future postretirement benefits expected to be paid. The **accumulated postretirement benefit obligation (APBO)** is the actuarial present value of future postretirement benefits attributed to an employee's service rendered to a particular date (measurement date). APBO is the more important liability measure for reporting purposes because it reflects service through a measurement date. Neither is recognized as a balance sheet liability, but APBO is disclosed in the footnotes.

Before the full eligibility date, APBO is the portion of the EPBO attributed to service rendered to a measurement date. If the benefit formula includes expected salary increases, both the APBO and the EPBO reflect them.[37] On the full eligibility date, APBO and EPBO are equal.

Exhibit 18A–2 illustrates both liability measures. In that exhibit, EPBO is $5,580 at December 31, 1997, because this amount is the present value of benefits expected to be paid, as of that date. An equal amount of EPBO for each employee is attributed to each year of service, from the date of hire to the full eligibility date, unless the benefit formula attributes a disproportionate share of the benefits to early years of service.[38] Therefore, the APBO at that measurement date reflects the portion of the total required period served, or $^{21}/_{25}$ in Michael's case.

Assuming that there are no changes in expected health care costs, both EPBO and APBO equal $7,877 at December 31, 2001, when Michael has served 25 years and is fully eligible for the benefits. The two obligation measures are reestimated (but remain equal) at the end of each year until payments are no longer required.

Postretirement Benefit Expense

Postretirement benefit expense, a current operating expense, is the cost of a postretirement benefit plan recognized in a reporting period.[39] The expense has six components, similar to accounting for pensions:

1. Service cost.
2. Interest cost.
3. Actual return on plan assets.

---

[37]Therefore, APBO is more comparable to PBO than to ABO for pension plans. If the plan is pay related, APBO is affected by changes in future salary levels. Both APBO and PBO are based on services rendered to a measurement date.

[38]Given the complexity of many plans, the FASB chose to attribute an equal amount of EPBO to each year of service, rather than to base attribution on the benefit formula, which may define different benefits for different years of service and have multiple age and service requirements for eligibility.

[39]If the full eligibility date occurs before retirement, postretirement benefit expense is recognized only to the full eligibility date. However, the measurement of the obligation considers periods beyond that date because benefit payments do not commence until retirement.

EXHIBIT 18A–2

Determining Expected
Postretirement Benefit Obligation
and Accumulated Postretirement
Benefit Obligation

Michael Reni works for a firm with a postretirement plan that provides health-care benefits to employees who render 15 years of service and retire after age 60. Michael was hired January 1, 1977, just after turning age 35. He must serve 25 years to reach his full eligibility date, December 31, 2001.

Michael is expected to leave the firm at age 65 (at the end of 2006) and live to age 70. The first benefit payment ($3,000 in the table below) is expected to be paid December 31, 2007. Assume a 9 percent discount rate. The health benefit payments for Michael estimated at the measurement date, December 31, 1997 (age 56), follow:

Age	Expected Net Incurred Claims Cost by Age*	Present Value of Claims Cost at Age	
		56 (12/31/97)	60 (12/31/01)
66	$3,000	$1,267†	$1,789‡
67	3,500	1,356§	1,915‖
68	2,700	960	1,355
69	1,900	620	875
70	4,600	1,377	1,943
	Total present value	$5,580	$7,877

At December 31, 1997:

Michael is 56 and has served 21 years, or $^{21}/_{25}$ of the period required for full eligibility.
EPBO = $5,580, the present value of payments expected under plan.
APBO = $5,580($^{21}/_{25}$) = $4,687.

*Assume end-of-year payments; these amounts reflect anticipated health-care cost trend rates and the other factors listed in Exhibit 18A–1.

†$3,000(PV1, 9%, 10) = $3,000(.42241) = $1,267**

‡$3,000(PV1, 9%, 6) = $3,000(.59627) = $1,789

§$3,500(PV1, 9%, 11) = $3,500(.38753) = $1,356

‖$3,500(PV1, 9%, 7) = $3,500(.54703) = $1,915

**The present value of the first benefit payment ($3,000) at December 31, 1997, 10 years before payment, is $1,267.

4. Amortization of prior service cost.
5. Gains and losses to the extent recognized.
6. Amortization of transition asset or liability.

Service cost for a period is the actuarial present value of benefits attributed to service rendered by employees during the period. It is the portion of EPBO attributed to service in the period. Actuaries calculate service cost from the per capita claims cost and other information.

Interest cost is the increase in APBO during the period resulting from the passage of time, and it is obtained by multiplying beginning APBO by the discount rate.

The **actual return on plan assets** is the change in the fair value of plan assets during the period, adjusted for contributions and benefit payments. As with pension accounting, the expected return on plan assets, found by multiplying the expected long-term rate of return by beginning plan assets at fair value, is the amount used for postretirement benefit expense. The expected long-term rate of return on plan assets reflects the average rate of earnings expected on plan assets. In contrast to pensions, this return reflects a reduction for income tax because nonpension postretirement benefit funds are not tax-exempt.

When postretirement benefit expense and annual funding are not equal, accrued or prepaid postretirement benefit cost is recognized for the difference.

Example   Assume that postretirement benefit expense is $30,000 in the first year of a plan and that $20,000 is funded by contribution to the plan fund. The entry to record the expense and obligation is as follows:

To record annual postretirement benefit expense:

Postretirement benefit expense	30,000	
Accrued postretirement benefit cost		10,000
Cash		20,000

The $10,000 accrued postretirement benefit cost balance (a liability) represents recognized, but unfunded, postretirement benefit expense. The liability (or asset if overfunded) is classified as current or long term, depending on the expected period of payment (or reduction in future payment). Because prior service cost, gains and losses, and transition amount are subject to delayed recognition, the balance in accrued or prepaid postretirement benefit cost is generally not equal to the plan's funded status (difference between APBO and plan assets at fair value).

Transition Amount

The transition amount is the difference between the firm's accrued or prepaid postretirement benefit cost account (if any) and the plan's funded status, at the date of transition to *SFAS No. 106:*

Accrued or prepaid postretirement benefit cost + Transition asset or liability
$$= APBO - \text{Plan assets at fair value}$$

For example, at transition, a plan with a $400,000 APBO and $210,000 in plan assets at fair value is underfunded by $190,000. If the firm recognized $100,000 of accrued postretirement benefit cost (liability) before transition, the firm has a $90,000 transition liability (L is used for liability and A for asset):

$$\$100,000 \text{ L} + \text{Transition liability} = \$400,000 \text{ L} - \$210,000 \text{ A}$$
$$\text{Transition liability} = \$190,000 \text{ L} - \$100,000 \text{ L} = \$90,000 \text{ L}$$

The transition liability generally represents nonrecognition of service cost, interest cost, prior service cost, and net unrecognized losses before transition.

The transition amount can be recognized in net income immediately (in the transition period, not in later periods) as a cumulative effect of a change in accounting principle or on a delayed basis as a component of postretirement benefit expense.[40] If delayed recognition is elected, the transition amount is amortized on a straight-line basis over the average remaining service period of active plan participants. If that average is less than 20 years, the employer can elect to use 20 years for amortization.[41] If almost all plan participants are inactive, the average life expectancy of those participants is used for amortization.

Amortization of a transition liability increases postretirement benefit expense; the reverse is true for a transition asset. However, delayed recognition of the transition liability should not result in slower recognition of the postretirement obligation than under the pay-as-you-go approach. Therefore, after transition, if the cumulative benefit payments exceed the cumulative recognized postretirement benefit expense, additional amortization of the transition liability is recognized for the difference. An example later in this appendix illustrates this provision.

Accounting for the transition amount is of particular concern to employers. The transition liability is substantial for firms that used the cash basis of accounting before transition.[42] For many firms the transition liability equals APBO at transition because no plan assets or previously recognized balance sheet liability exists. Therefore, delayed recognition of the transition liability means delayed recognition of the entire obligation for such firms. For this reason, the FASB does not require recognition or disclosure of a minimum liability for postretirement benefits. Also, whereas the minimum liability for pensions approximates the statutory U.S. liability for vested benefits, no such statutory requirement exists for postretirement benefits.

Prior Service Cost

Prior service cost arises from plan amendments that increase benefits for employee service rendered in prior periods. Amendments are granted on the assumption that the employer will realize future economic benefits. Therefore, the prior service cost (the increase in the APBO) is amortized by allocating an equal amount to each remaining year of service to the full eligibility date. Consistent use of a more rapid amortization method, such as straight-line amortization, is allowed over the average remaining years of service to full eligibility. Amortization increases postretirement benefit expense. Employees who are already fully eligible for the increased benefits and employees hired after the amendment date are not included in the calculation.

If most participants are fully eligible for the amended benefits, prior service cost is amortized over the remaining life expectancy of those plan participants. If an amendment reduces APBO, that reduction is first used to reduce any existing unrecognized prior service cost from previous amendments, then any unrecognized transition liability is reduced, and then any remainder is amortized. Exhibit 18A–3 illustrates amortization of prior service cost.

---

[40]The portion of the transition amount attributable to the effects of a plan initiation or benefit improvement adopted after December 21, 1990, is treated as prior service cost and excluded from the transition amount immediately recognized.

[41]In a field test of the exposure draft preceding *SFAS No. 106,* the FASB found that a majority of participating companies had an average remaining service period between 18 and 21 years.

[42]One study of 25 companies found that interest cost would average approximately 50 percent of postretirement benefit expense because the transition obligation is so large. See M. Akresh, B. Bald, and H. Dankner, "Results of OPEB Field Test Show Impact on Corporate Expenses," *Financial Executive,* July–August 1989, pp. 33–36.

EXHIBIT 18A–3
Amortization of Prior Service Cost

On January 1, 1998, a firm amended its postretirement benefit plan by increasing the benefits attributable to service performed before the amendment date. The accumulated postretirement benefit obligation increased $93,000 as a result (prior service cost). The remaining years of service for employees who have not yet reached full eligibility follow:

Number of Employees	Remaining Years to Full Eligibility at January 1, 1998	Total Service Years for Each Remaining Year to Full Eligibility					Total
		1998	1999	2000	2001	2002	
3	1	3*					3
6	2	6	6				12
9	3	9	9	9			27
4	4	4	4	4	4		16
7	5	7	7	7	7	7	35
29		29	26	20	11	7	93

Note: Average remaining years of service to full eligibility: 3.207 (93 total years/29 employees).

Amortization under the two approaches for each year is as follows:

Year	Amortization of Prior Service Cost	
	Allocating an Equal Amount to Each Remaining Year to Full Eligibility	Using Average Remaining Years of Service to Full Eligibility
1998	$29,000 ($93,000 × 29/93)	$29,000 ($93,000/3.207)
1999	26,000 ($93,000 × 26/93)	29,000 ($93,000/3.207)
2000	20,000 ($93,000 × 20/93)	29,000 ($93,000/3.207)
2001	11,000 ($93,000 × 11/93)	6,000 (remaining)
2002	7,000 ($93,000 × 7/93)	
	$93,000	$93,000

*Three employees have one remaining year to full eligibility.

Gains and Losses

Gains and losses arise from changes in assumptions affecting APBO or from a difference between experience and assumptions, as well as from differences between expected and actual return on plan assets. As with pensions, these gains and losses are allowed to cancel out to a considerable extent before they are recognized in postretirement benefit expense.

Minimum (corridor) amortization of the net unrecognized gain or loss is the same for postretirement benefits and pensions. The amortization period is the average remaining service period of active plan participants. Any systematic alternative amortization method can be used if:
- The minimum is recognized when the alternative method results in a smaller amount.
- The method is applied consistently.
- The method is disclosed.

In contrast to pensions, immediate recognition of gains and losses also is allowed. However, the amount of any net gain exceeding a net loss previously recognized in income is first offset against any unrecognized transition liability, and the amount of any net loss in excess of a net gain previously recognized in income is first offset against any unrecognized transition asset.[43] Therefore, the gain or loss component of postretirement benefit expense consists of these values:
- The difference between actual and expected return on plan assets for the current period.
- Any gain or loss immediately recognized at the discretion of the employer *or* amortization of net unrecognized gain or loss.
- Any gain or loss required to be recognized immediately.[44]

Footnote 14 to the financial statements of the Coca-Cola Company, reproduced at the end of the text, illustrates many of the points discussed here. The statement details the components of postretirement benefit expense and funded status. Coca-Cola recognized the entire transition liability in 1992 earnings.

---

[43]This provision was added to avoid recognizing gains (losses) before the underlying underfunded (overfunded) accumulated postretirement benefit obligation is recognized.

[44]If an employer forgives a retroactive adjustment of current or past years' cost-sharing provisions relating to benefit costs already incurred by employees, or if an employer deviates from the provisions of the substantive plan to increase or decrease the employer's share of the benefit costs incurred in current or past periods, the effect is recognized immediately as a gain or loss.

Three-Year Example of Postretirement Accounting

A three-year example illustrates accounting for postretirement benefits. Exhibit 18A–4 provides background information and first-year results for Waldorf Corporation. Exhibits 18A–5 and 18A–6 illustrate the second and third years.

Required Disclosures   Disclosures required under *SFAS No. 106* include these items. Relevant amounts for Waldorf Corporation at December 31, 2000, are also given.

- A description of the substantive plan and planned changes, the employee groups covered, types of benefits provided, funding policy, and types of assets held.
- The amount of postretirement benefit expense showing service cost, interest cost, actual return, amortization of transition amount, and the net of other components (2000 postretirement benefit expense, $84,104; service cost, $40,000; interest cost, $31,403; actual return, $5,000; amortization of transition liability, $10,000; net of other components, $7,701).
- A schedule reconciling the plan's funded status with amounts disclosed in the balance sheet (the 2000 reconciliation for Waldorf is given in Exhibit 18A–6).
- The assumed health care cost trend rates used to measure the gross eligible charges for the next year, and a description of the direction and change in the trend rate.
- The weighted-average discount rate (9 percent) and rate of compensation increase (for pay-related plans) used to measure APBO, the expected long-term rate of return on plan assets (10 percent), and estimated income tax rates included in the rate of return.
- The effect of a 1 percent increase in assumed health-care cost trend rates for each future year on the sum of service cost and interest cost and on APBO.[45]

Recognition of Additional Amortization of Transition Liability

Although delayed recognition is allowed for the transition liability, *SFAS No. 106* does not allow cumulative postretirement benefit expense to be exceeded by cumulative benefit payments *as a result of delayed recognition*. Otherwise, the cumulative expense on a pay-as-you-go basis would exceed cumulative expense on the accrual basis. If this situation exists, additional amortization of the transition liability is required.

Exhibit 18A–7 uses some of the Waldorf Corporation results to illustrate additional amortization.

Reaction to *SFAS No. 106*

SFAS No. 106 was issued amid considerable controversy. Concerns focus on its effect on corporate annual reports and retiree benefit plans. The statement requires estimates of many factors spanning decades, casting doubt on the accuracy of the results. The length of time increases the sensitivity of the expense and obligation to changes in assumptions. Unforseeable events can render last year's estimates meaningless, in some cases more so than for pension accounting.

Employee turnover, for example, can completely erase postretirement benefits, while only reducing pension benefits. Health-care costs often increase dramatically with a person's age, while pension benefit payments remain constant. Other postretirement benefits are reduced less than pension benefits by early retirement.

Some accountants believe that *SFAS No. 106* allows too much latitude in measuring the expense and related liability. These two amounts may be manipulated easily by changing the factors giving rise to the annual cost estimates. The estimation problem is compounded by questions concerning the existence of the postretirement liability:

> There is the question of whether there is a liability at all. Many companies extend health benefits to retirees but change them often. Recent court cases indicate that the employer's right to change or terminate the benefit will be upheld.[46]

Some evidence suggests that *SFAS No. 106* directly or indirectly contributed to a lowering of retiree health-care benefits.

Example   A poll of 220 companies providing retiree medical benefits found that 74 percent have made changes, while 16 percent are considering modifications to cope with rising medical costs and the cost of new accounting rules.[47]

The analysis of retiree health-care programs and costs required to comply with the new standard has raised the awareness of managers concerning the magnitude of the related liabilities.

---

[45]The reason for this requirement is that postretirement costs are very sensitive to small changes in future health care costs. See H. Dankner and N. Ford, "Postemployment Benefits: Key Measurement Issues," *Financial Executive,* November–December 1987, pp. 24–27.

[46]"Ignore the Retiree Health Benefits Rule," *The Wall Street Journal,* February 21, 1992, p. A16.

[47]"By the Numbers: Why Retiree Medical Benefits Are Changing," *Journal of Accountancy,* September 1993, p. 20.

WALDORF CORPORATION

Three-Year Postretirement Benefit Accounting Example

Background Information

Transition date: January 1, 1993.   Transition liability: $250,000.

Waldorf used pay-as-you-go accounting before transition and had no fund or accrued liability at 1/1/93.

Average remaining service period at transition was 25 years. This value is used to amortize the transition amount. Since then, the average remaining service period has steadily declined. Assume as of January 1, 1998, the value is 12 years and is constant for the case.

1998 is the first year of the case. APBO at January 1, 1998, is $200,000. More benefits were paid to retirees between 1993 and 1998 than were earned (at present value) by current employees, causing APBO to decline during this period.

The fund was exhausted at January 1, 1998. The firm has been unable to maintain a positive fund balance due to the high level of benefit payments. However, beginning in 1998, the firm has committed to increase funding levels.

For simplicity, assume accrued postretirement benefit cost at January 1, 1998, is also zero.

Discount rate: 9 percent.

1998: Service Cost, Interest Cost, and Amortization of Transition Obligation

Information for 1998:

Waldorf contributed $35,000 to the fund on December 31, 1998

Benefit payments (to retirees), December 31, 1998: $20,000

Service cost: $30,000

Postretirement benefit expense, 1998:

Service cost	$30,000
Interest cost ($200,000 × .09)	18,000
Amortization of transition liability ($250,000/25)	10,000
Postretirement benefit expense, 1998	$58,000

To record 1998 postretirement benefit expense:

Postretirement benefit expense	58,000	
Accrued postretirement benefit cost		23,000
Cash		35,000

Return on plan assets is not a component of the expense because a benefit fund does not exist at the beginning of 1998. The following report reveals why the recognized liability ($23,000) does not equal the plan's funded status (underfunded $213,000):

Reconciliation of Funded Status

December 31, 1998

APBO	$(228,000)*
Plan assets at fair value	15,000†
Underfunded APBO (funded status)	(213,000)
Unrecognized transition liability	190,000‡
Accrued postretirement benefit cost	$ (23,000)

The unrecognized transition liability is that part of APBO not yet recognized in expense and therefore not yet recognized in accrued postretirement benefit cost.

*APBO, 1/1/98	$200,000		†Plan assets, 1/1/98	$ 0
Service cost	30,000		Contributions	35,000
Interest cost	18,000		Benefit payments	(20,000)
Benefit payments	(20,000)		Plan assets, 12/31/98	$15,000
APBO, 12/31/98	$228,000			

‡$250,000 − ($10,000 amortization per year × 6 years)

EXHIBIT 18A–5
Postretirement Benefit Expense
and Liabilities, 1999

WALDORF CORPORATION
1999: Plan Amendment, Amortization of Prior Service Cost, Actual and Expected Return on Plan Assets

Information for 1999:

On January 1, 1999, the plan is amended to increase benefits attributed to service performed before the amendment date; the amendment causes APBO to increase $60,000.

Average remaining years of service to full eligibility for active plan participants: 10 years. (Waldorf chooses the straight-line amortization method for prior service cost.)

An increase in estimated health-care cost trend rates at December 31, 1999 results in a $50,000 increase in APBO.

Service cost: $30,000

Contribution to fund, December 31, 1999: $75,000

Benefit payments, December 31, 1999: $45,000

Expected rate of return on plan assets: 10 percent

Actual return on plan assets in 1999: $1,000

The plan amendment is a voluntary change in the provisions of the postretirement benefit plan. The change in the estimated health-care costs is involuntary and represents an unrecognized loss on the plan. Both events cause APBO to increase.

Postretirement benefit expense, 1999:

Service cost	$30,000
Interest cost ($228,000 + $60,000*)(.09)	25,920
Expected return ($15,000 × .10)	(1,500)
Amortization of prior service cost ($60,000/10)	6,000
Amortization of transition liability ($250,000/25)	10,000
Postretirement benefit expense, 1999	$70,420

*Prior service cost, determined at January 1, 1999

Interest cost reflects the immediate increase in APBO caused by the plan amendment. The $50,000 loss does not affect interest cost in 1999, nor is it amortized in 1999, because it occurred at the end of the year. Expected return reduces postretirement benefit expense.

To record 1999 postretirement benefit expense:

Postretirement benefit expense	70,420	
Accrued postretirement benefit cost	4,580	
Cash		75,000

Waldorf contributed more to the fund than it recognized as expense during the year. Therefore, the accrued postretirement benefit cost account decreased $4,580 at the end of 1999, although the unrecognized APBO increased significantly during the period. The unrecognized portion of this increase is represented by unrecognized prior service cost and the unrecognized loss, as shown in the funded status report:

Reconciliation of Funded Status
December 31, 1999

APBO	$(348,920)*
Plan assets at fair value	46,000†
Underfunded APBO (funded status)	(302,920)
Unrecognized prior service cost	54,000‡
Unrecognized net loss	50,500§
Unrecognized transition obligation	180,000‖
Accrued postretirement benefit cost	$ (18,420)

*APBO, 1/1/99	$228,000		†Plan assets, 1/1/99	$15,000
Service cost	30,000		Contributions	75,000
Interest cost	25,920		Actual return	1,000
Prior service cost	60,000		Benefit payments	(45,000)
Loss on rate change	50,000		Plan assets, 12/31/99	$46,000
Benefit payments	(45,000)			
APBO, 12/31/99	$348,920			

‡$60,000 beginning-of-year amount − $6,000 amortization.

§$50,000 loss on rates + ($1,500 expected return − $1,000 actual return).

‖$190,000 beginning-of-year amount − $10,000 amortization.

EXHIBIT 18A–6
Postretirement Benefit Expense
and Liabilities, 2000

WALDORF CORPORATION
2000: Amortization of Unrecognized Loss

Information for 2000:
Service cost: $40,000
Contribution to fund, December 31, 2000: $80,000
Benefit payments, December 31, 2000: $60,000
Actual return on plan assets in 2000: $5,000
Waldorf recognizes minimum amortization of gains and losses:

Minimum (corridor) amortization:

Unrecognized net loss, 1/1/00:		$50,500
APBO, 1/1/00	$348,920	
Plan assets, 1/1/00	46,000	
Greater of APBO or plan assets, 1/1/00	348,920	
10% of greater of APBO or plan assets, 1/1/00		34,892
Amount in excess of corridor, subject to amortization		15,608
Amortization of net unrecognized loss, ($15,608/12)		$ 1,301

Postretirement benefit expense, 2000:

Service cost	$40,000
Interest cost ($348,920 × .09)	31,403
Expected return ($46,000 × .10)	(4,600)
Amortization of prior service cost ($60,000/10)	6,000
Amortization of net unrecognized loss	1,301
Amortization of transition liability ($250,000/25)	10,000
Postretirement benefit expense, 2000	$84,104

To record 2000 postretirement benefit expense:

Postretirement benefit expense	84,104	
Accrued postretirement benefit cost		4,104
Cash		80,000

The funded status report explains the $22,524 ($18,420 + $4,104) ending 2000 balance in accrued
postretirement benefit cost:

Reconciliation of Funded Status
December 31, 2000

APBO	$(360,323)*
Plan assets at fair value	71,000†
Underfunded APBO (funded status)	(289,323)
Unrecognized prior service cost	48,000‡
Unrecognized net loss	48,799§
Unrecognized transition obligation	170,000‖
Accrued postretirement benefit cost	$ (22,524)

*APBO, 1/1/00	$348,920	†Plan assets, 1/1/00	$46,000
Service cost	40,000	Contributions	80,000
Interest cost	31,403	Actual return	5,000
Benefit payments	(60,000)	Benefit payments	(60,000)
APBO, 12/31/00	$360,323	Plan assets, 12/31/00	$71,000

‡$54,000 beginning-of-year amoumt − $6,000 amortization

§Unrecognized net loss, 1/1/00	$50,500
Amortization, 2000	(1,301)
Gain: actual return ($5,000) − expected return ($4,600)	(400)
Unrecognized net loss, 12/31/00	$48,799

‖$180,000 beginning-of-year amount − $10,000 amortization

EXHIBIT 18A–7

Additional Amortization of
Transition Liability, 2001

Assume the following for the Waldorf Corporation in 2001:

On January 1, 2001, the firm contributes $230,000 to the fund.
At December 31, 2001, postretirement benefit expense before additional amortization of transition liability
    (but including the usual $10,000 amortization): $90,000
Benefit payments, December 31, 2001: $200,000
For simplicity, assume that total benefit payments and total postretirement benefit expense for the five years
    1993–1997 inclusive both equal $200,000.

Schedule to Determine Additional Amortization and Final Postretirement Benefit Expense

Year	Postretirement Benefit Expense	Benefit Payments
1993–1997	$200,000	$200,000
1998	58,000	20,000
1999	70,420	45,000
2000	84,104	60,000
2001, before additional transition amortization	90,000	200,000
Cumulative benefit payments		525,000
Cumulative expense through 2001 before additional transition liability amortization	$502,524 ⟶	(502,524)
Required additional amortization of transition liability		22,476
2001 expense before additional amortization of transition liability		90,000
Final 2001 postretirement benefit expense		$112,476
Unrecognized transition liability, 1/1/01		$170,000
Amortization of transition liability, 2001 ($10,000 + $22,476)		(32,476)
Unrecognized transition liability, 12/31/01, to be amortized over the remaining 16-year term (25 years − 9 years of amortization) in equal amounts per year		$137,524

For some firms, the increase in balance sheet debt arising from recognition of retiree health-care
costs has increased the cost of obtaining capital and correspondingly may have contributed to
lowered benefits. Another hypothesis is that some firms used the resulting increase in reported
debt as a justification for lowering benefits.

Despite the concerns about the effect of the new standard, the FASB concluded that disclosures about postretirement benefits are useful. The statement does not require changes in funding or benefit payments and has no immediate direct cash flow consequences other than the cost
of compliance. Further, many believe that a reasonable estimate of health care costs is better
than no estimate at all. If decisions as to the allocation of resources to health care and other
postretirement benefits are improved, the standard will have been beneficial.[48] The long-term
effect of the statement on retiree benefit plans remains to be assessed.

UNDERSTANDING AND APPLYING CONCEPTS AND STANDARDS

QUESTIONS

1. Distinguish between a defined contribution pension plan and a defined benefit pension plan.
2. Distinguish the three parties involved in accounting and reporting for a pension plan.
3. What are the primary actuarial factors related to a pension plan?
4. Explain the three funding approaches that the employer can use for pension plans.
5. Distinguish between a contributory pension plan and a noncontributory pension plan.
6. Employer Max has a defined benefit pension plan. The estimated pension expense for 1998 is $100,000.
   Explain and give the 1998 journal entry for each of the following cases: Case A—Max pays 100 percent
   of the pension expense; Case B—Max pays 80 percent of the expense; Case C—Max pays 120 percent
   of the expense.

---

[48]However, the FASB attempts to be neutral with respect to economic consequences when it sets accounting standards. Standards
are not set with the objective of achieving a specific economic objective.

7. Employee Jax will receive an annual pension benefit of $12,000 for five years, starting on December 31, 1998. Assuming an interest rate of 8 percent, how much must be in the pension fund on January 1, 1998? Explain why the answer is not $60,000.

8. Employer Wendy must build a pension fund of $50,000 by December 31, 2001. Five equal annual payments are made into the fund starting on December 31, 1997. The fund will earn 8 percent. What is the amount of each payment? Explain why it is not $10,000.

9. Explain why pension accounting must be based on assumptions and estimates.

10. What is the pension benefit formula?

11. Explain the application of the matching principle in accounting for pensions.

12. What does attribution mean in pension accounting?

13. Three special features of pension accounting are (*a*) delayed recognition, (*b*) net cost, and (*c*) offsetting. Explain each feature.

14. What is the vested benefit obligation?

15. List and define the six components of net periodic pension expense.

16. Explain the additional minimum pension liability.

17. Vana Company recorded an additional minimum pension liability as follows (000s):

Intangible pension asset	15
Unrealized pension cost	3
Additional minimum pension liability	18

Explain each line in the above entry.

18. Define and explain the projected benefit obligation (PBO).

19. What information is typically found in the report from the trustee on plan assets?

20. Explain what is meant by *underfunded (overfunded) PBO.*

21. Explain the difference between the projected benefit obligation and the accumulated benefit obligation.

22. Explain the primary approaches for amortizing unrecognized pension costs.

23. Explain the purpose and application of the additional minimum pension liability. Illustrate its computation with the following data: Prepaid pension cost, $10; accumulated benefit obligation, $300; and plan assets at fair value, $240.

24. In the case of the unrecognized pension costs, such as prior service cost, that are first incurred during 1998, amortization may or may not be appropriate at the end of 1998. Explain why.

25. Why did many firms experience a large one-time earnings reduction upon their transition to the current accounting standard on postretirement benefits other than pensions?

26. Explain the difference between expected postretirement benefit obligation (EPBO) and accumulated postretirement benefit obligation (APBO) in accounting for postretirement benefits other than pensions.

27. Explain how accounting for the transition amount for postretirement benefits is similar to and different from that for pensions.

EXERCISES

E 18–1
(L.O. 1, 2)

Understanding Pension Terminology   Match the brief definitions with the terms by entering one letter in each space provided.

Terms	**Brief Definition**
_______ 1. Projected benefit obligation	A. Amount reported as total pension expense for the period; has six components
_______ 2. Expected return on plan assets	
_______ 3. Amortization of gains and losses	B. Allocation of the cost of retroactive pension benefits to periodic expense
_______ 4. Pension plan assets	
_______ 5. Net periodic pension expense	C. Actuarial present value of all future pension benefits at the measurement date excluding the effects of expected future compensation levels
_______ 6. Fair market value (of plan assets)	
_______ 7. Amortization of prior service costs	
_______ 8. ERISA (1974)	D. Employee Retirement Income Security Act of 1974
_______ 9. Prepaid pension cost	E. Cost of future pension benefits earned during the current accounting period
_______ 10. Accumulated benefit obligation	
_______ 11. Interest cost	F. The interest rate used by the actuary to adjust for the time value of money
_______ 12. Discount rate	
_______ 13. Service cost (pensions)	G. Present value of the employee's benefits at the measurement date not contingent on remaining an employee
_______ 14. Amortization of transition cost	
_______ 15. Vested benefit obligation	H. Allocation of the difference between expected and actual return on plan assets and changes in actuarial assumptions to periodic expense
_______ 16. Actual return on plan assets	

> I. Cumulative fund assets plus unrecognized pension costs in excess of the PBO
>
> J. Difference between plan assets at fair market value at the beginning and end of the period minus contributions and plus distributions during the accounting period.
>
> K. The value of plan assets between a willing buyer and a willing seller (not a forced sale)
>
> L. Attribution (allocation) to accounting periods of the costs recognized when *SFAS No. 87* is first applied
>
> M. Actuarial present value of all future pension benefits at the measurement date, including the effects of current and future compensation levels
>
> N. Projected benefit obligation at the beginning of the current accounting period multiplied by the actuary's discount rate
>
> O. Resources set aside to provide future pension benefits to retirees
>
> P. Beginning market-related value of pension plan assets multiplied by the expected rate of return on plan assets

E 18–2
(L.O. 2, 3, 4, 5)

Multiple Choice   Choose the best answer from among the alternatives.

1. Service cost for 1998 for a pension plan whose pension benefit formula incorporates estimates of future compensation levels is
    a. The present value of benefits earned by employees in 1998 based on current salary levels.
    b. The increase in ABO for 1998 less interest cost on the beginning balance in ABO.
    c. The nominal value of benefits earned by employees in 1998 based on future salary levels.
    d. The present value of benefits earned by employees in 1998 based on future salary levels.

2. The following statements describe some aspect of accounting for defined benefit pension plans. Choose the incorrect statement.
    a. When only the first three components of pension expense have occurred to date for a plan, and actual return has always equaled expected return, underfunded PBO at a reporting date equals the balance in the accrued pension liability.
    b. When only the first three components of pension expense have occurred to date for a plan, and actual return has always equaled expected return, pension expense reflects the true annual cost to the company of providing future benefits earned in the current period, assuming all the actuarial assumptions are correct.
    c. Because the last three components of pension expense are derived from amortizing initial present values on a straight-line or similar basis, the true total cost of these items is not reflected in pension expense.
    d. Pension expense can be negative.

3. Choose the correct relationship among off-balance-sheet values and values reported in a balance sheet, relative to a pension plan.
    a. Underfunded PBO less amortization of unrecognized PSC equals the balance in accrued pension cost.
    b. Unrecognized PSC is an item that reconciles the balance in accrued pension cost and overfunded PBO.
    c. Sum of pension expense to date equals PBO.
    d. PBO less ABO equals balance in accrued pension cost.

4. For external reporting purposes, assuming an underfunded ABO, the liability that must be reported in the balance sheet is
    a. PBO less plan assets at fair value.
    b. Balance in accrued pension cost.
    c. The underfunded ABO.
    d. Additional minimum pension liability.

5. Choose the correct statement concerning amortization of unrecognized gain or loss:
    a. Some amortization must be recognized in a year that begins with a nonzero unrecognized gain or loss.
    b. The corridor is the maximum amortization allowed.
    c. The corridor amount for 1998 is 10 percent of the greater of these two December 31, 1998, values: PBO and plan assets at fair value.
    d. The amortization of an unrecognized gain yields a reduction in pension expense and a reduction in that unrecognized gain.

6. Defined contribution plans and defined benefit plans are two common types of pension plans. Choose the correct statement concerning these plans.
    a. The required annual contribution to the plan is determined by formula or contract in a defined contribution plan.
    b. Both plans provide the same retirement benefits.

    c. The retirement benefit is usually determinable well before retirement in a defined contribution plan.

    d. In both types of plans, pension expense is generally the amount funded during the year.

7. PBO and plan assets at fair value are two values critical to the determination of the financial status of defined benefit plans. Choose the correct statement regarding items to be included in each (none of these statements is necessarily complete).

    a. Ending PBO includes total service cost to date, interest cost to date, net initial unamortized actuarial gain or loss to date, and initial PSC.

    b. Ending PBO includes total service cost to date, interest cost to date, net initial unamortized actuarial gain or loss to date, initial PSC, and initial transition cost.

    c. Ending fair value of plan assets includes funding to date and expected return to date, reduced by benefits paid to date.

    d. Ending PBO includes service cost to date, gross differences between expected and actual returns to date, and net initial unamortized actuarial gain or loss to date, all less contributions to date.

8. Which of the following is not one of the six components of pension expense (or part of a component)?

    a. Initial transition asset.

    b. Amortization of unrecognized gain or loss.

    c. Actual return on plan assets.

    d. Growth (interest cost) in PBO since the beginning of the period.

E 18–3
(L.O. 2, 3)

Prepaid Pension Cost   Rico Corporation initiated a defined benefit pension plan on January 1, 1998. The plan does not provide any retroactive benefits for existing employees. The pension funding payment is made to the trustee on December 31 of each year. The following information is available for 1998 and 1999.

	1998	1999
Service cost	$75,000	$82,500
Funding payment (contribution)	85,000	92,500
Interest on projected benefit obligation		7,500
Actual return on plan assets		9,000

Required

In its December 31, 1999, balance sheet, Rico should report what amount of prepaid pension cost? (Prepare the journal entry to record pension expense for 1999.)

(AICPA adapted)

E 18–4
(L.O. 4)

Amortization of Transition Amount   As of December 31, 1987, the projected benefit obligation and plan assets of a noncontributory defined benefit plan sponsored by Neeni, Inc., were

Projected benefit obligation	$390,000
Plan assets at fair value	300,000

Neeni elected to apply the provisions of *SFAS No. 87* in its financial statements for the year ended December 31, 1988. As of December 31, 1987, all amounts accrued as net periodic pension cost had been contributed to the plan. The average remaining service period of active plan participants expected to receive benefits was estimated to be 10 years at the date of transition. Some participants' estimated service periods are 20 and 25 years.

Required

To minimize 1998 pension expense, what amount of amortization of the transition amount should Neeni recognize?

(AICPA adapted)

E 18–5
(L.O. 2, 3)

Pension Plan, One Employee: Compute Funding Payment   Fisher Company initiated a noncontributory defined benefit pension plan on January 1, 1998. The accounting period ends December 31. This exercise relates to one employee, V. R. Able. The pension formula specifies that Able will receive five annual retirement benefits of $50,000 at the end of each year, starting on December 31, 2008. Fisher Company will fully fund the pension plan by contributing 10 equal annual amounts starting on December 31, 1998. The pension fund will earn 8 percent annual interest during Able's service period and 7 percent during the retirement (payment) period.

Required

Compute the equal annual funding payment that must be made by Fisher Company.

E 18–6
(L.O. 2, 3)

Pension Plan, Five Employees: Compute Funding Payment   Plans are being made to fund the prospective pension benefits of a group of employees of Farr Company due to retire in nine years and to be paid in these amounts from one to five years after retirement:

End of year 1	$ 90,000
End of year 2	50,000
End of year 3	30,000
End of year 4	15,000
End of year 5	5,000
Thereafter	–0–
Total of pension payments	$190,000

Funds deposited with the pension fund trustee will earn 6 percent per annum. The pension plan contract calls for deposit of an amount sufficient to fund all of the expected payments from the fund by the date the employees retire.

Required

Round amounts to nearest dollar.

1. Compute the amount required by the trustee on the employees' retirement date, assuming that the first pension payment is one year after retirement, and prepare a proof schedule reflecting the 6 percent earnings on unused funds and pension payout by the trustee.
2. Assuming that eight equal payments are made to the trustee, with the last payment coinciding with the retirement date, compute the amount of the equal payment.

E 18–7
(L.O. 2, 3)

Understanding the PBO, Plan Assets, and Underfunding or Overfunding   Bello Company has a noncontributory, defined benefit pension plan. Data available for 1998 were the following:

Projected benefit obligation (PBO):	
Balance, January 1, 1998	$164,000
Balance, December 31, 1998	214,000
Plan assets (at fair value):	
Balance, January 1, 1998	$80,000
Balance, December 31, 1998	140,000

Required

1. How much did the PBO increase during 1998? Give five items that could have caused the PBO to change.
2. How much did the pension plan assets change during 1998? Give three items that could have caused the change in plan assets.
3. Compute the amount of the underfunded (overfunded) PBO at (*a*) January 1, 1998, and (*b*) December 31, 1998. Explain what these amounts mean.

E 18–8
(L.O. 2, 3, 4)

Understanding the Relations between the Actuary's Report and the Trustee's Report   The following listed items are shown on the 1999 PBO actuary's report (AR) or the trustee's report, status of plan assets (TR). Enter one check mark to the left for each item to indicate the report on which it appears. If a single item appears in both reports, enter two check marks. If the item does not appear on either report do not enter a check mark on that line.

AR	TR	Items (1999 unless stated otherwise)
____	____	1. December 31, 1998, ending pension obligation
____	____	2. Interest cost
____	____	3. Loss (gain) related to changes in actuarial assumptions
____	____	4. Unrecognized pension costs
____	____	5. Cash funding by the employer
____	____	6. Prior service cost (increase)
____	____	7. Net periodic pension expense
____	____	8. Actual return on plan assets
____	____	9. Accrued/prepaid pension costs
____	____	10. Underfunded (overfunded) PBO
____	____	11. December 31, 1998, balance of pension plan asset
____	____	12. Pension benefits paid to retirees
____	____	13. Transition cost (increase or decrease)
____	____	14. PBO balance, January 1, 2000
____	____	15. Expected return on plan assets
____	____	16. Pension plan assets, January 1, 2000
____	____	17. Service cost
____	____	18. Accumulated benefit obligation

E 18–9
(L.O. 2, 3)

Prepare Trustee's Report, Analysis, Prepare Employer's Entries   Mason Company has a noncontributory, defined benefit pension plan. On December 31, 1998, (end of the accounting period and the measurement date) information about the pension plan included the following:

a. Projected benefit obligation (actuary):

January 1, 1998	$ 40,000
Service cost	60,000
Interest cost	3,600
Pension benefits paid	–0–
December 31, 1998	$103,600

Interest (discount) rate used by actuary, 9 percent.

b. The trustee's report on plan assets showed a beginning balance of $50,000, cash received from the employer of $37,000, and an actual return and expected return on plan assets of $10,000.

c. Unamortized prior service cost, gains and losses, transition costs, and additional minimum pension liability: none (from company records).

Required

1. Prepare the trustee's report on the status of the plan assets (that is, a list of the beginning asset balance, changes and the ending balance).
2. Compute the amount of the underfunding (overfunding) of the PBO on the beginning and ending dates.
3. Give the 1998 entry for Mason Company to record net periodic pension expense.
4. Give the same entry, assuming cash funding of $55,000 (instead of $37,000).
5. Show how the interest of $3,600 was computed.

E 18–10
(L.O. 2, 3)

Compute Net Periodic Pension Expense and Underfunded or Overfunded PBO; Entries   The 1998 records of Jax Company provided the following data related to its noncontributory, defined benefit pension plan (amounts in $000s):

a. Projected benefit obligation (report of actuary):

Balance, January 1, 1998	$3,000
Service cost	1,200
Interest cost	240
Pension benefits paid	(400)
Balance, December 31, 1998	$4,040

Discount rate used by actuary, 8 percent.

b. Plan assets at fair value (report of trustee):

Balance, January 1, 1998	$2,408
Actual return on plan assets	168
Contributions, 1998	1,016
Pension benefits paid, 1998	(400)
Balance, December 31, 1998	$3,192

Expected long-term rate of return of plan assets, 7 percent.

c. January 1, 1998, balance of unrecognized prior service cost, gains and losses, and transaction cost, zero.

Required

1. Compute 1998 net periodic pension expense. Show the correct amount for each of the six components.
2. Give the 1998 entry(s) for Jax Company to record pension expense and funding.
3. Compute the under- or overfunded PBO at the beginning and end of 1998.

E 18–11
(L.O. 2, 3)

Compute Net Periodic Pension Expense and Underfunding or Overfunding of the PBO; Entries   Fox Company has a noncontributory, defined benefit pension plan. On December 31, 1998 (end of the accounting period and measurement date), the following data are available:

a. Projected benefit obligation (actuary's report):

Balance, December 31, 1997	$45,000
Prior service cost (due to plan amendment on January 1, 1998)	5,000
Balance, January 1, 1998	50,000
Service cost	32,500
Interest cost	4,000
Pension benefits paid	–0–
Balance, December 31, 1998	$86,500

Interest (discount) rate used by actuary, 8 percent.

b. Funding report of the trustee:

Balance, January 1, 1998	$52,500
Actual return on plan assets*	2,500
Cash received from employer	25,000
Pension benefits paid to retirees	–0–
Balance, December 31, 1998	$80,000

*Same as the expected return.

Required

1. Show how the interest cost was computed.
2. Compute net periodic pension expense. Assume that prior service cost will be amortized over a 10-year average remaining service period. Show the correct amounts for each component.
3. Give the 1998 entry for Fox Company to record net periodic pension expense.
4. Give the same entry assuming cash funding from the employer of $35,500 and no other changes.
5. Compute the underfunding (overfunding) of the PBO for (3) and (4), at December 31, 1998.

E 18–12
(L.O. 2, 3)

Compute Net Periodic Pension Expense and Underfunded or Overfunded PBO; Entries   New Company started a noncontributory, defined benefit pension plan on January 1, 1997. Data available for 1998 were as follows:

a. Projected benefit obligation, 1998 (actuary's report):

Balance, January 1, 1998	$30,000
Service cost	10,000
Interest cost (interest rate, 10%)	3,000
Prior service cost	–0–
Losses (gains) due to change in actuarial assumptions (amortization to start in 1999)	(2,000)
Pension benefits paid	(500)
Balance, December 31, 1998	$40,500

b. Status of fund assets (trustee's report):

Balance, January 1, 1998	$27,500
Actual earnings on plan assets (same as expected return)	2,500
Payments received from employer during 1998	15,000
Pension benefits paid	(500)
Balance, December 31, 1998	$44,500

c. Company records: Unamortized gain from 1997 due to changes in assumptions, $1,500 (this amount was included in the 1997 PBO). There are no gains or losses on plan assets. Unamortized (unrecognized) prior service cost and transition cost from 1997 are zero.

Required

1. Compute net periodic pension expense for 1998 assuming that the 1997 losses (gains) are amortized for 1998 over a 15-year average remaining service period.
2. Give the 1998 pension expense and funding entry for New Company.
3. Give the same entry assuming the 1998 cash payment by employer was $9,000 instead of $15,000.
4. Compute the underfunded (overfunded) PBO for (2) and (3).

E 18–13
(L.O. 2, 3, 4)

Pension Spreadsheet: Underfunded and Accrued Pension Cost; Entries   Gecko Company has a defined benefit pension plan. At the end of the current reporting period, December 31, 1998, the following information was available:

a. Projected benefit obligation (actuary's report):

Balance, January 1, 1998	$2,400
Service cost	312
Interest cost ($2,400 × 7% actuary's rate)	168
Loss (gain) change in actuarial assumptions*	72
Pension benefits paid	(160)
Balance, December 31, 1998	$2,792

*Amortization to start in 1999.

b. Status of fund assets (trustee's report):

Balance, January 1, 1998	$2,000
Actual return on plan assets (same as expected)	120
Cash received from employer company	280
Pension benefits paid to retirees	(160)
Balance, December 31, 1998	$2,240

c. From company records, unamortized pension cost from prior years (amortize over a nine-year average remaining service period):

Transition cost	$ 72
Prior service cost	108
Losses (gains)	144
Total	$ 324

Required

1. Set up and complete a spreadsheet or format of your choice to develop the pension data required at the end of 1998.
2. Give the employer's pension entry at December 31, 1998.

E 18–14
(L.O. 2, 3, 4)

Pension Spreadsheet: Underfunded and Accrued Pension Cost; Entry   Avis Company has a defined benefit pension plan. At the end of the current reporting period, December 31, 1998, the following information was available:

a. Projected benefit obligation, (actuary's report):

Balance, January 1, 1998	$750
Service cost	80
Interest cost ($750 $\times$ 10% actuary's rate)	75
Loss (gain) change in actuarial assumptions*	(7)
Pension benefits paid	(34)
Balance, December 31, 1998	$864

*Amortization to start in 1999.

b. Status of fund assets (trustee's report):

Balance, January 1, 1998	$600
Actual return on plan assets (same as expected)	54
Cash received from employer company	150
Pension benefits paid to retirees	(34)
Balance, December 31, 1998	$770

c. From company records, unamortized pension cost from prior years (amortize over a 10-year average remaining service period):

Transition cost	$100
Prior service cost	30
Losses (gains)	(20)
Total	$110

Required

1. Set up and complete a spreadsheet or format of your choice to develop the pension data required at the end of 1998.
2. Give the employer's pension entry at December 31, 1998.

E 18–15
(L.O. 2, 3, 4, 5)

Understanding Pension Accounting Terminology   Match the following items with the financial statements by entering the appropriate letter in each blank.

<table>
<tr><td>Items</td><td>Reported on the Financial Statements</td></tr>
</table>

Items	Reported on the Financial Statements
______ 1. Accumulated benefit obligation	A. Income statement expense
______ 2. Unrealized pension cost	B. Income statement gains and losses
______ 3. Unrecognized gains (losses)	C. Balance sheet assets
______ 4. Additional minimum pension liability	D. Balance sheet liabilities
______ 5. Unrecognized prior service cost	E. Balance sheet owners' equity
______ 6. Pension benefits paid	F. None of the above
______ 7. Expected return on pension plan assets	
______ 8. Unrecognized transition cost	
______ 9. Accrued pension cost	
______ 10. Net periodic pension expense	
______ 11. Vested benefit obligation	
______ 12. Unfunded accumulated benefit obligation	
______ 13. Pension plan assets at fair value	
______ 14. Prepaid pension cost	
______ 15. Pension plan assets used in operations of the plan (furniture and fixtures)	

E 18–16
(L.O. 1, 2, 4, 5)

Multiple Choice: Accounting for Pensions   Choose the correct statement for each question.

1. Which of the following defined benefit pension plan disclosures should be made in a company's financial statements?

   I. A description of the company's funding policies and types of assets held.
   II. The amount of net periodic pension cost for the period.
   III. The fair value of plan assets.

   a. I and II.
   b. I, II, and III.
   c. II and III.
   d. I only.

2. Interest cost included in the net pension cost recognized by an employer sponsoring a defined benefit pension plan represents the
   a. Amortization of the discount on unrecognized prior service cost.
   b. Increase in the fair value of plan assets due to the passage of time.
   c. Increase in the projected benefit obligation due to the passage of time.
   d. Shortage between the expected and actual returns on plan assets.

3. On July 31, 1998, Tumwater Company amended its single-employer defined benefit pension plan by granting increased benefits for services provided prior to 1998. This prior service cost will be reflected in the financial statement(s) for
   a. Years before 1998 only.
   b. 1998 only.
   c. 1998 and years before and after 1998.
   d. 1998 and the following years only.

4. An employer sponsoring a defined benefit pension plan is subject to the minimum pension liability recognition requirement. An additional liability must be recorded equal to the unfunded
   a. Accumulated benefit obligation plus the previously recognized accrued pension cost.
   b. Accumulated benefit obligation less the previously recognized accrued pension cost.
   c. Projected benefit obligation plus the previously recognized accrued pension cost.
   d. Projected benefit obligation less the previously recognized accrued pension cost.

(AICPA adapted)

E 18–17
(L.O. 4)

Minimum Amortization of Unrecognized Losses or Gains   Temblor Company is preparing the 1998 entry to record pension expense, funding, and the change in accrued/prepaid pension cost. The company has a noncontributory, defined benefit plan. The date is the end of the annual accounting year. The company has the reports of the actuary and the fund trustee. The company is preparing a spreadsheet.

Concern has been expressed about the three unrecognized pension costs: transition, prior service, and gains and losses. The first two costs will be properly amortized based on the average remaining service period (currently 10 years). The concern in this exercise is about the amortization of losses and gains. Separate data maintained by the company showed the following at December 31, 1998:

Company record of unrecognized losses (gains):

		Case A	Case B
a.	Losses (gains):		
	Balance loss (gain) Jan. 1, 1998	$ 30,000	$ 16,000
	Increase (decrease) during 1998	–0–	–0–
	Total	30,000	16,000
	Amortization during 1998*	?	?
	Balance, December 31, 1998	$?	$?

*Included in pension expense.

b.	Additional data on January 1, 1998:		
	Projected benefit obligation (actuary)	$200,000	$200,000
	Plan assets at market-related value	160,000	160,000
	Average remaining service years	10	10

Required   For each case complete the above schedule using the minimum method. Show computations.

E 18–18
(L.O. 4)

Unrecognized Gains and Losses   On January 1, 1998, a company reported a $6,000 unrecognized gain in the informal record of its pension plan. During 1998, the following events occurred:

a. Actual return on plan assets was $8,000, and expected return was $10,000.

b. A gain of $4,000 was determined by the actuary at December 31, 1998, based on changes in actuarial assumptions.

The company amortizes unrecognized gains and losses on the straight-line basis over the average remaining service life of active employees (20 years). It does not recognize the minimum amortization. Further information on this plan follows:

	Values At	
	January 1, 1998	**December 31, 1998**
PBO	$50,000	$56,000
Fair value of plan assets	30,000	34,000

Required   Compute amortization of unrecognized gain or loss for 1998 and 1999.

E 18–19
(L.O. 4)

Transition Asset or Liability   Maxfield Corporation made its transition to *SFAS No. 87* for its pension plan on January 1, 1987. At that date, its PBO was $120,000 and plan assets at fair value were $140,000. Accounting for pensions under *APB Opinion No. 8* produced an accrued pension liability of $30,000 as of January 1, 1987.

Required   1. Determine the transition asset or liability for Maxfield on January 1, 1987.

2. If the transition item relates to an employee group with an average remaining service life of 20 years, how is pension expense in 1998 affected by the amortization of the item?

E 18–20
(L.O. 4)

Apply Minimum Amortization of Unrecognized Losses or Gains   West Corporation initiated a noncontributory, defined benefit pension plan on January 1, 1989, and applied the provisions of *SFAS No. 87*. Information is available for the reporting year ended December 31, 1998, for the following independent cases (amounts in $000s):

	Case A	Case B
Projected benefit obligation, January 1, 1998	$500	$700
Plan assets at fair value, January 1, 1998*	400	800
Unrecognized (gain) or loss, January 1, 1998	(50)	30
Average remaining service period of active employees	10 years	15 years

*Same as market-related value.

Required   West uses the straight-line method, based on the average remaining service period of active employees, to amortize unrecognized gain or loss (subject to required minimum amortization).

1. Compute the amount of straight-line amortization of unrecognized gain or loss in each case. Round all amounts to the nearest $ thousand.

2. For each case, determine whether minimum amortization is required.

E 18–21
(L.O. 5)

Minimum Pension Liability: Four Years; Entries   Goode Corporation established a noncontributory, defined benefit pension plan for its employees in 1989. The following information is available for the reporting years ended December 31, (in $000s):

Items	1998	1999	2000	2001
Projected benefit obligation	$1,100	$1,500	$2,000	$2,500
Accumulated benefit obligation	900	1,050	1,400	1,900
Plan assets at fair value	800	1,100	1,300	1,400
(Accrued) prepaid pension cost	100	25	(90)	(180)
Unrecognized prior service cost	150	180	160	200

Required

1. Compute the required additional minimum liability for each year, 1998 through 2001.
2. Give the entry to recognize the additional minimum liability for each year, 1998 through 2001.

E 18–22
(L.O. 5)

Minimum Liability: Three Cases; Entries   Yates Company has a noncontributory, defined benefit pension plan. It is December 31, 1998, end of the accounting year and measurement date for the pension plan. The following are the data for three separate cases, as of the measurement dates (in $000s):

Items (at December 31, 1998)	Case A	Case B	Case C
a. Projected benefit obligation	$1,000	$1,000	$1,000
b. Accumulated benefit obligation	800	800	800
c. Vested benefit obligation	360	360	360
d. Pension plan assets at book value	550	550	550
e. Pension plan assets at fair value	600	840	600
f. (Accrued) prepaid pension cost	0	80	(20)
g. Unrecognized prior service cost	220	180	150

Required

1. For each case, compute the additional minimum pension liability that should be reported.
2. For each case (*a*) explain whether a minimum liability must be reported and why, and (*b*) if one must be reported, give the entry.

E 18–23
(L.O. 2, 3, 4, 5)

Prepare Pension Spreadsheet: Additional Minimum Pension Liability; Entries   Fox Company has a noncontributory, defined benefit pension plan. The following data are available at December 31, 1998, which is the end of the accounting period and the measurement date:

a. Projected benefit obligation, 1998 (actuary):

Balance, January 1, 1998	$223,000
Service cost	80,000
Interest cost	?
Prior service cost	–0–
Losses (gains) due to changes in assumptions (begin amortizing in 1999)	8,000
Pension benefits paid	(30,000)
Balance, December 31, 1999	?

Average remaining service period, 10 years.
Actuary's discount rate, 8 percent.
Accumulated benefit obligation, $292,000.

b. Pension plan assets (trustee):

Balance, January 1, 1998, at fair value	$200,000
Contributions to the pension plan by Fox	70,000
Actual return on plan assets	10,000
Benefits paid to retirees	(30,000)
Balance, December 31, 1998, at fair value	$250,000

Long-term expected rate of return on plan assets, 7 percent

c. Other balances at December 31, 1998: Unrecognized pension costs (total), $3,000, only prior service has a balance; accrued pension cost, $20,000.

Required

1. Prepare a spreadsheet or format of your choice to develop the required pension data.
2. Give the annual pension entry for Fox.
3. Compute the additional minimum pension liability and give the related entry.
4. Give the entry for the next year assuming that additional minimum pension liability is $10,000.

E 18–24   **Appendix: Accounting for Postretirement Benefits Other than Pensions**   Choose the correct statement for each question.

1. The balance in the accrued postretirement benefit cost account generally reflects which of the following?
   a. The underfunded accumulated postretirement benefit obligation.
   b. The underfunded expected postretirement benefit obligation.
   c. The excess of cumulative postretirement benefit expense over cumulative funding.
   d. The excess of cumulative employer contributions over cumulative benefit payments.

2. Which of the following statements correctly describes the relationship between expected postretirement benefit obligation (EPBO) and accumulated postretirement benefit obligation (APBO)?
   a. EPBO can be less than or equal to APBO but never more.
   b. EPBO and APBO are never equal.
   c. EPBO and APBO are always equal.
   d. APBO can be less than or equal to EPBO but never more.

3. A firm has a transition obligation for postretirement benefits. The average remaining service period of active plan participants is 15 years. Which of the following options for recognizing the transition obligation is open to this firm?

   > I. Immediate recognition in transition year.
   > II. Amortization over 15 years.
   > III. Amortization over 20 years.
   > IV. Amortization over 40 years.

   a. I, II, and III only.
   b. I, II, III, and IV.
   c. I and II only.
   d. I only.
   e. II only.

4. At the end of the current year, a firm's accumulated postretirement benefit obligation exceeds plan assets by $20,000. However, the firm is reporting $10,000 of prepaid postretirement benefit cost. Which of the following might explain why the firm can report an asset while having an underfunded plan?
   a. The transition obligation was recognized immediately in the year of transition.
   b. The firm has significant unrecognized amounts for past service cost and transition obligation.
   c. The firm has a large recognized transition asset.
   d. The firm's annual funding amount has never exceeded the amount recognized as annual postretirement benefit expense.

5. A firm reports an underfunded accumulated postretirement benefit obligation in its report of funded status. This amount generally equals the
   a. Amount by which cumulative postretirement benefit expense exceeds cumulative funding since transition.
   b. Amount by which the present value of benefit payments expected to be made exceeds the plan assets at fair value.
   c. Prepaid pension cost balance less amounts funded to date.
   d. Amount by which the present value of benefit payments earned to date exceeds the plan assets at fair value.

E 18–25   **Prepare Spreadsheet: Additional Minimum Pension Liability; Entries**   Saxon Company has a noncontribu-
(L.O. 2, 3, 4, 5)   tory, defined benefit pension plan. The accounting period ends December 31, 1998 (also the pension measurement date). Pension plan data for 1998 are as follows:

a. Projected benefit obligation:

Balance, January 1, 1998	$5,000
Service cost	3,000
Interest cost	402
Loss (gain) due to changes in assumptions, January 1, 1998.	25*
Pension benefits paid	(60)
Balance, December 31, 1998	$8,367

Accumulated benefit obligation, $8,367.
Actuary's discount rate, 8 percent.
Average remaining service period, 10 years.

*Begin amortizing in 1998

b. Pension plan assets:

Balance, January 1, 1998, at fair value	$4,000
Actual return; gain (expected return $160; 4%)	150
Contribution to pension fund by Saxon	3,200
Benefits paid to retirees	(60)
Balance, December 31, 1998	$7,290

c. Company records:

(1) January 1, 1998, Unamortized amounts:

Unrecognized prior service cost	$ 500
Unrecognized gain/loss	300 (gain)
Unrecognized transition cost	200
(2) (Accrued) prepaid pension cost at January 1, 1998.	(600) cr.

Amortize all unrecognized items over the average service period (for problem purposes).

Required

1. Prepare a spreadsheet or other format of your choice for the pension plan for 1998.
2. Based on (1), give the December 31, 1998, entry to record pension expense and funding for Saxon.
3. Test to determine whether additional minimum pension liability is required. Show computations and give the related entry.
4. Give the related entry for the next year assuming that the additional minimum pension liability is $200.

E 18–26   **Appendix: Postretirement Benefit Liabilities**   At December 31, 1998, Gypsum, Inc., estimated the following net incurred claims costs for one of its employees, for each year of the employee's retirement period to which the plan applies:

At Age	Estimated Net Incurred Claims Cost by Age
64	$4,194
65	4,640
66	1,284
67	1,421
68	1,577

The postretirement plan of Gypsum provides no benefits after age 68. For full eligibility, an employee must serve 20 years. The employee in question is 51 years old at December 31, 1998, and has served 15 years at that date. The employee is expected to retire at age 63. Gypsum's discount rate for postretirement benefit accounting purposes is 8 percent.

Required

1. Determine the expected postretirement benefit obligation and accumulated postretirement benefit obligation at December 31, 1998, for this employee.
2. Assuming that the employee works another five years after December 31, 1998, and that there are no changes in expected net incurred claims costs, determine the expected postretirement benefit obligation and accumulated postretirement benefit obligation at December 31, 2003, for this employee.

E 18–27    **Appendix: Full Eligibility Date and Attribution Period**   The following situations relate to an employee's eligibility for postretirement benefits.

a. A postretirement benefit plan provides 25 percent of full postretirement health coverage in return for 15 years of service to the firm after age 30, 50 percent coverage for 25 years of service after age 30, and 100 percent (full) coverage for 35 years of service after age 30. What is the full eligibility date for an employee hired at age 25 if she's expected to retire at age 57? And what percentage of full coverage will she receive?

b. Another plan provides life insurance benefits to employees who serve 20 years and reach age 50. The benefit equals 30 percent of final salary. A 45-year-old employee who currently earns $100,000 has worked 15 years for the firm. He is expected to retire at age 65 and is expected to be earning $200,000 at that time. What is the full eligibility date for this employee?

c. Bob joined a firm at age 25. The firm has a postretirement benefit plan. Five years later, Tom joined the firm at age 30. The postretirement plan specifies that employees are eligible for full benefits after rendering 20 years of service after age 30. What are the full eligibility dates for Bob and Tom?

d. A postretirement plan promises 100 percent health care coverage for all employees who retire after age 62. It is expected that participants will have rendered an average of 15 years of service at age 62. What is the full eligibility date for a participant? What is the attribution period (the period to which the expected postretirement benefit obligation is assigned)?

Required   Answer each question independently.

E 18–28   **Appendix: Amortization of Prior Service Cost**   A firm amended its postretirement plan on January 1, 1998, by increasing health-care benefits attributable to service rendered by employees before the amendment date. The accumulated postretirement benefit obligation increased $90,000 (prior service cost). The three employees affected, and their remaining years to full eligibility, follow:

	Remaining Years to Full Eligibility at Date of Amendment (January 1, 1998)				
Employee	**1998**	**1999**	**2000**	**2001**	**2002**
Robert	1	1	1	1	1
Susan	1	1			
William	1	1			
	3	3	1	1	1

The average remaining service period for all active plan participants is 10 years.

Required
1. Determine the amortization of prior service cost for each remaining year to full eligibility by allocating an equal amount to each remaining year to full eligibility.
2. Determine the amortization of prior service cost for each remaining year to full eligibility using the average remaining years to full eligibility.

E 18–29   **Appendix: Transition Item and Amortization**   The following cases relate to the transition to *SFAS No. 106* for postretirement benefit accounting. The average remaining service period for active plan participants is 15 years. Assume that the firm does not choose to recognize the obligation or asset in income immediately.

	At Transition Date		
Case	**Accumulated Postretirement Benefit Obligation**	**Plan Assets at Fair Value**	**Balance Sheet Account: (Accrued) Prepaid Postretirement Benefit Cost**
I	$100,000	$ 0	$ 0
II	100,000	200,000	30,000
III	100,000	50,000	(60,000)
IV	100,000	40,000	(40,000)

Required   For each case, determine the two permitted annual amortization amounts for the unrecognized transition asset or liability.

PROBLEMS

P 18–1
(L.O. 3)   **Present Value: PBO and ABO**   Felco company sponsors a pension plan with the following pension benefit formula:

Benefit paid at end of each year of retirement

= (number of years worked)(Annual salary at retirement)/25

Credit for service began January 1, 1988, Bob Johnson's first day with the company. Bob is expected to work a total of 30 years with an annual salary at retirement of $100,000. He is expected to draw 10 years of retirement benefits. The discount rate is 10 percent.

Required
1. Compute PBO on January 1, 1998, if Bob's current salary is $30,000.
2. Compute ABO on January 1, 1998.

P 18–2
(L.O. 4)   **Prior Service Cost Amortization**   On January 1, 1998, Oracle Company amended its pension plan by granting retroactive pension benefits for work performed before that date. The present value of those benefits was

determined to be $100,000 at that date. The following employees expect to receive benefits under the plan, and they have the indicated expected number of years remaining in their careers at January 1, 1998:

Bob: three years.

Barbara: five years.

Required   Determine the amortization of prior service cost to be recognized in 2002 under:

1. The method that associates an equivalent amount of prior service cost to each service year.
2. The straight-line method based on the average remaining service period of employees.

P 18–3   **Pension Expense**   The following data relate to a pension plan:
(L.O. 2, 4)

PBO, 1/1/98	$30,000
Initial total PSC awarded 1/1/96	10,000
(relates to an employee group with an average remaining	
service period of 10 years, use SL method)	
Initial total transition liability	8,000
(transition occurred 1/1/89, use SL method, 15 years)	
Discount rate	8%
Unrecognized gain (use SL method), 1/1/98	5,000
Service cost	7,000
Contributions	9,000
Expected return	2,000
Actual return	3,000
Average remaining service period	15 years

Required   Provide the entry to record pension expense for 1998.

P 18–4   **Unrecognized Gains and Losses**   Information for a pension plan follows:
(L.O. 4)

Unrecognized gain, 1/1/98	$ 8,000
Years used to amortize unrecognized gain or loss	10
Fair value of plan assets, 1/1/98	200,000
Expected rate of return on plan assets	12%
Fair value of plan assets, 12/31/98	220,000
1998 funding	40,000
Benefits paid in 1998	32,000
Actuarial loss computed in 12/31/98	8,000

The SL method is used for all amortizations. The firm does not use the minimum amortization for unrecognized gains and losses.

Required   Compute the net unrecognized gain or loss at January 1, 1999.

P 18–5   **Pension Expense**   The following information pertains to a pension plan for a company that always recognizes
(L.O. 2, 4)   only the minimum amortization of unrecognized gains and losses:

Unrecognized gain or loss, 1/1/97	$ 0
PBO, 1/1/97, not considering items below	60,000
Discount rate	10%
Fair value of plan assets, 1/1/97	24,000
Initial PSC value, from a grant on 1/1/89	40,000
Unrecognized PSC, 1/1/97	8,000
Average remaining service life of employees covered under initial PSC grant	10 years
Actuarial loss, 1/1/97	$12,000
Expected rate of return on fund assets	12%
Average remaining service life used to amortize unrecognized gain or loss	12 years
Service cost, 1997	$12,000
Service cost, 1998	14,000
Funding amount, end of 1997	16,000
Funding amount, end of 1998	20,000
Actual return on fund in 1997	1,800
Actual return on fund in 1998	2,400

    PART III LIABILITIES

No benefits were paid in either year.

Required   Compute pension expense for 1997 and 1998.

P 18–6
(L.O. 2, 5)

Multiple Choice: Accounting for Pensions   Choose the correct statement for each question.

1. The following information pertains to Lara Corporation's defined benefit pension plan for 1998:

Service cost	$160,000
Actual and expected gain on plan assets	35,000
Unexpected increase in PBO incurred during 1998	40,000
Amortization of unrecognized prior service cost	5,000
Annual interest on pension obligation	50,000

What amount should Lara report as pension expense in its 1998 income statement?
   a. $250,000.
   b. $220,000.
   c. $210,000.
   d. $180,000.

2. Nion Company sponsors a defined benefit plan covering all employees. Benefits are based on years of service and compensation levels at the time of retirement. Nion determined that, as of September 30, 1998, its accumulated benefit obligation was $380,000 and its plan assets had a $290,000 fair value. Nion's September 30, 1998, trial balance showed prepaid pension cost of $20,000. As of September 30, 1998, what is the balance of additional minimum pension liability?
   a. $110,000.
   b. $360,000.
   c. $ 90,000.
   d. $400,000.

3. Nebb Company implemented a defined benefit pension plan for its employees. During 1996 and 1997, Nebb's contributions fully funded the plan. The following data are provided for 1999 and 1998:

	1999 Estimated	1998 Actual
Projected benefit obligation, December 31	$187,500	$175,000
Accumulated benefit obligation, December 31	130,000	125,000
Plan assets at fair value, December 31	168,750	150,000
Pension expense	22,500	18,750
Employer's contribution	?	12,500

What amount should Nebb contribute in order to report an accrued pension liability of $3,750 in its December 31, 1999, balance sheet?
   a. $12,500.
   b. $15,000.
   c. $18,750.
   d. $25,000.

4. On June 1, 1996, Ware Corporation established a defined benefit pension plan for its employees. The following information was available on May 31, 1998:

Projected benefit obligation	$3,625,000
Accumulated benefit obligation	3,000,000
Unfunded accrued pension cost	50,000
Plan assets at fair market value	1,750,000
Unrecognized prior service cost	637,500

To report the proper pension liability in Ware's May 31, 1998, balance sheet, what is the required balance in additional minimum pension liability?
   a. $562,500.
   b. $1,187,500.
   c. $1,200,000.
   d. $1,825,000.

(AICPA adapted)

P 18–7
(L.O. 3, 4)

Three-Year Pension Accounting Case, Components 1–5   This problem is amenable to a group or individual solution. Refer to the preface for additional details on using group items.

This problem involves three years of accounting for the defined benefit pension plan of Americo's Inc., a calendar-year firm. The problem is a good vehicle for reviewing the first five components of pension expense and associated changes in both the formal and informal pension records over several years. The pension plan for the firm has been in existence for several years before January 1, 1998, the first year of the case. Small dollar amounts are used for convenience.

Pension plan data from actuaries and fund trustee

Discount rate and expected long-term rate of return	10%
PBO, January 1, 1998, amount does not include	
prior service cost noted below	$1,965.00
Plan assets at fair value, January 1, 1998	2,094.50
Prepaid pension cost balance, January 1, 1998	129.50
Average remaining service period (assume constant each year) . . .	10 years

	1998	1999	2000
Service cost	$ 800.00	$1,400.00	$1,700.00
Funding (end of year)	1,100.00	1,600.00	1,700.00
Actual return	209.45	300.00	600.00

On January 1, 1998, the firm retroactively granted three employees an increase in benefits based on work performed before that date. The immediate present value of those benefits is $1,200. The three employees have estimated remaining service periods at the grant date as follows: Nick (5 years remaining), Jo (4), and Pat (3). The firm elects to amortize this grant using the service method.

On January 1, 1998, the actuaries inform the firm that, on the basis of new estimates, turnover is expected to be higher than previously anticipated. The immediate effect on the actuarial present value of benefits based on the budget formula is $1,500. The firm elects minimum amortization of the net unrecognized gain or loss.

On January 1, 2000, the actuaries inform the firm that, on the basis of new estimates, average life expectancy of retirees and current employees is expected to be higher than previously anticipated. The immediate effect on the actuarial present value of benefits based on the budget formula is $1,400.

Required

Record pension expense and prepare the reconciliation of funded status for the three years 1998–2000. Show all computations and round to the nearest penny.

P 18–8
(L.O. 2, 3, 4)

Pension Spreadsheet: Overfunded and Prepaid Pension Cost; Entry   Waters Company has a defined benefit pension plan. At the end of the current reporting period, December 31, 1998, the following information was available:

a. Projected benefit obligation (actuary's report):

Balance, January 1, 1998	$150,000
Service cost	40,000
Interest cost ($150,000 × 10% actuary's rate)	15,000
Loss (gain) change in actuarial assumptions*	(400)
Pension benefits paid	(42,000)
Balance, December 31, 1998	$162,600
Accumulated benefit obligation	$120,000
Vested benefit obligation	40,000
Average remaining service period, 10 years.†	

*At December 31, 1998.

†Assume this is appropriate for all amortizations

b. Status of fund assets (trustee's report):

Balance, January 1, 1998	$160,000
Actual return on plan assets (same as expected)	16,000
Cash received from employer company	30,000
Pension benefits paid to retirees	(42,000)
Balance, December 31, 1998	$164,000

c. From company records—unrecognized pension costs:

Transition cost	$ 10,000
Prior service cost	20,000
Losses (gains)	(2,000)
Total	$ 28,000
Accrued (prepaid) pension cost	$ (38,000)

Required

1. Set up and complete a spreadsheet or other format of your choice to develop the pension data required at the end of 1998.
2. Give the employer's pension entry at December 31, 1998.

P 18–9
(L.O. 2, 3, 4)

Prepare a Spreadsheet and Respond to a Query about the Use of Cash   Stoney Company first applied the provisions of *SFAS No. 87* to its noncontributory, defined benefit pension plan on January 1, 1998. The annual accounting period ends on December 31. Data about the pension plan for 1999 follow.

a.   Projected benefit obligation (actuary's report):

Balance, January 1, 1999	$16,000
Service cost	1,920
Interest cost ($16,000 × 8% actuary's rate)	1,280
Loss (gain) change in actuarial assumptions*	660
Pension benefit paid to retirees	(1,600)
Balance, December 31, 1999	$18,260

*At December 31, 1999.

Accumulated benefit obligation	$16,000
Vested benefit obligation	6,000
Actuary's estimated discount rate	8%
Average remaining service period (assumed apprpriate for all amortizations)	11 years

b.   Status of fund assets (trustee's report):

Balance, January 1, 1999	$12,600
Actual return on plan assets	1,000
Cash received from employer company	3,000
Pension benefits paid to retirees	(1,600)
Balance, December 31, 1999	$15,000
Expected return on plan assets	$ 1,000

c.   Company data of July 1, 1999

Unrecognized transition cost	$ 660
Unrecognized prior service cost	1,980
Unrecognized losses (gains)	(440)
Total unrecognized	$ 2,200
(Accrued) prepaid pension cost	$(1,200)

Required

1. Prepare a pension spreadsheet or other format of your choice and give Stoney's 1999 journal entry for the pension plan.
2. The company president asked the following question: We paid $3,000 cash to the pension fund, but the pension liability was reduced by only $600. Why? Prepare a written response with data and explanation.

P 18–10
(L.O. 2, 3, 4)

Comparative Cases: Prepare Two Spreadsheets and Employer's Entry   Art Company first applied the provisions of *SFAS No. 87* to its noncontributory, defined pension plan in 1998. The annual accounting period ends December 31. Data about the pension plan for 1999 follow for two comparative cases to emphasize how losses versus gains affect the results.

	Case A	Case B

a.   Actuary's PBO report at December 31, 1999:

Projected benefit obligation (actuary's report):

	Case A	Case B
Balance, January 1, 1999	$500	$500
Service cost	100	100
Interest cost ($500 × 10% actuary's rate)	50	50
Loss (gain) change in actuarial assumptions*	8	(8)
Pension benefit paid to retirees	(10)	(15)
Balance, December 31, 1999	$648	$627

*At December 31, 1999; amortizations start in 2000.

	Case A	Case B
Accumulated benefit obligation	$500	$484
Vested benefit obligation	200	184
Actuary's estimated interest rate	10%	10%
Average remaining service period†	8 years	8 years

   b. Status of fund assets (trustee's report):

Balance, January 1, 1999	$450	$450
Actual return on plan assets	20	20
Cash received from employer company	150	120
Pension benefits paid to retirees	(10)	(15)
Balance, December 31, 1999	$610	$575
Expected return on plan assets	$ 24	$ 25

       †Assume that a period of eight years is appropriate for all amortizations

   c. Company data of January 1, 1999

Unrecognized transition cost	$ 8	$ 8
Unrecognized prior service cost	16	16
Unrecognized losses (gains)‡	24	(24)
Total recognized	$ 48	$–0–
(Accrued) prepaid pension cost	$ (2)	$ (50)

       ‡Due only to changes in actuarial assumptions.

Required Prepare a spreadsheet or other format of your choice and give the employer's journal entry for the pension plan for Case A and Case B. When preparing these two spreadsheets or formats, focus on the effects of losses versus the effects of gains.

P 18–11
(L.O. 2, 3, 4, 5)

Spreadsheet: Additional Minimum Pension Liability; Entries Frazier Company has a noncontributory, defined benefit pension plan. The company must record its pension expense for the year ended December 31, 1998. The following data are available (in $000s):

   a. Actuary's report: PBO

Balance, January 1, 1998	$600
Service cost	60
Interest cost (at 8%)	48
Loss (gain) in actuarial changes*	20
Pension benefit paid to retirees	(200)
Balance, December 31, 1998	$528
Accumulated benefit obligation, end of 1998	$494

       *At December 31, 1998.

   b. Fund trustee's report:

Balance, January 1, 1998 (at fair value)†	$400
Actual return on plan assets	36
Payments received from Frazier	120
Pension benefits paid	(200)
Balance, December 31, 1998	$356
Expected return on plan assets, 10%	

       †Same as market-related value

   c. Data from company records:

Unrecognized transition cost (January 1, 1998)	$ 54
Unrecognized prior service cost (January 1, 1998)	72
Unrecognized loss (January 1, 1998)	8
Total unrecognized	$134

   Amortization periods, for problem purposes only:
     Transition cost 9 years; prior service cost, 10 years; and
     losses (gains), 4 years.
   (Accrued) prepaid pension cost January 1, 1998, $(66).

Required 1. Prepare a pension spreadsheet or other format of your choice and give the 1998 entry for Frazier Company.
2. Compute any additional minimum pension liability to be recorded for 1998 and give the related entry.
3. Give the related entry for 1999 assuming that the ending balance of additional minimum pension liability for 1999 is $20.

P 18–12
(L.O. 2, 3, 4, 5)

Spreadsheet: Additional Minimum Pension Liability; Entries Jacks Company has a noncontributory, defined benefit pension plan. The company will record its pension expense for the year ended December 31, 1998. The following data are available (in 000s):

a.   Actuary's report: PBO

Balance, January 1, 1998	$300
Service cost	50
Interest cost (at 8%)	24
Loss (gain) actuarial changes (December 31, 1998)	(10)
Pension benefit paid to retirees	(124)
Balance, December 31, 1998	$240
Accumulated benefit obligation, end of 1998	$237

b.   Fund trustee's report:

Balance, January 1, 1998 (at fair value)*	$170
Actual return on plan assets	27
Payments received from Jacks	110
Pension benefits paid	(124)
Balance, December 31, 1998	$183

Expected return on plan assets, 12%

*Same as market-related value

c.   Data from company records:

Unrecognized transition cost (January 1, 1998)	$ 60
Unrecognized prior service cost (January 1, 1998)	40
Unrecognized loss (gain) (January 1, 1998)	–0–
Total unrecognized	$100

Average remaining service period is 10 years (for problem purposes use this for amortizing each of the three unrecognized pension costs).
(Accrued) prepaid pension cost, January 1, 1998, $30 accrued.

Required

1. Prepare a pension spreadsheet or other format of your choice and give the 1998 entry for Jacks Company.
2. Compute any additional minimum pension liability for 1998 and give the related entry.
3. Give the related entry for the next period, 1999, assuming that the additional minimum liability required for 1999 is $40 and that the amortization of PSC and transition cost is the same as in 1998.

P 18–13
(L.O. 2, 3, 4, 5)

Prepare Pension Spreadsheet and Additional Minimum Pension Liability for Two Consecutive Years Andros Company has a noncontributory, defined benefit pension plan. This problem focuses on the accounting required at December 31, 1998 and 1999, with emphasis on the PBO, plan assets, unrecognized pension costs, net periodic pension expense, accrued/prepaid pension cost, and the additional minimum pension liability. The data for the two years are as follows (in $000s):

	1998	1999
a. Actuary's (PBO):		
Projected benefit obligation beginning	$1,700	$2,196
Service cost	180	210
Interest cost	136	198
Prior service cost	240	
Loss (gain), actuarial changes, December 31	20	5
Loss (gain), plan assets		
Pension benefits paid	(80)	(125)
Projected benefit obligation, ending	$2,196	$2,484
Accumulated benefit obligation	$1,775	$2,109
Average remaining service period*	10 years	9 years
Actuary's interest rate	8%	9%

*For problem purposes, assume that minimun amortization of unrecognized loss/gain does not apply; therefore, use these periods for all amortization.

	1998	1999
b. Trustee's report (plan assets at fair value):†		
Balance at beginning	$1,000	$1,210
Actual return on plan assets	90	110
Contribution from employer	200	440
Pension benefits paid to retirees	(80)	(125)
Balance at ending	$1,210	$1,635
Expected return on plan assets	10%	10%

†Same as market-related value.

c. Company records:

Unrecognized cost at beginning:

Prior service cost	$ –0–	$ 216
Transition cost	300	270
Loss (gain)	150	165
Total	$ 450	$ 651

Required

1. Prepare a pension spreadsheet or format of your choice and give the related pension entry for Andros Company for (*a*) 1998 and (*b*) 1999.
2. Compute the additional minimum pension liability for 1998 and 1999 and give any related entry for (*a*) 1998 and (*b*) 1999. Also, give the 1999 ending balances in the three related accounts.

P 18–14
(L.O. 5)

Additional Minimum Pension Liability   The following information (amounts in $000s) applies to 1998 through 2000 for a pension plan. The sponsor has no balance in either the additional minimum pension liability or intangible pension asset at January 1, 1998.

	1998	**1999**	**2000**
ABO at end of year	$80	$90	$120
Plan assets at fair value at end of year . . .	60	62	96

The next two values are stated at the end of each year, after the pension expense entry but before the entry to adjust additional minimum pension liability.

Balance in accrued pension cost (cr.)	8	14	18
Unrecognized PSC	8	6	4

Required

Provide the entry adjusting additional minimum pension liability for each year. Assume that the maximum intangible balance is the lower of unrecognized PSC and balance in additional minimum pension liability.

P 18–15

Appendix: Postretirement Benefit Expense and Funded Status   The following information pertains to a firm with a postretirement benefit health care plan:

Transition date: January 1, 1993
Accumulated postretirement benefit liability at transition: $100,000
The firm has no plan assets or balance sheet account relating to the plan at transition
Discount rate: 12 percent
Amortization period for unrecognized transition liability: average remaining service period of active plan participants, 15 years
Service cost, 1993: $25,000
Contribution to benefit fund, December 31, 1993: $35,000
Benefit payments, December 31, 1993: $10,000

Required

Provide the entry to record 1993 postretirement benefit expense, and the reconciliation of funded status and (accrued) prepaid postretirement benefit cost at December 31, 1993.

P 18–16

Appendix: Postretirement Benefit Expense and Funded Status   The December 31, 1997, reconciliation of funded status and accrued postretirement benefit cost for a firm with a postretirement benefit plan is as follows:

APBO	$(224,000)
Plan assets at fair value	63,000
Underfunded APBO (funded status)	(161,000)
Unrecognized transition liability	61,000
Accrued postretirement benefit cost	$(100,000)

At the beginning of 1998, the plan was amended to increase future health-care benefits for retirees. The increase is attributable to service performed before 1998. As a result, APBO increased $56,000. The discount rate is 12 percent, and the expected long-term rate of return on plan assets is 10 percent. There are 10 years remaining in the amortization period for the unrecognized transition liability. The average remaining years of service to full eligibility for active plan participants is 15 years.

Additional information for 1998:

Service cost	$50,000
Actual return on plan assets	6,000
Contributions (end-of-year)	75,000
Benefit payments (end-of-year)	85,000

Required   Provide the entry to record 1998 postretirement benefit expense and the reconciliation of funded status and (accrued) prepaid postretirement benefit cost at December 31, 1998.

P 18–17   **Appendix: Postretirement Benefit Expense and Funded Status**   The December 31, 1999, reconciliation of funded status and accrued postretirement benefit cost, and additional information, for a firm with a postretirement benefit plan is as follows:

APBO	$(450,000)
Plan assets at fair value	125,000
Underfunded APBO (funded status)	(325,000)
Unrecognized prior service cost	48,000
Unrecognized net loss	62,000
Unrecognized transition liability	180,000
Accrued postretirement benefit cost	$ (35,000)

Additional information:

Expected return on plan assets: 10 percent
Discount rate: 8 percent
Remaining years to amortize prior service cost: 8
Average remaining service period: 10
Remaining years to amortize unrecognized transition liability: 18
The firm recognizes the minimum amortization of gains and losses.
Service cost, 2000: $80,000
Actual return on plan assets, 2000: $30,000
APBO increased $100,000 on December 31, 2000, due to an increase in health-care cost trend rates.
Contributions to fund, December 31, 2000: $100,000
Benefit payments, December 31, 2000: $80,000

Required   Provide the entry to record 2000 postretirement benefit expense and the reconciliation of funded status and accrued (prepaid) postretirement benefit cost at December 31, 2000.

P 18–18
(L.O. 2, 3, 4, 5)   **Comprehensive Problem: Prepare Pension Spreadsheet for Two Years with Corridor (minimum) Amortization Test; Entries**   Voss Company has a noncontributory, defined benefit pension plan for its employees. The data available at year-end, December 31, 1998 and 1999, are as follows ($000s):

	1998	1999
a. Actuary's report (PBO):		
Projected benefit obligation, beginning	$1,520	$1,752
Service cost	200	238
Interest cost	152	140
Prior service cost	20	13
Loss (gain), actuarial changes, December 31	10	6
Pension benefits paid	(150)	(170)
Projected benefit obligation, ending	$1,752	$1,979
Accumulated benefit obligation	$ 920	$1,000
Average remaining service period*	10 years	9 years

     *For problem purposes, use this for all unrecognized pension costs.

	1998	1999
b. Trustee's report (plan assets at fair value):		
Balance at beginning	$ 940	$1,084
Actual return on plan assets	84	92
Contributions from employer	210	320
Pension benefits paid to retirees	(150)	(170)
Balance at ending	$1,084	$1,326
Expected return on plan assets	10%	10%

c. Voss Company records:

Unrecognized costs at beginning:

Prior service cost	$ 100	$ 110
Transition cost	40	36
Loss (gain)	182	184
Total	$ 322	$ 330

Required

1. Prepare a spreadsheet or other format of your choice and give the related pension entry for Voss Company for (*a*) 1998 and (*b*) 1999. Use the straight-line method to amortize unrecognized gains and losses in your format. Also compute the minimum amortization.
2. Explain why additional minimum pension liability does not apply in this situation.
3. Provide the following footnote disclosures required by *SFAS No. 87* for both years: (*a*) the amount of pension expense for each period with separate disclosure of service cost, interest cost, actual return on plan assets, and net total of other components; and (*b*) the reconciliation of funded status.

ANALYSIS, JUDGMENT, AND COMMUNICATION

CASES

C 18–1
(L.O. 2, 4, 5)

Components of Pension Expense and Minimum Liability   At December 31, 1998, as a result of its single-employer defined benefit pension plan, Big Company had an unrecognized net loss and an unfunded accrued pension cost. Big's pension plan and its actuarial assumptions have not changed since it began operations in 1991. Big has made annual contributions to the plan. Write a short report addressing the following questions:

Required

1. Identify the components of net pension cost that should be recognized in Big's 1998 financial statements.
2. What circumstances caused Big's (*a*) unrecognized net loss and (*b*) unfunded accrued pension cost?
3. How should Big compute its minimum pension liability and any additional pension liability?

(AICPA adapted)

C 18–2
(L.O. 1–5)

Is *SFAS No. 87* Workable?   *SFAS No. 87*, "Employers' Accounting for Pensions," was one of the most controversial standards issued by the FASB, as illustrated by the following excerpts from an article in *The Wall Street Journal* about the *Standard* shortly before its release ("Accounting Proposal Troubles Firms," *The Wall Street Journal*, December 6, 1985, p. 6):

> Corporate financial executives are fuming about a controversial pension-accounting rule that the Financial Accounting Standards Board is expected to issue soon.
>
> They say the proposed rule is vexing on two counts: It would burden corporate balance sheets by placing a hefty new liability on the books, and it would make bottom-line financial results more volatile.
>
> The FASB sets the four-year phase-in period to cushion the rule's effects. But some financial executives in depressed smoke-stack industries argue that boosting liabilities simply by a bookkeeping change is like kicking them when they're down.

This debate continues unabated. For example, an interesting article in the *Financial Executive Magazine* (September–October 1987) contained an interesting dialogue in "Is FASB 87 Workable?" The dialogue was summarized as follows:

No!

1. The rule-making body of the accounting profession has issued the *Statement* despite objections by the overwhelming majority of their own profession, clients, and related professions. This is either admirable or foolish. Only time will tell.
2. The *Statement* is much too complex. Simpler solutions exist.
3. It does not accomplish its objectives of presenting a more meaningful measure of pension expense and introducing balance sheet items helpful to readers of financial statements.
4. The FASB based its decisions on conceptualizations, rather than on user needs.

The authors of the article continue with comments to support these statements.

Yes!

The four myths concerning the *Statement* are as follows:

1. *SFAS No. 87* represents bad accounting.
2. The new standards eliminate management's ability to tailor financial reporting to individual facts and circumstances.

3. The accounting and disclosure requirements do not provide the information that users need.

4. As a result of all of the above, corporate financial managers are badly served.

The authors of the article continue with comments to deflate these myths.

Required

1. In a brief report, discuss the requirements of *SFAS No. 87* that might cause concern to companies affected by it. Give reasons why companies might be upset.
2. Be prepared to discuss this controversy, including your opinion. Also, focus on delayed recognition and its implications.

C 18–3
(L.O. 4)

You Make the Call   Delayed Recognition in Pension Accounting   The FASB made significant changes to pension accounting when it mandated *SFAS No. 87*. However, do you think it went far enough? The *Statement* has been criticized by those who maintain that it provides a wealth of opportunity for sponsors to manipulate and smooth earnings. Would you have closed these loopholes?

Required

Briefly discuss the provisions of *SFAS No. 87* that contribute to opportunities for income smoothing or manipulation. For each point, give your opinion as to whether the provision is appropriate in terms of optimal measurement and reporting (as opposed to the economic consequences of such reporting).

C 18–4
(L.O. 1, 2)

You Make the Call   Pension Expense Based on Funding   The cost approach to pension expense, an alternative conceptualization of pension expense that had been proposed at various times before *SFAS No. 87,* would have based annual pension expense on the required annual contribution needed to fully fund the estimated total pension benefit at retirement. It is called the cost approach because pension expense for a period is considered to be the contribution (annuity amount) required in that year to fund the plan. This approach is not allowed under GAAP.

Required

1. Using the Nicole Whitney example developed in the text, determine 1998 pension expense using the cost approach.
2. Determine the amount necessary to fund only the pension benefits she earned in her last year of service using the same approach.
3. Based on your findings above and your knowledge of GAAP as it pertains to pensions, give your opinion as to whether the cost approach would be a better approach to measuring pension expense.

C 18–5
(L.O. 1, 2)

Appendix: Differences between Accounting for Pensions and Nonpension Postretirement Benefits   Accounting for pensions is similar to accounting for nonpension postretirement benefits in many ways. However, there are some significant differences. In an E-mail message to a fellow student, list and discuss some of these differences and their financial statement effects.

C 18–6
(L.O. 2, 3, 4, 5)

Ethical Considerations and Opportunities for Managing Pension Expense and Liabilities   You are the senior auditor for the audit of a client firm in considerable financial difficulty. In particular, debt covenants may be violated if liabilities are increased. In addition, the client's balance in retained earnings is minimal as a result of excessively high dividends and diminished earnings in the past several years.

The client firm is dominated by its CEO, a person who has worked his way up the ladder and has served the firm for 30 years. The CEO makes most of the major decisions in the firm. This person is the firm's primary representative working with the audit staff. At present there is no organized audit committee. The CEO is very aggressive with respect to earnings.

From the minutes, you have discovered that extreme emphasis has been placed on meeting earnings projections. Department officers have been fired for not meeting earnings goals for two successive years. The firm uses FIFO, straight-line depreciation, and other accounting techniques that reduce or delay expense recognition. The firm has resisted using the installment sales method for customers with questionable credit ratings.

You know that, through *Statement on Auditing Standards No. 53,* "The Auditor's Responsibility to Detect and Report Errors and Irregularities," part of your responsibility as an auditor is to develop an audit plan that is sensitive to audit risk. Audit risk is the probability that you may unknowingly fail to modify your audit report on financial statements that are materially misstated. Your audit plan should be designed to provide reasonable assurance that material errors and irregularities are detected.

Required

You understand that the pressures faced by this firm may create incentives for unethical and fraudulent financial reporting. In a report of not more than two pages, discuss the aspects of pension accounting that should be considered with special care. What pension-related variables might be changed, and in what direction, to achieve reduced pension expense and liabilities? Include in your discussion reasons why you chose these variables.

C 18–7
(L.O. 2)

Pension Expense; Assumed Rate of Salary Increase   Jenner, Inc., has a defined benefit pension plan for its 2,000 employees. It provides covered employees with a pension equal to 1.5 percent of their average salary during the two calendar years of highest pay times the number of years of service, with a maximum of 30 years. Benefits are based on an assumed retirement age of 65 and are reduced or increased to their actuarial equivalents for those employees who retire before or after age 65. The projected benefit obligation of Jenner's plan on December 31, 1995, was $180 million and the market value of assets in the fund was $207 million.

Early in 1996 Jennifer Jasko, CFO of Jenner, Inc., received a report from the actuaries of Jenner's pension plan that recommended an increase in the assumed rate of increase in future salaries among other things. An annual rate of 3 percent per year had been used for several years; according to the actuaries' experience during the last five years, a period of relatively low inflation, average salaries increased considerably more than that. Actuaries recommended a 6 percent rate that would increase Jenner's year-end projected benefit obligation by 40 percent. The actuaries also sent a copy of the report to Jason Jenner, CEO of Jenner, Inc.

Several days after receiving the report, Jenner and Jasko were having lunch when the subject of the report came up. Jenner began by saying that initially he feared a 40 percent increase in the pension obligation would wipe out 1995 profits, but after discussing the astronomical rise in the stock market in 1995 with his friend, John Jacob Jinglehimer Schmidt, he began to think that since Jenner, Inc.'s pension fund is heavily invested in equities, the effect of the increase in the salary increase rate might be offset to some extent by the large increase in return on plan assets in 1995. Schmidt had mentioned to him that the bull market of 1995 caused his company's plan to go from underfunded to overfunded. Jenner then asked Jasko what she thought a revision of the salary increase rate would do to 1995 profits, but before she had a chance to respond, they were interrupted and did not have a chance to get back to the subject.

Later that day Jasko received an E-mail from Jenner asking her to write him a memo explaining what the proposed revision in the salary increase rate would do to profits. Jasko will be out of town for several days so she has asked you, her assistant, to prepare a memo to Jenner for her signature. (Prepared by Dr. Loyd Heath, University of Washington.)

Required

Prepare a draft of the requested memo, using not more than two printed pages.

ANALYZING FINANCIAL STATEMENTS

All questions in this section are based on information taken from the financial statements of actual companies.

A 18–1
(L.O. 3, 4, 5)

Pension Disclosures   Refer to the 1995 financial statements of the Coca-Cola Company that appear at the end of this text, and respond to the following questions:

1. What are the main variables affecting the amount a Coke employee receives in annual pension benefits? Based only on information about Coke's pension benefit formula, would you expect PBO and ABO to differ?
2. As a whole, describe the funded status of Coke's defined benefit plans at December 31, 1995.
3. What type of pension plan (defined contribution or benefit) is the most prevalent at Coke?
4. For Coke's U.S. defined benefit plans, how would you characterize the magnitude of the difference between current salaries and those used to compute pension benefits?
5. For U.S. defined benefit plans, was amortization of unrecognized net gain or loss required in 1995?
6. What was the contribution of return on U.S. plan assets to the amount of ending 1995 unrecognized net gain or loss?
7. Explain (*a*) why the $81 million unrecognized net gain is subtracted from funded status for U.S. plans with assets exceeding benefits in 1995, and (*b*) the general composition of this amount.
8. Verify the $54 million adjustment to additional minimum pension liability for U.S. plans with benefits exceeding assets in 1995, and explain what this amount represents.

A 18–2
(L.O. 1, 4)

Funding and Pension Expense Components   The Dole Food Company is one of the largest international food processing and distribution companies. Portions of footnote 8 (pension benefits) to its 1995 annual report appear below.

The Company has qualified defined benefit pension plans covering most full-time employees. The status of the plans was as follows (amounts in $ thousands):

	1995	1994
Projected benefit obligation	$239,855	$223,082
Plan assets at fair value, primarily		
stocks and bonds	238,730	206,326
Projected benefit obligation in excess		
of plan assets	(1,125)	(16,756)
Unrecognized net transition obligation	(942)	(1,087)
Unrecognized prior service cost	2,662	1,714
Unrecognized net (gain) loss	(83)	17,866
Additional minimum liability	(1,941)	(10,917)
Accrued pension liability	$ (1,429)	$ (9,180)

The expected long-term rate of return on assets was 9 percent in both years.
Pension expense included the following components:

	1995	1994
Service cost-benefits earned during		
the year	$ 8,114	$ 7,158
Interest cost on projected benefit		
obligation	21,270	20,112
Actual (return) loss on plan assets	(46,944)	4,656
Net amortization and deferral	28,337	(22,980)
Pension expense	$10,777	$ 8,946

<table>
<tr><td>Required</td><td>

1. What was Dole's contribution to the pension fund in 1995?
2. What might have caused the change from an unrecognized net loss in 1994 to an unrecognized net gain in 1995?

</td></tr>
</table>

<table>
<tr><td>

A 18–3
(L.O. 5)

</td><td>

Additional Minimum Pension Liability   Westinghouse Electric Corporation, a large technology company, separates its reporting of pension plans according to those with benefits exceeding assets, and those with assets exceeding benefits. Information adapted from the firm's financial statements for those plans with benefits exceeding assets follows. These plans account for 89 percent of the total defined benefits earned as of 1995.

</td></tr>
</table>

	1995	1994
	(millions)	
Accumulated benefit obligation	$(5,272)	$(4,731)
Projected benefit obligation	(5,533)	(5,004)
Plan assets at fair value	3,407	3,557
Projected benefit obligation in excess		
of plan assets	(2,126)	(1,447)
Unrecognized net loss	2,120	1,736
Prior service benefit not yet recognized		
in net periodic pension cost	(95)	(136)
Unrecognized net transition obligation	161	250
Prepaid pension cost	60	403
Minimum pension liability	(1,925)	(1,577)
Pension asset (liability) included in		
consolidated balance sheet	$(1,865)	$(1,174)

<table>
<tr><td>Required</td><td>

1. Explain why an additional minimum pension liability is needed at the end of 1995.
2. What might cause the firm to report a prepaid pension cost account when both PBO and ABO are underfunded?
3. Assuming the firm maintains the maximum balance in its intangible pension asset account, reconstruct the entry adjusting the additional minimum pension liability at the end of 1995.

</td></tr>
</table>

<table>
<tr><td>

A 18–4
(L.O. 2)

</td><td>

Pension Expense   Refer to the 1995 financial statements of the Coca-Cola Company reproduced at the end of this text and answer the following questions regarding the firm's reconciliation of funded status for its defined benefit pension plans.

</td></tr>
</table>

<table>
<tr><td>Required</td><td>

1. Compute 1995 pension expense for all of Coke's defined benefit plans using expected return for component 3 of pension expense rather than actual return as is shown by Coke. Show how you determined each

</td></tr>
</table>

of the six components, aggregating as needed across U.S. and international plans. The amortization of net unrecognized gain or loss (component 5) cannot be directly computed. Treat this component as a derived or plug figure. Comment on the magnitude of this derived amount.

2. From your results in question 1, estimate the net actuarial gain or loss experienced by the firm in 1995.

A 18–5

Appendix: Postretirement Benefits Other than Pensions   Refer to the 1995 financial statements of the Coca-Cola Company at the end of this text and respond to the following questions. Coke had a large OPEB transition liability when it adopted *SFAS No. 106,* in 1992. Answer the following questions:

1. From the 1995 statements, can you determine how Coke recognized its transition liability? Did this choice affect cash flows?
2. Although this amount is not shown in the current statements, why did Coke add the transition amount to net income in its 1992 statement of cash flows?
3. What type of account does the transition effect of change in accounting for postretirement benefits other than pensions represent?
4. Why was the *other* component of postretirement benefit expense so small in relation to total expense in 1995? Explain in terms of the components of postretirement benefit expense.
5. Why is interest cost so large relative to the other components of postretirement benefit expense in 1995?

A 18–6

 **Appendix: Postretirement Benefits Other than Pensions—The Dole Food Company**   Portions of footnote 5 (postretirement benefits) to the 1992 annual report of the Dole Food Company appear below.

In 1992, the Company implemented *Statement of Financial Accounting Standards No. 106,* "Employer's Accounting for Postretirement Benefits Other than Pensions." This statement, among other changes, requires companies to accrue for postretirement benefits during the employee's active service period. The Company elected to immediately recognize the accumulated postretirement benefit obligation as of December 29, 1991 of $82.5 million ($49.5 million, net of tax).

The status of the plans at January 2, 1993 was as follows (in $ thousands):

Accumulated postretirement benefit obligation	$85,885
Unrecognized net loss	(299)
Accrued postretirement benefit cost	$85,586

Net periodic postretirement benefit cost for 1992:

Service cost—benefits earned during the year	$ 926
Interest cost on APBO	7,622
Postretirement benefit cost	$ 8,548

In prior years, the cost of postretirement benefits was recognized as payments were made. These costs totaled $4.9 million and $4.3 million during 1991 and 1990, respectively.

This is a portion of Dole's comparative income statement:

	1992	1991	1990
Income before cumulative effect of change in accounting principle.	$65,213	$133,726	$120,455
Cumulative effect of change in accounting principle	(49,492)		
Net income	$15,721	$133,726	$120,455

Required

1. Why might Dole Food Company have decided to recognize the postretirement benefit transition amount immediately?
2. What was the approximate effect of implementing *SFAS No. 106* on 1992 earnings before taxes?
3. What was the amount funded for the postretirement benefit plan in 1992?

A 18–7
(L.O. 3, 4, 5)

Using the World Wide Web: Pension Accounting   This problem requires access to the World Wide Web portion of the Internet. The data required for this problem are in the most recent 10-K annual report of PepsiCo, Inc. To obtain that information, use the Securities and Exchange Commission's Electronic Data Gathering, Analysis and Retrieval System (EDGAR) to retrieve PepsiCo's report.

Steps to access EDGAR on the World Wide Web:

a. URL: http://www.sec.gov/index.html (the SEC's home page)
b. Click on EDGAR Database of Corporate Information
c. Click on Search the EDGAR Database
d. Click on Search the EDGAR Archives
e. Enter the company name in the search dialog box
f. Click on the listing for the most recent 10-K annual report
g. Use Edit, Find in the toolbar to locate the pension footnote.

Required   Answer the following questions related to PepsiCo's defined benefit pension plans for the most recent year available or for the period specified by your instructor:

1. Describe PepsiCo's plans: are they contributory, do they cover only U.S. employees, what is the firms funding policy, what is the primary composition of the pension fund, and what percentage of the fund for U.S. plans consists of PepsiCo stock?
2. Which plans appear to cover more employees, the U.S. plans or the international plans?
3. Did the firm have an asset gain or loss for the year for its U.S. plans?
4. Was PepsiCo's pension expense for U.S. plans increased or decreased by delayed recognition of pension-related costs?
5. Are PepsiCo's U.S. plans over- or underfunded in total?
6. Is an additional minimum pension liability required or reported for U.S. plans?
7. For U.S. plans, what is the net pension asset or liability reported in the balance sheet?
8. What proportion of U.S. funded status is reported in the balance sheet?
9. What proportion of U.S. plan benefits was vested?
10. Describe the relative economic burden of the pension plans in total to PepsiCo's financial situation and performance for the current year.

COMPARATIVE ANALYSIS

(L.O. 2, 3, 4)   **Pension Accounting and Ratio Analysis**   This item is amenable to a group or individual solution. Refer to the preface for additional details on using group items. This problem provides a vehicle for reviewing important aspects of pension plan accounting and disclosure, within the context of two firms in the same industry. The following excerpts are from the pension plan footnotes to the 1995 annual statements of Anheuser Busch Companies and Adolph Coors Company. Both companies are large U.S. brewers, although Anheuser Busch is a substantially larger enterprise.

ANHEUSER-BUSCH COMPANIES, INC.

1995 Information	*(millions)*
Service cost	$ 41.0
Interest cost on projected benefit obligation	64.4
Assumed return on assets)	(80.6)
Amortization of prior service cost, actuarial gains/losses and the excess of market value of plan assets over projected benefit obligation at January 1, 1986	4.8
Net pension expense	$ 29.6
Actual return on plan assets	$(140.9)
Accumulated benefit obligation	$(786.2)
Projected benefit obligation	$(924.8)
Plan assets at fair market value—primarily corporate equity securities and publicly traded bonds	935.8
Plan assets in excess of projected benefit obligation	11.0
Unamortized excess of market value of plan assets over projected benefit obligation at January 1, 1986	(33.6)
Unrecognized net actuarial (losses)	21.9
Prior service costs	81.4
Prepaid pension cost	$ 80.7

1994 Information

Plan assets at fair value, end of 1994 . . . . $ 791.2

ADOLPH COORS COMPANY
1995 Information

Service cost	$ 9.9
Interest cost	29.3
Actual gain on plan assets	(69.3)
Net amortization and deferral	47.0
Net pension expense	$ 16.9
Accumulated benefits	$341.6
Projected benefit obligations.	$423.6
Plan assets available for benefit	330.8
Plan assets less than projected benefit obligation	92.8
Unrecognized net loss	(62.5)
Prior service cost not yet recognized	(20.9)
Unrecognized net asset being recognized over 15 years	7.5
Net accrued pension liability	$ 16.9

1994 Information

Plan assets at fair value, end of 1994 . . . . $262

OTHER 1995 FINANCIAL STATEMENT INFORMATION

	Anheuser-Busch	Adolph Coors
Total assets	$10,591	$1,386
Current liabilities.	1,242	323
Long-term liabilities	4,915	368
Total owners' equity	4,434	695
Income from continuing operations before tax	1,462	73
Net income	642	43

Required

1. Write a short report comparing the status of these two firms' pension plans. Include in your report a discussion of funding policy, cost and relative burden of the plan, and any differential earnings effects related to the plans.
2. For each firm, compute the following ratios:
   - Total liabilities to total equity (debt to equity).
   - Total liabilities to total assets (debt to assets).
   - Rate of return on assets.
   - Rate of return on owners' equity.

   For the rates of return, use ending assets and owners' equity for reasonable approximations to these ratios. Ignore interest expense in the return on assets calculation.
3. Analyze the effect of (*a*) nonrecognition of PBO, and (*b*) delayed recognition, on each firm's financial position, earnings, and any of the ratios above that would be affected. Compare the effects across the two firms. Ignore income tax effects for this section of the problem and evaluate the effects on the rates of return using pretax income.

19

ACCOUNTING FOR INCOME TAXES

LEARNING OBJECTIVES

After you have studied this chapter, you will:

1   Appreciate the problems in accounting for income taxes.

2   Understand the theory and application of the asset/liability method of accounting for income taxes.

3   Be familiar with the disclosure requirements as they relate to accounting for income taxes.

4   Be able to account for and provide the required disclosures for tax loss carrybacks and carryforwards.

INTRODUCTION

In 1995, Coca-Cola Company reported income before income taxes of $4,328 million. The statutory federal income tax rate for corporations is 35 percent. This suggests Coke's 1995 federal income tax should be .35 × $4,328, or $1,515 million. However, the income statement reports income tax expense of only $1,342 million, nearly $200 million less than what would appear to be the correct amount. It would seem that an interesting question is: *Why is Coca-Cola paying taxes at a rate less than 35 percent?*

Now look at Note 15 to the Coca-Cola financial statements at the end of the book. The second schedule in the note shows that Coca-Cola pays income taxes at the federal (United States) level, at the state and local level, and at the international level. It also shows that income tax expense is either current or deferred. Another interesting question: *Why are some taxes current and others deferred?*

These two questions often arise when studying the income tax expenses of almost any company. Accounting for income taxes is complicated because the rules for determining what is a taxable revenue and what is a tax deductible expense can and often do differ from what are defined as revenues and expenses by GAAP. In addition, different tax jurisdictions or authorities have different rules for determining taxable revenues and tax deductible expenses.[1] The major topic covered in this chapter is how to account for income taxes when income measured for tax reporting differs from the income measured for financial reporting.

---

[1]This chapter focuses on accounting for *income* taxes. There are a number of other types of taxes paid by firms, including real estate taxes, personal property taxes, sales taxes, and excise taxes. These non-income taxes are accounted for under the general principles of accrual accounting and are not subject to the principles discussed in this chapter.

CONCEPTUAL ISSUES

For-profit corporations are required to file income tax returns with the Internal Revenue Service (IRS), an agency of the federal government. When a firm has taxable income as measured by the rules found in the Internal Revenue Code and other IRS regulations and pronouncements, the firm must pay income taxes. If the firm operates in a state that levies an income tax on corporations, a similar procedure is followed to determine the amount of state income tax to be paid.

Why Income Taxes?

A primary purpose for taxing income is to raise funds for government activities, such as providing for national defense; building and maintaining a national infrastructure of roads, airports, dams, and so on; and making transfer payments established by elected government representatives. A secondary purpose—one that sometimes influences the measurement rules used for determining taxable income—is to shift the tax burden in ways that influence various types of economic activity.

Example   A number of years ago the government decided to encourage firms to invest more in plant and equipment, thereby increasing employment in the economy by putting people to work building plants and equipment. The government encouraged such behavior by changing the Internal Revenue Code to allow firms investing in plant and equipment to deduct the cost for tax purposes at a very rapid rate and over a shorter period than the expected useful life of the assets. This change allowed the firms to recover the investment rapidly by reducing the amount of income taxes paid early in the asset's life. For financial reporting purposes, however, GAAP required firms to depreciate the assets over their estimated useful life. This is an example of the measurement rules for determining taxable income being different from GAAP rules because of government's desire to influence economic behavior.

Defining Taxable Income and Pretax Accounting Income

Taxable income is the income determined by applying the measurement rules found in the tax laws. Taxable income is computed to determine the amount of income taxes a firm must pay. The left column of Exhibit 19–1 diagrams the process and some of the factors that can affect the computation of taxable income. As noted, the sources of guidance are the Internal Revenue Code and other IRS regulations. These rules often allow firms to choose different ways to compute taxable revenues and allowed expenses (generally called **deductions** on a tax return). Most firms choose among the alternatives allowed by tax laws to minimize the firm's long-term tax obligation. The amount of income taxes to be paid for a tax period is the product of taxable income and the applicable tax rate:

Taxable income $\times$ Applicable income tax rate $=$ Income taxes currently payable

Pretax accounting income is the amount of income before income taxes determined under GAAP. The right side of Exhibit 19–1 diagrams the process and some of the factors that can affect the computation of pretax accounting income. Computed for financial reporting purposes, pretax accounting income has no effect on the amount of income taxes actually paid. Because it is part of the information provided to financial statement users for decision making, and because alternative measurement rules can be chosen to measure pretax accounting income, we again might expect management to choose among reporting choices with certain objectives in mind, as suggested in Exhibit 19–1.

After pretax accounting income is determined, the amount of income tax expense must be computed and deducted to compute net income. A central conceptual issue is how to determine income tax expense. Before we address this issue, we consider in more detail why taxable income and pretax accounting income might be different.

Two Types of Differences

The two basic types of differences between taxable income and pretax accounting income are permanent differences and temporary differences.

EXHIBIT 19–1
Purposes and Influences in Tax Reporting and Financial Reporting

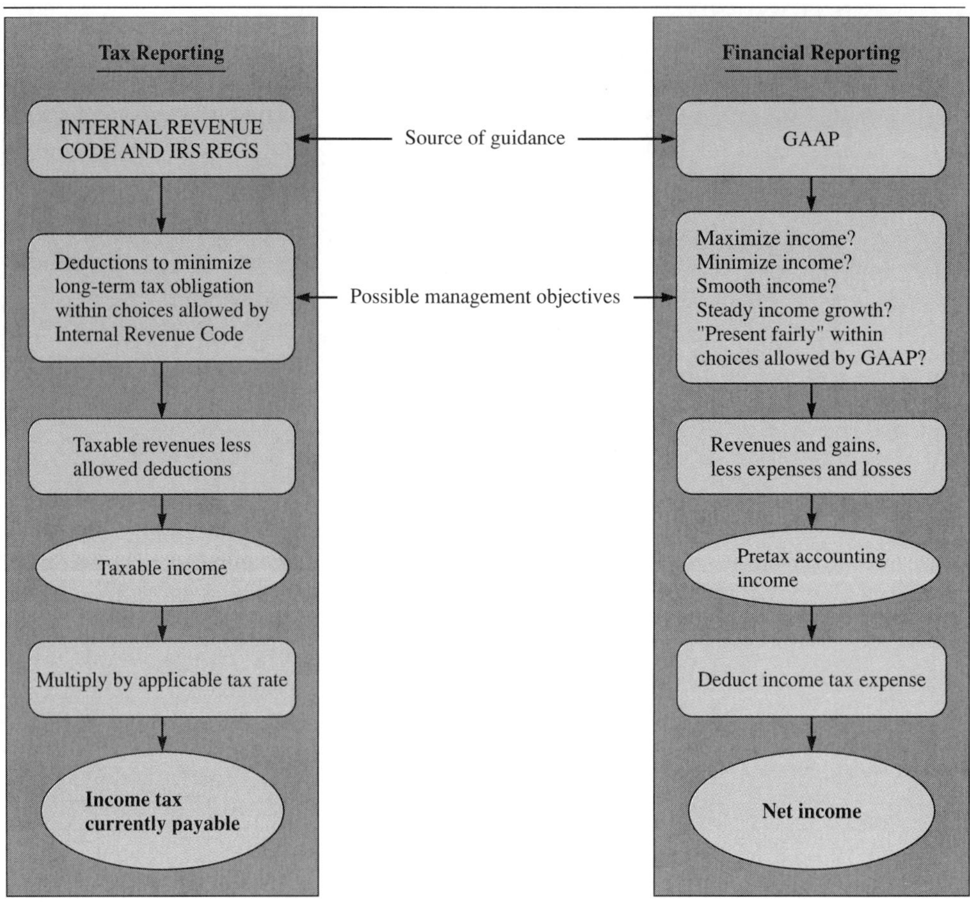

Permanent Differences   A permanent difference is created when an income element—a revenue, gain, expense, or loss—enters the computation of either taxable income or pretax accounting income, but never enters into the computation of the other.

Example   Watts Inc. invests in local or municipal bonds and receives $10,000 interest. The interest is revenue for financial reporting. However, interest received on investments in tax exempt municipal bonds is not taxable by the federal government. The interest appears as a revenue for financial reporting, but because it is tax exempt income, it is never reported as a revenue for federal tax purposes:

	1997	1998 and All Years Thereafter
Accounting records	Record the $10,000 as a revenue.	No effect of interest received in 1997.
Tax records	The $10,000 is not recorded as taxable income.	No effect since it is tax-free interest income.
Difference between pretax accounting income and taxable income	Pretax accounting income is $10,000 greater than taxable income.	Pretax accounting income is the same as taxable income.

This is a **permanent difference** item. The tax-free interest income increases Watts' pretax accounting income in 1997, but is never recorded as taxable income. The first four items in Exhibit 19–2 are examples of permanent differences.

Accounting for Permanent Differences   For financial reporting, the effect a permanent difference has on taxes currently payable, as determined on the tax return, also is included

EXHIBIT 19–2

Items that Result in Differences between Taxable Income and Pretax Accounting Income

Items that Cause Permanent Differences

1. **Tax-free interest income** Most state and local government bonds and other obligations pay interest that is not taxable at the federal level.
2. **Corporate dividend exclusion** When a firm owns shares of a second corporation, a portion of the dividends received from the investee company is not taxable for the investor company.
3. **Amortization of goodwill** Any goodwill that arose from acquisitions and mergers prior to August 11, 1993, cannot be deducted for tax purposes. However, the Revenue Reconciliation Act of 1993 (passed in August 1993) makes certain types of goodwill recorded in acquisitions or mergers occurring after August 11, 1993, deductible for tax purposes under some circumstances. In this chapter, assume goodwill is a permanent difference unless stated otherwise.
4. **Fines** Fines and related expenses resulting from violation of the law are not tax-deductible items.

Items that Cause Temporary Differences

5. **Accelerated depreciation** The modified accelerated cost recovery system (MACRS) is used for tax reporting, and some alternative method (such as the straight-line method) is used for financial reporting. Larger amounts are deducted for tax purposes in the early years of an asset's life, and vice versa in the later years.
6. **Installment sales** Sales are recorded for financial reporting on an accrual basis with revenue recognition at delivery of goods, but revenues are recorded on a cash basis for tax reporting.
7. **Warranty expenses** Warranty obligations are expensed and accrued when sales are recorded for accounting purposes, but are not deducted for tax purposes until warranty costs are actually incurred.
8. **Prepaid expenses** Prepaid rent, insurance, and similar items are reported as assets and expensed over the period of usage for financial reporting, but are deducted for tax purposes on a cash basis.

in the determination of income tax expense reported in the financial statements. If a permanent difference is the only difference between taxable income and pretax accounting income, income tax expense for financial reporting is equal to the amount computed as taxes payable on the tax return for the period.

Example   Assume that Watts Inc. has taxable revenues of $100,000 and tax-deductible expenses of $60,000. In addition, Watts Inc. receives interest from municipal bonds in the amount of $10,000, which is not subject to income taxation. All these revenues and expenses are included in pretax accounting income for the period. Assume that the tax rate is 35 percent. The computation of income taxes payable is as follows:

Simplified Tax Return for Watts Inc. for 1997

Taxable revenues	$100,000
Tax deductible expenses	60,000
Taxable income	40,000
Tax rate	× .35
Income taxes payable	$ 14,000

For financial reporting Watts includes the tax-free interest as revenue. Assuming there are no other differences, income tax expense equals income taxes payable. The income statement for financial reporting purposes shows the following:

Simplified Income Statement (for financial reporting) for Watts Inc. for 1997

Revenues (includes tax-free interest revenue)	$110,000
Expenses	60,000
Pretax accounting income	50,000
Income tax expense	14,000
Net income	$ 36,000

The **effective tax rate** is the tax rate that the company appears to be paying. It equals income tax expense divided by pretax accounting income. When a company has nontaxable revenue (e.g., interest revenue from municipal bonds) or deductions for tax purposes not reportable in the financial statements, the effective tax rate is reduced. The effective tax rate for Watts Inc. is

$$\text{Effective tax rate} = \$14,000/\$50,000 = 28\%$$

Thus, Watts Inc. has an effective tax rate lower than the statutory rate of 35 percent because its pretax accounting income is increased by a nontaxable revenue item.

Another reason the effective tax rate might differ from the U.S. federal statutory rate of 35 percent is that some income might be taxable in other tax jurisdictions such as states or foreign countries.

Example   Suppose that all of Watts' revenues and expenses were in a foreign country where the statutory tax rate is only 30 percent. Assume further that this income is not now or ever taxable in the United States. In this case, the income taxes payable would be only $12,000 ($40,000 \times .30$); thus the income statement would be:

Simplified Income Statement for Watts Inc.

Revenues	$110,000
Expenses	60,000
Income before income taxes	50,000
Income tax expense	12,000
Net income	$ 38,000

In this example the effective tax rate is 24 percent ($12,000/$50,000). One reason the effective tax rate is less than the statutory rate is that Watts has tax-free revenue. A second reason is that a portion (actually all in this case) of its taxable income is taxed at a rate different than the 35 percent U.S. statutory rate. There are two reasons why a company's effective tax rate might differ from the U.S. statutory rate (currently 35%):

- There is a permanent difference in which a revenue (or expense) is not taxable (deductible).
- A portion of the taxable income is taxed at a rate different than the U.S. statutory income tax rate.

As discussed in the introduction, Coca-Cola reports an effective tax rate of 31 percent in 1995. Looking more closely at Note 15, we see that the cause is a combination of the two reasons illustrated above:

- Much of Coca-Cola's income is earned in foreign countries where the tax rate is lower than in the United States, and this results in a reduction of the effective rate by 3.9 percent.
- Equity income is an example of income that is not taxable.[2] The income Coca-Cola records from its equity basis companies results in a reduction in the effective tax rate of 1.7 percent.

State income taxes cause an increase in the effective tax rate of 1 percent, and there are other effects that increase the rate by 0.6 percent.

Temporary Differences   A temporary difference arises when the measurement rules for financial reporting (GAAP) differ from tax reporting rules (the Internal Revenue Code) as to the *timing* of recognition of various revenues, gains, expenses, losses, assets, or liabilities. Temporary differences affect the computation of either taxable income or pretax accounting income in one period, and in some subsequent period or periods they affect the computation of the other type of income. The differences are temporary because they originate in one (or more) periods, then reverse and have the opposite effect in one (or more) future periods.

---

[2]We do not cover in any detail the tax code that defines what are taxable revenues and tax deductions, except for some often-encountered examples. In intercompany investments, equity in the earnings of an unconsolidated affiliated company not received in cash (i.e., as dividends) is not a taxable revenue. Moreover, cash dividends received by corporations are taxed at a lower rate than the 35 percent statutory rate. This gives rise to a permanent difference.

Example   Watts Inc. pays a fire insurance premium of $20,000 on December 31, 1997, for the following year. GAAP requires that the firm record a prepaid expense rather than expense the payment. Tax laws, however, generally would allow a tax deductible expense to be taken because an actual cost has been incurred. Watts would show fire insurance expense of $20,000 in 1998, but would have taken the tax deduction for this item in 1997:

	1997	**1998**
Accounting records	Record the $20,000 outlay as an asset. No expense this year.	Record $20,000 as fire insurance expense
Tax records	Take tax deduction of $20,000, reducing taxable income.	No deduction since it was taken in 1997.
Difference between pretax accounting income and taxable income	Pretax accounting income is $20,000 *greater* than taxable income.	Pretax accounting income $20,000 *less* than taxable income.

Items 5 through 8 in Exhibit 19–2 are examples of temporary differences. Temporary differences give rise to two effects:

1. Taxable income is different from pretax accounting income in one or more periods, but this effect is reversed in one or more subsequent periods.
2. Assets or liabilities have a **tax basis** different from their amounts reported in the financial statements.

The tax basis of an asset is the cost that remains to be deducted in computing taxable income. If a firm takes a tax deduction for insurance paid in advance but records it as a prepaid expense for financial reporting, the tax basis of the prepaid insurance is zero because it already has been deducted for tax purposes.

Example   Assume that Watts Inc. (in 1997 and 1998, its first two years of operation) has revenue of $100,000 for both book (financial reporting) and tax purposes. In 1997, however, Watts has expenses of $60,000 for financial reporting purposes, and $80,000 for tax purposes. Assume that the difference arises because in 1997 Watts Inc. prepaid fire insurance for 1998 in the amount of $20,000, and that this outlay is tax deductible in 1997. For financial reporting, fire insurance payments are an expense as the insurance period expires. Thus, in 1998 the prepaid insurance becomes an expense for financial reporting and is included in the $60,000 of expenses for 1998. Assume a corporate income tax rate of 35 percent and that Watts Inc. does not prepay its 1999 fire insurance in 1998.[3] With the above information, Watts Inc. would calculate pretax accounting income and taxable income for each of the two years to be:

	Financial Statements		**Tax Returns**	
	1997	**1998**	**1997**	**1998**
Revenues	$100,000	$100,000	$100,000	$100,000
Expenses	60,000	60,000	80,000	40,000
Pretax accounting income	$ 40,000	$ 40,000		
Taxable income.			$ 20,000	$ 60,000

The calculation of income taxes payable for each of the two years is as follows:

	1997	**1998**
Taxable income.	$20,000	$60,000
Tax rate	× .35	× .35
Income taxes payable	$ 7,000	$21,000

---

[3] A flat income tax rate is assumed in this and all examples. A graduated rate could be used, but the results do not change significantly, and the computations are unnecessarily complex.

On the balance sheet dated December 31, 1997, Watts would report an asset, prepaid insurance, in the amount of $20,000. However, the tax basis is zero because the $20,000 was deducted in computing taxable income in 1997. The 1998 financial statements treat the $20,000 as an expense, but the 1998 tax return cannot include it as a deduction because it was deducted in 1997. The prepaid insurance transaction gives rise to $20,000 less taxable income in 1997 and $20,000 more taxable income in 1998 relative to pretax accounting income. The prepaid rent is a temporary difference that arises in 1997 and reverses in 1998.

There are two questions in this area with which the accounting profession has wrestled for several decades:

- Should the **future tax consequences** of temporary differences be recognized in current period financial statements?
- If they are to be recognized, how and in what amount should they be recognized?

In the last example, should the potential increased income tax obligation in 1998, which occurs because of the temporary difference arising in 1997 and reversing in 1998, be included in the determination of income tax expense in 1997? If the potential income tax obligation is to be recognized in 1997, how should it be computed, and how should it be presented on the income statement and balance sheet? Consider first the question of whether the tax consequences of temporary differences should be recognized. There are two possible answers to the question:

- Disregard the future potential tax effects created by the temporary difference and recognize the amount of income taxes payable as determined on the tax return as the amount of income tax expense (the no-allocation method).
- Recognize the future tax effects of the temporary difference and develop a method for allocating these effects to current and future periods (interperiod tax allocation methods).

We illustrate the no-allocation method first even though it is not GAAP at the present time.

THE NO-ALLOCATION METHOD

The no-allocation approach to determining income tax expense simply ignores temporary differences. Under this approach, income tax expense for financial reporting is recorded as the amount of income taxes payable as computed on the period tax return. This **no-allocation method** is not acceptable under current GAAP, but it is important to understand its application and why it was rejected as an acceptable method.

The no-allocation method is easy to apply: income tax expense under this method is equal to the income taxes currently payable. In the Watts Inc. example, the no-allocation method income statements for 1997 and 1998 would report:

Income Statements for Years Ending December 31

	1997	1998
Revenues	$100,000	$100,000
Expenses other than income taxes	60,000	60,000
Income before income taxes	40,000	40,000
Income tax expense (taxes		
payable from tax return)	7,000	21,000
Net income	$ 33,000	$ 19,000

One appealing aspect of the no-allocation method is that income tax expense approximates the cash flow for income tax payments during the period, differing only by the change in accrued income taxes payable. The no-allocation approach would be conceptually appropriate if income taxes were viewed as a distribution of income rather than as an expense. There would be no need to measure the future tax consequences of current period transactions.

Many accountants and users of financial statements take the position that the no-allocation method is misleading. Returning again to the Watts Inc. example, the firm operated as effectively and efficiently in 1998 as it did in 1997 (revenues of $100,000 and expenses before tax of $60,000) but the income statement under the no-allocation method shows a large decline in net income from 1997 to 1998. Also, the balance sheet is potentially misleading. Because Watts took the tax deduction on prepaid insurance in 1997, there is no insurance expense that can be deducted on the tax return in 1998. By taking the deduction in 1997, Watts has an increased tax obligation in 1998 as a result of past transactions, yet no tax liability is shown on the balance sheet.

There is strong support in the accounting community for recognizing and allocating the future tax consequences of temporary differences on an appropriate accrual basis to current-period income tax expense. This procedure assures that the above potentially misleading interpretations are avoided.

THE ALLOCATION METHOD OF ACCOUNTING FOR TEMPORARY DIFFERENCES

The alternative to no allocation is some form of **interperiod tax allocation.** There are several alternative approaches to implementing interperiod tax allocation. We initially consider the method currently required by *SFAS No. 109,* "Accounting for Income Taxes," interperiod tax allocation using the asset/liability method.

The conceptual framework presented in Chapter 2 provides the rationale for the approach required by *SFAS No. 109,* which superseded *APB Opinion No. 11* in 1992. In fact, accounting for income taxes as required by *SFAS No. 109* is an excellent example of an application of the framework to arrive at a measurement rule. In *SFAC No. 6,* assets are defined as probable future economic benefits resulting from past transactions or events, and liabilities are defined as probable future economic outlays or sacrifices due to past transactions or events. Temporary differences arise because a past transaction or event is recorded in the financial statements or the tax return, but not both. The conceptual basis underlying *SFAS No. 109* is the measurement of the future economic tax effect (benefit or obligation) that arises from the current temporary difference.

The specific procedure used to achieve interperiod tax allocation under current GAAP is the *asset/liability method,* the only acceptable method of accounting for temporary differences.

Asset/Liability Method

Under the asset/liability method, the future tax consequences arising from temporary differences existing at the end of the accounting period are recorded as **deferred tax assets** or **deferred tax liabilities.**

- Deferred tax assets are expected future tax benefits arising from temporary differences existing at the end of the accounting period that will reduce taxable income relative to pretax accounting income in future periods.
- Deferred tax liabilities are expected future tax obligations arising from temporary differences existing at the end of the accounting period that will increase taxable income relative to pretax accounting income in future periods.

The deferred tax asset or liability measures are estimates of the future tax cash flow consequences of existing temporary difference. Moreover, if enacted future tax rates are different from current tax rates, the future tax rates are used in determining the amount of the asset or liability. The future enacted rate is the rate at which the deferred tax accounts will be realized or settled.

Example   In applying the asset/liability method to Watts Inc., income taxes payable are $7,000 in 1997 and $21,000 in 1998. The future tax consequences of the temporary difference existing at December 31, 1997, must be analyzed. In what period or periods will the temporary difference be reversed, and what will be the income tax rate in those periods? There is a temporary difference of $20,000. Not having the $20,000 of prepaid insurance as a tax deduction in 1998 causes 1998 taxable income to increase by this amount relative to pretax accounting income. It is known in 1997 that the tax rate will be 35 percent in 1998. Increasing 1998 taxable income by $20,000 will cause taxes payable to increase by this amount times the 1998 tax rate:

Increase in future income taxes arising
because prepaid insurance was tax-deducted = Future income tax rate $\times$ \$20,000
in 1997

$\qquad\qquad\qquad\qquad\qquad\qquad\qquad\qquad = .35\ \$(20,000)$

Increase in deferred tax liability $\qquad\qquad\qquad = \$7,000$

This amount is recognized as a **deferred tax liability** at December 31, 1997.

Income Tax Expense   Income tax expense is computed as the algebraic sum of the income taxes payable and the change (increase or decrease) in the deferred tax liability (and deferred tax asset, if there is any). Because the beginning balance in the deferred tax liability account for Watts Inc. was zero, the change is an increase of $7,000, and therefore income tax expense is $14,000 for 1997:

Compute 1997 income tax expense:

Income taxes payable	$ 7,000
Increase in deferred tax liability	7,000
Income tax expense	$14,000

The journal entry to record the income taxes using the asset/liability method for 1997 is as follows:

Income tax expense	14,000	
Deferred tax liability		7,000
Income tax payable		7,000

The preceding entry is required by GAAP and reflects the asset/liability approach to interperiod tax allocation. The $14,000 of income tax expense recognized in 1997 reflects the total income tax consequences of transactions occurring in 1997, even though only $7,000 is currently payable. The deferred tax liability meets the conceptual framework's definition of a liability in that it is a future obligation to transfer resources as a result of past transactions.

Had the 1998 tax rate been increased to 40 percent during the 1997 legislative session, the deferred tax liability would be recorded at $8,000 ($20,000 $\times$ .40) and income tax expense would be recorded at $15,000 ($7,000 payable + $8,000 deferred). Enacted future tax rates are used because they represent the rate at which the future tax benefit or cost stemming from 1997 transactions will be measured.

In 1998, taxes payable are $21,000. During 1998 the prepaid insurance is expensed, and there are no other temporary differences at December 31, 1998. Therefore, the deferred tax liability at December 31, 1998, is zero. The beginning balance in the deferred tax liability account of $7,000 must be adjusted to zero. The result is income tax expense for 1998 of $14,000:

Income taxes payable	$21,000
Decrease in deferred tax liability	(7,000)
Income tax expense	$14,000

The entry to record income taxes payable, adjust the deferred tax liability account, and record income tax expense for 1998 is:

Income tax expense	14,000	
Deferred tax liability	7,000	
Income tax payable		21,000

Simplified income statements for 1997 and 1998 prepared using the asset/liability method would show:

WATTS INC.

Interperiod Tax Allocation Using the Asset/Liability Method
Income Statements for the Years Ending December 31,

	1997	1998
Revenues	$100,000	$100,000
Expenses	60,000	60,000
Income before income taxes	40,000	40,000
Income tax expense	14,000	14,000
Net income	$ 26,000	$ 26,000

At December 31, 1997, the Watts Inc. balance sheet would show a deferred tax liability of $7,000. As mentioned earlier, the asset/liability method as required by *SFAS No. 109* has the appealing feature of being consistent with the FASB's conceptual framework. The objective is to measure and report accurately the future tax consequences of temporary differences. Thus it focuses on *asset and liability measurement,* rather than on *matching* income tax expense with pretax accounting income. A consequence of this focus is that income tax expense is a derived amount, computed as the sum of the income taxes currently payable plus the net change in the deferred tax asset and liability amounts from the beginning to the end of the year. As a result, income tax expense often does not equal the tax rate times pretax accounting income. We consider this again in a later section. Now, however, we examine in greater detail the procedures for determining income tax expense under the asset/liability method.

Terminology and Definitions Temporary differences *originate* in the financial statements in one period and are sometimes referred to as originating differences at this time. Temporary differences turn around, or *reverse,* in one or more future periods. When temporary differences reverse, sometimes they are referred to as reversing differences. Temporary differences are of two possible types:

- **Future taxable amounts** are temporary differences that increase taxable income relative to pretax accounting income in future periods when reversal occurs.
- **Future deductible amounts** are temporary differences that decrease taxable income relative to pretax accounting income in future periods when reversal occurs.

Future taxable amounts result in a future tax obligation (a **deferred tax liability**) because they cause an increase in future taxable income relative to pretax accounting income. Future deductible amounts result in a reduced future tax obligation (a **deferred tax asset**) because they cause future taxable income to decrease relative to pretax accounting income.

The following table summarizes some general sources of future taxable (deductible) amounts, and the relationship between future taxable (deductible) amounts and deferred tax liabilities (assets):

Future Taxable Amounts ⟶ Future Taxable Income Greater than Future Pretax Accounting Income

Common Sources	Examples	Result in
Revenues (gains) included in pretax accounting income *before* taxable income	Unrealized holding gains on investment in trading securities	Deferred tax liability
Expenses (losses) included in pretax accounting income *after* taxable income	Prepaid expenses	Deferred tax liability

Future Deductible Amounts ⟶ Future Taxable Income Less than Future Pretax Accounting Income

Common Sources	Examples	Result in
Revenues (gains) included in pretax accounting income *after* taxable income	Advances from customers	Deferred tax asset
Expenses (losses) included in pretax accounting income *before* taxable income	Warranty expenses	Deferred tax asset

The first example of future taxable amounts in the previous table has a balance sheet effect of causing the carrying value of the asset (investment in trading securities) to be greater than the tax basis, which is the original cost. The second item also causes the carrying value to be greater than the tax basis, which is zero after it is deducted for tax purposes. The first example under the future deductible amounts section has the balance sheet effect of creating a liability (advances from customers) that will not be taxed when it is taken into accounting income. This is equivalent to saying the tax basis is equal to the carrying amount. If it becomes earned and is included in pretax accounting income, there are no income taxes payable on it because it was taxed in the period when it was received. The final example also creates a liability that has a tax basis equal to its carrying amount. When it is paid, the full amount becomes a tax deduction.

Other Sources of Future Taxable (Deductible) Amounts   In the preceding examples, an income item is recognized for GAAP in a different period than for tax purposes, causing the amount of taxable income (on the tax return) to be different from pretax accounting income for the period. Another type of temporary difference occurs when assets or liabilities have a different tax basis from their carrying value in the financial statements, but the effect is not created with income items.

Example   An investment in securities of another company classified as a security available for sale would be carried at fair value in the financial statements, but the tax basis continues to be the original cost of the shares to the investor company. There has been no income statement effect in recording the investment at fair value, but there is a temporary difference because the tax basis differs from the carrying value. There are several examples of these more complex temporary differences:

Future taxable amounts:
- Reductions in the tax basis of assets, usually due to **tax credits,** that do not have the same effect on the financial statements. A tax credit is a direct reduction in the amount of income taxes payable. For example, a tax law change in 1982 gave taxpayers the option to take a tax credit in a specified situation, but if they did so, the amount of the tax credit would reduce the tax basis (depreciable amount for taxes) of the related asset. Firms choosing this option would depreciate the total cost of the asset (less salvage value) for financial reporting purposes, but the total allowed tax deduction would be the asset's cost reduced by the amount of the tax credit.[4]

Future deductible amounts:
- Increases in the tax basis of assets that are not considered in financial reporting. For example, in some foreign tax jurisdictions, the tax basis of assets is adjusted for the effects of inflation, but historical cost is used for financial reporting.
- Intercompany sales of inventory or an asset at a profit between a parent and a subsidiary that prepare separate tax returns. In the consolidated financial statements the intercompany profit is eliminated, but it would not be eliminated in the two separate tax returns.[5]

IMPLEMENTATION PROCEDURES

SFAS No. 109 requires the asset/liability method to be used in accounting for income taxes, and also requires recognition on the balance sheet of
- The current income taxes payable or refundable at the balance sheet date.
- The deferred tax assets and liabilities arising from temporary differences existing at the balance sheet date.

All temporary differences are to be considered in determining current or future tax consequences, and the tax consequences are to be measured using enacted current and future tax rates. Income tax expense is composed of a current portion and a deferred portion.

Current Portion Income Tax Expense   The income tax return computes income taxes payable for the current period in conformity with tax laws and regulations. The tax liability (or refund) for the year is the current portion of income taxes expense (savings). The accrual of this liability, less any payments made, is reported on the balance sheet as income taxes payable.

Deferred Portion of Income Tax Expense   The total deferred tax asset and the total deferred tax liability existing at year-end are determined based on temporary differences at

---

[4]For example, suppose a firm purchases an asset for $1,000, and the tax law allows the firm to take a tax credit in the year the asset is acquired in the amount of 10 percent of the purchase price of the asset. Moreover, the tax law requires that if the firm takes the tax credit, the tax basis of the asset is reduced an equal amount. The asset has a salvage value of zero. If the firm elects to use the tax credit, the credit reduces the amount of taxes payable in the year the asset is acquired by $100 (10% $\times$ $1,000), but the firm is allowed only $900 (the cost of the asset less the tax credit) as the total amount of tax deduction over the life of the asset. For financial reporting, however, the firm would depreciate the full $1,000 cost of the asset.

[5]These last two sources of future deductible amounts are beyond the scope of this text. Both international accounting and intercompany transactions are covered in advanced accounting texts.

that time. This computation usually involves both a deferred tax liability and a deferred tax asset. Future deductible amounts and future taxable amounts are not offset or netted together. Separate computations are made to determine the deferred tax liability resulting from the gross future taxable amount, and the deferred tax asset resulting from the gross future deductible amount. The changes in the balances of the deferred tax asset and the deferred tax liability accounts from the beginning to the end of the accounting period are included as the deferred component of income tax expense:[6]

	Deferred Tax	
	Asset	**Liability**
Temporary differences at end of year times appropriate tax rates	End balance	End balance
Less: Balances brought forward from opening balance sheet	− Beg. balance	− Beg. balance
Two components of deferred portion of income tax expense	Deferred tax	Deferred tax

Thus the deferred portion of income tax expense can be represented algebraically as:

Deferred portion of income tax expense or (benefit) = Increase (decrease) in deferred tax liability + Decrease (increase) in deferred tax asset

Total Income Tax Expense   Income tax expense for the period is the sum of the current portion and the deferred portion. The total income tax expense also is called provision for income taxes. Its current and deferred components must be disclosed on the face of the income statement or in the notes to the financial statements. Note that income tax expense is a derived amount. It is not computed directly, but is as the sum of income taxes currently payable and the net change in the deferred tax accounts over the period.

Example   Consider again the Watts Inc. example. The facts for 1997:

Statutory income tax rate 35%
Pretax accounting income . . . . $40,000   Taxable income $20,000

Temporary difference: prepaid fire insurance totaling $20,000
Income taxes payable = $20,000 × .35   7,000
Deferred tax liability at end of year = $20,000 × .35   7,000
Deferred tax liability as of beginning of year   0

The firm makes the following journal entry to record income taxes in 1997:

Income tax expense 14,000
   Deferred tax liability ($20,000 × .35)   7,000
   Income taxes payable ($20,000 × .35)   7,000

1998   Assume now that Watts has the following new information for 1998 after recording the above entry for 1997:

Pretax accounting income $70,000
Temporary differences existing at December 31, 1998:
   Prepaid rent (an asset for the books but deducted for tax purposes), ... $24,000
   Installment sale receivable (a revenue for the books
     but not for tax purposes), ... $6,000
Tax rate for 1998 and thereafter . . . . 35 percent

Both the above temporary differences are future taxable amounts—that is, both will cause future taxable income to increase relative to future pretax income. The determination

---

[6]If it is likely that some or all of the future benefit measured by the deferred tax asset will not be realized, *SFAS No. 109* requires that the deferred tax asset be reduced to the amount more likely than not to be realized. This topic is covered in a later section.

of income tax expense for 1998 proceeds as follows. First, determine the amount of taxable income, and compute the amount of income taxes currently payable. The determination of taxable income begins with pretax accounting income, and adjusts for temporary differences that originate or reverse during the period. For example, the prepaid fire insurance becomes an expense for accounting purposes in 1998, reducing pretax accounting income. However, it is not tax deductible in 1998 as it was taken as a tax deduction in 1997. This item *by itself* would cause taxable income to be $20,000 greater than pretax accounting income. The computation of taxable income from pretax accounting income is as follows:

Pretax accounting income	$70,000
Reversing temporary difference:	
Prepaid fire insurance at beginning of year	20,000
Originating temporary differences:	
Prepaid rent at end of year	(24,000)
Installment sales receivable	(6,000)
Taxable income	60,000
Current income tax rate	× .35
Income taxes currently payable	$21,000

Prepaid rent at year-end is subtracted from pretax accounting income because it was not an expense for GAAP but is currently deductible for tax purposes. Likewise, the installment sale was included in pretax accounting income but is not taxable in 1998.

Second, compute the deferred tax liability and deferred tax asset balances at December 31, 1998, based on temporary differences existing at that time:

Future taxable amounts existing at December 31, 1998:	
Prepaid rent	$24,000
Installment sales receivable	6,000
Total future taxable amount	30,000
Future tax rate	× .35
Deferred tax liability, December 31, 1998	$10,500

There are no future deductible amounts in this example. If there were, the computations to determine the deferred tax asset balance would be analogous to the procedure above.

Third, compute the change in the deferred tax liability and deferred tax asset accounts that must be recorded:

	Deferred Tax	
	Liability	**Asset**
Balance required, December 31, 1998	$10,500	0
Balance, December 31, 1997	7,000	0
Adjustment needed (credit) debit	$(3,500)	0

Finally, record income taxes payable and any changes to the deferred tax liability or deferred tax asset accounts and income tax expense:

Income tax expense	24,500	
Income taxes payable		21,000
Deferred tax liability		3,500

Steps in the Process   The previous example demonstrates both the accounting for temporary differences and a general process to follow in determining income tax expense. The general process can be summarized in four basic steps after collecting the essential data: Collect essential data including

- Pretax accounting income.
- Taxable income (or originating and reversing temporary differences for the period that can be used to compute taxable income from pretax accounting income).
- Enacted current and future tax rates.

- Temporary differences as of year-end, identified as future taxable amounts or as future deductible amounts.
- Deferred tax asset and liability account balances as of the beginning of the year.

Step 1. Compute income taxes currently payable.   This amount can be taken from the tax return or computed as taxable income times the current income tax rate.

Step 2. Compute end-of-period deferred tax asset and liability account balances.   These amounts are based on end-of-period future taxable amounts (for any deferred tax liability), future deductible amounts (for any deferred tax assets), and future enacted tax rates.

Step 3. Determine the adjustments to the deferred tax liability and asset accounts.   These are the amounts needed to adjust the beginning balances to the appropriate (computed) ending balances.

Step 4. Prepare the journal entry.   Record income taxes payable, adjustments to deferred tax asset and liability accounts, and income tax expense.

A possible addition to step 4 is discussed in detail in a later section of this chapter. This additional step deals with reducing the carrying value of deferred tax assets (with a valuation allowance account) when there is a greater than 50 percent probability that some portion of it will not be realized.

Identifying Future Taxable and Deductible Amounts

Step 1 includes the important task of finding all the temporary differences at the end of the accounting period and determining whether each is a future taxable or future deductible amount. This is accomplished by analyzing the various balance sheet accounts and transactions and, with information from tax returns, determining the tax status of each.[7] Tax returns also must be examined to identify any existing operating loss or tax credit carryforwards that can be used to reduce future taxable income and future income taxes. An operating loss is a loss for tax purposes that can be used to reduce future taxable income (discussed later).

The basic process for finding temporary differences begins with examining the asset and liability accounts to find those amounts that have already been recorded as a revenue or expense (or deduction) on either the income statement or on the tax return, but not both, and that will be recorded on the other statement in future periods. Any permanent differences are not used in the process of determining the changes in the deferred tax accounts.

Among the assets, there are two kinds:

1. Assets that have been recorded as a revenue on the income statement but have not been included on the tax return (such as installment sale receivables).
2. Assets that have been deducted on the tax return but have not been expensed on the income statement (such as prepaid expenses).

Among the liabilities, there are also two kinds of accounts:

1. Accrued liabilities that have been expensed on the income statement but will be tax deductible in a later period (such as accrued warranty obligation).
2. Unearned revenues that have been included in taxable income but will be included on the income statement in future periods (such as advances from customers).

These asset and liability accounts represent temporary differences.

Another type of item that gives rise to a temporary difference is an asset whose carrying value on the balance sheet differs from its tax basis. The most frequently encountered account of this type is a depreciable asset that has a remaining depreciable amount for book purposes different from the remaining deductible amount for tax purposes (the tax basis of

---

[7]Tax accounting is more involved than the simplified examples found in this chapter. Individuals responsible for preparing tax returns may need to be consulted to determine the tax status of various items.

the asset). The amount by which the remaining depreciable amount for book purposes exceeds the tax basis of the depreciable asset is a future taxable amount. A second type of item in this category is an investment or other asset for which unrealized holding gains or losses have been recorded on the financial statements but have not yet been deducted for tax purposes.

Example   The reduction of inventory through use of the lower-of-cost-or-market method to a market value that is lower than cost results in a future deductible amount. Also, the amount of any unrealized gain (loss) included in recording investments at fair value is a future taxable (deductible) amount.

Operating loss carryforwards can be used to offset (reduce) taxable income in future periods and hence have the same effect as future deductible amounts. Similarly, tax credit carryforwards can be used to offset (reduce) a portion of the tax liability, and therefore are equivalent to deferred tax assets. Both these items are discussed in later sections of this chapter.

│CONCEPT REVIEW

1. Why are there differences between taxable income and pretax accounting income? What are two basic types of differences?
2. How are permanent differences handled in determining income tax expense? What are some examples of permanent differences?
3. What is a temporary difference? What are some examples of temporary differences?

Illustrations of Deferred Tax Assets and Deferred Tax Liabilities

The four steps discussed previously are illustrated by an extended two-year example leading to the income tax accrual entry in each year. Each year in the example introduces a new complexity to the computational process. We assume the enacted income tax rate for 1998 is 30 percent but a different enacted tax rate of 40 percent applies for all future periods. Using different rates in the example shows the effect of rate changes, which can occur from time to time, on the computations.

Example: Max Company—Year One   Assume that Max Company is a retailer with credit sales of $90,000 in 1998, its first year of operations. All credit sales are outstanding as accounts receivable as of December 31, and these amounts will not be taxable in 1998. Max also records a provision for warranty costs of $30,000 as an expense. This amount is expensed for financial reporting in 1998 but is not deductible for tax purposes until incurred. However, $10,000 of the estimated warranty costs are incurred in 1998. Pretax accounting income is $100,000. We proceed by carefully following the four steps outlined earlier (after repeating the basic data). Essential accounting and income tax data for the year:

Pretax accounting income $100,000
Temporary differences:

Account	Beginning Balance	Ending Balance	Increase (Decrease)	Type of Difference
Accounts receivable	$0	$90,000	$90,000	Taxable
Warranty liability.	0	(20,000)	20,000	Deductible

Warranty costs of $30,000 were expensed for financial reporting and were incurred in the amount of $10,000. The $10,000 amount is deductible for tax purposes in 1998, but the remaining $20,000 is a future deductible amount.

Steps 1 and 2   Compute the first amount of income taxes payable for the year, and, second, the end-of-year deferred tax liability and end-of-year deferred tax asset based on future enacted tax rates.

	Temporary Differences, Taxes Payable, Deferred Tax Balances, Effect on Future Years' Income			
	Current Year 1998	Total for Future Years	1999 and Thereafter Deductible	1999 and Thereafter Taxable
Pretax accounting income (loss)	$100,000			
Temporary differences:				
Credit sales	(90,000)	$90,000	$ 0	$90,000
Warranty costs	20,000	(20,000)	20,000	
Net taxable income	30,000			
Total temporary difference		70,000	20,000	90,000
Enacted tax rate	× 0.30		× 0.40	× 0.40
Taxes currently payable	$ 9,000			
Deferred tax asset balance, December 31, 1998			$ 8,000	
Deferred tax liability balance, December 31, 1998				$36,000

Future deductible and taxable amounts are not netted to determine a net deferred tax asset or liability. Rather, all future taxable amounts are aggregated to compute a total deferred tax liability, and all future deductible amounts are aggregated to compute a total deferred tax asset. The classification of the deferred tax accounts is discussed later. The future tax rate is used to calculate the deferred tax asset/liability because this is the rate at which future deductible/taxable differences will cause taxes to decrease/increase in future years.

Step 3   Compute the change in the deferred tax asset and deferred tax liability accounts:

	Deferred Tax Asset*	Deferred Tax Liability*
Ending balance (computed in step 2 above)	$8,000	$(36,000)
Less: Beginning balance (taken from opening balances)	0	0
Adjustment amount	$8,000	$(36,000)

*Debit (credit)

Step 4   Prepare the journal entry to record income tax payable, all changes in the deferred tax asset and liability accounts, and income tax expense. The journal entry to record 1998 income taxes is:

Income tax expense (current portion)	9,000	
Income tax expense (deferred portion)	28,000	
Deferred tax asset	8,000	
Deferred tax liability		36,000
Income tax payable		9,000

The total income tax expense is $37,000 ($9,000 current + $28,000 deferred).

At December 31, 1998, the Max Company balance sheet and income statement would reflect the following balances relating to the above activities:

MAX COMPANY

Balance Sheet Excerpts

As of December 31, 1998

Assets		Liabilities	
Accounts receivable	$90,000	Warranty liability	$20,000
Deferred tax asset	8,000	Deferred tax liability	36,000

MAX COMPANY

Income Statement Excerpts

For Year Ending December 31, 1998

Income before income taxes		$100,000
Income tax expense:		
Current portion	$ 9,000	
Deferred portion	28,000	37,000
Net income		$ 63,000

The accounts receivable and the warranty liability are the two temporary differences existing at December 31. The warranty liability of $20,000 gives rise to the deferred tax asset of $8,000, and the accounts receivable of $90,000 gives rise to the deferred tax liability of $36,000.[8] Both of the deferred tax items were computed using the **enacted future** tax rate of 40 percent. Note that the effective tax is not equal to the current statutory rate (30%) because the deferred tax asset and liability were measured using 40 percent rate.

Continuing Example: Max Company—Year 2   In 1999, Max continues to sell on credit and to warrant its products. Credit sales in 1999 total $120,000 and warranty expense is $40,000. Collections in 1999 on credit sales total $50,000 (assume all for 1998 sales) and actual warranty costs incurred total $15,000. Pretax accounting income totals $80,000 for 1999. Essential accounting and income tax data for the year:

Pretax accounting income $80,000
Temporary differences:

Account	Beginning Balance	Ending Balance	Increase (Decrease)	Type of Difference
Accounts receivable	$90,000	$160,000*	$70,000	Taxable
Warranty liability.	(20,000)	(45,000)†	25,000	Deductible

*Beginning balance + Credit sales − Cash collections = $90,000 + $120,000 − $50,000 = $160,000

†Beginning balance + Current period warranty provision − Cash payments for warranties during the period = $20,000 + $40,000 − $15,000 = $45,000

The increase (decrease) column amounts are used to reconcile pretax accounting income to taxable income in the current year. Pretax accounting income is $70,000 greater than taxable income in 1999 because of the increase in the accounts receivable and $25,000 less because of the increase in the warranty liability. At the end of 1999, however, there is a total of $160,000 in future taxable amounts related to the accounts receivable. This latter amount is used to compute the amount of the deferred tax liability at the end of 1999.

Steps 1 and 2   Compute the amount of income taxes payable for the year and the end-of-year deferred tax liability and end-of-year deferred tax asset based on future enacted tax rates.

	Temporary Differences, Taxes Payable, Deferred Tax Balances, Effect on Future Years' Income			
	Current Year 1999	Total for Future Years	2000 and Thereafter Deductible	2000 and Thereafter Taxable
Pretax accounting income (loss)	$80,000			
Temporary differences:				
Credit sales	(70,000)	$160,000	$ 0	$160,000
Warranty costs	25,000	(45,000)	45,000	
Net taxable income	35,000			
Total temporary difference		$115,000	45,000	160,000
Enacted tax rate	× 0.40		× 0.40	× 0.40
Taxes currently payable	$14,000			
Deferred tax asset balance, December 31, 1999			$18,000	
Deferred tax liability balance, December 31, 1999				$64,000

---

[8]There are circumstances when, after computing these balances for deferred tax asset and deferred tax liability, the two balances would be netted together for presentation on the balance sheet.

Step 3 Compute the change in the deferred tax asset and liability accounts:

	Deferred Tax	
	Asset*	Liability*
Ending balance (computed in step 2 above)	$18,000	$(64,000)
Less: Beginning balance (taken from opening balances)	8,000	(36,000)
Adjustment amount	$10,000	$(28,000)

*Debit (credit)

This is an important step. Only the *future* temporary differences at the end of 1999 contribute to the ending deferred tax accounts. Previous amounts that have now reversed no longer contribute to these accounts. The future temporary differences at the end of 1999 require $18,000 and $64,000 of deferred tax asset and liability to be recognized, respectively. Because Max has $8,000 and $36,000 in these accounts, only the $10,000 and $28,000 increases in each account are necessary.

Step 4 Prepare the journal entry to record income tax payable, all changes in the deferred tax asset and liability accounts, and income tax expense. The journal entry to record income taxes is:

Income tax expense (current portion)	14,000	
Income tax expense (deferred portion)	18,000	
Deferred tax asset	10,000	
Deferred tax liability		28,000
Income tax payable		14,000

The total income tax expense is $32,000 ($14,000 current + $18,000 deferred). At December 31, 1999, the Max Company balance sheet and income statement would reflect the following balances relating to the above activities:

MAX COMPANY

Balance Sheet Excerpts

As of December 31, 1999

Assets		**Liabilities**	
Accounts receivable	$160,000	Warranty liability	$45,000
Deferred tax asset	18,000	Deferred tax liability	64,000

MAX COMPANY

Income Statement Excerpts

For Year Ending December 31, 1999

Income before income taxes		$80,000
Income tax expense:		
Current portion	$14,000	
Deferred portion	18,000	32,000
Net income		$48,000

This extended example illustrates the procedures for computing income tax expense. The example also demonstrates how income tax expense for a period is determined indirectly. Income tax expense is the sum of taxes payable and the change in deferred tax asset and deferred tax liability accounts for the period. Each of these amounts is computed directly.

This example also demonstrates a common effect of interperiod tax allocation—the growth in deferred tax accounts, particularly the deferred tax liability. Growing firms typically increase the deferred tax liability each year because more future taxable differences are generated each year than reverse. Although earlier taxable differences do reverse, there often is no *net* reversal (a net decrease in the deferred tax liability). For Max, this effect in 1999 is:

**Deferred Tax Liability
(Decrease) Increase**

1999 reversal of taxable difference originating in 1998, $50,000
    of collections in 1999 of 1998 credit sales. $50,000(.40) . . . . $(20,000)
1999 originating difference, $120,000 credit sales. $120,000(.40)   48,000
Net increase in deferred tax liability during 1999 . . . . $ 28,000

Only when firms reduce their growth rate or reduce a particular type of transaction is a *net* reversal experienced.

Another aspect of interperiod tax allocation demonstrated by the Max Company example is the larger magnitude of deferred tax liabilities relative to deferred tax assets. Firms take advantage of Internal Revenue Code provisions that minimize their *current* taxable income. In so doing, future taxable amounts are more likely to be created than are future deductible amounts. Depreciation is a common example. Tax depreciation deductions are greater than book depreciation expense amounts early in the life of a depreciable asset, but that situation reverses in later years. For future deductible differences to be created, *current* taxable revenues must exceed book revenues, or tax deductions must be less than book expenses. These situations are less common than the opposite case and firms actively avoid them within the limits of the tax law.

Depreciation   Some temporary differences require more than one period to fully originate. For these temporary differences, an overall netting approach is appropriate.

Example   A plant asset purchased in 1988 is to be depreciated as follows:

Year	Tax Depreciation	Book Depreciation
1998	$ 40,000	$ 20,000
1999	30,000	20,000
2000	20,000	20,000
2001	10,000	20,000
2002	0	20,000
	$100,000	$100,000

At the end of 1998, the future taxable difference of $20,000 equals the excess of book depreciation for the years 1999–2002 ($80,000) over tax depreciation for the same period ($60,000). The $20,000 difference at the end of 1998 is taxable because future taxable income over the four remaining years of the asset's life will be increased relative to pretax income by the depreciation differences reversing in those years. The overall period 1999–2002 is used to determine the future temporary difference at the end of 1998. The differences are not analyzed on an individual-year basis.

For the asset depicted above, the difference for 1999 alone appears to be a deductible difference because taxable income will decline relative to pretax income as a result of depreciation. However, the overall temporary difference is completing its origination phase in 1999. Even if enacted tax rates are different during the reversal period, the overall difference is treated as a taxable difference. The different tax rates would be applied to each year's difference in determining the net taxable difference.

| CONCEPT REVIEW

1. What is a future taxable amount? What is a future deductible amount? Why are they important in determining income tax expense?
2. How are deferred tax assets and liabilities determined?
3. Suppose the statutory tax rate is increased from 35 to 40 percent during 1998, effective for 1999 and all years thereafter. What rate is used to determine deferred tax asset and liability amounts at December 31, 1998? Why?

▍REVIEW PROBLEM

Lake Company has the following results of operations at December 31, 1997:
- Pretax accounting income in 1997, its first year of operations, totals $100,000. Taxable income is $90,000.
- Lake Company has credit sales included in pretax accounting income totaling $60,000, none of which is included in taxable income. This amount will be included in taxable income in future years.
- The firm expensed in its financial statements $50,000 as a provision for future warranty costs in 1997. This amount was not deductible for tax purposes in 1997, but will be deductible in future years.
- The enacted marginal tax rate for 1997 and all future years is 40 percent.

Required

Determine income taxes payable, any deferred tax account amounts, and show the journal entry to record income tax expense for 1997.

▍SOLUTION

The determination of deferred tax assets and liabilities proceeds by the steps outlined earlier. Essential accounting and income tax data for the year:

Pretax accounting income $100,000
Temporary differences:

Account	Beginning Balance	Ending Balance	Increase (Decrease)	Type of Difference
Accounts receivable	$0	$60,000	$60,000	Taxable
Warranty liability.	0	(50,000)	50,000	Deductible

Steps 1 and 2   Compute the amount of income taxes payable for the year, and compute the end-of-year deferred tax liability and end-of-year deferred tax asset based on future enacted tax rates.

	Temporary Differences, Taxes Payable, Deferred Tax Balances, Effect on Future Years' Income			
	Current Year 1997	Total for Future Years	1998 and Thereafter Deductible	1998 and Thereafter Taxable
Pretax accounting income (loss)	$100,000			
Temporary differences:				
Credit sales	(60,000)	$60,000	$ 0	$60,000
Warranty costs	50,000	(50,000)	50,000	
Net taxable income	90,000			
Total temporary difference		$10,000	50,000	60,000
Enacted tax rate	× 0.40		× 0.40	× 0.40
Taxes currently payable	$ 36,000			
Deferred tax asset balance, December 31, 1997			$20,000	
Deferred tax liability balance, December 31, 1997				$24,000

Step 3   Compute the change in the deferred tax asset and liability accounts:

	Deferred Tax	
	Asset*	Liability*
Ending balance (computed in step 2 above)	$20,000	$(24,000)
Less: Beginning balance (taken from opening balances)	0	0
Adjustment amount	$20,000	$(24,000)

*Debit (credit)

Step 4   Prepare the journal entry to record income tax payable, all changes in the deferred tax asset and liability accounts, and income tax expense. The journal entry to record 1998 income taxes is:

```
Income tax expense (current portion) . . . . . . . . . . . . . . . . . . . . . . . . . .   36,000
Income tax expense (deferred portion) . . . . . . . . . . . . . . . . . . . . . . . . .    4,000
Deferred tax asset  . . . . . . . . . . . . . . . . . . . . . . . . . . . . . . . . . . . .   20,000
    Deferred tax liability  . . . . . . . . . . . . . . . . . . . . . . . . . . . . . . .            24,000
    Income tax payable  . . . . . . . . . . . . . . . . . . . . . . . . . . . . . . . . .            36,000
```

NET OPERATING LOSSES

An additional aspect of tax law can affect the amount of income taxes payable in any given year and provides another source of deferred tax assets. Specifically, tax laws allow a firm that experiences a loss for tax purposes to use the loss to offset taxable income in either earlier or subsequent years, and thus receive either a refund of taxes paid or a reduction of taxes payable in future years. We first discuss how this feature of the tax law works, and then consider how to account for it in the financial statements.

Carrybacks and Carryforwards of Net Operating Losses

When a for-profit firm has negative taxable income in a period, it has a **net operating loss (NOL).** As a result, the firm has no income tax obligation in the current period. Moreover, current federal tax law allows the firm to obtain a refund of income taxes paid in recent years by applying for an **operating loss carryback,** or to reduce the amount of income taxes payable in future years that have positive taxable income by applying for an **operating loss carryforward.** Under current federal tax laws, a firm with an NOL must, at the end of the year of the loss, irrevocably choose between two options:

Carryback and Carryforward (Option 1)   Losses are carried back *three years* (in order of years, starting with the earliest year) in order to secure a refund of prior years' taxes on income of an equivalent amount. If the NOL is so large that the carryback to the prior three years does not fully absorb it, the remaining loss may be carried forward a maximum of 15 years to reduce taxable income in future years until it is fully absorbed. With this option, there are a total of 18 years available to absorb the NOL. The earliest NOL is used completely before considering a later NOL.

Carryforward-Only (Option 2)   A firm with an NOL may choose a carryforward-only option again for up to 15 years, to reduce taxable income and thus taxes payable in future years. This option is chosen if management thinks the benefit will be greater than if the carryback and carryforward option were chosen.

Example   Assume that Watters Tent Company began operations in 1994 and has taxable income of $20,000, $10,000 and $5,000 in years 1, 2, and 3 of its operations, respectively. During this period it pays income taxes at a statutory rate of 20 percent. In 1997, Watters experiences an operating loss of $65,000. Suppose further that an enacted tax law will increase the statutory tax rate to 40 percent in 1999. The above information and Watters management's estimates of taxable income for the period 1998 through 2001 follow:

Year	Taxable Income	Tax Rate	Taxes Paid or Payable
1994	$20,000	20%	$ 4,000
1995	10,000	20%	2,000
1996	5,000	20%	1,000
1997 (current year)	**(65,000)**	**20%**	**–0–**
1998	10,000 Est.	20%	2,000
1999	5,000 Est.	40%	2,000
2000	50,000 Est.	40%	20,000
2001	60,000 Est.	40%	24,000

Watters must decide whether to choose option 1 (carryback and carryforward) or option 2 (carryforward only). Exhibit 19–3 diagrams the two choices. If option 1 is chosen, Watters can request a tax refund of $7,000 ($35,000 of taxable income in years 1994 through 1996, multiplied by the 20 percent tax rate) and will have $30,000 of NOL ($65,000 total NOL, less $35,000 carried back to 1994 through 1996) to carryforward to future years. If this

EXHIBIT 19–3 Comparison of Estimated Effects of NOL Options for Watters Company (in thousands)

	Prior Years			Current Year	Future Years (Estimated)				
Year	−3	−2	−1	1997	1	2	3	4	5 . . . 15
Taxable Income	$20	$10	$ 5		$10	$ 5	$50	$60	
Tax rate	20%	20%	20%		20%	40%	40%	40%	
Taxes paid	4	2	1						
Operating loss (NOL)				$(65)					

Option 1: Carryback–Carryforward

Carryback amount to this period	$65	$45	$35	Carryforward amount to this period	$30	$20	$15	
Used in this period	20	10	5	Used in this period	10	5	15	
Remaining NOL	45	35	30		20	15	0	
Tax refund or savings*	**$ 4**	**$ 2**	**$ 1**		**$ 2**	**$ 2**	**$6**	**Total benefit = $17**

Option 2: Carryforward Only

Carryforward	$65	$55	$50	
Used this period	10	5	50	
Remaining	55	50	0	
Tax savings*	**$ 2**	**$ 2**	**$20**	**Total benefit = $24**

*Amount of NOL used × tax rate for the period.

option is chosen and the estimates of future taxable income are realized, Watters will have tax savings of $2,000, $2,000, and $6,000 in 1998, 1999, 2000, respectively. The total amount of tax refund and future tax savings is $17,000.

If option 2 is chosen and the estimates of future taxable income are realized, the total benefit is $24,000, as shown in Exhibit 19–3. In this case the benefit is greater under option 2 because of the increased tax rate starting in 1999. The $35,000 that was carried back under option 1 generates a refund at a tax rate of 20 percent, but if the $35,000 is carried forward (as it is under option 2), it generates tax savings at 40 percent. Since the cash flows of tax refunds and future tax savings occur in different amounts and in different periods, a complete analysis would take into account the present value of the cash flows of the two options and the risk associated with estimates of future taxable income. Looking again at Exhibit 19–3, the alternatives for Watters are to

- Accept a certain $7,000 tax refund today and an uncertain carryforward worth an estimated $10,000 (at nominal value).
- Wait and apply for a carryforward worth an estimated $24,000 (nominal value).

Is the present value of the uncertain $14,000 difference in carryforward amounts greater than the certain $7,000 refund?

Accounting for NOLs

Accounting for the effects of NOLs is straightforward regardless of whether a firm chooses option 1 or option 2. Under option 1, some or all of the benefit is in the form of a tax refund. Under option 2, and for the portion of the NOL not absorbed by carryback under option 1, the benefit is in the form of future tax savings. Future deductible amounts from temporary differences also create future tax savings; therefore, we can think of tax loss carryforwards as analogous to future deductible amounts. Carryforwards of NOLs result in deferred tax assets in the same manner as future deductible amounts. The accounting under option 1 and option 2 follows:

Carryback–Carryforward (Option 1) Continuing the Watters Company example, suppose the carryback and carryforward option is chosen. Assume that Watters has no other future taxable or deductible amounts (taxable income or loss equals pretax accounting income or loss) and therefore files a tax return requesting a tax refund of $7,000 in 1997. Based on known future tax rates and estimates of future taxable income, Watters estimates that the remaining $30,000 NOL carryforward will result in future tax savings of $10,000. *SFAS No. 109* requires that this estimated future tax savings from the carryforward be recorded as a deferred tax asset. The entry to be made by Watters in 1997 to record the effects of the NOL is:

Receivable for income tax refund	7,000	
Deferred tax asset	10,000	
Income tax expense		17,000

The after-tax loss reported on the income statement is the $65,000 NOL, less the total tax refund and tax savings of $17,000, for a net loss of $48,000.

Carryforward-Only (Option 2) If Watters elects the carryforward-only option, the accounting is similar to the above except that there is no tax refund. The entire $65,000 NOL is carried forward and is expected to result in future tax savings of $24,000, as is shown in Exhibit 19–3. The entry to record the effects of the NOL is:

Deferred tax asset	24,000	
Income tax expense		24,000

The after-tax loss reported on the income statement is the $65,000 NOL, less the total future tax savings of $24,000, for a net loss of $41,000.

Regardless of whether option 1 or option 2 is chosen, the deferred tax asset is based on estimates of future taxable income and enacted future tax rates. If the future benefit of the NOL carried forward is unlikely to be realized, *SFAS No. 109* requires that a valuation allowance be established to reduce the carrying value of the deferred tax asset to an amount that is likely to be realized. The establishment of a valuation allowance is covered in a later section. For the moment we assume no valuation allowance is required.

Accounting in subsequent periods reflects the asset/liability method, with the remaining NOL carryforward amount treated as a future deductible amount. Suppose that in 1998 Watters has taxable income of $15,000 before adjusting for the NOL carryforward. Assuming option 2 has been chosen, the NOL is used to absorb taxable income in 1998, leaving an NOL carryforward amount of $50,000. Assuming no changes in estimates of taxable income in future years, this amount will generate future tax savings as follows:

Year	Remaining NOL	Taxable Income	Tax Rate	Tax Savings
1999	$50,000	$ 5,000	40%	$ 2,000
2000	45,000	50,000	40%	18,000*
Total				$20,000

*$45,000(.40)

Thus the NOL remaining at December 31, 1998, is expected to generate future tax savings of $20,000. The deferred tax asset balance created at December 31, 1997, was $24,000; hence, the deferred tax asset account is reduced by $4,000. There are no income taxes currently payable, since $15,000 of the NOL is used to reduce taxable income to zero in 1998. The entry to record income taxes in 1998 is:

Income tax expense	4,000	
Deferred tax asset		4,000

The effect of the above accounting procedures is to recognize the benefit of NOL carrybacks and carryforwards in the year in which the NOL occurs.

A LIMITATION ON DEFERRED TAX ASSETS

To realize the benefit of a deferred tax asset, either there must be future taxable income against which the future deductible amounts (or NOLs) are offset to reduce taxes payable, or there must be a way to obtain a refund of taxes paid previously. If these situations are not likely, *SFAS No. 109* provides for reducing the carrying value of the deferred tax asset. Realization of the benefit of an existing deductible amount or an NOL carryforward (which result in deferred tax assets) depends on the existence of taxable income within the period of carryback and carryforward available under tax law.

If, based on the weight of available evidence, it is *more likely than not* that some portion of the deferred tax asset will *not* be realized, the deferred tax asset is reduced by a **valuation allowance.** The valuation allowance is a contra account sufficient to reduce the deferred tax asset to the amount more likely than not to be realized. Any *change* in the balance of the valuation allowance from the beginning to the end of the accounting period also is included in the deferred component of income tax expense.

Evidence to Consider in Determining Whether a Valuation Allowance Is Needed

A firm must consider all available evidence, both positive and negative, to make the determination of whether a valuation allowance is necessary. Such evidence includes information about the firm's:
- Current financial position.
- Results of operations for the current and preceding years.
- Future operations.

Negative Evidence   A recent history of several years of losses is strong evidence that suggests a valuation allowance is needed. Other evidence suggesting the need for a valuation allowance includes, but is not limited to:
- A history of operating loss carryforwards that expire unused.
- Losses expected in future years.
- Circumstances that if unfavorably resolved would adversely affect future operations.
- A remaining carryback or carryforward period so short it is of limited use in realizing tax benefits if a large deductible temporary difference is expected to reverse in a single year or if the firm operates in a highly cyclical business.

Positive Evidence   Positive evidence that a valuation allowance is not needed includes the following:
- A history of profitability.
- Existing contracts or firm sales backlog that will produce more than enough taxable income to realize the deferred tax asset.
- An excess of appreciated asset value over the tax basis of the assets sufficiently large to realize the deferred tax asset.

Each of the above items provides information useful for estimating future taxable income. If the amount expected for future taxable income is large enough to realize the deferred tax asset, no valuation allowance is needed. Even if it is not large enough, a valuation allowance may still not be required. If the deductible temporary difference that is creating the deferred tax asset will reverse soon enough that it can be carried back to the current and prior years to realize the benefit, no valuation allowance is required. Also, if the future reversals of taxable temporary differences can offset deductible temporary differences by carryback and carryforward procedures, and the taxable temporary differences are large enough to cause the deferred tax assets to be realized, no valuation allowance is needed. Finally, if there are prudent and feasible tax-planning strategies that a firm could implement to prevent an operating loss or tax credit carryforward from expiring or that in general would result in the realization of the deferred tax asset, then once again a valuation allowance is not needed.

Strong positive evidence from *any one* of these sources is sufficient to support a conclusion that a valuation allowance is not necessary. If such evidence is available from one source, other sources need not be considered. Thus, a firm with a history of strong profitability need not consider the other sources of evidence, assuming it is more likely than not that it will generate sufficient taxable income from sources exclusive of the temporary differences to realize the benefits of the deferred tax assets.

SFAS No. 109 does not require conclusive evidence of realizability. *SFAS No. 109* uses the phrase *more likely than not* in referring to the strength of evidence required. Thus, the requirement is that a firm must conclude there is a better than 50–50 chance that the benefit will be realized in order to avoid recording a valuation allowance. Alternatively, if there is a 50–50 chance or less that all or a portion of the deferred tax asset will be realized, a valuation allowance must be recorded for that portion.

Sources for Realizing Deferred Tax Assets   To summarize the above discussion, three basic sources may be used to realize the tax benefit of deferred tax assets:

1. Future taxable income exclusive of future temporary differences and carryforwards.
2. Taxable income in prior (carryback) years.
3. Future reversals of existing taxable amounts.

In addition, a firm might pursue tax-planning strategies that would, if implemented, result in future taxable income. If some or all of the future benefit of a deferred tax asset is not expected to be realized, a valuation allowance, a contra account to the deferred tax asset, is established for the amount not expected to be realized. The first three basic sources are illustrated in the following example.

Example   Western Company is in its second year of operations. In each of the following independent cases, the tax law provides for a 3-year carryback and 15-year carryforward of NOLs, and the income tax rate is a constant 40 percent. The question is whether Western can expect to realize the benefit of its deferred tax asset in each case.

Case A: Using Estimates of Future Taxable
Income Exclusive of Future Temporary Differences

Taxable income in first year	$ 0
Taxable income in second (current) year	0
Future deductible amounts, end of second year	$50,000
Times future tax rate	× .40
Deferred tax asset at end of second year	$20,000
Deferred tax liabilities at end of second year.	0
Expected taxable income in year 3	$80,000

Western cannot use the carryback provision of the tax law because it had no taxable income in the carryback years. However, since Western expects to have taxable income from its operations in year 3 in excess of $50,000, this source of expected taxable income is sufficient to realize the tax benefit of the deferred tax asset. No valuation allowance is required.

Now assume that expected future taxable income in year 3 is expected to be only $40,000, and the firm is unable to reasonably expect taxable income in later years. Here, a valuation allowance of $4,000 [($50,000 − $40,000) × .40] is required. The net deferred tax asset, after deducting the valuation allowance, is $16,000 ($20,000 − $4,000) at the end of year 2.

Case B: Using Taxable Income from Prior Years

Taxable income in first year	$40,000
Taxable income in second (current) year	$50,000
Future deductible amounts, end of second year	$50,000
Times future tax rate	× .40
Deferred tax asset at end of second year.	$20,000
Deferred tax liabilities at end of second year	0
Estimated future taxable income exclusive of	
temporary differences	0

The company does not expect to be profitable, but it could consider the carryback provision of the tax law as a source of taxable income that could be used to realize the benefit of the deferred tax asset if it is expected to reverse within the carryback period. Suppose, for example, the entire $50,000 of the deductible amount associated with the deferred tax asset is expected to reverse in year 3. Even if the company does not expect to have taxable income in the third year, it could realize the tax benefit by carrying back the deductible amount as a NOL to years 1 and 2 and obtain a tax refund. No valuation allowance would be required because the benefit of the tax asset is expected to be realized.

Case C: Using Future Reversals of Taxable Amounts

Taxable income in first year	$ 0
Taxable income in second (current) year	0
Future deductible amounts, end of second year	$50,000
Times future tax rate	× .40
Deferred tax asset at end of second year.	$20,000
Future taxable amounts, end of second year	$75,000
Times future tax rate	× .40
Deferred tax liability at end of second year	$30,000
Estimated future taxable income exclusive of	
temporary differences	0

Western cannot use the carryback provision of the tax law because it had no taxable income in the carryback years. Also, Western is uncertain whether future operations will generate taxable income exclusive of reversals of taxable amounts. Assume that the timing of future reversals of taxable amounts is such that they can be used to offset the reversals of the deductible amounts through the carryback-carryforward period: the taxable amount is due to reverse in year 3 and the deductible difference is due to reverse in year 4. Even if the firm had no other transactions in year 4, the deductible difference (an NOL under these circumstances) could be carried back to year 3 to absorb the taxable income in year 3 represented by the taxable difference reversing in that year. These taxable amounts are considered a source of future taxable income that will result in the realization of the tax benefit of the deferred tax asset. Once again, no valuation allowance is required.

The three cases above illustrate situations in which one of the three sources of taxable income could be used to support the conclusion that no valuation allowance is needed because the benefit of the deferred tax asset is more likely than not to be realized.

Adjusting the Valuation Allowance

Annual adjustments to the valuation allowance and deferred tax accounts are handled the same way. At the end of each period, the ending required balance in each account is compared to the beginning balance to determine the required increase or decrease for the period. Income tax expense is derived from the income taxes payable amount and the net change in deferred tax and valuation allowance accounts. The following examples illustrate the use of the valuation allowance.

Example 1—Realization Sources: Future Taxable Income and Taxable Income in Prior Years

1998

Azure, Inc., has no deferred tax accounts at the beginning of 1998.

Pretax accounting income	$20,000
Taxable income	45,000
Future deductible difference, unearned revenue taxed in 1998. $9,000 of the difference is expected to reverse in 2002, and $16,000 is expected to reverse in 2003. Total deductible difference	25,000
Amount of future taxable income more likely than not to be earned	15,000
Tax rate	40%

No additional sources for realizing the deferred tax asset are available.

1998 tax accrual entry:

Income tax expense	12,000	
Deferred tax asset ($25,000 × .40)	10,000	
Income taxes payable ($45,000 × .40)		18,000
Valuation allowance ($25,000 − $15,000).40		4,000

The only source for realizing the deferred tax asset as of the end of 1998 is future taxable income. The $25,000 deductible difference cannot be carried back to 1998 which is more than three years previous to 2002 (earliest expected reversal) and therefore outside the limit for carrybacks. Also, only $15,000 of future taxable income is more than likely. Therefore, the remaining $10,000 cannot be used to support the deferred tax asset. Thus, a valuation allowance of $4,000 ($10,000 × .40) is needed. The net deferred tax asset is computed as:

1. $10,000 deferred tax asset less $4,000 valuation allowance = $6,000, or
2. $15,000 (expected usable deductible difference) × .40 = $6,000.

The valuation allowance is a separate account and is subtracted from the deferred tax asset in the balance sheet or footnotes. At the end of 1998, the net value of Azure's deferred tax asset is $6,000 because only that much of a reduction in future taxes can be anticipated based on the information available at the end of 1998.

1999

Pretax and taxable income	$22,000
Tax rate	40%
Amount of future taxable income more likely than not to be earned	$ 8,000

No additional temporary differences are generated in 1999.

Computations leading to the tax accrual entry:

1. At the end of 1999, the full $25,000 of deductible difference originating in 1998 has yet to reverse. However, the $9,000 portion of this difference expected to reverse in 2002 could be carried back to 1999 as an NOL. The reversing deductible difference, even if it were the only item in Azure's 2002 tax return, can be carried back at most three years. The earliest year within the three-year limit must be used first. Taxable income in 1999 exceeds the $9,000 reversal. Thus $9,000 of the deductible difference is supported by prior taxable income.

2. $8,000 of future taxable income is more likely than not to be earned. This supports an additional $8,000 of the deductible difference.

Now there are two sources of support: prior and future taxable income. In total, $17,000 ($9,000 + $8,000) of the $25,000 future deductible difference is supported.

	Deferred Tax Asset	Valuation Allowance
Ending 1998 balances:	$10,000	$4,000
Ending 1999 balances:		
$25,000(.40).	10,000	
($25,000 − $17,000).40.		3,200
Decrease in account	$　　0	$　800

1999 tax accrual entry:

Income tax expense	8,000	
Valuation allowance	800	
Income taxes payable ($22,000 $\times$ .40)		8,800

At the end of 1999, only $3,200 of valuation allowance is needed. This represents the tax effect of the $8,000 ($25,000 − $17,000) of deductible difference that is expected not to be usable as the foundation for the deferred tax asset.

Example 2—Realization Source: Taxable Income in Prior Years

Azure, Inc., has no deferred tax accounts at the beginning of 1998.

1998 pretax accounting loss	($18,000)
1998 taxable income	7,000
Future deductible difference, unearned revenue taxed in 1998.	
$10,000 of the difference is expected to reverse in 1999, and $15,000	
is expected to reverse in 2000. Total deductible difference	25,000
Taxable income earned in each of the prior years 1994–1997	2,000
Tax rate	40%
No additional sources for realizing the deferred tax asset are available.	

In this example, part of the $25,000 deductible difference originating in 1998 could be carried back as an NOL to 1997, and 1998, absorbing the taxable income in those years.

Schedule of support for realization of deferred tax asset, end of 1998:

1. Carryback of $2,000 of the 1999 ($10,000) reversal of deductible difference to 1996	$2,000
2. Carryback of $2,000 of the 1999 ($10,000) reversal of deductible difference to 1997	2,000
3. Carryback of the remaining $6,000 of the 1999 ($10,000) reversal of deductible difference to 1998	6,000
4. Carryback of $1,000 of the year 2000 ($15,000) reversal of deductible difference to 1998 (only $1,000 of the 1998 taxable income remains after step 3)	1,000
Total amount of 1998 future deductible difference that can be used to absorb prior years' taxable income	$11,000

Azure has only $11,000 of prior year taxable income available within the three-year carryback limit on NOLs. The remaining $14,000 of the $25,000 deductible difference originating in 1998 will not be realized under the assumptions given. Therefore, the required valuation allowance balance is $5,600 ($14,000 $\times$ .40).

1998 tax accrual entry:

Deferred tax asset ($25,000 $\times$ .40)	10,000	
Income taxes payable ($7,000 $\times$ .40)		2,800
Valuation allowance		5,600
Income tax expense (benefit)		1,600

Income tax expense is negative in this case. Taxes are paid on positive taxable income, but Azure has an accounting loss.

Example 3—Realization Source: Future Reversals of Existing Taxable Differences

Azure, Inc. has no deferred tax accounts at the beginning of 1998.

1998 pretax accounting income	$20,000
1998 taxable income	25,000
Future temporary differences at the end of 1998:	
Taxable, $10,000; half is expected to reverse in 1999, the rest in 2003	
Deductible, $15,000 expected to reverse in 2002	
Tax rate	40%
No additional sources for realizing the deferred tax asset are available.	

1998 tax accrual entry:

Income tax expense	10,000	
Deferred tax asset ($15,000 × .40)	6,000	
Income taxes payable ($25,000 × .40)		10,000
Valuation allowance ($5,000 × .40)		2,000
Deferred tax liability ($10,000 × .40)		4,000

The deferred tax accounts are recorded as usual, based on the future temporary differences existing at the end of 1998. The valuation allowance is computed as follows:

1. $5,000 of the deductible difference can be carried back from 2002 to the reversal of the $5,000 of taxable difference reversing in 1999 (a source of taxable income), three years earlier. Note that the deductible difference cannot absorb the taxable income in 1998, which is four years previous to 2002.
2. Another $5,000 of the deductible difference can be carried forward to the reversal of the $5,000 of taxable difference in 2003.
3. The remaining $5,000 of deductible difference cannot be used. The valuation allowance is based on this unusable amount: $2,000 = $5,000 × .40.

Tax-planning strategies also provide ways that, when implemented, ensure the realization of the benefit of a deferred tax asset.

Tax-Planning Strategies

In the normal course of business, a firm's management undertakes many actions, pursues strategies, and makes elections designed to minimize the firm's long-run tax obligation.

Example A firm might structure its credit sales activities so that sales qualify as installment sales for tax purposes, allowing the deferral of a taxable revenue until cash is received. While this is a kind of tax-planning strategy in the normal or traditional sense, it is not the meaning of the term as intended by *SFAS No. 109.*

For purposes of *SFAS No. 109,* a **tax-planning strategy** is an action meeting these criteria:
- The action would result in the realization of deferred tax assets.
- The firm might not take the action in the ordinary course of business, but would be expected to take it to prevent an operating loss or tax credit carryforward from expiring unused.
- The action is prudent and feasible; management must have the ability to implement the strategy and be expected to do so unless the need to do so is eliminated.

Tax-planning strategies can assist in the realization of deferred tax assets in a number of ways.

Example A tax-planning strategy might shift future taxable income between future years. A firm facing a need for taxable income to realize the benefit of deferred tax assets might structure its sales contracts to include them in taxable income in the current period rather than defer them. Other actions of this nature include changing depreciation schedules and procedures for tax purposes, thereby increasing taxable income in the current year. A firm might even change from the LIFO to the FIFO inventory method to shift taxable income from one period to another.

Alternatively, tax-planning strategies might shift the pattern and timing of future reversal of temporary differences in ways that realize the deferred tax assets. Factoring or selling installment sales receivables accelerates the future reversal of a taxable temporary difference to the period of the sale. Accelerating the reversal of future deductible temporary differences might be an appropriate action in some circumstances.

Example Disposing of obsolete inventory that is reported at net realizable value for book purposes (and at historical cost for tax purposes) would accelerate a tax deduction for the amount of the difference.

A firm might incur a significant expense or significant loss as a result of a tax-planning strategy. The expense or loss reduces the net benefit realized from the tax-planning strategy. The actual amount of the expense or loss is not important so long as the three criteria listed are met. The benefit from the deferred tax asset must be greater than the expense or loss; otherwise, the tax-planning strategy would not be prudent.

Example Suppose the Tasha Sports Company has an operating tax loss carryforward of $10,000 that will expire on December 31, 1998. The current date is December 31, 1997. The enacted marginal tax rate is 30 percent, so the tax loss carryforward results in a deferred tax asset of $3,000 if its realization is more likely than not. Assume the following additional information:

- Management expects taxable income in 1998 to be $2,000 exclusive of the operating tax loss carryforward and any reversal of existing temporary differences.
- At December 31, 1997, a taxable temporary difference totaling $9,000 exists from an installment sale. It is expected to reverse in equal amounts for the next three years.
- Tasha could sell the installment accounts receivable to a financing company for cash and accelerate the reversal of the taxable temporary difference. Tasha would incur legal and other expenses of approximately $1,000 to implement this tax-planning strategy.

If Tasha did not implement the tax-planning strategy, the firm would have taxable income in 1998 of only $5,000 (a reversal of the taxable temporary difference of $3,000 resulting from collection of a portion of the installment sale, and the $2,000 of taxable income expected from operations). Half of the tax loss carryforward would be used to offset taxes payable, but the remaining $5,000 of tax loss carryforward would expire unused. If Tasha did not expect to implement the tax-planning strategy at December 31, 1997, the firm would have to record a valuation allowance of $5,000 times 30 percent, or $1,500 to reflect the amount of the deferred tax asset not expected to be realized.

If Tasha could implement the tax-planning strategy described above, enough taxable income would be generated in 1995 to fully use the tax loss carryforward. The full amount of the installment sale ($9,000) plus the regularly expected taxable income ($2,000) is more than enough to offset the tax loss carryforward. However, the cost of implementing the tax-planning strategy is $1,000, which on an after-tax basis is $700. If the tax-planning strategy meets all the preceding criteria, the strategy can be used as a plan to realize the deferred tax asset benefit. However, the after-tax cost of $700 of the strategy must be recorded as a valuation allowance, because it will have to be incurred if the tax-planning strategy is implemented. The net gain from the tax-planning strategy is $800, which is the difference between the valuation allowance without the strategy ($1,500) and with the strategy ($700). Assuming that the tax-planning strategy is used for the realization of the deferred tax asset, Tasha would report the following in its December 31, 1997, financial statements:

- A deferred tax liability of $2,700, relating to the taxable temporary difference of $9,000.
- A deferred tax asset of $3,000, relating to the tax loss carryforward.
- A valuation allowance of $700, relating to the after-tax expense that would be incurred to implement the tax-planning strategy.
- Income tax expense for 1997 would include the $700 amount recorded as a valuation allowance.

|CONCEPT REVIEW

1. What is a valuation allowance? When is one required?
2. Do taxable temporary differences give rise to deferred tax assets or deferred tax liabilities? What about deductible temporary differences?
3. What is a tax-planning strategy? When is one considered?

|REVIEW PROBLEM   Lake Company (used in an earlier Review Problem in this chapter) continues operations in 1998, with the following activities and results:

- Pretax accounting income in 1998 totals $180,000. This includes $100,000 of installment sales that are not included in taxable income. Collections during 1998 of prior year installment sales total $30,000.
- Included in expenses for financial reporting are estimated warranty costs of $120,000. Warranty costs actually incurred during 1998 total $10,000.
- On January 1, 1998, Lake Company purchases machinery at a cost of $100,000. The machinery has a five-year estimated useful life with zero salvage value. Straight-line depreciation will be used for financial reporting. For tax reporting, the machinery will be depreciated in the amounts of $45,000, $35,000, and $20,000 in 1998, 1999, and 2000, respectively (an accelerated schedule).
- Lake Company sublets a portion of its warehouse to another company and requires rent to be paid in advance. Lake received an advance rent payment of $20,000. This amount is included in taxable income in 1998 but will be included in pretax accounting income in 1999.
- During 1998 a new tax law is enacted, decreasing the marginal tax rate to 35 percent beginning January 1, 1999. (Taxable income in 1998 is taxed at the 40 percent rate.)
- Management is confident the company will continue to be profitable in the future.
- Beginning 1998 deferred tax asset: $20,000; deferred tax liability: $24,000.

Required

Determine income taxes payable, any deferred tax account amounts, and show the journal entry to record income tax expense for 1998.

SOLUTION

The second year has several complications over the first year. The analysis, however, is the same as before. The four steps presented earlier provide the structure for the analysis. Essential accounting and income tax data for the year:

Pretax accounting income $180,000
Temporary differences:

Account	Beginning Balance	Ending Balance	Increase (Decrease)	Type of Difference
Accounts receivable	$60,000	$130,000*	$ 70,000	Taxable
Warranty liability.	(50,000)	(160,000)†	110,000	Deductible
Advances from customers	0	(20,000)	20,000	Deductible
Accumulated tax over book depreciation	0	25,000§	25,000	Taxable

* Beginning balance + Credit sales − Cash collections = $60,000 + $100,000 − $30,000 = $130,000

†Beginning balance + Current period warranty provision − Cash payments for warranties during the period = $50,000 + $120,000 − $10,000 = $160,000

§Tax depreciation in 1998, $45,000. Book depreciation in 1998, $100,000 divided by 5 years, or $20,000. This is a taxable difference because future tax depreciation is $25,000 less than future book depreciation. Future taxable income will increase relative to pretax accounting income.

Steps 1 and 2 Compute the amount of income taxes payable for the year, and compute the end-of-year deferred tax liability and end-of-year deferred tax asset based on future enacted tax rates

Temporary Differences, Taxes Payable, and Deferred Tax Balances

	Current Year 1998	Total for Future Years	Effect on Future Years' Income 1999 and Thereafter Deductible	Effect on Future Years' Income 1999 and Thereafter Taxable
Pretax accounting income (loss)	$180,000			
Temporary differences:				
Credit sales	(70,000)	$130,000	$ 0	$130,000
Warranty costs	110,000	(160,000)	160,000	
Advances from customers	20,000	(20,000)	20,000	

(continued)

Tax over book depreciation.	(25,000)	$25,000		25,000
Net taxable income	215,000			
Total temporary difference		($25,000)	180,000	155,000
Enacted tax rate	**× 0.40**		**× 0.35**	**× 0.35**
Taxes currently payable	$ 86,000			
Deferred tax asset balance, December 31, 1998			$ 63,000	
Deferred tax liability balance, December 31, 1998				$ 54,250

Step 3   Compute the change in the deferred tax asset and liability accounts:

	Deferred Tax	
	Asset*	Liability*
Ending balance (computed in step 2 above)	$63,000	$(54,250)
Less: Beginning balance (taken from opening balances)	20,000	(24,000)
Adjustment amount	$43,000	$(30,250)

*Debit (credit)

Step 4   Prepare the journal entry to record income tax payable, all changes in the deferred tax asset and liability accounts, and income tax expense. The journal entry to record 1998 income taxes is as follows:

Income tax expense (current portion)	86,000	
Deferred tax asset	43,000	
Income tax expense (deferred portion)		12,750
Deferred tax liability		30,250
Income tax payable		86,000

FINANCIAL STATEMENT PRESENTATION AND DISCLOSURES

SFAS No. 109 specifies the required presentation of items related to income taxes. Income taxes payable (or income tax refund receivable) is reported as a current liability (current asset) on a classified balance sheet. Deferred tax assets and deferred tax liabilities are merged into net current and net noncurrent amounts for reporting on a classified balance sheet. The components of deferred tax assets or liabilities are classified as current or noncurrent depending on the classification of the related asset or liability giving rise to the deferred tax item.

Example   Suppose the only temporary difference Elloit Company reports arises from an installment receivable, $100,000 of which is classified as a current asset and $300,000 of which is classified as a noncurrent. Assuming a marginal tax rate of 30 percent and a total deferred tax liability of $120,000 ($400,000 × .30), the firm would report a current deferred tax liability of $30,000 and a noncurrent deferred tax liability of $90,000.

If a deferred tax asset or liability is not related to a specific asset or liability, including a deferred tax asset related to tax loss carryforwards, the classification as current or noncurrent depends on the expected period of reversal. Thus a deferred tax asset arising from a tax loss carryforward is classified as current if management expects the tax benefit to be realized in the following year (assuming an operating cycle of one year or less). If the expectation is that the realization of the benefit will occur in later years, it is classified as noncurrent.

Example   Suppose that O'Hara, Inc., has the following items that give rise to deferred tax assets and liabilities. The tax rate is 30 percent for the current and all future periods.

Items creating deferred tax assets and liabilities at December 31, 1997

Assets—current:

- Prepaid expenses of $40,000. The entire amount has been deducted for tax purposes.

Assets—noncurrent:

- Investment in securities available for sale, classified as a noncurrent asset, has an original cost of $100,000 and a current carrying value (fair value) of $90,000.
- Cumulative tax over book depreciation totals $150,000.

Liabilities—current:

- Warranty liability of $30,000

Liabilities—noncurrent:

- A long-term accrued liability for postretirement benefits other than pensions of $200,000 has not been deducted for tax purposes.

Not related to a classified item on the balance sheet:

- The firm has a tax loss carryforward of $50,000. The benefit relating the NOL carryforward is not expected to be realized in 1998.

We can determine the ending deferred tax asset/liability balances and classify each as current or noncurrent based on the information given above:

Item	Taxable (Deductible) Temporary Difference Amount	Deferred Tax Assets (Liabilities) Current	Noncurrent	Total
Prepaid expenses	$ 40,000	$(12,000)		$(12,000)
Investment in SAS	(10,000)		$ 3,000	3,000
Tax over book depreciation	150,000		(45,000)	(45,000)
Warranty liability	(30,000)	9,000		9,000
Postretirement liability	(200,000)		60,000	60,000
NOL carryforward	(50,000)		15,000	15,000
Net deferred tax asset (liability)		$ (3,000)	$33,000	$30,000

The total deferred tax asset amount is $87,000 ($9,000 + $3,000 + $60,000 + $15,000). The total deferred tax liability amount is $57,000 ($12,000 + $45,000). On the balance sheet, however, O'Hara would present a current deferred tax liability of $3,000 and a noncurrent deferred tax asset of $33,000.

SFAS No. 109 is silent on how valuation allowances are to be classified. The valuation allowance classification is likely to be linked to the timing of when the opportunity to utilize the deferred tax asset would expire.

Example   A valuation allowance established because a tax loss carryforward that will expire in the coming year is not likely to be realized, would be classified as current. The valuation allowance should be associated with the part of the deferred tax asset not expected to be realized.

Additional Disclosures   In addition to the above presentation, footnotes to the financial statements should provide the following supplemental disclosures regarding deferred tax assets and liabilities:

> The total of all deferred tax liabilities ($57,000).
> The total of all deferred tax assets ($87,000).

A publicly held company also must disclose the approximate tax effect of each major source of temporary difference and carryforward that gives rise to significant portions of deferred tax assets and liabilities. If a firm has NOL carryforwards or other tax credit carryforwards, it must disclose their amounts and expiration dates. For the preceding example, the following presentations and disclosures are appropriate:

> On the balance sheet:
> Noncurrent assets: Deferred tax assets $33,000
> Current liabilities: Deferred tax liabilities   3,000

The notes to the 1997 financial statements would include the following disclosures:

Temporary differences give rise to significant portions of deferred tax
assets and liabilities at December 31, 1997:

Source	Deferred Tax Assets	Deferred Tax Liabilities
Prepaid expenses		$12,000
Accrued warranties liability	$ 9,000	
Excess of tax over book depreciation		45,000
Excess cost over carrying value of investments	3,000	
Postretirement liability	60,000	
Net operating loss carryforward	15,000	
Totals	$87,000	$57,000

Finally, the notes must provide a reconciliation between the effective tax rate (computed by dividing income tax expense by income before taxes) to the U.S. statutory rate (currently 35 percent). This reconciliation would identify permanent differences that affect the effective tax rate, and also the effects of paying taxes in jurisdictions other than the United States. The reconciliation can be either in percentage format (as is found in Coca-Cola's Note 15) or in a dollar amount format.

Example   Fowler Inc. has pretax accounting income of $100,000 and the federal statutory tax rate is 35 percent. Fowler has no temporary differences, so there is no deferred tax component to income tax expense. However, Fowler has the following permanent difference items:
- Interest income of $20,000 resulting from an investment in tax-exempt municipal bonds.
- Fines paid of $30,000 relating to several environmental laws that were violated. The fines are not tax deductible.

Since there are no temporary differences, income tax expense will be equal to income taxes payable. The first issue is to determine the amount of income taxes payable in 1998:

Pretax accounting income		$100,000
Adjustments:		
Less: Tax-exempt income	$(20,000)	
Addback: Expenses not tax deductible	30,000	10,000
Taxable income		$110,000
U.S. federal tax rate		$\times$ .35
Income taxes payable		$ 38,500

Again since there are no temporary differences, income tax expense is $38,500. The required reconciliation could be in either of the following two formats:

A reconciliation of the statutory U.S. federal tax rate and effective rates

	Dollar Format	Percentage[‖] Format
Income taxes at statutory rate* · · · · · · · · · · · ·	$35,000	35%
Tax-exempt income† · · · · · · · · · · · · · · · · ·	(7,000)	(7)
Non-deductible expense§ · · · · · · · · · · · · · ·	10,500	10.5
Income taxes payable (Effective tax rate) · · · · · ·	$38,500	38.5%

*$100,000 $\times$ .35
†$20,000 $\times$ .35
§$30,000 $\times$ .35
‖Percent of pretax accounting income, $100,000

Intraperiod Tax Allocation

SFAS No. 109 requires intraperiod tax allocation for items such as income from continuing operations, discontinued operations, extraordinary items, certain accounting changes, and other items charged or credited directly to shareholders' equity (for example, prior-period adjustments). The amount allocated to continuing operations includes the tax effect of the pretax income or loss from continuing operations for the year, plus or minus the income tax effect of

- Changes in tax laws or rates.
- Changes in tax status.
- Changes in estimates about the realization of deferred tax assets.
- Tax-deductible dividends paid to shareholders.

If only one item subject to intraperiod tax allocation remains after the above allocation to continuing operations, the remainder of the unallocated income tax expense is allocated to it. If more than one item remains, the tax effect of each item is determined and the remaining unallocated income tax expense is allocated ratably to each item.

Example   Seeley Corporation reports pretax accounting income of $6,000, resulting from a loss of $3,000 from continuing operations and an extraordinary gain (taxable at capital gain rates) of $9,000. Taxable income is $4,000. The difference is a future taxable temporary difference, and it gives rise to a deferred tax liability of $800. The tax rate is 40 percent on ordinary income and 30 percent on capital gains. The capital gain is used to offset the operating loss, so income taxes payable are $4,000 times the capital gains tax rate of 30 percent, or $1,200. Income tax expense totals $2,000 ($1,200 plus the $800 deferred tax liability).

The allocation of income tax expense begins with the loss from continuing operations of $3,000. The normal tax rate would be 40 percent, but in this instance the tax benefit from the loss has been to offset a capital gain. Therefore, the tax rate used to determine the allocation to continuing operations is the capital gains rate:

Total income tax expense	$2,000
Tax benefit allocated to loss from continuing operations: $3,000 × .30	900
Incremental tax expense allocated to extraordinary gain	$2,900

Additional Disclosures

The following significant components of income tax expense attributable to continuing operations must be disclosed, either in the financial statements or in disclosure notes:

- The current portion of income tax expense or benefit.
- The deferred portion of income tax expense or benefit.
- Any investment tax credits.
- Government grants to the extent they are used as reductions of income tax expense.
- The benefits of operating loss carryforwards.
- Adjustments of deferred tax assets or liabilities as a result of enacted tax law or rate changes or changes in the tax status of the firm.

If income tax expense or benefit is allocated to items in addition to continuing operations, the amounts allocated separately to these additional items must be disclosed for each year for which those items are presented.

SUMMARY OF KEY POINTS

(L.O. 1)   1. Taxable income and pretax accounting income usually differ. Income measurement for financial reporting results from applying generally accepted accounting principles. Income measurement for purposes of determining income taxes payable is governed by the tax laws and their interpretation by the Internal Revenue Service and state income tax authorities.

(L.O. 1)   2. There are two types of differences between pretax accounting income and taxable income. The first is permanent differences, in which a revenue or expense item is included in the determination of either pretax accounting income or taxable income, but does not and will not ever appear in the computation of the other. Permanent differences have no future tax consequences. Thus they do not require the recognition of deferred tax assets or deferred tax liabilities.

(L.O. 1)   3. The second type of difference is a temporary difference. Temporary differences are items that are included in the current- or past-period determination of either pretax accounting income or taxable income, but not both, and are expected to be included in the other at a later date.

(L.O. 2)   4. Under GAAP, the tax consequences of temporary differences are measured and included in the computation of income tax expense. GAAP requires the asset/liability method be used for interperiod tax allocation.

(L.O. 2)   5. Under the asset/liability method, the tax consequences of temporary differences are analyzed to determine what the tax effects will be in the future periods in which the temporary differences reverse. The enacted tax rates for those future periods are applied to the temporary differences to determine the future (deferred) tax asset and liability. The income tax expense for the period is income taxes payable plus the net change in deferred tax asset and liability amounts during the period.

(L.O. 4)   6. A tax benefit related to a taxable loss can be realized by carrying back the loss to three immediately prior periods, oldest period first, for a refund of taxes previously paid on amounts of taxable income equal to the amount of the net operating loss. Benefits also can be realized in the future by carrying the loss forward up to 15 years to offset taxable income in future periods.

(L.O. 4)   7. At the time a net operating loss occurs, a firm can either elect to carry back the loss (and also use the carryforward provision for any amounts of the loss not recovered by the carryback provision), or the firm can elect only to carry forward the net operating loss to offset future taxable income. The choice must be made in the period of the loss, and it is irrevocable.

(L.O. 2, 3)   8. *SFAS No. 109* imposes a limitation on the net amount of a deferred tax asset that can be reported. After any deferred tax asset is recorded, a determination is made regarding the likelihood that the benefit of the deferred tax asset will be realized. If it is more likely than not that some portion of the deferred tax asset will not be realized as a benefit, a valuation allowance is established as a contra account to the deferred tax asset. Changes in the valuation allowance are a component of income tax expense.

(L.O. 3)   9. Deferred tax assets and liabilities are classified as either current or noncurrent, depending on the classification of the asset or liability giving rise to the deferred tax item. Current deferred tax assets and current deferred tax liabilities are offset, and a net current deferred tax asset or liability is reported. The same type of offset is applied to noncurrent deferred tax assets and liabilities.

▌REVIEW PROBLEM

The Duesing Company began operations in 1992, engaging in a number of business activities ranging from manufacturing and marketing durable goods to writing technical business textbooks on which the firm collects royalty income. The accounting for these many activities resulted in a number of differences between reporting for book and tax purposes. For financial reporting purposes, the company accrued estimated warranty costs when it sold products under warranty, deferred advance royalty payments it received, and prepaid many operating expenses. For tax purposes it recognized warranty costs when paid, royalty income when cash was received, and operating expenses when cash was paid. The opening and closing balances in these accounts for 1997 were as follows:

Balance: Debit (credit)	January 1	December 31	Change during Year
Accrued warranty costs	$(50,000)	$(40,000)	$10,000
Deferred royalty income	(10,000)	(40,000)	(30,000)
Prepaid expenses	33,000	25,000	(8,000)

All three accounts are classified as current items on the balance sheet. The company depreciates its manufacturing equipment using an accelerated method for tax purposes and straight line for financial reporting. The schedule of book and tax depreciation for 1997 and all remaining years for the company's existing equipment is as follows:

Year	Book Depreciation	Tax Depreciation
1997 (current year)	$ 9,000	$14,000
Future years:		
1998	$9,000	$ 9,000
1999	9,000	6,000
2000	9,000	3,000
Totals	$27,000	$18,000

The company's 1997 pretax accounting income was $8,000. This includes $2,000 of interest income on municipal bonds that is not taxable. The history of taxable income reported by the company since it began operations is as follows:

Year	Taxable Income (Loss)
1992	$ 2,000
1993	17,000
1994	(78,000)
1995	24,000
1996	9,000

The company elected the carryback–carryforward option for the 1994 loss. As of January 1, 1997, $52,000 of the NOL had been used, leaving a carryforward balance of $26,000.

The marginal tax rate the company expected to be effective in 1997 and 1998 (and for all prior years) is 34 percent. However, during 1997 a tax law was enacted that will change the tax rate to 40 percent for 1999 and subsequent years.

There are no prior taxes currently payable, nor any prior tax refunds currently receivable. At January 1, 1997, there are opening balances in the deferred tax asset account of $29,240, in the valuation allowance of $5,100, and in the deferred tax liability account of $15,980.

Required

1. Determine the 1997 income tax expense assuming that the company expects taxable income exclusive of temporary differences to be $20,000 in 1998 but that it cannot support a forecast of taxable income for subsequent years.
2. Prepare the journal entry to record the company's income tax expense for 1997, and determine the net current and noncurrent deferred tax asset and deferred tax liability to be reported in the balance sheet.

|SOLUTION

The solution to this problem begins with the worksheet computation of income taxes payable and the ending deferred tax asset and liability balances as presented in Exhibit 19–4. Because of the NOL in 1994 of $78,000, there are tax loss carrybacks and carryforwards that must be considered in addition to the temporary differences.

The temporary differences are identified and categorized on the top portion of the worksheet under the columns for 1997, 1998, and 1999 and thereafter. The 1997 column computes taxable income starting from pretax accounting income. The adjustments begin with subtraction of the nontaxable permanent difference (municipal interest income of $2,000). The next four items in the 1997 column are the current-year effects of either originating or reversing temporary differences. After these adjustments are made, taxable income for 1997 is $29,000. Carryforward of the remaining $26,000 of the 1994 NOL reduces the taxable income to $3,000.

The columns for 1998 and 1999 and thereafter are further divided into deductible and taxable columns in order to determine the deferred tax asset and deferred tax liability amounts. The two different future period columns are needed because there is a known, enacted change in the tax rate for 1999 and thereafter. The new tax rate must be used for temporary differences reversing in 1999 and thereafter in determining the deferred tax asset or liability.

Once the taxable income and temporary differences are determined, the worksheet proceeds to compute taxes payable in 1997 of $1,020 and gross amounts of deferred tax assets and liabilities at December 31, 1997, of $27,200 and $12,100 (equal to $8,500 plus $3,600) respectively.

The top portion of Exhibit 19–5 computes the amount of the valuation allowance under the assumption that taxable income exclusive of temporary differences will be $20,000 in 1998 and zero thereafter. On the valuation allowance worksheet, the gross amounts of future deductible temporary differences are entered, and then sources of income are considered. Three sources are used:

1. Future reversing taxable temporary differences: $25,000 in 1998 and $9,000 in 1999 and thereafter. A deductible difference—a potential future NOL—can be carried forward 15 years and be offset against reversing taxable differences.
2. Estimated taxable income: $20,000 in 1998 and $0 thereafter.
3. A tax loss carryback of $3,000 to 1997, recovering taxes paid in 1997 of $1,020. The worksheet shows that $23,000 of the deductible temporary difference is not expected to be realized; therefore, a valuation allowance balance of $7,820 is required at December 31, 1997.

EXHIBIT 19–4   Worksheet to Compute Deferred Tax Asset and Liability for Duesing Company

							Effect on Future Years' Income			
	1992	1993	1994	1995	1996	1997	1998 Deductible	1998 Taxable	1999 and Thereafter Deductible	1999 and Thereafter Taxable
Pretax accounting income (loss)						$ 8,000				
Less: Nontaxable income						(2,000)				
Temporary differences:										
Warranty costs						(10,000)	$40,000			
Royalty income						30,000	40,000			
Prepaid expenses						8,000		$25,000		
Depreciation						(5,000)				$9,000
Net taxable income before carryback and carryforward	$ 2,000	$17,000	($78,000)	$24,000	$9,000	29,000				
Total temporary differences							80,000	25,000	0	9,000
Net operating loss carrybacks and carryforwards	($2,000)	($17,000)	$78,000	($24,000)	($9,000)	(26,000)* 3,000				
Total future taxable and deductible amounts							80,000	25,000	0	9,000
Marginal tax rate						×0.34	×0.34	×0.34	×0.40	×0.40
Taxes currently payable						$ 1,020				
Gross deferred tax asset at December 31, 1997							$27,200		$ 0	
Gross deferred tax liability at December 31, 1997								$ 8,500		$ 3,600

*Remaining NOL to be applied to 1997 taxable income.

The worksheet in the second portion of Exhibit 19–5 presents the computation of the amounts to be recorded in the deferred tax asset and liability accounts and in the valuation allowance account to adjust these accounts to their correct ending balances. In each case, the other side of the entry is to income tax expense. The worksheet also determines the classification of current and noncurrent amounts of deferred tax assets and liabilities and presents the journal entry to record income tax expense, taxes payable, changes in the deferred tax asset and liability accounts, and change in the valuation allowance. The income tax expense for the period can be computed as:

Computation of Income Tax Expense

Income taxes payable (from Exhibit 19–4)	$1,020
Less: Decrease in deferred tax liability (from Exhibit 19–5)	(3,880)
Add: Decrease in deferred tax asset (from Exhibit 19–5)	2,040
Add: Increase in valuation allowance (from Exhibit 19–5)	2,720
Income tax expense	$1,900

The current portion of income tax expense is $1,020, and the deferred portion is $880.

The classification of the deferred tax asset and liability amounts as current and noncurrent is determined by the classification of the related balance sheet items giving rise to them. After these amounts are determined and the ending valuation allowance determined, the current asset and liability amounts are netted for presentation on the balance sheet as a net current deferred tax asset of $10,880. The same netting concept applies to noncurrent asset and liability amounts, resulting in a noncurrent liability of $3,600 for Duesing Company.

EXHIBIT 19–5
Valuation Allowance and Balance Sheet Classification Worksheet

Valuation Allowance Worksheet
Assumption: Expect Taxable Income of $20,000 in 1998, and Zero in 1999 and Thereafter

		1998	1999 and Thereafter
Gross deductible temporary difference		$80,000	$ 0
Less:			
Gross taxable temporary difference	$25,000		$ 9,000
Estimated taxable income before temporary differences	20,000	45,000	0
			9,000
Excess deductible (taxable)		35,000	(9,000)
Carryforward of future deductible amounts to offset future taxable amounts		(9,000)	9,000
Carryback of future deductible amounts to offset 1997 taxable income		(3,000)	
Excess deductible amounts not expected to be realized		23,000	
Marginal tax rate		×0.34	
Valuation allowance		$ 7,820	

Adjustments and Balance Sheet Classification—Debit (credit)

Debit (credit)	Gross Amount	Current	Noncurrent
Deferred tax asset, December 31, 1997	$ 27,200	$ 27,200	$ 0
Deferred tax asset, January 1, 1997	29,240		
Adjustment (include in income tax expense)	$ (2,040)		
Valuation allowance, December 31, 1997	$ (7,820)	(7,820)	
Valuation allowance, January 1, 1997	(5,100)		
Adjustment (include in income tax expense)	$ (2,720)		
Net deferred tax asset after valuation allowance		19,380	0
Deferred tax liability, December 31, 1997 ($8,500 plus $3,600)	$(12,100)	(8,500)	(3,600)
Deferred tax liability, January 1, 1997	(15,980)		
Adjustment (include in income tax expense)	$ 3,880		
Net deferred tax asset (liability) reported on balance sheet		$ 10,880	$(3,600)

Journal Entry

Deferred tax liability	3,880	
Income tax expense	1,900	
Income taxes payable		1,020
Deferred tax asset		2,040
Valuation allowance		2,720

APPENDIX   *Investment Tax Credit and Additional Conceptual Issues*

Investment Tax Credit

The **investment tax credit (ITC)** is an income tax provision implemented from time to time by the federal government to encourage investments in new productive assets such as plant and equipment. First enacted as part of the federal tax regulations in 1962, it has been repealed and restored seven times in the past 30 years. Prior to its repeal in the Tax Reform Act of 1986, the law provided that taxpayers could receive a tax credit equal to 10 percent of the purchase price of qualifying new asset purchases as a direct offset to income tax payable. The tax credit was important because it was an immediate tax savings in the year of purchase. A tax credit, as opposed to a tax deduction, results in a direct dollar-for-dollar tax saving. A tax deduction decreases income tax only by the deduction amount multiplied by the income tax rate. Also, the ITC did not reduce the tax basis of the asset to which it applied.

The first investment tax credit was provided by the Revenue Act of 1962. Its provisions were revised by the 1964 act, suspended in 1966, and restored in 1967. The Revenue Act of 1978 set the credit permanently at 10 percent of the cost of qualifying property; however, the Tax Reform Act of 1986 again suspended the ITC.

Accounting rules for the ITC have been issued and are still in effect. Because the financial statements of some companies still report deferred investment tax credits, and the ITC might be restored at some future time, the accounting standards applicable to the ITC are briefly discussed next.

Two alternative methods are acceptable under GAAP for recording and reporting the ITC:

1. **Flow-through (or current reduction) method** Under the **flow-through method for ITC,** the full amount of the ITC is recorded and reported as a direct reduction of income tax expense in the period in which the related asset is acquired. Income taxes payable is debited and income tax expense is credited for the amount of the ITC. The full amount of the ITC *flows through* the current-period income statement. As a result, it increases the reported income in the period of acquisition on a dollar-for-dollar basis. This method relates the ITC to the purchase, rather than to the use, of the asset.

2. **Deferral (or allocated reduction) method** Under the **deferral method for ITC,** the total amount of the ITC is recorded (credited) to an account labeled *deferred investment tax credit.* This account may appear among the liabilities on the balance sheet or, less frequently, as a contra account to the related asset account. The ITC is allocated to each period over the life of the asset as a direct reduction of periodic income tax expense. The ITC amount decreases reported income tax expense over the estimated useful life of the asset that caused it. This method relates the ITC to the use, rather than to the purchase, of the asset.

Example   Suppose in 1985 Trans National Airways (TNA) purchased 10 Boeing 747 airplanes for a total purchase price of $400 million, and the purchase qualified for a 10 percent investment tax credit. The airplanes have an estimated useful life of 20 years. TNA had taxable income of $200 million in the year of the purchase, and the income tax rate was 30 percent. TNA has no other permanent or temporary differences.

The income tax payable in 1985 by TNA is computed as follows:

Taxable income		$200 million
Tax rate		× .30
Income taxes payable before investment tax credit		60 million
Less: Investment tax credit:		
Qualified assets acquired	$400 million	
ITC rate	× .10	40 million
Taxes payable (after ITC)		$ 20 million

The two alternative methods of accounting for the $40 million of ITC are shown in the 1985 entries for TNA.

A. Flow-through method
   1. To record income taxes payable and income tax expense before consideration of the ITC:

Income tax expense	60 million	
Income taxes payable		60 million

   2. To record the ITC:

Income taxes payable	40 million	
Income tax expense		40 million

The entire amount of the ITC flows through to reduce income tax expense in the current period.

B. Deferral method
   1. To record income taxes payable and income tax expense before consideration of the ITC:

Income tax expense	60 million	
Income taxes payable		60 million

2. To record the ITC:

Income tax payable . . . . 40 million
    Deferred investment tax credit . . . .   40 million

3. To record the first year of amortization of the deferred ITC:

Deferred investment tax credit ($40 million/20 years) . . . . 2 million
    Income tax expense . . . .   2 million

For the flow-through method, the entire $40 million is recognized as a reduction of income tax expense in the year in which the ITC arises, thus increasing net income by this amount in the year of the acquisition. Under the deferral method, the ITC is deferred and recognized as a reduction of income tax expense in the amount of $2 million for each year during the airplanes' useful lives.

Many accountants believe the deferral method to be conceptually preferable. They view the benefit of the ITC (immediate reduction of taxes payable) as attaching to the assets that gave rise to it, not to the period in which the IRS allows the tax reduction. The tax code has generally provided for recapture of the ITC if the firm sells the assets that generated the ITC in the immediate future (generally within five years). Nonetheless, the majority of firms used the flow-through method to account for investment tax credits, thus recognizing the immediate increase in earnings.

<table>
<tr><td>

Additional Conceptual Issues in Interperiod Tax Allocation

</td><td>

Two additional conceptual issues relate to how interperiod tax allocation might be accomplished.

Comprehensive or Partial Allocation   Assume a company must always pay its rent one year in advance. Thus, when there is a reversal of the temporary difference that arose in the prior year, there is also a new and equal temporary difference arising in the current year that exactly offsets the reversal. In cases such as this, an argument could be made for not allocating income taxes. Because of the recurring nature of the activity, a deferred tax amount is recorded on the balance sheet that is never removed. Under **partial allocation,** temporary differences that are not expected to experience a net reversal in the foreseeable future are not allocated. The logic is that when regular, similar, and recurring transactions occur that continually create temporary differences that offset subsequent reversals of the temporary differences and indefinitely postpone the tax payments, no allocation is needed.

</td></tr>
</table>

Many transactions might be considered in this category, such as depreciation for manufacturing companies that are continually making investments in capital equipment, or merchandising companies that have continuous installment sales. Taking the continuous investment in capital goods as an example, the firm can, under current tax law, depreciate those assets over a period considerably shorter than their estimated useful lives. This gives rise to a temporary difference. However, as the firm replaces worn-out assets (especially if it increases its level of investment in the assets and the assets are viewed as a group), the deferred taxes arising from the new assets offsets the reversing deferred taxes arising from earlier-period assets.

The alternative to partial allocation is **comprehensive allocation.** Under comprehensive allocation, all the temporary differences entering into the determination of pretax accounting income are considered in the computation of deferred taxes and income tax expense, regardless of their size or recurrent nature.

Arguments in favor of partial interperiod tax allocation include the following:

- Income tax temporary differences are not like other accounting items, such as accounts payable. Accounts payable roll over with actual payment transactions, whereas recurring deferred tax items do not result in tax payments.
- Comprehensive allocation is not a good representation of tax assets and liabilities. The tax regulations creating temporary differences are expected to continue indefinitely; thus, future originating differences are likely to continue to offset reversing temporary differences.
- Partial allocation improves the ability to predict future cash flows for the firm because future tax payments are more closely related to these amounts than to comprehensive tax allocation amounts.
- Accounting results should not be distorted by using a rigid, mechanical method for computing deferred income taxes.

All GAAP pronouncements to date, however, have required comprehensive interperiod tax allocation. The primary arguments for this point of view are as follows:

- All individual temporary differences do eventually reverse. They are not permanent. Financial statements should not be prepared under the assumption that reversal will not take place. (The manufacturing firm may wish to decrease its investment in capital equipment, which would cause a reversal.) The focus is on the individual items giving rise to temporary differences, not on the group.
- Partial allocation violates the matching concept. It is not proper to offset the income tax effects of current transactions with possible future transactions.
- Matching requires that the effects of transactions, including temporary differences, be reported in the period in which they arose.

Current GAAP requires comprehensive allocation and currently there is not much support in the accounting and business communities for moving to partial allocation.

Discounting   A second conceptual issue is the possibility of discounting the deferred tax amount on the balance sheet to reflect its present value. This possibility seems to be consistent with the framework and rationale that underlie the asset/liability method. The discounting concept takes into account the expected time of payment of the deferred tax and would record the deferred tax amount at its present value. If temporary differences do not reverse until many years in the future, the deferred tax balance reflects the present value of the expected future cash flows. Proponents of discounting argue that discounting is consistent with the accounting principles used in accounting for long-term notes receivable and payable and for pensions and leases. Others argue that discounting results in a mismatching of the full tax effects of taxable transactions with the transactions themselves. The basic transaction giving rise to taxes occurs in one period, and the related tax effects are recorded over subsequent periods as the interest on the deferred tax balance is recorded. Opponents of discounting also argue that discounting would tend to hide the true tax consequences of transactions because they become buried in the subsequent interest expense. Finally, opponents argue that deferred taxes are essentially an interest-free loan from the government; hence, the appropriate interest rate to use in discounting is zero, and a zero interest rate results in no discounting.

Current GAAP does not allow for discounting of deferred taxes, and discounting is not likely to be accepted in the near future. None of the examples in this chapter used discounting. The computational complexities are also formidable.

UNDERSTANDING AND APPLYING CONCEPTS AND STANDARDS

QUESTIONS

1. Briefly distinguish between interperiod tax allocation and intraperiod tax allocation.
2. Relate the matching principle to interperiod tax allocation.
3. Explain why deferred income tax can be either an asset or a liability.
4. Briefly define pretax accounting income and taxable income.
5. Define an income tax difference. Identify and briefly define the two types of differences.
6. XTE Corporation (*a*) uses straight-line depreciation for its financial accounting and uses accelerated depreciation on its income tax return, and (*b*) holds a $50,000 investment in tax-free municipal bonds. What kind of tax difference is caused by each of these items? Explain.
7. Does the word *deferred* in *deferred tax liability* mean that deferred income tax is always a long-term (noncurrent) item? Explain.
8. ATW Corporation has completed an analysis of its accounting income, taxable income, and the temporary differences. Taxable income is $100,000, and there are several temporary differences, which result in (*a*) a deferred tax asset of $15,000 and (*b*) a deferred tax liability of $20,000. The income tax rate for the current and all future periods is 32 percent. There were no deferred tax assets or deferred tax liabilities as of the beginning of the current year. Give the entry to record income taxes and indicate how the amounts were determined.
9. Explain the difference between a taxable temporary difference and a deductible temporary difference.
10. Briefly explain how the asset/liability method links to the conceptual framework found in the *Statements of Financial Accounting Concepts*.
11. Suppose Wilson Company has one item that gives rise to a temporary difference, and that item is expected to continue indefinitely. Specifically, Wilson prepays the following year's annual rent of $100,000 each

December 31. In years subsequent to the first year, what will the effects be of (*a*) no allocation and (*b*) the asset/liability method on the income statement and the balance sheet? Assume a constant tax rate of 40 percent.

12. Explain the difference between a deferred tax liability and a deferred tax asset.

13. Define net operating loss (NOL), carrybacks, and carryforwards. Briefly explain the options available to taxpayers.

14. With respect to NOL carrybacks and carryforwards, which one involves greater certainty of realization? How does this difference in uncertainty affect the accounting treatment for loss carrybacks and carryforwards?

15. Is deferred tax arising from an NOL carryforward classified as current or noncurrent?

16. Explain the limitation on the carrying value of deferred income tax assets under *SFAS No. 109.*

17. RVA Corporation's accounting and income tax records provided the following data at the end of 1997: pretax accounting income, $60,000; deductible temporary differences, $14,000; taxable income, $50,000; and taxable temporary differences, $23,000. Prepare a reconciliation of pretax accounting income and taxable income.

18. Bye Corporation is preparing its 1997 financial statements. Its pretax amounts are income before extraordinary items, $300,000; extraordinary gain, $20,000; and prior-period adjustment, $16,000 (a loss). Interperiod income tax computations showed income tax expense (including the prior-period adjustment) of $104,880. How much income tax should be allocated to each of the three intraperiod amounts?

▌*EXERCISES*

E 19–1
(L.O. 1, 2)

Analysis of Interperiod Income Tax Deferrals   Listed below are six independent situations that require interperiod income tax allocation. For each item indicate with a check mark whether the deferred income tax account would be an asset or a liability.

	The Deferred Income Tax Account Would Be	
Item	**Asset**	**Liability**
a. Construction contracts: percentage of completion for accounting and completed contract for income tax	______	______
b. Estimated warranty costs: accrual basis for accounting and cash basis for income tax	______	______
c. Straight-line depreciation for accounting and accelerated depreciation for income tax	______	______
d. Unrealized gain on investments: fair value recognized for accounting, but gain recognized only on disposal of the asset for income tax	______	______
e. Rent revenue collected in advance: accrual basis for accounting, cash basis for income tax	______	______
f. Unrealized loss on investments: fair value recognized for accounting but loss recognized only on disposal of the asset for income tax	______	______

E 19–2
(L.O. 1, 2)

Terminology Overview   Listed below to the left are some terms frequently used in *SFAS No. 109*. Brief definitions are listed to the right. Match the definitions with the terms by entering the appropriate letters in the blanks.

______ 1. Deferred tax asset.

______ 2. Taxable amount.

______ 3. Permanent difference.

______ 4. Valuation allowance.

______ 5. Temporary difference.

______ 6. Taxable income.

______ 7. Net current deferred tax liability.

______ 8. Income tax expense.

______ 9. NOL carryback/carryforward

______ 10. Intraperiod income tax allocation.

A. Income tax payable plus net changes in the deferred tax liability, deferred tax asset, and valuation allowance accounts.

B. An amount used to compute income tax payable.

C. The difference between a current deferred tax asset and a current deferred tax liability when the latter is higher.

D. May result in a cash refund or a reduction of income tax payable in future periods.

E. An amount used to compute deferred tax assets and liabilities, and a portion of income tax expense.

F. A deferred tax amount that has a debit balance.

G. A tax difference that does not reverse, or turn around.

H. An allocation of tax among the components in the income statement.

I. A contra account used to reduce deferred tax assets to the portion more likely than not to be realized.

J. An amount that represents a difference between financial accounting and tax accounting that will increase taxable income in future periods.

E 19–3
(L.O. 3)

Reporting Deferred Income Tax on the Balance Sheet   At the end of 1998, Raleigh Corporation had a $90,000 credit balance in its deferred tax liability account. The income tax rate was 30 percent. This credit balance was due to the following two temporary differences:

a. Depreciation for accounting purposes, $200,000, and for income tax purposes, $300,000. The related asset has a five-year remaining life.
b. Installment sale revenue for accounting purposes, $600,000, and for income tax purposes, $400,000. The collection period for the $200,000 receivable is the following four years with equal amounts each year.

Required   Show how the deferred tax amounts would be reported on the 1998 balance sheet. Show computations.

E 19–4
(L.O. 2, 3)

Recording and Reporting Income Tax Consequences for a Two-Year Period   The records of Star Corporation provided the following data related to accounting and taxable income:

	1997	1998
Pretax accounting income	$200,000	$220,000
Taxable income (tax return)	220,000	200,000
Income tax rate	35%	35%

There are no existing temporary differences other than those reflected in this data.

Required
1. Give the journal entry to record the income tax consequences for each year.
2. Show how income tax expense, income tax payable, and deferred income tax should be reported on the financial statements each year.

E 19–5
(L.O. 2, 3)

Interperiod Tax Allocation, a Revenue and an Expense   The records of TNA Corporation, at the end of 1997, provided the following data related to income taxes:

a. Gain on disposal of an asset, $50,000; recorded for accounting purposes at the end of 1997; to be reported for income tax purposes at the end of 1999.
b. Estimated expense, $30,000; accrued for accounting purposes at the end of 1997; to be reported for income tax purposes when paid at the end of 1998.
c. Taxable income (from the tax return) at the end of 1997, $100,000; the enacted income tax rate is 35 percent. There were no deferred tax amounts as of the beginning of 1997.

Required
1. Did the gain and expense cause temporary differences? Explain why. Classify each item as deductible or taxable and explain why.
2. Prepare the following for 1997: (*a*) reconciliation of taxable income with pretax accounting income and compute income taxes payable, (*b*) schedule of temporary differences, and (*c*) entry to record income taxes at the end of the year.
3. Show the amounts that will be reported on (*a*) the balance sheet and (*b*) the income statement for 1997.

E 19–6
(L.O. 2, 3)

Analyze a Tax Difference, Deferred Asset: Entries and Reporting   Beetle Corporation reported accounting income before taxes as follows: 1997, $150,000; 1998, $176,000. Taxable income for each year would have been the same as pretax accounting income except for the tax effects, arising for the first time in 1997, of $600 per month rent revenue collected in advance on October 1, 1997, for the six months ending March 31, 1998. Rent revenue is taxable in the year collected. The tax rate for 1997 and 1998 is 30 percent, and the year-end for both accounting and tax purposes is December 31. The rent revenue collected in advance is the only difference, and it is not repeated in October 1998.

Required
1. Is this a temporary difference? Why or why not?
2. Reconcile accounting income with taxable income, calculate income tax payable, prepare a schedule of temporary differences, compute the balance in the deferred tax asset account, and prepare journal entries for each year-end.
3. Prepare a partial income statement for each year starting with pretax accounting income.
4. What amount of deferred income tax asset or liability would be reported on the 1997 and 1998 balance sheets?

E 19–7
(L.O. 2, 3)

Analyze a Tax Liability: Entries and Reporting   Stacy Corporation would have had identical income before taxes on both its income tax returns and income statements for the years 1997 through 2000 except for an operational asset that cost $120,000. The asset was depreciated for income tax purposes using the following amounts: 1997, $48,000; 1998, $36,000; 1999, $24,000; and 2000, $12,000. However, for accounting

purposes the straight-line method was used (that is, $30,000 per year; this is the only temporary difference). The accounting and tax periods both end December 31. The operational asset has a four-year estimated life and no residual value. Accounting income amounts before income taxes for each of the four years were as follows:

	1997	1998	1999	2000
Accounting income before taxes	$30,000	$50,000	$40,000	$40,000

Assume that the average and marginal income tax rate for each year was 30 percent.

Required

1. Is this a temporary difference? Explain why.
2. Reconcile pretax accounting and taxable income, calculate income tax payable, compute the balance in the deferred tax liability account, and prepare journal entries for each year-end.
3. For each year show the deferred income tax amount that would be reported on the balance sheet.

E 19–8
(L.O. 1, 2)

Asset/Liability Method with Change in Tax Rates   Wittco Company reports pretax accounting income in 1997, its first year of operations, of $100,000. Taxable income is $70,000, with temporary differences arising in 1997 from the following sources:

a. Prepayment of 1998 rent in the amount of $24,000 in 1997.

b. An installment sale in the amount of $36,000, with cash collections expected in two equal amounts in 1999 and 2000.

The enacted tax rates all known in 1997 are 30 percent in 1997, 30 percent in 1998, and 40 percent in 1999 and thereafter.

Required

1. Prepare the journal entry to record income taxes.
2. Repeat (1) above, assuming that a new tax law is passed in 1997 raising the statutory tax rate to 40 percent for 1997 and all years thereafter.

E 19–9
(L.O. 1, 2)

Asset/Liability Method: Beginning Balance and Change in Tax Rate   The Beeville Company has a deferred tax liability in the amount of $12,000 at December 31, 1997, relating to a $40,000 installment sale receivable, $20,000 of which is collected in 1998. The tax rate in 1998 is 30 percent. However, the rate for 1999 and thereafter is changed during 1998 to 40 percent. Warranty expense in 1998 included in the determination of pretax accounting income is $100,000, with these amounts expected to be incurred and deductible for tax purposes in 1999. Pretax accounting income is $280,000 in 1998.

Required

Prepare the journal entry to record income taxes in 1998.

E 19–10
(L.O. 4)

Operating Carryback–Carryforward (NOL) Options: Choices, Entries, and Reporting   Tyson Corporation reported pretax income from operations in 1997 of $80,000 (the first year of operations). In 1998, the corporation experienced a $40,000 pretax loss from operations (NOL). Management is very confident the firm will have taxable income in excess of $50,000 in 1999. Assume an income tax rate of 20 percent in 1997, increasing to 30 percent in 1998 and thereafter. Tyson has no other temporary differences.

Required

1. Assess Tyson's income tax situation for 1997 and 1998 separately. How should Tyson elect to handle the loss in 1998? Which carryback/carryforward option should Tyson choose?
2. Based on your assessments in (1), give the 1997 and 1998 income tax entries that Tyson should make.
3. Show how all tax-related items would be reported on the 1997 and 1998 income statement and balance sheet.

E 19–11
(L.O. 4)

Operating Carryback–Carryforward (NOL) Options: Entries   Toner Corporation reported the following taxable income and loss: 1997 income, $10,000 (tax rate 20 percent); and 1998 income, $40,000 loss (tax rate 20 percent). At the end of 1998, Toner made the following estimates: 1999 income, $4,000 (tax rate 20 percent); 2000 income, $11,000 (tax rate 30 percent); and 2001 income, $50,000 (tax rate 30 percent). On the basis of these estimates, which the company considered to be conservative, Toner elected the carryforward-only option and believes the full amount of tax loss carryforward benefit is more likely than not to be realized. There are no other temporary differences. Assume that no valuation allowance is needed.

Required

1. Give the income tax entry for 1997.
2. Give the income tax entry for 1998. Explain the basis for your response.
3. Give the income tax entry for 1999, assuming that the actual income was $6,000 (tax rate, 20 percent).

4. Give the income tax entry for 2000, assuming 1999 results were as described in 3, and that the actual 2000 income was $13,000 (tax rate, 30 percent).
5. Give the entry for 2001, assuming results for 1999 and 2000 as described above, and that the actual 2001 income was $45,000 and the tax rate increases to 35 percent.
6. Did Toner make a wise choice? Explain.

E 19–12
(L.O. 2, 3, 4)

Valuation Allowance, NOL Carryforward   At December 31, 1997, Allsoap Corporation has a deferred tax asset of $25,000, all of which arose as a result of temporary differences occurring in 1997. Allsoap began operations in 1996. In its first year the company had a net operating loss of $10,000, which was carried forward and used to reduce income taxes payable in 1997. In 1997, Allsoap had taxable income before the use of the NOL carryforward of $40,000. The income tax rate is 40 percent. No valuation allowance has been established.

Required

1. Compute income taxes payable and income tax expense for 1997 before any consideration of recording a valuation allowance. Show the journal entry to record income taxes assuming that no valuation allowance is required.
2. Now assume Allsoap has encountered stiff competition and is uncertain whether it will have any taxable income in the foreseeable future. Assume that the temporary differences that give rise to the deferred tax asset are expected to reverse in 1998 and 1999. Determine what amount, if any, should be recorded as a valuation allowance at December 31, 1997, and make the appropriate entry.
3. Show how the December 31, 1997, balance sheet and income statement would disclose the information above, assuming that a valuation allowance is recorded.

E 19–13
(L.O. 1, 2)

Multiple Depreciable Assets, Temporary Differences, Tax Rate Change   On January 1 of each of the first four years of its existence, Allway Company purchases a new unit of equipment. Each unit has a four-year life and zero salvage value, costs $100,000, and is depreciated for book and tax purposes as shown below. The income tax rate is 35 percent. Allway has a deferred tax liability of $17,500 ($50,000 of future taxable amount × 35 percent) at the end of year 3. The current year is year 4, and pretax accounting income is $30,000. Amounts are in thousands.

	1	2	3	Current Year 4	5	Future Years 6	7
Equipment:							
Beginning balance	$ 0	$100	$200	$300			
Purchases at January 1	100	100	100	100			
Retirements at December 31	0	0	0	(100)			
Ending balance	100	200	300	300			
Accumulated book depreciation	25	75	150	150			
Book depreciation:							
Machine 1	$ 25	$ 25	$ 25	$ 25			
Machine 2		25	25	25	$ 25		
Machine 3			25	25	25	$ 25	
Machine 4				25	25	25	$ 25
Annual total	$ 25	$ 50	$ 75	$100	$75	$ 50	$ 25
Tax depreciation:							
Machine 1	$ 40	$ 30	$ 20	$ 10			
Machine 2		40	30	20	$ 10		
Machine 3			40	30	20	$ 10	
Machine 4				40	30	20	$ 10
Annual total	$ 40	$ 70	$ 90	$100	$ 60	$ 30	$ 10
Annual increase (decrease) in future taxable amount	$ 15	$ 20	$ 15	$ 0	$(15)	$(20)	$(15)
Cumulative future taxable amount remaining at year-end	$ 15	$ 35	$ 50	$ 50	$ 35	$ 15	$ 0

Required

1. Show the entry to record income taxes payable, income tax expense, and changes in deferred tax amounts as of the end of year 4.

2. Assume that during year 4 the tax rate is increased to 40 percent effective as of the beginning of year 4. Repeat (1) under this assumption.

3. Assume that during year 4 the tax rate is increased to 40 percent effective in year 5 and to 45 percent thereafter. Repeat (1) under this assumption.

E 19–14
(L.O. 4)

Operating Carryforward–Carryback (NOL) Options: Entries and Reporting   The financial statements of Gibson Corporation for the first two years of operations reflected the following amounts:

	1997	1998
Revenues	$295,000	$330,000
Expenses	320,000	315,000
Pretax income (loss)	$ (25,000)	$ 15,000

Assume an average tax rate of 20 percent for 1997 and 1998.

Required

Gibson will have to apply the NOL carryforward-only option because there are no prior earnings. Estimates of future earnings at the end of 1997 and 1998 are very uncertain, therefore assume them to be zero. There are no temporary differences.

1. Restate Gibson's financial statements incorporating the income tax effects.
2. Give entries to record the NOL income tax effects for 1997 and 1998. Explain the basis for your entries.

PROBLEMS

P 19–1
(L.O. 4)

Operating Carryback–Carryforward (NOL) Options: Entries   The financial statements of Bixler Corporation for the first four years of operations reflected the following pretax amounts:

	1997	1998	1999	2000
Income statement (summarized):				
Revenue	$125,000	$155,000	$180,000	$250,000
Expenses	120,000	195,000	160,000	200,000
Pretax income (loss)	$ 5,000	$ (40,000)	$ 20,000	$ 50,000

There are no temporary differences other than those created by tax loss carryforwards. Assume an income tax rate of 30 percent during 1997 and 1998 and 40 percent in 1999 and 2000. Assume that future incomes are very uncertain at the end of each year, so a valuation allowance is needed for any deferred tax asset. In 1998, management of Bixler Corporation elects the carryback–carryforward option in order to obtain the immediate cash refund on the NOL carryback.

Required

1. Recast Bixler's statements to incorporate the income tax effects as required by *SFAS No. 109*. Show computations.
2. Give entries to record the NOL income tax effects for each year.
3. Explain the alternative option that Bixler might have considered. What are the primary considerations that Bixler should assess in making its choice?

P 19–2
(L.O. 2, 3)

Income Tax Allocation: Depreciation   The financial statements of Dakar Corporation for a four-year period reflected the following pretax amounts:

	1997	1998	1999	2000
Income statement (summarized):				
Revenues	$120,000	$134,000	$154,000	$174,000
Expenses other than depreciation	(80,000)	(92,000)	(95,000)	(128,000)
Depreciation expense (straight-line)	(20,000)	(20,000)	(20,000)	(20,000)
Pretax accounting income	$ 20,000	$ 22,000	$ 39,000	$ 26,000
Balance sheet (partial):				
Machine (four-year life, no residual value), at cost	$ 80,000	$ 80,000	$ 80,000	$ 80,000
Less: Accumulated depreciation	(20,000)	(40,000)	(60,000)	(80,000)

Dakar has an average and marginal tax rate of 40 percent each year and deducts accelerated depreciation for income tax purposes as follows: 1997, $32,000; 1998, $24,000; 1999, $16,000; and 2000, $8,000. There are no deferred tax assets or liabilities at January 1, 1997.

Required

1. Is this a temporary difference? Explain your answer.
2. Prepare the following for each year: (*a*) schedule to reconcile accounting and taxable incomes, (*b*) schedule to compute income tax payable, (*c*) schedule to compute deferred income tax, and (*d*) journal entry at each year-end to record income taxes.
3. For each year show the deferred income tax amount that should be reported on the balance sheet.

P 19–3
(L.O. 2, 3)

Analyze Three Income Tax Items: Entries and Reporting   The income statements for Lemond Corporation for two years (summarized) were as follows:

	1997	1998
Revenues	$180,000	$200,000
Expenses	152,000	181,000
Pretax accounting income	$ 28,000	$ 19,000
Taxable income (per tax return)	$ 56,000	$ 11,000

Income tax rate is 40 percent for both years.

For tax purposes, the following differences existed:

a. Expenses (given above) on the 1997 and 1998 income statements include goodwill amortization of $10,000. Assume this is not deductible for income tax purposes.
b. Revenues (given above) on the 1998 income include $10,000 rent revenue, which was taxable in 1997 but was unearned at the end of 1997.
c. Expenses (given above) on the 1997 income statement include $8,000 of estimated warranty costs, which are not deductible for income tax purposes until 1998.

There were no other differences.

Required

1. Write a brief memo explaining why each one of the three income tax consequences given above is or is not a permanent or temporary difference.
2. Prepare the following for each year: (*a*) schedule to reconcile accounting and taxable incomes, (*b*) schedule to compute income tax payable, (*c*) schedule to compute deferred income tax, and (*d*) journal entry at each year-end to record income taxes.
3. Show how the deferred income tax asset or liability would be reported on the income statement and balance sheet for 1997 and 1998.

P 19–4
(L.O. 1, 2, 3)

Recording and Reporting the Income Tax Consequences of a Deferred Asset and a Deferred Liability   The records of Lollie Corporation provided the following income tax-related information:

	1997	1998	1999	2000
Pretax accounting income	$ 90,000	$ 92,000	$ 95,000	$ 98,000
Taxable income (tax return)	63,000	101,000	104,000	107,000

Income tax rate is 30 percent.

The above amounts include only two temporary differences, as follows:

a. Installment sales—for accounting purposes in 1997, $30,000; included in the tax return, $10,000 each year, 1998 through 2000.
b. Cost of warranties—for accounting purposes, $4,000 in 1997; deducted for income tax $1,000 each year, 1997 through 2000.

Required

1. Prepare the following for each year: (*a*) schedule to reconcile accounting and taxable income and to compute taxes payable, (*b*) schedule of temporary differences, (*c*) schedule to compute deferred income taxes, and (*d*) journal entry at the end of each year to record income taxes.
2. Show how income tax expense, deferred income tax asset or liability, and income taxes payable should be reported on the financial statements for each year.

P 19–5
(L.O. 2, 3)

Interperiod Tax Allocation: Temporary and Permanent Differences, Tax Rate Change Fox Corporation purchased a machine on January 1, year 1, that cost $40,000. The machine had an estimated service life of five years and no residual value. Fox uses straight-line depreciation for accounting purposes, and accelerated depreciation for the income tax return as follows: year 1, 30 percent; year 2, 25 percent; year 3, 20 percent; year 4, 15 percent; and year 5, 10 percent. Taxable income on the tax return for year 1 was $150,000. The year 1 income statement also showed a $15,000 deduction for amortization of goodwill (assume that income tax regulations do not permit the amortization of this goodwill for income tax purposes). There were no other factors to complicate the company's income tax computations during year 1. The income tax rate is 20 percent in year 1 and 40 percent in all subsequent years.

Required

1. Identify any temporary difference and explain the basis for your decisions. Also, identify any taxable amounts and deductible amounts and explain their effects on the analysis of the income tax differences.
2. Prepare the following at the end of year 1: (*a*) schedule to reconcile accounting income and taxable income and to compute income tax payable, (*b*) schedule of temporary differences, (*c*) schedule to compute deferred income taxes, and (*d*) journal entry to record income taxes at year-end.

P 19–6
(L.O. 2, 3)

Recording and Reporting Income Tax Consequences for Temporary Differences The records of Hicks Corporation provided the following information: taxable income based on tax return, 1997, $47,600; income tax rate, 30 percent. There were two temporary differences, as follows:

a. December 31, 1997, collected $5,000 rent in advance for 1998. The $5,000 is included on the 1997 tax return.
b. On December 31, 1997, the company recorded a $10,000 estimated expense, accrued as a liability to be paid in 1998 and included in the 1998 income tax return.

Required

1. Prepare a reconciliation of taxable income with pretax accounting income for 1997.
2. Prepare a schedule of temporary differences for 1997.
3. Give the entry to record income taxes at the end of 1997. Show computations for each amount.
4. Show how the income tax consequences should be reported on the three required financial statements for 1997 assuming that 75 percent of the income tax payable was paid by the end of 1997.

P 19–7
(L.O. 2, 3)

Recording and Reporting a Deferred Tax Liability and Change in Tax Rate The records of Morgan Corporation provided the following data at the end of years 1 through 4 relating to income tax allocation:

	Year 1	Year 2	Year 3	Year 4
Pretax accounting income	$58,000	$70,000	$80,000	$88,000
Taxable income (tax return)	28,000	80,000	90,000	98,000

The above amounts include only one temporary difference; no other changes occurred. At the end of year 1, the company prepaid an expense of $30,000, which will be amortized for accounting purposes over the next three years (straight line). The full amount is included in year 1 for income tax purposes. At the end of year 1, the enacted tax rate was 35 percent. During year 2, the enacted tax rate was changed to 30 percent, retroactive to the beginning of year 2, and was to remain in effect through year 4.

Required

1. Prepare a schedule of temporary differences at the end of year 1.
2. Give the entry to record income taxes at the end of year 1.
3. Give any entry that should be made in year 2 to reflect the change in the enacted income tax rate. If none is required, explain why.
4. Give the entry at the end of each year for years 2 through 4 assuming that the new enacted tax rate is not changed.
5. Complete the following tabulation:

	Year 1	Year 2	Year 3	Year 4
Income statement:				
Income tax expense				
Balance sheet:				
Liabilities:				
Income tax payable				
Deferred tax liability				

P 19–8
(L.O. 2, 4, 6)

Recording and Reporting Income Tax: Consequences for a Four-Year Period The records of Cross Corporation provided the following income tax allocation data:

	1997	1998*	1999*	2000
Taxable income (tax return)	$60,000	$80,000	$85,000	$ 75,000
Pretax accounting income	40,000	70,000	90,000	100,000
Income tax rate, 30%				

*Estimated amounts

The deferred tax account has a zero balance at the start of 1997. There was only one source of temporary differences, estimated warranty expenses, which were recorded (i.e., accrued) for accounting purposes in 1997 and 1998 but were deductible for tax purposes in 1999 and 2000.

Required

1. Prepare schedules to reconcile taxable and accounting income and to compute the temporary differences, deferred tax assets and deferred tax liabilities, for each year.
2. Give the entry at the end of each year for 1997 through 2000 assuming that the enacted tax rate is not changed.
3. Complete the following tabulation:

	Estimated			
	1997	1998	1999	2000
Income statement:				
Income tax expense				
Balance sheet:				
Deferred tax liability				

P 19–9
(L.O. 1, 2, 3)

Asset/Liability Method Applied to Depreciation   On January 1, 1997, Keefe Corporation purchased a machine at a cost of $100,000. The machine has a five-year life and no salvage value. The depreciation for tax and accounting purposes follows:

Year	Book Depreciation	Tax Depreciation	Annual Difference	Cumulative Difference
1997	$20,000	$25,000	$ 5,000	$ 5,000
1998	20,000	38,000	18,000	23,000
1999	20,000	37,000	17,000	40,000
2000	20,000	–0–	(20,000)	20,000
2001	20,000	–0–	(20,000)	–0–

At the end of 1997, there is $5,000 of temporary difference that will result in increased taxable income in the future. However, there are two years in the future in which the amount of tax depreciation exceeds book depreciation: in 1998, tax depreciation exceeds book depreciation by $18,000, and in 1999, tax depreciation exceeds book depreciation by $17,000. Assume that pretax accounting income in 1997 totals $20,000 and the statutory tax rate is 30 percent.

Required

1. Prepare the following for 1997: (*a*) a schedule to reconcile accounting and taxable income; (*b*) a schedule of income taxes payable, temporary differences, and deferred tax balances; and (*c*) the journal entry to record income taxes.
2. Show how income taxes would be shown on the income statement and balance sheet for the year ending December 31, 1997.

P 19–10
(L.O. 1, 2, 3)

Depreciable Assets and Changes in Tax   Refer to the data and information given in P 19–9 for Keefe Corporation. Assume that the tax rate for 1997 through 1999 is known to be 30 percent but that a new law is passed in 1997 that will raise the tax rate in 2000 and thereafter to 40 percent.

Required

Prepare the tax accrual entry for 1997 and 1998 assuming pretax accounting income equals $20,000 in each year.

P 19–11
(L.O. 1, 2)

Analysis of Temporary Differences and Deferred Tax Classifications   Triple Corporation started operations on January 1, 1997. At the end of 1997, the following income tax–related data were available:

	1997	1998	1999
Taxable income (tax return)	$116,500		
a. Gross margin on installment sales:			
Accounting	175,000		
Tax return	65,000	$70,000	$40,000
b. Rent revenue collected in advance:			
Accounting (earned)	8,000	24,000	
Tax return (cash collected)	32,000		
c. Estimated warranty expense:			
Accounting (accrued)	25,000		
Tax return	12,000	10,500	2,500
Income tax rate	30%	30%	30%

The gross margin of the installment sale receivable expected to be collected in 1998 was classified as a current asset; the remainder was classified as noncurrent. Rent collected in advance and estimated warranty obligations are both classified as current liabilities.

Required

1. What kind of tax difference is represented by each one of the three income tax consequences given above? Explain. Also, identify the taxable and deductible amounts.
2. Prepare the following schedules related to income tax allocation for 1997:
   a. Schedule to reconcile taxable accounting and taxable income.
   b. Schedule of temporary differences.
3. Give the entry at the end of 1997 to record income taxes as required by *SFAS No. 109.* Show computations. Assume that no valuation allowance is needed.
4. Show the items that should be reported on the 1997 financial statements assuming that 75 percent of taxes payable were paid.

P 19–12
(L.O. 2, 3)

Analysis of Two Temporary Differences   Cruse Corporation started operations on January 1, 1997. At the end of 1997 the data related to income taxes were as follows (in $000s):

Taxable income from the tax return $2,850

Income tax consequences:

a. Profit on installment sale, $330—recognized for accounting purposes in 1997 and will be
included on tax return equally over 1998, 1999, and 2000 . . . . $330
b. Litigation loss, $270—accrued as expense for accounting purposes in 1997 and will be
included in the tax return in 2000 . . . . $270
Income tax rate is 30 percent.

Required

1. In a brief memo, analyze each of the income tax consequences given above to determine whether each one is a temporary difference, a taxable or deductible amount, and a deferred tax liability or asset. Explain each determination.
2. Prepare the following schedules for 1997: (*a*) reconciliation of taxable income and pretax accounting income and (*b*) temporary differences.
3. Give the entry to record income taxes at the end of 1997. Show computations.
4. Show the amounts that should be reported on the financial statements at the end of 1997. Assume that none of the 1997 income tax liability is paid before the end of 1997. The amount to be collected in 1998 on the installment sale is classified as a current asset. All other items giving rise to temporary differences are classified noncurrent.

P 19–13
(L.O. 1, 2, 3)

Accounting for Deferred Taxes, Changes in Tax Rate   The first year of operations for Blair Corporation is 1997. The accounting and income tax periods end on December 31. The records of the company provided the following income tax–related data at the end of 1997 in $000s:

Marginal income tax rate is 40 percent for 1997–1999 and becomes 30 percent in 2000. All of these rates are
enacted as of 1997.
Taxable income $150

Temporary differences:

a. A $300 estimated expense was accrued (that is, recognized) at the end of 1997 for accounting purposes and recorded as a liability; expected settlement date, year-end 2000 for income tax purposes.

b. A $200 gain on a special installment sale, recognized for accounting purposes at the end of 1997; to be included in income tax return as collected in equal amounts for 1998 through 2001.

c. A depreciable asset that cost $200 (estimated useful life five years and no residual value) is depreciated as follows:

	1997	1998	1999	2000	2001
Accounting purposes	$40	$40	$40	$40	$40
Income tax purposes	66	54	40	26	14
Differences	($26)	($14)	$ 0	$14	$26

d. Rent revenue collected in advance at the end of 1997, $40; recognized for accounting purposes in 1998 and 1999. The full amount must be included in the 1997 income tax return.

Required

1. Analyze each of the four income tax consequences given above to determine whether each one is a taxable or deductible temporary difference.
2. Use the procedures shown in the Review Problem to determine the entry for income taxes in 1997.
3. Give the entry to record income taxes at the end of 1997. Show computations.
4. Show the amounts that should be reported on the financial statements at the end of 1997. Assume that 75 percent of the 1997 income tax liability was paid before the end of 1997.

P 19–14
(L.O. 1, 2, 4)

Operating Carryback–Carryforward (NOL) Options: Entries and Reporting   Decker Corporation experienced a loss in 1997. The company reported taxable income (loss) for 1994 to 1997 and had average tax rates as follows:

	1994	1995	1996	1997
Taxable income (loss)	$8,000	$32,000	$15,000	($65,000)
Income tax rate	30%	30%	35%	40%

There were no temporary differences from 1994 to 1997.

Required

1. Record income taxes for 1997 and 1998 assuming that Decker elects the carryback–carryforward option. Also assume the following:
   a. For 1997, any tax refund receivable is collected early in 1998.
   b. For 1998, the company reported taxable income of $45,000 and pretax accounting income of $50,000 (a $5,000 temporary difference). The income tax rate for 1998 is 45 percent.
2. List the accounts and amounts that should be reported on the income statements and balance sheet for each of the above requirements.
3. Repeat (1) and (2) assuming that Decker elects the carryforward-only option, and no valuation allowance is deemed necessary.

P 19–15
(L.O. 1, 2, 3, 4)

Taxable and Deductible Amounts with NOL Carryback and Carryforward, Valuation Allowance   (This item is amenable to a group or individual solution. Refer to the preface for additional details on using group items.) Coleman Computer Company started operations on January 1, 1996. The accounting period ends December 31. This problem encompasses a four-year period, 1996 through 1999. During this period, the company has several temporary differences and incurs an operating loss in 1997. The data are given in the following table. The enacted tax rate for all periods is 40 percent, and all amounts are given in thousands of dollars.

	1996	1997	1998	1999
a. Pretax accounting income (loss)	$400	$(700)	$100	$200
b. Temporary differences:				
Gross margin on installment sales				
Accounting basis (when sold)	200	50	150	100
Tax basis (when collected)	0	125	75	125
Deferred gross margin, December 31	200	125	200	175
Accrued estimated warranty costs:				
Accounting basis	100	100	180	160
Tax basis	0	80	110	130
Accrued warranty costs, December 31	100	120	190	220

Assume that one-half of the end-of-period deferred gross margin is classified as a current asset in each year, and that 25 percent of the ending accrued provision for warranty costs is classified as a current liability. Also assume that Coleman elects the carryback–carryforward option for any NOL that occurs, and that management cannot expect positive taxable income exclusive of reversals of temporary differences in any year. That is, in determining whether a valuation allowance is needed, assume that future taxable income exclusive of temporary differences is zero. Assume that future taxable amounts can be utilized to realize the tax benefit of an equal amount of any future deductible amounts. Also assume that the carryback option can be used to realize the tax benefit of any future deductible amount up to the amount of the current period taxes paid.

Required

1. Complete the appropriate schedules and prepare the journal entry to record income taxes for each year under the provisions of *SFAS No. 109*.
2. For each year, show how the income tax information would be reported on the income statement and balance sheet, including the current and noncurrent classifications.

ANALYSIS, JUDGMENT, AND COMMUNICATIONS

CASES

C 19–1
(L.O. 2)

Change in the Statutory Rate   The statutory federal tax rate had been 35 percent for a number of years. Late in the third quarter of 1997, a new rate, 40 percent, was approved as the new statutory rate, effective as of January 1, 1997. You are an assistant controller with Zenics Inc., a manufacturer of laser printers. The CEO of the company is concerned about what effect, if any, the new tax rate will have on 1997 earnings.

At the beginning of the year, Zenics had a deferred tax asset of $10 million and a deferred tax liability of $6 million. There was no need for a valuation allowance, nor is it expected that any will be needed this year. You estimate that pretax accounting income will be approximately $5 million in 1997 and that taxable income will be about $7 million. The company is publicly traded, with 500,000 shares outstanding all year.

Required

Write a memorandum to the CEO, J. C. Blades, explaining what effect the tax rate increase will have on the balance sheet and income statement for the company for 1997. Be as specific as you can, especially with regard to the effect the change will have on earnings per share. If there is likely to be a negative impact on earnings, the CEO would like your advice on what actions the company might consider taking in the last few days of 1997 to minimize the impact. You should also comment on what effect, if any, you think the tax rate change will have on the company's stock price.

C 19–2
(L.O. 1)

Interperiod Tax Allocation   A friend overhears you talking about accounting for income taxes with a colleague. She hears you say that the company you are analyzing had a tax refund of $2,000 but that it reported an income tax expense of $5,000 on its income statement. Being a social studies major, she is furious and shouts at you:

> "That's just what I've always suspected—big business keeps two sets of books. In the one for tax purposes they always report low earnings and losses, and in the other for shareholders they show big profits. This has got to be illegal. How can you be a part of this by being an accounting major?"

Required

1. Explain to your friend how it is perfectly appropriate and legal for a company to keep two sets of books.
2. Explain to your friend how a company might have an income tax refund at the time it is reporting an income tax expense.

C 19–3
(L.O. 4)

Operating Losses   The Internal Revenue Code allows a corporation to carry back or carry forward an operating loss occurring in a given year.

Required

1. In a brief memo, describe an operating loss carryback and a carryforward. What are the effects of each of these actions?
2. Briefly summarize the current generally accepted accounting principles for the financial reporting of operating loss carrybacks and for reporting operating loss carryforwards.
3. Explain why a firm might forgo the opportunity to obtain a tax refund with a carryback, choosing instead the carryforward only option.

C 19–4
(L.O. 3)

Classifying Deferred Income Taxes   Rimes Inc. has each of the following items on its balance sheet at December 31, 1997:

<pre>
Current assets: Prepaid expenses $50,000
Noncurrent assets: Goodwill*   200,000
Current liabilities: Warranty liability   100,000
Noncurrent liabilities: Postretirement
    liability other than pensions   1,000,000
</pre>

*Not tax deductible

The prepaid expenses have already been deducted for tax purposes; none of the other items have yet been deducted. The current and future income tax rate is 35 percent.

Required

In a two-page or less memo addressed to your instructor:
- Explain which of the above items requires a deferred tax amount to be recorded, in what amount, and whether it is a deferred tax asset or deferred tax liability.
- Determine the amounts of deferred tax asset and deferred tax liability that would be reported on the balance sheet for Rimes and the current or noncurrent classification of each. Explain your reasoning in each case.

C 19–5
(L.O. 2)

Valuation Allowance for Deferred Tax Assets   Soderstrom Company has a deferred tax asset of $1,000,000 at December 31, 1997, arising from its recording of its liability for postretirement benefits other than pensions. Soderstrom's CPA asks management whether a valuation allowance to reduce the deferred tax asset to zero should be recorded.

Required

1. Why would Soderstrom not want to report a valuation allowance? Outline what evidence, assuming it existed, that Soderstrom might use to argue against recording a valuation allowance.
2. Suppose in the final analysis, it is determined that a valuation allowance of $400,000 is needed. How would the company have arrived at this determination, and what effect will it have on net income in fiscal 1997?

| ANALYZING FINANCIAL STATEMENTS

All cases in this section are based on information taken from the actual financial statements of real companies.

A 19–1
(L.O. 2, 3)

Deferred Taxes.   In the notes to its 1995 financial statements, Texaco Inc., a major U.S. oil producer, provides the following disclosure regarding the deferred tax asset and liability accounts at December 31, 1995 (amounts in millions):

	Asset (liability)
Depreciation	$ (912)
Depletion	(327)
Intangible drilling costs	(501)
Other deferred tax liabilities	(343)
Total	(2,083)
Employee benefit plans	524
Tax loss carryforwards	907
Tax-related reserves	36
Tax credit carryforwards	388
Environmental reserves	211
Other deferred tax assets	383
Total	2,449
Total before valuation allowance	366
Valuation allowance	(901)
Total—net	$(535)

Required

1. What is the total amount of deferred tax liability at December 31, 1995? The total amount of deferred tax asset? The net amount of deferred tax asset or liability?
2. Assuming a federal tax rate of 35 percent, estimate the amount of temporary difference arising from depreciation that exists for Texaco at December 31, 1995.
3. On December 31, 1995, Texaco shows a noncurrent liability on its balance sheet, captioned *deferred income taxes,* in the amount of $634 million. What other deferred tax account, if any, is included in the balance sheet? In what amount?

A 19–2
(L.O. 1, 2, 4)

Applied Technology Laboratories (ATL)   ATL a medical equipment manufacturer, reported a loss before income taxes of $20.9 million in 1994, yet the income tax effect was a savings of only $0.7 million. The effective income tax rate is only 3.3 percent (0.7/20.9). ATL reported a loss before income taxes of $1.7 million in 1993, yet had income tax expense of $1.6 million—an effective tax rate of 94.1 percent! Assume a statutory income tax rate of 35 percent.

This schedule from the notes to the 1994 ATL annual report explains its deferred tax assets and deferred tax liabilities (in thousands):

	1994	1993
Deferred tax assets		
Receivables	$ 3,230	$ 2,936
Inventories	11,564	8,800
Net operating loss carryforwards	3,969	3,157
State taxes	3,106	2,087
Compensation	2,623	2,171
Provision for litigation claim	1,700	—
Research and experimentation credit carryforwards	6,602	6,425
Other	3,032	3,107
Gross deferred tax assets	$35,826	$28,683
Less valuation allowance	(27,249)	(19,709)
Net deferred tax assets	$ 8,577	$ 8,974
Deferred tax liabilities, primarily depreciation and intangible assets	(4,472)	(4,628)
Net deferred income taxes	$ 4,105	$ 4,346

Required

1. What are some reasons why ATL's effective tax rate might be so low in 1994?
2. Why might ATL show an income tax expense in a year when it has a loss before income taxes for financial reporting?
3. In general terms, explain why ATL has such a large amount reported as a valuation allowance.
4. What effect did the increase in the valuation allowance from 1993 to 1994 have on ATL's income tax expense computation in fiscal 1994?
5. Using a tax rate of 35 percent, estimate the amount of net operating loss carryforwards that ATL has as of December 31, 1994.
6. Using a tax rate of 35 percent, estimate the amount of "research and experimentation credit carryforwards" that ATL has as of December 31, 1994.
7. Using a tax rate of 35 percent, estimate the amount of accrued liability for litigation claim that ATL has as of December 31, 1994.

A 19–3
(L.O. 3)

Coca-Cola   Refer to the 1995 Coca-Cola financial statements at the back of this book, especially Note 15, and answer the following questions:

1. If Coca-Cola had no permanent or temporary differences and all earnings were subject to the federal statutory income tax rate, in what amount would Coca-Cola record income tax expense in 1995?
2. Identify three sources and their percentage effects on income taxes that caused Coca-Cola's effective tax rate in 1995 to differ from the federal statutory rate of 35 percent.
3. By how much did Coca-Cola increase or decrease its valuation allowance in 1995? What effect did this change by itself have on income tax expense? On net income?
4. At December 31, 1995, Coca-Cola disclosed a deferred tax liability of $125 million after deducting the valuation allowance. In what amount are deferred tax assets included on the balance sheet as a component of total assets? Show a reconciliation of the net deferred tax liability of $125 million to the deferred income taxes shown on the December 31, 1995, balance sheet of $194 million.

IV

OWNER'S EQUITY

20 CORPORATIONS: CONTRIBUTED CAPITAL

After you have studied this chapter, you will:

1 Be able to describe the characteristics, advantages, and disadvantages of the corporate form of business organization.

2 Know the different types of investments shareholders make in firms and the rights of each.

3 Be able to describe and demonstrate accounting and reporting practices for the issuance of various forms of capital stock.

4 Understand the accounting and reporting practices for the issuance of subscription stock.

5 Understand the accounting and reporting practices for treasury stock, including both the cost method and the par value method.

6 Understand the accounting and reporting practices for the retirement of callable and redeemable stock and for the conversion of convertible preferred stock.

INTRODUCTION

With total assets of $90.5 billion, Banc One is one of the largest banks in the United States. This excerpt is from the stockholders' equity section of a balance sheet in Banc One Corporation's 1995 annual report. It is a typical stockholders' equity section of a balance sheet for a corporation.

	December 31	
$ *(thousands, except per share amounts)*	**1995**	**1994**
Stockholders' equity:		
Preferred stock, 35,000,000 shares authorized:		
Series C convertible, no par value 4,992,694 and 4,997,999 shares issued and outstanding, respectively	**$ 249,635**	$ 249,900
Common stock, no par value, $5 stated value, 600,000,000 shares authorized, 451,741,054 and 408,985,564 shares issued, respectively (December 31, 1995 shares reflect the 10% stock dividend payable March 6, 1996 to shareholders of record on February 21, 1996)	**2,258,705**	2,044,928
Capital in excess of aggregate stated value of common stock.	**5,157,763**	3,796,746
Retained earnings	**1,100,345**	1,921,256

Net unrealized holding gains (losses) on securities available for sale, net of tax	**91,804**	(111,517)
Treasury stock (24,090,000 and 11,999,500 shares, respectively), at cost	**(660,774)**	(336,453)
Total stockholders' equity	**8,197,478**	7,564,860
Total liabilities and stockholders' equity	**$90,453,963**	$88,922,586

Banc One has two kinds of capital stock issued and outstanding—preferred stock and common stock. Several questions come to mind in looking over Banc One's stockholders' equity section:

- What is the difference between preferred stock and common stock?
- The preferred stock is convertible. What is implied by the word *convertible?*
- Both the preferred stock and the common stock have no par value. What does no par mean?
- The common stock has a stated value of $5 per share. What does stated value mean?
- What is the meaning of capital in excess of aggregate stated value of common stock?
- What is treasury stock? Why is it a negative component of stockholders' equity?

You may have other questions, but this list provides a sense of some of the topics we cover in this chapter. Our purpose is to cover accounting for stockholders' equity (except for retained earnings, which is covered in Chapter 21).

SFAC No. 6 defines **owners'** or **stockholders' equity** for corporations as the difference between the recorded assets and recorded liabilities of an entity. Stockholders' equity is a residual interest and has no existence without the presence of assets. Stockholders' equity is not a claim on specific assets, but rather a claim on total assets after liabilities are recognized. It is sometimes referred to as *net assets*. Stockholders' equity is the net contribution to the firm by the owners, plus the firm's cumulative earnings retained in the business, less any reacquisition of the company's stock.

Generally accepted accounting principles apply to all forms of business organization, whether sole proprietorship, partnership, or corporation. Corporations, however, have legal and contractual implications that result in different accounting and reporting requirements for owners' equity.

CONTRIBUTED CAPITAL AT THE FORMATION OF A CORPORATION

Formation of a Corporation

In the United States, the incorporation process follows the laws of the state in which the corporation is organized. There are no federal incorporation laws. Most states have adopted many of the principles recommended in the Model Business Corporation Act, resulting in many common legal provisions.

Corporation laws have an impact on accounting for stockholders' equity. These laws specify such items as:

- Requirements for stock issuance.
- Definition of legal capital.
- Limitations on dividends.
- Constraints on treasury stock.
- Provisions for the retirement of capital stock.

It is impractical to describe the legal requirements of each state, but we can make some reasonable generalizations. In most states:

- Articles of incorporation are prepared by the organizers to meet the legal requirements of the state. These articles specify the purpose of the business, its location, the names of the organizers, the classes and numbers of shares of capital stock authorized, and the consideration to be paid in by the organizers for their respective shares.
- The articles of incorporation are filed with a designated state official, usually the secretary of state.
- After approving the articles of incorporation, the state issues a corporate charter, which makes the articles of incorporation operative.
- A board of directors is selected. It meets and approves (*a*) corporate bylaws to supplement, but not change, the provisions of the charter, and (*b*) corporate officers.

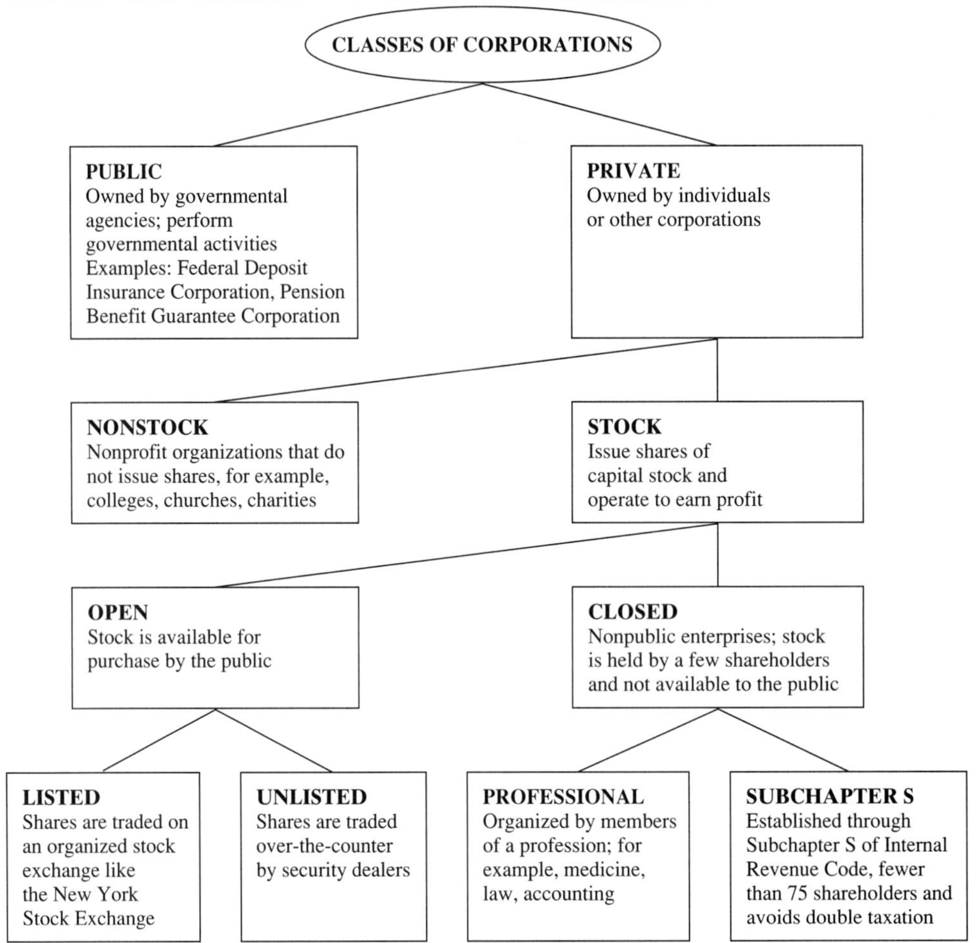

Classification of Corporations   There are many different types of corporations, each organized by different parties for different purposes. The general classes of corporations are shown in Exhibit 20–1.

Our focus in this chapter is on private stock corporations because they issue shares and operate to earn a profit. Secondarily, our focus is on open corporations because their shares are available to the public. The stockholders' equity topics covered here also apply to closed corporations.

Characteristics of Capital Stock

Shares of capital stock, represented by stock certificates, evidence ownership in a corporation. Shares may be bought, sold, or otherwise transferred by the stockholders without the consent of the corporation (unless there is an enforceable agreement not to do so). Ownership of common stock usually entitles the holder to:

- The **right to vote** in stockholder meetings and influence the management of the corporation.
- The **right to participate in the earnings** of the corporation through dividends declared by the board of directors.
- The **right to share in the distribution of assets** of the corporation at liquidation.
- The **right to purchase shares** of the common stock of the corporation on a pro rata basis when new issues are offered for sale. This **preemptive right** is designed to provide each stockholder the opportunity to maintain a proportional ownership in the corporation.

The first three rights are basic and generally hold in all states. The fourth right is less consistently required across states, and in some instances it may not exist. These basic rights are shared proportionately by all stockholders of each class of stock unless the charter or

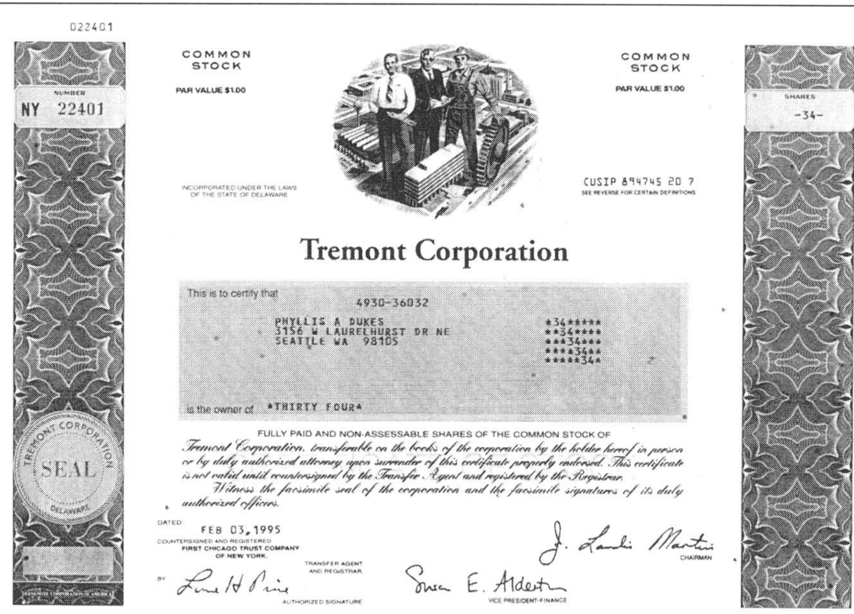

bylaws (as noted on the stock certificates) specifically provide otherwise. When there are two or more classes of stock, ownership rights vary depending on the class.

A typical stock certificate is shown in Exhibit 20–2 for the Tremont Corporation.

Concepts and Definitions Fundamental to Corporate Equity Accounting

The fundamental concepts that underlie the accounting and reporting of stockholders' equity are summarized here:

1. **Separate legal entity** A corporation is a nonpersonal entity that may own assets, owe debts, and conduct operations as a separate accounting entity, independent of the stockholders.[1]

2. **Categories of stockholders' equity** Primarily for historical legal reasons, there are several categories of stockholders' equity that are organized, accounted for, and reported separately on the balance sheet. The specific categories and subcategories of stockholders' equity include:

   a. **Contributed capital** (often referred to as *paid-in capital*):
      (1) Capital stock:
          (*a*) Preferred stock.
          (*b*) Common stock.
      (2) Other contributed capital or **additional paid-in capital.** Subcategories include contributed capital in excess of par or stated value (sometimes called *premium on capital stock*) and contributed capital from treasury stock and stock retirement transactions.

   b. **Retained earnings**   Two common subcategories of retained earnings are:
      (1) Unappropriated retained earnings.
      (2) Appropriated retained earnings (amounts not available for dividends); discussed in the next chapter.

   c. **Unrealized capital**   Increases or decreases in stockholders' equity that do not arise from contributions from stockholders or from the retention of earnings. Exhibit 20–3 illustrates a typical stockholders' equity section in a balance sheet. Stockholders'

---

[1] The issue of what is a separate legal entity becomes more complex when one corporation is the majority shareholder of a second corporation, or when there are reciprocal holdings of shares. Complex ownership structures are covered in advanced accounting texts.

EXHIBIT 20–3
Stockholders' Equity Section
of a Balance Sheet

Stockholders' Equity

Contributed capital:
Capital stock:

Preferred stock, 6 percent, par $10, cumulative and nonparticipating, 20,000 shares authorized; 15,000 issued and outstanding	$150,000	
Preferred stock subscribed, 100 shares	1,000	
Total preferred stock outstanding and subscribed	151,000	
Common stock nopar value, 10,000 shares authorized; 8,000 shares issued and outstanding, stated value $5.	40,000	$191,000
Additional contributed capital:*		
In excess of par value, preferred stock.	12,000	
In excess of stated value, common stock	8,000	20,000
Total contributed capital		211,000
Retained earnings:†		
Appropriated for bond sinking fund	50,000	
Unappropriated	170,000	
Total retained earnings		220,000
Unrealized capital:		
Unrealized loss on investments in securities available for sale		(6,000)
Total stockholders' equity		$425,000

*The additional contributed capital accounts often are aggregated into a single amount on the balance sheet with detailed disclosure in the notes or a supporting schedule.

†Total retained earnings often is reported on the balance sheet with disclosure of the appropriation in a supporting note.

equity generally is reported by category: contributed capital, retained earnings, and unrealized capital items.

3. **Issuance of capital stock** The issuance of capital stock is recorded in conformity with the **cost principle.** The issue price recorded is the cash consideration received plus the market value of all noncash consideration received.

4. **Sale and repurchase of shares** Transactions of a corporation involving the sale, purchase, or resale of its own shares do not directly affect periodic net income. When shares are reissued, the consideration received is recorded as an adjustment to an appropriate contributed (paid-in) capital account.

5. **Classification of capital stock** Following are definitions of various classifications of capital stock:

   a. **Authorized:** the number of shares of stock that can be issued legally, as specified in the charter of the corporation.

   b. **Issued:** the number of shares of authorized capital stock that have been issued to stockholders.

   c. **Unissued:** the number of shares of authorized capital stock that have not been issued; that is, the difference between authorized and issued shares.

   d. **Treasury stock:** shares previously issued and later repurchased by the corporation that are still held (also, the difference between issued shares and outstanding shares).

   e. **Outstanding:** the number of shares issued, less the number of shares repurchased and currently held by the company as treasury stock.

   f. **Subscribed:** unissued shares of stock set aside to meet subscription contracts (that is, shares sold on credit and not yet paid for). Subscribed stock is usually not issued until the subscription price is paid in full.

6. **Equity versus debt** Stockholders' equity is reported separately from the liabilities of the corporation.

**Stockholders' Equity:
Terminology Issues**

There are some potentially misleading terms and expressions in common use regarding stockholders' equity. Many who are more familiar with accounting will find the following comments self-evident, but others are sometimes misled by these terms and statements.

1. Stockholders' equity is sometimes called the *net assets* of the corporation. Although stockholders' equity is equal to assets minus liabilities, it is inappropriate to think of stockholders' equity as *assets*. Rather, stockholders' equity represents the claim by shareholders on the assets of the firm.

2. The term *contributed* or *paid-in capital* is used to identify a category of stockholders' equity. This label would seem to imply that shareholders contributed this amount of cash or other assets to the corporation. This is not necessarily true. As we will see, amounts are often transferred (reclassified) from retained earnings to the contributed capital category, but there is no inflow of assets to the corporation when this happens. An example of an action that increases contributed capital with no increase in the assets of the firm is a stock dividend.

3. The term *retained earnings* is also subject to misunderstanding. First, it may not represent the total amount of earnings retained since the inception of the corporation, because of item 2 above. Second, we sometimes read or hear the statement "Dividends were paid out of retained earnings." Dividends are usually a distribution of cash and are "paid out" of the cash account. They are charged (debited) to retained earnings because they reduce the amount of the remaining stockholders' claim. To declare and pay cash dividends, a corporation must have cash available to distribute, regardless of the amount of retained earnings. Also, legal requirements may limit dividend payments. For example, there must be a balance in the retained earnings account equal to or greater than the amount of dividends to be paid, but dividends are not paid out of retained earnings.

4. The word *capital* sometimes has different meanings in accounting and finance. For example, in finance, capital sometimes means total owners' equity. For our purposes capital often identifies only that portion of stockholders' equity that relates to capital stock, including additional contributed capital. It excludes retained earnings. We use the terms *contributed capital* and *paid-in capital* interchangeably.

Advantages and Disadvantages of the Corporate Form of Organization

The corporate form of business is the dominant form of U.S. business organization in terms of total capital invested. It has both advantages and disadvantages over partnerships and sole proprietorships:

Advantages

- **Limited liability** Stockholders are at risk for the corporation's actions only to the extent of their proportionate share of investment in total shareholders' equity. Stockholders can only lose the amount of their investment, or the legal capital of the shares they own, whichever is greater.
- **Capital accumulation** Large accumulations of funds from investors with diverse investment objectives give the corporation access to the investment market (such as stock exchanges). This accumulation enables a firm to invest large amounts in equipment or facilities in order to achieve manufacturing or other efficiencies and to support activities that might not be affordable by partnerships or proprietorships.
- **Ease of ownership transfer** Continuity, transfer, expansion, and contraction of ownership interests are facilitated.

Disadvantages

- **Increased taxation** Corporate earnings are subject to double taxation. Earnings are taxed first as corporate income and again after distribution in the form of stockholder dividends. This can result in a high overall rate of taxation.
- **Difficulties of control** The large size and impersonal nature of a corporation complicate stockholder control. Since ownership is usually separated from management and can become quite dispersed, owners may be unable to exercise active control over management actions. There can be communication difficulties. Owners may have difficulty gaining comprehensive information about the activities of the firm.
- **Regulation** Public companies are subject to greater regulatory scrutiny and incur additional costs in complying with regulatory mandates.

> *CONCEPT REVIEW*
>
> 1. How is a public corporation different from a private corporation? How is an open corporation different from a closed corporation? What type of corporation may not have the characteristic of limited liability?
> 2. Explain the differences between authorized stock, issued stock, outstanding stock, subscribed stock, and treasury stock.
> 3. Most corporations will have two primary categories of stockholders' equity. What are they? How are they distinguished on the balance sheet?

FEATURES OF EQUITY SECURITIES

The term *equity security* refers to all classifications of capital stock issued by corporations. These are usually divided into two basic types of stock: common and preferred. More than one class of common or preferred stock may be issued by a corporation, and even within each type the contractual characteristics can vary greatly. In the extreme, some preferred stock has many of the characteristics of debt.

Par Value Stock

State corporation laws usually provide for the issuance of **par value stock:** shares of stock with a designated dollar amount per share as stated in the corporate charter and printed on the stock certificates. Either par value common or par value preferred stock may be issued.

Par value stock sold initially at less than par is issued at a *discount*. Today, the issuance of par value stock at a discount is illegal in most states.[2] Par value stock sold initially above par is issued at a *premium*. A discount liability protects creditors and holds the original stockholders liable unless the liability is contractually transferred to subsequent stockholders.

In the early history of corporations in the United States, only par value stock was authorized. Because the owners of a corporation are not personally liable to the corporation's creditors, statutes allowing only par value stock were intended to protect creditors. The courts' view was that stockholders of a corporation who paid less than par value for stock could be assessed an amount equal to the discount if it were deemed necessary to satisfy creditors' claims.

Par value has little significance in most states. In the case of insolvency, stockholders cannot be held personally liable to creditors if the par value of all outstanding shares was fully paid in (or an equivalent amount of retained earnings was capitalized as in a stock dividend). Par value establishes the minimum amount of owners' equity the law requires to be contributed by shareholders to the firm when the shares are initially issued. Also, par value of preferred stock is often the basis on which preferred dividends are declared. To avoid a real or implied discount on capital stock, many corporations use a low par value, such as $1 per share, but sell the stock at a much higher price.

Par value has no particular relationship to the market value of a company's stock. Market value is a function of future expected earnings and opportunities available to the company.

Nopar Stock

Nopar stock was first permitted by statute in New York in 1912. Today many states permit its issuance. True nopar stock is designated in the charter and does not carry a stated or assigned value per share. Some states authorize the issuance of nopar stock with a *stated,* or *assigned,* value per share that is established permanently by the corporate directors and is stated in the bylaws. Most companies use a stated value for nopar stock.

Assignment of a stated value makes nopar stock equivalent to par value stock for accounting purposes. The chief advantages claimed for nopar stock are that

- A contingent liability of stockholders for stock discount is avoided.
- In some jurisdictions, there is less tax on nopar shares.

---

[2] Issuance of par value stock at a discount sometimes happens de facto when promoters and others receive shares of stock in exchange for noncash assets or services that are overvalued.

The chief disadvantage is that some states levy high franchise tax (a state tax) and other taxes (such as registration taxes) on nopar stock.

Legal Capital

Legal capital is that portion of stockholders' equity, specified by the laws of the state in which the corporation receives its charter, that must be contributed to the firm at the issuance of shares. Generally, corporation laws prohibit a distribution of assets to shareholders if the distribution would reduce the remaining total capital below legal capital. In the case of par value stock, legal capital is specified in most states as the par value of the issued or outstanding shares, including subscribed shares.[3] In the case of nopar stock, legal capital is

- The full amount paid in at issuance if it is true nopar stock.
- The stated or assigned value per share as initially established by the corporate directors if it is other than true nopar stock.

In some states, preferred stock is not included in legal capital.

Maintenance of legal capital provides a measure of protection for creditors. A corporation must refrain from paying dividends when the effect would be to impair legal capital. Also in some states, treasury stock cannot be purchased if the distribution would exceed retained earnings. However, legal capital is sometimes impaired as a result of operating losses. Stockholders are not legally liable to creditors when this happens.

Common Stock

Common stock is the primary issue of shares, normally entitling holders to all the basic rights listed earlier. When there is only one class of stock, all the shares are common stock (whether so designated or not).

Common stockholders are the residual owners of the corporation. Their position is less secure than that of creditors and preferred stockholders. The corporation owes its creditors contractual payments on specified dates, and preferred stockholders usually have a priority as to dividend and liquidation amounts per share. Thus, common stockholders have the greatest exposure to the risks of corporate failure because their right to cash flows comes after creditor and preferred stockholder claims have been met.

Although common stock is usually voting stock, some corporations issue two (or more) classes of common stock: one class has voting rights (often identified as Class A), and any other (Class B and other classes) is nonvoting. When two or more classes of common stock are issued, the Class B stock usually is traded publicly, while the Class A stock is often held by a small group and traded privately. This arrangement permits control by a small group (perhaps as protection against takeovers) and still allows access to capital markets.

Preferred Stock

Preferred stock confers *preferences,* or specific rights, that distinguish it from common stock. The most common preference is a priority claim on dividends, usually at a stated rate or amount. In exchange for this preference, the preferred stockholders often sacrifice voting rights and the right to dividends beyond the stated rate or amount.

In general, these preferences affect a variety of rights:

- Voting.
- Cumulative or noncumulative dividends.
- Nonparticipating, partially participating, or fully participating with common stockholders in dividends in excess of the stated preferred dividend.
- Assets in liquidation.
- Convertibility to other securities.
- Call features, under specified conditions.
- Redemption.

Preferred stock usually is par value stock with dividend preference expressed as a percentage of par. For example, 6 percent preferred stock has a dividend of 6 percent of the par value of each share. Preference does not guarantee a dividend, but when the

---

[3]Whether legal capital at a specific date is based on shares issued or shares outstanding depends on the state's laws of incorporation. It appears that using outstanding shares as a basis is prevalent, especially when there is a treasury stock restriction on retained earnings.

corporation declares a dividend, preferred stockholders must get a 6 percent dividend before common stockholders receive any dividends. In the case of nopar preferred stock, the dividend preference is expressed as a specific dollar amount per share, such as $5 per preferred share.

Voting Privileges on Preferred Stock   Because the right to vote is a basic right, preferred stockholders have full voting rights unless specifically prohibited in the charter. However, preferred stock is often nonvoting because the corporation issues it specifically to obtain resources without diluting the voting strength of the common stock.

Cumulative Dividend Preferences on Preferred Stock   The **cumulative dividend preference** on preferred stock provides that dividends not declared in a given year accumulate at the preference rate for the stock. This accumulated amount must be paid in full before dividends can be paid on the common stock. If preferred dividends are not declared in a given year, they are said to have been *passed* and are called *dividends in arrears* on the cumulative preferred stock. If only a part of the preferred stock dividend is paid for any year, the remainder of the cumulative dividend is in arrears. Cumulative preferred stock normally is entitled, in dissolution of the corporation, to dividends in arrears to the extent that the corporation has retained earnings. Different provisions for dividends in arrears may be stipulated in the charter and bylaws.

Assume in this text that preferred stock is cumulative unless stated otherwise. This is reasonable because courts have ruled that when the charter is silent as to the cumulative feature, preferred stock dividends are cumulative. *APB Opinion No. 9* requires that when cumulative preferred dividends are in arrears, the per share and aggregate amounts be disclosed. They are not recorded as liabilities until they are declared.

Noncumulative preferred stock provides that dividends not declared (that is, dividends passed) for any prior year or years are lost permanently. The noncumulative feature has a negative effect for the preferred stock investor. Noncumulative preferred stock is seldom issued.

Participating Dividend Preferences on Preferred Stock   There are several types of *participating dividend preferences* on preferred stock. *Nonparticipating* preferred stock limits the dividends for any year to the specified dividend preference (plus any dividends in arrears if preference is cumulative). For example, 5 percent preferred stock, par $10, noncumulative, nonparticipating, would limit the holder to a $.50 dividend per share in any one year.

Partially participating preferred stock allows the preferred stockholders to receive dividends above the preferential rate on a pro rata basis with the common stockholders. This participation is limited to an additional rate specified in the charter and on the stock certificate.

Example   A corporation may issue 5 percent preferred stock with participation up to a total of 7 percent. In this case, participation privileges with the common stockholders would be limited to an additional 2 percent dividend.

Fully participating preferred stock means that the preferred stockholders have a preference for the current year at a stated preference rate, and that they will also share on a pro rata basis in any dividends declared beyond that rate.

Example   Five percent preferred stock, par $10, fully participating, would receive its 5 percent preference ($.50 per share) plus a pro rata share (based on total par or stated value of the common and preferred stock) of any excess dividends after the common stockholders have received a matching amount (that is, 5 percent of the par or stated value of the common stock in this case). *Most preferred stock is not fully participating.*

Three cases illustrate various combinations of cumulative/noncumulative rights and of participating/nonparticipating rights. Assume the same capital structure for all cases, with contractual rights of the preferred shareholders varying case by case:[4]

Preferred stock, 5 percent, $10 par, 10,000 shares issued and outstanding	$100,000
Common stock, $5 par, 40,000 shares issued and outstanding	200,000

Case A   The preferred stock is *cumulative* and *nonparticipating,* and dividends are in arrears for the two preceding years. Cash dividends of $28,000 are declared.

	Preferred	Common
Step 1: Preferred dividends in arrears ($100,000 × .05 × 2 years)	$10,000	
Step 2: Preferred, current dividends ($100,000 × .05)	5,000	
Step 3: Balance of declared dividends to common ($28,000 − $15,000)		$13,000
	$15,000	$13,000

Case A shows the allocation of dividend payments as required by the rights attached to the preferred stock. First, payment of dividends in arrears is made. Next, current preferred dividends are paid. The remainder, no matter how large or small, accrues to the common shareholders.

Case B   The preferred stock is *noncumulative* and *partially participating,* up to an additional 4 percent. Cash dividends of $28,000 are declared.

	Preferred	Common
Step 1: Preferred, current dividends ($100,000 × .05)	$5,000	
Step 2: Common, current dividends (matching) ($200,000 × .05)		$10,000
Step 3: Allocation up to limit of participation:		
Preferred ($100,000 × .04)	4,000	
Common ($200,000 × .04)		8,000
Step 4: Balance of declared dividends to common ($28,000 − $27,000)		1,000
	$9,000	$19,000

In this case the dividends declared are sufficient to pay dividends to preferred shareholders up to the limit of their participation and then to pay the common shareholders a matching amount. If the amount of dividends declared is not sufficient (in this example, if dividends declared are less than $27,000), the dividends after step 2 are allocated proportionately between the preferred and common shareholders.

Case C   The preferred stock is *cumulative* and *fully participating.* Dividends are in arrears for the preceding two years. Cash dividends of $28,000 are declared.

	Preferred	Common
Step 1: Preferred, dividends in arrears ($100,000 × .05 × 2 years)	$10,000	
Step 2: Preferred, current dividends ($100,000 × .05)	5,000	
Step 3: Common, current dividends, matching ($200,000 × .05)		$10,000
Step 4: Allocation of remainder of $3,000 based on total par value:		
Preferred ($100,000/$300,000 × $3,000)	1,000	
Common ($200,000/$300,000 × $3,000)		2,000
	$16,000	$12,000

In Cases B and C, common stockholders receive a matching allocation after the basic dividend preference for the preferred shares has been satisfied. Once participation begins, dividends are allocated based on the total par value of the class of stock. If either the com-

---

[4]Dividends are discussed in more detail in Chapter 21. Cases A, B, and C are given here only to help illustrate the definition and features of preferred stock. The declaration of a dividend involves more than merely selecting a total amount.

mon or preferred stock is nopar and the preferred stock has participating privileges (partial or full), a specified dollar amount per share must be established in the charter to replace the percent and par value for the participation matching computations.

Asset Preference in Liquidation   In case of corporate dissolution, preferred stock that has a liquidation preference gives the preferred stockholders a priority on the assets of the corporation up to the stated liquidation preference amount per share. When this amount is satisfied, the remainder of the assets are distributed to the common stockholders. *APB Opinion No. 10* (par. 10) requires that "the liquidation preference of the preferred stock be disclosed in the equity section of the balance sheet in the aggregate . . . rather than on a per share basis or by disclosure in notes."

Preferred Stock Convertible to Other Securities   Preferred stock may carry a *convertibility* provision, allowing the preferred shares to be exchanged for (converted to) other securities, usually common stock. Because the conversion privilege offers a valuable option, convertible preferred stock is favored by investors. Convertibility privileges should be disclosed in the financial statements (tabular portion or notes) of the issuing corporation.

Callable Preferred Stock   Preferred stock may also be *callable,* which means that the issuer can call it in for cancellation at a specified price and date(s). When callable stock is called by the issuer, the stockholder must forward the stock (usually through a stockbroker) to the issuer and receive payment as specified in the call agreement. All dividends in arrears on cumulative stock also must be paid. The call price is usually above par and sometimes above the original issue price. *APB Opinion No. 10* (par. 11) states that the corporation should disclose "on the face of the balance sheet or in notes pertaining thereto, the aggregate or per share amounts at which preferred shares may be called."

Redeemable Preferred Stock   Some corporations have issued *redeemable preferred stock,* preferred stock with the unique feature of *redemption.* This stock allows either (1) mandatory redemption at a specified date and price or (2) redemption at the option of the shareholder, who has a right to redeem the shares at a specified date and price. The latter feature allows the shareholder to sell the shares back to the issuing corporation, which must purchase them. In the case of mandatory redemption, the corporation must redeem all shares of the issue at the specified date and price. Preferred shares that are redeemable solely at the option of the issuer (i.e., callable preferred stock) are viewed as *nonredeemable preferred shares* by the SEC.[5]

Debt or Equity?   Redeemable preferred shares have financial characteristics of both debt and equity. They are similar to debt in that they must be either retired or refunded at the option of the holder at a specified date. They also resemble equity securities in that
- If a dividend is passed, the shareholder does not have the right to initiate default proceedings (as would a debt holder whose interest payments were passed).
- Redeemable preferred shares are subordinate to debt in the event of liquidation.

Preferred stock with mandatory redemption has increased in popularity. It carries with it a commitment to use the firm's future cash flows to redeem the preferred stock and is therefore more like debt than equity. Some accountants believe that preferred stock with such debt-like characteristics should be reported as debt rather than as stockholders' equity. However, current GAAP does not directly recognize any preferred stock as debt.[6] On the other hand, the SEC prohibits the inclusion of redeemable preferred stock in the general category of stockholders' equity.[7] Amounts for redeemable preferred stock, nonredeemable preferred stock, and common stock cannot be combined in financial statements filed with the SEC.

---

[5] *Securities and Exchange Commission Release No. 33-6097* (Washington, DC: SEC, July 27, 1979).

[6] However, a few accounting standards have distinguished between redeemable and nonredeemable preferred stock. *SFAS No. 115* excludes redeemable preferred stock from the definition of *equity security,* and *SFAS No. 47* requires the same disclosures for capital stock redeemable at fixed or determinable prices as for long-term debt.

[7] *SEC Release No. 33-6097.*

The FASB may someday require such issues to be accounted for as debt rather than as equity, consistent with the SEC's position, but it is not currently an agenda topic for the Board.

Required SEC Presentation   *Accounting Series Release No. 268* (Washington, DC: SEC, July 1979) requires that the redeemable preferred stock amount be reported immediately before stockholders' equity for SEC reporting.

If redeemable preferred stock is really debt, why don't corporations just issue debt in the first place? After all, preferred dividends are not tax deductible, and interest payments normally are. One answer may lie in requirements affecting debt capacity in debt agreements and covenants. The issuance of redeemable preferred stock may be possible without violating a debt covenant, when issuing debt securities would not be.

A second incentive is the desire to raise capital at rates below the market rate of interest. Corporate buyers are willing to accept a dividend rate on redeemable preferred stock that is less than the market rate of interest because corporations can exclude a significant portion of their dividend income from taxable income. No such exclusion is available for interest income.

Disclosures for Capital Stock   *SFAS No. 129,* "Disclosure of Information about Capital Structure," requires disclosure of the rights associated with a firm's outstanding securities. Dividend and liquidation preferences, participation rights, call prices and dates, and conversion rates are examples of the information to be disclosed. The statement also lists the following additional specific required disclosures, several of which pertain to preferred stock.

1. The number of shares issued from the conversion or exercise of securities during the period.
2. The liquidation preference of preferred of other senior stock must be disclosed in the *equity section of the balance sheet* when that preference is significantly greater than par or stated value.
3. The aggregate or per-share amounts at which preferred stock may be called or is subject to redemption.
4. The aggregate and per-share amounts of preferred stock dividends in arrears.
5. The redemption requirement for all capital stock redeemable at fixed or determinable prices on fixed or determinable dates in each of the five years following the date of the balance sheet.

|CONCEPT REVIEW

1. What are the fundamental differences between common stock and preferred stock?
2. Why would a firm issue redeemable preferred stock?
3. A firm has issued an outstanding 1,000 shares of $100 par, cumulative, nonparticipating shares of 5 percent preferred stock, and 20,000 shares of $5 par common stock. Dividends are in arrears for the past year (not including the current year). The board of directors of the firm declares dividends of $25,000 to be paid to shareholders at the end of the fiscal year. How will the $25,000 be shared between the preferred and common shareholders?

ACCOUNTING FOR STOCK ISSUANCE AND RELATED TRANSACTIONS

Accounting for stockholders' equity emphasizes the various categories of equity. If there is only one class of stock, an account titled *capital stock* is usually used. Where there are two or more classes of stock, more descriptive account titles such as *common stock, preferred stock, 5 percent,* and *common stock, nopar* are used. The additional (or other) capital stock accounts represent the remaining contributed capital of the corporation.

The sequence of transactions related to the issuance of stock is

1. Authorization of shares.
2. Sale for cash or subscriptions (that is, the sale of shares on credit).
3. Collections on subscriptions (when applicable).
4. Issuance of the shares.

Accounting for the Issuance of Par Value Stock

Authorization   The charter authorization to issue a specified number of shares may be recorded as a memo entry in the general journal and in the ledger account by the following notation:

Common stock—Par value $10 per share (authorized 50,000 shares)

Par Value Stock Issued for Cash   When stock is issued, a stock certificate specifying the number of shares represented is prepared for each stockholder. An entry reflecting the number of shares held by each stockholder is made in the stockholder ledger, a subsidiary ledger of the capital stock account.

Example   A firm issues 10,000 shares of common stock, par $10, for cash of $10.20 per share. The transaction would be recorded as follows:

Cash	102,000	
Common stock, par $10 (10,000 shares)		100,000
Contributed capital in excess of par, common stock		2,000

The common stock account is credited for the par value of the stock issued. The excess over par is credited to an account named *contributed capital in excess of par* or *additional paid-in capital* to record the source in detail. If in the rare instance when par value stock is sold at a discount (less than par), a negative stockholders' equity account, *discount on common* (or *preferred*) *stock,* is debited for the amount of the discount.

Accounting for the Issuance of Nopar Stock

Authorization of nopar stock may be recorded in the same way shown for par value stock. Most states require that the total number of shares authorized be shown on each stock certificate, in addition to the number of shares represented by that particular stock certificate.

Many state statutes permit either of two types of nopar stock, *true* nopar stock and *stated value* nopar stock. True nopar stock, when sold, is recorded as a credit to the capital stock account in accordance with the legal requirements of the state of incorporation. If the statute provides that all proceeds represent legal capital, the capital stock account should be credited for the full amount received. If the statutes establish a minimum amount per share, at least this amount should be credited to the capital stock account, with any remainder credited to an account labeled *contributed capital in excess of stated value*. In the absence of legal requirements, the total amount received should be credited to the nopar capital stock account. In this case, no contributed capital in excess of par (or additional paid-in capital) is recorded.

Nopar stock with a stated (or assigned) value is accounted for in the same manner as par value stock with a stated value used on essentially the same basis as par value stock. The amount of the sale (issue) price in excess of stated value should be credited to an account with a title such as *contributed* (or *additional paid-in*) *capital in excess of stated value, nopar common stock.*

Capital Stock Sold on a Subscription Basis

During the start-up of a corporation, prospective stockholders may sign a contract to purchase a specified number of shares on credit, with payment due at one or more specified future dates. This may be done because the newly formed corporation does not need the capital all at once, or because the stockholders need time to accumulate funds to pay for shares. A corporation may sell capital stock on credit anytime after incorporation. Such contractual agreements are known as *stock subscriptions,* and the stock involved is called *subscribed capital stock.*

Although most stock is marketed through intermediaries, some firms sell directly to investors, often through stock subscriptions as discussed below. Some firms even market their stock on the Internet.

Example   Spring Street Brewing, a small beer brewing firm, posted a page on the World Wide Web facilitating trading in its stock. This medium allows firms to access the capital market without paying underwriters or brokers.

When a legal contract is involved, accounting recognition must be given to these transactions. The agreed or contractual purchase price is debited to stock subscriptions receivable. Capital stock subscribed is credited for the par, stated, or assigned amount per share. The difference is credited to contributed capital in excess of par (or stated value) as though the subscriber had paid for the subscribed shares in full.

Example   Assume that 120 shares of Bee Corporation common stock, par $10, are subscribed for at $12 by J. Doe. The total is payable in three installments. The entry by Bee Corporation would be as follows:

Stock subscriptions receivable—Common stock (Doe)	1,440*	
Common stock subscribed, par $10 ($120 shares)		1,200
Contributed capital in excess of par, common stock		240

*Payable in three installments of $480 each.

The excess contributed capital is recognized when the subscription is recorded, rather than later when the cash is collected. In this way, the full legal claim (the stock subscription receivable) the corporation has on the subscriber is recognized. Similar to capital leases, this is an example of recognition of an executory contract.

The credit balance in common stock subscribed reflects the corporation's obligation to issue the 120 shares on fulfillment of the terms of the agreement by the subscriber. This account is reported on the balance sheet similar to the related capital stock account (see Exhibit 20–3).

There are two ways to present stock subscriptions receivable acceptable under GAAP:
- As an asset.
- As a contra to stockholders' equity.

If the receivable is treated as an asset, it is reported as a current asset if collection is expected within one year of the balance sheet date. Otherwise it is a noncurrent asset under the category *other assets*.

If the receivable is treated as a contra account to stockholders' equity, it is offset against the common stock subscribed account in the stockholders' equity section of the balance sheet. Since it is not possible in many states to obtain a judgment against a subscriber for failure to pay the unpaid balance of a subscription receivable, this treatment is reasonable. Moreover, the SEC requires the contra equity approach.

In some cases, subscription contracts call for installment payments. In such cases, separate accounts may be set up for each installment. If the corporation has a number of subscriptions, it is usually desirable to maintain a subscribers' ledger as a subsidiary record to the stock subscriptions receivable account, similar to that maintained for trade accounts receivable.

Collections on stock subscriptions receivable may be in cash, property, or services. The appropriate account is debited, and subscriptions receivable is credited. If a noncash asset or a service is received, the amount recorded is based on the market value of that asset or service.

Stock certificates are generally not issued until the subscription price is paid in full. In the Bee Corporation example, when the final payment of $480 is received, the issuer makes two entries as follows:

To record receipt of final payment:

Cash	480	
Stock subscriptions receivable—Common stock (Doe)		480

EXHIBIT 20–4 Entries for Sales and Subscriptions for Nopar Stock

Case Data and Accounts	Stated Value Stock		True Nopar Value Stock	
1. To record authorization of 10,000 shares of nopar stock:				
Notation—10,000 shares of nopar common stock authorized	Stated value, $5		No stated value	
2. To record cash sale and issuance of 5,000 shares at $6:				
Cash	30,000		30,000	
Common stock, nopar, stated value $5		25,000		
Common stock, nopar				30,000
Contributed capital in excess of stated value, nopar common stock		5,000		
3. To record subscription taken for 5,000 shares at $6; 20% collected in cash:				
Cash (5,000 × $6 × .20)	6,000		6,000	
Stock subscriptions receivable, nopar common stock	24,000		24,000	
Nopar common stock subscribed (5,000 shares)		25,000		30,000
Contributed capital in excess of stated value, nopar common stock		5,000		
4. To record collection of subscription receivable and issuance of all of the subscribed shares:				
Cash	24,000		24,000	
Stock subscriptions receivable, nopar common stock		24,000		24,000
Nopar common stock subscribed	25,000		30,000	
Common stock, nopar, stated valued $5 (5,000 shares)		25,000		
Common stock, nopar (5,000 shares)				30,000

To record issuance of stock:

Common stock subscribed	1,200	
Common stock, par $10 (120 shares)		1,200

Accounting for cash sales and for stock subscriptions of true nopar stock and stated value nopar stock is illustrated in Exhibit 20–4.

Default on Subscriptions Subscriber defaults are treated in several different ways, depending on the subscription contract and state law. The corporation may
- Return all payments received to the subscriber.
- Issue shares equivalent to the number paid for in full.
- Simply keep the monies received.

The first two options do not penalize the subscriber. The third option is unusual, although state statutes generally do not prevent it. State laws vary considerably; two contrasting possibilities are:

1. The subscribed stock and all payments made are forfeited. The forfeited amount is credited to the contributed capital of the corporation. The corporation is free to resell the shares. Provisions of this type favor the corporation and seldom occur. In the Bee Corporation example, assume that Subscriber Doe has made one $480 payment, and then defaults. The entry to remove the related account balances is as follows:

Common stock subscribed (120 shares)	1,200	
Contributed capital in excess of par, common stock	240	
Subscriptions receivable (Doe)		960
Contributed capital from defaulted subscriptions (amount paid in by Doe)		480

The corporation recognizes a contribution of $480 to stockholders' equity.

2. The stock is forfeited, and the corporation resells the stock under a lien providing reimbursement to the original subscriber to the extent that the net receipts for the stock (both from the subscriber and from subsequent resale of the stock to another investor, less the cost incurred in making the later sale) exceed the original subscription price. To remove any incentive to default, the refund cannot exceed the amount paid to the date of default less resale costs.

Exhibit 20–5 illustrates the accounting under this provision.

EXHIBIT 20–5
Default on Stock Subscriptions—Shares Resold under Lien

1. Bee Corporation received from Subscriber Doe a subscription for 120 shares of common stock, par $10, at $12 per share:

Stock subscription receivable, common stock (120 shares × $12)	1,440	
Common stock subscribed, par $10 (120 shares × $10)		1,200
Contributed capital in excess of par, common stock (120 shares × $2)		240

2. Bee Corporation received a $480 installment on the subscription from Subscriber Doe:

Cash	480	
Stock subscription receivable, common stock		480

3. Subscriber Doe defaults on the subscription. Bee Corporation records the default under the lien provision:

Common stock subscribed, par $10 (120 shares)	1,200	
Contributed capital in excess of par, common stock	240	
Stock subscription receivable, common stock ($1,440 − $480)		960
Payable to Subscriber Doe (pending resale of formerly subscribed shares)		480

4. Bee Corporation resells the formerly subscribed shares for $15 per share. Bee Corporation pays the cost of resale, $50, and debits this amount to the payable to Subscriber Doe account.

Resale of shares:

Cash (120 shares × $15) − $50	1,750	
Payable to Subscriber Doe (resale costs)	50	
Common stock, par $10 (120 shares)		1,200
Contributed capital in excess of par, common stock (120 shares × $15 = $1,800) − $1,200		600

5. Bee Corporation pays stipulated amount to Subscriber Doe:

Payable to Subscriber Doe*	430	
Cash		430

*Computation:
Amount to be paid to Subscriber Doe based on lien provisions:

Net receipts for the stock:		
Cash collected from Subscriber Doe	$ 480	
Cash collected from resale of shares	1,800	
Less: Cost of resale	(50)	
Net receipts		$2,230
Original subscription price		1,440
Remainder payable to Subscriber Doe, subject to limitation		$ 790
Limitation—total actual payments made by Subscriber Doe, less resale costs ($480 − $50)		$ 430

Therefore, Subscriber Doe is paid $430.

Issuance of Capital Stock for Noncash Assets

Corporations sometimes issue capital stock for noncash assets. In one example, Butterfield Equities Corporation privately placed 1.8 million shares of its new preferred stock and 100,000 new common shares, primarily in exchange for real estate. (In a private placement a corporation arranges to sell an issue to a limited number of specific buyers, and the issuer need not meet all the SEC disclosure requirements of a public offering.)

The current market value of the stock issued or the noncash consideration received, *whichever is the most reliably determinable,* is used to record the transaction.[8] If the

---

[8]"Business Combinations," *APB Opinion No. 16* (New York: AICPA, 1970), par. 67; and *FASB Technical Bulletin 84–1* (Norwalk, CT: FASB, 1984), par 7.

current market value of neither the capital stock issued nor the noncash consideration received can be reliably determined, appraised values are used. If neither market values nor appraisals are reliable, values are established by the corporation's board of directors. Should a reliable market value for the capital stock be subsequently established, the value set by the corporation's board may be revised.

Watered Stock or Secret Reserves?   The issuance of capital stock for noncash considerations can involve questionable valuations. Some companies have not used market values or independent appraisals, and instead permitted directors to set arbitrary values. In some cases, the over-valuation of assets received results in overvaluation of stockholders' equity. This is referred to as *watered stock*. The value of the resources received for the issued stock is less than (i.e., it waters down) the recorded value of the stock issued. In contrast, some companies undervalue the assets received and understate stockholders' equity—resulting in a condition often called *secret reserves*. Secret reserves also are created by depreciating or amortizing an asset over a period less than its useful life.

Special Sales of Capital Stock

A corporation may sell two or more classes of capital stock for one lump-sum amount (often referred to as a *basket sale*). The total proceeds must be allocated logically among the several classes of securities. Two methods used are (1) the **proportional method,** where the lump sum received is allocated proportionately among the classes of stock on the basis of the relative market value of each security, and (2) the **incremental method,** where the market value of one security is used as a basis for that security, with the remainder of the lump sum allocated to the other class.

The method selected should be the one that produces the most reliable results for the data available.

Example   Assume Vax Corporation issues 1,000 shares of common stock, par $10, and 500 shares of preferred stock, par $8, in two different situations.

Situation 1—Proportional Method Applied   The common stock is selling at $40 per share and the preferred at $20. Assume that the total cash received is $48,000. Because reliable market values are available, the proportional method is preferable as a basis for allocating the lump-sum amount as follows:

Proportional allocation:

Market value of common (1,000 shares × $40)	$40,000	(⅘)
Market value of preferred (500 shares × $20)	10,000	(⅕)
Total market value	$50,000	(⁵⁄₅)

Allocation of the lump-sum sale price of $48,000:

Common stock ($48,000 × ⅘)	$38,400
Preferred stock ($48,000 × ⅕)	9,600
Total	$48,000

The journal entry to record the issuance:

Cash	48,000	
Common stock, par $10 (1,000 shares)		10,000
Preferred stock, par $8 (500 shares)		4,000
Contributed capital in excess of par, common ($38,400 − $10,000)		28,400
Contributed capital in excess of par, preferred ($9,600 − $4,000)		5,600

Situation 2—Incremental Method Applied   The common stock of Vax Corporation is selling at $40; a market for the preferred stock has not been established. The market value of the common is used as a basis for the following entry:

```
Cash . . . . . . . . . . . . . . . . . . . . . . . . . . . . . . . .   48,000
    Common stock, par $10 (1,000 shares)   . . . . . . . . . . . . . . . . . . . .        10,000
    Preferred stock, par $8 (500 shares)   . . . . . . . . . . . . . . . . . . . .         4,000
    Contributed capital in excess of par, common
        [1,000 shares × ($40 − $10)] . . . . . . . . . . . . . . . . . . . .               30,000
    Contributed capital in excess of par, preferred (remainder)  . . . . . . . . . . . .    4,000
```

Assessments on Capital Stock

Some states permit the issuance of *assessable stock*. A stock assessment is the collection of cash from each stockholder in proportion to the shares held without the issuance of additional stock. In some states and under certain conditions, the board of directors may assess the stockholders a certain amount per share, even though the stock is not identified as assessable stock. However, such an assessment usually requires stockholder approval. Stock assessments may be made when a corporation needs cash or is facing insolvency, or when the stock originally was issued at a discount. In the last case, the assessment (up to the amount of the discount) should be credited to the discount account. If no stock discount is carried in the accounts, the credit is to a contributed capital account with an appropriate caption, such as *contributed capital from stock assessments.*

Stock assessments are not often used. To the extent that such assessments are required to be paid, the feature of limited liability has been compromised. Investors would have reduced interest in owning such stock, especially if they have little direct control over the firm.

Stock Issue Costs

Issues of capital stock can entail substantial expenditures. These expenditures include registration fees, underwriter commissions, attorney and accountant fees, printing costs, clerical costs, and promotional costs. These expenditures are called *stock issue costs.* While stock issue costs are usually not large compared with the total funds received, they are large enough to require careful accounting. Two methods of accounting for stock issue costs are used:

1. **Offset method** Stock issue costs are treated as a reduction of the amount received from the sale of the related capital stock. The rationale to support this method is that these one-time costs cannot reasonably be assigned to future period revenues and that the net cash received is the actual issue price of the stock. Stock issue costs are debited to contributed capital in excess of par.

2. **Deferred charge method** Stock issue costs are recorded as a deferred charge and amortized over a reasonable period. The argument for this method is that these costs create an intangible asset that contributes to the earning of future revenues. They are allocated against future period revenues in conformity with the matching principle.

Although the offset method dominates in practice, both methods are used. After the issuance of capital stock, administrative costs required to maintain stockholder records, transfer costs, and dividend payment costs are expensed when incurred.

Unrealized Capital

A third category of stockholders' equity, found in many financial statements, is *unrealized capital.* Unrealized capital represents special and separately identified items that are an increment (increase) or decrement (decrease) in stockholders' equity not arising from earnings, dividend payment, or changes in contributed capital. An example is cumulative unrealized holding gain or loss on investments classified as securities available for sale (SAS). *SFAS No. 115* requires that these gains/losses be classified as unrealized capital rather than as income. Accounting for unrealized gains and losses from SAS investments is covered in Chapter 14. A second, frequently encountered source of unrealized capital is the gain or loss arising from translating foreign-denominated financial statements into U.S. currency for financial reporting. *SFAS No. 52* covers this accounting issue; it is usually covered in advanced accounting courses. Several additional sources of unrealized capital are only infrequently encountered. These include:

- Guarantees of ESOP debt.
- Pension liability adjustments.
- Deferred compensation related to employee stock award plans.

These various sources of unrealized capital have the effect of increasing or decreasing stockholders' equity, usually from items that are held in suspense until recognized as an income statement element. For example, unrealized holding gains and losses on SAS investments are held in suspense as unrealized capital until the investment is sold, at which time the realized holding gain or loss is included in income. Each source of unrealized capital is covered by various accounting pronouncements or is accepted practice. Further discussion regarding the measurement and recording of each source is found in relevant chapters of this text or, in the case of translation gains and losses, in advanced accounting texts.

CONCEPT REVIEW

1. When capital stock is sold on a subscription basis, what are the arguments for and against accounting for the stock subscription receivable as an asset?
2. Why is the transaction in (1) recorded at all?
3. A bundle or unit of securities consisting of one share of common stock and one share of new-issue preferred stock is sold for $50. There is a current market price for the firm's publicly traded common stock, but not for the preferred stock. Describe how to account for the issue.

ACCOUNTING FOR REACQUISITION OF STOCK

Treasury Stock

Treasury stock is a corporation's preferred or common stock that (1) has been issued, (2) is reacquired by the issuing corporation, and (3) has not been resold or retired. The purchase of treasury stock does not reduce the number of *issued* shares, but does reduce the number of *outstanding* shares. Treasury shares subsequently may be resold or, in some cases, retired.

In general, treasury stock is acquired for any of the following reasons:

- To use for employee stock options, bonus plans, and direct sale to employees.
- To establish a market for the company's stock.
- To use the shares acquired to purchase other securities or assets.
- To use the shares acquired for a stock dividend.
- To increase earnings per share by reducing the number of shares outstanding.
- To buy out one or more specific stockholders.
- To thwart takeover attempts.
- To reduce dividend payments by reducing the number of shares outstanding.

The purchase of treasury stock decreases both assets and stockholders' equity; a sale of treasury stock increases both assets and stockholders' equity. Treasury stock usually does not carry voting, dividend, preemptive, or liquidation rights and is not an asset. It is accounted for as a contra account to stockholders' equity. Treasury stock transactions do not affect the income statement. They may, however, cause retained earnings to decrease.

Accounting Trends and Techniques—1996 reports that 384 of the 600 corporations surveyed disclosed treasury stock in 1995. This fact indicates the prevalence of the purchase and sale of treasury stock, which is almost always common stock. Some purchases of treasury stock have dramatically reduced the size of the purchasing firm.

Example   Anheuser-Busch Companies, Inc., the world's largest brewer and a company with total assets of $10,591 million, shows the following stockholders' equity section at December 31, 1995 (in millions of dollars):

Common stock, $1.00 par value, authorized 800,000,000 shares	$ 347.3
Capital in excess of par	1,012.2
Retained earnings	6,869.6
Foreign currency translation adjustment	(12.1)
	$8,217.0
Treasury stock, at cost	(3,435.0)
ESOP debt guarantee offset	(347.1)
Total	$4,434.9

In a note to the statements, Anheuser-Busch reports that 347,265,124 shares of common stock are issued at December 31, 1995, and 93,288,622 of those have been reacquired and are treasury stock at December 31, 1995. The company has reacquired and holds nearly 27 percent of the common stock it has issued. By purchasing over one-fourth of its outstanding shares, Anheuser-Busch has substantially reduced its size ($3,435.0 million has been paid out to acquire these shares).

There are a number of consequences of such a stock repurchase:

- Ownership is concentrated with the remaining shareholders (a desirable result if there is concern that other investors or investor groups might attempt a takeover).
- The firm distributes cash to shareholders on a self-selection basis (to those who sold their shares), and does not have to increase its dividend to accomplish this.
- There are fewer shares outstanding, thus earnings per share may increase.
- Assuming no similar decrease in the amount of debt, the leverage of the company is increased.

Insider Information and Stock Transactions   Companies must exercise care in transactions involving their stock (including treasury stock) because corporate management is legally prohibited from using insider information to the detriment of stockholders. For example, oil company management with knowledge of a profitable oil discovery cannot withhold this news and acquire stock at a low market price. Alternatively, a company cannot withhold bad news and sell its stock (including treasury stock) at an artificially high market price. The securities laws (particularly Rules 10b–5 and 10b–6 of the Securities and Exchange Act of 1934) prohibit corporations from engaging in deceptive conduct, including acts related to transactions involving their stock.

Classification   The repurchase by a corporation of shares of its own capital stock poses a conceptual question about its classification. Should treasury stock be accounted for as an asset (that is, an investment in equity securities) or as a contraction of the stockholders' equity of the corporation? Although treasury stock has some of the attributes of an asset, it is viewed as a reduction of stockholders' equity because:

- A corporation cannot own itself (the separate entity assumption).
- The purchase of treasury stock is a payment to the selling stockholders for their investment interest in the corporation.
- Treasury stock is similar to the unissued stock of the corporation, and unissued stock is not an asset.
- Treasury stock may be retired by the corporation. When this is done, the number of shares issued is reduced.

Recording and Reporting Treasury Stock Transactions

Two methods are used to account for treasury stock:

1. Cost method (one-transaction concept).
2. Par value method (dual-transaction concept).

Both methods are acceptable. The two methods yield different results for individual accounts within the stockholders' equity section of the balance sheet, but the *total* amount of stockholders' equity is the same under both methods.

Cost Method   The cost method is referred to as the one-transaction method because the purchase and subsequent sale of the treasury stock are viewed as one transaction with two parts. First, at acquisition, the cost of the treasury stock is debited to a contra stockholders' equity account called **treasury stock.**[9] Separate treasury stock accounts are established for each class of stock. At the subsequent resale, the treasury stock account is credited for the cost of the treasury stock. When treasury stock is acquired at different costs, specific shares may be identified. Otherwise, a FIFO or average cost per share must be used to determine the credit to the treasury stock account (at cost) at resale date.

When treasury stock accounted for using the cost method is sold (usually resulting in a debit to cash) for more than its acquisition cost, the difference is credited to a contributed capital account called **contributed capital from treasury stock transactions.** If treasury stock is sold for an amount less than its acquisition cost, the difference is debited to the same account if the credit balance in that account is sufficient to absorb the debit. Any excess is debited to retained earnings.

The journal entries and reporting under both the par value and the cost method are illustrated in Exhibit 20–6. Under the cost method, the treasury stock account at the end of the accounting period is reported as an unallocated reduction of the total amount of stockholders' equity. The original contributed capital accounts are unaffected. The account *contributed capital from treasury stock transactions* is reported infrequently as a separate account.

Par Value Method   The par value method is called the dual-transaction method because the purchase and sale of treasury stock are treated as two separate, independent transactions. The objectives of the par value method are:
- At acquisition date of treasury stock—To make a final accounting with the stockholder selling the stock, and to adjust the capital accounts on a constructive stock retirement basis.
- At resale date of treasury stock—To record the sale in essentially the same manner as for the sale and issuance of unissued stock.

To accomplish these two objectives, the treasury stock account is carried at the par or stated value per share (thus the designation *par value method*). Accounting for treasury stock under the par value method is described below.

Date of Acquisition   The acquisition of the stock for cash is recorded as a debit to treasury stock for the par value in the case of par value stock, for the stated value in the case of nopar stock with a stated value, or for the average amount previously credited to the capital stock account in the case of true nopar stock. Contributed capital in excess of par is debited for the proportionate amount of any excess over par or stated value that was paid by the stockholders when the shares were originally issued. If a debit or credit balance still remains, this excess is allocated as follows:

1. When there is a debit difference to be allocated:
    a. Step 1—debit contributed capital from treasury stock transactions (to the extent needed, but not in excess of any credit balance in that account from the same class of stock).
    b. Step 2—allocate any remainder as a debit to retained earnings. The purpose of this step allocation is to maintain a distinction among the sources of contributed capital. Alternatively, *APB Opinion No. 6* (par. 12a) states that "the excess [debit difference] may be charged entirely to retained earnings in recognition of the fact that a corporation can always capitalize or allocate retained earnings for such purposes." Some companies are reluctant to debit retained earnings because they wish either to protect the cumulative retained earnings amount or to be able to declare dividends in the future.

---

[9]*FASB Technical Bulletin 85–6* specifies that if the price paid for treasury stock exceeds the current market price, the excess should be attributed to the other elements of the transaction if identifiable. An example occurs when the selling shareholder agrees not to buy additional shares of the issuing company. In this case the excess is expensed; treasury stock is recorded at market value. However, in routine transactions involving prices exceeding current market value, such as in a tender offer to all or most shareholders, the entire price is used as the cost of the treasury stock.

Case Data (initial sale of stock)

To record the initial sale and issuance of 10,000 shares of common stock, par $25, at $26 per share:

Cash (10,000 shares × $26). 260,000
  Common stock, par $25 (10,000 shares) 250,000
  Contributed capital in excess of par, common stock (10,000 shares × $1) 10,000

Assume a beginning balance of $40,000 in retained earnings.

Entries to Record Treasury Stock Transactions

Cost Method	Par Value Method

1. Acquisition—To record the acquisition of 2,000 shares of treasury common stock at $28 per share:

Cost Method		Par Value Method	
Treasury stock, common stock:		Treasury stock, common stock	
(2,000 shares × cost, $28)	56,000	(2,000 shares × par, $25).	50,000
Cash	56,000	Contributed capital in excess of	
		par, common stock (at $1)	2,000
		Contributed capital from treasury	
		stock transactions, common stock	–0–*
		Retained earnings	4,000
		Cash	56,000

*There is no credit balance to absorb a debit, so the remaining $4,000 is debited to retained earnings. Alternatively, if the 2,000 shares had been acquired for $46,000, contributed capital from treasury stock transactions would have been credited for $6,000.

2. Sale—To record sale of 500 shares of the treasury stock at $30 per share (above cost and above par):

Cost Method		Par Value Method	
Cash (500 shares × $30).	15,000	Cash (500 shares × $30)	15,000
Treasury stock, common stock		Treasury stock, common stock	
(500 shares × cost, $28)	14,000	(500 shares × par, $25)	12,500
Contributed capital from treasury		Contributed capital in excess of par,	
stock transactions, common stock*.	1,000	common stock	2,500

*If this sale had been at cost ($28 per share), no entry would have been made to contributed capital from treasury stock transactions, common stock.

3. Sale—To record the sale of another 500 shares of the treasury stock at $19 per share (below cost and below par, which would be an unusual occurrence):

Cost Method		Par Value Method	
Cash (500 shares × $19).	9,500	Cash (500 shares × $19).	9,500
Contributed capital from treasury		Contributed capital from treasury	
stock transactions, common stock‡	1,000	stock transactions, common stock†	–0–
Retained earnings	3,500	Retained earnings	3,000
Treasury stock, common stock		Treasury stock, common stock	
(500 shares × cost, $28).	14,000	(500 shares × par, $25)	12,500

‡Debit limited to the credit balance in this account (entry 2); any remainder is debited to retained earnings.

†Debit limited to the credit balance in this account, which is zero, because there were no prior purchases of treasury stock below original issue price. Any remainder is debited to retained earnings.

Financial Statement Reporting (after all transactions)

Cost Method		Par Value Method	
Contributed capital:		Contributed capital:	
Common stock, par $25, authorized 50,000		Common stock, par $25, authorized 50,000	
shares, issued 10,000 shares	$250,000	shares, issued 10,000 shares	$250,000
Contributed capital in excess of par,		Less: Treasury stock, 1,000 shares at par $25	(25,000)
common stock.	10,000	Total common stock outstanding, 9,000	
Contributed capital from treasury stock		shares	225,000
transactions, common stock	–0–	Contributed capital in excess of par, common	
Total contributed capital	260,000	stock ($10,000 − $2,000 + $2,500).	10,500
Retained earnings ($40,000 − $3,500)	36,500	Contributed capital from treasury stock	
Total contributed capital and retained		transactions, common stock	–0–
earnings	296,500	Total contributed capital	235,500
Less: Treasury stock, 1,000 shares at cost, $28	28,000	Retained earnings ($40,000 − $4,000 −	
Total stockholders' equity	$268,500	$3,000).	33,000
		Total stockholders' equity	$268,500

2. When there is a credit difference to be allocated, the excess should be credited in full to contributed capital from treasury stock transactions.

Date of Resale   Under the par value method, the entry for resale of treasury stock is essentially the same as the entry for the original sale (see exception below). Cash is debited for the amount of cash received, and treasury stock is credited for the par value, stated value, or average paid in (in the case of true nopar stock). If the sale price (the debit to cash) of the treasury stock is more than its par value, stated value, or average paid in for nopar stock originally (the usual case), the full amount of the difference should be credited to contributed capital in excess of par. If the sale price of the treasury stock is less than its par value, stated value, or average paid in for nopar stock, the usual debit is to contributed capital from treasury stock transactions. If the credit balance in that account cannot absorb the difference, the remainder is debited to retained earnings. It is acceptable to debit the full amount to retained earnings, but most companies prefer not to reduce retained earnings any more than is required.

The section titled *Financial Statement Reporting* in Exhibit 20–6 shows how the two methods report treasury stock on the balance sheet. The par value method is conceptually preferable because it maintains the reporting of capital by source. Treasury stock is reported as a negative element of contributed capital. By contrast, under the cost method, treasury stock is reported as a separate, unallocated negative component of total stockholders' equity. Nevertheless, probably because of its simplicity, the cost method is used more often. Of the 385 companies reporting treasury stock in *Accounting Trends and Techniques—1996,* 355 companies used the cost method, while only 27 companies used the par value method.

The use of contributed capital from treasury stock transactions can be confusing because the account is increased and decreased under different circumstances depending on whether the cost or par value method is used. The following table summarizes the use of this account:

	Cost Method	**Par Method**
Increase Contributed Capital from Treasury Stock Transactions	When *reissue* treasury stock at more than cost	When *purchase* treasury stock at less than original issue price
Decrease Contributed Capital from Treasury Stock Transactions	When *reissue* treasury stock at less than cost	When *purchase* treasury stock at more than original issue price

Stock Received by Donation   Stockholders occasionally donate shares to the corporation. *SFAS No. 116* requires that donated stock be recorded as a revenue or gain and included in income for the period. The donated stock continues to be identified as treasury stock.

Example   Assume that Snow Company has 10,000 shares of $10 par common stock issued and outstanding. On May 15, a stockholder donates 1,000 shares of her stock to the company. On that date the market price of the stock is $15 per share. Snow Company plans to resell the donated shares in the near future, and it uses the cost method to account for treasury stock.

The entry Snow Company would make, under *SFAS No. 116* requirements, would be the following:

Treasury stock	15,000	
Gain from receipt of donated stock		15,000

Suppose Snow sold the donated stock on June 15 for $17 per share. The entry to record the resale of the donated shares is the same as the sale of any treasury stock:

Cash	17,000	
Treasury stock		15,000
Contributed capital from treasury stock transactions, common		2,000

The receipt of donated capital shares is a rare event for most corporations. There is only one example of this transaction in the three most recent issues of *Accounting Trends and*

Techniques. Corporations are more frequently the recipient of other types of donated assets (such as land for a plant); the accounting requirements for these types of donations are covered in Chapter 11.

Formal Retirement of Treasury Stock

Firms may retire treasury stock and return it to authorized but unissued status. A corporation may retire treasury shares (by amending its charter) and have the shares revert to unauthorized (that is, not subject to resale or reissuance) status. In either case, when treasury stock is retired, the treasury stock account is credited and contributed capital from treasury stock transactions is reduced (debited) on a proportional basis. Any difference, if a credit, is recorded in contributed capital from stock retirement; if a debit, retained earnings is reduced.

Example   The bottom panel of Exhibit 20–6 shows financial statement presentation of 1,000 shares of treasury stock acquired at $28 per share and accounted for under the cost and the par value methods. Suppose the 1,000 shares are to be retired and returned to unissued status. The entries under each method are:

a. Retirement when accounted for by the cost method:

Common stock, par $25	25,000	
Retained earnings	3,000	
Treasury stock, at cost		28,000

b. Retirement when accounted for by the par value method:

Common stock, par $25	25,000	
Treasury stock, at par		25,000

The retirement of the stock does not affect the net balance in stockholders' equity. However, it does reduce the number of shares issued by the number of shares retired.

Restriction of Retained Earnings for Treasury Stock

The purchase of treasury stock involves disbursement of assets (usually cash) to the owners of the shares purchased. This may jeopardize creditor interests (or those of another class of stockholders), even though legal capital is technically maintained. Some states therefore limit the amount of treasury stock that may be held at any one time to a specified amount, usually the total amount of retained earnings. This provision has the effect of requiring a restriction (often called an *appropriation*) of retained earnings equal to the cost of treasury stock held, which reduces the amount of retained earnings that may be used for dividends until the treasury shares are resold. Debt covenants may also limit the amount of treasury stock a corporation may purchase. Some states impose no limits on amounts of treasury stock that can be acquired.

Retained earnings restrictions (that is, appropriations) related to treasury stock usually are reported by a disclosure note in the financial statements. An alternative is to use appropriation entries, as is discussed in Chapter 21.

Retirement of Callable and Redeemable Stock

Callable preferred stock provides the issuing corporation the option, after a certain date, to call in the shares at a specified price. **Redeemable** stock gives the stockholder the option under certain conditions to tender the shares to the company at a specified price. These preferences can be illustrated as follows:

Preferred Stock	Preference
Callable	**Issuing corporation** has the option to recall at specified dates at specified prices. Investor must comply.
Redeemable	**Investor** has the option to require the issuing corporation to reacquire shares at specified dates and specified prices. Issuing corporation must comply.

The terms *callable* or *redeemable* are used with the above definitions in this text. In practice, however, they are sometimes defined somewhat ambiguously. For example, the term *redeemable* is sometimes used to mean callable.

The exercise of a call or redemption option usually involves acquisition and formal retirement of the stock by the issuing corporation. Shares called or redeemed have the status of unissued shares. They are not classified as treasury stock.

When callable or redeemable stock is acquired and formally retired, cash is credited and all capital balances relating to the specific shares are removed from the accounts. Any remaining debit difference is recorded in retained earnings. Any remaining credit difference is credited to a contributed capital account, such as contributed capital from retirement of stock. If the preferred stock is cumulative and there are dividends in arrears, such dividends must be paid and debited to retained earnings at the date of the call or redemption.

Example   Assume that a corporation has outstanding 2,500 shares of 5 percent callable preferred stock (par value $100) that was issued at $104 per share. Stockholders' equity accounts include 5 percent callable preferred stock, par $100, $250,000; contributed capital in excess of par, preferred stock, $10,000; and retained earnings, $45,000. Assume that the corporation calls and formally retires the preferred stock:

Assumption 1   The preferred stock is noncumulative and callable at the original issue price of $104 per share.

Preferred stock (2,500 shares at par, $100)	250,000	
Contributed capital in excess of par, preferred stock ($4 per share)	10,000	
Cash (2,500 shares × $104)		260,000

Assumption 2   The preferred stock is noncumulative and callable at $110 per share—$6 per share above the original issue price of $104.

Preferred stock (2,500 shares at par, $100)	250,000	
Contributed capital in excess of par, preferred stock ($4 per share)	10,000	
Retained earnings	15,000	
Cash (2,500 shares × $110)		275,000

Assumption 3   The preferred stock is cumulative; three years' dividends are in arrears. The stock is callable at $101. The dividends in arrears must be paid:

To recognize payment of dividends in arrears:

Retained earnings ($250,000 × .05 × 3 years)	37,500	
Cash		37,500

To record the retirement of called preferred shares:

Preferred stock (2,500 shares at par, $100)	250,000	
Contributed capital in excess of par, preferred stock ($4 per share)	10,000	
Contributed capital from retirement of preferred stock [($104 − $101) × 2,500 shares]		7,500
Cash (2,500 shares × $101)		252,500

If true nopar stock is formally retired, the average price per share originally credited to the stock account is removed from the capital stock account, cash is credited, and any net debit or credit is accounted for as illustrated above. If nopar stock with a stated or assigned value is retired, the procedures illustrated above for par value stock are followed.

To ensure adequate disclosure of future cash outflows related to redeemable stock, *SFAS No. 47* (par. 10) states that the balance sheet should disclose "the amount of redemption requirements for all issues of capital stock that are redeemable at fixed or determinable prices on fixed or determinable dates, separately by issue or combined."

CONCEPT REVIEW

1. Describe two methods of accounting for treasury stock. How do they differ with respect to treatment of amounts in the individual contributed capital accounts in the stockholders' equity section of the balance sheet?

> 2. What effect does choosing one method over the other have on the total balance reported in stockholders' equity?
> 3. A firm receives shares of its $100 par value common shares as a donation from a stockholder. At the time the shares are received, they have a market value of $140 per share. The shares were originally issued for $110 per share. Describe the method of accounting for this transaction.

ACCOUNTING FOR CONVERSIONS, CHANGES IN PAR VALUE, AND CONTRIBUTED CAPITAL

Corporations sometimes issue convertible preferred stock that gives stockholders an option, within a specified time period, to exchange their preferred shares for other classes of capital stock, usually common stock, at a specified rate. The accounting treatment for conversion of preferred stock is analogous to that for convertible bonds. The converted shares usually are formally retired when received by the corporation. Conversion privileges require the issuing corporation to set aside enough of the other security to fulfill the conversion privileges until they are exercised or the conversion option expires.

Conversion of Convertible Preferred Stock

At date of conversion, all account balances related to the converted shares are removed, and the new shares issued are recorded at their par or stated value. Any credit difference is recorded in an appropriately designated contributed capital account (such as contributed capital from conversion of preferred stock). If there is a debit difference, retained earnings is reduced.

Example   To illustrate three typical cases, assume the following data, and that the converted stock is retired:

Preferred stock, convertible, noncumulative, par $2, shares outstanding, 100,000	$200,000
Contributed capital in excess of par, preferred stock	20,000
Common stock, par $1, shares authorized, 500,000; shares outstanding, 150,000	150,000
Contributed capital in excess of par, common stock	50,000

Case 1   The conversion privilege specifies the issuance of one share of common stock for each share of preferred stock. Assume that stockholders tender, that is, turn in 10,000 shares of preferred stock for conversion.

Preferred stock (10,000 shares at par, $2)	20,000	
Contributed capital in excess of par, preferred stock		
($20,000 ÷ 100,000 shares = $.20 per share)	2,000	
Common stock (10,000 shares at par, $1)		10,000
Contributed capital from conversion of preferred stock		12,000

Case 2   The conversion privilege specifies the issuance of two shares of common stock for each share of preferred stock. Stockholders turn in 10,000 shares of preferred stock for conversion.

Preferred stock (10,000 shares at par, $2)	20,000	
Contributed capital in excess of par, preferred stock ($.20 per share)	2,000	
Common stock (20,000 shares at par, $1)		20,000
Contributed capital from conversion of preferred stock		2,000

Case 3   The conversion privilege specifies the issuance of three shares of common stock for each share of preferred stock. Stockholders turn in 10,000 shares of preferred stock for conversion.

Preferred stock (10,000 shares at par, $2)	20,000	
Contributed capital in excess of par, preferred stock ($.20 per share)	2,000	
Retained earnings	8,000	
Common stock (30,000 shares at par, $1)		30,000

In Case 3, $8,000 of retained earnings must be capitalized as contributed capital in order to maintain the common stock account at its legal capital amount.

EXHIBIT 20–7
Transactions that Affect
Additional Contributed Capital

Decreases Additional Contributed Capital	Increases Additional Contributed Capital
1. Issuance of stock below par or stated value.	1. Issuance of stock above par or stated value.
2. Sale of treasury stock below cost, cost method.	2. Sale of treasury stock above cost, cost method.
3. Acquisition of treasury stock above par and/or average paid in originally, par value method.	3. Acquisition of treasury stock below par and/or average paid in originally, par value method.
4. Conversion of convertible preferred stock.	4. Conversion of convertible preferred stock.
5. Retirement of callable or redeemable preferred stock.	5. Retirement of callable or redeemable preferred stock.
6. Payment of a liquidating dividend.	6. Conversion of convertible bonds.
7. Quasi reorganizations.	7. Distribution of a stock dividend.

Changing Par Value

Companies sometimes want to increase the number of shares outstanding, perhaps to reduce the market price per share in the hope of increasing market activity in the stock. One way to increase the number of shares outstanding is to reduce the par value per share and issue additional shares to shareholders on a pro rata basis with the end result that total legal capital is unchanged but more shares are outstanding. This is a form of *stock split,* which is covered in detail in Chapter 21. Briefly, a corporation may amend its charter and bylaws to change the par value (or the number of authorized shares) of one or more classes of authorized stock. Par value stock may be called in, formally retired, and replaced with nopar stock or stock of a different par value; conversely, nopar stock may be replaced with par value stock. This is not allowed in all states.

To record changes in par value, all capital account balances that relate to the stock retired are removed from the accounts, and the new stock issued is recorded. If an additional credit is needed, an appropriately designated contributed capital account is credited; if an additional debit is needed, retained earnings is debited. The entries are similar to those for recording the conversion of convertible preferred stock.

Additional Contributed Capital

Legal capital, defined earlier, is recorded in the specific capital stock accounts—common stock and preferred stock. All **additional contributed capital** [often called *additional paid-in* (or *contributed*) *capital* or *paid-in capital in excess of par* (or *stated value*)] is recorded in appropriately designated additional (or other) contributed capital accounts.

Additional contributed capital is created by a number of transactions that involve the corporation and its stockholders. Several accounts for additional contributed (or additional paid-in) capital were introduced in this chapter. Exhibit 20–7 summarizes some of the types of transactions that can cause increases or decreases in additional contributed capital. For financial reporting, the various types of additional paid-in capital accounts are aggregated and reported as one item in the contributed capital section of stockholders' equity. Contributed capital does not include retained earnings or unrealized capital. No operating or extraordinary gains and losses or prior period adjustments may be recorded as contributed capital.

Stockholders' Equity and Financial Statement Analysis

When investors are attempting to evaluate the strengths and weaknesses of a company, stockholders' equity is an important component of the analysis. Commonly, they use several ratios to assess financial strength and long-run solvency.

Debt to Equity Ratios   Debt to equity ratios provide a direct reading of the relationship between debt and owners' equity. They measure the balance between resources provided by creditors and resources provided by owners (including retained earnings). The debt to equity ratio is defined in several ways, but the most common version is:

$$\text{Total Debt to Equity} = \frac{\text{Total liabilities}}{\text{Total owners' equity}}$$

The higher this ratio is, the more leverage the firm is using, and the more risk that is borne by owners. Since interest payments are a required expense and creditors have a priority claim on the assets of the company, investors are concerned if this ratio is high relative to the inherent risk of the operations of the company. On the other hand, a company also may have too low a ratio if management is not using debt financing to an appropriate level.

Debt to Total Assets   A second ratio used to assess financial strength is debt to total assets. This ratio measures the portion of total assets supplied by creditors:

$$\text{Total Debt to Total Assets} = \frac{\text{Total liabilities}}{\text{Total assets}}$$

$$= \frac{\text{Total liabilities}}{\text{(Total liabilities + Owners' equity)}}$$

It is important to know which of these two forms of debt to equity ratio is being computed when doing an analysis. Also, there are other forms of the ratio found in the literature. For example, if the focus is on long-term forms of financing of the company, the ratios are computed substituting long-term borrowings for total liabilities.

Book Value per Share of Common Stock   Another ratio commonly computed for analysis is book value per share of common stock. This ratio was defined in Chapter 5 and is computed as:

$$\text{Book Value per Share of Common Stock} = \frac{\text{Common stock equity}}{\text{Number of common shares outstanding}}$$

When more than one class of stock is outstanding, total stockholders' equity is allocated among the various classes according to the legal and statutory claims that are effective if the company is liquidated. The usual case requires an allocation based on the preferential rights of the preferred stockholders.

Example   Suppose a company's total stockholders' equity is $120 million, and it has 10 million shares of common stock issued. It also has reacquired 2 million shares as treasury stock and has outstanding 10 million shares of 8 percent, $1 par cumulative preferred stock. The preferred stock has a liquidation preference of $3 per share and the preferred shares are in arrears for two years including the current year.

Computation of book value per share would be as follows (in millions except per share amounts):

Total stockholders' equity.		$120.0
Allocated to preferred stock:		
Liquidation value (10 shares × $3 liquidation preference)	$30.0	
Cumulative dividends in arrears (10 shares × .08 × $1 × 2).	1.6	
Total allocated to preferred stock.		31.6
Balance applicable to common stock.		$ 88.4
Total common shares outstanding (10 shares − 2 shares)		8.0
Book value per share of common stock ($88.4/8)		$11.05 per share

The $11.05 per common share amount represents the liquidation value per share of common stock based on historical cost and other accounting principles affecting measurement and recognition in the financial statements. It is interesting to note that, at the time this text was written, the average market price per share of the Standard & Poor's 500 is almost *four* times book value per share.

Numerous ratios can be computed per share of common stock. These ratios should be computed based on shares of common stock *outstanding* and not shares *issued*. Examples include cash flow per share and earnings per share.

SUMMARY OF KEY POINTS

(L.O. 1) 1. For corporations, owners' equity is called *stockholders' equity* or *shareholders' equity*. Claims to ownership are represented by shares of stock providing differing contractual rights for the holder. Shareholders' equity has three main categories: contributed capital, retained earnings, and unrealized capital.

(L.O. 1) 2. The principal advantages of the corporate form of organization over proprietorships and partnerships include separation of ownership and management so that large amounts of capital can be acquired, and limited liability for the shareholders. The principal disadvantage of the corporate form is the likelihood of double taxation.

(L.O. 2) 3. Two basic types of stock are common stock and preferred stock. Holders of common stock generally have the residual claim on the firm's assets and accept greater investment risk. Preferred stock has one or more contractually specified preferences over common stock.

(L.O. 2) 4. Preferred stock can be convertible, fully participating, noncumulative and redeemable.

(L.O. 3) 5. Authorized stock is the total number of shares that can legally be issued. The term *issued shares* refers to the number of shares sold or otherwise issued to shareholders. Treasury shares are shares that have been reacquired by the corporation. Outstanding shares equal issued shares less treasury shares. Subscribed stock is unissued shares that are to be used to meet subscription contracts.

(L.O. 3) 6. Par value generally establishes the legal capital amount that stockholders must contribute to the corporation when the shares are issued. Because capital stock almost always sells for a premium over par value, par value has little economic meaning. Nevertheless, it is used to record the stock issuance in the stock account specific to the type of stock issued. Proceeds received in excess of par value are recorded in a *contributed capital in excess of par,* also called *additional paid-in capital* account, for the specific type of stock issued.

(L.O. 3) 7. Nopar stock, whether preferred or common, is accounted for at issuance by first crediting the appropriate capital stock account with the stated value if there is one, otherwise with an amount required by state law. Any additional amount is credited to an additional paid-in capital account.

(L.O. 3) 8. The issue of stock for assets or for services rendered to the corporation requires determination of the appropriate amount at which to record the transaction. The most reliably determinable amount, whether it is the market value of the shares issued or the current market value of the asset or service received, is used to record the transaction.

(L.O. 3) 9. Stock issue costs are either offset against the proceeds received, resulting in only the net proceeds being recorded in stockholders' equity, or are treated as a deferred charge to be amortized over future periods. Both methods are acceptable under GAAP.

(L.O. 4) 10. Stock subscriptions are contractual agreements specifying the number of shares to be acquired by specified buyers. The subscribed stock receivable account can be reported as an asset of the corporation, or treated as a contra to stockholders' equity. The latter method is required by the SEC.

(L.O. 5) 11. Treasury stock is accounted for either by the cost method or by the par value method. Both have the same total effect on total stockholders' equity but result in different amounts being recorded in the various accounts within stockholders' equity. The cost method is the more commonly used method.

(L.O. 5) 12. When the cost method of accounting for treasury stock is used, the acquisition cost of the stock acquired is debited to a contra stockholders' equity account, often labeled *treasury stock, at cost*. When the stock is resold, the difference between the acquisition price and the resale price is debited or credited as appropriate to an additional paid-in capital account.

(L.O. 5) 13. When the par value method of accounting for treasury stock is used, the transaction effectively treats the acquired stock as being retired. When the shares are resold, the sale is treated in the same manner as the sale and issuance of unissued stock.

(L.O. 6) 14. When shares are retired, either through the call or redeemable feature, or simply by retirement through treasury stock acquisitions, all capital balances relating to the specific stock are removed. Any remaining balance is either debited to retained earnings as a de facto dividend or is credited to an additional paid-in capital account.

(L.O. 6) **15.** If convertible preferred stock is converted, all account balances related to the converted shares are removed, and newly issued shares are recorded at their par value. Any difference is either debited to retained earnings or credited to an appropriate additional paid-in account.

REVIEW PROBLEM

On January 2, 1998, Fleury Corporation was chartered in the state of Delaware. The corporation was authorized to issue 100,000 shares of $5 par value common stock, and 10,000 shares of $100 par value, cumulative, and nonparticipating preferred stock. During 1998 the firm completed the following transactions:

Jan.   8 Accepted subscriptions for 40,000 shares of common stock at $12 per share. Down payment on the subscribed stock totaled $150,000.

     30 Issued 4,000 shares of preferred stock in exchange for the following assets: machinery with a fair value market value of $35,000, a factory with a fair market value of $110,000, and land with an appraised market value of $295,000.

Apr. 25 Collected the balance of the subscription receivable and issued the shares.

Jun. 30 Purchased 2,200 shares of common stock at $18 per share. Use the cost method to account for treasury stock.

Sep. 20 Sold the 2,200 shares of treasury stock at $21 per share.

Dec. 31 Closed the income summary to retained earnings. The income for the period was $88,000.

Required

1. Prepare the journal entries to record the above transactions up to closing the books on December 31, 1998.

2. Prepare the stockholders' equity section of the balance sheet for Fleury Corporation for December 31, 1998.

SOLUTION

1. Jan. 8—Account for subscription of common stock:

Cash	150,000	
Stock subscription receivable	330,000	
Common stock subscribed		200,000
Additional paid-in capital, common		280,000

Jan. 30—Issue preferred stock in exchange for assets:

Machinery	35,000	
Factory	110,000	
Land	295,000	
Preferred stock, $100 par		400,000
Additional paid-in capital, preferred stock		40,000

Note: Since there is no market price established for the preferred shares prior to this transaction, the transaction is recorded at the fair market values of the assets received.

April 25—Record receipt of cash for subscribed stock and issuance of stock:

Cash	330,000	
Stock subscription receivable		330,000

Common stock subscribed	200,000	
Common stock, $5 par		200,000

June 30—Record acquisition of treasury stock:

Treasury stock, at cost	39,600	
Cash		39,600

Sept. 20—Record sale of treasury stock:

Cash	46,200	
Treasury stock, at cost		39,600
Additional paid-in capital from treasury stock transactions		6,600

Dec. 31—To close income summary to retained earnings:

Income summary	88,000	
Retained earnings		88,000

2. The stockholders' equity section of the balance sheet for Fleury Corporation for December 31, 1998:

FLEURY CORPORATION

Stockholders' Equity

At December 31, 1998

Contributed capital:

Common stock, $5 par value (100,000 shares authorized; 40,000 shares issued)	$ 200,000
Preferred stock, $100 par value (10,000 shares authorized; 4,000 shares issued)	400,000
Additional paid-in capital, common stock*	280,000
Additional paid-in capital, preferred stock*	40,000
Additional paid-in capital, treasury stock transactions*	6,600
Retained earnings	88,000
Total stockholders' equity	$1,014,600

*For financial reporting purposes, the various additional paid-in capital accounts are usually aggregated into one account.

UNDERSTANDING AND APPLYING CONCEPTS AND STANDARDS

QUESTIONS

1. Define public, private, open, closed, and publicly traded corporations.
2. Identify four basic rights of stockholders. How may one or more of these rights be withheld from the stockholders?
3. Explain the meaning of: authorized capital stock, issued capital stock, unissued capital stock, outstanding capital stock, subscribed capital stock, and treasury stock.
4. Describe the three main categories of stockholders' equity in accounting for corporate capital.
5. Explain how the cost principle relates to the issuance of capital stock.
6. Define the term *capital* as it is usually applied in accounting.
7. Define legal capital.
8. Distinguish between par and nopar stock. Distinguish between common and preferred stock.
9. Identify and explain a transaction that causes contributed capital to increase but does not result in any increase in the assets or decrease in the liabilities of the corporation.
10. Explain the difference between cumulative and noncumulative preferred stock.
11. Explain the differences between nonparticipating, partially participating, and fully participating preferred stock.
12. Explain asset preference as it relates to preferred stock.
13. Distinguish between callable and redeemable preferred stock.
14. Under what circumstances should stock subscriptions receivable be reported (*a*) as a current asset, (*b*) as a noncurrent asset, and (*c*) as a deduction in the stockholders' equity section of the balance sheet?
15. How should premium and discount on capital stock be accounted for and reported?
16. How are assets valued when shares of stock are given in payment to acquire these assets?
17. Briefly explain the two methods of accounting for stock issue costs.
18. What is the difference between unrealized capital increases and unrealized capital decreases? How might each arise?
19. Define treasury stock.
20. What is the effect on the amounts of assets, liabilities, and stockholders' equity of (*a*) the purchase of treasury stock and (*b*) the sale of treasury stock?
21. Explain the theoretical difference between the one-transaction concept and the dual-transaction concept in accounting for treasury stock.
22. Total owners' equity is not affected by the use of the cost or par value method of accounting for treasury stock, yet some components of owners' equity are affected. Is this statement correct? Explain.
23. Why have many states limited purchases of treasury stock to the amount reported as retained earnings? How may the restriction on retained earnings be removed?
24. In recording treasury stock transactions, explain why gains are recorded in a contributed capital account, whereas losses may involve a debit to retained earnings.

25. How is treasury stock reported on the balance sheet (*a*) under the cost method and (*b*) under the par value method?
26. How is stock donated to the corporation recorded?
27. When treasury stock is formally retired, retained earnings may be affected. Explain how this situation may occur.
28. One sometimes hears the statement "Dividends are paid out of retained earnings." Criticize this statement. What is the source of cash dividends?

| EXERCISES

E 20–1
(L.O. 3)

Stock Issuance: Effects on the Balance Sheet   Nay Corporation received a charter authorizing 200,000 shares of $1 par value stock. During the first year, 120,000 shares were sold at $8 per share. One thousand additional shares were issued in payment for legal fees. At the end of the first year, reported net income was $46,000. Dividends of $20,000 were paid on the last day of the year. Liabilities at year-end amounted to $60,000.

Required

Complete the following tabulation (show calculations); state any assumptions that you make.

	Items	Amount	Assumptions
a.	Total assets	$_______	___________________________
b.	Owners' equity	$_______	___________________________
c.	Contributed capital	$_______	___________________________
d.	Issued capital stock	$_______	___________________________
e.	Outstanding capital stock	$_______	___________________________
f.	Unissued capital stock	$_______	___________________________
g.	Treasury stock	$_______	___________________________

E 20–2
(L.O. 2, 3, 4)

Prepare Stockholders' Equity: Two Classes of Stock and Subscribed Stock   The charter of Ray Corporation authorized 200,000 shares of nopar common stock and 20,000 shares of 6 percent, cumulative and nonparticipating preferred stock, par value $10 per share. Stock issued to date: 80,000 shares of common sold at $540,000 and 10,000 shares of preferred stock sold at $21 per share. In addition, subscriptions for 2,000 shares of preferred have been received, and 30 percent of the purchase price of $21 has been collected. The stock will be issued upon collection in full. The retained earnings balance is $288,000. At year-end, there was a cumulative unrealized loss of $20,000 on investments in securities available for sale.

Required

Prepare the stockholders' equity section of the balance sheet.

E 20–3
(L.O. 2, 3, 4)

Prepare Stockholders' Equity: Subscriptions and Unrealized Gain   Prepare, in good form, the stockholders' equity section of the balance sheet for Warren Corporation. Treat receivables for subscribed stock as a contra to stockholders' equity.

Retained earnings	$ 390,000
Premium on common stock	40,000
Preferred stock subscribed, but not yet issued (3,000 shares)	30,000
Preferred stock, 6 percent, par $10, authorized 25,000 shares (20,000 shares issued)	200,000
Common stock, par $20, authorized 500,000 shares (110,000 shares issued)	2,200,000
Stock subscriptions receivable, preferred	4,000
Premium on preferred stock	30,000
Unrealized gain on investment classified as securities available for sale	10,000

E 20–4
(L.O. 2, 3, 4)

Analysis of Stockholders' Equity: Prepare Statement   The following data are from the accounts of Mitar Corporation at December 31, 1998 (amounts in thousands):

Subscriptions receivable (noncurrent)	$ 10
Retained earnings, 1/1/1998	900
Capital stock, par ?, authorized 100,000 shares	1,000
Capital stock subscribed, 1,000 shares (to be issued upon collection in full)	20
Premium on capital stock	400
Subscriptions receivable, capital stock (due in three months)	4
Bonds payable	200
Net income for 1998 (not included in retained earnings above)	190
Dividends declared and paid during 1998	80

Required

1. Respond to the following (state any assumptions that you make):
   a. Total retained earnings at end of 1998 is . . . . $______
   b. Retained earnings on 1/1/1998 was . . . . $______
   c. Par value per share is . . . . $______
   d. Number of shares outstanding is . . . . ______
   e. Legal capital is . . . . $______
   f. Total stockholders' equity is . . . . $______
   g. Number of shares issued is . . . . ______
   h. Average selling price per share including any shares subscribed was . . . . $______
   i. Number of shares sold including any shares subscribed was . . . . ______
2. Prepare the stockholders' equity section of the balance sheet at December 31, 1998. Use good form, complete with respect to details. Subscriptions receivable is to be recorded as an asset.

E 20–5
(L.O. 2, 3)

Compute Dividends: Preferred Stock, Cumulative and Partially Participating   Darby Corporation has the following stock outstanding:

Preferred, 6 percent, par $10, cumulative and partially participating up to an additional 2 percent; outstanding, 5,000 shares. No dividends were declared during the prior two years.

Common stock, nopar, outstanding, 10,000 shares; participating matching dividend, $1.50 per share.

The board of directors has just declared a total cash dividend of $43,000.

Required

Complete journal entries to record the dividend declaration for both the preferred and common shares. Show computations.

E 20–6
(L.O. 2, 3)

Compute Dividends: Preferred Stock, Four Cases   Able Corporation has the following stock outstanding:

Common, $50 par value—6,000 shares.

Preferred, 6 percent, $100 par value—1,000 shares.

Required

Compute the amount of dividends payable in total and per share on the common and preferred stock for each separate case:

Case A Preferred is cumulative and nonparticipating; two years in arrears; dividends declared, $34,000.

Case B Preferred is noncumulative and fully participating; dividends declared, $40,000.

Case C Preferred is cumulative and partially participating up to an additional 3 percent; three years in arrears; dividends declared, $60,000.

Case D Preferred is cumulative and fully participating; three years in arrears; dividends declared, $50,000.

E 20–7
(L.O. 2, 3)

Compute Dividends: Preferred Stock, A Legal Constraint   Polaris Corporation has the following account balances:

Common stock, par $5, 40,000 shares outstanding	$200,000
Preferred stock, par $20, 9 percent cumulative and nonparticipating, 5,000 shares outstanding	100,000
Contributed capital in excess of par:	
Common	120,000
Preferred	15,000
Retained earnings	220,000

Total cash dividends were limited to the balance in retained earnings; no dividends were paid during the two prior years.

Required

Show your computations in answering the following questions:

1. The average issue price per share for (*a*) common was $______ and (*b*) preferred was $______.
2. Compute dividends for each class of stock under each of the following proposals:
   a. The dividend declaration is $50,000.
   b. The dividend declaration specifies that (1) the same amount of dividends per share will be paid for each class of stock and (2) all preferences of the preferred stock are met. Does this situation pose a problem? Explain.

E 20–8
(L.O. 2, 4)

Stock Issuance: Nopar with Stated Value versus True Nopar, Subscriptions   The charter of Rainier Corporation authorized the issuance of 400,000 shares of nopar common stock. Give journal entries for the following transactions, assuming Case A—the board of directors set a stated value of $2 per share; and Case B—the stock is true nopar. Set up two pairs of columns so that Case A is to the left and Case B is to the right. Explain and justify any assumptions that you make. Assume that all transactions occurred within a short time span.

a. Authorization recognized (memorandum).
b. Sold 150,000 shares at $5 and collected in full; the shares were issued.
c. Received subscriptions for 12,000 shares at $5 per share; collected 40 percent of the subscription price. The shares will be issued upon collection in full.
d. Issued 500 shares for legal services related to the charter. Use the deferred charge method.
e. Issued 2,000 shares and in addition paid $80,000 cash for some used machinery.
f. Collected balance of subscriptions in (c).

E 20–9
(L.O. 4)

Stock Issuance: Subscriptions, Default   The charter of Maly Corporation authorized 100,000 shares of $1 par value common stock. A. B. Cook subscribed for 1,000 shares at $25 per share, paying $5,000 down, the balance to be paid $2,000 per month. The stock will not be issued until collection in full. After paying for three months, Cook defaulted. Six months later, the corporation sold the stock for $33 per share.

Required

1. Give all journal entries related to the 1,000 shares originally subscribed for by Cook, assuming Maly refunded all collections made to date of default.
2. Give the journal entry for the default, assuming that shares equivalent to the collection were issued to Cook (at $25 per share). Also give the entry for the sale of the remaining shares at $33 six months later.
3. Give the journal entries, assuming
   a. The stock is true nopar.
   b. The subscriber paid in full as scheduled over the 10-month period.

E 20–10
(L.O. 3)

Noncash Sale of Stock: Three Cases   The charter for Kay Manufacturing Corporation authorized 100,000 shares of common stock ($10 par value) and 10,000 shares of preferred stock ($50 par value). The company issued 600 shares of its common and 100 shares of its preferred stock for used machinery.

Required

For each separate situation, give the entry to record the purchase of the machinery, assuming the following: Case A—the common stock has been selling at $70 per share and the preferred stock at $80 per share; Case B—the common stock has been selling at $70, there have been no recent sales of the preferred stock, and no reliable value can be placed on the used machinery; and Case C—there is no current market price for either class of stock (however, the machinery has been independently appraised at $44,000).
State and justify any assumptions made.

E 20–11
(L.O. 2, 3)

Common and Preferred Stock Issued: Four Transactions   The charter of Gilmore Company authorized 20,000 shares of common stock, par $2, and 20,000 shares of preferred stock, par $10. The following transactions were completed. Assume that each is completely independent.

a. Sold 400 shares of common and 200 shares of preferred stock for a lump sum of $12,300. The common had been selling during the current week at $25 per share, and the preferred at $12 per share.
b. Issued 180 shares of preferred stock for some used equipment. The equipment had been appraised at $2,400 and the book value shown by the seller was $1,200. A reliable market value on the preferred stock has not been established.
c. A 10 percent assessment on par value was voted on both the common and preferred when 12,000 shares of common and 8,000 shares of preferred were outstanding. The assessment was collected in full.
d. Sold 600 shares of common and 400 shares of preferred stock in one transaction for a total cash price of $20,000. The common recently had been selling at $26; there were no recent sales of the preferred.

Required

Give the journal entry for each transaction. State and justify any assumptions that you make.

E 20–12
(L.O. 3)

Changes in Stockholders' Equity: An Overview   Each numbered item below changes the amount of stockholders' equity.

Required

Identify which category of stockholders' equity is affected by each item, and briefly explain how it is affected.

1. Donation of a plant site to the company.
2. Purchased treasury stock (cost method).
3. Declaration of cash dividend payable next period.
4. Unrealized loss on investment in securities available for sale.
5. Sale of additional common stock of the corporation.
6. Sold the company's capital stock on credit.
7. Corrected an accounting error (expense) from a prior period.
8. Default on a stock subscription.
9. Collected a stock assessment.
10. Restricted retained earnings by making an entry equal to the cost of treasury stock purchased.
11. Exchanged the corporation's capital stock for land.
12. Investors tendered their convertible preferred stock for the common stock of the corporation.

E 20–13
(L.O. 5)

Treasury Stock, Cost and Par Value Methods; Entries and Reporting   Han Tire Corporation had outstanding 10,000 shares of preferred stock, par value $10, and 10,000 shares of nopar common stock sold initially for $20 per share. Contributed capital in excess of par on the preferred stock amounted to $40,000; the retained earnings balance was $81,600. The corporation purchased 200 shares of its preferred at $25 per share and 500 shares of its common at $30 per share. Subsequently, 100 shares of the common treasury stock were sold for $26 per share.

Required

1. Give entries to record the treasury stock transactions, assuming the cost method is used.
2. Prepare the resulting stockholders' equity section of the balance sheet subsequent to the above transactions.

E 20–14
(L.O. 5)

Treasury Stock, Cost and Par Value Methods Compared; Entries and Account Balances   On January 1, 1997, Johnson Soap Corporation issued 20,000 shares of $20 par value common stock at $50 per share. On January 15, 1997, Johnson purchased 50 shares of its own common stock at $55 per share. On March 1, 1997, 20 of the treasury shares were resold at $58. The balance in retained earnings was $25,000 prior to these transactions.

Required

1. Give all entries indicated in parallel columns, assuming application of (*a*) the cost method and (*b*) the par value method.
2. Give the resulting balance in each one of the stockholders' equity accounts for each method.
3. Assume that on March 30, 1997, all remaining treasury stock shares are retired. Show the journal entries for (*a*) the cost method and (*b*) the par value method.

E 20–15

Treasury Stock: Analysis and Entries   During 1998, Crown Corporation had several changes in stockholders' equity. The comparative balance sheets for 1997 and 1998 reflect the following amounts in stockholders' equity:

	Balances December 31	
	1997	**1998**
Common stock, par $10, issued	$600,000*	$700,000[†]
Contributed capital in excess of par	180,000	230,000
Contributed capital, treasury stock transactions		1,000
Retained earnings	120,000	146,000
Treasury stock	36,000	2,800

*Includes 2,000 shares of treasury stock.

[†] Includes 200 shares of treasury stock (the 2,000 shares held at the end of 1997 were sold, and the 200 shares held at the end of 1998 were purchased during 1997).

Required

1. What method was used to account for treasury stock? Explain the basis for your conclusion.
2. Give the required entry for each transaction that affected stockholders' equity during 1998. Show how you determined the amounts used in each entry.

E 20–16
(L.O. 5)

Treasury Stock: Reporting, Restrictions, Cost and Par Value Method Compared   The records of Pincoff Corporation at December 31, 1997, show the following (assume that the cost method was used for treasury stock):

Assets	$139,000
Liabilities	32,000
Stockholders' equity:	
Common stock, par $10, 7,000 shares	70,000
Treasury stock, 1,000 shares (at cost)	17,000
Contributed capital in excess of par	14,000
Retained earnings	40,000

Required

Prepare balance sheets (including any disclosure notes) for the corporation with special emphasis on the stockholders' equity section assuming that the state law places a restriction on retained earnings equal to the cost of treasury stock held if:

1. The cost method is used.
2. The par value method is used. *Hint:* Certain of the above account balances must be modified for the par value method.

PROBLEMS

P 20–1
(L.O. 2, 3)

Stockholders' Equity: Appropriations and Unrealized Capital   Use appropriate information from the data to prepare the stockholders' equity section of a balance sheet for Croton Corporation at December 31, 1997:

Stock subscriptions receivable, preferred stock	$ 8,000
Retained earnings appropriated for bond sinking fund	40,000
Preferred stock, 6 percent, authorized 1,000 shares, par $100 per share, cumulative and fully participating	90,000
Bonds payable, 7 percent	200,000
Common stock, nopar, 5,000 shares authorized and outstanding	250,000
Premium on preferred stock	15,000
Discount on bonds payable	1,000
Retained earnings	250,000
Preferred stock subscribed (to be issued upon collection in full)	10,000
Unrealized gain on investments classified as SAS	5,000

P 20–2
(L.O. 2, 3, 4)

Entries and Reporting, Par and Nopar, Subscriptions, and Unrealized Gain   Gill Corporation was granted a charter that authorized 10,000 shares of 6 percent preferred stock, par value $10 per share, and 100,000 shares of common stock, nopar value. No stated or assigned value was identified with the common stock. During the first year, the following transactions occurred:

a. 40,000 shares of common stock were sold for cash at $12 per share.

b. 2,000 shares of preferred stock were sold for cash at $25 per share.

c. Subscriptions were received for 2,000 shares of preferred stock at $25 per share; 20 percent was received as a down payment, and the balance was payable in two equal installments. The shares will be issued upon collection in full.

d. 5,000 shares of common stock, 500 shares of preferred stock, and $37,500 cash were given as payment for a small plant that the company needed. This plant originally cost $40,000 and had a depreciated value on the books of the selling company of $20,000. Assume that the prior market price per share did not change.

e. The first installment on the preferred subscriptions was collected.

Required

1. Give journal entries to record the above transactions. State and justify any assumptions you make.
2. Prepare the stockholders' equity section of the balance sheet at year-end. Retained earnings at the end of the year amounted to $121,500. There was a $10,000 balance in the account labeled unrealized gain on investments classified as securities available for sale.

P 20–3
(L.O. 4)

Subscription and Default under Two Assumptions: Entries   Ace Corporation was issued a charter that authorized 500,000 shares of $5 par value common stock. A. B. Rye subscribed for 20,000 shares at $20 per share and paid a 30 percent cash down payment. The remaining 70 percent was payable in four equal quarterly amounts. After paying the first quarterly amount, Rye defaulted. The stock is issuable at date of full payment.

Required

1. Give the journal entries to record (*a*) the subscription and (*b*) collection of the first quarterly payment.
2. Assumption A—Give the journal entries to record (*a*) the default by Rye and the issuance to Rye of shares equivalent to the cash paid by Rye and (*b*) the sale one month later of the remaining subscribed shares to another party for cash at $22 per share (the cost of reselling was 40 cents per share).
3. Assumption B—Give the journal entries to record (*a*) the default by Rye and (*b*) the resale one month later under lien of all of the subscribed shares to another party for cash at $22 per share (the cost of reselling was 40 cents per share), including any cash refunded to Rye.

P 20–4
(L.O. 3, 4)

Entries and Reporting: Subscriptions, Noncash Sale   The charter of Day Corporation, a manufacturing business, authorized 300,000 shares of common stock, nopar value, and 50,000 shares of 6 percent preferred stock, which is cumulative and nonparticipating with par value per share of $10. During the early part of the first year, the following transactions occurred:

a. Six individuals each subscribed to 2,000 shares of Day Corporation common at $18 per share and 1,000 shares of the preferred at $12 per share. Half the subscription price was paid, and half the subscribed shares issued.

b. Another individual purchased 1,000 shares of Day common and 200 shares of preferred stock, paying $18,560 cash.

    c. One of the stockholders purchased a used machine for $40,000 and immediately transferred it to the corporation for 2,000 shares of common stock, 200 shares of preferred stock, and a one-year, 15 percent interest-bearing note for $8,000. Assume 15 percent is the market rate of interest.

    d. The investors paid the subscriptions, and the remaining stock was issued.

Required
1. Give all journal entries indicated for Day Corporation.
2. Prepare the stockholders' equity section of the balance sheet. Assume retained earnings of $55,040 at year-end.

P 20–5
(L.O. 2, 3, 4)

Entries and Reporting: Subscriptions, Noncash Sale—Par, Nopar, and Stated Value Compared   The charter for Wiley Corporation authorized 500,000 shares of common stock. During the first year of operations, the following transactions affected stockholders' equity:

    a. Immediately after incorporation, the corporation sold 400,000 shares of its capital stock at $10 per share; collected cash.

    b. Immediately after incorporation, Wiley received a subscription for 10,000 shares of capital stock from one individual at $10 per share. It collected 40 percent of the subscription, and the balance is due at the end of one year. The shares will be issued upon collection in full.

    c. Near year-end, Wiley exchanged 6,000 shares of capital stock for a plant site. The site was carried on the books of the seller at $25,000, and it had been independently appraised within the past month at $70,000. The market value of the stock is $10 per share.

    d. Wiley collected $12,000 on the subscription in (*b*).

Required
1. Give journal entries for the above transactions, assuming Case A—par value stock, $4 par value per share; Case B—true nopar value stock; Case C—nopar value stock with a stated value of $2 per share. Set up parallel amount columns for each case. State and justify any assumptions you make.
2. Prepare the stockholders' equity section of the balance sheet at the end of the first year for each case. Assume a $94,000 ending balance in the retained earnings account, a reserve for bond sinking fund of $27,000, and unrealized loss of $11,000 on investments classified as securities available for sale.

P 20–6
(L.O. 4)

Entries and Reporting: Par and Nopar, Subscriptions, and Deferred Charge   The charter of Koke Corporation authorized the issuance of 20,000 shares of 6 percent cumulative, nonparticipating preferred stock, par $10 per share, and 100,000 shares of common stock, nopar value. During the first year of operations, the following transactions affecting stockholders' equity were completed:

    a. The company sold 9,000 shares of the preferred stock at $25 per share for cash; the stock was issued.

    b. Subscriptions were received for an additional 1,000 shares of preferred stock at $25 per share; 20 percent was collected, and the balance is to be paid in four equal installments; the stock will be issued upon collection in full.

    c. Each of three promoters was issued 1,000 shares of common stock (only the common stock has voting privileges) at $20 per share; each paid one-fifth in cash. The remainder was considered to be appropriate reimbursement for promotional activities; the shares were issued.

    d. An individual purchased 100 shares of preferred and 100 shares of common stock and paid a single sum of $4,400. The stock was issued. Assume a current market price of $25 for the preferred stock and assume that at this date no current market price for the common was established.

    e. Collected cash from the subscribers in (*b*) for the first installment.

    f. Koke issued 5,000 shares of common stock for a used plant. The plant had been independently appraised during the past month at $110,000 and was reported by the seller at a book value of $60,000. Assume that at this date no current market price for the common was established.

Required
1. Prepare journal entries to record these transactions. State and justify any assumptions you make.
2. Prepare the stockholders' equity section of the balance sheet; assume retained earnings at year-end of $32,200 and an unrealized loss of $6,600 on an investment classified as securities available for sale.

P 20–7
(L.O. 3)

Reconstruct Entries Based on Stockholders' Equity   The stockholders' equity section of the balance sheet of Star Corporation at the end of its first accounting year was reported as follows:

Contributed capital:
  Capital stock:
    Preferred, 6 percent, cumulative, nonparticipating, $100 par value, redeemable at
      $125 per share, authorized 10,000 shares; issued and outstanding 8,370 shares . . . . . . $ 837,000
      Preferred stock subscribed, 930 shares . . . .   93,000 $ 930,000

Common stock, stated value $8 per share, authorized 1,500,000 shares; issued and		
outstanding 954,000 shares	7,632,000	
Common stock subscribed, 106,000 shares	848,000	8,480,000
Other contributed capital:		
In excess of par, preferred	30,000	
In excess of stated value, common	21,200	51,200
Retained earnings		110,000
Total stockholders' equity		$9,571,200

Required

Prepare journal entries during the first year as indicated by the above report. Use the memorandum approach to record the authorization and assume that all stock was purchased through subscriptions under terms of 30 percent cash down payment and 70 percent payable six months later. Also assume that of the 70 percent, all but 10 percent of the subscribers had paid in full by year-end. Shares are not issued until collection in full from the subscriber.

P 20–8
(L.O. 3)

Compute Dividends; Five Cases   The charter of Crew Corporation authorized 5,000 shares of 6 percent preferred stock, par value $20 per share, and 8,000 shares of common stock, par value of $50 per share. All of the authorized shares have been issued. In a five-year period, annual dividends paid in chronological order were $4,000, $40,000, $32,000, $5,000, and $36,000, respectively.

Required

Compute the amount of dividends that would be paid to each class of stock for each year under the following separate cases: Case A—preferred stock is noncumulative and nonparticipating; Case B—preferred stock is cumulative and nonparticipating; Case C—preferred stock is noncumulative and fully participating; Case D—preferred stock is cumulative and fully participating; Case E—preferred stock is cumulative and partially participating up to an additional 2 percent; also assume that the dividend for year 5 was $42,000 instead of $36,000.

P 20–9
(L.O. 5)

Treasury Stock, Cost and Par Value Methods Compared: Entries and Account Balances   At January 1, 1997, the records of Frazer Corporation provided the following:

Capital stock, par $10, 60,000 shares outstanding	$600,000
Contributed capital in excess of par	240,000
Retained earnings	160,000

During the year, the following transactions affecting shareholders' equity were recorded:

a. Purchased 1,000 shares of treasury stock at $20 per share.
b. Purchased 1,000 shares of treasury stock at $22 per share.
c. Sold 1,200 shares of treasury stock at $25.
d. Net income for 1997 was $45,000.

State law places a restriction on retained earnings equal to the cost of treasury stock held.

Required

1. Give entries for each of the above transactions, in parallel columns, assuming application of (*a*) the cost method and (*b*) the par value method. Assume FIFO flow for treasury stock.
2. Give the resulting balances in each capital account. Include any required disclosure note related to the treasury stock.

P 20–10
(L.O. 5)

Treasury and Donated Stock, Cost Method: Entries and Stockholders' Equity   Monet Corporation had 30,000 shares of $10 par value capital stock authorized, of which 20,000 shares were issued three years ago at $15 per share. During the current year, the corporation received 500 shares of the capital stock as a bequest from a deceased stockholder; in addition (at approximately the same date), 1,000 shares were purchased by Monet at $14 per share. State law places a restriction on retained earnings equal to the cost of treasury stock held. At the end of the year, a cash dividend of 85 cents per share was paid; prior to the dividend, retained earnings amounted to $40,000.

Required

1. Prepare entries to record all of the transactions; assume that the cost method for recording treasury stock is used. Record the donated stock at its market value.
2. Prepare the stockholders' equity section of the balance sheet at year-end and include any required disclosure notes related to the treasury stock.

P 20–11
(L.O. 5)

Treasury Stock Retired: Entries, and Cost and Par Value Compared   On December 31, 1997, the records for Macrosoft, Inc., provided the following data on stockholders' equity:

a. Preferred stock, par $50, issued 2,000 shares.
b. Preferred treasury stock, 200 shares (cost $54 per share).
c. Premium on preferred stock at original issue, $2 per share.
d. Common stock, par $10, issued 30,000 shares.
e. Common treasury stock, 3,000 shares (cost $9.80 per share).
f. Premium on common stock at original issue, $0.30 per share.

The stockholders voted to retire all of the treasury stock immediately and to purchase for retirement another 4,000 shares of common stock that could be purchased currently at $12.50 per share.

Required

Give entries in parallel columns for the following transactions, assuming application of (*a*) the cost method and (*b*) the par value method:

1. Purchase of the 4,000 shares of outstanding common stock and their immediate retirement. This transaction does not affect treasury stock.
2. Retirement of all of the treasury shares. Give separate entries for the preferred and common stock.

P 20–12
(L.O. 5)

Treasury Stock: Entries and Reporting, Cost and Par Value Methods Compared   On January 1, 1997, Dawn Steel Corporation reported the following summarized data prior to these transactions (amounts in thousands):

Assets	$1,320
Less: Liabilities	200
	$1,120
Stockholders' equity:	
Preferred stock, $10 par.	$600
Common stock, $5 par	300
Contributed capital in excess of par, preferred stock	60
Retained earnings.	160
	$1,120

State law places a restriction on the retained earnings equal to the cost of treasury stock held.
During 1997, the following transactions affecting stockholders' equity were recorded:

a. Purchased preferred as treasury stock, 1,200 shares at $15.
b. Purchased common as treasury stock, 2,000 shares at $20.
c. Sold preferred treasury stock, 200 shares at $17.
d. Sold common treasury stock, 800 shares at $14.

Required

1. Give entries in parallel columns for these treasury stock transactions assuming application of (*a*) the cost method and (*b*) the par value method.
2. Prepare the resulting December 31, 1997, balance sheet for each method with emphasis on stockholders' equity. Include any required note disclosure.

P 20–13
(L.O. 6)

Exchange of Old Shares for New Shares: Entries for Seven Cases   Rather Corporation had authorized an outstanding 100,000 shares of capital stock, par value $2 per share. The stockholders approved the exchange of two new shares for each share of the old stock.

Required

Give the journal entries to record the change under each of the following independent cases (assume a sufficient balance in retained earnings):

Case A The old stock was sold at par, and the new stock was nopar stock with no stated or assigned value.

Case B The old stock was sold at a premium of $3 per share, and the new stock was nopar stock with a stated value of $2 per share.

Case C The old stock was sold at a premium of $1.50 per share, and the new stock was nopar stock with a stated value of $2 per share.

Case D The old stock was sold at par, and the new stock was nopar stock with a stated value of $1.50 per share.

Case E The old stock originally was sold at a premium of $1.50 per share, and the new stock was $1 par value.

Case F The old stock was sold at a premium of $3 per share, and the new stock was nopar stock with no stated or assigned value.

Case G The old stock was sold at a premium of $1 per share, and the new stock was nopar stock with no stated or assigned value.

P 20–14
(L.O. 2, 3, 5)

Preferred and Common Stock Transactions, Treasury Stock Transactions   At the end of 1998, the comparative balance sheets for Sirmon Corporation reported the following stockholders' equity amounts:

	Balance December 31	
	1997	**1998**
Preferred stock, par $10, shares authorized 20,000	$150,000	$200,000
Common stock, nopar, shares authorized 100,000: issued (near the end of 1997), 30,000; 1998, 31,000	210,000	218,000
Contributed capital in excess of par, preferred stock.	74,000	155,600
Treasury stock, preferred.	2,000	1,000
Treasury stock, common	2,100	3,500*
Retained earnings.	60,074	97,974[†]
Restriction on retained earnings at the end of 1997 equal to the cost of treasury shares held: Preferred stock, $5,124; common stock, $1,950 (300 shares).		

*Increased by 200 shares during 1998 at $8 per share.

[†] No dividends were declared during 1998.

Required

1. What method is being used to account for the treasury stock? Explain.
2. At the end of 1997, what had been the average selling price per share (by the corporation) of (*a*) the preferred and (*b*) common shares?
3. Complete the following tabulation for the treasury stock held at December 31, 1997 (show your computations):

	Number of Treasury Shares Held	**Average Cost per Share**
Preferred	_______	_______
Common	_______	_______

4. How many shares were outstanding at December 31, 1997, for (*a*) preferred and (*b*) common?
5. What was the total amount of stockholders' equity at December 31, 1997?
6. Give the required entry for each transaction that affected stockholders' equity during 1998 (exclude consideration of net income). The preferred stock sold for $26 per share in 1998.
7. Explain the reasons for a possible disclosure concerning treasury stock sometimes required by state laws.

P 20–15
(L.O. 3)

Compute, Interpret, and Evaluate Equity Ratios   The balance sheets for Wooten Inc. and Thompson Company reflect the following:

	Wooten Inc.	**Thompson Company**
Current liabilities	$ 30,000	$ 30,000
Long-term liabilities	30,000	230,000
Stockholders' equity:		
Common stock, par $5.	170,000	46,000
Preferred stock, par $10, liquidation preference, $10	50,000	20,000
Retained earnings	60,000	30,000
Total liabilities and stockholders' equity.	$340,000	$356,000
Net income, included in the above retained earnings amount	40,000	20,000

Required

1. Compute the following two ratios and interpret the result:
   a. Debt to equity
   b. Debt to total assets
2. Compute book value per share of common stock.
3. Interpret and evaluate the situation for both companies.

ANALYSIS, JUDGMENT, AND COMMUNICATIONS

CASES

C 20–1
(L.O. 5)

? *YOU MAKE THE CALL*   **Conceptual: Classification of Treasury Stock**   Arguments are made that treasury stock is an asset because it is purchased, owned, and paid for in cash like any other asset. Further, as with other assets, it can be sold for cash at any time in an established market. Conclusion: because treasury stock has the overriding attributes of an asset, it should be reported and classified on the balance sheet as an asset.

Required

1. Assuming that you have no GAAP constraints to consider, explain in a memo how you think treasury stock should be classified and why.
2. Assume that the issuing company has a bond sinking fund being accumulated to retire outstanding bonds payable at maturity date. It is administered by an independent outside trustee in accordance with the bond agreement. Assume that the sinking fund investments include stock of the issuing company. How should that particular stock be classified? Explain the basis for your conclusions.

C 20–2
(L.O. 3)

Issuance of Capital Stock to Organizers: Valuation   C. Banfield, an engineer, developed a special safety device to be installed in backyard swimming pools; when turned on, it would set off an alarm if anything should fall into the water. Over a two-year period, Banfield's spare time was spent developing and testing the device. After receiving a patent, three of Banfield's friends, including a lawyer, considered plans to produce and market the device. Accordingly, a charter was obtained, which authorized 200,000 shares of $10 par value stock. Each of the four organizers contributed $20,000, and each received in return 2,000 shares of stock. They also agree that, for other consideration, each would receive 5,000 additional shares. The remaining shares were to be held as unissued stock. Each organizer made a proposal concerning how the additional 5,000 shares would be paid for. These individual proposals were made independently; then the group considered them as a package. The four proposals were:

Banfield: The patent would be turned over to the corporation as payment for the 5,000 shares. An independent appraisal of the patent could not be obtained.

Lawyer: 1,000 shares would be received for legal services already rendered during organization, 1,000 shares would be received as advance payment for legal retainer fees for the next three years, and the balance would be paid for in cash at par.

Friend No. 2: A small building, suitable for operations, would be given to the corporation for the 5,000 shares of stock. It was estimated that $20,000 would be needed for renovation prior to use. The owner estimates that the market value of the building is $750,000 and there is a $580,000 loan on it to be assumed by the corporation.

Friend No. 3: To pay $10,000 cash on the stock and to give a 12 percent (the going rate) interest-bearing note for the total price of $40,000 (subscriptions receivable) to be paid out of dividends over the next five years.

Required

Write a short report answering the following questions.

1. How would the above proposals be recorded in the accounts? Assess the valuation basis for each, including alternatives.
2. What are your recommendations for an agreement that would be equitable to each organizer? Explain the basis for such recommendations.

C 20–3
(L.O. 2)

A Reporting Issue Concerning Preferred Stock: Equity versus Debt   Onray Corporation reported the following items on its balance sheet dated December 31, 1998:

Liabilities:	
Long-term note payable, 12 percent interest payable each June 30 and December 31	
(maturity date December 31, 2003)	$ 500,000
Stockholders' equity:	
Common stock, nopar	6,000,000
Preferred stock, par $100, nonvoting, 9 percent cumulative, nonparticipating, and	
mandatory redemption at par no later than December 31, 2003; 4,000 shares	
authorized and outstanding	400,000
Retained earnings	800,000

Required

1. In one page, critically evaluate the reporting classifications applied by Onray. Did Onray violate current GAAP? Explain.
2. Disregarding all current accounting rules, how do you think Onray should report the four items shown above? Explain why.

C 20–4
(L.O. 2)

Equity versus Debt Agreements: Asset Purchased   Ellis Corporation purchased equipment (cash price of $144,000) for $107,000 cash and a promise to deliver an indeterminate number of shares of its $5 par common stock, with a market value of $15,000, on January 1 of each year for the next four years. Hence, $60,000 in market value of shares will be required to discharge the $37,000 balance due on the equipment.

The corporation then acquired 5,000 shares of its own stock (which became treasury shares) in the expectation that the market value of the stock would increase substantially before the delivery date.

Required

1. Discuss in one page the propriety of recording the equipment at the following values:
   a. $107,000 (the cash payment).
   b. $144,000 (the cash price of the equipment).
   c. $167,000 (the $107,000 cash payment plus the $60,000 market value of treasury stock that must be transferred to the vendor in order to settle the obligation according to the terms of the agreement). Assume an ordinary annuity.
2. Discuss the arguments for treating the balance due as the following:
   a. A liability.
   b. Treasury stock subscribed.
3. Assuming that legal requirements do not affect the decisions, discuss the arguments for treating the corporation's treasury shares as follows:
   a. An asset awaiting ultimate disposition.
   b. A capital element awaiting ultimate disposition.

(AICPA adapted)

C 20–5
(L.O. 2)

Conceptual: Debt versus Equity Securities Used to Purchase an Asset   (This item is amenable to a group or individual solution. Refer to the preface for additional details on using group items.) On January 1, 1997, Crefax Corporation purchased a tract of land, for long-term use as a possible future plant site, in exchange for $50,000 cash plus a five-year note with no interest, even though the current interest for similar debt is 15 percent. The note is to be paid in $20,000 annual amounts; the first $20,000 is due one year from the date of the land purchase, and the last $20,000 is due at the end of five years. The note also specifies (quite unusually) that instead of being payable in cash, each $20,000 annual amount is to be settled by issuance of 20,000 shares of Crefax common stock, par $1, to the holder of the note. On the date land was purchased, the market value of the stock set aside to be issued on the five dates by Crefax Corporation was $180,000.

Required

1. Develop and explain the basis for the journal entry that Crefax should make on January 1, 1997.
2. Give, and explain the basis for, the entry or entries that Crefax should make on December 31, 1997.
3. Explain how the following items should be reported on the 1997 financial statements of Crefax Corporation: (*a*) interest expense, (*b*) land, (*c*) debt, and (*d*) contributed capital.

C 20–6
(L.O. 3, 5)

Coca-Cola   The 1995 annual report of Coca-Cola is shown at the end of the book. The following questions relate to 1995 unless stated otherwise:

a. What types of capital stock does the company use? Give the par value per share.
b. At the end of 1995, how many shares were (1) authorized, (2) issued, (3) held as treasury stock, (4) unissued, and (5) outstanding?
c. What is the average per-share amount of capital in excess of par value for the shares outstanding at the end of 1995?
d. What overall percentage of total capital (total assets) was provided by stockholders' equity at the end of 1995?
e. What percentage of the shares of common stock issued was held as treasury stock at the end of 1995?
f. What was the ratio of 1995 dividends declared to earnings?
g. Explain any changes in authorized capital stock in 1995.
h. Explain any changes in treasury stock during 1995.
i. What was the annual percentage change in the balance of retained earnings from December 31, 1993, through December 31, 1995?

ANALYZING FINANCIAL STATEMENTS

All questions in this section are based on information taken from the financial statements of actual companies.

A 20–1
(L.O. 3, 4)

Starbuck's Corporation   Starbucks's Corporation, a high-quality national coffee retailer, provides the following information in its fiscal 1995 annual report:

(*In thousands*)	October 1, 1995	October 2, 1994
Shareholders' equity		
Common stock—Authorized, 100,000,000 shares; issued		
and outstanding, 70,956,990 and 57,936,988 shares	$265,679	$ 93,532
Less stock subscription notes receivable	—	(3,671)
	265,679	89,861
Retained earnings	46,552	20,037
Total stockholders' equity	$312,231	$109,898

The Consolidated Statement of Shareholders' Equity provides this additional information:

	Common Stock		Retained Earnings	Treasury Stock		Total
	Shares	Amount		Shares	Amount	
Balance, October 2, 1994	57,936,988	$ 89,861	$20,037	—	—	$109,898
Exercise of stock options including tax benefit of $4,754	945,780	7,911	—	—	—	7,911
Sale of common stock	12,050,000	163,873	—	—	—	163,873
Stock subscription notes repayments	—	3,671	—	—	—	3,671
Conversion of convertible debentures, net	6,798	100	—	—	—	100
Sale of common stock under employee stock purchase plan	17,424	263	—	—	—	263
Net earnings	—	—	26,102	—	—	26,102
Unrealized holding gains, net	—	—	141	—	—	141
Translation adjustment	—	—	272	—	—	272
Balance, October 1, 1995	70,956,990	$265,679	$46,552	—	—	$312,231

Required

1. Show the entry to record the sale of common stock during fiscal 1995. What was the average price per share for which this stock was sold?
2. Does Starbucks have a par value for its common stock that you can determine from the information provided? If so, what is it?
3. Show the entry to record the conversion of convertible debentures into common stock. What is the conversion rate in terms of the price per share of common stock?
4. Compute Starbucks's book value per share at October 2, 1994, and again at October 1, 1995. Why has it increased so much?
5. What alternative treatment might have been used with the stock subscription notes receivable?

A 20–2
(L.O. 3, 5)

Statement of Owners' Equity   The General Dynamics Corporation, a high-technology company, shows the following statement of shareholders' equity for the period from December 31, 1994, to December 31, 1995.

(*Dollars in millions, except per share amounts*)	Common Stock		Capital Surplus	Retained Earnings	Treasury Stock	
	Shares	Amount			Shares	Amount
Balance, December 31, 1994	84,387,336	$84	3	$1,860	21,391,547	$631
Net earnings				321		
Cash dividends declared ($1.50 per share)				(94)		
Shares issued under Incentive Compensation Plan			11		(249,586)	(6)
Balance, December 31, 1995	84,387,336	$84	14	$2,087	21,141,961	$625

Required

1. What appears to be the par value, if any, of General Dynamics Corporation common stock? What amount of proceeds was received for common stock issued under the Corporation's Incentive Compensation Plan? What was the average proceeds per share for these issued shares?
2. What is the book value per common share of General Dynamics at December 31, 1994? At December 31, 1995?
3. At December 31, 1995, General Dynamics common stock had a market price of approximately $57 per share. Briefly discuss why investors might pay so much, relative to the company's book value per share, for General Dynamics Corporation common stock.

A 20–3
(L.O. 3, 5)

Owners' Equity Statement, Stock Issue Costs   Gtech Holdings Corporation is a computer and communications services company. Its consolidated statements of shareholders' equity for the three-year period ending February 27, 1993, follow:

(*Dollars in thousands*)	Common Stock		Additional Paid-In Capital	Other	Retained Earnings (deficit)	Treasury Stock	Total
	Shares	**Amount**					
Balance at February 24, 1990	30,060,003	$301	$ 22,199	$(6,978)	$ (4,281)	—	$ 11,241
Common stock issued	4,529,040	45	3,345	—	—	—	3,390
Common stock issuance cost	—	—	(182)	—	—	—	(182)
Purchase of 40,090 shares of common stock	—	—	—	—	—	$ (30)	(30)
Net loss	—	—	—	—	(3,986)	—	(3,986)
Foreign currency translation	—	—	—	734	—	—	734
Balance at February 23, 1991	34,589,043	346	25,362	(6,244)	(8,267)	(30)	11,167
Common stock issued	133,600	1	99	—	—	—	100
Common stock issued under stock award plans	1,570,999	16	6,109	—	—	—	6,125
Net income	—	—	—	—	13,862	—	13,862
Foreign currency translation	—	—	—	(539)	—	—	(539)
Balance at February 29, 1992	36,293,642	363	31,570	(6,783)	5,595	(30)	30,715
Purchase of 73,463 shares of common stock	—	—	—	—	—	(113)	(113)
Common stock issued	5,900,000	59	90,294	—	—	—	90,353
Common stock issued under stock award plans	765,867	8	8,747	—	—	—	8,755
Tax benefit from stock compensation	—	—	17,467	—	—	—	17,467
Net income	—	—	—	—	21,694	—	21,694
Foreign currency translation	—	—	—	(816)	—	—	(816)
Balance at February 27, 1993	42,959,509	$430	$148,078	$(7,599)	$27,289	$(143)	$168,055

Required

1. What is the par value of Gtech common stock?
2. During the fiscal year ending February 23, 1991, Gtech issued 4,529,040 shares of common stock. Describe how the stock issue costs were accounted for. Is there an acceptable alternative treatment? If so, describe it. What were the net proceeds from the issuance? What were the net proceeds per share?
3. What was the average price per share paid for treasury stock acquired during 1990? How is treasury stock accounted for by Gtech?
4. What is the book value per share of Gtech at February 23, 1991? At February 27, 1993? Briefly describe why book value per share changed so much from February 23, 1992, to February 27, 1993.
5. What was the average price per share paid for common shares acquired during the year ending February 27, 1993? What were the average proceeds per share for shares issued, other than those issued under stock award plans, during the year ending February 27, 1993? List any possible reasons why these amounts might differ greatly.

A 20–4
(L.O. 5)

T. Rowe Price (TRP) Stock Split, Treasury Stock   T. Rowe Price's primary business is providing investment information services to Price Funds and individual private accounts. The 1995 annual report for the company included the following Consolidated Statement of Stockholders' Equity:

(Dollars in thousands)	Common Stock		Capital in Excess of Par Value	Retained Earnings	Unrealized Security Holdings Gains	Total Stockholders' Equity
	Shares	Par Value				
Balance at December 31, 1992	14,429,315	$2,886	$1,171	$150,141		$154,198
Common stock issued under						
stock-based compensation plans	254,629	51	2,963			3,014
2-for-1 stock split	14,491,095	2,898	(1,997)	(901)		—
Purchases of common stock.	(80,000)	(16)	(940)	(1,295)		(2,251)
Net income				48,539		48,539
Dividends declared				(12,892)		(12,892)
Unrealized security holding gains.					$ 5,345	5,345
Balance at December 31, 1993	29,095,039	5,819	1,197	183,592	5,345	195,953
Common stock issued under						
stock-based compensation plans	366,880	74	4,277			4,351
Purchases of common stock.	(892,500)	(179)	(3,539)	(22,831)		(26,549)
Net income				61,151		61,151
Dividends declared				(15,876)		(15,876)
Decrease in unrealized security						
holding gains					(2,791)	(2,791)
Balance at December 31, 1994	28,569,419	5,714	1,935	206,036	2,554	216,239
Common stock issued under						
stock-based compensation plans	465,553	93	5,555	(2)		5,646
Purchases of common stock.	(369,500)	(74)	(4,578)	(8,789)		(13,441)
Net income				75,409		75,409
Dividends declared				(19,720)		(19,720)
Increase in unrealized security						
holding gains					10,099	10,099
Balance at December 31, 1995	28,665,472	$5,733	$2,912	$252,934	$12,653	$274,232

Required

1. From the information provided at December 31, 1992, estimate the par value of a share of common stock on that date. From the information provided at December 31, 1993, estimate the par value of a share of common stock on that date. Did TRP really split the par value of its shares 2 for 1?

2. When TRP purchases common stock, is it held as treasury stock or as retired stock? If as treasury stock, is TRP using the cost method or the par value method or some variation of one of these for accounting for treasury stock? Discuss.

3. Determine the average price per share TRP paid for common stock repurchased during 1995. Determine the average price per share TRP received for common stock issued under the stock-based compensation plans.

4. On December 31, 1995, TRP common stock had a market price of $48 per share. What is the company's total market value on this date? What is the company's net book value on this date? Why do these two amounts differ?

A 20–5
(L.O. 3)

Unocal Corporation Unocal is the parent company of Union Oil, a fully integrated energy resources company. In its 1995 annual report, Unocal shows the following regarding stockholders' equity:

	December 31,	
(Millions of dollars)	1995	1994
Stockholders' equity		
Preferred stock ($0.10 par value; stated at liquidation value of $50 per share;		
authorized: 100,000,000 shares)		
Shares outstanding 10,250,000 in 1995 and 1994		
Common stock ($1 par value).	$513	$513
Shares authorized: 750,000,000		
Shares outstanding: 247,310,376 in 1996; 244,198,701 in 1994	247	244
Capital in excess of par value	319	237

In notes to the financial statements, the following is provided regarding the preferred stock:

Preferred Stock

The company has authorized 100,000,000 shares of preferred stock with a par value of $0.10 per share. In July 1992, the company issued 10,250,000 shares of $3.50 convertible preferred stock. The convertible preferred stock is redeemable on and after July 15, 1996, in whole or in part, at the option of the company, at a redemption price of $52.10 per share declining to $50 per share on and after July 15, 2002, together with accumulated but unpaid dividends. The convertible preferred stock has a liquidation value of $50 per share and is convertible at the option of the holder into common stock of the company at a conversion price of $30.75 per share, subject to adjustment in certain events. Dividends on the preferred stock at an annual rate of $3.50 per share are cumulative and are payable quarterly in arrears, when and as declared by Unocal's Board of Directors (the Board). Holders of the preferred stock have no voting rights. However, there are certain exceptions including the right to elect two additional directors if the equivalent of six quarterly dividends payable on the preferred stock are in default.

Required

1. Suppose Unocal decides to redeem the outstanding preferred stock on July 15, 1996. Show the entry to record the transaction. Assume dividends for the quarter ending June 30, 1996, have not been paid, and that the shares were originally issued at their liquidation value.
2. Assume all the preferred stock is converted to common stock on January 1, 1996. Show the entry to record the transaction.
3. Suppose that Unocal passes (does not declare and pay) the preferred dividends for the year 2001 and the first half of 2002. On July 15, 2002, Unocal calls and redeems the preferred stock. Show the entry to record the redemption.

A 20–6
(L.O. 3, 6)

Consolidated Edison Company (Con Ed) Preferred Stock   Con Ed is a large public utility company that provides New York City with electric service. As many other public utilities do, Con Ed uses preferred stock for a portion of its financing. In its 1995 annual report, Con Ed provided the following schedule regarding its capitalization:

CONSOLIDATED STATEMENT OF CAPITILIZATION
Consolidated Edison Company of New York, Inc.

At December 31 (Thousands of Dollars)	Shares Outstanding		1995	1994
	December 31, 1995	December 31, 1994		
Common shareholders' equity (Note B)				
Common stock, $2.50 par value,				
authorized 340,000,000 shares.	234,956,299	234,905,235	$1,464,305	$1,463,913
Retained earnings.			4,097,035	3,888,010
Capital stock expense.			(38,606)	(38,926)
Total common shareholders' equity			5,522,734	5,312,997
Preferred stock (Note B)				
Subject to mandatory redemption				
Cumulative Preferred, $100 par value,				
7.20% Series I	500,000	500,000	50,000	50,000
6⅛% Series J.	500,000	500,000	50,000	50,000
Total subject to mandatory redemption.			100,000	100,000
Other preferred stock				
$5 Cumulative Preferred, without par value,				
authorized 1,915,319 shares	1,915,319	1,915,319	175,000	175,000
Cumulative Preferred, $100 par value,				
authorized 6,000,000 shares*				
5¾% Series A	600,000	600,000	60,000	60,000
5¼% Series B	750,000	750,000	75,000	75,000
4.65% Series C.	600,000	600,000	60,000	60,000
4.65% Series D.	750,000	750,000	75,000	75,000
5¾% Series E	500,000	500,000	50,000	50,000
6.20% Series F	400,000	400,000	40,000	40,000
Cumulative Preference, $100 par value,				
authorized 2,250,000 shares 6%				
Convertible Series B	49,174	53,102	4,917	5,310
Total other preferred stock			539,917	540,310
Total preferred stock			$ 639,917	$ 640,310

*Represents total authorized shares of cumulative preferred stock, $100 par value, including preferred stock subject to mandatory redemption.

In the notes to the financial statements Con Ed provides the following information regarding its preferred stock:

Note B Capitalization

Common Stock and Preferred Stock Not Subject to Mandatory Redemption   Each share of Series B preference stock is convertible into 13 shares of common stock at a conversion price of $7.69 per share. During 1995, 1994 and 1993, 3,928 shares, 4,176 shares and 5,208 shares of Series B preference stock were converted into 51,064 shares, 54,288 shares and 67,704 shares of common stock, respectively.

At December 31, 1995, 639,262 shares of unissued common stock were reserved for conversion of preference stock. The preference stock is subordinate to the $5 Cumulative Preferred Stock and Cumulative Preferred Stock with respect to dividends and liquidation rights.

Redemption prices of preferred stock other than Series I and Series J (in each case, plus accrued dividends) are as follows:

$5 Cumulative Preferred Stock	$105.00
Cumulative Preferred Stock:	
Series A	$102.00
Series B	102.00
Series C	101.00
Series D	101.00
Series E	101.00
Series F	102.50
Cumulative Preference Stock:	
6% Convertible Series B	$100.00

Preferred Stock Subject to Mandatory Redemption   The Company is required to redeem 25,000 of the Series I shares on May 1 of each year in the five-year period commencing with the year 2002 and to redeem the remaining Series I shares on May 1, 2007. The Company is required to redeem the Series J shares on August 1, 2002. In each case, the redemption price is $100 per share plus accrued and unpaid dividends to the redemption date. In addition, the Company may redeem Series I shares at a redemption price of $105.04 per share, plus accrued dividends, if redeemed prior to May 1, 1996 (and thereafter at prices declining annually to $100 per share, plus accrued dividends, after April 30, 2002); provided, however, that prior to May 1, 1997, the Company may not redeem any Series I shares with borrowed funds or proceeds from certain securities issuances having a cost to the Company of less than 7.20 percent per annum.

Required

1. Outline the preference differences between the various types of preferred stock issued by Con Ed. Which of these issues is most like a debt issue? Which is most like a common equity issue? Why?
2. What were the proceeds per share for the preferred stock identified as $5 Cumulative Preferred, without par value? What were the proceeds per share for each of the Cumulative Preferred, $100 par value series (A through F)?
3. Show the entry Con Ed would have made if it elects to redeem the entire Series I preferred stock on April 30, 1996. Assume all preferred dividends are paid as of April 30.
4. If Con Ed had not redeemed the preferred stock as stated in requirement 3, show the entry Con Ed would make on May 1, 2002, when it begins the mandatory redemption of its Series I Cumulative Preferred Stock.
5. Suppose that during 1996, a total of 5,000 shares of the 6 percent Convertible Series B preference stock is tendered to the company for conversion into common stock. Show the entry to record this transaction.
6. Con Ed shows a contra equity item in the common stockholders' equity portion of the statement identified as capital stock expense. What is the nature of this item? Has it been expensed already? If not, how much was expensed in 1995? What is an alternative treatment of this item?

21 CORPORATIONS: RETAINED EARNINGS AND STOCK OPTIONS

LEARNING OBJECTIVES

After you have studied this chapter, you will:

1. Understand the nature of dividends and retained earnings.

2. Be able to account for cash dividends, property dividends, liquidating dividends, and scrip dividends.

3. Know how to account for stock dividends and stock splits.

4. Understand appropriations of retained earnings and how they are reported.

5. Know the accounting and reporting standards for fixed and performance stock option plans under both *APB Opinion No. 25* and *SFAS No. 123*.

6. Be able to account for stock appreciation rights.

INTRODUCTION

On January 1, 1995, two new companies were formed to develop, produce, and market personal computer software. Both firms issue 100,000 shares of $1 par value common stock at a price of $3 per share. Immediately after issuing the shares, the two companies have identical stockholders' equity sections:

	Splitz Co.	Divz Co.
Stockholders' Equity:		
Common stock, $1 par value	$100,000	$100,000
Additional paid in capital.	200,000	200,000
Total.	$300,000	$300,000

Splitz and Divz are equally successful; both firms have earnings of exactly $100,000 in each of the next five years. Thus, at December 31, 1999, both companies have earned income totaling $500,000 since their inception. Now assume neither company pays any cash dividends, nor do they acquire any of their own shares or issue any additional shares in a public sale. Nevertheless, at December 31, 1999, the two companies have significantly different stockholders' equity sections:

	Splitz Co.	Divz Co.
Stockholders' Equity:		
Common stock, $0.50 par value	$100,000	
Common stock, $1 par value		$200,000
Additional paid in capital	200,000	600,000
Retained earnings	500,000	–0–
Total	$800,000	$800,000

How can this situation be? What actions could each company have taken to result in these different stockholders' equity sections? More importantly, does the underlying cause for the difference matter to an investor or creditor? In which firm would you prefer to invest, assuming again that future earnings are going to continue to be the same? Finally, are you concerned that Divz has no retained earnings?

You may have some idea as to how Splitz achieved its ending stockholders' equity section. If the firm declared a pure two-for-one stock split, each share of $1 par value stock would be split into two shares, each with a new par value of $0.50. Because the firm paid no cash dividends, the entire amount of earnings since inception of the company is retained earnings.

But how did Divz achieve its ending stockholders' equity? As we will see, it may have declared annual small stock dividends of less than 20 percent. As it issued the shares of the stock dividend, Divz would be required to capitalize a portion of its retained earnings as common stock and as additional paid-in capital. Under the right circumstances, the annual stock dividends would result in the above stockholders' equity figures.

Do these differences between the two firms' stockholders' equity sections matter? Your authors think they matter very little, if at all. At December 31, 1999, both firms have 200,000 shares outstanding. The firms' past performance has been identical and is expected to continue in the future. These are the factors that should influence the value of each company's stock. We believe the firms would be of approximately equal value. The amount of retained earnings a firm has may tell us something about the firm's past success, but it tells us little, if anything, about the financial condition of the company or its future prospects. While there may be restrictions on Divz with respect to declaring and paying cash dividends because the firm has no retained earnings, the firm has additional paid-in capital that could be distributed, depending on legal constraints.

This chapter covers the concepts and procedures used in measuring, recording, and reporting retained earnings. Procedures for declaring and paying all kinds of dividends are covered, as well the accounting procedures for stock rights and stock options. An important topic in this chapter is accounting for compensation-based stock options, a controversial accounting issue during the past several years.

Disposition of Earnings

When a corporation earns a profit, management advises the board of directors on two alternative uses of the firm's earnings:

1. Reinvest the earnings in operations of the firm.
2. Distribute the earnings to shareholders in the form of a dividend.

If the company has investment opportunities in which it expects to earn profits, management may advise that the earnings be retained and used as capital for financing the investment. Retaining earnings is a common way for a firm to provide capital for growth. Many start-up companies pay little or no dividends. Generally, investors are not disappointed when a firm retains earnings and reinvests them, so long as the investment earns a high return. Once the earnings are reinvested, however, generally they are not available for distribution through cash dividends to shareholders. For example, Splitz's $500,000 in retained earnings could not easily be distributed to shareholders as cash dividends: the earnings have been invested in property and equipment, in inventory, accounts receivable, and other assets. These assets would have to be liquidated to raise the case needed to distribute a $500,000 cash dividend. If the decision is to reinvest earnings in the business, the financial statements reflect the reinvestment as a claim by shareholders in the form of retained earnings.

When the decision is to pay out earnings through a cash dividend, cash is distributed to shareholders. Cash dividends depend on the corporation having sufficient cash available for distribution. Another form of dividend, called a stock dividend, can also be declared. When a stock dividend is declared, the company is essentially signaling to shareholders its intention to retain the earnings permanently. This portion of retained earnings is transferred to the contributed capital portion of stockholders' equity. If Divz, for example, declared stock dividends each year in amounts equal to annual earnings, all its (retained) earnings would have been transferred to contributed capital.

CHARACTERISTICS OF RETAINED EARNINGS

Retained earnings are sometimes called *reinvested earnings* or *earned surplus*. Retained earnings represent the firm's accumulated net income or net loss (including prior period adjustments) less accumulated cash dividends, property dividends, stock dividends, and other amounts transferred to the contributed capital accounts. If the accumulated losses and distributions of retained earnings exceed the accumulated earnings, a *deficit* exists (represented by a debit balance) in retained earnings.

The following T-account summarizes the items affecting retained earnings:

Retained Earnings

Decreases (debits)	Increases (credits)
■ Net loss (including extraordinary losses)	■ Net income (including extraordinary gains)
■ Prior period adjustments (correction of accounting errors of prior periods)	■ Prior period adjustments (correction of accounting errors of prior periods)
■ Cash dividends	■ Removal of deficit by quasi reorganization
■ Property dividends	■ Retroactive accounting principle changes
■ Scrip dividends	
■ Stock dividends	
■ Treasury stock and stock retirement transactions	
■ Retroactive accounting principle changes	

NATURE OF DIVIDENDS

A **dividend** is a distribution of earnings to shareholders in the form of assets or shares of the issuing company's stock. A dividend is accounted for by a credit to the account that represents the item distributed (cash, noncash asset, or capital stock) and a debit to retained earnings (some exceptions are explained later). Types of dividends include:
- Most common:
    Cash dividends (cash disbursed).
    Property dividends (noncash assets disbursed).
    Stock dividends (corporation's own stock distributed).
- Special:
    Liquidating dividends (return of contributed capital).
    Scrip dividend (creation of a liability by declaring a dividend to be paid at a specific future date).

Corporations are not required to pay dividends. It is rare that 100 percent of a firm's earnings are distributed as dividends. Instead of paying a dividend, the corporation may
- Conserve cash for immediate use.
- Expand, grow, and modernize by investing in new assets.
- Provide a cushion of resources to minimize the effect of recessions and other unforeseen contingencies.

Furthermore, some state laws and bond covenants restrict the amount of retained earnings that can be distributed as cash and property dividends.

Relevant Dividend Dates

Prior to payment, dividends must be *declared* by the board of directors of the corporation. Four dates are important in accounting for dividends:

1. Date of declaration.
2. Date of record.

3. Ex-dividend date.
4. Date of payment.

These dates occur chronologically as shown on this time line:

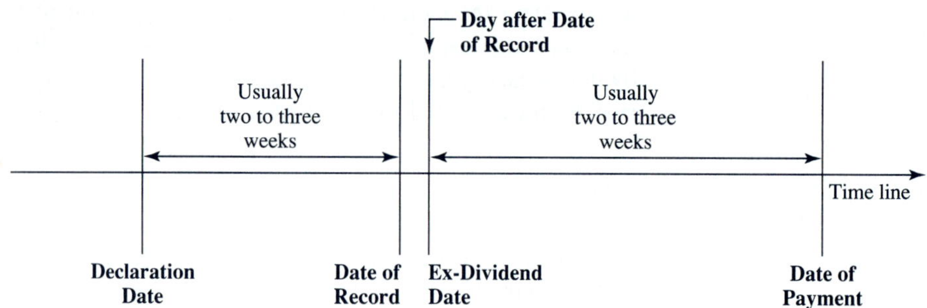

Date of Declaration   On this date, the corporation's board of directors formally approves and announces the dividend declaration. In the case of a cash or property dividend, the declaration is recorded as a debit to retained earnings and a credit to dividends payable. In the absence of fraud or illegality, the courts have held that formal declaration of a cash, property, or scrip dividend constitutes an enforceable contract between the corporation and the stockholders. For such dividends, a liability, dividends payable, is recognized on the dividend declaration date, with a corresponding debit to retained earnings.

In the case of a stock dividend, no distribution of corporate assets is involved, and thus the courts have held that a stock dividend declaration is revocable up to the date of issuance. Because there is no liability, no entry is required on the declaration date.

Date of Record   On the record date the list of current stockholders is prepared. Those holding stock at this date receive the dividend, regardless of sales or purchases of stock after the record date. No entry is made in the accounts on this date. The record date selected by the board of directors is stated in the declaration. Usually the record date follows the declaration date by two to three weeks.

Ex-Dividend Date   In theory, the ex-dividend date is the day following the date of record. This day is the first day on which the shares are traded without the right to receive the declared dividends. As a practical matter, stock exchanges advance the effective ex-dividend date by three or four days before the date of record to provide adequate time for transfer of the stock. Thus, holders of the stock on the day prior to the stipulated ex-dividend date receive the dividend. Investors who buy shares on and after the ex-dividend date do not receive the dividend.

Between the declaration date and the ex-dividend date, the market price of the stock reflects the dividend. On the stipulated ex-dividend date, the price of the stock usually drops because purchasers of the stock will not receive the dividend. The recipient of the dividend already has been identified. Under the revenue principle, dividend revenue is earned on the declaration date. The importance of the ex-dividend date is indicated by a section in *The Wall Street Journal,* "Dividend News," which lists stocks that are ex-dividends effective as of the *Journal*'s publication date.

Date of Payment   This date also is determined by the board of directors and is usually stated in the declaration. The date of payment typically follows the declaration date by four to six weeks. At the date of payment of cash or property dividends, the liability recorded at date of declaration is debited and the appropriate asset account is credited. A stock dividend distribution usually is recorded on the date of issue.

Legality of Dividends

State laws require that there be sufficient retained earnings (which in some states can be augmented by elements of contributed capital) before dividends can be declared. Requirements differ from state to state, but at least two provisions appear to be uniform:

1. Dividends may not be paid from *legal capital* (usually represented in the capital stock accounts—par value, stated value, and average paid-in on nopar stock).
2. Retained earnings are available for dividends unless there is a contractual or statutory restriction.

Beyond these two provisions, numerous variations exist, depending on state statutes and the type of dividend. Possibilities include:

- All contributed capital, other than legal capital, is available for dividends.
- Specified items of contributed capital, other than legal capital, are available for dividends.
- Contributed capital, other than legal capital, is available for dividends on preferred stock but not on common stock.
- Unrealized capital is not available for any kind of dividend.
- Unrealized capital is available for stock dividends only.
- Debits must be made to the additional contributed capital accounts in order to restore a deficit in retained earnings before payment of any dividends.
- Dividends debited to retained earnings must not reduce the retained earnings balance below the cost of treasury stock held.

When the legality of the accounting treatment of dividends is at issue the accountant has a responsibility to ensure that such matters are referred to an attorney and that the financial statements disclose all material facts concerning such dividends.

TYPES OF DIVIDENDS

Cash dividends are the usual form of distributions to stockholders. Before a cash dividend can be paid to common shareholders, any preference dividends (including those in arrears) must be paid to preferred stockholders.

Cash Dividends

To illustrate a cash dividend, assume the board of directors of Bass Company, at its meeting on January 20, 1998, declares a dividend of 50 cents per share, payable March 20, 1998, to stockholders of record on March 1, 1998. There are 10,000 shares of nopar capital stock outstanding.

At date of declaration (January 20, 1988):

Retained earnings* (10,000 shares × $.50)	5,000	
Cash dividends payable		5,000

*Or dividends declared, which is later closed to retained earnings.

At date of record (March 1, 1998):
No entry. The list of dividend recipients is prepared as of this date.

At date of payment (March 20, 1998):

Cash dividends payable	5,000	
Cash		5,000

Dividends payable is classified as current or noncurrent consistent with the definition of current liabilities. Generally, dividends payable is a current liability.

Property Dividends

Corporations occasionally pay dividends with noncash assets, called **property dividends** or **dividends in kind.** The property may be securities of other companies held by the corporation, real estate, merchandise, or any other noncash asset designated by the board of directors. A property dividend is recorded at the current market value of the assets transferred in conformity with *APB Opinion No. 29,* "Accounting for Non-Monetary Transactions." When the corporation's book value of the property to be distributed as the dividend is different from its market value on the declaration date, the corporation recognizes a gain or loss on disposal of the asset as of the declaration date.

Most property dividends are the securities of other companies held as an investment. This kind of property dividend reduces the problem of indivisibility of units that would occur with most other noncash assets.

An alternative transaction similar to a property dividend is a **spin-off,** which is a distribution of the shares of a wholly or substantially owned subsidiary to shareholders. The shareholders then own the subsidiary directly, rather than indirectly through the corporation. A spin-off is a form of reorganization and conceptually different from a property dividend. A spin-off usually is recorded at the book value of the spun-off organization, not at its market value.

The following excerpt from the disclosure notes in the 1988 financial report of Sun Company, Inc., describes a spin-off:

> On November 1, 1988, the Company distributed on a pro rata basis to holders of its issued and outstanding common stock substantially all of the issued and outstanding shares of common stock of Sun E&P Co., with no consideration being paid by such holders of Sun Company Stock. Each holder of Sun Company common stock on October 14, 1988, the record date for the Distribution, received one share of common stock of Sun E&P Co. for each share of Sun Company common stock owned.
>
> The Distribution has been accounted for as a "spin-off" with a pro rata reduction in Sun's earnings employed in the business . . . in an aggregate amount equivalent to the stockholders' equity of Sun E&P.

The statement of changes in stockholders' equity shows a debit to retained earnings of $1,458 million, which is labeled as "distribution of Sun E&P Co. common stock." This debit entry indicates that the book value of the distributed stock was $1,458 million. The following entries record the transaction.

At the declaration date:

Retained earnings (distribution of Sun E&P Co. common stock) . . .	1,458,000,000	
Property dividend payable		1,458,000,000

At the distribution date (November 1, 1988):

Property dividend payable	1,458,000,000	
Investment in stock of Sun E&P Co.		1,458,000,000

Suppose this transaction were to be accounted for as a property dividend. Assume that Sun Company currently records its interest in Sun E&P at $1,458 million, but that the current market value of the Sun E&P common shares to be distributed is $1,800 million. This latter amount could be determined easily if the shares of Sun E&P were publicly traded. If the transaction is to be treated as a property dividend, Sun Company must recognize the gain in market value over book value ($1,800 million less $1,458 million, or $342 million) before recording the distribution:

At the declaration date:

Investment in stock of Sun E&P Co.	342,000,000	
Gain on disposal of investment		342,000,000
Retained earnings	1,800,000,000	
Property dividend payable		1,800,000,000

At the distribution (payment) date:

Property dividend payable	1,800,000,000	
Investment in stock of Sun E&P Co.		1,800,000,000

The balance sheet is unaffected by treatment of the transaction as a spin-off or as a property dividend, assuming there are no taxes on the gain. The income statement for the year of the transaction, however, will reflect the amount of the gain if the transaction is treated as a property dividend. There may be tax reasons for preferring the spin-off treatment over the property dividend treatment; a spin-off transaction can be tax-free. There is no apparent reason to prefer one treatment over the other for financial reporting except for the convenience of using one method for both purposes.

Liquidating Dividends

Liquidating dividends are a return of additional contributed capital rather than retained earnings. Owners' equity accounts other than retained earnings are debited. Any dividend not based on retained earnings is a liquidating dividend to the extent that it is not debited to retained earnings. Liquidating dividends may be either intentional or unintentional.

Liquidating dividends are intentional when the board of directors knowingly declares dividends that will represent a return of investment, in whole or in part, to the stockholders. In most states, intentional liquidating dividends are not legal until creditors' claims have been met.

Liquidating dividends are appropriate when there is no intention to conserve resources for asset replacement. A mining company might pay such a liquidating dividend when it is exploiting a nonreplaceable asset. Such a dividend would be an intentional liquidating dividend equal to the amount of depletion. Stockholders should be informed of the portion of any dividend that represents a return of capital. The liquidation portion of the dividend is not income to the investor and is usually not taxable as income. The dividend reduces the cost basis of the stock.

Example   Ignoring taxes, total depreciation on an asset with a depreciable cost of $100 reduces earnings by $100 over the asset's life. Retained earnings also are reduced by $100. By limiting dividends to the balance of retained earnings, resources are conserved for the eventual replacement of the asset, maintaining the total capital of the firm.

Depletion of a $100 **depletable** resource has the same total effect as the depreciable asset has on income and retained earnings. However, if the depletable asset will not be replaced, there is no need to restrict dividends to the amount of retained earnings. Over the depletable asset's life, a liquidating dividend of $100 could be declared. Such a dividend is a return of the investment in the depletable resource to the shareholders. The liquidating dividend in any year is restricted to total depletion expensed to date less any previous liquidating dividends.

A contributed capital account, rather than retained earnings, is debited for liquidating dividends because a portion of contributed capital is returned. Rather than debiting the capital stock accounts, which would be debited if shares were being retired, other contributed capital accounts, such as the "in excess of par" accounts, may be debited. In some cases, a special account, "capital repayment," is set up to report a deduction (contra account) in the contributed capital section of the balance sheet.

Example   Assume that Dako Corporation declares a cash dividend of $40,000 and informs the stockholders that 75 percent of it is a liquidating dividend. The entries are:

At declaration date:

Retained earnings ($40,000 × .25)	10,000	
Capital repayment ($40,000 × .75)	30,000	
Dividends payable		40,000

At payment date:

Dividends payable	40,000	
Cash		40,000

Unintentional liquidating dividends can occur when the balance of retained earnings is overstated and dividends are declared and paid. Any error that overstates revenue or understates expense can cause retained earnings to be overstated. In such cases, if reported retained earnings (prior to correction) are used in full for dividends, part of the dividend would be a liquidating dividend. Unintentional liquidating dividends paid, and later discovered, require an entry to correct the retained earnings account and any other affected accounts.

Scrip Dividends

A corporation that has a temporary cash shortage may issue a scrip dividend to maintain its continuing dividend policy. A **scrip dividend** (also called a *liability dividend*) is represented by promissory notes, called *scrip*. A scrip declaration generally means that a relatively long time (six months to a year) will elapse between declaration and payment. The scrip can become a marketable financial instrument. A stockholder may hold the scrip until the due date and collect the dividend, or sell the scrip to obtain immediate cash.

A scrip issue specifies the due date and rate of interest. Scrip usually is payable at a specified date, with the interest period usually the time from the declaration date to the payment date. If a dividend is payable as part cash and part scrip, the interest period may start on the cash dividend payment date. A scrip dividend is recorded by a debit to retained earnings and a credit to a liability account titled "scrip dividends payable." Because interest paid on a scrip dividend is not a part of the dividend, any interest payments should be debited to interest expense. In other respects, accounting for a scrip dividend is the same as for a cash dividend.

Example   Assume that Mexis Corporation declares a dividend of 25 cents per share on its 200,000 outstanding shares of nopar capital stock. Scrip is issued in full for the dividend, specifying a 10 percent interest rate and a maturity date six months after declaration date. the entries are:

At declaration date:

Retained earnings (200,000 × $.25)	50,000	
Scrip dividends payable		50,000

At scrip payment date (six months after declaration date):

Scrip dividends payable	50,000	
Interest expense ($50,000 × .10 × %12)	2,500	
Cash		52,500

Stock Dividends

A **stock dividend** is a proportional distribution of additional shares of the corporation's common or preferred stock to stockholders. It is not a real, or true, dividend, because there is no distribution of assets to stockholders. A stock dividend changes neither the assets, liabilities, or total stockholders' equity of the issuing corporation, nor the proportionate ownership of any stockholder. It merely increases the number of shares.

A stock dividend usually is accompanied by a transfer of an amount from retained earnings to the contributed capital accounts (capital stock and contributed capital in excess of par). Sometimes a stock dividend is recorded as a transfer from additional paid-in capital to capital stock. In either case, total stockholders' equity is unchanged.

A stock dividend may be issued from either treasury stock or unissued stock. When a stock dividend is of the same class as that held by the recipients, it is an *ordinary* stock dividend. When a class of stock other than the one already held by the recipients is issued, it is a *special* stock dividend (such as preferred shares issued to the common stockholders).

Companies issue stock dividends for several reasons, including:

- To indicate that the firm plans to retain a portion of earnings permanently in the business. The effect of a stock dividend, through a debit to retained earnings and offsetting credits to permanent capital accounts, is to increase the contributed capital and thereby shelter it from future declarations of dividends.
- To continue dividend distributions without disbursing cash needed for operations. Stockholders may be willing to accept a stock dividend representing accumulated earnings because they can sell these additional shares. Ordinary stock dividends are not taxable to stockholders. Instead, they reduce the investment cost per share.
- To increase the number of shares outstanding, reducing the market price per share and possibly leading to increased trading of shares in the market. This is a frequently cited reason.

Accounting for Ordinary Stock Dividends   The three primary issues in accounting for stock dividends are:

1. The amounts to be recognized.
2. The accounts and dates to be used.
3. The manner of disclosure.

Accountants disagree about the amounts that should be used in recognizing stock dividends. The basic issue is whether the stock issued for the dividend should be recorded at market value, at par or stated value, or at some other value.

A stock dividend is usually based on the availability of retained earnings. The question is what amount of retained earnings to capitalize as contributed capital. State laws and GAAP do not establish a specific amount, so the board of directors generally has the authority to determine the amount to be capitalized, subject to certain constraints. A few states permit any type of additional contributed capital to be used as a basis for a stock dividend. Other states prohibit it, while others permit only the use of additional contributed capital in excess of the par or stated value of the stock. The statutory *minimum* amount that must be capitalized from whatever source in most states is par or stated value. If the stock is true nopar, the minimum amount is the average amount per share originally paid in.

Because of the lack of agreement about capitalization of the market value or just the par value, the AICPA Committee on Accounting Procedures, in *ARB No. 43,* described two distinct approaches to accounting for stock dividends:

1. Market value method
2. Par value method

Situation 1—Small Stock Dividend, Market Value Method   When the proportion of the additional shares issued is small in relation to the shares previously outstanding, the *current market value* of the additional shares should be capitalized. *Small* is defined as less than 20 percent to 25 percent of the outstanding shares. The market price per share immediately after the stock dividend is issued is used to record the dividend. The Committee on Accounting Procedures rationalizes this position as follows:

> Many recipients of stock dividends look upon them as distributions of corporate earnings and usually in an amount equivalent to the [market] value of the additional shares received. Furthermore, it is to be presumed that such views of recipients are materially strengthened in those instances, which are by far the most numerous, where the issuances are so small in comparison with the shares previously outstanding that they do not have any apparent effect upon the share market price and, consequently, the market value of the shares previously held remains substantially unchanged. The committee therefore believes that where these circumstances exist the corporation should in the public interest account for the transaction by transferring from [retained earnings] to the category of permanent capitalization . . . an amount equal to the [market] value of the additional shares issued [that is, the market value immediately after issuance].[1]

Situation 2—Large Stock Dividend, Par Value Method   When the proportion of the additional shares issued is large in relation to the total shares previously outstanding (more than 20 percent to 25 percent), no less than the legal minimum (usually par, or stated value, or average paid in for nopar stock) should be capitalized. When the stock dividend is between 20 and 25 percent, judgment is required. The Committee continues its rationalization as follows:

> Where the number of additional shares issued as a stock dividend is so great that it has, or may reasonably be expected to have, the effect of materially reducing the share market value, the committee believes that the implications and possible constructions discussed in the [above quotation] are not likely to exist. . . .

> Consequently, the committee considers that under such circumstances there is no need to capitalize [retained earnings], other than to the extent occasioned by legal requirements.[2]

Although *ARB No. 43* was intended to settle the issue for GAAP purposes, there is still lack of agreement. Arguments supporting the par value method are:
- Legal capital is preserved.
- The corporation's assets, liabilities, and total stockholders' equity are not changed.
- Stockholders' proportionate ownership is not changed.

Arguments based on market value lack persuasive validity partly because of measurement problems. In support of the par value method, it is generally recognized that if a company

---

[1]*Accounting Research Bulletin No. 43,* "Restatement and Revision of *Accounting Research Bulletins Nos. 1–42,*" (New York, 1953), Chapter 7, Sec. B, par. 10.

[2]Ibid.

doubles the number of shares outstanding by issuing a stock dividend, the competitive market price will fall to one-half its previous level, absent any other market factors.

Recording a Stock Dividend   A stock dividend is usually recorded by a debit to retained earnings and a credit to common stock. Occasionally the dividend is recorded by a debit to an additional contributed capital account.

Stock dividend declarations are revocable prior to issuance date. Given this fact and the market-price measurement date problem, many accountants do not make a journal entry on the declaration date but wait until the issuance date. If an entry is made on the declaration date, it is made at the par value amount, then adjusted to market value on the issuance date when market value is known. Either way, a disclosure note is needed for financial statements prepared between the two dates. Either recording approach produces the same results, and both satisfy GAAP.

Example   Assume a 10 percent common stock dividend is declared on 100,000 shares of $1 par common stock issued and outstanding; market price on the declaration date is $4 per share, and immediately after the issue date it is $5 per share. Entries under both approaches are as follows:

	Originating Entry Date			
	Declaration		Issuance	
Declaration date (par value used):				
Retained earnings	10,000		None	
Stock dividends distributable*		10,000		
*Reported as a credit in stockholders' equity until issuance.	Also use disclosure note		Use disclosure note	
Issuance date (record transaction at $5 market price):				
Retained earnings	40,000		50,000*	
Stock dividends distributable	10,000			
Common stock		10,000		10,000
Contributed capital in excess of par (or stated) value . .		40,000		40,000†

*100,000 (.10) ($5)   †100,000 (.10) ($5 − $1)

│CONCEPT REVIEW

1. What dates are important in accounting for cash dividends? What does each represent?
2. What is a liquidating dividend? How is a liquidating dividend accounted for?
3. Describe two methods of recording stock dividends. Under what circumstances is each used?

Special Stock Dividends

A **special stock dividend** is a dividend in a class of stock different from the class held by the recipients.

Example   A stock dividend consisting of preferred stock issued to common stockholders is a special stock dividend. In this case, the market value of the dividend (the preferred shares) should be capitalized. Issuance of such a dividend should not have much impact, if any, on the market value of the common stock. Stockholders would appear to receive a dividend equal to the market value of the shares received.

Exhibit 21–1 provides examples of the issuance of ordinary and special stock dividends:
■ Case A—a small stock dividend, market value method.
■ Case B—a large stock dividend, par value method.
■ Case C—a special stock dividend.

Dividends and Treasury Stock

Cash and property dividends are not paid on treasury stock. Stock dividends, however, may be paid on treasury stock in certain situations, although some states prohibit the practice. Even where state statutes allow stock dividends to be paid on treasury stock, not all

EXHIBIT 21–1

Stock Dividend Entries:
Small Dividend, Large
Dividend, Special Dividend

Data Prior to the Dividend (same for each case)

Preferred stock, par value $20, 10,000 shares authorized, 5,000 shares outstanding	$100,000
Common stock, par value $10, 20,000 shares authorized, 10,000 shares outstanding.	100,000
Contributed capital in excess of par, preferred stock.	10,000
Contributed capital in excess of par, common stock.	15,000
Retained earnings.	150,000
Total stockholders' equity	$375,000

Stock Dividend Entry at Date of Issuance of Dividend Shares (each situation is independent)

Case A—A small stock dividend, market value method: A 10 percent common stock dividend is declared on the common stock. The stock dividend is capitalized at market value, which is $24 immediately after issuance.

Retained earnings (10,000 × .10) $24.	24,000	
Common stock, par $10 (1,000 shares).		10,000
Contributed capital in excess of par, common stock		14,000

Case B—A large stock dividend, par value method: A 50 percent common stock dividend is declared on the common stock. The market value per share drops to $16 on the ex-dividend date from $24 before issuance. The stock dividend is capitalized at par value.

Retained earnings [(10,000 × .50) × $10]	50,000	
Common stock, par $10 (5,000 shares).		50,000

Case C—A special stock dividend: A 20 percent common stock dividend is issued to both common and preferred stockholders. The market price per common share after issuance is $24.

Retained earnings (3,000 shares* × $24).	72,000	
Common stock, par $10 (3,000 shares).		30,000
Contributed capital in excess of par, common stock		42,000

*(10,000 shares + 5,000 shares) × 20% = 3,000 shares.

---

corporations do so. The decision depends, in part, on why the treasury stock is held. If treasury stock is held primarily in connection with a stock option plan, the corporation is likely to issue a stock dividend on the treasury stock. This is because stock options are usually adjusted for stock dividends and stock splits. Issuing stock dividends on the firm's treasury stock allows the firm to maintain its position with regard to the number of shares available when stock options are exercised. Unless treasury stock is held for such a specific purpose, the firm will seldom issue stock dividends on treasury stock.

Issuing Treasury Stock as a Stock Dividend If treasury stock is used for the issuance of a small stock dividend, the stock dividend is recorded as a debit to retained earnings (or other appropriate account) for the market value of the treasury stock issued and a credit to treasury stock for the book value of the treasury stock issued. Any difference is debited or credited to an appropriate additional contributed capital account. If additional contributed capital is insufficient to make up any debt difference, the excess is debited to retained earnings.

Fractional Share Rights

When a stock dividend is issued, not all shareholders may own exactly the number of shares needed to receive whole shares.

Example If a firm issues a 5 percent stock dividend and a shareholder owns 30 shares, the stockholder is entitled to 1½ shares (30 × .05). One way for the issuing firm to deal with this problem is to distribute **fractional share rights.**

Example Assume Moon Company has 1,000,000 outstanding shares of common stock, par $5. Moon declares a 5 percent stock dividend. The market value of the common shares before the stock dividend is $80 per share. The number of shares to be issued as the stock dividend is 5 percent of the number of shares outstanding, or 50,000 shares.

Assume the firm's shareholder ownership is such that 42,000 whole or complete shares can be issued. The firm would issue fractional share rights for the remaining shares to be issued. Each fractional share right would entitle the holder to acquire $\frac{1}{20}$ of a share. Since there are 8,000 shares yet to be issued, there would be 160,000 (8,000 $\times$ 20) fractional share rights issued. A market could develop for the fractional share rights, with each having a market value of approximately one-twentieth of a whole share ($80/20), or $4. Shareholders could buy or sell fractional share rights to the point where whole shares can be acquired. A holder would turn in 20 fractional share rights to Moon to receive 1 share of common stock.

The entries for recording the issuance of the stock dividend and fractional share rights are:
To record the 42,000 shares issued as a stock dividend (at market value):

Retained earnings (42,000 $\times$ $80)	3,360,000	
Common stock, at par (42,000 $\times$ $5)		210,000
Additional paid-in capital (42,000 $\times$ $75)		3,150,000

To record the issuance of 160,000 fractional share rights:

Retained earnings (8,000 $\times$ $80)	640,000	
Common stock fractional share rights		640,000

The *common stock fractional share rights* account is included in paid-in capital. When rights are turned in to the company for redemption, the common stock fractional share rights account is debited, and common stock, as well as additional paid-in capital (if needed), is credited. Suppose, for example, that 2,000 fractional share rights are turned in for 100 shares of common stock. The entry to record the transaction would be

Common stock fractional share rights (2,000 $\times$ $4)	8,000	
Common stock, $5 par (100 shares)		500
Additional paid-in capital		7,500

Cash Payments in Lieu of Fractional Share Rights

An alternative to the issuance of fractional share rights is to pay cash to shareholders for the fractional shares to which they are entitled. For example, suppose a shareholder of Moon Company owns 30 shares of common stock; the shareholder is entitled to $1\frac{1}{2}$ shares when the 5 percent stock dividend is issued. The firm would sell enough shares in the market to represent fractional ownership, and then distribute the proceeds to shareholders, as appropriate. Thus, Moon would sell 8,000 shares at a market price of $80:

Cash	640,000	
Common stock, $5 par (8,000 shares)		40,000
Additional paid-in capital		600,000

Shareholders with fractional share holdings would receive a cash dividend in lieu of fractional share rights. Thus the above shareholder would receive one share from the firm, plus a cash payment of $40 ($80 per share $\times$ .5 shares), representing the value of the one-half share at current market value. The entry to record the cash payment is a debit to retained earnings and a credit to cash (essentially a cash dividend). This procedure is simpler for the stockholder, as there is no need to buy or sell fractional shares. Stockholders' equity accounts have the same ending balances whichever procedure is followed.

STOCK SPLITS

A **stock split** is a change in the number of shares outstanding accompanied by an offsetting change in the par or stated value per share. A stock split is implemented either by calling in all the old shares and concurrently issuing the split shares, or by issuing the additional split shares and notifying stockholders of the change in par or stated value per share of all shares.

The primary purpose of a stock split is to increase the number of shares outstanding and decrease the market price per share. This often increases the market activity of the stock and may cause the stock's price to rise. Increasing the number of shares outstanding also reduces earnings per share.

The lower market price after a stock split also increases potential investor participation by appealing to budget-minded investors. In addition, the split makes it easier for the price to rise again. Also there is evidence that stock splits reduce stock volatility and presage cash dividend increases. Lastly, firms generally do not split their stock in bad times because decreases in the stock price *after* the split could cause embarrassingly low stock prices. The lower price increases the number of shares required to obtain a given amount of investor capital in the future.

In a *pure* stock split, no accounting entry is needed because there is no change in the dollar amounts in capital stock, additional contributed capital, or retained earnings. The increase in the number of shares is exactly counterbalanced by a proportional reduction in the par or stated value per share. The only items changed are

- Par, or stated, value per share.
- Shares issued, outstanding, in treasury, and subscribed.

Example   We illustrate a two-for-one, pure stock split (two new shares for each old share called in). Assume that Split Corporation is authorized to issue 200,000 shares of common stock, par $10, of which 40,000 shares were issued initially at par, and retained earnings has a balance of $450,000. In the following table, a 100 percent stock dividend and stock split are compared for Split Corporation. Both events double the number of shares outstanding, but have different effects on the components of total owners' equity.

| | | | | Total Par Value | | |
| | | | | | After Recording | |
Transaction	Shares Outstanding	Par per Share	Prior to Stock Dividend or Stock Split	100% Stock Dividend	2-for-1 Stock Split
Initial issue	40,000	× $10 =	$400,000		
100% stock dividend	80,000	× 10 =		$800,000*	
Two-for-one stock split	80,000	× 5 =			$400,000
Total contributed capital			400,000	800,000	400,000
Retained earnings			450,000	50,000[†]	450,000
Total stockholders' equity			$850,000	$850,000	$850,000

*Retained earnings capitalized: 40,000 shares × $10 = $400,000. Entry: Debit retained earnings $400,000; credit common stock $400,000.

[†] $450,000 − $400,000.

The stock dividend capitalizes retained earnings as contributed capital, but the stock split does not. Total stockholders' equity is the same for either the stock dividend or the stock split treatment.

Occasionally financial statements refer incorrectly to a stock dividend as a stock split. *ARB No. 43* uses the phrase "stock split effected in the form of a dividend" to describe large stock dividends, which may be the source of confusion.

Some stock splits are issued that do not maintain the offsetting relationship between the split shares and the change in the par or stated value per share. An example is a two-for-one split on $10 par value stock and a reduction of par value per share to $6 (rather than to $5). Such a transaction is a combined stock split and stock dividend.

A *reverse stock split* involves a proportional increase in the par or stated value per share and reduction in the number of shares issued and outstanding. One new share for every two held is an example of a reverse split.

APPROPRIATIONS AND RESTRICTIONS OF RETAINED EARNINGS

Appropriated retained earnings and **restricted retained earnings** constrain a specified portion of accumulated earnings for a specified purpose. Appropriated retained earnings are the result of discretionary management action. Restricted retained earnings are the result of a legal contract or law.[3]

Retained earnings are appropriated and restricted primarily to protect the cash position of the corporation by reducing the amount of cash dividends that otherwise might be paid. Appropriations and restrictions of retained earnings arise in the following situations:

---

[3] Although accountants traditionally use the term *appropriation of retained earnings* to cover both appropriations and restrictions, it is important to know whether retained earnings are appropriated or restricted.

- To fulfill a legal requirement, as in the case of a state law requiring a restriction on retained earnings equivalent to the cost of treasury stock held.
- To fulfill a contractual agreement, as in the case of a debt covenant restricting the use of retained earnings for dividends that would result in the disbursement of assets.
- To report a discretionary appropriation made to constrain a specified portion of retained earnings as an aspect of financial planning.
- To report a discretionary appropriation of a specified portion of retained earnings in anticipation of possible future losses.

For reporting purposes appropriations and restrictions may be reported any one of three ways:

- Report each appropriation and restriction as a separate item in the retained earnings statement.
- Report appropriations and restrictions parenthetically in the retained earnings statement.
- Disclose appropriations and restrictions in the notes to the financial statements.

When the need for an appropriation or restriction no longer exists, the appropriated balance is returned to the unappropriated retained earnings account.

Appropriation or restriction of retained earnings made by transferring an amount from retained earnings to an appropriated retained earnings account has no effect on assets, liabilities, or total stockholders' equity. An appropriation is an administrative identification that does not set aside specific assets. This effect would occur only if, as a management action, cash is set aside in a separate fund, such as a bond sinking fund.

The primary purpose of an appropriation is to communicate to statement users management's judgment that the appropriated amounts are not available for dividends. Exhibit 21–2 shows an example of the disclosure of appropriations and restrictions (see note 5).

RETAINED EARNINGS STATEMENTS

Retained earnings statements are not required to be reported, but when a retained earnings statement is presented, it should include

- Beginning balance of retained earnings.
- Restatement of the beginning balance for any prior period adjustments (discussed in Chapter 24).
- Restatement of beginning balance for any retroactive accounting changes (discussed in Chapter 24).
- Net income or loss for the period.
- Dividends declared for the period.
- Appropriations and restrictions of retained earnings.
- Any adjustments made pursuant to a quasi reorganization (discussed in the first appendix to this chapter).
- Ending balance of retained earnings.

STOCK RIGHTS AND WARRANTS

Corporations often issue **stock rights** that give the holder an option to acquire a specified number of shares of capital stock under prescribed conditions and within a stated period. These rights are similar to fractional share rights in that more than one right may be required to acquire an additional share of stock.

Evidence of ownership of stock rights is a certificate called a **stock warrant.** Stock rights

EXHIBIT 21–2

Retained Earnings Statement:
Reporting Prior Period
Adjustments and
Appropriations

Basic Case Data (May Corporation)

1. For the year ended December 31, 1998, May Corporation reported
   a. Retained earnings beginning balance, $158,000.
   b. Net income, $52,000.
   c. Dividends declared and paid, $30,000.
2. During 1998, it was discovered that 1997 depreciation expense had been understated by $20,000 (the applicable tax rate during 1997 was 30 percent) for both books and income taxes. An amended tax return was submitted for 1997.

Reported Retained Earnings

MAY CORPORATION

Retained Earnings Statement
For Year Ended December 31, 1998

Balance in retained earnings, 12/31/1997	$158,000
Prior period adjustment (a debit):	
Correction of accounting error in 1997, net of $6,000 income tax saving	
(see Note 4).	(14,000)
Balance in retained earnings, 12/31/1997 as corrected	144,000
Add: Net income for 1998.	52,000
Total	196,000
Deduct: Dividends for 1998	(30,000)
Balance in retained earnings, 12/31/1998 (see Note 5)	$166,000

Note 4: During 1997 the company inadvertently understated depreciation expense by $20,000. This accounting error caused an overstatement of the reported income of 1997 and of the balance in retained earnings at December 31, 1997, by $14,000, which reflects the $6,000 tax effect of the error. The error was detected and corrected during 1998 by debiting retained earnings for a prior period adjustment in the after tax amount of $14,000. To correct other affected accounts, an income tax receivable was set up for the $6,000 tax saving and accumulated depreciation was increased by $20,000.

Note 5: Appropriation and restrictions:

Appropriations for investment in plant	$ 35,000
Restriction for cost of treasury stock	25,000
Unappropriated retained earnings	106,000
Total retained earnings	$166,000

---

sometimes are referred to simply as stock warrants. A stock warrant typically specifies

- The number of rights represented by the warrant.
- The option price (which may be zero) per share of the specified stock.
- The number of rights required to obtain a share of the stock.
- The expiration date of the rights.
- Instructions for exercising the rights.

When more than one right is required to obtain one share of stock in the future, the rights represent fractional shares and are called *fractional share rights*.

Corporations issue stock rights and options for several reasons:

- As a preemptive right that gives existing stockholders the first chance to buy additional shares when the corporation decides to raise additional equity capital by selling a large number of unissued shares.
- To compensate outside parties (such as underwriters, promoters, and professionals) for services provided to the corporation.
- To represent fractional shares when a stock dividend is declared and issued. The option price for these rights is zero (as was discussed under fractional shares earlier in this chapter).
- To compensate officers and other employees of the corporation. These rights often are referred to as **stock options** or stock incentive plans (discussed later).
- To enhance the marketability of other securities issued by the corporation. An example is issuing common stock rights with convertible bonds.

Three dates are important regarding stock rights issued to shareholders:

1. *Announcement date* of the rights offering.
2. *Issuance date* of the rights.
3. *Expiration date* of the rights.

Between the announcement date and the issuance date, the stock will sell *rights on. Rights on* means the price of the stock includes the value of the rights because the stock and the rights are not separable during that period of time. After the issuance date and until expiration of the rights, the shares and rights are sold separately. During this time the shares sell *ex rights* and the *rights* have a separate price.

A stockholder or other party receiving stock rights may

- Exercise them by purchasing additional shares of the specified stock from the corporation.
- Sell them at the market value of the rights.
- Allow them to lapse on the expiration date.

Accounting for Stock Rights

Issuance of stock rights raises the accounting issues for both the recipient and the issuing corporation. For the recipient, stock rights received on capital stock held have no additional cost, so the current carrying value of the shares already owned is allocated between the original shares and the rights received, based on the current market values of each.

The issuing corporation must account for stock rights by either a memorandum entry or a regular journal entry on each relevant date: (1) announcement date, (2) issuance date, and (3) expiration date. The accounting under the first two of the five reasons for issuing stock rights listed above are discussed next. Accounting for stock options is covered later in this chapter. Chapter 16 discusses accounting for warrants attached to bond issues.

Issue of Stock Rights to Existing Stockholders Related to a Planned Sale of Unissued Stock   Stock rights may be issued in advance of the planned sale date to give current stockholders the opportunity to maintain their proportional share of ownership in the firm. These are preemptive rights.

Example   Sax Corporation's stockholders' equity on January 1, 1998, is:

Common stock, par $10, authorized 100,000 shares, issued and outstanding, 30,000 shares	$300,000
Additional paid-in capital	150,000
Retained earnings	70,000

Assume that on January 1, 1998, Sax decides to raise equity capital and increase its outstanding common shares 50 percent by issuing 15,000 additional shares. The current shareholders have preemptive rights, so Sax issues stock rights to current shareholders, one right for every share held. Two stock rights entitle the holder to purchase one share of common stock at a price of $30 per share (the market price on January 1, 1998). The rights are formally issued on March 1, 1998, and expire on September 1, 1998. On the issue date of the rights, the stock price is $32 per share. The rights trade at an average price of $5 per share between the issue and expiration dates. On the expiration date of the rights, the stock price is $34 per share.

These journal entries reflect various transactions involving the stock rights.

January 1, 1998—Announcement date: no entry because the transaction is not completed.

March 1, 1998—Issuance date: memorandum only, because there is no inflow of resources. There is only a commitment to issue shares contingent on the future actions of the party holding the rights. The following memo expresses that commitment:

> Memo—Issued 30,000 stock rights to current stockholders for 15,000 shares of stock to be sold. Each share will be sold for $30 cash plus the receipt of two stock rights. After September 1, 1998, all outstanding rights will expire and the remaining shares will be sold in the market at the then-current market price.

July 1, 1998—Assume that 1,000 stock rights are exercised by a stockholder. There is now a completed transaction. An entry is required:

```
Cash (1,000 rights ÷ 2 = 500 shares) × $30  . . . . . . . . . . . . . . . . . . . .    15,000
    Common stock, par $10 (500 shares)   . . . . . . . . . . . . . . . . . . . .                    5,000
    Additional paid-in capital, common stock   . . . . . . . . . . . . . . . . . . .                  10,000
```

Subsequent exercises of stock rights would be recorded similarly. No entry is required if a shareholder allows rights to lapse.

Compensation to Outside Parties   A company sometimes wants to conserve cash during the early stages of its life and therefore issues shares or stock rights as payment for professional services.

Example   Assume the same data for Sax Corporation, with a decision to issue Laurena Brown 100 stock rights that specify a $30 option price as payment for legal services. As before, two rights entitle the holder to purchase one share of common stock at $30. The rights were issued on March 1, 1998, expire on December 31, 1998, and were exercised by Brown on July 1, 1998. Assume that at the time of issuance of the stock rights, the market value of the stock is $35 and on the exercise date the market value is $38. The required journal entries are as follows:

March 1, 1998—Issue date (recognition of service cost):

```
Expense (legal services)   . . . . . . . . . . . . . . . . . . . . . . . . . . . . .    250
    Stock rights outstanding [(100 rights ÷ 2 = 50 shares) × ($35 − $30)]   . . . . . . . .           250
```

Brown was awarded the right to acquire for $30 each shares having a market value of $35; her compensation is $5 for each of the shares she can acquire with her rights, or $250.

July 1, 1998—Exercise date:

```
Cash (50 shares × $30)   . . . . . . . . . . . . . . . . . . . . . . . . .   1,500
Stock rights outstanding (50 shares × $5)   . . . . . . . . . . . . . . . . . . . .    250
    Common stock, par $10 (50 shares)   . . . . . . . . . . . . . . . . . . . .                  500
    Additional paid-in capital, common stock ($35 − $10) × 50 shares   . . . . . . . . .          1,250
```

During the period the stock rights are outstanding, the account labeled *stock rights outstanding* should be reported in stockholders' equity as a credit item along with the capital stock account to which it relates. The stock price at the exercise date is not used in accounting for the options.

|REVIEW PROBLEM

The Gilmore Company has the following stockholders' equity section as of December 31, 1997:

Stockholders' Equity

Preferred stock, $100 par, 8 percent cumulative, voting, 10,000 shares issued and outstanding	$1,000,000
Common stock, $20 par, 100,000 shares authorized, 70,000 shares issued and outstanding	1,400,000
Additional paid-in capital	800,000
Total paid-in capital	3,200,000
Retained earnings	3,000,000
Total stockholders' equity	$6,200,000

There are no dividends in arrears on the preferred shares. During 1998 the following events or transactions occurred:

a. Earnings during 1998 total $600,000. The board of directors declares a cash dividend totaling $280,000 to be paid as appropriate to preferred and common shareholders. Later, a stock dividend of 10 percent is declared on common stock. The market value of common stock is $68 per share on the date the stock dividend is declared.

b. In order to familiarize stockholders with one of the company's new products, the board declares a property dividend of one ounce of a new perfume the company produces for every share of outstanding common stock (before the above stock dividend). The cost of the perfume is 60 cents per ounce, and has a wholesale market value of $1 per ounce. Any gain or loss on this transaction is already included in the earnings reported above.

c. At the end of 1998, the board declares a three-for-two stock split. With the split, the number of common shares authorized to be issued is increased to 150,000. At the date of the stock split, the market value of common stock is $75 per share.

Required

1. Show all computations and entries to record the above transactions.
2. Show the stockholders' equity section as of December 31, 1998.
3. Assume the three-for-two stock split was accounted for as a stock dividend. Show the computations and entries to record it, and the stockholders' equity section as of December 31, 1998.

SOLUTION

1. Computations and entries:

To close the 1998 earnings to retained earnings:

Income summary	600,000	
Retained earnings		600,000

To compute and record cash dividends payable to preferred and common shareholders:

Total amount of dividends to be paid	$280,000
Preferred shareholder dividends ($1,000,000 × .08)	80,000
Common stock dividends	$200,000

The entry to record dividends payable:

Retained earnings	280,000	
Dividends payable (preferred)		80,000
Dividends payable (common)		200,000

To compute and record stock dividend:

The number of shares issued as a stock dividend is

$$70,000 \text{ shares outstanding} \times .10 = 7,000 \text{ shares}$$

Since the stock dividend is less than 20 percent, it is recorded at market value. The amount to be capitalized as permanent capital is

$$7,000 \text{ shares} \times \$68 \text{ per share} = \$476,000$$

Retained earnings	476,000	
Common stock (at par) (7,000 × $20)		140,000
Additional paid-in capital		336,000

Computations and entries to record the property dividend:

The property dividend is recorded at market value, with the gain being recorded for the amount by which the market value of the perfume exceeds the book value:

Market value of property dividend (70,000 × $1.00)	$70,000
Cost of property dividend (70,000 × $.60)	42,000
Gain on disposal of inventory	$28,000

These entries record the property dividend.

Record the gain when the dividend is declared:

Inventory held for property dividend	70,000	
Inventory, at cost		42,000
Gain on disposal of inventory		28,000

Record declaration of dividend:

Retained earnings	70,000	
Property dividend payable		70,000

When property dividend is distributed:

Property dividend payable	70,000	
Inventory held for property dividend		70,000

The three-for-two stock split occurs after all the above transactions; therefore, the number of common shares to be split is 70,000 plus the 10 percent stock dividend (7,000 shares), or a total of 77,000 shares with a par value totaling $1.54 million. Every two shares outstanding will become three new shares; hence, there will be 77,000 times ³⁄₂, or 115,500 new shares outstanding after the split. The new par value per share is

$$\text{\$1.54 million (the amount in the par value of outstanding shares)} \div$$
$$\text{115,500 new shares outstanding} = \text{\$13.33 per share}$$

This new par value also can be determined by noting that each existing share with a par value of $20 becomes one and one-half new shares. The $20 in par value is allocated to the one and one-half new shares, or each share has a new par value of $20/1.5, or $13.33 per share. A memo entry can be made to record the stock split, or a formal entry can be made in the accounting records as follows:

Common stock ($20 par)	1,540,000	
Common stock ($13.33 par)		1,540,000

There is no change in paid-in capital and no capitalization of retained earnings for this transaction.

2. The Gilmore Company has the following stockholders' equity section as of December 31, 1998:

Stockholders' Equity

Preferred stock, $100 par, 8 percent cumulative, voting, 10,000 shares issued and outstanding	$1,000,000
Common stock, $13.33 par, 150,000 shares authorized, 115,500 shares issued and outstanding	1,540,000
Additional paid-in capital	1,136,000
Total paid-in capital	3,676,000
Retained earnings	2,774,000
Total stockholders' equity	$6,450,000

The retained earnings balance is determined as follows:

Stockholders' Equity

Cash dividend	280,000	3,000,0000	Beg. bal.
Stock dividend	476,000	600,000	1998 Earnings
Property dividend	70,000		
		2,774,000	End. bal.

3. The three-for-two stock split is equivalent to a 50 percent stock dividend, which would be recorded at par value.

$$\text{Number of shares to be issued} = 77,000 \times .5 = 38,500 \text{ shares}$$

The entry to record the stock split accounted for as a 50 percent stock dividend:

Retained earnings	770,000	
Common stock, at par		770,000

The stockholders' equity section is:

Preferred stock, $100 par, 8 percent cumulative, voting, 10,000 shares issued and outstanding	$1,000,000
Common stock, $20 par, 150,000 shares authorized; 115,500 shares issued and outstanding	2,310,000
Additional paid-in capital	1,136,000
Retained earnings	2,004,000
Total stockholders' equity	$6,450,000

STOCK-BASED COMPENSATION PLANS

Over the past couple of decades an increasing number of firms have established plans under which employees receive:

- Shares of stock.
- Options to acquire shares of stock at a specified price during a specified time period.
- Other financial instruments of the employer.
- Compensation based on the price of the employer's stock.

  These plans come in many different formats and have many different titles, including:

- Employee stock purchase plans.
- Equity participation plans.
- Stock option plans.
- Restricted stock plans.
- Stock appreciation rights plans.

We refer to the entire set of such plans as *stock-based compensation plans*. Whatever the firm's description of the plan, the issuing corporation is the *grantor* and the employee receiving the stock, rights, or options is the *grantee*. Examples of different kinds of grants illustrate some of the difficulties in accounting for stock-based compensation plans.

Example   Jax Inc. grants to each of its five senior corporate officers options to acquire 1,000 shares of its common stock. They cannot exercise the options for four years, and the options expire if not exercised within seven years. The price the grantees will pay for the stock, called the **exercise price,** is equal to the stock price on the date the options are granted. This is an example of a **fixed stock option** plan because vesting is based solely on the employee continuing to render service. The option price and number of shares awarded are fixed at the grant date.

Example   All the facts are the same as above for Jax Inc. except that the exercise price is determined by the following formula:

$$\text{Exercise price} = \text{Current market price} \times 1.2 \times (1 - \text{growth rate of earnings over next three years})$$

This is an example of a **variable** (also called a **performance**) **stock option** plan. The exercise price is variable and will not be known until the three-year earnings growth rate is known. It is a performance plan in that the employees holding these options benefit if earnings growth is increased, thus they have an incentive to perform to increase earnings growth. The higher the growth rate, the lower the exercise price.

Example   Max Inc. awards rights to each of its five senior officers: Each officer will receive in three years either a cash payment or shares of common stock of equivalent value equal to the increase in common stock share price between the grant date and three years hence, multiplied by 1,000. This is an example of a **stock appreciation right (SAR)** plan.

Overview of Accounting Issues

Accounting for these plans involves a number of decisions, and can be complex. The purpose of these plans can vary across firms. They can be used to help recruit and retain outstanding employees. They also can encourage employee ownership. Stock-based plans are often awarded to particular groups of employees to encourage superior performance. As such they are incentive plans. The contract or agreement regarding the conditions under which the employee can take advantage of the plan provides information useful in determining the purpose of the plan. Fundamentally, the plans may be providing a form of compensation to employees, or they may simply encourage employees to have an ownership interest in the firm. The latter plans are not considered compensatory plans. Thus the first important question to be addressed is:

1. Is the stock-based plan providing the employees compensation, or is it noncompensatory?

If the plan is deemed noncompensatory, no compensation cost or expense is recorded.[4] If the plan is considered to be a compensatory plan, a second accounting question arises:

---

[4]We use the term *compensation cost* rather than *compensation expense* because it is the more general term. In some instances the compensation cost would be accrued as a component of inventory costs rather than treated as a period expense. However, we assume the compensation cost arising in a period is treated as a period expense unless stated otherwise.

2. What amount of compensation cost should be recognized?

Finally, if the plan is considered compensatory and the total amount of compensation is determined, the question is:

3. In what period or periods is the compensation cost to be expensed?

What Is GAAP Regarding These Issues?   *SFAS No. 123* was issued in October 1995 and is effective for fiscal years beginning after December 15, 1995. However, it is an unusual Standard in that it is *not* required to be used as the method for measuring compensation cost for recognition in the financial statements. While *SFAS No. 123* encourages firms to adopt the method of accounting contained in the Standard, it explicitly allows firms to continue using the method established by *APB Opinion No. 25*. The decision not to require *SFAS No. 123* was a compromise made by the FASB after it received significant opposition to the proposed Standard. As of the end of fiscal 1996, few firms appear to be adopting *SFAS No. 123* as their method for accounting for stock option plans.

However, a firm that continues using the method provided in *APB Opinion No. 25* also must provide pro forma disclosures of net income and earnings per share as if *SFAS No. 123* were used. A firm that adopts *SFAS No. 123* cannot revert back to the *APB Opinion No. 25* accounting treatment in the future. This means the accountant must understand both the *SFAS No. 123* and the *APB Opinion No. 25* methods. A firm that adopts *SFAS No. 123* cannot revert back to the *APB Opinion No. 25* method, and must use the same method for all plans.

Essentially, *APB Opinion No. 25* applies an **intrinsic-value-based method** in determining the value of the stock options granted. When stock options are granted with the exercise price set equal the market price of the stock on the grant date, the intrinsic value of the options, defined as the market price on the grant date less the exercise price times the number of shares optioned, is zero.[5] No compensation cost is recorded even though this could be a compensatory plan.

SFAS No. 123 rejects the intrinsic-value-based method in favor of a **fair-value method,** where fair value is determined at the grant date. The procedures by which fair value is determined are outlined in the Statement and beyond the coverage of this text. However, fixed stock options with an exercise price set equal to the current market price on the grant date, which have an intrinsic value of zero, will often have a fair value greater than zero.

After the value of the granted fixed options is determined, both *APB Opinion No. 25* and *SFAS No. 123* allocate this amount as compensation cost over the service period (usually the period from the grant date to the date the stock options vest with the employee).

The decision process described to this point is diagrammed:

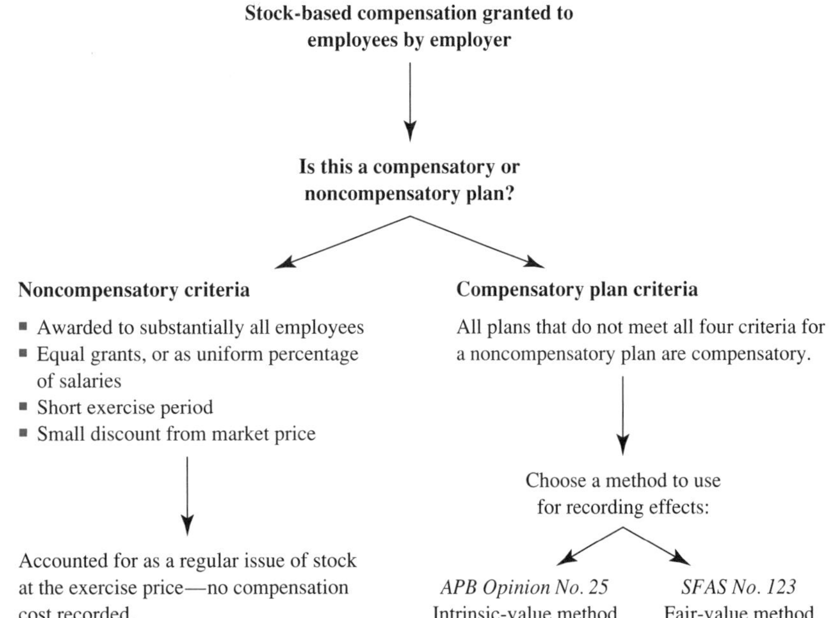

---

[5]In some instances, the exercise price is set above the market price on the grant date. Under the intrinsic-value-based method, these options are defined as having an intrinsic value of zero.

First, we examine the criteria for determining whether a plan is compensatory or noncompensatory as they are found in the two pronouncements, and cover accounting for noncompensatory plans. Second, we cover the accounting measurements as found in *APB Opinion No. 25*, because many firms are continuing to use this method. Finally, we cover accounting for stock-based plans as outlined in *SFAS No. 123*. Since pro forma disclosures are required even if a firm does not adopt the *SFAS No. 123* method, it is essential to understand the new Standard.

Compensatory or Noncompensatory   The initial key determination is whether the stock-based plan is a compensatory plan or a noncompensatory plan for accounting purposes. If it is determined to be noncompensatory, no compensation cost is recorded for the plan.

APB Opinion No. 25 and *SFAS No. 123* have slightly different criteria for determining whether a plan is noncompensatory. All criteria must be met for a plan to be considered noncompensatory.

APB Opinion No. 25	*SFAS No. 123*

■ Substantially all full-time employees are included.
■ Stock is offered to eligible employees either equally or on the basis of a uniform percent of salary.
■ The period permitted for exercise is limited to a reasonable period.
■ The discount from market price of the stock is no greater than would be reasonable to offer to current stockholders. Discounts of up to 15 percent are permitted in practice.
	■ Employees are permitted to enroll during a period not exceeding 31 days after the purchase price is fixed.
	■ The purchase price is based solely on the stock price at the date of purchase.
	■ The discount from the market price does not exceed:
	  1. A per-share discount that would be reasonable to regularly offer to shareholders.
	  2. The per-share amount of stock issuance costs avoided by not having to raise capital in the market.
	■ Substantially all full-time employees can participate on an equitable basis.

SFAS No. 123 has tighter criteria for qualifying the plans as noncompensatory relative to *APB Opinion No. 25*. Perhaps the biggest difference is that *APB Opinion No. 25* allows up to a 15 percent discount, while *SFAS No. 123* states, "a discount of 5 percent or less from the market price is considered to comply with this criterion without further justification." *SFAS No. 123* limited the option period to 31 days, while *APB Opinion No. 25* specifies only that exercise is limited to a reasonable period. Another tight restriction found in *SFAS No. 123* and not in *APB Opinion No. 25* has to do with the basis for determining the price employees will pay for the stock, namely that the price is based solely on the market price of the stock on the day it is purchased. These differences can lead to a plan being considered noncompensatory under *APB Opinion No. 25* but compensatory under *SFAS No. 123*.

So which applies, whichever the firm is using to account for this? [

Example   The following is taken from the notes to the fiscal 1996 financial statements of Microsoft Corporation:

> **Employee stock purchase plan.**   The Company has an employee stock purchase plan for all eligible employees. Under the plan, shares of the Company's common stock may be purchased at six-month intervals at 85 percent of the lower of the fair market value on the first or last day of each six-month period. Employees may purchase shares having a value not exceeding 10 percent of their gross compensation during the offering period. During 1994, 1995, and 1996, employees purchased 10.0 million, 1.1 million, and 0.9 million shares at average prices of $34.16, $48.76, and $75.44 per share.

Under *APB Opinion No. 25,* Microsoft Corporation accounts for this plan as a noncompensatory plan. Under *SFAS No. 123,* however, it would have to be treated as a compensatory plan, as it fails the 5 percent discount test, and the purchase price is not based solely on the fair market price of the stock at the purchase date.

Accounting for Noncompensatory Stock Option Plans

Noncompensatory stock option plans involve no expense recognition by the granting company. Stock issued under such a plan is recorded in conformity with the cost principle, with the price being the amount per share paid by the employee.

Example   Assume Microsoft Corporation has nopar common stock. The entry to record the issuance of employee stock purchases in 1996 based on the information provided in the above note follows. Total proceeds are computed as 0.9 million shares times the average price paid per share ($75.44), a total of $67.9 million. Assuming the employees paid cash for the purchased stock, the entry is:

```
Cash  . . . . . . . . . . . . . . . . . . . . . . . . . . . . . . .    67,900,000
   Capital stock, no par  . . . . . . . . . . . . . . . . . . . . . . . .              67,900,000
```

Typically employees sign up to have voluntary payroll deductions taken to accumulate the funds needed to purchase stock. Thus, as wages and salaries are earned some portion is not paid as the firm accrues a liability to the employees for the employee stock purchase plan.

Example   Suppose the employees of Microsoft earn wages and salaries totaling $700 million for fiscal 1996. The summary journal entry, ignoring withholding income tax and other payroll items, is:

```
Wages and salaries expense  . . . . . . . . . . . . . . . . . . . . . .   700,000,000
   Wages payable . . . . . . . . . . . . . . . . . . . . . . . . . . .                632,100,000
   Liability for employee stock purchase plan  . . . . . . . . . . . . . .               67,900,000
```

When the shares are issued the entry is:

```
Liability for employee stock purchase plan . . . . . . . . . . . . . . .    67,900,000
   Capital stock, no par  . . . . . . . . . . . . . . . . . . . . . . .                 67,900,000
```

In the first entry, the employees have earned $700 million in compensation and are simply allocating $67.9 million of that amount to the purchase of stock. The stock is not a form of compensation in this case, *but the discount on stock is not considered compensation—hence the term "non-compensatory."*

Accounting for Compensatory Stock Option Plans under *APB Opinion No. 25*

A stock option plan for employees that does not meet all the criteria for a noncompensatory plan is accounted for as a compensatory stock option plan. These are often called *incentive stock option plans,* or *incentive plans,* because they are designed to provide incentives to employees to increase productivity and the share price of the stock. For example, an option awarded to an employee to purchase stock at the current market price that is exercisable in five years provides an incentive to increase the market price of the stock over the next five years. The employee reaps a reward equal to the increase in the share price times the number of shares optioned.

A compensatory stock option incentive plan for employees may involve an expense to the grantor corporation in addition to the regular wage and salary expense and additional compensation income to the grantee. However, in many instances the option price is set equal to the market price of the stock on the grant date. In these instances, no compensation expense is recorded under *APB Opinion No. 25.*

Accounting for compensatory stock option plans requires application of the intrinsic value method and the cost principle to measure and record the total amount of compensation cost. During the relevant service period, application of the matching principle allocates the total compensation cost as periodic expense throughout the service period of the grantee.

There are numerous types of compensatory stock option plans in use. They provide a wide range of specifications. The measurement, recording, and reporting reflect that variety. We discuss here only the basic distinctions and recording requirements.

The various stock option incentive plans can be classified as:

- **Stock options**   Stock options give the grantee the right to buy a specified number of shares of the common stock of the grantor at a specified price per share.
- **Stock appreciation rights (SARs)**   Stock appreciation rights provide a cash bonus to the employee based upon the change in the market value of the specified shares of capital stock from the date of grant to the exercise date.
- **Restricted (or nonvested) stock plans**   Restricted (or nonvested) stock plans give the employee shares of stock that cannot be sold because the employee has not satisfied vesting requirements. A nonvested stock can be described as a nonvested stock option with a cash exercise price of zero.

EXHIBIT 21–3

Data for Compensatory Stock
Option Plan: Abat Corporation

Plan Specifications and Data for Stock Option Transactions

1. Abat Corporation—plan specification—executive stock options:
   a. Options approved for 10 designated executives.
   b. 5,000 shares of common stock, par $5, for each executive.
   c. Nontransferable, exercisable 5 years after grant and prior to expiration date, which is 10 years from date of grant.
   d. Option price, $20 per share (Note: This is also called the exercise price).
2. On January 1, 1998, an executive covered by the plan (I. Goode), is granted an option for 5,000 shares:
   a. For services to be performed from date of grant to the earliest possible exercise date (the earliest possible exercise is referred to as the *vesting date**) at December 31, 2002 (approximately equal services each year).
   b. At January 1, 1998, the quoted market price was $30 per share.
   c. The option was exercised by I. Goode on December 31, 2002, when the quoted market price per share was $60 (the stock price experienced steady increases from 1998 through 2002).

*The vesting date is important because as of that date the employee can exercise the option to acquire the stock with no constraints as to continued employment or disposition of the shares.

Accounting for any plan requires answering five basic questions. Exhibit 21–3 presents data to illustrate these five questions and how they are resolved.

Question 1: Is the plan compensatory?   A plan that fails to meet any one of the four criteria for a noncompensatory plan is classified as compensatory.

According to the data given in Exhibit 21–3, Abat Corporation's plan is compensatory because it does *not* meet all four of the criteria for a *noncompensatory* plan. The plan is limited to 10 executives (not substantially all the full-time employees), and the discount from the market price of the stock is 33⅓ percent, that is, ($30 − $20) ÷ $30. Also, the exercise period is substantial (5 years).

Question 2: When should the total compensation cost be measured?   Conceptually, compensation costs are measured when the grantor forgoes alternative uses (for example, sale) of the optioned shares. This date is called the *measurement date*. Under *APB Opinion No. 25,* the measurement date is the first date on which both (1) the number of shares that an individual employee is entitled to receive and (2) the option price are known. Both specifications are necessary to measure total compensation cost.

The measurement date may be the *date of grant*. However, a compensation plan may allow both the number of shares and the option price to be determined at a later date. If this is the case, the measurement date is the first date on which the two specifications are known.

For Abat Corporation, the measurement date is the grant date. On that date, January 1, 1998, both the number of optioned shares (5,000) and the option price per share ($20) are known (see Exhibit 21–3). Plans for which the measurement date is the grant date are known as **fixed option plans** under *APB Opinion No. 25*.

Question 3: What is the amount of total compensation cost?   Under the intrinsic-value method of *APB Opinion No. 25,* total compensation cost for Goode is the difference between the market value of the stock on the measurement date and the option price per share, multiplied by the number of optioned shares.[6] If the market value of the stock is less than or equal to the option price on the measurement date, no compensation cost is recorded for the option plan, even though the plan meets the definition of a compensatory plan. If there is no quoted market price, the best estimate of the market value of the stock is used to measure compensation.

---

[6]Conceptually, compensation cost should be the fair value of stock option rights (not the shares themselves). *APB Opinion No. 25* was issued before methods for determining the fair value of options had been developed. It therefore uses the simpler intrinsic-value approach.

For Abat Corporation (Exhibit 21–3), total compensation cost on the measurement date (date of grant, January 1, 1998) is $50,000, which equals the market value of the stock on measurement date, $30, minus option price, $20, times number of optioned shares, 5,000. If the market price were less than or equal to $20 per share on the grant date, no compensation cost would be recorded.

Question 4: To what service period should the total compensation cost be assigned as periodic expense?

Total compensation cost is allocated over a **service period** that is from the date of grant to the date on which the employee has no further service obligations or constraints imposed by the stock option incentive plan. Usually the service period ends at the first date that the option is exercisable, which is the **vesting date.** From that date forward, if the option is exercised, the employee controls the disposition of the shares. The compensation plan may specify the service period; otherwise, the grantor must use a best estimate. The assignment of total compensation cost to period expense begins in the first year and extends to the end of the service period. The service period is not reduced in length by early exercise of the options. When estimates of the service period are used, revisions are accounted for as a change in accounting estimate.

For Abat Corporation, the total compensation cost of $50,000 should be allocated to expense equally to each year of the five-year service period from date of grant (January 1, 1998) to the first exercise date (December 31, 2002). Executive Goode is required to work full-time for the company during that period.

Question 5: What journal entries should be made by the grantor?

The journal entries to record the effects of a compensatory stock option plan vary depending upon whether the measurement date is on or after the date of grant.

Measurement Date Same as Grant Date   The measurement date is the *grant date* if the number of optioned shares, the option price, and the market price of the stock are known at that date. Total compensation cost is recorded on the grant date as a debit to deferred compensation cost and a credit to executive stock options outstanding. As of the grant date, these two accounts are reported on the balance sheet in the stockholders' equity section, as follows:

Contributed capital:		
Executive stock options outstanding	$ 50,000	
Less: Deferred compensation cost	(50,000)	–0–

Deferred compensation cost, a contra owners' equity account, is subtracted from executive stock options outstanding because the stock options have been issued to the employee but the stock has not been issued. The employee has not yet earned the stock options, and consequently no owners' equity has been created for the unearned stock options.[7]

For each subsequent period in the employee's service period, total compensation cost is allocated on a straight-line basis. Straight-line allocation is used because it is reasonable to assume that the employee will provide equal service each period.

Exhibit 21–4 illustrates the accounting for the Abat Corporation plan when the measurement date is the grant date. The exhibit gives the entries required

1. On the measurement date.
2. At each year-end to record the assignment of periodic expense.
3. On the exercise date for the stock option granted to Goode.

The related reporting is also presented.

In the Exhibit 21–4 example, the actual value of Goode's stock option on December 31, 2002, is ($60 − $20) × 5,000 shares, or $200,000. The total compensation expense reported

---

[7]*APB Opinion No. 25* (par. 14) also states (italics added), "If stock is issued in a plan before some or all of the services are performed, part of the consideration recorded for the stock issued is unearned compensation and should be shown as a *separate reduction of stockholders' equity.* The unearned compensation should be accounted for as expense of the period or periods in which the employee performs service."

EXHIBIT 21–4

Accounting for Compensatory
Stock Options, Abat
Corporation—Measurement
Date Is Date of Grant

Case Data—See Exhibit 21–3.

Entries of Abat Corporation for Executive Goode Stock Option

1. January 1, 1998 (date of grant)—to record total deferred compensation cost and the issuance of stock options to Executive Goode:

Deferred compensation cost [($30 − $20) × 5,000 shares]	50,000	
Executive stock options outstanding (for 5,000 shares of		
common stock).		50,000

2. December 31, 1998 through 2002—to record the annual allocation of deferred compensation cost to compensation expense (equal amount for each of the five years):

Compensation expense	10,000	
Deferred compensation cost		10,000

$50,000 ÷ 5 years = $10,000 per year (straight line because of approximately equal services each year).

3. December 31, 2002 (exercise date)—to record the stock rights tendered by Executive Goode and the issuance of the 5,000 shares (quoted market price, $60 per share):

Cash (5,000 shares × $20 option price)	100,000	
Executive stock options outstanding (for 5,000 shares)	50,000	
Common stock, par $5 (5,000 shares)		25,000
Contributed capital in excess of par, common stock		125,000

Reporting in the Financial Statements of 1998

Income Statement:
Expenses:

Compensation expense	$ 10,000

Balance Sheet:

Stockholders' Equity

Contributed capital:

Common stock, par $5, authorized 500,000 shares, issued and		
outstanding 200,000 shares (assumed)		$1,000,000
Executive stock options outstanding (for 5,000 shares of		
common stock)	$50,000	
Less: Deferred compensation cost	<u>40,000</u>	10,000
Other contributed capital	(not illustrated)	

Note: For additional disclosures required, see the last section of this chapter.

---

by the grantor, Abat Corporation, is ($30 − $20) × 5,000 shares, or $50,000. This result demonstrates a major reason for the popularity of stock option incentive plans. They provide incentives for management to maximize future stock price, since they benefit directly from price increases. Moreover, the plans provide for compensation in excess of the expense recognized on the books when the stock price rises.

Exercise Price Equal to Market Price on the Grant Date   When the exercise price for the option is set equal to the current market price of the stock as of the grant date (also the measurement date for fixed options), the intrinsic value of the option is zero. In this case, the options may well be classified as compensatory but the amount of compensation cost is zero. No entries are made to record deferred compensation cost (since it is zero), and there is no compensation cost allocated during the service period. When the option is exercised and the grantee pays the exercise price to the firm, cash is debited and the appropriate capital accounts are credited similar to a normal issue of common stock. The one difference from a normal issue of stock is that if the stock is issued for less than its current value, generally the firm is entitled to a tax deduction for the difference. This deduction is a form of permanent difference, but it has nothing to do with revenues or expenses. *APB Opinion No. 25* and *SFAS No. 123* both account for this tax effect as a contribution to additional paid-in capital and a reduction of income taxes currently payable. The tax effect is not included as an item affecting income tax expense.

Variable or Performance Stock Option Plans. Measurement Date after Grant Date   If on the date of grant either the number of optioned shares or the option price is not known, or if the appropriate market price is not known, the exact amount of total compensation expense cannot be computed. If this is the case, the measurement date is after the date of grant. However, periodic compensation expense must be recorded for each service year from the date of grant, so estimates of total compensation cost are used for accounting purposes. At the end of each service year, the best estimate must be revised according to the latest year-end price of the stock (the new best estimate).[8] New estimates may need to be made for the number of optioned shares, the option price, or both. Changes in accounting estimates are normally spread prospectively over the current and future periods.

Exhibit 21–5 illustrates the accounting for Abat Corporation when the measurement date is later than the date of grant. This exhibit shows the entries at (1) date of grant, January 1, 1998, (2) year-end to record periodic expense (for the periods of service between the grant date and the later measurement date), and (3) exercise date. In this example the measurement date is the first date that the options can be exercised, December 31, 2000.

The exhibit also illustrates the related financial reporting. Abat Corporation has to estimate total compensation cost at the end of 1998 and 1999, and then subsequently determines the actual amount at the end of 2000 (the measurement date). To compute estimated total compensation expense at the end of 1998 and 1999, Abat uses the year-end market price of the stock as the best estimate of future stock price, and the best estimate for the option price. The expense amounts for 1999 and 2000 are computed using the prospective method.

<table>
<tr><td>**Lapse of Stock Options**</td><td>

Employee stock options outstanding may lapse because of

1. Failure to complete service obligations.
2. The exercise price never exceeds the market price of the stock.

</td></tr>
</table>

An employee may fail to fulfill the service obligations because of severance, disability, or death. Such situations should be accounted for as changes in accounting estimates. Two items are removed from the accounts: the credit balance relating to the particular lapsed option carried in the stock options outstanding account, and any related debit balance carried in the deferred compensation cost account. The difference should be accounted for as a reduction of compensation expense in the period of forfeiture (*APB Opinion No. 25*, par. 15).

Example   Suppose Executive Jones (in Exhibit 21–5) dies on January 2, 2000, and the stock options awarded to him lapse. The entry to record the lapse of the stock options is

Executive stock options outstanding	35,000	
Deferred compensation expense		22,500
Compensation expense		12,500

Failure to exercise may also occur because the option price of the stock is always higher than the quoted market price of the stock. Assume that Executive Jones (Exhibit 21–5) did not exercise the stock rights by December 31, 2007. All compensation expense has been recorded, and there is a remaining credit balance of $50,000 in executive stock options outstanding. What should be the disposition of this balance on the date of lapse, December 31, 2007? *APB Opinion No. 25* and *FASB Interpretation No. 28* are silent on this question.

---

[8]"Accounting for Stock Appreciation Rights and Other Variable Stock Option or Award Plans," *FASB Interpretation No. 28,* (Norwalk, CT: FASB, December 1978). There is some misunderstanding of this interpretation because par. 18 prescribes "prospective application" (which is how a change in estimate is treated), but its Appendix B illustrates the catch-up (retroactive approach). The change in estimate approach spreads the catch-up amounts over the remaining periods on a straight-line basis. The change in estimate approach appears to be conceptually and practically preferable, especially when significant increases followed by significant decreases in market prices occur. The prospective method is used in our illustrations.

Case Data

1. Basic data as given in Exhibit 21–3, but the option price is as specified below.
2. Date of grant to Executive Jones—January 1, 1998:
   a. A stock option for 5,000 shares of common stock, par $5, is granted to Executive Jones, exercisable after 5 years from date of grant and within 10 years from date of grant, at which time the option expires.
   b. Option price—to be established on December 31, 2000, by reducing the basic option price of $20 by the percentage increase in net income for 1998 through 2000 (a three-year period).
   c. Additional compensation will be for services to be rendered from date of grant, January 1, 1998, to the first exercise date, December 31, 2002, assuming approximately equal services each year.
   d. Market price per share of stock on date of grant, $20.
3. Estimates made on December 31, 1998, and December 31, 1999, of the amounts for December 31, 2000, measurement date:
   a. Estimated percentage increase in net income for 1998 through December 31, 2000: 15 percent.
   b. Resulting estimated option price on December 31, 2000, measurement date: $20 × (1 − .15) = $17 per share.
   c. Market price estimated for December 31, 2000, measurement date: for 1998, use the actual market price on December 31, 1998—$22 per share; for 1999, use the actual market price on December 31, 1999—$24 per share.
4. Actual amounts on December 31, 2000, the measurement date:
   a. Percentage increase in net income from January 1, 1998, through December 31, 2000: 10 percent.
   b. Resulting actual option price: $20 × (1 − .10) = $18 per share.
   c. Market price per share of stock quoted on December 31, 2000: $28.
5. December 31, 2002—Executive Jones exercised the option on December 31, 2002, when the quoted price per share was $60.

The above information is organized in a worksheet format, which leads to annual journal entries:

	December 31		
	1998 **Estimated**	**1999** **Estimated**	**2000** **Actual**
1. Adjustments to deferred compensation cost:			
Earnings growth	15%	15%	10%
Option price: $20 × (1 − Earnings growth)	$ 17	$ 17	$ 18
Estimate of market price at measurement date (equal to current market price)	22	24	28
Estimated market price at measurement date minus estimated option price	5	7	10
Number of shares optioned	× 5,000	× 5,000	× 5,000
Total deferred compensation cost at year-end	**$25,000**	**$35,000**	**$50,000**
Less: Total deferred compensation cost recorded in prior periods	0	25,000	35,000
Additional deferred compensation cost to be recorded	**$25,000**	**$10,000**	**$15,000**
2. Annual amortization (straight line over five years):			
Total deferred compensation cost at year-end	$25,000	$35,000	$50,000
Less: Accumulated amortization to date	0	5,000	12,500
Net deferred compensation cost to be amortized	$25,000	$30,000	$37,500
Years remaining in amortization period	5	4	3
Annual amortization based on unamortized deferred compensation	**$ 5,000**	**$ 7,500**	**$12,500**
Cumulative amortization to date	$ 5,000	$12,500	$25,000

EXHIBIT 21–5
(concluded)

Abat's journal entries for Executive Jones stock option:
January 1, 1998 (date of grant): No entry. Measurement and recording will begin on December 31, 1998.

December 31, 1998:
a. Record estimated total deferred compensation cost as of this date:

Deferred compensation cost	25,000	
Executive stock options outstanding.		25,000

b. Record current year amortization of deferred compensation cost:

Compensation expense	5,000	
Deferred compensation cost		5,000

December 31, 1999:
a. Record adjustment to estimated total deferred compensation cost as of this date:

Deferred compensation cost	10,000	
Executive stock options outstanding.		10,000

b. Record current year amortization of deferred compensation cost (includes adjustment for change in estimate):

Compensation expense	7,500	
Deferred compensation cost		7,500

December 31, 2000:
a. Record adjustment to estimated total deferred compensation cost as of this date:

Deferred compensation cost	15,000	
Executive stock options outstanding.		15,000

b. Record current year amortization of deferred compensation cost (includes adjustment for change in estimate):

Compensation expense	12,500	
Deferred compensation cost		12,500

December 31, 2001 and December 31, 2002:
a. Record current year amortization of deferred compensation cost:

Compensation expense ($50,000 − $25,000)/2 years	12,500	
Deferred compensation cost		12,500

December 31, 2002:
Executive Jones exercises option to acquire 5,000 shares at $18 per share:

Cash (5,000 × $18).	90,000	
Executive stock options outstanding	50,000	
Common stock, par $5.		25,000
Additional paid-in capital, common stock.		115,000

Excerpts from Abat's financial statements for 1998, 1999, and 2000.

	1998	1999	2000
Income statement:			
Compensation expense	$ 5,000	$ 7,500	$ 12,500
Balance sheet:			
Contributed capital:			
Common stock, par $5, authorized 500,000			
shares, issued and outstanding, 80,000 shares			
(assumed)	$400,000	$400,000	$400,000
Executive stock options outstanding	25,000	35,000	50,000
Less: Deferred compensation expense	(20,000)	(22,500)	(25,000)
Net	$ 5,000	$ 12,500	$ 25,000
Other contributed capital (not illustrated)			

Two approaches to account for the remaining credit balance are used in practice:

1. The firm may transfer the credit balance of executive stock options outstanding to an appropriately designated account, such as *contributed capital from lapsed stock options.* This approach increases permanent capital by the amount of compensation expense. Conceptually, the employee has made a contribution to permanent capital.
2. Alternatively, the firm may allocate the credit balance of executive stock options outstanding to compensation expense of the current period and a reasonable number of future periods as a change in estimate. This approach does not assume that the employee makes a contribution to permanent capital. Rather, it assumes that the prior debits to compensation expense (which decreased retained earnings) should be corrected as a change in estimate. This method increases retained earnings rather than contributed capital.

STOCK APPRECIATION RIGHTS UNDER *APB OPINION NO. 25*

Stock appreciation rights (SARs) were developed primarily to provide cash incentives to employees and to take advantage of favorable income tax provisions. Upon exercise, stock appreciation rights require the grantor to pay cash (or, in some cases, common stock) to the grantee. The amount of cash to be paid is based on the difference between the grant price and the market price of the company's common stock on the exercise date.

From the point of view of the employee, stock appreciation rights have two potential advantages over stock options. First, the employee does not have to purchase shares of stock as is required with stock options. If a large number of shares are involved, amassing the cash necessary to exercise a stock option may be difficult for the employee. Second, the difference between the market price and the exercise price for the acquired shares is usually taxable income for the employee when the shares are acquired. The employee must have the resources to pay this income tax, which presents another cash flow problem, especially if the employee plans to hold the newly acquired shares. SARs minimize these cash flow problems. While this receipt of cash is taxable income, the employee has the cash with which to pay the income tax.

Accounting for SAR plans involves dates similar to stock option incentive plans: grant date, measurement date, and exercise date. Total compensation cost must be allocated to years within the service period (from date of grant). Neither the market price nor the exercise date is known in advance; estimates must be used each year to record annual compensation expense. Also, because cash will be paid, an account titled *stock appreciation plan liability* replaces the executive stock options outstanding account that is typically used with stock incentive plans.[9]

Example   On January 1, 1997, Soker Corporation began a stock appreciation rights plan. For each stock appreciation right, the grantee receives cash for the difference between the market value per share of the company's common stock on the date the SARs are exercised and the market price per share on the grant date. The rights require continuing employment and may be exercised at any time between the end of the fourth year after the grant date and the expiration date. The rights expire at the end of the sixth year after the grant date, or when employment is terminated, whichever is earlier. The service period is from the grant date to the earliest exercise date (the vesting date), or in this case, four years.

On January 1, 1998, the company's common stock has a market price of $10 per share, and Ann Killian, CEO of Soker, is granted 5,000 SARs under the incentive plan. Killian exercises the SARs on December 31, 2001. Year-end market prices of Soker common stock are

Year-end	Price per Share
1998	$11.00
1999	13.50
2000	12.00
2001	14.00

---

[9]The entries used for stock option incentive plans usually are set up on the deferral basis (see Exhibit 21–5). In contrast, SARs usually are set up on the accrual basis as illustrated here. Either approach may be used in either situation because the entries can be made so that their net effects (but not detailed effects) are the same.

First, a determination must be made as to whether this is a compensatory plan or a noncompensatory plan. Because the plan does not apply to all employees, it is a compensatory plan. The plan creates compensation expense for the grantor and compensation income for the grantee. Second, the earliest possible measurement date must be determined to establish a service period. Since the earliest exercise date is four years after the grant date, the service period is four years and the earliest measurement date is December 31, 2001. On the date Killian exercises her SARs, the total actual compensation is computed to be $20,000, which is 5,000 times the difference between the price on the exercise date ($14 per share) and the price on the grant date ($10 per share), or $5,000 \times (\$14 - \$10)$.

To compute the compensation expense for each year, the year-end market price of the common stock and the portion of the service period that has expired are used. The total compensation expense that must be accrued to the end of the current year is also the ending stock appreciation rights liability balance:

$$\begin{bmatrix} \text{Balance of} \\ \text{stock appreciation} \\ \text{rights liability} \\ \text{(to date)} \end{bmatrix} = \begin{bmatrix} \text{No. of} \\ \text{SARs} \\ \text{granted} \end{bmatrix} \times \begin{bmatrix} \text{(Market price/} \\ \text{share at end of} - \\ \text{current year)} \end{bmatrix} \begin{matrix} \text{(Market price/} \\ \text{share at} \\ \text{grant date)} \end{matrix} \times \begin{bmatrix} \text{Percentage} \\ \text{of service} \\ \text{period} \\ \text{completed} \end{bmatrix}$$

After the amount to be accrued as the SAR liability at the end of the current year is computed, the current year compensation expense equals the accrual at the end of the current year less the accrual at the end of the prior year. A schedule of these computations for Killian is:

(1)	(2)	(3)	(4)	(5)	(6)	(7)
			Aggregate Compensation to Date	**Percent Accrued (percentage of**	**Total SAR Liability Accrued**	**Annual Compensation Expense (ending liability**
Year	**Year-End Market Price**	**Difference from Grant Date Price**	**(col. 3 × 5,000 SARs granted)**	**service period expired)**	**to Year-End (col. 4 × col. 5)**	**minus prior year liability)**
1998	$11.00	$1.00	$ 5,000	25%	$ 1,250	$ 1,250
1999	13.50	3.50	17,500	50%	8,750	7,500
2000	12.00	2.00	10,000	75%	7,500	(1,250)
2001	14.00	4.00	20,000	100%	20,000	12,500

The annual compensation expense equals the SAR liability at the end of the current year less the SAR liability at the end of the prior year. When the market price of common stock declines, as it does in 2000, the total accrued liability is reduced. In 2000, there is a credit to compensation expense and a debit entry to the SAR liability. In the extreme event that the market price falls below the market price at the grant date, the stock appreciation plan liability account is reduced to zero with an offsetting credit to compensation expense. The method required by *FASB Interpretation No. 28* for determining annual compensation expense for SARs is a retroactive approach; it is different from the prospective approach used for employee stock option plans.

The journal entries to record the compensation expense resulting from the SARs for the four years are:

1998:

Compensation expense	1,250	
Stock appreciation plan liability		1,250

1999:

Compensation expense	7,500	
Stock appreciation plan liability		7,500

2000:

Stock appreciation plan liability	1,250	
Compensation expense		1,250

2001:

Compensation expense	12,500	
Stock appreciation plan liability		12,500

Under *APB Opinion No. 25* the accounting for fixed stock options, variable stock options, and stock appreciation rights plans are inconsistent. SARs compute total compensation expense based on market price at the exercise date; fixed stock options use the grant date, and variable stock options use the first possible measurement date. With essentially the same economic effects, fixed stock option plans, variable stock plans, and SAR plans report significantly different (1) total compensation expense, (2) patterns of compensation expense for each year in the service period, and (3) amounts and items on the balance sheet.

CONCEPT REVIEW

1. When is a stock option plan compensatory?
2. Is it possible for a stock option plan to qualify as a compensatory plan according to the criteria, yet require no compensation expense to be recorded? Explain.
3. Is total compensation expense recorded for a compensatory plan for a grantee typically equal to the actual compensation received by the grantee?

ACCOUNTING FOR STOCK OPTIONS UNDER *SFAS NO. 123*

SFAS No. 123 alters the measurement rules for *variable* stock options (also known as performance stock options) and for stock appreciation rights in several ways, but the overall effect is generally not great. However, *fixed* stock options, by far the most popular type of employee stock option used, are greatly affected. Fixed options with the exercise price set equal to the market price of the stock on the grant date result in no compensation cost under *APB Opinion No. 25,* but there is usually some positive compensation cost under *SFAS No. 123.* We start by providing a quick overview of the process for determining the fair value of the option. We then show how the estimated compensation cost is revised under *SFAS No. 123,* resulting in revised periodic compensation cost. Finally, we provide an illustration comparing the intrinsic-value method and the fair-value method for fixed stock options.

Overview: Measuring the Fair Value of Fixed Stock Options

Consider the time line from the issuance to the expiration of stock options. The following time line shows a number of parameters that must be taken into account when using the fair-value method of *SFAS No. 123:*

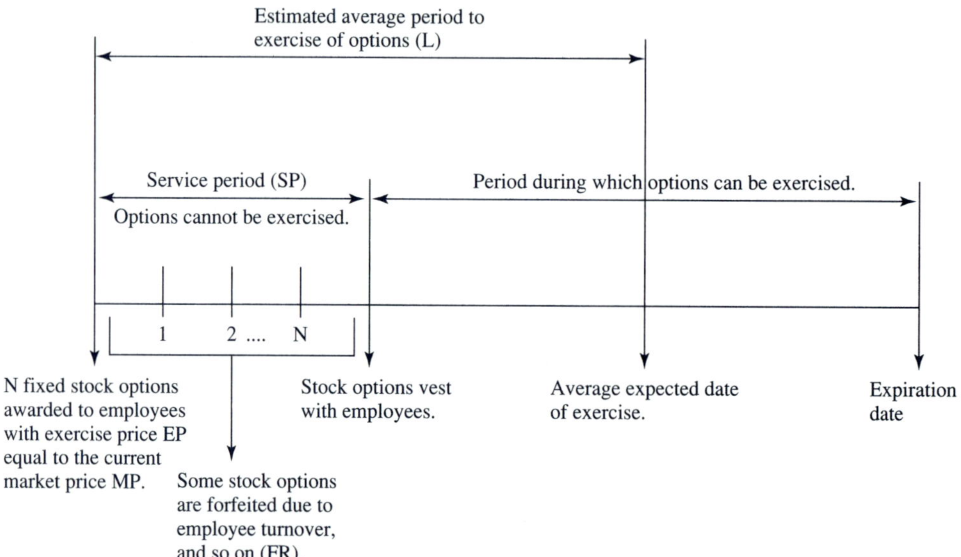

At the grant date, the agreement awarding the fixed stock options specifies:

- The exercise price, EP.
- The period before the options vest with employee (referred to as the service period), SP.
- The expiration date of the options, which is generally some time after the vesting date.

SFAS No. 123 requires that the fair value of the stock options be determined by applying an option pricing model to the data. Appendix 21B to this chapter outlines how the fair value is to be determined. A complex option pricing model is used, and it requires six inputs:

1. Exercise price, EP.
2. Current market price of the stock, MP.
3. Risk-free rate of interest, R_f.
4. Expected life of the options, L.
5. Expected volatility of the stock price, (δ^2).
6. Expected dividend yield of the stock, DY.

With these inputs and an option pricing model, the fair value of an option can be determined. Although alternative option pricing models can be used, the most popular is the Black-Scholes model. Nevertheless, some firms have elected to use another option pricing model, the binomial model.

The actual computation of fair values of options is beyond the coverage of this text. In this text we assume the fair value has been computed using an acceptable option pricing model. Again, Appendix 21B provides an overview of the intuition underlying how each of the above parameters enter into the determination of the fair value of an option.

<table>
<tr><td>

Total Compensation Cost under *SFAS No. 123*

</td><td>

Once the option's fair value is known, the total compensation cost of the options can be determined. Four values are needed:

</td></tr>
</table>

1. Fair value of a single option, FV.
2. Service period, SP (in years).
3. Number of options awarded, N.
4. Expected annual rate of forfeiture of the options, FR.

With these data, the estimated total compensation cost is:

$$\text{Estimate of total compensation cost} = \text{TCC} = \text{FV} \times [\text{N} \times (1 - \text{FR})^{\text{SP}}]$$

The term $[\text{N} \times (1 - \text{FR})^{\text{SP}}]$ above is an estimate of the total options that will vest for the awarded options. This term is revised over time as better estimates of FR become available, hence the estimated total compensation cost is revised periodically. The final amount is the actual number of shares that vest multiplied by the fair value of an option.

With an estimate of the total compensation cost, the amount to be recognized in the current period is a function of the amount recognized in prior periods and the service period. Let the cumulative compensation cost recognized in the prior $(T - 1)$ periods be CCC. The cumulative amount of compensation cost at the end of T periods is

$$\text{Cumulative compensation cost to recognize at the end of T periods} = (\text{T/SP}) \times \text{TCC}$$

$$\text{Therefore, the amount of compensation cost recognized in period T} =$$
$$[(\text{T/SP}) \times \text{TCC}] - \text{CCC}$$

This is a catch-up approach to recognizing compensation cost as opposed to a prospective approach. With a prospective approach, the total amount of compensation cost yet to be recognized would be allocated straight-line over all remaining periods including period T. Many changes in estimates are accounted for using the prospective approach, but *SFAS No. 123* specifies the catch-up approach for stock-based compensation.

Compare the formula for determining the total compensation cost of granting options under *SFAS No. 123* with the formula used in *APB Opinion No. 25*. First, *SFAS No. 123* has replaced the intrinsic value of an option with its fair value. Second, *APB Opinion No. 25* computes compensation cost based on the number of options issued, while *SFAS No. 123* adjusts this cost to the estimated options expected to vest. There are several ways to provide for this estimate. The format shown above is the one recommended by *SFAS No. 123*.

However, it is also acceptable to disregard the estimated forfeiture rate in the initial computation and to periodically update the computation of compensation cost based on actual forfeitures. If this latter method were used, the estimate of total compensation cost would be

$$\text{Estimated total compensation cost} =$$
$$\text{TCC} = \text{FV} \times [\text{N} - \text{Actual number of forfeitures to date}]$$

This is a more conservative approach, as all the options are treated as if they were going to vest, and only when it is certain that they will not vest are they removed from the computation of total compensation cost. TCC is thus updated each period as new information becomes available.

Accounting for Fixed Stock Options under *SFAS No. 123*

SFAS No. 123 encourages but does not require firms to adopt the above method of accounting for fixed stock options. However, if a firm does not adopt this method, it must still determine and disclose pro forma information *as if* the method had been adopted. Thus, firms that adopt *SFAS No. 123* will actually make the journal entries shown in the following illustrations. Firms that report only the required pro forma information need to make the same fair value determinations but not actually record these effects. Assuming the intrinsic-value method of *APB Opinion No. 25* results in compensation cost of zero (the most likely situation), the adjustment to reported net income and earnings per share to obtain the required pro forma disclosures reflects the full amount computed as compensation cost under *SFAS No. 123*. If the intrinsic-value method results in compensation cost greater than zero, the adjustment to reported net income and earnings per share to obtain the required pro forma disclosures reflect only the difference between the amount reported under *APB Opinion No. 25* and the amount of *SFAS No. 123* computed compensation cost.

Income Tax Effects of Stock Options   The granting of stock options by themselves do not have income tax consequences. However, when the options are exercised and the exercise price is less than the market price of the stock on the exercise date, the difference is generally a tax deductible item for the grantor firm and a taxable income item for the grantee. When stock options to employees result in compensation cost that is expensed, there is a temporary difference that gives rise to deferred tax assets.

When the options are exercised, the benefit of the deferred tax asset is realized, but the benefit may be more or less than the deferred tax asset. The actual tax deduction is a function of the exercise price and the market price of the stock on the exercise date. Moreover, the actual tax benefit may differ from the amount of the deferred tax asset, and this difference is not related to any income item. As a result, the tax savings are first credited to reduce the deferred tax asset to zero, and any additional amount is an adjustment directly to the additional paid-in capital account in stockholders' equity.

The following covers the reporting of compensatory stock options under *SFAS No. 123*, including the recording of tax effects related to the options. These same tax effects apply to the stock options accounted for using *APB Opinion No. 25*.

Example   Assume International Software Corporation (ISC) awards stock options to 1,000 employees on January 1, 1996. Each employee is awarded options to acquire 1,000 shares of common stock at an exercise price of $50 per share. The market price of ISC common stock on the grant date is $50 per share. The options are exercisable after January 1, 1999, and expire when the employee leaves the company or on December 31, 2005, whichever is first. Management estimates annual forfeitures will be 3 percent, and that the expected life of the options is six years. Finally, it is determined that the appropriate estimate of the risk-free rate of interest is 7.5 percent, that the estimate of stock price volatility is 30 percent, and that the expected dividend yield in the future is 2.5 percent. To summarize:

Exercise price	$50
Current market price	$50
Service period	3 years
Expiration period	10 years
Number of grantees	1,000
Number of options to each grantee	1,000

Example   Macro Systems has a performance stock option plan. Under this plan, differing numbers of shares vest three years after being awarded depending on the growth rate of Macro System's market share. This is Macro's schedule:

Market share percent increase over the three years following award of options	Shares vesting with grantee at end of three years
Less than 5 percent	0 options
At least 5% but less than 10%	100 options
At least 10% but less than 20%	200 options
20% or more	300 options

On January 1, 1998, Macro Systems awards options with the above terms to 1,000 employees. The options have a 10-year life from the grant date, and the exercise price is set equal to $50, which was the grant date market price of the Macro Systems common stock.

Management estimates that the expected life of the options will be six years and makes the additional estimates needed to determine the fair value of these options. The fair value of an option is determined to be $15. Since the options vest in three years, the service period is three years.

The unknown in this example is the number of options that will actually vest with grantees. This number must be estimated, and the estimate is updated as new information convinces management a revision is needed. The number of shares that will actually vest depends on the forfeiture rate of grantees and the growth in market share over the next three years.

End of 1998   At December 31, 1998, Macro Systems must record compensation cost for this stock based plan. Assume the following actual results are known at that date:

$$
\begin{array}{ll}
\text{Actual forfeitures (grantees no longer employed)} \dots \dots & 33 \\
\text{Actual growth in market share to date} \dots \dots \dots \dots & 5\%
\end{array}
$$

With this information, management estimates that the forfeiture rate will be 3 percent per year and that total market share growth over the three-year period will be between 10 and 20 percent. Note that one year's actual forfeitures may not be indicative of the overall rate for the service period. From the schedule shown above, the market share growth estimate translates into an expectation that each vesting grantee will vest options for 200 shares.

The number of grantees expected to vest, given the forfeiture rate of 3 percent:

$$
\text{Expected number of grantees to vest} =
$$
$$
1,000 \text{ grantees} \times (1 - .03) \times (1 - .03) \times (1 - .03) = 913 \text{ grantees}
$$

Thus the estimated total compensation cost is:

$$
\text{Fair value of an option} \times \text{number of options expected to vest} \times \text{number of grantees vesting} = \text{Estimated total compensation cost} = \$15 \times 200 \text{ options} \times 913 \text{ grantees} = \$2,739,000
$$

One-third of this is the compensation cost recognized in 1998:

$$
\text{Compensation cost recognized in 1998} = \$2,739,000/3 = \$913,000
$$

The journal entry to recognized compensation cost in 1998 is:

Compensation cost	913,000	
Additional paid-in capital—stock options		913,000

End of 1999   At the end of 1999, management knows the following:

$$
\begin{array}{ll}
\text{Actual forfeitures to date (grantees no longer employed)} \dots \dots & 118 \\
\text{Actual growth in market share to date} \dots \dots \dots \dots \dots & 12\%
\end{array}
$$

With this information, assume management continues to estimate the market share growth will be between 10 and 20 percent for the three-year period, but revises its estimated forfeiture rate to 6 percent per year. Again, 200 options are expected to vest with each grantee. The new estimate of grantees expected to vest, however, is

$$1{,}000 \text{ grantees} \times (1 - .06) \times (1 - .06) \times (1 - .06) = 831 \text{ grantees}$$

The new estimate of the total compensation cost is:

$$\text{Revised estimated total compensation cost} = \$15 \times 200 \text{ options} \times 831 \text{ grantees} = \$2{,}493{,}000$$

Under the accounting procedures of *SFAS No. 123,* two-thirds of this total must be recognized by the end of the second year of the three-year service period. Because $913,000 has been recognized in prior periods, the amount to be recognized in 1999 is:

$$\text{Compensation cost recognized in 1999} = \$2{,}493{,}000(2/3) - \$913{,}000 = \$749{,}000$$

The journal entry is:

Compensation cost	749,000	
Additional paid-in capital—stock options		749,000

The amount recognized in 1999 has decreased because Macro Systems increased its estimate of the forfeiture rate. Fewer grantees are expected to vest, thus the estimate of the total compensation cost is decreased.

End of 2000   At December 31, 2000, assume the following actual forfeitures and actual growth rate in market share are known:

Actual forfeitures as of December 31, 2000	143 grantees
Actual growth in market share to date	22%

The growth in market share has exceeded management's prior estimates, and each of the remaining 857 grantees (1,000 original grantees less the 143 forfeitures) now has 300 options vested. The total compensation cost that must be recognized is:

$$\text{Total compensation cost} = \$15 \text{ per option} \times 300 \text{ options} \times 857 \text{ grantees} = \$3{,}856{,}500$$

The amount of compensation cost to be recognized in 2000 is $3,856,500 less the cumulative amount recognized in prior periods:

$$\text{Compensation cost recognized in 2000} = \$3{,}856{,}500 - (\$913{,}000 + \$749{,}000) = \$2{,}194{,}500$$

The entry is:

Compensation cost	2,194,500	
Additional paid-in capital—stock options		2,194,500

At December 31, 2000, the total amount recorded as additional paid-in capital—stock options is $3,856,500, which also is the cumulative compensation cost recognized over the three-year period. We have not made the deferred tax entries that would accrue for this temporary difference, but a cumulative deferred tax asset would have been recorded over the three-year period in the amount of the future income tax rate times $3,856,500.

If and when these options are exercised, the entries would be the same as those presented for the fixed option example. If the options expired unexercised, the Additional Paid-in Capital—Stock Options account balance is transferred to an Additional Paid-in Capital account. As it becomes more likely than not that the deferred tax asset will not be realized, a valuation allowance to reduce its carrying value is created with the offsetting entry closed to income tax expense.

Performance Options with Exercise Price Not Fixed at Grant Date   The previous example used the number of options as part of the incentive to the employee. Another kind of performance option is one where the exercise price is a function of some future performance index. Suppose, for example, the exercise price of Micro Wizards is to be equal to the grant date market price of Micro Wizard common stock increased or decreased by the percent change in an index of the stock price of its competitors. If the index increases 10 percent, the exercise price for Micro Wizard options is increased by 10 percent. It turns out that the procedures used with an option pricing model become a bit more complex, but again it is possible to compute a fair value for this performance option.[14] Once it has been computed, the accounting procedures used for fixed options are followed.

Other Stock-Based Compensation Plans   It is not possible to cover all possible stock-based compensation plans in this text. The major types have been covered, but there are many modifications and variations to these plans. Appendix B to *SFAS No. 123* illustrates the accounting procedures for a number of such variations. Among the types of plans discussed in that appendix are:
- Options with the exercise price increasing a fixed amount or a fixed percentage annually.
- Modifications of either vested or nonvested plans, either before or after adoption of *SFAS No. 123*.
- Cash settlements of vested or nonvested options.
- Options granted by nonpublic firms.
- Tandem plans in which a grantee has a choice regarding options or cash.
- Tandem plans in which a grantee has a choice regarding options or shares.

   The underlying framework used in accounting for each of these more complex plans is the same as is presented above. The illustrations are useful, however, in understanding the application of the framework in these more complicated settings.

REQUIRED DISCLOSURES

Regardless of whether a firm uses the intrinsic-value method of *APB Opinion No. 25* or the fair-value method of *SFAS No. 123* for recognizing compensation cost in the financial statements, the following disclosures must be made:
- A description of the plan or plans, including general terms describing:
    Vesting requirements.
    Maximum terms of the options.
    The number of shares authorized for granting of options.
- For each year for which an income statement is provided in the financial statements:
    The number and weighted-average exercise prices for options in the following categories:
        Options outstanding at the beginning of the year.
        Options outstanding at the end of the year.
        Options exercisable at the end of the year.
    The number of options granted, exercised, forfeited, or expiring during the year.
    The number and weighted-average grant date fair value of equity instruments other than options granted during the year.
    A description and the important assumptions used in estimating fair value, including specifically:
        The risk-free rate of interest.
        The expected life of the options.
        The volatility of the stock price.
        The expected dividends.
    The total amount of compensation cost recognized in income for stock-based compensation awards, and terms of any significant modifications to outstanding awards.
- For options outstanding at the latest balance sheet date presented, disclose:
    The range of exercise prices.
    The weighted-average remaining contractual life of the awards.[15]

---

[14]A new factor, the cross-volatility between the stock price for which the options are granted and the performance index, becomes another input to the option pricing model. It is beyond the scope of this text to cover, but the grant-date option price can be as accurately determined as for a fixed option.

[15]*SFAS No. 123*, para. 45–48.

EXHIBIT 21–6

Excerpts for Note Disclosures from the 1996 Financial Statements of 1st Source Corp.

Note H—Common Stock

Effective January 1, 1996, 1st Source adopted *SFAS No. 123,* "Accounting for Stock-Based Compensation," on a disclosure basis only. The disclosure requirements include reporting the pro forma effect on net income and earnings per share of compensation expense that is attributable to the fair value of stock options and other stock-based compensation that have been issued to employees under the Stock Option Plans and the Employee Stock Purchase Plan. 1st Source will continue to apply *APB Opinion No. 25* in accounting for these plans. The Special Long-Term Incentive Award Plan, the Restricted Stock Award Plan, and the Executive Incentive Award Plan are already being accounted for as compensatory plans in accordance with the provisions of *SFAS No. 123.* Compensation cost that has been charged against income for these plans was $1.52 million, $1.93 million and $1.17 million for the years ended December 31, 1996, 1995, and 1994, respectively.

Stock Option Plans

1st Source's incentive stock option plans include the 1992 Stock Option Plan (the "1992 Plan") and certain stock option agreements which became effective March 1, 1988, and January 1, 1992. As of December 31, 1996, an aggregate of 1,978,972 shares of common stock are reserved for issuance under the above plans. Under the 1992 Plan, the exercise price of each option equals the market price of 1st Source stock on the date of grant and an option's term is 10 years. Options under the 1992 Plan generally vest in one to five years from date of grant. Options are granted on a discretionary basis by the Executive Compensation Committee (the "Committee") of the 1st Source Board of Directors.

The fair value of each option grant is estimated on the date of grant using the Black-Scholes option pricing model with the following weighted-average assumptions used for grants in 1996: dividend yield of 1.54 percent; expected volatility of 24.25 percent; risk-free interest rate of 6.60 percent; and expected life of 8.43 years.

The following is a summary of the activity with respect to 1st Source's stock option plans for the years ended December 31, 1996 and 1995:

	Number of Shares	Weighted-Average Exercise Price
Options outstanding, January 1, 1995	697,079	$ 8.42
Options granted	—	—
Options exercised	(2,501)	10.94
Options outstanding, December 31, 1995	694,578	8.42
Options exercisable, December 31, 1995	608,760	8.29
Options granted	146,633	16.60
Options exercised	(7,232)	10.94
Options outstanding, December 31, 1996	833,979	9.83
Options exercisable, December 31, 1996	675,330	8.34

The following table summarizes information about stock options outstanding at December 31, 1996:

	Options Outstanding		
Range of Exercise Prices	Number Oustanding at 12/31/96	Weighted-Average Remaining Contractual Life (Years)	Weighted-Average Exercise Price
$ 3.00 to $ 9.99	360,794	5.54	$ 5.86
10.00 to 14.99	326,552	7.09	11.17
15.00 to 16.60	146,633	9.58	16.60

Within the range of exercise prices, if the highest exercise price is more than 1.5 times the lowest exercise price, the exercise prices must be segregated into ranges to enable an assessment of the number and timing of additional shares that may be issued and the cash that may be received as a result of option exercises.

These disclosure requirements became effective for fiscal years beginning after December 15, 1995. The first significant group of such disclosures appeared in the financial statements of firms reporting their December 31, 1996, results. An example of such a disclosure for 1st Source Corp. is in Exhibit 21–6.

EXHIBIT 21–6
(concluded)

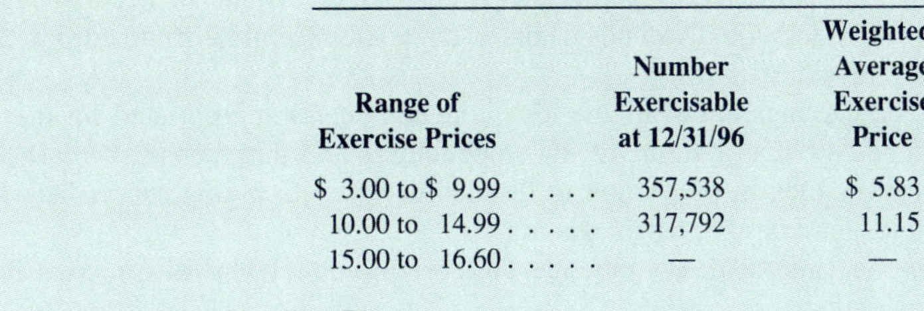

Earnings per Share

	Options Exercisable	
Range of Exercise Prices	Number Exercisable at 12/31/96	Weighted-Average Exercise Price
$ 3.00 to $ 9.99	357,538	$ 5.83
10.00 to 14.99	317,792	11.15
15.00 to 16.60	—	—

Employee Stock Purchase Plan

1st Source also has an employee stock purchase plan for substantially all employees with at least two years of service on the effective date of an offering under the plan. Eligible employees may elect to purchase any dollar amount of stock so long as such amount does not exceed 25 percent of their base rate of pay and the aggregate stock accrual rate for all offerings does not exceed $25,000 in any calendar year. Payment for the stock is made through payroll deductions over the offering period, and employees may discontinue the deductions at any time and exercise the option to take the funds out of the program. The most recent offering began June 1, 1995, and runs through May 31, 1997, with $415,817 in stock value to be purchased at $15.11 per share. The fair value of the employees' purchase rights for the 1995 offerings was estimated using the Black-Scholes model with the following assumptions: dividend yield of 1.48 percent; expected volatility of 18.03 percent; risk-free interest rate of 5.80 percent; and, expected life of two years.

Pro forma net income and earnings per share, reported as if compensation expense had been recognized under the fair value provisions of *SFAS No. 123* for the stock option and employee stock purchase plans are as follows:

	1996	1995
Net income (000s)		
As reported	$23,203	$21,042
Pro forma	$23,049	$20,984
Earnings per share		
As reported	$1.45	$1.31
Pro forma	$1.44	$1.31

Concluding Remarks   It is unfortunate that the accounting standards provide for two radically different methods of accounting for stock-based compensation. When it was issued in 1972, *APB Opinion No. 25* was a reasonable accounting compromise. There were a limited number of financial contracts that provided options and other forms of incentive compensations to employees. Such programs were generally limited to a very few high-level executives, hence the overall impact of alternative accounting treatments was probably small. The science of assessing the value of an option had not yet been developed.

All this has changed. Many forms of stock-based compensation programs now exist. Awards are made to a wide range of employees, and we can accurately compute the value of an option at the grant date. Valuing a transaction at its cost is a fundamental principle of accounting. There is little question that options have a cost to the grantor and value to the grantee, even when awarded with an exercise price below the stock's current market price. Many academic accountants believe that the method found in *SFAS No. 123,* while not ideal, is still a superior accounting treatment to the older intrinsic-valued method.

The solution of allowing firms to use either method but requiring disclosure of the impact on net income of the *SFAS No. 123* method is an unfortunate example of the compromises that can happen under our current standard setting system. Not only does it make the work of accountants more time consuming and complex, it also introduces additional difficulty for readers of financial statements as they attempt to understand just what impact the granting of stock-based compensation has on the current and future cash flows of the firm. It is our hope that in the near future *SFAS No. 123* will be accepted as the preferred method and applied uniformly.

SUMMARY OF KEY POINTS

(L.O. 1) 1. Retained earnings represents the accumulated net income or net loss and prior period adjustments of a corporation, less the dividends declared since the inception of the corporation. Other adjustments also may affect retained earnings.

(L.O. 1) 2. Retained earnings are available for dividends unless appropriated for a specific purpose.

(L.O. 2) 3. Dividends are distributions to the stockholders and may consist of cash, noncash assets, or the corporation's own stock in proportion to the number of outstanding shares held by each stockholder.

(L.O. 2) 4. The relevant dates for dividends are
   a. The declaration date—the date the corporation's board of directors formally announces the dividend declaration.
   b. The date of record—the date on which the list of stockholders of record will be prepared.
   c. The ex-dividend date—the date before the date of record at which the shares of stock will trade without the right to receive the declared dividend.
   d. The day of payment—that date on which payment of cash or property dividends to the list of stockholders of record actually occurs.

(L.O. 2) 5. The declaration of dividends other than stock dividends by the board of directors creates a liability for the corporation as of the date of declaration.

(L.O. 2) 6. Liquidating dividends are a return of capital rather than a return on capital. They represent a reduction of the paid-in capital of the corporation.

(L.O. 2) 7. Scrip dividends are a declaration of an intention to pay a cash dividend at some specified date in the future. Scrip, in the form of a promissory note, is issued to shareholders at the date of declaration.

(L.O. 3) 8. Stock dividends are proportional issuances of additional shares of stock in lieu of distributions of cash or noncash property to shareholders. Small stock dividends, those less than 20 percent to 25 percent, are recorded at the market value of the stock just after the stock dividend distribution. Large stock dividends, those in excess of 20 percent to 25 percent, are recorded at par or legal capital amounts.

(L.O. 3) 9. A stock split is a change in the number of shares outstanding accompanied by an offsetting change in the par or stated value per share.

(L.O. 4) 10. Appropriations of retained earnings are the result of management action to constrain a portion of retained earnings for some specific purpose. Restrictions of retained earnings result from contractual or legal agreements prohibiting a portion of retained earnings from being paid out.

(L.O. 5) 11. Stock rights are privileges awarded to shareholders and others to acquire a specified number of shares at a specified price during a specified period of time.

(L.O. 5) 12. Corporate stock option incentive plans for employees are either compensatory or noncompensatory. If the plans are compensatory, they may result in compensation cost for the grantor. Noncompensatory plans do not result in compensation expense to the grantor or income to the grantee.

(L.O. 5) 13. Noncompensatory stock option plans must meet four criteria under *APB Opinion No. 25*:
   a. Substantially all employees must be included.
   b. Stock is offered to all eligible employees either equally or on the basis of a percentage of salary or wages.
   c. The period for exercising the option is of reasonable length. (*SFAS No. 123* specifies this period to be less than 31 days.)
   d. The discount on the purchase price is small, generally 15 percent or less.

(L.O. 5) 14. Stock-based compensation plans can be accounted for by using *either APB Opinion No. 25 or SFAS No. 123*. If *APB Opinion No. 25* is used, pro forma net income and earnings per share amounts must be disclosed as if *SFAS No. 123* were used.

(L.O. 5) 15. *APB Opinion No. 25* uses an intrinsic value approach to measure compensation cost for stock-based compensation plans. Compensation cost is allocated to periods over the service period for earning the grant. For any given period within the service period, an estimate of total compensation cost is used to determine the allocation unless it is a fixed option plan. A prospective method of allocating changes in the estimates is used.

(L.O. 5) 16. *SFAS No. 123* uses a fair value approach to measure compensation cost for stock-based compensation plans. The fair value of awarded options is computed at the grant date. Other estimates regarding the number of options are made to determine total compensation cost. These latter estimates are revised and the estimated total compensation cost adjusted as new information on forfeiture rates is obtained. The compensation cost is allocated to service periods in the same manner as specified in *APB Opinion No. 25,* although the catch-up approach is required.

(L.O. 6) 17. Stock appreciation rights require the grantor to pay cash or common stock to the grantee based on the difference between the grant price and the market price of the common stock on the exercise date. SARs are usually compensatory and result in compensation expense for the corporation.

REVIEW PROBLEM

In late 1997, the board of directors of Advanced Communications Corporation (ACC) approved a stock option plan to be awarded to select employees containing the following general terms:
- Each option is to acquire one share of ACC common stock.
- The exercise price is set equal to the grant-day market price of the common stock.
- The options are exercisable two years from the grant date.
- The options expire on the earlier of the following two dates:
  Seven years after the grant date.
  The date the grantee leaves the employment of ACC without exercising the options.

The board authorized that up to 2,000,000 shares of common stock could be issued through this option plan.

On January 1, 1998, the board awarded options to acquire 1,000 shares to each of 500 employees. On that date the shares price was $80 per share. The exercise price was set equal to this amount. Management developed the necessary option pricing model to compute the fair value of the options. It was determined that each option had a fair value of $8.

Management did not think it could estimate the forfeiture rate in advance, so it elected to use an initial rate of zero, and to revise this rate over time based on actual forfeitures.

On January 1, 1998, ACC reported the following stockholders' equity accounts:

Common stock, par $1, 10,000,000 shares issued and outstanding	$ 10,000,000
Additional paid-in capital	390,000,000
Retained earnings	100,000,000
Total stockholders' equity	$500,000,000

For both 1998 and 1999, ACC had income of $40,000,000 before any stock-based compensation expense and before income taxes. The company has paid no dividends, and the current and future income tax rate is 40 percent.

During 1998, 15 stock option grantees forfeited their options by leaving the company. In 1999, an additional 20 grantees left the company.

Note: As was stated in the text, there are two acceptable methods for estimating forfeitures under the fair value method. The first involves estimating a forfeiture rate over the service period, and using it to estimate total compensation cost. This method was illustrated in the example in the text. The second method, which was not illustrated, is initially to assume a forfeiture rate of zero, and then to revise it based on actual forfeitures as they occur. Each year total compensation cost is revised. Use this alternative method in this review problem.

Required

1. Show the entries for 1998 and 1999 to record the above stock option plan under *APB Opinion No. 25*.
2. Show the entries for 1998 and 1999 to record the above stock option plan under *SFAS No. 123*.
3. Show the deferred tax account balance and the stockholders' equity section as they would appear at December 31, 1999, under both the *APB Opinion No. 25* method and the *SFAS No. 123* method.
4. Assume that on January 2, 2000, all vested stock options are exercised. On that date the market price of ACC common stock is $110 per share. Show the stockholders' equity section immediately after the options are exercised under both methods.

SOLUTION

1. Under *APB Opinion No. 25,* an option under this plan has an intrinsic value of zero, thus no compensation cost is recorded. There would be no entries other than a memo entry to note the granting of the options.
2. **For 1998:**
   Determine the total compensation cost as of December 31, 1998, after 15 grantees have forfeited their options:

$$\text{Total estimated compensation cost} =$$
$$(500 - 15) \text{ grantees} \times 1,000 \text{ options} \times \$8/\text{option} = \$3,880,000$$

The service period is two years, and the annual compensation cost is $3,880,000/2 = $1,940,000.

The journal entry to record this cost, assuming the entire amount is expensed:

Compensation expense from stock-based plans	1,940,000	
Additional paid-in capital—stock options		1,940,000

The deferred tax asset arising from this temporary difference is .40 × $1,940,000 = $776,000

Deferred tax asset	776,000	
Income tax expense—deferred portion		776,000

For 1999:

An additional 20 grantees forfeit their options, leaving $500 - (15 + 20) = 465$ grantees that have the options vested.

The total compensation cost = 465 grantees × 1,000 options × \$8/option = \$3,720,000

The annual compensation expense to be recorded in 1999 = \$3,720,000 − \$1,940,000 = \$1,780,000

The journal entry to record this cost, assuming the entire amount is expensed:

Compensation expense from stock-based plans	1,780,000	
Additional paid-in capital—stock-options		1,780,000

The deferred tax asset arising from this temporary difference is .40 × \$1,780,000 = \$712,000

Deferred tax asset	712,000	
Income tax expense—deferred portion		712,000

3. December 31, 1999, balance sheet excerpts under:

	APB Opinion No. 25	SFAS No. 123
Deferred tax assets	−0−	\$ 1,488,000
Stockholders' equity		
Common stock, par \$1	\$ 10,000,000	\$ 10,000,000
Additional paid-in capital (common)	390,000,000	390,000,000
Additional paid-in capital (stock options)	−0−	3,720,000
Retained earnings*	148,000,000	145,768,000
Total	\$548,000,000	\$549,488,000

*Computation of retained earnings at 12/31/99:

	APB Opinion No. 25	SFAS No. 123
Retained earnings at 1/1/98	\$100,000,000	\$100,000,000
Net income in 1998:		
Earnings before taxes and compensation expense	40,000,000	40,000,000
Stock-based compensation expense	−0−	(1,940,000)
Income tax expense:		
Current portion (40,000,000 × .40)	(16,000,000)	(16,000,000)
Deferred portion	−0−	776,000
Net income	24,000,000	22,836,000
Retained earnings, 12/31/98	\$124,000,000	\$122,836,000
Net income in 1999:		
Earnings before taxes and compensation expense	40,000,000	40,000,000
Stock-based compensation expense	−0−	(1,780,000)
Income tax expense:		
Current portion (40,000,000 × .40)	(16,000,000)	(16,000,000)
Deferred portion	−0−	712,000
Net income	24,000,000	22,932,000
Retained earnings, 12/31/99	\$148,000,000	\$145,768,000

4. Entries to record exercising of all vested options on January 2, 2000:

	APB Opinion No. 25	SFAS No. 123
Cash (\$80 × 1,000 × 465)	37,200,000	37,200,000
Income taxes payable*	5,580,000	5,580,000
APIC (stock options)	-0-	3,720,000
Common stock at par	465,000	465,000
APIC (common stock)	42,315,000	44,547,000
Deferred tax asset	−0−	1,488,000

*Reduction in income taxes due to issuing stock for proceeds less than its fair value = [(\$110 − \$80) × 1,000 shares × 465 grantees] × .40 = \$5,580,000. This is credited to additional paid-in capital.

If the stockholders' equity section were to be shown immediately after the above entries, the total amount of stockholders' equity is the same regardless of which method had been used. However, the amounts in the various categories differ because of the expense that was recognized under the fair-value method:

Stockholders' equity

Common stock, par $1	$ 10,465,000	$ 10,465,000
Additional paid-in capital (common)	432,315,000	434,547,000
Additional paid-in capital (stock options)	–0–	–0–
Retained earnings*	148,000,000	145,768,000
Total	$590,780,000	$590,780,000

*Retained earnings under *SFAS No. 123* = $148,000,000 − .6($3,720,000) = $145,768,000

APPENDIX 21A: *Quasi Reorganizations*

Heavy losses over an extended period of time can produce a significant *deficit* in retained earnings. Typically, unrealistic carrying values for a corporation's assets are associated with these losses. In these situations, a quasi reorganization is desirable. Quasi reorganization allows a corporation, without formal court proceedings of dissolution, to establish a new basis for accounting for assets, liabilities, and stockholders' equity. A quasi reorganization provides a fresh start with respect to certain assets, liabilities, legal capital, and retained earnings.

The Committee on Accounting Procedure of the AIPCA recognized the procedure, provided it is properly safeguarded.[16] The Securities and Exchange Commission also recognizes quasi reorganization with certain conditions:

- Retained earnings immediately after the quasi reorganization must be zero.
- Upon completion of the quasi reorganization, there can be no deficit in any corporate capital account.
- The effects of the procedure must be made known to all stockholders entitled to vote, and appropriate approval obtained in advance from them and creditors.
- A fair and conservative balance sheet must be presented as of the date of the reorganization, and the readjustment of values should be reasonably complete in order to obviate as far as possible future readjustments of like nature.[17]

The accounting guidelines to record a quasi reorganization require restatement of (1) the recorded values relating to relevant assets and (2) the capital accounts (and occasionally the liabilities), with retained earnings restated to a zero balance. The corporate entity itself is unchanged.[18] There must be full disclosure of the reorganization and its effects. Also, the retained earnings amount must be dated for a period of 3 to 10 years after the reorganization date, as illustrated in note 1 of Exhibit 21A–1, which is an example of the procedure.

The company described in Exhibit 21A–1 has two alternatives. The corporation could be *dissolved,* pay creditors, and then form a new corporation, which would receive the remaining assets and report their total amount as the stockholders' equity of the new corporation.

Alternatively, the corporation may undergo a quasi reorganization (without dissolution). This alternative is less cumbersome and less expensive than legal reorganization. A corporation that complies with the four above conditions, including creditor and stockholder approval, can effect a quasi reorganization without paying off its creditors. The entries needed are shown in Exhibit 21A–1. The exhibit also shows the restated balance sheet amounts immediately after the quasi reorganization. Specific account balances are transferred to retained earnings. Retained earnings is then restated to a zero balance, and legal capital is reduced accordingly.

In general, a quasi reorganization is justified when (1) a large deficit from operations exists, (2) it is approved by the stockholders and creditors, (3) the cost basis of accounting for operational assets becomes unrealistic in terms of going-concern values,[19] (4) a break in continuity of the historical cost basis is needed so that realistic financial reporting is possible, (5) the retained earnings balance is inadequate to absorb the decrease in going-concern asset values, and (6) a fresh start in the accounting sense appears to be desirable or advantageous to all

---

[16]*ARB No. 43,* chapter 7, section A.

[17]Securities and Exchange Commission, *Accounting Series Release 25.*

[18]For a detailed treatment of quasi reorganization, see J. Schindler, *Quasi Reorganization,* in Michigan Business Studies, vol. 13, no. 5 (Ann Arbor: Bureau of Business Research, University of Michigan, 1958).

[19]The AICPA *Technical Aids* (CCH, sec. 4220.01) states, "Thus, the official statements of the SEC and the APB can be interpreted as indicating that a quasi-reorganization, if otherwise appropriate, could result in a write-up as well as a write-down of assets." *APB Opinion No. 6* (par. 17) states, "The Board is of the opinion that property, plant and equipment should not be written up by an entity to reflect appraisal, market or current values which are above cost. This statement is not intended to change the accounting practice followed in connection with quasi-reorganizations or reorganizations."

EXHIBIT 21A–1   Accounting for Quasi Reorganization

Case Data

1. Balance sheet at January 1, 1998, immediately prior to quasi reorganization:

Current assets	$ 200,000
Operational assets	1,300,000
Total assets	$1,500,000
Liabilities	$ 300,000
Capital stock	1,500,000
Contributed capital in excess of par	100,000
Retained earnings	(400,000)
Total liabilities and owners' equity	$1,500,000

2. The inventories are overvalued by $50,000, and the carrying value of the operational assets should be reduced by $350,000.

Entries and Balances

Accounts	Balance before Quasi Reorganization	January 1, 1998 Entries to Record Quasi Reorganization*		Balance after Quasi Reorganization
Current assets	$ 200,000		(a) $ 50,000	$ 150,000
Operational assets	1,300,000		(b) 350,000	950,000
Total assets	$1,500,000			$1,100,000
Liabilities	$ 300,000			$ 300,000
Capital stock	1,500,000	(d) $700,000		800,000
Contributed capital in excess of par	100,000	(c) 100,000		–0–
Retained earnings	(400,000)	(a) 50,000 (b) 350,000	(c) 100,000 (d) 700,000	(Note 1)
Total liabilities and stockholders' equity	$1,500,000			$1,100,000

Note 1 (on balance sheet): Retained earnings represents accumulations since January 1, 1998, at which time a $400,000 deficit was eliminated as a result of a quasi reorganization.

*Explanations of entries:
 (a) To write down a current asset (inventory) by $50,000.
 (b) To write down operational assets by $350,000.
 (c) To write off contributed capital in excess of par as a partial offset to the deficit in retained earnings, $100,000.
 (d) To bring retained earnings up to a zero balance and to restate legal capital by the same amount (that is, $400,000 + $50,000 + $350,00 − $100,000 = $700,000). This leaves legal capital at $800,000, the amount necessary to reconcile the basic accounting model after quasi reorganization. Legal capital can be restated by (1) reducing par value per share (requires a charter change) or (2) reducing the shares outstanding (no charter change required).

parties who are concerned with the corporation. A quasi reorganization is usually supervised by a court to assure adequate protection of the interests of all parties and to avoid future litigation.

APPENDIX 21B: *Determining Fair Value of Options*

SFAS No. 123 requires that the fair value of the stock options be determined by applying an option pricing model to the data. Appendix B to *SFAS No. 123* outlines in some detail how the fair value is to be determined. A complex pricing model is used, and it requires a number of inputs:

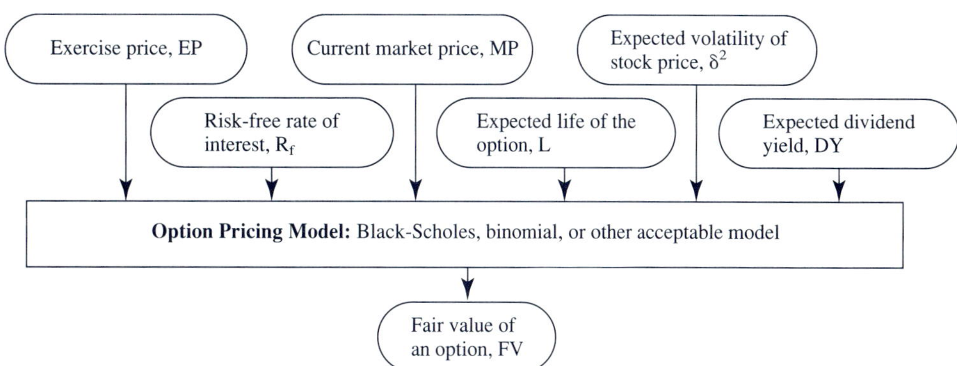

Option Pricing Models   A complete discussion of how option pricing models work is beyond the scope of this text. In this text we assumed the fair value of the option had been determined. We provide, however, a brief intuitive discussion of the factors that affect the fair value of an option.

Exercise Price (EP) and Current Market Price (MP)   The magnitude of the fair value of an option is a function of EP and MP. More specifically, the higher the magnitudes of EP and MP, the higher the fair value. The easiest way to see this is by way of an illustration. Suppose a manager is awarded options for 1,000 shares of a firm's common stock with MP and EP of $80. The value of the award can be determined as the fair value of an option multiplied by 1,000 shares. Now suppose the shares are split 2 for 1, and the manager now has 2,000 options for the newly split shares with a price of $40 (1/2 the original EP). There has been no economic change to the manager or the firm, so the total value of the award should be unchanged. That is, the new fair value times 2,000 options should equal the old fair value times 1,000 options. This is the case if at the $40 EP and MP the fair value of an option is exactly one-half of what it was at the $80 EP and MP.

Risk-Free Interest Rate (R_f)   Option pricing models compute the fair value of options by building theoretical investment portfolios that are risk-free. Risk-free portfolios should theoretically earn the risk-free rate of interest. Thus, the risk-free rate must be known to establish the return on a risk-free portfolio, and then compute the fair value of the option. This factor is constant across firms: *SFAS No. 123,* paragraph 19 states that it is to be estimated as the implied yield on a zero coupon U.S. government issue with a remaining term equal to the expected life of the option. In general, the higher the risk-free rate, the higher the fair value, but this effect is small when compared to the other factors affecting the fair value of the option.

Expected Life of the Option (L)   Consider two options to acquire Microsoft common stock. Both are issued today, and the EP is set equal to MP. The first is exercisable anytime over the next 30 days, but expires on the 31st day. The second is exercisable anytime in the next 10 years. The second is the more valuable because there is a greater likelihood that Microsoft stock's market price will exceed the EP over the next 10 years than over the next 30 days.

Options awarded to employees generally contain a period during which they are exercisable. For example, Microsoft grants options that can be exercised in three years and expire in seven years. Because an option's fair value is a function of time until it is exercised, the issue becomes which date during the three- to seven-year exercisable window should be used in determining fair value. The FASB recognized that some options will be exercised early, near the first date that a grantee needs cash and thus will exercise the option and immediately sell the stock at market price. Other grantees will wait until the last day before the option expires to exercise. Perhaps they don't have the funds to invest, want to hold the stock, and want to defer paying any income taxes that will arise when the option is exercised. Thus the average expected life of options is somewhere between the two extremes of the first day that they can be exercised and the day before they expire. Management must estimate the expected average life of the options granted; this is a factor in determining the fair value of the options.

Volatility of Stock Price (δ^2)   The volatility of a stock price is its variance over time. The volatility is assumed to be constant. Typically, data for a year or more is used to estimate volatility.

The greater the variance or volatility in the stock price, the more likely it is that the stock price will exceed EP at some time in the future. Consider two companies: Consolidated Edison (Con Ed), a large public utility that supplies New York City with electricity, and United Airlines (UAL), the largest commercial airline company in the United States. Assume for the moment the stock price of both companies is $50 per share, and that they both issue stock options to you with the same parameters (EP, vesting date, and expiration date). Which would you think the more valuable? In considering this question, recall that utilities are a regulated industry, thus profits are stable and grow slowly because of the regulation. As a result, the stock price of Con Ed is quite stable—very rarely does it make large movements up or down. UAL, on the other hand, is in an unregulated, very volatile business. Travel increases or decreases frequently with the state of the economy, and fare wars greatly affect periodic profitability. As a result, the price of UAL stock has frequent large movements up and down. Because the UAL stock is more likely to have large movements over time (i.e., it is more volatile) it is more likely to have periods at when the EP is less than the current market price of the stock. It is the more valuable option. Thus the fair value of an option increases with increasing stock price volatility. Stock price volatility has a large effect on the fair value of the option.

Expected Future Dividend Yield (DY)   If a company reinvests all of its earnings in new projects that are expected to generate high future profits, the prospects for increasing its stock price are enhanced. If its projects are successful and profits increase, the firm's stock price is also likely to increase. On the other hand, companies that pay out all of their earnings in dividends have nothing to reinvest in high potential projects. Expectations of future growth in earnings are less for such firms, relative to a company that reinvests its earnings. Thus future stock price increases are less likely. Because the stock price is expected to increase when a firm increases the amount of reinvestment of earnings, the fair value of options increases as a function of the amount of earnings reinvested in the company.

In the following illustration of option pricing using the Black-Scholes option pricing model, we demonstrate the effects of these various inputs.

| | | Changes to Base Option | | | | |
Input Item	Base Option	Double Price	Double Life	Double Variance	Increase Dividends	Higher Risk-free Rate
Current price	$40	$80	$40	$40	$40	$40
Exercise price	$40	$80	$40	$40	$40	$40
Estimated life	5	5	10	5	5	5
Volatility	30%	30%	30%	60%	30%	30%
Dividend yield	0%	0%	0%	0%	4.0%	0%
Risk-free rate	7.5%	7.5%	7.5%	7.5%	7.5%	8.0%
Resulting option price (fair value)	$16.29	$32.58	$23.93	$23.53	$10.73	$16.68

The base option, the one used to compare with all others, is shown in the left column and has an option price of $16.29 per option. The next column shows that if this same option were issued by a firm with the same inputs except that its stock price and exercise price were double that of the base option, the value of the option doubles.

The third column shows that when the estimated life of the base option is doubled, the option is more valuable. The fourth column illustrates that doubling the variance results in an increase in option value similar to the doubling of the life. The base option firm pays no dividends. That is, its dividend yield is zero. The fifth column shows the effect of having a dividend that results in a dividend yield (annual dividend divided by market price) of 4.0 percent. The value of the option declines because fewer resources are being reinvested in the company. Finally, the right column shows the effect of an increased risk-free rate estimate. Increasing the risk-free rate causes the value of the option to increase slightly.

It is possible to construct a template in a Microsoft EXCEL spreadsheet for computing the above estimates.[20] The input variables are self-explanatory except for the annual rate of quarterly dividends. Since most firms pay dividends quarterly (if at all), the model assumes this is the case. The model assumes a constant quarterly dividend yield (dividends divided by stock

---

[20]The template was written by J Mountain, *"FASB 123:* Putting Together the Pieces," *Journal of Accountancy,* January 1996, pp. 73–78.

price) of one-fourth the annual rate. Thus, if a firm has an annual rate of 3 percent, the model treats this as a quarterly dividend yield of 3 percent divided by 4, or .75 percent each quarter. If a firm were to pay dividends annually rather than quarterly, this model would have to be modified to reflect annual rather than quarterly compounding.

The results shown above were computed using this Microsoft EXCEL spreadsheet.

	A	B
1		
2	Template for determining option price using Black-Scholes model.	
3	Input data and assumptions in boxed area.	
4	**INPUT VARIABLE:**	
5	Stock price (MP)	
6	Exercise price (EP)	
7	Estimated term (L)	
8	Volatility (δ^2)	
9	Annual rate of quarterly dividends (DY)	
10	Risk-free discount rate—Bond equivalent yield (R_f)	
11		
12	INTERMEDIATE COMPUTATIONS	
13	Present value of stock ex-dividend	=B5/(1+B9/4)^(B7*4)
14	Present value of exercise price	=B6/(1+B10/2)^(B7*2)
15	Cumulative volatility	=B8*SQRT(B7)
16		
17	**CALL OPTION**	
18	Proportion of stock present value	=NORMSDIST(LN(B13/B14)/B15+B15/2)
19	Proportion of exercise price PV	=−NORMSDIST(LN(B13/B14)/B15−B15/2)
20	**Call option value**	**=B13*B18+B19*B14**
21		
22	**PUT OPTION**	
23	Proportion of stock present value	=B18−1
24	Proportion of exercise price PV	=B19+1
25	**Put option value**	**=+B13*B23+B14*B24**

UNDERSTANDING AND APPLYING CONCEPTS AND STANDARDS

QUESTIONS

1. Explain what an appropriation of retained earnings is, and why it is made.
2. What are the principal sources and uses of retained earnings?
3. Differentiate between total retained earnings and the balance of the retained earnings account, assuming some amount of appropriated retained earnings.
4. What are the four important dates relative to dividends? Explain the significance of each.
5. Distinguish among cash dividends, property dividends, and liability or scrip dividends.
6. What is a liquidating dividend? What are the responsibilities of the accountant with respect to such dividends?
7. Explain the difference between intentional and unintentional liquidating dividends.
8. What is the difference between a cash or property dividend and a stock dividend?
9. Explain this statement: When property dividends are declared and paid, a loss or gain often must be reported.
10. Explain how interest paid on a liability or scrip dividend is recorded.
11. Contrast the effects of a stock dividend (declared and issued) versus a cash dividend (declared and paid) on assets, liabilities, and total stockholders' equity.
12. Contrast the effects of a typical small stock dividend (declared and issued) versus a typical cash dividend (declared and paid) on the components of stockholders' equity.
13. Explain why the amount of retained earnings reported on the balance sheet is often not the net amount of all accumulated earnings (and losses) less all accumulated cash and property dividends.
14. Distinguish between a large stock dividend and a pure stock split.
15. What are the primary reasons for appropriating and for restricting retained earnings?
16. Explain the distinction between (*a*) a bond sinking fund and (*b*) an appropriation of retained earnings for a bond sinking fund.

17. What items are properly reported on the retained earnings statement?
18. Is the following statement correct? "Retained earnings was reduced by the $10,000 appropriated for plant expansion." Explain.
19. Does a bond sinking fund cause a restriction on retained earnings? Explain.
20. What is the difference between stock rights and stock warrants?
21. Can stock rights usually be bought and sold? Explain.
22. List the three important dates with respect to stock rights. When will the related stock sell (*a*) rights on and (*b*) ex rights?
23. List the five primary situations when stock rights are used.
24. Explain how the following account should be reported: "Stock rights outstanding (for 100 shares), $3,000."
25. Stock option incentive plans for employees may be either noncompensatory or compensatory. Briefly explain each.
26. Describe the two accounting methods that can be used to account for stock-based compensation plans for employees.
27. What is the measurement date for a compensatory stock option incentive plan under *APB Opinion No. 25?* Why is it sometimes later than the date of grant?
28. What is the amount of total compensation expense in a stock option plan under *SFAS No. 123?*
29. What estimates are necessary after the grant date of a fixed stock option under *SFAS No. 123?*
30. What are stock appreciation rights?
31. Discuss how *SFAS No. 123,* "Accounting for Stock-Based Compensation," differs from *APB Opinion No. 25* in recording the compensation cost of fixed stock options with the exercise price set equal to the grant-date market price of the stock.
32. When is the fair value of options and other equity financial instruments determined under *SFAS No. 123?* How does this differ from the treatment under *APB Opinion No. 25?*

EXERCISES

E 21–1
(L.O. 1)

Overview: Subclassifications of Stockholders' Equity   Stockholders' equity has the following subclassifications:

A. Capital stock.
B. Additional contributed capital.
C. Retained earnings.
D. Retained earnings appropriated.
E. Unrealized capital.
F. Contra to stockholders' equity.

Match each item below with the letter above that corresponds to its proper classification within stockholders' equity. Use *NA* if the above classifications are not applicable (give explanations if needed):

1. _____ Net loss.
2. _____ Restriction on retained earnings.
3. _____ Goodwill.
4. _____ Extraordinary item.
5. _____ Cash dividends declared, not paid.
6. _____ Bond sinking fund.
7. _____ Treasury stock, cost method.
8. _____ Unrealized gain on securities available for sale.
9. _____ Net income.
10. _____ Correction of accounting error affecting prior years' net income.
11. _____ Legal capital.
12. _____ Premium on capital stock.
13. _____ Subscribed stock.
14. _____ Stock dividends declared, but not issued.
15. _____ Prior period adjustment.

E 21–2
(L.O. 2)

Property Dividend Recorded: Common and Preferred Stock   The records of Frost Corporation showed the following at the end of 1998:

Preferred stock, 6 percent cumulative, nonparticipating, par $20	$200,000
Common stock, nopar value (50,000 shares issued and outstanding)	240,000
Contributed capital in excess of par, preferred stock	30,000
Retained earnings	125,000
Investment in stock of Ace Corporation (500 shares at cost)	10,000

The preferred stock has dividends in arrears for 1996 and 1997. On January 15, 1998, the board of directors approved the following resolution: "The 1998 dividend, to stockholders of record on February 1, 1998, shall be 6 percent on the preferred stock and $1.00 per share on the common stock; the dividends in arrears are to be paid on March 1, 1998, by issuing a property dividend using the requisite amount of Ace Corporation stock. All current dividends for 1998 are to be paid in cash on March 1, 1998." On January 15, 1998, the stock of Ace Corporation was selling at $60 per share, on February 1, at $61 per share, and at $62 on March 1, 1998.

Required

1. Compute the amount of the dividends to be paid to each class of stockholders, including the number of shares of Ace Corporation stock and the amount of cash required by the declaration. Assume that divisibility of the shares of Ace Corporation poses no problem.
2. Give journal entries to record all aspects of the dividend declaration and its subsequent payment.

E 21–3
(L.O. 1, 2)

Cash Dividend Recorded: Error in Retained Earnings   On November 1, 1997, Toni Corporation declared the 1997 cash dividend of $3.00 per share on its 20,000 outstanding shares of common stock (par $1, originally sold at $10 per share). The dividend is payable on January 5, 1998, to its stockholders of record as of December 30, 1997. On declaration date, the balance in the retained earnings account was $46,000; this balance had not been corrected for a $6,000 overstatement of the 1996 net income (caused by an understatement of 1996 depreciation expense). The annual accounting period ends December 31.

Required

1. Give all entries required for the declaration and payment in full of the dividend as declared. Include any additional disclosure notes.
2. Were any problems posed by this cash dividend? Explain.

E 21–4
(L.O. 2)

Cash Dividend Recorded: Return of Capital and Entries   On December 1, 1997, the board of directors of Jax Mining Company declared the maximum cash dividend permitted by state law. The company had never declared a dividend before this time. There were 100 stockholders, each holding 400 shares of stock with a par value of $5 per share. The laws of the state provide that "dividends may be paid equal to all accumulated profits prior to the depletion amount." Retained earnings showed a correct balance of $120,000; depletion for the year amounted to $24,000 (accumulated depletion was $40,000). The dividend was payable 60 days after declaration date.

Required

1. Give all entries related to the dividend through the payment date.
2. What special notification, if any, should be given the stockholders?
3. What items related to the dividend declaration would be reported on a balance sheet dated December 31, 1997, assuming net income for 1997 of $15,000 (included in the $60,000 balance of retained earnings given above)? Write any note that may be needed to fully disclose the dividend.

E 21–5
(L.O. 2)

Cash and Scrip Dividend: Entries   On September 1, 1997, Fox Corporation declared a cash dividend of $1 per share on its 800,000 outstanding shares of common stock (par $1). The dividend is payable on December 1, 1997, to stockholders of record as of October 1, 1997, as follows: one-fourth cash and the balance with scrip, which will be paid on June 30, 1998, plus 12 percent annual interest starting on the cash payment date. The annual accounting period ends December 31. The amount in the retained earnings account is adequate for payment of the dividend.

Required

Give all required journal entries, through final payment, directly related to this dividend.

E 21–6
(L.O. 3)

Stock Dividend Recorded: Dates Cross Two Periods   The records of Round Corporation showed the following balances on November 1, 1998:

Capital stock, par $10	$300,000
Contributed capital in excess of par	102,000
Retained earnings	200,000

On November 5, 1998, the board of directors declared a stock dividend to the stockholders of record as of December 20, 1998, of one additional share for each five shares already outstanding; issue date, January 10, 1999. The market value of the stock immediately after the issuance was $18 per share. The annual accounting period ends December 31.

Required

1. Give entries in parallel columns for the stock dividend assuming, for problem purposes, Case A—market value is capitalized; Case B—par value is capitalized; and Case C—average paid in is capitalized.
2. Explain when each value in (1) should be used.
3. With respect to the stock dividend, what should be reported on the balance sheet at December 31, 1998, assuming no intervening dividend transactions?

E 21–7
(L.O. 3)

Stock Dividend with Fractional Share Rights: Entries and Reporting   The accounts of Amick Corporation provide the following data at December 31, 1996:

Capital stock, par $5, authorized shares 100,000, issued and outstanding 40,000 shares $200,000
Contributed capital in excess of par   160,000
Retained earnings   300,000

On May 1, 1997, the board of directors of Amick Corporation declared a 50 percent stock dividend (for every two shares already outstanding, one additional share is to be issued) to be issued on June 1, 1997. The stock dividend is to be capitalized at the average of contributed capital per share at December 31, 1996.

On June 1, 1997, all of the required shares were issued for the stock dividend except for those required by 1,300 fractional share rights (representing 650 full shares) issued.

On December 1, 1997, the company honored 1,000 of the fractional share rights by issuing the requisite number of shares. The remaining fractional share rights were still outstanding at the end of 1997.

Required

1. Give the required entries by Amick Corporation at each of the following dates:
   a. May 1, 1997.
   b. June 1, 1997.
   c. December 1, 1997.
2. Prepare the stockholders' equity section of the balance sheet at December 31, 1997, assuming net income for 1997 was $30,000.
3. Assume instead that the fractional share rights specified (*a*) that two such rights could be turned in for one share of stock without cost or (*b*) that each right could be turned in for $2.50 cash. As a result, 900 rights were turned in for shares, 200 rights for cash, and the remainder lapsed. Give the entry to record the ultimate disposition of all the fractional share rights.

E 21–8
(L.O. 3)

Stock Dividend and Stock Split: Effects Compared   Bailey Corporation has the following stockholders' equity:

Capital stock, par $12; 20,000 shares outstanding $240,000
Contributed capital in excess of par   70,000
Retained earnings   500,000
Total stockholders' equity $810,000

The corporation decided to triple the number of shares currently outstanding (to 60,000 shares) by taking one of the following alternative and independent actions:

a. Issue a 200 percent (2-for-1) stock dividend (40,000 additional shares) and capitalize retained earnings on the basis of par value.
b. Issue a pure stock split (3-for-1; that is, three new shares are issued for each old share replaced) by changing par value per share proportionately.
c. Issue a 3-for-1 stock split and change the par value per share to $5.

Required

1. Give the journal entry that should be made for each alternative action. If none is necessary, explain why. On the stock splits, the old shares are called in and the new shares are issued to replace them.
2. For each alternative, prepare a schedule that reflects the stockholders' equity immediately after the change. For this requirement, complete the following schedule that compares the effects of the three alternative actions:

Item	Before Change	Stock Dividend	Pure Stock Split (par $4)	Stock Split (par $5)
Shares/par value				
Capital stock	$	$	$	$
Additional paid-in capital in excess of par				
Total contributed capital				
Retained earnings				
Total stockholders' equity	$	$	$	$

Be prepared to explain and compare the effects among the four columns in the above schedule.

E 21–9
(L.O. 4)

Appropriations and Restrictions of Retained Earnings: Entries Watters Corporation carries separate accounts for appropriations and restrictions of retained earnings. One such account is entitled "reserve for profits invested in operational assets, $420,000." Capital stock outstanding, par value $20, amounted to $400,000.

The company had bonds payable outstanding of $200,000. The following accounts were also carried: bond sinking fund, $100,000, and bond sinking fund reserve, $100,000.

The board of directors voted a 10 percent stock dividend and directed that the market value of the stock, $130 per share, be capitalized, using as a basis "the reserves for profits invested in operational assets" to the extent possible.

Required

Give entries for the following, using preferable titles:

1. To originally establish the reserve related to fixed (operational) assets.
2. To record the issuance of the stock dividend.
3. To originally establish the bond sinking fund.
4. To originally establish the reserve for the bond sinking fund.
5. To record payment of the bonds, assuming that the bond sinking fund and the reserve each have a balance of $180,000 at retirement date.

E 21–10
(L.O. 1)

Prepare Comparative Income Statements and Retained Earnings Statements Using the simplified data for Fey Corporation given below, construct comparative statements of (1) income (single step) and (2) retained earnings for 1997 and 1998. Assume that all amounts are material, the data are annual, and there is an average tax rate of 40 percent on all items. Disregard EPS.

	1997	1998
Current items (pretax):		
a. Sales	$110,000	$120,000
b. Cost of goods sold	45,000	50,000
c. Expenses	25,000	29,000
d. Extraordinary gain	3,000	
e. Extraordinary loss		6,000
f. Dividends declared and paid	12,000	10,000
g. Appropriation for profits invested in operational assets	10,000	
h. Prior period adjustment—correction of accounting error made in prior period; income tax was understated and no additional tax effect	2,200	
Beginning balances:		
Unappropriated retained earnings	130,000	?
Appropriation for profits invested in operational assets	–0–	?

E 21–11
(L.O. 5)

Stock Sale—Stock Rights Issued, Some Lapses: Entries Snowden Corporation has outstanding 200,000 shares of common stock, par $5. On January 15, 1997, the company announced its decision to sell an additional 100,000 shares of unissued common stock at $15 per share and to give the current stockholders first chance to buy shares proportionally equivalent to the number now held. To facilitate this plan, on February 1, 1997, each stockholder was issued one right for each common share currently held. Two rights must be submitted to acquire one additional share for $15. Rights not exercised lapse on June 30, 1997.

Required

Give any entry or memorandum that should be made in the accounts of Snowden Corporation on each of the following dates:

1. January 15, 1997, the date of the announcement.
2. February 1, 1997, issuance of all the rights. At this date, the stock of Snowden Corporation was quoted on the market at $12.50 per share.
3. June 27, 1997, exercise by current stockholders of 98 percent of the rights issued.
4. June 30, 1997, the remaining rights outstanding lapsed because of the deadline.

E 21–12
(L.O. 5)

Employee Stock Purchase Plan—Compensatory or Noncompensatory? Entries Rice Corporation has a stock purchase plan with the following provisions:

Each full-time employee with a minimum of one year's service may acquire, from Rice Corporation, its common stock, par $10, through payroll deductions at 10 percent below the market price on the date selected by the employee for a stock purchase (the exercise date). The exercise decision must be made within one year from the payroll deduction date.

Assume Rice Corporation uses *APB Opinion No. 25* as its method to account for stock-based compensation plans. Employee H. Adams signed a payroll deduction form on January 1, 1997, for $60 per month. At that date, the market price of the stock was $27. Assume a monthly salary of $2,000 and other payroll deductions in the aggregate of 18 percent. At the end of 1997, Adams requested that stock be purchased equal to the amount accumulated to Adams' credit. At that date, the market price of the stock was $25.

Required

1. Is this a compensatory plan under *APB Opinion No. 25?* If so, how much should be recorded as additional compensation for Adams? Explain.
2. How many shares will Adams acquire for the 1997 deductions? Show computations.
3. Give entries to record (*a*) one monthly payroll and (*b*) issuance of the shares for the year, assuming unissued shares are used.
4. If Rice Corporation were using *SFAS No. 123,* would this plan result in compensation cost? Why or why not?

E 21–13
(L.O. 5)

Stock Incentive Plan—*APB Opinion No. 25:* Analysis and Entries   Rex Corporation is authorized to issue 300,000 shares of common stock, par $1, of which 140,000 shares have been issued. The corporation initiated a stock bonus plan during 1998 for designated managers. Each manager will receive stock options to purchase 1,000 shares of Rex common stock, and the options vest with the grantee if still employed by the company two years from the date of grant. The rights are nontransferable and expire immediately after December 31, 2002. The option price is $20 per share; the market price on date of grant was $24. Assume that manager Ruth Roe receives the stock options on January 1, 1998.

Rex uses *APB Opinion No. 25* to account for stock-based compensation plans.

Required

1. Is this a noncompensatory plan? Explain.
2. What is the measurement date? Explain.
3. What is the amount of total compensation cost for manager Roe?
4. Over what period should this compensation cost be assigned as expense? How much should be assigned to 1998 and 1999? Explain.
5. What entry should be made on the date of grant to Roe?
6. What entry should be made on December 31, 1998 for Roe?
7. Give the entry to record the exercise of the option by Roe on December 31, 2002, when the market price of the common stock was $80 per share.
8. How much actual value did manager Roe receive? How much additional compensation expense did Rex Corporation report?

E 21–14
(L.O. 5)

Stock Incentive Plan—*SFAS No. 123:* Analysis and Entries   Assume all the data given in Exercise 21–13 with the following modification and additional fact:
- Rex Corporation used *SFAS No. 123* to account for stock-based compensation plans.
- Using an option pricing model and management estimates for input factors, the fair value of the options granted to Ms. Roe is computed to be $12 per option.
- Ignore income tax considerations.

Required

1. Compute the estimated total amount of compensation cost for the grant made to Ms. Roe.
2. What entry should be made on the date of the grant?
3. What entry should be made at December 31, 1998?
4. Give the entry to record the exercising of the options held by Ms. Roe on December 31, 2002.

E 21–15
(L.O. 5)

Performance Option Plan—*APB Opinion No. 25:* Analysis and Entries   In October 1997, Meno Corporation announced a stock option incentive plan for its six top executives. The plan provided each executive 3,000 stock options for Meno's common stock, par $1, at a standard option price of $36 per share reduced by the percentage increase in EPS from December 31, 1997, to December 31, 1999. The rights are nontransferable and are exercisable three years after the grant date and prior to five years from the grant date. Continuing employment is required through exercise date, and the service period ends on the first possible exercise date.

On January 1, 1998, Martha Smith was granted 3,000 options when the market price was $30 per share. On December 31, 1998, Meno's management believed that the EPS increase would be met and that Smith would exercise her options at the first exercise date. By December 31, 1999, Meno's EPS had increased by 20 percent. On December 31, 1999, Meno's stock was selling at $40. For simplification, assume that total compensation cost at the end of 1998 was estimated to be $24,000.

Smith exercised her option on December 31, 2000, when the market price of the stock was $60 per share. Assume Meno uses *APB Opinion No. 25* to account for its stock-based compensation plans.

Required

1. Is this a compensatory plan under *APB Opinion No. 25?* Explain.
2. What is the measurement date? Explain.
3. What is total compensation cost?

4. What is the service period? Explain.
5. Explain how total compensation cost is allocated to periodic expense in this situation.
6. Give all entries related to Smith's stock option.
7. How much actual value did Smith receive? How much additional compensation expense did Meno Corporation report?

E 21–16
(L.O. 5)

Performance Stock Incentive Plan—*SFAS No. 123*: Analysis and Entries   Assume all the data given in Exercise 21–15 with the following modification and additional fact:

- Meno Corporation uses *SFAS No. 123* to account for stock-based compensation plans.
- Using an option pricing model and management estimates for input factors, the fair value of the options granted to Ms. Smith computed to be $9 per option.
- Ignore income tax considerations.

Required

1. Compute the estimated total amount of compensation cost for the grant made to Ms. Smith.
2. What entry should be made on the date of the grant?
3. What entry should be made at December 31, 1998?
4. Give the entry to record the exercising of the options held by Ms. Smith on December 31, 2000.
5. Compare the total compensation expense computed in Exercise 21–15 (if this exercise is assigned) with the amount computed here. Which method results in the greater cost, and by how much?

E 21–17
(L.O. 7)

Stock Appreciation Rights—*APB Opinion No. 25*: Analysis, Estimates, and Entries   On January 1, 1997, Kelly Corporation established a stock appreciation rights plan that offers to selected executives rights (SARs) that can be redeemed for cash equal to the difference between the market price of the company's common stock at grant date and market price at the first exercise date. The rights can be exercised three years from grant date and expire four years from grant date or when employment is terminated, if earlier. The service period is considered to be three years because exercise is expected (highly probable) to occur on December 31, 1999.

Executive Brown was granted 2,000 SARs on January 1, 1997 (when the common stock price was $20) and exercised the rights on December 31, 1999. Relevant market prices at year-end on Kelly common stock were 1997, $23; 1998, $27; 1999, $30; and 2000, $26.

Assume Kelly Corporation uses the intrinsic-value method of *APB Opinion No. 25* to account for its stock-based compensation plan.

Required

1. Answer the following questions:
    a. Is this plan compensatory? _____ Yes _____ No
    b. The measurement date is _____.
    c. The service period is _____.
    d. Total compensation cost is $_____.
    e. Total cash paid by grantor to grantee is $_____.
2. Give the appropriate journal entries from January 1, 1997, through December 31, 1999.

E 21–18
(L.O. 5)

Stock Incentive Plan—Lapse of Rights: Analysis and Entries   Stacy Corporation offered a stock option incentive plan to six of its top executives. During the second year from date of grant, but prior to the permissible exercise date, one of the six executives resigned and accepted employment with a competitor. In accordance with the provisions of the incentive plan, the stock option for the resigned executive lapsed. At the date of lapse, the relevant account balance for all six executives combined were deferred compensation expense, $675,000; and executive stock options outstanding, $900,000. The service period extends for three more years, including the second year.

Required

1. Briefly explain what account treatment should be accorded the one-sixth of these balances that relate to the one resigned executive.
2. Give all journal entries directly related to the lapsed options.

| PROBLEMS

P 21–1
(L.O. 1)

Analysis and Correction of Stockholders' Equity: Entries   Toomey Corporation was organized on January 1, 1995, and began operations immediately. Unfortunately, the company hired an incompetent bookkeeper. For the years 1995 through 1997, the bookkeeper presented an annual balance sheet that reported only one amount for stockholders' equity: 1995, $137,700; 1996, $156,600; and 1997, $185,000. Also, the condensed income statement reported as follows: 1995, net loss, $17,500; 1996, net profit, $12,000; and 1997, net profit, $40,930 (cumulative earnings of $35,430). Based on the $35,430, the president has recommended to the board of directors that a cash dividend of $35,000 be declared and paid during January 1998. The outside director on the board has objected on the basis that the company's financial statements contain major errors (there has never been an audit). You have been engaged to clarify the situation. The single stockholders' equity account, provided by the bookkeeper, appeared as follows:

Stockholders' Equity

1995	Stock issue costs	$ 1,300	1995	Common stock, par $5, 20,000 shares issued		$160,000
1995	Net loss	17,500				
1996	Bought 100 shares of company stock from unhappy stockholder Doe	700	1996	Net profit (including $10,000 land write-up to appraisal)		22,000
	Depreciation expense* (1995, $1,500; 1996, $1,700; 1997, $2,300)	5,500	1996	Common stock, 200 shares issued		1,800
	Cash shortages* (1995, $2000; 1996, $2,500; 1997, $500)	5,000	1997	Sold 30 of the Doe shares		270
1997	Cash loan to the company president	10,000	1997	Net profit		40,930
		$40,000				$225,000

*Recorded as expense but not shown on the income statement.

Required   Based on the concerns of the outside director, you must address three major questions:

1. What amount of retained earnings would be available to support a cash dividend? (Assume that the above figures have been found to be arithmetically accurate and that there is no change in income tax.)
2. Based on your calculations in requirement 1, what journal entries should be made for declaration, and later payment of the full amount available as a cash dividend?
3. What entry, prior to the dividend entries in requirement 2, is necessary (*a*) to close the above single stockholders' equity account and (*b*) to record the various components of stockholders' equity in separate accounts? Use the cost method for treasury stock and the offset method for stock issue costs.

P 21–2
(L.O. 2)

Dividend of Property and Scrip: Entries   On June 1, 1998, Ward Corporation had outstanding 10,000 shares of capital stock, par value $10 per share. The shares were held by 10 stockholders, each having an equal number of shares. The retained earnings account showed a credit balance of $60,000, although the company was short of cash. The company owned 20,000 shares (2 percent) of the common stock of Carson Corporation that had been purchased as a long-term investment for $20,000 and classified as a security available for sale. The current market value of this stock is $1.25 per share. On June 1, 1998, the board of directors of Ward Corporation declared a dividend of $4 per share "to be paid with the Carson stock 30 days after declaration date and scrip to be issued for the difference. The scrip will be payable at the end of 12 months from payment date of the property dividend and will earn 12 percent interest per annum." The accounting period ends December 31.

Required

1. Give all entries related to the dividends through date of payment of the scrip, including accounts relating to the investment in Carson.
2. Illustrate how all items related to the dividend declaration should be reported by Ward on (*a*) the balance sheet and (*b*) income statement at the end of 1998, including any notes needed for full disclosure (that is, write the notes as they should appear in the statements).

P 21–3
(L.O. 2)

Common and Preferred Dividends; Property and Scrip   The summarized balance sheet at December 31, 1997, for Saxon Corporation is shown below.

Cash	$ 28,000
Receivables	30,000
Inventory	110,000
Investment in Mita Corporation, 4,000 shares, at cost (equal to fair value)	12,000
Operational assets (net)	80,000
Other assets	10,000
Total	$270,000
Current liabilities	$ 26,000
Bonds payable	50,000
Preferred stock, 6 percent, par $10, cumulative	20,000
Common stock, nopar (5,000 shares)	100,000
Contributed capital in excess of par, preferred	5,000
Retained earnings	69,000
Total	$270,000

The investment in Mita Corporation was made on December 31, 1997, at a purchase price of $3 per share. The dividends on preferred stock are three years in arrears (excluding the current year, 1998). On November 1, 1998, the board of directors of Saxon declared dividends, payment date December 1, as follows:

a. Preferred stock: all dividends in arrears plus the current year dividend; payment to be made by transferring the requisite number of shares of Mita stock at its current market value of $5 per share.

b. Common stock: $4 per share for the current year; payment to be made by transferring the remainder of the Mita stock and issuing a scrip dividend for the balance. The scrip will earn 10 percent annual interest. The scrip, including interest, will be paid at the end of five months from date of declaration.

Required
1. Compute the amount of dividends payable on each class of stock and the amount of the scrip dividend.
2. Give entries to record the transfer of the Mita stock and the issuance of the scrip dividend. Use separate accounts for the common and preferred stock.
3. Give the adjusting entry at December 31, 1998, for the interest on the scrip dividend.
4. Give the entry to record payment of the scrip dividend and interest on April 30, 1999.
5. Prepare the stockholders' equity section of the balance sheet as of December 31, 1998. Assume reported net income of $26,000 for 1998 (does not yet include the interest on the scrip dividend and gain on disposal of Mita stock; assume no change in income tax expense for these items).

P 21–4
(L.O. 2, 3)

Cash and Stock Dividends—Fractional Shares: Entries and Reporting   On December 31, 1997, the accounts for Quality Food Corporation (QFC) showed the following balances:

Stockholders' Equity

(in thousands)

Preferred stock, 7 percent, par value $25, noncumulative, authorized 20,000 shares, outstanding 16,000 shares	$400
Common stock, nopar, stated value $10, authorized 40,000 shares, outstanding 24,000 shares	240
Additional paid-in capital, preferred	30
Additional paid-in capital, common	60
Retained earnings	350

During 1998, the following transactions, in order of date, were recorded relating to the capital accounts:

a. Apr. 1   A stock dividend was issued whereby (1) each holder of 10 preferred shares received 1 share of common stock and (2) each holder of 6 shares of common stock received 1 additional share of common. The market price of the common stock was $15 per share immediately after issuance of the stock dividend. In the issuance of the stock dividend, 5,400 shares of common stock and 2,000 fractional share rights were issued. Each fractional share right represents one-tenth of a share of stock.

b. Nov. 1   All of the rights were redeemed except 200, which remained outstanding.

c. Dec. 15   A 7 percent cash dividend on the preferred shares and a $2.00 per share dividend on the common shares were declared and paid.

d. Dec. 31   Reported net income was $140,000.

Required
1. Give the journal entries for each of the above transactions during 1998.
2. Prepare the stockholders' equity section of the balance sheet at December 31, 1998.
3. Assume QFC paid cash to the stockholders in lieu of issuing fractional share rights. The cash distribution was based on the market value of $15 per common share. Give the entry on April 1, 1998, to record the dividend transaction. What would be the total stockholders' equity of QFC on December 31, 1998, in this situation if all other factors remain as they were given above?

P 21–5
(L.O. 2, 3)

Property and Scrip Dividends—Fractional Shares: Entries and Reporting Dawn Corporation records reflect the following data at the end of 1997:

Current assets		$ 167,000
Operational assets (net)		960,000
Other assets		300,000
Investment in AC Corp. stock* (5,000 shares, at cost)	5,000	
Valuation allowance.	12,500	
Long-term investment, at fair value.		17,500
		$1,444,500
Current liabilities		$ 60,000
Long-term liabilities.		100,000
Preferred stock, 6%, par $100.		300,000
Common stock, nopar, 100,000 shares outstanding		800,000
Contributed capital in excess of par, preferred		12,000
Retained earnings		160,000
Cumulative unrealized holding gain on long-term investments*		12,500
		$1,444,500

*Securities available for sale

To date, 3,000 shares of the preferred stock (6 percent, $100 par value, cumulative, nonparticipating) have been issued. Authorized shares were as follows: common, 200,000; preferred, 3,000. No dividends were declared or paid for 1997. During the subsequent two years, the following transactions affected stockholders' equity:

1998

a. Feb. 1 Declared and immediately issued one share of the AC Corporation stock for each share of preferred stock as a property dividend to pay the dividends in arrears from 1998 to date. The current market value of the AC stock was $3.50 per share. In addition, a cash dividend was paid to complete payment of the dividends in arrears.

b. Oct. 1 Declared and immediately issued scrip dividends amounting to 6 percent on the preferred and $1.00 per share on the common stock. Interest on the scrip is 7 percent per year (maturity date, September 30, 1999).

c. Dec. 31 Reported 1998 net income was $150,000, including all effects of the above transactions.

1999

d. Sept. 30 Paid the scrip dividends including 7 percent per annum interest for 12 months.

e. Nov. 1 Declared and issued a stock dividend, payable in common stock to holders of both preferred and common stock. The preferred holders are to receive value equivalent to 6 percent, and the common holders are to receive one share for each five shares held. The value and the amount to be capitalized per share as a debit to retained earnings are the market value. The price per share of the common stock immediately after the stock dividend was $1.50. The stock dividend was issued in full to the preferred. Fractional share rights for 500 shares (that is, 2,500 rights) were issued to common stockholders.

f. Dec. 1 The fractional rights specified that five such rights could be turned in for one share of common stock. On this basis, 1,800 of the outstanding fractional share rights were turned in. The remaining 700 rights remain outstanding.

g. Dec. 31 Reported 1999 net income was $95,000, including all effects of the above transactions.

Required

1. Give the journal entries for each of the above transactions (round to the nearest dollar).
2. Prepare the stockholders' equity section of the balance sheet at December 31, 1999, after recognition of the above transactions.

P 21–6
(L.O. 4)

Retained Earnings—Appropriations and Restrictions: Reporting   The following annual data were taken from the records of Bender Boat Corporation at December 31, 1998.

Current items (pretax):

a. Sales revenue	$450,000
b. Cost of goods sold	230,000
c. Expenses	85,000
d. Extraordinary gain	30,000
e. Stock dividend issued	80,000
f. Cash dividend declared and paid	25,000
g. Correction of accounting error involving understatement of income tax expense from prior period (not subject to income tax)	8,000
h. Current restriction for bond sinking fund	10,000
i. Current appropriation for plant expansion	40,000

Income taxes:

Assume an average income tax rate of 40 percent on all items except the prior period adjustment.

Retained earnings balances, debit (credit), January 1, 1998:

j. Unappropriated retained earnings	$(120,000)
k. Restriction for bond sinking fund	(20,000)
l. Appropriation for plant expansion	(60,000)

Required

1. Prepare a single-step income statement for the year ended December 31, 1998. Disregard EPS.
2. Prepare a statement of retained earnings for the year ended December 31, 1998, that separately discloses each restriction on total retained earnings.
3. Give any entries related to the appropriations and restrictions that would have been made, assuming subdivisions of retained earnings are recorded in separate accounts.
4. Assume that Bender Boat Corporation set up a bond sinking fund to pay off the bonds payable at maturity. Also assume that the bonds ($200,000 principal) mature when the bond sinking fund has a balance of $194,000 and that the restriction for bond sinking fund has a balance of $190,000. Give all related entries to record the bond payment at maturity date (assume that all interest has already been paid).

P 21–7
(L.O. 4)

Comparative Retained Earnings: Appropriations and Reporting   Hawken Supply Corporation records provided the following annual data at December 31, 1997, and 1998 (assume all amounts are material):

	1997	1998
Current items (pretax):		
a. Sales revenue	$240,000	$260,000
b. Cost of goods sold	134,000	143,000
c. Expenses	71,000	77,000
d. Extraordinary loss (before tax effects)	7,000	2,000
e. Cash dividend declared and paid	20,000	
f. Stock dividend issued		30,000
g. Restriction for bond sinking fund	10,000	10,000
h. Increase in bond sinking fund	10,000	10,000
i. Prior period adjustment—error correction, salary expense understated	6,000	
j. Income taxes—assume an average rate of 45 percent on all items including extraordinary items and prior period adjustments.		
Balances, January 1:		
k. Restriction for bond sinking fund	70,000	?
l. Unappropriated retained earnings	160,000	?
m. Appropriation for plant expansion	65,000	?
n. Bonds sinking fund	75,000	?
o. Bonds payable	100,000	?

Required

1. Prepare a single-step income statement for 1997 and 1998. Common stock outstanding is 10,000 shares.
2. Prepare a comparative statement of retained earnings for 1997 and 1998 that sets out separately each of the restrictions and appropriations of retained earnings.

P 21–8
(L.O. 2, 3, 4)

Analysis and Correction of Retained Earnings Account   Didrickson Computer Corporation is undergoing an audit. The books show an account entitled *surplus,* which is reproduced on the next page, covering the five-year period from January 1, 1995, to December 31, 1999.

Credits

1995–1998	Net income carried to surplus	$ 800,000
1995	Offset with debit to goodwill—authorized by management	50,000
12/31/1996	Contributed capital in excess of par	6,000
1/1/1997	Correction of prior accounting error*	2,000
1/1/1997	Donation to company—operational asset	5,000
3/31/1997	Refund of prior years' income taxes due to carryback of a 1996 net operating loss to 1995	9,000
7/1/1998	Reduction in capital stock from par value, $100, to par value, $50, with no change in	
	number of shares outstanding (10,000); approved by stockholders	500,000
12/31/1999	Net income, 1999	170,000
		$1,542,000

*Not included in net income 1995–1998.

Debits

1995–1998	Cash dividends declared	$ 520,000
12/31/1995	To reserve for bond sinking fund (required annually 1994–1996)	20,000
12/31/1997	Reserve for bond sinking fund	20,000
12/31/1998	Reserve for bond sinking fund	20,000
9/1/1999	50 percent stock dividend	250,000
		$ 830,000

Required

1. The above account is to be closed and replaced with appropriate accounts. Complete a worksheet analysis of the above account to reflect the correct account balances and the corrections needed. It is suggested that the worksheet carry the following columns: (*a*) surplus account per books; (*b*) net income, 1999; (*c*) corrected unappropriated retained earnings, December 31, 1999; and (*d*) columns for debits and credits to any other specific accounts needed.
2. Give the entry or entries to close this account as of December 31, 1999, and to set up appropriate accounts in its place.

(AICPA adapted)

P 21–9
(L.O. 5)

Fixed Option Incentive Plan—*SFAS No. 123*: Entries and Reporting   Baxter Furniture Corporation is authorized to issue 30,000,000 shares of common stock, par $5, of which 16,000,000 are outstanding; issue price $8 per share. On January 1, 1997, the company initiated a stock incentive plan for many employees. The plan provides for each qualified executive to receive options for 2,000 shares of the common stock. Subject to continued employment, the option is exercisable at any time after four years and prior to expiration, which is five years from the date of grant. The options are nontransferable, and the specified exercise price for the options is to be set equal to the grant date market price of the stock. The option is compensation, and any compensation cost is to be prorated equally for the period from the date of grant to the first exercise (vesting) date, which is four years. Baxter uses *SFAS No. 123* to account for stock-based compensation plans.

On January 1, 1997, 1,000 employees were each granted options to acquire 2,000 shares under the plan when the market price of the stock was $30. Management expects a forfeiture rate of approximately 4 percent per year over the service period. The Black-Scholes option pricing model is used, with estimates provided by management, to compute the fair value of an option. The fair value at the grant date is $12 per option.

All vested options are exercised just prior to their expiration on December 28, 2001, when the market price of the stock was $50 per share. Assume an income tax rate of 40 percent.

Required

1. Show the computation of the estimated total compensation cost as of the grant date.
2. Show the entries to record compensation cost, all of which is expensed, for 1997. Include the tax effects for this item.
3. Show the balances that would be in the Additional Paid-in Capital—Stock Options and the Deferred Tax accounts as of December 31, 1999. Assume the only item affecting deferred taxes for Baxter is the stock options.
4. At December 31, 2000, 840 grantees are still employed and will vest with 2,000 options each. Show the entries to record compensation cost for the year 2000. Again include the tax effects for this item.
5. Given the above, by how much is Baxter's retained earnings more or less than it would have been if Baxter had used the intrinsic value method and *APB Opinion No. 25* to account for this stock-based compensation plan? Explain.
6. Show the entries to record the exercising of all vested options on December 28, 2001. Include all tax-related effects.

P 21–10
(L.O. 5)

Performance Stock Option Incentive Plan—*SFAS No. 123*: Entries and Reporting   Sanchez Corporation has authorized 100,000 shares of common stock, par $20, of which 40,000 shares are outstanding. The company has a stock option plan that provides the following:

a. On January 1, 1997, 100 qualified managers receive options for a computed number of shares of common stock at a computed option price per share. The exercise price is $40, which is the market price of Sanchez common on the grant date. The computation of the number of options awarded will be made three years after the option is granted and will be related to the increase in net income over the three-year period. The formula for determining the number of options each grantee will receive is:

$$\text{Number of options} = 1,000 \times (1 + \text{growth rate of earnings per share from 1996 to 1999})$$
$$= 1,000 \times (1 + \text{EPS in 1999/EPS in 1996})$$

b. The options are nontransferable and must be exercised not earlier than three years, and not later than five years, from date of grant. Employment with the company is required through the exercise date.

Assume that all the vested options are exercised near the end of 2001, when the price of the stock was $70. The following additional information is available:

> Management estimates that earnings growth over the three-year period will be approximately 25 percent. It also expects that forfeitures will be approximately 2 percent per year from the grant date to the vesting date. A consultant is hired to assist management in estimating the fair value of these options. They use the binomial model and, based on the required estimates provided by management, compute the fair value to be $10 per option. Finally, the income tax rate is 40 percent.

At December 31, 1997, earnings per share have grown 10 percent over the 1996 EPS, but management continues to believe that the 25 percent growth amount over the three-year period is accurate. Two of the grantees have left the firm. The stock price has increased to $44 per share.

Required

1. Determine total estimated compensation cost based on grant date data and estimates and using *SFAS No. 123*. Take into account the estimated forfeitures in determining this amount. (Round the number of grantees expected to vest to a whole number.)
2. Show the entries to record any compensation cost to recognize for 1997 under *SFAS No. 123*, including the tax-related entries.
3. There are no changes in estimates during 1998. Earnings growth for the two-year period is 15 percent, and the market price of stock has increased to $51 per share. An additional three grantees have left the company. Show the entries to record any compensation cost to be recognized for 1998 under *SFAS No. 123*, including the tax-related entries.
4. At December 31, 1999, it is determined that the three-year growth in earnings is only 20 percent. Only 90 of the grantees are still with the company, and thus vest with their options. Stock price is now $48 per share. Show the entries to record any compensation cost to be recognized for 1999 under *SFAS No. 123*, including the tax-related entries.
5. Give appropriate entries reflecting the exercising of all options on December 28, 2001. Include entries for all income tax effects. On this date the market price of Sanchez common stock is $70 per share.

P 21–11
(L.O. 5)

Performance Stock Option Incentive Plan—*APB Opinion No. 25:* Entries and Reporting   Use the data found in Problem 21–10, but now assume that Sanchez uses *APB Opinion No. 25* to account for stock-based compensation. Initially assume all grantees will vest and revise this estimate annually for actual forfeitures in that period.

Required

1. Can you determine an estimate of total compensation cost as of the grant date from the data given and using the measurement methods of *APB Opinion No. 25?* If so, what is the amount? If you cannot, why not?
2. Show the entries to record any compensation cost to be recognized for 1997 under *APB Opinion No. 25*, including the tax-related entries.
3. Show the entries to record any compensation cost to be recognized for 1998 under *APB Opinion No. 25*, including the tax-related entries.
4. Show the entries to record any compensation cost to be recognized for 1999 under *APB Opinion No. 25*, including the tax-related entries.
5. Give appropriate entries reflecting the exercising of all options on December 28, 2001. Include entries for all income tax effects.

P 21–12
(L.O. 5)

Fixed Stock Incentive Plan—*SFAS No. 123:* Pro Forma Disclosures   Lavin Productions Incorporated (LPI) had the following stockholders' equity section on December 31, 1997:

($ in thousands)

Common stock, $1 par, 10,000,000 shares issued	$10,000
Additional paid-in capital	20,000
Retained earnings	50,000
Total stockholders' equity	$80,000

On January 1, 1998, the LPI Board of Directors awarded fixed stock options to 1,000 key employees to acquire up to 2,000 shares each under the following terms:
- The exercise price was to be $50 per share, which was the current market price of the stock.
- The options were exercisable on or after December 31, 1999, and would expire on December 31, 2002, if unexercised. Grantees must remain employed with LPI to exercise their stock options.
  Additional information:
- It is determined that fair value of the options is $15 each based on the Black-Scholes model and the following estimates: risk-free interest rate, 6 percent; stock price volatility, 30 percent; expected dividend payout rate, 0 percent; estimated life of the options, four years.
- Management elects to use an estimated forfeiture rate of zero. This estimate will be revised when actual forfeitures occur.
- The income tax rate is 40 percent. The only possible item affecting temporary or permanent differences is the accounting for stock-based compensation.
- LPI has elected not to adopt *SFAS No. 123,* but rather to continue reporting using *APB Opinion No. 25.* During 1998 and 1999, LPI has the following results:
- In 1998 and 1999, earnings before the effects of any stock-based compensation cost and income taxes is a profit of $18,000,000 and $30,000,000, respectively.
- In 1998, 10 grantees leave the employ of LPI. An additional grantees forfeit their option rights in 1999.
- LPI pays no dividends in either 1998 or 1999.

Required

1. What is the estimated total compensation cost as of January 1, 1998, under *APB Opinion No. 25?* Under *SFAS No. 123?*
2. For the year ending December 31, 1998, show what pro forma amounts LPI would compute and disclose to comply with the requirements of *SFAS No. 123.*
3. For the year ending December 31, 1999, show what pro forma amounts LPI would compute and disclose to comply with the requirements of *SFAS No. 123.*
4. Assume all outstanding options are exercised on January 2, 2000, when the current market price of LPI common stock is $120 per share. Show all the entries to record this transaction, including any tax effects.
5. Show the LPI stockholders' equity section immediately after the above transaction is recorded.
6. If LPI had been using *SFAS No. 123* to account for stock-based compensation, show how the stockholders' equity section would appear immediately after the options are exercised.

P 21–13
(L.O. 5)

Fixed Stock Option Incentive Plan—Required Disclosures   Use the data and information found in Problem 21–12. Assume that LPI uses *APB Opinion No. 25.* The current market price of LPI stock on December 31, 1998, is $70 per share.

Required

Write a sample footnote providing all the disclosures required by *SFAS No. 123* as of December 31, 1998. (If you did not work Problem 21–12, assume that the application of *SFAS No. 123* would reduce the 1998 net income by $9,000,000.) If additional information is needed, identify the needed items and make realistic assumptions.

P 21–14
(L.O. 6)

Stock Appreciation Rights: Analysis, Entries   On January 1, 1995, McClain Control Corporation employed a new president, Serina Miller, with the following compensation package: (1) salary, $200,000 per year (minimum employment period, three years); (2) an annual bonus of 10 percent of the dollar increase in accrual basis income before extraordinary items; and (3) 10,000 stock appreciation rights (SARs) tied to the market price of McClain's common stock. This problem focuses on the SARs granted to Miller on January 1, 1995, when the market price per share was $30. Four other executives also participate in this SAR plan.

The SAR plan specifies that each SAR will earn for the grantee cash equal to the difference between the market price of McClain's common stock on the grant date and on the exercise date. The SARs may be exercised at any time after the end of the fourth year from the grant date, and they expire at the end of the fifth year from the grant date, or at date of termination of employment, if before the end of the fifth year. The service period is from the grant date to the expected (a high probability) exercise (vesting) date, December 31, 1998.

Assume that McClain uses *APB Opinion No. 25* in accounting for these grants.

Miller exercised the SARs on January 4, 1999, when the market price per share was $40. Relevant year-end market prices of McClain's common stock: 1995, $33; 1996, $38; 1997, $38; 1998, $40; and January 4, 1999, $40. The accounting period ends December 31.

Required

1. Respond to the following questions:
   a. Is this plan compensatory? Why?
   b. What is the measurement date? Explain.
   c. What is total compensation cost?
   d. What is the service period? Explain.
   e. How is total compensation expense allocated to annual periodic expense?
2. Give all entries related to the SARs granted to Miller from the grant date through the exercise date.

<table>
<tr><td style="vertical-align:top">P 21–15
(L.O. 2, 3, 4, 5)</td><td>An Overview of Stockholders' Equity Chapters   Haywood Publishing Corporation is a publicly owned company whose shares are traded on a national stock exchange. At December 31, 1997, Haywood had 50,000,000 shares of $10 par value common stock authorized, of which 30,000,000 shares were issued and 28,000,000 shares were outstanding.</td></tr>
</table>

The stockholders' equity accounts at December 31, 1997, had the following balances:

	($ in millions)
Common stock	$300
Contributed capital in excess of par	160
Retained earnings	100
Treasury stock (at cost)	(36)

During 1998, Haywood had the following transactions:

a. On February 1, 1998, a secondary distribution of 4,000,000 shares of $10 par value common stock was completed. The stock was sold to the public at $18 per share, net of issue costs.

b. On February 15, 1998, Haywood issued, at $110 per share, 200,0000 shares of $100 par value, 8 percent cumulative preferred stock with 200,000 detachable warrants. Each warrant contained one right, which with $20 could be exchanged for one share of $10 par value common stock. On February 15, 1998, the market price for one stock right was $1.

c. On March 1, 1998, Haywood reacquired 40,000 shares of its common stock for $18.50 per share. Haywood uses the cost method to account for treasury stock.

d. On March 15, 1998, when the common stock was trading for $21 per share, a major stockholder donated 20,000 shares, which are appropriately recorded as treasury stock.

e. On March 31, 1998, Haywood declared a semiannual cash dividend on common stock of 10 cents per share, payable on April 30, 1998, to stockholders of record on April 10, 1998. State law prohibits cash dividends on treasury stock.

f. On April 15, 1998, when the market price of the stock rights was $2 each and the market price of the common stock was $22 per share, 60,000 stock rights were exercised. Haywood issued new shares to settle the transaction.

g. On April 30, 1998, employees exercised 200,000 options that were granted in 1996 under a noncompensatory stock option plan. When the options were granted, each option had a preemptive right and entitled the employee to purchase one share of common stock for $20 per share. On April 30, 1998, the market price of the common stock was $23 per share. Haywood issued new shares to settle the transaction.

h. On May 31, 1998, when the market price of the common stock was $23 per share, Haywood declared a 5 percent stock dividend distributable on July 1, 1998, to stockholders of record on June 1, 1998. Immediately after issuance of the dividend shares, the market price of the common stock was $20.

i. On June 30, 1998, Haywood sold the 40,000 treasury shares reacquired on March 1, 1998, and an additional 560,000 treasury shares costing $11.2 million that were on hand at the beginning of the year. The selling price was $25 per share.

j. On September 30, 1998, Haywood declared a semiannual cash dividend on common stock of 10 cents per share and the yearly dividend on preferred stock, both payable on October 30, 1998, to stockholders of record on October 10, 1998. State law prohibits cash dividends on treasury stock.

k. On December 31, 1998, the remaining outstanding rights expired.

l. Net income for 1998 was $50.0 million.

<table>
<tr><td style="vertical-align:top">Required</td><td>Prepare a schedule to be used to summarize, for each transaction, the changes in Haywood's stockholders' equity accounts for 1998. The columns on this schedule should have the following 11 headings:

Date of transaction (or beginning date); common stock—number of shares; common stock—amount; preferred stock—number of shares; preferred stock—amount; common stock warrants—number of rights; common stock warrants—amount; additional contributed capital (including contributed capital in excess of par, and so on); retained earnings; treasury stock—number of shares; and treasury stock—cost amount.</td></tr>
</table>

(AICPA adapted)

<table>
<tr><td style="vertical-align:top">P 21–16</td><td>Appendix 21A—Quasi Reorganization: Entries and Reporting   The following account balances were shown on the books of Overton Corporation at December 31, 1997:</td></tr>
</table>

Noncumulative preferred stock, 5 percent par $100, 2,000 shares outstanding	$200,000
Common stock, par $50, 5,000 shares outstanding	250,000
Retained earnings (deficit)	(45,000)

At a stockholders' meeting (including holders of preferred shares) the following actions related to a quasi reorganization were decided upon:

a. Amendment to the charter shall be obtained authorizing a total of 5,000 shares of preferred stock, 6 percent, par $100 per share, cumulative; and 40,000 shares of nopar common stock.

b. All outstanding stock shall be returned in exchange for the new stock as follows:

   (1) For each share of the old preferred stock, one share of new preferred. Purchased for cash at par 20 shares of old preferred stock from a dissatisfied stockholder. All that remained was exchanged.

   (2) For each share of the old common stock, two shares of the new common stock; the credit to the nopar stock account shall be at an amount that creates a credit balance in contributed capital from conversion sufficient exactly to eliminate the deficit in retained earnings. All the old common shares were exchanged.

c. The retained earnings deficit shall be written off against the credit created by the conversion of the common stock. The above actions were subsequently approved by Overton's creditors.

During the ensuing year, 1998, the following additional transactions and events were completed:

d. Sold 200 shares of the new preferred stock at $112 per share.

e. The company issued 1,200 shares of nopar common stock in payment for a patent tentatively valued by the seller at $20,000. (The current market value of a share of the common stock was $15.)

f. The company sold 50 shares of nopar common stock at $19 per share, receiving cash. Overton also issued 100, $1,000 bonds at 102; one share of common stock, as a bonus, was given with each bond.

g. At the end of 1998, the board of directors was informed that the new income before deductions for bonuses to officers was $100,000. The directors approved the following actions:

   (1) 500 shares of nopar common stock (from authorized but unissued shares) shall be issued to the officers as a bonus (at no cost to the officers). The market price of a nopar common share on this date was $16.

   (2) Declared and paid cash dividends (for one year) on the preferred stock outstanding.

Required

1. Prepare journal entries to record the above transactions, including the quasi reorganization.
2. Prepare the stockholders' equity section of the balance sheet after all the above transactions were provided.

P 21–17

Appendix 21A—Quasi Reorganization: Entries and Reporting   During the last five years, Norwood Corporation experienced severe losses. A new president has been tentatively employed who is confident the company can be saved from bankruptcy (and dissolution). Working with an independent CPA, the new president has proposed a quasi reorganization with the constraints that (*a*) the capital structure must be changed to eliminate the deficit in retained earnings and (*b*) it must be approved by the stockholders and creditors. The Norwood board of directors approved the proposal and submitted it to a vote of the stockholders and obtained approval of the creditors.

Prior to quasi reorganization, Norwood's balance sheet (summarized) reflected the following:

Cash	$ 20,000
Accounts receivable	94,000
Allowance for doubtful accounts	(4,000)
Inventory	150,000
Operational assets	800,000
Accumulated depreciation	(300,000)
Deferred charges	40,000
	$ 800,000
Current liabilities	$ 150,000
Long-term liabilities	240,000
Common stock, par $50	500,000
Preferred stock, par $100	100,000
Contributed capital in excess of par, preferred stock	30,000
Retained earnings, deficit	(220,000)
	$ 800,000

The quasi reorganization proposal, as approved by the stockholders and creditors, provided the following:

a. To adequately provide for probable losses on accounts receivable, increase the allowance to $6,000.

b. Write down the inventory to $100,000 because of obsolete and damaged goods.

c. Reduce the book value of the operational assets to $400,000 by increasing accumulated depreciation.

d. With the agreement of the creditors, reduce all liabilities by 5 percent.

e. Reduce the par value of the preferred shares to $60.

f. Eliminate the contributed capital in excess of par on the preferred stock.

g. Call in the old common stock and issue a new common stock, nopar. Set up a new nopar common stock account reduced by the amount needed to adjust retained earnings to zero.

Required

1. Give a separate entry for each of the above changes.
2. Prepare a balance sheet immediately after the quasi reorganization.

ANALYSIS, JUDGMENT AND COMMUNICATIONS

CASES

C 21–1
(L.O. 1, 2)

 **Recommendations about Dividends**   Tranor Corporation's accounts on January 1 showed the following balances (summarized):

Cash	$ 35,000
Other current assets	25,000
Operational assets (net)	235,000
Other assets	55,000
	$350,000
Current liabilities	$ 30,000
Long-term liabilities	60,000
Capital stock, par $10 (20,000 shares)	200,000
Contributed capital in excess of par	10,000
Retained earnings	50,000
	$350,000

The board of directors is considering a cash dividend, and you have been requested to provide assistance as an independent CPA.

Required

a. Write a short memo to the CEO explaining the maximum amount of cash dividends that can be paid on January 1. Also explain what amount of dividends you would recommend based upon the data from the accounts.
b. Give the entries that should be made assuming that a $26,000 cash dividend is declared, with the following dates specified: (1) declaration date, (2) record date, and (3) payment date.
c. Assuming that a balance sheet is prepared between declaration date and payment date, how should the dividend declaration be reported?

C 21–2
(L.O. 3)

Financial Shares: Analysis   Tudor Corporation made the following entry to record the final disposition of all fractional share rights issued in connection with a small stock dividend:

Fractional share rights outstanding	3,750	
Common stock, par $10		2,000
Contributed capital, lapsed stock rights		1,250
Cash		500

Required

1. What dispositions were made of the total of the fractional share rights, as evidenced by the above entry? State specifically what the stockholders did with their fractional share rights to dispose of them.
2. On what date would Tudor have known the number of fractional share rights it would have to issue as a part of the stock dividend distribution?
3. How would the above entry be altered if the stock dividend had been large instead of small?

C 21–3
(L.O. 1, 2, 3)

Should the Board of Directors Declare a Dividend?   This item is amenable to a group or individual solution. Drake Company was started in 1983 to manufacture a wide range of plastic products from three basic components. The company was originally owned by 23 stockholders; however, in late 1993 the capital structure was expanded considerably, at which time preferred stock was issued. The preferred is nonvoting, cumulative, nonparticipating, 6 percent stock. The company has experienced a substantial growth in business over the years. This growth was due to two principal factors: (*a*) the dynamic management and (*b*) the geographic location. The firm served a rapidly expanding area with relatively few regionally situated competitors.

The December 31, 1998, audited balance sheet showed the following (summarized):

Cash	$ 11,000	Current liabilities	$ 38,000
Other current assets	76,000	Long-term notes payable	60,000
Investment in Kile Co. stock (at cost)	30,000	Preferred stock, par $100 (500 shares)*	50,000
Plant and equipment (net)	310,000	Common stock, $15 par value (10,000	
Intangible assets	15,000	shares)*	150,000
Other assets	8,000	Premium on preferred stock	2,000
	$450,000	Retained earnings	25,000
		Profits invested in plant	125,000
			$450,000

*Authorized shares—preferred, 2,000; common, 20,000.

The board of directors has not declared any dividends since organization; instead, the profits were used to expand the company. This decision was based on the fact that the original capital was small and the number of stockholders was limited. At the present time, the common stock is held by slightly fewer than 50 individuals. Each of these individuals also owns preferred shares; their total holdings approximate 46 percent of the outstanding preferred. The preferred was issued at the time of the capital expansion.

The board of directors had been planning to declare a dividend during the early part of 1999, payable June 30. However, the cash position as shown by the balance sheet has raised serious doubts about the advisability of a dividend in 1999. The president has explained that most of the cash will be needed shortly to pay for inventory already purchased.

The company has a chief accountant but no controller. The board relies on an outside CPA for advice concerning financial management. The CPA was asked to advise about the contemplated dividend declaration. Four of the seven members of the board felt very strongly that some kind of dividend must be declared and paid, and that all stockholders "should get something."

Required

You have been asked to analyze the situation and make whatever dividend proposals that appear worthy of consideration by the board. Present amounts to support your recommendations in a written form suitable for consideration by the board in reaching a decision. Provide the basis for your proposals and indicate any preferences that you may have in a memorandum to the board.

C 21–4

Appendix: Quasi Reorganization   Marks Corporation, a medium-size manufacturer, has experienced operating losses for the past five years. Although operations for the current year ended also resulted in a loss, several important changes made the fourth quarter a profitable one; as a result, future operations of the company are expected to be profitable.

The treasurer suggested a quasi reorganization to (*a*) eliminate the accumulated deficit of $325,000 in retained earnings, (*b*) write up the $600,000 cost of operating land and buildings to their current market value of $800,000, and (*c*) set up an asset of $175,000 representing the estimated future tax benefit of the losses accumulated to date.

Required

1. What are the characteristics of a quasi reorganization?
2. List the conditions under which a quasi reorganization would generally be justified.
3. Discuss the propriety of the treasurer's proposals to do the following:
   a. Eliminate the deficit of $325,000.
   b. Write up the value of the operating land and buildings of $600,000 to their current market value.
   c. Set up an asset of $175,000 representing the future tax benefit of the losses accumulated to date.

(AICPA adapted)

| *ANALYZING FINANCIAL STATEMENTS*

A 21–1
(L.O. 5)

Davon Corporation   The following is excerpted from the income statement and the notes to the financial statements of Davon Corporation's 1996 Form 10-K filed with the SEC:

	Year Ending December 31,		
	1996	**1995**	**1994**
Net income (loss)	$9,114,607	$4,806,247	($5,749,956)
Net income (loss) per common and common equivalent share	$1.11	$0.62	($1.01)

From the note on stock-based compensation:

The Company accounts for its stock-based compensation under *Accounting Principles Board Opinion No. 25,* "Accounting for Stock Issued to Employees." In October 1995, the Financial Accounting Standards Board issued *SFAS No. 123,* "Accounting for Stock-Based Compensation," which is effective for fiscal years beginning after December 15, 1995. *SFAS No. 123* establishes a fair-value-based method of accounting for stock-based compensation plans. The Company has adopted the disclosure-only alternative under *SFAS No. 123,* which requires the disclosure of the pro forma effects on earnings and earnings per share as if *SFAS No. 123* had been adopted, as well as certain other information.

The Company has computed the pro forma disclosures required under *SFAS No. 123* for all stock options granted (including the employee stock purchase plan) as of December 31, 1996, using the Black-Scholes option pricing model prescribed by *SFAS No. 123.* The assumptions used and the weighted average information for the years ended December 31, 1996 and 1995, are as follows:

	Years ended December 31,	
	1996	**1995**
Risk-free interest rates	5.36%–6.64%	5.86%–7.7%
Expected dividend yield	—	—
Expected lives	5.5 years	5.5 years
Expected volatility	71%	71%
Weighted-average grant date fair value of options granted during the period	$19.20	$5.94
Weighted-average exercise price.	$ 9.31	$3.58
Weighted-average remaining contractual life of options outstanding	7.45 years	7.63 years
Weighted-average exercise price of 429,949 and 546,147 options exercisable at December 31, 1996 and 1995, respectively	$ 3.76	$3.08

The effect of applying *SFAS No. 123* would be as follows:

	Years ended December 31,	
	1996	**1995**
Pro forma net income	$8,290,265	$4,703,345
Pro forma net income per share.	$ 0.99	$ 0.61

Required

1. Assume a corporate income tax rate of 35 percent in all computations. Show the journal entries Davon would have made in 1996 had it adopted *SFAS No. 123.*
2. Independent of 1 above, assume Davon granted 200,000 options during 1996. Further assume that the service period is three years and that the estimated forfeiture rate is 3 percent per year. Compute the estimated total compensation cost for the options granted in 1996.

22 EARNINGS PER SHARE

After you have studied this chapter, you will:

1   Understand why financial statement users pay close attention to a company's reported earnings per share (EPS) and why EPS is difficult to interpret.

2   Know how to calculate EPS for companies with simple capital structures.

3   Be able to define diluted EPS (DEPS) and know how and when to compute DEPS for companies with complex capital structures.

4   Be able to identify which securities are dilutive securities for purposes of computing DEPS.

5   Know how to apply the treasury stock method to stock options, rights, and warrants in the computation of diluted EPS.

6   Know how to apply the if-converted method to convertible securities.

7   Know how to test for dilution/antidilution (D/A) in calculating EPS when more than one potential common stock is present.

INTRODUCTION

As of January 1, 1997, the Emerson Electric Company has reported increasing earnings calculated on a per share basis (EPS) for over 160 consecutive quarters (40 years), longer than any other major firm! Emerson is very proud of its performance as measured by the continued and uninterrupted growth in EPS, having made such a growth pattern a company objective. In this chapter you learn not only why EPS is an important measure to investors and company management but also some of the difficulties encountered in its use, interpretation, and calculation.

In its most elementary form, earnings per share for a period of time is calculated as:

$$\frac{\text{Net income to common stockholders for the time period}}{\text{Average number of shares of common stock outstanding during the time period}}$$

One implication of this expression is that any preferred dividends declared in the period (whether or not paid) must be deducted from net income because these dividends are a part of net income that does not belong to common stockholders.

Earnings per share is an important measure to many investors. For the average investor with no employment ties to the company, a corporation's reported earnings per share may well be all that matters. Earnings per share values appear to correlate highly with the market price of the company's common stock. Given the importance of EPS figures to investors, it is no surprise that the FASB, the SEC, and other investment regulatory agencies are concerned with how this corporate financial statistic is calculated.

With the passage of its new accounting standard on EPS, the FASB may be making some investors and firms happy with the change in the way this all important statistic is computed.[1] Before the new standard, many companies did not report basic EPS, the amount based only on actual outstanding shares during the period. Rather their EPS would reflect the potential dilution of warrants, options, and convertible securities that could be considered equivalent to common shares, which would cause the statistic to decline. Under the new standard, basic EPS *as well as* diluted EPS is reported. As a result, many firms are expected to show significant increases in reported EPS (and welcome decreases in their PE ratios).

Example   According to a large brokerage firm and based on the most recent EPS reports, the following firms are among the many expected to experience increases in EPS: TII Industries (up 20%), Safeway (up 19%), Robotic Vision (up 17%), Sterling Software (up 16%), and RJR Nabisco (up 15%).[2]

EPS under *SFAS No. 128* is now significantly easier to compute than it used to be. Although companies typically do not look forward to new FASB statements, any standard that adds 15 percent or more to the calculation of earnings on a per share basis is likely to be welcomed.

SIGNIFICANCE OF EARNINGS PER SHARE

Before 1960, reporting earnings per share was left to the discretion of company management. Emphasis tended to be on total earnings rather than on EPS, leading to a bias in favor of large companies. Another earnings measurement system was needed—one that compensated for the fact that even though big corporations are capable of generating dollar earnings that dwarf a smaller company's, the smaller company might offer the better investment return on a per share basis.

The majority of Americans own common stock either directly, through an intermediary such as a mutual fund or an insurance company, or by participating in employer-sponsored profit-sharing and pension programs. Common stock investors, and the brokers, advisors, and analysts who support them, evaluate companies and often make decisions to buy, sell, or hold on the basis of the company's EPS and the stock's current price. Together they form the price-earnings (PE) ratio, which is the number of times the stock's market price exceeds the company's last reported EPS figure.

Example   If a company is reporting an EPS of $3.25 and the market price of the stock is quoted at 48 and ¾, the stock is selling at 15 times earnings ($48.75 ÷ $3.25 = 15).

The significance of PE ratios becomes clear if the same company reports increased earnings per share of $3.50, up 25 cents from the last earnings report. All other factors remaining the same, the stock can be expected to advance in market price to $52.50 ($3.50 × 15), which is a $3.75 rise in price (or a $375 gain per 100 shares).[3]

The point is that changes in market prices are sensitive to changes in EPS figures. EPS figures therefore should be computed according to procedures designed to prevent accidental

---

[1] This chapter is based on *SFAS No. 128, Earnings per Share*, issued February 1997 and effective for financial statements for periods ending after December 15, 1997. The statement applies to all firms whose common stock, or securities that may become common stock in the future, are traded in a public market. Nonpublic entities are excluded from the scope of this statement as well as firms whose only securities traded publicly are debt securities.

[2] "Proposed Accounting Rule Could Boost Per-Share Earnings of Some Companies," *The Wall Street Journal*, April 10, 1996, p. C1.

[3] Rather than remaining constant, PE ratios are in fact quite elastic. They tend to rise in response to positive developments, in the expectation that future earnings will show improvement, and they drop in response to negative developments, in the expectation of still lower earnings in the future. Also, PE ratios respond to general market conditions, independent of a given company's earnings outlook. PEs tend to rise during bull markets and fall during bear markets.

or deliberate misstatement. Potential causes of misstatements in published reports include:

- Failure to deduct cash dividends on preferred stock from total earnings to determine earnings available to common stockholders. This error overstates income available to common stockholders on which EPS is based.
- Failure to account for changes in the number of shares outstanding during the accounting period. This error distorts comparisons of EPS between yearly reporting periods and between interim reporting periods.
- Failure to account for stock dividends and splits for the full year in which such distributions are made. This error also distorts comparisons of EPS between periods. For example, the DeVry Corporation declared a two-for-one stock split in 1995 and reported earnings per share of $0.89. Without the stock split, earnings per share would have been $1.78.

Shareholders also have concerns about possible dilution of their holdings due to convertible securities, corporate stock options, warrants, subscription rights, and any corporate commitments to issue common stock at some future time. Such matters include:

1. **Unconditional conversions and exercises** These commitments allow an increase in the number of common shares outstanding to occur at any time and without restriction, at the discretion of the security holder or the holder of a corporate commitment. When making current-period earnings evaluations and projecting earnings trends from today's base point, common stockholders should be able to assume that all unconditional conversions and exercises have, in fact, already taken place and that reported EPS figures reflect all such imminent conversions and exercises.

2. **Conditional conversions and exercises** These commitments allow an increase in the number of common shares outstanding at some future date if certain conditions are met. For EPS reporting purposes, conditional conversions and exercises are reported differently, depending on whether the conditions have been met or not. When making earnings per share projections, and for contingency planning purposes, stockholders should know about all conditional events that may reduce (i.e., dilute) EPS.

One objective of EPS calculations is to show the worst case, lowest EPS value possible. In this regard, the approach reflects conservatism. Unfortunately, EPS calculations are subject to numerous assumptions, making their interpretation difficult at best. These assumptions are covered in this chapter as they arise in conjunction with the related calculations. Securities that entitle the holder to obtain common stock are called **potential common stock** or **potentially dilutive securities.** Potential common stock whose conversion into common would reduce EPS are called *dilutive securities.*

A FRAMEWORK FOR CALCULATING EPS

Earnings per share calculations can be divided conveniently into two presentation formats based on the capital structure of the firm:

1. Simple capital structure (single EPS presentation).
2. Complex capital structure (dual EPS presentation).

These two divisions are shown at the top of Exhibit 22–1. This exhibit provides both an overview of the chapter and a schematic to help you keep the chapter's ideas organized. We refer to this exhibit frequently.

Types of Capital Structures

SFAS No. 128 prescribes different EPS disclosure requirements depending on whether a firm's capital structure is simple or complex. The basic distinction between simple and complex capital structures is the presence of dilutive or potentially dilutive securities; that is, securities that are exercisable or convertible into common stock and that may reduce EPS if included in the computation.

1. **Simple capital structure** A firm has a simple capital structure if stockholders' equity consists only of common stock or if no potential common stock exists that on conversion

EXHIBIT 22–1   Schematic of EPS Computations

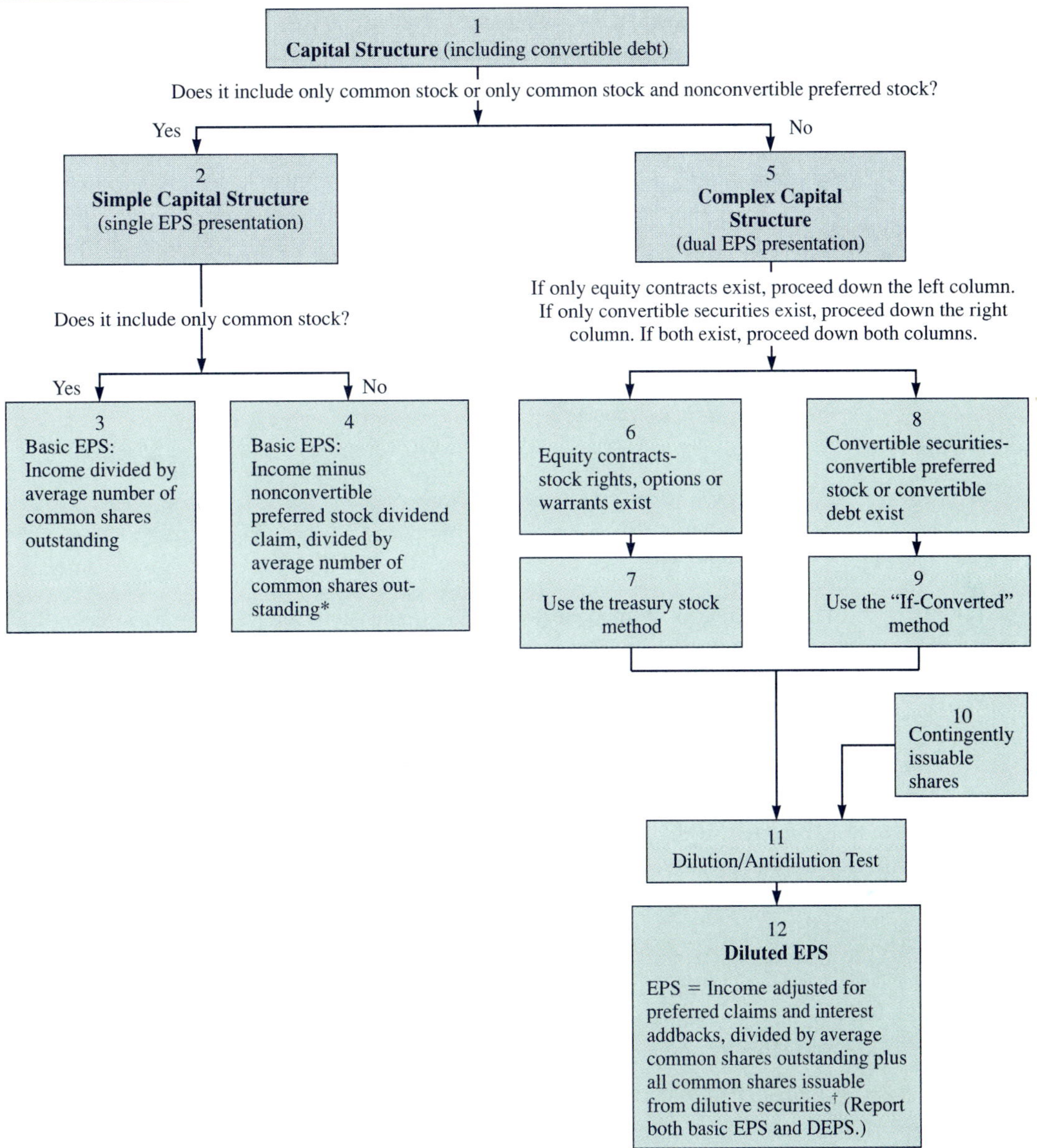

*If the preferred stock is cumulative, deduct the dividends for the current year whether declared or not; if noncumulative, deduct for current year only if declared during the current year.

†Dilutive securities are securities whose inclusion in earnings per share computations would decrease the DEPS figure computed excluding these same securities. Antidilutive securities are securities whose inclusion in earnings per share computations would increase the EPS figure computed excluding these same securities. Antidilutive securities are not included in diluted EPS computations.

or exercise could dilute (decrease) earnings per common share.[4] For simple capital structures, a single EPS presentation showing *basic* EPS is appropriate.

Example   Earnings per common share (amounts assumed):

Income before cumulative effect of accounting change	$1.40
Cumulative effect of accounting change	(.10)
Net income	$1.30

[4]This category includes capital structures involving only common stock and nonconvertible preferred stock.

The objective of basic EPS is to measure the performance of a firm over the reporting period. While the term *basic EPS* is used in this text (and in *SFAS No. 128*) to refer to the EPS calculation when a simple capital structure exists, this terminology is not required. The reported EPS figure may be referred to as simply earnings (or net income) per common share or other descriptive term.

2. **Complex capital structure** All capital structures other than those described as simple are complex. The firm has a complex capital structure if it has outstanding potentially dilutive securities including convertible preferred stock, convertible bonds, contingent common stock issues, stock rights, stock options, and other securities that provide for conversion into or purchase of common stock. For complex capital structures, a dual EPS presentation is required that reports the dilutive effects. Two EPS amounts are reported: basic and *diluted EPS*. This dual presentation must be made even if the two amounts are the same. The term *earnings per common share* should not be used without the appropriate qualifier when the dual presentation is necessary. (Complex capital structures are discussed in a later section.)

To illustrate the reporting (amounts assumed):

	Basic EPS	Diluted EPS
Income before cumulative effect of accounting change	$1.40	$1.25
Cumulative effect of accounting change	(.10)	(.09)
Net income	$1.30	$1.16

The objective of diluted EPS (DEPS) is consistent with that of basic EPS. This historical value, like basic EPS, measures the performance of a firm over a period, while also giving effect to all dilutive potential common shares outstanding during the period.

Calculations for Earnings per Share

The term *earnings per share* applies only to common stock, the fundamental equity investment medium that all corporations use to generate economic wealth. This change in wealth is reported in the form of after-tax income available to the shareholders. These resources are either paid out to the shareholders or retained by the company for reinvestment and generation of more wealth. Preferred stockholders, like bond holders, do not share in the wealth retained by the company, but are paid a constant return on their investments (similar to interest payments).

The calculation of basic EPS is based on the net income generated by a company during the accounting period, less preferred dividends for the period. Expressed as a formula, basic EPS is computed as:

$$\text{EPS} = [\text{Net income (after-tax)} - \text{Preferred dividends}] \div [\text{Weighted average of outstanding common shares}]$$

Example If a company has 300,000 weighted-average common shares outstanding (the term *weighted-average* is explained below), 50,000 shares of preferred stock outstanding paying $10 in dividends per share, and after-tax net income of $2 million, basic EPS would be $5:

$$[\$2,000,000 - 50,000(\$10)] \div 300,000 = \$5$$

If dividends equal to current-period earnings available to common stock were paid on each share of common stock outstanding for the entire year, each share could be paid a dividend of $5. However, dividends of $5 per common share are not required to be paid, nor are total dividends limited to $5 per share if earnings from previous years have been retained. Dividends actually declared on common stock do not enter into the calculation of EPS.

EPS Disclosures

For both simple and complex capital structures, earnings per share must be reported on the face of the income statement for:
- Income from continuing operations.
- Net income.

Entities that report extraordinary items, discontinued operations, or the cumulative effect of an accounting change in a period must present per-share amounts for these items either on the face of the income statement or in the notes to the financial statements, on a net-of-tax basis.

COMPUTING EARNINGS PER SHARE FOR SIMPLE CAPITAL STRUCTURES: BASIC EARNINGS PER SHARE

Following Exhibit 22–1 (boxes 2, 3, and 4), if the answer to the question immediately under box 1 (Does it include only common stock or only common stock and nonconvertible preferred stock?) is yes, the capital structure is simple. In this situation four issues need to be considered:

1. Adjustments to the numerator of the EPS calculation.
2. Adjustments to the denominator of the EPS calculation (the weighted-average shares).
3. Treatment of stock dividends and stock splits.
4. Contingent shares.

Adjustments to the Numerator

If the answer to the question in Exhibit 22–1 immediately below box 2 (Does it include only common stock?) is yes, no adjustment to the numerator is required. In this case:

$$\text{EPS} = \text{(Net income after tax)} \div \text{(Weighted-average outstanding shares)}$$

since there are no preferred dividends to deduct.

If the answer to the question is no, an adjustment to the numerator is required. The preferred dividend claim is subtracted from net income in computing EPS. The amount to be subtracted depends on whether the preferred stock is cumulative, and whether a dividend was declared. At most, one year's claim is subtracted.

If the preferred stock is noncumulative, only the dividends declared for the current period are subtracted. If no dividends are declared for the current year, they will not be paid in a future year because of the noncumulative feature; therefore, they are not subtracted from earnings in determining current-year EPS in this case.

For cumulative preferred stock, one year's dividend claim is subtracted from earnings whether or not declared. Undeclared cumulative preferred dividends must be paid before current common dividends, which is why they are subtracted even if not declared. However, only the current-year claim is subtracted. Prior years' cumulative preferred stock dividends were subtracted in computing EPS in prior years and should not be subtracted again. Declaration and payment of arrear dividends in the current year do not increase the preferred dividend claim on the current year's earnings.

Preferred Stock Dividend Adjustment to
EPS Numerator

	Preferred Stock	
	Cumulative	**Noncumulative**
Current period dividends were declared	Full year's dividend amount is subtracted	Amount of dividends declared is subtracted
Current period dividends were not declared	Full year's dividend amount is subtracted	No adjustment

Example   Assume that a firm issued $100,000 of 6 percent nonconvertible preferred stock several years ago. If the stock is noncumulative, and $6,000 of dividends were declared in the current year, then the $6,000 claim is subtracted from earnings in computing basic EPS. If the dividends were not declared, then there is no subtraction. If an amount less than $6,000 was declared, then the lesser amount is subtracted. The undeclared portion would never be subtracted in computing basic EPS.

Now assume that the preferred stock is cumulative. The full $6,000 is subtracted in computing current-year EPS whether or not declared. If $18,000 of dividends were declared in the current year (this amount includes two years of arrear dividends), again only $6,000 would be subtracted for the current year in computing basic EPS.

Adjustments to the Denominator: The Weighted-Average Calculation

Before basic EPS can be calculated, the denominator must be adjusted to reflect the average number of shares outstanding over the period. The resources made available by the issuance of shares during the period were available only for the part of the year for which the shares were outstanding.

Corporations often issue new shares of common stock, either as public offerings or to meet the exercise of corporate stock options and warrants to purchase stock. A corporation may also buy back outstanding common stock to be held either as treasury shares or for permanent retirement. Any changes in the number of common shares outstanding must be reflected in the calculation of EPS because they change the investment base on which the firm earns profit.

Example Assume that a company reports basic EPS of $3 for 1997, computed on the basis of net after-tax income of $300,000 and 100,000 common shares outstanding the entire year (no preferred stock). During the next year, on October 1, 1998, the company issues an additional 50,000 shares. At the end of 1998, net income after taxes of $337,500 is reported for the full year, with 150,000 shares outstanding. How should the company report its basic EPS figure for 1998?

The calculation uses a weighted-average schedule to show that 100,000 shares were outstanding for nine months (January through September) and 150,000 shares were outstanding for three months (October through December). The firm had the resources from the new issue for only one-quarter of a year. The correct EPS figure in this case is $3:

Inclusive Dates	Shares Outstanding	Months Outstanding	Weighted Shares Outstanding (Share-months)
January–September	100,000	9	900,000
October–December	150,000	3	450,000
		12	1,350,000

The weighted-average number of shares outstanding is $112,500 = (1,350,000 \div 12)$ and basic EPS is $3 = (\$337,500 \div 112,500)$, the same as in the prior year.

Another way to calculate the weighted-average shares is:

$$100,000 \ (12/12) + 50,000 \ (3/12) = 112,500.$$

The weights reflect the number of months the indicated number of shares were outstanding.

Example To illustrate the weighted-average computation process further, assume the following changes in common stock outstanding in 1998:

Transaction	Shares Issued (Repurchased)	Total Shares Outstanding
January 1: Balance outstanding	100,000	100,000
March 1: Additional stock issued	25,000	125,000
May 1: Stock purchased for treasury	(50,000)	75,000
July 1: Additional stock issued	100,000	175,000
September 1: Additional stock issued	25,000	200,000

The following weighted-average schedule is then developed:

Inclusive Dates	Shares Outstanding	Months Outstanding	Weighted Shares Outstanding (Share-months)
January–February	100,000	2	200,000
March–April	125,000	2	250,000
May–June	75,000	2	150,000
July–August	175,000	2	350,000
September–December	200,000	4	800,000
		12	1,750,000

The weighted-average number of shares outstanding is $145,833 = 1,750,000/12$.

Stock Dividends and Splits

Stock dividends and stock splits are not treated the same as the issuance of new stock because stock dividends and splits do not generate additional capital for the company. Reverse splits are contractions in the number of shares previously outstanding. Shares issued as dividends or split shares are treated as subdivisions of the shares already outstanding. As such, stock dividends and splits are taken into consideration by adjusting the number of shares outstanding retroactively to the beginning of the period of the earliest financial statements presented. Thus, they are treated as if the new shares had always been outstanding.

Example If a company has 100,000 common shares outstanding as of January 1 and declares a three-for-one stock split on May 1, for EPS purposes, the weighted-average number of shares is 300,000. If net income after taxes is $600,000, EPS is $2.

Although the 300,000 shares after adjustment for the stock split were not outstanding the entire year, they are equivalent to the 100,000 shares before the split. The stock split merely changes the measurement basis. An investor with 100 shares before the split is in the same position with 300 shares after the split. Then, each share's claim on earnings is only one-third that of a share before the split, but each investor has three times as many shares. For comparability, reported EPS figures for prior years also are adjusted for the split.

Example Assume that Gridley Inc., a calendar-year firm, earns $1,000,000 in 1997 and in 1998. During all of 1997, 1,000,000 shares of common stock were outstanding. Then at the beginning of 1998, Gridley split the stock two-for-one. As reported in the 1998 income statement, EPS for *both* 1997 and 1998 is $.50:

$$\$1,000,000 \div (1,000,000 \times 2) = \$.50$$

If the stock split were not applied retroactively, 1997's EPS would be $1:

$$\$1,000,000 \div 1,000,000 = \$1,$$

and 1998's would be $.50 as computed above. This result would imply a 50 percent decline in EPS when, in fact, Gridley has experienced the same earnings performance in both years. Further, common stockholders are just as well off with their two shares in 1998 as they were in 1997 with one share. Inter-year comparisons of EPS figures would not be meaningful without the retroactive adjustment.

EPS computations for stock dividends and splits are more involved when they occur during an accounting period when new shares are also issued or share retirements occur. In such cases, new-issue shares and retirements are calculated using a weighted-average schedule, with stock dividends and splits applied retroactively in proportion to the number of shares outstanding at the particular time during the accounting period. Only stock transactions occurring *before* a stock dividend or split are adjusted.

Example Assume the following example for Cloverleaf Dairy for the year ended December 31, 1998:

Transaction	Shares Issued	Total Shares Outstanding
January 1: Balance outstanding	10,000	10,000
April 1: Additional stock issued	1,000	11,000
June 1: 100 percent stock dividend	11,000	22,000
September 1: Additional stock issued	2,000	24,000

The weighted-average schedule in Exhibit 22–2 gives an accounting of how the 100 percent stock dividend is applied retroactively to January 1 and how the weighted-average number of shares of common stock outstanding for the year is computed.

An alternative way to compute the weighted average in Exhibit 22–2 is:

$$[10,000\ (12/12) + 1,000\ (9/12)]2^* + 2,000\ (4/12) = 22,167$$

*Effect of the 100 percent stock dividend—the calculation for a two-for-one split would be identical.

EXHIBIT 22–2   Computation of Weighted-Average Number of Shares of Common Stock Outstanding When Stock Dividends or Stock Splits Occur: Cloverleaf Dairy

Inclusive Dates	Actual Shares Outstanding	Retroactive Restatement for 100% Stock Dividend on June 1		Equivalent Shares Outstanding	Months Outstanding		Weighted Shares Outstanding (Share-months)
Jan. 1–March 31	10,000	× 2	=	20,000	× 3	=	60,000
April 1–May 31	11,000	× 2	=	22,000	× 2	=	44,000
June 1–August 31	22,000*		=	22,000	× 3	=	66,000
Sept. 1–Dec. 31	24,000*		=	24,000	× 4	=	96,000
Totals					12		266,000

Weighted-average number of shares outstanding: 266,000 ÷ 12 = 22,167.

*These numbers already reflect the stock dividend.

Weighted-average schedules can be compiled with greater precision based on share-days rather than share-months. A base of 365 days substitutes for 12 months.

To report EPS figures in comparative financial statements, a weighted-average schedule of changes in capitalization plus retroactive restatement of stock dividends and splits (if any) is needed. The schedule preparation process is essentially the same as that shown in Exhibit 22–2. EPS figures for each year shown are adjusted for all stock dividends and splits since the firm started operations. Thus, all stock dividends and splits are automatically taken into account when EPS is computed for prior years. This procedure eliminates the need to restate prior-year share amounts manually.

Sometimes stock dividends and splits occur after the balance sheet date but before the issuance of the financial statements. In this situation, all EPS amounts (both basic and diluted) shown for the period just ended and for any previous periods shown comparatively must reflect the stock dividend or split. Restatement provides the most current and relevant information for the user. A description of the effects of such dividends and splits is disclosed in the notes.

Contingent Shares

The FASB considers certain shares issuable by a corporation in the *future* to be outstanding for purposes of computing *current* EPS. In paragraph 10 of *SFAS No. 128* the Board states:

> Shares issuable for little or no cash consideration upon the satisfaction of certain conditions (contingently issuable shares) shall be considered outstanding common shares and included in the computation of basic EPS as of the date that all necessary conditions have been satisfied (in essence, when issuance of the shares is no longer contingent).

Contingent issuable shares are included in basic EPS only when there is no circumstance under which those shares would not be issued. Issuable shares are weighted for the fraction of the period for which the conditions are met. Calculations are made on a quarterly basis and then weighted for the interim periods affected.

Example   The terms of a contingent share agreement for a recent business combination requires that Mega, Inc., issue 100 shares to the stockholders of Rega, Inc., a firm recently acquired by Mega, for each new store opened by Rega during the current year. One new store was opened August 1 and another on October 1. Shares under the agreement are to be issued the following year. The contingent shares to be included in the denominators of *quarterly* basic EPS are:

Quarter 1:		0
Quarter 2:		0
Quarter 3:	100(2/3) =	67
Quarter 4:	200(3/3) =	200

The denominator effect for *annual* basic EPS can be computed in two ways:

$$(0 + 0 + 67 + 200)/4 = 67 \text{ or } 100(5/12) + 100(3/12) = 67$$

When contingent shares are based on a future earnings level, no contingent shares are included in basic EPS because the earnings level may not be reached. Furthermore, if issuance of the shares is contingent on meeting an earnings goal in the *current* year, again no contingent shares are included in basic EPS even if the earnings level is met. The contingency in this case is definitely met only on the last day of the year.

Example   If the required earnings level were $200,000, even though income through quarter three exceeds $200,000, the contingency period has not ended. The firm could experience a loss in the fourth quarter causing income to decline below $200,000. Therefore, the portion of the period for which the condition is met is negligible. However, assuming the required earnings level is reached in the current period, these shares would be included in EPS the *following* year, regardless of when actually issued, because the contingency has been met.

The same treatment is appropriate for contingencies based on the market price of a firm's stock. The ending price is not definite until the close of the last day's trading.

| **REVIEW PROBLEM** | Compute basic EPS using the following data for the Palmento Corporation involving non-convertible cumulative preferred stock: |

	Shares
Capital stock:	
Common stock, par $1, outstanding on January 1, 1998.	90,000
Common stock sold and issued May 1, 1998	6,000
Preferred stock, par $20, 6 percent (cumulative, nonconvertible)	
outstanding on January 1, 1998	2,500
Income data for the year ending December 31, 1998:	
Net income before extraordinary item	$134,000
Extraordinary gain (net of tax).	10,000
Net income	$144,000

| **SOLUTION** | 1. For the numerator (income): preferred dividend claim, for the current year only. |

$$\$50,000 \text{ (total par value; 2,500 shares} \times \$20) \times .06 = \underline{\$3,000}$$

2. For the denominator (shares): computation of weighted-average number of common shares outstanding during 1998:

Inclusive Dates	Actual Shares Outstanding	Months Outstanding		Weighted Shares Outstanding
Jan. 1–Apr. 30, shares outstanding	90,000	× 4	=	360,000
May 1, sold additional shares	6,000		=	
May 1–Dec. 31, shares outstanding	96,000	× 8	=	768,000
Dec. 31, shares outstanding	96,000		=	
Totals		12		1,128,000

Weighted-average number of shares outstanding during 1998: $1,128,000 \div 12 = \underline{94,000}$.

Earnings per Common Share

Earnings per common share outstanding:
  Income before extraordinary items: ($134,000 − $3,000 = $131,000) ÷

94,000 shares.	$1.39
Extraordinary gain: $10,000 ÷ 94,000 shares	.11
Net income: ($134,000 − $3,000 + $10,000) ÷ 94,000 shares	$1.50

> ### CONCEPT REVIEW
>
> 1. Why are preferred dividends deducted from net income after taxes for EPS computation purposes?
> 2. When a stock dividend is distributed, why is the resulting increase in shares outstanding considered to be in effect for the entire year?
> 3. If additional shares of common stock are issued and sold to the public for cash midway through the current accounting period, what impact is there on EPS for the current period?

COMPUTING EARNINGS PER SHARE FOR COMPLEX CAPITAL STRUCTURES: DILUTED EARNINGS PER SHARE

Again following Exhibit 22–1, if the answer to the question under box 1 (Does it include only common stock or only common stock and nonconvertible preferred stock?) is no, the firm has a complex capital structure requiring a dual EPS presentation. The EPS computational process deducts preferred dividends and computes the weighted-average shares, just as in the case of a simple capital structure. However, additional adjustments must be made. These adjustments allow for convertible securities or equity contracts (warrants and options) outstanding by assuming exercise or conversion. These instruments can lead to issuance of more shares of common stock in the future, thereby causing a dilution of stockholders' interest in the firm's earnings. This dilution is reflected in a decrease in EPS.

Besides actual outstanding common, only *dilutive* potential common stock is entered into the calculation of **diluted earnings per share (DEPS).**

- A security is **dilutive** if DEPS is *decreased* as a result of incorporating into DEPS the common shares from the assumed conversion or exercise of the potential common stock.
- A security is **antidilutive** if DEPS is *increased* as a result of incorporating into DEPS the common shares from the assumed conversion or exercise of the potential dilutive common stock. Antidilutive securities are *not* entered into the DEPS calculation.

The prohibition against antidilution reflects a conservative approach to reporting. The test for determining whether securities are dilutive or antidilutive is based on income from continuing operations. Thus, the number of potential common shares used in computing DEPS for income from continuing operations (or income before extraordinary items or the cumulative effect of an accounting change, for firms without discontinued operations) is used in computing DEPS for all other diluted per share amounts even if the result is antidilutive to these other per share amounts.

Example   When a firm has a loss from continuing operations, including potential shares in the denominator of DEPS for continuing operations is antidilutive because the loss per share would decrease. This is so *even if* it would not be antidilutive for other per-share amounts (such as the cumulative effect of an accounting change). In this situation, "no potential common shares shall be included in the computation of any diluted per-share amount when a loss from continuing operations is present, even if the firm reports a positive net income" (*SFAS No. 128* par 16). Numerical examples later in this chapter illustrate this effect, and also show that in some cases, antidilution results from using income from continuing operations as the control number for antidilution testing.

The dual presentation of EPS requires two computations, one for basic EPS, whose calculation we have already addressed, and one for diluted EPS (DEPS).

Diluted EPS (DEPS) reflects the *maximum dilution* of EPS that would occur if conversion or exercise of all dilutive securities took place at the beginning of the period (or date of issuance of the dilutive security, if later). Diluted EPS includes the effects of outstanding common shares, and potentially dilutive securities.

Although potentially dilutive securities have not been converted or exercised as of the end of the reporting period, their potential effect on EPS can be material. Analysts often use past EPS as a basis for their predictions of future EPS. Thus, potentially dilutive securities are an important factor in computing EPS. If the securities have a dilutive effect, they are entered into EPS based on *assumed* conversion or exercise.

EXHIBIT 22–3

Relationships among Simple Capital Structures (Basic EPS) and Complex Structures (Diluted EPS)

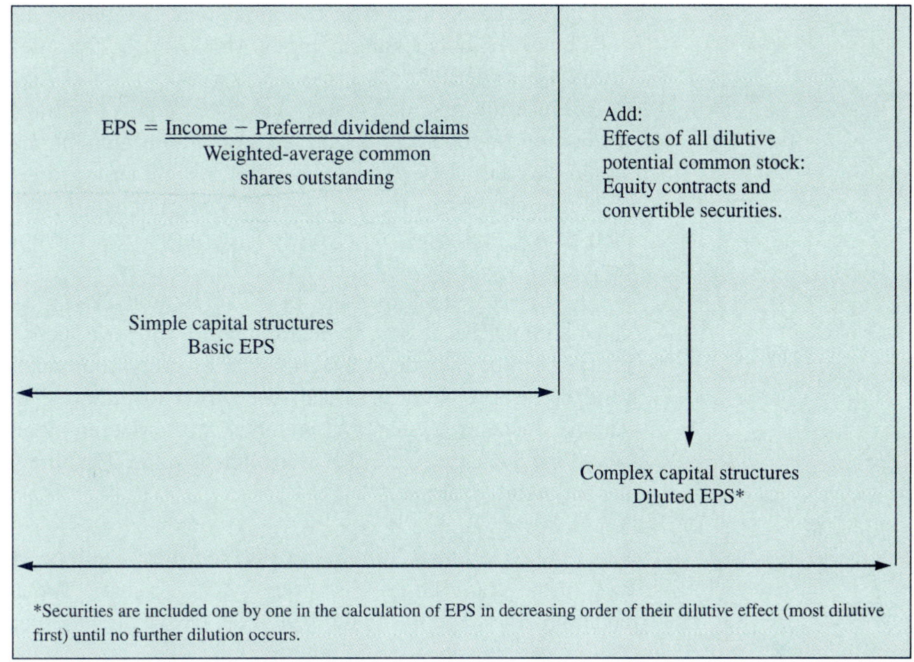

By reporting both basic EPS and DEPS, firms with complex capital structures show a range of values for EPS. This range reflects the effect that potentially dilutive securities will have if exercised or converted into common stock in the future. Because future conversion and exercise may or may not take place, a range of EPS amounts may be more relevant to financial statement users than a single amount.

The EPS relationships among simple and complex capital structures are shown in Exhibit 22–3.

The calculation of diluted EPS involves the following three steps:

1. Determination of the number of *potentially issuable shares* (boxes 6 through 10 in Exhibit 22–1).
2. A *test to determine dilution;* that is, which of the potentially issuable shares from conversion of the outstanding securities or equity contracts, if any, are dilutive (box 11 in Exhibit 22–1).
3. Calculation of DEPS (box 12 in Exhibit 22–1).

Potentially Issuable Shares

Potentially issuable shares (potential common stock) arise from three sources:

1. Equity contracts (stock rights, warrants, and options), see box 6 in Exhibit 22–1.
2. Convertible securities (preferred stock and debt), see box 8 in Exhibit 22–1, and
3. Contingently issuable shares, see box 10 in Exhibit 22–1.

Equity Contracts   Equity contracts, including common stock rights, options, subscribed stock that is partially paid, and other common stock purchase contracts are typically exercisable at the option of the holder. These contracts enter into the calculation of DEPS if they are dilutive.

The exercise of common stock rights has two effects. First, exercise increases the number of common shares outstanding and hence the denominator of the DEPS calculations. Second, the firm receives cash from the investor. The additional cash can be used for several purposes, including:

- To acquire productive assets or passive investments that would be used to increase earnings and therefore the numerator of the DEPS calculation.
- To retire nonconvertible debt, again increasing income (by reducing interest expense) and increase DEPS.

- To pay extra dividends on common stock that would have no effect on DEPS.
- To buy back outstanding common stock for the treasury that would reduce the impact of exercise on DEPS.

Because the assumed conversion of an equity contract has not, in fact, occurred as of the end of the reporting period, an assumption must be made about how any cash received would be used. Under *SFAS No. 128,* firms are assumed to use the funds to repurchase their own common shares for the treasury. The calculation of shares acquired is called the **treasury stock method.** Requiring the treasury stock method results in consistent treatment across firms and thereby increases comparability.

The treasury stock method (box 7 of Exhibit 22–1), a hypothetical calculation made in calculating DEPS, is used to determine the number of potentially issuable shares from equity contracts to be included in DEPS. When equity contracts are assumed to be exercised, the resulting proceeds are assumed to be used to purchase the firm's shares for the treasury. The net increase in shares is included in the denominator of DEPS for the portion of the year for which the securities were outstanding. The three-step calculation is illustrated in the following example:

Example   Options to purchase 1,000 shares of common stock are outstanding at the beginning of the year. The exercise price is $30 per share. The average market price of the firm's common stock is $50 for the year. Net income for the year is $4,000; and 2,000 common shares were outstanding the entire year.
- Step 1: Determine the new shares from assumed exercise: 1,000 shares.
- Step 2: Compute shares purchased for the treasury:
    Proceeds from assumed exercise ÷ Average price of the stock
    = 1,000($30) ÷ $50 = 600 shares
- Step 3: Compute the incremental shares assumed outstanding, the increase in the denominator of DEPS: 1,000 − 600 = 400 shares.

$$\begin{array}{ll} \text{Basic EPS: } \$4,000/2,000. \dots \dots \dots & \underline{\underline{\$2.00}} \\ \text{Diluted EPS: } \$4,000/(2,000 + 400) \dots \dots & \underline{\underline{\$1.67}} \end{array}$$

The options are dilutive because DEPS declined as a result of assuming the exercise of the options.

For DEPS, 400 shares are added to the weighted-average shares outstanding (the denominator effect). There is no numerator effect. Rather than use the entire 1,000 shares as the incremental shares, the assumed proceeds are used to purchase treasury shares. Increases in the average market price enhance the dilutive effect of options because the number of treasury shares (step 2) declines. This result is consistent with the higher probability of exercise as the market price increases.

The exercise of an equity contract such as a warrant brings cash from the exercise into the firm. Since the exercise has not occurred as of the reporting date, it is not clear what specific use the firm would make of the exercise proceeds. Step 2 above provides a reasonable and uniform use of the proceeds. In addition, by assuming treasury stock purchases, the total dilution in DEPS is reduced. In the example, rather than increasing the denominator 1,000 shares, only 400 additional shares are assumed outstanding. Without step 2, purchase of shares for the treasury, the dilution in EPS could be excessive.

When are options and similar contracts dilutive? They are dilutive only when the exercise price is less than the market price. When the exercise price exceeds the market price, the options are antidilutive. That is, the number of new shares from assumed exercise (step 1) is less than the number of treasury shares purchased (step 2). Under this condition, the options would not be exercised and, hence, should not be included in calculating DEPS.

Example   If the market price were $10 in the above example, the number of treasury shares purchased would be 3,000 [(1,000 × $30) ÷ $10], resulting in a negative 2,000 incremental shares (step 3), thereby causing EPS to increase. Furthermore, such options would not be exercised under such conditions by the investor. Therefore, equity contracts are not assumed to be exercised when the market price is less than or equal to the exercise price.

In using the treasury stock method, the average price over the period the options (or similar contracts) are outstanding is used to determine whether there is dilution. The average price of the stock for the period is used because it is assumed that exercise of the options would take place throughout the period rather than only at one point in the period. The use of an average price is consistent with the objective of reporting EPS figures, namely to produce a measure of performance of the firm *for the period*. As a practical matter, a simple average of weekly or monthly prices may be used if prices do not fluctuate significantly. (In practice, these calculations are made for each quarter. Examples of the quarterly calculations are given in the appendix to this chapter.)

Stock Subscriptions   Stock subscriptions outstanding are included in DEPS using the treasury stock method. The same three steps are used:

Step 1: Number of shares.

Step 2: Unpaid balance is used as the proceeds to determine the number of treasury shares purchased.

Step 3: The incremental shares equal the difference between the amounts determined in steps 1 and 2.

Numerator Effect   In most situations there is no numerator effect when using the treasury stock method. No amount is added to the numerator of basic EPS on the assumed exercise of most options and warrants. Sometimes an option permits the holder to pay the option price in debt securities of the issuer, in effect retiring the securities. In this case, the numerator effect is the after-tax interest on the debt tendered in payment by the holders of the options on assumed exercise. The denominator effect is the number of shares under option. Steps 2 and 3 of the treasury stock method are not applied.

Stock-Based Compensation Awards   Many firms award employees stock under stock-based compensation arrangements. These stock-based awards are considered the same as options for the purpose of determining DEPS. All such stock awards are considered as potential common stock as of the grant date in computing DEPS even if their exercise depends on vesting or whether the employee receives or is unable to sell the stock until a later date. The shares included in DEPS are weighted to reflect only the portion of the period the award is outstanding. Firms use the treasury stock method to compute the dilutive effect.

In applying the treasury stock method, the firm assumes the proceeds upon issue are the sum of:

- The amount the employees must pay on exercise.
- The amount of compensation cost attributed to future services but not yet recognized.
- The amount of deferred and current tax benefits that would be credited to additional paid-in capital assuming exercise of the options.

CONCEPT REVIEW

1. How does a complex capital structure differ from a simple capital structure?
2. Why is it important for a firm with a complex capital structure to report DEPS which includes the effects of potentially dilutive securities?
3. What are the steps required in calculating DEPS?

| REVIEW PROBLEM

Options to purchase 10,000,000 shares of common stock of Midus Electric are outstanding on December 31, 1998. The options were issued on July 1, 1998. The average price of the stock over the year was $25, but only $20 over the last half of the year. The exercise price is $12.50. What is the effect on the calculation of DEPS?

SOLUTION

Step 1: Shares from exercise: 10,000,000
Step 2: Shares purchased for the treasury: $10,000,000(\$12.50)/\$20 = 6,250,000$
Step 3: Denominator share increase: $(10,000,000 - 6,250,000) \times 1/2 = 1,875,000$

The price for only the half year for which the options are outstanding is used. The share calculation is adjusted further because the options are outstanding for only one-half year.

Convertible Securities   Convertible debentures (bonds) and convertible preferred stocks are potentially convertible into common stock. Therefore, the effect of conversion must be considered in computing DEPS. This is accomplished by using the **if-converted method** to determine whether the convertible securities are dilutive or not (see box 9 in Exhibit 22–1), and, if so, the amount needed to adjust DEPS.

The if-converted method assumes that conversion occurs as of the beginning of the period or at date of issue, if later. The assumed conversion of convertible bonds or preferred stock has two effects:

1. Assumed conversion increases the number of common shares outstanding and hence the denominator of the DEPS calculation.
2. Assumed conversion also decreases interest expense for convertible bonds and decreases preferred dividends for convertible preferred stock; both conversion effects increasing the DEPS numerator. Since both the numerator and the denominator of DEPS increase, the resulting DEPS may be higher or lower after conversion.

If the result of the conversion would decrease DEPS, the convertible is dilutive and the security is considered converted. If the result of the conversion would increase DEPS, the result is antidilutive and the security is not considered converted. Only dilutive securities are used to calculate DEPS. The distinction between dilutive and antidilutive securities is critical to computing DEPS in complex capital structures and applies to convertibles, equity contracts, and other potentially dilutive securities.

The if-converted method, like the treasury stock method, is a hypothetical calculation used for DEPS computation purposes only. Its premises are:

- The securities to be tested for their dilutive impact on DEPS are assumed to have been converted at the beginning of the current accounting period or at the date of issue during the current period, if later. In the latter case, the number of from conversion shares is weighted by the period over which the new shares are assumed outstanding. The number of total shares used in computing DEPS includes both the weighted average of common shares outstanding and the conversion shares.
- The interest expense incurred on convertible bonds is eliminated if the bonds are considered converted into common stock, as are the dividends paid on convertible preferred issues. Net income after tax available to common is adjusted upward to include interest expense savings (net of any tax effect) and preferred dividend savings (there is no tax effect adjustment since dividends do not reduce earnings).

Example   Convertible Bonds—If-Converted Method.   Current year net income for Gridley, Inc., is $600,000. All year 1,000, 6 percent, $1,000 debentures were outstanding, each convertible into 20 common shares. The weighted-average shares outstanding before considering potentially dilutive securities is 200,000, and the tax rate is 40 percent.

Steps:

1. Compute basic EPS: $\$600,000/200,000 = \$3.00$
2. Assume conversion of the convertible debentures at the beginning of the year, computing the numerator and denominator effect:

   Numerator effect: after-tax interest saved assuming conversion =
   $1,000(.06)(\$1,000)(1 - .40) = \$36,000$. (Had the bonds been converted at the beginning of the year, no interest would have been paid causing earnings after tax to increase $36,000.)

Denominator effect: common shares issued assuming conversion = $1,000(20) = 20,000$.

3. Incorporate the numerator and denominator effects into basic EPS. If the resulting DEPS is less than basic EPS, the debentures are dilutive and both basic EPS and DEPS are reported:

$$\text{DEPS} = (\$600,000 + \$36,000)/(200,000 + 20,000) = \$2.89$$

Because $2.89 is less than $3.00, dual presentation is required. If DEPS were computed to be more than $3.00 (for example, if the denominator effect were only 10,000 thus causing DEPS to be $3.03), then the convertible preferred would be antidilutive. In this case only basic EPS would be reported.

Had the debentures been issued during the year, both the numerator and denominator effects would be weighted by the portion of the year outstanding.

Example   Assume the debentures in the previous example were issued October 1 of the current year:

Basic EPS remains at $3.00
Numerator effect $= \$36,000(3/12) = \$9,000$.
Denominator effect $= 20,000(3/12) = 5,000$
DEPS $= (\$600,000 + \$9,000)/(200,000 + 5,000) = \$2.97$. Dual presentation is again required because DEPS $<$ basic EPS.

Convertible Bonds Issued at a Premium or Discount   When convertible bonds are issued at a price other than 100 (face value), a premium or discount results. Interest expense on convertible bonds (the numerator effect from assumed conversion) must reflect periodic amortization of the premium or discount. The numerator effect in this case is:

1. (Periodic cash interest $-$ premium amortization) $\times$ (1 $-$ tax rate)
2. (Periodic cash interest $+$ discount amortization) $\times$ (1 $-$ tax rate)

The amortization amount depends on the method used to amortize the discount and premium. Chapter 16 discusses the available methods in detail.

Convertible Preferred Stock   Preferred dividends are subtracted from earnings in the computation of basic EPS. When the if-converted method is applied to convertible preferred stock, the dividends are added back on assumed conversion for DEPS. There is no tax effect because dividends do not reduce earnings.

Example   Convertible Preferred Stock—If-Converted Method   Current year net income for Gridley, Inc., is $600,000. All year 10,000 shares of 4 percent, $100 par cumulative convertible preferred stock were outstanding, each convertible into five common shares. Dividends are paid at the end of each quarter. The weighted-average shares outstanding before considering potentially dilutive securities is 200,000, and the tax rate is 40 percent.

Steps:

1. Compute basic EPS:

   Annual preferred stock dividend $= 10,000(.04)(\$100) = \$40,000$
   Basic EPS $= (\$600,000 - \$40,000)/200,000 = \$2.80$

2. Assume conversion of the convertible preferred stock at the beginning of the year, computing the numerator and denominator effect:

   Numerator effect: dividends saved $= \$40,000$

   Denominator effect: common shares issued assuming conversion $= 10,000(5) = 50,000$.

3. DEPS $= (\$600,000 - \$40,000 + \$40,000)/(200,000 + 50,000) = \$2.40$

   $2.40 is less than $2.80; therefore dual presentation is required.

Stock Dividends and Splits—Effect on Dilution   When a company issues a stock dividend or splits its stock while dilutive securities are outstanding, the number of shares resulting from assumed conversion or exercise of convertibles and options are adjusted for the stock dividend or split. The reason for this adjustment is that the contracts underlying dilutive securities specify that the conversion rate and number of options be adjusted for stock dividends and splits. Otherwise the interests of the security holders would be compromised.

Example   Using the information in the previous example for convertible preferred stock, assume Gridley split the stock two-for-one late in the year, after all other transactions in common stock. The denominator effect would double to 100,000 shares $(10,000 \times 5 \times 2)$.

$$\text{Basic EPS} = (\$600,000 - \$40,000)/(200,000 \times 2) = \$1.40$$
$$\text{DEPS} = (\$600,000 - \$40,000 + \$40,000)/(200,000 \times 2 + 100,000) = \$1.20$$

Incremental shares for options under the treasury stock method also are adjusted for stock dividends and splits.

Actual Conversions of Convertible Securities   When dilutive convertible securities are *actually* converted into common stock during a period, the securities are treated as convertibles for the portion of the reporting period *before* conversion, and as actual common shares *after* the conversion. Appropriate weights are assigned to the assumed shares before conversion, and actual shares after conversion.

Example   Current year net income for Gridley, Inc., is $600,000. At the beginning of the year, 10,000 shares of 4 percent, $100 par cumulative convertible preferred stock were outstanding, each convertible into two common shares. Dividends are paid at the end of each quarter. The weighted average shares outstanding before considering potentially dilutive securities is 200,000, and the tax rate is 40 percent. On October 1, 2,000 preferred shares are converted.

1. Basic EPS:

   Actual preferred dividends declared for the year:
   $(\$100)(10,000)(.04)(3/4) + (\$100)(8,000)(.04)(1/4) = \$38,000$
   Weighted-average shares for the year:
   $200,000 + 2,000(2)(1/4) = 201,000$
   Basic EPS $= (\$600,000 - \$38,000)/201,000 = \$2.80$

2. Determine numerator and denominator effect:

   Numerator effect, the dividends avoided assuming conversion $= \$38,000$
   Denominator effect, the common shares issued assuming conversion:
   $\quad 10,000(2)(3/4) + 8,000(2)(1/4) = 19,000$

(For the last quarter of the year, only 8,000 convertible shares were outstanding.)
3. DEPS $= (\$600,000 - \$38,000 + \$38,000)/(201,000 + 19,000) = \$2.73$

The actual conversion of *options and warrants* is discussed in this chapter's appendix.

Contingent Common Stock   EPS also may be subject to dilution from **contingent stock issue agreements,** which can arise with corporate acquisitions, buyouts, and business combinations. Dilution is most likely if an acquiring company's offer includes an exchange of stock (acquired company's shares exchanged for shares in the acquiring company) or bonus shares to the acquired company's shareholders as an inducement.

Bonus shares in the acquiring company are referred to as **contingent-issue shares,** to be distributed to the acquired company shareholders at some future time contingent on the performance of the acquired company.

As discussed previously, contingently issuable shares are included in basic EPS if the conditions are met at the end of the reporting period. Such shares also are included in DEPS but the weighting of contingent shares may be different for DEPS.

Contingent shares are included in DEPS on a quarterly basis, and then weighted for the interim periods affected.

1. If the conditions are met in a period, the contingent shares are included in DEPS as of the *beginning* of the period (in contrast to basic EPS, which reflects the shares only for the portion of the period for which the conditions are met).
2. If the conditions are *not* met in a period, the number of shares included in DEPS is the number that would be issuable if the end of the period were also the end of the contingency period. Predictions of future income or market prices are not used to compute the number of included shares. (For basic EPS, no shares are included if the conditions are not met.)

The following examples illustrate these principles.

Example   Using the previous example on contingent shares for basic EPS, Mega, Inc. is required to issue 100 contingent shares to the stockholders of Rega, Inc. for each new store opened by Rega in the current year. Rega opened one store on August 1, and another on October 1. Contingent shares to be included in the denominators of *quarterly* DEPS are:

Quarter 1:	0
Quarter 2:	0
Quarter 3:	100
Quarter 4:	200

For DEPS, the shares are assumed to be outstanding as of the beginning of the period for which the condition is met. The denominator of annual DEPS includes 75 shares from the contingent share agreement (compared to 67 for basic EPS):

$$(0 + 0 + 100 + 200)/4 = 75$$

When an income level or a stated market price for the stock is the specified condition, DEPS includes the shares that would be issued based on the assumption that the current income or ending market price will remain unchanged until the end of the agreement. (For basic EPS, no shares are included because income or the market price could change.)

Example   Mega, Inc. is required to issue 100 shares to the shareholders of Rega for each $1,000 of earnings of the combined enterprise in excess of $200,000 for the current year. Consolidated earnings for the year were:

Quarter 1:	$ 70,000
Quarter 2:	150,000
Quarter 3:	(90,000)
Quarter 4:	180,000
Total:	$310,000

Contingent shares to be included in the denominator of quarterly DEPS are:

Quarter 1:	0 (earnings level not reached)
Quarter 2:	2,000 [= ($70,000 + $150,000 − $200,000)/$1,000] 100
Quarter 3:	0 (earnings level declined below $200,000)
Quarter 4:	11,000 [= ($310,000 − $200,000)/$1,000] 100

The denominator of annual DEPS includes 3,250 shares from the contingent share agreement:

$$(0 + 2,000 + 0 + 11,000)/4 = 3,250$$

The use of the current level of earnings, market price, or other variable is consistent with the objective of EPS: to measure the performance of a firm for a period. The use of predicted amounts would be inconsistent with the objective of reporting an historic, "for-the-period," performance measure.

REVIEW PROBLEM

A company has outstanding $1 million of 8 percent convertible debentures due in five years. Each $1,000 convertible debenture is convertible into 40 shares of common. Under the if-converted method, what is the effect on the numerator and the denominator of the diluted EPS calculation? Assume a 40 percent tax rate.

SOLUTION

Numerator effect: The after-tax interest will be added back to the numerator. If the debentures are assumed converted, the interest will no longer be paid but the firm will also not receive the tax deduction for interest expense. Add back $.08 \times \$1,000,000 \times (1 - .4) = \$48,000$.

Denominator effect: Add the common shares due to the conversion: $(\$1,000,000 \div \$1,000) \times 40 = 40,000$.

DEPS is computed by adding the numerator and denominator effects to basic EPS, if and only if the result is a final figure less than basic EPS.

Dilution-Antidilution (D/A) Method

To this point, we have considered only one potentially dilutive security at a time: the numerator and denominator effects are entered into DEPS only if it causes DEPS to decline relative to basic EPS.[5] If not, the security is antidilutive and not considered further.

In practice, firms often have several potentially dilutive securities outstanding at any one time. The order by which the securities are included into DEPS can affect the final amount reported. One ordering might result in the inclusion of a particular security in DEPS, while another ordering might result in that security being antidilutive and thus excluded.

In response to this issue, the FASB requires that potentially dilutive securities be considered for inclusion in DEPS in sequence *from the most dilutive to the least dilutive*. It can be shown that this approach achieves maximum dilution (lowest DEPS). We call this approach the *dilution-antidilution method*. The following steps describe the method:

1. Compute basic EPS for income from continuing operations (or before extraordinary items or cumulative effects if there is no discontinued operation). This amount is the benchmark for determining whether the first security to be considered is dilutive.
2. Compute the numerator and denominator effects for each potentially dilutive security as illustrated in the previous examples. The D/A ratio is the ratio of these two amounts:

$$D/A = \text{numerator effect/denominator effect}$$

3. Rank the securities from lowest D/A (ranked first) to highest D/A (ranked last). (The most dilutive security is considered for inclusion in DEPS first.)
4. If the D/A ratio of the first-ranked security $\geq$ basic EPS, then DEPS = basic EPS. No securities are dilutive because entering any of the securities into basic EPS would cause it to increase. Do not proceed further.
5. If the D/A ratio of the first-ranked security $<$ basic EPS, then DEPS is less than basic EPS. Incorporate this security into DEPS by adding its numerator effect to the numerator of basic EPS and the denominator effect to the denominator of basic EPS. The result is called *tentative DEPS,* the new benchmark for the next potentially dilutive security.
6. If the D/A ratio of the next highest-ranked security $\geq$ tentative DEPS, there are no more dilutive securities and tentative DEPS = final DEPS. Do not proceed further.

---

[5]For both convertible securities and equity contracts, the most advantageous conversion rate or exercise price available to the security holder is used in calculating DEPS. This increases the potential dilution.

7. If the D/A ratio of the next highest-ranked security < tentative DEPS, incorporate this security into tentative DEPS as before. Tentative DEPS is now a smaller amount because of the dilutive effect of the security.

8. Repeat steps 6 and 7 until (*a*) all potentially dilutive securities have been incorporated, or (*b*) the remaining securities are antidilutive because their D/A ratios exceed tentative DEPS (as signaled by step 6).

We illustrate the D/A method by continuing the Palmento example introduced earlier in a review problem.

Example   This example considers multiple potentially dilutive securities and extends the Palmento Corporation illustration by considering the order by which such securities are entered into EPS using the D/A method. The initial data are repeated below and the additional data are given afterward.

Initial Data: Palmento Corporation	**Shares**
Capital stock:	
Common stock, par $1, outstanding on January 1, 1998.	90,000
Common stock, sold and issued May 1, 1998	6,000
Preferred stock, par $20, 6 percent (cumulative, nonconvertible)	
outstanding on January 1, 1998	2,500
Income data for year ending December 31, 1998:	
Income before extraordinary item	$134,000
Extraordinary gain (net of 40 percent tax)	10,000
Net income	$144,000

Additional Data

1. Stock rights that entitle stockholders to purchase 2,000 common shares for $20 per share. The market price of the shares has averaged $25 over the current accounting period. The rights have been outstanding for the entire accounting period.

2. Convertible preferred, no par, with a $7 annual dividend per share. The stock is cumulative and each preferred share is convertible into eight shares of common. The stock has been outstanding over the entire accounting period. One thousand shares issued at $108 per share are outstanding.

3. Series A convertible bonds, $200,000 outstanding, 8 percent interest payable annually. Each $1,000 bond is convertible into 30 shares of common. The bonds were issued at par and were outstanding the entire year.

4. Series B convertible bonds, $500,000 outstanding, 10 percent interest payable annually. Each $1,000 bond is convertible into 50 shares of common. The bonds were issued at par and were outstanding the entire year.

Using this data, we calculated basic EPS for income before extraordinary items to be:

$$[\$134,000 - (2,500 \times \$20 \times .06) - (1,000 \times \$7)] \div [90,000 + 6,000(8/12)]$$
$$= (\$134,00 - \$3,000 - \$7,000) \div (90,000 + 4,000)$$
$$= \$124,000 \div 94,000$$
$$= \$1.32$$

Basic EPS makes no distinction between convertible and nonconvertible preferred stock; both are included in the calculation. The numerator and denominator effects of each potentially dilutive security are computed next.

Determining the Numerator Effect   The numerator effects of conversion for the four dilutive securities are:

- Stock rights: there is no numerator effect $ 0
- Convertible preferred: 1,000($7)   7,000
- Series A convertible bonds: ($200,000)(.08)(1 − .40)   9,600
- Series B convertible bonds: ($500,000)(.10)(1 − .40)   30,000

Determining the Denominator Effect   The stock rights are dilutive because the option price is less than average market price. The use of the treasury stock method to establish the number of common stock equivalent shares for the Palmento Corporation's stock rights yields 400 shares:

	Shares
Shares that would be issued upon exercise of rights (step 1)	2,000
Cash proceeds if rights were exercised, 2,000 rights $\times$ \$20 (option price) = \$40,000.	
Treasury stock shares that could be purchased: \$40,000 $\div$ \$25, at the average market price (step 2).	(1,600)
Incremental number of common shares that would be outstanding for DEPS—denominator effect (step 3)	400

The number of common shares under the if-converted method for the three convertibles is shown along with the shares from the rights:

- Stock rights (see above calculation)   400
- Convertible preferred stock (1,000 $\times$ 8)   8,000
- Series A convertible bonds (200 $\times$ 30)   6,000
- Series B convertible bonds (500 $\times$ 50) 25,000

D/A Ratios Based on these two sets of calculations, the D/A ratios for each security in order from most to least dilutive are:

Security	Numerator Effect	Denominator Effect	D/A Ratio	Rank
Stock rights	\$ 0	400	\$ 0	1
Convertible preferred	7,000	8,000	.88	2
Series B bonds	30,000	25,000	1.20	3
Series A bonds	9,600	6,000	1.60	4

The rights are ranked first. The D/A ratio for rights is 0, which is less than basic EPS of \$1.32. Therefore the rights are dilutive. The calculation to determine the first *tentative* DEPS is:

$$(\$124,000 + \$0) \div (94,000 + 400) = \$1.31$$

The D/A ratio of \$0.88 for the convertible preferred (ranked second) is less than the tentative DEPS figure of \$1.31. Therefore, the convertible debentures are dilutive and must be included in the computation. Doing so yields:

$$(\$124,000 + \$0 + \$7,000) \div (94,000 + 400 + 8,000) = \$1.28$$

as the new *tentative* DEPS.

Because the \$1.20 D/A ratio for the series B convertible bonds (ranked third) is less than the current tentative DEPS of \$1.28, the series B convertible bonds must now be included in the computation yielding:

$$(\$124,000 + \$0 + \$7,000 + \$30,000) \div (94,000 + 400 + 8,000 + 25,000)$$
$$= \$161,000 \div 127,400 = \$1.26$$

This is the final value for DEPS for income before extraordinary items because the \$1.60 D/A ratio for the remaining Series A convertible bonds (ranked fourth) exceeds \$1.26 and would create a larger EPS figure if added to the calculation. Including the series A bonds would be antidilutive.

Disclosure of earnings on a per-share basis in the income statement for the year ended December 31, 1998:

Basic earnings per share:

Income before extraordinary item	\$1.32
Extraordinary gain	.11*
Net income	\$1.43[†]

*(\$10,000 extraordinary gain) $\div$ 94,000. (May be reported in the notes.)

[†] (\$144,000 − \$3,000 − \$7,000)/94,000

Diluted earnings per share:

Income before extraordinary item.	$1.26
Extraordinary gain.	.08*
Net income.	$1.34†

*($10,000 extraordinary gain) ÷ 127,400. (May be reported in the notes.)

†($144,000 − $3,000 − $7,000 + $7,000 + $30,000) ÷ 127,400

CONCEPT REVIEW

1. What types of potentially dilutive securities are considered when computing DEPS?
2. If a convertible preferred stock is assumed considered, what impact does this have on the DEPS calculation assuming the conversion effect is dilutive?
3. What is the purpose of the D/A method?

REVIEW PROBLEM

Rio Oso Inc. provides the following data related to its EPS calculation for the year:

Common shares outstanding at the beginning of the year	200,000
Purchase of treasury shares on October 1	30,000
Net income	$600,000
Annual dividend on nonconvertible cumulative preferred stock	$20,000

The accountant for Rio Oso has developed the following preliminary amounts for the firm's four potentially dilutive securities:

Potentially Dilutive Security	Numerator Effect	Denominator Effect
1	$23,000	8,250 shares
2	19,000	17,000 shares
3	7,000	14,000 shares
4	0	3,000 shares

Compute basic EPS and DEPS.

SOLUTION

Basic EPS = ($600,000 − $20,000)/[200,000 − 30,000(3/12)] = $580,000/192,500 = $3.01

Potentially Dilutive Security	Numerator Effect	Denominator Effect	D/A Ratio	Rank
1	$23,000	8,250 shares	$2.79	4
2	19,000	17,000 shares	1.12	3
3	7,000	14,000 shares	.50	2
4	0	3,000 shares	0	1

The D/A ratio for security 4 ($0) < basic EPS ($3.01), therefore tentative DEPS = ($580,000 + $0)/(192,500 + 3,000) = $2.97

The D/A ratio for security 3 ($.50) < tentative DEPS ($2.97), therefore the new tentative DEPS = ($580,000 + $0 + $7,000)/(192,500 + 3,000 + 14,000) = $2.80

The D/A ratio for security 2 ($1.12) < tentative DEPS ($2.80), therefore the new tentative DEPS = ($580,000 + $0 + $7,000 + $19,000)/(192,500 + 3,000 + 14,000 + 17,000) = $2.68

The D/A ratio for security 1 ($2.79) > tentative DEPS ($2.68). Therefore, security 1 is not entered into DEPS because it would cause tentative DEPS to increase. Reported DEPS = $2.68.

EARNINGS PER SHARE AND RELATED DISCLOSURES

EPS disclosures Firms with simple capital structures (no dilutive common shares) must disclose basic EPS on the face of the income statement for the following, net of tax:

1. Income from continuing operations.
2. Net income.

Firms with complex capital structures must disclose *both* basic EPS and DEPS on the face of the income statement *with equal prominence* for the following, net of tax:

1. Income from continuing operations.
2. Net income.

EPS data must be presented for all periods for which an income statement or summary of earnings is presented. In comparative disclosures, if any period reports DEPS, then all periods reported must report DEPS even if it is the same as basic. If basic and diluted EPS are the same, dual presentation can be accomplished in one line on the income statement.

The following also must be disclosed on a per share basis (net of tax), either on the face of the income statement or in the footnotes, for simple capital structures (single presentation only) and for complex capital structures (dual presentation):

1. Discontinued operations.
2. Extraordinary items.
3. Cumulative effects of accounting change.

The terms *basic* and *diluted* EPS are not required terms. Other captions including *earnings per common share* and *earnings per common share—assuming dilution* are appropriate as well. Comprehensive income is not reported on a per-share basis.

Income from Continuing Operations—The Control Number for Antidilution   When reporting the required EPS amounts, income from continuing operations (or income before extraordinary items or cumulative effects for firms without discontinued operations) is the **control number** for purposes of testing for antidilution. In other words, the denominator value used for income from continuing operations must be used for all other per share amounts. Two situations arise that cause certain reported EPS amounts to change as a result of requiring the use of this control number.

1. When income from continuing operations is *positive,* but one or more amounts to be reported on a per share basis including net income are negative, the negative diluted per share amounts exceed their basic EPS counterparts. That is, they are less negative and, therefore, an antidilutive effect occurs. Furthermore, net income may be positive as well and including the dilutive shares in the calculation may cause DEPS for net income to exceed its basic EPS counterpart. These situations are instances for which antidilutive effects are reported.
2. When income from continuing operations is *negative* (or when the amount available to common is negative after considering preferred dividends), including the effects of potentially dilutive securities in DEPS for income from continuing operations would cause it to be less negative. The result would be a smaller loss per share, an antidilutive result. To avoid this circumstance, no potential common shares are included in DEPS for income from continuing operations. Basic EPS = DEPS for income from continuing operations. Furthermore, *no other* per share amount includes shares from potentially dilutive securities, even though to do so would be dilutive. This is the case even if the firm has positive income. This is an example of reducing the maximum dilution otherwise possible (another is the use of the treasury stock method).

Example   Income from continuing operations is *positive*. The bottom portion of Martingale Inc.'s income statement shows the following:

Income from continuing operations	$200,000
Discontinued operations (net)	20,000
Extraordinary loss	(12,000)
Net income	$208,000
Weighted average shares outstanding for the year	100,000
Denominator effect of potentially dilutive securities . . .	10,000
(Assume no numerator effect for simplicity.)	

Reported EPS	Basic		Diluted	
Income from continuing operations	$2.00	($200,000/100,000)	$1.82	($200,000/110,000)
Discontinued operations.	.20	($20,000/100,000)	.18	($20,000/110,000)
Extraordinary loss	(.12)	($12,000/100,000)	(.11)	($12,000/110,000)
Net income	$2.08	($208,000/100,000)	$1.89	($208,000/110,000)

The 11 cent diluted extraordinary loss per share is less negative (larger) than the 12 cent loss per share for basic EPS. This antidilutive result occurs because the control number, 110,000 shares, must be used for all per share amounts.

Example   **Income from continuing operations is *negative*.** Assume the same information for Martingale except that income from continuing operations is a $200,000 loss. Net income then is a $192,000 loss ($-$ $200,000 + $20,000 - $12,000 = - $192,000).

Reported EPS	Basic		Diluted	
Income from continuing operations (loss). .	($2.00)	($200,000/100,000)	($2.00)	(same as basic)
Discontinued operations.	.20	($20,000/100,000)	.20	(same as basic)
Extraordinary loss	(.12)	($12,000/100,000)	(.12)	(same as basic)
Net loss	($1.92)	($192,000/100,000)	($1.92)	(same as basic)

In this example, the 10,000 shares from assumed exercise or conversion is not used in the calculation of DEPS. To do so would cause income from continuing operations on a per share basis to increase:

$$($200,000 \text{ loss})/110,000 \text{ shares} = ($1.82 \text{ loss})/\text{share}$$

This amount exceeds the basic EPS counterpart per share ($2.00 loss per share), an antidilutive effect. Therefore, both basic and diluted EPS are reported at negative $2.00 per share. The requirement is the same even for firms with negative income from continuing operations but positive net income. Even though the denominator effect of assumed conversion or exercise would cause diluted net income per share to decline, no dilution is assumed.

In choosing income from continuing operations as the control number, the FASB avoided a problem that occurs when income from continuing operations is positive but net income is negative. In this situation, if net income were the control number, basic and diluted EPS for income from continuing operations would be equal because including assumed shares from conversion or exercise in diluted net income per share would be antidilutive. Firms would be reporting no dilution in income from continuing operations merely because discontinued operations, extraordinary items or cumulative effects caused earnings to turn negative.

Other Disclosures   Additional information required to be disclosed for each period reported includes:
- A reconciliation of the numerators and the denominators of the basic and diluted per share computations for income from continuing operations. (This reconciliation provides the same information as in our example of the D/A approach.)
- The effect of any preferred shares on basic EPS.
- Securities that could potentially dilute basic EPS but that are currently antidilutive.
- A description of any transaction that occurred after the end of the current reporting period but before the issuance of the financial statements that would have changed materially the number of common shares or potential common shares outstanding at the end of the period if the transaction had occurred before the end of the period.

The last two disclosures above allow users to assess the effects on EPS of transactions that have already taken place, and those that might take place in the future.

A FINAL COMMENT

Despite the attention given to EPS numbers, it is extraordinarily difficult to evaluate just what the numbers mean. For example, does the magnitude or the trend of EPS amounts indicate the effectiveness with which management uses the resources entrusted to its care?

GLOBAL VIEW

SFAS No. 128 is the result of an unprecedented cooperative effort between the FASB and the IASC (International Accounting Standards Committee). The goal of both groups was to achieve greater international comparability of reported EPS data. The EPS effort was an opportunity to achieve broad international agreement in a reasonable time. The Board saw EPS as an area with considerable potential for international harmony because measurement and recognition questions were not at issue. Most respondents to the FASB's prospectus detailing the goal of international cooperation were favorable to the effort.

One of the goals of *SFAS No. 128* is to increase the compatibility of U.S. EPS reporting with that of other countries. Before the new standard, many U.S. firms reported primary and fully diluted EPS but not basic EPS. Both EPS figures reflected dilution. Only two other countries required presentation of primary EPS. All other countries with EPS reporting requirements demand presentation of only basic EPS, or both basic and diluted EPS. With the adoption of *SFAS No. 128,* U.S. EPS reporting has moved much closer to the global norm.

The FASB and the IASC did not initially agree on all issues however. The treasury stock method was one area of initial disagreement. The IASC initially proposed using the ending market price for computing the number of shares to be purchased for the treasury (step 2 of the treasury stock method). The logic was that the ending prices provided a better warning signal of future potential dilution. Although the FASB considered this to be a useful objective, their preference was to use the average price, a value more representative of performance for the entire period.

The respondents to the exposure draft of both the FASB and the IASC also indicated a preference for the average market price. After considerable discussion, the IASC agreed to the FASB's position on this issue. On the other hand, the FASB agreed to the IASC's proposal to adopt the D/A method to maximize dilution for DEPS. *APB Opinion No. 15,* the forerunner of *SFAS No. 128,* had no such provision. Another area of agreement is the if-converted method for convertible securities. The IASC issued its *Accounting Standard 33, Earnings per Share,* concurrently with *SFAS No. 128.* The provisions of these two standards are substantially the same.

A firm's asset structure changes over time, making comparisons difficult. Mergers and divestitures compound the problem of making accurate inter-year comparisons. Reported EPS is not simply the earnings per share of common stock outstanding. Instead, weighted averages are used, and some contingent securities may be considered as if they were outstanding common shares. Moreover, firms may execute transactions merely to influence the year's EPS figures. One firm sold land each year so that the gains on sale produced a constant EPS growth rate year by year. The need felt by some firms to attain their own EPS goals and those of analysts adds to the pressures. Recall Emerson's nearly 40 years of quarterly increases in EPS. This firm's management considers it important to report continued increases.

EPS calculations are complex, and their meaning is sufficiently uncertain that many accountants believe the level of reliance on them is unwarranted. Further, using EPS as an important element in a firm's goal structure can contribute to a short-term management attitude. Such attitudes can lead to decisions that are detrimental to the long-term productivity and financial health of the firm. Nevertheless, EPS computations continue to be reported by companies and anticipated by stockholders, analysts, and management. Therefore, knowledge of how EPS amounts are calculated is essential if intelligent use is to be made of the resulting figures.

CONCEPT REVIEW

1. What income amounts must be reported in EPS form?
2. How are stock dividends and splits handled in EPS computations when they occur during the accounting period?
3. Do EPS figures necessarily indicate how effectively a firm is managing its resources?

SUMMARY OF KEY POINTS

(L.O. 1)   1. Investors and regulators watch earnings per share figures because they have an important impact on the movement of stock market prices.

(L.O. 2)   2. EPS computations are based on whether a firm has a simple or complex capital structure. Simple capital structures involve only common stock.

(L.O. 2)   3. Basic EPS equals return to common divided by the weighted-average outstanding common shares. For simple capital structures this result is called basic EPS.

(L.O. 3)   4. Convertible securities that are dilutive are included in diluted EPS using the if-converted method.

(L.O. 4)   5. The treasury stock method is used to incorporate dilutive options and warrants in the denominator of the DEPS calculation. The number of shares resulting from the assumed exercise of the options is reduced by using the funds obtained on exercise to purchase shares in the market at the period's average market price.

(L.O. 5)   6. The efficient procedure for calculating dilutive EPS is the dilution-antidilution (D/A) method. This method assures that antidilutive securities do not inadvertently lead to an increase in reported EPS and results in the maximum possible dilution.

▌REVIEW PROBLEM

1. Knight Company, a calendar-year firm, with 100,000 shares of common stock outstanding at the start of the year, declares a three-for-one stock split halfway through the year. The next day, Knight issues 200,000 new shares in conjunction with the acquisition of a new plant. What is the effect of these transactions on EPS?

2. On March 31, Knight issues:

   a. 10,000 shares of 10 percent nonconvertible, noncumulative preferred stock at par. The firm receives $1,000,000. Knight paid the appropriate dividend at year-end.

   b. $500,000 of 9 percent convertible bonds at par. Each $1,000 bond is convertible into 20 shares of common. The tax rate is 35 percent.

   If Knight reports on a calendar-year basis, what is the impact on EPS, assuming that the bonds are dilutive?

3. 5,000 warrants are outstanding all year that allow holders immediately to purchase one common share for $25. The average market price of the stock during the year was $40. What is the effect on DEPS?

▌SOLUTION

1. The effect is entirely on the denominator. The stock split means that 300,000 shares are now outstanding. Since no new assets are involved, the 300,000 shares are assumed to be outstanding the entire year. The issue of 200,000 shares for the new plant is outstanding for only half the year because only during this period does management have additional assets on which to earn profits. The denominator for EPS for the year is

$$300,000 + 1/2(200,000) = 400,000.$$

2. a. The nonconvertible preferred is not a potentially dilutive security. The only effect for EPS calculations is to subtract the dividend from net income in computing basic and diluted EPS. Thus, $1,000,000(.10)(3/4) = $75,000 is subtracted from the numerator in this year's EPS calculations. The preferred dividend is paid for three-fourths of the year (nine months), April 1 to December 31.

   b. Because the 9 percent convertible bond is dilutive by assumption, the effects of assumed conversion on DEPS only are:

   Add to the numerator of basic EPS: .09($500,000)(3/4)(1 − .35) = $21,938

   Add to the denominator of basic EPS: 20($500,000 ÷ $1,000)(3/4) = 7,500

   The convertible bond is outstanding for only three-fourths of the year resulting in the weighting of three-fourths. The numerator and the denominator effects would be added to basic EPS in computing DEPS.

3. The warrants are dilutive because the option price is less than the average market price. The effect on this year's DEPS is obtained using the treasury stock method. The number of shares added to the denominator in the calculation of this year's DEPS is:

Shares from issuance:.	5,000
Treasury shares purchased: 5,000($25) ÷ $40	3,125
Incremental shares:	1,875

There is no numerator effect. If income from continuing operations is positive, 1,875 shares would be added to the denominator of DEPS.

APPENDIX   *A Closer Look at the Treasury Stock Method*

EPS is reported for any period for which net income is reported. If the treasury stock method is in use and the reporting period exceeds three months, a separate computation must be made for each quarter for which the options are outstanding and for which a dilutive effect is present.

Then the quarterly results are weighted by one-fourth of a year in computing the annual incremental shares.

Example   Assume that a firm has 25,000 shares of common stock outstanding for the year and granted options at the end of the first quarter that result under the treasury stock method in the following:

First quarter:	No incremental shares (options not issued).
Second quarter:	500 incremental shares.
Third quarter:	No incremental shares (effect antidilutive due to option price exceeding the average market price).
Fourth quarter:	1,100 incremental shares.

The incremental shares for quarters 2 and 4 are included in quarterly DEPS. The weighted average of shares for *annual* DEPS would be 25,400:

$$(25,000 + 25,500 + 25,000 + 26,100) \div 4 = 25,400$$

Now consider an extended example of the necessary calculations.

Example   Suppose a firm has outstanding stock options for 5,000 shares of common at an exercise price of $10 per share. The options were outstanding the entire year. The average quarterly market prices were:

First quarter:	$11.11
Second quarter:	9.75
Third quarter:	13.89
Fourth quarter:	12.50

For diluted EPS, the calculation of the quarterly incremental shares to reflect the dilutive effect is:

First quarter:	$5,000 - [(5,000 \times \$10) \div \$11.11] = 500$
Second quarter:	Antidilutive because market price < option price
Third quarter:	$5,000 - [(5,000 \times \$10) \div \$13.89] = 1,400$
Fourth quarter:	$5,000 - [(5,000 \times \$10) \div \$12.50] = 1,000$

Incremental shares are $(500 + 0 + 1,400 + 1,000) \div 4 = 725$. This is the denominator effect for annual DEPS.

Actual Exercise of Options   When options are exercised during a quarter, the treasury stock method is applied to those shares for the portion of the period up to the exercise date. The average market price during the period up to the exercise date is used. Incremental shares are weighted for the period they are outstanding but not exercised. (Actual shares from exercise of options are weighted by the period they are outstanding.)

Example   Assume the information in the previous example with the following modification:

1. 2,000 options were exercised on September 1.
2. The average market price of common stock from July 1 to September 1 was $13.50.

Basic EPS   The denominators of *quarterly* basic EPS would include the following as a result of the actual exercise on September 1:

First quarter:	0
Second quarter:	0
Third quarter:	$2,000(1/3) = 667$
Fourth quarter:	$2,000(3/3) = 2,000$

The denominator of *annual* basic EPS includes 667 shares actually outstanding from exercise. This amount can be computed in two ways:

1. Based on the quarterly results: $0 + 0 + 667(1/4) + 2,000(1/4) = 667$
2. Based on the annual period: $2,000(4/12) = 667$

DEPS   The incremental shares from assumed exercise (denominator effects) for *quarterly* DEPS would include the following. These amounts are in addition to those computed above for basic EPS.

First quarter:	$5,000 - [(5,000 \times \$10) \div \$11.11] =$	500
Second quarter:	Antidilutive because average market price $<$ option price	
Third quarter:	$2,000 - [(2,000 \times \$10) \div \$13.50] = 519; 519(2/3) =$ 346	
	$3,000 - [(3,000 \times \$10) \div \$13.89] =$ <u>840</u>	
		1,186
Fourth quarter:	$3,000 - [(3,000 \times \$10) \div \$12.50] =$	600

During the third quarter, the 2,000 exercised options were options only for two-thirds of the quarter. Therefore, the application of the treasury stock method weights the 519 incremental shares by two-thirds of a quarter. The 3,000 unexercised options were options the entire period and receive a weighting of 3/3 or 1. The same holds for the fourth quarter in which only 3,000 options were outstanding. The incremental shares for quarters 1, 3, and 4 as calculated above are included in the respective quarterly DEPS figures.

Incremental shares (denominator effect) for *annual* DEPS is 572: $(500 + 0 + 1,186 + 600) \div 4$. In general, the sum of quarterly EPS amounts need not equal the annual EPS amounts for either basic or diluted EPS.

UNDERSTANDING AND APPLYING CONCEPTS AND STANDARDS

QUESTIONS

1. What is the fundamental difference in EPS computations and reporting between a simple capital structure and a complex capital structure?
2. Is the annual dividend on cumulative convertible preferred stock outstanding all year subtracted from net income in computing basic EPS? If so, why?
3. Explain the treasury stock method.
4. Is the treasury stock method's use of average market price consistent with the overall objective of EPS reporting? Explain.
5. Briefly, how are stock dividends and splits reflected in the calculation of basic EPS if the dividend or split occurs (a) before the balance sheet date, or (b) after the balance sheet date but before the issuance of the statements?
6. Why are dividends from dilutive convertible preferred stock added back to the numerator of basic EPS without tax effect, but interest recognized on dilutive convertible bonds is added back to the numerator on an after-tax basis?
7. What is the difference between a dilutive security and an antidilutive security? Why is the distinction important in EPS computations?
8. A company split its common stock two for one on June 30 of its accounting year, ended December 31. Before the split, there were 4,000 shares of common stock outstanding. How many shares of common stock should be used in computing EPS? How many shares of common stock should be used in computing a comparative EPS amount for the preceding year?
9. Explain why nonconvertible securities do not cause a complex capital structure, whereas convertible securities do cause a complex capital structure.
10. Explain why and when dividends on nonconvertible preferred stock must be subtracted from income to compute EPS in both simple and complex capital structures.
11. If income from continuing operations is a loss but net income is positive, describe the proper reporting for DEPS.
12. Suppose a firm has a convertible bond outstanding. What calculations must be made to establish an impact on EPS?
13. What is the D/A method, and why is it useful?
14. What are contingent shares, and do they need to be considered in figuring EPS?
15. A dilutive convertible bond was issued at a premium. Explain how to compute the numerator effect for such a bond when computing dilutive EPS.
16. Explain in general how to handle actual conversions of convertible dilutive securities for basic and diluted EPS purposes (denominator effect only).
17. Shares of a parent corporation will be issued in the future based on the number of retail outlets opened by a recently acquired subsidiary. The subsidiary predicts that 10 new outlets will be opened in the next three years. However, to date, no outlets have been opened. Describe how the contingent shares would be calculated for the parent firm's diluted EPS in this situation.

18. A firm has six potentially dilutive securities. They are entered into the calculation of diluted EPS in the proper manner. After entering two securities, tentative DEPS is less than the D/A ratio of the third-ranked security. What should the accountant do next?
19. A firm has a complex capital structure. What is the maximum number of per share amounts that must be disclosed, and where must they be disclosed?
20. Although antidilutive EPS reporting generally is not allowed, under what conditions would a diluted per share amount exceed its basic counterpart?
21. The International Accounting Standards Committee (IASC) initially preferred using the ending market price for a period in the treasury stock method. What was the rationale for this preference?
22. Briefly explain how *SFAS No. 128* on EPS has brought U.S. GAAP closer to international accounting standards.

APPLYING CONCEPTS AND STANDARDS

EXERCISES

E 22–1
(L.O. 2, 3)

EPS Calculations

1. On December 31, 1997, Case, Inc., had 300,000 shares of common stock issued and outstanding. Case issued a 10 percent stock dividend on July 1, 1998. On October 1, 1998, Case purchased 24,000 shares of its common stock for treasury and recorded the purchase using the cost method. What is the number of shares that should be used in computing primary earnings per share for the year ended December 31, 1998?
   a. 306,000.
   b. 309,000.
   c. 324,000.
   d. 330,000.
2. Seco Corporation was incorporated on January 2, 1997. The following information pertains to Seco's common stock transactions:

1997

January 2	Number of shares authorized	80,000
February 1	Number of shares issued	60,000
July 1	Number of shares reacquired but not canceled	5,000
December 1	Two-for-one stock split	

At December 31, 1997, the number of shares of Seco's common stock outstanding is
   a. 150,000.
   b. 120,000.
   c. 115,000.
   d. 110,000.
3. At December 31, 1998, and 1997, Gow Corporation had 100,000 shares of common stock and 10,000 shares of 5 percent, $100 par value cumulative preferred stock outstanding. No dividends were declared on either the preferred or the common stock in 1998 or 1997. Net income for 1998 was $1,000,000. For 1998, earnings per common share amounted to
   a. $10.00.
   b. $9.50.
   c. $9.00.
   d. $5.00.
4. Earnings per share data must be reported on the face of the income statement for which of the following, assuming the firm has an accounting principle change it reports?

	Income from Continuing Operations	**Cumulative Effect of a Change in Accounting Principle**
a.	Yes	Yes
b.	Yes	No
c.	No	No
d.	No	Yes

5. Mann, Inc., had 300,000 shares of common stock issued and outstanding at December 31, 1996. On July 1, 1997, an additional 50,000 shares of common stock were issued for cash. Mann also had unexercised stock options to purchase 40,000 shares of common stock at $15 per share outstanding at the beginning and end of 1997. The average market price of Mann's common stock was $20 during 1997. What is the

number of shares that should be used in computing diluted earnings per share for the year ended December 31, 1997?

a. 325,000.

b. 335,000.

c. 360,000.

d. 365,000.

(AICPA adapted)

E 22–2
(L.O. 4, 5, 6, 7)

Calculating Diluted EPS

1. Jones Corporation's capital structure is:

	December 31	
	1997	**1996**
Outstanding shares of stock:		
Common	110,000	110,000
Convertible preferred	10,000	10,000
8 percent convertible bonds	$1,000,000	$1,000,000

During 1997, Jones paid dividends of $3.00 per share on its preferred stock. The preferred shares are convertible into 20,000 shares of common stock. The 8 percent bonds are convertible into 30,000 shares of common stock. Net income for 1997 is $850,000. Assume that the income tax rate is 30 percent. The diluted earnings per share for 1997 is

a. $5.48.

b. $5.66.

c. $5.81.

d. $6.26.

2. Antidilutive stock options would generally be used in the calculation of

	Basic Earnings per Share	**Diluted Earnings per Share**
a.	Yes	Yes
b.	Yes	No
c.	No	No
d.	No	Yes

3. Cox Corporation had 1,200,000 shares of common stock outstanding on January 1 and December 31, 1997. In connection with the acquisition of a subsidiary company in June 1996, Cox is required to issue 50,000 additional shares of its common stock on July 1, 1998, to the former owners of the subsidiary. Cox paid $200,000 in preferred stock dividends in 1997 and reported net income of $3,400,000 for the year. Cox's diluted earnings per share for 1997 should be

a. $2.83.

b. $2.72.

c. $2.67.

d. $2.56.

4. Newt Corporation had earnings per share of $12.00 for 1998, before taking any dilutive securities into consideration. No conversion or exercise of dilutive securities took place in 1998. However, possible conversion of convertible preferred stock would have reduced earnings per share to $11.90. The effect of possible exercise of common stock warrants would have reduced earnings per share by an additional $0.05. For 1998, what must Newt report as diluted earnings per share?

a. $12.00.

b. $11.95.

c. $11.90.

d. $11.85.

(AICPA adapted)

E 22–3
(L.O. 4, 5, 6)

Diluted EPS

1. Dilutive stock options would generally be used in the calculation of which of the following?

	Basic Earnings per Share	**Diluted Earnings per Share**
a.	No	No
b.	No	Yes
c.	Yes	Yes
d.	Yes	No

2. The if-converted method of computing earnings per share data assumes conversion of convertible securities as of the
   a. Beginning of the earliest period reported (or at time of issuance, if later).
   b. Beginning of the earliest period reported (regardless of time of issuance).
   c. Middle of the earliest period reported (regardless of time of issuance).
   d. Ending of the earliest period reported (regardless of time of issuance).
3. Suppose a company's convertible debt is dilutive in determining earnings per share. What would be the effect of considering the convertible debt in calculating the following?

	Basic Earnings per Share	**Diluted Earnings per Share**
a.	Decrease	Decrease
b.	Increase	No effect
c.	No effect	Decrease
d.	Decrease	Increase

4. In determining basic or diluted earnings per share, dividends on nonconvertible cumulative preferred stock should be
   a. Disregarded.
   b. Added back to net income whether declared or not.
   c. Deducted from net income only if declared.
   d. Deducted from net income whether declared or not.

(AICPA adapted)

E 22–4
(L.O. 2)

Analyze the Capital Structure: Average Shares, Compute EPS   At the end of 1997 the records of Block Corporation reflected the following:

Common stock, par $5, authorized 500,000 shares:	
Outstanding 1/1/1997, 400,000 shares	$2,000,000
Sold and issued 4/1/1997, 2,000 shares	10,000
Issued 5% stock dividend, 9/30/1997, 20,100 shares	100,500
Preferred stock, 6%, par $10, nonconvertible, noncumulative, authorized 50,000 shares,	
outstanding during year, 20,000 shares	200,000
Contributed capital in excess of par, common stock	180,000
Contributed capital in excess of par, preferred stock	100,000
Retained earnings (after the effects of current preferred dividends declared during 1997)	640,000
Bonds payable, 6½%, nonconvertible, issued at par 1/1/97	1,000,000
Income before extraordinary items	182,000
Extraordinary loss (net of tax)	(18,000)
Net income	164,000
Average income tax rate, 40%.	

Required

1. Is this a simple or complex capital structure? Explain.
2. What kind of EPS presentation is required? Explain.
3. Compute the required EPS amounts (show computations).
4. Compute the required EPS amounts, assuming that the preferred is cumulative.

E 22–5
(L.O. 2)

Analyze the Capital Structure: Average Shares, Compute EPS   The records for Potter Corporation, at the end of 1997, reflected the following:

Common stock, nopar, authorized 500,000 shares:	
Outstanding at beginning of year, 100,000 shares	$200,000
Sold and issued during the year, September 1, 3,000 shares	8,000
Preferred stock, 9%, par $10, nonconvertible, cumulative, authorized 20,000 shares, outstanding	
during the year, 6,000 shares	60,000
Contributed capital in excess of par, preferred stock	5,000
Retained earnings	150,000
Bonds payable, 6½%, nonconvertible, issued at par in 1994	400,000
Income before extraordinary items	130,000
Extraordinary gain (net of tax)	20,000
Net income	150,000

Required

1. Is this a simple or a complex capital structure? Explain.
2. What kind of EPS presentation is required? Explain.
3. Compute the required EPS amounts (show computations).

4. Compute the required EPS amounts, assuming that the preferred stock is noncumulative, the current year's dividend has not been declared, and the preceding year's dividend was passed (that is, not declared).

E 22–6
(L.O. 2)

Compute EPS for Three Years: Stock Dividend and Split   Rambo Corporation's accounting year ends on December 31. During the following three years, its common shares outstanding changed as follows:

	1998	1997	1996
Shares outstanding, January 1	150,000	120,000	100,000
Sales of shares, 4/1/1996			20,000
25% stock dividend, 7/1/1997		30,000	
2-for-1 stock split, 7/1/1998	150,000*		
Shares sold, 10/1/1998	50,000		
Shares outstanding, December 31	350,000	150,000	120,000
Net income	$375,000	$330,000	$299,000

*For each share turned in, two new shares were issued so that the shares doubled.

Required

1. For purposes of calculating EPS at the end of each year, for each year independently, determine the number of shares outstanding.
2. For purposes of calculating EPS at the end of 1998, when comparative statements are being prepared on a three-year basis, determine the number of shares outstanding for each year.
3. Compute EPS for each year based on year computations in (2).

E 22–7
(L.O. 2)

Analyze the Capital Structure: Stock Dividend, Compute EPS   At the end of 1997 the records of Bostix Corporation showed the following:

Common stock, nopar, authorized 250,000 shares:
Outstanding 1/1/1997, 84,000 shares $420,000
Purchased treasury shares 4/1/1997, 2,000 shares (at cost) . . . . (46,000)
Issued a 100% stock dividend on 12/1/1997 on outstanding shares (82,000 additional shares)

Preferred stock, par $10:
Class A, 6% nonconvertible, noncumulative, outstanding 20,000 shares 200,000
Class B, 8% nonconvertible, cumulative, outstanding 40,000 shares 400,000
Contributed capital in excess of par, preferred stock 200,000
Retained earnings (no dividends declared in 1997) 570,000
Bonds payable, 7%, nonconvertible, issued at par in 1993 120,000
Income before extraordinary items 360,000
Extraordinary gain (net of tax) 24,000
Net income 384,000
Average income tax rate, 40%.

Required

1. Is this a simple or a complex capital structure? Explain.
2. What kind of EPS presentation is required? Explain.
3. Compute the required EPS amounts (show computations).

E 22–8
(L.O. 3)

Compute Basic EPS: Different Kinds of Gains and Losses   To illustrate EPS reporting for various combinations of gains and losses, assume that 1,000 weighted-average shares of common stock for basic EPS are outstanding for the six cases given below.

Items	Case A (all gains)	Case B (all losses)	Case C (mixed)	Case D (mixed)	Case E (mixed)	Case F (mixed)
Income (loss) from continuing operations	$10,000	$(10,000)	$10,000	$(10,000)	$(10,000)	$10,000
Discontinued operations (loss)	3,000	(3,000)	(3,000)	3,000	(3,000)	(6,000)
Extraordinary gain (loss)	6,000	(6,000)	(6,000)	6,000	6,000	(6,000)
Net income (loss)	$19,000	$(19,000)	$ 1,000	$ (1,000)	$ (7,000)	$ (2,000)

Required

Compute basic EPS for each case.

E 22–9
(L.O. 4)

Computing and Reporting Basic EPS: Different Kinds of Gains and Losses   Using the data in Exercise 22–8, assume that the capital structure is complex, the weighted-average number of shares outstanding for basic EPS is 1,500, and the income and loss from continuing operations amounts are $12,000 instead of $10,000 for Cases A to F. In Case F assume an extraordinary gain of $9,000.

Required

1. Compute basic EPS for each case.
2. Give a proof for each result in requirement 1.
3. Suppose that extraordinary items produced a gain of $9,000 in Case D. What is the proper reporting?

E 22–10
(L.O. 3, 4)

Complex Capital Structure and Reporting EPS   The Omega Company reports the following:

Income from continuing operations	$1,000,000
Extraordinary item	3,000,000
Net income	$4,000,000

Shares outstanding:

For basic EPS	1,000,000
For diluted EPS	1,500,000

Income adjustments to be made:

	Income before Extraordinary Item	Net Income
For diluted EPS	$200,000	$200,000

Required   What EPS figures would Omega report? What are their values?

E 22–11
(L.O. 3, 4)

Complex Capital Structure and Reporting EPS   The Jones Company reports the following:

Income before extraordinary item	$1,000,000
Extraordinary item.	(20,000)
Net income.	$ 980,000

Shares outstanding:

For basic EPS	1,000,000
For diluted EPS	1,100,000

Income adjustments to be made:

	Income before Extraordinary Item	Net Income
For diluted EPS	$80,000	$80,000

Required   What EPS figures would Jones report? What are their values?

E 22–12
(L.O. 3, 4)

Contingent Shares and Computing EPS   In 1997, Xonacs acquired Realtest Service. The acquisition agreement included a commitment by Xonacs to the shareholders of Realtest that if 1998 net income exceeded $250,000, an additional 50,000 shares of Xonacs stock would be issued to the shareholders in 1999. Realtest's net income in 1997 was $250,000.

Required

1. Must Xonacs recognize the contingent shares in its 1997 EPS calculations?
2. Suppose Realtest's earnings in 1997 were $200,000. Would your answer be different?

E 22–13
(L.O. 3, 4, 5)

Options and the Computation of EPS   Rand Inc. had a net income from continuing operations of $800,000. During the year in question, 200,000 shares were outstanding on average. During the year, Rand's common stock sold at an average market price of $50. In addition, Rand had 20,000 options outstanding to purchase a total of 20,000 shares at $25 for each option exercised.

Required

1. Are the options dilutive? Compute basic EPS for income from continuing operations.
2. Compute diluted EPS.

E 22–14
(L.O. 1, 2, 6)

Convertible Bonds and the Calculation of Diluted EPS   Shaffer Corporation issued 100, $1,000, 10 percent convertible bonds in 1996 at face value. Each bond is convertible into 100 shares of common. Shaffer's net income from continuing operations for 1997 is $1,824,000 ($3,040,000 before tax). The $1,824,000 reflects one year's interest after tax. If you consider all factors except convertible bonds, average common shares outstanding for 1997 are 1,010,000.

Required

1. Compute DEPS (test for dilution).
2. How would you answer (1) if the bonds were issued July 1, 1997?
3. Ignoring (2), how would the answer to (1) change if half the bonds were converted July 1, 1997?

E 22–15
(L.O. 3, 4, 6)

Analyze Capital Structure: Stock Split, Convertible Securities, Compute EPS   At the end of 1997, the records of Ruso Corporation reflected the following:

Common stock, nopar, authorized 250,000 shares: issued and outstanding throughout the period to 12/1/1997, 60,000 shares. A stock split issued 12/1/1997 doubled outstanding shares	$840,000
Preferred stock, 5%, par $10, nonconvertible, cumulative, nonparticipating, shares authorized, issued, and outstanding during year, 10,000 shares	100,000
Contributed capital in excess of par, preferred stock	30,000
Retained earnings (no cash or property dividends during year)	570,000
Bonds payable, 8%, issued 1/1/1997; each $1,000 bond is convertible into 60 shares of common stock after the stock split on 12/1/1997 (bonds initially sold at par)	200,000
Income before extraordinary items	86,000
Extraordinary loss	(14,000)
Net income	72,000

Average income tax rate, 30%.

Required

1. Is this a simple or a complex capital structure? Explain.
2. What kind of EPS presentation is required? Explain.
3. Compute the required EPS amounts (show computations, rounded to two decimal places, and assume that all amounts are material).

E 22–16
(L.O. 3, 4, 5, 6)

Analyze Capital Structure: Nonconvertible Preferred, Stock Rights, Compute EPS   The records of Seedin Corporation as of December 31, 1997, showed the following:

Common stock, par $10, authorized 400,000 shares: issued and outstanding during 1997, 200,000 shares	$2,000,000
Contributed capital in excess of par, common stock	300,000
Common stock rights outstanding (for 20,000 shares of common stock)	200,000
Preferred stock, 6%, par $100, nonconvertible, cumulative: authorized, 40,000 shares, outstanding during 1997, 15,000 shares	1,500,000
Contributed capital in excess of par, preferred stock	400,000
Retained earnings	7,000,000
Net income	2,000,000

Additional data: Common stock rights issued on April 1, 1997; option price, $15 per share; average market price of common stock during the period (i.e., 4/1/1997–12/31/1997) the rights were outstanding, $25.

Required

1. Is this a simple or a complex capital structure? Explain.
2. Prepare the required EPS presentation for 1997. Show all computations.

E 22–17
(L.O. 3, 4, 5, 6, 7)

Analyze Capital Structure: Stock Rights, Preferred Stock, Compute EPS   At the end of 1997 the records of Wolverine Corporation reflected the following:

Common stock, par $10; authorized 100,000 shares: issued and outstanding throughout the year, 50,000 shares	$500,000
Stock rights outstanding (all year for 10,000 shares of common stock at $15 per share)	100,000
Preferred stock, par $50, 7%, cumulative, convertible into common stock share for share, authorized, 10,000 shares; issued and outstanding throughout year, 2,000 shares	100,000
Contributed capital in excess of par, common stock	80,000
Retained earnings (no dividends declared during the year)	470,000
Bonds payable, 10% nonconvertible, issued at par in 1993	150,000
Income before extraordinary items	85,000
Extraordinary gain (net of tax)	35,000
Net income	120,000

Average income tax rate, 30%.
Average market price of the common stock during 1997, $25 per share.
Aa bond interest rate at date of issuance of preferred stock, 10%.

Required

1. Is this a simple or complex capital structure? Explain.
2. What kind of EPS presentation is required? Explain.
3. Compute the required EPS amounts (show computations and assume that all amounts are material).

E 22–18
(L.O. 6, 7)

Convertible Securities, D/A Method   Spencer Inc.'s 1998 earnings of $500,000 reflect a combined tax rate of 40%. During the entire year, Spencer had the following securities outstanding:

120,000 shares of common stock
5,000 shares of 6%, $100 par, nonconvertible, cumulative preferred stock
5,000 shares of 6%, $100 par, cumulative preferred stock, each convertible into 1.75 shares of common stock
500 bonds, $1,000 face value, 8% coupon interest, each convertible into 30 shares of common stock (issued at face value)
200 bonds, $1,000 face value, 6% coupon interest, each convertible into 20 shares of common stock (issued at face value)

Required

Compute the 1998 per share amounts that Spencer must report.

▌ *PROBLEMS*

P 22–1
(L.O. 3, 4, 6, 7)

Analyze Capital Structure: Stock Dividend, Convertible Securities, Compute EPS   At the end of 1997, the records of Richardson Corporation showed the following:

Common stock, nopar, authorized 400,000 shares:	
Outstanding 1/1/1997, 200,000 shares	$1,650,000
Treasury shares acquired 6/1/1997, 1,000 shares (at cost)	(15,000)
Stock dividend issued, 11/1/1997, 19,900 shares (10%, one additional share for each 10	
shares outstanding)	398,000
Preferred stock, 4%, par $20, noncumulative, nonconvertible, authorized, issued, and	
outstanding throughout the year, 10,000 shares	200,000
Contributed capital in excess of par, preferred stock	75,000
Retained earnings (no cash or property dividends declared during 1997)	942,000
Bonds payable, Series A, 7%, each $1,000 bond is convertible to 20 shares of common stock	
after stock dividend (bonds issued at par in 1994)	50,000
Bonds payable, Series B, 6%, each $1,000 bond is convertible to 57 shares of common stock	
after stock dividend (bonds issued at par in 1995)	400,000
Income before extraordinary gain	380,000
Extraordinary gain (net of tax)	15,000
Net income	395,000
Average income tax rate for 1997, 30%.	
Both bond series were issued prior to January 1, 1997.	

Required

1. Is this a simple or a complex capital structure? Explain.
2. Prepare the EPS presentation with all supporting computations.

P 22–2
(L.O. 3, 4, 5, 6, 7)

Analyze Capital Structure: Stock Rights and Convertible Securities, Compute EPS   Jiffie Corporation is developing its EPS presentation at December 31, 1997. The records of the company provide the following information:

Liabilities

Convertible bonds payable, 7% (each $1,000 bond is convertible to 100 shares of common stock)	$150,000

Stockholders' Equity

Common stock, nopar, authorized 100,000 shares:	
Outstanding 1/1/1997, 59,000 shares	214,000
Sold and issued 10,000 shares on 4/1/1997	40,000
Common stock rights outstanding (all year for 4,000 shares of common stock)	16,000
Preferred stock, par $10, 6%, cumulative, convertible (each share is convertible into ½ of 1	
share of common stock), authorized 10,000 shares, outstanding during 1997, 5,000 shares	50,000
Contributed capital in excess of par, preferred stock	15,000
Retained earnings	452,000
Income before extraordinary items	110,000
Extraordinary gain (net of tax)	20,000
Net income	130,000

Additional data:

a. Stock rights: option price, $4 per share; average market price of the common stock during 1997, $6.
b. Convertible bonds: issue price, par.
c. Average income tax rate, 30 percent.

Required

1. Is this a simple or a complex capital structure? Explain.
2. What kind of EPS presentation is required? Explain.
3. Prepare the required EPS presentation for 1997. Show all computations.

P 22–3
(L.O. 3, 4, 5, 6)

Complex Capital Structure: Partial Year, Compute EPS for Two Alternatives   Falcon Company has a compensatory stock option plan under which options to buy 255,000 common shares were issued in 1997. These options are exercisable during 1998 and 1999 at $16 per share. In 1998, Falcon reported net income of $500,000; the company's capital structure remained unchanged that year.

Outstanding stock consists of 1 million common shares, which traded at an average price of $20 per share throughout 1998. The company's long-term debt consists of a $2,500,000 bond issue sold at par, which pays 12 percent annual interest and was outstanding throughout 1998. Falcon had no other indebtedness. Falcon's average income tax rate is 30 percent.

Required

1. Compute basic and diluted EPS for 1998.
2. Suppose the facts given above are modified as follows: Falcon issued the stock options on July 1, 1998. The per share market price of Falcon's stock also averaged $20 throughout the last half of 1998. Compute diluted EPS for 1998.

P 22–4
(L.O. 3, 4, 6, 7)

Analyze Capital Structure: Convertible Bonds Sold at a Premium, Compute EPS   At the end of 1997, the records of Watson Corporation reflected the following information:

Common stock, nopar, authorized 500,000 shares:	
Outstanding 1/1/1997, 150,000 shares	$256,000
Sold and issued on 8/1/1997, 15,000 shares	30,000
Bonds payable, 6% convertible	150,000
Premium on bonds payable	13,800
Retained earnings	900,000
Net income	360,000

The convertible bonds were issued on July 1, 1997 to yield 4.03 percent. Interest is paid semiannually, on January 1 and July 1. Each $1,000 bond is convertible to 20 shares of common stock. Premium amortization related to the bonds during 1997 was $1,200. Watson's average income tax rate during 1997 was 40 percent.

Required

1. Is this a simple or a complex capital structure? Explain.
2. Prepare the required EPS presentation for 1997. Show all computations.

P 22–5
(L.O. 3, 4, 5, 6, 7)

Analyze Capital Structure: Stock Warrants, Nonconvertible Securities, Compute EPS   The records of Jefferson Corporation reflected the following data at the end of 1997:

Liabilities

Bonds payable, 5%, convertible (each $1,000 bond is convertible to 40 shares of common stock)	$150,000

Stockholders' Equity

Common stock, par $2, authorized 400,000 shares:	
Outstanding 1/1/1997, 150,000 shares	300,000
Sold and issued on 10/1/1997, 20,000 shares	40,000
Common stock warrants outstanding (all year for 6,000 shares)	12,000
Preferred stock, 6%, par $5, nonconvertible, cumulative; authorized 100,000 shares;	
outstanding during 1997, 20,000 shares	100,000
Contributed capital in excess of par, common stock	375,000
Contributed capital in excess of par, preferred stock	45,000
Retained earnings	280,000
Income before extraordinary items	170,000
Extraordinary loss (net of tax)	(20,000)
Net income	150,000

Additional data:

a. Stock warrants: option price, $3 per share; average market price of common stock during 1997, $3.60 per share.

b. Convertible bonds: issue price, par.

c. Average income tax rate, 30 percent.

Required

1. Is this a simple or complex capital structure? Explain.
2. What kind of EPS presentation is required? Explain.
3. Prepare the required EPS presentation for 1997. Show all computations.

P 22–6
(L.O. 3, 4, 6, 7)

Analyze Capital Structure: Stock Dividend, Convertible Securities, Compute EPS   At the end of 1997, the records of Luholtz Corporation reflected the following:

Common stock, nopar, authorized 500,000 shares; issued and outstanding throughout period, 100,000 shares	$680,000
Stock dividend issued, 12/31/1997, 50,000 shares (not included in the 100,000 shares above)	340,000
Retained earnings (after effect of dividends on all shares)	500,000
Bonds payable, 4½%; each $1,000 bond is convertible to 80 shares of common stock after the stock dividend (bonds issued at par in 1995)	100,000
Bonds payable, 6½%; each $1,000 bond is convertible to 90 shares of common stock after the stock dividend (bonds issued at par in 1995)	300,000
Income before extraordinary items	210,000
Extraordinary gain	12,000
Net income	222,000
Average income tax rate, 40%.	

Required

1. Is this a simple or a complex capital structure? Explain.
2. What kind of EPS presentation is required? Explain.
3. Prepare the required EPS disclosures.

P 22–7
(L.O. 3, 4, 6)

Computing a Loss per Share   Wilson Corporation's financial statements at December 31, 1998, reported:

Accrued interest payable	$ 1,000
Long-term notes payable, 10%, due in 2001	50,000
Bonds payable, 7%; each $1,000 of face value is convertible into 90 shares of common stock; bonds mature in 2010, issued at par in 1996	800,000
Preferred stock, 5%, nonconvertible, cumulative, par value $100, issued in 1989	300,000
Common stock, par value $5 outstanding all year	700,000
Common stock rights outstanding all year entitling holders to acquire 40,000 shares of common stock at $9 per share	200,000
Net loss for 1998	125,000

Additional data:

a. During 1998, 1,000 shares of preferred stock were issued at par on July 1. Dividends are paid semiannually, on May 31 and November 30. Declaration precedes payment by three weeks. On newly issued shares, dividends are prorated from issue date.

b. Average market price of common stock during 1998 was $10.

c. Wilson's income tax rate is 30 percent.

Required

Compute the EPS amount that Wilson must report on the income statement for 1998. Show all computations.

P 22–8
(L.O. 2, 3, 4, 5, 6)

Compute Average Number of Shares Outstanding and EPS   Zolar Corporation reported basic earnings per share of $22,875,000 ÷ 10,500,000 = $2.18 based on the following data:

Net income	$22,875,000
Common shares:	
January 1, 1997	12,000,000
December 31, 1997	9,000,000
Average number of shares outstanding	10,500,000

After examining Zolar's records, you note that Zolar acquired and retired 4 million shares on April 1, 1997, and issued 1,000,000 shares to satisfy all employee options outstanding on September 30, 1997. No equity securities besides common are outstanding, and Zolar has no convertible securities or other options outstanding.

Required

1. Is Zolar's EPS calculation correct or not? Explain.
2. Revise the EPS figure if you think it is in error.
3. Suppose the facts above are altered thus:
   a. An additional 500,000 options allowing holders to subscribe to 500,000 shares at $25 a share are outstanding all of 1997. The average stock price during the year is $30.
   b. Zolar has outstanding 100,000 shares of $100 par, 5 percent cumulative preferred, issued to yield 5 percent on September 9, 1991. The dividend was paid in 1997.

   What changes are required in the EPS calculations for diluted EPS?

P 22–9
(L.O. 3, 4)

Determine Capital Structure; Calculate and Report EPS Taft Corporation had net income from continuing operations of $6.7 million for 1997. Taft also settled legal claims of $1 million, which it shows as an extraordinary item of $.74 million after tax. Taft also reported a $1.23 million after-tax loss on the disposal of its textile subsidiary. Taft uses a calendar year reporting period.

Taft's capital structure consists of:

Preferred: 100,000 shares of $100 par, 8 percent cumulative nonconvertible preferred issued in 1991. The dividend was passed this year.

Common: Outstanding January 1, 1997, 4,271,865 shares, $1 par. Dividends of 25 cents per share were paid in 1997. On July 1, 1997, a three-for-one stock split was declared and the shares issued.

Required

1. What type of capital structure does Taft have (simple or complex)?
2. Compute and label the relevant EPS figures.
3. Must the EPS figures for the law settlement and discontinued operations be reported?

P 22–10
(L.O. 2, 3, 4, 6, 7)

Compute Basic and Diluted EPS Zorbas Inc. needs to establish its EPS figures for its 1997 reports. The following information is available to Deb Its, Zorbas' controller:

a. Net income $30 million (before tax, $50 million).
b. Common stock (20 million shares authorized; 15 million shares outstanding January 1, 1997).
c. Cumulative convertible preferred stock (2 million shares issued August 1, 1994, and outstanding January 1, 1997). The stock was issued at $50 a share with a yearly $4 dividend paid semiannually June 30 and December 31. The stock is convertible on a share-for-share basis adjusted automatically for any stock dividends or splits. Dividends are paid for time stock is held.
d. March 1, 1997: Half the preferred was converted to common.
e. April 1, 1997: Zorbas declared a 10 percent stock dividend.
f. July 1, 1997: One million shares of stock were issued in the acquisition of the Tande Corporation. The stock's market value at this time was $15 a share.
g. October 1, 1997: Zorbas purchased and retired 600,000 shares of its common stock for $700,000.
h. All preferred dividends were declared and paid.

Required

1. Establish the number of shares to be used in computing basic EPS for 1997.
2. Establish the number of shares to be used in computing diluted EPS for 1997.
3. Compute basic EPS.
4. Compute diluted EPS.
5. What additional considerations are required if Zorbas had issued convertible debt?

P 22–11
(L.O. 4, 6, 7)

Computing and Reporting DEPS A medium-sized retailer provided the following abbreviated financial data for its most recently ended fiscal year (amounts in thousands including shares).

Income before extraordinary loss	$10,000
Extraordinary loss, net of tax	(8,000)
Net income.	$ 2,000

The weighted average of shares of common stock outstanding for the period were 5,000.

Outstanding were convertible bonds that were issued several years before at a discount. These bonds provide a significant portion of the long-term financing for this firm. The accountant for the firm provides you with intermediate results that can help you determine the required EPS reporting for the firm:

After-tax interest on the convertible bonds for the period:	$1,800
Shares of common stock that would be issued upon conversion:	1,000

Required

1. Prepare the EPS figures that must be reported by this firm for the current year.
2. Did you allow for any antidilution in your answer in (1)? If so, what is the rationale for allowing antidilutive reporting in this instance?

P 22–12
(L.O. 5)

Appendix: Computing the Average Market Price of Common Stock   The treasury stock method requires that an average market price for the common be established. This average can be calculated in several ways. Two commonly used computations, based on the weekly prices for a three-month period, are provided following the basic data.

Basic Data: Three-Month Stock Price Data

	Week	High	Low	Close	Shares Traded
Month 1	1	21	19	20	300
	2	24	20	23	700
	3	24	22	22	500
	4	23	21	21	500
Month 2	5	26	22	23	1,000
	6	27	23	26	1,200
	7	29	27	28	1,500
	8	31	29	31	2,000
Month 3	9	28	26	26	2,500
	10	26	22	23	1,500
	11	24	22	22	1,000
	12	22	20	21	800
	13	20	20	20	500

1. A simple average of monthly prices is normally adequate unless prices fluctuate greatly, in which case weekly (or even daily) prices are preferable.
2. The average of the market's closing price, used consistently, is satisfactory unless, again, prices fluctuate widely, in which case an average of the high and low prices for the period would be preferable.

Required

1. Compute a simple average price for the three-month period using monthly closing prices.
2. Compute a simple average for the three-month period using the averages of the weekly high–low prices.
3. Which of the two methods seems most appropriate in this case? Why?

P 22–13
(L.O. 5)

Appendix: Application of Treasury Stock Method for Options   The Elax Company has 200,000 common shares outstanding along with 20,000 options that are exercisable at $40 per share. Each option allows the holder to obtain one share upon exercise. The average market prices for the common over the last three years were:

Quarter	Year 1 Average Price	Year 2 Average Price	Year 3 Average Price
1	36	48	40
2	40*	44	36
3	44	40	48
4	48	36	44

*Assume market prices exceeded $40 for substantially all of the previous quarter.

Required

Compute the number of incremental shares for diluted EPS for each quarter, and the year for each year.

P 22–14
(L.O. 1–7)

 **Calculating Earnings per Share**   (This problem can be worked as a group problem.) The following facts pertain to Conway Company:

Year Ended December 31, 1997

From the income statement:
  Net Income $10,500,000

From the balance sheet:
  Long-term debt:
    10% convertible debentures, due October 1, 2006 . . . . $10,000,000

Stockholders' equity (Note 1):

   Convertible voting preferred stock of $1 par value, 20-cent cumulative dividend.

     Authorized, 600,000 shares; issued and outstanding, 600,000. Liquidation value $22 per

      share, aggregating $13,200,000   600,000

   Common stock of $1 par value per share; authorized, 5,000,000 shares; issued and

     outstanding, 3,400,000 for the entire year 3,400,000

Note 1

The 20-cent convertible preferred stock is callable by the company after March 31, 1996, at $53 per share. Each share is convertible into one share of common stock.

Warrants to acquire 500,000 shares of the company's stock at $60 per share were outstanding at the end of 1997.

Other information:

a. The average market value of the common stock during 1997 was:

	Average
First quarter	$50
Second quarter	$60
Third quarter	$70
Fourth quarter	$70

b. Cash dividends of 12½ cents per common share were declared and paid for each quarter of 1997.

c. 10 percent convertible debentures with a principal amount of $10,000,000 due October 1, 2006, were sold for cash at a price of $98 on October 1, 1996. Each $100 debenture is convertible into two shares of common stock. Discount is amortized on a straight-line basis.

d. The 600,000 shares of convertible preferred stock were issued for assets in a purchase transaction on April 1, 1997. The annual dividend on each share of this convertible preferred stock is 20 cents. Each share is convertible into one share of common stock. The market value of the convertible preferred stock was $53 at the time of issuance.

e. Warrants to buy 500,000 shares of common stock at $60 per share for a period of five years were issued along with the convertible preferred stock mentioned in (*d*).

f. 3.3 million shares of common stock were outstanding at the end of 1996. There have been no conversions or warrants exercised in 1997.

g. An average tax rate of 40 percent is assumed.

Required

1. Determine whether dilutive securities exist and if so, compute the number of potentially dilutive shares. Use quarterly calculations for warrant shares.
2. Calculate basic EPS.
3. Calculate diluted EPS.

P 22–15
(L.O. 6)

Convertible Bonds, Amortization   Wonder Company began 1998 with 200,000 shares of common stock outstanding. The following data pertain to Wonder's EPS disclosures for 1998:

1. Purchased 40,000 shares of common stock for the treasury on April 1.
2. Issued 2,000 convertible bonds at 104 on June 1. Each 8%, $1,000 bond is convertible into 15 shares of common stock. The bond term is twenty years.
3. Net income for 1998 was $620,000 which included an $80,000 after-tax cumulative effect of an accounting change (cr.).
4. The tax rate is 40%.

Required

Prepare Wonder's EPS disclosures for 1998. Assume Wonder discloses all per share amounts on the face of the income statement.

P22–16
(L.O. 6)

Convertible Securities, Actual Conversion, Antidilution   Bridgeman Company, a large national baking firm headquartered in San Francisco, reported the following data for the current year:

Net income, $2,220,000

Extraordinary loss (after tax), $2,200,000

Common shares outstanding at the beginning of the year, 800,000

Nonconvertible cumulative preferred stock, $100 par, $8 dividend per year, 100,000 shares outstanding all year

Issued 200,000 shares of common stock on October 1

Convertible cumulative preferred stock, $100 par, $7 dividend per year, 50,000 shares outstanding at the beginning of the year. 20,000 shares converted on March 31. 40,000 shares of common stock were issued on conversion.

For both preferred stock issues, assume dividends are paid for time held.

Required

1. Prepare the EPS presentation. Assume all per share amounts are disclosed in the income statement.
2. Explain the reason for any antidilutive reporting required in this situation.

P 22–17
(L.O. 7)

D/A Method McLaughlin's, Inc., an international tea merchant, has a complex capital structure with several potentially dilutive securities. Outstanding for the entire current year were the following:

> Common stock, 10,000 shares
> Options to purchase 2,000 shares at $8. The average market price of common stock for the year was $12
> 500, 6%, $1,000 bonds, each convertible into 10 shares of common stock (issued at face value)
> 200, 8%, $1,000 bonds, each convertible into 30 shares of common stock (issued at face value)
> 1,000 shares of 9%, $100 par cumulative preferred stock, each convertible into 6 shares of common stock
> No options or warrants were exercised or converted during the period.
> The tax rate is 40%.
> Net income from continuing operations, $60,000
> Net gain from discontinued operations, $10,000

Required

Prepare the required EPS presentation for the current year. Assume all per share amounts are shown in the income statement.

P 22–18
(L.O. 5)

Appendix: Treasury Stock Method by Quarters Josh Jeans Company, a direct competitor of New Mexico Jeans Inc., earned $1,000,000 for the current year. Net income was earned evenly throughout the year. Josh had 450,000 shares of common stock outstanding all year. Also, 1,000,000 options to buy Josh common stock for $10 per share were outstanding all year. The average market prices of Josh common stock per share for the current year by quarter were:

Quarter 1	$20
Quarter 2	12
Quarter 3	8
Quarter 4	13

Required

Compute basic and diluted EPS for each quarter, and for the year as a whole.

P 22–19
(L.O. 4)

Contingent Share Agreement PellCo is subject to an agreement whereby it must issue shares to shareholders of a firm it recently acquired, if certain conditions are met. These shares are issuable the year following the year in which the relevant conditions are met. The agreement specifies:

1. PellCo will issue 20 shares for each $1,000 in net income of the combined enterprise in excess of $100,000.
2. PellCo will issue 1,000 shares for each new patent awarded to the recently acquired subsidiary (a research enterprise) during the year.
3. PellCo will issue 50 shares for each $5 increase in the market price of PellCo's stock above the price at the beginning of the year.

> Data for the current year:
> Beginning stock price: $30
> Patent awards:

Quarter	Patents Awarded*	Ending Stock Price	Earnings
1	0	$37	$120,000
2	2	42	130,000
3	1	28	(180,000)
4	0	41	120,000
			$190,000

*Patents are awarded at mid-quarter.

Required

Determine the quarterly and annual contingent shares to be included in basic and diluted EPS for the current year.

CASES

C 22–1
(L.O. 1)

Importance of EPS Figures On July 24, 1990, the Financial Accounting Standards Advisory Council (FASAC) met with SEC Commissioner Philip Lochner and SEC Chief Accountant Edward Coulson to discuss the effect of accounting standards on U.S. competitiveness. At that meeting, Dennis Dammerman, senior vice president for finance of General Electric Company and a member of FASAC, stated, "The chief executive officers of America, right or wrong, get their report card at least once a quarter and it's generally called earnings per share and that report card reflects accounting."

What relevance do you believe this statement has to US competitive strengths? What is your position on the relationship between US competitiveness and accounting standards concerning EPS? Why do you think the issue was raised with the FASAC?

C 22–2
(L.O. 1)

The Logic for Some EPS Calculations   Many people believe that earnings per share is the single most salient fact most financial statement readers examine. Together with earnings, it is also the most commonly reported statistic about a company's yearly activities. Discuss the following issues.

Required

1. If a convertible debenture exists,
    a. When is it considered in calculating EPS? Why?
    b. If it reduces EPS to consider it (as if) converted, what calculations need to be made?
2. In applying the treasury stock method, why must the firm first use the funds to repurchase common shares for the treasury?
3. If a 10 percent stock dividend is issued halfway through the year, how many additional shares are added to the denominator of the EPS calculation? Does the answer change if the same number of shares are issued for cash? Why?

C 22–3
(L.O. 1–7)

Coca-Cola   This problem refers to the financial statements for the Coca-Cola Company given at the end of this book.

1. What EPS values for net income from continuing operations and net income did Coca-Cola report for 1995?
2. The Coca-Cola Company Board authorized a two-for-one split on December 21, 1995. What numbers would the company have reported for EPS in 1995 if this event had occurred much earlier in 1995?
3. Does Coca-Cola have any convertible securities? Does it have any stock options outstanding on December 31, 1995?
4. Does Coca-Cola have a simple or complex capital structure?

| *ANALYSIS, JUDGMENT & COMMUNICATION*

| *ANALYZING FINANCIAL STATEMENTS*

All questions in this section are based on information taken from the financial statements of actual companies. Assume *SFAS No. 128* is in effect.

A 22–1
(L.O. 2, 3, 4, 6)

EPS Disclosures   American Home Products Corporation (AHP), a large company in the health care field, reported the following information (dollar amounts in thousands) in its December 31, 1995, consolidated statement of income:

Net income.	$1,680,418
Net income per share of common stock	$ 5.42

Required

1. Estimate the average number of common shares outstanding for 1995. Assume that AHP has outstanding the entire year $108 thousand of $2 preferred stock, par value $2.50; 5 million shares authorized. Indicate any assumptions you are making. The stock is not convertible.
2. Does AHP have a simple or complex capital structure?
3. Is AHP required to report EPS figures for the cumulative effect of an accounting change, if present, in their income statement?

| *COMPARATIVE ANALYSIS*

CA 22–1
(L.O. 1)

Comparison of PepsiCo and Coca-Cola   (This problem can be worked as a group problem.) This problem requires using the World Wide Web. The problem should be worked using the most recent available statements on the Web. You can find the statements under the SEC's Electronic Data Gathering, Analysis and Retrieval System (EDGAR). Use the following steps:

1. URL: http://www.sec.gov/index.html
2. Click on EDGAR Database of Corporate Information
3. Click on Search the EDGAR Database
4. Click on Search the EDGAR Archives
5. Enter the company name in the search dialog box
6. Click on the listing for the most recent 10K annual report
7. Use the Edit Find, in the toolbar, (or page down) to locate the financial statements

Consider the data on each firm's EPS. If you were constrained to consider only the EPS data, how would you respond to the query as to which firm appears to be more successful? If, as would be the case in practice, you could consider the additional material in the financial statements, what would you conclude? Can you identify other sources of relevant data?

V

SPECIAL TOPICS

23 STATEMENT OF CASH FLOWS

After you have studied this chapter, you will:

1. Have a familiarity with the evolution, development, and usefulness of the statement of cash flows.

2. Know the main provisions of *SFAS No. 95,* "Statement of Cash Flows."

3. Be able to analyze transactions to identify disclosures in the statement of cash flows.

4. Know how to prepare a statement of cash flows by analyzing transactions.

5. Be familiar with the spreadsheet approach to preparing a statement of cash flows.

INTRODUCTION

The previous chapter discussed earnings per share, a widely used measure of business performance. However, positive earnings do not necessarily imply a positive cash flow. Operations ultimately must provide enough cash to pay the bills. Many firms have ceased operations because they could not satisfy their creditors, while reporting positive earnings. A third required statement, the **statement of cash flows,** helps financial statement users assess the ability of a firm to generate cash in amounts sufficient to pay its debts, pay dividends, and take advantage of growth opportunities.

One of the more important uses of the statement of cash flows is to help financial statement users understand the difference between net income, an *accrual* measure, and net cash provided by operations, a *cash-basis* measure. In many cases these two amounts are significantly different.

Example   For fiscal 1996, Apple Computer Inc. reported a net *loss* of $816 million, yet received $519 million *more* in cash from sales and other operating activities than it paid out. In other words, Apple generated a significant amount of cash from operations but reported negative earnings. What caused the difference between these two amounts? A closer look at Apple's income statement reveals no significant unusual noncash charges. The answer is found in the statement of cash flows. During 1996, Apple's inventories and accounts receivable decreased a combined total of $1.55 billion, an amount that explains most of the difference between the negative *earnings* and positive *net operating cash flow.* Apple drew down its inventories causing cost of goods sold to increase without any related cash outflow, and collected much more accounts receivable than it established through sales.[1]

---

[1]Apple is by no means unusual. Many companies report vast differences between earnings and net operating cash flow.

The annual reports of large firms typically disclose cash flow statements for the most recent three years. This information allows users to spot trends and trouble spots in a firm's ability to generate cash. Cash flow problems often create considerable concern for management, shareholders, and stock analysts.

Example   Lawrence Bossidy, chairman of Allied-Signal, the aerospace-automotive engineering and materials conglomerate, was quite concerned with a prediction of negative cash flow for his firm, as his memo to his unit general managers and presidents indicates:

> Cash flow is a critical issue for the company. Not only is it the fuel for our growth, but it is an indication of operational efficiency. Our second-quarter cash flow, coupled with the results of the first quarter, may cause the analysts who follow Allied-Signal to question our performance. Please make cash flow a priority.[2]

The statement of cash flows also supplies information not disclosed in the income statement, balance sheet, or footnotes. For example, how much did Microsoft spend on software development? What was Coca-Cola's cash outlay for capital expenditures? How much did Chrysler receive when it issued new stock? Answers to these and other questions often are found in the statement of cash flows. Cash flow information is a vital part of a complete set of financial statements. This chapter discusses the use and preparation of the statement of cash flows. In doing so, it extends our introductory discussion of cash flows in Chapter 5.

CASH FLOW REPORTING: DEVELOPMENT AND USEFULNESS

The **statement of cash flows (SCF)** is a report listing cash inflows and outflows by category. It explains the change in cash during the period. Firms have not always been required to present a cash flow statement. Before *APB Opinion No. 19,* "Reporting Changes in Financial Position," (1971) some firms voluntarily disclosed the sources and uses of funds in a variety of formats.

The *Opinion* required a statement of changes in financial position and allowed several fund definitions, including working capital and cash. *SFAS No. 95,* "Statement of Cash Flows," (1987) superseded *APB Opinion No. 19* by requiring business enterprises to provide a statement of cash flows whenever a balance sheet and income statement are reported.[3] Separate disclosure of operating, investing, and financing cash flows is required.

The Trend toward Cash Flows

Between 1980 and 1986, the percentage of 600 surveyed firms defining funds as cash in the statement of changes in financial position grew from 10 percent to 66 percent.[4] Investors and creditors found cash flow information increasingly valuable for assessing a firm's liquidity and risk.[5]

Increased Business Risk   Beginning in the mid-1970s, an increase in business failures and suits against auditors for not adequately warning of those impending failures contributed to an increased interest in cash flow information. A growing bankruptcy rate, as well as general economic indicators, pointed to an overall increase in risk.

Example   The average current ratio of U.S. manufacturing firms fell from 2.67 to 1.71 between 1947 and 1979, suggesting a general deterioration in financial condition.[6] More

---

[2]"Allied-Signal Cash Flow Falls Short," *The Wall Street Journal,* July 10, 1996, p. C1.

[3]*SFAS No. 102,* which amends *SFAS No. 95,* exempts defined benefit pension plans and investment companies, subject to certain requirements.

[4]*Accounting Trends and Techniques—1987* (New York: AICPA, 1987), p. 109. The 1984 edition reflected a threefold increase in the number of firms categorizing cash flows into operating, investing, and financing from the year before.

[5]Louis Harris and Associates, *A Study of the Attitudes toward and an Assessment of the Financial Accounting Standards Board* (Stamford, CT: FASB, April 1980, p. 13), found that 67 percent of those interviewed rated cash flow information as highly important.

[6]FASB, *Reporting Funds Flows, Liquidity, and Financial Flexibility, Discussion Memorandum* (Norwalk, CT: FASB, 1980), p. 27.

recently, a nationwide survey of 350 companies found that uneven cash flow was the most pressing financial problem facing small companies.[7]

Example   The W. T. Grant bankruptcy demonstrates the value of cash flow information in assessing risk. W. T. Grant filed for bankruptcy in 1975. In 1973, Grant's common stock was selling for 20 times earnings per share, a high level by historical standards. Income and working capital provided by operations were positive from 1966 through 1974, and the company paid regular dividends in that period. Yet, during the decade before bankruptcy, the company generated almost no cash from *operations*. Except for two years when net operating cash flow was minimal, operations consumed, rather than provided cash between 1966 and 1974. The decline in operating cash flows preceded bankruptcy by a decade. Those investors acting on cash flow information, rather than income and other traditional financial ratios, avoided losses.[8]

Previous Funds Statements   A lack of uniformity in format and content of funds statements and the variety of fund definitions also contributed to an increased interest in standardizing cash flow information. Specifically, a strong working capital position does not necessarily imply a strong cash flow. A firm with healthy working capital but also with large inventories, prepaids, and receivables might be in a weak cash position. W. T. Grant is an example.

Differences between Cash and Accrual Accounting   Another factor in the trend toward cash flow reporting is the increased complexity of financial accounting principles. Accounting pronouncements on leases, pensions, foreign exchange, tax allocation, and investments have made financial statements more complicated. The inherent complexity of current accounting principles, along with management's flexibility to choose among several reporting choices allowing manipulation of earnings under current GAAP, and the lack of a general relationship between earnings and cash flow, leads to a preference by many financial statement users for cash flow information.

Accrual accounting matches efforts (costs) and results (revenues). The resulting earnings figure reflects changes in financial position, rather than the immediate cash consequences. Financial statement users find earnings information valuable because, in the long run, profits determine the success of a company.

In the shorter run, however, cash flow information is significant. It indicates whether a borrower will produce sufficient cash to pay its liabilities. Business creditors are interested in the historical record of cash inflows and outflows, for the same reasons that a mortgage lender insists on knowing the borrower's credit history and cash income.

Usefulness of Cash Flow Information

Many analysts use cash flow information in making recommendations about buying and selling. For example, operating cash flow is a primary performance measure for cable television companies.[9] Investors often avoid companies without **free cash flow,** generally defined as operating cash receipts less necessary operating and capital expenditures, and debt service payments.[10] Free cash flow can be used to repurchase stock, pay dividends, expand, acquire other businesses, pay debts, or to invest in securities. If free cash flow is negative, the deficiency must be made up with additional debt or equity financing.

The trend of cash flows over several periods allows an assessment of **financial flexibility,** the ability to use cash flows to meet unexpected needs and opportunities. A firm able to raise additional capital in the debt and equity markets, to sell nonoperating assets, and

---

[7]"Private Companies Practice Section Small Business Poll Finds Concern over Cash Flow," *Journal of Accountancy,* July 1990, p. 16.

[8]J. Largay and C. Stickney, "Cash Flows, Ratio Analysis, and the W. T. Grant Company Bankruptcy," *Financial Analysts Journal,* July–August, 1980, p. 51.

[9]"New York Cable Firm Posts Narrower Loss for Quarter," *The Wall Street Journal,* October 19, 1992, p. B4.

[10]The Coca-Cola Company defines free cash flow as cash from operations remaining after deducting net investment expenditures. The management discussion and analysis section of the firm's annual report, reproduced at the end of this text, explains how free cash flow is calculated and used.

to increase cash inflows by increasing efficiency and lowering costs is financially flexible. Healthy operating cash flows imply financial flexibility.

Cash flow information helps users to understand the relationship between income and cash flow and to forecast future operating cash flows. Cash flow information also provides feedback about past decisions, such as the cash flow effects of previous investment decisions, how capital expenditures were financed, and the amount of debt issued or retired.

Cash flow information also helps explain changes in balance sheet accounts, such as increases in long-term debt, and whether cash was affected. Cash flow reporting answers these questions as well as provides information about investing and financing activities.

THE STATEMENT OF CASH FLOWS AND THE REQUIREMENTS OF *SFAS No. 95*

The purpose of the SCF is to provide relevant information about cash receipts and disbursements. Cash flow information helps users assess

- A firm's ability to generate cash.
- A firm's ability to meet its obligations.
- The reasons for differences between income and associated cash flows.
- The effect of cash and noncash investing and financing activities on a firm's financial position.

By listing cash flows in meaningful categories and disclosing significant noncash investing and financing activities, the SCF details the cash consequences of operations and the changes in balance sheet accounts arising from investing and financing activities.

Exhibit 23–1 categorizes the 1998 cash flows of Simple Company, a hypothetical firm, into operating, investing, and financing classifications. The reasons why Simple's cash and cash equivalents increased $34 (amounts in thousands) during 1998 is explained by the SCF. Cash and **cash equivalents**—highly liquid, short-term securities readily convertible into cash—are the reporting basis for the SCF. Cash and cash equivalents are normally combined for balance sheet reporting.

Reporting Methods

The SCF can be prepared under either of two acceptable methods: the **direct method** or the **indirect method.** The two methods present operating activities in different ways but lead to the same subtotal, **net cash flow from operations.** This subtotal represents the net difference between cash receipts and cash disbursements related to operations. For Simple Company, operating receipts exceeded operating disbursements by $20. Simple's operating activities generated $20 more than it consumed in 1998. This subtotal is an important input into investor assessments of future cash flows. The investing and financing activities sections of the SCF are *identical* for both methods.

Direct method   Shown in the top half of Exhibit 23–1, the direct method lists the actual operating cash flows resulting in a net cash flow from operating activities. The boxed section of the exhibit for the direct method shows cash received from customers, payments to employees, and other operating cash flows. Net cash flow from operations is computed *directly* under this method.

Indirect method   Shown in the bottom half of Exhibit 23–1, the indirect method derives the same net operating cash flow amount by adjusting net income for items whose operating cash flow and income effects are unequal. For example, depreciation expense reduced income $4 but caused no cash outflow. The boxed section of the exhibit for the indirect method shows other adjustments causing income and operating cash flow to be different, but no actual cash flows. Net cash flow from operations is derived *indirectly* under this method.

Earnings and net cash inflow from operating activities for Simple Company are similar ($22 and $20, respectively). For many firms (Apple Computer was one), the two amounts are vastly different. The operating activities section under the indirect method explains the difference between earnings and operating cash flows. For firms using the direct method, a supporting schedule equivalent to the operating activities section under the indirect method is a required disclosure. This schedule is called the reconciliation of net income and operating cash flows.

EXHIBIT 23–1
Statement of Cash Flows

SIMPLE COMPANY

Statements of Cash Flows, Direct and Indirect Methods
For the Year Ended December 31, 1998
(in thousands)

Direct Method Statement of Cash Flows

Cash flows from operating activities:		
Cash received from customers	$ 58	
Payments to employees	(26)	
Payments for administrative and selling activities	(12)	
Net cash inflow from operating activities		$20
Cash flows from investing activities:		
Cash paid for acquisition of plant assets	$(30)	
Cash received from sale of plant assets	21	
Net cash outflow from investing activities		(9)
Cash flows from financing activities:		
Cash received from long-term debt issuance	$ 40	
Cash paid on long-term debt (principal only)	(46)	
Cash paid for treasury stock purchased	(8)	
Cash paid for dividends	(11)	
Cash received from sale of common stock	48	
Net cash inflow from financing activities		23
Effect of foreign exchange rates on cash		0*
Net increase in cash and cash equivalents during 1998		34
Cash and cash equivalents, January 1, 1998		42
Cash and cash equivalents, December 31, 1998		$76

Indirect Method Statement of Cash Flows

Cash flows from operating activities:†		
Net income	$ 22	
Add (deduct) to reconcile net income to net operating cash inflow:		
Accounts receivable increase	(8)	
Salaries payable increase	2	
Depreciation expense	4	
Net cash inflow from operating activities		$20
Cash flows from investing activities:		
Cash paid for acquisition of plant assets	$(30)	
Cash received from sale of plant assets	21	
Net cash outflow from investing activities		(9)
Cash flows from financing activities:		
Cash received from long-term debt issuance	$ 40	
Cash paid on long-term debt (principal only)	(46)	
Cash paid for treasury stock purchased	(8)	
Cash paid for dividends	(11)	
Cash received from sale of common stock	48	
Net cash inflow from financing activities		23
Effect of foreign exchange rates on cash		0*
Net increase in cash and cash equivalents during 1998		34
Cash and cash equivalents, January 1, 1998		42
Cash and cash equivalents, December 31, 1998		$76

*Effects of foreign currency exchange rate changes are listed here for firms with foreign operations or transactions in foreign currencies. The effect of exchange rate changes on foreign currencies held is not a cash flow, but affects the change in the cash balance, as measured in dollars, during the period. Advanced accounting courses discuss foreign currency issues in detail.

†This reconciliation schedule is also a required supplemental disclosure for firms choosing to report under the direct method.

Except for the operating section of the indirect method, each line item in the SCF describes a cash flow. The change in cash and cash equivalents for the period from the comparative balance sheets equals the change disclosed in the SCF. Through the double-entry accounting system, the change in cash is algebraically equal to the net change in all other accounts.

A firm can experience a cash decrease during the year yet generate considerable income and operating cash flow. The explanation is found in the SCF. Large investing cash outflows for equipment purchases or large financing cash outflows for debt retirement or for dividend payments would explain the cash decrease.

CONCEPT REVIEW

1. What were some of the major factors leading to the requirement of a statement of cash flows?
2. What does net operating cash flow represent, and what are the two different ways of computing it?
3. What is the purpose of the statement of cash flows?

Cash and Cash Equivalents

SFAS No. 95 standardizes the definition of the term *funds* by requiring that the SCF explain the change in cash and cash equivalents. Cash includes only those items immediately available to pay obligations. Cash equivalents are short-term, highly liquid investments with two additional characteristics:

1. They are readily convertible to known and fixed amounts of cash.
2. They are so near maturity that there is insignificant risk of market value fluctuation from interest rate changes.

Generally, only investments with an *original* maturity (to the purchasing firm) of three months or less qualify.

Example   A two-year U.S. Treasury note purchased three months before maturity is a cash equivalent because it is readily convertible into a known amount of cash and is very near maturity. The same note purchased four months before maturity is not, and it does not become a cash equivalent one month later because its original maturity to the purchaser is four months.

Securities that qualify as cash equivalents include money market funds, commercial paper, and Treasury bonds, notes, and bills.[11] An investment in equity securities cannot be a cash equivalent because it has no maturity date and is not convertible into a known (unchanging) amount of cash.

Cash equivalents are merged with cash for SCF purposes because a security that fulfills the criteria for cash equivalents is economically equivalent to cash. Their known value is not likely to change significantly, and they are readily convertible to cash. Cash has these characteristics. The three-month rule minimizes the risk of security price fluctuation from changes in interest rates and usually ensures that the face (or recorded value if different) of the investment is essentially equal to its market value during the holding period.

The assessment of a firm's cash flows would be incomplete without consideration of cash equivalents. Typically, firms invest idle cash in cash-equivalent securities to earn a return higher than is available from savings accounts. Purchases and sales of cash equivalents are a normal part of cash management practices.

SFAS No. 95 requires reporting the change in cash and cash equivalents as an item that reconciles the beginning and ending balances of cash and cash equivalents. The bottom

---

[11]Treasury bills have maturities of one year or less and constitute the largest component of the money market, the market for short-term debt. Treasury notes have maturity periods of 2 to 10 years. Treasury bonds have maturity periods exceeding 10 years.

portions of both statements in Exhibit 23–1 illustrate this reconciliation. Simple Company's net increase in cash and cash equivalents, $34, equals the net sum of net operating cash inflow, $20, net investment cash outflow, $9, and net financing cash inflow, $23. This increase is added to the beginning cash balance, $42, yielding the ending balance, $76.

A firm need not classify as cash equivalents all securities fulfilling the definition. Many companies invest in cash equivalents as long-term investments, rolling large quantities of securities over as they mature. Such securities are part of a larger pool of investment securities appropriately treated as other investments. *SFAS No. 95* requires disclosure of the classification policy. The beginning and ending cash and cash equivalent amounts disclosed in the SCF correspond to those shown in the balance sheet. Throughout this chapter, we use the term *cash* to describe both cash and cash equivalents unless there is a need to distinguish between the two.

Cash Flow Categories

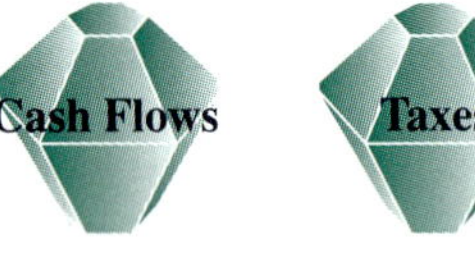

All cash inflows and outflows are classified into one of three categories:

1. Operating.
2. Investing.
3. Financing.

Classification of cash flows is important for evaluating past cash flows and predicting future flows. For example, the ability of a firm to generate positive cash flow from operations is critical to its survival. A firm cannot indefinitely sell its assets or incur additional debt if it is not operating successfully. Classification enables the user to distinguish between repetitive ongoing activities and long-term strategic changes.

Operating Cash Flows

Operating Cash Flows   Operating cash flows are associated with producing and delivering goods, providing services, and other transactions entering into the determination of income. Operating cash flows are all flows not defined as investing or financing activities.[12] Operating cash flows include the following:

Inflows	Outflows
▪ Receipts from customers*	▪ Payments to suppliers
▪ Interest received	▪ Payments to employees
▪ Dividends received	▪ Interest payments (net of amounts capitalized)
▪ Income tax refunds	▪ Income and other tax payments
▪ Refunds from suppliers	▪ Other payments related to income-producing activities, including prepayments and expenses
▪ Other receipts related to income-producing activities, such as revenues received in advance	▪ Payments on operating leases
▪ Receipts from lawsuits	▪ Settlements of lawsuits†
▪ Insurance proceeds from health, life, and business interruption insurance	▪ Principal payments on long- and short-term loans from suppliers‡
▪ Proceeds from sales and maturities of trading securities§	▪ Purchases of trading securities
	▪ Payments for fines and penalties
	▪ Charitable contributions

*Includes receipts of principal amounts from both short- and long-term receivables from the sale of goods and services.

†However, the cost of a successful legal defense of a patent is capitalized to patents and therefore treated as an investing cash outflow.

‡Suppliers provide the raw materials for the firm's business. Principal payments are considered a necessary cost of operations, regardless of the term of the loan.

§*SFAS No. 115*, par. 18. Trading securities are securities purchased principally for resale in the near term. They are carried at market value.

The association with income is the reason for classifying these flows as operating. For example, interest received and paid and dividends received are associated with expenses or revenues. All income tax payments are operating cash outflows, including those resulting

---

[12]*SFAS No. 95*, par. 21.

from extraordinary items, discontinued operations, accounting changes, and prior-period adjustments.

Cash flows from other transactions that may at first appear to be investing or financing flows are classified as operating if related to the main business activity. For example, if a real estate developer acquires land for subdivision, improvement, and resale as individual lots, the cash payment used to purchase the land is appropriately classified as operating. In this case, land is similar to the inventory of other types of businesses. Operating cash flows also include cash flows from originating, purchasing, and collecting principal amounts on loans carried at market value and held for a short time for resale.[13]

The direct method lists the operating cash flows resulting in net operating cash flow. Simple Company (Exhibit 23–1, direct method) received $58 from customers, paid $26 to employees, and paid $12 for administrative and selling expenses. Sales and expenses, the accrual counterpart of these receipts and payments, are listed in the income statement. A comparison of the income statement and SCF reveals the degree to which cash flows lead or lag revenue and expense recognition. The indirect method determines net operating cash flow indirectly, but does not list the individual operating cash flows.

Investing Cash Flows   Investing cash flows are associated with investing in and disposing of plant assets and certain debt and equity securities, making and collecting loans, and other strategic activities. This category is important for identifying a firm's growth plans. Capital expenditures and acquisitions of subsidiaries are important strategic decisions for a firm. This category includes the following:

Inflows	**Outflows**
▪ Proceeds from plant asset sales	▪ Payments to purchase plant assets
▪ Proceeds from sales and maturities of debt and equity securities not classified as cash equivalents or as trading securities*	▪ Purchases of debt and equity securities not classified as cash equivalents or as trading securities
▪ Collections of principal amounts of loans made to other parties and not held principally for resale	▪ Loans made to other parties and not held principally for resale
▪ Sale of real estate	▪ Payments to purchase real estate
▪ Casualty insurance proceeds (related to involuntary disposal of plant assets)	▪ Payments for capitalized interest (increases plant assets)
	▪ Down payments, advance payments, and other payments before or soon after purchase of plant assets (subsequent principal payments on debt financing are financing cash outflows)

*For example, *SFAS No. 115* defines debt securities held to maturity as those the investor intends and has the ability to hold to maturity. Securities available for sale are defined as those not classified as trading securities or held to maturity (par. 12b). This category in the list also includes investments accounted for under the cost and equity methods.

The difference between the investing cash inflows and outflows is **net cash inflow (outflow) from investing activities.** In Exhibit 23–1, Simple Company received $21 from plant asset sales and paid $30 for capital expenditures. The net cash outflow from investing activities is $9, indicating that Simple Company used more cash than it received from investing activities.

A fundamental distinction between operating and investing cash outflows is the anticipated benefit period. Inventory purchases are operating cash outflows because the benefits from inventory sales are expected in the short term. Plant assets provide benefits over longer periods of time.

Gains and losses from discontinued operations and transactions producing extraordinary items are often associated with investing cash flows. For example, the sale of assets from discontinued operations produces an investing inflow. The gains and losses from extraordinary items and discontinued operations appear as adjustments to net income in the reconciliation of net income and operating cash flows. Later examples illustrate the disclosure.

---

[13]*SFAS No. 102*, par. 9.

Financing Cash Flows   Financing cash flows are associated with obtaining resources from owners and providing a return on their investment, borrowing money, and repaying principal. Frequently, long-term debt or owners' equity accounts are involved in the transactions that give rise to financing cash flows. Examples of financing cash flows include the following:

Inflows	**Outflows**
▪ Proceeds from stock issuance	▪ Payments to purchase treasury stock
▪ Proceeds from bond issuance	▪ Payments to retire bonds
▪ Proceeds from debt for specific investing activities	▪ Dividends paid to shareholders
▪ Proceeds from loans from financial institutions*	▪ Principal payments on loans from financial institutions
	▪ Principal payments on capital leases
	▪ Principal payments on debt used to purchase productive assets financed by dealers or third parties

*Regardless of the use of the proceeds, borrowings from financial institutions are financing cash flows. Proceeds of a bank loan represent a financing cash inflow, even if used to buy inventory. If the firm finances the inventory purchase with a supplier, however, repayment of the loan is an operating outflow.

The difference between the financing cash inflows and outflows is **net cash inflow (outflow) from financing activities.** Exhibit 23–1 shows that Simple Company was active in the financing area in 1998. The company sold common stock and incurred new long-term debt for a total $88 cash inflow. Simple Company retired long-term debt, purchased treasury stock, and paid dividends to its shareholders. The company netted $23 from financing activities.

Noncash Activities

SFAS No. 95 requires disclosure of significant noncash investing and financing activities in a supporting schedule or in the footnotes, clearly identified as noncash transactions. Common noncash transactions include bond retirement by issuing stock, conversion of bonds to stock, settlement of debt by transferring noncash assets, receipt of donated property, and incurrence of capitalized lease obligations. Disclosure of significant noncash transactions, together with the cash flow amounts in the SCF, helps explain changes in balance sheet accounts.

Some noncash transactions are economically similar to cash transactions.

Example   Settling a $50,000 debt by issuing stock with a $50,000 fair market value has the same effect as issuing the stock for cash and using the proceeds to settle the debt. This transaction is recorded in the noncash schedule as follows:

Stock with a $50,000 fair market value was issued in payment of $50,000 of long-term debt.

Transactions can have both cash and noncash components. The cash flow is disclosed in the SCF, and the schedule or footnote discloses both components.

Example   If a plant asset costing $400,000 is acquired by paying $100,000 cash and issuing a $300,000 long-term note, the SCF discloses the $100,000 cash payment as an investing cash outflow and references the following footnote or supporting schedule:

A plant asset was acquired as follows:
Cost of asset acquired	$400,000
Cash paid	(100,000)
Long-term note issued	$300,000

SFAS No. 95 provides no guidance on disclosure of events such as retained earnings appropriations, stock dividends, and stock splits either issued or received. Typically, these transactions were not disclosed in prior funds statements because they did not represent significant financing activities or changes in capital structure.

Gross and Net Cash Flows

To maximize the information content of cash flow disclosures, *SFAS No. 95* generally requires that firms report gross cash flows. These flows may be grouped by similar type, for example,

Proceeds from bond issuance $120,000

which can represent several individual bond issues. The effects of fundamentally different transactions, however, are not netted; that is, the proceeds from a bond issue are not netted against payments to retire other bond issues. Netting different types of cash flows would obscure the very information the SCF is designed to disclose.

However, *SFAS No. 95* allows netting in certain situations:
- Transactions involving only cash and cash equivalents.
- Operating activities under the indirect method.
- Demand deposits of a bank, customer accounts of a broker–dealer, and other items that, for its customers, the firm holds or pays cash for.
- Investments, loans receivable and debt if turnover is quick, amounts are large and maturities are at most three months.

For these transactions, gross reporting is considered unnecessary to the understanding of the nature of the cash flows.[14]

Cash Flow per Share

SFAS No. 95 specifically prohibits disclosure of cash flow per share statistics, except for contractually determined cash flow per share amounts. Cash flow per share could be confused with earnings per share and might be taken as an amount available for cash dividends.

However, many analysts are interested in **cash flow per share,** an amount defined in several ways, including net operating cash flow divided by weighted average common shares outstanding during the year. Many other ratios involving cash flow are in common use. For example, the ratio of net operating cash flow to net income is one measure of the quality of earnings.[15]

CONCEPT REVIEW

1. How is the interest portion of a capital lease payment classified in the SCF? How is the principal portion classified?
2. Why are noncash activities disclosed?
3. Why does the basis for reporting in the SCF include cash equivalents?

REVIEW PROBLEM

Classify the following 10 items by writing one of the following letters to the left of each item:

O Operating cash flow   F Financing cash flow
I Investing cash flow   N None of the preceding categories applies

___ 1. Payment on an operating lease.
___ 2. Purchase of treasury stock.
___ 3. Principal portion of a payment on a loan from a bank; proceeds of the loan were used to purchase inventory for resale.
___ 4. Dividend payments.
___ 5. Dividends received on an investment accounted for by the equity method.
___ 6. Interest paid and capitalized to construction in process.

---

[14]*SFAS No. 104,* which amends *SFAS No. 95,* allows banks, savings institutions, and credit unions to report certain cash flows net or gross.

[15]See C. Carslaw and J. Mills, "Developing Ratios for Effective Cash Flow Statement Analysis," *Journal of Accountancy,* November 1991, p. 63.

___ 7. Income tax paid on extraordinary gain from debt retirement.
___ 8. Cost of goods sold.
___ 9. Purchase of another firm's stock.
___ 10. Payment to employee pension fund.

SOLUTION

1. O	6. I
2. F	7. O
3. F	8. N*
4. F	9. I
5. O	10. O

*This item is an expense, not a cash flow.

PREPARING THE SCF

Several approaches for preparing the SCF are used in practice. The objective of each is to identify, through analysis of transactions, the following:
- The operating, investing, and financing cash flows.
- Significant noncash investing and financing transactions.
- Items that reconcile income and net operating cash flow.

This chapter uses two approaches for preparation:

1. A format-free approach that uses no specific format for analysis.
2. A spreadsheet approach.

Both make use of T-accounts and reconstructed journal entries to analyze transactions. Although the spreadsheet dominates in industry and public accounting, many preparers combine features from these and other approaches.

Format-Free Approach: Direct Method

The direct method SCF, prepared under the format-free approach, is appropriate for companies with a small number of transactions and accounts. We use Simple Company to illustrate this approach.

Order of Information Search

Various information sources are searched for data relating to the period's transactions. Journal entries may be reconstructed to identify the components of transactions more clearly. The information sources are consulted in the order indicated:

1. The income statement: for information about noncash gains and losses, depreciation, and operating revenues and expenses helpful in determining operating cash flows. This source is searched in conjunction with related operating balance sheet accounts and additional information.
2. Additional information (including the retained earnings statement or owners' equity statement): for data on transactions such as debt issuance and retirement, stock transactions, and extraordinary items.
3. The comparative balance sheets: for account changes not explained by 1 or 2 above and that suggest additional transactions for analysis.

As cash flows are identified, they are classified into one of the three cash flow categories. For example, if the firm purchased land during the year for $200,000, the cash outflow is placed in the investing activities section. Noncash transactions are placed in a supporting schedule. Amounts reconciling income and net operating cash flow are discussed in a later section on the indirect method.

Exhibit 23–2 gives the background information behind Simple Company's SCFs, and Exhibit 23–3 repeats the direct method SCF. As transactions are analyzed, keep track of the balance sheet account changes that are explained.

Transaction Analysis for the Direct Method SCF

We start with the income statement and convert each item (except noncash charges and credits) to a cash flow amount, using related balance sheet account changes and, where relevant, additional information.

SIMPLE COMPANY

Case Data for Preparing the Statements of Cash Flow
Illustrated in Exhibits 23–1, 23–3, and 23–4
(in thousands)

A. Income statement for the year ended December 31, 1998:

Sales (all on credit)	$66
Salaries expense	(28)
Depreciation expense	(4)
Administrative and selling expenses (excluding salaries)	(12)
Net income	$22

B. Comparative balance sheets:

	December 31 1997	December 31 1998
Cash (no cash equivalents)	$ 42	$ 76
Accounts receivable	31	39
Plant assets	82	81
Accumulated depreciation	(20)	(14)
Total assets	$135	$182
Salaries payable	$ 3	$ 5
Notes payable, long term	46	40
Common stock, par $10	61	101
Contributed capital in excess of par	9	17
Treasury stock (at cost)	0	(8)
Retained earnings	16	27
Total liabilities and stockholders' equity	$135	$182

C. Additional information:
  1. Plant assets account:
     (*a*) Purchased plant assets for cash, $30.
     (*b*) Sold plant assets for $21 cash; recorded as follows:

Cash	21	
Accumulated depreciation	10	
Plant assets		31

  2. Long-term notes payable account:
     Borrowed cash, $40.
     Payments on note principal, $46.
  3. Treasury stock account—purchased treasury stock for $8 cash.
  4. Retained earnings statement:

Balance, 1/1/1998	$16
Net income for 1998	22
Cash dividend paid in cash at end of 1998	(11)
Balance, 12/31/1998	$27

  5. Issued common stock for $48 cash.

Income Statement Accounts

1. **Sales** Credit sales ($66) increase accounts receivable. A quick scan of additional information indicates no related data (for example, a write-off listed in additional information would be relevant here).

   The related cash flow is collections on accounts receivable. This amount can be derived in several ways. If Simple Company's accounting system permits, the total cash receipts amount is obtained from the cash receipts journal. Alternatively, a T-account can be used to identify collections on accounts receivable:

Accounts Receivable

Bal. 1/1/98	31		*Cash collections*
Sales in 1998	66	58	*in 1998 (derived)*
Bal. 12/31/98	39		

SIMPLE COMPANY

Statement of Cash Flows, Direct Method

For the Year Ended December 31, 1998

(in thousands)

Italic letters refer to the text discussion.

Cash flows from operating activities:		
(a) Cash received from customers	$ 58	
(b) Payments to employees	(26)	
(c) Payments for administrative and selling activities	(12)	
Net cash inflow from operating activities		$20
Cash flows from investing activities:		
(d) Cash paid for acquisition of plant assets	$(30)	
(e) Cash received from sale of plant assets	21	
Net cash outflow from investing activities		(9)
Cash flows from financing activities:		
(f) Cash received from long-term debt issuance	$ 40	
(g) Cash paid on long-term debt (principal only)	(46)	
(h) Cash paid for treasury stock purchase	(8)	
(i) Cash paid for dividends	(11)	
(j) Cash received from sale of common stock	48	
Net cash inflow from financing activities		23
Effect of foreign exchange rates on cash		0
Net increase in cash and cash equivalents during 1998		34
Cash and cash equivalents, January 1, 1998		42
Cash and cash equivalents, December 31, 1998		$76

Another alternative is to convert the accrual information (sales) to the cash basis (collections on account):[16]

$$\text{Cash collections} = \text{Accrual-basis revenue} \begin{cases} + \text{ Decrease in associated receivable} \\ - \text{ Increase in associated receivable} \end{cases}$$

$58 cash collections = $66 sales − $8 accounts receivable increase

Either way, the resulting disclosure in the SCF (Exhibit 23–3) is

(a) Cash received from customers $58

2. **Salaries expense** Salaries expense ($28) is related to salaries payable, which increased $2 during 1998. No additional information applies. The related cash flow is salary payments, determined in two ways:

a. T-Account Approach

Salaries Payable

Salary payments (derived)	26	Bal. 1/1/98	3
		Salaries expense	28
		Bal. 12/31/98	5

b. Formula Approach

$$\text{Cash payment} = \text{Accrual-basis expense} \begin{cases} + \text{ Decrease in associated payable} \\ - \text{ Increase in associated payable} \end{cases}$$

$26 salary payments = $28 salaries expense − $2 salaries payable increase

The resulting disclosure in the SCF (Exhibit 23–3) is

(b) Payments to employees .... ($26)

---

[16]These and other expressions facilitate preparation and embody the same logic as the use of the T-account.

3. **Depreciation expense** Depreciation expense ($4) is not a cash flow and is not disclosed in the operating section of the direct method SCF, although this amount appears in the reconciliation of net income and net operating cash flow.
4. **Administrative and selling expenses** There is no related additional information or balance sheet account. Therefore, the cash and accrual amounts are the same for this expense (Exhibit 23–3):

> (*c*) Payments for administrative and selling activities . . . . ($12)

Additional Information

1. Simple Company purchased plant assets for $30 cash. This is an investing cash outflow (Exhibit 23–3):

> (*d*) Cash paid for acquisition of plant assets . . . . ($30)

Simple Company also sold plant assets; the reconstructed entry is illustrated in the additional information, Exhibit 23–2. The $21 proceeds is an investing cash inflow:

> (*e*) Cash received from sale of plant assets $21

The two transactions listed in this item of additional information help explain the changes in accumulated depreciation and plant assets accounts during 1998.
2. Simple Company borrowed $40 cash (financing cash inflow) and paid $46 principal (financing cash outflow) on its long-term notes payable:

> (*f*) Cash received from long-term debt issuance $40
> (*g*) Cash paid on long-term debt (principal only) . . . . (46)

3. The treasury stock purchase is a financing outflow:

> (*h*) Cash paid for treasury stock purchased . . . . ($8)

4. The retained earnings statement reveals $11 of dividends declared and paid in 1998, a financing cash outflow. There is no dividends payable account, meaning all dividends declared were paid.

> (*i*) Cash paid for dividends . . . . ($11)

5. The last item is common stock issuance for $48, a financing cash inflow:

> (*j*) Cash received from sale of common stock $48

At this point, all additional information is incorporated, and the last information source is considered.

Comparative Balance Sheet   All balance sheet account changes are explained by the transaction analysis above, so there are no further items to disclose in the SCF. For example, the decrease in plant assets of $1 in 1998 is explained by the $30 purchase and sale of assets originally costing $31. Accumulated depreciation decreased $6, which equals depreciation expense (an increase of $4) less the decrease from equipment disposal ($10). The $11 retained earnings increase is explained by the $22 of net income less $11 of dividends.

Example   Now, let's add one more item to illustrate why the comparative balance sheets should be used as the *last* source of information. For this example only, after entering items *a* through *j* into the SCF as discussed above, assume that Simple Company had one other account listed in the balance sheet:

	1997	1998
Long-term investment in stock	$ 0	$12

There is no item listed under additional information referring to this account and all other account balances (except cash) have been explained. Under these circumstances, Simple Company would disclose another investing cash outflow in the SCF:

Purchase of long-term investment in stock . . . . ($12)

With all other account balance changes explained (except for cash), Simple must have purchased the investment in stock with cash. Such assumptions about a firm's transactions should be made only after all other information sources have been examined.

Completing the Direct Method SCF   All cash flows have been identified and classified as operating, investing, or financing. To complete the SCF, the change in cash (an increase of $34) and the beginning and ending cash balances are entered as shown in Exhibit 23–3. The net increase in cash from the SCF agrees with the cash account balance change.

Additional Examples of Operating Cash Flows: Direct Method

The Simple Company example focuses on the sequence of information search and transaction analysis. Additional examples of determining operating cash flows illustrate transactions not present in the Simple Company example.

Deferred Revenues   Determining the cash receipts related to deferred revenues such as unearned rent revenue is accomplished with a T-account or formula. The analysis follows the same reasoning applied to the accrual revenues and expenses of Simple Company.

$$\text{Cash collections} = \text{Accrual-basis revenue} \begin{cases} + \text{ Increase in associated deferred revenue} \\ - \text{ Decrease in associated deferred revenue} \end{cases}$$

Suppose a firm reports $12,000 in fee revenue and a $2,000 decrease in unearned fee revenue:

$$\$10,000 \text{ fees collected} = \$12,000 \text{ fee revenue} - \$2,000 \text{ decrease in unearned fee revenue}$$

Using T-accounts, and reconstructing the summary transactions, also explains the result:

Unearned Fee Revenue

Decrease	2,000		
Revenue earned	12,000	*Fees collected (derived)*	10,000

Some accountants prefer to reconstruct full summary worksheet journal entries to determine the cash flow. For this example, the first entry is as follows:

Unearned fee revenue	12,000	
Fee revenue		12,000

The second entry is implied by the first and the decrease in the unearned fee revenue account:

Cash	10,000	
Unearned fee revenue		10,000

Fees collected is an operating inflow.

Prepaid Expenses   The expression used to determine cash payments related to prepaids is

$$\text{Cash payment} = \text{Accrual-basis expense} \begin{cases} + \text{ Increase in associated prepaid} \\ - \text{ Decrease in associated prepaid} \end{cases}$$

Assume that a firm reports $4,000 rent expense and a $1,000 increase in prepaid rent. Cash payments are therefore determined as follows:

$$\$5,000 \text{ cash paid for rent} = \$4,000 \text{ rent expense} + \$1,000 \text{ increase in prepaid rent}$$

Rent payments exceed rent expense because prepaid rent increased during the period. Rent payments is an operating outflow. The T-account analysis also can be applied.

Payments for Inventory Purchases   Purchases of inventory are normally made on account. Therefore, accounts payable, cost of goods sold, and inventory are analyzed to determine the associated cash flow:

$$\text{Cash paid for inventory purchases} = \text{Cost of goods sold} \begin{cases} + \text{ Inventory increase} \\ - \text{ Inventory decrease} \\ + \text{ Accounts payable decrease} \\ - \text{ Accounts payable increase} \end{cases}$$

An inventory increase implies that the cash outflow exceeds cost of goods sold. Therefore, the increase is added to derive cash payments. An accounts payable increase implies that purchases exceed payments. Therefore, the increase is subtracted to derive cash payments. Assume that cost of goods sold is $10,000 for the year, accounts payable increased $3,000, and inventory increased $2,000. Payments for inventory purchases are therefore determined as follows:

$$\begin{array}{ccccc} \$9,000 \text{ cash paid} & = & \$10,000 \text{ cost of} & + & \$2,000 \text{ inventory} & - & \$3,000 \text{ accounts payable} \\ \text{for purchases} & & \text{goods sold} & & \text{increase} & & \text{increase} \end{array}$$

A T-account analysis is especially useful for deriving cash flows when more than one account is involved:

Inventory

Increase	2,000		
Purchases (derived)	12,000	Cost of goods sold	10,000

Accounts Payable

		Increase	3,000
Cash payments (derived)	9,000	Purchases (from inventory)	12,000

This analysis assumes that accounts payable is used only for inventory purchases. Payments for inventory purchases is an operating outflow.

Format-Free Approach: Indirect Method and Reconciliation of Net Income and Operating Cash Flow

The investing and financing sections of the indirect and direct method SCFs are identical. Therefore, this section discusses only the operating section for the indirect method, using Simple Company as an example. The operating section of the indirect method is the reconciliation of net income and net operating cash flow. The reconciliation begins with net income, and discloses the items that reconcile net income and net operating cash flow (see Exhibit 23–4, which reproduces the Simple Company indirect SCF). The indirect method SCF does *not* disclose the individual operating cash flows.

The reconciliation of net income and operating cash flows is another approach to converting accrual income to cash-basis income. Rather than seeking to uncover the operating cash flows, however, the search is for amounts that explain why net income is not equal to net operating cash flow. These amounts are called reconciling adjustments. The order of information search followed in the direct method also is used in the indirect method.

A useful generalization for identifying reconciling adjustments is

If a transaction's effect on *operating* cash flow is not equal to its effect on net income, a reconciling adjustment is needed for the difference.

Simple Company's $4 of depreciation expense is an example. In Exhibit 23–4, the $4 addition adjustment (*c*) for depreciation reconciles the earnings effect ($4 decrease) and the operating cash flow effect (zero). Because the reconciliation begins with net income, which is reduced by depreciation, a noncash expense, a $4 addition adjustment is needed to prevent understatement of net operating cash flow.

SIMPLE COMPANY

Statement of Cash Flows, Indirect Method

For the Year Ended December 31, 1998

(in thousands)

Italic letters refer to the text discussion.

Cash flows from operating activities:		
Net income	$ 22	
Add (deduct) to reconcile net income to net operating cash inflow:		
(a) Accounts receivable increase	(8)	
(b) Salaries payable increase	2	
(c) Depreciation expense	4	
Net cash inflow from operating activities		$20
Cash flows from investing activities:		
Cash paid for acquisition of plant assets	$(30)	
Cash received from sale of plant assets	21	
Net cash outflow from investing activities		(9)
Cash flows from financing activities:		
Cash received from long-term debt issuance	$ 40	
Cash paid on long-term debt (principal only)	(46)	
Cash paid for treasury stock purchased	(8)	
Cash paid for dividends	(11)	
Cash received from sale of common stock	48	
Net cash inflow from financing activities		23
Effect of foreign exchange rates on cash		0
Net increase in cash and cash equivalents during 1998		34
Cash and cash equivalents, January 1, 1998		42
Cash and cash equivalents, December 31, 1998		$76

Transaction Analysis for the Indirect Method SCF

Income Statement Accounts

1. **Sales** Credit sales ($66) increased accounts receivable, yet accounts receivable increased a net of $8, implying $58 of collections on account. Therefore, the net income effect (increase $66) exceeds the operating cash flow effect (increase $58), necessitating an $8 reconciling adjustment. The $8 accounts receivable increase is *subtracted* from net income to remove the excess of accrual revenue over cash received, adjustment (*a*) in Exhibit 23–4.
2. **Salaries expense** Salaries expense ($28) increased salaries payable, yet salaries payable increased a net of $2, implying $26 of salary payments. The net income effect (decrease $28) exceeds the operating cash flow effect (decrease $26).

Therefore, the $2 increase in salaries payable is added to net income to offset the excess of accrual expense deducted over salary payments made, adjustment (*b*) in Exhibit 23–4.

3. **Depreciation expense** As discussed before, the $4 expense is added to net income, adjustment (*c*) in Exhibit 23–4.
4. **Administrative and selling expenses** There is no related additional information or balance sheet account, and the cash payments equal the accrual expense. Therefore, no reconciling adjustment is needed.

Additional Information   None of the items in additional information affects net income or operating cash flow. Therefore, no additional reconciling adjustments are required. (The investing and financing cash flows are identified and entered as under the direct method.)

1. Adjustments for changes in working capital accounts related to operations (accounts receivable, inventory, prepaids, interest receivable, investments in trading securities, accounts payable, interest payable, income taxes payable, short-term payables to suppliers and others) and long-term accounts such as payables to suppliers for inventory purchases, and other operating activities:

Change in Account Balance during Year

	Increase	**Decrease**
Asset	*Subtract* increase from net income	*Add* decrease to net income
Liability	*Add* increase to net income	*Subtract* decrease from net income

The following working capital accounts are excluded from this category of adjustment:
- Cash and cash equivalents (the SCF is explaining the net change in this fund).
- Short-term investments in securities available for sale (associated cash flows are investing).
- Dividends payable (dividend payments are financing).
- Short-term payables to financial institutions (associated cash flows are financing).

2. Noncash expenses, including depreciation, depletion, amortization of intangibles, and amortization of discount on bonds payable, are *added* to net income as reconciling adjustments because they do not cause cash to decrease.

   Also *add* to income:
   - Increase in deferred tax liability and decrease in deferred tax asset.
   - Negative investment revenue from equity method investments.
   - Amortization of premium on bond investments held to maturity.
   - Dividends received from equity method investments.

3. Noncash revenues, including investment revenue from equity method investments and revenues realized by receipt of noncash resources (settlement of liabilities, receipt of long-term assets for services) are *subtracted* from income because they do not cause cash to increase.

   Also *subtract* from income:
   - Amortization of premium on bonds payable.
   - Amortization of discount on bond investments held to maturity.
   - Decrease in deferred tax liability and increase in deferred tax asset.

4. Noncash gains are *subtracted* from net income, and noncash losses are *added* to net income. Gains and losses on disposals of plant assets, extraordinary gains and losses on casualties and bond retirements, and gains and losses from discontinued operations are examples.

Comparative Balance Sheets   After the investing and financing sections of the SCF are completed, all balance sheet account balance changes were explained for Simple Company. The indirect method SCF is completed when the change in cash for the period and the beginning and ending cash balances have been entered.

Additional Examples of Reconciling Adjustments

Refer to Exhibit 23–5 for common reconciling adjustments. In this section, several of these reconciling adjustments are discussed in detail.

Changes in Operating Working Capital Accounts   The Simple Company case provides two examples of this type of adjustment: the increase in accounts receivable (subtracted from net income) and the increase in salaries payable (added to net income). These adjustments are required because the operating cash effect is not equal to the related income effect. Changes in working capital accounts, such as dividends payable, are not related to operating cash flows and are not reconciling adjustments.

Amortization of Bond Discount   Information pertaining to bond discount is found in additional information or in the comparative balance sheets. An example entry amortizing bond discount is:

Interest expense	12,000	
Discount on bonds payable		2,000
Cash		10,000

Interest expense reduces income $12,000, yet only $10,000 cash was paid. Therefore, the $2,000 amortization is added to income in the reconciliation. Amortization of bond *premium* is subtracted from net income.

Noncash Revenues   Revenues recognized on collection of noncash resources or in settlement of liabilities are subtracted from net income because they provide no cash. The income statement is the source of information for these revenues. For example, assume a firm extinguishes a $10,000 long-term note payable by performing a service for the creditor:

Long-term note payable	10,000	
Service revenue		10,000

The income effect ($10,000) exceeds the operating cash flow effect (zero); therefore, the $10,000 revenue is subtracted from income.

Gain on Sale of Land   The income statement (or additional information) is the information source for gains and losses on disposal of plant assets and investments. The following entry records such a gain:

Cash	200,000	
Land (cost)		150,000
Gain on sale of land		50,000

The $200,000 proceeds is an investing cash inflow. This cash flow completely explains the cash consequences of the transaction. However, net income reflects the $50,000 gain and consequently overstates net operating cash flow by that amount. The gain does not represent an additional cash inflow, nor is it related to operations. Therefore, the $50,000 gain is subtracted from net income in the reconciliation.

Comparison of Direct and Indirect Methods

The investing and financing sections for both methods are identical. However, the direct method SCF and related disclosures supply all the information found in the indirect method SCF, and more. The direct method SCF and related disclosures provide more information by supplying *both*
- The individual operating cash flows within the statement.
- Reconciliation of income and operating cash flows in a supporting schedule.

The indirect method provides only the reconciliation, which appears in the operating section of the SCF or in a supporting schedule. In effect, an indirect method SCF is prepared whenever a direct method SCF and related disclosures are prepared. The following diagram illustrates these points and compares the two methods:

Direct Method	**Indirect Method**
Operating Activities	
Operating cash flows	Reconciliation of earnings and net operating cash flow
Investing Activities	
Investing cash flows	Investing cash flows
Financing Activities	
Financing cash flows	Financing cash flows
Supplemental Schedule	
Reconciliation of earnings and net operating cash flow	

Thus, the main difference between the two methods is that the direct method reports the operating cash flows and the reconciliation. The indirect method reports only the reconciliation.

SIMPLE COMPANY
Reconciliation of Net Income and Operating Cash Flows:
Supporting Schedule to the Direct Method SCF

Reconciliation of Net Income and Operating Cash Flows (in thousands)

Net income	$22
Add (deduct) to reconcile net income to net cash inflow:	
Accounts receivable increase	(8)
Salaries payable increase	2
Depreciation expense	4
Net cash flow from operating activities	$20

Operating cash flows, in SCF
   Minimum breakdown of reporting for operating cash flows:
      Collections from customers (including lessees, licensees)
      Interest and dividends received
      Other operating receipts
      Payments to employees and suppliers of all goods and services
      Interest payments, net of amounts capitalized
      Income tax payments
      Other operating payments
Reconciliation of net income and net operating cash flow in supporting schedule

Investing cash flows, in SCF
Financing cash flows, in SCF
Minimum breakdown of reporting for reconciliation (reconciling items to be clearly
   identified as such to avoid inference that they are cash flows):
   Change in receivables related to operations
   Change in inventories
   Change in payables related to operations
   Other categories including amortization, depreciation, and noncash gains and
     losses
Noncash investing and financing activities disclosure
Cash and cash equivalents: the change during the period reconciles beginning and
   ending balances; policy regarding securities included in cash equivalents is
   disclosed

Disclose income tax payments and interest payments (net of amounts capitalized),
   in schedule or notes
Reconciliation of net income and net operating cash flow in SCF, or disclose in one
   line the net operating cash flow in the SCF with supporting schedule showing
   detail

Key:
   Required under the direct method: ——————
   Required under the indirect method: – – – – –

Exhibit 23–6 illustrates the required reconciliation of income and operating cash flows for Simple Company under the direct method. The reconciliation is identical to the operating section of Simple Company's SCF under the indirect method (Exhibit 23–4).

Disclosure Requirements of SFAS No. 95

Exhibit 23–7 presents the disclosure requirements for both the direct and indirect methods. The central part of the exhibit illustrates the considerable overlap between the two methods.

The lack of operating cash flow reporting under the indirect method led to the required disclosure of interest and income tax payments. The minimum disclosure of reconciliation items under the indirect method allows users to approximate certain operating cash flows when used with income statement information.

REVIEW PROBLEM

For each of the following independent items, indicate the required disclosure in the direct method statement of cash flows. If the reconciliation of net cash flow from operating activities and net income is affected, indicate that effect. Also indicate any noncash activities.

1. Prepaid rent decreased $20,000 during the year. Rent expense recognized for the year amounted to $30,000.
2. Patent amortization recognized amounted to $30,000.
3. Net income was $100,000; retained earnings increased $60,000; and dividends payable decreased $20,000.
4. Wages payable decreased $12,000 and wages expense for the year amounted to $48,000.
5. The balance in salaries payable increased $50 for the year.
6. Sales on account for the year are $1,000 and the balance in accounts receivable increased $200 during the year. All sales are on account.
7. Plant assets costing $4,000 were purchased by paying $1,000 down, and signing a long-term note for the remainder.
8. The balance in accumulated depreciation increased $100 for the year. No disposals of plant assets occurred during the year.
9. Rent expense is $400; no prepaid rent or rent payable accounts appeared in the comparative balance sheets.
10. Sold for $1,000 a long-term investment in another firm's stock. The stock had been purchased for $1,000 one year earlier.

SOLUTION

1. Operating cash outflow: rent payment $10,000.
   ($20,000 of the rent expense was the expiration of prepaid rent paid for in an earlier period; only $10,000 of rent was paid in the current period.)
   Reconciliation: add prepaid rent decrease $20,000.
2. Reconciliation: add patent amortization $30,000.
3. Financing cash outflow: dividends paid $60,000.
   (Dividends declared equals $100,000 − $60,000 = $40,000. Dividends payable decreased $20,000, thus $60,000 of dividends must have been paid.)
4. Operating cash outflow: wage payments $60,000.
   (For wages expense to be $48,000 and wages payable to decrease $12,000, $60,000 of wages must have been paid.)
   Reconciliation: subtract wages payable decrease $12,000.
5. Reconciliation: add salaries payable increase $50.
6. Operation cash inflow: collections from customers $800.
   (Sales exceeded cash collections by $200 because accounts receivable increased.)
   Reconciliation: subtract accounts receivable increase $200.
7. Investing cash outflow: down payment on plant asset $1,000.
   Noncash activity schedule: purchase of $4,000 plant asset, paid $1,000 in cash and financed the remaining $3,000 with a long-term note.
8. Reconciliation: add depreciation expense $100.
9. Operating cash outflow: rent payments $400.
10. Investing cash inflow: proceeds from sale of investment $1,000.

The Spreadsheet Approach

A computerized (or manual) columnar format can be used for analyzing transactions and identifying SCF disclosures. The spreadsheet (or worksheet) approach

- Provides an organized format for documenting the preparation process for subsequent analysis, review, and evaluation (accountants use spreadsheets and other working papers in legal proceedings to substantiate their work).
- Provides several proofs of accuracy.
- Formally keeps track of the changes in balance sheet accounts and ensures that all account changes are explained.

The spreadsheet is the most involved format for preparing the SCF, and a certain amount of practice is required for proficiency. For complex preparation problems, however, the benefits of the spreadsheet are worth the effort. Even so, no format, spreadsheet or otherwise, eliminates the need to analyze transactions carefully.

The spreadsheet developed for the accounting cycle in Chapter 3, resulting in the income statement and balance sheet, cannot be used for the SCF, which requires information beyond the ending adjusted ledger account balances.[17] Most spreadsheet formats currently in use are variations on a common theme. The spreadsheet format we discuss is concise, and results in simultaneous preparation of both direct and indirect method SCFs.[18]

Although the format-free and spreadsheet approaches use the same order of information search and logic for identifying disclosure items, the spreadsheet formalizes the process. In many cases, a transaction entry is reconstructed and entered into the spreadsheet to explain changes in account balances (for the purposes of the spreadsheet only).

Exhibit 23–8 illustrates the complete spreadsheet for the Simple Company. As cash flows are located, they are entered into one of the cash flow activity sections in the lower half of the spreadsheet. Inflows are debits (a cash inflow is a debit to cash), and outflows are credits (a cash outflow is a credit to cash). The corresponding debit or credit is entered into the appropriate balance sheet account in the upper half of the worksheet.

Example   The spreadsheet entry corresponding to the purchase of plant assets for $30 is entry (f). The debit of $30 helps to explain the change in plant assets in the upper half, and the credit of $30 appears in the investing section of the worksheet as a cash outflow in the lower half.

In the operating activities section, the debit and credit columns reflect the reconciliation of income and net operating cash flow. These columns are labeled *indirect method* because their entries are used for the operating section under the indirect method. Debit adjustments are added to net income, and credits are subtracted in the reconciliation. Going across rows, the debits and credits adjust the accrual revenue or expense to yield the operating cash flow for the direct method. The process is completed when all balance sheet account changes are explained. The information from the three activity sections is transferred to the direct method or indirect method SCF.

<table>
<tr><td>Spreadsheet Approach
Example: The Simple
Company</td><td>

The explanation for each cash flow and reconciling adjustment mirrors the format-free approach (the italic letters, however, do not correspond). Except for entering net income first, the information sources are searched in the usual order.

</td></tr>
</table>

(a)   The $22 debit (positive net income, implying cash increase) in the operating section of the indirect method columns begins the reconciliation schedule (Exhibit 23–8). Net income is the starting figure for net operating cash flow. The credit partially explains the change in retained earnings. Net income is not a cash flow and is not extended to the direct method columns.

(b)   The $8 debit explains the increase in accounts receivable. In the indirect method columns (the reconciliation), the $8 credit is subtracted from net income. Increases in operating current assets are subtracted from net income. The credit is also subtracted from sales (going across the row) to yield cash collected from customers, under the direct method. When used as adjustments across rows, credits result in cash decreases (either a decrease in a cash inflow as in this item, or an increase in a cash outflow). The direct method column lists the $58 operating cash inflow.

(c)   The $2 credit explains the increase in salaries payable. The debit (indirect method columns) increases net income because an operating payable increased. The debit also adjusts salaries expense to yield cash paid to employees. When used as adjustments across rows, debits result in cash increases (either an increase in a cash inflow, or a

---

[17]If it did not require further information, the SCF would only repeat the information in the balance sheet and income statement.

[18]This format is adapted from an article by W. Collins that appeared in the "Practitioners Forum" of the *Journal of Accountancy,* May 1990, p. 124.

EXHIBIT 23–8
Spreadsheet Approach

EXHIBIT 23–8
Spreadsheet Approach

SIMPLE COMPANY
Spreadsheet for Direct and Indirect Method SCFs
For the Year Ended December 31, 1998
(in thousands)

Italic letters refer to the text discussion.

Comparative Balance Sheets	12/31/97		Dr.	Cr.		12/31/98
Cash	42	(m)	34			76
Accounts receivable	31	(b)	8			39
Plant assets	82	(f)	30	31	(g)	81
Accumulated depreciation	(20)	(g)	10	4	(d)	(14)
Total assets	135					182
Salaries payable	3			2	(c)	5
Notes payable	46	(i)	46	40	(h)	40
Common stock	61			40	(l)	101
Contributed capital in excess of par	9			8	(l)	17
Treasury stock		(j)	8			(8)
Retained earnings	16	(k)	11	22	(a)	27
Total liabilities and owners' equity	135					182
Total changes			147	147		

Adjustments Leading to SCF			Indirect Method			Direct Method (operations)
			Dr.	Cr.		
Operating activities:						
Net income	22	(a)	22			
Sales	66			8	(b)	58 customer collections
Salary expense	28	(c)	2			26 salary payments
Depreciation	4	(d)	4			
Administrative and selling	12				(e)	12 payments
Investing activities:						
Purchase plant assets				30	(f)	
Sale of plant assets		(g)	21			
Financing activities:						
Issue notes payable for cash		(h)	40			
Payments on notes payable				46	(i)	
Purchase treasury stock				8	(j)	
Dividends paid				11	(k)	
Issue common stock		(l)	48			
				103		
Net cash increase				34	(m)	
			137	137		

decrease in a cash outflow as in this item). The direct method column lists the $26 operating cash outflow.

(*d*) Depreciation affects only the reconciliation (indirect method columns). This spreadsheet entry is the first to reconstruct an actual journal entry. The $4 credit explains part of the accumulated depreciation change, and the debit implies an addition to net income for the reconciliation.

(*e*) This is not a formal spreadsheet entry because no balance sheet account requires explanation. Administrative and selling expenses were paid entirely in cash. No reconciling item appears, but the direct method column lists the $12 operating cash outflow.

(*f*) At this point, the operating section is completed; both methods now use only the indirect method columns. The $30 debit for the plant asset purchase in this reconstructed journal entry helps explain the change in plant assets. The investing section lists the credit, or cash outflow.

(*g*) This reconstructed entry records the removal of $10 accumulated depreciation on disposal, removes the $31 original asset cost, and records the $21 investing cash inflow.

(*h*) The $40 credit of this reconstructed entry records the issuance of a long-term note payable. The financing section records the debit, or cash inflow.

(*i*) The $46 debit of this reconstructed entry records the decrease or principal payment for a long-term note. The financing section records the credit, or cash outflow.

(*j*) The reconstructed entry to record the treasury stock purchase includes an $8 debit, which completely explains the treasury stock account change, and the credit (outflow) listed in the financing section of the spreadsheet.

(*k*) The reconstructed entry to record dividends paid results in the $11 credit (cash outflow) listed in the financing section.

(*l*) The stock issue is the only transaction affecting common stock. The reconstructed entry explains that account change, with a $48 debit (cash inflow) in the financing section.

(*m*) This is a balancing entry, not a reconstructed journal entry. At this point, all balance sheet account changes except cash are explained, and all relevant information is incorporated. The $34 debit explains the cash change, and the $34 credit reconciles the cash credit change total with the cash debit change total.

The three operating cash flows (direct method column) are transferred to the direct method SCF (Exhibit 23–3). The three reconciling items (indirect method columns) are transferred to the operating section of the indirect method SCF, *and* to the reconciliation for the direct method. The two investing cash flows and five financing cash flows are transferred to both direct and indirect method SCFs. The spreadsheet easily accommodates either method.

The spreadsheet provides several accuracy checks. The changes in all balance sheet accounts are explained. The debit and credit balance sheet change column totals agree ($147), although this amount is meaningful only for checking purposes. Entry (*m*), the $34 cash change, reconciles the total of cash increases and decreases. Furthermore, the net operating cash flow ($20) agrees for both methods. Disagreement between these two totals is a common problem when the spreadsheet approach is applied for the first time.

CONCEPT REVIEW

1. Explain why a gain on a sale of equipment is subtracted in the reconciliation of income and operating cash flows.
2. Why is depreciation added in the reconciliation?
3. Why is an increase in net accounts receivable subtracted in the reconciliation?

Analyzing More Complex Situations

The purpose of the Simple Company example is to describe preparation of a complete SCF. However, more involved situations often arise when actual SCFs are prepared. The examples in this section show both the direct and indirect method disclosures separately from the reconciliation adjustments because the reconciliation of income and net operating cash flow is reported under both methods.

Purchase and Sale of Cash Equivalents   Transactions involving only cash and cash equivalents are operating activities.[19] When cash equivalents are acquired or sold at cost, no disclosure in the SCF is necessary because total cash and cash equivalents are unaffected. However, a gain or loss on sale of cash equivalents changes total cash and cash equivalents by the amount of the gain or loss, requiring disclosure.

Example   Assume that Niko Inc. sold cash equivalents costing $50,000 for $52,000. The $2,000 gain represents an increase in cash and cash equivalents.

---

[19]*SFAS No. 95*, par. 16.

Direct Method	$2,000 operating cash inflow, gain on sale of cash equivalents.
Indirect Method	No disclosure.
Reconciliation	No adjustment. (The $2,000 gain is reflected in earnings.)

Income Taxes, Current and Deferred   Income tax expense on income from continuing operations is recorded in income taxes payable and a deferred tax account. Assume the following information:

From comparative balance sheets:

	1997	1998
Income taxes payable	$20,000	$27,000
Deferred tax liability	18,000	23,000

Income tax expense for 1998: $45,000

The reconstructed entries for taxes are as follows:

```
Income tax expense  . . . . . . . . . . . . . . . . . . . . . . . . . . . . . . . . . . . . . .   45,000
    Deferred tax liability ($23,000 − $18,000)  . . . . . . . . . . . . . . . . . . . . . . .            5,000
    Income taxes payable . . . . . . . . . . . . . . . . . . . . . . . . . . . . . . . . . .           40,000
Income taxes payable ($20,000 + $40,000 − $27,000)  . . . . . . . . . . . . . . .   33,000
    Cash . . . . . . . . . . . . . . . . . . . . . . . . . . . . . . . . . . . . . . .           33,000
```

The following disclosures are required in the SCF:

Direct Method	$33,000 operating cash outflow, tax payments.
Indirect Method	Disclose income tax payments, $33,000, in a supporting schedule.

Reconciliation		
Net income	$	xxx
Income taxes payable increase	+	7,000
Deferred tax liability increase	+	5,000
Net cash flow from operations	$	xxx

Earnings is reduced $45,000 by income tax expense, but cash provided by operations is reduced only $33,000. The two reconciling adjustments explain the $12,000 difference.

Trading Securities and Securities Available for Sale   Under *SFAS No. 115*, cash flows from purchases and sales of trading securities (TS) are classified as operating cash flows. For securities available for sale (SAS), the cash flows are classified as investing. This classification scheme leads to significant differences in cash flow reporting, as the next few examples illustrate. Cash inflows from interest and dividends are classified as operating for both TS and SAS.

Example   Assume Medico Company purchased common stock of HMO, Inc., for $3,000 in 1998. The market value of the stock on December 31, 1998, is $4,000. (The unrealized gain is included in income for TS, in owners' equity for SAS.) In 1999, Medico sold the entire investment for $3,800.

1998 SCF: HMO Securities Classified as TS

Direct Method	$3,000 operating cash outflow, purchase of TS.
Indirect Method	No disclosure other than in the reconciliation.

Reconciliation		
Net income	$	xxx
Net investment in TS increase	−	4,000
Net cash flow from operations	$	xxx

The investment in HMO is carried at the $4,000 market value on December 31, 1998, and has increased $4,000 during 1998. Net income reflects the unrealized $1,000 gain, but operating cash flows have been reduced $3,000 on the purchase. The $4,000 subtraction adjustment reconciles this difference.

1998 SCF: HMO Securities Classified as SAS

Direct and Indirect Methods	$3,000 investing cash outflow, purchase of SAS.
Reconciliation	No adjustment.

The unrealized gain on the SAS bypasses the income statement. Because the market value change in HMO stock did not affect earnings or operating cash flow, a reconciliation adjustment is not required.

In 1999, the investment in HMO declined $200 in value to $3,800, and was then sold. If the investment is a TS, a $200 realized loss is recognized. If it is a SAS, an $800 realized gain is recognized ($3,800 − $3,000).

1999 SCF: HMO Securities Classified as TS

Direct Method	$3,800 operating cash inflow, proceeds from sale of TS.
Indirect Method	No disclosure other than in the reconciliation.
Reconciliation	Net income . . . . $ xxx Net investment in TS decrease . . . . + 4,000 Net cash flow from operations . . . . $ xxx

The balance in the net TS account has decreased from $4,000 to zero (assuming no additional purchases of TS during 1999). The $4,000 addition adjustment reconciles the earnings effect ($200 decrease) and the operating cash flow effect ($3,800 increase). A separate reconciliation adjustment for the realized loss is not necessary because the loss is included in earnings.

1999 SCF: HMO Securities Classified as SAS

Direct and Indirect Methods	$3,800 investing cash inflow, proceeds from sale of SAS.
Reconciliation	Net income . . . . $ xxx Realized gain on sale of SAS . . . . − 800 Net cash flow from operations . . . . $ xxx

The $800 subtraction adjustment reconciles the earnings effect ($800 increase) and the operating cash flow effect ($0).

Equity Method of Accounting for Investments   Under the equity method, the investor records its share of investee earnings as an increase in the investment and investment revenue accounts. Dividends received, an operating cash inflow, decreases the investment.

Example   Assume Emmet Company owns 30 percent of Sandoval Company. Sandoval earned $400,000 and paid $300,000 in dividends the current year. Emmet records the following entries:

Investment in stock (.30 × 400,000)	120,000	
Investment revenue		120,000
Cash (.30 × $300,000)	90,000	
Investment in stock		90,000

The SCF disclosures are as follows:

Direct Method	$90,000 operating cash inflow, dividends received from investment.
Indirect Method	No disclosure other than in the reconciliation.
Reconciliation	Net income . . . . $ xxx Investment revenue, equity method investment . . . . . −120,000 Dividends received, equity method investment* . . . . . + 90,000 Net cash flow from operations . . . . $ xxx

*The adjustment for dividends received on equity method investments is one of the few cash flows appearing in the reconciliation.

The two adjustments together reconcile Emmet's earnings increase of $120,000 and net operating cash flow increase of $90,000 (dividends received).

An alternative reconciliation disclosure frequently found in practice also is acceptable: $30,000 subtraction adjustment, excess of equity method investment revenue over dividends.

Example   The Coca-Cola Company chose this alternative by including a $25 million subtraction adjustment, equity income net of dividends, in its 1995 SCF, shown at the end of this text.

Short-Term and Long-Term Notes Payable to Suppliers   Principal payments on both short- and long-term notes to suppliers for purchases of inventory are operating cash outflows.

Example   Assume that notes payable to suppliers increased from $10,000 to $15,000 during the year, and $25,000 was paid on notes during the year. The following disclosures are required:

Direct Method	$25,000 operating cash outflow, payments to suppliers.
Indirect Method	No disclosure other than in the reconciliation.
Reconciliation	Net income . . . . $ xxx
	Notes payable to suppliers (short or long term) increase . . + 5,000
	Net cash flow from operations . . . . $ xxx

Short- and Long-Term Notes Payable to Banks   Principal payments on loans from financial institutions, whether short or long term, are financing cash outflows.

Example   Assume that notes payable to banks increased from $10,000 to $15,000 during the year and that $25,000 of principal payments were made on loans during the year. This implies that $30,000 was borrowed during the year. The following disclosures are required:

Direct and Indirect Methods	$30,000 financing cash inflow, borrowings from banks; $25,000 financing cash outflow, principal payments to banks.
Reconciliation	No adjustment. (There is no earnings or operating cash flow effect.)

Accounts Receivable, Bad Debts, and Write-Offs   Uncollectible accounts complicate the analysis of cash flows related to accounts receivable. Transaction analysis helps to determine the necessary cash flow and reconciliation disclosures. Assume the following information:

From the comparative balance sheets:

	1997	1998
Accounts receivable	$ 600,000	$175,000
Allowance for doubtful accounts	20,000	35,000

Information for 1998:

Bad debt expense	$ 40,000
Accounts written off	25,000
Collections on account	1,400,000
Sales on account	1,000,000

T-accounts are used to reconstruct the relevant events for determining cash flows and earnings effects:

Accounts Receivable

Beg. bal.	600,000		
Sales	1,000,000	Collections	1,400,000
		Write-offs	25,000
End. bal.	175,000		

Allowance for Doubtful Accounts

		Beg. bal.	20,000
Write-offs	25,000	Bad debt expense	40,000
		End. bal.	35,000

Net accounts receivable 12/31/97: $600,000 − $20,000 = $580,000
Net accounts receivable 12/31/98: $175,000 − $35,000 =   140,000

   Decrease in net accounts receivable $440,000

Change in gross accounts receivable before write-offs:
  Sales ($1,000,000) − Collections ($1,400,000) = $400,000 decrease
Net income effect:
  Sales ($1,000,000) − Bad debt expense ($40,000) = $960,000 increase

The following disclosures would appear in the SCF:

Direct Method $1,400,000 operating cash inflow, collections on account.

Indirect Method   No disclosure other than in the reconciliation.

Reconciliation   Two options are available:

1. Net income . . . . $ xxx
      Net accounts receivable decrease . . . . +440,000
      Net cash flow from operations . . . . $ xxx

2. Net income . . . . $ xxx
      Gross accounts receivable decrease before write-offs . . +400,000
      Bad debt expense . . . . + 40,000
      Net cash flow from operations . . . . $ xxx

Both alternatives yield a net $440,000 addition adjustment.[20] This amount reconciles the earnings effect ($960,000 increase) and the operating cash inflow ($1,400,000 cash collections).

Extraordinary Items   Extraordinary items generally are not cash flows, but they do affect income. Therefore, they usually appear as reconciling adjustments in their pretax amounts. The cash flow associated with the transaction usually is classified as investing or financing. Tax payments (or reduction in payments) resulting from extraordinary items are operating cash flows. The reconciling adjustments for the change in income taxes payable and deferred taxes automatically include the tax effects of extraordinary items.

Example   Suppose Angeles Company retires a bond issue before maturity by paying $330,000, excluding accrued interest. The firm recognizes a $20,000 extraordinary gain before tax ($4,000 tax effect) on the retirement. The following are the SCF disclosures:

Direct and $330,000 financing cash outflow, bond retirement.
Indirect
Methods

Reconciliation   Net income . . . . $ xxx
      Extraordinary gain on bond retirement . . . . −20,000
      Net cash flow from operations . . . . $ xxx

---

[20] The second option is not appropriate when accounts written off in previous periods are collected.

There is no operating cash flow associated with the $20,000 extraordinary gain; hence the subtraction adjustment. SCF disclosures for discontinued operations are similar to those for extraordinary items.

The appendix provides a longer example of preparing a complete SCF under both direct and indirect methods, and incorporates additional transaction examples.

> **CONCEPT REVIEW**
>
> 1. What is the effect on total cash and cash equivalents of selling cash equivalents at a $3,000 loss?
> 2. Explain how transactions giving rise to extraordinary items are disclosed in the SCF.
> 3. Explain why dividends received from equity method investments are added in the reconciliation.

ISSUES IN CASH FLOW REPORTING

Cash or Accrual Information

Researchers looking at the relative usefulness of cash flow versus accrual information can reach different conclusions. In one study of 98 firms, the authors found that cash flow information increases the overall information content of financial statements.[21] Another study provides evidence to suggest that cash flow variables supply risk assessment information beyond that provided by earnings information.[22]

But other researchers report less favorable predictive results for cash flow. Authors in one study of 290 companies found that operating cash flow information from a five-year period was not a good discriminator between healthy firms and firms that declared bankruptcy.[23] Accrual measures, including traditional financial accounting ratios, seemed to be more accurate predictors of business failure. Firms with poor operating cash flows can survive for an extended period if creditors are willing to renegotiate and restructure debt. Massey-Ferguson and International Harvester (now Navistar) are examples.[24] Growing companies also may have negative cash flow because they invest heavily in capital expenditures.

Neither accrual nor cash flow information alone is sufficient for a complete understanding of a company's performance. The relationships between revenues and cash inflows and between expenses and cash outflows can be understood only by studying both types of information.

Classification of Cash Flows

How cash flows are to be classified remains a controversial issue. Historically, accountants have viewed operating activities as those that are repetitive in nature and are related to income-producing activities. Under *SFAS No. 95,* the association with earnings justifies classifying a cash flow as operating. Consequently, net cash flow from operating activities may include amounts that are nonrepetitive and that result from investing and financing activities.

Example   All income tax payments are classified as operating cash outflows, although this results in classifying taxes on gains and losses from extraordinary items, discontinued operations, and plant asset disposals as operating. The FASB concluded that the cost of requiring allocation of income tax payments among the three cash flow categories exceeded its benefit.

---

[21]R. Bowen, D. Burgstahler, and L. Daley, "The Incremental Information Content of Accrual versus Cash Flows," *Accounting Review,* October 1987, pp. 723–47.

[22]B. Ismail and M. Kim, "On the Association of Cash Flow Variables with Market Risk: Further Evidence," *Accounting Review,* January 1989, pp. 125–36.

[23]C. Casey and N. Bartczak, "Cash Flow—It's Not the Bottom Line," *Harvard Business Review,* July–August 1984, p. 61.

[24]Ibid.

Interest received and paid, and dividends received are also classified as operating. An alternative view maintains that interest and dividends *received* result from lending money and investing in stock, which are investing activities. Interest *paid* results from incurring debt, a financing activity. This issue is related to the decision to classify all income tax payments as operational. If these amounts were classified as financing or investing, the associated income tax payments would be classified similarly.

An unintended consequence of classifying interest payments as an operating activity arises when zero coupon bonds are retired at maturity. Most of the maturity amount paid represents interest, yet many firms report the entire cash outflow in the financing category. As a result, net operating cash flow is overstated, significantly in some cases. If interest payments were defined as a financing outflow, this problem would be avoided.[25] At least four different methods of reporting cash flows related to discounted debt have been detected in practice, confounding interfirm comparability.[26]

The FASB stated that a distinction must be made between return *of* investment (return of principal) and return *on* investment (interest and dividends). Return on investment is a component of income. The Board decided that inclusion in income is a stronger argument than association with a previous investing transaction, for classifying return on investment. In addition, the Board noted that most firms reported interest received and paid as an operating fund flow in the statement of changes in financial position, which preceded the SCF. Also, under both direct and indirect methods, interest and income tax payments must be disclosed and can therefore be reclassified by the user.

Principal payments on long-term notes to suppliers also are classified as operating. An alternate view maintains that these flows are actually financing cash outflows. Under this view, the operating classification is inconsistent with that of payments on notes to financial institutions and other creditors.

Direct or Indirect Method?

Is the additional information disclosed under the direct method worth its cost? The actual operating cash flows may be more useful for predicting future net operating cash flow. The indirect method does not report collections from sales and other operating cash inflows that analysts need to assess cash-generating ability.

The direct method presents cash flows in all three cash flow categories; the indirect method provides only indirect information concerning operating cash flows. Bankers responding to the exposure draft preceding *SFAS No. 95* overwhelmingly favored the direct method, while (according to one study) 82 percent of surveyed CPAs favored the indirect method.[27] Familiarity with the statement of changes in financial position contributed to the preference of CPAs for the indirect method.

The FASB recommends the direct method but permits either. Tradition played a part in this decision. The indirect method of reporting fund flows had been used for more than four decades. Industry has more experience with the indirect method, and it is less expensive. Ledger account balances provide most of the reconciling adjustments. The indirect method enables financial statement users to approximate operating cash flows from the reconciliation and the income statement and balance sheet accounts.

Companies are reluctant to divulge more information than required, especially about cash flows, and some report that their accounting systems do not readily provide gross operating cash receipts and payments.[28] Only 2½ percent of 600 surveyed companies used the direct method.[29] Thus far, creditors have been unable to persuade their corporate clients to use the direct method.

---

[25] H. Nurnberg, "Inconsistencies and Ambiguities in Cash Flow Statements under *FASB Statement No. 95*," *Accounting Horizons,* June, 1993, p. 67.

[26] G. Vent, J. Cowling, and S. Sevalstad, "Cash Flow Comparability: Accounting for Long-Term Debt under *SFAS No. 95*," *Accounting Horizons* 9, no. 4 (December 1995), pp. 88–96.

[27] C. Gibson, T. Klammer, and S. Reed, "The Cash Flow Statement," *CPA Journal,* November 1986, pp. 18–38.

[28] *SFAS No. 95,* par. 109.

[29] *Accounting Trends and Techniques—1996* (New York: AICPA, 1996), p. 461.

GLOBAL VIEW

Most of the world's large companies report **funds flow** information along with the income statement and balance sheet, although the specific content and format vary. *Funds flow* is a generic term that can include cash and cash equivalents, working capital (current assets less liabilities), and net quick assets (working capital less inventories and prepaids). For example, before *SFAS No. 95,* many U.S. firms reported a statement of changes in financial position based on funds defined as working capital.

The International Accounting Standards Committee (IASC), as part of its Comparability and Improvement project, revised its *Standard No. 7,* "Cash Flow Statements," effective January 1, 1994. The Statement previously had required a statement of changes in financial position but did not specify the fund definition, and was similar in content to *APB Opinion No. 19.* Now, in keeping with the international trend toward cash flow reporting, the IASC requires a statement of cash flows as an integral part of a set of financial statements.

The major provisions of *IAS No. 7* and *SFAS No. 95* are in agreement. Cash and cash equivalents are the reporting basis of the statement, and the definition of cash equivalents is the same under both standards. Cash flows are classified according to the three categories of cash flows: operating, investing, and financing; the format is essentially the same under both standards. As with U.S. GAAP, both the direct and indirect methods are allowed, with the direct method also being recommended by the IASC.

The two standards are not identical however. For example, *IAS No. 7* allows the reporting firm to choose how interest and dividends received and paid are classified, provided that the classification is based on the nature of the underlying transaction and is made consistently. The IASC recognizes that, except for financial institutions that generally tend to classify these cash flows as operating, there is no general agreement as to the classification of these cash flows for other types of firms.

The international standard also allows (but does not require) classification of income tax payments as financing and investing cash flows, depending on the underlying transaction. In addition, noncash activities are not combined with cash flow information under *IAS No. 7.* Such transactions are disclosed elsewhere in the annual report, based on the principle that cash flow disclosures should emphasize cash transactions.

Although some differences exist between U.S. and international cash flow reporting standards, a financial statement user accustomed to U.S. GAAP would have no difficulty understanding a cash flow statement prepared under IASC standards. But funds flow statements based on noncash fund definitions continue to be found in international settings, *IAS No. 7* notwithstanding. For example, firms in the United Kingdom generally issue a cash flow statement, whereas in France the working capital funds flow statement is more prevalent.

Internationally, the trend toward cash flow reporting is exemplified by six countries that have issued standards requiring cash flow statements: Canada, New Zealand, South Africa, the United States, the United Kingdom, and the Republic of Ireland. Other countries, including Japan and Australia, are exploring the issue of whether to require a cash flow statement.[30]

The perceived objectivity of cash is an important reason for the growth in popularity of cash flow statements. Although there is concern that the variety of definitions of cash and cash equivalents across international borders may reduce the effectiveness of cash flow reporting, such differences are probably smaller than those under the present assortment of allowable funds flow definitions. We believe that the international trend toward cash flow statements is one step toward more understandable financial statements and a more uniform international accounting language.

SUMMARY OF KEY POINTS

(L.O. 1)   1. Cash flow information is used to predict future cash flows, to assess liquidity, to evaluate the ability of a firm to pay dividends and extinguish obligations, to assess the ability of a firm to adapt to changes in the business environment, and for other purposes.

(L.O. 1)   2. The SCF is one of three required financial statements. Its primary purpose is to provide relevant information about cash receipts and disbursements.

(L.O. 2)   3. Cash and cash equivalents are the reporting basis for the SCF. Cash equivalents are investments readily convertible into a known amount of cash and having an original maturity of three months or less.

---

[30]R. Wallace and P. Collier, "The 'Cash' in Cash Flow Statements: A Multi-Country Comparison," *Accounting Horizons,* December 1991, p. 44.

(L.O. 2)   4. Cash flows fall into three categories. Operating flows are those associated with the earnings process. Investing flows involve long-term purposes to which cash is applied, and the proceeds from sale of long-term assets. Financing flows are the sources of short- and long-term financing other than operations, repayments of short- and long-term liabilities not related to operations, and equities.

(L.O. 2)   5. *SFAS No. 95* permits two different methods of preparing the SCF: the direct and the indirect methods. They differ only with respect to cash flows from operating activities. The direct method reports the operating cash flows. The indirect method reports adjustments that reconcile net income and net cash flow. Investing and financing activities are reported the same way under both methods.

(L.O. 2)   6. The reconciliation of net income and net operating cash flow is required for both methods. The operating activity sections of both the direct and indirect SCFs convert accrual income to cash-basis income.

(L.O. 2)   7. Significant noncash transactions are disclosed in a supplementary schedule for a description of investing and financing activities.

(L.O. 3)   8. There are several approaches to preparing the SCF. The same objective applies to all: analyzing transactions to identify all cash flows, reconciling items, and noncash transactions.

(L.O. 4)   9. The format-free approach to preparing the SCF emphasizes transaction analysis and uses no particular format. The sources of information for cash flows are the income statement, additional information, and the comparative balance sheets.

(L.O. 5)   10. The spreadsheet is an organized format for preparing the SCF. Both the direct and indirect method SCFs can be prepared with the same spreadsheet.

REVIEW PROBLEM

The Phillies Company prepared the following information relevant to its 1998 SCF:

Comparative Balance Sheets

	December 31	
	1997	**1998**
Cash	$200,000	$ 62,000
Accounts receivable, net	60,000	80,000
Inventory	12,000	20,000
Prepaids	6,000	10,000
Equipment, net	300,000	500,000
Patent, net	90,000	70,000
Total assets	$668,000	$742,000
Accounts payable	$ 40,000	$ 60,000
Salaries payable	60,000	50,000
Interest payable	6,000	9,000
Income tax payable	12,000	20,000
Mortgage payable	120,000	110,000
Bonds payable	200,000	100,000
Premium on bonds payable	8,000	3,000
Common stock, no par	150,000	170,000
Retained earnings	72,000	220,000
Total liabilities and owners' equity	$668,000	$742,000

Income Statement Accounts, 1998

Sales	$820,000
Cost of goods sold	(380,000)
Depreciation expense	(100,000)
Amortization of patent	(20,000)
Other expenses	(46,000)
Gain, excess of insurance proceeds over book value of equipment destroyed	10,000
Interest expense	(22,000)
Income tax expense	(72,000)
Extraordinary loss, bond retirement, net of $1,000 tax	(2,000)
Net income	$188,000

Additional information:

1. Phillies declared $40,000 of dividends in 1998.
2. Equipment (cost $100,000, accumulated depreciation $60,000) was destroyed by fire. Proceeds from insurance: $50,000.

3. Bonds were retired on January 1, 1998, at 107. Applicable taxes: $1,000.

Required

Prepare the 1998 SCF for Phillies; use the direct method. The spreadsheet is used to illustrate the solution. You also may use the format-free approach.

SOLUTION

Spreadsheet

Comparative Balance Sheets	12/31/97	Dr.		Cr.		12/31/98
Cash	200,000			138,000	*(q)*	62,000
Accounts receivable, net	60,000	*(b)*	20,000			80,000
Inventory	12,000	*(c)*	8,000			20,000
Prepaids	6,000	*(g)*	4,000			10,000
Equipment, net	300,000	*(h)*	60,000	100,000	*(e)*	500,000
		(n)	340,000	100,000	*(h)*	
Patent, net	90,000			20,000	*(f)*	70,000
Total assets	668,000					742,000
Accounts payable	40,000			20,000	*(d)*	60,000
Salaries payable	60,000	*(g)*	10,000			50,000
Interest payable	6,000			3,000	*(i)*	9,000
Income tax payable	12,000			8,000	*(k)*	20,000
Mortgage payable	120,000	*(o)*	10,000			110,000
Bonds payable	200,000	*(l)*	100,000			100,000
Premium on bonds payable	8,000	*(l)*	4,000			3,000
		(j)	1,000			
Common stock, no par	150,000			20,000	*(p)*	170,000
Retained earnings	72,000	*(m)*	40,000	188,000	*(a)*	220,000
Total liabilities and owners' equity	668,000					742,000
Total changes			597,000	597,000		

Adjustments Leading to SCF

		Indirect Method			Direct Method (operations)
		Dr.		Cr.	
Operating activities:					
Net income	188,000	*(a)* 188,000			
Sales	820,000			20,000 *(b)*	800,000 customer collections
Cost of goods sold	380,000	*(d)* 20,000		8,000 *(c)*	368,000 payments to suppliers
Depreciation expense	100,000	*(e)* 100,000			
Amortization of patent	20,000	*(f)* 20,000			
Other expenses	46,000			14,000 *(g)*	60,000 other operating payments
Gain on equipment	10,000			10,000 *(h)*	
Interest expense	22,000	*(i)* 3,000		1,000 *(j)*	20,000 interest payments
Income tax expense	72,000	*(k)* 8,000			64,000 tax payments
Extraordinary loss	3,000	*(l)* 3,000			
Tax	1,000				1,000 reduce tax payments
Investing activities:					
Insurance proceeds, equipment		*(h)* 50,000			
Purchase of equipment				340,000 *(n)*	
Financing activities:					
Retirement of bonds				107,000 *(l)*	
Dividends paid				40,000 *(m)*	
Principal payment, mortgage				10,000 *(o)*	
Issue stock		*(p)* 20,000			
		412,000			
Net cash decrease		*(q)* 138,000			
		550,000		550,000	

Explanations for spreadsheet entries:

(*a*) Net income.

(*b*) Accounts receivable increase.

(*c*) Inventory increase.

(*d*) Accounts payable increase.

(*e*) Depreciation expense.

(*f*) Amortization of patent.

(*g*) Prepaids increase, and salaries payable decrease (related to other expenses).

(*h*) Equipment fire—gain is subtracted from income because the investing cash inflow completely explains the cash effect. The original cost and accumulated depreciation are removed from the net equipment account.

(*i*) Interest payable increase.

(*j*) Amortization of bond premium in 1998—one-half the premium was removed from the accounts at the beginning of the year upon retirement of one-half the bond issue. The remaining $1,000 decrease in bond premium is amortization.

(*k*) Increase in income taxes payable.

(*l*) Extraordinary loss does not decrease cash, yet it decreased net income. The associated tax reduction decreases the initial amount of tax payments computed after entry (*k*).

Entry to record the bond retirement, January 1, 1998:

Bonds payable	100,000	
Bond premium (1/2 of $8,000)	4,000	
Extraordinary loss	3,000	
Cash (1.07 × $100,000)		107,000

(*m*) Dividends declared equal dividends paid (no dividends payable account).

(*n*) There remained a $340,000 unexplained increase in net equipment after all available information was incorporated.

(*o*) Decrease in mortgage payable implies a principal payment, in the absence of other information.

(*p*) Increase in common stock implies issuance of additional shares, in the absence of other information.

(*q*) Net cash decrease (to balance).

PHILLIES COMPANY

Statement of Cash Flows

For the Year Ended December 31, 1998

Cash flows from operating activities:		
Collections from customers	$800,000	
Payments to suppliers	(368,000)	
Other payments	(60,000)	
Interest payments	(20,000)	
Tax payments	(63,000)	
Net cash inflow from operating activities		$289,000
Cash flows from investing activities:		
Insurance proceeds—equipment fire	(50,000)	
Purchase of equipment	(340,000)	
Net cash outflow from investing activities		(290,000)
Cash flows from financing activities:		
Bond retirement	(107,000)	
Dividends paid	(40,000)	
Principal payment, mortgage	(10,000)	
Issue stock	20,000	
Net cash outflow from financing activities		(137,000)
Net cash decrease		(138,000)
Cash, January 1, 1998		200,000
Cash, December 31, 1998		$ 62,000

Reconciliation of Net Income and Net Cash Inflow from Operating Activities

Net income	$188,000
Reconciling items:	
Accounts receivable increase	(20,000)
Accounts payable increase	20,000
Inventory increase	(8,000)
Depreciation	100,000
Patent amortization	20,000
Salaries payable decrease	(10,000)
Prepaids increase	(4,000)
Gain on equipment fire	(10,000)
Interest payable increase	3,000
Amortization of bond premium	(1,000)
Income taxes payable increase	8,000
Extraordinary loss	3,000
Net cash inflow from operating activities	$289,000

APPENDIX   *Comprehensive Example*

This appendix provides a more involved example of preparing a complete SCF. The spreadsheet approach is used to determine both the direct and indirect method SCFs. Exhibit 23A–1 furnishes the case data for Complex Company. Exhibit 23A–2 is the complete spreadsheet.

Income Statement Accounts   The accounts are analyzed in order of appearance in the income statement. Amounts are in thousands of dollars:

(a) Net income of $15 begins the reconciliation of net income and net operating cash flows.

(b) Reconciliation: gross $3 accounts receivable decrease (related to sales and services) is added to net income. Bad debt expense is a separate adjustment, in (i).

Direct method: cash collections exceed sales by $3 because accounts receivable decreased $3. In terms of the spreadsheet, the $96 sales (initial cash inflow estimate) is increased by the $3 entry in the debit column (a debit to cash increases cash), yielding the $99 cash inflow.

(c) Reconciliation: no adjustment for $1 dividends on short-term investments is necessary because the increase in net income equals the cash inflow.

Direct method: $1 dividend is an operating cash inflow.

(d) Reconciliation: subtract the $3 gain on sale of plant assets.

Both methods: using related additional information, proceeds on sale of plant assets, $15, is an investing cash inflow. The related changes in plant assets and accumulated depreciation are entered. These amounts serve as a partial explanation of the account balance changes.

(e) Reconciliation: no adjustment is needed for the gain on sale of cash equivalents because the $2 gain equals the cash increase.

Direct method: the gain is a $2 operating cash inflow.

(f), (g) Reconciliation: the adjustments related to cost of goods sold include the $4 accounts payable increase added to net income and $7 inventory increase subtracted from net income.

Direct method: in terms of the spreadsheet, the $42 cost of goods sold (initial cash outflow estimate) is decreased by the $4 entry in the debit column (a debit to cash increases cash or decreases the cash outflow) and is increased by the $7 credit entry (a credit to cash increases the cash outflow).

(h) Reconciliation: $8 depreciation is added to net income.

(i) Reconciliation: $3 bad debt expense is added to net income. Alternatively, the reconciliation adjustments in (b) and (i) can be combined into one adjustment for the decrease in net accounts receivable: add $6.

(j) Reconciliation: subtract the $1 interest payable decrease (related to interest expense), and add the $1 amortization of bond discount.

Direct method: $5 operating cash outflow. A summary entry explains this outflow and the changes in relevant accounts.

EXHIBIT 23A–1
Case Information
Complex Company

COMPLEX COMPANY
Case Data for Preparing Statements of Cash Flow
(in thousands)

Income Statement, 1998

Revenues and gains:

Sales and services	$96
Dividends (Xenon Corp.)	1
Gain on sale of plant assets	3
Gain on sale of cash equivalents	2

Expenses:

Cost of goods sold	(42)
Depreciation expense	(8)
Bad debt expense	(3)
Interest expense (on bonds)	(5)
Remaining expenses	(13)
Income tax expense (continuing operations)	(9)
Income before extraordinary items and discontinued operations	22
Discontinued operations, gain $10 (tax expense, $3)	7
Extraordinary loss, land condemnation $20 (tax saving, $6)	(14)
Net income	$15

Comparative Balance Sheets

	December 31 1997	December 31 1998
Cash	$ 30	$ 61
Cash equivalents	6	0
Total	36	61
Investment, short term (stock of Xenon Corp.)*	12	17
Accounts receivable	32	29
Allowance for doubtful accounts	(2)	(5)
Inventory (perpetual system)	30	37
Prepaid insurance	4	2
Land	60	41
Plant assets	80	96
Accumulated depreciation	(20)	(26)
Other assets (includes discontinued operations, $13)	35	22
Total assets	$267	$274
Accounts payable	$ 26	$ 30
Interest payable	2	1
Income tax payable	11	4
Notes payable, long term	0	10
Bonds payable	80	60
Unamortized bond discount	(3)	(2)
Common stock, nopar	100	130
Retained earnings	51	41
Total liabilities and stockholders' equity	$267	$274

*Classified as securities available for sale.

Interest expense	5	
Interest payable	1	
Unamortized bond discount		1
Cash (derived)		5

(*k*) Reconciliation: add the $2 prepaid insurance decrease (the only balance sheet account related to remaining expenses).

Direct method: the $11 cash payment equals the $13 remaining expenses less the $2 decrease in prepaid insurance.

EXHIBIT 23A–1
(*concluded*)

COMPLEX COMPANY
Case Data for Preparing Statements of Cash Flow
(in thousands)

Additional Information

1. Sold cash equivalents in January 1998 for $8 cash.
2. Cash borrowed on long-term note at the end of 1998, $10.
3. Retained earnings statement, year ended December 31, 1998:

Beginning balance	$51
Net income for 1998	15
Cash dividend declared and paid in 1998	(15)
Stock dividend issued in 1998 (capitalize par value)	(10)
Ending balance	$41

	Asset	Accumulated Depreciation
4. Plant asset account:		
Beginning balance	$80	$20 credit
Disposal of asset (for cash, $15)	(14)	(2)
Acquisition of new asset (machine)*	30	
Depreciation		8
Ending balance	$96	$26

*Paid cash $10 and issued common stock in full settlement, $20 (market value).

	Bonds	Discount, Unamortized Balance
5. Bonds payable account:		
Beginning balance	$80	$3 debit
Discount amortization for 1998		(1)
Bonds retired at end of 1998 at face value	(20)	—
Ending balance	$60	$2

6. Land account:	
Beginning balance	$60
Sale due to condemnation (extraordinary loss); cash received in full payment, $40	(60)
Land acquisition (paid cash, $41)	41
Ending balance	$41

7. Discontinued operations:
   Closed out a segment completely by selling all related assets for cash, $23.
   The $13 cost of these assets is included in the account other assets at the
   beginning of 1998. Assume no accumulated depreciation.

8. Income tax payable account:

Beginning balance		$11
Additions for current income taxes:		
Tax on continuing operations	$9	
Extraordinary loss ($20), tax saving	(6)	
Discontinued operations ($10), tax expense	3	
Increase in payable (net)		6
Cash payments made during 1998		(13)
Ending balance		$ 4

(*l*) Reconciliation: subtract the $7 income tax payable decrease (related to income tax expense).
Direct method: $16 income tax payment exceeds $9 income tax expense by the $7 income
tax payable decrease. This is an initial tax payment amount, adjusted by the tax related to
the extraordinary loss and discontinued operations gain (see (*m*) next).

EXHIBIT 23A–2
Spreadsheet

COMPLEX COMPANY

Spreadsheet for Direct and Indirect Method SCFs
For the Year Ended December 31, 1998
(in thousands)*

Comparative Balance Sheets	12/31/97	Dr.		Cr.		12/31/98
Cash	30	(v)	31			61
Cash equivalents	6			6	(v)	
Investment in Xenon	12	(u)	5			17
Accounts receivable	32			3	(b)	29
Allowance for doubtful accounts	(2)			3	(i)	(5)
Inventory	30	(g)	7			37
Prepaid insurance	4			2	(k)	2
Land	60	(t)	41	60	(n)	41
Plant assets	80	(r)	30	14	(d)	96
Accumulated depreciation	(20)	(d)	2	8	(h)	(26)
Other assets	35			13	(m)	22
Total assets	267					274
Accounts payable	26			4	(f)	30
Interest payable	2	(j)	1			1
Income taxes payable	11	(l)	7			4
Notes payable				10	(o)	10
Bonds payable	80	(s)	20			60
Unamortized bond discount	(3)			1	(j)	(2)
Common stock	100			10	(q)	130
				20	(r)	
Retained earnings	51	(p)	15	15	(a)	41
		(q)	10			
Total liabilities and owners' equity	267					274
Total changes				169	169	

*Italic letters refer to text discussion.

(m) Reconciliation: subtract the $10 gain from discontinued operations.

Both methods, using related additional information, the $23 proceeds from sale of assets from discontinued operations is an investing cash inflow. The original cost of assets is entered into the spreadsheet.

Direct method: the $3 tax on the gain increases tax payments.

(n) Reconciliation: add the $20 extraordinary loss to net income.

Both methods: using related additional information, the $40 proceeds from sale of land due to condemnation is an investing cash inflow. The original cost of land is entered into the spreadsheet.

Direct method: the $6 tax savings reduces tax payments. Total tax payments equal $13 ($16 on continuing operations plus $3 on discontinued operations less $6 on extraordinary loss).

Additional Information

The additional information not already incorporated into the spreadsheet is analyzed in order of appearance in Exhibit 23A–1:

(o) Both methods: financing cash inflow, $10 proceeds from issuing long-term note.

(p) Both methods: financing cash outflow, $15 dividend payments.

(q) Stock dividends are not disclosed in the SCF.

(r) Both methods: investing cash outflow, $10 payment to purchase plant assets. Note A to the SCF (Exhibit 23A–3) describes the noncash aspects of the acquisition: issuance of $20 of common stock for the remaining portion of the purchase price.

(s) Both methods: financing cash outflow, $20 payment to retire bonds.

(t) Both methods: investing cash outflow, $41 payment to acquire land.

EXHIBIT 23A–2
(*concluded*)

COMPLEX COMPANY
Spreadsheet for Direct and Indirect Method SCFs
For the Year Ended December 31, 1998
(in thousands)

Adjustments Leading to SCF

Italic letters refer to the text discussion.

		Indirect Method				Direct Method (operations)
		Dr.		Cr.		
Operating activities:						
Net income	15	(a)	15			
Sales and services	96	(b)	3		99	customer collections
Dividends	1			(c)	1	dividends received
Gain, sale of plant asset	3		3 (d)			
Gain on sale of cash equivalents	2		(e)		2	cash equivalent sale
Cost of goods sold	42	(f)	4	7 (g)	45	payments to suppliers
Depreciation	8	(h)	8			
Bad debt expense	3	(i)	3			
Interest expense	5	(j)	1	1 (j)	5	interest payments
Remaining expenses	13	(k)	2		11	payments for other expenses
Income tax expense	9		7 (l)		16	tax payments
Gain on discontinued operations	10		10 (m)			
Less tax	3				3	increase tax payments
Extraordinary loss	20	(n)	20			
Less tax savings	6				6	reduce tax payments
Investing activities:						
Sale of plant assets		(d)	15			
Proceeds from sale of discontinued assets		(m)	23			
Proceeds from land condemnation		(n)	40			
Purchase of plant assets				10 (r)		
Acquisition of land				41 (t)		
Purchase of Xenon stock				5 (u)		
Financing activities:						
Issue long-term note		(o)	10			
Dividend payment				15 (p)		
Bond retirement				<u>20</u> (s)		
				119		
Net increase in cash and cash equivalents			—	25 (v)		
			<u>144</u>	<u>144</u>		

Remaining Unexplained Balance Sheet Accounts

(*u*) At this point, all additional information is incorporated, and all balance sheet account changes are explained except for investment in Xenon stock, which increased $5 during 1998. This implies a purchase of additional stock.

Both methods: investing cash outflow, $5 payment to acquire Xenon stock. There was

COMPLEX COMPANY

Statement of Cash Flows, Direct Method
For the Year Ended December 31, 1998
(in thousands)

Cash flows from operating activities:		
Cash inflows:		
From customers	$99	
From dividends received on short-term investments	1	
From gain on cash equivalents sold	2	
Cash outflows:		
Paid to suppliers (for cost of goods sold)	(45)	
Paid for interest	(5)	
Paid for remaining expenses	(11)	
Paid for income taxes	(13)	
Net cash inflow from operating activities		$28
Cash flows from investing activities:		
Cash inflows:		
From sale of plant assets	15	
From discontinued operations	23	
From sale of land (condemnation)	40	
Cash outflows:		
Paid for plant assets (Note A)	(10)	
Paid for purchase of land	(41)	
Paid for purchase of investment in Xenon	(5)	
Net cash inflow from investing activities		22
Cash flows from financing activities:		
Cash inflows:		
Borrowing on long-term note	10	
Cash outflows:		
Paid cash dividend	(15)	
Payment on bond principal	(20)	
Net cash outflow for financing activities		(25)
Net increase in cash and cash equivalents during 1998		25
Cash and cash equivalents, January 1, 1998		36
Cash and cash equivalents, December 31, 1998		$61

Note A: The company purchased an operational asset (machine); payment was in cash and the company's common stock as follows:

Cash paid	$10
Common stock issued	20
Total asset cost recorded	$30

no change in the market value of the securities available for sale, as evidenced by the lack of a valuation account or unrealized gain or loss in owners' equity.

(*v*) Balancing entry: cash increased $31 during 1998, and cash equivalents decreased $6. The net increase in cash and cash equivalents is therefore $25. This amount reconciles total cash increases and total cash decreases.

The spreadsheet is totaled to confirm its accuracy. The direct method SCF is prepared by transferring the operating cash flows in the direct method columns of the spreadsheet to the operating activities section of the SCF. The investing and financing cash flows are transferred to their respective sections in the SCF. The complete direct method SCF is illustrated in Exhibit 23A–3, which also shows the noncash footnote, or schedule.

The reconciliation of net income and net operating cash flow for both methods is prepared by transferring the 12 reconciling adjustments from the indirect method columns in the operating section of the spreadsheet. The reconciliation appears in Exhibit 23A–4. To prepare the indirect method SCF (not illustrated), replace the operating section of the direct method SCF with the reconciliation. The policy for cash equivalents and the supporting schedule for income tax payments and interest payments for the indirect method also are not illustrated.

EXHIBIT 23A–4
Reconciliation

COMPLEX COMPANY

Reconciliation of Net Income to Net Cash Inflow
(outflow) from Operating Activities
For the Year Ended December 31, 1998
(in thousands)

Net income (accrual basis, from income statement)	$15
Add (deduct) to reconcile net income to net cash flow from operating activities:	
Accounts receivable decrease	3
Gain on sale of operational assets	(3)
Inventory increase	(7)
Accounts payable increase	4
Depreciation expense	8
Bad debt expense	3
Interest payable decrease	(1)
Amortization of bond discount	1
Prepaid insurance decrease	2
Income tax payable decrease	(7)
Discontinued operations, gain (pretax)	(10)
Extraordinary loss (pretax)	20
Net cash inflow from operating activities	$28

UNDERSTANDING AND APPLYING CONCEPTS AND STANDARDS

QUESTIONS

1. Compare the purposes of the balance sheet, income statement, and statement of cash flows.
2. Explain the basic difference between the three activities reported in the SCF: operating, investing, and financing.
3. List three major cash inflows and three major cash outflows under (*a*) operating activities, (*b*) investing activities, and (*c*) financing activities.
4. Define a noncash investing activity. Give examples of two possible cases.
5. Define a noncash financing activity. Give examples of two possible cases.
6. Define a cash equivalent for SCF purposes.
7. What policy must a company adopt about cash equivalents? What accounting procedure must the company follow if the policy is changed?
8. Explain the basic difference between the direct and indirect methods of reporting on the SCF. Use net income, $5,000, sales revenue, $100,000, and an increase in net accounts receivable, $10,000, to illustrate the basic difference. Which method provides the most relevant information to investors and creditors?
9. Explain why cash paid during the period for purchases and for salaries is not specifically reported on the SCF, indirect method, as cash outflows.
10. Explain why a $50,000 increase in inventory during the year must be considered when developing disclosures for operating activities under both the direct and indirect methods.
11. What three reconciling amounts must be reported at the bottom of the SCF? Which one must agree with a key amount in another financial statement? Use assumed amounts for illustrative purposes.
12. One of the criticisms of the SCF, indirect method, is that it does not report each of the three activities consistently. Explain the basis for this argument.
13. Explain why an adjustment must be made to compute cash flow from operating activities for depreciation expense, bad debt expense, amortization of intangibles (e.g., patents, copyrights, franchises, goodwill), and bond discount.
14. Explain why gains and losses reported on the income statement usually must be omitted (or removed) from operating activities to compute cash flow from operating activities.
15. A corporation's records showed the following: sales, $80,000, and accounts receivable decrease, $10,000, after the write-off of a $3,000 bad debt. Assuming the direct method, compute the cash inflow from customers.

16. Explain the two ways that the SCF, indirect method, can be designed to report cash flows from operating activities.
17. Why are cash and cash equivalents grouped together for purposes of the SCF even though cash equivalents are not actually cash?
18. Why is a two-year Treasury note purchased three months before maturity a cash equivalent for SCF purposes, although the same security purchased one year before maturity is not?
19. If the intent is to hold an investment in common stock less than three months, why is the investment not a cash equivalent?
20. Is there an inconsistency in the classification of dividends received and dividends paid in the SCF? Discuss your answer.
21. How is a lease payment (after inception) on a capital lease classified in the SCF?
22. Trading securities and securities available for sale are treated differently in the statement of cash flows. What are the major differences in treatment?

23. What type of flow statement is required under International Accounting Standards? Internationally, is there a trend toward any particular fund definition?

EXERCISES

E 23–1
(L.O. 2)

SCF: Terminology, Format, and Requirements   Two lists are given below: key terms and brief descriptions. You are to match the descriptions with the terms by entering one letter in each blank.

Key Terms	Brief Description
_____ 1. Fundamental purpose of the SCF.	A. Net cash increase (decrease), beginning balance, and ending balance.
_____ 2. Basic components of the SCF.	B. Cash flows related to obtaining capital for the enterprise.
_____ 3. Three reconciling lines at the bottom of the SCF.	C. Cash flows primarily related to the income statement.
_____ 4. Must be disclosed in a separate SCF schedule.	D. Financial statements do not report this ratio.
_____ 5. Cash flows from operating activities.	E. Includes highly liquid investments, but not all short-term investments.
_____ 6. Cash flow per share.	F. Cash flows from three activities: operating, investing, and financing.
_____ 7. SCF, direct method.	G. Add (deduct) to adjust net income to net cash flows.
_____ 8. This amount must agree with the change in cash.	H. Noncash investing and financing activities.
_____ 9. Cash flows from investing activities.	I. Two approaches to prepare the SCF.
_____ 10. This is a special item on the SCF.	J. To help investors, creditors, and others to assess future cash flows.
_____ 11. SCF, indirect method.	K. Cash flows related to obtaining productive facilities and other noncash assets.
_____ 12. Format-free and spreadsheet.	L. Report cash flows for each major revenue and expense.
_____ 13. Cash equivalents.	M. Effect of foreign exchange rates on cash.
_____ 14. Cash flows from financing activities.	N. Net increase (decrease) in cash during the period.
_____ 15. This item on the SCF, indirect method, must be clearly identified as a reconciliation.	O. Does not report cash flows for revenues and expenses, but reconciles net income with cash flows.

E 23–2
(L.O. 3)

SCF: Cash Flow Analysis of Sales   The records of ZZ Hat Company showed sales revenue of $100,000 (on the income statement) and a change in the balance of accounts receivable. To demonstrate the effect of changes in accounts receivable on cash inflows from customers, five independent cases are used. Complete the following tabulation for each independent case:

Case	Sales Revenue (from income statement)	Accounts Receivable Increase (decrease)	Computations	Cash Inflow
A	$100,000	$ –0–		
B	100,000	10,000		
C	100,000	(10,000)		
D	100,000	9,000*		
E	100,000	(9,000)*		

*Includes the effect of a $1,000 write-off of an uncollectible account.

E 23–3
(L.O. 3)

SCF: Cash Flow Analysis of Cost of Goods Sold   The records of Atlas Company showed cost of goods sold (on the income statement) of $60,000 and a change in the inventory and accounts payable balances. To demonstrate the effect of these changes on cash outflow for cost of goods sold (i.e., payments to suppliers), eight independent cases are used. Complete the following tabulation for each case:

Case	Cost of Goods Sold	Inventory Increase (decrease)	Accounts Payable Increase (decrease)	Computations	Cash Outflow*
A	$60,000	$ –0–	$ –0–		
B	60,000	6,000	–0–		
C	60,000	(6,000)	–0–		
D	60,000	–0–	4,000		
E	60,000	–0–	(4,000)		
F	60,000	6,000	4,000		
G	60,000	(6,000)	(4,000)		
H	60,000	(6,000)	(6,000)		

* This is the amount of cash paid during the current period for past and current purchases.

E 23–4
(L.O. 3)

SCF, Direct Method: Analysis of Cash Inflows and Outflows   The records of Easie Company provided the following data:

a. Sales revenue, $190,000; accounts receivable decreased, $10,000.
b. Cost of goods sold, $84,000; inventory decreased, $6,000; accounts payable, no change.
c. Wage expense, $32,000; wages payable decreased, $3,000.
d. Depreciation expense, $8,000.
e. Purchased productive asset for $36,000; paid one-third down and gave a two-year, interest-bearing note for the balance.
f. Borrowed $40,000 cash on a note payable.
g. Sold an old operational asset for $6,000 cash; original cost, $20,000; accumulated depreciation, $18,000.
h. Paid a $5,000 note payable (principal).
i. Paid a cash dividend, $8,000.

Required

For each of the above transactions give (1) its SCF activity (operating, investing, financing) and (2) the SCF (direct method) inflow or outflow amount. Also, give any disclosure schedules required.

E 23–5
(L.O. 2, 3)

Multiple Choice: Statement of Cash Flows   Choose the correct response for each question.

1. In the statement of cash flows, which of the following would increase reported cash flows from operating activities under the direct method? Ignore tax considerations.
   a. Dividends received from investments.
   b. Gain on sale of equipment.
   c. Gain on early retirement of bonds.
   d. Change from straight-line to accelerated depreciation.
2. Which of the following cash flows per share should be reported in a statement of cash flows?
   a. Primary cash flows per share only.
   b. Fully diluted cash flow per share only.
   c. Both primary and fully diluted cash flows per share.
   d. Cash flows per share should not be reported.
3. Cantova Company sold used equipment for a cash amount equaling its carrying amount for both book and tax purposes. A few days later, Cantova replaced the equipment by paying a cash down payment and signing a note payable for new equipment. The cash down payment exceeded the cash received for the old equipment. How should these equipment transactions be reported in Cantova's statement of cash flows?
   a. Cash outflow equal to the downpayment less the cash received.
   b. Cash outflow equal to the downpayment and note payable less the cash received.
   c. Cash inflow equal to the cash received and a cash outflow equal to the downpayment and note payable.

d. Cash inflow equal to the cash received and a cash outflow equal to the downpayment.

4. How should a gain from the sale of used equipment for cash be reported in a statement of cash flows using the indirect method?

  a. In investment activities as a reduction of the cash inflow from the sale.

  b. In investment activities as a cash outflow.

  c. In operating activities as a deduction from income.

  d. In operating activities as an addition to income.

5. Would the following be added back to net income in the reconciliation of net income and net operating cash flow?

Excess of Treasury Stock Acquisition Cost over Sales Proceeds (cost method)	Bond Discount Amortization
a. Yes	Yes
b. No	No
c. No	Yes
d. Yes	No

6. Malli Manufacturing Company purchased a three-month U.S. Treasury bill, to be classified as a cash equivalent. In the preparation of Malli's statement of cash flows, this purchase would

  a. Not be reported.

  b. Be treated as an outflow from financing activities.

  c. Be treated as an outflow from investing activities.

  d. Be treated as an outflow from lending activities.

(AICPA adapted)

E 23–6
(L.O. 2)

SCF: Format and Disclosure Requirements   Place an X in the blanks when the item listed must be reported in the SCF or in other required disclosures for the format indicated.

	Indirect Method	Direct Method
1. Change in cash and cash equivalents for the period	______	______
2. Reconciliation of earnings and net operating cash flow	______	______
3. Investing cash flows	______	______
4. Financing cash flows	______	______
5. Most operating expenses	______	______
6. Operating cash flows	______	______
7. Significant noncash transactions	______	______
8. Disclosure of interest and income tax payments outside the SCF	______	______
9. Cash flow per share	______	______
10. Changes in operating working capital accounts	______	______

E 23–7
(L.O. 4)

SCF: Indirect Method   Calexico Inc. reported the following comparative balance sheets for the current year:

Balance Sheets	January 1	December 31
Cash	$ 4,000	$10,750
Accounts receivable	3,000	2,000
Equipment	10,000	15,000
Accumulated depreciation	(1,000)	(2,000)
Total assets	$16,000	$25,750
Salaries payable	$ 1,000	$ 2,000
Long-term notes payable	5,000	5,000
Capital stock	8,000	8,000
Retained earnings	2,000	10,750
Total liabilities and owners' equity	$16,000	$25,750

Additional information:

1. Net income for the current year was $9,750.

2. No purchases or disposals of equipment took place during the year.

Required

1. Prepare the indirect method statement of cash flows for Calexico.

2. What additional information would you need to prepare the *direct method* statement of cash flows for this firm?

E 23–8
(L.O. 4)

SCF, Direct Method　The accounting records of Jones and Williamson provided the following data for the current year:

Balance Sheets	January 1	December 31	Income Statement	
Cash	$ 100	$ 65	Sales.	$3,000
Accounts receivable, net	300	200	Cost of goods sold	(1,700)
Inventory	100	300	Gross margin	1,300
Equipment, net	1,800	2,200	Salary expense	(125)
Total assets	$2,300	$2,765	Interest expense	(60)
			Depreciation expense.	(400)
Accounts payable	200	150	Loss on equipment sale	(200)
Salaries payable	50	25	Net income	$ 515
Dividends payable	75	90		
Bonds payable	600	700		
Common stock	1,100	1,200		
Retained earnings	275	600		
Total liabilities and Owners' equity	$2,300	$2,765		

Additional information:
The book value of equipment sold was $300. All dividends declared were cash dividends.

Required

Prepare the direct method statement of cash flows (including the reconciliation of earnings and net operating cash flow) for the current year.

E 23–9
(L.O. 3)

Cash Flows and Reconciling Items　For each of the items indicated, determine the *complete* required disclosure in the statement of cash flows (direct method) including the reconciliation of earnings and net operating cash flow. Place the required dollar amount and a + or − in the appropriate blank. More than one blank may be needed for certain items. Use the following key:

R Reconciling item　　　I Investing cash flow
O Operating cash flow　　F Financing cash flow

The first item is completed for you.

	R	O	I	F
1. $200 increase in accounts payable for the period.	+200	___	___	___
2. Sales were $500, accounts receivable increased $200.	___	___	___	___
3. Purchase $300 of treasury stock.	___	___	___	___
4. Disposed of equipment with $500 book value, received $300.	___	___	___	___
5. Paid $200 interest of which $60 was capitalized.	___	___	___	___
6. Interest payable increased $100, interest expense is $400.	___	___	___	___
7. Retired bonds early by paying $5,000, resulted in $600 extraordinary loss.	___	___	___	___
8. Pension expense of $1,000 is recognized, $800 was funded.	___	___	___	___
9. A $120 payment was made on an operating lease.	___	___	___	___
10. A $120 payment was made on a capital lease of which $40 is interest.	___	___	___	___

E 23–10
(L.O. 3)

Transaction Analysis　The following five situations involve transactions and account changes:

1. The current income statement discloses $30,000 of utility expense for electricity consumption. The comparative balance sheets show a decrease of $6,000 in accrued utilities payable for the current year.
2. Short-term notes payable to banks increased $80,000 during the current year.
3. The following end-of-year adjusting entry was recorded. No other interest-related transactions or entries occurred during the year.

Interest expense	12,000	
Premium on bonds payable	800	
Interest payable		12,800

4. A $500 payment was made to reduce the principal balance of a loan from a bank; the loan had been obtained for the purpose of purchasing inventory for resale.
5. The gross equipment account increased $20,000 during the year, accumulated depreciation increased $8,000, and depreciation expense for the period is $10,000. One item of equipment (cost $10,000, accumulated depreciation $2,000) was sold during the year; a gain of $1,000 on the sale was recognized.

Required

For each item, describe the required disclosure for the direct method SCF including any reconciliation amounts. If you are unable to determine the disclosure, indicate what additional information you need.

E 23–11
(L.O. 3)

Transaction Analysis   You are requested by the controller of a large company to determine the appropriate disclosure for the following transactions in the SCF. Assume that all adjusting entries were recorded.

a. The company wrote off a $4,000 account. During the year, gross accounts receivable increased $100,000, and the allowance for doubtful accounts increased $10,000. All sales ($600,000) are on account.
b. Pension expense is $100,000; the balance of accrued pension cost (cr.) increased $24,000.
c. Deferred tax liability increased $80,000, income taxes payable decreased $20,000, and income tax expense was $220,000.
d. $20,000 of interest was capitalized. Interest expense is $100,000. There is no change in interest payable.
e. The company sold short-term investments (cash equivalents) at a $4,000 gain, proceeds $16,000.
f. The company sold short-term investments in securities classified as available for sale at a $4,000 gain, proceeds $16,000. There was no valuation allowance balance on the securities, and market value equaled cost at the beginning of the period.

Required

Indicate the complete disclosure of each item in the SCF under (1) the direct method and (2) the indirect method.

E 23–12
(L.O. 3)

Cash Flow Categories: Transaction Analysis   Denton Corporation's balance sheet accounts as of December 31, 1997 and 1998, and information relating to 1998 activities are presented below.

	December 31	
	1998	**1997**
Assets:		
Cash	$ 230,000	$ 100,000
Short-term investments	300,000	—
Accounts receivable (net)	510,000	510,000
Inventory	680,000	600,000
Long-term investments	200,000	300,000
Plant assets	1,700,000	1,000,000
Accumulated depreciation	(450,000)	(450,000)
Goodwill	90,000	100,000
Total assets	$3,260,000	$2,160,000
Liabilities and stockholders' equity:		
Accounts payable and accrued liabilities	$ 825,000	$ 720,000
Short-term debt to financial institutions	325,000	—
Common stock, $10 par	800,000	700,000
Additional paid-in capital	370,000	250,000
Retained earnings	940,000	490,000
Total liabilities and stockholders' equity	$3,260,000	$2,160,000

Information relating to 1998 activities:

a. Net income for 1998 was $690,000.
b. Cash dividends of $240,000 were declared and paid in 1998.
c. Equipment costing $400,000 and having a carrying amount of $150,000 was sold in 1998 for $150,000.
d. A long-term investment was sold in 1998 for $135,000. There were no other transactions affecting long-term investments in 1998. These investments are in securities classified as available for sale. Their market value had not changed before 1998.
e. 10,000 shares of common stock were issued in 1998 for $22 per share.
f. Short-term investments consist of treasury bills maturing on June 30, 1999, and are classified as available for sale.

Required   Determine the following for Denton for 1998:

1. Net cash provided by operating activities.
2. Net cash used in investing activities.
3. Net cash provided by financing activities.

(AICPA adapted)

E 23–13
(L.O. 4)

SCF, Direct Method   The following data were provided by the accounting records of Smiley Company at year-end, December 31, 1998:

Income Statement

Sales	$70,000
Cost of goods sold	(42,000)
Depreciation expense	(5,000)
Remaining expenses	(18,000)
Gain on sale of investments	3,000
Loss on sale of operational assets	(1,000)
Net income	$ 7,000

Comparative Balance Sheets

	December 31	
Debits	**1997**	**1998**
Cash	$ 34,000	$ 33,500
Accounts receivable (net)	12,000	17,000
Inventory	16,000	14,000
Long-term investments	6,000	
Operational assets	80,000	98,000
Treasury stock		11,500
Total debits	$148,000	$174,000

Credits		
Accumulated Depreciation	$ 48,000	$ 39,000
Accounts payable	19,000	12,000
Bonds payable	10,000	30,000
Common stock, nopar	50,000	65,000
Retained earnings	21,000	28,000
Total credits	$148,000	$174,000

Analysis of selected accounts and transactions:

a. Sold operational assets for $6,000 cash; cost, $21,000, and two-thirds depreciated (the loss or gain is not an extraordinary item).
b. Purchased operational assets for cash, $9,000.
c. Purchased operational assets; exchanged unissued bonds of $30,000 (face value and market value) in payment.
d. Sold the long-term investments for $9,000 cash (assume that the gain or loss is an extraordinary item). The investment is in securities classified as available for sale. Their market value had not changed until 1998.
e. Purchased treasury stock for cash, $11,500.
f. Retired bonds payable at maturity date by issuing common stock, $10,000.
g. Sold unissued common stock for cash, $5,000.

Required   Prepare the SCF, direct method.

E 23–14
(L.O. 2)

SCF, Direct Method   The accounting records of Pall-Mall Company provided the following data:

Income Statement for Year Ended December 31, 1998

Sales	$600,000
Cost of goods sold	(360,000)
Depreciation expense	(8,000)
Remaining expenses	(128,000)
Net income	$104,000

Comparative Balance Sheets

Debits	December 31 1997	1998	Increase (decrease)
Cash	$ 16,000	$ 68,000	$ 52,000
Accounts receivable (net)	20,000	36,000	16,000
Inventory	40,000	48,000	8,000
Investment, long-term	8,000		(8,000)
Operational assets	120,000	188,000	68,000
Total debits	$204,000	$340,000	$136,000

Credits			
Accumulated Depreciation	$ 20,000	$ 28,000	$ 8,000
Accounts payable	12,000	20,000	8,000
Notes payable, short-term (nontrade)	16,000	12,000	(4,000)
Notes payable, long-term	40,000	72,000	32,000
Common stock, nopar	100,000	160,000	60,000
Retained earnings	16,000	48,000	32,000
Total credits	$204,000	$340,000	$136,000

Analysis of selected accounts and transactions:

a. Sold the long-term investment at cost, for cash. The securities were classified as available for sale, and the market value had not changed since acquisition.
b. Declared and paid a cash dividend of $28,000.
c. Purchased operational assets that cost $68,000; gave a $48,000 long-term note payable and paid $20,000 cash.
d. Paid a $16,000 long-term note payable by issuing common stock; market value, $16,000.
e. Issued a stock dividend, $44,000.

Required Prepare the SCF, direct method.

E 23–15
(L.O. 4)

SCF, Indirect Method: Prepare the Reconciliation for Operating Activities The data given below were provided by the accounting records of Darby Company. Prepare the reconciliation of net income with cash flow from operations for inclusion in the SCF, indirect method.

Net income (accrual basis)	$40,000
Depreciation expense	$ 8,000
Decrease in wages payable	$ 1,200
Decrease in trade accounts receivable	$ 1,800
Increase in merchandise inventory	$ 2,500
Amortization of patent	$ 100
Increase in long-term liabilities	$10,000
Sale of capital stock for cash	$25,000
Amortization of premium on bonds payable	$ 200
Accounts payable increase	$ 4,000
Stock dividend issued	$10,000

E 23–16
(L.O. 4)

SCF, Indirect Method: Prepare the Reconciliation for Operating Activities The data given below were provided by the accounting records of Sileo Company. Prepare the reconciliation of net income with cash flow from operating activities for inclusion in the SCF, indirect method.

Net income (accrual basis)	$25,000
Depreciation expense	$ 3,000
Increase in wages payable	$ 500
Increase in trade accounts receivable	$ 900
Decrease in merchandise inventory	$ 1,150
Amortization of patent	$ 100
Decrease in long-term liabilities	$ 5,000
Sale of capital stock for cash	$12,500
Amortization of discount on bonds payable	$ 150

E 23–17
(L.O. 4)

SCF, Indirect Method Zepo Corporation's recent comparative balance sheet and income statement follow:

Comparative Balance Sheets
December 31

	1998	1997
Assets:		
Cash	$ 59,000	$ 60,000
Accounts receivable	34,000	24,000
Plant assets	277,000	247,000
Accumulated depreciation	(178,000)	(167,000)
Total assets	$192,000	$164,000
Liabilities and stockholders' equity:		
Bonds payable	$ 49,000	$ 46,000
Dividends payable	8,000	5,000
Common stock, $1 par	22,000	19,000
Additional paid-in capital	9,000	3,000
Retained earnings	104,000	91,000
Total liabilities and stockholders' equity	$192,000	$164,000

Income Statement
For Year Ended December 31, 1998

Sales Revenue	$155,000
Cost of goods sold	(107,000)
Gross margin	48,000
Depreciation expense	(33,000)
Gain on sale of equipment	13,000
Net income	$ 28,000

Additional information:

1. During 1998, equipment costing $40,000 was sold for cash.
2. During 1998, $20,000 of bonds payable were issued in exchange for property, plant, and equipment. There was no amortization of bond discount or premium.

Required

Prepare Zepo's statement of cash flows under the indirect method.

(AICPA adapted)

E 23–18
(L.O. 2, 3)

Cash Flow Disclosure for Retirement of Debt On June 30, 1995, Camellia Florist issued 15-year 12 percent bonds at a premium (effective rate 10 percent). On November 30, 1998, Camellia transferred both cash and property to the bondholders to extinguish the entire bond issue. The fair value of the transferred property equaled its carrying amount but exceeded the bonds' carrying amount. Ignore income taxes.

Required

How should Camellia report the effects of the bond retirement in its 1998 statement of cash flows using the indirect method?

(AICPA adapted)

E 23–19
(L.O. 3)

Analysis of Changes in Accounts Receivable The following information pertains to Medicoil, Inc., producers of medical hardware, for the current year just ended.

From the balance sheet:

	January 1	December 31
Accounts receivable	$20,000	$35,000
Allowance for doubtful accounts	1,000	2,000
Net accounts receivable	$19,000	$33,000

From the income statement:

Net credit sales	$80,000
Bad debt expense	5,500

Additional information:

a. $6,000 of accounts receivable were written off during the year.
b. $1,500 was collected on accounts receivable written off in previous years.

Required

1. Determine which items pertain to accounts receivable and would appear in the statement of cash flows for the current year under both the direct and indirect methods.
2. The amount of cash collected from customers is not disclosed by firms using the indirect method. Write a general expression for determining collections on accounts receivable for a period given the change in net accounts receivable during the period, net credit sales, accounts written off during the period, and any other information relevant to accounts receivable. Verify your expression using data from this exercise.

E 23–20
(L.O. 3)

Multiple Choice: Statement of Cash Flows   The adjusted trial balances for Garboz Company, an industrial recycler, at December 31, 1998 and 1997, are as follows:

	December 31	
Debits	**1998**	**1997**
Cash	$ 35,000	$ 32,000
Accounts receivable	33,000	30,000
Inventory	31,000	47,000
Property, plant, and equipment	100,000	95,000
Unamortized bond discount	4,500	5,000
Cost of goods sold	250,000	380,000
Selling expenses	141,500	172,000
General and administrative expenses	137,000	151,300
Interest expense	4,300	2,600
Income tax expense	20,400	61,200
	$756,700	$976,100

Credits		
Allowance for doubtful accounts	$ 1,300	$ 1,100
Accumulated depreciation	16,500	15,000
Trade accounts payable	25,000	17,500
Income taxes payable	21,000	27,100
Deferred income tax liability	5,300	4,600
Callable bonds payable, 8 percent	45,000	20,000
Common stock	50,000	40,000
Additional paid-in capital	9,100	7,500
Retained earnings	44,700	64,600
Sales	538,800	778,700
	$756,700	$976,100

Additional information:

a. Garboz purchased $5,000 of equipment in 1998.
b. Garboz allocated one-third of its depreciation expense to selling expenses and the remainder to general and administrative expenses.

Required

What amounts should Garboz report in its statement of cash flows for the year ended December 31, 1998, for the following?

1. Cash collected from customers.
   a. $541,800.
   b. $541,600.
   c. $536,000.
   d. $535,800.
2. Cash paid for goods to be sold.
   a. $258,500.
   b. $257,500.
   c. $242,500.
   d. $226,500.

   3. Cash paid for interest.
     a. $4,800.
     b. $4,300.
     c. $3,800.
     d. $1,700.
   4. Cash paid for income taxes.
     a. $25,800.
     b. $20,400.
     c. $19,700.
     d. $15,000.
   5. Cash paid for selling expenses.
     a. $142,000.
     b. $141,500.
     c. $141,000.
     d. $140,000.

(AICPA adapted)

E 23–21
(L.O. 5)

SCF, Direct Method: Optional Spreadsheet   Analysis of accounts and other information for 1998: (*a*) purchased an operational asset, $60,000; issued capital stock in full payment; (*b*) purchased a long-term investment in securities classified as available for sale for cash, $20,000; (*c*) paid cash dividend, $20,000; (*d*) sold operational asset for $10,000 cash (cost, $36,000; accumulated depreciation, $32,000); and (*e*) sold capital stock, 1,000 shares at $11 per share cash.

Item	Balance 12/31/1997	Analysis Debit	Analysis Credit	Balance 12/31/1998
Income statement accounts:				
Sales			240,000	
Cost of goods sold		96,000		
Depreciation		12,000		
Wage expense		44,000		
Income tax expense		20,000		
Interest expense		14,000		
Remaining expenses		4,600		
Gain on sale of operational asset			6,000	
Net income		55,400		
Balance sheet accounts:				
Cash	39,000			63,800
Accounts receivable (net)	68,000			68,000
Merchandise inventory	156,000			170,000
Investments, long term				20,000
Property, plant, and equipment	337,000			361,000
Total	600,000			682,800
Accumulated depreciation	88,000			68,000
Accounts payable	42,000			38,000
Wages payable	3,000			1,000
Income taxes payable	4,000			7,000
Bonds payable	200,000			200,000
Premium on bonds payable	8,000			7,400
Common stock, nopar	240,000			311,000
Retained earnings	15,000			50,400
Total	600,000			682,800

Required

Prepare the SCF, direct method.

E 23–22
(L.O. 5)

SCF, Direct Method: Optional Spreadsheet   Analysis of accounts and other information for 1998: (*a*) retired bonds paying $40,000 cash; (*b*) bought long-term investment in securities classified as available for sale, $20,000 cash; (*c*) purchased operational asset, $14,000 cash; (*d*) purchased short-term investment in securities classified as available for sale, $6,000 cash; (*e*) paid cash dividend, $8,000; and (*f*) issued capital stock, 1,000 shares at $19 cash per share.

Item	Balance 12/31/1997	Analysis		Balance 12/31/1998
		Debit	**Credit**	
Income statement accounts:				
Sales			208,000	
Cost of goods sold		110,000		
Depreciation expense		16,000		
Patent amortization		600		
Remaining expenses		35,400		
Net income		46,000		
Balance sheet accounts:				
Cash	30,000			43,000
Investments, short term				6,000
Accounts receivable	34,000			42,000
Inventory (perpetual)	20,000			30,000
Investments, long term				20,000
Property, plant, and equipment	120,000			118,000
Patent (net)	6,000			5,400
Other assets	14,000			14,000
Total	224,000			278,400
Accounts payable	24,000			44,000
Accrued expenses payable				17,400
Bonds payable	80,000			40,000
Common stock, par $10	70,000			80,000
Contributed capital in excess of par				9,000
Retained earnings	50,000			88,000
Total	224,000			278,400

Required   Prepare the SCF, direct method.

E 23–23
(L.O. 5)

SCF, Direct Method: Optional Spreadsheet   Shown below are the income statement, comparative balance sheet, and additional information useful in preparing the 1998 SCF for Sells Company.

Income Statement
For Year Ended December 31, 1998

Net sales		$300,000
Cost of goods sold		80,000
Gross margin		220,000
Depreciation expense	$45,000	
Amortization	2,000	
Other expenses	44,000	
Interest expense	3,000	
Income tax expense	65,000	159,000
Net income		$ 61,000

Comparative Balance Sheets

		December 31	
Debits		**1997**	**1998**
Cash		$ 16,000	$ 32,000
Accounts receivable		56,000	52,000
Allowance for doubtful accounts		(6,000)	(5,000)
Other receivables		3,000	2,000
Inventory		30,000	32,000
Equipment		80,000	77,000
Accumulated depreciation		(6,000)	(5,000)
Intangibles, net		55,000	53,000
Total assets		$228,000	$238,000
Accounts payable		50,000	60,000
Income taxes payable		70,000	50,000
Interest payable		2,000	1,000
Bonds payable		32,000	
Discount on bonds payable		(2,000)	
Common stock, no par		70,000	80,000
Retained earnings		6,000	47,000
Total liabilities and owners' equity		$228,000	$238,000

Additional information:

1. $20,000 of dividends were declared in 1998.
2. Equipment costing $66,000, with a book value of $20,000, was sold at book value. New equipment also was purchased; common stock was issued in partial payment.
3. The bonds were retired at book value; $500 of bond discount was amortized in 1998.
4. Assume no bad debt expense in 1998.

Required   Prepare the 1998 SCF, direct method, for Sells Company.

PROBLEMS

P 23–1
(L.O. 2)

Correcting Erroneous Cash Flow Statement   The accountant for Mentor Company prepared the following cash flow statement and additional information.

MENTOR COMPANY

Cash Flow Statement
December 31, 1998

Cash inflows:		
Net income (loss)	$ (40,000)	
Extraordinary gain on bond retirement	20,000	
Dividends received on equity method investment	80,000	
Issue stock	120,000	
Total cash inflows		$ 180,000
Cash outflows:		
Market value of bonds retired	160,000	
Cost of treasury stock acquired	32,000	
Dividends paid	50,000	
Acquisition of property, plant, and equipment	60,000	
Issuance of bonds for real estate	86,000	
Total cash outflows		388,000
Net cash decrease during 1998		$(208,000)

The accountant was sure that cash decreased $208,000 during 1998, but was not sure whether all relevant information was incorporated into the statement. Also, the accountant admitted knowing very little about cash flow statements. Therefore, the accountant made available the additional information:

Beginning cash balance	$408,000
Depreciation	70,000
Amortization of premium on bonds	10,000
Gain on equipment sale (not extraordinary)	8,000
Stock dividend declared and distributed	40,000
Mentor's share of income from equity method investment	130,000
Retained earnings appropriation	30,000

The following accounts changed by the amount noted, during 1998:

Increased	**Decreased**
Accounts payable, $36,000	Prepaids, $12,000
Revenue received in advance	Inventory, $10,000
(current liability), $14,000	
Accounts receivable, $40,000	

Required

Using the above information, prepare a revised SCF, indirect method. Assume that all values are correct in both the statement and additional information. Ignore taxes.

P 23–2
(L.O. 4)

SCF, Direct Method   The records of Easy Trading Company provided the following information for the year ended December 31, 1998:

Income Statement

Sales revenue	$80,000
Cost of goods sold	(35,000)
Depreciation expense	(5,000)
Bad debt expense	(1,000)
Insurance expense	(1,000)
Interest expense	(2,000)
Salaries and wages expense	(12,000)
Income tax expense	(3,000)
Remaining expenses	(13,000)
Loss on sale of operational assets	(2,000)
Net income	$ 6,000

Balance Sheet	**January 1, 1998**	**December 31, 1998**
Cash	$ 15,000	$ 31,000
Accounts receivable	30,000	28,500
Allowance for doubtful accounts	(1,500)	(2,000)
Inventory	10,000	15,000
Prepaid insurance	2,400	1,400
Operational assets	80,000	81,000
Accumulated depreciation	(20,000)	(16,000)
Land	40,100	81,100
Total	$156,000	$220,000
Accounts payable	$ 10,000	$ 11,000
Wages payable	2,000	1,000
Interest payable		1,000
Notes payable, long term	20,000	46,000
Common stock, nopar	100,000	136,000
Retained earnings	24,000	25,000
Total	$156,000	$220,000

a. Wrote off $500 accounts receivable as uncollectible.
b. Sold operational asset for $4,000 cash (cost, $15,000; accumulated depreciation, $9,000).
c. Issued common stock for $5,000 cash.
d. Declared and paid a cash dividend, $5,000.
e. Purchased land, $20,000 cash.
f. Acquired land for $21,000 and issued common stock as payment in full.
g. Acquired operational assets, cost $16,000; issued a $16,000, three-year, interest-bearing note payable.
h. Paid a $10,000 long-term note installment by issuing common stock to the creditor.
i. Borrowed cash on long-term note, $20,000.

Required   Prepare the SCF, direct method.

P 23–3   **SCF, Indirect Method**   This problem uses the data given in P 23–2. No additional information is needed.
(L.O. 4)

Required   Prepare the SCF, indirect method.

P 23–4   **SCF, Indirect Method**   The income statement and balance sheet of Kenwood Company and related analysis
(L.O. 4)   are given below.

KENWOOD COMPANY
Income Statement
For the Year Ended December 31, 1998

Sales revenue	$1,000,000
Expenses and losses:	
Cost of goods sold	560,000
Salaries and wages	190,000
Depreciation	20,000
Patent amortization	3,000
Loss on sale of equipment	4,000
Interest expense	16,000
Miscellaneous expenses	8,000
Total expenses	801,000
Income before income taxes and extraordinary item	199,000
Income tax expense (continuing operations)	86,000
Income before extraordinary item	113,000
Extraordinary item—gain on early extinguishment of long-term bonds payable (net of $4,000 tax)	8,000
Net income	$ 121,000

Analysis of selected accounts and transactions:

a. On February 2, 1998, Kenwood issued a 10 percent stock dividend to stockholders of record on January 15, 1998. The market price per share of the common stock on February 2, 1998, was $15.

b. On March 1, 1998, Kenwood issued 3,800 shares of common stock for land. The common stock had a current market value of approximately $40,000 on March 1, 1998.

c. On April 15, 1998, Kenwood repurchased its long-term bonds payable with a face value of $50,000 for cash. The gain of $12,000 was correctly reported as an extraordinary item on the income statement.

d. On June 30, 1998, Kenwood sold equipment that cost $53,000, with a book value of $23,000, for $19,000 cash.

e. On September 30, 1998, Kenwood declared and paid a 4 cents per share cash dividend to stockholders of record on August 1, 1998.

f. On October 10, 1998, Kenwood purchased land for $85,000 cash.

KENWOOD COMPANY

Comparative Balance Sheets

	December 31	
Assets	**1998**	**1997**
Current assets:		
Cash	$ 100,000	$ 90,000
Accounts receivable (net of allowance for doubtful		
accounts of $10,000 and $8,000, respectively)	210,000	140,000
Inventory	260,000	220,000
Total current assets	570,000	450,000
Land	325,000	200,000
Plant and equipment	580,000	633,000
Less: Accumulated depreciation	(90,000)	(100,000)
Patents	30,000	33,000
Total assets	$1,415,000	$1,216,000
Liabilities and Stockholders' Equity		
Liabilities:		
Current liabilities:		
Accounts payable	$ 260,000	$ 200,000
Salaries and wages payable	200,000	210,000
Income tax payable	140,000	100,000
Total current liabilities	600,000	510,000
Bonds payable (due 12/15/2007)	130,000	180,000
Total liabilities	$ 730,000	$ 690,000
Stockholders' equity:		
Common stock, par value $5, authorized 100,000		
shares, issued and outstanding 50,000 and 42,000		
shares, respectively	250,000	210,000
Additional paid-in capital	233,000	170,000
Retained earnings	202,000	146,000
Total stockholders' equity	685,000	526,000
Total liabilities and stockholders' equity	$1,415,000	$1,216,000

Required   Prepare the SCF, indirect method.

(AICPA adapted)

P 23–5
(L.O. 4)

SCF, Direct Method   This problem uses the data given in P 23–4. No additional information is needed.

Required   Prepare the SCF, direct method.

P 23–6
(L.O. 4)

SCF, Indirect Method   The following is Orem Corporation's comparative balance sheets for 1998 and 1997.

	December 31	
	1998	**1997**
Cash	$ 400,000	$ 350,000
Accounts receivable	564,000	584,000
Inventories	925,000	857,500
Property, plant, and equipment	1,653,500	1,483,500
Accumulated depreciation	(582,500)	(520,000)
Investment in Belle Co.	152,500	137,500
Loan receivable	135,000	
Total assets	$3,247,500	$2,892,500
Accounts payable	$ 507,500	$ 477,500
Income taxes payable	15,000	25,000
Dividends payable	40,000	45,000
Capital lease obligation	200,000	
Capital stock, common, $1 par	250,000	250,000
Additional paid-in capital	750,000	750,000
Retained earnings	1,485,000	1,345,000
Total liabilities and stockholders' equity	$3,247,500	$2,892,500

Additional information:

1. On December 31, 1997, Orem acquired 25 percent of Belle Company's common stock for $137,500. On that date, the carrying value of Belle's net assets and liabilities, which approximated fair value, was $550,000. Belle reported income of $60,000 for the year ended December 31, 1998. No dividend was paid on Belle's common stock during the year.
2. During 1998, Orem loaned $150,000 to Chase Company, an unrelated company. Chase made the first semi-annual principal repayment of $15,000, plus interest at 10 percent, on October 1, 1998.
3. On January 2, 1998, Orem sold equipment costing $30,000, with a carrying value of $17,500, for $20,000 cash.
4. On December 31, 1998, Orem entered into a capital lease for an office building. The present value of the annual rental payments is $200,000, which equals the fair value of the building. Orem made the first rental payment of $30,000 when due on January 2, 1999.
5. Orem's net income for 1998 was $180,000.
6. Orem declared and paid cash dividends for 1998 and 1997 as follows:

	1998	1997
Declared	Dec. 15, 1998	Dec. 15, 1997
Paid	Feb. 28, 1999	Feb. 28, 1998
Amount	$40,000	$45,000

Required   Prepare the 1998 statement of cash flows for Orem using the indirect method. Prepare relevant supplemental schedules.

(AICPA adapted)

P 23–7
(L.O. 4)

SCF, Indirect Method   The differences between the Boole Inc. balance sheet accounts of December 31, 1997 and 1998, are presented below:

Assets	Increase (decrease)
Cash and cash equivalents	$ 60,000
Short-term investments	150,000
Accounts receivable, net	—
Inventory	40,000
Long-term investments	(50,000)
Plant assets	350,000
Accumulated depreciation	—
	$550,000

Liabilities and Stockholders' Equity

Accounts payable and accrued liabilities.	$ (2,500)
Dividends payable	80,000
Short-term bank debt	162,500
Long-term debt	55,000
Common stock, $10 par	50,000
Additional paid-in capital	60,000
Retained earnings	145,000
	$550,000

Additional information for 1998:

1. Both short- and long-term investments are classified as available for sale. The market value of the short-term investments did not change during 1998; the market value of the long-term investments did not change until 1998. There was no associated valuation allowance for either account.
2. A building costing $300,000 and having a carrying amount of $175,000 was sold for $175,000.
3. Equipment costing $55,000 was acquired through issuance of long-term debt.
4. A long-term investment was sold for $67,500. There were no other transactions affecting long-term investments.
5. 10,000 shares of common stock were issued for $11 a share.
6. Net income was $395,000.

Required   Prepare Boole's statement of cash flows under the indirect method.

(AICPA adapted)

P 23–8
(L.O. 3)

Transaction Analysis   Internode, an international technology transfer firm, entered into the transactions described below during the current year. For each, describe the disclosure required for the statement of cash flows under both the direct and indirect methods. Include in your answer the effect on the reconciliation of net income and net operating cash flow and any noncash effects.

1. Internode made the following two entries related to a capital lease in the current year:

January 1:

Lease receivable	60,000	
Plant asset		50,000
Unearned interest		10,000

December 31:

Cash	12,000	
Unearned interest	4,000	
Interest revenue		4,000
Lease receivable		12,000

2. Internode's current-year comparative balance sheet discloses:

	January 1	December 31
Dividends payable	$80,000	$120,000

Assume that $140,000 of dividends were declared during the current year.

3. Internode made the following entry at the end of the current year:

Cash surrender value of life insurance	4,000	
Life insurance expense	36,000	
Cash		40,000

(Of the annual $40,000 premium, $4,000 is applied to the cash surrender value of the policy—an investment account.)

4. Internode decided to purchase new equipment for its plant. A $20,000 down payment was made to acquire equipment at the beginning of the current year, and a 7 percent, $180,000 note payable from a bank was used to finance the remaining acquisition cost. The note calls for five equal annual payments to be made at the end of each of the next five years. Provide the SCF disclosures for both the acquisition of the equipment and the payment on the note at the end of the first year.
5. Internode purchased shares of Geneco, Inc., common stock for $60,000 during the current year. The securities are classified as trading securities. At the end of the current year, the securities were worth $54,000. No securities were sold during the current year; this is the only purchase of securities ever for Internode.

6. Assume that the securities in (5) are classified as available for sale.

P 23–9
(L.O. 3)

Transaction Analysis   As the junior accountant for Hondo, Inc., a retailing firm, you are assisting the controller in preparing the statement of cash flows. The controller has finished the analysis for all but the following items. Advise the controller, who has not yet decided whether to use the direct or indirect method, on the appropriate disclosures for the current year's statement of cash flows for each of these items.

1. Hondo borrowed $80,000 from a financial institution, signing a six-month note. The proceeds were used to purchase merchandise inventory. Hondo paid $84,800 in full payment of the note and interest, when due, during the current year.
2. Hondo purchased $80,000 worth of merchandise from a supplier, signing a six-month note. Hondo paid $84,800 in full payment of the note and interest, when due, during the current year.
3. Hondo reported an $18,000 (dr.) balance in its valuation allowance account for its investment in Aland Company bonds, classified as trading securities, at the beginning of the year. The bonds originally cost $72,000. During the year, Hondo sold one-third of the bonds for $28,000. (Provide the SCF disclosure for the sale.)
4. The market value of the remaining bonds in part (3) at the end of the year was $56,000. (Provide any additional SCF disclosures required, using information in part (3) if needed.)
5. Assume now that the bonds in part (3) are classified as available for sale. (Provide the SCF disclosure for the sale.)
6. The market value of the remaining bonds in part (5) (classified as available for sale) at the end of the year was $56,000. (Provide any additional SCF disclosures required, using information in part (5) if needed.)

P 23–10
(L.O. 5)

SCF, Direct Method: Optional Spreadsheet   At December 31, 1998, the following data for Lincoln Company were available:

Balance Sheet

Debits	December 31 1997	December 31 1998	Increase (decrease)
Cash	$ 8,000	$ 22,000	$ 14,000
Accounts receivable (net)	18,000	24,000	6,000
Inventory	16,000	10,000	(6,000)
Long-term investments	4,000		(4,000)
Plant	60,000	60,000	
Equipment	40,000	44,000	4,000
Land	20,000	80,000	60,000
Patents	16,000	14,000	(2,000)
	$182,000	$254,000	$ 72,000

Credits	December 31 1997	December 31 1998	Increase (decrease)
Accumulated depreciation—plant	$ 14,000	$ 20,000	$ 6,000
Accumulated depreciation—equipment	20,000	16,000	(4,000)
Accounts payable	16,000	4,000	(12,000)
Wages payable	2,000		(2,000)
Notes payable, long term	20,000	38,000	18,000
Common stock, nopar	100,000	150,000	50,000
Retained earnings	10,000	26,000	16,000
	$182,000	$254,000	$ 72,000

Income Statement

Sales revenue	$180,000
Cost of goods sold	(110,000)
Depreciation expense, plant	(6,000)
Depreciation expense, equipment	(4,000)
Patent amortization	(2,000)
Remaining expenses	(40,000)
Loss on sale of equipment	(2,000)
Income tax expense (continuing operations)	(4,000)
Income from continuing operations	12,000
Extraordinary item: gain on sale of long-term investment (net of $4,000 tax)	12,000
Net income	$ 24,000

Analysis of selected accounts and entries:

a. At the end of the year, sold equipment that cost $16,000 (50 percent depreciated) for $6,000 cash (this was not an extraordinary item).
b. Purchased land that cost $20,000; paid $4,000 cash, gave long-term note for the balance.
c. Paid $8,000 to retire long-term note payable at maturity.
d. Sold $20,000 common stock at par.
e. Purchased equipment costing $20,000; paid half in cash, balance due in three years (interest-bearing note).
f. Issued 3,000 shares of common stock, market value $30,000, for land that cost $40,000; the balance was paid in cash.
g. Sold the long-term investments for $20,000 cash. The investments were securities classified as available for sale. The securities were purchased December 31, 1997; therefore, no valuation allowance was established.
h. Declared and paid dividends, $8,000.

Required Prepare the SCF, direct method.

P 23–11 **SCF, Indirect Method** This problem uses the data given in P 23–10. No additional information is needed.
(L.O. 4)

Required Prepare the SCF, indirect method.

P 23–12 **SCF, Direct Method: Optional Spreadsheet** The records of Arizona Company provided the following
(L.O. 5) data for the accounting year ended December 31, 1998:

Comparative Balance Sheets

Debits	December 31 1997	1998	Increase (decrease)
Cash	$ 30,000	$ 69,000	$39,000
Investment, short term (Sun Co. stock)	10,000	8,000	(2,000)
Accounts receivable	56,000	86,000	30,000
Inventory	20,000	30,000	10,000
Prepaid rent		2,000	2,000
Land	60,000	25,000	(35,000)
Machinery	80,000	90,000	10,000
Other assets	29,000	39,000	10,000
Discount on bonds payable	1,000	900	(100)
Total debits	$286,000	$349,900	$63,900

Credits			
Allowance for doubtful accounts	$ 6,000	$ 7,000	$ 1,000
Accumulated depreciation	20,000	26,900	6,900
Accounts payable	33,000	45,000	12,000
Salaries payable	5,000	2,000	(3,000)
Income taxes payable	2,000	8,000	6,000
Bonds payable	70,000	55,000	(15,000)
Common stock, nopar	100,000	131,000	31,000
Preferred stock, nopar	20,000	30,000	10,000
Retained earnings	30,000	45,000	15,000
Total credits	$286,000	$349,900	$ 63,900

Income Statement 1998

Sales revenue	$180,000
Cost of goods sold	(90,000)
Depreciation expense	(6,900)
Bad debt expense	(1,000)
Salaries	(32,900)
Interest expense	(6,100)
Remaining expenses	(4,000)
Income tax expense	(7,000)
Extraordinary gain on sale of land, condemnation (net of income tax, $5,400)	12,600
Extraordinary loss on bond retirement (net of tax saving, $300)	(700)
Net income	$ 44,000

Analysis of selected accounts and transaction:

a. Issued bonds payable for cash, $5,000. The bonds payable account represents more than one bond issue.

b. Sold land due to condemnation for $53,000 cash; book value, $35,000; extraordinary item.

c. Purchased machinery for cash, $10,000.

d. Purchased short-term investments for cash, $2,000.

e. Declared a property dividend on the preferred stock and paid it with a short-term investment (Sun Company stock); market value and carrying value are the same, $4,000.

f. Prior to maturity date, retired $20,000 (face) of bonds payable by issuing common stock; the common stock had a market value of $21,000. The bonds retired had been issued at face value.

g. Acquired other assets by issuing preferred stock with a market value of $10,000.

h. Retained earnings statement:

Balance, January 1, 1998	$30,000
Net income for 1998	44,000
Dividends paid, cash	(15,000)
Stock dividend issued, common stock	(10,000)
Property dividend, Sun Company stock	(4,000)
Balance, December 31, 1998	$45,000

Required

Prepare the SCF, direct method.

P 23–13
(L.O. 4)

SCF, Indirect Method: This problem uses the data given in P 23–12. No additional information is needed.

Required

Prepare the SCF, indirect method.

P 23–14
(L.O. 5)

SCF, Indirect Method: Optional Spreadsheet   The income statement, balance sheet, and analysis of selected accounts of Summer Company are given below.

Balance Sheet

		December 31		Increase
Debits		**1997**	**1998**	**(decrease)**
Cash plus short-term investments*	$	80,000	$ 89,800	$ 9,800
Accounts receivable (net)		120,000	105,000	(15,000)
Merchandise inventory (perpetual)		360,000	283,200	(76,800)
Prepaid insurance		4,800	2,400	(2,400)
Investments, long term		60,000		(60,000)
Land		20,000	76,800	56,800
Plant assets		500,000	518,000	18,000
Patent (net)		3,200	2,800	(400)
		$1,148,000	$1,078,000	$(70,000)

*Cash equivalents

Credits				
Accumulated depreciation	$	130,000	$ 158,000	$ 28,000
Accounts payable		100,000	106,000	6,000
Wages payable		4,000	3,000	(1,000)
Income taxes payable		18,000	26,800	8,800
Bonds payable		200,000	100,000	(100,000)
Premium on bonds payable		10,000	3,400	(6,600)
Common stock, par $10		600,000	612,000	12,000
Contributed capital in excess of par		30,000	36,000	6,000
Retained earnings		56,000	32,800	(23,200)
		$1,148,000	$1,078,000	$(70,000)

Income Statement 1998

Sales revenue	$800,000
Cost of goods sold	(448,800)
Depreciation expense	(28,000)
Patent amortization	(400)
Remaining expenses (including interest)	(287,800)
Extraordinary gain, net of $5,000 tax	15,000
Net income	$ 50,000

Analysis of selected accounts and entries:

a. Purchased operational asset; cost, $18,000; payment by issuing 1,200 shares of stock.
b. Payment at maturity date to retire bonds payable, $100,000.
c. Sold the long-term investments for $80,000. The market value of these securities classified as available for sale had not changed until 1998.
d. Purchased land, $56,800; paid cash.
e. Further information:

Retained earnings, beginning balance	$56,000
Prior period adjustment, income tax, paid in 1998	(13,200)
Net income, 1998	50,000
Cash dividend paid	(60,000)
Ending balance	$32,800

Required   Prepare the SCF, indirect method.

P 23–15
(L.O. 2, 3, 4, 5)

SCF, Direct Method, Optional Spreadsheet   This item is amenable to a group or individual solution. Refer to the preface for additional details on using group items. The comparative balance sheets and income statement for Gamme Company follow:

Comparative Balance Sheets

	December 31	
	1997	**1998**
Cash	$ 35,000	$ 49,582
Cash equivalents	20,000	10,000
Short-term investments in equity securities	8,000	5,000
Accounts receivable	50,000	75,000
Allowance for doubtful accounts	(2,000)	(3,000)
Inventory	120,000	40,000
Prepaid insurance	20,000	30,000
Long-term investment, equity	40,000	45,000
Land	250,000	350,000
Equipment	100,000	130,000
Leased building		75,816
Accumulated depreciation (including leased building)	(50,000)	(80,000)
Intangible assets, net	45,000	35,000
Total assets	$636,000	$762,398
Accounts payable	40,000	70,000
Income tax payable	5,000	8,000
Dividends payable	6,000	12,000
Lease liability, long term		63,398
Deferred tax liability	20,000	25,000
Mortgage payable		80,000
Note payable		100,000
Bonds payable	180,000	
Unamortized bond discount	(12,000)	
Common stock	300,000	300,000
Retained earnings	97,000	104,000
Total liabilities and owners' equity	$636,000	$762,398

(continued)

Income Statement, 1998

Sales		$620,000
Cost of goods sold		400,000
Gross margin		220,000
Bad debt expense	(18,000)	
Interest expense	(23,000)	
Depreciation	(42,000)	
Amortization of intangibles	(10,000)	
Other expenses	(85,000)	
Gain on sale of short-term investments	3,000	
Gain on equipment sale	7,000	
Investment revenue	30,000	
Income tax expense (continuing operations)	(20,000)	(158,000)
Income before extraordinary item		62,000
Extraordinary gain, bond retirement, net of $5,000 tax		15,000
Net income		$ 77,000

Additional information about events in 1998:

1. On January 1, 1998, the market value of the portfolio of short-term investments in equity securities, classified as available for sale, equaled cost. During 1998, investments costing $3,000 were sold for $6,000. No securities were purchased during 1998. At December 31, 1998, the market value of the portfolio is $5,000.
2. Cash equivalents were continually purchased and sold at cost. No gains or losses were incurred.
3. $20,000 of accounts receivable were written off in 1998, and $3,000 was collected on an account written off in 1996. All sales are on account.
4. The long-term equity investment represents a 25 percent interest in Wickens Company. During 1998, Wickens paid $100,000 of dividends and earned $120,000.
5. At the end of 1998, Gamme acquired land for $100,000 by assuming an $80,000 mortgage and paying the balance in cash.
6. Equipment (cost, $20,000; book value, $8,000) was sold for $15,000.
7. Gamme started and completed construction of equipment for its own use in 1998. The cost of the finished equipment, $50,000, includes $5,000 of capitalized interest.
8. Gamme entered into a capital lease on January 1, 1998. The interest rate used to capitalize the lease is 10 percent. Equal annual payments of $20,000 are due each December 31 for five years.
9. The bonds were retired before maturity at a $20,000 gain, before taxes. Applicable taxes, $5,000; discount amortized in 1998, $4,000.
10. Gamme declared $70,000 of dividends in 1998.

Required   Prepare the 1998 SCF, direct method, for Gamme Company.

ANALYSIS, JUDGMENT, AND COMMUNICATION

CASES

C 23–1
(L.O. 2)

SCF: Direct or Indirect?   During the FASB deliberations on the SCF, there was considerable debate and disagreement about the direct and indirect methods of reporting operational activities in the SCF. There was pressure on the Board from various groups. The following quotations from *SFAS No. 95* suggest the diversity of views (the numbers refer to *SFAS No. 95* paragraphs):

107. The principal advantage of the direct method is that it shows operating cash receipts and payments. Knowledge of the specific sources of operating cash receipts and the purposes for which operating cash payments were made in past periods may be useful in estimating future operating cash flows. The relative amounts of major classes of revenues and expenses and their relationship to other items in the financial statements are presumed to be more useful than information only about their arithmetic sum—net income—in assessing enterprise performance.

108. The principal advantage of the indirect method is that it focuses on the differences between net income and net cash flow from operating activities.

109. Many providers of financial statements have said that it would be costly for their companies to report gross operating cash receipts and payments. They said that they do not presently collect information in a manner that will allow them to determine amounts such as cash received from customers or cash paid to suppliers directly from their accounting systems.

111. A majority of respondents to the Exposure Draft asked the Board to require use of the direct method. Those respondents, most of whom were commercial lenders, generally said that amounts of operating cash receipts and payments are particularly important in assessing an enterprise's external borrowing needs and its ability to repay borrowings. They indicated that creditors are more exposed to fluctuations in net cash flow from operating activities than to fluctuations in net income and that information on the amounts of operating cash receipts and payments is important in assessing those fluctuations in net cash flow from operating activities. They also pointed out that the direct method is more consistent with the objective of a statement of cash flows—to provide information about cash receipts and cash payments—than the indirect method, which does not report operating cash receipts and payments.

As a basis for your analysis of the two methods, make appropriate check marks on each line in the following overview.

	Reported On		
	SCF Method		
Cash Inflows and Outflows **(and related changes)**	**Direct***	**Indirect**	**Comparative** **Balance Sheet**
1. Cash inflow from sales			
2. Cash inflow from services			
3. Cash inflow from interest			
4. Cash inflow from dividend received			
5. Accounts receivable increase or decrease			
6. Interest receivable increase or decrease			
7. Payments to suppliers (cash purchases)			
8. Inventory increase or decrease			
9. Accounts payable increase or decrease			
10. Payments for salaries and wages			
11. Wages and salaries payable increase or decrease			
12. Payments for income tax			
13. Income taxes payable increase or decrease			
14. Net income			
15. Net cash flow from operating activities			
16. Investing activities			
17. Financing activities			
18. Net increase or decrease in cash during the period			
19. Cash, beginning balance			
20. Cash, ending balance			

*Statement only, and not the reconciliation.

Required   Consider the above comments and your checkmarked responses. Prepare a memo on the advantages of each method.

C 23–2
(L.O. 1)

Ethical Considerations: Interpretation of the SCF   Honore Company has competed for many years in product lines that have recently experienced a great increase in global competition. These products have long been dominated by U.S. firms. Honore has no foreign operations and few personnel with experience in international trade. Honore has made few product changes in recent years and is not actively engaged in product innovation or research and development.

The following information is selected from the company's financial statements and notes for the period 1996 to 1998 (in thousands):

	1996	1997	1998
Net income	$50,000	$30,000	$10,000
Net accounts receivable (ending)	40,000	12,000	6,000
Inventory (ending)	19,000	14,000	7,000
Net cash inflow from operations	15,000	7,000	4,500
Capital expenditures	9,000	7,000	6,000
Proceeds from sale of plant assets	15,000	10,000	18,000
Net gain on sales of plant assets and net extraordinary gains	16,000	12,000	15,000

The company
- Recently negotiated with banks to extend payment terms on short-term loans.
- Has maintained very low levels of accounts payable during this period.
- Has significant investments in corporate bonds (interest revenue on bonds in 1999 was $3,000).
- Paid no dividends during this period.
- Issued no stock or bonds during this period.

HONORE COMPANY

Statement of Cash Flows

For the Year Ended December 31, 1999

(in thousands)

Cash flows from operating activities:		
Net income		$ 7,000
Items reconciling net income and net cash inflow from operating activities		
Accounts receivable decrease	1,000	
Inventory decrease	1,500	
Extraordinary loss, building fire	8,000	
Dividends received (equity investment)	6,000	
Investment revenue (equity investment)	(10,000)	
Gains on sales of plant assets	(14,000)	
Depreciation, amortization	4,000	
Net cash inflow from operating activities		$ 3,500
Cash flows from investing activities:		
Purchase of plant assets	(4,000)	
Insurance proceeds on building fire	20,000	
Sale of plant assets	25,000	
Purchase of corporate bonds	(5,000)	
Purchase of corporate stocks	(10,000)	
Net cash inflow from investing activities		26,000
Cash flows from financing activities:		
Principal payments on short-term notes to financial institutions	(15,000)	
Purchase of treasury stock	(6,000)	
Net cash outflow from financing activities		(21,000)
Net cash increase		8,500
Beginning cash balance		12,000
Ending cash balance		$ 20,500

Required   Provide an interpretation of the SCF in light of Honore's situation. Weigh ethical considerations in terms of company strategy and financial disclosure.

C 23–3
(L.O. 3)

Cash Flow Reporting for Investments in Securities   *SFAS No. 115,* "Accounting for Certain Investments in Debt and Equity Securities," (1993) changed the classification of cash flows resulting from investments in securities not accounted for under the cost method, amortized cost method, equity method, or consolidation method.

Specifically, the *Statement* requires that cash flows from purchases and sales of securities be classified as operating cash flows if the securities are trading securities, and as investing cash flows if the securities are securities available for sale.

The following transactions and end-of-year market values refer to investments of Troy, Inc., in equity securities of Classic Art Company.

a. Troy purchased securities of Classic Art Company for $10,000 during 1998. Troy, a dealer in antiquities, is a calendar-year firm.
b. The December 31, 1998, market value of Troy's investments in Classic Art is $12,000 (adjusting entry needed).
c. During 1999, Troy sold half of the Classic Art securities for $5,500.
d. The December 31, 1999, market value of Troy's remaining investment in Classic Art is $5,200 (adjusting entry needed).

Required

For each of the above transactions and end-of-year adjusting entries, describe the disclosures required in the statement of cash flows and in the reconciliation of net income and net operating cash flow, under both the direct and indirect methods, for the following two cases:

1. The securities are classified as trading securities.
2. The securities are classified as available for sale.

Include in your answer an explanation or defense of your classification of cash flows and your reconciliation adjustment.

C 23–4
(L.O. 2, 3)

Reconciliation of Net Income and Net Operating Cash Flow   The reconciliation of a firm's earnings and its net cash flow from operating activities is a required disclosure regardless of the method chosen to prepare the statement of cash flows. If the direct method is used, the reconciliation appears as a supporting schedule. If the indirect method is used, the reconciliation appears either as the operating activity section of the SCF or as a supporting schedule. This case asks you to look more closely at the reconciliation.

Required

Answer the following questions about the reconciliation.

1. What is the purpose of the reconciliation?
2. Why does the reconciliation yield the same amount for net operating cash flow as does the list of operating cash flows found in the operating activities section under the direct method?
3. One of the most common adjustments found in the reconciliation is the change in operating working capital accounts, such as accounts receivable and prepaid expenses. Why are changes in dividends payable and short-term notes to financial institutions not found in the reconciliation?
4. Are the changes referred to in (3) limited to changes in current assets and liabilities? Explain.
5. Why is a cash flow not a common adjustment to be found in the reconciliation? Can you think of any cash flows that would appear in the reconciliation?

C 23–5
(L.O. 2)

YOU MAKE THE CALL   **The Statement of Cash Flows**   By issuing *SFAS No. 95,* "Statement of Cash Flows," the FASB established the accounting principles governing the disclosures to be placed in the statement, the classification of cash flows, the format of the statement, and the required supporting information. Many respondents to the exposure draft preceding the final statement indicated disagreement with various provisions. Obtaining complete agreement by all interested parties on the content and format of such an important financial statement is probably impossible, and the FASB may revisit this issue in the future.

Do you feel that the principles governing the SCF have produced the most useful statement possible? If you were a member of the FASB, would you have argued for a different set of principles? Provide your thoughts to the Board on how the SCF might be improved.

ANALYZING FINANCIAL STATEMENTS

All questions in this section are based on information taken from the financial statements of actual companies.

A 23–1
(L.O. 3)

Interpreting the Statement of Cash Flows: Ameritech Corporation is the parent corporation of five Bell companies serving the Great Lakes region. A portion of the operating activities section of the firm's 1995 statement of cash flows is reproduced below (in millions):

Net income (loss)	$ 2,007.6
Adjustments to net income (loss)	
Restructuring (credits) charges, net of tax	(78.7)
Deferred income taxes, net	149.0
Investment tax credits, net	(47.9)
Capitalized interest	(19.7)
Provision for uncollectibles	209.5
Change in certain noncurrent assets and liabilities	(154.3)

Ameritech uses the deferral method to account for investment tax credits: the firm amortizes part of the deferred ITC account as a reduction in income tax expense over the lives of related plant assets.

Required

Using only the information provided, explain why each of the reconciling items above appears in the operating section and why it is added or subtracted as the case may be.

A 23–2
(L.O. 3, 4)

Reconstruct Direct Method Operating Section: The Dole Food Company is one of the largest international food processing and distribution companies. Partial information from the 1995 annual report appears below (amounts in thousands):

DOLE FOOD COMPANY, INC.
Consolidated Statement of Income
For the Year Ended December 31, 1995

Revenue	$3,803,846
Cost of products sold	3,217,869
Gross margin	585,977
Selling, marketing and administrative expenses	392,694
Operating income	193,283
Interest expense	(81,186)
Interest income	7,501
Net gain on assets sold or held for disposal	61,655
Other expense—net	(5,429)
Income from continuing operations before income taxes	175,824
Income taxes	(56,000)
Income from continuing operations	119,824
Discontinued operations:	
Income (loss) from discontinued operations, net of income taxes . . . $(93,543)	
Distributions expenses, net of taxes . . . (2,950)	
Income (loss) from discontinued operations	(96,493)
Net income	$ 23,331

Portions of the balance sheets

	December 31	
	1995	**1994**
Current assets		
Cash and short-term investments	$ 72,151	$ 45,162
Receivables—net	462,303	494,755
Inventories	559,660	552,523
Prepaid expenses	43,087	46,569
Total current assets	$1,137,201	$1,139,009
Current liabilities		
Notes payable	$ 21,778	$ 50,366
Current portion of long-term debt	1,779	3,450
Accounts payable	182,152	173,463
Accrued liabilities	451,181	416,987
Total current liabilities	$ 656,890	$ 644,266

Additional assumptions:

1. *Other operating payments* may be determined by analyzing *selling, marketing, and administrative expenses,* and *other expense—net,* and the change in prepaid expenses and accrued expenses.
2. The notes payable are due to financial institutions.
3. The net deferred tax liability increased $30,429 during 1995 and was not affected by the discontinued operations.

Required

Dole uses the indirect method to prepare its SCF. Sufficient information to recast the operating section under the direct method is not available from the report. However, using the information presented in this case, prepare a rough draft of the 1995 direct method operating section.

A 23–3
(L.O. 3)

Interpreting the Statement of Cash Flows: Johnson Products, Inc., is a leading personal care products manufacturer. The firm's 1991 SCF, prepared under the indirect method, disclosed the following two reconciling adjustments in the operating activity section (amounts in thousands):

Imputed interest on note $134
Increase in cash surrender value of life insurance   . . .   (251)

Required   Explain why the reconciliation includes these two adjustments and why they are added to or subtracted from net income.

A 23–4   **Reconstructing an Income Statement from the SCF:**   Collins Industries, Inc., based in Missouri, is a manu-
(L.O. 3, 4)   facturer of specialty vehicles, such as ambulances, school and shuttle buses. The firm uses the direct method to prepare its SCF. Reproduced below from the 1995 SCF are (1) the operating activities section and (2) the reconciliation schedule.

Operating Activities

Cash received from customers	$141,425,892
Cash paid to suppliers and employees	(132,956,101)
Interest paid, net	(3,209,818)
Cash provided by operations	$ 5,259,973

Reconciliation of Net Loss to Net Cash Provided by Operations

Net loss	$ (340,759)
Depreciation and amortization	2,513,541
Common stock issued for benefit of employees	106,365
Decrease in receivables, net	700,827
Decrease in inventories	1,614,442
Decrease in prepaid expenses	329,517
Increase (decrease) in accounts payable	276,782
Increase (decrease) in accrued expenses	(261,519)
Gain on sale of vacant land	(99,667)
Loss on early extinguishment of debt	420,444
Cash provided by operations	$ 5,259,973

Required   Assuming that accrued and prepaid expenses do not relate to interest or to income taxes and that Collins had no interest income in 1995, reconstruct the 1995 income statement for Collins Industries. You need to aggregate certain expense categories.

A 23–5   **Interpreting the Coca-Cola Company Statement of Cash Flows**   Refer to the 1995 financial statements of the
(L.O. 2, 3, 4)   Coca-Cola Company that appear at the end of this text, and respond to the following questions:

1. Is Coke's statement of cash flows prepared under the direct method or the indirect method?
2. Provide an estimate of cash receipts from sales for 1995, assuming that all net operating revenues are credit sales and that there were no write-offs of receivables in 1995.
3. Were all 1995 declared dividends paid in 1995?
4. What is the company's policy with respect to classification of investments fulfilling the definition of cash equivalent for *SFAS No. 95?*
5. Did the firm fulfill the requirement to disclose certain operating cash flows for 1995?
6. Why is the first adjustment in the operating activities section of the *1993* SCF added to net income?
7. Can you estimate the amount of dividends received from investments accounted for under the equity method in 1995? Why is this amount not shown in the SCF?
8. Comment on trends you see in the SCFs for 1993–1995.

A 23–6   **Using the World Wide Web: Statement of Cash Flows**   This problem requires access to the World Wide Web
(L.O. 2)   portion of the Internet. The data for use in this problem is the most recent 10–K annual report of Cisco Systems. To obtain that information, use the Securities and Exchange Commission's Electronic Data Gathering, Analysis and Retrieval System (EDGAR) to retrieve Cisco's report. Steps to access EDGAR on the World Wide Web:

a. URL: http://www.sec.gov/index.html (the SEC's home page).
b. Click on EDGAR Database of Corporate Information.
c. Click on Search the EDGAR Database.
d. Click on Search the EDGAR Archives.
e. Enter the company name in the search dialog box.
f. Click on the listing for the most recent 10–K annual report.
g. Use Edit, Find in the toolbar to locate the statement of cash flows.

Required   Answer the following questions related to Cisco's statement of cash flows for the most recent year available or for the period specified by your instructor:

1. What method does Cisco use to present its statement of cash flows?
2. Comment on the difference between net income and net operating cash flow for the three years presented in the annual report. Which items caused the most significant differences between earnings and net operating cash flow?
3. Describe Cisco's investment behavior, both in short-term investments and in other longer-term investments.
4. How does Cisco report the difference between the earnings and the cash flow effects of accounts receivable?
5. Comment on Cisco's use of leverage, and whether there is a trend in the use of long-term debt financing.
6. Comment on the trend in capital expenditures and depreciation amounts shown in the SCF. Is there a relationship between the two?

COMPARATIVE ANALYSIS

CA 23–1
(L.O. 1, 2)

Analysis of SCFs for The Coca-Cola Company and PepsiCo Inc., Cash Flow Ratios This item is amenable to a group or individual solution. Refer to the preface for additional details on using group items.

The following information is excerpted from the 1995 annual report of PepsiCo, Inc. This information is to be used in conjunction with the Coca-Cola Company's annual report reproduced at the end of this text.

PEPSICO, INC. and SUBSIDIARIES

Consolidated Statement of Cash Flows

Fiscal Years Ended December 30, 1995, December 31, 1994, and December 25, 1993

(in millions)

Cash Flows—Operating Activities	**1995**	**1994**	**1993**
Income before cumulative effect of accounting changes	$1,606	$1,784	$1,588
Adjustments to reconcile income before cumulative effect of accounting changes to net cash provided by operating activities:			
Depreciation and amortization	1,740	1,577	1,444
Impairment of long-lived assets	520	—	—
Deferred income taxes	(111)	(67)	83
Other noncash charges and credits, net	398	391	345
Changes in operating working capital, excluding effects of acquisitions:			
Accounts and notes receivable	(434)	(112)	(161)
Inventories	(129)	(102)	(90)
Prepaid expenses, taxes, and other current assets	76	1	3
Accounts payable	133	30	143
Income taxes payable	(97)	55	(125)
Other current liabilities	40	159	(96)
Net Cash Provided By Operating Activities	3,742	3,716	3,134

Cash Flows—Investing Activities			
Acquisitions and investments in unconsolidated affiliates	(466)	(316)	(1,011)
Capital spending	(2,104)	(2,253)	(1,982)
Sales of property, plant and equipment	138	55	73
Sales of restaurants	165	—	7
Short-term investments, by original maturity:			
More than three months—purchases	(289)	(219)	(579)
More than three months—maturities	335	650	846
Three months or less, net	18	(10)	(8)
Other, net	(247)	(268)	(117)
Net Cash Used for Investing Activities	(2,450)	(2,361)	(2,771)

Cash Flows—Financing Activities			
Proceeds from issuances of long-term debt	2,030	1,285	711
Payments of long-term debt	(928)	(1,180)	(1,202)
Short-term borrowings, by original maturity:			
More than three months-proceeds	2,053	1,304	3,034
More than three months-payments	(2,711)	(1,728)	(2,792)
Three months or less, net	(747)	114	839
Cash dividends paid	(599)	(540)	(462)
Purchases of treasury stock	(541)	(549)	(463)
Proceeds from exercises of stock options	252	97	69
Other, net	(42)	(43)	(37)
Net Cash Used for Financing Activities	(1,233)	(1,240)	(303)
Effect of Exchange Rate Changes on Cash and Cash Equivalents	(8)	(11)	(3)
Net Increase in Cash and Cash Equivalents	51	104	57
Cash and Cash Equivalents—Beginning of Year	331	227	170
Cash and Cash Equivalents—End of Year	$ 382	$ 331	$ 227

Selected information from PepsiCo's 1995 annual report (ending 1995):

Total current assets	$ 5,546
Total current liabilities	5,230
Net income	1,606
Total assets	25,400
Total owners' equity	7,300
Outstanding common shares, Dec. 30	863

Required   Answer the following questions using the annual report information for both Coke and Pepsi.

1. Which method of reporting cash flows is used by each firm? Does the answer surprise you?
2. Compute the following three cash flow ratios for each firm for 1995 and comment on your results: (*a*) net operating cash flow to current liabilities, (*b*) net operating cash flow per share (use ending common shares outstanding), and (*c*) net operating cash flow to earnings. In particular, discuss any differences in the quality of earnings you find between the two firms.
3. Comment on differences in cash flow activity between the two firms in nonoperating areas over the three years 1993–1995.

CA 23–2
(L.O. 2)

Direct versus Indirect Methods: Mosinee Paper Company and Oxford Industries   The following information is excerpted from the 1992 financial statements of Mosinee Paper Company, a Wisconsin paper products manufacturer, and Oxford Industries, Inc., a clothing manufacturer. Mosinee prepares its statement of cash flows using the direct method, while Oxford uses the indirect method. The objective of this problem is to highlight the differences between the two methods from a user perspective. The investing and financing sections of the two cash flow statements are not provided in order to focus on the operating activity section of the SCF.

MOSINEE PAPER CORPORATION AND SUBSIDIARIES

Consolidated Statements of Cash Flows
(operating activities section only)
For the Year Ended December 31, 1992
(amounts in thousands)

Increase (decrease) in Cash and Cash equivalents:	
Cash flows from operating activities:	
Cash received from customers	$222,274
Cash paid to suppliers and employees	(202,722)
Interest received	146
Interest paid—net of amount capitalized	(7,774)
Income taxes refunded	4,277
Net cash provided by operating activities	$ 16,201
Reconciliation of Net Income (loss) to Net Cash Provided by Operating Activities:	
Net loss	$ (8,500)
Provision for depreciation, depletion and amortization	15,839
Provision for postretirement benefits other than pensions	14,242
Recognition of deferred revenue	(40)
Provision for losses on accounts receivable	247
Gain on property, plant, and equipment disposals	(558)
Deferred income taxes	(3,312)
Changes in operating assets and liabilities:	
Accounts receivable	(3,238)
Refundable income taxes	2,744
Inventories	(3,919)
Other assets	(2,032)
Accounts payable and other liabilities	4,611
Accrued income taxes	117
Net cash provided by operating activities	$ 16,201

Selected information from Mosinee Paper's 1991 and 1992 comparative balance sheets, and 1992 income statement:

1992 cost of goods sold $197,390

	1992	**1991**
Accounts payable balance	$16,997	$14,173

OXFORD INDUSTRIES, INC.

Consolidated Statement of Cash Flows
(operating activities section only)
For the Year Ended May 29, 1992
(amounts in thousands)

Cash Flows from Operating Activities:	
Net earnings	$12,532
Adjustments to reconcile net earnings to net cash provided by operating activities:	
Depreciation and amortization	6,254
Loss (gain) on sale of property, plant and equipment.	33
Changes in working capital: (Increase) decrease in:	
Receivables	(7,470)
Inventories	(15,359)
Prepaid expenses	(1,200)
Increase (decrease) in:	
Trade accounts payable	8,353
Accrued expenses and other current liabilities	1,122
Income taxes payable	(324)
Increase (decrease) in deferred income taxes	250
(Increase) decrease in other noncurrent assets	(374)
Net cash provided by operations	$ 3,817

Supplemental Disclosures of Cash Flow Information. Cash Paid (received) for:

Interest	$ 1,701
Income taxes	9,592
Income taxes refunded	(168)

OXFORD INDUSTRIES, INC.

Income Statement
For the Year Ended May 29, 1992

Net sales		$527,673
Costs and expenses:		
Cost of goods sold	$420,960	
Selling, general and administrative	84,466	
Interest	1,703	507,129
Earnings before income taxes		20,544
Income taxes		8,012
Net earnings		$ 12,532

OXFORD INDUSTRIES, INC.

Comparative Balance Sheets

	May 29, 1992	May 31, 1991
Current assets		
Cash and cash equivalents	$ 8,409	$ 19,156
Receivables, less allowance for doubtful accounts of		
$1,892 and $1,871 in 1992 and 1991, respectively	67,158	59,688
Inventories	82,021	66,662
Prepaid expenses	9,847	8,647
	167,435	154,153
Property, plant and equipment, net	30,754	32,351
Other assets, net	1,065	710
Total assets	$199,254	$187,214
Current liabilities		
Trade accounts payable	$ 38,363	$ 30,010
Accrued compensation	11,285	9,741
Other accrued expenses	10,141	10,564
Dividends payable	1,321	1,109
Income taxes	402	726
Current maturities of long-term debt	4,693	4,653
	66,205	56,803
Long-term debt, less current maturities	22,693	27,309
Deferred income taxes	2,142	1,892
Total liabilities	91,040	86,004
Stockholders' equity		
Common stock	8,810	8,855
Additional paid-in capital	5,054	4,828
Retained earnings	94,350	87,527
Total stockholders' equity	108,214	101,210
Total liabilities and stockholders' equity	$199,254	$187,214

Required
1. For each firm, determine (or approximate) the following operating cash flows for 1992:
   a. Cash collected from customers
   b. Cash paid to suppliers and other operating payments
   c. Interest paid
   d. Income taxes paid
2. Comment on the relative usefulness of the direct and indirect methods from a financial statement user's perspective, given your response in (1).

24 ACCOUNTING CHANGES AND ERROR CORRECTIONS

LEARNING OBJECTIVES

After you have studied this chapter, you will:

1 Recognize the issues in reporting for accounting changes.

2 Know how to identify the three types of accounting changes.

3 Understand the three approaches to reporting for accounting changes and error corrections and when to apply each.

4 Be able to prepare the required entries and disclosures for the current approach to reporting for accounting changes.

5 Be able to prepare the required entries and disclosures for the retroactive approach to reporting for accounting changes.

6 Be able to prepare the required entries and disclosures for the prospective approach to reporting for accounting changes.

7 Recognize several types of accounting errors and know when to record a prior period adjustment.

INTRODUCTION

Generally accepted accounting principles allow some flexibility with regard to making accounting changes. Accounting changes are not uncommon.

In 1996, America Online Inc. (AOL) disclosed a second-quarter charge of $385 million in conjunction with a change in its method of accounting for deferred subscriber acquisition costs. The charge was reported as part of income from continuing operations. AOL's net loss for the first two quarters of that year was $509 million. The $385 million charge involved no cash outlay and was added back to earnings in the statement of cash flows.

AOL explained in the footnotes that it had previously deferred the cost of certain marketing activities aimed at increasing its subscriber base, and then amortized them based on revenues recognized. Changing market dynamics and other factors prompted AOL to change its method of accounting to immediately recognize these costs as incurred.

Was this a change in accounting principle, or a change in accounting estimate? For similar accounting changes, such as a change in the method of depreciation, a special gain or loss (cumulative effect of an accounting principle change) would be recognized below income from continuing operations in the income statement.

AOL did not retroactively apply the new method of accounting to prior years. Normally firms disclose income statements for the current year and two preceding years in annual reports. Thus, AOL reported 1996 earnings computed under the new method, and 1995 and 1994 earnings computed under the old method, shown comparatively with 1996. Given the magnitude of the costs involved, this reporting does not foster the consistency characteristic of financial accounting information. However, it avoids the problems associated with restatement of prior earnings.

Example   Mitchell Energy & Development Corp., a Texas oil firm, retroactively applied a new method of accounting when it changed to the successful efforts method from the full cost method of accounting for oil exploration costs in 1995. As a result, Mitchell restated earnings it had previously reported under the full costing method. Consistency in the comparative income statements was achieved by this reporting. However, how do investors feel when earnings of prior years are restated? Were they misled in the past? What does this do to their confidence in the financial reporting process?

This chapter considers the issues underlying accounting changes and methods of reporting them. The reporting principles governing accounting changes apply to most of the topics covered in previous chapters of this text. Many accounting methods can be changed, and accounting estimates are frequently subject to change. This chapter also discusses the rationale for the reporting principles and illustrates accounting for error corrections.

ACCOUNTING CHANGES: REPORTING ISSUES AND APPROACHES

Accounting changes are made for many reasons. New FASB pronouncements often require changes in accounting principles. Since 1985, for example, the FASB has issued statements affecting the accounting for pensions and other postemployment benefits, changing prices, regulated enterprises, business combinations, the statement of cash flows, income taxes, and investments.

Firms may change accounting principles to adapt to changing economic conditions, as AOL did. For another example, increasing tax burdens and rising prices provide an incentive for firms to change to LIFO. Changing internal circumstances also may trigger accounting changes. Technological change and obsolescence, for example, may necessitate revisions in the useful lives of plant assets, in turn affecting depreciation expense.

Unfortunately, accounting changes obscure the meaning of net income for casual financial statement users. Critics charge that accounting changes undermine the usefulness and credibility of financial statements because the changes affect income but not the value of the firm. To enhance consistency, comparability, confidence in financial reporting, and full disclosure, *APB Opinion No. 20,* "Accounting Changes," (1971) was issued. This opinion, as amended, allows changes in accounting methods and estimates under certain circumstances and establishes reporting standards.

APB Opinion No. 20 addresses the essential issues in reporting accounting changes:
- Whether an accounting change is allowed.
- Whether to restate prior period financial statements to reflect the new principle or estimate.
- Whether to recognize the effect of the change on prior years' income as an adjustment to current net income, or to the beginning retained earnings balance in the year of the change.

Types of Accounting Changes

The reporting principles applied to accounting changes depend on the type of change. *APB Opinion No. 20* defines three types of **accounting changes** and specifies how to correct errors in previously issued financial statements. The three types of accounting changes are as follows:

1. A **change in accounting principle** replaces one generally accepted accounting principle with another. A change from straight-line to declining-balance depreciation is an example.

2. A **change in accounting estimate** substitutes one good-faith estimate for another, according to new information or conditions. A change in the estimated useful life or estimated residual value of a depreciable asset is an example.
3. A **change in reporting entity** (a special category of accounting principle change classified separately for purposes of *Opinion No. 20*) results in financial statements of a different reporting entity. Substitution of consolidated statements for individual company financial statements is an example.

A fourth item, **error corrections,** affects the income of prior periods and requires special treatment. The discovery and correction in 1998 of depreciation overstated in 1995 is an example. *Opinion No. 20* does not classify error corrections as accounting changes, but reporting principles similar to certain accounting changes apply to error corrections.

Objectives of Reporting Accounting Changes

Relevance   Maintaining the **relevance** of financial accounting information in light of new information and changing circumstances is one objective of reporting for accounting changes. In some instances, an accounting change can improve the relevance of reported information. For example, increasing inventory prices may prompt a change to the LIFO method of accounting for inventories, which matches more recent inventory costs against sales.

Consistency   Maintaining consistency is a second objective of reporting for accounting changes. Consistency, the conformity of accounting principles and procedures across periods, makes accounting information more useful by facilitating an understanding of information and relationships across time periods and firms. Financial statement users expect consistent application of accounting principles.

Comparability, the quality of information enabling users to identify similarities and differences between two sets of reports, is related to consistency. Information is more useful if it can be compared with similar data of the same firm for different time periods and with similar data from other firms.

Example   To determine whether $2 million of net income for a firm is a favorable result, an investor might examine previous income data from the same firm and other firms.

Consistency is a necessary but not sufficient condition for comparability. Significant inflation reduces the comparability of sales revenue over time even though the same recognition method is used consistently. If different accounting methods are used in consecutive reporting periods, comparability suffers. Consistency and comparability are secondary qualities of accounting information that enhance relevance and reliability, the primary qualities.

Yet consistency and comparability are no guarantee of relevance and reliability, and they should not prevent necessary change. "And you can't blame the accountants, either, unless you think accountants should stop trying to discover more accurate ways of describing the financial health of a company."[1]

Public Confidence   Maintaining public confidence in the financial reporting process is a third objective. Inconsistent use of accounting principles, disparity between disclosures and underlying firm value, and restatement of previously published financial statements all erode confidence. Many users expect that, except for error corrections, financial statements are final. "If companies were forever changing their earnings retroactively, investors would quickly lose whatever faith they once had in financial reports."[2]

Accounting Principle Changes

Accounting principles include methods, techniques, and procedures applied to transactions or information for purposes of measurement, recognition, or disclosure. When a firm makes a change in an accounting principle, it substitutes one generally accepted accounting principle for another. Examples include changing from FIFO to the weighted-average method, and straight-line to accelerated depreciation.

---

[1] "Solutions, Anyone?" *Forbes,* April 18, 1988, p. 72.
[2] "Add a Dash of Cumulative Catch-up," *Forbes,* June 6, 1983, p. 98.

Accounting principle changes also include less obvious modifications in measurement and reporting.

Example   Under *FASB Interpretation No. 1,* "Accounting Changes Related to the Cost of Inventory," a change in the composition of inventory cost is an accounting change.

Accounting principle changes are distinguished from accounting estimate changes in that the former involve a change in procedure or method of measurement. A change from the direct method to the allowance method of recognizing bad debts is an example. On the other hand, an estimate change involves only the value of parameters or variables affecting an accounting measurement. A change in the percentage of expected uncollectible accounts is an example.

The procedures for accounting changes are applied to existing assets and liabilities and to those that would exist under a new accounting principle. The required disclosures are limited to the financial statements presented on a comparative basis.

Although the following changes appear similar to accounting principle changes, they are not so considered under *APB Opinion No. 20:*

1. Initial adoption of an accounting principle for new transactions or for transactions that were previously immaterial. Immaterial prepaid advertising costs that were previously expensed but are now capitalized in an expanded advertising program is an example.
2. Adopting an accounting principle for a new group of assets or liabilities. For example, a firm begins applying accelerated depreciation to new equipment but continues to use straight-line depreciation for old equipment.
3. A change from an inappropriate accounting principle to an allowed method. For example, switching from capitalizing research and development costs to immediate expensing is an error correction.
4. A *planned* change to straight-line depreciation from accelerated depreciation at a particular future date to avoid overdepreciating plant assets.
5. A change in accounting principle that cannot be distinguished from a change in accounting estimate. Such a change is treated as a change in estimate.

Example   The America Online accounting change discussed in the introduction is an accounting principle change that cannot be distinguished from an estimate change. When AOL changed its method of accounting for its subscriber costs from capitalization and amortization to immediate expensing, the change had the same effect as if AOL revised its estimate of remaining useful life to zero for the costs capitalized in the past. Either approach results in immediate write-off of the previously capitalized costs. Because the two approaches are indistinguishable as to earnings effect, the write-off is treated as an estimate change and included *in* earnings from continuing operations, rather than as an accounting principle change that would disclose a cumulative effect account *below* earnings from continuing operations.

Approaches to Reporting Accounting Changes

Meeting the three reporting objectives simultaneously is challenging. Applying a new accounting method to current and future periods is in conflict with the consistency objective. Restating previously issued financial statements to reflect a new accounting method results in comparative statements based on the same accounting principles but conflicts with the public's expectation that previous financial statements should not be changed.

However, the disclosure requirements of *APB Opinion No. 20* attempt to satisfy these objectives. The APB appealed to the need to maintain public confidence when it decided that previous financial statements should not be restated for most accounting principle changes. But to promote consistency, prior period income as measured under the new accounting principle is also disclosed for most principle changes.

There are three approaches to recognizing and reporting accounting changes.

1. Current Approach The **current approach** recognizes in current period earnings the cumulative difference ("catch-up" adjustment) between the total expense or revenue under the old and new accounting principles for all affected prior periods up to the beginning of the current period.[3] This amount is disclosed (net of tax) in the income statement between extraordinary items and net income in an account titled **cumulative effect of change in accounting principle.** Prior financial statements shown comparatively with the current period are not restated, however. **Pro forma income** amounts (income computed under the new accounting principle) are disclosed for each year presented.[4]

Example   Ansel Company changes its depreciation method from double-declining balance (DDB) to straight-line (SL) in 1998 and applies the current approach. Applying SL to years before 1998 would have resulted in $500,000 *less* depreciation than actually recognized under DDB in those years. Ignoring income taxes, Ansel records the accounting change as of January 1, 1998:

Accumulated depreciation	500,000	
Cumulative effect of change in accounting principle		500,000

Financial statement effects of this accounting change:

- The cumulative effect account, a special type of gain in this case, increases 1998 income and is disclosed in the income statement just above net income. Thus the total effect of the change on the income of all prior years affected by the change is recognized in 1998 income.
- The accumulated depreciation balance after this entry reflects the use of SL depreciation on the assets affected, to the beginning of 1998.
- The 1997 financial statements, shown comparatively with those of 1998, continue to reflect the DDB method (no retroactive restatement):

Financial Statements	**1998**	**1997**
Method applied	SL	DDB

- Earnings for 1997 and 1998, recomputed under the SL method, are disclosed (pro forma earnings amounts) in the 1998 annual report.
- Depreciation for 1998 is computed under the SL method.

The APB concluded that most accounting principle changes should be reported under the current approach. The pro forma amounts support the consistency objective, enabling users to see a trend in income computed under the same (new) method for all periods presented.

2. Retroactive Approach For a few accounting principle changes, the advantages of retroactive restatement outweigh the disadvantages. The **retroactive approach** restates all prior financial statements presented on a comparative basis to conform to the new principle. The cumulative income difference for prior periods (net of tax), computed as in the current approach, adjusts the current beginning retained earnings balance. This cumulative income difference does not affect current income.

Example   Ansel Company changes its method of accounting for revenue on long-term construction contracts in 1998 from the completed contract method (CC) to the percentage of completion method (PC) and applies the retroactive approach. Ansel has recognized $1 million of earnings to the beginning of 1998 using the completed contract method. Under the percentage of completion method, that figure would have been $2.5 million. Ignoring income taxes, Ansel records the accounting change as of January 1, 1998:

Construction in process inventory	1,500,000	
Retained earnings, adjustment for accounting change		1,500,000

Financial statement effects of this accounting change:

- The effect of the change on prior year earnings is recorded in retained earnings, bypassing the income statement. The beginning 1998 balance in retained earnings now reflects

---

[3] Throughout this chapter, the *current* reporting period is the period in which an accounting change or error correction is made.

[4] Pro forma financial statements and amounts show the effect of transactions, conditions, or principles that have not yet occurred or been applied. They are as-if amounts.

the use of the new method in prior years. The $1,500,000 amount is disclosed as an adjustment to the beginning balance of retained earnings.
- The construction in process inventory balance after this entry reflects the use of percentage of completion on the contracts affected to the beginning of 1998.
- The 1997 financial statements, shown comparatively with those of 1998, are *retroactively* restated to reflect the new method. Net income for 1997 as reported in the 1998 comparative income statements is restated, and thus does not equal the amount reported in the 1997 annual report.

Financial Statements	**1998**	**1997**
Method applied	PC	PC

- Percentage of completion is used to account for revenue on long-term contracts in 1998.

Both the current and retroactive approaches compute a cumulative catch-up amount. However, the retroactive approach applies the same method consistently to each year shown in the comparative statements. This contrasts with the current approach that applies the new method to the current year, and the old method to the prior years. The retroactive approach also is applied to corrections of errors in prior year earnings.

3. Prospective Approach The **prospective approach** applies revised accounting *estimates* to current and future periods affected by the change.[5] Prior financial statements remain unchanged, and no cumulative effect on prior years' income is computed. Estimate changes are the most common accounting change. Estimates are subject to error and require periodic revision over time. The prospective approach is not applied to accounting principle changes.

Example Ansel Company changes its estimate of useful life and residual value on equipment purchased January 1, 1996, costing $440,000. The original useful life and residual value estimates were 10 years and $40,000, respectively. During 1998, Ansel revises the remaining useful life and residual value estimates to five years and $0 as a result of changes in technology. Assume straight-line depreciation.

The new salvage value and remaining useful life estimates are applied to the book value of equipment remaining at the beginning of 1998:

Original cost, January 1, 1996	$440,000
Depreciation per year: ($440,000 − $40,000)/10 = $40,000	
Accumulated depreciation, January 1, 1998: 2($40,000)	80,000
Book value, January 1, 1998	$360,000
Depreciation, 1998: ($360,000 − $0)/5	$ 72,000

Financial statement effects of this accounting change:
- An estimate change is not applied to prior years; the change affects only the current year and possibly future years. Thus there is no special entry to record the accounting change.
- The accumulated depreciation balance at the end of 1998, after recording depreciation, reflects both the old and new estimates. The new estimates are applied as of the beginning of 1998.
- The 1997 financial statements, shown comparatively with those of 1998, continue to reflect the old estimates (no retroactive restatement).

Financial Statements	**1998**	**1997**
Estimates applied	New	Old

- Pro forma earnings amounts are not disclosed.

The prospective approach is supported by the notion that good-faith estimates are valid until conditions change. New estimates are not applied to the results of previous periods

---

[5] This approach also is referred to as the current and prospective approach.

because the information supporting the estimate change was not available or applicable until the current period. Although the results of previous periods reflect different estimates, disclosing the effect of the change on current income partially offsets the reduced consistency.

The following diagram compares the three approaches to accounting changes, emphasizing the periods that recognize the impact of the change. In each case, 1998 is the year the accounting change is made.

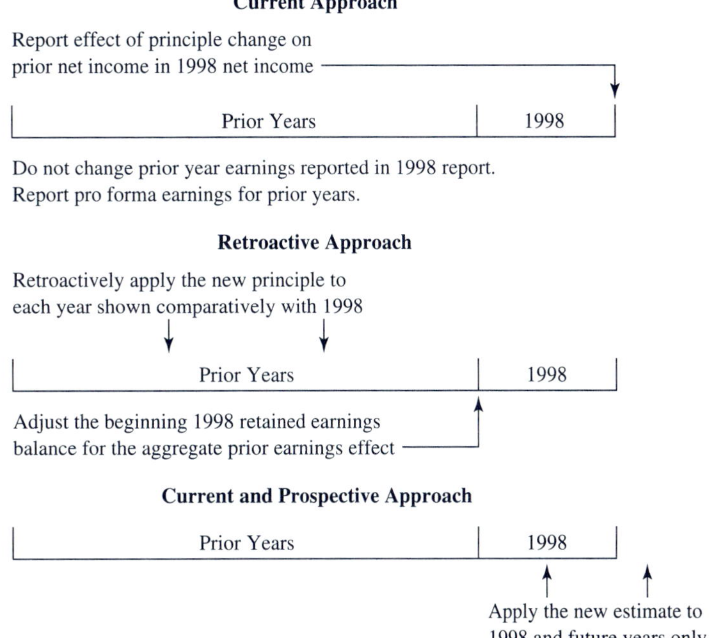

> **CONCEPT REVIEW**
>
> 1. How does the current approach maintain a measure of consistency in financial reporting?
> 2. Why are estimate changes treated prospectively?
> 3. Explain the major differences between the current and retroactive approaches.

General Application of the Three Approaches

Exhibit 24–1 summarizes the application of the three approaches to accounting changes. Changes in accounting principles, estimates, and error corrections are often made during the closing process. However, entries to record accounting changes and error corrections affecting prior years are made *as of the beginning* of the current year and thus reflect the new principle or estimate for the entire year. The entries to record the change are not affected by the number of prior years shown comparatively with the current period.

The cumulative effect on prior years' income under the current and retroactive approaches, and prior period adjustments (for errors), are disclosed in the financial statements net of tax. Intraperiod tax allocation separates the tax effects on these three items from tax on income from continuing operations.

Changes in Reporting Entity

Changes in reporting entity result in financial statements that, in effect, are those of a different reporting entity. They occur mainly in
- Reporting consolidated or combined statements in place of individual company statements.
- Reporting the effects of changing the composition of the consolidated group.
- Reporting the effects of changing the composition of the group of companies included in combined financial statements.

EXHIBIT 24–1   Summary of Accounting Changes and Reporting Approaches

Type of Accounting Change or Error Correction	Reporting Approach Required	Summary of the Approach	
		Cumulative Adjustment Reported as	**Comparative Statements (results of prior years)**
Accounting changes: 1. Changes in accounting principles a. Most principle changes.*	Current	A separate income statement item below income from continuing operations.	Prior years' results remain unchanged (pro forma income amounts disclosed).
b. Specified exceptions.†	Retroactive	An adjustment to retained earnings, beginning balance.	Prior years' results restated to reflect new principle.
2. Changes in accounting estimates.	Prospective	None	Prior years' results remain unchanged. New estimates applied prospectively.
3. Changes in reporting entity.	Retroactive	None‡	Prior years' results restated.
Correction of accounting errors affecting income of prior years.	Retroactive	An adjustment to retained earnings, beginning balance (a prior period adjustment).	Prior years' results correctly restated.

*The change to LIFO typically does not require reporting a cumulative effect of a change in accounting principle, but is otherwise treated as a current change.

†Three examples are (1) change in method of natural resource exploration costs, (2) change in method of revenue recognition for long-term contracts, and (3) change from LIFO.

‡Discussed in advanced accounting courses.

To allow meaningful comparisons across reporting periods, the retroactive approach is applied to these changes. The results of all prior periods presented are restated as if the consolidated group represented the current combination of entities during those periods. The nature and justification for the change are reported, as well as the effect on income before extraordinary items, net income, and related per share amounts for all periods presented. Subsequent financial statements need not repeat the disclosures. Advanced accounting courses treat consolidations in detail.

Justification for Accounting Changes

There is a presumption that an accounting principle should not be changed in accounting for transactions of a similar type. Under GAAP, only if the firm justifies the use of a new principle on the basis that it is preferable may a change be made. The nature of the accounting principle change and its justification appear in a footnote. The justification should clearly explain why the new principle is preferable. Common justifications for accounting changes as disclosed in company footnotes include:

- To improve matching of expenses and revenues.
- To enhance asset valuation.
- To provide new information.
- To respond to changed economic or market conditions.
- To comply with new reporting standards.

Example   A firm justifies its change from the completed contract method to the percentage of completion method by citing improved reliability of total construction cost estimates.

SFAS No. 111, "Rescission of *FASB Statement No. 32* and Technical Corrections," specifies that a pronouncement recognized as GAAP and establishing a new accounting principle, interpreting an existing principle, expressing a preference for a specific accounting principle, or rejecting a previous principle is sufficient support for a change in accounting principle required by the pronouncement.

SFAS No. 111 recognizes the hierarchy of GAAP as specified in auditing standards.[6] This hierarchy has four levels, with the highest being the most authoritative:

Level A: FASB *Statements and Interpretations,* APB *Opinions,* and AICPA *Accounting Research Bulletins.*

Level B: FASB *Technical Bulletins,* AICPA *Industry Audit and Accounting Guides,* and AICPA *Statements of Position.*

Level C: Consensus positions of the FASB Emerging Issues Task Force, and AICPA *Practice Bulletins.*

Level D: AICPA *Accounting Interpretations, "Qs and As"* published by the FASB staff, and industry practices widely recognized and prevalent.

A firm making an accounting change in conformance with a new pronouncement should report the change as specified in the pronouncement. Otherwise, *APB Opinion No. 20* guidelines apply.

Comparative Statements

Annual reports generally include financial statements for the current year and for one or two previous years. Comparative financial statements increase the usefulness of annual reports by increasing the quantity of information available and by establishing a basis for comparison with current results. This dynamic portrayal is more useful for predictions than single-year statements because it indicates whether reported accounting data are increasing or decreasing.

Comparative financial statements are recommended under GAAP,[7] and the SEC requires firms under its jurisdiction to report more than one year's data. Creditors also typically require comparative financial statements for lending purposes. Later sections provide more detailed examples and reporting guidelines involving comparative financial statements and footnote disclosures. The previous discussion emphasized the main accounting objectives and procedures for reporting accounting changes.

SUMMARY OF ACCOUNTING CHANGES

The three approaches to reporting changes have certain similarities. Each approach requires disclosures designed to reduce the loss of consistency caused by the accounting change. The current and retroactive approaches recognize the effect of the change on prior years' income directly in the accounts; and they either modify prior statements presented comparatively or add disclosures related to them. The pro forma amounts (current approach) and the restated net income amounts (retroactive approach) supply the same *income* information. All three approaches disclose the effect of the change on current income. In addition, the change is effective at the beginning of the current year. Exhibit 24–2 summarizes the effects of accounting principle and estimate changes.

CORRECTION OF ACCOUNTING ERRORS

An accounting error occurs when a transaction or event is recorded incorrectly or is not recorded at all. All of the following are examples of accounting errors:

1. Use of an inappropriate or unacceptable accounting principle and mistakes in applying GAAP. For example, the use of the fair value method to account for an investment when the equity method is appropriate is an error. Changing from an unacceptable accounting principle, or one incorrectly applied, to a generally accepted one is an error correction.
2. Intentional use of an unrealistic accounting estimate or gross negligence in making estimates. For example, adopting an unrealistic depreciation rate requires an error correction.

---

[6] The hierarchy appears in *Statement of Auditing Standards No. 69,* "The Meaning of 'Present Fairly in Conformity with Generally Accepted Accounting Principles' in the Independent Auditor's Report." *SFAS No. 32* had specified only certain AICPA pronouncements as justifications for accounting changes. With the hierarchy established in *SAS No. 69, SFAS No. 32* is no longer needed.

[7] "Restatement and Revision of Accounting Research Bulletins Nos. 1–42," *Accounting Research Bulletin No. 43* (New York: AICPA, 1953), chapter 2, section A, par. 2.

EXHIBIT 24–2
Accounting Changes and
Reporting Approaches:
Summary Table

Attribute	Estimate Change	Most Accounting Principle Changes	Specified Accounting Principle Changes, Prior Period Adjustments
Accounting approach	Prospective	Current	Retroactive
Entry to record effect of change on prior years' income	None	Recognize cumulative effect in current income	Cumulative effect adjusts beginning retained earnings balance
Restate prior statements	No	No	Yes
Pro forma income disclosures	No	Yes	No
Report effect of change on net income	Yes, current period only	Yes, current period only	Yes, for all years presented and affected
Repeat disclosures in subsequent statements	Continue to use new estimates	Yes	No
Maintain consistency by	Disclosing effect on net income	Disclosing pro forma amounts	Restating prior statements
Confidence in reporting process maintained by	Leaving prior statements unchanged	Leaving prior statements unchanged	Disclosing effect on net income

3. Misstating or misclassifying an account balance.
4. Delay in or failure to recognize accruals, deferrals, and other transactions.
5. Arithmetic mistakes.
6. Fraud or gross negligence in financial reporting.

Material errors are not a common occurrence. Larger firms discover most material errors before completing the financial statements.

Classification of Accounting Errors

Accounting and reporting for error corrections depends on several factors:
- Whether the error affects prior financial statements.
- Whether the error affects prior net income.
- Whether the error counterbalances (automatically self-corrects) within two accounting periods.
- When the error was made and discovered.[8]
- The periods presented in the comparative financial statements.

To facilitate the discussion, errors are classified as follows:

I. Errors that occur and are discovered in the same accounting period.
II. Errors that occur in one accounting period and are discovered in a later accounting period.
   A. Errors affecting prior period financial statements but not prior period income.
   B. Errors affecting prior period net income.
      1. Counterbalancing errors.
      2. Noncounterbalancing errors.

Errors that Occur and Are Discovered in the Same Accounting Period   This type of error does not affect prior financial statements and is corrected by reversing the incorrect

---

[8] In the examples to follow, errors are discovered before closing the books in the year of discovery, and before preparing the financial statements.

entry and then recording the correct entry, or by making an entry to correct the account balances. For example, assume that the collection of $4,000 cash in advance from a customer at the end of the reporting period is credited to a revenue account as $400:

Incorrect entry:

Cash	400	
Revenue		400

The correcting entry, when combined with the incorrect entry, yields the correct ending balance for all affected accounts.[9]

Correcting entry:

Cash	3,600	
Revenue	400	
Unearned revenue		4,000

After this entry is recorded as part of the adjusting process, cash, revenue, and unearned revenue are correctly stated.

Errors Affecting Prior Financial Statements but Not Income   This type of error involves incorrect classification of permanent or temporary accounts. Neglecting to classify the current portion of a long-term liability as current is an example. Another example is crediting a gain rather than revenue. Neither error affects prior years' income.

APB Opinion No. 20 requires that previously issued statements that contain errors and are presented with the current period statements be corrected. Applying the retroactive approach to these is not complex because income is not affected. An entry reclassifying accounts affected is recorded. A footnote discloses the nature of the error.

Errors Affecting Prior Period Net Income (counterbalancing)   An accounting error is a counterbalancing error if it self-corrects over a two-year period. The income for the period of error is misstated as is the income of the second period, but in the opposite direction. Many errors that affect both the income statement and balance sheet are self-correcting over a two-year period.[10]

Example   Assume that 1997 ending inventory is overstated $4,000 through an arithmetic error in applying unit costs to inventory items. The error causes the following effects, assuming a 30 percent tax rate:

	Effect of Error			
	1997		**1998**	
Beginning inventory	Unaffected		Overstated	$4,000
Ending inventory	Overstated	$4,000	Unaffected	
Cost of goods sold	Understated	$4,000	Overstated	$4,000
Pretax income	Overstated	$4,000	Understated	$4,000
Income tax expense (30 percent)	Overstated	$1,200	Understated	$1,200
Net income (70 percent)	Overstated	$2,800	Understated	$2,800
Ending retained earnings	Overstated	$2,800	Unaffected	

The inventory error is a counterbalancing error because the overstatement of 1997 income and ending retained earnings is offset by the understatement of 1998 income. Ending 1998 retained earnings is corrected automatically as is the inventory account.

The counterbalancing feature does not imply that financial statements are correct, however. If the 1998 report presents both years comparatively, all the errors (understatements or overstatements) remain in the statements if not corrected. Net income for both years is

---

[9] A useful way to determine the correcting entry is as follows: incorrect entry + correcting entry = correct entry.

[10] Practically all errors eventually counterbalance, but many require more than two years to reverse. For example, a depreciation error on an operational asset self-corrects but only at disposal. However, a more meaningful classification is achieved when the term *counterbalancing* is restricted to a two-year cycle.

in error. In addition, if the income tax rate changes in 1998, the effects of the error do not completely counterbalance. Assume that the tax rate changes to 40 percent in 1998. Then, in 1998, beginning inventory and pretax income are misstated by $4,000, but income tax expense and payable are now understated $1,600 ($4,000 × .40). Net income is understated by $2,400. Therefore, 1998 ending retained earnings remains overstated $400 ($2,800 overstatement in 1997 less $2,400 understatement in 1998).

Discovery after Self-Correction   Counterbalancing errors discovered two or more years after the year of error do not require a correcting entry. If the above 1997 ending inventory error is discovered in 1999 (assume the original 30 percent tax rate), no correcting entry is required because all relevant 1999 beginning account balances are correct. The ending balances of inventory and retained earnings are no longer affected, and the temporary account balances (containing errors) were closed at the end of 1998. The financial statements for 1997 and 1998 should be restated if presented.

Discovery before Self-Correction   If counterbalancing errors are discovered during the second year of the two-year cycle, a correcting entry is required. If the error in the inventory example is discovered in 1998, an entry is recorded that corrects the beginning 1998 retained earnings balance for the effect of the 1997 error (assume the original 30 percent tax rate):

As of January 1, 1998—To correct error made in 1997:

Prior period adjustment, inventory correction	2,800	
Income tax receivable	1,200*	
Inventory		4,000

*Assuming that 1997 income tax is paid.

A **prior period adjustment** is the after-tax adjustment required to correct an error in prior period income ($2,800 in our example). This account is closed to retained earnings and revises the beginning retained earnings balance in the discovery year. The errors in the 1997–1998 comparative statements are corrected under the retroactive approach. Income tax receivable is debited because the error was made for both accounting and tax purposes.[11]

Typical accounts involved in counterbalancing errors include inventories, prepayments and deferrals, and accruals. Inventory errors involve omitting, miscounting, and misclassifying items, nonrecording of purchases, and costing errors. Errors involving prepayments and deferrals are caused by failing to recognize the expirations applicable to the current year. Because accruals precede cash flows, accrual errors are caused by failing to recognize expense and revenue accruals.

Errors Affecting Prior Period Net Income (noncounterbalancing)   An accounting error is not counterbalancing if it does not automatically self-correct within two consecutive accounting periods. The error continues to affect account balances for a longer period. One or more balance sheet accounts remain in error.

Over- or understating depreciation expense is an example of a noncounterbalancing error. The accumulated depreciation and retained earnings balances are in error until corrected or until the asset is sold or fully depreciated.

Another example is the immediate expensing of a large purchase of plant assets. The effects include incorrect asset balances, expense amounts, and retained earnings until corrected or until the asset is sold or fully depreciated. Correcting a noncounterbalancing error usually requires a prior period adjustment.

---

[11]An accounting error need not necessarily imply a tax error. Furthermore, if an error is made for both accounting and tax, the effects on income may be different. For example, if a plant asset is not depreciated, the annual depreciation errors are not the same for the two systems if different depreciation methods are used in each.

CONCEPT REVIEW

1. If an error is discovered in the year after it counterbalances, why must certain account balances in comparative statements be corrected?
2. What is a prior period adjustment?
3. Do all errors require prior period adjustments?

The All-Inclusive Concept of Income and Prior Period Adjustments

Most profit and loss items are disclosed in the income statement. *SFAC No. 6* defines comprehensive income as the net of all changes in equity except those resulting from investments by, and distributions to, owners. Although a few items other than transactions with owners are currently excluded from earnings, income measurement continues to evolve toward a more all-inclusive concept.

The following items are currently excluded from income:
- Changes in the market value of investments in securities available for sale (affects owners' equity).
- The effect on prior years' income of accounting principle changes under the retroactive approach (adjusts retained earnings).
- Certain foreign currency translation adjustments.
- Prior period adjustments.

At one time, prior period adjustments included items such as income tax adjustments of prior years and the costs and proceeds of lawsuits initiated in prior years. If an item fulfilled the criteria of a prior period adjustment as given in *APB Opinion No. 9,* "Reporting the Results of Operations," it was excluded from current income.

SFAS No. 16, "Prior Period Adjustments," as amended by *SFAS No. 109,* "Accounting for Income Taxes," considerably narrows the definition of prior period adjustment to include only errors affecting prior period income.

Errors are caused by misusing or omitting information known at the time the error was committed. The prior statements *could have* reflected the correct information.

Example   All the information to correctly report 1998 depreciation is present in 1998. Therefore, the correction of an error in recording 1998 depreciation should not affect income of years other than 1998, even if discovered after 1998. A prior period adjustment, which adjusts retained earnings, is consistent with this rationale.

Other items previously included in prior period adjustments are not measurable until later periods.

Example   The cost of a lawsuit brought in 1996 and concluded in 1998 is not known until 1998. Therefore, it is reasonable to reflect the cost in 1998 income.

FASB's rationale is that the all-inclusive concept is less confusing than allowing special treatment for some profit and loss items and not for others. To reinforce this stance, the FASB reviewed approximately 6,000 annual reports of the mid-1970s and found that items reported as prior period adjustments (before *SFAS No. 16*) were not sufficiently different from items included in net income to warrant treatment as prior period adjustments.

Correcting Entries and Analysis

The number and variety of possible errors is unlimited. We illustrate five examples of errors and correcting entries. Income taxes are ignored for simplicity.

Example 1 Error in Purchases and Inventory   Coe Company purchases $2,000 of inventory in 1997 but records the purchase in 1998 when paid. Coe did not include the goods in the 1997 ending inventory although they were on hand at December 31, 1997.

Case A: Coe discovers the error in 1998.

Analysis: In 1997, both purchases and ending inventory are understated by the same amount. Because they have opposite effects on cost of goods sold and income, 1997 income is correctly stated, although ending 1997 inventory and payables balances are understated $2,000. Both beginning inventory and purchases for 1998 are also in error. The 1997 statements are restated.

Correcting entry in 1998:

Inventory	2,000	
Purchases		2,000

Case B: Coe discovers the error in 1999.

Analysis: At the beginning of 1999, all account balances are correct. Neither 1997 nor 1998 income was misstated. Therefore, no correcting entry is needed in 1999. The 1997 and 1998 financial statements are restated if shown on a comparative basis with 1999 statements.

Example 2 Error in Prepaid Expense

Coe acquires a five-year fire insurance policy on January 1, 1997, pays the entire $500 premium, and debits insurance expense in 1997. Coe does not make an adjusting entry to recognize prepaid insurance at the end of 1997.

Case A: Coe discovers the error in 1998.

Analysis: In 1997, insurance expense is overstated and income understated by $400 ($500 expense recognized less $100 correct expense). At the end of 1997, both prepaid insurance and retained earnings are understated by $400. The 1997 statements are restated.

Correcting entry in 1998:

Prepaid insurance (1999–2001)	300	
Insurance expense (1998)	100	
Prior period adjustment, insurance correction		400

Case B: Coe discovers the error in 1999.

Analysis: The error in beginning 1999 retained earnings is now only $300, because at January 1, 1999, $200 of insurance expense should have been recognized (1997 and 1998), but $500 was recognized. (Eventually, this error self-corrects.) The 1997 and 1998 statements are restated.

Correcting entry in 1999:

Prepaid insurance (2000–2001)	200	
Insurance expense (1999)	100	
Prior period adjustment, insurance expense correction		300

Example 3 Error in Accrued Expense

Coe fails to record $100 accrued property tax payable for 1997. Coe pays the tax early in 1998 and records an expense at that time.

Case A: Coe discovers the error in 1998.

Analysis: In 1997, property tax expense is understated and income overstated. Also, liabilities are understated by $100. Property tax expense for 1998 is overstated by $100. The 1998 payables balance is correct because taxes were paid in 1998. The 1997 statements are restated.

Correcting entry in 1998:

Prior period adjustment, property tax correction	100	
Property tax expense		100

Case B: Coe discovers the error in 1999.

Analysis: The errors counterbalanced in 1998 because 1997 income is overstated and 1998 income is understated by the same amount. No correcting entry is needed for 1999. The 1997 and 1998 statements are restated.

Example 4 Error in Revenue Earned but Not Yet Collected

Coe fails to accrue $75 interest receivable earned to the end of 1997. Coe collects the interest in 1998 and records revenue at that time.

Case A: Coe discovers the error in 1998.

Analysis: In 1997, interest revenue, net income, and receivables are understated. In 1998, interest revenue is overstated. Because the interest was collected, 1998 receivables are correctly stated. The 1997 statements are restated.

Correcting entry in 1998:

```
Interest revenue  . . . . . . . . . . . . . . . . . . . . . . . . . . . . . . . . . . . . . . . . . . .   75
    Prior period adjustment, interest revenue correction  . . . . . . . . . . . . . . . . . . .        75
```

Case B: Coe discovers the error in 1999.

Analysis: The error counterbalanced in 1998 because 1997 income is understated and 1998 income is overstated by the same amount. No correcting entry is needed in 1999. The 1997 and 1998 statements are restated.

Example 5 Error in Capitalizing an Asset

On January 1, 1997, Coe pays $500 for ordinary repairs and debits the machinery account. Depreciation is 10 percent per year.

Case A: Coe discovers the error in 1998.

Analysis: For 1997, repair expense is understated and depreciation expense overstated. Also, income is overstated by the difference. Assets and retained earnings are overstated by $450 [$500 − (.10 × $500)]. The 1997 statements are restated.

Correcting entry in 1998:

```
Accumulated depreciation ($500 × .10) . . . . . . . . . . . . . . . . . . . . . . . . . .         50
Prior period adjustment, repair expense correction  . . . . . . . . . . . . . . . . . . . .       450
    Machinery  . . . . . . . . . . . . . . . . . . . . . . . . . . . . . . . . . . . . . . . . . . . . .            500
```

Case B: Coe discovers the error in 1999.

Analysis: Retained earnings is overstated $400 because $500 expense should have been recognized but only $100 depreciation is recognized by the end of 1998. The 1997 and 1998 statements are restated.

Correcting entry in 1999:

```
Accumulated depreciation ($500 × .10 × 2) . . . . . . . . . . . . . . . . . . . . . . . .        100
Prior period adjustment, repair expense correction  . . . . . . . . . . . . . . . . . . . .       400
    Machinery  . . . . . . . . . . . . . . . . . . . . . . . . . . . . . . . . . . . . . . . . . . . . .            500
```

DETAILED REPORTING GUIDELINES AND EXAMPLES

The next four sections provide more detailed reporting guidelines and examples to supplement the previous discussion. The emphasis here is on comparative financial statements.

Current Approach

Reporting Guidelines   The following guidelines apply to accounting principle changes subject to the current approach. They apply to all accounting principle changes except those subject to the retroactive approach (the specified exceptions).

1. Prior year financial statements reported on a comparative basis remain unchanged.
2. The cumulative income difference between the two methods for all affected prior periods is reported net of tax between extraordinary items and net income in the income statement. The entry to record the cumulative effect also involves a real account (such as accumulated depreciation or inventory) and often an income tax account.[12]
3. The effects of the new principle on current year's income before extraordinary items and on net income (and related per share amounts) are disclosed.
4. Pro forma income before extraordinary items and net income (and related per share amounts) are disclosed on the face of the income statement (or noted prominently and cross-referenced) for all prior periods presented and for the current year as if the new accounting principle were in effect during those periods. If only the current period is presented, the actual and pro forma amounts for the immediately preceding period and the current period are disclosed.

---

[12] If the change is also made for tax purposes, income taxes payable or receivable is recorded, and an amended tax return is filed. If not, a change in a deferred income tax account is recorded. In most cases, however, changes are not made for both purposes.

5. The new principle is applied as of the beginning of the current year. The current year's financial statements reflect the new principle; the prior years' statements reflect the old principle.
6. Future annual reports repeat the disclosures until the year of change is no longer presented.

Example   Exhibit 24–3 presents case information for a detailed example of the current approach applied to a change in depreciation method. In that exhibit, the cumulative income difference before tax ($37,600) is also the difference in the accumulated depreciation balance between the two methods. If the DDB method were used during the previous three years, the accumulated depreciation balance would be $97,600 at the end of 1997, rather than $60,000. The entries Sunrise makes in 1998 to record the accounting change, and depreciation expense are as follows:

As of January 1, 1998—To record accounting change:

Cumulative effect of change in accounting principle, depreciation	22,560	
Deferred tax liability ($37,600 × .40)	15,040	
Accumulated depreciation		37,600

December 31, 1998—To record depreciation expense (DDB):

Depreciation expense ($200,000 − $97,600)(.20)	20,480	
Accumulated depreciation		20,480

The cumulative effect account is similar to a loss or expense in this instance, and reduces income $22,560 after tax because DDB recognizes depreciation expense faster than SL during the asset's early years.[13] Depreciation expense for 1998 reflects the DDB method.

The January 1, 1998, entry to record the accounting change reduces the deferred tax liability because *future* book depreciation is reduced relative to tax depreciation (the change was made for book purposes only). Although the deferred tax consequences of the accounting change are dependent on the specific schedule of future temporary differences, for simplicity we assume an existing deferred tax liability. Alternatively, a firm may record the accounting change in pretax amounts and postpone the income tax allocation until the end of the year.

Exhibit 24–4 shows Sunrise's 1997 statements under the old method (SL) and the 1998 statements under the new method (DDB). The reported net income amounts for 1997 and 1998 are not comparable to the extent that depreciation expense is material. However, this lack of consistency is somewhat offset by the reporting of pro forma earnings amounts for each year, which are computed under the new depreciation method.

Pro forma income before extraordinary items in the current year equals its actual counterpart because both values reflect the new method. Pro forma net income for the current year equals the reported net income plus or minus the cumulative effect. If DDB were used previously, there would be no cumulative effect. Therefore, 1998 pro forma income equals reported net income plus the cumulative effect, because the cumulative effect reduced reported income.

The footnote in Exhibit 24–4 describes the change, its justification, and the effect on 1998 income. These disclosures supplement the pro forma disclosures and help users understand the change.

Direct and Indirect Effects of Changes in Accounting Principle   Many firms that change accounting principles under the current approach report both direct and indirect effects. The direct effects of the change are those adjustments made to account balances and earnings amounts to reflect the new principle, such as those illustrated in the Sunrise Company example.

---

[13]A credit cumulative effect increases income.

1. In 1998, Sunrise Company changes from straight-line (SL) depreciation to double-declining balance (DDB) for financial reporting purposes. The new method affects machinery purchased January 1, 1995, costing $200,000. The machinery has no salvage value; its estimated useful life is 10 years. The reporting year ends December 31. A 40 percent tax rate is assumed.
2. Sunrise reports 1997 and 1998 results on a comparative basis. Summary financial information for both years follows. (The order of years presented facilitates the discussion; normally the most recent statements are on the left.)

	Reported in 1997	1998 Adjusted Trial Balance before Accounting Change and Depreciation
Balance sheet, December 31:		
Assets (not detailed)	$700,000	$823,400
Machinery	200,000	200,000
Accumulated depreciation (straight line)	(60,000)	(60,000)
Total	$840,000	
Liabilities (including deferred income tax)	$340,000	$291,112
Contributed capital (100,000 shares)	300,000	300,000
Retained earnings	200,000	200,000
Total	$840,000	
Income statement, year ended December 31:		
Revenues	$700,000	$770,000
Expenses (includes 40 percent income tax)	(550,000)	(607,712)
Depreciation expense	(20,000)	
Income before extraordinary items	130,000	
Extraordinary gain (loss), net of tax	(6,000)	10,000
Net income	$124,000	
Earnings per share:		
Income before extraordinary items	$1.30	
Extraordinary gain (loss)	(.06)	
Net income	$1.24	

Analysis of the Accounting Change

1. This is a change in accounting principle (not a specified exception); the current approach must be applied.
2. Computation of the cumulative adjustment before tax:

From SL depreciation: depreciation recorded to date for years 1995–1997 ($200,000 × .10 × 3 years)		$60,000
To DDB depreciation: depreciation that would have been recorded under DDB:		
1995: $200,000 × .20*	$40,000	
1996: ($200,000 − $40,000) × .20	32,000	
1997: ($200,000 − $40,000 − $32,000) × .20	25,600	97,600
Cumulative adjustment—increase in accumulated depreciation to DDB basis (pretax), 1995–1997		$37,600
Cumulative adjustment, net of tax [$37,600 × (1.00 − .40)]		$22,560

*.20 = 2/(10 years).

Had the new accounting principle been in effect in prior years, certain nondiscretionary items based on earnings, including bonus arrangements and royalties, would have been different. These are the indirect effects of the accounting principle change. For example, Sunrise's depreciation change decreased 1997 net income $3,360 on a pro forma basis ($124,000 − $120,640). If Sunrise's executive compensation arrangement includes a bonus based on income, the 1997 bonus would have been lower under the new method.

EXHIBIT 24–4
Sunrise Company's Comparative Financial Statements and Related Disclosures

	1997—From Prior Year; No Change	1998—Based on New Principle; DDB
Balance Sheet:		
Assets	$700,000	$823,400
Machinery (cost)	200,000	200,000
Accumulated depreciation (SL).	(60,000)	
DDB: ($60,000 + $37,600 + $20,480)		(118,080)
Total	$840,000	$905,320
Liabilities (1998: $291,112 − $15,040* − $8,192[†])	$340,000	$267,880
Contributed capital (100,000 shares)	300,000	300,000
Retained earnings	200,000	
1998: ($200,000 + $137,440 income)		337,440
Total	$840,000	$905,320

*Reduction in deferred tax liability

[†] Tax effect of 1998 depreciation: $20,480(.40)

	1997—From Prior Year; No Change	1998—Based on New Principle; DDB
Income statement:		
Revenues	$700,000	$770,000
Expenses (including 40 percent income tax)	(550,000)	(599,520)[‡]
Depreciation expense	(SL) (20,000)	(DB) (20,480)
Income before extraordinary items and accounting change.	130,000	150,000
Extraordinary gain (loss), net of tax	(6,000)	10,000
Cumulative effect of accounting change		(22,560)
Net income	$124,000	$137,440

[‡] $607,712 − $8,192 (tax effect of depreciation)

	1997—From Prior Year; No Change	1998—Based on New Principle; DDB
Earnings per share (100,000 shares):		
Income before extraordinary items	$1.30	$1.50
Extraordinary items	(.06)	.10
Effect of accounting change		(.23)
Net income	$1.24	$1.37

Pro Forma Income under DDB

	1997—From Prior Year; No Change	1998—Based on New Principle; DDB
Income before extraordinary items and accounting change:		
1997: $130,000 − [($25,600, DDB − $20,000, SL) × .60].	$126,640	
1998: Actual and pro forma amounts equal		$150,000
Earnings per share	$1.27	$1.50
Net income:		
1997: $124,000 − [($25,600, DDB − $20,000, SL) × .60].	$120,640	
1998: $137,440 net income above + $22,560 cumulative effect.		$160,000
Earnings per share	$1.21	$1.60

Footnote: As of the beginning of 1998, the company changed from the straight-line method to double declining balance for depreciation. In management's opinion, the new method better measures income. The effect of the change on 1998 results is to increase depreciation expense and decrease net income before extraordinary items $480 ($20,480 − $20,000) before tax ($288 after tax and less than $.01 per share), and decrease net income $22,848 ($22,560 cumulative effect plus $288 after tax depreciation increase, or $.23 per share).

The cumulative effect account reflects *only* direct effects unless the indirect effects are actually recorded.[14] The pro forma amounts reflect *both* direct and indirect effects. Therefore, the pro forma income amounts reflect the assumed bonuses and royalties under the new method even though such amounts did not occur in the past.

The direct and indirect effects may interact. For example, if Sunrise grants a bonus based on income, the accounting change causes Sunrise's 1997 calculated bonus to decrease because income decreased. The decreased bonus in turn serves to increase 1997 income on a pro forma basis, partially offsetting the effect of the accounting change.

Cumulative Effect of Change Not Determinable Sometimes it is too expensive or impossible to determine the cumulative income difference for prior years' income between the old and new methods. In this case, the reporting requirements are reduced to the following:

1. Disclose the effect of the change on income before extraordinary items and net income (and related per share amounts) for the current year only.
2. Disclose the nature and justification for the change.
3. Explain why the cumulative effect and pro forma amounts are not disclosed.

Generally, firms that change to the LIFO method report only the reduced disclosures because reconstructing LIFO inventory layers is prohibitively expensive or impossible. Past costs and purchase prices necessary for reconstructing inventory layers are typically unavailable. For example, a firm whose annual unit production exceeded unit sales each year during the last decade requires cost information dating back 10 years to make the change under the current approach.

Instead, the beginning inventory balance in the current year serves as the base layer or beginning balance for LIFO. The current year's financial statements use LIFO. If the firm produces more than it sells in the current year, the entire base year layer remains in ending inventory.

CONCEPT REVIEW

1. Verify that the effect of Sunrise's accounting change on income before extraordinary items in 1998 is $288 (see footnote to Exhibit 24–4).
2. Explain how the cumulative effect of a change in accounting principle is computed.
3. How are the following current year (year of change) pro forma amounts computed: net income before extraordinary items and net income?

Retroactive Approach

Some accounting principle changes are subject to the retroactive approach because they create catch-up amounts that would greatly increase income if the current approach were applied. The sheer size of the income difference argues for the retroactive approach for these specified exceptions.

The following specific changes in accounting principle are required to be reported under the *retroactive approach* rather than the current approach:

1. A change *from* the LIFO inventory method to another inventory method.
2. A change in the method of accounting for long-term construction contracts (from percentage of completion to completed contract or vice versa).
3. A change to or from the full-cost method in extractive industries.
4. The retroactive approach *may* be applied to all changes in accounting principle made in conjunction with the initial public offering of equity securities for obtaining additional

---

[14] Whether the firm retroactively adjusts the actual bonus or royalty payments based on an accounting change depends on the underlying agreement.

equity capital, effecting a business combination, or registering securities. This exemption from the current approach is available only once (*APB Opinion No. 20, par. 29*).

5. A change from retirement/replacement accounting to depreciation accounting for railroad track structures.

6. A change to a principle required by a new pronouncement recognized as GAAP that requires retroactive application.

7. A change to the equity method of accounting for investments in common stock.[15]

Changes in reporting entity and prior-period adjustments are also reported under the retroactive approach. Each of the seven listed changes is discussed next.

1. For some firms, the change from LIFO to FIFO would cause serious distortion in income under the current approach. LIFO layers can be many years or even decades old. FIFO would recognize in income the old (lower) cost layers, rather than the more recent (higher) cost layers expensed under LIFO, resulting in a potentially large increase in income.

2., 3. The methods allowed for long-term construction contracts and natural resource exploration costs are among the accounting principles that produce the greatest income differences. The percentage-of-completion method gradually recognizes income on long-term construction projects. The completed-contract method recognizes no income until projects are completed. Use of the completed-contract method has decreased because its use for tax purposes has been significantly restricted in recent years. Substantial differences also occur between immediate expensing of unsuccessful exploration efforts (successful-efforts method) and gradual amortization (full costing).

4. For initial public offerings of equity securities, retroactively restating financial statements for periods before the first public share offering better serves the investing public. Applying the same accounting principles to all presented statements allows meaningful comparisons, and no loss in public confidence occurs because the statements were not previously issued.

5. Regulatory changes resulted in the requirement that changes by railroads to depreciation accounting be applied retroactively. Beginning in 1983, railroads were required to depreciate railroad track structures in reports to the Interstate Commerce Commission. Many railroads adopted the practice for general-purpose financial reporting. In *SFAS No. 73,* "Reporting a Change in Accounting for Railroad Track Structures," the FASB concluded that the comparability advantages of retroactive restatement outweigh the disadvantages in this case. Analysts at the time expected a general increase of 20 percent to 30 percent in railroad net income as a result of the change.[16]

6. Many recent SFASs require that mandated new accounting principles be applied retroactively. This requirement reinforces consistency as an important quality of accounting information. This category of accounting change is involuntary, in contrast to the other changes discussed.

7. A change to the equity method can affect investor income materially because undistributed investee net income from previous periods is immediately recognized by the investor. This change is sometimes categorized as a change in reporting entity.

Reporting Guidelines   The following guidelines are followed when an accounting principle change subject to the retroactive approach is reported.

1. Prior year financial statements reported on a comparative basis are restated to conform to the new accounting principle. All affected account balances are restated. Therefore, all periods presented reflect the new accounting principle.

---

[15] "The Equity Method of Accounting for Investments in Common Stock," *APB Opinion No. 18,* par. 19 (*m*).

[16] "Add a Dash of Cumulative Catch-up," *Forbes,* June 6, 1983, p. 98.

EXHIBIT 24–5

Application of Retroactive
Approach—Case Information
for Sunset Company: Change
from LIFO to FIFO

1. In 1998, Sunset Company changes its inventory cost method from LIFO to FIFO for financial reporting and tax purposes. The reporting years end on December 31, and the average income tax rate is 40 percent. Sunset reports 1997 and 1998 results on a comparative basis.
2. To provide data for the change, a computer run generated selected data:

	1997		1998—Year of Change	
	FIFO	**LIFO***	**FIFO[†]**	**LIFO**
a. Beginning inventory	$47,000	$ 45,000	$ 60,000	$50,000
b. Ending inventory	60,000	50,000	80,000	68,000
c. Income before extraordinary items (after tax)			160,000	176,000
d. Retained earnings, beginning balance			86,000	
e. Extraordinary gains (losses), net of tax			3,000	(2,000)
f. Dividends declared and paid			80,000	88,000
g. Common shares outstanding all year			100,000	100,000

*Reporting method in 1997.

[†]Reporting method in 1998.

2. The cumulative income difference between the two methods for all affected prior periods is recorded as an adjustment to the beginning retained earnings balance for the current period, net of tax. The entry to record the cumulative adjustment involves a real account and often an income tax account.
3. For each year presented in the retained earnings statement, the beginning retained earnings balance is adjusted by the after-tax effect of the change attributable to prior years (whether or not presented). The adjustment for the current year (only) equals the recorded cumulative adjustment in (2) above.
4. The effects on income before extraordinary items and on net income (and related per share amounts) are disclosed for all periods presented (if affected by the change).
5. Subsequent financial statements need not repeat the disclosures.

Example   Exhibit 24–5 presents case data for a change from LIFO to FIFO.

The change from LIFO to FIFO, a retroactive change, affects 1997 and 1998. The effect on both years must be determined, as well as the overall change to the beginning of both years, to fulfill the reporting requirements.

Effect of the Accounting Change on Pretax Income

To the beginning of 1997:

$47,000 (FIFO) − $45,000 (LIFO) = $2,000 ($1,200 after tax)

(FIFO pretax income is higher by $2,000 through December 31, 1996, because $2,000 less cost of goods sold is recognized.)

To the beginning of 1998:

$60,000 (FIFO) − $50,000 (LIFO) = $10,000 ($6,000 after tax)

(FIFO pretax income is higher by $10,000 through December 31, 1997, because $10,000 less cost of goods sold is recognized.)

For 1997:

Beginning inventory effect:
  FIFO has higher beginning inventory, higher cost of
    goods sold, and lower income, by $47,000 − $45,000 = ($2,000)
Ending inventory effect:
  FIFO has higher ending inventory, lower cost of
    goods sold, and higher income, by $60,000 − $50,000 = 10,000
Change to FIFO increases 1997 pretax income by $8,000 ($4,800 after tax)

For 1998:

Beginning inventory effect:
   FIFO has higher beginning inventory, higher cost of
     goods sold, and lower income, by $60,000 − $50,000 = ($10,000)
Ending inventory effect:
   FIFO has higher ending inventory, lower cost of
     goods sold, and higher income, by $80,000 − $68,000 =   12,000

Change to FIFO increases 1998 pretax income by $ 2,000   ($1,200 after tax)

To compute the pretax income effect of an inventory change to a particular date (the first two computations above), only the inventory amounts on that date need be considered. The inventory cost flow assumptions do not affect purchases, and no beginning inventory existed when the firm was organized. Therefore, the difference between LIFO and FIFO inventory at January 1, 1997, represents the difference between total LIFO and FIFO pretax earnings to that date. The first two effects are the adjustments to the beginning retained earnings balances, shown comparatively. The $10,000 effect on pretax income to the beginning of 1998 is the pretax cumulative difference recognized in 1998, the year of change.

To compute the effect for individual years (the last two computations above), both beginning and ending inventories are considered because both affect cost of goods sold for a period. These amounts are needed for the footnote describing the income effect for each year presented.

As of January 1, 1998—To record accounting change:

Inventory	10,000	
Income taxes payable ($10,000 × .40)		4,000
Retained earnings, adjustment for accounting change		6,000

The total pretax income increase from changing to FIFO for all years before January 1, 1998, is $10,000. This amount is also the difference between ending 1997 inventories under the two methods ($60,000 − $50,000). The $4,000 increase in taxes reflects the tax on profits avoided by using LIFO in the past. Upon including the $6,000 after-tax increase, beginning 1998 retained earnings reflects FIFO. The 1998 income statement does not reflect this cumulative catch-up amount because the change from LIFO is a retroactive change.

Exhibit 24–6 shows the 1997 and 1998 comparative statements. The 1997 statements originally reported under LIFO are restated to reflect FIFO. Some firms title the retained earnings adjustment *cumulative effect of accounting change.*

The comparative statements reflect the FIFO method after restating the 1997 results. Net income for 1997 is increased $4,800, and the 1997 balance sheet discloses ending inventory under FIFO, not LIFO.

The retained earnings statements for each year contains a cumulative adjustment, because income before both 1997 and 1998 is affected by the change. The $1,200 adjustment to the beginning 1997 retained earnings balance accounts for the income effect for all years before 1997. The $6,000 adjustment to the beginning 1998 balance accounts for the income effect for all years before 1998 and equals the adjustment in the entry to record the accounting change. Therefore, the $6,000 amount includes the $1,200. The 1998 adjustment equals the effect on all years before 1997 ($1,200) plus the effect on 1997 ($4,800). The adjustments in the retained earnings statements thus overlap.

The beginning retained earnings balance is not adjusted if prior years are not affected. For example, assume that the years 1994 to 1998 are shown comparatively, but only the years 1995 to 1998 are affected by a retroactive accounting principle change. The beginning retained earnings balances for 1996 to 1998 are adjusted. No retained earnings adjustment is needed for 1995 because 1995 net income is adjusted for the change, and no year before 1995 is affected.

In the Sunset Company retained earnings statement, the ending 1997 retained earnings balance ($175,000) does not equal the beginning 1998 retained earnings balance as previously reported under LIFO ($169,000) for two reasons:

	1997 FIFO Basis	1998 FIFO Basis
Balance sheet:		
Inventory (FIFO)	$ 60,000	$ 80,000
Income statement:		
Income before extraordinary items	$164,800*	$176,000
Extraordinary item, net of tax	3,000	(2,000)
Net income	$167,800	$174,000
Earnings per share (100,000 shares):		
Income before extraordinary items	$1.65	$1.76
Extraordinary items	.03	(.02)
Net income	$1.68	$1.74
Retained earnings statement:		
Beginning balance, as previously stated	$ 86,000	$169,000†
Add: Adjustment for accounting change net of $800 and $4,000 tax	**1,200**	**6,000**
Beginning balance as restated	87,200	175,000
Add: Net income (from above)	167,800	174,000
Deduct: Dividends declared and paid	(80,000)	(88,000)
Ending balance	$175,000	$261,000

Note: During 1998 the company changed from LIFO to FIFO for inventory accounting purposes because FIFO more realistically measures net income. The change increased 1997 net income $4,800 ($.048 per share). The change increased 1998 net income $1,200 ($.012 per share). The 1997 statements are restated to reflect the change.

*$164,800 = $160,000 + $4,800 (after-tax increase in 1997 income due to accounting change)

†$169,000 = ending 1997 retained earnings under LIFO
= $86,000 + $160,000 + $3,000 − $80,000
(All from Exhibit 24–5 under 1997 LIFO column.)

- Income for 1997 now reflects the change to FIFO.
- The beginning 1997 retained earnings balance as restated also reflects the change to FIFO.

But the $175,000 ending 1997 balance equals the 1998 beginning balance *as restated.* In general, the restated ending balance for any year equals the next year's restated beginning balance.

An alternative to reporting overlapping adjustments that is sometimes used adjusts only the earliest beginning retained earnings balance shown if previous years are affected by the change. Under this alternative, Sunset discloses the following:

	1997	1998
Retained earnings statement:		
Beginning balance	$ 86,000	
Add: Adjustment for accounting change	1,200	
Beginning balance as restated	87,200	$175,000
Add: Net income	167,800	174,000
Deduct: Dividends declared and paid	(80,000)	(88,000)
Ending balance	$175,000	$261,000

The first approach is preferable because it discloses the previously reported retained earnings balance for each year, and the adjustment for the current year equals the total adjustment to retained earnings for the change (recognized in the entry to record the change). This approach also has authoritative support.

|CONCEPT REVIEW

1. How is the entry to record an accounting principle change under the retroactive approach different from the entry for the current approach?
2. Why are pro forma income amounts not necessary under the retroactive approach?
3. Explain how the adjustments to the beginning comparative retained earnings balances are computed under the retroactive approach.

Prospective Approach

Accounting estimates are necessary when future events that affect current measurement and disclosure are not known with certainty. Examples include estimated uncollectible accounts, estimated useful lives and residual values of plant assets, and estimated turnover and mortality in accounting for pensions. Estimates are judgments based on assumptions and projections concerning future events.

As time passes, new information requires revision of the original estimates. Revision of estimates requires no special entry because prior years are not affected. However, a change in an estimate not made in good faith or one that did not consider all the relevant information at the time is treated as an error.

Reporting Guidelines   The following guidelines apply to accounting estimate changes.

1. An estimate change affects reporting for the current and future periods only.
2. Prior year statements shown on a comparative basis are not restated.
3. The effects of the change on income before extraordinary items and on net income (and related per share amounts) for the current period are disclosed for a change in estimate affecting future periods. For changes affecting only the current period (e.g., a change in expected uncollectible accounts), this disclosure is not required, although recommended if material.
4. The new estimate is applied as of the beginning of the current period, generally based on the book value of the relevant real account remaining at that time.
5. No entry is made for prior year effects; only the normal current year entry incorporating the new estimate is made.
6. Future years, if affected by the change, continue to use the new estimate.

Estimate Change Affecting Only the Current Year   Assume that during the first two years of Tenaya Company's operations, the actual and estimated uncollectible accounts receivable rates varied widely as collection experience was gained and credit policies developed. At the end of the third year (1998), Tenaya changed its estimated uncollectible percentage, applied to the ending gross accounts receivable balance, from 2 percent to 4 percent reflecting an upturn in delinquent accounts.

Tenaya's December 31, 1998, unadjusted trial balance showed the following:

Accounts receivable	$300,000
Allowance for doubtful accounts	5,000 (dr. balance)

The debit balance in the allowance account reflects the unexpectedly high rate of write-offs. Tenaya records the uncollectible accounts:

Bad debt expense (.04 × $300,000 + $5,000)	17,000	
Allowance for doubtful accounts		17,000

This entry reflects the estimate change for 1998. A similar change is possible in subsequent years. Under the old estimate, bad debt expense would be $11,000 (.02 × $300,000 + $5,000). The following footnote is typical (assuming a material effect on income):

> In 1998, the Company changed its estimate of uncollectible accounts to provide a better estimate of bad debt expense. Net income in 1998 declined $4,200 [after 30 percent income tax, .70($17,000 − $11,000)], or $.42 per share, based on 10,000 shares outstanding, as a result of the change.

Estimate Change Affecting Current and Future Years   Assume that LeMond Company purchased equipment with no residual value and a 10-year useful life for $120,000 on January 1, 1994. New information available during 1998 indicates that a 12-year total useful life appears more realistic and that the estimated residual value is now $8,000. LeMond uses straight-line depreciation.

The book value of the machine on January 1, 1998, represents a new starting point for subsequent depreciation:

Original cost	$120,000
Depreciation through December 31, 1997 ($120,000/10)4 years	48,000
Book value, January 1, 1998	$ 72,000
Annual depreciation beginning in 1998 ($72,000 − $8,000)/(12 − 4)	$ 8,000

December 31, 1998—To record depreciation expense:

Depreciation expense	8,000	
Accumulated depreciation		8,000

LeMond reports the following in its 1997–1998 comparative financial statements:

	1997	**1998**
Income statement:		
Depreciation expense	$ 12,000	$ 8,000
Balance sheet:		
Machine	120,000	120,000
Accumulated depreciation	(48,000)	(56,000)*
Net book value	$ 72,000	$ 64,000

*$56,000 = $48,000 + $8,000 (1998 depreciation).

The following footnote would be appropriate (assuming material amounts):

> In 1998, the company changed its estimate of useful life and residual value on major equipment. This change was made in response to new information about the benefits to be derived from the equipment and about estimated residual value. Net income increased $2,800 [after 30 percent tax, .70($12,000 − $8,000)] as a result of the change, or $.28 per share based on 10,000 shares outstanding.

The 1997 statements reflect the old estimates, and the 1998 statements reflect the new. The inconsistency is unavoidable because conditions have changed. Future years continue to use the new estimates until the asset is sold or until further new information becomes available, requiring another estimate change.

CONCEPT REVIEW

1. If the estimated useful life of equipment is reduced and residual value is not changed, what is the effect on annual depreciation?
2. Explain how book value is used when changing the estimated useful life of a plant asset.
3. If an estimate was not made in good faith, how is the change in estimate treated?

Analysis and Reporting of Prior Period Adjustments

The general reporting guidelines for prior period adjustments are essentially the same as those for retroactive accounting principle changes.

Exhibit 24–7 presents the case data for an example of error correction with comparative statements. The error overstates January 1, 1998, retained earnings by $6,000, the total after-tax effect on 1996 and 1997 income ($10,000 × .60). This is not a counterbalancing error.

1. The accounting records of Emory Company reflect the following data:

	1997	1998
Sales revenue	$450,000	$480,000
Cost of goods sold	(300,000)	(310,000)
Depreciation expense	(20,000)	(25,000)
Remaining expenses	(55,000)	(65,000)
Income tax (40 percent average rate)	(30,000)	(32,000)
Net income (for year ended December 31)	$ 45,000	$ 48,000
Balance in retained earnings, January 1	$135,000	$165,000
Dividends declared and paid	15,000	17,000

2. During June 1998, the company discovers that depreciation expense for 1996 and 1997 was understated each year by $5,000 for both accounting and income tax purposes;* total pretax understatement, $10,000. Depreciation for 1998 is correct.

*Assume that Emory uses the same depreciation method for accounting and tax purposes.

The following entry is required for correction:

As of January 1, 1998:

Prior period adjustment, depreciation correction	6,000	
Income tax receivable (amended return)	4,000	
Accumulated depreciation		10,000

The entry corrects all account balances stated incorrectly as of January 1, 1998. The prior period adjustment is closed to retained earnings, thus correcting the beginning balance. Exhibit 24–8 shows the corrected comparative statements for 1997 and 1998.

The adjusted 1997 statements show correct depreciation expense, income tax expense, net income, and beginning retained earnings. Income tax expense is decreased because pretax income decreased as a result of the error correction. The error did not affect 1998.

The adjustments to the beginning retained earnings balances overlap, as in accounting principle changes under the retroactive approach. The 1998 adjustment ($6,000), the amount from the correcting entry, accounts for both 1996 and 1997 effects and therefore includes the 1996 adjustment ($3,000). Both adjustments decrease retained earnings because income was overstated.

ACCOUNTING CHANGES: AN EVALUATION

APB Opinion No. 20 was not endorsed by the entire APB. Some members believed that all accounting principle changes should be applied retroactively. The cumulative income effect of the change is not relevant to current income measurement in their view. Accountants have expressed concerns about the effect on comparability:

> It is the worst of all worlds. Not only is the current year incompatible with past years, the change rips the current year's figures away from any link with reality. Why such a ridiculous method? "I think some members of the APB felt the catch-up method would be punitive and would reduce the number of capricious accounting changes," says Price Waterhouse partner Raymond Lauver.[17]

Board members also feared that allowing alternative approaches to reporting principle changes would dilute public confidence more than requiring retroactive restatement for all principle changes.

Certain board members contended that once an income item is reported, it is final. Changes should be made only prospectively, except for error corrections. They argued that *Opinion No. 20* tends to encourage changes, especially if the cumulative effect increases net income.

Others argued that the cumulative effect on prior years' income cannot be computed

---

[17] Ibid., Lauver later served as a member of the FASB.

	1997	1998
Comparative income statement:		
Sales revenue	$450,000	$480,000
Cost of goods sold	(300,000)	(310,000)
Depreciation expense	(25,000)*	(25,000)
Remaining expenses	(55,000)	(65,000)
Income tax expense	(28,000)†	(32,000)
Net income	$ 42,000	$ 48,000
Comparative retained earnings statement:		
Beginning balance, as previously stated	$135,000	$165,000
Prior period adjustment, depreciation, net of $2,000 ($5,000 × .40) and $4,000 ($10,000 × .40) tax	(3,000)	(6,000)
Beginning balance, as restated	132,000	159,000
Net income	42,000	48,000
Dividends declared and paid	(15,000)	(17,000)
Ending balance	$159,000	$190,000

Note: Prior period adjustment: in 1998, the company discovered that depreciation expense for 1996 and 1997 was understated. Accordingly, the 1997 statement is restated. The error overstated net income $3,000 after tax ($.03 per share, based on 100,000 shares outstanding) in both years.

*$25,000 = $20,000 + $5,000 error correction.

†$28,000 = $30,000 − ($5,000 × .40).

accurately. Certain accounting principles influence operating decisions and pricing. These effects cannot be approximated simply by the arithmetic effect of the new accounting principle on net income. In addition, evidence suggests that accounting changes reduce the predictive ability of accounting information. One study found that the accuracy of analysts' earnings forecasts declined when accounting changes were made.[18]

The variety of reporting approaches reflects disagreement concerning which method provides the most useful information. Future deliberations by the FASB on this issue may evaluate the motivations for making changes. Why do firms choose specific accounting principles, and later make accounting changes?

Motivations for Accounting Changes

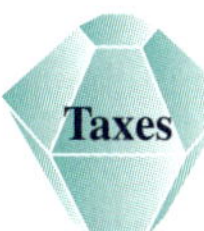

Many explanations are advanced to explain initial accounting method choices and later changes. Traditional motivations are

- To adhere to established firm practice.
- To conform to industry practice.
- To minimize accounting costs.
- To correspond with tax accounting.
- To maximize income and facilitate capital formation.
- To report the most advantageous accounting ratios, particularly for rates of return and debt ratios.
- To achieve the closest match between reporting and economic reality.

One theory holds that accounting choices are made to achieve objectives such as increased bonus compensation, compliance with debt covenants, and reduced government interference.[19]

The findings of several studies confirm the notion that firms with bonus plans based on earnings choose accounting methods that increase current income.[20] Even if no structured bonus agreement exists, some managements may make accounting choices that increase income because an implicit link exists between income and compensation. Furthermore, a

[18] J. Elliot and D. Philbrick, "Accounting Changes and Earnings Predictability," *Accounting Review,* January 1990, pp. 157–74.

[19] R. Watts and J. Zimmerman, "Positive Accounting Theory: A 10-Year Perspective," *Accounting Review,* January 1990, p. 150.

[20] See R. Watts and J. Zimmerman, *Positive Accounting Theory* (Englewood Cliffs, NJ: Prentice Hall, 1986), chapter 11.

study of bonus agreements found that if earnings are not expected to reach the minimum income level necessary to achieve a bonus, managers tend to recognize discretionary losses, including plant asset write-downs.[21] Future years' earnings are thus relieved of these losses.

Debt covenants requiring minimum income levels provide another incentive for methods that report higher income. A change to a method that increases current income is desirable under these circumstances. Furthermore, increases in income ease the burden imposed by debt covenants that stipulate minimum retained earnings balances.

A broad study of 3,231 voluntary accounting changes during the period 1969–1988 found evidence supporting the theory that accounting changes are made to achieve a reporting objective or economic benefit.[22] Specific findings include:

- Most changes other than LIFO adoptions cause earnings to increase.
- Firms making income-increasing changes have significantly lower sales and earnings growth before making the change, and have lower interest coverage ratios and higher debt-to-equity ratios, compared to a random sample of firms.
- The adoption of LIFO is the most common accounting change; the frequency of such changes increases with the rate of inflation, implying that tax minimization is the primary reason for making the change.

The theory does not imply a unilateral preference for standards that increase net income, however. Larger firms may reduce reported income in an attempt to avoid antitrust and other regulatory restrictions. Reduced income may lessen media exposure and scrutiny by regulators, politicians, and labor unions.

Another apparent motivation for accounting choices and changes is **income smoothing,** also known as *earnings management, cooking the books,* and *paper entrepreneurialism.* This refers to choosing accounting methods or making accounting principle changes to produce a specified income level or trend. In particular, reducing the volatility of income and reporting relatively gradual and continual increases in income are alleged to be common company goals. The implicit assumption is that the investing public values a smooth and predictable income trend. Investors perceive an erratic earnings trend as more risky than a smooth trend.

To smooth income, firms must increase reported earnings during a downturn and decrease reported earnings during prosperous times. Excessively high income often invites unfriendly press, government intervention, and increased demands for dividends. Furthermore, large income increases are difficult to sustain, and they create increased expectations.

Stock Prices and Economic Consequences

By choosing methods that increase income, many firms seek to avoid the unfavorable economic consequences of lowered earnings, such as reduced stock prices, higher borrowing costs, and noncompliance with debt covenants. Research suggests, however, that stock prices usually do not react to the changes in earnings caused by accounting changes unless those changes affect cash flows, through tax or indirect effects. Indirect effects include changes in bonuses, royalties, and other arrangements based on income, and changes in borrowing costs and regulation. In spite of the evidence, however, many firms continue to manage income to avoid earnings reductions.

Example   The controversy over accounting for oil exploration costs shows how firms seek to influence accounting standards, in part because of concerns over economic consequences. *SFAS No. 19,* "Financial Accounting and Reporting by Oil and Gas Producing Companies" (1977), required the successful efforts method that capitalizes exploration costs only for successful wells and expenses all other exploration costs. Small and medium-size oil companies lobbied the FASB, claiming their income would be reduced drastically under the standard, thus impairing their ability to raise capital. These firms were using the full-cost

[21]P. Healy, "The Effect of Bonus Schemes on Accounting Decisions," *Journal of Accounting & Economics,* April 1985, pp. 85–107.

[22]M. Pincus and C. Wasley, "The Incidence of Accounting Changes and Characteristics of Firms Making Accounting Changes," *Accounting Horizons,* 8, no. 2 (June 1994), pp. 1–24.

GLOBAL VIEW

The United States is not the only country with GAAP allowing for changes in accounting methods. Although the specific measurement rules and constraints may vary, the incentives for making the changes often are similar.

Example   Japan Airlines, the largest airline in Japan, reported a positive operating profit in 1996, the first time since 1991. Operating profit was ¥15.4 billion ($143 million). A significant part of this profit was derived from changing its method of depreciation from an accelerated method to straight-line. JAL's justification? Like many of its U.S. counterparts, JAL indicated that the change was made to more faithfully reflect the costs and benefits of large cash outlays recently made for new airports and other facilities.

---

method, which allows capitalizing all exploration costs, with subsequent expensing through cost of goods sold.

> They claimed that the FASB's ruling would have the effect of rendering their reported earnings meaningless, of impeding their access to the capital markets and ultimately of reducing their ability to be competitive in their own exploration arena.[23]

These lobbying efforts contributed to the reversal of *SFAS No. 19*. Following the SEC's permission to use either method, the FASB suspended its requirement to use the successful efforts method in *SFAS No. 25*, "Suspension of Certain Accounting Requirements for Oil and Gas Producing Companies" (1979).

SUMMARY OF KEY POINTS

(L.O. 1)   1. Firms change accounting principles and estimates to adapt to changing economic conditions, to implement new accounting principles, to improve financial reporting, and to fulfill other reporting objectives. Major reporting considerations include the effect of changes on consistency, public confidence in financial reporting, and the need to adapt to changing environments. Financial reporting of accounting changes emphasizes comparability, consistency, and full disclosure.

(L.O. 2)   2. Accounting changes include changes in accounting principle, changes in estimate, and changes in reporting entity. An accounting error is an incorrect recording (or omission) of a transaction and is not classified as an accounting change.

(L.O. 3)   3. Most accounting principle changes are reported under the current approach; specified exceptions are reported under the retroactive approach. Estimate changes are reported under the prospective approach. Errors affecting prior years' income are reported under the retroactive approach.

(L.O. 4)   4. The current approach recognizes the cumulative effect of the change on prior years' income as a separate item in the income statement for the year of the change between extraordinary items and net income. Pro forma income amounts for all prior years presented are reported as if the new principle had been applied in those periods.

(L.O. 5)   5. The retroactive approach recognizes the cumulative effect of the change on prior years' income as an adjustment to the beginning balance in retained earnings in the year of the change. The beginning balance in retained earnings for all years shown comparatively is adjusted by the effect of the change attributable to previous years.

(L.O. 6)   6. Only current and future reporting periods are affected by estimate changes. No cumulative catch-up amount is recognized. In many cases, the book value of the affected account at the beginning of the current year is the starting amount to which new estimates are applied.

(L.O. 7)   7. The net effect of an error on prior years' income is recorded and reported as a prior period adjustment to the beginning retained earnings balance. Accounting errors are counterbalancing if they self-correct over two consecutive reporting periods, such as an error in the ending inventory. Noncounterbalancing errors, such as errors in depreciation, do not self-correct in two reporting periods.

REVIEW PROBLEM

The following cases are independent.

1. Change in Estimated Useful Life and Residual Value   Phelps Company purchases equipment on January 1, 1997, for $36,000 and decides to use the sum-of-years'-digits method for depreciation. The equipment has a residual value of $6,000 and useful life of three years. On

---

[23] "Storm Brewing over Oil Accounts." *The Wall Street Journal*, February 22, 1978, p. 22.

July 1, 1998, Phelps decides that the machine has an original total useful life of four years and $3,000 salvage value.

Required

What is depreciation in 1998?

2. Retroactive Change in Accounting Principle Rhein Company changes its method of accounting for long-term construction contracts from the percentage-of-completion method to the completed-contract method in 1999. Income for the years affected by the change appear below (ignore income taxes):

Year	Percentage of Completion	Completed Contract
1997	$400	$200
1998	300	150
1999	500	200

Required

If comparative financial statements for 1998 and 1999 are shown, what are the adjustments to the January 1 balances of retained earnings for 1998 and 1999?

3. Current-Type Change in Accounting Principle Gear Company records $2,000 of depreciation under the sum-of-years'-digits method (SYD) in 1997, the firm's first year of operations. In 1998, the firm decides to change to the straight-line method (SL) for accounting purposes. If SL were used in 1997, depreciation would have been $1,500. Depreciation in 1998: SYD, $2,200; SL, $1,800. The tax rate is 30 percent. Net income from continuing operations before tax and before deducting depreciation in 1998 is $12,000.

Required

Provide the 1998 entry to record this change and calculate 1998 net income and 1998 pro forma net income.

4. Error Correction and Prior Period Adjustment Helms Company purchases a delivery truck for $12,000 on January 1, 1997. Helms expects to use the truck only two years and to sell it for $4,000. The accountant is instructed to use straight-line depreciation but neglects to record any depreciation in 1997. Rather, the accountant charges the entire cost to delivery expense in 1997. The controller discovers the error late in 1998.

Required

Provide the 1998 entries to record depreciation and the error correction, and indicate the amounts of the prior period adjustments appearing in the 1997 and 1998 comparative retained earnings statements. The tax rate is 30 percent.

5. Error Correction, Prior Period Adjustment, and Comparative Statements On July 1, 1996, a full year's insurance premium of $2,400, covering the period July 1, 1996, to June 30, 1997, was paid and debited to insurance expense. Assume the following:
- The firm has a calendar fiscal year.
- January 1, 1996, retained earnings is $20,000.
- 1996 reported net income (assuming the error is not discovered) is $22,800.
- 1997 net income (assuming the error is not discovered) is $30,000.
- 1998 net income is $40,000. Ignore taxes.

Required

a. List the effects of the error on affected accounts and on net income in 1996 and 1997, assuming no adjusting entry is made on December 31, 1996.
b. Prepare the entry to record the error if discovered in 1996.
c. Prepare the entry to record the error if discovered in 1997, and the 1996 and 1997 comparative retained earnings statements.
d. Prepare the entry (if needed) to record the error if discovered in 1998, and the 1997 and 1998 comparative retained earnings statements.

|SOLUTION

1.
$$\text{Book value, January 1, 1998} = \$36,000 - (\$36,000 - \$6,000)3/6$$
$$= \$21,000$$
$$\text{1998 depreciation} = (\$21,000 - \$3,000)3/6 = \$9,000$$

(Three years remain in the asset's useful life on January 1, 1998, the date on which the estimate change becomes effective.)

2. The adjustment for the change in accounting principle for the 1998 retained earnings statement is the effect of the change for all years before 1998: $200 decrease (dr.) ($400 − $200). For 1999, this amount is a $350 decrease (dr.) [($400 + $300) − ($200 + $150)]. These amounts decrease the balance in retained earnings as previously reported.

3. 1998 entry to record accounting change:

Accumulated depreciation	500	
Cumulative effect of change in account principle,		
depreciation ($2,000 − $1,500).70		350
Deferred tax liability		150

1998 net income:		
Net income before tax, depreciation, and cumulative effect	$12,000	
Depreciation expense (SL)	(1,800)	
Net income from continuing operations before tax	10,200	
Income tax expense (30 percent)	(3,060)	
Net income from continuing operations	7,140	
Cumulative effect of accounting change	350	
Net income	$ 7,490	

1998 pro forma net income is $7,140. If SL were used in previous years, there would be no cumulative effect, and 1998 results would reflect SL depreciation.

4. 1998 entry to record error correction:

Equipment	12,000	
Prior period adjustment, depreciation $8,000 × .70		5,600
Income taxes payable $8,000 × .30		2,400
Accumulated depreciation ($12,000 − $4,000)/2		4,000

Pretax income for 1997 is understated $8,000 ($12,000 erroneous delivery expense less $4,000 omitted depreciation).

1998 entry to record depreciation:

Depreciation expense	4,000	
Accumulated depreciation		4,000

Only the 1998 retained earnings statement reports a prior period adjustment ($5,600 cr.). This is the effect of the error on income in years before 1998. The 1997 statement does not report a prior period adjustment because years before 1997 are not affected by the error.

5. *a.* Effects of error if not discovered:

	1996	1997
Insurance expense	+ $1,200	− $1,200
Ending prepaid insurance	− 1,200	no effect
Net income	− 1,200	+ $1,200
Ending retained earnings	− 1,200	is now correct

Note: − = understated; + = overstated.

b. If error is discovered in 1996:

Prepaid insurance	1,200	
Insurance expense		1,200

c. If error is discovered in 1997:

Insurance expense	1,200	
Prior period adjustment		1,200

	1996	1997
Retained earnings, Jan. 1, as previously stated	$20,000	$42,800[‡]
Prior period adjustment	0*	1,200
Retained earnings, Jan. 1, as adjusted	20,000	44,000
Net income	24,000[†]	28,800[§]
Retained earnings, Dec. 31	$44,000	$72,800

*No year before 1996 was affected by the error.

[†] Correct 1996 net income = $22,800 + $1,200 = $24,000.

[‡] This balance reflects erroneous 1996 income:
$42,800 = $20,000 + $22,800.

[§] $30,000 erroneous income − $1,200 (1997 income was overstated).

d. No entry is needed because the error counterbalanced.

	1997	1998
Retained earnings, Jan. 1, as previously stated	$42,800*	$ 72,800‡
Prior period adjustment.	1,200†	0
Retained earnings, Jan. 1, as adjusted	44,000	72,800
Net income	28,800	40,000
Retained earnings, Dec. 31	$72,800	$112,800

*$20,000 + $22,800.

†To correct the error's effect on 1996 net income.

‡Equals the ending adjusted retained earnings from 1997 because by January 1, 1998, the error has counterbalanced.

UNDERSTANDING AND APPLYING CONCEPTS AND STANDARDS

QUESTIONS

1. Distinguish among the following: (*a*) change in principle, (*b*) change in estimate, (*c*) change in reporting entity, and (*d*) accounting error.
2. What are the three basic ways to account for the effects of accounting changes and error corrections?
3. Complete the following schedule:

Method of Reflecting the Effect*

	(1) ______	(2) ______	(3) ______
a. Change in estimate	______	______	______
b. Change in principle	______	______	______
c. Correction of error	______	______	______

*Identify these three captions; then enter appropriate checkmark on each line.

4. What are pro forma amounts? Why are they used for some accounting changes?
5. Explain the basic difference between an accounting change and an error correction.
6. Why are the effects of changes from LIFO to other inventory flow methods accounted for retroactively when changes to LIFO from another method are reflected as changes in the income of the year the change is made?
7. Other than changing from LIFO to another inventory flow method (which must be reflected retroactively), what other types of accounting changes must be accorded retroactive treatment rather than being accounted for using the current approach?
8. *APB Opinion No. 20* deals with three types of accounting changes in addition to error corrections. The three types of accounting changes involve (*a*) principles, (*b*) estimates, and (*c*) reporting entities. Using these letters and (*d*) for error corrections, identify each of the following changes:
   (1) A lessor discovers during the term of a capital lease that an estimated material unguaranteed residual value of the leased property has probably become zero.
   (2) A corporation with foreign subsidiaries has used the cost method of accounting for its investments in the subsidiary companies because economic conditions in the countries in which the subsidiary companies operate have been unstable and exchange of foreign currency into dollars has been restricted. Under changed, improved conditions, it has become feasible for the controlling entity to prepare consolidated statements instead, thereby eliminating the foreign investment account from the balance sheet of the corporation.
   (3) After five years of use, an asset originally estimated to have a 15-year life is now to be depreciated on the basis of a 20-year life.
   (4) Because of inability to estimate reliably, a contractor began business using the completed-contract method. Now that reliable estimates can be made, the percentage-of-completion method is adopted.
   (5) Office equipment purchased last year is discovered to have been debited to office expense when acquired. Appropriate accounting is to be applied at the discovery date.
   (6) A company that has been using the FIFO inventory method is changing to LIFO.
   (7) A company that used 1 percent of sales to estimate its bad debt expense discovers that losses are running higher than expected and changes to 2½ percent.
9. How is the book value of a plant asset at the beginning of the year of a change in estimated life used in the accounting for the change?

10. Explain why (*a*) net income before extraordinary items in the year of a current-type accounting principle change equals its pro forma counterpart, and (*b*) why net income does not equal its pro forma counterpart.

11. What is the difference between a counterbalancing and a noncounterbalancing error? Why is the distinction significant in the analysis of errors?

12. Complete the schedule below by entering a plus sign to indicate overstatement, a minus sign to indicate understatement, or a zero for no effect.

	Effect of Error On			
	Net Income	**Assets**	**Liabilities**	**Owners' Equity**
a. Ending inventory for 1997 understated:				
1997 financial statements	______	______	______	______
1998 financial statements	______	______	______	______
b. Ending inventory for 1998 overstated:				
1998 financial statements	______	______	______	______
1999 financial statements	______	______	______	______
c. Failed to record depreciation in 1997:				
1997 financial statements	______	______	______	______
1998 financial statements	______	______	______	______
d. Failed to record a liability resulting from revenue collected in advance at end of 1997; instead, credited revenue in full erroneously:				
1997 financial statements	______	______	______	______
1998 financial statements	______	______	______	______

13. Give two examples of each of the following types of errors:
    a. Affects the income statement only.
    b. Affects the balance sheet only.
    c. Affects both income statement and balance sheet.

14. A company failed to accrue $12,000 of wages at the end of 1997. Explain (*a*) why the discovery of the error in 1998, after the issuance of the 1997 statements, requires a correcting entry, and (*b*) why discovery of the error in 1999, after the issuance of the 1998 statements, does not require a correcting entry.

EXERCISES

E 24–1
(L.O. 2, 3)

Multiple Choice: Accounting Changes   Choose the correct answer to each question.

1. Which of the following is a change in accounting principle?
    a. Correction of an error using the retroactive approach.
    b. Change from an incorrect method to a correct method.
    c. Change in the application of an accounting principle.
    d. Change in the number of total expected service miles for depreciating a truck.

2. Which of the following is not the type of accounting change that reports a cumulative effect in the income statement?
    a. Change to the successful-efforts method of accounting for natural resources.
    b. Change to LIFO for a firm in its second year that is able to reconstruct LIFO inventory layers.
    c. Change in depreciation method.
    d. Change in method of amortizing bond discount.

3. Retroactive accounting treatment is used for which of the following?
    a. Correcting errors and making estimate changes.
    b. Changing to LIFO and correcting errors affecting income of prior years.
    c. Changing to the completed-contract method of accounting for long-term contracts.
    d. Correcting errors affecting prior years' income, but only if those prior years are disclosed on a comparative basis with the current year.

4. A company changed from percentage of completion (PC) to completed contract (CC) for financial accounting purposes during 1998. Therefore:
    a. Beginning January 1, 1998, CC should be used for construction accounting, and the difference between the income under the two methods for years before 1998 is disclosed in the 1998 income statement.
    b. Beginning January 1, 1998, CC should be used for construction accounting, but no entry is made for the effects of the change on years before 1998.

    c. Beginning January 1, 1998, CC should be used for construction accounting, and the difference between the income under the two methods for years before 1998 is an adjustment to the January 1, 1998, retained earnings balance.

    d. Pro forma income amounts are disclosed in a schedule to the income statement for all years before 1998 shown in the 1998 annual report.

5. Choose the correct statement concerning comparative financial statements.

    a. They are required by the APB.

    b. They are required by the SEC.

    c. The number of statements presented comparatively affects the recorded amount of a cumulative effect of a change in accounting principle.

    d. Firms generally do not disclose more than one year because financial statement users already have access to the reports of previous years.

6. One of the advantages of the current, or cumulative effect, change is

    a. Consistency is maintained.

    b. Prior years' income effects do not affect income in the year of change.

    c. The statements of previous years shown comparatively do not disclose any information about the effect of the change in those previous years.

    d. Prior years' financial statements are not altered.

7. Pro forma income numbers

    a. Somewhat reduce the loss of comparability inherent in current, or cumulative effect, accounting principle changes.

    b. Are required only for the year of change.

    c. Are required for changes in estimates.

    d. Equal the effect of the accounting change on income for each year shown.

8. Pro forma net income for the year of a change in accounting principle equals

    a. Net income for the year of change.

    b. Net income for the year of change under the new method.

    c. Net income before extraordinary items for the year of change.

    d. Net income before cumulative effect of changes in accounting principle for the year of change.

E 24–2
(L.O. 2, 3)

Overview: Types of Accounting Changes and Errors   Analyze each case and enter a letter code in each column (type and approach) to indicate the basic accounting.

	Type	Approach
	P = Principle	
	E = Estimate	C = Current
	R = Entity	R = Retroactive
Case (event or transaction)	AE = Error	P = Prospective
1. Recorded expense, $870; should be $780.	______	______
2. Changed useful life of a machine.	______	______
3. Changed from single-company to consolidated financial statements.	______	______
4. Changed from straight-line to accelerated depreciation.	______	______
5. Change in residual value of an intangible operational asset.	______	______
6. Changed from cash basis to accrual basis in accounting for bad debts.	______	______
7. Changed from percentage of completion to completed contract for long-term construction contracts.	______	______
8. Changed from LIFO to FIFO for inventory.	______	______
9. Changed to a new accounting principle required by the FASB.	______	______

E 24–3
(L.O. 2, 3)

Identifying Accounting Changes and Accounting Approach   For items A through J, fill in the two blanks to indicate the type of accounting change and accounting application that applies. The first item (O) is completed for you. Use the following abbreviations:

Type of Accounting Change

Accounting principle change	PRN
Accounting estimate change	EST
Error correction	COR
Not applicable	NA

Accounting Approach

Current treatment

(cumulative effect to income) . . . .   CU

Retroactive treatment

(cumulative effect or correction to RE) . . . . .   RE

Current and prospective treatment

(no effect on prior years) . . . .   CP

Not applicable . . . .   NA

For each item, assume the change affects earnings of prior years unless the change is an estimate change.

	Type of Change	Accounting Approach
O. Changed the residual value of an asset.	EST	CP
A. Changed from SL depreciation to accelerated.	______	______
B. Changed from aging to credit sales method of bad debts estimation.	______	______
C. Changed to LIFO (layers can be costed).	______	______
D. Changed from LIFO (layers were costed).	______	______
E. Changed from an erroneous method to the required method.	______	______
F. Changed to a new accounting method mandated by a new SFAS that requires retroactive application.	______	______
G. Reestimated total petroleum reserves.	______	______
H. Changed to SL at a prespecified date, from DDB.	______	______
I. Change in accounting method indistinguishable from an estimate change.	______	______
J. Application of accelerated depreciation to a newly acquired building; all previously acquired buildings use SL.	______	______

E 24–4
(L.O. 4)

Change in Depreciation Method   Four-H, Inc., changed from straight-line to an accelerated depreciation method for book purposes only in 1998. Data for years affected by the change:

	1998	1997	1996
Increase in depreciation due to change	$ 20,000	$25,000	$ 30,000
Income computed under the SL method*	100,000	90,000	120,000

*After tax; the tax rate is 40%. The income amount shown for 1998 was computed before considering the accounting change.

Required

1. Provide the 1998 entry to record the accounting change.
2. What is reported net income for 1998?
3. What is the 1997 pro forma net income amount?

E 24–5
(L.O. 4)

Change in Method of Depreciation   The 1997 annual report of Goodspeed Inc. reported earnings of $50,000. During 1998, the firm changed from accelerated depreciation to straight-line depreciation for reporting purposes only. Depreciation amounts for the years affected follow:

	SL	Accelerated
1998	$10,000	$12,000
1997	8,000	11,000
1996	6,000	8,000
1995	4,000	5,500

The tax rate is 30 percent. The firm reports 1997 and 1998 results on a comparative basis in its 1998 annual report.

Required

1. Provide the entry to record the accounting change.
2. In the 1998 annual report, what amount will be shown for 1997 earnings?
3. How will the effect of the change on 1997 net income be disclosed in the 1998 annual report, if at all? Be specific and show dollar amounts.

E 24–6
(L.O. 4)

Change in Revenue Recognition Method   As of the beginning of 1998, Ames Inc. changed its method of accounting for revenue recognition on certain types of installment sales contracts. Reported net income for

1997 was $80,000. Net income from continuing operations for 1998 under the old method would have been $100,000. The effect of the change on net income from continuing operations is as follows:

**Effect of Change on Net Income from
Continuing Operations**

On years before 1997	Increase $70,000
On 1997	Increase 20,000
On 1998	Increase 30,000

Assume that the permanent or real account affected by the change is Current Receivables.

Required

1. Provide the entry to record the accounting change.
2. Fill in the following schedule of amounts that would be found in the comparative 1997 and 1998 income statements.

	1997	1998
Net income	_______	_______
Pro forma net income	_______	_______

E 24–7
(L.O. 4)

Change in Depreciation Method: Entries and Reporting   Gunnard Company changed from double-declining-balance depreciation (DDB) to the straight-line method (SL) for both accounting and tax purposes in 1998. Had SL been used before 1998, total depreciation for all prior years would have been $20,000 less than under DDB. Gunnard discloses 1997 and 1998 results comparatively in its 1998 annual report. The tax rate is 30 percent in both years. Assume a calendar fiscal year.

Depreciation expense for 1997 and 1998 under both methods:

	SL	DDB
1997	$4,000	$6,000
1998	4,000	5,000

Additional information for Gunnard:

	1997	1998
Revenues	$80,000	$120,000
Expenses other than depreciation and tax	50,000	60,000
Extraordinary loss after tax		7,000

Required

1. Prepare the 1998 entry(ies) for depreciation and the accounting change.
2. Prepare the comparative income statements, and include disclosures related to the accounting change.

E 24–8
(L.O. 6)

Change in Estimated Useful Life and Salvage Value for a Plant Asset   Bellico Company, which has a calendar fiscal year, purchased its only depreciable plant asset on January 1, 1997, which has the following characteristics:

Original cost	$10,000
Estimated residual value	1,000
Estimated useful life	three years
Depreciation method	sum-of-years'-digits

In 1998, Bellico increased the estimated residual value to $2,000 and increased the total estimated useful life to five years for financial accounting purposes. Additional information:

	1997	1998
Revenue	$ 40,000	$ 50,000
Expenses other than depreciation and tax	25,000	30,000
Extraordinary loss before tax		5,000
Tax rate	30%	30%
Common shares outstanding entire year	100,000	100,000

Required

1. Provide the 1998 entry(ies) for depreciation and the ending 1998 accumulated depreciation balance.
2. Provide the comparative 1997 and 1998 income statements, including disclosures related to the accounting change.

E 24–9
(L.O. 6)

Change in Estimated Useful Life: Entries, Reporting   Stacy Corporation has been depreciating equipment over a 10-year life on a straight-line basis. The equipment, which cost $24,000, was purchased on January 1, 1994. The equipment has an estimated residual value of $6,000. On the basis of experience since acquisition, the management has decided to depreciate it over a total life of 14 years instead of 10, with no change in the estimated residual value. The change is to be effective on January 1, 1998. The annual financial statements are prepared on a comparative basis (1997 and 1998 are presented). 1997 and 1998 income before depreciation and accounting changes for 1997 and 1998 were $49,800 and $52,800, respectively. Disregard income tax considerations.

Required

1. Identify the type of accounting change involved and analyze the effects of the change. Which approach should be used—current, prospective, or retroactive? Explain.
2. Prepare the entry, or entries, to appropriately reflect the change in the accounts for 1998, the year of the change.
3. Illustrate how the change should be reported on the 1998 financial statements, which are accompanied by the 1997 results for comparative purposes (shares of common stock outstanding, 100,000).

E 24–10
(L.O. 6)

Change in Depreciation Method: Entries, Reporting   Bite Corporation has been depreciating equipment over a 10-year life using the SYD method. The equipment was acquired January 1, 1994, and cost $68,000 (estimated residual value, $13,000). The company decided to change to straight-line depreciation, effective the beginning of 1998, with no change in the estimated useful life or the residual value. The annual accounting period ends December 31. The annual financial statements are prepared on a comparative basis (1997 and 1998 are presented). Income before depreciation and prior to giving effect to this change was $55,000 in 1997 and $57,500 in 1998. Shares of stock outstanding were 100,000. Disregard income tax considerations.

Required

1. Identify the type of accounting change involved and analyze the effects of the change. Which approach should be used—current, prospective or retroactive? Explain.
2. Prepare the entry, or entries, to appropriately reflect the change in the accounts in 1998, the year of the change, including the 1998 adjusting entry.
3. Show how the change should be reported on the 1998 financial statements, which include 1997 results for comparative purposes.

E 24–11
(L.O. 4)

Change from SYD to Straight-Line Depreciation and Change Useful Life: Entries   Backlog Sales Company has made several accounting changes to improve the matching of expenses with revenue. Assume that it is the end of 1998 and that the accounting period ends on December 31. The books have not been adjusted or closed at the end of 1998. Among the changes are the following:

a. Machinery that cost $50,000 (estimated useful life 10 years, residual value $6,000) has been depreciated using the SYD method. Early in the eighth year (1998), it was decided to change to straight-line depreciation (with no change in residual value or estimated life).
b. A patent that cost $17,000 is being amortized over its legal life of 17 years. Early in the sixth year (1998), it was decided that the economic benefits would not last longer than 13 years from date of acquisition.

Required

1. For each of the above situations, identify the type of accounting change that was involved, and briefly explain how it should be accounted for.
2. Give the appropriate entry to record the change and the 1998 adjusting entry in each instance. Show computations and disregard income tax considerations. If no entry is required in a particular instance, explain why.

E 24–12
(L.O. 5)

Change from LIFO to FIFO: Entries, Reporting   On January 1, 1998, Baker Company decided to change the inventory costing method used from LIFO to FIFO. The annual reporting period ends on December 31. The average income tax rate is 30 percent. The following related data were developed:

	LIFO Basis	FIFO Basis
Beginning inventory, 1997	$ 20,000	$30,000
Ending inventory:		
1997	40,000	70,000
1998	44,000	76,000
Net income:		
1997: LIFO basis	80,000	
1998: FIFO basis		90,000
Retained earnings:		
1997 beginning balance	120,000	
Dividends declared and paid:		
1997	64,000	
1998		70,000

Common shares outstanding, 10,000.

Required

1. Identify the type of accounting change involved. Which approach should be used—current, prospective, or retroactive? Explain.
2. Give the entry(ies) to record the effect of the change, assuming that the change was made only for accounting purposes.
3. Prepare a schedule to indicate the relevant effects on the 1997 and 1998 comparative balance sheet, income statement, and retained earnings statement.
4. Provide the footnote describing the accounting change assuming that 1997 and 1998 results are shown comparatively.

E 24–13
(L.O. 7)

Analysis of Seven Errors: Correcting Entries, Correct Pretax Income   The 1997 income statement of Burke Corporation has just been tentatively completed. It reflects pretax income for 1997 of $85,000. The accounts have not been closed for the year ended December 31, 1997. A review of the company's files and records revealed the following errors that have not been corrected:

a. Patent amortization of $3,000 per year was not recorded in 1996 and 1997.
b. The 1995 ending inventory was overstated by $4,000.
c. Machinery acquired on January 1, 1993, at a cost of $26,000 is being depreciated by the straight-line method over 10 years. The good-faith estimate of its residual value of $6,000 has not been included in the computation of depreciation expense.
d. Accrued wages of $1,500 at December 31, 1996, were not recognized.
e. A $1,000 cash shortage during 1997 was debited to retained earnings.
f. Ordinary repairs on the machinery in (*c*) above of $7,000, incurred during January 1997, were debited to the machinery account.
g. During 1997, treasury stock that cost $8,000 was sold for $11,000. The difference was credited to extraordinary gain. The company uses the cost method to account for treasury stock.

Required

1. Give the correcting entry, if needed, for each of the above errors. Explain the basis and show computations for each item. Ignore income tax considerations.
2. Compute the correct pretax income amount for 1997. Set up an appropriate schedule that reflects each change and the correct 1997 pretax income.

E 24–14
(L.O. 7)

Analysis of Four Errors: Correcting Entries and Correct Pretax Income   Travis Corporation has just completed its financial statements for the reporting year ended December 31, 1998. The pretax income amount is $160,000. The accounts have not been closed for December 31, 1998. Further consideration and review of the records revealed the following items related to the 1998 statements:

a. On January 1, 1994, a machine was acquired that cost $10,000. The estimated useful life was 10 years, and the residual value was $2,000. At the time of acquisition, the full cost of the machine was incorrectly debited to the land account. Use straight-line depreciation.
b. On January 1, 1996, a long-term investment of $18,000 was made by purchasing a $20,000, 8 percent bond of Watch Corporation. The investment account was debited for $18,000. Each year, starting on December 31, 1996, the company has recognized and reported investment revenue on these bonds of $1,600. The bonds mature in 10 years from date of purchase. Assume that any amortization would be straight line, that the net method is used to record the investment, and that Travis intends to hold the bonds to maturity.
c. The 1997 ending inventory was overstated by $7,000 (periodic inventory system).
d. An $11,000 credit purchase of merchandise occurred on December 18, 1997. Because the merchandise was on hand on December 31, 1997, it was included in the 1997 ending inventory. The purchase was recorded on January 18, 1998, when the invoice was paid.

Required

1. Prepare any correcting and adjusting entries that should be made on December 31, 1998, and reported on the 1998 income statement. Ignore income tax.
2. Compute the correct income for 1998. Set up an appropriate schedule that reflects each change and the correct 1998 pretax income.

E 24–15
(L.O. 7)

Error, Comparative Statements, Correcting Entry, and Reporting   Bar Corporation had never been audited before December 31, 1997, the current year. Before the arrival of the auditor, the company accountant prepared comparative financial statements showing the results of 1996 and 1997. The accounts for 1997 have not been closed. The auditors discovered that an invoice dated January 1994 for $9,000 (paid in cash at the time) was debited to 1994 operating expenses, although it was for the purchase of equipment. The equipment has an estimated useful life of 10 years and no estimated residual value.

Reported incomes reflected on the financial statements prepared by the company (before discovery of the error) were 1994, $11,000; 1995, $22,000; 1996, $30,000; and 1997, $33,000. Shares of common stock outstanding, 100,000. Disregard income tax considerations, and assume that Bar uses straight-line depreciation.

Required

1. Identify the type of change or correction involved and analyze the effects of the change or correction, as appropriate.
2. Give the entry, or entries, to appropriately record the change or correction in the accounts for 1997, the year of the change.
3. Show how the change or correction should be reported on the 1997 comparative financial statements.

E 24–16
(L.O. 7)

Errors, Prior Years Adjustments Not Recorded, and Entries to Correct for Current Year   You are auditing the accounts of Sun Merchandising Corporation for the year ended December 31, 1998. You discover that the adjustments made in the previous audit for the year 1997 were not entered in the accounts by Sun's bookkeeper; therefore, the accounts are not in agreement with the audited amounts as of December 31, 1997. The following adjustments were included in the 1997 audit report:

a. Invoices for merchandise purchased on credit in December 1997 were not entered on the books until payment of $12,000 was made in January 1998. The merchandise was not included in the December 31, 1997, inventory. The company uses a periodic inventory system.
b. Invoices for merchandise received on credit in December 1997 were not recorded in the accounts until payment was made in January 1998; the goods were included in the 1997 ending inventory, $18,000.
c. Allowance for doubtful accounts for 1997 was understated by $2,000 because bad debt expense in 1997 was not recorded.
d. Selling expense for 1997, $5,000, was not recorded in the accounts until paid in January 1998.
e. Accrued wages of $4,000 at December 31, 1997, were not recorded in the accounts until paid in January 1998.
f. Prepaid insurance at December 31, 1997, was understated by $600 because this amount was included in 1997 expense. The insurance policy expires on December 31, 1998.
g. Income tax expense of $2,400 for the last part of the year ended December 31, 1997 was not recorded until paid in January 1998.
h. Depreciation of $9,000 was not recorded for 1997.

Required

You have the uncorrected and unadjusted trial balance dated December 31, 1997. Give the journal entry for each of the above items that should be made to the trial balance before using it for further 1998 audit purposes.

PROBLEMS

P 24–1
(L.O. 3, 4, 5, 6)

Multiple Choice: Accounting Changes   Choose the correct answer to each of the following questions:

1. Immutable Company changed from the sum-of-years'-digits method (SYD) to the straight-line method (SL) of depreciation in 1998. Depreciation under each method for the years affected follows:

Year	SYD	SL
1995	$200	$150
1996	240	160
1997	600	450
1998	450	500

Ignoring taxes, Immutable reports which of the following amounts in cumulative effect of change in accounting principle in 1998?

   a. $280 cr.

   b. $230 cr.

   c. $50 dr.

   d. $320 dr.

2. Quick Company changed depreciation methods for accounting purposes and correctly computed a cumulative effect before tax of $600 (reduces income). The tax rate is 30 percent. The entry to record the change in accounting principle includes

   a. Cr. accumulated depreciation $420.

   b. Dr. deferred tax liability $180.

   c. Dr. income taxes payable $420.

   d. Dr. cumulative effect $600.

3. Fido Dog Food Company changed its method of accounting for inventory from LIFO to FIFO in 1998 for both tax and financial accounting purposes. The 1997 ending inventory was $40,000 under LIFO and $55,000 under FIFO. Fido discloses 1997 and 1998 results comparatively. The tax rate is 30 percent. The entry to record the change in accounting principle includes

   a. Cr. inventory $15,000.

   b. Cr. retained earnings $10,500.

   c. Cr. cumulative effect of change in accounting principle $10,500.

   d. Insufficient information.

4. An asset purchased January 1, 1994, costing $10,000 with a 10-year useful life and no salvage value was depreciated under the straight-line method during its first three years. During 1997, the total useful life was reestimated to be 17 years. What is depreciation in 1998?

   a. $462.

   b. $412.

   c. $464.

   d. $500.

5. A company made a retroactive accounting change in 1998. Only the net incomes of 1997 and 1998 were affected. Therefore, the comparative retained earnings statements featuring both years disclose which of the following?

   a. A cumulative effect adjusting the January 1, 1997, retained earnings balance.

   b. A cumulative effect adjusting the January 1, 1997, and 1998 retained earnings balances.

   c. A cumulative effect adjusting the January 1, 1998, retained earnings balance.

   d. No cumulative effect.

P 24–2
(L.O. 4)

Change from Declining-Balance to Straight-Line Depreciation: Entries and Reporting   On January 1, 1994, Klamath Corporation purchased equipment that cost $23,000; the estimated useful life was 10 years with no estimated residual value. The company uses 200 percent declining-balance depreciation; however, at the start of 1999, the company decided to switch to straight-line depreciation (no change in useful life or residual value). At December 31, 1998, the annual financial statements reported the following correct amounts:

Depreciation expense (DB) $1,884*

Accumulated depreciation (DB)   15,463

Shares of common stock outstanding, 10,000.

*1999, $1,507.

Net income before depreciation and before the effects of the accounting change was $40,000 in 1998 and $47,000 in 1999. Disregard income tax considerations.

Required

1. What type of accounting changes is this? What approach should be used—current, prospective, or retroactive? Explain.
2. Prepare the 1999 (i.e., the year of change) entry to appropriately reflect the change; also prepare the 1999 adjusting entry.
3. Show how the change and the amount of accumulated depreciation should be reported on the 1998 and 1999 comparative balance sheet and the relevant portions of the comparative income statement, including any required pro forma disclosure.

P 24–3
(L.O. 4)

Change to SYD: Income Tax, Entries, and Reporting   Cathode Company purchased a machine on January 1, 1994, for $240,000. At the date of acquisition, the machine had an estimated useful life of 10 years with an estimated residual value of $20,000. The machine is being depreciated on a straight-line basis for financial reporting purposes, but for income tax purposes an accelerated method is used because of its cash flow advantage.

On January 1, 1997, Cathode changed, for financial reporting purposes, to an accelerated method of depreciation for this machine (with no change in estimated useful life or residual value). The accelerated depreciation amounts were 1994, $40,000; 1995, $36,000; 1996, $32,000; and 1997, $28,000. The annual accounting period ends December 31. The annual financial statements are presented on a comparative basis (1996 and 1997 presented). Cathode has an average income tax rate of 40 percent. Pretax income before depreciation and prior to making this change was $90,000 in 1996 and $98,000 in 1997. There are 10,000 shares of common stock outstanding.

Required

1. Identify the type of accounting change involved. Which approach should be used—current, prospective, or retroactive? Explain.
2. Give the entry to appropriately reflect the accounting change in 1997, the year of change, including the 1997 adjusting entry.
3. Show how the change should be reported on the 1997 comparative balance sheets (1996 and 1997).
4. Prepare the comparative income statements for 1996 and 1997, starting with pretax income before depreciation and prior to the effects of the change.

P 24–4
(L.O. 5)

Change in Method of Accounting for Long-Term Contracts   Gillespi, Inc., changed from the completed contract method of accounting for long-term contracts to the percentage of completion method, during 1998. Reported earnings in 1997 were $50,000, and the beginning 1997 retained earnings balance was $150,000. Net income for 1998 under the completed contract method would have been $140,000. No dividends were declared during 1997 or 1998.

Effect of Change on Net Income

On years before 1997	Increase $100,000
On 1997	Increase 30,000
On 1998	Increase 60,000

Required

Prepare the 1997 and 1998 comparative retained earnings statements.

P 24–5
(L.O. 5)

Change in Method of Accounting for Natural Resources   The Endil Company changed from the successful efforts method to the full costing method for its exploration costs related to natural resources. The change occurred early in 1998. The ending 1996 balance sheet reported retained earnings of $40,000. Previously reported 1997 earnings were $18,000. The accounting change increased 1997 earnings by $7,000 and increased 1996 earnings by $8,000. 1998 earnings were $30,000. No other years were affected by the change, and no dividends have been declared during the last several years.

Required

Provide the comparative 1997 and 1998 retained earnings statements. Ignore income tax effects.

P 24–6
(L.O. 5)

Change in Inventory Accounting Method   Bennz, Inc., changed from LIFO to FIFO in 1998. Earnings amounts for the two most recent years and inventory balances under both methods follow:

Year	Net income
1998	$30,000 (computed under FIFO)
1997	20,000 (computed under LIFO)

Inventory Balances	1998	1997	1996
Ending inventory, FIFO	$15,000	$10,000	$8,000
Ending inventory, LIFO	9,000	7,000	4,000

Required

1. Provide the 1998 entry to record the accounting change.
2. What amount of net income will the 1997 retained earnings statement disclose?

P 24–7
(L.O. 5)

Change in Method of Accounting for Natural Resources: Entries and Reporting   In 1997, Digger Oil Company changes its method of accounting for oil exploration costs from the successful-efforts method (SE) to the full-costing method (FC) for financial reporting. Digger has been in operation since January 1994.

Pretax income under each method:

	SE	FC
1994	$ 5,000	$15,000
1995	22,000	25,000
1996	25,000	35,000
1997	40,000	60,000

Digger reports the results of years 1995 to 1997 in its 1997 annual report and has a calendar fiscal year. The tax rate is 30 percent.

Additional information:

	1994	**1995**	**1996**	**1997**
Ending retained earnings (SE basis)	$18,000	$23,000	$31,000	
Dividends declared	9,000	10,400	9,500	18,000

Required

1. Prepare the entry in 1997 to record the accounting change. Use natural resources as the depletable asset. For simplicity, assume the difference in accounting for exploration costs accounts for the entire income difference in all years.
2. Prepare the comparative retained earnings statements.

P 24–8
(L.O. 5)

Change from Completed Contract to Percentage of Completion: Entries and Reporting Modern Construction Company began operations on January 1, 1994. During 1994 and 1995, the company used the completed-contract (CC) basis to account for its long-term construction contracts for financial reporting purposes. At the start of 1996, the company changed to the percentage-of-completion (PC) basis.

The following data are available:

	1994	**1995**	**1996**
Income (net of 30 percent income tax)	$70,000 (CC)	$120,000 (CC)	$185,000 (PC)
Dividends	–0–	50,000	90,000
Retained earnings (ending balance)	70,000 (CC)	140,000 (CC)	

	CC	**PC**	**CC**	**PC**	**CC**	**PC**
Inventory of construction in process, net of billings (ending balance)	$150,000	$165,000	$250,000	$350,000	$280,000	$360,000

Shares outstanding, 100,000.

Required

1. Identify the type of accounting change involved. How should it be accounted for—current, retroactive, prospective? Explain.
2. Give the entry on January 1, 1996, to record this accounting change in 1996 (net of income tax).
3. Show how the following should be reported on the 1995 and 1996 comparative
   a. Balance sheet—inventory of construction in process and ending balance of retained earnings.
   b. Income statement—starting with income before extraordinary items.
   c. Retained earnings statements—starting with beginning balance (CC). The ending 1996 balance of retained earnings is $305,000.

P 24–9
(L.O. 7)

Eight Errors: Analysis and Correction, Entries General Sales Company recently was acquired by a new owner who has decided to clean up the prior accounting records during the current reporting period, which ends December 31, 1998. The accounts have been partially adjusted but not closed for 1998. The following additional items have been discovered:

a. The merchandise inventory at December 31, 1997, was overstated by $10,000 (periodic inventory system).
b. During January 1996, extraordinary repairs on machinery were debited to repair expense; the $15,000 should have been debited to machinery, which is being depreciated 15 percent per year on cost (no residual value).
c. A patent that cost $9,350 has been amortized (straight line) for the past 7 years (excluding 1998) over its legal life of 17 years. It is now clear that its economic life will not be more than 12 years from the initial acquisition date.
d. At the end of 1997, sales revenue collected in advance of $3,000 was included in 1997 sales revenue. It was earned in 1998.
e. Paid $8,000 during January 1996 for ordinary repairs on a machine that was acquired during January 1996. The repairs were erroneously capitalized. The machine has an estimated life of five years and no residual value. Assume straight-line depreciation.

f. The rate used for bad debts has been ½ percent of credit sales, which has proven to be too low; therefore, for 1998 and thereafter, the rate used will be 1 percent of credit sales. The amount of the expense recorded per year under the old rate was $800 in 1996 and $1,000 in 1997. (The amount for 1998 has not been entered in the accounts because the adjusting entries have not been made). Credit sales for 1998 exceeded 1997 credit sales by 20 percent.

g. During January 1996, a five-year insurance premium of $750 was paid, which was debited in full to insurance expense at that time.

h. At the end of 1997, accrued wages payable of $1,800 were not recorded; they were first recorded when paid early in 1998. Unpaid wages at the end of 1998 were $2,100.

Required

1. For each of the above items, identify whether it is an error correction or an accounting change and briefly explain how each should be accounted for.
2. Give the appropriate pretax entry to record any change or correction and give any adjusting entry needed in each instance at the end of 1998. Show computations. If no entry is needed, explain why.

P 24–10
(L.O. 7)

Error Correction: Entry and Reporting   In 1997, Arrow Company, which has a calendar fiscal year, discovered that depreciation expense was erroneously overstated $2,000 in both 1995 and 1996 for financial reporting purposes. The tax rate is 30 percent.

Additional information:

	1996	1997
Beginning retained earnings, as previously reported	$36,000	—
Net income (as previously reported for 1996)	32,000	$36,000
Dividends declared	12,000	16,000

Required

1. Record the entry in 1997 to correct the error.
2. Provide the comparative retained earnings statements for 1996 and 1997, including any required footnote disclosure.

P 24–11
(L.O. 4, 6, 7)

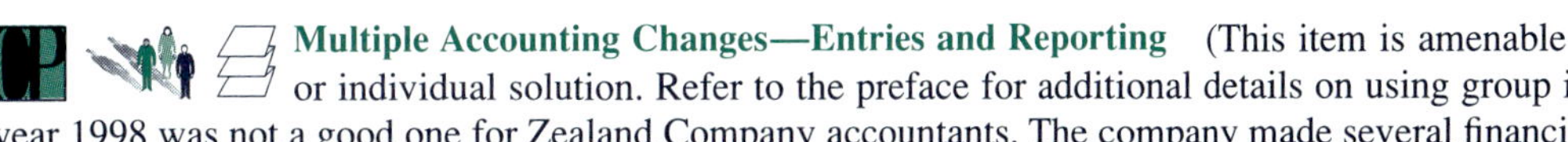 **Multiple Accounting Changes—Entries and Reporting**   (This item is amenable to a group or individual solution. Refer to the preface for additional details on using group items.) The year 1998 was not a good one for Zealand Company accountants. The company made several financial accounting changes that year.

First, the company changed the total useful life from 20 years to 13 years on an asset purchased January 1, 1995, for $350,000. The asset was originally expected to be sold for $50,000 at the end of its useful life, but that amount also was changed in 1998 to $200,000. Zealand applies the straight-line method of depreciation to this asset.

Second, the company changed from FIFO to LIFO but is unable to recreate LIFO inventory layers. The FIFO 1998 beginning and ending inventories are $30,000 and $45,000, respectively. Under LIFO, the 1998 ending inventory is $35,000. The company expects LIFO to render income numbers more useful for prediction, given inflation.

Third, the company changed to the straight-line method from the sum-of-years'-digits method on equipment purchased for $650,000 on January 1, 1994. The equipment has a $100,000 residual value and 10-year useful life. These values were not changed. The change in depreciation method was made to provide a better measure of expired equipment cost because the annual benefits derived from the asset have been relatively constant.

Fourth, an error in amortizing patents was discovered in 1998. Patents costing $510,000 on January 1, 1996, were amortized over their legal life (17 years). The accountant neglected to obtain an estimate of the patent's economic life, which totals only 5 years.

Additional information: Zealand has a calendar fiscal year, is subject to a 30 percent tax rate, and has had 10,000 shares of common stock outstanding since 1993.

	1997 (previously published)	1998
Beginning retained earnings	$319,000	—
Income before extraordinary items, after tax	220,000	$325,000*
Extraordinary gain, net of tax		10,000
Dividends declared	50,000	70,000

*This is the correct reported amount and includes the appropriate amounts related to the accounting changes.

Required   1. Record the entries in 1998 necessary to make the accounting changes.
               2. Prepare the 1997 and 1998 comparative income statement (lower portion) and retained earnings statement, including footnote disclosures for the accounting changes.

ANALYSIS, JUDGMENT, AND COMMUNICATION

CASES

C 24–1
(L.O. 2, 3)

Analysis of Three Accounting Changes   A business entity may change its method of accounting for certain items. The change may be classified as a change in accounting principle, accounting estimate, or reporting entity. Listed below are three independent, unrelated situations.

Situation 1:

Able Company determined that the depreciable lives currently used for its operational assets were too long to best match the cost of using the assets with the revenue produced. At the beginning of the current year, the company decided to reduce the depreciable lives of all its existing operational assets by five years.

Situation 2:

On December 31, 1997, Baker Company owned 51 percent of the voting stock of Allen Company. At that time Baker reported its investment using the cost method due to political uncertainties in the country in which Allen was located. On January 2, 1998, the management of Baker Company was satisfied that the political uncertainties had been resolved and that the assets of the company were in no danger of nationalization. Accordingly, Baker will prepare consolidated financial statements for Baker and Allen for the year ended December 31, 1998.

Situation 3:

Charlie Company decides in January 1998 to adopt the straight-line method of depreciation for plant equipment. The straight-line method will be used for new acquisitions as well as for previously acquired plant equipment for which depreciation in the past has been provided on a declining-balance basis (DB).

Required   For each of the situations described above, write in a memo to the CFO the information indicated below:

               1. Type of accounting change.
               2. Manner of reporting the change under current GAAP, including a discussion, for situations 1 and 3 only, of how amounts are computed.
               3. Effect of the change on the balance sheet and income statement (situations 1 and 3 only).
               4. Note disclosures which would be necessary.

                                                                                          (AICPA adapted)

C 24–2
(L.O. 1)

Ethical Considerations: Accounting Changes   In 1982, RTE Corporation, a manufacturer of electric power transmission and distribution equipment, more than doubled its EPS by changing depreciation methods. In justifying the change, the controller said, "We realized that, compared to our competitors, our conservative method of depreciation might have hurt us with investors because of its negative impact on net earnings" ("Double Standard," *Forbes,* November 22, 1982, p. 178).

   Although difficult to prove, there is considerable evidence that accounting changes are made for reasons other than improved financial reporting. GAAP is flexible in the initial selection of accounting methods and in making subsequent changes. However, *APB Opinion No. 20* specifically requires that only changes to preferable accounting methods be made.

Required   Comment on the appropriateness of making accounting changes to fulfill financial reporting objectives. Consider relevant ethical issues in your response.

C 24–3
(L.O. 1)

Conflicting Issues in Accounting Changes   Consistency, comparability, and the need to maintain public confidence in the financial reporting process (defined in terms of the expectation that prior financial statements not be changed except for error) are conflicting objectives.

Required   Write a memo to a new accounting employee discussing the extent to which the three approaches to accounting changes (current, retroactive, and prospective) fulfill these objectives.

25 DISCLOSURES, SEGMENT REPORTING, AND INTERIM REPORTING

LEARNING OBJECTIVES

After you have studied this chapter, you will:

1 Understand the full disclosure principle.

2 Know the financial disclosures in the 10-K report to the SEC.

3 Be aware of the rationale for and components of the Summary of Significant Accounting Policies, and other related disclosures.

4 Understand the rationale and implementation requirements for segment reporting disclosures.

5 Be familiar with the alternative concepts that may be applied in preparing interim reports and how to select the appropriate concept.

INTRODUCTION

Suppose you were to inherit shares of common stock of Hilo Electric Switching Products, Inc. The company manufactures telephone switching and networking equipment and has been in business for nearly 50 years. Recently the company has been trying to expand its businesses into more sophisticated computer communications and switching technology, but their success to date is unknown. Hilo pays a small dividend annually, and the company's stock price has not been increasing as fast as the market in recent years. The company's annual report suggests that its performance has been modest at best (amounts in thousands):

Year	1992	1993	1994	1995	1996
Sales	$10,100	$10,150	$10,225	$10,338	$10,506
Profit	1,000	1,001	1,012	1,038	1,088
Growth in profit		0.1%	1.1%	2.6%	4.8%

The company appears to be stodgy with a rather unexciting future. Hilo is growing, but not at a rate that would cause excitement among investors.

If this were all the information available, you might be tempted to sell the stock and find a more interesting investment. Indeed, the above summary information on sales and profits might be all the detail you could obtain on Hilo. But suppose that Hilo provided supplemental information in its financial statements about its two businesses: its traditional telephone switching equipment business, and its efforts in the relatively new computer

"

communications area. Suppose the breakdown of sales and profits for the two lines of business are:

Year	1992	1993	1994	1995	1996
Sales by line of business					
Telephone equipment	$10,000	$10,000	$10,000	$10,000	$10,000
Computer equipment	100	150	225	338	506
Total sales	$10,100	$10,150	$10,225	$10,338	$10,506
Profit by line of business					
Telephone equipment	$960	$941	$922	$903	$885
Computer equipment	40	60	90	135	203
Total profit	$1,000	$1,001	$1,012	$1,038	$1,088
Growth in profit by line of business					
Telephone equipment		(2%)	(2%)	(2%)	(2%)
Computer equipment		50%	50%	50%	50%

Breaking out the sales, profits and growth in profits by line of business provides considerably more insight into what is happening at Hilo than the company-wide aggregated data provided. Hilo's traditional telephone business is not growing at all, and in fact is losing profit margin over time. The company's new computer communications business, however, is growing at 50 percent per year with a 40 percent profit margin. If this trend continues, in a few short years the computer communications business would dominate the company's sales and profits. In the year 2000 profits from the computer communications business will exceed those of the telephone switching business, and total firm profit growth will exceed 20 percent per year. Most of us would like to know this line-of-business information when evaluating Hilo as a potential investment.

Is Hilo required to provide this line-of-business information? We discuss the relevant accounting rules in this chapter, but for the moment you should know that the answer is probably no, at least until 1995 when the profit margin from the computer equipment business is more than 10 percent of the total. A recently enacted Standard, *SFAS No. 131,* will require companies like Hilo to provide the segment information shown above if the internal organization of the company requires this kind of information be used by management.

Segment reporting is an important topic covered in this chapter. The guidelines for interim reporting for firms electing or required to provide quarterly financial statements also are covered in this chapter. Finally, the required disclosures that augment and help to clarify the interpretation of financial statements are covered. We begin with the broad issue of clarifying disclosures before turning specifically to segment reporting and interim reporting.

FULL DISCLOSURE

The primary objective of financial reporting is to provide present and potential investors, creditors, and other users with information that is useful in making investment, credit, and other decisions. Many different user groups want information about the firm, and different groups may desire different information. *General-purpose financial statements* prepared in conformity with generally accepted accounting principles are assumed to be the most cost-effective way to provide the desired information. In an attempt to make such statements as comprehensive as possible, the tendency has been to require disclosure of virtually any item of information that may be of interest to financial statement users.

On the other hand, it is impossible to present all the information about a firm essential for decision making in a balance sheet, income statement, statement of cash flows, and statement of stockholders' equity. *Statement of Financial Accounting Concepts No. 5* outlines various types of information beyond financial statement information used in investment, credit, and similar decisions. The basic framework of the different types of information is presented in Exhibit 25–1.

The **full-disclosure principle** calls for the disclosure of all financial information that has the potential to influence the judgment of an informed reader. It is subject to a cost–

EXHIBIT 25–1   Types and Sources of Information Useful for Investment, Credit, and Similar Decisions

All information useful for investment, credit, and similar decisions

Financial reporting

Area directly affected by FASB standards

Basic financial statements

Scope of recognition and measurement Concepts Statement

Financial statements	Notes to financial statements (& parenthetical disclosures)	Supplementary information	Other means of providing financial information	Other information
- Balance sheet - Statements of earnings and comprehensive income - Statement of cash flows - Statement of investments by and distribution to owners	Examples: - Accounting policies - Contingencies - Inventory methods - Number of shares of stock outstanding - Alternative measures (market values of items carried at historical cost)	Examples: - Segment information (*SFAS No. 14*) - Oil and gas reserves information (*SFAS No. 69*)	Examples: - Management discussion and analysis - Letters to stockholders - SEC Form 10-K disclosures	Examples: - Discussion of competition - Order backlogs - Analysts' reports - Economic statistics - News articles about company

benefit evaluation, but making such an evaluation is usually difficult. Firms claiming that the cost of implementing a particular standard is too high relative to the benefit it provides often cite specific cost estimates. More difficult for the Board to determine is the benefit to users of required disclosures. Until a method is developed to better quantify the costs and benefits of disclosure, the Board will continue to hear the argument that the cost of many required disclosures exceeds their benefit.

Many in the business community and in the accounting profession are concerned about the ever-increasing number and complexity of authoritative accounting pronouncements. Indeed, there has been a substantial increase in the amount of required disclosures in the past two decades. Most *Standards* issued by the FASB require various disclosures in addition to providing guidance on accepted methods of measurement. This trend is expected to continue. Perhaps the most important reason for the increased disclosure requirements is the increasing complexity of business transactions and the difficulty of describing them in simple accounting terms. An example is the increased complexity of financial instruments developed in recent years, primarily used in business acquisitions and in risk management. These instruments often have characteristics of both debt and equity. Increased disclosure in the notes to the financial statements is one way to provide detailed information on the specific debt and equity characteristics of a particular financial instrument.

Another reason for increased disclosure lies in the desire to monitor and control the activities of large public corporations. Thus, government regulations require increased disclosure regarding management compensation, insider trading transactions, related party transactions, environmental issues, and potentially illegal activities. Many of these disclosures are required by the SEC, but they are implemented by the accounting profession.

FINANCIAL REPORTING REQUIREMENTS OF THE SEC

The Securities and Exchange Commission (SEC) is a governmental agency that administers various securities acts under the Securities Act of 1933 and the Securities Exchange Act of 1934. Congress established the SEC to regulate the disclosures of financial information by publicly traded companies. Although it has delegated authority for prescribing accounting principles and reporting practices to the FASB, the SEC maintains legal responsibility and final authority in these matters.

The SEC is administered from its headquarters in Washington, DC, by five commissioners. It is organized into several administrative offices. The Office of the Chief Accountant oversees administrative policies regarding accounting matters and is directly responsible for *Regulation S-X* which establishes guidelines for financial statements filed with the SEC. The Chief Accountant also is responsible for *Financial Reporting Releases (FRRs)* (called *Accounting Series Releases (ASRs)* prior to 1982). *FRRs* and *ASRs* prescribe accounting principles for reporting companies. The Chief Accountant is a member of the Financial Accounting Standards Advisory Committee (FASAC) and is in regular contact with the FASB to provide counsel on the impact of proposed standards on business reporting.

The Division of Corporate Finance also plays a major role in financial reporting. It is responsible both for assisting in establishing reporting standards other than those dealing directly with financial statements, and for compliance with the standards. This division also reviews submitted financial reports.

Of the many forms and reports required to be filed with the SEC, two of particular importance are

- Form 10-K.
- Form 10-Q.

The 10-K is the annual report, including all financial reporting information, required to be submitted to the SEC. The 10-Q is the quarterly report, is based on the 10-K, and contains much of the same information, although usually in more summarized form. Only the 10-K is discussed here.

Form 10-K

The 10-K must be filed with the SEC within 90 days of a company's fiscal year-end. It is organized into four major parts, each providing information on specified topics or items. Part II is especially relevant to accounting because all the items required there must also be included in the company's annual report to shareholders. The five items included in Part II are:

SEC Item No.	Heading	Description
5	Market for Common Stock	Identification of market(s) where common stock is traded, including number of shares, frequency of trading, and amounts of dividends.
6	Selected Financial Data	Five-year summary, including net sales, income (loss) from continuing operations, EPS, total assets, cash dividends, and long-term obligations.
7	Management Discussion and Analysis	Discussion of liquidity, capital resources, results of operations, and impact of inflation as needed to understand the company's financial condition, change in financial condition, and operating results.
8	Financial Statements and Supplementary Data	Consolidated financial statements, including balance sheets for two years, income statements, cash flow statements, and statements of changes in stockholders' equity for three years, and related notes. Also selected quarterly data and the auditor's opinion.
9	Disagreements on Accounting Disclosures	If and when auditors are changed due to disagreements on accounting principles, a description of the disagreement and summary of the effects on the financial statements.

Exhibit 25–2 lists additional items of disclosure required in the Form 10-K. These items are not required to be included in the annual report to stockholders, although companies often include many of them.

Most of the preceding items in Part II of the 10-K are self-explanatory. Many have been discussed in other sections and chapters of this text. Some of the disclosures are straightforward, such as information on where the company's securities are traded. Item 6, Selected Financial Data, requires a five-year historical record on key financial variables. Item 8 relates to the financial statements and related notes that are the primary focus of an annual report to shareholders. Items 7 and 9 require additional explanation.

Management Discussion and Analysis

The management discussion and analysis (MDA) section, item 7, is intended to describe the company from the perspective of management. The MDA is somewhat forward-looking and deals with near-term and long-term analysis. The SEC's *Regulation S-K* and *Finan-*

EXHIBIT 25–2

Form 10-K Required Disclosures except Disclosures in Annual Report (part II disclosures)

Item No.	Heading	Description
PART I		
1	Business	History and description of business, recent developments, principal products and services, major industry segments.
2	Properties	Locations and general descriptions of plants and other physical properties.
3	Legal Proceedings	Description of pending legal proceedings, principal parties to the proceedings, dates, allegations, and relief sought.
4	Voting Matters	Description of matters submitted to voting shareholders for approval.
PART III		
10	Directors and Officers	Names, ages, and positions of directors and officers.
11	Executive Compensation	Salaries, stock options, and other benefits for corporate officers and selected others.
12	Security Ownership	List of beneficial owners and management owners of corporate securities.
13	Certain Relationships	Description of transactions with managers and related parties, and for certain other business relationships.
PART IV		
14	Exhibits, Schedules, and Reports	Detailed supporting schedules, often specified in *Regulation S-K*. Examples are marketable securities; property, plant, and equipment (including accumulated depreciation); short-term borrowings, and a list of subsidiaries.
15	Signatures	The report must be signed by the chief executive officer, the chief financial officer, and a majority of the board of directors.

cial Reporting Release No. 36 provide guidance for MDA disclosures. Basically, a firm must provide information needed to understand its financial condition and changes in its financial condition. Some disclosures are required; others are encouraged. The voluntary disclosures tend to involve anticipation of trends or events. The MDA is not required to be audited by the independent auditor.

An example of an MDA is included in the Coca-Cola Company annual report, found at the end of this text. The complete Coca-Cola MDA covers seven pages.

Disagreements on Accounting Disclosures

Disclosures regarding disagreements on accounting (item 9) occur infrequently, in part because management and auditors work hard to find an appropriate middle ground that both find acceptable when a disagreement arises. When a compromise position is reached, disclosure is not required. A disagreement disclosure occurs only when there is no acceptable solution to a disagreement between management and the auditor. In this case, the financial statements are prepared and disclosures made that are contrary to the wishes of one party.

NOTES TO FINANCIAL STATEMENTS

Notes to the financial statements are an integral part of the financial statements and are audited. Notes provide quantitative and descriptive explanations of various items included (or not included) in the body of the statements that are deemed to be potentially meaningful to users. Readers can make their own assessments of the potential quantitative ramifications of the information presented. Notes sometimes are complex and highly technical, and provide very valuable information.

Summary of Significant Accounting Policies

A knowledge of the various accounting policies used in generating a set of financial statements is essential to developing an understanding of the statements. For example, knowing that a firm is using LIFO rather than FIFO provides a basis for interpreting both the inventory value and the cost of goods sold amount.

APB Opinion No. 22 requires the disclosure of accounting policies used to present the financial position, cash flows, and results of operations in accordance with GAAP. Accounting

policies include both specific accounting principles and the methods of applying these principles. A description of all significant accounting policies is required. The disclosures must include those accounting principles and methods that involve the following factors:
- A selection from existing acceptable alternatives.
- Principles and methods peculiar to the industry.
- Unusual or innovative applications of GAAP.

The summary of significant accounting policies is presented either as a separate section or as the first note to the financial statements. The summary included as Note 1 to the Philip Morris Companies' Inc. 1995 financial statements is shown as Exhibit 25–3. The specific items in the disclosure vary from firm to firm. Another example is the first Note to the Coca-Cola financial statements reproduced at the end of this volume.

Other Notes to Financial Statements

In addition to the Summary of Significant Accounting Policies, many additional note disclosures are either required by the specific accounting standards or voluntarily provided in compliance with the full-disclosure principle. Reflecting back over most of the topics covered in this text, recall many had specific disclosure requirements in addition to the guidance provided on how to account for a particular item.

Rather than review all disclosure notes that can appear, we would again consider the Coca-Cola financial statements at the back of the text, and in particular the 19 Notes included as part of the financial statements. Nearly all these notes are required, but a few are voluntary disclosures; for example, Note 5 on Accounts Payable and Accrued Expenses.

Often industry specific practices result in specific disclosures for the firms in an industry. Boeing, for example, manufactures and sells airplanes, but selling takes on different forms:
- Outright sale for cash.
- Outright sale, but provide the customer with credit (customer financing).
- Sales type leases.
- Operating leases.

Boeing provides the following disclosure concerning customer financing in Note 4 to its 1995 annual report (partially excerpted):

Note 4 (amounts in millions)

Customer Financing

Long-term customer financing, less current portion, at December 31 consisted of the following:

	1995	1994
Notes receivable	$ 721	$1,189
Investment in sales-type leases	351	1,235
Operating lease aircraft, at cost, less		
accumulated depreciation of $326 and $269	688	747
	1,760	3,171
Less valuation allowance	(100)	(100)
	$1,660	$3,071

Financing for aircraft is collateralized by security in the related asset, and historically, the Company has not experienced a problem in accessing such collateral. The operating lease aircraft category includes new and used jet and commuter aircraft, spare engines and spare parts.

The total of $1,660 million is reported in the balance sheet as a noncurrent asset. The breakdown in Note 4 provides valuable supplementary information on what is included in the broad term *long-term customer financing.*

Special Transactions and Events

Some transactions and events are so unusual and sensitive that they create difficult reporting problems for the firm. These include
- Related party transactions.
- Illegal acts.
- Errors and irregularities.

EXHIBIT 25–3   Philip Morris Companies Inc. 1995 Financial Statements: Note 1—Summary of Significant Accounting Policies

---

Note 1. Summary of Significant Accounting Policies:

Basis of presentation:

The consolidated financial statements include all significant subsidiaries. The preparation of financial statements in conformity with generally accepted accounting principles requires management to make estimates and assumptions that affect the reported amounts of assets and liabilities and disclosure of contingent assets and liabilities at the dates of the financial statements and the reported amounts of operating revenues and expenses during the reporting periods. Actual results could differ from those estimates.

Balance sheet accounts are segregated by two broad types of business. Consumer products assets and liabilities are classified as either current or non-current, whereas financial services and real estate assets and liabilities are unclassified, in accordance with respective industry practices.

Cash and cash equivalents:

Cash equivalents include demand deposits with banks and all highly liquid investments with original maturities of three months or less.

Inventories:

Inventories are stated at the lower of cost or market. The last-in, first-out ("LIFO") method is used to cost substantially all domestic inventories. The cost of other inventories is determined by the average cost or first-in, first-out methods. It is a generally recognized industry practice to classify the total amount of leaf tobacco inventory as a current asset although part of such inventory, because of the duration of the aging process, ordinarily would not be utilized within one year.

Advertising costs:

Advertising costs are expensed generally as incurred.

Depreciation, amortization and goodwill valuation:

Depreciation is recorded by the straight-line method. Substantially all goodwill and other intangible assets are amortized by the straight-line method, principally over 40 years. The Company periodically evaluates the recoverability of goodwill and measures any impair-

ment by comparison to estimated undiscounted cash flows from future operations.

Financial instruments:

Derivative financial instruments are used by the Company to manage its foreign currency and interest rate exposures. Realized and unrealized gains and losses on foreign currency swaps that are effective as hedges of net assets in foreign subsidiaries are offset against the foreign exchange gains or losses as a component of stockholders' equity. The interest differential to be paid or received under the currency and related interest rate swap agreements is recognized over the life of the related debt and is included in interest and other debt expense, net. Unrealized gains and losses on forward contracts that are effective as hedges of assets, liabilities, and commitments are deferred and recognized in income as the related transaction is realized.

Accounting changes:

Effective January 1, 1995, the Company adopted Statement of Financial Accounting Standards ("SFAS") No. 116, "Accounting for Contributions Received and Contributions Made." This Statement requires the Company to recognize an unconditional promise to make a contribution as an expense in the period the promise is made. The Company had previously expensed contributions when payment was made. The cumulative effect at January 1, 1995 of adopting SFAS No. 116 reduced 1995 net earnings by $7 million ($.01 per share), net of $4 million of income tax benefits. The application of SFAS No. 116 did not materially reduce earnings before cumulative effect of accounting changes.

The Company's adoption of SFAS No. 106 for non-U.S. postretirement benefits other than pensions, effective January 1, 1995, is discussed in Note 14. The Company's adoption of SFAS No. 112 for postemployment benefits, effective January 1, 1993, is discussed in Note 13.

SFAS No. 121, "Accounting for the Impairment of Long-Lived Assets and for Long-Lived Assets to be Disposed of" will be adopted by the Company on January 1, 1996. The Company estimates that the effect of adoption will not be material.

To balance the rights of reporting entity and the rights of the potential users of the financial statements, there is some guidance for reporting on each of these issues.

Related Party Transactions   When a firm engages in a transaction where one of the parties has the ability to influence the actions and policies of the other, or when a nontransacting third party has the ability to influence the policies of the transacting parties, the transaction is termed a **related party transaction.** Such transactions cannot be assumed to be at arm's length because the conditions necessary for a competitive, free-market interaction are not likely to be present. Examples of related party transactions include transactions between

- A firm and its principal owners, its management, members of families of owners or management, or its affiliates.
- A parent firm and its subsidiaries.
- Subsidiaries of a common parent firm.
- A firm and the trusts it controls or manages for the benefit of employees.
  For related party transactions, *SFAS No. 57* requires the following disclosures
- The nature of the relationship(s) involved.
- A description of the transaction, even when no amounts or nominal amounts were involved, for each period for which income statements are presented.

- The dollar amounts of transactions for each period for which income statements are presented.
- Any amounts due to or from related parties as of the balance sheet date, and the terms and manner of settlement planned.

Note 3 to the Coca-Cola financial statements under the Coca-Cola Enterprises (CCE) section contains an example of a related party disclosure in the paragraphs that describe activities that Coca-Cola undertakes for CCE.

Illegal Acts   Bribes, kickbacks, illegal political contributions, and other violations of statutes and regulations constitute **illegal acts.** Congress enacted the Foreign Corrupt Practices Act of 1977 largely to discourage illegal acts and to require their disclosure when discovered. The Foreign Corrupt Practices Act has affected business practices as well as the accounting profession. The auditor must ensure complete disclosure of relevant information when an illegal act is discovered. For example, if the auditor discovers that revenue is the result of an illegal act such as bribery, the amount must be disclosed, along with all the known facts about the bribe.

Errors and Irregularities   Errors are defined as "incorrect recording and reporting of the facts about the business that existed at the time an event or transaction was recorded." They are, essentially, unintentional mistakes. Irregularities, however, are intentional distortions of the financial statements. Irregularities should be corrected in the same manner as errors, but they are more serious than errors. Attempts by companies to mislead readers of financial statements intentionally are of sufficient concern that a national commission was appointed to study the problem and recommend actions for dealing with it.[1]

Fraudulent Financial Reporting

From time to time there are instances of fraudulent financial reporting, defined by the *Report of the National Commission on Fraudulent Financial Reporting* as financial reporting that is "intentional or reckless, whether act or omission, that results in materially misleading financial statements." The report, often referred to as the *Treadway Report,* for the Commission's chairperson James Treadway, provides useful information on the causes of fraudulent financial reporting and suggests ways to prevent it.

Recently the AICPA issued *Statement on Auditing Standards No. 82,* "Consideration of Fraud in a Financial Statement Audit." The new Statement articulates the independent auditor's responsibility to plan and perform the audit to obtain reasonable assurance about whether the financial statements are free of material misstatement, whether caused by error or fraud. The AICPA's Auditing Standards Board issued the new standard to enhance audit performance and to provide auditors with additional operational guidance on the consideration of material fraud in conducting a financial statement audit. Specifically, the standard describes two types of fraud:

1. Fraudulent financial reporting and
2. Misappropriation of assets

Both are relevant to the auditor's consideration of fraud in a financial statement audit. The Statement was issued in February 1997 with an effective date for audits of financial statements for periods ending on or after December 15, 1997.

Fraudulent financial reporting generally can be traced to poor internal control or to poor industry or overall business conditions. Extreme pressures on management, such as a major decline in revenue, unrealistic profit or other performance goals, or bonus plans that depend on short-term performance, can also lead to fraudulent financial reporting.

The opportunity to engage in fraudulent financial reporting is present when

- The board of directors or an audit committee of the board does not carefully review the reporting process.

---

[1]National Commission on Fraudulent Financial Reporting, *Report of the National Commission on Fraudulent Financial Reporting* (Washington, DC: 1987).

- The firm has engaged in unusual or complicated transactions.
- The system of internal control is weak.
- Internal audit staffs are small or poorly trained and underfunded.
- There is extensive need for judgment in making accounting estimates.

The ethical climate of an organization can either contribute to or inhibit fraudulent financial reporting. The attitude top management conveys about issues of honesty in general and truthful reporting in particular influences the actions of other managers in positions of responsibility.

The accounting profession must try to prevent fraudulent financial reporting, and it must determine responsibility when it occurs. The AICPA's Audit Standards Board frequently considers standards for prevention and detection of fraudulent reporting, and a number of new auditing standards have been issued in response to the recommendations of the Treadway Report. Disclosures required by the SEC, such as the item on disagreements on accounting disclosures, are another attempt at preventing the issuance of potentially misleading financial statements.

The auditor's responsibility to detect fraudulent reporting has not been fully resolved. The profession is generally of the opinion that it is not the responsibility of the auditor to detect fraud, beyond what is revealed with the diligent application of generally accepted auditing standards. In litigation, however, the auditor is often one of the parties sued. The issue is what the auditor should have detected in the audit and what is beyond the scope of detection through normal procedures. The legal system will continue to play a leading role in defining auditor responsibility in this area.

｜CONCEPT REVIEW

1. Describe what might appear in a summary of significant accounting policies. Why is this summary important?
2. What are the disclosures required for a related party transaction?
3. Under what kinds of circumstances might fraudulent financial reporting occur?

｜SEGMENT REPORTING

Before studying the procedures for segment reporting and why segment information might be important, we reproduce a portion of Coca-Cola Company's line-of-business and operations disclosures Note 18:

(amounts in millions)

Line of Business	Beverages	Foods
1995 Operating Revenues	$16,350	$1,613
1995 Operating Income	4,594	(14)

Perhaps it is not surprising to learn that over 90 percent of Coke's total revenues are from the beverages line of business, but it might be somewhat surprising to learn that Coke has a $1.6 billion foods line of business (primarily the Minute Maid fruit juice business), that lost $14 million in 1995. Knowing these facts and recalling the example that opened this chapter, we see why analysts consider line-of-business reporting very important.

In June 1997, the FASB issued *SFAS No. 131*, "Disclosures about Segments of an Enterprise and Related Information." This Standard supersedes the earlier pronouncement on this topic, *SFAS No. 14*, and is effective for fiscal years beginning after December 15, 1997. *SFAS No. 131* also supersedes several other Standards dealing with specific segment reporting issues.

SFAS No. 131 applies to public companies that have issued debt or equity securities that are traded in a public market, or that provide financial statements for the purpose of issuing any class of securities in a public market. It does not apply to not-for-profit organizations or nonpublic companies.

Definition of Reportable Operating Segments

SFAS No. 131 uses a modified management approach to identify potentially reportable segments. The fundamental idea is that the way a company is organized for management of its various business activities and the financial information that is used for managing those operations should determine the segment information to be reported. The focus is on the financial information that a company's management uses to make decisions about the operations of the company. This management approach is modified so as to require reporting on a reasonable number of segments. If too many segments are identified, aggregation criteria are used to develop a smaller number of reportable segments. Quantitative thresholds are used to determine the minimum size of operating segments that must be reported.

Defining Operating Segments   The business components that are established by management for making operating decisions and assessing performance are called **operating segments.** More specifically, *SFAS No. 131* defines an operating segment as a component of a company:

- That engages in business activities from which it may earn revenues and incur expenses (including transactions with other components of the company).
- Whose operating results are regularly reviewed by the company's "chief operating decision maker" to make segment resource allocation decisions and to assess segment performance.
- For which discrete financial information is available.

Not every part of a company is necessarily part of an operating segment. For example, components that do not earn revenues (e.g., corporate headquarters) or that earn revenues that are only incidental to the central activities of the company are not operating segments.

The term "chief operating decision maker" is not a job title, but rather is used to identify the manager whose function is to allocate resources and assess the performance of the segment. It may be the chief executive officer or the chief operating officer, or it may consist of a group including the company's president, executive vice presidents, and others.

Usually an operating segment will have a *segment manager* who is directly accountable to and maintains regular contact with the chief operating decision maker to discuss operating activities, financial results, forecasts or plans for the segment. A chief operating decision maker may be a segment manager. A single manager might be the segment manager for more than one operating segment. Sometimes there are overlapping sets of components for which managers are responsible. An example is where one set of managers is responsible for various products and services worldwide, while other managers are responsible for sales by geographic areas. In this case, *SFAS No. 131* suggests that components based on products and services be regarded as the operating segments.

Reportable Segments   A firm must report separate and specific information about each operating segment identified by the above definition, subject to several aggregation criteria and quantitative thresholds.

Aggregation Criteria   First, there are criteria for aggregating operating segments when the number of operating segments resulting from the above definition is so excessive that the level of detail is not useful to readers of financial statements and may be cumbersome to present. When this is the case, *SFAS No. 131* provides for aggregating the information from operating segments if the segments have similar economic characteristics and are similar in *each* of the following areas:

- The nature of the products and services.
- The nature of the production processes.
- The type or class of customer for the products and services.
- The methods used to distribute products and services.
- If applicable, the nature of the regulatory environment.

Example   A retail chain has 9 stores, each of which meets the definition of an operating segment, but each store is essentially the same as the others. In this case it would be appropriate to aggregate the results of the 9 stores into a single reportable segment.

Quantitative Thresholds   In addition to meeting the definition of an operating segment, there also are several quantitative thresholds which determine the operating segments that must be separately *reported*. A company must report information about an operating segment if the segment meets *any* of the following three thresholds:

1. Its reported revenue, including both sales to external and internal customers, is 10 percent or more of the combined revenue, internal and external, of all reported operating segments.
2. The absolute amount of its reported profit or loss is 10 percent or more of the greater, in absolute amount, of
   a. the combined reported profit of all operating segments that did not report a loss, or
   b. the combined reported loss of all operating segments that did report a loss.
3. Its assets are 10 percent or more of the combined assets of all operating segments.

Additional Aggregation   A company may combine information about operating segments not meeting the quantitative thresholds with information about other such segments to produce a reportable segment, but only if the operating segments share a majority of the aggregation criteria listed above. However, if the total of the external revenue reported by operating segments is less than 75 percent of the total revenue, additional operating segments must be individually identified as reportable segments until at least 75 percent of total consolidated revenue is included in reportable segments.

Information about operating segments that are not reportable segments, and other business activities are combined and disclosed in an "all other" category. The sources of revenue for the "all other" category must be described.

There is a practical limit to the number of reportable segments beyond which segment information is overly detailed. *SFAS No. 131* does not establish a precise limit, but does suggest that when the number of reportable segments increases above 10, a company should consider whether a practical limit has been reached.

Example   (adapted from Appendix B of *SFAS No. 131*)   In 1998 Diversified Products Incorporated as a company has total revenue of $31,000, profit before income taxes of $3,070, and total assets of $85,000. Assume Diversified Products has identified eight operating segments as candidates for reporting, based on the definition of an operating segment, with the following segment specific financial information:

Operating Segment	Intersegment Revenue	External Segment Revenue	Total Segment Revenue	Pretax Operating Profit (Loss)	Identifiable Assets
Auto parts	$ —	$ 8,000	$ 8,000	$ 270	$ 7,000
Software production and sales	3,000	6,500	9,500	900	3,000
Software consulting	—	200	200	100	100
Electronics production and sales	1,500	10,500	12,000	2,300	12,000
Electronics equipment rental	—	300	300	100	1,000
Real estate	—	400	400	(150)	600
Warehouse leasing	—	100	100	50	300
Finance	—	5,000	5,000	500	57,000
Totals	$4,500	$31,000	$35,500	$4,070	$81,000

The quantitative threshold tests are:

Revenue Test   Any operating segment with revenue equal to or greater than $3,550 (10% × $35,500) meets the test. Auto parts, Software production and sales, Electronics production and sales, and Finance meet the threshold and are required to be separately reported.

Operating Profit Test   The criterion for this test is 10% of the greater of (1) the absolute value of combined profit for segments reporting a profit: 10% × ($4,070 + $150) or $422, and (2) the absolute value of the combined loss for segments reporting a loss: 10% × $150 or $15. Therefore, the criterion amount is $422. Segments with operating profit (loss) greater than $422 must be reported separately. Software production and sales, Electronics production and sales, and Finance meet the threshold and are required to be separately reported. The only segment to report a loss is real estate. The absolute value of the loss, $150, does not exceed $422. Therefore, the real estate segment does not meet the operating profit test.

Identifiable Assets Test   Any operating segment with identifiable assets greater than $8,100 (10% × $81,000) must be separately reported, thus Finance must be reported.

The four reporting segments thus are: Auto parts, Software production and sales, Electronics production and sales, and Finance. Four operating segments do not meet the threshold amounts and do not need to be reported separately.

However, if combined external operating segment revenues are less than 75 percent of total external company revenue, or $23,250 (75% × $31,000) for Diversified, then additional segments must be identified. The sum of the external revenues for the reportable segments is $30,000 ($8,000 + $6,500 + $10,500 + $5,000), thus 96.8% ($30,000/$31,000) of the total reported revenue is included in the reportable segments. The 75 percent requirement is met without considering additional aggregation of operating segments in this case. If the 75 percent test were not met, management must identify additional individual segments, even though they do not meet any of the three quantitative thresholds, until the 75 percent test is met.

The segments and other business activities that are not separately reported are combined into an "all other" category for reporting purposes.

Required Segment Disclosures

A firm must provide several descriptive and quantitative disclosures of information about its reportable segments:

1. The factors used to identify the company's reportable segments must be described, including the company's basis or organization. The disclosure would describe whether the company is organized around products and services, geographic areas, regulatory environments, or a combination of factors, and whether operating segments have been aggregated.

2. A description of the types of products and services from which each segment derives its revenues.

3. A measure of profit or loss, and total assets is required for each reportable segment. To support these disclosures, information about the measurement of segment profit or loss and of segment assets also is required. These include an explanation of:
- The basis of accounting for any transactions between reportable segments.
- The nature of any differences between the measurement of segment profit or loss and the firm's reported income before income taxes.
- The nature of any difference between the measurement of segment assets and the firm's assets.
- The nature of any change from measurement methods used in prior periods to determine reported segment profit or loss (including the effect of the change).
- The nature and effect of any asymmetrical allocations to segments (such as allocating depreciation expense to a segment without allocating the related depreciable assets to that segment).

Example   The following is an illustration of the kinds of descriptive information that would be disclosed by Diversified Products:

Factors used to identify reportable segments   Diversified Products' reportable segments are strategic business units that offer different products and services. They are managed separately because each business requires different technology and marketing strategies.

Description of products and services   Diversified Products has four reportable segments: auto parts, software, electronics, and finance. The auto parts segment produces replacement parts for sale to auto parts retailers. The software segment produces application software for sale to computer manufacturers and retailers. The electronics segment produces integrated circuits and related products for sale to computer manufacturers. The finance segment is responsible for portions of the company's financial operations including financing customer purchases of products.

Measurement of segment profit (loss) and segment assets   The accounting policies of the segments are the same as those described in the summary of significant accounting policies except that pension expense for each segment is recognized and measured on the basis of cash payments to the pension plan.

Diversified Products accounts for intersegment sales and transfers as if the sales or transfers were to independent third parties at current market prices.

Quantitative Information   The required quantitative information that must be disclosed includes a measure of profit or loss and of total assets for each reportable segment. Any of the following items that are included in the measure of segment profit or loss that is reviewed by the chief operating decision maker must also be reported:

- Revenues from external customers.
- Revenues from transactions with other operating segments.
- Interest revenue.
- Interest expense.
- Depreciation, depletion, and amortization expenses.
- Any unusual items as defined by *APB Opinion No. 30*.
- Equity in the net income of investees accounted for by equity method.
- Income tax expense or benefit.
- Extraordinary items.
- Significant noncash items other than depreciation, depletion and amortization expense.

In addition, the following are to be disclosed for each reportable segment if the chief operating decision maker uses the amounts in determining the amount of segment assets:

- The amount of investment in equity method investees.
- Total expenditures for additions to long-lived assets (other than financial instruments, long-term customer relationships of a financial institution, mortgage and other servicing rights, deferred policy acquisition costs, and deferred tax assets).

Example   The following is an illustration of the quantitative information that would be disclosed by Diversified Products:

Operating profit (loss) information   Diversified does not allocate income taxes or unusual items to segments. Amounts reported to the chief operating decision maker include:

	Auto Parts	Software	Electronics	Finance	All Other	Totals
Total segment revenues.	$8,000	$9,500	$12,000	$ 5,000	$1,000*	$35,500
Intersegment revenues	—	3,000	1,500	—	—	4,500
Interest revenue.	1,250	1,000	1,500	—	—	3,750
Interest expense	950	700	1,100	—	—	2,750
Net interest revenue	—	—	—	1,000	—	1,000
Depreciation and						
amortization	300	50	1,500	1,100	50	3,000
Segment profit	270	900	2,300	500	100	4,070
Segment assets	7,000	3,000	12,000	57,000	2,000	81,000
Expenditures for						
segment assets	1,000	500	800	600	—	2,900

*Revenues from segments below the quantitative thresholds are attributable to four operating segments: a small real estate business, an electronics equipment rental business, a software consulting practice, and a warehouse leasing operation.

Reconciliations   Several reconciliations between the reportable segment amounts and firm reported amounts must be disclosed:

- The total of the segments' revenues to the firm's total revenues.
- The total of the segments' assets to the firm's total assets.
- The total of the segments' measures of profit or loss to the firm's income before income taxes.[2]
- The total of the segments' amount for any other significant items of information that the firm discloses to the firm's corresponding amount.

All significant reconciling items must be separately identified and disclosed.

Example   The following is an illustration of the reconciliations that would be disclosed by Diversified Products:

Reconciliations

Reconciliations for revenues, income before income taxes, total assets and other significant items are:

Revenues

Total revenues for reportable segments	$34,500
Other revenues	1,000
Less: intersegment revenues	(4,500)
Total company reported revenues	$31,000

Profit or Loss

Total profit for reportable segments	$ 3,970
Other profit or loss	100
Elimination of intersegment profits	(500)
Unallocated amounts:	
Litigation settlement received	500
Other corporate expenses	(750)
Adjustment to pension expense	(250)
Company total income before income taxes	$ 3,070

Assets

Total assets for reportable segments	$79,000
Other assets	2,000
Elimination of receivables from corporate headquarters	(1,000)
Goodwill not allocated to segments	4,000
Other unallocated amounts	1,000
Company total assets	$85,000

Other Significant Items	Segment Totals	Adjustments[†]	Company Totals
Interest revenue	$3,750	$ 75	$3,825
Interest expense	2,750	(50)	$2,700
Net interest revenue	1,000	—	1,000
Expenditures for assets	2,900	1,000	3,900
Depreciation and amortization	3,000	—	3,000

[†]Adjustments relate to items earned by or incurred for corporate headquarters. These items are not allocated to segments.

Other Firmwide Disclosures

All firms, including firms that have only one reportable segment, are required to provide additional information about revenues from its products and services, about its geographic areas of operation, and about its major customers, unless this information is already provided as part of the reportable segment information.

Products and Services Information   A firm must report the revenues from external customers for each product and service or each group of similar products and services unless

---

[2] If a firm allocates items such as income taxes or extraordinary items to segments, it may choose to reconcile the total of the segments' measures of profit or loss to the firm's income after those items.

it is impractical to do so. If providing this information is impractical, this fact is to be disclosed.

Geographic Area Information   A firm must also report revenues from external customers (*a*) from the home country of the firm, and (*b*) from all foreign countries in total. If the revenues are material from any one foreign country, those revenues are to be disclosed separately. Likewise, the firm must disclose the total of long-lived assets (*a*) located in the firm's home country, and (*b*) located in foreign countries. If the assets in an individual foreign country are material, they are to be disclosed separately. A firm can also provide subtotals for groups of countries if it so chooses.

Example   The following is an illustration of the geographic information that would be disclosed by Diversified Products:

Geographic Disclosures

	Revenues	Long-lived Assets
United States.	$19,000	$11,000
Canada	4,200	—
Taiwan	3,400	6,500
Japan	2,900	3,500
Other foreign countries	1,500	3,000
Totals	$31,000	$24,000

Major Customers   If revenues from a single customer amount to 10 percent or more of the firm's revenues, the firm must disclose this fact, including the total amount of revenues from each such customer, and the identity of the segment or segments reporting the revenues. It is not necessary to report the identity of the major customers.

Example   The following is an illustration of the major customer information that would be disclosed by Diversified Products:

Major Customers

Revenues from one customer of Diversified Products' software and electronics segments represents approximately $5,000 of the company's consolidated revenues.

Concluding Comments   *SFAS No. 131* should result in more useful segment information because it uses the management approach rather than a line of business approach. General Motors, for example, would likely have treated all of its automobile divisions as one line of business under the superseded *SFAS No. 14*. If the management approach is used, it may be the case that General Motors will treat its various divisions (Buick, Cadillac, Chevrolet, Oldsmobile, and Pontiac) as reported operating segments if the company is organized this way and the divisions meet the threshold criteria.

On the other hand, some of the reported segment information may not be easily understood if it is prepared using measurement rules that are not GAAP. The FASB attempts to minimize the cost to the firm of preparing segment information by requiring disclosure of information on revenues, operating profit (loss) and segment assets measured on the same basis used by the chief operating decision maker for allocating resources and assessing performance. If firms use a wide range of measurement bases other than GAAP for internal reporting, and these various measurement bases are used for presenting segment information, the segment information may not be comparable across firms. It is important for the financial statement reader to understand the measurement basis used in preparing segment information.

INTERIM REPORTS

The accounting period required for financial reporting is the fiscal year of the firm. *Annual* financial statements, however, do not generally provide the most timely information for investors. Firms often issue **interim reports,** usually quarterly, to provide more timely information.

Reporting more frequently than once each fiscal year gives rise to a new set of financial reporting problems. For example, many retailers do a large percentage of their business in the fourth quarter of the calendar year, the holiday season. Results of the fourth quarter often determine whether the firm will make a profit. In preparing quarterly reports for such a firm, the accountant must decide which costs to expense in the first three quarters and which costs are more appropriately capitalized and expensed in the fourth quarter.

APB Opinion No. 28, "Interim Financial Reporting," was issued in 1973 to provide guidance. It does not require firms to prepare interim financial statements, although the SEC requires quarterly Form 10-Q for publicly traded companies. Various exchanges also require listed firms to prepare interim financial reports for public distribution.

Interim financial statements, if they are reported, may consist of only summarized financial data. The minimum data to be reported include

- Sales, income taxes, and net income.
- Disposal of a segment of a business, extraordinary items, and unusual or infrequently occurring items.
- Basic and diluted earnings per share.
- Seasonal revenue, costs, or expenses.
- Significant changes in estimates or provisions for income taxes.
- Changes in accounting principles or estimates.
- Significant changes in financial position.

Interim Reporting and Segment Reporting

When a company with reportable segments issues interim condensed financial statements, *SFAS No. 131* requires that the interim reports provide the following segment information for each reportable segment:

- Revenues for external customers.
- Intersegment revenues.
- A measure of segment profit or loss.

In addition, a reconciliation of total reportable segment profit or loss to the firm's income before taxes is required. When there has been a material change in segment total assets from the amount disclosed in the last annual report, the new total assets amount is to be disclosed. Also, a description of differences, if any, in the basis of segmentation or in basis of measurement of segment profit or loss is to be described and disclosed.

Issues in Interim Reporting

Preparing interim reports presents difficulties for several reasons, including

- Seasonality of revenues, costs, and expenses.
- Major costs that occur in one interim period but benefit other interim periods within the same reporting year.
- Seasonality of production activities.

- Extraordinary items and accounting changes that occur in one interim period.
- Selection of appropriate income tax rates for each interim period.
- LIFO inventory that is liquidated during one or more interim periods but is expected to be restored before the end of the reporting year.

There are two opposing conceptual views on treatment of the interim period:

1. **Discrete view.** Each interim period is viewed as a basic reporting period. It stands alone and not as a part of a longer (that is, annual) reporting period. According to this view, revenue and expense recognition, accruals, and deferrals for the interim period follow the same principles and procedures as for an annual period. There are no interim-period allocations. Thus, an expense incurred in one interim period would not be allocated to other interim periods.

2. **Integral-part view.** Each interim period is viewed as an integral part of the annual reporting period. Revenue and expense recognition, deferrals, and accruals are affected by judgments made at the end of each interim period about the results of operations for the remainder of the reporting period. Thus, an expense incurred in one interim period may be allocated among other interim periods within the reporting year.

APB Opinion No. 28 basically adopts the second conceptual perspective and states that "each interim period should be viewed primarily as an integral part of the annual period." The *Opinion* does, however, make some practical concessions on this point.

Guidelines for Preparing Interim Financial Reports

APB Opinion No. 28 provides guidelines for preparing interim reports:
- The accounting principles and practices used by the firm in preparing its annual financial statements should be used for interim reports, with certain modifications (discussed below).
- Revenue from products and services sold should be recognized as earned during the interim period on the same basis as followed for the annual period.
- Costs and expenses for interim periods:
    Costs *directly* associated with interim revenue are reported in the interim period.
    Costs and expenses *not directly* associated with interim revenue must be allocated to interim periods on a reasonable basis.

Costs Directly Associated with Revenue

The discrete view is used to report revenue. Costs directly associated with revenue, such as costs of goods sold, wages, salaries, fringe benefits, and warranties, should be expensed in the interim period in which the related revenue is recognized, with some exceptions and disclosure:
- Use of the gross margin method (discussed in Chapter 10) for computing cost of goods sold must be disclosed.
- If LIFO is used and if inventory is liquidated during an interim period and is expected to be restored by year-end, cost of goods sold for the interim period should reflect the anticipated replacement cost of the units liquidated, and an estimated liability account should be recognized.
- Declines in inventory value, unless temporary, should not be deferred to future interim periods; recovery in later interim periods should be recognized as gains, but not in excess of the previously recognized losses.

Costs Not Directly Associated with Revenue

All costs not directly associated with revenue should be reported for interim periods as follows:
- A cost should be recognized as an expense in the interim period in which it was incurred, or be allocated among interim periods on the basis of an estimate of time expired, benefit received, or activity associated with the periods.
- Arbitrary allocation of such costs should not be made. Costs that cannot be allocated reasonably should be assigned to the interim period in which they were incurred.
- Gains and losses that arise in an interim period should be recognized in the interim period in which they arise if they would not normally be deferred at year-end.

- Income tax expense for each interim period should be based on an estimate of the annual rate as of the end of each quarter. The income tax expense for the current interim period is the difference between the income tax expense computed on year-to-date income from operations and the total income tax expense reported on prior interim reports for the fiscal year.

Unusual or infrequently occurring items and extraordinary items should be recognized in the interim period in which they occur. Similarly, contingent losses not directly associated with revenue and the related liabilities, should be recognized in the interim period in which they occur. Accounting changes are accounted for and reported in essentially the same manner as in annual periods.

Interim Reporting Illustrated

Assume these data for the first quarter (ended March 31, 1998) for the Gilmore Corporation:

Selected Items	Amount
Sales of products and services	$500,000
Interest revenue	1,000
Extraordinary loss	15,000
Correction of 1997 accounting error (credit)	6,000
Cost of goods sold	241,000
Operating assets, cost (10-year remaining useful life, no residual value, straight-line)	480,000
Salary and wage expense	89,000
Inventory allowance change, LCM (temporary)	4,000
Advertising expense (benefits first and second quarters equally)	18,000
Annual property tax for 1998 (estimated)	12,000
Contribution to United Fund for 1998	6,000
Shipping expense	7,000
Unusual loss	4,000
Retained earnings, 12/31/97	100,000
Estimated average annual income tax rate, 30 percent, reporting period ends December 31	
30,000 common shares outstanding	

Exhibit 25–4 illustrates quarterly interim statements that meet the reporting requirements of *APB Opinion No. 28*. The statements distinguish between costs directly related to interim revenue and other costs not directly related to interim revenue. Both sales of products and interest revenue are direct and thus recognized in full in the interim period. Cost of goods sold and salaries and wages are recognized in full because they relate directly to the revenues recognized. Depreciation expense is allocated on the basis of time. There is no recognition of the inventory decline because it is viewed as temporary. If it were viewed as permanent, the full amount would be recorded as an expense in the current interim period. Advertising expense is allocated over the two periods expected to benefit from this item. The remaining $9,000 of advertising outlay is capitalized as an asset on the interim balance sheet. Similarly, the property tax item is allocated equally to each of the four quarters: ($12,000 × 1/4), or $3,000 per quarter. The contribution is expensed for the quarter because it is not related to operations and there is no reasonable basis for allocation. The shipping expense and unusual loss are both recognized in the current quarter. The estimate of the annual tax rate is used to determine income tax expense for the interim period. The income statement shows intraperiod tax allocation of the income tax expense of $34,500: $39,000 to continuing operations, and $4,500 tax savings with the extraordinary loss.

While *APB Opinion No. 28* provides some guidance for interim reporting, many issues remain. One is the auditor's role in interim reporting. Most auditors are reluctant to express an opinion on interim financial statements because the data are subjective and involve more estimation and allocation than is required for annual reports. Yet more users of interim financial statements want the auditor to provide assurance that the published data are accurate and in accordance with generally accepted accounting standards. As information processing costs continue to decrease, the effect will likely be an increasing demand for interim financial reporting. Interim reports are becoming increasingly important as a valuable source of information for investors.

EXHIBIT 25–4

Interim (quarterly) Income Statement and Retained Earnings Statement for Gilmore Corporation

GILMORE CORPORATION
Income Statement
For Quarter Ending March 31, 1998

Revenues:	
Sales of products and services	$500,000
Interest revenue	1,000
Total revenue	501,000
Expenses:	
Cost of goods sold	241,000
Salaries and wages	89,000
Depreciation expense ($480,000 ÷ 10)(3/12)	12,000
Inventory decline, LCM	–0–
Advertising expense	9,000
Contributions	6,000
Property tax expense	3,000
Shipping expense	7,000
Unusual loss	4,000
Income tax expense*	39,000
Total expenses	410,000
Income before extraordinary item	91,000
Extraordinary loss (net of $4,500 income tax)	10,500
Net income	$ 80,500
Basic and diluted earnings per share (30,000 common shares outstanding):	
Income before extraordinary items ($91,000/30,000 shares)	$ 3.03
Extraordinary loss ($10,500/30,000)	(.35)
Net income ($80,500/30,000)	$ 2.68

Retained Earnings Statement
For Quarter Ending March 31, 1998

Beginning balance (given)	$100,000
Prior period adjustment, error correction (net of $1,800 tax)	4,200
Balance, as adjusted	104,200
Net income	80,500
Ending balance	$184,700

*(Revenues − Expenses before Income Tax) × 0.30 = ($501,000 − $371,000) × 0.30 = $39,000

CONCEPT REVIEW

1. Explain the difference between the discrete view and the integral-part view of accounting measurement in interim reporting.
2. Suppose a firm that operates a ski resort is preparing to issue a second-quarter interim report. The firm has just completed a $100,000 advertising campaign, which it expects to generate revenues in the third and fourth quarters. How would this item be accounted for under the discrete view? Under the integral-part view?
3. Provide two examples of costs not directly associated with revenues.

SUMMARY OF KEY POINTS

(L.O. 1)

1. The principle of *full disclosure* calls for the disclosure of any financial information potentially significant enough to influence the judgment of an informed reader. There is some danger in taking this principle too far, which can result in *information overload* for the reader.

(L.O. 2)   2. The SEC is the final authority for determining reporting standards for publicly traded companies. Form 10-K is the primary annual financial report that publicly traded companies must file with the SEC.

(L.O. 3)   3. Notes to financial statements are an integral part of the statements. Financial statements are incomplete without the appropriate note disclosures.

(L.O. 3)   4. *APB Opinion No. 22* requires firms to include in the financial statements a summary of significant accounting policies. The disclosure must include a description of selections made from acceptable alternatives, principles and methods of accounting measurement particular to the industry, and any unusual or innovative application of GAAP.

(L.O. 3)   5. There are special disclosure requirements for related party transactions, errors and irregularities, and illegal acts.

(L.O. 4)   6. *SFAS No. 131* requires that publicly held firms organized in operating segments report various information on the activities of its segments meeting several quantitative thresholds.

(L.O. 4)   7. If any one of the following thresholds is met by an operating segment, the segment must be separately reported: (*a*) the segment revenue, including sales to external customers and intersegment sales is 10 percent or more of the combined revenue, external and internal for all segments, (*b*) the operating segment assets are 10 percent or more of the combined assets of all operating segments, or (*c*) the operating segment reported profit or loss is 10 percent or more of the greater of the absolute total of all segment reported profit or the absolute total of all segment reported losses.

(L.O. 4)   8. *SFAS No. 131* requires disclosure of (*a*) revenues from and (*b*) long-lived assets located in (i) the firm's country of domicile, and (ii) all foreign countries in total. When revenues or long-lived assets located in any individual foreign country are material, these revenues and long-lived assets must be separately reported.

(L.O. 4)   9. Segment reporting is not required for nonpublic firms.

(L.O. 5)   10. Interim reports are required by the SEC and some stock exchanges, but are not required by accounting standards. If they are presented, they should be prepared according to the same accounting policies used for annual reports. The interim report can contain summary information that is less comprehensive than that presented in an annual financial statement. The information required for an interim report is specified in *APB Opinion No. 28*.

(L.O. 5)   11. *APB Opinion No. 28* primarily requires the integral-part view in preparing interim reports. This view results in allocations of items between interim periods that are not normally allocated across fiscal periods in annual financial statements.

UNDERSTANDING AND APPLYING CONCEPTS AND STANDARDS

QUESTIONS

1. What are some sources of information about a company other than the financial statements?
2. What is information overload? Why is it a problem?
3. What is the full disclosure principle? Why has note disclosure increased substantially over the past decade?
4. What is the purpose of notes to the financial statements?
5. What is the purpose of the Securities and Exchange Commission? Which specific offices and divisions are concerned with accounting matters?
6. What is Form 10-K? What firms must prepare a Form 10-K? When must Form 10-K be filed? What information items must be included in Form 10-K?
7. In recent years, many firms regulated by the SEC have included a management discussion and analysis section in the annual report to shareholders. Describe what is included in the MDA section.
8. What are the accounting policies of a company? What, if any, are the requirements for disclosing information about accounting policies?
9. What must a firm disclose about related party transactions?
10. What is the basic rationale for requiring segment reporting? What are the arguments against segment reporting?
11. *SFAS No. 131* requires disclosures in three areas: operating segments, geographic areas, and major customers. Are these three areas independent of each other? When might they be? When might they not be?
12. What is the difference, if any, between the terms *operating segment* and *reportable segment?* Explain how each is determined.
13. What are the criteria used to determine whether operating segments can be combined into a single segment? When the reportable segments do not account for at least 75 percent of the firm's reported revenue, how are these aggregation criteria used to increase the amount of revenue included in reportable operation segments?

14. Briefly describe the alternative tests for determining a reportable segment.
15. What is interim reporting? Why is it potentially important?
16. What is the difference between the discrete view and the integral-part view of interim financial reporting periods?
17. Should income statement items that are separately classified, such as extraordinary items, be prorated over interim reporting periods or recognized in a single interim period?
18. What items are required to be included in both the Form 10-K and the annual report to shareholders?
19. At a minimum, what information items should be included in an interim financial report?

| EXERCISES

E 25–1
(L.O. 5)

Interim Reporting   In January 1998, management of Clip Inc. estimates that its year-end bonus to executives will be $500,000 for 1998. The amount paid in 1997 was $440,000. The final determination of the amount to be paid is made at the conclusion of the fiscal year.

Required

Determine the amount, if any, of bonus expense that should be reflected in Clip's quarterly income statement for the three months ending March 31, 1998. Justify and explain your answer.

E 25–2
(L.O. 5)

Interim Reporting   In September 1998, Crystal Mountain Ski Resorts spent $300,000 for advertising for the coming ski season. The ski season lasts from October through the following March, with business expected to be spread evenly over this period. The fiscal year for Crystal Mountain ends March 31, 1999.

Required

Determine the amount of expense that should be included in Crystal Mountain's interim financial statements for September 30 and for December 31, 1998. Justify and explain your answer.

E 25–3
(L.O. 5)

Interim Reporting   The Proctor Company reported income before income taxes of $100,000 and $150,000 in the first two quarters of 1998. Management's estimate of the annual effective tax rate was 35 percent at the end of the first quarter and 30 percent at the end of the second quarter.

Required

Determine the income tax expense for the first two quarters of 1998.

E 25–4
(L.O. 4)

Segment Reporting: Major Customer Disclosure   Montgomery Company operates as a single operating segment, but it has large sales to a small number of customers. In 1998, Montgomery had sales to customers as follows:

California Company	$16,000,000
Oregon Inc.	8,000,000
Montana Corp.	5,000,000
Arizona Company	4,000,000
Texas Inc.	3,000,000
Domestic governments	19,000,000
Foreign governments	14,500,000
Other sales	40,000,000

Additional information:
a. Other sales include sales to many customers, none of which exceeds $1,000,000.
b. Oregon Inc. and Arizona Company are both subsidiaries of Utah Incorporated. Direct sales to Utah total $1,000,000 and are included in *other sales*.
c. Sales to domestic governments include $14,000,000 to federal governmental agencies, with the remainder being to local governmental agencies.
d. Sales to foreign governments include $8,500,000 in sales to the Canadian government, with the remainder being to various other foreign governments, none more than $1,000,000.

Required

Determine the major customer disclosures that must be made in accordance with *SFAS No. 131*. Write a one-page memo to the chief financial officer, Georgia O'Keefe, explaining your answer and providing a sample disclosure to be included in the Montgomery Company financial statements.

E 25–5
(L.O. 4)

Segment Reporting   The Ullrich Products Corporation is organized in three major product divisions: Health care products, Agricultural products, and Food products. Within the Health care products division are three separately organized groups: pharmaceuticals, consumer health care, and medical devices. The Health care products division manager receives separate financial information from each group within the division for purposes of allocating resources and assessing performance. The chief executive officer of the company, Jan Ullrich, make similar decisions for all three divisions. In 1998 the company has revenues of $12,300,000, which includes interest revenue of $100,000 that is not allocated to any of the divisions. Total companywide income before taxes is $1,500,000 after deducting all expenses, including some that are not allocated to the divisions. The corporation has total assets of $22,000,000, some of which are headquarters facilities not included in any of the divisions. Intercompany sales are priced at market prices, and profits on intersegment sales total $50,000 in 1998. The same accounting procedures used for corporate financial reporting are used in measuring sales, profits, and assets at the division and group level of the organization. Specific division and group level financial information provided to management for 1998 is as follows (all amounts are in thousands):

Health Care Products Groups

	Pharmaceuticals	Consumer Health Care	Medical Devices	Total Health Care Products Division
Sales to external customers	$ 6,000	$3,000	$1,200	$10,200
Intersegment sales	500	0	0	500
Income (loss) before taxes	1,800	200	(400)	1,600
Segment assets as of Dec. 31.	10,000	3,500	1,500	15,000
Depreciation & amortization	300	100	100	500
Capital expenditures	400	200	100	700

	Agricultural Products Division	Food Products Division
Sales to external customers	$1,000	$1,000
Intersegment sales	0	700
Income (loss) before taxes	200	100
Segment assets as of Dec. 31.	4,000	2,000
Depreciation & amortization[†]	150	100
Capital expenditures*	200	200

[†]An additional depreciation of $50 on headquarters facilities is not included in segment amounts.

*An additional $200 of capital expenditures was incurred for facilities for headquarters.

Required

1. Assume all the groups within the Health care products qualify as operating segments, as do the Agricultural products and the Food products divisions. Determine which are the reportable operating segments.
2. Show the quantitative information that is required to be reported under *SFAS No. 131* for Ullrich for 1998. All revenues, expenses, or assets not included above as part of an operating segment are unallocated corporate items.

E 25–6
(L.O. 4)

Identify Reporting Segments and Major Customers   Keefe Corporation has expanded rapidly, and segment reporting has become an accounting issue. The company has no intersegment sales. The following data are available for the 1998 fiscal year which ended on December 31 (amounts in millions):

Operating Segments	Total Segment Revenues	Operating Profit (Loss)	Identifiable Assets
A	$620	$200	$400
B	100	20	80
C	340	70	300
D	190	(30)	140
E	180	(25)	180
F	70	10	120
G	120	(20)	140
All others	380	(25)	140

The "all others" includes five operating segments, none with revenues or assets greater than $80 million and none with an operating profit.

Operating segments A and B have very similar products and production processes, but serve different customer types and use quite different product distribution systems. This is partly because operating segment B is in a regulated environment but operating segment A is not. Also, operating segments F and G have very similar products, production processes, and product distribution systems, but are organized as separate divisions because they serve substantially different types of customers. Neither F or G is in a regulated environment.

Required

1. Determine what are reportable segments without regard to aggregation criteria.
2. If the requirements for reportable segments are not yet met, apply appropriate aggregation criteria to identify additional reportable segments.
3. Assume Keefe has sales totaling $220 million to the U.S. Federal government primarily from operating segments A and C. Other significant customers include annual revenues of $190 million from Ikon Tech-

nology (primarily sales of segment D), and $100 million in sales by segment E to the French government. What, if any, disclosures must Keefe make regarding major customers? Show the disclosure Keefe must make.

E 25–7
(L.O. 5)

Interim Reporting: Application of Guidelines   In the context of interim reporting, items may (*a*) be recognized in the interim statements of the current interim period, (*b*) be recognized in the current interim period but require special disclosure, (*c*) be deferred in their entirety (that is, not recognized until some later interim period, or not recognized at all), or (*d*) be amortized or accrued (recognized partly in the current interim period and partly in subsequent interim periods). A number of items are listed below that require a decision on how they should be incorporated on interim statements. Match the letters given above with the numbered items given below to indicate how each item should be incorporated on the interim statements.

1. Salaries allocable to services rendered during the current period.
2. Inventories estimated by use of the gross margin method.
3. Temporary declines in market value of inventories.
4. Short-term stock investment gains from recoveries of market value (not in excess of previously recognized market declines).
5. Materials and wages allocable to products sold this period.
6. Costs benefiting two or more interim periods.
7. Increase in gross margin due to liquidation of a layer of LIFO-based inventory expected to be replenished by year-end.
8. Quantity discounts allowed to customers based on the annual volume of their purchases.
9. Contingencies and other uncertainties that may affect fairness of presentation.
10. Income tax on income of first quarter where total income for the first quarter puts the company in a low tax bracket; subsequent operations are expected to be sufficiently profitable that by end of second quarter, and thereafter taxable income of the company will be in a higher bracket.

E 25–8
(L.O. 4)

Industry Segment Disclosure   Operating profit and loss figures for the seven industries in which the Sheets Company operates are:

	1997 Operating Profit (Loss)
Industry 1	$1,075,000
Industry 2	200,000
Industry 3	550,000
Industry 4	(208,000)
Industry 5	(18,000)
Industry 6	5,000
Industry 7	(2,000)
	$1,602,000

Required

Identify those industries that meet the operating profit or loss criteria to be a reportable segment for 1997.

E 25–9
(L.O. 5)

Interim Reporting   *APB Opinion No. 28,* "Interim Financial Reporting" states that "each interim period should be viewed primarily as an integral part of an annual period." It goes on to state

In general, the results for each interim period should be based on the accounting principles and practices used by an enterprise in the preparation of its latest annual financial statements unless a change in an accounting practice or policy has been adopted in the current year. However, the [APB] concluded that certain accounting principles and practices followed for annual reporting purposes may require modification at interim reporting dates so that the reported results for the interim period may better relate to the results of operations for the annual period.

Required

Below are six independent cases on how accounting facts might be reported on a company's interim financial reports. State whether the proposed method would be acceptable under generally accepted accounting principles applicable to interim financial data. Support your answer with a brief explanation.

1. Cup Company management was reasonably certain it would have an employee strike in the third quarter. As a result, it shipped heavily during the second quarter but plans to defer the recognition of the sales in excess of the normal sales. The deferred sales will be recognized as sales in the third quarter, when the strike is in progress. Management thinks this is more representative of normal second- and third-quarter operations.

2. Glass Company takes a physical inventory at year-end for annual financial statement purposes. Inventory and cost of sales reported in interim quarterly statements are based on estimated gross profit rates because a physical inventory would result in a temporary shutdown of operations. Glass Company has reliable perpetual inventory records.
3. Taylor Company is planning to report one-fourth of its annual pension expense each quarter.
4. Temple Company wrote down inventory to reflect lower of cost or market in the first quarter of this year. At year-end, the market exceeds the original acquisition cost of this inventory. Consequently, management plans to write the inventory back up to its original cost as a year-end adjustment.
5. Tall Company realized a large gain on the sale of investments at the beginning of the second quarter. The company wants to report one-third of the gain in each of the remaining quarters.
6. Dill Company has estimated its annual audit fee. Management plans to prorate this expense equally over the four quarters.

(CMA adapted)

E 25–10
(L.O. 5)

Interim Reporting   The Dunn Manufacturing Company budgeted activities for 1998 are:

	Amount
Net sales (1,000,000 units)	$6,000,000
Cost of goods sold	(3,600,000)
Gross margin	2,400,000
Selling, general, and administrative expenses	(1,400,000)
Operating earnings	1,000,000
Nonoperating income	100,000
Earnings before income taxes	1,100,000
Estimated income taxes (current and deferred)	(385,000)
Net earnings	$ 715,000
Earnings per share of common stock	$7.15

Dunn has operated profitably for many years and has experienced a seasonal pattern of sales volume and production. Sales volume for 1998 is expected to follow a quarterly pattern of 10 percent, 20 percent, 35 percent, and 35 percent because of the seasonality of the industry. Due to production and storage capacity limitations, it is expected that production will follow a pattern of 20 percent, 25 percent, 30 percent, and 25 percent during the four quarters of 1998.

At the end of the first quarter of 1998, the controller of Dunn has prepared and issued the following interim report for public release:

	Amount
Net sales (100,000 units)	$ 600,000
Cost of goods sold	(360,000)
Gross margin	240,000
Selling, general, and administrative expenses	(290,000)
Operating loss	(50,000)
Loss from warehouse fire	(175,000)
Loss before income taxes	(225,000)
Estimated income taxes	0
Net loss	$(225,000)
Loss per share of common stock	$(2.25)

The following additional information is available for the first quarter, just completed, but was not included in the public information released:

a. The company uses a standard cost system in which standards are set at currently attainable levels on an annual basis. At the end of the first quarter, there was underapplied fixed factory overhead (volume variance) of $50,000 that was treated as an asset at the end of the quarter. Production during the quarter was 200,000 units, of which 100,000 were sold.
b. The selling, general, and administrative expenses were budgeted on a basis of $1,000,000 fixed expenses for the year plus 40 cents of variable expenses per unit of sales.

c. The warehouse fire loss met the conditions of an extraordinary loss. The warehouse had an undepreciated cost of $475,000, and $300,000 was recovered from insurance on the warehouse. No other gains or losses are anticipated this year from similar events or transactions, nor has Dunn had any similar losses in preceding years. The full loss will be deductible as an ordinary loss for income tax purposes.

d. The effective income tax rate, for federal and state taxes combined, is expected to average 35 percent of earnings before income taxes during 1998. There are no permanent differences between pretax accounting income and taxable income.

e. Earnings per share were computed on the basis of 100,000 shares of capital stock outstanding. Dunn has only one class of stock issued, no long-term debt outstanding, and no stock option plan.

Required

1. Do you agree and approve of the way Dunn has prepared its interim income statement? Why or why not?
2. Identify any weaknesses in the form and content of Dunn's interim report without reference to the additional information.
3. Without reference to the specific situation of Dunn Manufacturing, what are the standards of disclosure for interim financial data (published interim financial reports) for publicly traded companies? Explain.

ANALYSIS, JUDGMENT, AND COMMUNICATION

CASES

C 25–1
(L.O. 4)

Segment Reporting   Many financial analysts and professional accountants argue that firms should report segment data, while many managers argue strongly against such disclosures.
In a one- to two-page report, briefly outline:

a. The reasons for requiring financial reporting by segments.
b. The reasons against requiring financial reporting by segments.
c. The accounting difficulties in implementing segment reporting.

C 25–2
(L.O. 5)

Interim Reporting   The unaudited quarterly financial statements issued by many corporations are prepared on the same basis as annual statements, with some minor exceptions.

a. Under what circumstances would there be a difference between the basis used to prepare interim statements and that for annual statements?
b. Why are there problems in using interim statements to predict annual income?
c. How might quarterly income be affected by the behavior of costs incurred in the *repairs and maintenance of manufacturing equipment* account?

C 25–3
(L.O. 4)

Coca-Cola   Study the information in Notes 18 and 19 to the Coca-Cola financial statements. Answer the following questions, stating the reasoning and analysis that support your conclusions.

1. Does Coca-Cola appear to be expanding its Foods business? In what business does Coca-Cola appear to be investing most heavily? Why would the company be doing this?
2. For 1995, do all segments shown in Note 18 meet all the criteria for requiring a segment to be reported? Show your computations.
3. For 1995, in what geographic area does the firm earn the largest margin on sales? In what geographic area is the firm increasing its level of investment the fastest?

ANALYZING FINANCIAL STATEMENTS

A 25–1
(L.O. 4)

PepsiCo Inc.   Excerpts from the Industry Segments disclosures in the 1995 PepsiCo Inc. annual report follow:

Industry Segments

Net Sales		Growth Rate 1990–1995	1995	1994	1993
Beverages:	U.S.	7%	$ 6,977	$ 6,541	$ 5,918
	International	19%	3,571	3,146	2,720
		10%	10,548	9,687	8,638
Snack Foods:	U.S.	10%	5,495	5,011	4,365
	International	19%	3,050	3,253	2,662
		12%	8,545	8,264	7,027
Restaurants:	U.S.	11%	9,202	8,694	8,026
	International	25%	2,126	1,827	1,330
		13%	11,328	10,521	9,356

Combined Segments

	Growth Rate 1990–1995	1995	1994	1993
U.S.	9%	$21,674	$20,246	$18,309
International	20%	8,747	8,226	6,712
	12%	30,421	28,472	25,021
By U.S. Restaurant Chain				
Pizza Hut	8%	$ 3,977	$ 3,712	$ 3,595
Taco Bell	15%	3,503	3,340	2,855
KFC	9%	1,722	1,642	1,576
	11%	$ 9,202	$ 8,694	$ 8,026

Operating Profit

		Growth Rate 1990–1995	1995	1994	1993
Beverages:	U.S.	11%	$ 1,145	$ 1,022	$ 937
	International	19%	164	195	172
		12%	1,309	1,217	1,109
Snack Foods:	U.S.	9%	1,132	1,025	901
	International	14%	300	352	289
		10%	1,432	1,377	1,190
Restaurants:	U.S.	10%	451	659	685
	International	8%	(21)	71	93
		9%	430	730	778

Combined Segments

	Growth Rate 1990–1995	1995	1994	1993
U.S.	10%	$ 2,728	$ 2,706	$ 2,523
International	14%	433	618	554
	10%	3,171	3,324	3,077
Equity (Loss) Income		(3)	38	30
Unallocated Expenses, Net		(181)	(161)	(200)
Operating Profit	11%	$ 2,987	$ 3,201	$ 2,907
By U.S. Restaurant Chain				
Pizza Hut	9%	$ 308	$ 285	$ 338
Taco Bell	12%	105	273	256
KFC	7%	38	101	91
	10%	$ 451	$ 659	$ 685

	Net Sales			Segment Operating Profit (Loss)			Identifiable Assets		
Geographic Areas	1995	1994	1993	1995	1994	1993	1995	1994	1993
United States	$21,674	$20,246	$18,309	$2,728	$2,706	$2,523	$14,505	$14,218	$13,590
Europe	2,783	2,177	1,819	(65)	17	47	3,127	3,062	2,666
Mexico	1,228	2,023	1,614	80	261	223	637	995	1,217
Canada	1,299	1,244	1,206	86	82	102	1,344	1,342	1,364
Other	3,437	2,782	2,073	342	258	182	2,629	2,196	1,675
Combined Segments	$30,421	$28,472	$25,021	$3,171	$3,324	$3,077	22,242	21,813	20,512
Investments in Unconsolidated Affiliates							1,635	1,295	1,091
Corporate							1,555	1,684	2,103
							$25,432	$24,792	$23,706

Identifiable Assets

	Growth Rate 1990–1995	1995	1994	1993		Growth Rate 1990–1995	1995	1994	1993
Beverages	9%	$10,032	$ 9,566	$ 9,105	**By U.S. Restaurant Chain**				
Snack Foods	7%	5,451	5,044	4,995	Pizza Hut	8%	$1,700	$1,832	$1,733
Restaurants	14%	6,759	7,203	6,412	Taco Bell	19%	2,276	2,327	2,060
Investments in					KFC	7%	1,111	1,253	1,265
Unconsolidated Affiliates	9%	1,635	1,295	1,091	Total U.S.	12%	5,087	5,412	5,058
Corporate		1,555	1,684	2,103	International	27%	1,672	1,791	1,354
	8%	$25,432	$24,792	$23,706		14%	$6,759	$7,203	$6,412

<table>
<tr><td>Required</td><td>

1. In what different lines of business does PepsiCo report? For 1995, which line of business earned the largest profit margin (operating profit as a percent of revenues)? The smallest profit margin? Which of the restaurant chains has the highest profit margin?
2. In what lines of business does PepsiCo appear to be growing the most rapidly? How does this growth relate to the profit margins of the various lines of business?
3. In general how important is international operations to PepsiCo? Comment on the relative profit margin of U.S. versus international operations.
4. Consider another measure of profitability such as operating income divided by identifiable assets. Evaluate the profitability of PepsiCo's various businesses.

</td></tr>
</table>

TABLE A–1   Future Value of 1: $FV1 = (1 + i)^n$, also expressed as $(FV1, i, n)$

This table shows the compound amount (future value) of $1 at various interest rates and for various time periods. It is used to compute the future value of single payments.

Number of Periods

n	2%	2½%	3%	4%	5%	6%	7%	8%	9%	10%
1	1.02000	1.02500	1.03000	1.04000	1.05000	1.06000	1.07000	1.08000	1.09000	1.10000
2	1.04040	1.05063	1.06090	1.08160	1.10250	1.12360	1.14490	1.16640	1.18810	1.21000
3	1.06121	1.07689	1.09273	1.12486	1.15763	1.19102	1.22504	1.25971	1.29503	1.33100
4	1.08243	1.10381	1.12551	1.16986	1.21551	1.26248	1.31080	1.36049	1.41158	1.46410
5	1.10408	1.13141	1.15927	1.21665	1.27628	1.33823	1.40255	1.46933	1.53862	1.61051
6	1.12616	1.15969	1.19405	1.26532	1.34010	1.41852	1.50073	1.58687	1.67710	1.77156
7	1.14869	1.18869	1.22987	1.31593	1.40710	1.50363	1.60578	1.71382	1.82804	1.94872
8	1.17166	1.21840	1.26677	1.36857	1.47746	1.59385	1.71819	1.85093	1.99256	2.14359
9	1.19509	1.24886	1.30477	1.42331	1.55133	1.68948	1.83846	1.99900	2.17189	2.35795
10	1.21899	1.28008	1.34392	1.48024	1.62889	1.79085	1.96715	2.15892	2.36736	2.59374
11	1.24337	1.31209	1.38423	1.53945	1.71034	1.89830	2.10485	2.33164	2.58043	2.85312
12	1.26824	1.34489	1.42576	1.60103	1.79586	2.01220	2.25219	2.51817	2.81266	3.13843
13	1.29361	1.37851	1.46853	1.66507	1.88565	2.13293	2.40985	2.71962	3.06580	3.45227
14	1.31948	1.41297	1.51259	1.73168	1.97993	2.26090	2.57853	2.93719	3.34173	3.79750
15	1.34587	1.44830	1.55797	1.80094	2.07893	2.39656	2.75903	3.17217	3.64248	4.17725
16	1.37279	1.48451	1.60471	1.87298	2.18287	2.54035	2.95216	3.42594	3.97031	4.59497
17	1.40024	1.52162	1.65285	1.94790	2.29202	2.69277	3.15882	3.70002	4.32763	5.05447
18	1.42825	1.55966	1.70243	2.02582	2.40662	2.85434	3.37993	3.99602	4.71712	5.55992
19	1.45681	1.59865	1.75351	2.10685	2.52695	3.02560	3.61653	4.31570	5.14166	6.11591
20	1.48595	1.63862	1.80611	2.19112	2.65330	3.20714	3.86968	4.66096	5.60441	6.72750
21	1.51567	1.67958	1.86029	2.27877	2.78596	3.39956	4.14056	5.03383	6.10881	7.40025
22	1.54598	1.72157	1.91610	2.36992	2.92526	3.60354	4.43040	5.43654	6.65860	8.14027
23	1.57690	1.76461	1.97359	2.48472	3.07152	3.81975	4.74053	5.87146	7.25787	8.95430
24	1.60844	1.80873	2.03279	2.56330	3.22510	4.04893	5.07237	6.34118	7.91108	9.84973
25	1.64061	1.85394	2.09378	2.66584	3.38635	4.29187	5.42743	6.84848	8.62308	10.83471

n	11%	12%	14%	15%	16%	18%	20%	22%	24%	25%
1	1.11000	1.12000	1.14000	1.15000	1.16000	1.18000	1.20000	1.22000	1.24000	1.25000
2	1.23210	1.25440	1.29960	1.32250	1.34560	1.39240	1.44000	1.48840	1.53760	1.56250
3	1.36763	1.40493	1.48154	1.52088	1.56090	1.64303	1.72800	1.81585	1.90662	1.95313
4	1.51807	1.57352	1.68896	1.74901	1.81064	1.93878	2.07360	2.21533	2.36421	2.44141
5	1.68506	1.76234	1.92541	2.01136	2.10034	2.28776	2.48832	2.70271	2.93163	3.05176
6	1.87041	1.97382	2.19497	2.31306	2.43640	2.69955	2.98598	3.29730	3.63522	3.81470
7	2.07616	2.21068	2.50227	2.66002	2.82622	3.18547	3.58318	4.02271	4.50767	4.76837
8	2.30454	2.47596	2.85259	3.05902	3.27841	3.75886	4.29982	4.90771	5.58951	5.96046
9	2.55804	2.77308	3.25195	3.51788	3.80296	4.43545	5.15978	5.98740	6.93099	7.45058
10	2.83942	3.10585	3.70722	4.04556	4.41144	5.23384	6.19174	7.30463	8.59443	9.31323
11	3.15176	3.47855	4.22623	4.65239	5.11726	6.17593	7.43008	8.91165	10.65709	11.64153
12	3.49845	3.89598	4.81790	5.35025	5.93603	7.28759	8.91610	10.87221	13.21479	14.55192
13	3.88328	4.36349	5.49241	6.15279	6.88579	8.59936	10.69932	13.26410	16.38634	18.18989
14	4.31044	4.88711	6.26135	7.07571	7.98752	10.14724	12.83918	16.18220	20.31906	22.73737
15	4.78459	5.47357	7.13794	8.13706	9.26552	11.97375	15.40702	19.74229	25.19563	28.42171
16	5.31089	6.13039	8.13725	9.35762	10.74800	14.12902	18.48843	24.08559	31.24259	35.52714
17	5.89509	6.86604	9.27646	10.76126	12.46768	16.67225	22.18611	29.38442	38.74081	44.40892
18	6.54355	7.68997	10.57517	12.37545	14.46251	19.67325	26.62333	35.84899	48.03860	55.51115
19	7.26334	8.61276	12.05569	14.23177	16.77652	23.21444	31.94800	43.73577	59.56786	69.38894
20	8.06231	9.64629	13.74349	16.36654	19.46076	27.39303	38.33760	53.35764	73.86415	86.73617
21	8.94917	10.80385	15.66758	18.82152	22.57448	32.32378	46.00512	65.09632	91.59155	108.42022
22	9.93357	12.10031	17.86104	21.64475	26.18640	38.14206	55.20614	79.41751	113.57352	135.52527
23	11.02627	13.55235	20.36158	24.89146	30.37622	45.00763	66.24737	96.88936	140.83116	169.40659
24	12.23916	15.17863	23.21221	28.62518	35.23642	53.10901	79.49685	118.20502	174.63064	211.75824
25	13.58546	17.00006	26.46192	32.91895	40.87424	62.66863	95.39622	144.21013	216.54199	264.69780

TABLE A–2 Present Value of 1: $PV1 = 1/(1 + i)^n$, also expressed as $(PV1, i, n)$

This table shows the present value of $1 discounted at various rates of interest and for various time periods. It is used to compute the present value of single payments.

Number of Periods

n	2%	2½%	3%	4%	5%	6%	7%	8%	9%	10%
1	.98039	.97561	.97087	.96154	.95238	.94340	.93458	.92593	.91743	.90909
2	.96117	.95181	.94260	.92456	.90703	.89000	.87344	.85734	.84168	.82645
3	.94232	.92860	.91514	.88900	.86384	.83962	.81630	.79383	.77218	.75131
4	.92385	.90595	.88849	.85480	.82270	.79209	.76290	.73503	.70843	.68301
5	.90573	.88385	.86261	.82193	.78353	.74726	.71299	.68058	.64993	.62092
6	.88797	.86230	.83748	.79031	.74622	.70496	.66634	.63017	.59627	.56447
7	.87056	.84127	.81309	.75992	.71068	.66506	.62275	.58349	.54703	.51316
8	.85349	.82075	.78941	.73069	.67684	.62741	.58201	.54027	.50187	.46651
9	.83676	.80073	.76642	.70259	.64461	.59190	.54393	.50025	.46043	.42410
10	.82035	.78120	.74409	.67556	.61391	.55839	.50835	.46319	.42241	.38554
11	.80426	.76214	.72242	.64958	.58468	.52679	.47509	.42888	.38753	.35049
12	.78849	.74356	.70138	.62460	.55684	.49697	.44401	.39711	.35553	.31863
13	.77303	.72542	.68095	.60057	.53032	.46884	.41496	.36770	.32618	.28966
14	.75788	.70773	.66112	.57748	.50507	.44230	.38782	.34046	.29925	.26333
15	.74301	.69047	.64186	.55526	.48102	.41727	.36245	.31524	.27454	.23939
16	.72845	.67362	.62317	.53391	.45811	.39365	.33873	.29189	.25187	.21763
17	.71416	.65720	.60502	.51337	.43630	.37136	.31657	.27027	.23107	.19784
18	.70016	.64117	.58739	.49363	.41552	.35034	.29586	.25025	.21199	.17986
19	.68643	.62553	.57029	.47464	.39573	.33051	.27651	.23171	.19449	.16351
20	.67297	.61027	.55368	.45639	.37689	.31180	.25842	.21455	.17843	.14864
21	.65978	.59539	.53755	.43883	.35894	.29416	.24151	.19866	.16370	.13513
22	.64684	.58086	.52189	.42196	.34185	.27751	.22571	.18394	.15018	.12285
23	.63416	.56670	.50669	.40573	.32557	.26180	.21095	.17032	.13778	.11168
24	.62172	.55288	.49193	.39012	.31007	.24698	.19715	.15770	.12640	.10153
25	.60953	.53939	.47761	.37512	.29530	.23300	.18425	.14602	.11597	.09230

n	11%	12%	14%	15%	16%	18%	20%	22%	24%	25%
1	.90090	.89286	.87719	.86957	.86207	.84746	.83333	.81967	.80645	.80000
2	.81162	.79719	.76947	.75614	.74316	.71818	.69444	.67186	.65036	.64000
3	.73119	.71178	.67497	.65752	.64066	.60863	.57870	.55071	.52449	.51200
4	.65873	.63552	.59208	.57175	.55229	.51579	.48225	.45140	.42297	.40960
5	.59345	.56743	.51937	.49718	.47611	.43711	.40188	.37000	.34111	.32768
6	.53464	.50663	.45559	.43233	.41044	.37043	.33490	.30328	.27509	.26214
7	.48166	.45235	.39964	.37594	.35383	.31393	.27908	.24859	.22184	.20972
8	.43393	.40388	.35056	.32690	.30503	.26604	.23257	.20376	.17891	.16777
9	.39092	.36061	.30751	.28426	.26295	.22546	.19381	.16702	.14428	.13422
10	.35218	.32197	.26974	.24718	.22668	.19106	.16151	.13690	.11635	.10737
11	.31728	.28748	.23662	.21494	.19542	.16192	.13459	.11221	.09383	.08590
12	.28584	.25668	.20756	.18691	.16846	.13722	.11216	.09198	.07567	.06872
13	.25751	.22917	.18207	.16253	.14523	.11629	.09346	.07539	.06103	.05498
14	.23199	.20462	.15971	.14133	.12520	.09855	.07789	.06180	.04921	.04398
15	.20900	.18270	.14010	.12289	.10793	.08352	.06491	.05065	.03969	.03518
16	.18829	.16312	.12289	.10686	.09304	.07078	.05409	.04152	.03201	.02815
17	.16963	.14564	.10780	.09293	.08021	.05998	.04507	.03403	.02581	.02252
18	.15282	.13004	.09456	.08081	.06914	.05083	.03756	.02789	.02082	.01801
19	.13768	.11611	.08295	.07027	.05961	.04308	.03130	.02286	.01679	.01441
20	.12403	.10367	.07276	.06110	.05139	.03651	.02608	.01874	.01354	.01153
21	.11174	.09256	.06383	.05313	.04430	.03094	.02174	.01536	.01092	.00922
22	.10067	.08264	.05599	.04620	.03819	.02622	.01811	.01259	.00880	.00738
23	.09069	.07379	.04911	.04017	.03292	.02222	.01509	.01032	.00710	.00590
24	.08170	.06588	.04308	.03493	.02838	.01883	.01258	.00846	.00573	.00472
25	.07361	.05882	.03779	.03038	.02447	.01596	.01048	.00693	.00462	.00378

TABLE A–3 Future Value of an Ordinary Annuity of n Payments of 1 Each: $FVA = \left[\dfrac{(1 + i)^n - 1}{i} \right]$, also expressed as (FVA, i, n)

This table shows the future value of an ordinary annuity of $1 at various rates of interest and for various time periods. It is used to compute the future value of a series of payments made at the end of each interest compounding period.

Number of Periods n	2%	2½%	3%	4%	5%	6%	7%	8%	9%	10%
1	1.00000	1.00000	1.00000	1.00000	1.00000	1.00000	1.00000	1.00000	1.00000	1.00000
2	2.02000	2.02500	2.03000	2.04000	2.05000	2.06000	2.07000	2.08000	2.09000	2.10000
3	3.06040	3.07563	3.09090	3.12160	3.15250	3.18360	3.21490	3.24640	3.27810	3.31000
4	4.12161	4.15252	4.18363	4.24646	4.31013	4.37462	4.43994	4.50611	4.57313	4.64100
5	5.20404	5.25633	5.30914	5.41632	5.52563	5.63709	5.75074	5.86660	5.98471	6.10510
6	6.30812	6.38774	6.46841	6.63298	6.80191	6.97532	7.15329	7.33593	7.52333	7.71561
7	7.43428	7.54753	7.66246	7.89829	8.14201	8.39384	8.65402	8.92280	9.20043	9.48717
8	8.58297	8.73612	8.89234	9.21423	9.54911	9.89747	10.25980	10.63663	11.02847	11.43589
9	9.75463	9.95452	10.15911	10.58280	11.02656	11.49132	11.97799	12.48756	13.02104	13.57948
10	10.94972	11.20338	11.46388	12.00611	12.57789	13.18079	13.81645	14.48656	15.19293	15.93742
11	12.16872	12.48347	12.80780	13.48635	14.20679	14.97164	15.78360	16.64549	17.56029	18.53117
12	13.41209	13.79555	14.19203	15.02581	15.91713	16.86994	17.88845	18.97713	20.14072	21.38428
13	14.68033	15.14044	15.61779	16.62684	17.71298	18.88214	20.14064	21.49530	22.95338	24.52271
14	15.97394	16.51895	17.08632	18.29191	19.59863	21.01507	22.55049	24.21492	26.01919	27.97498
15	17.29342	17.93193	18.59891	20.02359	21.57856	23.27597	25.12902	27.15211	29.36092	31.77248
16	18.63929	19.38022	20.15688	21.82453	23.65749	25.67253	27.88805	30.32428	33.00340	35.94973
17	20.01207	20.86473	21.76159	23.69751	25.84037	28.21288	30.84022	33.75023	36.97370	40.54470
18	21.41231	22.38635	23.41444	25.64541	28.13238	30.90565	33.99903	37.45024	41.30134	45.59917
19	22.84056	23.94601	25.11687	27.67123	30.53900	33.75999	37.37896	41.44626	46.01846	51.15909
20	24.29737	25.54466	26.87037	29.77808	33.06595	36.78559	40.99549	45.76196	51.16012	57.27500
21	25.78332	27.18327	28.67649	31.96920	35.71925	39.99273	44.86518	50.42292	56.76453	64.00250
22	27.29898	28.86286	30.53678	34.24797	38.50521	43.39229	49.00574	55.45676	62.87334	71.40275
23	28.84496	30.58443	32.45288	36.61789	41.43048	46.99583	53.43614	60.89330	69.53194	79.54302
24	30.42186	32.34904	34.42647	39.08260	44.50200	50.81558	58.17667	66.76476	76.78981	88.49733
25	32.03030	34.15776	36.45926	41.64591	47.72710	54.86451	63.24904	73.10594	84.70090	98.34706

Number of Periods n	11%	12%	14%	15%	16%	18%	20%	22%	24%	25%
1	1.00000	1.00000	1.00000	1.00000	1.00000	1.00000	1.00000	1.00000	1.00000	1.00000
2	2.11000	2.12000	2.14000	2.15000	2.16000	2.18000	2.20000	2.22000	2.24000	2.25000
3	3.34210	3.37440	3.43960	3.47250	3.50560	3.57240	3.64000	3.70840	3.77760	3.81250
4	4.70973	4.77933	4.92114	4.99338	5.06650	5.21543	5.36800	5.52425	5.68422	5.76563
5	6.22780	6.35285	6.61010	6.74238	6.87714	7.15421	7.44160	7.73958	8.04844	8.20703
6	7.91286	8.11519	8.53552	8.75374	8.97748	9.44197	9.92992	10.44229	10.98006	11.25879
7	9.78327	10.08901	10.73049	11.06680	11.41387	12.14152	12.91590	13.73959	14.61528	15.07349
8	11.85943	12.29969	13.23276	13.72682	14.24009	15.32700	16.49908	17.76231	19.12294	19.84186
9	14.16397	14.77566	16.08535	16.78584	17.51851	19.08585	20.79890	22.67001	24.71245	25.80232
10	16.72201	17.54874	19.33730	20.30372	21.32147	23.52131	25.95868	28.65742	31.64344	33.25290
11	19.56143	20.65458	23.04452	24.34928	25.73290	28.75514	32.15042	35.96205	40.23787	42.56613
12	22.71319	24.13313	27.27075	29.00167	30.85017	34.93107	39.58050	44.87370	50.89495	54.20766
13	26.21164	28.02911	32.08865	34.35192	36.78620	42.21866	48.49660	55.74591	64.10974	68.75958
14	30.09492	32.39260	37.58107	40.50471	43.67199	50.81802	59.19592	69.01001	80.49608	86.94947
15	34.40536	37.27971	43.84241	47.58041	51.65951	60.96527	72.03511	85.19221	100.81514	109.68684
16	39.18995	42.75328	50.98035	55.71747	60.92503	72.93901	87.44213	104.93450	126.01077	138.10855
17	44.50084	48.88367	59.11760	65.07509	71.67303	87.06804	105.93056	129.02009	157.25336	173.63568
18	50.39594	55.74971	68.39407	75.83636	84.14072	103.74028	128.11667	158.40451	195.99416	218.04460
19	56.93949	63.43968	78.96923	88.21181	98.60323	123.41353	154.74000	194.25350	244.03276	273.55576
20	64.20283	72.05244	91.02493	102.44358	115.37975	146.62797	186.68800	237.98927	303.60062	342.94470
21	72.26514	81.69874	104.76842	118.81012	134.84051	174.02100	225.02560	291.34691	377.46477	429.68087
22	81.21431	92.50258	120.43600	137.63164	157.41499	206.34479	271.03072	356.44323	469.05632	538.10109
23	91.14788	104.60289	138.29704	159.27638	183.60138	244.48685	326.23686	435.86075	582.62984	673.62636
24	102.17415	118.15524	158.65862	184.16784	213.97761	289.49448	392.48424	532.75011	723.46100	843.03295
25	114.41331	133.33387	181.87083	212.79302	249.21402	342.60349	471.98108	650.95513	898.09164	1054.79118

TABLE A–4   Present Value of an Ordinary Annuity of n Payments of 1 Each: $PVA = \left[\dfrac{1 - 1/(1 + i)^n}{i}\right]$, also expressed as (PVA, i, n)

This table shows the present value of an ordinary annuity of $1 at various interest rates and for various time periods. It is used to compute the present value of a series of payments made at the end of each interest compounding period.

Number of Periods n	2%	2½%	3%	4%	5%	6%	7%	8%	9%	10%
1	.98039	.97561	.97087	.96154	.95238	.94340	.93458	.92593	.91743	.90909
2	1.94156	1.92742	1.91347	1.88609	1.85941	1.83339	1.80802	1.78326	1.75911	1.73554
3	2.88388	2.85602	2.82861	2.77509	2.72325	2.67301	2.62432	2.57710	2.53129	2.48685
4	3.80773	3.76197	3.71710	3.62990	3.54595	3.46511	3.38721	3.31213	3.23972	3.16987
5	4.71346	4.64583	4.57971	4.45182	4.32948	4.21236	4.10020	3.99271	3.88965	3.79079
6	5.60143	5.50813	5.41719	5.24214	5.07569	4.91732	4.76654	4.62288	4.48592	4.35526
7	6.47199	6.34939	6.23028	6.00205	5.78637	5.58238	5.38929	5.20637	5.03295	4.86842
8	7.32548	7.17014	7.01969	6.73274	6.46321	6.20979	5.97130	5.74664	5.53482	5.33493
9	8.16224	7.97087	7.78611	7.43533	7.10782	6.80169	6.51523	6.24689	5.99525	5.75902
10	8.98259	8.75206	8.53020	8.11090	7.72173	7.36009	7.02358	6.71008	6.41766	6.14457
11	9.78685	9.51421	9.25262	8.76048	8.30641	7.88687	7.49867	7.13896	6.80519	6.49506
12	10.57534	10.25776	9.95400	9.38507	8.86325	8.38384	7.94269	7.53608	7.16073	6.81369
13	11.34837	10.98318	10.63496	9.98565	9.39357	8.85268	8.35765	7.90378	7.48690	7.10336
14	12.10625	11.69091	11.29607	10.56312	9.89864	9.29498	8.74547	8.24424	7.78615	7.36669
15	12.84926	12.38138	11.93794	11.11839	10.37966	9.71225	9.10791	8.55948	8.06069	7.60608
16	13.57771	13.05500	12.56110	11.65230	10.83777	10.10590	9.44665	8.85137	8.31256	7.82371
17	14.29187	13.71220	13.16612	12.16567	11.27407	10.47726	9.76322	9.12164	8.54363	8.02155
18	14.99203	14.35336	13.75351	12.65930	11.68959	10.82760	10.05909	9.37189	8.75563	8.20141
19	15.67846	14.97889	14.32380	13.13394	12.08532	11.15812	10.33560	9.60360	8.95011	8.36492
20	16.35143	15.58916	14.87747	13.59033	12.46221	11.46992	10.59401	9.81815	9.12855	8.51356
21	17.01121	16.18455	15.41502	14.02916	12.82115	11.76408	10.83553	10.01680	9.29224	8.64869
22	17.65805	16.76541	15.93692	14.45112	13.16300	12.04158	11.06124	10.20074	9.44243	8.77154
23	18.29220	17.33211	16.44361	14.85684	13.48857	12.30338	11.27219	10.37106	9.58021	8.88322
24	18.91393	17.88499	16.93554	15.24696	13.79864	12.55036	11.46933	10.52876	9.70661	8.98474
25	19.52346	18.42438	17.41315	15.62208	14.09394	12.78336	11.65358	10.67478	9.82258	9.07704

Number of Periods n	11%	12%	14%	15%	16%	18%	20%	22%	24%	25%
1	.90090	.89286	.87719	.86957	.86207	.84746	.83333	.81967	.80645	.80000
2	1.71252	1.69005	1.64666	1.62571	1.60523	1.56564	1.52778	1.49153	1.45682	1.44000
3	2.44371	2.40183	2.32163	2.28323	2.24589	2.17427	2.10648	2.04224	1.98130	1.95200
4	3.10245	3.03735	2.91371	2.85498	2.79818	2.69006	2.58873	2.49364	2.40428	2.36160
5	3.69590	3.60478	3.43308	3.35216	3.27429	3.12717	2.99061	2.86364	2.74538	2.68928
6	4.23054	4.11141	3.88867	3.78448	3.68474	3.49760	3.32551	3.16692	3.02047	2.95142
7	4.71220	4.56376	4.28830	4.16042	4.03857	3.81153	3.60459	3.41551	3.24232	3.16114
8	5.14612	4.96764	4.63886	4.48732	4.34359	4.07757	3.83716	3.61927	3.42122	3.32891
9	5.53705	5.32825	4.94637	4.77158	4.60654	4.30302	4.03097	3.78628	3.56550	3.46313
10	5.88923	5.65022	5.21612	5.01877	4.83323	4.49409	4.19247	3.92318	3.68186	3.57050
11	6.20652	5.93770	5.45273	5.23371	5.02864	4.65601	4.32706	4.03540	3.77569	3.65640
12	6.49236	6.19437	5.66029	5.42062	5.19711	4.79322	4.43922	4.12737	3.85136	3.72512
13	6.74987	6.42355	5.84236	5.58315	5.34233	4.90951	4.53268	4.20277	3.91239	3.78010
14	6.98187	6.62817	6.00207	5.72448	5.46753	5.00806	4.61057	4.26456	3.96160	3.82408
15	7.19087	6.81086	6.14217	5.84737	5.57546	5.09158	4.67547	4.31522	4.00129	3.85926
16	7.37916	6.97399	6.26506	5.95423	5.66850	5.16235	4.72956	4.35673	4.03330	3.88741
17	7.54879	7.11963	6.37286	6.04716	5.74870	5.22233	4.77463	4.39077	4.05911	3.90993
18	7.70162	7.24967	6.46742	6.12797	5.81785	5.27316	4.81219	4.41866	4.07993	3.92794
19	7.83929	7.36578	6.55037	6.19823	5.87746	5.31624	4.84350	4.44152	4.09672	3.94235
20	7.96333	7.46944	6.62313	6.25933	5.92884	5.35275	4.86958	4.46027	4.11026	3.95388
21	8.07507	7.56200	6.68696	6.31246	5.97314	5.38368	4.89132	4.47563	4.12117	3.96311
22	8.17574	7.64465	6.74294	6.35866	6.01133	5.40990	4.90943	4.48822	4.12998	3.97049
23	8.26643	7.71843	6.79206	6.39884	6.04425	5.43212	4.92453	4.49854	4.13708	3.97639
24	8.34814	7.78432	6.83514	6.43377	6.07263	5.45095	4.93710	4.50700	4.14281	3.98111
25	8.42174	7.84314	6.87293	6.46415	6.09709	5.46691	4.94759	4.51393	4.14742	3.98489

TABLE A–5 Future Value of an Annuity Due of n Payments of 1 Each: $\text{FVAD} = \left[\dfrac{(1 + i)^n - 1}{i}\right] \times (1 + i)$, also expressed as

$(\text{FVAD}, i, n) = (1 + i)\,(\text{FVA}, i, n)$

This table shows the future value of an annuity due of $1 at various rates of interest and for various time periods. It is used to compute the future value of a series of payments made at the beginning of each interest compounding period.

Number of Periods

n	2%	2½%	3%	4%	5%	6%	7%	8%	9%	10%
1	1.02000	1.02500	1.03000	1.04000	1.05000	1.06000	1.07000	1.08000	1.09000	1.10000
2	2.06040	2.07563	2.09090	2.12160	2.15250	2.18360	2.21490	2.24640	2.27810	2.31000
3	3.12161	3.15252	3.18363	3.24646	3.31013	3.37462	3.43994	3.50611	3.57313	3.64100
4	4.20404	4.25633	4.30914	4.41632	4.52563	4.63709	4.75074	4.86660	4.98471	5.10510
5	5.30812	5.38774	5.46841	5.63298	5.80191	5.97532	6.15329	6.33593	6.52333	6.71561
6	6.43428	6.54743	6.66246	6.89829	7.14201	7.39384	7.65402	7.92280	8.20043	8.48717
7	7.58297	7.73612	7.89234	8.21423	8.54911	8.89747	9.25980	9.63663	10.02847	10.43589
8	8.75463	8.95452	9.15911	9.58280	10.02656	10.49132	10.97799	11.48756	12.02104	12.57948
9	9.94972	10.20338	10.46388	11.00611	11.57789	12.18079	12.81645	13.48656	14.19293	14.93742
10	11.16872	11.48347	11.80780	12.48635	13.20679	13.97164	14.78360	15.64549	16.56029	17.53117
11	12.41209	12.79555	13.19203	14.02581	14.91713	15.86994	16.88845	17.97713	19.14072	20.38428
12	13.68033	14.14044	14.61779	15.62684	16.71298	17.88214	19.14064	20.49530	21.95338	23.52271
13	14.97394	15.51895	16.08632	17.29191	18.59863	20.01507	21.55049	23.21492	25.01919	26.97498
14	16.29342	16.93193	17.59891	19.02359	20.57856	22.27597	24.12902	26.15211	28.36092	30.77248
15	17.63929	18.38022	19.15688	20.82453	22.65749	24.67253	26.88805	29.32428	32.00340	34.94973
16	19.01207	19.86473	20.76159	22.69751	24.84037	27.21288	29.84022	32.75023	35.97370	39.54470
17	20.41231	21.38635	22.41444	24.64541	27.13238	29.90565	32.99903	36.45024	40.30134	44.59917
18	21.84056	22.94601	24.11687	26.67123	29.53900	32.75999	36.37896	40.44626	45.01846	50.15909
19	23.29737	24.54466	25.87037	28.77808	32.06595	35.78559	39.99549	44.76196	50.16012	56.27500
20	24.78332	26.18327	27.67649	30.96920	34.71925	38.99273	43.86518	49.42292	55.76453	63.00250
21	26.29898	27.86286	29.53678	33.24797	37.50521	42.39229	48.00574	54.45676	61.87334	70.40275
22	27.84496	29.58443	31.45288	35.61789	40.43048	45.99583	52.43614	59.89330	68.53194	78.54302
23	29.42186	31.34904	33.42647	38.08260	43.50200	49.81558	57.17667	65.76476	75.78981	87.49733
24	31.03030	33.15776	35.45926	40.64591	46.72710	53.86451	62.24904	72.10594	83.70090	97.34706
25	32.67091	35.01171	37.55304	43.31174	50.11345	58.15638	67.67647	78.95442	92.32398	108.18177

n	11%	12%	14%	15%	16%	18%	20%	22%	24%	25%
1	1.11000	1.12000	1.14000	1.15000	1.16000	1.18000	1.20000	1.22000	1.24000	1.25000
2	2.34210	2.37440	2.43960	2.47250	2.50560	2.57240	2.64000	2.70840	2.77760	2.81250
3	3.70973	3.77933	3.92114	3.99338	4.06650	4.21543	4.36800	4.52425	4.68422	4.76563
4	5.22780	5.35285	5.61010	5.74238	5.87714	6.15421	6.44160	6.73958	7.04844	7.20703
5	6.91286	7.11519	7.53552	7.75374	7.97748	8.44197	8.92992	9.44229	9.98006	10.25879
6	8.78327	9.08901	9.73049	10.06680	10.41387	11.14152	11.91590	12.73959	13.61528	14.07349
7	10.85943	11.29969	12.23276	12.72682	13.24009	14.32700	15.49908	12.76231	18.12294	18.84186
8	13.16397	13.77566	15.08535	15.78584	16.51851	18.08585	19.79890	21.67001	23.71245	24.80232
9	15.72201	16.54874	18.33730	19.30372	20.32147	22.52131	24.95868	27.65742	30.64344	32.25290
10	18.56143	19.65458	22.04452	23.34928	24.73290	27.75514	31.15042	34.96205	39.23787	41.56613
11	21.71319	23.13313	26.27075	28.00167	29.85017	33.93107	38.58050	43.87370	49.89495	53.20766
12	25.21164	27.02911	31.08865	33.35192	35.78620	41.21866	47.49660	54.74591	63.10974	67.75958
13	29.09492	31.39260	36.58107	39.50471	42.67199	49.81802	58.19592	68.01001	79.49608	85.94947
14	33.40536	36.27971	42.84241	46.58041	50.65951	59.96527	71.03511	84.19221	99.81514	108.68684
15	38.18995	41.75328	49.98035	54.71747	59.92503	71.93901	86.44213	103.93450	125.01077	137.10855
16	43.50084	47.88367	58.11760	64.07509	70.67303	86.06804	104.93056	128.02009	156.25336	172.63568
17	49.39594	54.74971	67.39407	74.83636	83.14072	102.74028	127.11667	157.40451	194.99416	217.04460
18	55.93949	62.43968	77.96923	87.21181	97.60323	122.41353	153.74000	193.25350	243.03276	272.55576
19	63.20283	71.05244	90.02493	101.44358	114.37975	145.62797	185.68800	236.98927	302.60062	341.94470
20	71.26514	80.69874	103.76842	117.81012	133.84051	173.02100	224.02560	290.34691	376.46477	428.68087
21	80.21431	91.50258	119.43600	136.63164	156.41499	205.34479	270.03072	355.44323	468.05632	537.10109
22	90.14788	103.60289	137.29704	158.27638	182.60138	243.48685	325.23686	434.86075	581.62984	672.62636
23	101.17415	117.15524	157.65862	183.16784	212.97761	288.49448	391.48424	531.75011	722.46100	842.03295
24	113.41331	132.33387	180.87083	211.79302	248.21402	341.60349	470.98108	649.95513	897.09164	1053.79118
25	126.99877	149.33393	207.33274	244.71197	289.08827	404.27211	566.37730	794.16526	1113.63363	1318.48898

TABLE A–6 Present Value of an Annuity Due of n Payments of 1 Each: $\text{PVAD} = \left[\dfrac{1 - 1/(1 + i)^n}{i} \right] \times (1 + i)$, also expressed as

$(\text{PVAD}, i, n) = (1 + i)\,(\text{PVA}, i, n)$

This table shows the present value of an annuity due of $1 at various rates of interest and for various time periods. It is used to compute the present value of a series of payments made at the beginning of each interest compounding period.

Number of Periods n	2%	2½%	3%	4%	5%	6%	7%	8%	9%	10%
1	1.00000	1.00000	1.00000	1.00000	1.00000	1.00000	1.00000	1.00000	1.00000	1.00000
2	1.98039	1.97561	1.97087	1.96154	1.95238	1.94340	1.93458	1.92593	1.91743	1.90909
3	2.94156	2.92742	2.91347	2.88609	2.85941	2.83339	2.80802	2.78326	2.75911	2.73554
4	3.88388	3.85602	3.82861	3.77509	3.72325	3.67301	3.62432	3.57710	3.53130	3.48685
5	4.80773	4.76197	4.71710	4.62990	4.54595	4.46511	4.38721	4.31213	4.23972	4.16987
6	5.71346	5.64583	5.57971	5.45182	5.32948	5.21236	5.10020	4.99271	4.88965	4.79079
7	6.60143	6.50813	6.41719	6.24214	6.07569	5.91732	5.76654	5.62288	5.48592	5.35526
8	7.47199	7.34939	7.23028	7.00205	6.78637	6.58238	6.38929	6.20637	6.03295	5.86842
9	8.32548	8.17014	8.01969	7.73274	7.46321	7.20979	6.97130	6.74664	6.53482	6.33493
10	9.16224	8.97087	8.78611	8.43533	8.10782	7.80169	7.51523	7.24689	6.99525	6.75902
11	9.98259	9.75206	9.53020	9.11090	8.72173	8.36009	8.02358	7.71008	7.41766	7.14457
12	10.78685	10.51421	10.25262	9.76048	9.30641	8.88687	8.49867	8.13896	7.80519	7.49506
13	11.57534	11.25776	10.95400	10.38507	9.86325	9.38384	8.94269	8.53608	8.16073	7.81369
14	12.34837	11.98318	11.63496	10.98565	10.39357	9.85268	9.35765	8.90378	8.48690	8.10336
15	13.10625	12.69091	12.29607	11.56312	10.89864	10.29498	9.74547	9.24424	8.78615	8.36669
16	13.84926	13.38139	12.93794	12.11839	11.37966	10.71225	10.10791	9.55948	9.06069	8.60608
17	14.57771	14.05500	13.56110	12.65230	11.83777	11.10590	10.44665	9.85137	9.31256	8.82371
18	15.29187	14.71220	14.16612	13.16567	12.27407	11.47726	10.76322	10.12164	9.54363	9.02155
19	15.99203	15.35336	14.75351	13.65930	12.68959	11.82760	11.05909	10.37189	9.75563	9.20141
20	16.67846	15.97889	15.32380	14.13394	13.08532	12.15812	11.33560	10.60360	9.95012	9.36492
21	17.35143	16.58916	15.87747	14.59033	13.46221	12.46992	11.59401	10.81815	10.12855	9.51356
22	18.01121	17.18455	16.41502	15.02916	13.82115	12.76408	11.83553	11.01680	10.29224	9.64869
23	18.65805	17.76541	16.93692	15.45112	14.16300	13.04158	12.06124	11.20074	10.44243	9.77154
24	19.29220	18.33211	17.44361	15.85684	14.48857	13.30338	12.27219	11.37106	10.58021	9.88322
25	19.91393	18.88499	17.93554	16.24696	14.79864	13.55036	12.46933	11.52876	10.70661	9.98474

Number of Periods n	11%	12%	14%	15%	16%	18%	20%	22%	24%	25%
1	1.00000	1.00000	1.00000	1.00000	1.00000	1.00000	1.00000	1.00000	1.00000	1.00000
2	1.90090	1.89286	1.87719	1.86957	1.86207	1.84746	1.83333	1.81967	1.80645	1.80000
3	2.71252	2.69005	2.64666	2.62571	2.60523	2.56564	2.52778	2.49153	2.45682	2.44000
4	3.44371	3.40183	3.32163	3.28323	3.24589	3.17427	3.10648	3.04224	2.98130	2.95200
5	4.10245	4.03735	3.91371	3.85498	3.79818	3.69006	3.58873	3.49364	3.40428	3.36160
6	4.69590	4.60478	4.43308	4.35216	4.27429	4.12717	3.99061	3.86364	3.74538	3.68928
7	5.23054	5.11141	4.88867	4.78448	4.68474	4.49760	4.32551	4.16692	4.02047	3.95142
8	5.71220	5.56376	5.28830	5.16042	5.03857	4.81153	4.60459	4.41551	4.24232	4.16114
9	6.14612	5.96764	5.63886	5.48732	5.34359	5.07757	4.83716	4.61927	4.42122	4.32891
10	6.53705	6.32825	5.94637	5.77158	5.60654	5.30302	5.03097	4.78628	4.56550	4.46313
11	6.88923	6.65022	6.21612	6.01877	5.83323	5.49409	5.19247	4.92318	4.68186	4.57050
12	7.20652	6.93770	6.45273	6.23371	6.02864	5.65601	5.32706	5.03540	4.77569	4.65640
13	7.49236	7.19437	6.66029	6.42062	6.19711	5.79322	5.43922	5.12737	4.85136	4.72512
14	7.74987	7.42355	6.84236	6.58315	6.34233	5.90951	5.53268	5.20277	4.91239	4.78010
15	7.98187	7.62817	7.00207	6.72448	6.46753	6.00806	5.61057	5.26456	4.96160	4.82408
16	8.19087	7.81086	7.14217	6.84737	6.57546	6.09158	5.67547	5.31522	5.00129	4.85926
17	8.37916	7.97399	7.26506	6.95423	6.66850	6.16235	5.72956	5.35673	5.03330	4.88741
18	8.54879	8.11963	7.37286	7.04716	6.74870	6.22233	5.77463	5.39077	5.05911	4.90993
19	8.70162	8.24967	7.46742	7.12797	6.81785	6.27316	5.81219	5.41866	5.07993	4.92794
20	8.83929	8.36578	7.55037	7.19823	6.87746	6.31624	5.84350	5.44152	5.09672	4.94235
21	8.96333	8.46944	7.62313	7.25933	6.92884	6.35275	5.86958	5.46027	5.11026	4.95388
22	9.07507	8.56200	7.68696	7.31246	6.97314	6.38368	5.89132	5.47563	5.12117	4.96311
23	9.17574	8.64465	7.74294	7.35866	7.01133	6.40990	5.90943	5.48822	5.12998	4.97049
24	9.26643	8.71843	7.79206	7.39884	7.04425	6.43212	5.92453	5.49854	5.13708	4.97639
25	9.34814	8.78432	7.83514	7.43377	7.07263	6.45095	5.93710	5.50700	5.14281	4.98111

THE COCA-COLA COMPANY 1995 ANNUAL REPORT

Financial Review Incorporating
Management's Discussion and Analysis

We exist for one reason: to maximize share-owner value over time. To accomplish this mission, The Coca-Cola Company and its subsidiaries (our Company) have developed a comprehensive business strategy focused on four key objectives: (1) increasing volume, (2) expanding share of worldwide beverage sales, (3) maximizing long-term cash flows, and (4) improving economic profit and creating economic value added. We achieve these objectives by investing aggressively in the high-return beverages business and by optimizing our cost of capital through appropriate financial policies.

Investments

With a global business system that operates in nearly 200 countries and generates superior cash flows, our Company is uniquely positioned to capitalize on profitable new investment opportunities. Our criterion for investment is simple but strict: We seek to invest in opportunities that strategically enhance our existing operations and offer cash returns that exceed the Company's long-term after-tax weighted average cost of capital, estimated by management to be approximately 11 percent.

Because it consistently generates high returns on capital, our beverages business is a particularly attractive area for investment. In new and emerging markets, where increasing the penetration of our products is our primary goal, the bulk of our investments is dedicated to infrastructure enhancements: facilities, distribution networks, sales equipment and technology. These investments are made by acquiring or forming strategic business alliances with local bottlers, and by matching local expertise with our Company's experience and focus. In highly developed beverage markets, where our primary goals include increasing consumer awareness and broadening the appeal of our products, the bulk of our expenditures is dedicated to marketing activities, such as creating new products and serving sizes, and improving the efficiency of production and distribution.

Currently, 60 percent of the world's population live in markets where the average person consumes less than 10 servings of our products per year, offering high-potential growth opportunities for our Company and its bottlers. In fact, the emerging markets of China, India, Indonesia and Russia represent approximately 44 percent of the world's population, but, on a combined basis, their average per capita consumption of our products is approximately 1 percent of the United States level. As a result, we will continue aggressively investing to ensure that our products are *pervasive*, *preferred* and offer the best *price* relative to value.

Our investment strategy focuses primarily on capital expenditures, bottling operations and marketing activities.

Capital Expenditures

Capital expenditures on property, plant and equipment and the percentage distribution by geographic area for 1995, 1994 and 1993 are as follows (dollars in millions):

Year Ended December 31,	**1995**	1994	1993
Capital expenditures	**$ 937**	$ 878	$ 800
United States	**33%**	32%	23%
Africa	**2%**	3%	1%
Greater Europe	**45%**	42%	51%
Latin America	**10%**	16%	19%
Middle & Far East and Canada	**10%**	7%	6%

Bottling Operations

We invest heavily in bottling operations to maximize the strength and efficiency of our production, distribution and marketing systems around the world. These aggressive investments result in increases in unit case volume, net revenues and profits at the bottler level, which in turn generate increased gallon shipments for the Company's concentrate business. As a result, both the Company and our bottlers benefit from long-term growth in volume, cash flows and share-owner value.

We designate certain bottling operations in which we have invested as anchor bottlers due to their level of responsibility and performance. Anchor bottlers, which include Coca-Cola Amatil Limited (Coca-Cola Amatil) and Coca-Cola Enterprises Inc. (Coca-Cola Enterprises), are strongly committed to the strategic goals of the Company and to furthering the interests of our worldwide production, distribution and marketing systems. They tend to be large and geographically diverse, and have strong financial and management resources.

In addition to our anchor bottlers, we will continue making investments in bottling operations of new and emerging markets and in existing bottling operations that require restructuring or rebuilding. Our investments in a bottler can represent either a noncontrolling or a controlling interest, depending on the bottler's capital structure and its available resources at the time of our investment.

Through noncontrolling investments in bottling companies, we provide expertise and resources to strengthen those businesses. Specifically, we help improve sales and marketing programs, assist in the development of effective business and information systems and help establish appropriate capital

Financial Review Incorporating
Management's Discussion and Analysis

structures. In 1995, we increased our economic interest in Panamerican Beverages, Inc. (Panamerican Beverages) from 7 to 13 percent and designated it as an anchor bottler. Panamerican Beverages owns bottling operations in Mexico, Brazil, Colombia and Costa Rica. Also in 1995, we contributed assets to a new joint venture, Coca-Cola Sabco (Proprietary) Limited (Coca-Cola Sabco), also an anchor bottler, in return for a 16 percent economic interest and notes receivable. Coca-Cola Sabco will strengthen our distribution system in south and east Africa. During 1994, we formed a joint venture known as the Coca-Cola Bottling Companies of Egypt following the privatization of the Egyptian public sector bottler. In 1993, our Company purchased a 30 percent economic interest in another anchor bottler, Coca-Cola FEMSA, S.A. de C.V. (Coca-Cola FEMSA), to assist in further strengthening strategic bottling territories in Latin America.

The following table illustrates the excess of the calculated fair values, based on quoted closing prices of publicly traded shares, over our Company's carrying values for selected equity method investees (in millions):

December 31,	Carrying Value	Fair Value	Excess
1995			
Coca-Cola Amatil Limited	$ 682	$ 1,579	$ 897
Coca-Cola Enterprises Inc.	556	1,513	957
Coca-Cola FEMSA, S.A. de C.V.	86	264	178
Coca-Cola Beverages Ltd.	11	123	112
Coca-Cola Bottling Co. Consolidated	84	97	13
			$ 2,157

Equity income, primarily from investments in unconsolidated bottling investments, reached $169 million in 1995.

In certain situations, it is advantageous to acquire a controlling interest in bottling operations. Although not our primary long-term business strategy, owning a controlling interest allows us to compensate for limited local resources or facilitate improvements in customer relationships while building or restructuring the bottling operations. While bottling businesses typically generate lower margins on revenue than our concentrate business, they can increase revenues and operating profits on a per-gallon basis. In 1995, we acquired controlling interests in certain bottling operations in Italy and Venezuela. By providing capital and marketing expertise to these newly acquired bottlers, we intend to strengthen our bottling territories and market positions in those countries.

In line with our long-term bottling strategy, we will consider options for reducing our ownership interest in a consolidated bottler. One such option is to sell our interest in a consolidated bottling operation to one of our equity investee bottlers. In these situations, we continue participating in the previously consolidated bottler's earnings through our portion of the equity investee's income.

Currently, we are holding preliminary discussions to sell our bottling and canning operations located in Belgium and France to Coca-Cola Enterprises. During 1995, we sold our controlling interests in certain bottling operations in Poland, Croatia and Romania to Coca-Cola Amatil. In 1994, our Company sold a controlling 51 percent interest in the previously wholly owned bottler in Argentina, Coca-Cola S.A. Industrial, Comercial y Financiera, to Coca-Cola FEMSA.

In 1995, consolidated bottling and fountain operations produced and distributed approximately 16 percent of our worldwide unit case volume. Bottlers in which we own a noncontrolling interest produced and distributed an additional 36 percent of our worldwide unit case volume.

Marketing Activities

In addition to investments in bottling and distribution infrastructure, we also make significant expenditures in support of our trademarks. Through prudent expenditures on marketing activities, we enhance global consumer awareness of our products. Enhancing consumer awareness builds consumer preference for our products, which produces growth in volume, per capita consumption of our products and our share of worldwide beverage sales.

We build consumer awareness and product appeal for our trademarks using integrated marketing programs. These programs include activities such as advertising, point of sale merchandising and product sampling. Each of these activities contributes to building consumer awareness and product preference.

Through our bottling investments and strategic alliances with other bottlers of Company products, we are able to develop and implement integrated marketing programs on a global basis. In developing a global strategy for a Company trademark, we perform product and packaging research, establish brand positioning, develop precise consumer communications and seek consumer feedback. Examples of recent successes with our global brand strategies include the Coca-Cola Classic theme, "Always," and, for Sprite, "Obey Your Thirst."

As part of our ongoing efforts to maximize the impact of our advertising expenditures, we recently began assigning specific brands to individual advertising agencies. This approach enables us to enhance each brand's global

Financial Review Incorporating
Management's Discussion and Analysis

positioning, increase accountability and use the Company's marketing expenditures more efficiently and effectively.

During 1995, our Company's direct marketing expenses, which include our expenditures on consumer marketing activities, increased 11 percent to reach $3,834 million.

Financial Strategies

We use several strategies to optimize our cost of capital, which is a key component of our ability to maximize share-owner value.

Debt Financing

We maintain debt levels considered prudent based on our cash flow, interest coverage and percentage of debt to total capital. We use debt financing to lower our overall cost of capital, which increases our return on share-owners' equity.

Our capital structure and financial policies have earned long-term credit ratings of "AA" from Standard & Poor's and "Aa3" from Moody's, and the highest credit ratings available for our commercial paper programs.

Financial Risk Management

We use derivative financial instruments to reduce our exposure to financial risks.

With approximately 82 percent of our 1995 operating income generated outside the United States, weakness in one particular currency is often offset by strengths in others.

Most of our foreign currency exposures are managed on a consolidated basis, which allows us to net certain exposures and thus take advantage of any natural offsets. We use forward exchange contracts to adjust the currency mix of our recorded assets and liabilities, which further reduces our exposure from adverse fluctuations in exchange rates. In addition, we enter into forward exchange and swap contracts and purchase options to hedge both firmly committed and anticipated transactions, as appropriate, and net investments in certain international operations.

We use primarily liquid spot, forward, option and swap contracts. Our Company does not enter into leveraged or structured contracts. Additionally, we do not enter into derivative financial instruments for trading purposes. As a matter of policy, all of our derivative positions are used to hedge underlying economic exposures by mitigating certain risks such as changes in currency, interest rates and other market factors on a matched basis. Gains or losses on hedging transactions are offset by gains or losses on the underlying exposures being hedged.

Share Repurchases

In July 1992, our Board of Directors authorized a plan to repurchase up to 100 million shares of our Company's common stock through the year 2000. In 1995, we repurchased 29 million shares under this plan at a total cost of approximately $1.8 billion. As of December 31, 1995, we have repurchased 67 million shares under the July 1992 plan.

Since the inception of our initial share repurchase program in 1984 through our current program as of December 31, 1995, our Company has repurchased 483 million shares, representing 30 percent of the shares outstanding as of January 1, 1984, at an average price per share of $18.21.

Dividend Policy

Because of our continually strong earnings growth, our Board of Directors has increased the cash dividend per common share by an average annual compound growth rate of 13 percent since December 31, 1985. Our annual common stock dividend was $.88 per share, $.78 per share and $.68 per share in 1995, 1994 and 1993, respectively. At its February 1996 meeting, our Board of Directors again increased our quarterly dividend per share to $.25, equivalent to a full-year dividend of $1.00 in 1996, the 34th consecutive annual increase.

Our 1995 dividend payout ratio was approximately 37 percent of our net income. It is the intention of our Board of Directors to gradually reduce our dividend payout ratio to 30 percent over time.

Measuring Performance

Economic profit and economic value added provide a framework for measuring the impact of value-oriented actions. We define economic profit as net operating profit after taxes in excess of a computed capital charge for average operating capital employed. Economic value added represents the growth in economic profit from year to year.

Recently, we began expanding the use of economic value added as a performance measurement tool. Both annual incentive awards and long-term incentive awards for most eligible employees are now determined, in part, by comparison against economic profit target levels. These changes in performance measures were made to ensure that our management team is clearly focused on the key drivers of our business. We intend to continue expanding the use of economic profit and the related concept of value creation in measuring performance. We believe that a clear focus on the components of economic profit, and the resultant growth in economic value added over time, leads to the creation of share-owner wealth.

Financial Review Incorporating Management's Discussion and Analysis

Over the last 10 years, we have increased our economic profit at an average annual compound rate of 23 percent, resulting in economic value added to the Company of $1.9 billion. Over the same period, our Company's stock price has increased at an average annual compound rate of 27 percent.

Total Return to Share Owners

Share owners of our Company have received an excellent return on their investment over the past decade. A $100 investment in our Company's common stock on December 31, 1985, together with reinvested dividends, was worth approximately $1,287 on December 31, 1995, an average annual compound return of 29 percent.

Management's Discussion and Analysis

Lines of Business

Beverages

Our beverages business is the largest manufacturer, marketer and distributor of soft drink and noncarbonated beverage concentrates and syrups in the world. We manufacture beverage concentrates and syrups, and in certain instances, finished beverages, which we sell to bottling and canning operations, authorized fountain wholesalers and some fountain retailers. In addition, we have substantial ownership interests in numerous bottling and canning operations.

Foods

Our foods business produces, markets and distributes principally juice and juice-drink products. It is the largest marketer of juice and juice-drink products in the world.

Volume

Beverages

We measure beverage volume in two ways: (1) gallon shipments of concentrates and syrups and (2) equivalent unit cases of finished product. Gallon shipments represent our primary business, since they measure the volume of concentrates and syrups we sell to our bottling system. Most of our revenues are based on this measure of "wholesale" activity. We also measure volume in unit cases, which represent the amount of finished product our bottling system sells to retail customers. We believe unit case volume more accurately measures the underlying strength of our business system because it measures trends at the retail level and is less impacted by inventory management practices at the wholesale level. Fountain syrups sold directly to our customers are included in both measures simultaneously.

Operations

Net Operating Revenues and Gross Margin

In 1995, revenues from our beverages business increased 13 percent, reflecting an increase in gallon shipments, selective price increases and continued expansion of our bottling and canning operations. Revenues from our foods business decreased 7 percent in 1995, resulting from implementation of a strategy to reduce short-term price promotions and increase long-term brand-building and marketing investments.

In 1994, revenues from our beverages business increased 18 percent, primarily due to increased gallon shipments, selective price increases, continued expansion of our bottling and canning operations and a weaker U.S. dollar versus key currencies. Revenues for our foods business increased 3 percent in 1994 as a result of price increases for orange juice products.

On a consolidated basis, our net revenues grew 11 percent and our gross profit grew 11 percent in 1995. Our gross margin declined to 61 percent in 1995 from 62 percent in 1994, primarily due to higher costs for materials such as sweeteners and packaging.

On a consolidated basis, our worldwide net revenues grew 16 percent in 1994, while gross profit grew 14 percent. Our gross margin contracted to 62 percent in 1994 from 63 percent in 1993, primarily due to the acquisition of bottling and canning operations, which typically have lower gross profit to net revenue relationships, but offer strong cash flows.

Selling, Administrative and General Expenses

Selling expenses were $5,399 million in 1995, $4,931 million in 1994 and $4,360 million in 1993. The increases in 1995 and 1994 were primarily due to higher marketing investments in support of our Company's volume growth.

Administrative and general expenses were $1,587 million in 1995, $1,366 million in 1994 and $1,335 million in 1993. The increase in 1995 reflects higher expenses related to stock-based employee benefits and a nonrecurring provision of $86 million to increase efficiencies in the Company's operations in the United States and Europe. The increase in 1994 was due primarily to expansion of our business, particularly newly formed Company-owned bottling operations. Administrative and general expenses, as a percentage of net operating revenues, were approximately 9 percent in 1995, 8 percent in 1994 and 10 percent in 1993.

Financial Review Incorporating Management's Discussion and Analysis

Operating Income and Operating Margin

On a consolidated basis, our operating income grew 10 percent in 1995, on top of a 20 percent increase in 1994. During 1995, operating income for our beverages business rose approximately 14 percent primarily as a result of increased revenues. Our foods business reported a modest loss of $14 million in 1995, due to its decline in net revenues and a nonrecurring provision for increasing efficiencies. Our consolidated operating margin was 23 percent in 1995 and 1994.

Margin Analysis

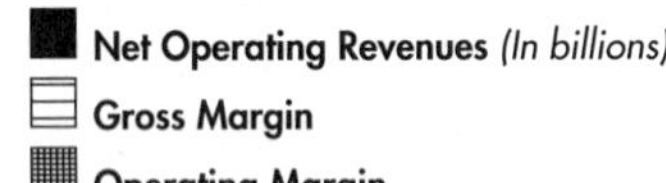

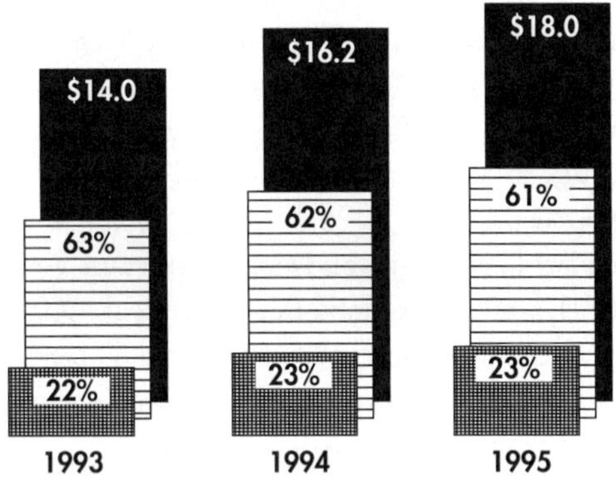

Our company's gross profit and operating income growth are a result of increasing revenues.

Interest Income and Interest Expense

In 1995, our interest income increased 35 percent as a result of higher average interest rates outside of the United States. Interest expense increased 37 percent in 1995, reflecting higher commercial paper balances.

Interest income increased 26 percent in 1994, due primarily to rising interest rates and higher average investments in cash equivalents and marketable securities. Interest expense increased 18 percent in 1994 as a result of rising interest rates.

Equity Income

Equity income increased 26 percent to $169 million in 1995, due primarily to improved results at Coca-Cola FEMSA, Coca-Cola Nestlé Refreshments, Coca-Cola Bottlers Philippines, Inc. and Coca-Cola Beverages Ltd.

Equity income increased 47 percent to $134 million in 1994, resulting from increased earnings from Coca-Cola

Enterprises and Coca-Cola & Schweppes Beverages Ltd. and improved results from Coca-Cola Beverages Ltd.

Other Income (Deductions)-Net

In 1995, other income (deductions)-net increased $124 million, and includes gains recorded on the sale of bottling operations in Poland, Croatia and Romania.

In 1994, other income (deductions)-net decreased $102 million, primarily due to recognition in 1993 of approximately $84 million of pretax gains on sales of real estate and bottling investments. These 1993 gains include a $50 million pretax gain recognized on the sale of citrus groves in the United States and a $34 million pretax gain recognized on the sale of property no longer required as a result of a consolidation of manufacturing operations in Japan. No transactions resulting in significant gains occurred in 1994.

Gain on Issuance of Stock by Coca-Cola Amatil

In July 1995, Coca-Cola Amatil completed a public offering in Australia of approximately 97 million shares of common stock. In connection with the offering, our ownership in Coca-Cola Amatil was reduced to approximately 40 percent. We recognized a non-cash pretax gain of approximately $74 million as a result of this transaction.

In the fourth quarter of 1993, Coca-Cola Amatil purchased a bottling operation in Indonesia by issuing approximately 8 million shares of common stock, resulting in a non-cash pretax gain of $12 million for our Company.

Income Taxes

Our effective tax rates of 31.0 percent in 1995, 31.5 percent in 1994 and 31.3 percent in 1993 reflect the tax benefit we derive from having significant operations outside the United States that are taxed at rates lower than the U.S. statutory rate of 35 percent.

Transition Effect of Changes in Accounting Principles

In 1995, the Financial Accounting Standards Board (FASB) issued Statement of Financial Accounting Standards No. 121, "Accounting for the Impairment of Long-Lived Assets and for Long-Lived Assets to be Disposed Of" (SFAS 121). We will adopt the provisions of SFAS 121 on January 1, 1996. SFAS 121 standardizes the accounting practices for the recognition and measurement of impairment losses on certain long-lived assets. We do not expect the adoption of SFAS 121 to have a material impact on our results of operations or financial position. However, the provisions of SFAS 121 will require certain charges historically recorded by our Company in other income (deductions)-net to be included in operating income.

Financial Review Incorporating
Management's Discussion and Analysis

We adopted Statement of Financial Accounting Standards No. 115, "Accounting for Certain Investments in Debt and Equity Securities" (SFAS 115) as of January 1, 1994, resulting in an after-tax increase to share-owners' equity of $60 million, with no effect on net income. SFAS 115 changed our method of accounting for certain debt and marketable equity securities from a historical cost basis to a fair value approach.

Income Per Share

Accelerated by our Company's share repurchase program, our net income per share grew 20 percent and 19 percent in 1995 and 1994, respectively. Income per share before changes in accounting principles grew 18 percent in 1994.

Liquidity and Capital Resources

Our ability to generate cash from operations in excess of our capital reinvestment and dividend requirements is one of our chief financial strengths. We anticipate that our operating activities in 1996 will continue to provide us with sufficient cash flows to capitalize on opportunities for business expansion and to meet all of our financial commitments.

Free Cash Flow

Free cash flow is the cash remaining from operations after we have satisfied our business reinvestment opportunities. We focus on increasing free cash flow to achieve our primary objective, maximizing share-owner value over time. We use free cash flow, along with borrowings, to pay dividends and make share repurchases. The consolidated statements of our cash flows are summarized as follows (in millions):

Year Ended December 31,	1995	1994	1993
Cash flows provided by (used in):			
Operations	$ 3,115	$ 3,183	$ 2,508
Investment activities	(1,013)	(1,037)	(885)
Free Cash Flow	2,102	2,146	1,623
Cash flows provided by (used in):			
Financing			
Share repurchases	(1,796)	(1,192)	(680)
Other financing activities	(482)	(600)	(860)
Exchange	(43)	34	(41)
Increase (decrease) in cash	$ (219)	$ 388	$ 42

Cash provided by operations amounted to $3.1 billion, a 2 percent decrease from 1994. This 1995 decrease primarily resulted from increases in accounts receivable and inventories related to the increase in our net revenues, and an increase in prepaid expenses and other assets. In 1994, cash from operations totaled $3.2 billion, a 27 percent increase over 1993, resulting primarily from growth in our net income before non-cash charges for depreciation and amortization and increased dividends from equity method investments.

As compared to 1994, net cash used in investment activities decreased in 1995, primarily attributable to an increase in proceeds from disposals of investments and other assets. Specifically, during 1995, we sold our interests in the bottling operations of Poland, Croatia and Romania.

While cash used for acquisitions and investments, principally bottling companies, declined in 1994, that decline was more than offset by a reduction in proceeds from disposals of property, plant and equipment and investments and other assets, resulting in a net increase in cash used in investment activities in 1994.

The 1995 increase in cost method investments includes an increased investment in Panamerican Beverages. In 1995, goodwill and other intangible assets increased in association with our acquisitions during the year, such as Barq's, Inc. and certain fountain syrup manufacturing operations. The increase in 1994 in marketable securities and the carrying value of cost method investments was due, in part, to our Company's adoption of SFAS 115, which reflects a non-cash adjustment to fair value. A portion of the 1994 increase was attributable to an increase in securities held in accordance with a negotiated income tax exemption grant for the Company's manufacturing facilities in Puerto Rico. The balance also increased due to deferred tax assets generated in 1994.

Financing Activities

Our financing activities include net borrowings, dividend payments and share repurchases. Net cash used in financing activities totaled $2.3 billion in 1995, $1.8 billion in 1994 and $1.5 billion in 1993. The change between years was due, in part, to net borrowings of debt in 1995 and 1994, compared to net reductions of debt in 1993. Cash used to purchase common stock for treasury increased to $1.8 billion in 1995, from $1.2 billion in 1994.

Our global presence and strong capital position afford us easy access to key financial markets around the world, enabling us to raise funds with a low effective cost. This posture, coupled with the aggressive management of our mix of short-term and long-term debt, results in a lower overall cost of borrowing. Our debt management policies, in conjunction with our share repurchase program and investment activity, typically result in current liabilities exceeding current assets.

Financial Review Incorporating
Management's Discussion and Analysis

We manage our debt levels based on the following financial measurements and ratios:

Year Ended December 31,	1995	1994	1993
Net debt (in billions)	$ 2.2	$ 1.5	$ 1.6
Net debt-to-net capital	29%	23%	26%
Free cash flow to net debt	96%	141%	100%
Interest coverage	16x	19x	18x
Ratio of earnings to fixed charges	14.5x	16.8x	15.7x

Net debt excludes the debt entered into on behalf of the Company's finance subsidiary, and is net of cash, cash equivalents and marketable securities in excess of operating requirements and net of temporary bottling investments.

Commercial paper is our primary source of short-term financing. On December 31, 1995, we had $3.3 billion in lines of credit and other short-term credit facilities available, under which $2.4 billion was outstanding. Included was $2.2 billion outstanding in commercial paper borrowings. The 1995 and 1994 increases in loans and notes payable were primarily attributable to additional commercial paper borrowings resulting from the management of our short-term and long-term debt mix.

Exchange

Our international operations are subject to certain opportunities and risks, including currency fluctuations and government actions. We monitor our operations in each country closely so that we can respond to changing economic and political environments quickly and decisively, and take full advantage of changing foreign currencies and interest rates.

We use approximately 48 functional currencies. In 1995, we expanded the calculation of the impact of weighted average exchange rates versus the U.S. dollar to include the Mexican and Philippine pesos and the South African rand. The 1994 and 1993 calculation for key currencies now reflects this change. In 1995, 1994 and 1993, the weighted average exchange rates for certain key foreign currencies strengthened (weakened) against the U.S. dollar as follows:

Year Ended December 31,	1995	1994	1993
Key currencies	Even	2 %	(3)%
Australian dollar	1 %	9 %	(7)%
British pound	3 %	2 %	(15)%
Canadian dollar	Even	(5)%	(8)%
French franc	13 %	(1)%	(3)%
German mark	13 %	2 %	(5)%
Japanese yen	9 %	9 %	15 %
Mexican peso	(46)%	(8)%	(1)%

The change in our foreign currency translation adjustment in 1995 was due primarily to the revaluation of net assets located in countries where the local currency significantly weakened versus the U.S. dollar. Exchange losses amounting to $21 million in 1995, $25 million in 1994 and $74 million in 1993 were recorded in other income (deductions)-net. Exchange losses include the remeasurement of certain currencies into functional currencies and the costs of hedging certain transaction and balance sheet exposures.

Additional information concerning our hedging activities is presented on pages 60 through 61.

Impact of Inflation and Changing Prices

Inflation is a factor that impacts the way we operate in many markets around the world. In general, we are able to increase prices to counteract the effects of increasing costs and generate sufficient cash flows to maintain our productive capability.

Outlook

As a global business that generates the majority of its operating income outside the United States, our Company is uniquely positioned to benefit from operating in a variety of currencies, as downturns in any one region are often offset by strengths in others. Additionally, we have various operational initiatives available to offset the unfavorable impact of such events.

While we cannot predict future economic events, we believe continued expansion into the developing population centers of the world presents further opportunity for growth. The strength of our brands, our broad global presence and our strong financial condition allow our Company the flexibility to take advantage of growth opportunities and to continue increasing share-owner value.

Additional Information

For additional information about our operations, cash flows, liquidity and capital resources, please refer to the information on pages 50 through 70 of this report. Additional information concerning our operations in different lines of business and geographic areas is presented on pages 67 and 68.

Selected Financial Data

(In millions except per share data, ratios and growth rates)	Compound Growth Rates		Year Ended December 31,	
	5 Years	10 Years	1995	1994[2]
Summary of Operations				
Net operating revenues	12.0%	11.9%	**$ 18,018**	$ 16,181
Cost of goods sold	10.5%	9.1%	**6,940**	6,168
Gross profit	12.9%	14.1%	**11,078**	10,013
Selling, administrative and general expenses	11.4%	12.4%	**6,986**	6,297
Operating income	16.0%	17.6%	**4,092**	3,716
Interest income			**245**	181
Interest expense			**272**	199
Equity income			**169**	134
Other income (deductions)-net			**20**	(104)
Gain on issuance of stock by equity investees			**74**	—
Income from continuing operations before income taxes and changes in accounting principles	16.5%	17.2%	**4,328**	3,728
Income taxes	16.3%	15.6%	**1,342**	1,174
Income from continuing operations before changes in accounting principles	16.7%	18.0%	**$ 2,986**	$ 2,554
Net income	16.7%	15.3%	**$ 2,986**	$ 2,554
Preferred stock dividends			**—**	—
Net income available to common share owners	17.0%	15.3%	**$ 2,986**	$ 2,554
Average common shares outstanding			**1,262**	1,290
Per Common Share Data				
Income from continuing operations before changes in accounting principles	18.4%	20.7%	**$ 2.37**	$ 1.98
Net income	18.4%	17.8%	**2.37**	1.98
Cash dividends	17.1%	13.4%	**.88**	.78
Market price on December 31	26.1%	26.6%	**74.25**	51.50
Total Market Value of Common Stock	24.5%	23.9%	**$ 92,983**	$ 65,711
Balance Sheet Data				
Cash, cash equivalents and current marketable securities			**$ 1,315**	$ 1,531
Property, plant and equipment–net			**4,336**	4,080
Depreciation			**421**	382
Capital expenditures			**937**	878
Total assets			**15,041**	13,873
Long-term debt			**1,141**	1,426
Total debt			**4,064**	3,509
Share-owners' equity			**5,392**	5,235
Total capital[1]			**9,456**	8,744
Other Key Financial Measures[1]				
Total debt-to-total capital			**43.0%**	40.1%
Net debt-to-net capital			**28.8%**	22.6%
Return on common equity			**56.2%**	52.0%
Return on capital			**34.9%**	32.7%
Dividend payout ratio			**37.2%**	39.4%
Economic profit[6]			**$ 2,172**	$ 1,881

[1] See Glossary on page 74.
[2] In 1994, the Company adopted SFAS No. 115, "Accounting for Certain Investments in Debt and Equity Securities."
[3] In 1993, the Company adopted SFAS No. 112, "Employers' Accounting for Postemployment Benefits."
[4] In 1992, the Company adopted SFAS No. 106, "Employers' Accounting for Postretirement Benefits Other Than Pensions."
[5] The Company adopted SFAS No. 109, "Accounting for Income Taxes," in 1992 by restating financial statements beginning in 1989.
[6] The calculation of economic profit has been simplified and amounts prior to 1995 have been restated.

1993[3]	1992[4,5]	1991[5]	1990[5]	1989[5]	1988	1987	1986	1985
$ 13,963	$ 13,074	$ 11,572	$ 10,236	$ 8,622	$ 8,065	$ 7,658	$ 6,977	$ 5,879
5,160	5,055	4,649	4,208	3,548	3,429	3,633	3,454	2,909
8,803	8,019	6,923	6,028	5,074	4,636	4,025	3,523	2,970
5,695	5,249	4,604	4,076	3,348	3,038	2,701	2,626	2,163
3,108	2,770	2,319	1,952	1,726	1,598	1,324	897	807
144	164	175	170	205	199	232	154	151
168	171	192	231	308	230	297	208	196
91	65	40	110	75	92	64	45	52
(2)	(82)	41	13	66	(33)	—	35	69
12	—	—	—	—	—	40	375	—
3,185	2,746	2,383	2,014	1,764	1,626	1,363	1,298	883
997	863	765	632	553	537	496	471	314
$ 2,188	$ 1,883	$ 1,618	$ 1,382	$ 1,211	$ 1,089	$ 867	$ 827	$ 569
$ 2,176	$ 1,664	$ 1,618	$ 1,382	$ 1,537	$ 1,045	$ 916	$ 934	$ 722
—	—	1	18	21	7	—	—	—
$ 2,176	$ 1,664	$ 1,617	$ 1,364	$ 1,516[7]	$ 1,038	$ 916	$ 934	$ 722
1,302	1,317	1,333	1,337	1,384	1,458	1,509	1,547	1,573
$ 1.68	$ 1.43	$ 1.21	$ 1.02	$ .86	$ .74	$ .57	$ .53	$ .36
1.67	1.26	1.21	1.02	1.10[7]	.71	.61	.60	.46
.68	.56	.48	.40	.34	.30	.28	.26	.25
44.63	41.88	40.13	23.25	19.31	11.16	9.53	9.44	7.04
$ 57,905	$ 54,728	$ 53,325	$ 31,073	$ 26,034	$ 15,834	$ 14,198	$ 14,534	$ 10,872
$ 1,078	$ 1,063	$ 1,117	$ 1,492	$ 1,182	$ 1,231	$ 1,489	$ 895	$ 843
3,729	3,526	2,890	2,386	2,021	1,759	1,602	1,538	1,483
333	310	254	236	181	167	152	151	130
800	1,083	792	593	462	387	304	346	412
12,021	11,052	10,189	9,245	8,249	7,451	8,606	7,675	6,341
1,428	1,120	985	536	549	761	909	996	801
3,100	3,207	2,288	2,537	1,980	2,124	2,995	1,848	1,280
4,584	3,888	4,239	3,662	3,299	3,345	3,187	3,479	2,948
7,684	7,095	6,527	6,199	5,279	5,469	6,182	5,327	4,228
40.3%	45.2%	35.1%	40.9%	37.5%	38.8%	48.4%	34.7%	30.3%
26.2%	31.9%	19.2%	23.7%	14.7%	18.9%	15.4%	10.9%	15.6%
51.7%	46.4%	41.3%	41.4%	39.4%	34.7%	26.0%	25.7%	20.0%
31.2%	29.4%	27.5%	26.8%	26.5%	21.3%	18.3%	20.1%	16.8%
40.6%	44.3%	39.5%	39.2%	31.0%[7]	42.1%	46.0%	43.1%	53.8%
$ 1,488	$ 1,300	$ 1,038	$ 918	$ 817	$ 717	$ 490	$ 331	$ 266

[7]Net income available to common share owners in 1989 included after-tax gains of $604 million ($.44 per common share) from the sales of the Company's equity interest in Columbia Pictures Entertainment, Inc. and the Company's bottled water business and the transition effect of $265 million related to the change in accounting for income taxes. Excluding these nonrecurring items, the dividend payout ratio in 1989 was 39.9 percent.

Consolidated Balance Sheets

December 31,	**1995**	1994
(In millions except share data)		
Assets		
Current		
Cash and cash equivalents	**$ 1,167**	$ 1,386
Marketable securities	**148**	145
	1,315	1,531
Trade accounts receivable, less allowances of $34 in 1995 and $33 in 1994	**1,695**	1,470
Finance subsidiary receivables	**55**	55
Inventories	**1,117**	1,047
Prepaid expenses and other assets	**1,268**	1,102
Total Current Assets	**5,450**	5,205
Investments and Other Assets		
Equity method investments		
Coca-Cola Enterprises Inc.	**556**	524
Coca-Cola Amatil Limited	**682**	694
Other, principally bottling companies	**1,157**	1,114
Cost method investments, principally bottling companies	**319**	178
Finance subsidiary receivables and investments	**351**	255
Marketable securities and other assets	**1,246**	1,163
	4,311	3,928
Property, Plant and Equipment		
Land	**233**	221
Buildings and improvements	**1,944**	1,814
Machinery and equipment	**4,135**	3,776
Containers	**345**	346
	6,657	6,157
Less allowances for depreciation	**2,321**	2,077
	4,336	4,080
Goodwill and Other Intangible Assets	**944**	660
	$ 15,041	$ 13,873

December 31,	**1995**	1994
Liabilities and Share-Owners' Equity		
Current		
Accounts payable and accrued expenses	**$ 2,894**	$ 2,564
Loans and notes payable	**2,371**	2,048
Current maturities of long-term debt	**552**	35
Accrued taxes	**1,531**	1,530
Total Current Liabilities	**7,348**	6,177
Long-Term Debt	**1,141**	1,426
Other Liabilities	**966**	855
Deferred Income Taxes	**194**	180
Share-Owners' Equity		
Common stock, $.25 par value		
Authorized: 2,800,000,000 shares		
Issued: 1,711,839,497 shares in 1995; 1,707,627,955 shares in 1994	**428**	427
Capital surplus	**1,291**	1,173
Reinvested earnings	**12,882**	11,006
Unearned compensation related to outstanding restricted stock	**(68)**	(74)
Foreign currency translation adjustment	**(424)**	(272)
Unrealized gain on securities available for sale	**82**	48
	14,191	12,308
Less treasury stock, at cost (459,540,663 shares in 1995; 431,694,661 shares in 1994)	**8,799**	7,073
	5,392	5,235
	$ 15,041	$ 13,873

See Notes to Consolidated Financial Statements.

Consolidated Statements of Income

Year Ended December 31, (*In millions except per share data*)	1995	1994	1993
Net Operating Revenues	**$ 18,018**	$ 16,181	$ 13,963
Cost of goods sold	**6,940**	6,168	5,160
Gross Profit	**11,078**	10,013	8,803
Selling, administrative and general expenses	**6,986**	6,297	5,695
Operating Income	**4,092**	3,716	3,108
Interest income	**245**	181	144
Interest expense	**272**	199	168
Equity income	**169**	134	91
Other income (deductions)-net	**20**	(104)	(2)
Gain on issuance of stock by Coca-Cola Amatil	**74**	—	12
Income before Income Taxes and Change in Accounting Principle	**4,328**	3,728	3,185
Income taxes	**1,342**	1,174	997
Income before Change in Accounting Principle	**2,986**	2,554	2,188
Transition effect of change in accounting for postemployment benefits	**—**	—	(12)
Net Income	**$ 2,986**	$ 2,554	$ 2,176
Income per Share			
Before change in accounting principle	**$ 2.37**	$ 1.98	$ 1.68
Transition effect of change in accounting for postemployment benefits	**—**	—	(.01)
Net Income per Share	**$ 2.37**	$ 1.98	$ 1.67
Average Shares Outstanding	**1,262**	1,290	1,302

See Notes to Consolidated Financial Statements.

Consolidated Statements of Cash Flows

Year Ended December 31, (*In millions*)	1995	1994	1993
Operating Activities			
Net income	$ 2,986	$ 2,554	$ 2,176
Transition effect of change in accounting principle	—	—	12
Depreciation and amortization	454	411	360
Deferred income taxes	157	58	(62)
Equity income, net of dividends	(25)	(4)	(35)
Foreign currency adjustments	(23)	(6)	9
Gains on sales of assets	—	—	(84)
Other noncash items	(29)	41	78
Net change in operating assets and liabilities	(405)	129	54
Net cash provided by operating activities	3,115	3,183	2,508
Investing Activities			
Additions to finance subsidiary receivables	(144)	(94)	(177)
Collections of finance subsidiary receivables	46	50	44
Acquisitions and investments, principally bottling companies	(338)	(311)	(611)
Purchases of securities	(190)	(201)	(245)
Proceeds from disposals of investments and other assets	580	299	690
Purchases of property, plant and equipment	(937)	(878)	(800)
Proceeds from disposals of property, plant and equipment	44	109	312
Other investing activities	(74)	(11)	(98)
Net cash used in investing activities	(1,013)	(1,037)	(885)
Net cash provided by operations after reinvestment	2,102	2,146	1,623
Financing Activities			
Issuances of debt	754	491	445
Payments of debt	(212)	(154)	(567)
Issuances of stock	86	69	145
Purchases of stock for treasury	(1,796)	(1,192)	(680)
Dividends	(1,110)	(1,006)	(883)
Net cash used in financing activities	(2,278)	(1,792)	(1,540)
Effect of Exchange Rate Changes on Cash and Cash Equivalents	(43)	34	(41)
Cash and Cash Equivalents			
Net increase (decrease) during the year	(219)	388	42
Balance at beginning of year	1,386	998	956
Balance at end of year	$ 1,167	$ 1,386	$ 998

See Notes to Consolidated Financial Statements.

Consolidated Statements of Share-Owners' Equity

Three Years Ended December 31, 1995	Number of Common Shares Outstanding	Common Stock	Capital Surplus	Reinvested Earnings	Outstanding Restricted Stock	Foreign Currency Translation	Unrealized Gain on Securities	Treasury Stock
(In millions except per share data)								
Balance December 31, 1992	1,307	$ 424	$ 871	$ 8,165	$ (100)	$ (271)	$ —	$ (5,201)
Stock issued to employees exercising stock options	7	2	143	—	—	—	—	—
Tax benefit from employees' stock option and restricted stock plans	—	—	66	—	—	—	—	—
Stock issued under restricted stock plans, less amortization of $19	—	—	6	—	15	—	—	—
Translation adjustments	—	—	—	—	—	(149)	—	—
Purchases of stock for treasury	(17)[1]	—	—	—	—	—	—	(680)
Net income	—	—	—	2,176	—	—	—	—
Dividends (per share–$.68)	—	—	—	(883)	—	—	—	—
Balance December 31, 1993	1,297	426	1,086	9,458	(85)	(420)	—	(5,881)
Transition effect of change in accounting for certain debt and marketable equity securities, net of deferred taxes	—	—	—	—	—	—	60	—
Stock issued to employees exercising stock options	4	1	68	—	—	—	—	—
Tax benefit from employees' stock option and restricted stock plans	—	—	17	—	—	—	—	—
Stock issued under restricted stock plans, less amortization of $13	—	—	2	—	11	—	—	—
Translation adjustments	—	—	—	—	—	148	—	—
Net change in unrealized gain on securities, net of deferred taxes	—	—	—	—	—	—	(12)	—
Purchases of stock for treasury	(25)[1]	—	—	—	—	—	—	(1,192)
Net income	—	—	—	2,554	—	—	—	—
Dividends (per share–$.78)	—	—	—	(1,006)	—	—	—	—
Balance December 31, 1994	1,276	427	1,173	11,006	(74)	(272)	48	(7,073)
Stock issued to employees exercising stock options	4	1	85	—	—	—	—	—
Tax benefit from employees' stock option and restricted stock plans	—	—	26	—	—	—	—	—
Stock issued under restricted stock plans, less amortization of $12	—	—	7	—	6	—	—	—
Translation adjustments	—	—	—	—	—	(152)	—	—
Net change in unrealized gain on securities, net of deferred taxes	—	—	—	—	—	—	34	—
Purchases of stock for treasury	(29)[1]	—	—	—	—	—	—	(1,796)
Treasury stock issued in connection with an acquisition	1	—	—	—	—	—	—	70
Net income	—	—	—	2,986	—	—	—	—
Dividends (per share–$.88)	—	—	—	(1,110)	—	—	—	—
Balance December 31, 1995	**1,252**	**$ 428**	**$ 1,291**	**$ 12,882**	**$ (68)**	**$ (424)**	**$ 82**	**$ (8,799)**

[1]*Common stock purchased from employees exercising stock options amounted to 280 thousand, 208 thousand and 2.7 million shares for the years ending December 31, 1995, 1994 and 1993, respectively.*

See Notes to Consolidated Financial Statements.

Notes to Consolidated Financial Statements

1. Accounting Policies

The significant accounting policies and practices followed by
The Coca-Cola Company and subsidiaries (the Company) are
as follows:

Organization

The Company is predominantly a manufacturer, marketer and
distributor of soft drink and noncarbonated beverage concentrates and syrups. Operating in nearly 200 countries worldwide, the Company primarily sells its concentrates and syrups
to bottling and canning operations, fountain wholesalers and
fountain retailers. The Company has significant markets for
its products in all of the world's geographic regions.

Consolidation

The consolidated financial statements include the accounts
of the Company and all subsidiaries except where control is
temporary or does not rest with the Company. The
Company's investments in companies in which it has the
ability to exercise significant influence over operating and
financial policies are accounted for by the equity method.
Accordingly, the Company's share of the net earnings of these
companies is included in consolidated net income. The
Company's investments in other companies are carried at
cost or fair value, as appropriate. All significant intercompany
accounts and transactions are eliminated.

Certain amounts in the prior years' financial statements have been reclassified to conform to the current
year presentation.

Advertising Costs

The Company generally expenses production costs of print,
radio and television advertisements as of the first date the
advertisements take place. Advertising expenses included
in selling, administrative and general expenses were
$1,333 million in 1995, $1,142 million in 1994 and
$1,002 million in 1993. As of December 31, 1995 and 1994,
advertising costs of approximately $299 million and
$259 million, respectively, were recorded primarily in prepaid
expenses and other assets in the accompanying balance sheets.

Net Income per Share

Net income per share is computed by dividing net income
by the weighted average number of shares outstanding.

On December 21, 1995, the Board of Directors authorized a two-for-one stock split. The stock split is subject to
share-owner approval in April 1996. If approved, the stock
split will be payable to share owners of record on May 1,
1996. These financial statements have not been restated to
reflect the proposed stock split.

Cash Equivalents

Marketable securities that are highly liquid and have maturities of three months or less at the date of purchase are classified
as cash equivalents.

Inventories

Inventories are valued at the lower of cost or market. In general, cost is determined on the basis of average cost or first-in,
first-out methods.

Property, Plant and Equipment

Property, plant and equipment are stated at cost and are
depreciated principally by the straight-line method over the
estimated useful lives of the assets.

Goodwill and Other Intangible Assets

Goodwill and other intangible assets are stated on the basis
of cost and are amortized, principally on a straight-line
basis, over the estimated future periods to be benefited (not
exceeding 40 years). Goodwill and other intangible assets are
periodically reviewed for impairment based on an assessment
of future operations to ensure that they are appropriately
valued. Accumulated amortization was approximately
$117 million and $77 million on December 31, 1995
and 1994, respectively.

Use of Estimates

The preparation of financial statements in conformity with
generally accepted accounting principles requires management
to make estimates and assumptions that affect the amounts
reported in the financial statements and accompanying notes.
Although these estimates are based on management's knowledge of current events and actions it may undertake in the
future, they may ultimately differ from actual results.

Changes in Accounting Principles

In 1995, the Financial Accounting Standards Board (FASB)
issued Statement of Financial Accounting Standards No. 121,
"Accounting for the Impairment of Long-Lived Assets and for
Long-Lived Assets to be Disposed Of" (SFAS 121). The
Company's required adoption date is January 1, 1996. SFAS
121 standardizes the accounting practices for the recognition
and measurement of impairment losses on certain long-lived
assets. The Company anticipates the adoption of SFAS 121 will
not have a material impact on its results of operations or financial position. However, the provisions of SFAS 121 will require
certain charges historically recorded by the Company in other
income (deductions)-net to be included in operating income.

Statement of Financial Accounting Standards No. 115,
"Accounting for Certain Investments in Debt and Equity
Securities" (SFAS 115), was adopted as of January 1, 1994.

Notes to Consolidated Financial Statements

SFAS 115 requires that the carrying value of certain investments be adjusted to their fair value. Upon adoption of SFAS 115, the Company recorded an increase to share-owners' equity of $60 million, which is net of deferred income taxes of $44 million.

Statement of Financial Accounting Standards No. 112, "Employers' Accounting for Postemployment Benefits" (SFAS 112), was adopted as of January 1, 1993. SFAS 112 requires employers to accrue the costs of benefits to former or inactive employees after employment, but before retirement. Upon adoption, the Company recorded an accumulated obligation of $12 million, which is net of deferred income taxes of $8 million.

Stock-Based Compensation

The Company currently accounts for its stock-based compensation plans using the provisions of Accounting Principles Board Opinion No. 25, "Accounting for Stock Issued to Employees" (APB 25).

In 1995, the FASB issued Statement of Financial Accounting Standards No. 123, "Accounting for Stock-Based Compensation" (SFAS 123). Under the provisions of SFAS 123, companies can elect to account for stock-based compensation plans using a fair-value-based method or continue measuring compensation expense for those plans using the intrinsic value method prescribed in APB 25. SFAS 123 requires that companies electing to continue using the intrinsic value method must make pro forma disclosures of net income and earnings per share as if the fair-value-based method of accounting had been applied. The adoption of SFAS 123 will be reflected in the Company's 1996 consolidated financial statements.

As the Company anticipates continuing to account for stock-based compensation using the intrinsic value method, SFAS 123 will not have an impact on the Company's results of operations or financial position.

2. Inventories

Inventories consist of the following (in millions):

December 31,	**1995**	1994
Raw materials and supplies	**$ 784**	$ 728
Work in process	**7**	4
Finished goods	**326**	315
	$ 1,117	$ 1,047

3. Bottling Investments

Coca-Cola Enterprises Inc.

Coca-Cola Enterprises is the largest soft drink bottler in the world. The Company owns approximately 44 percent of the outstanding common stock of Coca-Cola Enterprises, and accordingly, accounts for its investment by the equity method of accounting. A summary of financial information for Coca-Cola Enterprises is as follows (in millions):

December 31,	**1995**	1994
Current assets	**$ 982**	$ 809
Noncurrent assets	**8,082**	7,928
Total assets	**$ 9,064**	$ 8,737
Current liabilities	**$ 859**	$ 1,088
Noncurrent liabilities	**6,770**	6,310
Total liabilities	**$ 7,629**	$ 7,398
Share-owners' equity	**$ 1,435**	$ 1,339
Company equity investment	**$ 556**	$ 524

Year Ended December 31,	**1995**	1994	1993
Net operating revenues	**$ 6,773**	$ 6,011	$ 5,465
Cost of goods sold	**4,267**	3,703	3,372
Gross profit	**$ 2,506**	$ 2,308	$ 2,093
Operating income	**$ 468**	$ 440	$ 385
Operating cash flow	**$ 997**	$ 901	$ 804
Net income (loss)	**$ 82**	$ 69	$ (15)
Net income (loss) available to common share owners	**$ 80**	$ 67	$ (15)
Company equity income (loss)	**$ 35**	$ 30	$ (6)

The Company's net concentrate/syrup sales to Coca-Cola Enterprises were $1.3 billion in 1995, $1.2 billion in 1994 and $961 million in 1993. Coca-Cola Enterprises purchases sweeteners through the Company under a pass-through arrangement, and accordingly, related collections from Coca-Cola Enterprises and payments to suppliers are not included in the Company's consolidated statements of income. These transactions amounted to $242 million in 1995, $254 million in 1994 and $211 million in 1993. The Company also provides certain administrative and other services to Coca-Cola Enterprises under negotiated fee arrangements.

The Company's direct support for certain marketing activities of Coca-Cola Enterprises and participation with Coca-Cola Enterprises in cooperative advertising and other marketing programs amounted to approximately $343 million in 1995, $319 million in 1994 and $256 million in 1993. Additionally, in 1995 and 1994, the Company

Notes to Consolidated Financial Statements

committed to provide approximately $55 million and $34 million, respectively, to Coca-Cola Enterprises under a Company program which encourages bottlers to invest in building and supporting beverage infrastructure.

If valued at the December 31, 1995, quoted closing price of publicly traded Coca-Cola Enterprises shares, the calculated value of the Company's investment in Coca-Cola Enterprises would have exceeded its carrying value by approximately $957 million.

Other Equity Investments

On December 31, 1995, the Company owned approximately 40 percent of Coca-Cola Amatil Limited (Coca-Cola Amatil), an Australian-based bottler of Company products that operates in 16 countries. Accordingly, the Company accounts for its investment in Coca-Cola Amatil by the equity method.

In July 1995, Coca-Cola Amatil completed a public offering in Australia of approximately 97 million shares of common stock. This transaction resulted in a non-cash pretax gain of approximately $74 million for the Company.

In the fourth quarter of 1993, Coca-Cola Amatil issued approximately 8 million shares of stock to acquire the Company's franchise bottler in Jakarta, Indonesia. This transaction resulted in a pretax gain for the Company of approximately $12 million.

On December 31, 1995, the excess of the Company's investment over its equity in the underlying net assets of Coca-Cola Amatil was approximately $91 million, which is being amortized on a straight-line basis over 40 years.

During 1995, the Company's finance subsidiary invested $160 million in The Coca-Cola Bottling Company of New York, Inc. (CCNY), in return for redeemable preferred stock. As of December 31, 1995, the Company held a 49 percent voting and economic interest in CCNY. Accordingly, the Company accounts for its investment in CCNY by the equity method.

In 1993, the Company acquired a 30 percent equity interest in Coca-Cola FEMSA, S.A. de C.V. (Coca-Cola FEMSA), which operates bottling facilities in Mexico and Argentina, for $195 million. On December 31, 1995, the excess of the Company's investment over its equity in the underlying net assets of Coca-Cola FEMSA was approximately $31 million, which is being amortized over 40 years.

Operating results include the Company's proportionate share of income from equity investments since the respective dates of investment. A summary of financial information for the Company's equity investments, other than Coca-Cola Enterprises, is as follows (in millions):

December 31,	1995	1994
Current assets	$ 2,954	$ 2,747
Noncurrent assets	6,637	5,316
Total assets	$ 9,591	$ 8,063
Current liabilities	$ 2,944	$ 2,382
Noncurrent liabilities	2,849	2,669
Total liabilities	$ 5,793	$ 5,051
Share-owners' equity	$ 3,798	$ 3,012
Company equity investment	$ 1,839	$ 1,808

Year Ended December 31,	1995	1994	1993
Net operating revenues	$ 11,563	$ 9,668	$ 8,168
Cost of goods sold	7,646	6,397	5,385
Gross profit	$ 3,917	$ 3,271	$ 2,783
Operating income	$ 846	$ 783	$ 673
Operating cash flow	$ 1,403	$ 1,076	$ 984
Net income	$ 355	$ 323	$ 258
Company equity income	$ 134	$ 104	$ 97

Equity investments include certain non-bottling investees.

Net income for the Company's equity investments in 1993 reflects an $86 million after-tax charge recorded by Coca-Cola Beverages Ltd., related to the restructuring of its operations in Canada.

Net sales to equity investees other than Coca-Cola Enterprises were $1.4 billion in 1995 and $1.2 billion in 1994 and 1993. The Company also participates in various marketing, promotional and other activities with these investees, the majority of which are located outside the United States.

If valued at the December 31, 1995, quoted closing prices of shares actively traded on stock markets, the calculated value of the Company's equity investments in publicly traded bottlers other than Coca-Cola Enterprises would have exceeded the Company's carrying value by approximately $1.2 billion.

Notes to Consolidated Financial Statements

4. Finance Subsidiary

Coca-Cola Financial Corporation (CCFC) provides loans and other forms of financing to Coca-Cola bottlers and customers for the acquisition of sales-related equipment and for other business purposes. The approximate contractual maturities of finance receivables for the five years succeeding December 31, 1995, are as follows (in millions):

1996	1997	1998	1999	2000
$ 55	$ 39	$ 39	$ 33	$ 58

These amounts do not reflect possible prepayments or renewals.

CCFC has agreed to issue up to $50 million in letters of credit on CCNY's behalf, of which $24 million was committed on December 31, 1995.

5. Accounts Payable and Accrued Expenses

Accounts payable and accrued expenses consist of the following (in millions):

December 31,	1995	1994
Accrued marketing	$ 492	$ 425
Container deposits	130	112
Accrued compensation	198	189
Accounts payable and other accrued expenses	2,074	1,838
	$ 2,894	$ 2,564

6. Short-Term Borrowings and Credit Arrangements

Loans and notes payable consist primarily of commercial paper issued in the United States. On December 31, 1995, the Company had $3.3 billion in lines of credit and other short-term credit facilities available, under which $2.4 billion was outstanding. Included was $2.2 billion outstanding in commercial paper borrowings. The Company's weighted average interest rates for commercial paper were approximately 5.7 and 5.8 percent on December 31, 1995 and 1994, respectively.

These facilities are subject to normal banking terms and conditions. Some of the financial arrangements require compensating balances, none of which are presently significant to the Company.

7. Accrued Taxes

Accrued taxes consist of the following (in millions):

December 31,	1995	1994
Income taxes	$ 1,322	$ 1,312
Sales, payroll and other taxes	209	218
	$ 1,531	$ 1,530

8. Long-Term Debt

Long-term debt consists of the following (in millions):

December 31,	1995	1994
7¾% U.S. dollar notes due 1996	$ 250	$ 250
5¾% Japanese yen notes due 1996	292	301
5¾% German mark notes due 1998[1]	175	161
7⅞% U.S. dollar notes due 1998	250	250
6% U.S. dollar notes due 2000	252	—
6⅝% U.S. dollar notes due 2002	149	149
6% U.S. dollar notes due 2003	150	150
7⅜% U.S. dollar notes due 2093	116	116
Other, due 1996 to 2013	59	84
	1,693	1,461
Less current portion	552	35
	$ 1,141	$ 1,426

[1]*Portions of these notes have been swapped for liabilities denominated in other currencies.*

After giving effect to interest rate management instruments (see Note 10), the principal amount of the Company's long-term debt that had fixed and variable interest rates, respectively, was $1,017 million and $676 million on December 31, 1995 and $849 million and $612 million on December 31, 1994. The weighted average interest rate on the Company's long-term debt was 6.5 and 6.6 percent on December 31, 1995 and 1994, respectively.

Maturities of long-term debt for the five years succeeding December 31, 1995, are as follows (in millions):

1996	1997	1998	1999	2000
$ 552	$ 10	$ 435	$ 8	$ 255

The above notes include various restrictions, none of which are presently significant to the Company.

Interest paid was approximately $275 million, $197 million and $158 million in 1995, 1994 and 1993, respectively.

Notes to Consolidated Financial Statements

9. Financial Instruments

Fair Value of Financial Instruments

The carrying amounts reflected in the consolidated balance sheets for cash, cash equivalents, loans and notes payable approximate their respective fair values due to the short maturities of these instruments. The fair values for marketable equity securities, investments, receivables, long-term debt and hedging instruments are based primarily on quoted prices for those or similar instruments. A comparison of the carrying value and fair value of these financial instruments is as follows (in millions):

December 31,	Carrying Value	Fair Value
1995		
Current marketable securities	$ 148	$ 148
Finance subsidiary receivables and investments	406	410
Cost method investments, principally bottling companies	319	319
Marketable securities and other assets	1,246	1,245
Long-term debt	(1,693)	(1,737)
Hedging instruments (see Note 10)	54	(107)
1994		
Current marketable securities	$ 145	$ 145
Finance subsidiary receivables and investments	310	315
Cost method investments, principally bottling companies	178	236
Marketable securities and other assets	1,163	1,156
Long-term debt	(1,461)	(1,416)
Hedging instruments (see Note 10)	64	(293)

Certain Debt and Marketable Equity Securities

Investments in debt and marketable equity securities, other than investments accounted for by the equity method, are categorized as either trading, available for sale, or held to maturity. On December 31, 1995 and 1994, the Company had no trading securities. Securities categorized as available for sale are stated at fair value, with unrealized gains and losses, net of deferred income taxes, reported in share-owners' equity. Debt securities categorized as held to maturity are stated at amortized cost.

On December 31, 1995 and 1994, available-for-sale and held-to-maturity securities consisted of the following (in millions):

December 31,	Cost	Gross Unrealized Gains	Gross Unrealized Losses	Estimated Fair Value
1995				
Available-for-sale securities				
Equity securities	$ 128	$ 151	$ (2)	$ 277
Collateralized mortgage obligations	147	—	(5)	142
Other debt securities	26	—	—	26
	$ 301	$ 151	$ (7)	$ 445
Held-to-maturity securities				
Bank and corporate debt	$ 1,333	$ —	$ —	$ 1,333
Other debt securities	40	—	—	40
	$ 1,373	$ —	$ —	$ 1,373
1994				
Available-for-sale securities				
Equity securities	$ 48	$ 76	$ (4)	$ 120
Collateralized mortgage obligations	150	—	(11)	139
Other debt securities	32	—	—	32
	$ 230	$ 76	$ (15)	$ 291
Held-to-maturity securities				
Bank and corporate debt	$ 1,388	$ —	$ —	$ 1,388
Other debt securities	68	—	—	68
	$ 1,456	$ —	$ —	$ 1,456

Notes to Consolidated Financial Statements

On December 31, 1995 and 1994, these investments were included in the following captions on the consolidated balance sheets (in millions):

December 31,	Available-for-Sale Securities	Held-to-Maturity Securities
1995		
Cash and cash equivalents	**$ —**	**$ 900**
Current marketable securities	**74**	**74**
Cost method investments, principally bottling companies	**222**	**—**
Marketable securities and other assets	**149**	**399**
	$ 445	**$ 1,373**
1994		
Cash and cash equivalents	$ —	$ 1,041
Current marketable securities	87	58
Cost method investments, principally bottling companies	58	—
Marketable securities and other assets	146	357
	$ 291	$ 1,456

The contractual maturities of these investments as of December 31, 1995, were as follows (in millions):

	Available-for-Sale Securities		Held-to-Maturity Securities	
	Cost	Fair Value	Amortized Cost	Fair Value
1996	$ 22	$ 22	$ 974	$ 974
1997-2000	4	4	379	379
After 2000	—	—	20	20
Collateralized mortgage obligations	147	142	—	—
Equity securities	128	277	—	—
	$ 301	$ 445	$ 1,373	$ 1,373

For the years ended December 31, 1995 and 1994, gross realized gains and losses on sales of available-for-sale securities were not material. The cost of securities sold is based on the specific identification method.

10. Hedging Transactions and Derivative Financial Instruments

The Company employs derivative financial instruments primarily to reduce its exposure to adverse fluctuations in interest and foreign exchange rates. These financial instruments, when entered into, are designated as hedges of underlying exposures. Because of the high correlation between the hedging instrument and the underlying exposure being hedged, fluctuations in the value of the instruments are generally offset by changes in the value of the underlying exposures. The Company effectively monitors the use of these derivative financial instruments through the use of objective measurement systems, well-defined market and credit risk limits and timely reports to senior management according to prescribed guidelines. Virtually all of the Company's derivatives are "over-the-counter" instruments.

The estimated fair values of derivatives used to hedge or modify the Company's risks will fluctuate over time. These fair value amounts should not be viewed in isolation, but rather in relation to the fair values of the underlying hedged transactions and investments and the overall reduction in the Company's exposure to adverse fluctuations in interest and foreign exchange rates.

The notional amounts of the derivative financial instruments do not necessarily represent amounts exchanged by the parties and, therefore, are not a direct measure of the exposure of the Company through its use of derivatives. The amounts exchanged are calculated by reference to the notional amounts and by the other terms of the derivatives, such as interest rates, exchange rates or other financial indices.

The Company has established strict counterparty credit guidelines and only enters into transactions with financial institutions of investment grade or better. Counterparty exposures are monitored daily and any downgrade in credit rating receives immediate review. If a downgrade in the credit rating of a counterparty were to occur, the Company has provisions to require collateral in the form of U.S. government securities for transactions with maturities in excess of three years. To mitigate pre-settlement risk, minimum credit standards become more stringent as the duration of the derivative financial instrument increases. To minimize the concentration of credit risk, the Company enters into derivative transactions with a portfolio of financial institutions. As a result, the Company considers the risk of counterparty default to be minimal.

Interest Rate Management

Management of the Company has implemented a policy to maintain the percentage of fixed and variable rate debt within certain parameters. The Company enters into interest rate swap agreements that maintain the fixed/variable mix within these defined parameters. These contracts had maturities ranging from 2 to 8 years on December 31, 1995. Variable rates are predominantly linked to the LIBOR (London Interbank Offered Rate). Any differences paid or received on interest rate swap agreements are recognized as adjustments to interest expense over the life of each swap, thereby adjusting the effective interest rate on the underlying obligation.

Additionally, the Company enters into interest rate cap agreements that entitle the Company to receive from a financial institution the amount, if any, by which the Company's interest

Notes to Consolidated Financial Statements

payments on its variable rate debt exceed pre-specified interest rates through 1997. Premiums paid for interest rate cap agreements are included in prepaid expenses and other assets and are amortized to interest expense over the terms of the respective agreements. Payments received pursuant to the interest rate cap agreements, if any, are recognized as an adjustment of the interest expense on the underlying debt instruments.

Foreign Currency Management

The purpose of the Company's foreign currency hedging activities is to reduce the risk that the eventual dollar net cash inflows resulting from sales outside the U.S. will be adversely affected by changes in exchange rates.

The Company enters into forward exchange contracts and purchases currency options (principally European currencies and Japanese yen) to hedge firm sale commitments denominated in foreign currencies. The Company also purchases currency options (principally European currencies and Japanese yen) to hedge certain anticipated sales. Premiums paid and realized gains and losses, including those on terminated contracts, if any, are included in prepaid expenses and other assets. These are recognized in income along with unrealized gains and losses, in the same period the hedged transactions are realized. Approximately $27 million and $10 million of realized losses on settled contracts entered into as hedges of firmly committed transactions which have not yet occurred were deferred on December 31, 1995 and 1994, respectively. Deferred gains/losses from hedging anticipated transactions were not material on December 31, 1995 or 1994. In the unlikely event that the underlying transaction terminates or becomes improbable, the deferred gains or losses on the associated derivative will be recorded in the income statement.

Gains and losses on derivative financial instruments that are designated and effective as hedges of net investments in international operations are included in share-owners' equity as a foreign currency translation adjustment.

The following table presents the aggregate notional principal amounts, carrying values, fair values and maturities of the Company's derivative financial instruments outstanding on December 31, 1995 and 1994 (in millions):

December 31,	Notional Principal Amounts	Carrying Values	Fair Values	Maturity
1995				
Interest rate management				
Swap agreements				
Assets	$ **705**	$ **4**	$ **30**	**1997-2003**
Liabilities	**62**	**—**	**(2)**	**2000-2002**
Interest rate caps				
Assets	**400**	**2**	**—**	**1997**
Foreign currency management				
Forward contracts				
Assets	**1,927**	**25**	**36**	**1996**
Liabilities	**554**	**(17)**	**(15)**	**1996-1997**
Swap agreements				
Assets	**390**	**17**	**11**	**1996-2000**
Liabilities	**1,686**	**(46)**	**(262)**	**1996-2002**
Purchased options				
Assets	**1,823**	**62**	**90**	**1996**
Other				
Assets	**327**	**7**	**5**	**1996**
	$ **7,874**	$ **54**	$ **(107)**	
1994				
Interest rate management				
Swap agreements				
Assets	$ 626	$ 3	$ (30)	1995-2003
Liabilities	225	(1)	1	1995-2005
Interest rate caps				
Assets	400	3	5	1995-1997
Foreign currency management				
Forward contracts				
Assets	1,887	24	33	1995-1996
Liabilities	666	(10)	(9)	1995
Swap agreements				
Assets	399	23	22	1995-2000
Liabilities	2,104	(44)	(356)	1995-2002
Purchased options				
Assets	3,485	66	41	1995-1996
	$ 9,792	$ 64	$ (293)	

Maturities of derivative financial instruments held on December 31, 1995, are as follows (in millions):

1996	1997	1998	1999 through 2003
$ 5,343	$ 1,025	$ 534	$ 972

Notes to Consolidated Financial Statements

11. Commitments and Contingencies

On December 31, 1995, the Company was contingently liable for guarantees of indebtedness owed by third parties in the amount of $202 million, of which $48 million is related to independent bottling licensees.

The Mitsubishi Bank Limited has provided a yen denominated guarantee for the equivalent of $253 million in support of a suspension of enforcement of a tax assessment levied by the Japanese tax authorities. The Company has agreed to indemnify Mitsubishi if amounts are paid pursuant to this guarantee. This matter is being reviewed by the tax authorities of the United States and Japan under the tax treaty signed by the two nations to prevent double taxation. Any additional tax payable to Japan should be offset by tax credits in the United States and would not adversely affect earnings.

In the opinion of management, it is not probable that the Company will be required to satisfy these guarantees or indemnification agreements. The fair value of these contingent liabilities is immaterial to the Company's consolidated financial statements.

It is also the opinion of management that the Company's exposure to concentrations of credit risk is limited, due to the diverse geographic areas covered by the Company's operations.

Additionally, the Company has committed, under certain circumstances, to make future investments in bottling companies. However, none of these commitments is considered by management to be individually significant.

12. Restricted Stock, Stock Options and Other Stock Plans

The Company sponsors restricted stock award plans, stock option plans, Incentive Unit Agreements and Performance Unit Agreements.

Under the amended 1989 Restricted Stock Award Plan and the amended 1983 Restricted Stock Award Plan (the Restricted Stock Plans), 20 million and 12 million shares of restricted common stock, respectively, may be granted to certain officers and key employees of the Company.

On December 31, 1995, 17 million shares were available for grant under the Restricted Stock Plans. Participants are entitled to vote and receive dividends on the shares, and under the 1983 Restricted Stock Award Plan, participants are reimbursed by the Company for income taxes imposed on the award, but not for taxes generated by the reimbursement payment. The shares are subject to certain transfer restrictions and may be forfeited if a participant leaves the Company for reasons other than retirement, disability or death, absent a change in control of the Company.

On July 18, 1991, the Restricted Stock Plans were amended to specify age 62 as the minimum retirement age. The 1983 Restricted Stock Award Plan was further amended to conform to the terms of the 1989 Restricted Stock Award Plan by requiring a minimum of five years of service between the date of the award and retirement. The amendments affect shares granted after July 18, 1991.

Under the Company's 1991 Stock Option Plan (the Option Plan), a maximum of 60 million shares of the Company's common stock was approved to be issued or transferred to certain officers and employees pursuant to stock options and stock appreciation rights granted under the Option Plan. The stock appreciation rights permit the holder, upon surrendering all or part of the related stock option, to receive cash, common stock or a combination thereof, in an amount up to 100 percent of the difference between the market price and the option price. Options outstanding on December 31, 1995, also include various options granted under previous plans. Further information relating to options is as follows (in millions, except per share amounts):

	1995	1994	1993
Outstanding on January 1,	**33**	30	31
Granted	**9**	7	6
Exercised	**(4)**	(4)	(7)
Canceled	**(1)**	—	—
Outstanding on December 31,	**37**	33	30
Exercisable on December 31,	**23**	22	22
Shares available on December 31,			
for options that may be granted	**30**	38	45
Prices per share			
Exercised	**$6–$51**	$5-$44	$4-$41
Unexercised on December 31,	**$7–$76**	$6-$51	$5-$44

In 1988, the Company entered into Incentive Unit Agreements whereby, subject to certain conditions, certain officers were given the right to receive cash awards based on the market value of 1.2 million shares of the Company's common stock at the measurement dates. Under the Incentive Unit Agreements, the employee is reimbursed by the Company for income taxes imposed when the value of the units is paid, but not for taxes generated by the reimbursement payment. In 1993, 400,000 units were paid, leaving 800,000 units outstanding on December 31, 1993. No units were paid in 1994 or 1995, leaving the number of units outstanding unchanged on December 31, 1995.

In 1985, the Company entered into Performance Unit Agreements, whereby certain officers were given the right to receive cash awards based on the difference in the market

Notes to Consolidated Financial Statements

value of approximately 2.2 million shares of the Company's common stock at the measurement dates and the base price of $5.16, the market value as of January 2, 1985. In 1993, 780,000 units were paid, leaving approximately 1.4 million units outstanding on December 31, 1993. No units were paid in 1994 or 1995, leaving the number of units outstanding unchanged on December 31, 1995.

13. Pension Benefits

The Company sponsors and/or contributes to pension plans covering substantially all U.S. employees and certain employees in international locations. The benefits are primarily based on years of service and the employees' compensation for certain periods during the last years of employment. Pension costs are generally funded currently, subject to regulatory funding limitations. The Company also sponsors nonqualified, unfunded defined benefit plans for certain officers and other employees. In addition, the Company and its subsidiaries have various pension plans and other forms of postretirement arrangements outside the United States.

Total pension expense for all benefit plans, including defined benefit plans, amounted to approximately $81 million in 1995, $73 million in 1994 and $57 million in 1993. Net periodic pension cost for the Company's defined benefit plans consists of the following (in millions):

Year Ended December 31,	1995	1994	1993
U.S. Plans			
Service cost-benefits earned during the period	$ 20	$ 22	$ 17
Interest cost on projected benefit obligation	62	53	53
Actual return on plan assets	(184)	(4)	(77)
Net amortization and deferral	136	(44)	31
Net periodic pension cost	$ 34	$ 27	$ 24
International Plans			
Service cost-benefits earned during the period	$ 23	$ 24	$ 17
Interest cost on projected benefit obligation	27	25	22
Actual return on plan assets	(27)	(21)	(27)
Net amortization and deferral	9	5	13
Net periodic pension cost	$ 32	$ 33	$ 25

The funded status for the Company's defined benefit plans is as follows (in millions):

December 31,	Assets Exceed Accumulated Benefits		Accumulated Benefits Exceed Assets	
	1995	1994	1995	1994
U.S. Plans				
Actuarial present value of benefit obligations				
Vested benefit obligation	$ 562	$ 479	$ 137	$ 101
Accumulated benefit obligation	$ 613	$ 521	$ 144	$ 104
Projected benefit obligation	$ 705	$ 599	$ 169	$ 125
Plan assets at fair value[1]	785	597	3	2
Plan assets in excess of (less than) projected benefit obligation	80	(2)	(166)[2]	(123)[2]
Unrecognized net (asset) liability at transition	(26)	(30)	13	15
Unrecognized prior service cost	35	37	14	15
Unrecognized net (gain) loss	(81)	(30)	53	18
Adjustment required to recognize minimum liability	—	—	(54)	(28)
Accrued pension asset (liability) included in the consolidated balance sheet	$ 8	$ (25)	$ (140)	$ (103)
International Plans				
Actuarial present value of benefit obligations				
Vested benefit obligation	$ 169	$ 156	$ 149	$ 147
Accumulated benefit obligation	$ 177	$ 157	$ 172	$ 175
Projected benefit obligation	$ 214	$ 199	$ 225	$ 237
Plan assets at fair value[1]	259	235	109	110
Plan assets in excess of (less than) projected benefit obligation	45	36	(116)	(127)
Unrecognized net (asset) liability at transition	(18)	(18)	28	36
Unrecognized prior service cost	3	4	11	13
Unrecognized net (gain) loss	(3)	(1)	1	16
Adjustment required to recognize minimum liability	—	—	(6)	(9)
Accrued pension asset (liability) included in the consolidated balance sheet	$ 27	$ 21	$ (82)	$ (71)

[1]*Primarily listed stocks, bonds and government securities.*

[2]*Substantially all of this amount relates to nonqualified, unfunded defined benefit plans.*

Notes to Consolidated Financial Statements

The assumptions used in computing the preceding information are as follows:

Year Ended December 31,	1995	1994	1993
U.S. Plans			
Discount rates	7¼%	8¼%	7¼%
Rates of increase in compensation levels	4¾%	5¼%	4¾%
Expected long-term rates of return on assets	9½%	9½%	9½%
International Plans (weighted average rates)			
Discount rates	6¼%	6%	6½%
Rates of increase in compensation levels	4½%	4½%	5%
Expected long-term rates of return on assets	6%	6%	7%

14. Other Postretirement Benefits

The Company has plans providing postretirement health care and life insurance benefits to substantially all U.S. employees and certain employees in international locations who retire with a minimum of five years of service.

Net periodic cost for the Company's postretirement health care and life insurance benefits consists of the following (in millions):

Year Ended December 31,	1995	1994	1993
Service cost	$ 12	$ 12	$ 10
Interest cost	23	21	21
Other	(2)	(1)	(1)
	$ 33	$ 32	$ 30

The Company contributes to a Voluntary Employees' Beneficiary Association trust that will be used to partially fund health care benefits for future retirees. Generally, the Company funds benefits to the extent contributions are tax-deductible, which under current legislation is limited. In general, retiree health benefits are paid as covered expenses are incurred.

The funded status of the Company's postretirement health care and life insurance plans is as follows (in millions):

December 31,	1995	1994
Accumulated postretirement benefit obligations:		
Retirees	$ 122	$ 128
Fully eligible active plan participants	40	35
Other active plan participants	141	120
Total benefit obligation	303	283
Plan assets at fair value[1]	42	41
Plan assets less than benefit obligation	(261)	(242)
Unrecognized prior service cost	(3)	(3)
Unrecognized net gain	(9)	(7)
Accrued postretirement benefit liability included in the consolidated balance sheet	$ (273)	$ (252)

[1]Consists of corporate bonds, government securities and short-term investments.

The assumptions used in computing the preceding information are as follows:

Year Ended December 31,	1995	1994	1993
Discount rate	7¼%	8¼%	7¼%
Rate of increase in compensation levels	4¾%	5¼%	4¾%

The rate of increase in the per capita costs of covered health care benefits is assumed to be 8¼ percent in 1996, decreasing gradually to 5 percent by the year 2003. Increasing the assumed health care cost trend rate by 1 percentage point would increase the accumulated postretirement benefit obligation as of December 31, 1995, by approximately $39 million and increase the net periodic postretirement benefit cost by approximately $5 million in 1995.

15. Income Taxes

Income before income taxes and change in accounting principle consists of the following (in millions):

Year Ended December 31,	1995	1994	1993
United States	$ 1,270	$ 1,214	$ 1,035
International	3,058	2,514	2,150
	$ 4,328	$ 3,728	$ 3,185

Notes to Consolidated Financial Statements

Income tax expense (benefit) consists of the following (in millions):

Year Ended December 31,	United States	State & Local	International	Total
1995				
Current	**$ 204**	**$ 41**	**$ 940**	**$ 1,185**
Deferred	**80**	**10**	**67**	**157**
1994				
Current	$ 299	$ 38	$ 779	$ 1,116
Deferred	24	5	29	58
1993				
Current	$ 356	$ 34	$ 669	$ 1,059
Deferred[1]	(64)	5	(3)	(62)

[1]*An additional deferred tax benefit of $8 million in 1993 has been included in the SFAS 112 transition effect charge.*

The Company made income tax payments of approximately $1,000 million, $785 million and $650 million in 1995, 1994 and 1993, respectively.

A reconciliation of the statutory U.S. federal rate and effective rates is as follows:

Year Ended December 31,	1995	1994	1993
Statutory U.S. federal rate	**35.0%**	35.0%	35.0%
State income taxes-net of federal benefit	**1.0**	1.0	1.0
Earnings in jurisdictions taxed at rates different from the statutory U.S. federal rate	**(3.9)**	(4.3)	(5.1)
Equity income	**(1.7)**	(1.1)	(1.7)
Other-net	**.6**	.9	2.1
	31.0%	31.5%	31.3%

The Company's effective tax rate reflects the favorable U.S. tax treatment from manufacturing facilities in Puerto Rico that operate under a negotiated exemption grant that expires December 31, 2009. Changes to U.S. tax law enacted in 1993 limit the utilization of the favorable tax treatment from operations in Puerto Rico. The Company's effective tax rate also reflects the tax benefit derived from having significant operations outside the United States that are taxed at rates lower than the U.S. statutory rate of 35 percent. As a result of changes in U.S. tax law, the Company was required to record charges for additional taxes and tax-related expenses that reduced net income by approximately $51 million in 1993.

Appropriate U.S. and international taxes have been provided for earnings of subsidiary companies that are expected to be remitted to the parent company. Exclusive of amounts that would result in little or no tax if remitted, the cumulative amount of unremitted earnings from international subsidiaries that are expected to be indefinitely reinvested is approximately $577 million on December 31, 1995. The taxes that would be paid upon remittance of these indefinitely reinvested earnings are approximately $202 million based on current tax laws.

The tax effects of temporary differences and carryforwards that give rise to significant portions of deferred tax assets and liabilities consist of the following (in millions):

December 31,	1995	1994
Deferred tax assets:		
Benefit plans	**$ 369**	$ 324
Liabilities and reserves	**178**	169
Net operating loss carryforwards	**97**	108
Other	**151**	128
Gross deferred tax assets	**795**	729
Valuation allowance	**(42)**	(46)
	$ 753	$ 683
Deferred tax liabilities:		
Property, plant and equipment	**$ 414**	$ 362
Equity investments	**170**	188
Intangible assets	**89**	34
Other	**205**	72
	$ 878	$ 656
Net deferred tax asset (liability)[1]	**$ (125)**	$ 27

[1]*Deferred tax assets of $69 million and $207 million have been included in the consolidated balance sheet caption "marketable securities and other assets" at December 31, 1995 and 1994, respectively.*

On December 31, 1995, the Company had $265 million of operating loss carryforwards available to reduce future taxable income of certain international subsidiaries. Loss carryforwards of $107 million must be utilized within the next 5 years, and $158 million can be utilized over an indefinite period. A valuation allowance has been provided for a portion of the deferred tax assets related to these loss carryforwards.

Notes to Consolidated Financial Statements

16. Net Change in Operating Assets and Liabilities

The changes in operating assets and liabilities, net of effects of acquisitions and divestitures of businesses and unrealized exchange gains/losses, are as follows (in millions):

Year Ended December 31,	1995	1994	1993
Increase in trade accounts receivable	$ (255)	$ (169)	$ (151)
(Increase) decrease in inventories	(80)	43	(41)
Increase in prepaid expenses and other assets	(373)	(273)	(76)
Increase (decrease) in accounts payable and accrued expenses	214	197	(44)
Increase in accrued taxes	26	200	355
Increase in other liabilities	63	131	11
	$ (405)	$ 129	$ 54

17. Nonrecurring Items

During 1995, selling, administrative and general expenses include provisions of $86 million to increase efficiencies in the Company's operations in the United States and Europe.

Upon a favorable court decision in 1993, the Company reversed previously recorded reserves for bottler litigation, resulting in a $13 million reduction to selling, administrative and general expenses and a $10 million reduction to interest expense. Selling, administrative and general expenses for 1993 also include provisions of $63 million to increase efficiencies in the Company's operations in the United States and Europe, and Corporate. Also in 1993, equity income was reduced by $42 million related to restructuring charges recorded by Coca-Cola Beverages Ltd. Other income (deductions)-net for 1993 included a $50 million pretax gain recorded by the foods business upon the sale of citrus groves in the United States, and a $34 million pretax gain recognized on the sale of property no longer required as a result of a consolidation of manufacturing operations in Japan.

Net Operating Revenues by Line of Business

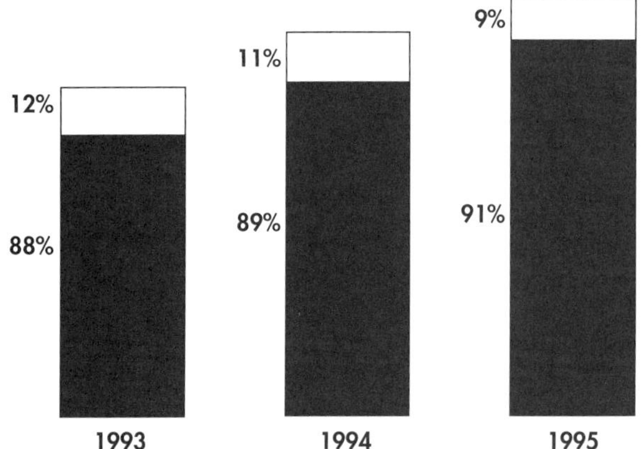

Operating Income by Line of Business

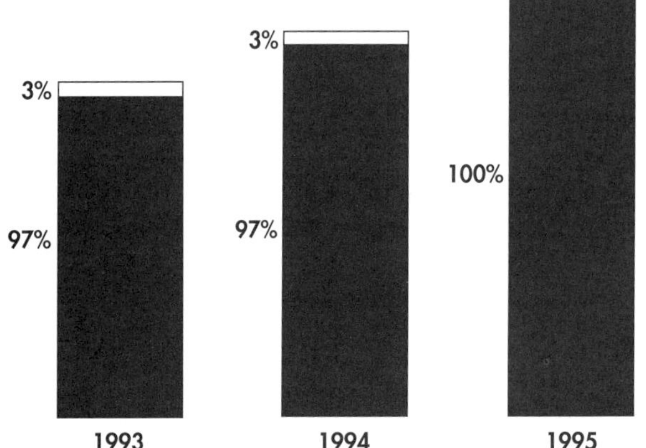

Notes to Consolidated Financial Statements

18. Lines of Business

The Company operates in two major lines of business: beverages and foods. Information concerning operations in these businesses is as follows (in millions):

	Beverages	Foods	Corporate	Consolidated
1995				
Net operating revenues	**$ 16,350**	**$ 1,613**	**$ 55**	**$ 18,018**
Operating income	**4,594[2]**	**(14)[2]**	**(488)**	**4,092**
Identifiable operating assets	**10,177**	**689**	**1,461[1]**	**12,327**
Equity income			**169**	**169**
Investments (principally bottling companies)			**2,714**	**2,714**
Capital expenditures	**795**	**65**	**77**	**937**
Depreciation and amortization	**350**	**38**	**66**	**454**
1994				
Net operating revenues	$ 14,412	$ 1,728	$ 41	$ 16,181
Operating income	4,022	123	(429)	3,716
Identifiable operating assets	9,176	731	1,456[1]	11,363
Equity income			134	134
Investments (principally bottling companies)			2,510	2,510
Capital expenditures	750	39	89	878
Depreciation and amortization	313	38	60	411
1993				
Net operating revenues	$ 12,257	$ 1,680	$ 26	$ 13,963
Operating income	3,433[3]	117	(442)[3]	3,108
Identifiable operating assets	7,765	761	1,280[1]	9,806
Equity income			91[3]	91
Investments (principally bottling companies)			2,215	2,215
Capital expenditures	693	30	77	800
Depreciation and amortization	263	38	59	360

Intercompany transfers between sectors are not material.

Certain prior year amounts related to net operating revenues and operating income have been reclassified to conform to the current year presentation.

[1]*Corporate identifiable operating assets are composed principally of marketable securities, finance subsidiary receivables and fixed assets.*

[2]*Operating income for the beverages and foods businesses was reduced by $49 million and $37 million, respectively, for provisions to increase efficiencies.*

[3]*Operating income for the beverages business and Corporate was reduced by $46 million and $17 million, respectively, for provisions to increase efficiencies. Equity income was reduced by $42 million related to restructuring charges recorded by Coca-Cola Beverages Ltd.*

Compound Growth Rates Ending 1995	Beverages	Foods	Consolidated
Net operating revenues			
5 years	14%	—%	12%
10 years	14%	2%	12%
Operating income			
5 years	16%	—%	16%
10 years	19%	—%	18%

Notes to Consolidated Financial Statements

19. Operations in Geographic Areas

Effective February 1, 1996, the Company's operating management structure will consist of five geographic groups and Coca-Cola Foods, and the International and North America Business Sectors will cease to exist. Information about the Company's operations by geographic area is as follows (in millions):

	United States	Africa	Greater Europe	Latin America	Middle & Far East & Canada	Corporate	Consolidated
1995							
Net operating revenues	$ 5,261	$ 595	$ 6,025	$ 1,920	$ 4,162	$ 55	$ 18,018
Operating income	840[2]	206	1,300[2]	797	1,437	(488)	4,092
Identifiable operating assets	3,384	348	4,301	1,294	1,539	1,461[1]	12,327
Equity income						169	169
Investments (principally bottling companies)						2,714	2,714
Capital expenditures	285	19	383	88	85	77	937
Depreciation and amortization	146	8	180	31	23	66	454
1994							
Net operating revenues	$ 5,092	$ 522	$ 5,047	$ 1,928	$ 3,551	$ 41	$ 16,181
Operating income	869	182	1,173	713	1,208	(429)	3,716
Identifiable operating assets	2,991	357	3,958	1,164	1,437	1,456[1]	11,363
Equity income						134	134
Investments (principally bottling companies)						2,510	2,510
Capital expenditures	252	27	330	129	51	89	878
Depreciation and amortization	128	6	160	36	21	60	411
1993							
Net operating revenues	$ 4,586	$ 255	$ 4,456	$ 1,683	$ 2,957	$ 26	$ 13,963
Operating income	782[3]	152	1,029[3]	582	1,005	(442)[3]	3,108
Identifiable operating assets	2,682	153	3,287	1,220	1,184	1,280[1]	9,806
Equity income						91[3]	91
Investments (principally bottling companies)						2,215	2,215
Capital expenditures	165	6	366	141	45	77	800
Depreciation and amortization	127	3	120	33	18	59	360

Intercompany transfers between geographic areas are not material.
Certain prior year amounts related to net operating revenues and operating income have been reclassified to conform to the current year presentation.
Identifiable liabilities of operations outside the United States amounted to approximately $2.7 billion on December 31, 1995, $2.5 billion on December 31, 1994, and $1.9 billion on December 31, 1993.

[1]Corporate identifiable operating assets are composed principally of marketable securities, finance subsidiary receivables and fixed assets.

[2]Operating income for the United States and Greater Europe was reduced by $61 million and $25 million, respectively, for provisions to increase efficiencies.

[3]Operating income for the United States, Greater Europe and Corporate was reduced by $13 million, $33 million and $17 million, respectively, for provisions to increase efficiencies. Equity income was reduced by $42 million related to restructuring charges recorded by Coca-Cola Beverages Ltd.

Compound Growth Rates Ending 1995	United States	Africa	Greater Europe	Latin America	Middle & Far East & Canada	Consolidated
Net operating revenues						
5 years	6%	24%	14%	19%	15%	12%
10 years	5%	9%	20%	16%	15%	12%
Operating income						
5 years	14%	16%	12%	22%	17%	16%
10 years	10%	9%	20%	24%	20%	18%

Report of Independent Auditors

Net Operating Revenues by Geographic Area

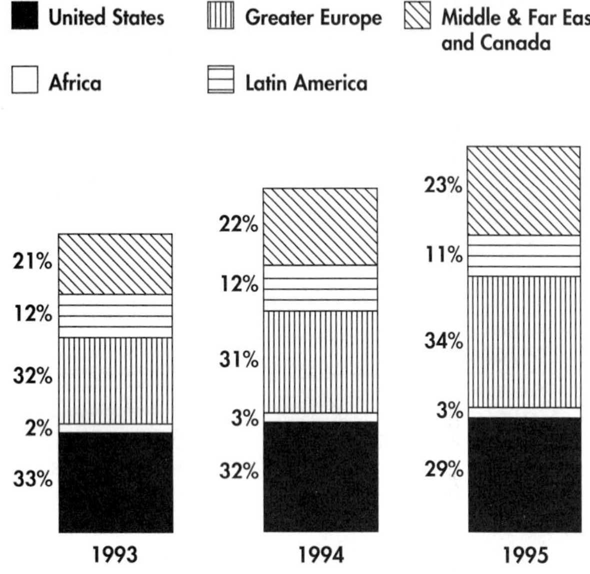

Operating Income by Geographic Area

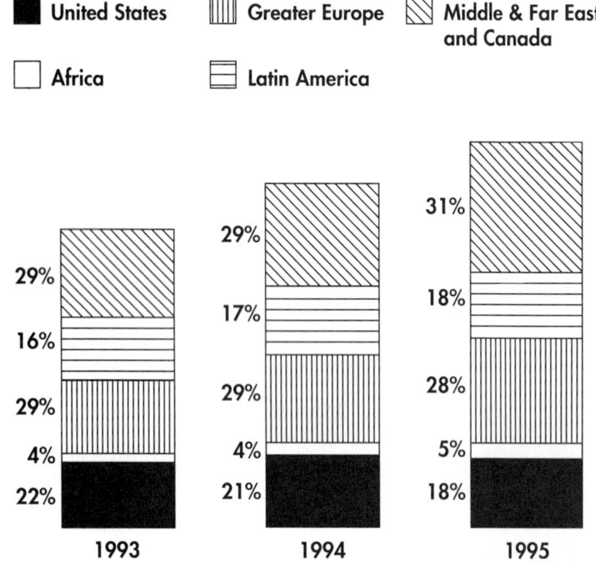

Board of Directors and Share Owners
The Coca-Cola Company

We have audited the accompanying consolidated balance sheets of The Coca-Cola Company and subsidiaries as of December 31, 1995 and 1994, and the related consolidated statements of income, share-owners' equity, and cash flows for each of the three years in the period ended December 31, 1995. These financial statements are the responsibility of the Company's management. Our responsibility is to express an opinion on these financial statements based on our audits.

We conducted our audits in accordance with generally accepted auditing standards. Those standards require that we plan and perform the audit to obtain reasonable assurance about whether the financial statements are free of material misstatement. An audit includes examining, on a test basis, evidence supporting the amounts and disclosures in the financial statements. An audit also includes assessing the accounting principles used and significant estimates made by management, as well as evaluating the overall financial statement presentation. We believe that our audits provide a reasonable basis for our opinion.

In our opinion, the financial statements referred to above present fairly, in all material respects, the consolidated financial position of The Coca-Cola Company and subsidiaries at December 31, 1995 and 1994, and the consolidated results of their operations and their cash flows for each of the three years in the period ended December 31, 1995, in conformity with generally accepted accounting principles.

Ernst & Young LLP

Atlanta, Georgia
January 23, 1996

Report of Management

Management is responsible for the preparation and integrity of the consolidated financial statements appearing in this Annual Report. The financial statements were prepared in conformity with generally accepted accounting principles appropriate in the circumstances and, accordingly, include certain amounts based on management's best judgments and estimates. Financial information in this Annual Report is consistent with that in the financial statements.

Management is responsible for maintaining a system of internal accounting controls and procedures to provide reasonable assurance, at an appropriate cost/benefit relationship, that assets are safeguarded and that transactions are authorized, recorded and reported properly. The internal accounting control system is augmented by a program of internal audits and appropriate reviews by management, written policies and guidelines, careful selection and training of qualified personnel and a written Code of Business Conduct adopted by the Board of Directors, applicable to all employees of the Company and its subsidiaries. Management believes that the Company's internal accounting controls provide reasonable assurance that assets are safeguarded against material loss from unauthorized use or disposition and that the financial records are reliable for preparing financial statements and other data and for maintaining accountability of assets.

The Audit Committee of the Board of Directors, composed solely of Directors who are not officers of the Company, meets with the independent auditors, management and internal auditors periodically to discuss internal accounting controls and auditing and financial reporting matters. The Committee reviews with the independent auditors the scope and results of the audit effort. The Committee also meets with the independent auditors and the chief internal auditor without management present to ensure that the independent auditors and the chief internal auditor have free access to the Committee.

The independent auditors, Ernst & Young LLP, are recommended by the Audit Committee of the Board of Directors, selected by the Board of Directors and ratified by the share owners. Ernst & Young LLP is engaged to audit the consolidated financial statements of The Coca-Cola Company and subsidiaries and conduct such tests and related procedures as it deems necessary in conformity with generally accepted auditing standards. The opinion of the independent auditors, based upon their audits of the consolidated financial statements, is contained in this Annual Report.

Roberto C. Goizueta
Chairman, Board of Directors,
and Chief Executive Officer

James E. Chestnut
Senior Vice President
and Chief Financial Officer

Gary P. Fayard
Vice President
and Controller

January 23, 1996

Quarterly Data (Unaudited)

(In millions except per share data)

Year Ended December 31,	First Quarter	Second Quarter	Third Quarter	Fourth Quarter	Full Year
1995					
Net operating revenues	**$ 3,854**	**$ 4,936**	**$ 4,895**	**$ 4,333**	**$ 18,018**
Gross profit	**2,409**	**3,060**	**2,946**	**2,663**	**11,078**
Net income	**638**	**898**	**802**	**648**	**2,986**
Net income per share	**.50**	**.71**	**.64**	**.52**	**2.37**
1994					
Net operating revenues	$ 3,352	$ 4,342	$ 4,461	$ 4,026	$ 16,181
Gross profit	2,110	2,675	2,701	2,527	10,013
Net income	521	758	708	567	2,554
Net income per share	.40	.59	.55	.44	1.98

The third quarter of 1995 includes provisions to increase efficiencies of $86 million ($.04 per share after income taxes) and a non-cash gain recognized on the issuance of stock by Coca-Cola Amatil of $74 million ($.04 per share after income taxes).

Stock Prices

Below are the New York Stock Exchange high, low and closing prices of The Coca-Cola Company's stock for each quarter of 1995 and 1994.

	First Quarter	Second Quarter	Third Quarter	Fourth Quarter
1995				
High	**$ 59.38**	**$ 66.00**	**$ 70.63**	**$ 80.38**
Low	**48.75**	**56.13**	**62.63**	**68.38**
Close	**56.38**	**63.75**	**69.00**	**74.25**
1994				
High	$ 44.75	$ 42.38	$ 50.00	$ 53.50
Low	40.13	38.88	41.00	48.00
Close	40.63	40.63	48.63	51.50

INDEXES

COMPANY NAME INDEX

SUBJECT INDEX

<table>
<tr><td>INT
No.</td><td>Date
Issued</td><td></td><td align="center">Financial Accounting Standards Board (FASB) Interpretations (1974–85)</td></tr>
<tr><td>1</td><td>June</td><td>1974</td><td>Accounting Changes Related to the Cost of Inventory</td></tr>
<tr><td>2</td><td>June</td><td>1974</td><td>Importing Interest on Debt Arrangements Made under the Federal Bankruptcy Act</td></tr>
<tr><td>3</td><td>Dec.</td><td>1974</td><td>Accounting for the Cost of Pension Plans Subject to the Employment Retirement Income Security Act of 1974</td></tr>
<tr><td>4</td><td>Feb.</td><td>1975</td><td>Applicability of FASB Statement 2 to Business Combinations Accounted for by the Purchase Method</td></tr>
<tr><td>5</td><td>Feb.</td><td>1975</td><td>Applicability of FASB Statement 2 to Development Stage Enterprises</td></tr>
<tr><td>6</td><td>Feb.</td><td>1975</td><td>Applicability of FASB Statement 2 to Computer Software</td></tr>
<tr><td>7</td><td>Oct.</td><td>1975</td><td>Applying FASB Statement 7 in Financial Statements of Established Operating Enterprises</td></tr>
<tr><td>8</td><td>Jan.</td><td>1976</td><td>Classification of a Short-Term Obligation Repaid Prior to Being Replaced by a Long-Term Security</td></tr>
<tr><td>9</td><td>Feb.</td><td>1976</td><td>Applying APB Opinions 16 and 17 When a Savings and Loan Association or a Similar Institution Is Acquired in a Business Combination Accounted for by the Purchase Method</td></tr>
<tr><td>10</td><td>Sept.</td><td>1976</td><td>Application of FASB Statement 12 to Personal Financial Statements</td></tr>
<tr><td>11</td><td>Sept.</td><td>1976</td><td>Changes in Market Value after the Balance Sheet Date</td></tr>
<tr><td>12</td><td>Sept.</td><td>1976</td><td>Accounting for Previously Established Allowance Accounts</td></tr>
<tr><td>13</td><td>Sept.</td><td>1976</td><td>Consolidation of a Parent and Its Subsidiaries Having Different Balance Sheet Dates</td></tr>
<tr><td>14</td><td>Sept.</td><td>1976</td><td>Reasonable Estimation of the Amount of a Loss</td></tr>
<tr><td>15</td><td>Sept.</td><td>1976</td><td>Translation of Unamortized Policy Acquisition Costs by a Stock Life Insurance Company</td></tr>
<tr><td>16</td><td>Feb.</td><td>1977</td><td>Clarification of Definitions and Accounting for Marketable Equity Securities That Become Nonmarketable</td></tr>
<tr><td>17</td><td>Feb.</td><td>1977</td><td>Applying the Lower of Cost or Market Rule in Translated Financial Statements</td></tr>
<tr><td>18</td><td>Mar.</td><td>1977</td><td>Accounting for Income Taxes in Interim Periods</td></tr>
<tr><td>19</td><td>Oct.</td><td>1977</td><td>Lessee Guarantee of the Residual Value of Leased Property</td></tr>
<tr><td>20</td><td>Nov.</td><td>1977</td><td>Reporting Accounting Changes under AICPA Statements of Position</td></tr>
<tr><td>21</td><td>Apr.</td><td>1978</td><td>Accounting for Leases in a Business Combination</td></tr>
<tr><td>22</td><td>Apr.</td><td>1978</td><td>Applicability of Indefinite Reversal Criteria to Timing Differences</td></tr>
<tr><td>23</td><td>Aug.</td><td>1978</td><td>Leases of Certain Property Owned by a Governmental Unit or Authority</td></tr>
<tr><td>24</td><td>Sept.</td><td>1978</td><td>Leases Involving Only Part of a Building</td></tr>
<tr><td>25</td><td>Sept.</td><td>1978</td><td>Accounting for an Unused Investment Tax Credit</td></tr>
<tr><td>26</td><td>Sept.</td><td>1978</td><td>Accounting for Purchase of a Leased Asset by the Lessee during the Term of the Lease</td></tr>
<tr><td>27</td><td>Nov.</td><td>1978</td><td>Accounting for Loss on a Sublease</td></tr>
<tr><td>28</td><td>Dec.</td><td>1978</td><td>Accounting for Stock Appreciation Rights and Other Variable Stock Option or Award Plans</td></tr>
<tr><td>29</td><td>Feb.</td><td>1979</td><td>Reporting Tax Benefits Realized on Disposition of Investments in Certain Subsidiaries and Other Investees</td></tr>
<tr><td>30</td><td>Sept.</td><td>1979</td><td>Accounting for Involuntary Conversions of Nonmonetary Assets to Monetary Assets</td></tr>
<tr><td>31</td><td>Feb.</td><td>1980</td><td>Treatment of Stock Compensation Plans in EPS Computations</td></tr>
<tr><td>32</td><td>Mar.</td><td>1980</td><td>Application of Percentage Limitations in Recognizing Investment Tax Credit</td></tr>
<tr><td>33</td><td>Aug.</td><td>1980</td><td>Applying FASB Statement 34 to Oil and Gas Producing Operations Accounted for by the Full Cost Method</td></tr>
<tr><td>34</td><td>Mar.</td><td>1981</td><td>Disclosure of Indirect Guarantees of Indebtedness of Others</td></tr>
<tr><td>35</td><td>May</td><td>1981</td><td>Criteria for Applying the Equity Method of Accounting for Investments in Common Stock</td></tr>
<tr><td>36</td><td>Oct.</td><td>1981</td><td>Accounting for Exploration Wells in Progress at the End of a Period</td></tr>
<tr><td>37</td><td>July</td><td>1983</td><td>Accounting for Translation Adjustments upon Sale of Part of an Investment in a Foreign Entity</td></tr>
<tr><td>38</td><td>Aug.</td><td>1984</td><td>Determining the Measurement Date for Stock Options, Purchase, and Award Plans Involving Junior Stock</td></tr>
<tr><td>39</td><td>Mar.</td><td>1992</td><td>Offsetting of Amounts Related to Certain Contracts</td></tr>
<tr><td>40</td><td>Apr.</td><td>1993</td><td>Applicability of Generally Accepted Accounting Principles to Mutual Life Insurance and Other Enterprises</td></tr>
<tr><td>41</td><td>Dec.</td><td>1994</td><td>Applicability of Generally Accepted Accounting Principles to Mutual Life Insurance and Other Enterprises (an interpretation of FASB Statements No. 12, 60, 97, and 113)</td></tr>
<tr><td>42</td><td>Sept.</td><td>1996</td><td>Accounting for Transfers of Assets in Which a Not-for-Profit Organization Is Granted Variance Power (an interpretation of FASB Statement No. 116)</td></tr>
</table>

<table>
<tr><td>TB
No.</td><td></td><td></td><td align="center">Financial Accounting Standards Board (FASB) Technical Bulletins (1979–87)</td></tr>
<tr><td>79–1</td><td>Dec.</td><td>1979</td><td>Purpose and Scope of FASB Technical Bulletins and Procedures for Issuance—To Provide Guidance Concerning the Application of Official Pronouncements of the FASB, APB, and ARBs</td></tr>
<tr><td>79–2</td><td>Dec.</td><td>1979</td><td>Computer Software Costs</td></tr>
<tr><td>79–3</td><td>Dec.</td><td>1979</td><td>Subjective Acceleration Clauses in Long-Term Debt Agreements</td></tr>
<tr><td>79–4</td><td>Dec.</td><td>1979</td><td>Segment Reporting of Puerto Rican Operations</td></tr>
<tr><td>79–5</td><td>Dec.</td><td>1979</td><td>Meaning of the Term "Customer" as It Applies to Facilities</td></tr>
<tr><td>79–6</td><td>Dec.</td><td>1979</td><td>Valuation Allowances Following Debt Restructure</td></tr>
<tr><td>79–7</td><td>Dec.</td><td>1979</td><td>Recoveries of a Previous Writedown under a Troubled Debt Restructuring Involving a Modification of Terms</td></tr>
<tr><td>79–8</td><td>Dec.</td><td>1979</td><td>Applicability of FASB Statements 21 and 33 to Certain Brokers and Dealers in Securities</td></tr>
<tr><td>79–9</td><td>Dec.</td><td>1979</td><td>Accounting in Interim Periods for Changes in Income Tax Rates</td></tr>
<tr><td>79–10</td><td>Dec.</td><td>1979</td><td>Fiscal Funding Clauses in Lease Agreements</td></tr>
<tr><td>79–11</td><td>Dec.</td><td>1979</td><td>Effect of a Penalty on the Term of a Lease</td></tr>
<tr><td>79–12</td><td>Dec.</td><td>1979</td><td>Interest Rate Used in Calculating the Present Value of Minimum Lease Payments</td></tr>
<tr><td>79–13</td><td>Dec.</td><td>1979</td><td>Applicability of FASB Statement 13 to Current Value Financial Statements</td></tr>
<tr><td>79–14</td><td>Dec.</td><td>1979</td><td>Upward Adjustment of Guaranteed Residual Values</td></tr>
<tr><td>79–15</td><td>Dec.</td><td>1979</td><td>Accounting for Loss on a Sublease Not Involving the Disposal of a Segment</td></tr>
</table>